COMPLETE
COLLECTED
ESSAYS

By the same author

COMPLETE COLLECTED ESSAYS

V.S. PRITCHETT

Random House
NEW YORK

All the essays that appear in this volume have been previously published. Some were originally published in *The New Statesman, The New York Review of Books*, and *The New Yorker*. These essays have also appeared in the following compilations by V. S. Pritchett: *In My Good Books, The Living Novel, Books in General, The Working Novelist, The Myth Makers, The Tale Bearers, A Man of Letters*, and *Lasting Impressions*.

This work was originally published in Great Britain by Chatto & Windus Ltd, London, in 1991.

Library of Congress Cataloging-in-Publication Data

Pritchett, V. S. (Victor Sawdon), 1900–
[Essays]
Complete collected essays/by V. S. Pritchett, – 1st ed.
p.   cm.
Published simultaneously under title: The complete essays.
I S B N 0-679-41112-7
I. Title.
PR6031.R7A6   1992   91-39919
824'.912 – dc20

Manufactured in the United States of America
23456789

First U.S. Edition

For my wife

Contents

COMPLETE
COLLECTED
ESSAYS

Gibbon and the Home Guard

'No war has had greater results on the history of the world or brought greater triumphs to England,' writes the historian Green when he comes to the Seven Years War, 'but few have had more disastrous beginnings'. To that familiar note we are now inured. Military preparedness appears to be an impossibility in these islands. At the beginning of 1756 there were only three regiments fit for service, and after the collapse of the Duke of Cumberland's army on the Elbe a year later 'a despondency without parallel in our history took possession of our coolest statesmen, and even the impassive Chesterfield cried in despair, "We are no longer a nation".' So often has the despondency been paralleled since, and so often survived, that one hesitates to repeat the old, old story for fear of encouraging the gloomy smugness of it once too often. There were 18,000 men waiting to cross the Channel at Quiberon in the summer of 1759, before Admiral Hawke scotched them. But now, in contrast to the despair of two years earlier, 'the national spirit most gloriously disproved the charge of effeminacy which, in a popular estimate, had been imputed to the times'.

Edward Gibbon wrote these words when he looked back upon the military ardour which penetrated to the sleepy hesitations of country life at Buriton, near Petersfield, and which impelled his father to drive both of them into the Militia:

> The country rings around with loud alarms,
> And raw in fields the rude Militia swarms.

Gibbon remembered his Dryden. Left to himself, removed from his notorious habit of 'obeying as a son', Gibbon (one suspects) would have stayed where he was with his nose in his books and raising an occasional eye to consider and dismiss the prospect of marrying the next imperfect West Sussex lady on the calling list. Perhaps if he had not joined the Home Guard of 1759 Gibbon might have married from lack of having anything

[1]

else to do, and then – who knows – we might be reading of the Birth and Rise, rather than of the Decline and Fall of the Roman Empire. A woman, even one of the West Sussex chatterboxes, might have prevailed against the eighteenth-century taste for ruins. But Gibbon *père* had always been the decisive partner in the life of Gibbon *fils*. The father had put his foot down once or twice to some effect already; and having sent the youth to the Continent in order to rid him of Popery, he was equally determined on effacing the Frenchified personality and mind which the young man had brought back in exchange for his religion. Edward Gibbon was to be made into an Englishman, and on June 12th Major and Captain Gibbon received their commissions in the South Battalion of the Hampshires.

The story of Gibbon's service with the Militia is well known. It can be read in his *Autobiography*, in his *Journal*, and in the various *Lives*, of which Mr D. M. Low's is especially thorough, sympathetic and readable. To the one-time Territorial, the conscript or the Home Guard of today, Gibbon's experiences are amusing, consoling and instructive. The peculiar torments which sting the amateur soldier seem to change very little from age to age. Joining to repel the invader at a moment's notice, the Gibbons were very soon to find that the Navy had done it for them – Hawke sank the French at Quiberon in the following November – and that their patriotism had led them into the demoralising trap of soldiering without an enemy. Gibbon's first impression confirmed the remaining lines of Dryden:

> Mouths without hands maintained at vast expense,
> In peace a charge, in war a weak defence.
> Stout once a month they march, a blust'ring band,
> And ever but in times of need at hand.
> This was the more when, issuing on guard,
> Drawn up in rank and file they stood prepar'd,
> Of seeming arms to make a short essay;
> Then hasten to be drunk – the business of the day.

As a writer, Gibbon found himself in charge of the battalion's administrative and even literary affairs, which meant mainly conducting the correspondence and piling up the dossier of a row – 'passionate and prolix' – a typical military row with a peer about precedence. When the danger of invasion had passed, the Major and the Captain hoped to be allowed to take their duties easily in Petersfield or Alton, but they were caught for two and a half years more and began an unheroic, tedious and often sordid progress round the South of England. Winchester was too near home for discipline; they went to Devon, where they were happy, to Devizes where the habits of the town were riotous – twenty-one courts martial – to Porchester, where they guarded the French prisoners and many of the men caught fevers or the smallpox in the swampy wildernesses nearby, to Alton, where they entered the camp 'indisputably the last and worst'.

To the Major this was all far less depressing than to the Captain. There was a vein of happy impetuosity and slackness in the Major's character. He had always been at home in either the highest or the lowest society. He frequently cut parades, and when he did turn up his drill was terrible. Gibbon writes: 'We had a most wretched field day. Major, officers and men seemed to try which should do worst.' The Captain did not claim to be perfect: 'The battalion was out, officers but no powder. It was the worst field day we had had a good while, the men were very unsteady, the officers very inattentive, and I myself made several mistakes.' Still, there were consolations: 'After going through the manual, which they did with great spirit, I put them . . . thro' a variety of evolutions . . . At the volley I made them recover their arms, not a piece went off.' Edward Gibbon was not one of those lackadaisical literary soldiers who hope their shufflings and errors will be lost in the crowd or that their sporadic brainwaves will impress the command. He was, as always, thorough, industrious and responsible; and some part of his suffering was due to his conscientiousness.

The qualities we expect of Gibbon are sense, balance and judiciousness. No man is more likely to give a more considered account of his experience, to extract the value from his disappointments, to gather in, perhaps complacently, all the compensations. The plump little man, only five feet high, with the bulging forehead and the bulbous cheeks, gazes like some imperturbable and learned baby at his life and can be trusted to give both sides of the question, if only for the sensuous pleasure of balancing a sentence:

> The loss of so many busy and idle hours was not compensated by any elegant pleasure; and my temper was insensibly soured by the society of our rustic officers who were alike deficient in the knowledge of scholars

and the manners of gentlemen. In every state there exists, however, a balance of good and evil. The habits of a sedentary life were usefully broken by the duties of an active profession; in the healthful exercise of the field I hunted with a battalion instead of a pack, and at that time I was ready at any hour of the day or night to fly from quarters to London, from London to quarters on the slightest call of private or regimental business. But my principal obligation to the militia was the making me an Englishman and a soldier. After my foreign education, with my reserved temper, I should long have continued a stranger in my native country, had I not shaken in this various scene of new faces and new friends; had not experience forced me to feel the characters of our leading men, the state of parties, the forms of office, and the operation of our civil and military system. In this peaceful service I imbibed the rudiments of the language and science of tactics which opened a new field of study and observation . . . The discipline and evolutions of a modern battalion gave me a clearer notion of the Phalanx and the Legions, and the Captain of the Hampshire Grenadiers [the reader may smile] has not been useless to the historian of the Roman Empire.

He took Horace with him on the march and read up the questions of Pagan and Christian theology in his tent. Sooner or later, the great men turn out to be all alike. They never stop working. They never lose a minute. It is very depressing.

Gibbon, like Francis Bacon, Swift and Dr Johnson, is a writer whose experience is digested and set forth like the summing-up of a moral judge. 'My temper is not very susceptible of enthusiasm' . . . that is not really quite true, as his sudden conversion to Rome, his first meetings with Suzanne Curchod, his occasional feats with the bottle at Lausanne and in the militia seem to show. But if not phlegmatic, he is formal. The truth is that his temper was far more susceptible to style. For him style was the small, ugly man's form of power. His shocking health as a child and youth, though astonishingly restored when he was sixteen years of age, must have inscribed on his heart and instincts the detachment, the reserve, the innate melancholy of invalid habits. The coldness which is alleged, the tepidity of feeling and the fixed air of priggishness and conceit, are misleading. Really, he is self-contained. In telling his own story he is not recklessly candid, but he is honest to a startling extent, and especially in disclaiming emotions which it is conventional to claim. His formality is comic, even intentionally so at times, and his detachment about himself may, of course, show an unconscionable vanity; but it also indicates the belief that a civilised man is one who ought to be able to stand the display of all the evidence. We think here particularly of his brief comment on Rousseau's dislike of his character and behaviour: Rousseau, Gibbon mildly remarks, ought not to have passed judgment on a foreigner. (Or did Gibbon mean that a continental enthusiast ought not to pass judgment on an English country gentleman? It is quite likely he did mean this.) Gibbon is not ashamed to record his constant concern about money and property, nor to admit that his father's recklessness about money alarmed him not only as a son, but as an heir. And after drawing the most gracious portrait of his father, he is careful not to end on the note of filial idolatry or remorse:

> The tears of a son are seldom lasting. I submitted to the order of Nature, and my grief was soothed by the conscious satisfaction that I had discharged all the duties of filial piety. Few perhaps are the children who, after the expiration of some months or years, would sincerely rejoice in the resurrection of their parents; and it is a melancholy truth, that my father's death, not unhappy for himself, was the only event that could save me from an hopeless life of obscurity and indigence.

It *is* a melancholy truth. Gibbon has a taste for the truth that is melancholy, for seeing life as a series of epitaphs. And yet in Reynolds' portrait the fat little scholar with the second roll of chin, and the lips which seem set for the discharge of some destructive epigram, is not as sober as he looks. He is, in fact, cutting a dash. With the amateur soldier's love of a splash and with a glance back at the heroic days when his Militia boldly exercised within sight of the French coast, he has put on his scarlet coat for the picture. 'For in England the red ever appears the favourite and, as it were, the national colour of our military ensigns and uniforms.'

A Conscript

Conscription for military service, in peace and war, has not a long history in Europe. It dates from the French Revolution and was the basis of Napoleon's enormous military achievement. No other general in Europe could say, as he did to Metternich: 'I can afford to lose 30,000 men per month.' But many years passed before a population who had been used to the unheroic pleasures of peaceful industry and were far removed from memory of the massacres of the religious wars became amenable to this pace of slaughter. Men fled from their houses in thousands, the Vendée rose in revolt. Nevertheless in times of revolutionary persecution and espionage, the army becomes the safest hiding-place; the glory of the Napoleonic conquests was irresistible and, with all Europe hungry, the discovery that you could pillage the conquered and live well off them was a final factor in making for the success of the new system. One has only to look at the memoirs of such rogues as Vidocq to see what a piping time the tougher conscripts had. Their European travels turned them into foreigners. They became a race apart. This is of course true of all soldiers. In his *Verdun* M. Jules Romains shows that the common daydream of the men in the trenches was of somehow melting away from the front in little bands, retiring to the woods and living a kind of Robin Hood life on the tribute they exacted from civilians.

What was the life of Napoleon's first European conscripts? Some idea can be got from that old school-book, *Histoires d'un Conscrit de 1813*, by Erckmann-Chatrian. (It is a pity one reads these two Alsatian authors at school, for while they are safe enough and exciting enough for schoolboys and inculcate a very sound and civilised moral repugnance to Cæsarism, they have a quality which schoolboys are not able to appreciate.) Neither Chatrian, the glassmaker who worked his way up in the world, and became a school teacher, nor Erckmann, the clever briefless lawyer, was actually a Napoleonic conscript. They were born a few years after Waterloo and

[6]

they wrote of the campaigns and the revolution itself as those events still lived in the memories of their elders, picking up the old boasts and lamentations from humble and ordinary folk. They look at the war from below, assume in their stories the point of view of some small tradesman or peasant, and view the scene from the vantage-point of a period of disillusion. This pretence of being eye-witnesses, and with it the circumstantial manner at which they excel, recalls Defoe's *Journal of the Plague Year*. Both books have that modest, trim, but firm respectability, the stoicism of the small trader. The meek shall inherit the earth. Joseph, the good, lame apprentice working overtime to save up money in order to marry his innocent little Catherine whose hand he holds all the evening like a sugar stick, is an early example of the pious, non-tough hero of the nineteenth century. He does not seem a prig to us because he is good without knowing it, or perhaps one should say that really his piety lies not in his religion but in an innate belief in the goodness of his class itself. (In popular belief class is the chief God.) Sainte-Beuve scornfully called this book 'L'Iliade de la peur', but if Joseph is often as frightened as any young soldier is, he is certainly no coward. He stands his ground in the French squares, terrified by the screaming, monkey faces of the Prussian Hussars as they charge down at the Battle of Leipzig, but he is savagely angry that any man on earth should try and take away his life without consulting him and in a cause to which he is indifferent. 'La gloire' did not intoxicate Joseph. Before he went to his medical examinations he swallowed a bottleful of vinegar, hoping to deceive the doctors, because he had been told this drink would make him look as pale as an invalid. In fact it gave him the violent flush of an enormous health, and he regards his failure to get out of military service as a just punishment for acting a lie. Mild, one would call Joseph, very mild, yet really he has the pathos which war gives to the sensible man:

> I wish those who love glory so much would go and find it themselves and not leave it to others.
> To tell you the truth [said Zebedee] I think the same as you do, but as they have got us it is better to say we are fighting for glory.

One reads all books on the Napoleonic period with one eye continually jumping forward to the present. The pacifist would naturally jump at a passage like the one I have quoted; but the moral of the book is not pacific. It is patriotic denunciation of despotism, and it is based upon descriptions of what the ordinary man and woman were saying and feeling at the time. Here I think those who are conducting anecdotal propaganda in Germany against Hitler might read the *Story of a Conscript* with advantage. It is a book full of fruitful murmurs and suggestive ironies. Joseph joins up after the retreat from Moscow, and a wonderful public statement is issued in the town admitting and indeed almost boasting of the catastrophe and calling for more sacrifices.

I quote from R. G. Gillman's translation in the Everyman Edition:

Harmentier, the police sergeant, came from the watch-house and stood on the top of the steps, with a large piece of paper in his hand, similar to that which was placed on the wall; some soldiers were with him. Everybody ran towards him, but the soldiers made them stand back. Harmentier began by reading the notice, which he called the 29th bulletin, in which the Emperor stated that, during the retreat from Moscow, the horses had died every night by thousands; he said nothing about the men. As the sergeant read slowly and more slowly, the listeners whispered never a word; even the old woman listened dumbly like the rest, although she could not understand French.

The silence was such that one could hear a pin drop. When the sergeant came to this passage: 'Our cavalry were so utterly disorganised that it was necessary to form the officers who still had a horse left, into four companies of one hundred and fifty men each; the generals and colonels acting as regimental officers, and those of lower rank as privates'. When he read this, which spoke more than anything for the sufferings of the Grande Armée, I heard groans and cries on every side, and two or three women fell to the ground and had to be helped away.

The notice terminated with these words: 'The health of his Majesty has never been better.' This was indeed one great consolation to us; unhappily, this consolation could not bring back to life the 300,000 men buried in the snow, and the people went away very, very sad.

Before the disaster in Russia became known the simple people of Alsace believed that, since Napoleon had conquered the whole of Europe, the war would be over. 'You forget,' the sardonic replied, 'that there is still the conquest of China.' One can imagine that being said in Germany. Erckmann-Chatrian were, it is true, writing tendenciously after the event; but after all, France had seen the Revolution betrayed, and had paid a frightful price for her Fuehrer. At the summit of conquest there is always uncertainty and guilt in the minds of the conqueror's followers. 'It can't last.' 'We shall have to pay.' But Joseph found himself shouting 'Vive l'Empereur' with the rest, and could not explain why he shouted with such fervour for the man who had enslaved him.

The conscripts of 1813 and the conscripts today have very much the same experiences. Joseph and his friends soon found themselves standing drinks to the old soldiers, whose thirst was boundless. The veterans were patronising and the conscripts were cocky. Duels between them were common. The second lesson was the foundation of military discipline:

> The corporal is always right when he speaks to the private soldier, the sergeant is right when he speaks to the corporal, the sergeant-major is right when speaking to the sergeant, the sub-lieutenant to the sergeant-major, and so on upwards to the marshal of France – even if he were to say that the moon shines in broad daylight or that two and two make five.
>
> This is not an easy thing to get into your head, but there is one thing which is a great help to you, and that is a great noticeboard fixed up in the rooms, and which is read out from time to time, to settle your thoughts. This noticeboard enumerates everything that a soldier is supposed to want to do – such as, for instance, to return to his native village, to refuse service, to contradict his superior officer, etc., and always ends by promising he shall be shot or at least have five years hard labour, with a cannon ball fastened to his leg if he does it.

You then sold your civilian clothing and stood the corporals more drinks 'as it is well to be friends with them, as they drilled us morning and afternoon in the courtyard'. And the drinks were served by one Christine, an eternal figure.

> She showed particular consideration for all young men of good family, as she called those who were not careful of their money. How many of us were fleeced to their last sou in order to be called 'men of good family'.

Joseph has no private adventures or affairs on the way. He is the normal prig, the prudent Mr Everyman, who keeps as far from trouble as he can. He is thinking all the time of his dear Catherine; but Catherine, you feel pretty certain, is not going to be like the rest of the Phalsbourg girls, who turn round and marry someone else the moment their young man joins up and goes away. Joseph's day-long hope is that he won't be in the advance guard, that he won't have to kneel in the front rank of the square when the cavalry charge; and when he get to billets he is worried about the state of his feet and always manages to awaken the sympathy of the household. The odd thing is that he has our sympathy too. Erckmann-Chatrian succeed in making us prefer Joseph to the rasher and more virile Zebedee who fights a duel with a veteran and kills him with his sabre. The reason for this preference is that Joseph, in his mildness, is exactly the right kind of narrator. His virtue after all is not that of the best boy in the Sunday School; it is the virtue of everyday life, the *virtu* of peace set against the *virtu* of war. Such a humble figure shows up the gaudy chaos of war in dramatic contrast. The excellence of Erckmann-Chatrian lies in their continual remembrance of the common human feelings; and in the midst of their battle pieces, as the grape-shot ploughs the ranks and the men take up positions in the upper rooms of cottages, or in the horrible scenes of surgery which occur afterwards, the authors are always exact about the feeling of the simple man. Who does not respond to Joseph's description of his first action when he came under artillery fire? –

A tremendous cloud of smoke surrounded us and I said to myself if we remain here a quarter of an hour longer we shall be killed without a chance of defending ourselves. It seemed hard that it should be so.

Another point that occurs to me when I read either this book or *L'Histoire d'un Paysan* (a book which describes all the phases of the Revolution as they affected a peasant) is that the modern literature of war and revolution has become too egotistical. What 'I' said, what 'I' did, what happened to 'me'. The modern books from Blunden to Hemingway are all far more horrifying than Erckmann-Chatrian and I wonder how much this is due to their exceptional, personal point of view. For I do not think that the entire explanation is that modern war has become more horrifying. Erckmann-Chatrian can be grim. There is the moment, for example, when a soldier will not believe he has lost his arm until he sees it lying among a pile of amputated arms and recognises it by the tattoo mark. But usually the authors are sparing with this kind of particularity. Although a conscript or a peasant is writing, the predominant pronoun is 'we' not 'I'; he is writing of *all* the peasants, *all* his friends, *all* the soldiers. The private sensibility is merged with the general and we get a sensibility to the feelings of crowds, classes and masses which was to become one of the marks of nineteenth-century literature and which we have lost. When Erckmann-Chatrian were writing, this had not degenerated into the only too convenient means of melodrama and the vague picturesque. The simplicity and sincerity of the eighteenth century gave the Erckmann-Chatrian 'we' a real humanity, a genuine sentiment, a moral charm. The tough, first-person-singular hero of today is rich in knowingness; he knows the ropes far better than a softie like Joseph; but the tough man is poor in feeling, for the Romantic movement has intervened to make his feelings seem both larger and more catastrophically injured than they really are . . . Morbidity and insincerity are never far off. This poverty of feeling has affected the tough man's awareness of his comrades, for he is afraid of betraying himself before them. Our impression, in fact, is that the tough man is more afraid of his friends than of his enemies – a falsification of soldierly character which the 'soft school' were incapable of making.

A Swiss Novel

The difficulty, in thinking about *Adolphe*, is to lay the ghost of Constant. One is listening to Mozart against a disruptive mutter of music-hall which has got on to almost the same wavelength. But this happens with all the Romantics; their passionate exaltation of the first person singular aimed at the solitary *cri de cœur* but it leaves one with a confusing impression of duet, in which life, with its subversive pair of hands, is vamping in jaunty undertone the unofficial version. Beside the broken heart of the imagined Ellenore, healed at last by death, stands Madame de Staël, in the full real flesh of her obstreperous possessiveness with no sign of mortality on her. She is off to Germany to write a damned good book. And as Adolphe, free at last, contemplates with horror the wilderness of his liberty, up bobs Constant, explanatory about his secret marriage, still hopelessly susceptible, still with a dozen duels before him on account of ladies' faces and with one leg out of the nuptial couch at the thought of the rather acid enticements of Madame Récamier. It is distressing that a man should obtrude so persistently on his own confessions.

One of the earliest psychological novelists, Constant is enmeshed in ambiguity. He is more than the surgeon of the heart; he is more than the poet of masochism. *Adolphe* is not the tragedy of unequal love created out of the comedy of his chronic amorousness: it is the tragedy of the imagination itself and rendered in words as melodiously and mathematically clear as the phrases of a Mozart quartet. One understands as one reads *Adolphe* why the tears streamed down Constant's face and why his voice choked when he read his book. But he did weep rather a lot. He went weeping about the Courts of Europe with it – taking his precautions. Would Madame de Staël object to this line? Had he sufficiently toned down the money difficulties? (One would like to write the financial side of *Adolphe*, but that kind of thing was left to the vulgar Balzac.) Had he beaten up his literary omelette so well that none of his wives and mistresses could put out a finger and exclaim, Lo! here, or Lo! there? He was very anxious and very evasive. Never can autobiography – disguised though it was – have emerged from the facts with such a creeping and peeping. There was even a special preface for the English edition, in which, knowing his England, he declared *Adolphe* was a cautionary tale to warn us of the wretchedness of love which tries to live outside the necessary conventions of society. There is a sort of sincerity in this, of course; Constant had the bullied free-lover's sneaking regard for marriage as a kind of patent medicine. The dictatorship of Napoleon and the despotism of Madame de Staël had given him a hunger for the constitutional. But for one who thought nobly of the soul he is – well, shall we say practical?

One looks up from the music of *Adolphe*, from the cool dissertation of that unfaltering violin, to the noble head of his portrait. At Holland House, when they watched him, aware that they were being entertained by one of the most intelligent scandals of exiled Europe, they must have noticed that he had none of the frank charlatanry of the Romantics. A dignified and even debonair forty, he was sensitive, witty and vivacious. The nose suggests firmness and probity. And yet one can understand that Constant was considered a shade tough. One detects the buried outline of the original human monkey under the half-smile of the small courtier. In the pose and in the eyes there is something of the mandrill's mask, something of that animal's vanity and temper. So gentle – and yet Ellenore and Madame de Staël, violent themselves, complain of the rasp of his tongue. The mouth is almost beautiful, a talker's mouth caught with the perpetual epigram, but it lifts at the corner with an upward twist of slyness. It hints at the hard malice of the inhibited. One does not altogether trust Constant even before one has read *Adolphe*. One foresees the danger of a cleverness which is indecisive, the peril of an elusiveness which is captivating but never revealing.

What is lacking in the portrait is any sign of the morbid apathy of his nature. M. Gustav Rudler, the most searching editor of *Adolphe*, says Constant lived in a sort of apathy which 'made crises of passion an essential need'. A cat-and-dog life with all those mistresses, duels with young Englishmen – he was still at it in his crippled old age, being carried to the ground to fire from his chair – a wicked senility at the gaming tables. 'I leave myself to Chance,' Constant wrote, 'I go where it puts me and stay

[13]

there until it sweeps me away again.' Brilliant and unrevealing in conversation, he buries his serious opinions which he can contemplate only when he is alone. And then the temperature is so cool that the sensibility is still thwarted and unmelted. He lives listlessly and constrained. This is Byronism once more, the beginning of the malady of the age; but Byronism turned analytical, without the guts, without also the hocuspocus. His world weariness has no sense of theatre; it is not so highly coloured; it is the fatigue which makes for the abstract mind and not for poetic journalism, the sickness of the *âme sèches*.

'Je ne puis que vous plaindre', the father of Adolphe writes when he observes that, as he expected, the young man's determination to break with Ellenore is going to weaken. 'Je ne puis que vous plaindre de ce qu'avec votre esprit d'indépendance, vous faites toujours ce que vous ne voulez pas.' But lovers of independence are like that; the love of liberty is more easily come by than the will to ensure it. Constant was inured to despotism; society conspired with Madame de Staël to reduce his will. Adolphe and Constant together both lament their lack of career. And if one can think of the writer of a masterpiece as a failure, the *âme sèche* of Constant was not the sole or even the chief cause of his disorientation. It is true that Madame de Staël's party was the wrong one to belong to; but it was anyway hopeless for Constant to be a liberal democrat, full of the ideas of the Edinburgh Whigs, under an unconstitutional regime; and one can only sympathise with him when, shut out of public life where he could excel, and kept in the backwaters of scholarship and dalliance by the Napoleonic dictatorship, he should find this backwater dominated by a female of the Napoleonic species. One hesitates, of course, to call any place that Madame de Staël inhabited a backwater. Maelstrom comes nearer to her disposition. 'Storm' was his word for her (modified to *bel orage* in *Adolphe*); warming up to 'earthquake' and settling finally on 'volcano'. And not extinct, either, like that crater to which Chateaubriand's René climbed, in a famous passage, to weep for the mere matter of an hour or two. The real Romantics were men of theatrical moments; a borrower like Constant had to endure the years. He was ten years among the explosions of Madame de Staël, and even Napoleon, it is said, could not withhold a breath of congratulation when he heard she had gone to Italy where the volcano, as he pointed out, is natural to the scenery.

Constant's own solution was simply liberal constitutionalism. Marriage, he seems to suggest, was devised by society precisely for this kind of malady, i.e. the fatigue of the imagination, the discovery that when you possessed your mistress you did not love her. Cynical – but the idea had been in his mind since he was a boy of thirteen. He seems to have thought that even Madame the Volcano in full eruption would become amenable after standing at the altar. He was obeying the instinct of the male who, drowning in the passion he has unwittingly roused, seeks to appease the storm by throwing off his lifebelt.

'Scène épouvantable avec Madame de Staël. J'annonce une rupture décisive. Deuxième scène. Fureur, reconciliation impossible, départ difficile. Il faut me marier.'

Départ difficile – that sums up the diminuendo of human love. And even when it was not *épouvantable* it went on quietly nagging:

'Minette est de mauvaise humeur, parceque je ne veux pas veiller le soir. Il est clair que je serai forcé de me marier pour pouvoir me coucher de bonne heure.'

Well, he had two good goes at it and marriage was not a success.

Adolphe is the intellectual in love, beginning it all out of *amour propre* and some fashionable imitation, creating love out of his head, rejoicing in the mind's freedom, and horrified to find that the heart desires slavery. The beauty of the book is that the theme is lived and not argued; not indeed lived with the accidental paraphernalia or even the embellishment with which life mercifully obscures fundamental human problems, but with the austere serenity of abstraction. There is a little of the Romantic foliage taken from the literature of the time – the presentiments, the solitary walks, the wintry landscape and some notes in the deathbed scene are *de rigueur* – but he is not lyrical, nor does he go back to the urbane generalities of the pure eighteenth-century manner. He is something new. The lives of the lovers are singled out like two trees in the winter, their branches articulated in exact and delicate skeleton against a clear and cloudless sky.

He was restless, it was noted. He could not keep still when he was in a room. The imagination is the most quickly wearied of our faculties; it craves for more and more stimulus. After its ecstasies it leaves a void; hollowness and listlessness lie like ashes after it has burned. Presently sentiment rewarms them and the tepid souls like Constant begin to live on the imagination's memories. They are not memories of real things; but a mistress abandoned twenty years ago begins to be clothed in a glamour which, mathematically speaking, is twice the glamour of a mistress abandoned ten years ago; and twenty times the attraction of one he happens to be living with at the moment. She, poor wretch, has to deal with him, stark naked. It is a familiar perversity. The oldest of Constant's ladies, now old enough to be his grandmother, seems almost proper for the magic state of marriageability. Alas, he had left it too late. She was dead. How far back would Constant's memories have to go before he hit upon the ultimate and assuaging woman?

At that question, out of malice to all, one wants to transplant him. One always wants to do this with the early liberals. One wants to show them where it was all leading, this exaltation of life, liberty and the pursuit of autobiography. Since that time there has been only one period in which the intellectuals have had it all their own way; when imagination and experiment were to be canonised, where liberty made its last if desiccated whoopee. One leads him into the Bloomsbury of the Twenties. The Lawrence wave catches him, as Chateaubriand and *Corinne* caught him before. Presently he is thrown among the psycho-analysts. They seize him and one hears (as he describes the ever-enrichening associations of his memory) the inevitable question: 'When did you last see your mother?' He has to confess he cannot remember: it was his father who had bothered him; *she* had died at his birth. And then one hears the shrill, scientific howl as Constant at last hears the cause of his trouble, the seat of that sullen willlessness. It was the charm of living 130 years ago that the psychological novelists did not have to know what their own trouble was.

The First Detective

T he time of the year and the year itself are unknown, but one day, well
before the French Revolution, a tall, good-looking, fair-haired youth was
hanging about dejectedly on the quay at Ostend seeking for a boat which
would take him to America. Arras was his native town, but Arras could not
hold him. His energy, his vitality, his hopes demanded a larger land.
Unhappily the only boats going to America were far too expensive for him,
and he stood on the quay lonely, homesick and in despair. He was in this
state when a stranger fell into conversation with him, a stranger who
turned out to be a shipping agent and who explained that once you knew
the ropes it was the simplest thing on earth to find a ship. He, personally,
would see to it. The two men went off to an inn to discuss the matter
further. What happened after that was never quite clear to the youth.
There had been good food and drink; there appeared to have been some
'dames fort aimables' whose hospitality was of 'the antique kind' which did
not stop at the table; he even had some recollection of being in a pleasant if
rotating room and under the same eiderdown as one of the ladies. All the
more astonishing therefore to wake up in the morning and find himself
lying half-naked on a pile of ropes – the only ones he was to learn about –
with only a couple of *écus* in his pockets. A sad story and, as the innkeeper
said, he ought to be grateful that worse had not happened. But this was not
the appropriate moral. The money with which Eugène-François Vidocq
had planned to pay his fare to America had been stolen from his mother's
baker's shop in Arras. The theft was the first major enterprise – hitherto he
had only tickled pennies out of the slot in the counter with feather dipped
in glue – in a picaresque career which was to lead Eugène-François into the
French, Austrian and revolutionary armies, into the perpetual company of
criminals, all over the roads of France and into most of the prisons, until at
last, an artist in escape and quick changes, he arrived at the Sûreté in Paris
not as a convict but as its Director. To his legend as a criminal was to be

added a new legend as a detective. He was to be the first of the Big Four.

The astonishing story of the life of Vidocq can be read in two French biographies, notably one by Jagot published in 1928; a far fuller and livelier account, however, is contained in the four volumes of Vidocq's own *Mémoires* published in 1829, of which, as far as I know, no complete or reliable English translation exists. A French edition in two volumes is published by the Librairie Grund. The *Mémoires* are said not to be his own work, but, whoever wrote them, the book is enormously readable, especially the opening volume. This early narrative has the rapidity, the nonchalance, the variety and crude intrigue of the good picaresque novels; and in it Vidocq is a living man and not a mere first person singular. If he touched up his own past or if someone else touched it up for him, introducing romantic coincidences – Vidocq was always running into his ex-wife, his discarded mistresses or ill-intentioned fellow prisoners, at the least desirable moments – the story gains in romance and ingenuity.

To describe Vidocq as a great criminal is inaccurate. Rather he was a reckless, adventurous young man with a gift for trouble, a true *tête brulée*. The Revolution, the war with Austria, the amateur and professional armies of the period, were his environment; the armies were recruited, dissolved, changed sides and, in default of pay, lived by their wits. Brussels was a hive of this knavery and there Vidocq found himself posing as an officer and plotting a bigamous marriage with an elderly baroness. There is some charm in his account of how his nerve went and of how he confessed to the lady. After the Ostend episode he had avoided theft and had tried to settle down with a circus. His employer tried to make him into an acrobat and failed; the alternative was the rôle of the noble savage, but he found this uncongenial, indeed terrifying: he was expected to eat birds alive and swallow stones. His next master was a wandering quack and knave who swindled farmers and who took Vidocq back to Arras, where his adventures and an orgy of forgiveness by his parents at once made him famous. Vidocq no doubt boasted. He was a great talker and something of an actor. Soon he had mistresses all over the town, was fighting duels or assaulting those who refused to fight. He found himself at last in prison.

Here one picks up the recurring pattern of Vidocq's life. Gaoled because of one woman, he intrigues with another to get him out – going this time to the length of marriage – but once he is out, the jealousy or unfaithfulness of the rescuing lady drives him again into hiding. It is a continually repeated story. Worse than his infidelity was his lack of tact. A girl called Francine, for example, risked everything to aid his escape from one gaol; yet, such was his crassness or his ill-luck, he walked straight out of the prison gates into the arms of an old mistress and unwisely spent the night with her instead of going to the woman who had rescued him. This was too much for the faithful, or at least sacrificial, Francine. It seemed to her – and to many others – that the best way to be assured of Vidocq was to get him back to prison as soon as possible. Vidocq made no pretence to virtue and delighted in the mystery which gradually grew around his character. He had the vanity of a child. Later on he was to describe with a proper sardonic agony how, when escaping from the police in Brittany and disguised as a nun, he was obliged by a farmer and his wife to occupy the same bed as their daughters, in the interests of propriety. Such a trial by fire is the kind of thing picaresque literature enjoys.

The other element in the Vidocq pattern is his faculty for escape. Vidocq always held that his big conviction was unjust and that he was 'framed' by a fellow prisoner. To escape was therefore a matter of justice and duty. There is something moving in this very vital man's continual struggles for liberty. The fame of his escapes eclipsed whatever other notoriety he had. At Arras the disconsolate police were driven to put out the legend that he was a werewolf. One gendarme swore that, as he laid hands on him, Vidocq turned into a bale of straw.

Awaiting trial, for example, he simply picked up the coat and helmet of the guard, which had been put on a bench near by, and walked unmolested out of court. On another occasion he locked the police up in his room. Over and over again he enjoyed the comedy of leading an unsuspecting police officer on to saying what he would do with Vidocq when he caught him. Jumping out of cabs when under escort, leaving prison by a rope at the window, sawing through manacles, digging tunnels out of gaol or making his guards drunk, became a routine. In Arras, where he was very much wanted, he lived for a year disguised as an Austrian officer and neither his family, the police nor the girl he lived with, who had known him well before, discovered his true identity.

For twelve years, while he was supposedly serving a long sentence,

Vidocq was more often out of prison than in it. But it was an exhausting life; freedom was constantly menaced by blackmailing associates, and just when he seemed to have settled down happily as a draper – such was his mild ambition – he met his divorced wife and found himself keeping her and her relatives in order to shut their mouths. The worm turned. He went to the Chief of Police and made him an offer. Pardon him, leave him in peace, Vidocq said, and he would help them to capture all the criminals they desired. It cannot be said that this second period of respectable fame makes entirely comfortable reading. He delivered 'the goods' of course; no one could approach his abilities as a detective, for no one else had his knowledge of the underworld. The vanity of criminals is as inexhaustible as their love of the great figure; a burglar or assassin, however great in his own esteem, was flattered if the great and mysterious Vidocq sat down with him at the table of some shabby *marchand de vin*. Vidocq decoyed them with charm or effrontery, as the case demanded. With a rather devilish gusto he will tell how, hearing So-and-so was wanted, he would go to the house of the man's mistress, announce her man had been caught, install himself with the lady for a few days and (his own mistress aiding him) would get to know the whole gang, and, at the right moment, strike. It is a little embarrassing. The authorities themselves became embarrassed. The law never feels very happy about the *agent provocateur*.

The *Mémoires* of Vidocq are by a man who was hugely proud of his life both as a fugitive and a pursuer of fugitives. He had an eye for character and there are some admirable farces of low life such as his adventures with the drunken colonial sergeant and their riotous visits to the brothels. The dialogue is racy and real. His portraits of the innumerable 'dames fort aimables' are very vivid. He is delighted with himself as a detective. There is a search, at one period, for a house where a hunchback girl lives in a quarter which at first seems to have no hunchbacks. Hunchbacks (Vidocq reasons) are natural gossips – especially about other people's love affairs; they are jealous and also very respectable. Where do the most respectable gossips meet? At the milk shops. Disguised as a respectable man of 60 he sets out to search the most popular creameries. Sure enough a hunchback appears, a very Venus of hunchbacks, of course, a great-eyed creature like a medieval fairy. Posing as a wronged husband, Vidocq soon discovers who is living in sin in the house and so traces his victims.

[20]

One can hardly call this subtle, but the methods of Vidocq were made for the chaotic period of the Napoleonic wars and their aftermath when France swarmed with criminals. Later on, more systematic and respectable means were wanted. His day came to an end and he had the mortification of seeing another reformed criminal, his secretary, one Coco Lacour, succeed him. Coco had reformed in earnest. He had gone to the Jesuits, who made him and his wife do public penance bare-footed in the streets. A coolness existed between Vidocq and Coco. Coco was a miserable man with no air of the gentleman about him and Vidocq had pointed out that a touch more polish in his conversation as a member of the Big Four would be an advantage. (After all, Vidocq had very nearly married a baroness, a Belgian baroness it is true, but still . . .) Coco resented his lessons in etiquette. Vidocq, in his jealousy, has drawn a very funny portrait of the little reformed sinner sitting all day by the Pont Neuf fishing while, at home, his wife is doing a good trade in clothes with prostitutes.

Once out of favour Vidocq is said to have faked a robbery and then to have made arrests to show how clever he was; but the trick was discovered and the words *agent provocateur* finally doomed him. He started a paper factory which failed, a detective agency which declined into triviality. He died at last in poverty. There is one sentence in the *Mémoires* which I like to think he really wrote:

> Les voleurs de profession [it says] sont tous ceux qui volontairement ou non, ont contracté l'habitude de s'approprier le bien d'autrui.

Germinal

In the portrayal of character for its own sake and of the sociable rather than the social man, the English novelists have always excelled. The social man, the creature of ideas who must sacrifice some of his idiosyncrasy to environment, movements or theories, appears in a few exceptional books, books like *The Pilgrim's Progress*, *Gulliver*, *Jonathan Wild* and later on in *Hard Times* and *The Way of All Flesh*. Elsewhere he is to be found mostly in the background. There is emotion about society (Dickens), but there is repugnance to ideas about it. It is remarkable how little the English novel was influenced in the nineteenth century by the political and scientific thought of the time, though some passages in George Eliot and Mrs Gaskell show the novelist dealing with concrete event. Vainly we look, for example, for any sign that Darwin had been read, at any rate with an eye to the reconsideration of society. Thomas Hardy merely changes the pronoun by which one usually addresses the Deity; and at the turn of the century, Arnold Bennett performs a typical feat in importing the methods of the French naturalists, and leaving out the whole philosophical and political impulse behind that movement. This repugnance is supposed to have changed now. Yet so blankly do the alternatives of sociability and society present themselves to the English novelist that Wells thought he had to abandon character altogther. Since then there has been a good deal of talk about Marx and social realism which may be fruitful but which so far has produced next to nothing in the novel. Why, I am not sure; perhaps because we left learning about the nineteenth century too late.

How late may be seen by reading Zola's *Germinal*. It was published in 1885. I do not know whether Zola ever read Marx, though I believe that at this time he certainly had not – but he had heard of the First International; he knew the doctrines of Anarchism and its personalities; he had read Darwin. He was familiar with those Siamese twins, the idea of the struggle for life and the struggle of the classes, contests so congenial to his dramatic temperament. He saw not indeed the grey trudge of economic man, but, more picturesquely and not a little mystically – mouths. Mouths wide open, groups of mouths, kinds of mouths; for his curiously divided personality the vision became an orgy of gluttony both gross and idealised. ('Seed' and 'gluttony' are the recurring keywords of *Germinal*.) Where is the English parallel to the bad dream of *Germinal*? There is none. The religious conscience of the English novelists was certainly troubled by Darwin, their social conscience not at all. The fittest, the English middle-classes and their writers seem to have assumed, had survived.

And, to be more particular, we not only had Darwin but we had the mines. Where still is the English *Germinal*? There have been English novels about the coal-mines in the last twenty years, novels concerned with the social question. There have been talent, experience, feeling. What has been lacking? Genius, except in the abortive case of D. H. Lawrence, of course; but above all a philosophy of life which could feed the kind of genius this novel calls for. Zola dug out of nineteenth-century speculation a theatrical but also profound view of mankind. He had temperament, will and curiosity. And he had the chronic ability to write novels on a variety of very different subjects. All these qualities the English mining novelists lack.

Comparing their books with *Germinal* one sees at once that they suffer also from a fatal moral simplicity. There is the choke of the hard-luck story in their throats. And from their chief fallacy Zola is entirely free: the fallacy that people who are starved, poor and oppressed are good and noble because they are poor and oppressed. And he is also free of the rider to the fallacy: that their sufferings and struggles make them more virtuous. Zola's drawing undoubtedly exaggerated – temperament *is* exaggeration – and in the way which his period tended to exaggerate. His inverted idealism idealised the monstrous. But his nineteenth-century preoccupation with corruption and nightmare did show him that poverty may lead to degradation, that souls may become exhausted, that the moral victories of poverty may be at the cost of humanity itself. This was not, it is true, Zola's final judgment. He appears in *Germinal* to back the *bête humaine*, and to admire the brute mob because they are bestial and brutal, or rather, because he sees in them a force of nature which is overthrowing, on Darwinian lines, the weaklier types and eventually transcending them. The miners are the seed sown in the horror of the dark earth and will one day germinate and rise through the mud to free themselves and the world. So there are positive and negative poles to Zola's philosophy. In the English novels on the subject there is no similar organic conception of the nature of men. They are not tragic figures because they are never struggling with themselves. What miner in an English novel ever misbehaved, unless he was a blackleg or a labelled villain? True, he may drink or fight a bit, but that is merely toughness. He never has evil in his nature. Zola's central character and hero bashes a man's brains out. He does this because of an hereditary poison in his soul. One smiles at Zola's topical little fuss about heredity, but the case shows the difference between the pieties of the political Sunday School and the freedom of imaginative literature.

The two great things in the main outline of *Germinal* are its romantic grasp of the scene – the sustained symbolism – and the handling of groups of people. As he approaches it at night through the freezing gale, the mine appears to Etienne first of all as two points of yellow light like the eyes of a night animal; then its dragon-like form takes shape, the gasp of steam from its engine is like a monster's breathing. The monster squats on the plain; the cages whirr down full of men; up comes the coal; the mine is a monster devouring men, excreting coal. That sombre opening character is un-forgettable. One is overpowered and frightened. What a relief to meet the sardonic old night-watchman, Bonnemort, the first character, the old man whom the mine cannot kill; and then how brilliant of Zola, a master of the strategy of story-telling, to show us that the relief we found in Bonnemort is deceptive. His is no sunny face to charm the visitor with; he is – the malice of the mine itself, the shrewd grin that remains on life when it is maimed. There are the gluttony of that animal the mine, the gluttony of those animals the Hennebeaus, the owning family with their terrible, overfed daughter; and this is set against the gluttony of the miners which is very different: the rabid gluttony of the starved. Zola's poetic symbolism no doubt gets out of hand at times, especially later on when the shouting mouths of the rioters are caught by the red light of the setting sun and seem to be blotched with guzzled blood. That is a bad moment; the fresco becomes as false as a poster; but, in general, the romanticism of Zola transfigures the enormous dossier which he collected. At the end, in that terrifying chapter where the underground landslides make the mine cave in, so that the monster, which has devoured so many, is itself devoured, the

[24]

preposterous symbolism comes off because Zola has prepared the way with extraordinary technical thoroughness. The engine goes:

And then a terrible thing was seen; the engine, dislocated from its massive foundation, with broken limbs was struggling against death; it moved; it straightened its crank, its giant's knee, as though to rise: but crushed and swallowed up, it was dying.

'Its crank, its giant's knee' – fact and symbol continue their fertile marriage to the end.

Too much nightmare, it has been said. Yes, but it is a nightmare of fact not of mere eloquence. Still it must be admitted that *Germinal* destroys one's capacity to feel. At least it does that to mine. Each agony wrings the neck of its predecessor. One is broken at the end, not by feeling, but by the unremittingly documented thunderclaps of the drama. Strangely enough it is the briefly drawn soldiers, rather than the miners, who move one most. This may be because they are silent; or simply because Zola, with his genius for getting the feeling of groups of people, has got their essential passive pathos. Then that copulation! The mines appear like an erotic gymnasium, and it gets a bit dubious after the first two or three hundred acts of rutting, though Zola's invariable note of the positions adopted by lovers is as professionally pernicketty as Casanova's and is a relief after Lawrence. (Is this realism or mania? Zola's personal anxiety about impotence?) And what a lot of dangling breasts and posturing bottoms!

The real stuff of *Germinal* is the documentation and the groups of people on which the nightmare throws its strange light. This most bourgeois of all the bourgeois gave himself six months to get up the facts for *Germinal*; in that time he seems to have assimilated not merely all the technical, economic and social details of mining – see, for example, his knowledge of the structure of the pit-shaft, which becomes important in that terrific chapter when Souvarine, the anarchist, goes down alone by the ladder to saw through the beams and wreck the mine – but to have fertilised them so that they are no longer dead stuff in a notebook, but life. I do not know whether it is a defect of our novels about mining that they are written by ex-miners. Zola, who came from outside, surpasses them, perhaps because what is thoroughly and consciously conquered by force of will is enor-mously stimulating to invention. The fault of the modern novelist in general is that he does not go outside his own world for his material and I think that the decline of the power to tell a story or of the interest in doing so is due to this. Zola is an example of the value of pure curiosity. It is said that he had no natural power of observation; he relied upon learned facts, and when a piece of observation is put in to clinch a picture – the woman bringing her children to enjoy the sight of the riot, another woman stopping and re-starting her work at the sink while she quarrels, so that potato peeling goes on half the morning, the soldier blinking just before he is provoked to fire at the crowd, the comical formal politeness of the Mme Raisseneur, a real tricoteuse, as she agrees with Souvarine's bloodiest theories – it is wonderful in its effect because it is exact. Zola's ability to describe the movements of crowds is due to the fact that, unlike natural observers, he had to study crowds like a statistician and is therefore not carried away. Timid and plump, fussing with pencil and paper, Zola stands on the outskirts, noting not only the leaf-like swirl of humanity, but those single eddies, those sudden arrivals and departures of individuals, which indicate more than anything the pulse of a crowd's unreason.

One Zola believed that evil existed in all men and also that man was an amoral natural force; another Zola – the plump little professor with a halo in Forain's funny caricature – believed in man's ideal aims. This duality enables him to make the agitator, Etienne, a complete human being. *Germinal* can be read as the case against the miners as well as the case for them and, looking at Etienne, you can say on the evidence, either that here is a man exploiting the workers in his own ambition to get out of the working class; or here is an idealist who, though he sacrifices the workers in fact, is in effect leading them to their emancipation. Working-class leaders are not commonly studied with Zola's candour; they are never presented as egotists unless the novelist's object is to denounce them.

Of course, one may read *Germinal* and think that its philosophical background is as dated as the bestial conditions it describes; the mines are no longer brothels; people no longer starve at work; they starve for lack of it. War has become the crux of the social problem. But the greatness of *Germinal* lies in the exalted thoroughness of its exposure of the situation as it was during Zola's time, and equally in the mastery of its story. Its lesson to English novelists is that their education is incomplete and sterile if it does not apply itself to reinterpreting contemporary history.

Sofa and Cheroot

W hen we ask ourselves what the heroes of novels did with themselves in their spare time, a hundred to a hundred and fifty years ago, there can be no hesitation in the answer. Novel after novel confirms it, from *Tom Brown at Oxford* back to Fielding and Smollett: they stretched themselves on a sofa, lit a cheroot and picked up again *The Adventures of Gil Blas*. Once more they were on the road with that hopeful young valet from the Asturias as he went from town to town in Old Castile in the reign of Philip IV, always involved in the love affairs and the money secrets of his employers, until, a model of Self-Help, he enters the valet-keeping classes himself and becomes secretary to the Prime Minister. Say your prayers (his loving parents advised him when he set out for the University of Salamanca which he never reached, at least not to become a student), avoid bad company, and above all keep your fingers out of other people's property. Gil Blas ignored this good advice from the beginning and returned home at last to a benign retirement as a rich man and a noble. Not exactly a sinner, not exactly virtuous, Gil Blas is a kind of public statue to what we would call the main chance and to what the Spaniards call *conformidad* or accepting the world for what it is and being no better than your neighbour.

English taste has always been responsive to Le Sage; his influence on English writers and his vogue were far greater among us than they were in France. Defoe probably read him; Smollett translated and copied him. Le Sage became the intermediary between ourselves and that raw, farcical, sour, bitter picaresque literature of Spain which, for some reason, has always taken the English fancy. Gil Blas took the strong meat of the rogues' tales and made it palatable for us. He put a few clothes on the awful, goose-fleshed and pimpled carnality of Spanish realism, disguised starvation as commercial anxiety, filled the coarse vacuum, which the blatant passions of the Spaniards create around them, with the rustle and crackle of intrigue. We who live in the north feel that no man has the right to be so utterly stripped of illusions as the Spaniard seems to be; Gil Blas covered that blank and too virile nakedness, not indeed with illusions, but with a degree of elegance. It was necessary. For though the picaresque novel appealed to that practical, empirical, rule-of-thumb strain in the English mind, to that strong instinct of sympathy we have for an ingenious success story – and all picaresque novels are really unholy success stories – we have not the nervous system to stand some of the things the Spaniards can stand. What is *Lazarillo de Tormes*, the most famous of the picaresque novels, but the subject of starvation treated as farce? We could never make jokes about starvation.

Compared to the real Spanish thing, *Gil Blas* is a concoction which lacks the native vividness. It belongs to the middle period of picaresque literature when the rogue has become a good deal of the puritan. Historically this transition is extraordinarily interesting. One could not have a clearer example of the way in which the form and matter of literature are gradually fashioned by economic change in society. The literature of roguery which Le Sage burgled for the compilation of *Gil Blas* is the fruit of that economic anarchy which early capitalism introduced into Spanish life. In England the typical character of the period is the puritan; in Spain his opposite number is the man who has to live by his wits. A system has broken down, amid imperialist war and civil revolt, poverty has become general among those who rely on honest labour. There is only one way for the energetic to get their living. They can rush to the cities and especially to the Court and help themselves to the conquered wealth of the New World, to that wealth or new money which has brought poverty to the rest of the population by destroying the value of the old money. I am not sure how far economists would confirm the generalisation, but it seems that Spain used foreign conquest and the gold of the New World to stave off the introduction of private capitalism, and the parallel with Nazi policy is close. At any rate, instead of the successful trader, Spain produces the trader frustrated, in other words, the rogue.

They are, of course, both aspects of the same kind of man, and that is one of the reasons why Defoe and English literature got so much out of the picaresque novel, so that it is hard to distinguish between Defoe's diligent nonconformists and his ingenious cheats and gold-diggers. Gil Blas himself represents the mingling of the types. He is not many hours on the road before he is adroitly flattered and cheated. It is the first lesson of the young and trusting go-getter in the ways of the world. Until he gets to Madrid his career is one long list of disasters. He is captured by robbers, robbed by cocottes in the jewel racket. The hopeful young man on the road to an estimable career at the university is soon nothing but a beggar and is well on the way to becoming a knave by the time he sets up in partnership with a provincial quack doctor. Madrid really saves him from the louder kinds of crime. Intrigue is, he learns, far more remunerative. He goes from one household to another as a valet, filling his pockets as he goes. The knave has given place to the young man with an eye for a good situation and whose chief social ambition is to become a *señorito* or *petit maître*, extravagantly dressed and practising the gaudy manners of the innumerable imitators of the aristocracy. No one is more the new bourgeois than Gil Blas – especially in his great scorn for the bourgeois. And there is something very oily about him. How careful he is to worm his way into his master's confidence so that he may become a secretary and rake off small commissions or in the hope that he will be left something in the old man's will! Much later, by his attention to duty, he becomes a secretary to a Minister, and sells offices and pockets bribes. What of it? – he is no worse, he says, than the Minister himself, or the heir to the throne who has dirty money dealings all round, or those old ladies who pose as aristocrats in order to palm off their daughters on wealthy lovers. There is a sentence describing an old actress which puts Gil Blas's ambition in a nutshell. She was

> Une de ces héroïnes de galanterie qui savent plaire jusque dans leur vieillesse et qui meurent chargées des depouilles de deux ou trois générations.

'To be loaded with the spoils' – that is very different from the fate of the real *picaro* of the earlier dispensation, and Gil Blas is not entirely cynical about it. 'After all' (he seems to say, his eyes sharp with that frantic anxiety which still exercises Spaniards when there is a question of money), 'after all, I worked for it, didn't I? I served my master's interest? I'm a *sort* of honest man.' And when he decides to keep a valet of his own and interviews the applicants, there is a clarm in the way he rejects the one who has a pious face and picks out one who has been a bit of a twister too.

[29]

The character of Gil Blas himself could hardly be the attraction of Le Sage's book, and indeed he is little more than a lay figure. The pleasures of picaresque literature are like the pleasures of travel. There is continuous movement, variety of people, change of scene. The assumption that secret self-interest, secret passions, are the main motives in human conduct does not enlarge the sensibility – Le Sage came before the sensibility of the eighteenth century awakened – but it sharpens the wits, fertilises invention and enlarges gaiety. But again, the book is poor in individual characters. One must get out of one's head all expectation of a gallery of living portraits. Le Sage belonged to the earlier tradition of Molière and Jonson and foreshadowed creations like Jonathan Wild: his people are types, endeared to us because they are familiar and perennial. You get the quack, the quarrelling doctors fighting over the body of the patient, the efficient robber, the impotent old man and his young mistress, the blue-stocking, the elderly virgin on the verge of wantonness, the man of honour, the jealous man, the poet, the actress, the courtier. Each is presented vivaciously, with an eye for self-deception and the bizarre. The story of the Bishop of Granada has become the proverbial fable of the vanity of authors. And that scene in the Escorial when the Prime Minister, in order to impress the King and the Court, takes his secretary and papers out into the garden and pretends to be dictating though he is really gossiping, is delicious debunking of that rising type – the great businessman.

The pleasure of *Gil Blas* is that it just goes on and on in that clear, exact, flowing style which assimilates the sordid, the worldly, or the fantastic romance with easy precision, unstrained and unperturbed. It is the pleasure of the perfect echo, the echo of a whole literature and of a period. You are usually smiling, sometimes you even laugh out loud; then boredom comes as one incident clutches the heels of another and drags it down. No one can read the novel of adventure for adventure's sake to the end; and yet, put *Gil Blas* down for a while, and you take it up again. It is like a drug. Self-interest, the dry eye, the low opinion, the changing scene, the ingenuity of success, the hard grin of the man of the world – those touch something in our natures which, for all our romanticism and our idealism, have a weakness for the *modus vivendi*. The puritan and the rogue join hands.

[30]

A Russian Byron

Mikhail Yurevich Lermontov was born in the year before Waterloo and was killed in a duel twenty-seven years later, a year after the publication of the novel which brought him fame throughout Europe. The extraordinary duel in the last chapter but one of *A Hero of Our Time* is said to have been exactly prophetic of the manner of his death. Lermontov had declared through his chief character that life was a bad imitation of a book; and the episode, if true, looks like some carefully planned Byronic legend.

A Hero of Our Time belongs to that small and elect group of novels which portray a great typical character who resumes the fashion and idiosyncrasy of a generation. Pechorin, the 'hero', is consciously a Russian Byron. He is cold, sensual, egoistical, elegant. He is neurotic, bored and doomed. Only one passion is unexhausted – and this is the making of him – the passion for personal freedom. He is the cold, experimental amorist celebrated by Pushkin (I quote from Oliver Elton's translation of *Evgeny Onegin*):

> Men once extolled cold-blooded raking
> As the true science of love-making:
> Your own trump everywhere you blew . . .
> Such grave and serious recreation
> Beseemed old monkeys, of those days . . .

Pechorin becomes the slave of perpetual travel, and finally fulfils himself not in love but in action. Byron goes to Greece. Pechorin becomes the soldier of the Caucasus who plays with life and death. He drives himself to the limit, whether it is in the duel on the edge of the precipice down which his absurd rival in love is thrown; or in the dramatic bet with Vulich where he draws a revolver and puts sixty roubles on the doctrine of predestination; or in the final episode when he goes in alone to collar the Cossack who has run amok. In its greater actors the Byronic pose of weariness is balanced by love of living dangerously in action, and here it is interesting to contrast the character of Constant's Adolphe with a man like Pechorin. Adolphe also is the imaginative man who loves from the head and then revenges himself secretively and cruelly upon the strong-minded woman who is devouring him and with whom he is afraid to break: Pechorin, more histrionic and less sensitive (more Byronic, in short), loves from the head also but takes special care to avoid strong-minded women. He possesses, but is not possessed. He prefers the weak and yielding who respond at once to cruelty and whom he can abandon quickly. Faced with the strong-minded, Pechorin becomes a man of action and makes his getaway. Readers of *A Hero of Our Time* will remember how Pechorin dealt with the determined duplicity of Taman, the smuggler's girl, when she took him out in her boat on a moonlight night. He threw her into the sea. What would not Adolphe have given for such decisiveness? What would he not have given for that Byronic ruthlessness in action, who knew only the cool vacillations of the mind? Of the two characters, Pechorin's is the more arrested and adolescent. He has not Adolphe's sensibility to the tragedy of the imagination. He does not suffer. Pechorin is sometimes a 17-year-old sentimentalist who blames the world:

> I have entered upon this life when I have already lived it in imagination, with the result that it has become tedious and vile to me. I am like a man who has been reading the bad imitation of a book with which he has been long familiar.

But perhaps the main difference between these lovers of freedom is merely one of age after all. Pechorin-Lermontov is young: Adolphe is the creation of an older man. Pechorin says:

> Now I only want to be loved, and that by a very few women. Sometimes (terrible thought) I feel as if a lasting tie would satisfy me.

Adolphe would have been incapable of this naïve Byronic jauntiness; but he would have raised a sympathetic eyebrow at that first hint of nostalgia for respectable marriage.

This was not a solution which Russian literature was yet to permit its Pechorins. Press on to the middle of the century and we find Turgenev's Rudin, all Byronism spent, and with no exciting war of Russian

Imperialism to occupy him, conducting an affair as heartless and disgraceful as Pechorin's affair with Princess Mary and very similar to it. But Rudin is reduced to the condition of an unheroic, rootless talker with no corresponding performance. Byronism, with its roots in the Napoleonic wars, was a fashion which fortunately could give the best of its followers something to do. For the maladjusted and the doomed there were duels; even better there was always a war and the cause of Liberty. The poseur of Venice attained some dignity at Missolonghi: and the sentimentalist of the Caucasus, reviving new trouble with an old mistress, and in the midst of the old trouble with a new one, could feel the heady contagion of that half-savage passion for freedom with which his enemies, the Tartar tribesmen, were imbued.

Travel is one of the great rivals of women. The officers and visitors at the garrison town of Narzan spend their time drinking the waters, making love, scandal-mongering and playing cards; and into this gossiping frontier outpost Pechorin brings something like the preposterous coldness, austerity and violence of the mountain scene outside the town. The coach arrives, he yawns, stays a night, throws his diaries to a friend in lieu of a renewal of friendship and drives on, another Childe Harold on an eternal Grand Tour of the battle fronts. The *Hero* is not one of the calculated, constructed, and balanced books of maturity; its virtues and defects are all of youth. The book appears to pour out of the Caucasus itself. It is one of those Romantic novels in which a place and not a woman has suddenly crystallised a writer's experience and called out all his gifts. 'I was posting from Tiflis' – that opening sentence of Lermontov's classically nonchalant prose takes the heart a stride forward at once. Like the traveller, we step out of ourselves into a new world. True, it is the fashionable step back to Rousseau, for the *Hero* is nothing if not modish; but who does not feel again with Lermontov, as he gazes at the ravines, breathes the rare, crisp, savage air and sees the golden dawn on the upper snows, who does not feel the force of the Romantic emotion? 'When we get close to Nature the soul sheds all that it has artificially acquired to be what it was in its prime and probably will be again some day.' One is captivated by such a nostalgia, by its youthful and natural idealism and by the artifice of its youthful melancholy.

The structure of the book is both ingenious and careless. Later novelists would have been tempted to a full-length portrait of Pechorin. Lermontov is episodic yet tells us all we need to know in a handful of exciting short stories. We first hear of Pechorin at two removes. The narrator meets a curt, humdrum officer who has known him and who tells the first story of Pechorin's capture and abandonment of Bela, the Tartar girl. Passion has ended in boredom. In the next episode, when Pechorin meets again the officer who had helped him fight the girl's murderers, one sees the Byronic mask go up at the mere hint of the 'incident'. After that Pechorin himself describes his adventures in his diaries. They tell, with sadistic detachment, of how he is playing with the despair of an old mistress while planning to convert another woman's fear and hatred of him to love. He succeeds. Which is all Pechorin wants – a victory for his vanity. He explains this quite candidly to her. And he is candid not because he is an honest man but because, of course, he is interested only in himself. Equally coolly, he plans that the duel he fights with her lover shall take place on the famous precipice.

Pechorin's notions are not merely the melodramatic. He is the enemy of simple, highfalutin romanticism; his taste is for the reserved, the complex and mysterious. The precipice is chosen, for example, as a masterpiece of vengeance, because he has discovered that his opponent intends to fool him with blank cartridges. The opposing faction at Narzan has perceived that Pechorin's vulnerable point is his pride; knock the Byronic mask off his face and there will stand an empty actor. Lermontov is an expert in subtleties like this. In the final episode, when Vulich, the gambler, proposes to discover whether he is or is not fated to die that day, by putting a revolver to his head and pulling the trigger, the suicide is abortive. But Vulich does die that day, and in a most unexpected manner. The Calvinist doctrine of predestination in Byron's Aberdeen has become the almost exotic Oriental Kismet in Lermontov's Caucasus.

To the modern novelist, tired of the many and overdone conventions of the novel, the apparently loose and unconnected construction of *A Hero of Our Time* offers a suggestion. Lermontov's method is to thread together a string of short stories about a central character, using an inside and an outside point of view. But before he did this Lermontov had decided what were the important things in Pechorin's character. They were, as it happened, all aspects of Byronism. Mr Desmond MacCarthy has said in an essay on Pushkin that from Byron and Pushkin 'men caught the infection of being defiantly themselves'; in so planning, however, they became other than themselves. They invented a simplified *persona*. It is this simplification of Pechorin's character which is exciting. The detailed realism of the modern novel tells us far too much, without defining the little that it is absolutely essential to know. In what modern novels are the main traits of a hero of *our* own times delineated? It is the measure of the failure of modern novelists that they have not observed and defined a characteristic man of these years; and the explanation of the failure is our lack of moral and political perceptiveness. Our novels would be shorter, more readable and more important if we had one or two more ideas about our times and far fewer characters.

A Comic Novel

The modern novel has reached such a pitch of competence and shapeliness that we are shocked at the disorderliness of the masterpieces. In the modern novel we are looking at a neatly barbered suburban garden; in the standard works how often do we have the impression of bowling through the magnificent gateway of a demesne only to find the house and gardens are unfinished or are patched up anyhow, as if the owner had tired of his money in the first few weeks and after that had passed his life in a daydream of projects for ever put off. We feel the force of a great power which is never entirely spent, but which cannot be bothered to fulfil itself. In short, we are up against the carelessness, the lethargy, the enormous bad taste of genius, its liability to accident, its slovenly and majestic conceit that anything will do. *Don Quixote* falls in half, the *Chartreuse* and *Le Rouge et le Noir* go shockingly to pieces, Tolstoy stuffs a history book into *War and Peace*, Fielding and Dickens pad and Dostoevsky wanders into ideological journalism. And then there is *Dead Souls.* You reach the second part of that masterpiece to find the editor's maddening note over and over again in the text: 'Here a hiatus occurs in the manuscript.' Worse, you discover that Gogol burned the manuscript of the last part and that the full story of Chichikov, the swindler, will never be known.

Perhaps it is as well that Gogol could not pull himself together for this second plunge. The remorse of comedians is painful, and it is pitiable to see an artist rounding upon his art or mistaking his ethical impulses for his artistic ones. The kind of virtue which has been successfully fought off until middle age is apt at that time to have its dull, industrious revenge if it has been fought too hard in youth. Given the choice, it would, ideally, be better for an artist to let his egotism drive him to madness as Goya's did, than for it to become apostolic. For all we know, therefore, we should be grateful that the second part of *Dead Souls* was not completed. The loss may mean something on the same noble level as the second part of *Quixote*, but we know that Gogol was worried about his humour and that he was planning to put everything right by following the model of the *Divine Comedy*! We could perhaps pin some hope on the fabulous medieval and heroic side to Gogol's genius – the tremendous story of *Taras Bulba* is the pre-eminent example of this vein; but knowing the curious guilt which ate into the latter part of Gogol's life and the peculiarities of his conversion at the hands of a contemporary Rasputin, it looks as though the starch of religiosity was stiffening him.

'Dead Souls – no, I'll never allow such a thing', said the Russian censor, 'our soul is immortal; there is no dead soul; the author rises against immortality.' (See Janko Lavrin's useful little book on *Gogol* published fifteen years ago.) The title *is* misleading. We have had a good deal of the Russian soul in our time and the idea of a dead Russian soul is doubly sombre. I wonder how many people have put the book back on the library shelf without realising that they were rejecting one of the world's great comic novels. Chichikov is not, I think, a comic character to be compared with Pickwick or Don Quixote – he belongs rather to the line of Gil Blas, to those whose antics spring from self-interest and not from the follies of the heart. But Chichikov is a superb comic device. The originality and farce of the idea which animates him take the breath away. One is paralysed by humorous expectation. Chichikov is any carpet-bagger, any bucket-shop proprietor, any prosaic commercial traveller of distressingly commonplace ambitions, whose gift of the gab is given an extra flight by Gogol's gift of fantasy. As a fraud Chichikov is mousey, but he understands the lower side of human nature and that one of the quickest ways to the human heart is to offer it something for nothing.

It is pleasant to roll his simple scheme over the tongue again. Since the previous census in which every landowner had to give a list of the serfs or 'Souls' on his estate and on whom he had to pay head tax, a number would have died. The landowner still had to pay the tax until the next census. Why not therefore (Chichikov argued) offer to buy these dead names – for that is all they were – pay the taxes himself, and then, taking the title deeds to a bank, pose as the owner of so many thousand serfs, raise a large mortgage on an apparently thriving estate, and make a rich marriage? For a novelist one cannot imagine a more useful device for collecting a variety of human character, for farcical interviews, for spying into strange interiors and the uncovering of stranger motives. Chichikov's scheme was a passport to the whole of Russia. As a servant, Gil Blas became an expert on the habits of the Spanish aristocracy and the demi-monde; as a buffoon and victim Pickwick travelled through England; as a disinterested lunatic and comic martyr Don Quixote travelled Spain. They are all the tools of circumstance, clowns who get slapped and come to grief. But Chichikov succeeds or almost succeeds. In chapter after chapter, he is the master of every situation. The clowns are his victims. Even when disaster temporarily singes him at N——— where he has triumphed for so long, we know that he will soon cook up something new. Puzzled at first by his dimness as a person, we perceive that his deadly seriousness and touchy anxiety about his scheme are in themselves comical. He is astonished when people hesitate to take the bait. The bluffer believes in his own bluff. He has, what we often observe, the fundamental stupidity of the over-ingenious and too original mind.

Novels which have been fitted to an idea usually run to the artifices of the theatre, and there is more than a note or two from the Molière farces in Gogol's situations. In his work as a playwright Gogol in fact followed Molière, and scene after scene in *Dead Souls* would have been pounced upon by the dramatist. Take the interview with Sobakevitch, the great hairy, cunning, and bear-like man who haggles over kopecks as if he were in an Eastern *souk*. Sobakevitch seeks to put up the price of his dead serfs by saying what a wonderful blacksmith or what a brilliant saddler poor So-and-so was. He must be worth an extra five roubles because he was a good workman. The unexpected capping of one absurd situation with another in this fashion is pure theatre. The interview with the stupid widow, who is eager to sell but who suspects all the time she is being swindled and tries hard to palm off lard or corn instead, has the same theatrical quality. Gogol has seized upon the stage value of a character who is so obstinate and suspicious that she can only go on repeating the same fixed idea. Her 'What troubles me is the fact that they are dead' is another: 'Mais qu'est ce qu'il fait dans cette galère?'

'In everything the will of God, madam,' said Chichikov with a sigh. 'Against the divine wisdom it is not for us to rebel. Pray hand them over to me, Natasia Petrovna.'

'Hand over whom?'

'The dead peasants.'

'But how could I do that?'

'Quite simply. Sell them to me, and I will give you some money in exchange.'

'But how am I to sell them to you? I scarcely understand what you mean. Am I to dig them up again from the ground?'

Chichikov perceived that the old lady was altogether at sea, and that he must explain the matter; wherefore in a few words he informed her that the transfer or purchase of the souls in question would take place merely on paper – that the said souls would be listed as still alive.

'And what good would they be to you?' asked his hostess, staring at him with her eyes distended.

'That is *my* affair.'

'But they are *dead* souls.'

'Who said they were not? The mere fact of their being dead entails upon you a loss as dead as the souls, for you have to continue paying the tax upon them, whereas *my* plan is to relieve you both of the tax and of the resultant trouble. *Now* do you understand? And I will not only do as I say but also hand you over fifteen roubles per soul. Is that clear enough?'

'Yes – but I do not know,' said his hostess diffidently. 'You see, never before have I sold dead souls.'

'Quite so. It would be a surprising thing if you had. But surely you do not think that these dead souls are in the least worth keeping?'

'Oh no, indeed! Why should they be worth keeping? I am sure they are not so. The only thing which troubles me is the fact that they are *dead*.'

'She seems a truly obstinate old woman!' was Chichikov's inward comment. 'Look here, madam,' he added aloud. 'You reason well, but you are simply ruining yourself by continuing to pay the tax upon dead souls as though they were still alive.'

'Oh, good sir, do not speak of it!' the lady exclaimed. 'Three weeks ago I took a hundred and fifty roubles to the Assessor, and buttered him up, and –'

'Then you see how it is, do you not? Remember that, according to my plan, you will never again have to butter up the Assessor, seeing that it

[39]

will be I who will be paying for those peasants – I, not *you*, for I shall have taken over the dues upon them, and have transferred them to myself as so many *bona fide* serfs. Do you understand *at last*?'

However, the old lady still communed with herself. She could see that the transaction would be to her advantage, yet it was one of such a novel and unprecedented nature that she was beginning to fear lest this purchaser of souls intended to cheat her. Certainly he had come from God only knew where, and at the dead of night, too!

'Let us shake hands over it,' advised Chichikov.

'But, sir, I have never in my life sold dead folk – only living ones. Three years ago I transferred two wenches to Protopopov for a hundred roubles apiece, and he thanked me kindly, for they turned out splendid workers – able to make napkins or anything else.'

'Yes, but with the living we have nothing to do, damn it! I am asking you only about *dead* folk.'

'Yes, yes, of course. But at first sight I felt afraid lest I should be in-curring a loss – lest you should be wishing to outwit me, good sir. You see, the dead souls are worth rather more than you have offered for them.'

'See here, madam. (What a woman it is!) *How* could they be worth more? Think for yourself. They are so much loss to you – so much loss, do you understand? Take any worthless, rubbishly article you like – a piece of old rag, for example. That rag will yet fetch its price, for it can be bought for paper-making. But these dead souls are good for *nothing at all*. Can you name anything that they *are* good for?'

'True, true – they *are* good for nothing. But what troubles me is the fact that they are dead.'

'What a blockhead of a creature!' said Chichikov to himself, for he was beginning to lose patience. 'Bless her heart, I may as well be going. She has thrown me into a perfect sweat, the cursed old shrew!'

In the main – and here it is like *Gil Blas* again – *Dead Souls* is a collection of genre portraits; it is a sort of provincial social anatomy of Russia based on universal types – the foolish credulous couple whose kisses are so long that you 'could smoke a small cigar before they had finished'; the town liar, the gambler, the drunkard, the miser, the crafty man, the jack-in-office, the settled official and the soldier.

The difference between farce and humour in literature is, I suppose, that farce strums louder and louder on one string, while humour varies its note, changes its key, grows and spreads and deepens until it may indeed reach tragic depths. Gogol's humour has not only the eye for the comic particularity, the ridiculous situation, but is based on a genius for humorous generalising. His generalisations are not facetious nor strained. They convey not fantastifications of life, but the full easy feeling of life itself, as though his humour was its breath, blood and natural condition and not a spectator's witty convulsions. Gogol's gallery is short of women to whom he was in life little attached; but this lack of experience or distaste for the subject is turned very cunningly to advantage by his generalising faculty. He is describing the ladies of N———:

> . . . I should need to say a great deal about the ladies themselves and to describe in most vivid of colours their social intercourse and spiritual qualities. Yet this would be a difficult thing for me to do since, on the one hand, I should be hampered by my boundless respect for the womenfolk of all Civil Service officials, and, on the other hand – well, simply by the innate arduousness of the task. The ladies of N——— were – But no, I cannot do it. My heart has already failed me. Come, come! The ladies of N——— were distinguished for – But it's no use; somehow my pen seems to refuse to move over the paper – it seems to be weighted as with a plummet of lead. Very well. That being so I will merely say a word or two concerning the most prominent tints of the feminine pallette of N——— merely a word or two concerning the outward appearance of its ladies . . . The ladies of N——— were pre-eminently 'presentable'.

And further on:

> In addition, I may say, like most of the female world of St. Petersburg, the ladies of N——— were careful and refined in their choice of words and phrases. Never did a lady say 'I blew my nose', or 'I perspired', or 'I spat'. No, it had to be 'I relieved my nose through the expedient of wiping it with my handkerchief' and so forth. Again, to say 'This glass, or this plate, smells badly' was forbidden. Rather, the proper phrase in such a case was 'This glass, or this plate, is not behaving very well' – or

some such formula. In fact, to refine the Russian tongue the more thoroughly something like half the words in it were cut out: which circumstance necessitated very frequent recourse to the tongue of France, since the same words, if spoken in French, were another matter altogether, and one could use even blunter ones than the ones originally objected to.

(This is from D. J. Hogarth's translation in *Everyman*: Mrs Garnett's rendering, which I have not by me as I write, is, I remember, far more spirited and fluent.) Gogol's generalisations, which link up the points of action, are never flat; some touch in them, like the comic personal reluctance of the first passage or a physical phrase like 'I blew my nose', in the end gives a human relief. They are the solid residue of a detailed observation of society. Gogol has selected the bold outline and essentials from a full notebook. He is writing about a town, a body of people. He is laughing at the Russian situation of the time. The book has significance beyond its laughter and yet laughter and pity engulf that significance too. There are two very moving passages – and Gogol is always surprising the reader by his changes of mood as well as by the changes of the antics of his characters – one when Chichikov takes home the list of 'dead peasants' and studies first the manner in which each landowner has written his list, this one casually, another with precision and remarks, and then meditates, Hamlet-like, on the fates and habits of the dead serfs. This passage deepens the joke until it touches the seriousness of men's lives and directs our eyes from the laughter of the moment to the irony of eternity. The other passage is the apostrophe to Russia and her mission in the world. From Gogol onwards this nostalgia for spiritual greatness is one of the most moving things in Russian literature. We are moved by it because of the strangeness of meeting a nationalism rooted not in pride but in humility. This humility and this disinterestedness have given the Russian novel its supreme place in European literature.

Dead Souls belongs to that group of novels which most novelists dream of writing. I mean the picaresque or novel of travel, in which the episodic adventures of a single character open up the world. Given the brilliant idea the task, it seems, should be easy. Yet has there been such a novel of any quality since, say, *David Copperfield*? I can think of none. It seems that the appearance of the picaresque literature depends on the existence of disorder in society. In *Pickwick*, we remember, 'boilers were busting and the minds of coachmen were unsettled'; in the Spain of Cervantes, the new gold wealth of the Spanish Empire had destroyed the value of money and had brought misery. In the Russia of *Dead Souls* tyranny was struggling to hold down the unrest of hope and vision which had followed the Napoleonic wars. What is necessary to this kind of novelist is a time of lethargy, cynicism and low comedy, a time when romantic idealism would be thwarted and when wry laughter at the roguery and fatuousness of people would be the only outlet. Our own society has been too prosperous for this kind of book, for a prosperous society is without humour or pity. Is that an explanation of the decline in the picaresque novel? Or is it simply that the kind has been done too often and is now exhausted?

A Hero of Our Time

In the February of 1848 Turgenev left Brussels for Paris where he joined Bakunin. They had come to see a revolution. Five months later, namely in the sultry afternoon of the 26th of July, Turgenev was out in the streets watching the Revolution collapse. He watched, he noted, he deplored. When it was over he did not, for all his love of Liberty, share that sense of personal tragedy which overcame the Herzen circle. Herzen wished now that he had taken a rifle which a workman had offered him and had died upon the barricades. 'I would then', he said, 'have taken with me to the grave one or two beliefs.' But Turgenev, who believed in 'the homeopathy of science and education', shrugged his shoulders. 'What is history, then? Providence, chance, irony or fatality?' he asked Pauline Viardot. He paid Bakunin his allowance, he made jokes to break the gloom of the Herzen household. The dogmas and violence of active politicians had little attraction for Turgenev though he liked to think that his *Sportsman's Sketches* had popularised the idea of freeing the serfs in Russian society.

But it was impossible in that decade for a Russian writer to escape from politics, and seven years later, when his lethargic nature stirred and he sat down to write his first political novel, Turgenev turned again to those sultry days in Paris. Always in doubt about his characters, subject to all the waverings of sensibility, running round to his friends for advice because he had no confidence in his own judgment, Turgenev managed, at last, and like a naturalist, to pin his hero to the paper. In his memory Turgenev saw once more the Faubourg St Antoine, the barricades and the broken revolutionaries dribbling away from them in furtive groups. As a line battalion came up and the last workmen ran for their lives, he imagined a solitary figure rising up on the barricade. He was 'a tall man in an old overcoat, with a red sash and a straw hat on his grey, dishevelled hair. In one hand he held a red flag, in the other a blunt curved sabre, and as he scrambled up he shouted something in a shrill, strained voice, waving his flag and sabre. A Viennese shooter took aim at him – fired.' The tall man fell with a bullet in his heart.

'"Tiens!"' said one of the escaping revolutionaries to another, '"on vient de tuer le polonais."' So, with an ineptitude for his epitaph, died the Russian Dimitri Rudin. He had died, cutting a figure on a foreign barricade for a cause not his own, futile to the end.

I first read *Rudin* during the Spanish Civil War. It was a good moment. For years we had been talking about the problem of the intellectual for whom society has no use – that is to say we had been talking about all the English intellectuals who had grown up since 1914 – for years we had argued the reasons for this isolation, its effects upon their minds and had speculated upon their future. The figure of Rudin seemed to crystallise the case. And when one more angry friend from Bloomsbury packed up his books and his chequered love affairs and went out to be killed in the Spanish war, we could picture the scene at once and swear we heard some Spanish soldier revise Rudin's insulting epitaph once more, with a 'God, they've killed the German'. The English have always been Germans in Spain.

It was thought at first that Bakunin had been Turgenev's model for Rudin, and Turgenev encouraged the belief; but Herzen observed that there was a good deal of Turgenev himself in this minor Hamlet. In fact, Rudin was drawn from several models. He was Bakunin on the barricades and luckier than his original in dying there; he was any gifted young Russian whom political tyranny at home had reduced to futility: and he was Turgenev in love. Perhaps Turgenev was getting the Bakunin family out of his system and all the philosophy of his German period too, for there are unflattering resemblances between Turgenev's affair with Bakunin's sister and Rudin's cold-hearted experiments with the heart of Natalya. There are really two Rudins in the book and the critic must decide for himself whether he is dealing with two irreconcilable beings, the idealist and the cad, or whether Turgenev is showing an eye for the variety and inconsistency of human nature. One thing is plain, as it always is when social types are analysed in fiction, that Turgenev had a theory. We must not ask why Rudin appeared in Russia, one of the characters says, one must merely examine him; but Turgenev leaves one in little doubt about the social and political reasons for his existence.

It is often assumed that tyranny can conquer everything except the intelligence, but the briefest glance at history shows that this residue of optimism is without foundation. The aim and effect of tyranny is to break up the normal social relations between people and to ensure that the only permitted social relationship shall be with the tyrant. Our duty is not to our neighbour, but to the leader, the tyrant, the ruling oligarchy, and this duty isolates us from each other whether we think of ourselves as individuals or as groups. Once isolated like this the mind degenerates, faculties stray and purpose falls to pieces. Upon the intelligence the effect is immediate, for the intellectual man, who seems to be so independent of the mass of mankind because of his brains, in fact needs the moral background of normal social relations more strongly than anyone else. Without them he is like a sculptor who, deprived of stone, is obliged to carve in the air. We see this plainly enough in the lives of the exiles from German and Italian fascism; we shall see it again if we consider the isolation of the English intellectuals in the Big Business tyranny which impoverished the material, spiritual and intellectual life of England in the years leading up to the present war. There was a choice between two evils: the futility of exile, the futility of a life at home which had been carefully unco-ordinated. In the Russia of the Forties despotism had driven the active into exile; those who would not or could not leave were obliged to preserve their ideas in a vacuum or to while away their time on mere personal speculation which grew more and more esoteric.

When Rudin arrives at Darya Mihailovna's country house, he is a man of 35. He is shy at first, sizing up his company. Soon he is drawn into argument with one of those strutting, professional sceptics who hide a general lack of information under the disguise of being plain, downright fellows who say, 'To hell with principles, give me the facts'. Rudin-Turgenev has not been a philosopher for nothing; he wipes the floor with this eccentric. Rudin's polish, his heart and his eloquence arouse a generous response in the company and in the reader. We are delighted with him. But he stays on with Darya Mihailovna, and as he stays we get to know him better. A longer acquaintance does not confirm the first favourable impression. Those glorious words of Rudin's, for example, were not his own; that passionate idealism has no recognisable earthly objective. He can settle to nothing. The enthusiasm which would be admirable in a man of 20 is suspect in a man of 35 who ought to have built up some stability. Bassistov, the young tutor, cries out that Rudin is a natural genius. 'Genius very likely he has,' replies Lezhnyov, 'but as for being natural – that's just his misfortune, that there's nothing natural in him . . .' He is a mere oracle of the boudoir and a fake.

In the next phase Turgenev strikes nearer home: Rudin is far too expert in the egoism of romantic love. He knows the whole keyboard from the evocation of 'pure souls' to the effectiveness of a melancholy hint at incurable fate:

> 'Look,' began Rudin with a gesture towards the window, 'do you see that apple tree? It is broken by the weight and abundance of its own fruit. True emblem of genius.'

Rudin is as cold as ice and he will do nothing unless his vanity is aroused; then he behaves like a pompous and meddlesome idiot and discovers he has done so half an hour too late. For he is introspective. Philosophy – we have exchanged it for psycho-analysis – has got into his blood and he is interested only in the doomed course of his own development. And this coldness of Rudin which leads him skilfully to awaken the feeling of inexperienced women and particularly those very young ones whose feeling is maternal, and then to take fright before their dullness, is of long standing. He had been too much adored by his mother.

The Rudin of our generation would have had more to say about this mother. The Russian Rudin says little or nothing, and Turgenev tells only that the cold youth dropped her, as he dropped all his friends. Did he hate her? Turgenev does not say. That field, so fruitful to our contemporaries, is neglected. We know simply that Rudin's lack of means and career is an excellent excuse for running away from marriage, and we can only guess at a deeper dread of reproducing the pattern that made him. Rudin is homeless politically and emotionally, and if he *had* had a career and a place in society, he would have had to retreat into more complex justifications – as nowadays the Rudin in us does.

But if he tortures others Rudin tortures himself, too. After the affair with Natalya, there is an interlude of desperate farce. Philosophy (to which he has retired) tells him he should allow himself to fall really in love and so wipe out his guilt, and in Germany he tries out a passion to order with a

French dressmaker. Alas, the old Adam remains. Seated in a boat Rudin gazes at the lady, pats her gently on the head – and tells her he feels like a father to her. He had been a brother to Natalya.

And now Rudin is nothing but a cad, Turgenev makes his severest critic, the mature and decent Lezhnyov, take everything back. This is the most exciting point in the novel. This new Rudin is not as vivid as the old one, he has the weakness – perhaps it is due to Turgenev's old-fashioned, hearsay technique as a story-teller – of being a point of view and an afterthought. But a warmth *is* put into the old outline and the figure is at last taken out of the psychologist's bottle and related to his environment:

> He has enthusiasm; and believe me, who am a phlegmatic person enough, that is the most precious quality of our times. We have all become insufferably reasonable, indifferent and slothful; we are asleep and cold, and thanks to anyone who will wake us up and warm us . . . He is not an actor, as I called him, nor a cheat, nor a scoundrel; he lives at other people's expense, not like a swindler, but like a child . . .

(Herzen had said almost these very words of Bakunin.)

> Who has the right to say that he has not been of use? That his words have not scattered good seeds in young hearts, to whom nature has denied, as she has to him, power for action and the faculty of carrying out their ideas?

This is all very nice, and Bassistov, for the younger generation, cries out, 'Bravo!' But is it nature that has denied Rudin the power for action? We come nearer truth (and nearer today) as Lezhnyov proceeds:

> Rudin's misfortune is that he does not understand Russia, and that, certainly, is a great misfortune. Russia can do without every one of us, but not one of us can do without her. Woe to him who thinks he can, and woe two-fold to him who actually does do without her! Cosmopolitanism is all twaddle, the cosmopolitan is a nonentity; without nationality is no art, nor truth, nor life, nor anything . . . It would take us too far if we tried to trace Rudin's origin among us.

It was not Rudin's fault that 1848 was not 1917. It was to his credit that he half-killed himself and his wretched companion when they went 'up to the river in the province of K.', with the hare-brained scheme of making it navigable, several generations before the Five Year Plan gave intelligent men something to do. Rudin not only sowed the seed, but with some courage he accepted the knowledge of foredoomed failure, the destiny and the ridicule that watches over the sower who cannot hope to reap. Mean in his egoism, he was not mean in his imagination.

Turgenev considered the figure of Rudin from an uneasy seat on the liberal fence. By nature timid and hesitant, he resisted the notion of dramatic choice. And we must remember, too, that he wrote of Rudin when there was no flush of belief in Europe. He was writing in 1855, seven years after the 'Viennese shooter' had taken aim, in the lethargy of disillusion. When Herzen's conversion to communism was complete Turgenev broke with him.

Faits Divers

=====

I have been reading Dostoevsky again: *The Possessed.* You know the sensation. You are sitting by the fire reflecting that one of the things which reconciles you to life, even at its most tragic, is the low clear daily monotone of its voice. Suddenly comes a knock at the door, there are cries. A man has been murdered at a house down the street. Dostoevsky again. Dostoevsky, 'the great sinner', the great literary murderer. You put on your thickest coat and go out. What a fog! What a melodramatic fog. You can see nothing. Such is the impression as one turns to those tortured novels again. But there's obviously a crowd somewhere down the road, you can hear voices, people go rushing by. Who is it this time? Shatov, you hear, the student, the ex-radical, the believer in the Russian Christ. Good heavens! There was no one more serious, more honest, more likeable than Shatov; rather difficult in argument because he had never got over a sort of angry awkwardness about his class. He was tongue-tied and shy one moment, violently angry the next. His anger soon passed, however, and then he smiled repentantly. There was absolutely no malice in Shatov. You hurry down the street, still seeing nothing. Shapes move about. They may be human. You call to them and they gesticulate but you can't hear what they're saying. Presently you make a disconcerting discovery, that you are in something like one of Kafka's nightmares; you are walking and yet making no progress. You begin to wonder which street you're in. People bump into you and don't answer questions. No one in Dostoevsky ever answers questions. You just detect a scowling face which shouts at you. This one (he says he's an engineer), shouts that he is going to commit suicide. It is necessary to commit suicide to show that he has overcome fear of pain and the beyond. When he has done this he will be God, the Man-God, the superman. He vanishes. A girl shape stands dumbly in front of you; she desires, you gather, to suffer. Which way to the murder? you ask. No answer. Terrible complications. The air full of the sounds of people talking. A drunken captain is beating his daughter and quoting poetry. You turn a corner and there is a young nobleman, handsome, cultivated, thoughtful, and what is he doing? He's biting the Governor's ear. And still, as in one of those anxiety dreams, your feet stick to the pavement, you make enormous, concentrated efforts of will, and you move about an inch instead of a yard. The fog chokes. 'Russia, the God-fearing nation,' someone shouts. 'Let us start an illegal printing press,' a girl says. 'Destroy everything', come other voices, 'and then a new man will be born, a new society, harmonious, communistic, brotherly.' Or 'Russia's mission is to save the world'. And another voice, 'Russia must save Germany first from the catastrophe which is coming inevitably in the West.' And what is the catastrophe? 'Socialism! Socialism is the despotism of materialism, the ally of the Roman Catholic Church in the destruction of the soul.' You struggle towards that voice only to be pulled in the opposite direction by another. 'Christianity, communism, through the People and the purification of the heart.' At this moment you very nearly fall over a man who is on his knees before a woman, abased, weak and weeping; she is pulling his hair out. 'Love-hate,' they are murmuring. 'Who', you ask, 'are all these people, all these voices?' A moan comes from the man: 'Relations,' he says, 'everyone has brought his relations.'

And then, the tension of the nightmare slackens, the fog clears and along come a middle-aged couple and you laugh for the first time. The humour in Dostoevsky always clears the fog. They are quarrelling, of course. The man is talking all the time. 'Chère amie,' he says, as she gives him a violent push to make him shut up. Scholarly, noble-looking, vague and slopping a glass of champagne, Stepan Trofimovitch is straying and tottering along, pouring out epigrams, tag ends of French and cultural chit-chat. He will stop to make a speech about his dangerous political past and is alarmed the moment afterwards lest a spy has heard him or, worse still, in case someone lets on that he has no political past whatever and certainly no political future. And behind him comes Varvara Petrovna, twenty years his protector and his 'amie' but only in the sense that he used to smoke a cigar under the lilac tree with her in the evenings. A female rolling-pin, a torment and manager, dusting him, cleaning him up, mocking his feeble-ness, rating him about his gambling debts, but paying them, awed by his brains. For the last twenty years he has talked of beginning his great book.

[51]

But there are the club, his cards, the perpetual apprehension of what Varvara Petrovna will do next. He must leave her; he can't leave her. Varvara Petrovna is another Madame de Staël whacking into her pet, Benjamin Constant. She pushes her tame intellectual and toy liberal along.

Man was born free, but not necessarily born with will or cash. What does man achieve? Nothing, except habits. On top of everything, Stepan has been married so many times. It is years since he has seen his son. How terrible the separation of father and son – and yet, just as well, for Stepan Trofimovitch has never been quite straight about money. So he goes on, speaking French, weeping, evading, making noble gestures, cheating, scenting his handkerchief, making 'final stands' about the intrigues of Varvara Petrovna – though not in her presence – while she, the masterful *intrigante*, frankly tells him he's a fool and that she's going to send a servant round to clean up, and then marry him off.

The nightmare, of course, again intercepts that comic intrigue. The fog comes down once more. But you have been distracted from the suicides, ear-biters, daughter-beaters and ideological murderers. As you grope once more it is the figure of Stepan Trofimovitch you seek, the bold voice of Varvara Petrovna you long to hear. He is in love and hates her, but with *them* the love-hate is nostalgia and comedy. And then the nightmare affects Stepan Trofimovitch, too. He *does*, to his own astonishment, make a 'last stand'. He walks out of the house. He is like that. He will take to the road. They said he had not the will to do anything for an idea! That his idealism was a fraud! He goes forth as exalted as Don Quixote (though far more rattled), follows a cow which is following some peasants, flabbergasts them by talking French, picks up with a Bible-seller, and rambles away, tragically, comically, but far from ignobly, to his death. Vanity is a friend to him to the end; it enables him to humbug on the very brink of eternity (this time about the Sacrament) and prevents him from realising he is dying. It is he who explains the whole nightmare to you, all that fog, talk, intrigue, violence; who all these people are. They are 'The Possessed', 'the devils', and with the detachment of a well-stocked intellect he announces half-nobly, half-cynically, that 'he and everyone else in Russian politics are the Gadarene swine of Russia which must all be cleared out and driven to the sea, so that the wonderful new future may be born'.

[52]

The Possessed is a novel which contains one of the great comic characters of all literature; and the first 150 pages contain the best writing in Dostoevsky's surprising comic vein. Lytton Strachey was the first to point out the individuality and importance of Dostoevsky's humour. It steadies those toppling and seemingly intoxicated monuments. Critics usually refer to this gift as satirical, but as Lytton Strachey said, the humour is not cruel. If it begins cruelly it grows, deepens and broadens into the humour of loving-kindness. But there are other reasons for reading *The Possessed*. It is a political novel which – though many of its premises are derived from inaccurate information – deals prophetically with some of the political issues of our time. Tolstoy, not very sensitive in his old age, once said to Gorky that Dostoevsky ought to have been a Buddhist; and Gorky said of Dostoevsky that 'you could tell a petit-bourgeois as surely as you could tell a goat'. These are amusing examples of a criticism which seems to be passing out of fashion now that the fanatical Freudians and the narrower kind of Marxist have discovered that they were not really interested in literature. The only proper general political criticism of Dostoevsky is, as a recent American critic, Mr Ernest Simmons, has said, that he expresses the confusion in Russian middle-class thought at the time, its ideals, its apprehension, its practice. We see the psychological discoveries of Dostoevsky in better perspective when we remember that Constant and many others had written more precisely about the ambivalence of human character. We cool down when we reflect that the Self-Willed Man, the meek and the famous 'doubles of Dostoevsky', are the fruits of the romantic movement which came to Russia late.

From the letters, diaries and notes of Dostoevsky which have been made available in Russia since the Revolution, the curious reader may discover that the fog he had been groping through is nothing to the personal fog in which Dostoevsky worked. (I recommend anyone interested in the intimate processes of literary creation to read Ernest Simmons's *Dostoevski: The Making of a Novelist*.*) The main character types are repeated with growing emphasis from novel to novel, but they emerge from a nightmare of rough drafts and notes. Dostoevsky worked in the greatest uncertainty and indecision. He was one of those writers who, having for a long time no

*John Lehmann, London, 1950.

clear and fixed idea of his intention, was obliged to lash himself into action by pious ejaculations. He worked, so to speak, on a stage, before an audience, delightfully unaware that there was something comic in his vociferations.

'I am planning' (when was he not 'planning'?) 'a huge novel' (they were always going to be 'huge' and transcendental) 'to be called *Atheism* – for God's sake between ourselves.'

The touch of persecution mania is part of the show. Then: 'the hero falls to the very depths of self-abasement and in the end he returns to find both Christ and the Russian soul. For God's sake do not tell anyone.' Tortured as the reader of the novels may be, lost in the wilderness of a dialogue which has eliminated none of the drooling and rambling of humanity's eternal tongue-wagging, worried by the involutions of the plot and the fact that no character seems to be able to appear without half his family and without at least one family skeleton, he is nevertheless far more certain than Dostoevsky himself was as he struggled at his desk. He chops and changes his characters and events. He has constantly to write down the theme of his novel again in order to remind himself of what he is doing; and the theme is always drifting off its course. The change has been noted in *Crime and Punishment*: Raskolnikov was intended to commit suicide. Ivan was thought of as the murderer of Karamazov. If Dostoevsky's life was a search for God, his novels are a search for a method. The higher synthesis which he laboured after and retreated from in religion, only to labour after it again, plagued him too in the art of writing. The thing that strikes one in Dostoevsky's novels is how, both in their ideas and their method of presentation, they convey the struggle, the search for something to be born, the longing to assume a shape. But perhaps it is not a longing for form. Perhaps the profound longing of Dostoevsky is to decide nothing for himself, but to be dominated. It is significant that a formal Westernised writer like Turgenev is hated, and that when Dostoevsky looks beyond Russia, his eye stops at Germany. That domineering race has attractive wastes of primitive myth behind the façade of its culture; and when the great catastrophe comes Russia, he says, will save Germany from the West and Germany and Russia will save the world. It is curious that the Nazis did not make use of Dostoevsky's mysticism, though it goes really far beyond nationalism into mysticism. The race myth is there:

'If a great people [Shatov cries in *The Possessed*] does not believe that the truth is to be found in it alone (in itself alone and exclusively in itself), if it does not believe that it alone is fit and destined to raise up and save all by its truth, it at once ceases to be a great nation, and at once turns into ethnographical material and not into a great people. A truly great people can never reconcile itself with a secondary rôle in humanity or even with the first, but without fail must exclusively play the first rôle. A nation which loses this belief ceases to be a nation.

The Russians are, in fact – God-bearing!

It is useless to try and disentangle the confusions from the subtleties of Dostoevsky's thought. The great prophets are always playing for both sides. And then Dostoevsky is a Victorian journalist. There is always a less exalted strain of compromise running through Dostoevsky's life, a sort of left-handed self-interest such as makes the comedy of Stepan Trofimovitch's character. There is frequently something disconcertingly practical if not disingenuous about the mystics. Ideologically, Dostoevsky is often in a panic. Yet, there are two perennial kinds of revolutionary thought; there is the political revolutionary who arises to change man by changing society, the religious who arises to change society by changing man. Dostoevsky is brought nearer to us also because the catastrophe has come, the problem of suffering has become real; and if we cannot believe in the absolute value of suffering, any more than Dostoevsky entirely did, it is arresting when we cry out egotistically against injustice to be reminded, as Zosima reminded Ivan Karamazov, of guilt.

Dostoevsky was a spiritual sensationalist, a man of God somewhat stained with the printing ink of the late night final. He lives at first in the upper air as he plans his novels, and gradually comes down to earth, still undetermined until he is pulled up – by what? 'Ordinary' life? No, a newspaper cutting. What a passion he has for the newspapers! What significance things had once they were in headlines! The report of the Nechaev affair clinches *The Possessed,* a *cause célèbre* sets the idea of *The Idiot* in motion. These court cases pinned down his restless mind. Early in *The Possessed* Liza asks Shatov to help her compile an annual collection of newspaper cuttings of all the court cases, trials, speeches, incidents and so on, the child-beatings, thefts, accidents, will-suits, etc., which would serve to give a real picture of the Russian situation year by year. Dostoevsky must often have longed for a book like that on his desk. For ordinary people were lost in an anonymity which thwarted the romantic temperament. In the *faits divers* they were transformed; give him the evidence and the process of mystification could begin. The *faits divers* could become the *faits universels.*

The Clown

For the civilised reader the psychological novel has been a most fascinating and flattering mirror, and egoism the delightful subject *par excellence*. But from Constant to Joyce and Proust the analysis of motive or of sensation has suffered from scientific priggishness and preciosity. Humour, in the sense of forgiveness, has not been the dominant trait. There is excellent humorous writing in Proust and Joyce, but the sustained note of those writers does not come from the dry, skipping, fiddle-strings of the comedians and buffoons. On the contrary, pitiless diagnosis is the note of Proust; and Joyce is driven on, not by laughter, but by a dishevelled hatred of the root of life. Disappointment and frustration seem to be inherent in the psychological approach, no doubt because the assumption that we stand alone is fallacious. And in the novelists who have isolated themselves or their subjects, we cannot but observe that the analysis of character or sensation tends to degenerate into the desiccation of character; the surgery upon motives turns into a medical search for the diseased and monstrous ones.

To those who are in danger of reacting too violently against the great botanists of our hidden flora, I recommend the cure offered by the works of Italo Svevo. Here is laughter at last. Here Hamlet raises a smile, Oedipus is teased away from his fate like some figure of light opera, the *malade imaginaire* of the fag-end of the Romantic movement is made to get out of bed and run about in his pyjamas. The absurdities of life rescue us from the illusions of the intellect, from the grim stepmotherdom of our egoism and our brains. I do not mean that Svevo is a mere joker. He is far from that. He is no less sensitive or subtle in the elucidation of our feelings than the great botanists. The advantage of his laughter is that it makes his science humane and prevents his intelligence from dragging up our moral roots. And this is a point of huge importance to the development of the psychological novel. Over and over again we feel in such novels that the novelist is too knowingly superior to his people, his intelligence is too penetrating for the muddle of human nature. We suspect the sin of pride. That sin is entirely absent from the work of Svevo. He is the first of the psychological novelists to be beatified by a spirit of humility which recalls the battered but serene humility of *Don Quixote*, the humility of the comic tradition.

Very little is known in England about the life of Italo Svevo. Such information as we have comes from the introductions to his novels which were translated in the late Twenties, and from the brother of James Joyce, who knew him well in Trieste. Joyce is said to have put something of Svevo into the portrait of Leopold Bloom. Svevo's real name was Ettore Schmitz; he was born in 1861 and died in 1928. He lived most of his life in Trieste and was half-Italian, half-Austrian by origin. At the age of 32 he published his first novel, *Una Vita*, which was well received; five years later another novel, entitled *Senilità*, which was totally ignored. The fact that Svevo wrote in an Italian speckled by the impurities of the Trentino dialect was against him. He gave up literature for a business career in which he was very successful. Not until he was in his sixties did he write *La Coscienza di Zeno* (In English, *The Confessions of Zeno*), his most remarkable work, which he is said to have dashed off in a fortnight. The writing of this book and the fame it brought to Svevo owe something to the encouragement of Joyce, who, as a teacher of English in Trieste, had by chance been engaged by the business man to teach him our language. In his life the epicurean Svevo seems to have been robust, genial, solid, successful and urbane, the complete antithesis of the stoic Zeno, the brilliant, erratic hypochondriac, who is palmed off with marvellous skill as a self-portrait in *The Confessions*. Zeno was the hidden artist, an agile piece of mystification by an expert in loquacity. One can see a clue to the link between the solid Schmitz and the restless, forever enquiring and ever-deluded egoism of Zeno in the fact of Svevo's divided birth. He was one of the frontier people of Europe, of divided temperament, and was therefore perfectly fitted for the analytical passion in which one part of our nature sits on the fence and observes the other.

Senilità is itself not a very original book. It is the usual *étude de mœurs* on the favourite Latin theme of the *p'tite maîtresse*, the working-class girl who can be kept cheaply. The interest of the story lies in the humility of Svevo before his characters, in a studied naïvety which foreshadows the manner of Kafka in the use of the method of unconscious revelation, i.e. of letting the psyche expose itself, and, finally, in Svevo's gift of writing epitaphs upon human feeling: 'The thought of death is like an attribute of the body, a physical malady. Our will can neither summon it nor drive it away.' The underlying subject of *Senilità* is illness – that is to say, the senility or second childishness of the illusions we live by, and this hidden subject gives the commonplace story its peculiar double plot.

But when *Zeno* was written, thirty years later, it was totally original and mature and, like *Adolphe*, contained the essence of a lifetime. Throwing chronology away, Svevo writes an autobiographical novel divided into subjects. The book is split up into reminiscent essays on his father, his marriage, his mistress and his business partnership, and, naturally, many of the episodes are concurrent. This unconventional method has the attractive carelessness of conversation. Moreover, the story is held to-gether by an amusing framework. Zeno writes in order to debunk his psycho-analyst. According to his analyst, all Zeno's troubles – his trouble-some love of his wife's sister, his hypochondria, his will-lessness, his nervous crises, his mad, restless brainwaves, heroic moral illusions, and his suspicions – are all due to the Oedipus complex. Zeno sets out to show life slipping like an eel through the stiff hands of this theory. At the end of the book he gives up psycho-analysis because, by chance, he runs across a doctor who tells him that his real disease is diabetes. Zeno is delighted. A régime at last, a new theory, a new order, the solution of all his problems! His wife remarks:

'My poor dear Zeno, you have talked so much during your life about illnesses that sooner or later you were bound to get one.' And she overwhelmed me with tenderness.

However, neither Freud nor diabetes saves Zeno in the end. Obliged by the death and debts of his partner to attend seriously to his business, Zeno is saved by work. The intellectual is a natural gambler. He slaves (successfully) on the Bourse.

On its formal side Svevo's originality springs from high spirits, from sheer wit and brain, such as are found in a comedy of Beaumarchais or Sheridan. When we turn to his matter, we see that Svevo belongs to that rare number of novelists – almost non-existent in modern literature – who like their characters and side with them instead of destroying them piecemeal. And in Zeno, Svevo is engaged in liking the kind of character who is most vulnerable to disapproval. For Zeno is the egoist of all the egoists. How Meredith would have detached the pomposity and complacency from that ubiquitous first person singular! Zeno is in love with explanation. He is perpetually button-holing and explaining. He would have been the supreme café bore of Trieste. Now he is fantasticating about his struggles to give up smoking; now he is being unguardedly complacent about his wife, his ideals as a seducer, his mental superiority to his more experienced business partner, and so on. But Zeno has one saving virtue; he never believes his own self-justifications. Zeno is just as happy when he is grotesquely wrong as when he is accidentally right. He is always on the damaging and humbling search for truth. Under the café gabble of Zeno's enthusiastic tongue there lies a personal humility and tenderness, an exquisite ear for the true tune of human living, an unshockable wonder at each transient mystery of our feelings. Zeno *appears* to be a weak and vacillating mad-hatter – and obtuse critics have attacked the figure of Zeno as an example of the neurotic bourgeois who suffers from a kind of intellectual diarrhœa – but, in fact, the abiding impression he leaves is one of moral gravity.

The exaggerations which spring from the tradition of Italian farce are the making of *The Confessions of Zeno*. The absurd is trained upon the serious in order to awaken our emotions from the conventional turgidity into which they habitually settle. Two episodes illustrate the macabre and disturbing effect of Svevo's use of bizarre incident. The first occurs in the very moving and faithful account of the death of Zeno's father. As usual, Zeno is overwrought, his emotions have got beyond him. In his love for the dying father with whom he has nothing in common, Zeno is quarrelling with everyone at the sick-bed. With the scorn of youth, he has always regarded his father as a weak man; but at the moment of dying the old man rises in his bed as if he is going at last to reveal the mystery of life and death to his son and to embrace him; instead, the old man inadvertently hits him a blow on the cheek and dies. It is unexpected, it is ridiculous, it is terrifying. Literature abounds in deathbed scenes. To this one Svevo has given a particularity which is memorable, not only because it is eccentric, but because its effect on Zeno's character is shown with real perspicacity. From that moment Zeno's haunting illusion of weakness is dated. It is as illusory, of course, as his earlier illusion of being stronger than his father.

The second episode is more truly farcical, and not macabre at all. Svevo is again observing how life does not play up to conventional emotion, nor indeed to any theory at all. Guido, Zeno's partner and brother-in-law, has died. Zeno has always disapproved of him because Guido was a chronic womaniser, but chiefly because Guido had married the sister whom Zeno had once wished to marry. Zeno could never in consequence be sure of the honesty of his disapproval, as indeed he could never be sure of anything in his life. But, obviously, now Guido was dead, the tangle had been cut. Moreover, to show that he was really devoted to Guido, Zeno slaves day after day at the office until the very hour of the funeral, in order to clear up the shady financial mess in which Guido had left his affairs and so preserve Guido's good name. Give Zeno an illusion to preserve and he works for it with the fever of a lover. And then, when he is exhausted, Zeno suddenly remembers the funeral. He dashes out, hires a cab and begins a frantic search of the city for the funeral procession. His sister-in-law, whom he has always loved, will never forgive him if he fails to turn up at the funeral. At last the procession is found. The cab joins it and Zeno and his clerk sit back and relax to talk about the Bourse. Thank heaven. They are doing the conventional thing, for Zeno, like so many of the aberrated, has a longing for the conventional. And then they discover they are in the Greek cemetery. Guido was a Catholic. Obviously, they have followed the wrong funeral.

Four books by Svevo are available in English and are admirably translated by Beryl de Zoete. They include two collections of short stories which suffer from being brief restatements of the longer books. They are *The Hoax* and *The Nice Old Man and the Pretty Girl.* I find the Svevo of the short stories too playfully charming and serene, though *The Hoax* does define his quality:

> . . . a humble life, endowed with a kind of strength that comes from absolute surrender . . .

Svevo sees our lives hanging in suspense from minute to minute; we appear, as we must do to the psychologist, to be in continual process of disintegration. And yet, surveying the scene again in longer stretches of time, there is, under the breathless chasing of illusions, a process of reintegration, too. The fool becomes the strong man, the younger son marries the ugly sister, who turns out to be the beautiful princess. And the business man of Trieste, ignored by literary society, is avenged by the brilliant, serious and hypochondriacal clown.

The Nobodies

If my guess is right, this year or next is the centenary of Mr Pooter and maybe of Mr Padge, Mr Gowing and Mr Cummings as well. The patriotic historians of Holloway should be at work, scheming for a plaque to be placed over the doorway of The Laurels (No 12), Brickfield Terrace. There Mr Pooter with his 'dear wife' Carrie and his atrocious son, Lupin, finally settled, and, in '91, when Mr Pooter's 'grand old master' presented the freehold of the place to his faithful clerk, he must have been 50. That, as the saying is, takes one back; indeed, it is so far back for some of us that we cross the frontier of comedy and enter into the wilderness where family ends and history begins. The joke dims and dims until it ceases to be a joke and becomes a fact.

The fact, neutral, normal, pathetic, is the essence of the humour of *The Diary of a Nobody*. Gentility was the illusion; the grim fact was that Mr Pooter was not very well off, that he tripped on doorscrapers, that he ate Wednesday's blancmange on Thursday and Friday in holy matrimonial privacy and was caught doing the same on Saturday by the brutal Gowing who shouted out *while the servant was in the room*, 'Hulloh! The remains of Wednesday.' Facts were the fly in Mr Pooter's ointment, the Gowing in the laurel bush. Off pops his made-up tie at the ball, out 'in Society' he is horrified to meet his ironmonger, the laundry returns his coloured handkerchief without the colour, and his wife violates the sanctity of marriage by complaining, 'in company', that every morning she has to listen to his 'blessed' dreams. For years he has laboured and reached that summit where a man can at last open a bottle of three-and-sixpenny champagne with an air both festive and refined, only to discover that this is not a summit but a foothill. Indeed he has to listen to Mr Hardfur Huttle saying that it is insult and murder to give your guests even a six-shilling champagne. Mr Pooter's life is one long humiliation at the hands of triviality and God gave him no gift of laughing at himself. Far from this, the only things he can laugh at are his own jokes – puns brought forth after long preparation which only 'dear Carrie' sees and then not always – and though as sensitive in the trills of decorum as the Cid was on the point of honour, he is doomed to be pestered all his life by the enraging bites of petty indignity. A boob, a fool, a tedious and touchy old bore, Mr Pooter has the innocence but not the stature of the comic martyrs; he is a study in the negative; he is a good man in the sense that the Devil evidently regards him as being too dull for temptation. The Evil One is content to put hard peas in the shoes of the pilgrim on the trim avenues of gentility and to leave him to it.

The foreigner who picked up *The Diary of a Nobody* would be bound to note that there must have been something especially dreary about English lower-middle-class life in the Nineties. I hear echoes of elderly relatives saying 'Poor So-and-so' was a 'cure' or 'a caution', that he or she was always saying and doing things which were 'too real'. Reality was the joke, its awful, dreary greyness. People who, like 'dear Carrie', turned the leg of mutton over and covered it with parsley so that the unexpected visitor would not notice the joint had been cut, laughed at the little comedy when they read about it or saw it on the stage. There is a pathos in a joke so small, a Cockney whine, a cringing suggestion of the prison house. Yet it would be a mistake to regard the humour of the Grossmiths as a sedative to its audience, an aid to complacency or resignation. Looking down upon snobbery, we see the comedy of snobbery; looking up to it, we see what a dynamic romantic force it has been in English middle-class life, how it is natural to an expanding society. The words 'too real' are not a pathetic acceptance of life's little domestic ironies only; they are an idealistic protest against reality, a call to push on with the illusion, to afford a really uncut shoulder of mutton in the house next time. The moral impulse in the English character takes peculiar and generally vulgar forms. Like the go-getting Japanese, we dare not lose face, and the cultivation of dignity, ambivalence and vulgarity to this end is automatic with us.

As 'too-realists' the Grossmiths were salutary historians. They recorded the paralysis of middle-class living, the horror when the preoccupation with etiquette, with good manners and bad manners, was upset by someone like Mr Padge who had no manners at all, not even bad ones. Mr Padge, that low man who seemed all moustache, who took the best chair and would not budge from it all the evening, who stared at everybody, smoked a dirty pipe and whose only words were 'That's right' and who had a coarse, vacuous laugh, is a great character:

> I was so annoyed at the conduct of Padge, I said: 'I suppose you would have laughed if he had poked Mr. Gowing's eye out?' to which Padge replied 'That's right', and laughed more than ever.

And yet the Grossmiths are just; they are never savage, never unkind; they trip Mr Pooter but they help him up afterwards; they leave to insipidity its native pathos. The fact that Mr Pooter himself is recording his daily hopes and disasters in all their shattering mildness keeps us on his side. One cannot kick a man when he is down; one cannot ridicule a man who is already making an ass of himself in his diary. One feels protective towards the Mr Pooter who is so childishly engaged in curling the whiskers and adjusting the coat-tails of the proprieties that, when life breaks through in the form of a slapstick bread fight, a row with the butcher or 'words' with his son, he is always helpless and hides his nakedness with indignation. And indignation, of course, makes it worse. English humour on its cheerfully vulgar course always ends in knockabout:

> They then commenced throwing hard pieces of crust, one piece catching me on the forehead, and making me blink. I said: 'Steady, please; steady!' Frank jumped up and said: 'Tum, tum, then the band played.'
> I did not know what this meant, but they roared and continued the bread battle. Gowing suddenly seized all the parsley off the cold mutton and threw it in my face. I looked daggers at Gowing who replied: 'I say, it's no good trying to look indignant, with your hair full of parsley.' I rose from the table and insisted that a stop should be put to this foolery at once. Frank Mutlar shouted, 'Time, gentlemen, please, time,' and turned out the gas, leaving us in complete darkness.

Yes, one feels protective to Mr Pooter; he is innocent. The truly comic character always is. From Don Quixote down to Pickwick, Pooter and Beachcomber's Mr Thake.

The Diary of a Nobody was the sane answer to the sentimental realism of

Gissing. The 'too real' had reached a stage in Gissing which was altogether too real. There is an incredible story of Gissing's which describes how a young lady from Balham broke off her engagement and ruined her life because of the shame of discovering that a photograph of herself as a baby had appeared in the public press to advertise a baby food. The need for laughter was obviously urgent. But each age provides its own antidote in the younger generation. In the *Diary* there is nothing so fascinating sociologically as the character of the awful son Lupin, that bouncing, insubordinate and loud young man who is always being sacked from his jobs only, against all desert, to get much better and also much shadier ones. Lupin is a symptom. The prim mid-Victorians have given birth to the effusively vulgar Edwardians, the exuberant business man is succeeding to the industrious clerk and 'the grand old master'; just as the stucco and yellow brick of Brickfield Terrace is to be abandoned – shortly to become a slum – and will be superseded by the red brick, balconies and Tudor of the next ring of suburbia. The sulking, the shiftiness, the flashiness of Lupin are perfect. He is of his time and yet he has touches of the eternal.

Much of *The Diary of a Nobody* is dated in fact and in general atmosphere. The happy ending, so natural, is quite dated. At 50 the present-day Pooters do not get a rise of £100 a year; they get the sack. They are too old. As for 'the grand old master', the Pooters of today never see their employers, hardly know who they are. Most of us would be glad to know our ironmongers. The humorous writing which was a kind of comic game of chess with the English class system survives in only the feeblest artificial comedy of the commercial stage, and the commercial stage is usually a generation behind the times. With the loss of class as a comic subject, kindness has gone because stability has gone. Our own humour is more cruel. It is speedier and prefers fantasy, as is shown by a glance at Beachcomber – the Grossmiths' successor. Why, then, does the *Diary* still amuse? Like an old fashion, of course; but also because it was the most economical, the least wordy, the most limpid and crystalline of its kind; because it anticipated the *sans commentaire* method which is characteristic of today. Its popularity with the older generation of whom Mr Pooter was the ridiculous father, where to us he is an archaic and hardly known grandparent, springs from the general relief it brought to the mid-Victorian strain; it was a new humour of the lower middle class which Wells and

Bennett (a pair of Lupins in their time) were to carry further, and which was disapproved of by the refined. It is interesting to read of the disgust which this new voice of the lower middle-class aroused when it became heard at the beginning of the century. The objection of the aristocratic critic of the *Morning Post*, for example, to Jerome's *Three Men in a Boat* was to the lowness of its people. The subtle *Diary* disarmed that critic by satirising the gentility he had taught them.

A Victorian Misalliance

The epic of the free speech and little things – so that heroic critic, the late G. K. Chesterton, described Robert Browning's *The Ring and the Book*. Here was a giant whom the great rescuer of giants in distress found irresistible. Twice as long as the *Æneid*, twice as long as *Paradise Lost*, twice as long as the *Odyssey* and one-third as long as the *Iliad*, Browning's poem is obviously a great something, if only a great miscarriage. An epic, I think, despite Chesterton's brilliant special pleading, it is not, and precisely for the reasons which he gives for the view. Epics deal with great things, not little things; they describe not humanity free but humanity bound by the primitive chains of Fate, ruled by some absolute tribunal of value or dogma. No such fixed or majestic background stands behind the Renaissance police-court story on which Browning based *The Ring and the Book*; on the contrary, the very nature of the search for Truth, which is Browning's substitute, is that it is fluid, restless, uncertain, evolutionary. The stepping-stones by which we rise from our dead selves to higher things ascend into a mist and disappear from sight.

What Browning did produce was a great Victorian novel or, more accurately, the child of a misalliance between poetry and the novel. The Franceschini murder was essentially a novelist's subject; it was as much concerned with intrigues of property as it was with the aspirations and corruption of the soul. One's mind wanders to another nineteenth-century writer who had also found his subject in the *faits divers*. Just as Flaubert patiently wrote out the dossier of a similar scandal from Rouen and added to it the alloy of his own love-affair with Louise Colet and made *Madame Bovary*, so Browning put something of Elizabeth Barrett into his seventeenth-century Pompilia, and from the memory of his unforgettable crisis of conscience at the time of the elopement – an adventure in which, he felt, he had been on the brink of murder – narrated that flight with Caponsacchi, the priest, which was to lead to Pompilia's death. Poetry abstracts drama from the dossier; Browning reverses the process. Finding the drama concise and abstract in the famous yellow book picked up on the second-hand bookstall in Rome, he multiplied and analysed it into the point of view of every possible spectator of the case. Not only were the leading characters given their say, but he collected the common gossip of the streets and even parodied his own subject in the two books which describe the esoteric high jinks of the lawyers. The poem is clamorous with rival voices of people; real people with characters, coats, hats, trades, names and addresses. This impression was not lost on Henry James. The great rival collector of Italian curiosities saw that *The Ring and the Book* was a Henry James novel gone wrong – not long enough among other things!

It is curious to note how these two Victorian connoisseurs moved instinctively towards a tale of scandal and spiritual corruption. The period's growing interest in crime, its love of melodrama and its feeling for corruption have considerable social interest. The preoccupation grows stronger as the great bourgeois period becomes self-confident. Flaubert spent his life collecting objects of disgust; Henry James had the shocked expression of a bishop discovering something unspeakable in a museum; Browning, the casuist, becomes in Chesterton's excellent words 'a kind of cosmic detective who walked into the foulest of thieves' kitchens and accused men publicly of virtue.' (If one resents Browning's optimism today it is because of this ingenious complacency; surely one should accuse thieves of being thieves.) To be more particular, the thieves' kitchens were a traditional interest of the Browning family. They had delicate consciences which were awkwardly allied to exuberant natures. Suburban Camberwell had been unable to contain the imaginations of the Bank of England clerk or of his precocious son. Sunday strollers, as they passed the Browning villa, could not have suspected that, inside, a child and his father were re-enacting the siege of Troy with chairs and tables, spouting epics and medieval romances to each other, re-arguing the battles of forgotten pedants, revelling in the dubious intrigue, the passion and the poisons of the Continent, and all the time keeping up to the minute on the crime story of the week. A man of the eighteenth century and a clerk, Browning's father easily kept this learned escapism cool. The heroic couplet, as practised by Pope, did a good deal to soothe his savage breast. But it was otherwise in the nineteenth-century son. Liberty was in the air, shape lost its symmetry, energy blew itself out into the sublime or the grotesque.

The Ring and the Book is one of those detective stories in which we are given the crime and the murderer at the beginning. We are given an event as we ourselves might read of it in the newspaper and the object is to discover what is true and what is false in everyone's story and in the crowd's conjecture. Browning's method complicates and recomplicates the suspense, shifts us from one foot to the other in growing agitation and excitement before the mystery.

Do we feel for Pompilia, still not dead, with twenty-five dagger-wounds in her? Very little. One is, of course, more moved than one is by the conventional corpse of a detective story; but not vastly more. The true incentive is to the brain, in watching this pile of evidence mount up and the next 'point of view' undermine it. Now we are thrown into the common gossip of Rome and no one excels Browning in the rendering of rumour, scandal and the tunnellings of common insinuation:

> At last the husband lifted an eyebrow – bent
> On day-book and the study how to wring
> Half the due vintage from the worn-out vines
> At the villa, tease a quarter the old rent
> From the farmstead, tenants swore would tumble soon –
> Picked up his ear a-singing day and night
> With 'ruin, ruin' – and so surprised at last –
> Why, what else but a titter? Up he jumps
> Back to mind come those scratchings at the grange,
> Prints of the paw about the outhouse; rife
> In his head at once again are word and wink,
> *Mum* here and *budget* there, the smell o' the fox,
> The musk of the gallant. 'Friends, there's
>   falseness here!'

The case for Pompilia and her priests never quite recovers from the effectiveness of Franceschini's defence. His story is a false one. He is as villainous as Iago; all the better he draws his own character: the down-at-heel noble, rich in tradition, empty in purse – 'a brainful of belief, the noble's lot' – cynical no doubt, but look how he has been treated; can he be blamed for bitterly resenting the trick played on him by Pompilia's ignoble parents?

With the cunning of an excellent story-teller Browning gradually demolishes our credulity about Franceschini. We hear Caponsacchi, the priest. Can we believe that this handsome, cultivated, worldly young man, known for the slackness of his vows, came to desire the salvation and not the seduction of Pompilia? But we know our Browning by now, the 'cosmic detective' nosing out virtue in our unlikeliest moments; and though Pompilia's lawyer appears to be much fonder of his diction than careful of the interest of his client, we know that the unravelling of motive and evidence will eventually lead to her innocence. Her simple story comes from her own lips, artless and pathetic, as she dies. One more of those Victorian innocents, fragile, wraith-like, childish, affecting at their best, sickly at their worst, breathes her last in the Victorian phantasmagoria where ogre-like villains and corrupted worldings nudge and snarl together in the smoke. How they liked suffering in women.

The realism, Browning's eye for the physical, conveys an extraordinary excitement. He cannot describe an emotion or sensation without putting a hat and coat on it:

> Till sudden at the door a tap discreet
> A visitor's premonitory cough,
> And poverty has reached him on her rounds.

Or

> . . . Guido woke
> After the cuckoo, so late, near noon day
> With an inordinate yawning of the jaws,
> Ears plugged, eyes gummed together, palate, tongue
> And teeth one mud-paste made of poppy milk.

Or

> The brother walking misery away
> O' the mountain side with dog and gun belike.

His people live, their thoughts live physically; indeed they live so physically that in the metaphors they breed a crowd of other things and other people, cramming the narrative until the main theme is blocked and obscured. A stuttering demagogue, said Chesterton. A crowd of thoughts, arguments, theories, casuistries, images, doubts and aspirations, in physical shape, are trying to get to the point of Browning's pen all at once and they reduce him to illegibility.

The Ring and the Book of the Seventies has become *The Waste Land* of today. The Browning bric-à-brac, the Browning personalities, the 'points of view', the arguments, have degenerated into a threadbare remnant:

These fragments I have shored against my ruins.

Shantih, shantih, the end of individualism and free speech. When one reads the heirs of Browning and especially the subjective, personal and obscure poets with their private worlds, their family jokes, their shop talk and code language, one sees what their work has lost in interest and meaning by the lack of that framework of dramatic realism which gives the cogency of event to Browning's poems. There is a reason for this loss. Private life in the nineteenth century had its public sanction; nowadays private life is something which we live against the whole current of our time. For the moment.

The First and Last of Hardy

———

How little a novelist's choice of story and character widens or changes between his first book and his last. In an obvious way there seems to be no kinship between Hardy's *Under the Greenwood Tree* and *Jude the Obscure*, but reading these books again we see their differences are on the surface. Only age separates the youthful pastoral from the middle-aged tract. One is the sapling, pretty in its April leafage, the other is the groaning winter oak, stark with argument; but the same bitter juice rises in both their stems. Sue Bridehead is one of the consequences of being Fancy Day, Jude is a Dick Dewy become conscious of his obscurity; the tantalised youth has become the frustrated man and, according to such biographical notes as I have seen, all is a variation on the theme of Hardy's first marriage. What has changed, of course, is the stretch of the scene. After the *Greenwood Tree*, we are always struck by the largeness of the panorama and by the narrowness of Hardy's single, crooked, well-trodden path across it. And if the path is narrow, so is the man. He stands like a small, gaitered farmer in his field, dry, set, isolated and phlegmatic, the most unlikely exponent of human passion, but somehow majestic because he is on the skyline.

There have been dozens of English rural novels like *Under the Greenwood Tree*, there have been none at all like the rest of Hardy's work. He is the only English novelist who knows what the life, speech and values of the cottager really are and who knows them from the inside. Unlike the urban novelists he is not secretly laughing at the countryman, nor blatantly poeticising him. From an urban point of view, indeed, Hardy is totally unpoetic. His verse, his prose and what poetic feeling he has are as awkward as the jerking and jangling of plough and harrow. Where, to the urban writer, the poetry of the countryside and the countryman lies in the sight of natural beauty and a feeling that here life is as sweet and sound as an apple, to Hardy the beauty is as bitter as grass. The native reek of shag and onions seems to come off his people's breath. You have the sense that

[73]

these people work and work for wages. And they speak like peasants, too, a speech which is not pure decorative dialect – the weakness of the poetic novelists who have tried to do for England what Synge did for the West of Ireland – but a mixture of dialect and the trite, sententious domestic phrase.

In rescuing the dying peasant of the empty and derelict countryside from cultured sentiment, Hardy put him where Burns and Piers Plowman had found him. Yet Hardy did not achieve this by giving up all outside standards and by attempting to merge spiritually with the peasant in the manner of modern mystical writers like Giono. So far from doing this, Hardy is even something of the Victorian antiquary who smacks of the local museum. His view of man is geological. What he did was not to merge but indeed to step aside from his subject and to look at the peasant again from the point of view of the characteristic thought of his day. Hardy is unique among Victorian novelists in this sense: he is not our first novelist to be influenced by scientific ideas – there was Swift – but he is the only Victorian novelist to have been influenced by them. He seems to be the only English novelist to have read his Darwin and, like Zola who had also done so, to have had his imagination enlarged, not by the moral conflicts which Darwinism started among English writers, but by the most striking material contribution of Darwinism to our minds: its enormous widening of our conception of time. A huge and dramatic new vista was added to the years and an emancipated imagination was now free to march beyond the homely Christian fables on to the bleak and endless plain of human history. Where other writers were left to struggle with their religious faith and were gradually to lose it or to compromise in the rather woolly world of 'Christian values', Hardy's imagination was stimulated to recreate the human ritual. Only in *Jude*, at the end of his career as a novelist, do we see that he, too, may have had his moral struggle with orthodox Christianity, but it seems quickly to have been settled. The very timidity of Hardy's nature, so obvious in every page, gave him a personal loneliness, an instinct to go more than half-way to accept the worst, and these readily made acceptable the great indifferent *It* and the long empty, frightening Eons of *It*'s life. In the competitive stampede of Victorian liberty the peasant was left behind, he was not the fittest to survive; under the iron stamp of Hardy's Victorian determinism, he became fixed, lonely and great.

This is said to be the weakness and not the strength of Hardy. And it is true that a novelist is usually ruined by his philosophy of life. Easily shown to be untenable, a philosophy is also easily shown to be the element by which an art and human nature are falsified. The world is not a machine. Knowing this and, under the influence of French and Russian novelists, and with the decline, too, of self-confidence in middle-class culture, the English novelist has tried letting life tell its own story or, as in the case of D. H. Lawrence, has made heavy borrowings from exotic cultures. When we compare the result of this with Hardy's achievement, our position is humiliating. Whatever else the English novel may have achieved during the last thirty years, it has not described English life. It has described the sensibility of Western cosmopolitana and has been the work of people who have been, essentially, expatriates in their own country. There is, of course, a curious passage in *Jude*, after the murder of the children, when the doctor wonders whether the unrest growing in society has not awakened a universal wish for death, a passage which shows that the disintegrating ferment was working in Hardy himself. But his beliefs were cast in the sober, native moralistic mould. Since Puritanism we have always had this worried gravity and our moral instinct has been social and practical, not intellectual. When we open Hardy again we are back to worry and moral conflict, the normal condition of the English nature. The nerves relax as we prepare for what in our bones we understand: liberty loved chiefly when manacled to an inordinate respect for circumstance, the cry of passion almost silenced by windy ruminations over right and wrong. The very prose of Hardy, heavy with a latinity which suggests a Milton reborn to drive a steamroller along the Wessex roads, has the effect of pressing men down among their neighbours and into the hills and towns where they live. Around the 'rages of the ages' assembles the rural district council and, beyond that body, a moral hierarchy of which the council is the awkward shadow. As in Ibsen, Fate works, with a revived gusto, among the sanitary engineers.

In the pastoral realism of *Under the Greenwood Tree* there is a visual vividness, despite some old-fashioned phrasing, which is what we es-pecially like today and the talk of the cottagers is taken, rich and crooked, as it comes from their mouths. If one discards the quaint scenes when the Mellstock worthies are together, there are passages which have the true, unpolished country look, in the plain comedy of Fancy's wedding at the end. The tranter is speaking of his marriage:

'Ay, 'twas a White Tuesday when I committed it. Mellstock Club walked the same day and we new-married folk went a-gaying round the parish behind 'em. Everybody used to wear something white at Whitsuntide in them days. My sonnies, I've got the very white trousers that I wore at home in a box now. Ha'n't, Ann?'
    'You had till I cut 'em up for Jimmy,' said Mrs. Dewy.

But long before *Jude*, the visual brightness had gone. There appeared instead that faculty of instant abstraction in Hardy's eye, whereby the people, the towns, the country, became something generalised in the mind as if Time had absorbed them. The light catches the vanes of Christminster and they glint the more brightly because they are seen against an abstract foreground 'of secondary and tertiary hues'. One is looking at things not seen by an eye but known by a mind, by tens of thousands of minds. If society in the mass could see, if a town or village could look, this is what they would see. Masses themselves, they would see beyond the surface to the mass beneath. The realism of Hardy is a realism of mass, you are aware all the time that hundreds of other people are passing and bumping into Jude and Sue Bridehead when they stand in the street or go to the train, carrying their passion with them. They are tired, not fired, by passion. It is something which has come out of the inherited human destiny, to use them. Jude confesses to his first marriage in a vegetable market, he is seen by his first wife in the crowd at an agricultural show. In streets, on railway platforms, in lodging houses, inns and empty churches, his tragedy is enacted. The fidelity of Hardy's descriptions of love-affairs does not really lie in his evocation of love itself, which is not especially good, but of its circumstances. The characters of Hardy, being rural people, are always on small local journeys, trailing their lives about with them, printing their history fragmentarily as they go upon vehicles and roads. Where the modern novelist uses journeys as a device in which, perhaps, to go into his characters' thoughts or to pick up scenes from the past, in Hardy the journeys themselves are tragic because they are bound into the business of his characters. The humdrum circumstance becomes a kind of social poetry. Hardy himself called it 'the low, sad music of humanity'.

[76]

The chief criticism of Hardy's technique as a novelist usually falls upon his use of coincidence, melodrama and fateful accidental meetings. He is said to overload the dice. Now the question of melodrama in Victorian life and fiction is not anything like as simple as it looks – I discuss this point later in dealing with Mrs Gaskell's novels about industrial unrest – but certain distinctions must be made. For example, the accidental meetings of Jude with his first wife after they have parted for years seem to me not only artistically permissible but, given Hardy's method, artistically desirable. We happen nowadays to be less interested than he in the irony of circumstance; our irony is altogether satirical. By it we disparage our characters personally because we are criticising their standards and behaviour. In Hardy there is no personal disparagement. He hates no one, disapproves of very few people. The disparagement – and it is all the more true and shattering because of this – comes not from a superior author but from the triviality of the circumstances in which people live. An agricultural show, the mere changing of trains at a junction, may start the poison in high human feeling. We are mocked by *things*; things themselves are but the expression of 'It'. We rightly object to this kind of coincidence in the cheap romantic literature of wishes, in them the convention is mechanical and worn out. In Hardy, on the other hand, coincidence is far from being the unreal literary trick of a commercial storyteller; such mechanism falls naturally into place in his mechanistic philosophy.

Far indeed from suffering from coincidence Hardy is the master of coincidence. He is its master because he is the master of the movement of people. What are the scenes we most vividly remember? They are, I think, the journeys. The whole burden of the story weighs upon them. The tragic idea of people circling further and further from the crux of their fate and yet mile by mile coming inescapably nearer to it is very familiar; Hardy fills in the provincial detail of this conception. Again, it is not tragic feeling which is his subject, but the burden of feeling. At a high moment like the murder of the children in *Jude*, Hardy completely fails to convince or move us, and this is not only because the whole episode is too much in itself; the failure owes something to the fact that in the preceding pages which describe how Jude and Sue are turned out of one lodging after another in Christminster, either because they are unmarried or because they have noisy children,

Hardy has described something far more real, more fated and more significant.

As so many Victorian novels do, *Jude* suffers at crucial moments from the intervention of the author. 'The poor fellow,' we are told, 'poor Jude', 'honest Jude', and so on. When a novelist pities a prig he is usually writing about himself and Jude walks stiffly and bookishly to his doom. Cynical critics have pointed out that if Jude had been born a little later he would have gone to Ruskin College and the whole tragedy would not have happened. This is a nonsensical criticism. There *is* a tragedy of the desire for knowledge. Hardy's analysis of the phases of Jude's intellectual development and disillusion is masterly and only fails when he makes Jude die with the bells of Remembrance Day at Christminster in his ears. That is as bad as the lovers kissing under the gibbet where ten years later one of them will be hanged. The reason, to my mind, why the book fails is that part of it is a tract on the marriage laws. It would have been perfectly fitting for Jude to be ruined by two women, one a sensual slut and the other a fey, half-sexed coquette posing as a creature of fastidious higher nature, without dragging the marriage laws in. Hardy was at his worst in attacking convention, because his interests were so narrow. What are his tragedies? Love stories only, the enormous Victorian preoccupation with sex. He seems never to have outgrown the tantalisation, the frustration which the Sue Brideheads brought down upon their husbands, making them expert, as only the true Puritan can be, on the pathetic subject of female vanity. So obsessed, the Victorians could never turn easily from sex to other dramas around them – as Zola could turn to the mines and the soil, Balzac to money, Dickens to the farces and tragedies of the law. The attack upon convention is one of the great bores of the late Victorian period, for all the attackers except Shaw thought they could get rid of conventions without altering the basis of the kind of society which produced them.

A Curate's Diary

A writer's humiliations come at every hour of the day and one of the greatest is the common failure of professional authors to write an interesting diary. Most of them try. The thing looks so easy, so indolent a labour, so casual and go-as-you-please. No shape to torture, no plot to drive one mad, no scheme to follow. One looks out of the window with an empty mind and lets the day pour in its news like the varieties of light coming in from the garden. Or so it seems. Yet, let the professional writer compare his jottings with those of the famous diarists. Let him look at Amiel or Pepys, Woodforde or Evelyn, and the discrepancy is shattering. Why such a coarseness of texture, such a failure in intimacy, even such an absence of newsiness? Obviously diary writing is *not* an affair of the idle moment, *not* a spare-time occupation. It must be a life-work, one's only literary work, one of the constant domestic arts like gossip, cookery or gardening which leave little mind for anything else. The diary is indeed the revenge of the secretive and of the failures upon the public self-importance of the world of letters. A mere schoolmaster, a piffling clergyman, an official limpet, may jump at once to permanent fame without the agony of an author's vanity.

And of course without an author's rewards. The one consolation to the regular professionals is that no diarist reaches fame in his own lifetime. He sows but he does not reap. We have had a recent example of this poetic injustice in the case of the Reverend Kilvert. We cannot know what this shy, gracious and strangely ecstatic Victorian curate would have thought if he had known that the eyes of the public would one day swarm like flies over the three volumes of his private diary. Perhaps he would have been pleased and had half hoped to be read. For it seems very doubtful that a man who takes an obvious trouble to write well should do so entirely for himself. There must be, one feels, a limit to the satisfactions of self-love; and Kilvert had that Victorian sense of duty or responsibility which would give him the need of an object for his daily record. He was very much

[79]

aware of recording history, if only with a small 'h', and he cannot have been so different from his contemporaries who lived in a society so set and with such an air of eternity about its conventions, practices and beliefs that they regarded themselves as a kind of communal phenomenon. That sense of belonging to a society is one which has been lost in the last thirty years – hence the awful fuss we make about it today when we try to set down our beliefs, speaking of it as something distant, revolutionary, Utopian – and it was that sense which made Kilvert an historian.

Diary writing is the most private of the arts. It is not really surprising therefore that the Wiltshire and Radnorshire curate should have stopped writing before his marriage. In any case he could not have experimented in the difficult task of combining diary keeping with marriage, for he died a month later. Privacy was going. For some time he had been too busy with marriage preparations to write many of those long lyrical entries of the earlier pages. We feel indeed that a phase had finished. Kilvert had given the best of himself and though his death was tragically sudden, he died, from a literary point of view, at the right time – at one of the two or three right times which a talented man has in his life.

What would marriage and family life have done to the innocent ardours of this susceptible bachelor? A difficult time, we suspect, awaited the lyrical idealist who was put in 'a state of continual bewitchment' (as Mr Plomer, his editor, says) and 'emotional upheaval' by every female he met, child, girl or young woman. A wife might not have understood this 'strange and terrible gift of stealing hearts and exciting such love' which was an instinct of his rapturous nature. And how rapturous it was! The little deaf and dumb girl who flings her arms round him makes him cry out, 'I have been loved; no one can take this from me'. An Irish girl sends him into ecstasy with her play-acting on a train journey. There are Ettie and 'the wild, mad trysts in the snow'. There is a procession of girls and girl children with 'glorious' hair or 'glorious' eyes and hosts of chaste but exciting kissings, as if his heart were a spring day. We love by the book and Kilvert had read his Tennyson; but it is the special triumph of Kilvert's sincerity that he has conveyed and made credible his kind of feeling to a generation whose notions of love are totally alien to those of a bubbling young mid-Victorian curate:

How delightful it is in these sweet summer evenings to wander from cottage to cottage and from farm to farm exchanging bright words and looks with the beautiful girls at their garden gates and talking to the kindly people sitting at their cottage doors or meeting in the lane when their work is done. How sweet it is to pass from house to house welcome and beloved everywhere by young and old, to meet the happy loving smile of the dear children at their evening play in the lanes and fields and to meet with no harsher reproach than this: 'It is a longful while since you have been to see us. We do all love to see you coming and we do miss you sorely when you are away.'

We have lost the art of rendering pure sentiment and the feeling for such a tenderness as Kilvert's. Echoes of the stage clergyman – 'the deah children' – run mocking along the lines as we read a passage like that. But Kilvert's *Diary* might be called the revenge of the comic curate. His sensibility and dignity show up the Edwardian horseplay at the expense of the clergy for the dated boorishness it is. When we contrast the note and rhythm of our lives with those of Kilvert's we see there is more than a change of fashions between the generations. We perceive with a shock that it is we who are unnatural because we do not live within the walls of a long period of civilisation and peace. It is we who are the abnormal, distorted people: creatures of revolutionary age who of all human types are the most passagery, and least characteristic, the most ill-fitting and bizarre.

Towards the end of his short life Kilvert was in Wiltshire acting as curate to his father. An account of Kilvert's father, who kept a school during his son's earliest childhood, is to be found in Augustus Hare's autobiography. Hare wrote: 'at nine years old I was compelled to eat Eve's apple quite up; indeed the Tree of Knowledge of Good and Evil was stripped absolutely bare: there was no fruit left to gather'. Was Kilvert's prolonged and limpid innocence the result of some early check of horror? There is one incident in the third volume which catches the prying eye of the modern reader and which makes him hesitate about that innocence. There would be no hesitation but for the fact that Kilvert's virginal innocence is phenomenal. At 38 it is a major feat of clerical sublimation. The incident concerns a village girl who had become hopelessly disobedient and uncontrollable. She had been reasoned with, prayed over, punished

[81]

without result. There was nothing for it, Kilvert said, but formally and solemnly to give her a good whipping and he offered to do it for the parents. The offer was refused but it was agreed to allow him to be present. There may be nothing in it. Kilvert records it exactly as he records any other village happening; but it gives one a shock, for he had no cruelty in his nature. The shock does not arise from the act alone. What shakes us is that, charmed by the Victorian felicity, we had forgotten for a moment the price the Victorians paid for their ignorance of themselves.

There was nothing spinsterly in Kilvert; his sensibility is masculine, or as the Victorians would have said 'manly'. After Wiltshire Kilvert went to the Border country once more where he was always happiest. He responded to the lively, imaginative and courteous Welsh people. The Border country provides many of his best characters. In Wiltshire the comedy is heavier. There was the row about Mrs Prodgers, for example; there was the campaign which raged between the vicar and the squire about the harmonium. And then so many of those little girls who jumped up to kiss the curate would suddenly die. The diary form lends itself even better than the novel or the short tale to rounding off character, for life is always adding its felicitous afterthought. Where art is selective and one-sided, the diary dips its net daily and brings out what is there. Take the Prodgers incident. Mrs Prodgers was one of those pushful, fecund and importunate parishioners who bring their umbrellas down with a firm tap on every vicarage doorstep. She came from Kingston St Michael, a village where droll things were always happening, and caused a lot of tittering when she insisted that she and the little Prodgerses should be used as models in the design of the new stained-glass window for the church. 'Suffer the little children' was the subject, and Mrs Prodgers had edged her brood of sufferers well into the foreground of the picture. Doubly immortal Mrs Prodgers to be done both by Kilvert and by stained glass. In a few lines there is the essence of a life-story. It is not worth more, it is not worth less. Outside a stained-glass window, a diary note is the perfect place for her. And then the Squire. He illustrates the aptitude of the diary form for collecting fragments day by day, for catching each day's contribution to the jigsaw of human character. The novelist must summarise, theorise and jump to conclusions; the diarist can take the more leisurely course of letting the character out piecemeal, as he makes himself. A vicar-baiter and a tyrant, the Squire ordered the tenor to be turned out of the choir and so spoiled the singing, but opposed 'with strong language' the proposal to introduce a harmonium. 'Distant from music' was one woman's description of him. 'He apprehended', he said, 'a chronic difficulty in finding someone to play the instrument.' The Kilverts won, but the Squire wouldn't pay a penny. That is not the end of the Squire. His portrait is perfected a few days later in the midst of a later and very affecting description of a child's funeral. Kilvert, familiar with rural sorrow and intensely observant, had a perceptiveness uncommon in literature. We see the mother's distracted face, her cries of guilt and helplessness, her hard, despairing eye. And then the afternoon sun shines in the church and the birds begin to sing as if in honour of the dead child and Kilvert, as he reads the service, catches sight of the Squire through the window. He is dressed in a white hat and a drab suit, dashing fussily across the churchyard and putting his stick into the grave to see that it is the right depth. Things must be done properly.

Kilvert has always these completing realistic touches so that a scene is never made top-heavy with the emotion it arouses. His eye and ear are acute; they seem always to be roving over the scene and to hit upon some sight or word which is all the more decisive for having the air of accident. And in literature, to convey the chance effects of life without being bizarre is everything. So he goes on his walking tours, has his holidays in Sussex, the Isle of Wight, marks his catalogue at Burlington House, loses his easy heart, preaches, consoles the sick, collecting the odd but never isolating it from the stream of living in the manner of the caricaturist. An old lady – you could meet her in the town if you wanted – was parachuted over the cliff hanging from her umbrella in a gale and alighted unhurt. Another 'grasped at vacancy' on the cellar stairs and fell to the bottom; the trouble began when her husband at the top explained that she couldn't have done so because you can't grasp at vacancy – a grotesque bit of domestic argument. An old man on his deathbed says, 'It is hard work dying,' and a fine farmer wrecked by illness in middle life says sadly, 'I shall never again be a big man like you with your strong body.' These things are too sharp when detached from Kilvert's context; in that, they are the windows of a way of rural life which is far from gone, though curates go no more to drink whey with dairymaids or dance Roger de Coverley at picnics with the prettiest girls of the parish.

Kilvert's account of his visit to Priscilla Price shows him at his dramatic best. The old lady was 77 and could remember the coronation of George IV. She lived with her step-daughter, a woman turned 50 who was an idiot. They were an astonishing pair, for the idiot added a touch of frightening parody to the picture. They were drinking tea in their cottage when Kilvert found them. What an excellent short story they make:

'Ar Tader, Ar Tader!' cried the idiot. 'She means "Our Father",' explained the stepmother. 'She has been wanting to see the clergyman, the gentleman that says "Our Father".' Prissy detailed to me the story of an illness she had suffered, illustrated by a dramatic performance by the idiot as a running accompaniment. Occasionally in addition to the acting of the details of the illness, the bursting of a blood vessel, the holding of the head of the invalid, and yelling to the neighbours for help, the idiot roared out an affirmative or negative according to the requirements of the tale. 'The blood spouted up,' said Prissy. 'Yes,' thundered the idiot. 'She held my head,' explained Prissy. 'Yes,' roared the idiot. 'There was no one here but her,' said Prissy. 'No!' shouted the idiot. 'They say that Mr. Davies heard her crying for help as far as Fine Street,' declared Prissy. 'Yes!' asseverated the idiot with a roar of pride and satisfaction. 'She had to run out into the deep snow,' said the stepmother. The idiot stepdaughter measured the depth of the snow upon her thigh.

Later Kilvert was asked to read the Testament and pray:

The reading was accompanied by a running fire of ejaculations and devout utterances from Prissy. She put a mat on the floor for me to kneel on and knelt down herself with some pain and difficulty, having sprained her knee. I begged her to be seated. 'No,' she said. 'I will kneel. I must punish the body. Kneel down, my dear,' she said reprovingly to the idiot. The idiot knelt humbly down in front of the fire with her head almost in the ashes.

There were other meetings like this. Priscilla collected old lore. She told the story of a man at Staunton-by-Wye who had seen the oxen kneel down at midnight on Christmas Eve and stay there moaning, the tears running down their faces.

Those especially Victorian words, words which bring back a whole period: 'radiant, glorious, infinite, innocence, picturesque,' are common in Kilvert's descriptions of scenery or of his sentiment. 'A splendid romp with Polly Taverner' – that is an authentic note from the time. His broken romances belong to the period too. Where Kilvert is superior to many of the novelists is that he is writing straight from nature, idealising often but never falsifying, for he moralises very little. His piety like his sentiment is firm but unprofessional. A being who feels, he does not go into the muddy introspections which many diary writers love, he has humour but he does not make insincere, defensive diary jokes against himself. One likes him in the end, I am convinced, because entirely without self-importance or self-consciousness, he is serious about himself. That supremely difficult art! Putting those three volumes down, one reflects that too many diarists are not content to work within a small field. A diary needs a frame and they are not willing to make it anything less than the universe. It is a pity, for the village is more interesting.

The Great Flunkey

Judged by their portraits, what a large number of the Victorian writers seem not to be writers at all, but creatures from the Green Room and the stage! There are the haggard, Irving-like grimaces of Dickens, the dank, baleful ringlets, so Siddonish, of George Eliot and Elizabeth Barrett. Tennyson glowers like the bearded villain from the Lyceum. They were a histrionic generation and in a way the habit embellishes them. But not all. Every prejudice we feel about Thackeray is confirmed by his disastrous portraits. Did ever a snob look more like a footman, was ever a man of the world more easily mistaken – as so often occurs to men of the world – for one of the servants? Take the very literary steel spectacles from Thackeray's nose in Samuel Lawrence's portrait, and what is more damning than that episcopal look of his, as if he were at once a bishop, bland and patronising, at a ducal christening, and Mr Yellowplush himself announcing, in the long soirée of Victorian letters, that the carriage has arrived? What a rôle to have chosen – to be the great flunkey of God and Mammon, the whited expert on the whited sepulchres.

There is, naturally, more in the portrait than that. Bishops and footmen have not that sensibility; his eyes have not the vacant stare of servitude; and the chin, which Thackeray raises so high, seems to be raised defensively rather than superciliously. Like an actor's, it suggests the pride of a personal style. People who knew Thackeray well said that they had never got to the bottom of him, and one can well believe it. One is held off. And yet one cannot escape him. Other novelists conceal themselves, but the figure of Thackeray is pushed forward in advance of his characters. We simply have to make up our minds about him personally because in all those novels 'without a hero' he is the hero himself, the compère of his own show. We are obliged to know the flow of his egoism better than we shall know the Osbornes and the Sedleys or any of his characters.

Re-reading *Vanity Fair* again, one realises what a brilliant innovation this was in the English novel. *Vanity Fair* is, as the traditional usually turns out to be, a new experiment. A new experiment in the manner of Sterne. Before everything, Thackeray was a versatile journalist, the author of clever sketches and short pieces which are still sharp and pungent in their satire after three generations. Egoistical but detached, he is alive to the current of life, the stream on which the curious fragments called human beings are borne. He observes. He does not appear to have a sustained imaginative power which can create a character larger than life, like one of Balzac's, though his interests resemble Balzac's. (He has more in common with Balzac than with Dickens.) Thackeray is like the modern novelists who derive from James and Proust, in his power of dissecting (and of desiccating!) character, in the refusal to inflate it. For a Victorian, we feel this had to be a fatal originality. The long novel, the great theme, the crowded canvas, were essential. Thackeray can see this, yet he must realise that his genius is for the fragmentary. And so he disguises his inability to create the proper paraphernalia of fiction, by introducing himself as the *raconteur*, who, having got you to listen, can distract, delude and beguile you with an atmosphere – an atmosphere which lifts like a haze from time to time upon one of those interludes of real talk, action and character which are as true as life itself. A voice talks on, going forward, winding backward, playing with scene and time. We see that this is not merely a new kind of narrative, but that Thackeray catches the illusion of living as none of his contemporaries ever did. They were inclined too much to be interested in the outsize thing called Life.

Another innovation – and Thackeray seems always to be innovating – is his attitude of character. There are no fixed characters in *Vanity Fair*. Amelia, Becky, that grim wreck Miss Crawley, the egotistical young soldier, George Osborne, old Sedley the virtuous bankrupt, and Jos, his son, the Regency dandy and glutton – they are not defined once and for all. They change with the story, they change in time, their view of one another changes. Thackeray makes them fluid and unexpected. It is a wicked concession to melodrama and humbug that Becky apparently murders Jos Sedley at the end. And yet, what is more perfect than the career of this buffoon? Comically drunk at Vauxhall at the beginning, then respectably in flight from his errors, he turns up dressed for the part in Brussels before Waterloo. Then panic again. Clothes, 'dashed fine gals and ices' become the ruling passions of this windy, fat and simple hypochondriac. Food-poisoning in low company is the fitting end, even if it is incredible that Becky had been studying Jos Sedley's liver all these years in order to commit the crime. Becky and Rawdon are greater examples of Thackeray's eye for the unexpected in character. It is a pity that Thackeray had to preach to us about Becky for, whether taking her side or not, he was capable of letting her live for herself. The stay at Crawley, when she is received into the family and listens to Lady Southdown's homilies, winds the wool and sings Haydn in the evenings, is made perfect by Becky's pleasure in it. It is a brief pleasure, for Becky is no fool. 'I could be good', she reflects, 'if I had £5,000 a year.' Then again there is Rawdon, the brainless Guardsman, the 'Mayfair playboy' with 'no harm' in him. His famous bequest of his horse to Becky as he goes off to battle is the crown of stumbling humanity upon his character:

'Look here,' said he. 'If I drop, let us see what there is for you. I have had a pretty good run of luck here, and here's two hundred and thirty pounds. I have got two Napoleons in my pocket. That is as much as I shall want; for the General pays everything like a prince; and if I'm hit, why you know I cost nothing. Don't cry, little woman; I may live to vex you yet. Well, I shan't take either of my horses, but shall ride the General's grey charger; it's cheaper, and I told him mine was lame. If I'm done, those two ought to fetch you something. Grigg offered ninety for the mare yesterday, before this confounded news came, and like a fool I wouldn't let her go under the two O's. Bullfinch will fetch his price any day, only you'd better sell him in this country, because the dealers have so many bills of mine, and so I'd rather he shouldn't go back to England. Your little mare the General gave you will fetch something, and there's no d——d livery-stable bills here, as there are in London,' Rawdon added with a laugh. 'There's that dressing-case cost me two hundred – that is, I owe two for it; and the Gold tops and bottles must be worth thirty or forty. Please to put *that* up the spout, ma'am, with my pins and rings, and watch and chain, and things. They cost a precious lot of money. Miss Crawley, I know, paid a hundred down for the chain and ticker. Gold tops and bottles, indeed! dammy. I'm sorry I didn't take more now. Edwards pressed on me a silver-gilt boot-jack, and I might have had a dressing-case fitted up with a silver warming-pan, and a service of plate. But we must make the best of what we've got, Becky, you know.'

And so, making his last dispositions, Captain Crawley, who had seldom thought about anything but himself until the last few months of his life, when Love had obtained the mastery over the dragoon, went through the various items of his little catalogue of effects, striving to see how they might be turned into money for his wife's benefit, in case any accident should befall him. He pleased himself by noting down with a pencil, in his big schoolboy handwriting, the various items of his portable property which might be sold for his widow's advantage – as, for example, 'My double-barril by Manton, say 40 guineas; my driving cloak, lined with sable fur, £50; my duelling pistols in rosewood case (same which I shot Captain Marker) £20; my regulation saddle-holsters and housings; my Laurie ditto' and so forth, over all of which articles he made Rebecca the mistress.

Faithful to his plan of economy, the Captain dressed himself in his oldest and shabbiest uniform and epaulets, leaving the newest behind under his wife's (or it might be his widow's) guardianship. And this famous dandy of Windsor and Hyde Park went off on his campaign with a kit as modest as that of a sergeant, and with something like a prayer on his lips for the woman he was leaving. He took her up from the ground, and held her in his arms for a minute, tight pressed against his strong-beating heart. His face was purple and his eyes dim as he put her down and left her. He rode by his General's side, and smoked his cigar in silence as they hastened after the troops of the General's brigade, which preceded them; and it was not until they were some miles on their way that he left off twirling his mustachio and broke silence.

The virtue of such incidents is not merely their comedy; it is their reality. With every line in these portraits – and, I say, in the portraits not in the disquisitions Thackeray wrote under them – there is an extension of reality, the excitement of the detective who goes from clue to clue. And still the honeymoon at Brighton with Becky being witty about the moon while her husband sharps at cards in the room behind her, and the Brussels chapters, stand out as a culminating height in English comic writing. The bullet in George Osborne's heart is not so good; but the rest – well, in the first year of this war we saw the whole Thackerean scene enacted again.

Thackeray and Balzac: they are like the opposite sides of the same penny. Here is young George Osborne speaking to Amelia:

> 'Ours is a ready money society. We live among bankers and city big-wigs, and be hanged to them, and every man as he talks to you jingles his guineas in his pocket.'

Money in Balzac is as dynamic as a passion; in Thackeray it is less massive; it is as ubiquitous as the senses. True, it is reduced in his philosophy to the common level of vanity, another factor which the moralist washes down with another glass of vintage sadness; but in the narrative Thackeray understands money and its place in the contemporary situation. Waterloo must have looked romantic in 1840, yet Thackeray also knew who won that battle. It is not an accident that Osborne and Sedley are Stock Exchange speculators, the newest representatives of middle-class finance. And in the cut-throat stage, too. He knows the anxiety of the aristocracy – 'make them pay up first and cut them afterwards' – and the anxiety of speculators to get their sons and daughters into the class above them. Thackeray's picture of the Regency aristocracy is a caricature, as we know from the memoirs of the time; it is a middle-class view which understands the aristocrats only when, like Lady Southdown, they catch the infection of middle-class piety. But how proper is the distinction he makes between the attitude of the various members of the Crawley family to Miss Crawley's fortune, and the attitude of old Osborne to *his* fortune. The portrait of Miss Crawley – the greatest character in the book to my mind – makes one wonder if Thackeray did always go wrong about aristocrats. (I take it she was one? An old-fashioned revolutionary aristocrat, already an anachronism before Waterloo.) She is the one character who understands Becky, and it is the older, shrewder feeling of her generation for money which sharpens Miss Crawley's eyes. One seems to see wills becoming deeds, deeds becoming notes, notes dissolving into coins and passing from above from hand to hand until they reach the dress-wiping palms of the servants, in nearly every page of this novel. It was a perception which was no doubt heightened in Thackeray by the taboo on sex; so that socially the background is perfect, where the individuals are castrated.

One does not say that the inability to write above love as a sexual passion is fatal to a novelist; but in Thackeray the people do become, as he says, 'Puppets'. They are small to the eye, figures seen through the wrong end of a telescope. As egotists, they are made mean by their sexlessness; for there is a generosity about sexual egotism. We recall the terrible crime of Becky, even in her schooldays: 'she was old in life and experience'. After the hush caused by that remark, we do not today rise, as we were intended to do, to nobler heights; on the contrary, we sink to that plane where the 'quid' dominates its unmentionable partnership with the 'pro quo'.

But the pleasure of Thackeray is in the sense of Style, in the intimacy with an educated mind. It is absurd to condemn the educated for being humbugs: they are merely more skilful humbugs. Since when have the educated been observed to 'know better', to be any more than a more self-conscious product of their times? Remove the vices of a novelist and his virtues vanish too. To us, and especially since the two wars, Thackeray is the great sedentary novelist, a moralist to whom adventure and physical action are alien; and that cuts him off. He is cut off by his melancholy – a peacetime luxury: our emotion is sharp, dramatic and tragic. But in *Vanity Fair*, in those hundreds of fragmentary pictures where scenes are crystallised and people talk, there is the original journalist Thackeray. Here are Rawdon and Becky again, first Thackeray the compère, then the reporter:

An article as necessary to a lady in this position as her brougham or her bouquet, is her companion. I have always admired the way in which the tender creatures, who cannot exist without sympathy, hire an exceedingly plain friend of their own sex from whom they are almost inseparable. The sight of that inevitable woman in her faded gown seated behind her dear friend in the opera-box, or occupying the back seat of the barouche, is always a wholesome and moral one to me, as jolly a reminder as that of the Death's-head which figured in the repasts of Egyptian *bons vivants*, a strange sardonic memorial of Vanity Fair. What? – even battered, brazen, beautiful conscienceless, heartless Mrs. Firebrace, whose father died of her shame; even lovely, daring Mrs. Mantrap, who will ride at any fence which any man in England will take, and who drives her greys in the Park, while her mother keeps a huckster's stall in Bath still; – even those who are so bold, one might fancy they could face anything, dare not face the world without a female friend. They must have somebody to cling to, the affectionate creatures! And you will hardly see them in any public place without a shabby companion in a dyed silk, sitting somewhere in the shade close behind them.

'Rawdon', said Becky, very late one night, as a party of gentlemen were seated round her crackling drawing-room fire (for the men came to her house to finish the night; and she had ice and coffee for them, the best in London): 'I must have a sheep-dog.'

'A what?' said Rawdon, looking up from an écarté table.

'A sheep-dog!' said young Lord Southdown. 'My dear Mrs. Crawley, what a fancy! Why not have a Danish dog? I know of one as big as a camel-leopard, by Jove. It would almost pull your brougham. Or a Persian greyhound, eh? (I propose, if you please); or a little pug that would go into one of Lord Steyne's snuff-boxes? There's a man at Bayswater got one with such a nose that you might – I mark the king and play, – that you might hang your hat on it.'

'I mark the trick,' Rawdon gravely said. He attended to his game commonly, and didn't much meddle with the conversation except when it was about horses and betting.

'What *can* you want with a shepherd's dog?' the lively little Southdown continued.

'I mean a *moral* shepherd's dog,' said Becky, laughing, and looking up at Lord Steyne.

'What the devil's that?' said his Lordship.

'A dog to keep the wolves off me,' Rebecca continued. 'A companion.'

'Dear little innocent lamb, you want one,' said the Marquis; and his jaw thrust out, and he began to grin hideously, his little eyes leering towards Rebecca.

The great Lord of Steyne was standing by the fire sipping coffee. The fire crackled and blazed pleasantly. There was a score of candles sparkling round the mantelpiece, in all sorts of quaint sconces, of gilt and bronze and porcelain. They lighted up Rebecca's figure to admiration, as she sat on a sofa covered with a pattern of gaudy flowers. She was in a pink dress, that looked as fresh as a rose; her dazzling white arms and shoulders were half-covered with a thin hazy scarf through which they sparkled; her hair hung in curls round her neck; one of her little feet peeped out from the fresh crisp folds of silk: the prettiest little foot in the prettiest little sandal in the finest silk stockings in the world.

The candles lighted up Lord Steyne's shining bald head, which was fringed with red hair. He had thick bushy eyebrows, with little twinkling bloodshot eyes, surrounded by a thousand wrinkles. His jaw was underhung, and when he laughed, two white buck-teeth protruded themselves and glistened savagely in the midst of the grin. He had been dining with royal personages, and wore his garter and ribbon. A short man was his Lordship, broad-chested, and bow-legged, but proud of the fineness of his foot and ankle, and always caressing his garter-knee.

'And so the Shepherd is not enough', said he, 'to defend his lambkin?'

'The Shepherd is too fond of playing at cards and going to his clubs,' answered Becky, laughing.

''Gad, what a debauched Corydon!' said my Lord – 'what a mouth for a pipe!'

'I take your three to two,' here said Rawdon, at the card-table.

'Hark at Melibeus,' snarled the noble Marquis; 'he's pastorally occupied too; he's shearing a Southdown. What an innocent mutton, hey? Damme, what a snowy fleece!'

Rebecca's eyes shot out gleams of scornful humour. 'My Lord,' she said, 'you are a knight of the Order.' He had the collar round his neck, indeed – a gift of the restored Princes of Spain.

Lord Steyne in early life had been notorious for his daring and his success at play. He had sat up two days and two nights with Mr. Fox at Hazard. He had won money of the most august personages of the realm; he had won his marquisate, it was said, at the gaming-table; but he did not like an allusion to those bygone *fredaines*. Rebecca saw the scowl gathering over his heavy brow.

She rose up from her sofa, and went and took his coffee-cup out of his hand with a little curtsey. 'Yes,' she said, 'I must get a watch-dog. But he won't bark at *you*.' And, going into the other drawing-room, she sat down to the piano, and began to sing little French songs in such a charming, thrilling voice, that the mollified nobleman speedily followed her into that chamber, and might be seen nodding his head and bowing time over her.

Rawdon and his friend meanwhile played écarté until they had enough. The Colonel won; but, say that he won ever so much and often, nights like these, which occurred many times in the week – his wife having all the talk and all the admiration, and he sitting silent without the circle, not comprehending a word of the jokes, the allusions, the mystical language within – must have been wearisome to the ex-dragoon.

'How is Mrs. Crawley's husband?' Lord Steyne used to say to him by way of a good-day when they met: and indeed that was now his avocation in life. He was Colonel Crawley no more. He was Mrs. Crawley's husband.

We cannot say 'reporter', but how actual, on the spot, caught in the casualness of the moment, those people are. Rawdon's slang, even Jos Sedley's jokes, Becky's startling opening sentences, George Osborne's exclamations – these are not jollifications of language; they are real. *Yellowplush*, the snob book, and all those curious phonetic dialogues of his – Joyce-like in their way – indicate something like the modern ear's curiosity. Cut *Vanity Fair* by a third and the rest moves at once into step with our lives.

The South Goes North

━━━━

The chief fault of the Victorian novelists, says Lord David Cecil, writing of Mrs Gaskell in his *Early Victorian Novelists*, is that they write beyond their range. This criticism is probably true, but it is one, I think, that must be applied with great caution. What is the range of a novelist? Even of Turgenev it has been objected that he went beyond his range in his portraits of the revolutionaries in *Virgin Soil*. There can be few novelists in any country who keep to the things they know in their bones. Opinion, beliefs collected and disputed, *weltanschauung*, are shovelled into all but the purely æsthetic novels; part of the impulse to write novels and a good deal of the material is in a sense the work of the period in which a novelist lives. It is a dangerous criticism which picks out from the past the fragments that appeal to us, and which suggests for example that the Victorian domestic charm can be separated from the Victorian sermon. And if, in picking up novels like Mrs Gaskell's *Wives and Daughters* or *North and South*, we say we prefer a self-regarding and captivating young flirt and hedonist like Cynthia Kirkpatrick to the worthy Molly Gibsons or the prim and reprimanding Margaret Hales, we have no right to say the latter are lay figures, sticks and prigs. All early and mid-Victorian fiction, with the exception perhaps of *Wuthering Heights*, inculcates the idea of responsibility, as our own novels seek to impress us with ideas of self-sufficiency and guilt, and if *we* find responsible characters heavy going, or too good to be true, there was a time in which they were considered passionately attractive.

What a sombre, violent and emotional scene these early Victorian novelists present. Did they create those melodramatic plots to relieve the peaceful boredom of prosperity? A glance at the social history of the nineteenth century shows that this cannot be so. It was a time of spiritual and material turbulence. Victorian melodrama was only a very slightly exaggerated picture of Victorian life. The riots, shipwrecks, fires, lunatic asylums and deportations we read of in the novels, the awful family splits about legacies and estates, the sons told never again to darken the door, the rejected lovers trekking off to the brutal colonies, all are real enough. In these novels one sees a panorama where women in childbed die like flies, where stepmothers are rampant, orphanages overflow and hordes of fallen women grovel helplessly in the wake of a seducer who has the devil-may-care air of a disguised Sunday School teacher. And beyond them, in the middle distance, the factory smoke rises, the workers herd into the workshops, the mob plunges in the streets. Everything we can learn of Victorian life confirms the picture. People did turn out to be the missing sons of earls, honest families *were* ruined in the markets, clergymen *were* able to work themselves up to crises of conscience on what seems to us a mere point of order. My own early impression of Victorian novels in childhood was of islands of domestic peace surrounded by a sea of moral peril. One read not for pleasure, but to worry and to be frightened. The truth is, I think, that a passionate and brutal age, intoxicated above all by the idea of power – not only Carlyle, but Mrs Gaskell too, had a weakness for the rough Teutonic ancestor, the Viking and the Nordic myth – could control itself only by moral violence. The castration of youth, the idealis-ation of middle age seem to indicate this. The Victorian novel not only put the heart in the mouth; it started the burglar alarm of conscience very loudly in the head, and conventions are strong when the passions are strong. The very complications of the plots and sub-plots, the stagey coincidences, the impossible innocence and the impossible vice, are photographs of the Victorian mind which carried its characteristic doctrine of the survival of the fittest even into the reader's task as he sat down to be tortured into taking life still more seriously by the latest serial instalment.

It is not on these grounds that we would praise Mrs Gaskell's *North and South* or *Mary Barton*, as the Victorian critics did; but it is on these grounds that we must defend her. They were didactic melodramas and best sellers in their time, and we must not forget this when we find *Cranford* or the social comedy of *Wives and Daughters* more to our taste.

North and South is dead now and that is a pity; for now that we have ceased to believe that the most important events in life occur only in the drawing-room, the bedroom or the psychologist's clinic, it is interesting to discover that Mrs Gaskell was intensely moved by the questions of her time. The idea of responsibility was not merely philanthropical; it sprang from a practical and religious sense of the coherence of society.

Like all her books, except *Cranford*, like all Victorian novels, *North and South* is too long; that it is stiff, stilted and lifeless no one who has lived in the industrial north will ever agree. And on this point I must differ with Lord David Cecil. Economics were outside her range, but the men and women of the industrial revolution were not. *North and South* succeeds where Mrs Gaskell always succeeds: in the simple essentials of character, in her skill at distinguishing and presenting manners, in her delightful eye for detail, the mild deftness of her satire. Ladylike though she was and very apt with a moral, she had an untroubled steadiness of eye when she faced human emotions. She shrank from investigating the passions, but she at least missed nothing from their outline. The motive of jealousy is lightly touched; it is never missed. Margaret Hale is a prig, no doubt, when she attacks John Thornton for abusing his workers. She is a snob also about tradesmen and manufacturers; but she is capable of strong feeling, her pride is not sick and self-consuming, but is directed outward upon her relationships with people, a firm consummate assertion of her personality. Margaret Hale is a prig, if you like, in the sense in which most of us are prigs; but it is more truthful to say that she is stubborn in her loyalties and decided in her affections. She is assured in her class, in her belief, for example, of the superiority of southern English culture when it is contrasted with the rougher manners of the north; but she has not simply inherited these things without inquiry. She has a strong mind and is prepared to argue. I take it that a novelist unwittingly draws a stick and a prig when he uses a character to express views he approves of and then, so to speak, publicly congratulates the character on being an example to us all, without building this upon the positives and negatives of human nature. Now Mrs Gaskell is quite clear about the nature of Margaret Hale. John Thornton's dour, jealous and terrifying old mother observes Margaret with detachment and judges her as one woman judges another. Mrs Thornton is reserved about the question of Margaret Hale's goodness; the quality the hard old lady notes with approval is not goodness; but the fundamental one of will. The plain north-country people are always quick to criticise Margaret's virtuousness. They tell her she is a mere social manner and that she fails to fulfil promises. There is, it is true, one of those awful self-sacrificial moments, so common in the early Victorian novels, when Margaret tells a lie to shield her brother. It is one of those lies which, apparently, could wreck love affairs because the Victorian belief in appearances seems to have prevented inquiry. (Obviously in a passionate age if you saw a lady walking unattended with a strange man, it was natural and stimulated more excitement if you assumed she was an abandoned woman.) Margaret Hale makes a terrible fuss about this fib of hers, treating it, in the best pious tradition, as if it were incest or adultery; but when you look at the matter more closely, you see that Mrs Gaskell never really neglected real human motive for long. It is Margaret Hale's pride, not her conscience, which is disturbed. She is afraid that she has exposed a weakness of will to a lover whom she has so far kept at arm's length. As the portrait of a normally prim young woman (and it was Fielding who, with real Englishness, spoke of the irresistible attraction of the prude) on the defensive in a hostile environment, Mrs Gaskell's picture of the conflicts in Margaret Hale's character is an accurate one.

John Thornton's mother is a wonderful sketch. One sees her in that too brilliant and ornate drawing-room which looks out upon the mill, a woman with a single passion, a primitive love for her son. 'Her face moved slowly from one decided expression to another equally decided.' Stiff and forbidding she is to the southerner, implacable, blankly insensitive and interfering, but the heart is there, now fierce, now yielding. Hard as she is, she is at her son's mercy. She is the first to see that he will fall for Margaret because of Margaret's pride, because he knows the affair will be a battle and probably will be lost. The obstinacy of the northern character, an aggressiveness in it which instinctively prefers enemies to friends, or resistance to acquiescence, is admirably displayed. This is brought out even more successfully in the tale of Thornton's relations with his workers. At first Margaret sees only the mutual hatred in the relationship; then she perceives that both sides like hating. Their hatred is a sort of independence with them, a sport, an animal instinct which on both sides seeks not moral solutions, but a master. The reconciliation of Thornton with the strike leader whom he has sacked and intends to victimise has the inevitable sugaring of Victorian domestic sentiment in it – 'remember the poor children' – but it is very truthful to northern manners.

Higgins did not turn round, or immediately respond to this. But when he did speak, it was in a softened tone, although the words were gruff enough.

'Yo've no business to go prying into what happened between Boucher and me. He's dead and I'm sorry. That's enough.'

'So it is. Will you take work with me? That's what I came to ask.'

Higgins's obstinacy wavered, recovered strength, and stood firm. He would not speak. Mr. Thornton would not ask again. Higgins's eye fell on the children.

'Yo've called me impudent, and a liar, and a mischief-maker, and you might ha' said wi' some truth, as I were now and then given to drink. An' I ha' called you a tyrant, and an oud bull-dog, and a hard, cruel master; that's where it stands. But for th' childer. Measter, do yo' think we can e'er get on together?'

'Well!' said Mr. Thornton, half-laughing, 'it was not my proposal that we should go together. But there's one comfort, on your own showing. We neither of us can think much worse of the other than we do now.'

'That's true,' said Higgins reflectively. 'I've been thinking, ever sin' I saw you, what a marcy it were yo' did na take me on, for that I ne'er saw a man whom I could less abide. But that's maybe been a hasty judgment; and work's work to such as me. So, measter, I'll come; and what's more I thank yo'; and that's a deal fro' me,' said he, more frankly, suddenly turning round and facing Mr. Thornton fully for the first time.

'And this is a deal from me,' said Mr. Thornton, giving Higgins's hand a good grip. 'Now mind, you come sharp to your time,' continued he, resuming the master. 'I'll have no laggards at my mill. What fines we have, we keep pretty sharply. And the first time I catch you making mischief, off you go. So now you know where you are.'

'Yo' spoke of me wisdom this morning. I reckon I may bring it wi' me; or would yo' rayther have me 'bout my brains!'

' 'Bout your brains if you use them for meddling with my business; with your brains if you can keep to your own.'

'I shall need a deal o' brains to settle where my business ends and yo'rs begins.'

'Your business has not begun yet, and mine stands still for me. So good afternoon.'

And in fact whenever Mrs Gaskell is among the lives of people – and the half-starving Darkshire workers with their deathbeds, their drunks and their touch of fantastic Methodism are a different human species from the ladies of Cranford – she has a true eye and ear.

In all her work from *Cranford* onwards, Mrs Gaskell is the neat social historian. First of all she is the historian of the impecunious genteel, then her net is thrown wider until, in *Wives and Daughters*, it catches a whole society from the aristocracy and the squirearchy down to the professions and trades. 'Why', Molly Gibson, the doctor's daughter, asks Lady Harriet, 'why do you speak of my class as if we were a strange kind of animal instead of human beings?' That question Mrs Gaskell put to all classes. In her own way, Mrs Gaskell was a Lady Harriet, an animal collector. She never gets speech wrong, from dialect to drawl. So that when she came to social strife in *North and South* – and it may be remembered that Dickens published her immediately after *Hard Times* – she had the practice of faithful record. The streets and, again, the manners of the streets in that northern town are down with the fidelity of a Dutch painting, though never overdone. She observes not only particular looks and phrases, but the general look, the drift of the common gossip. She contrasts the brutality of the mill atmosphere with the superstition of Margaret's beloved Hampshire village. With the reproachfulness of the good but detached Unitarian lady, she notes how both places go blindly on in the pursuit of their own magic. The chapters of discussion are not good, they stick out like lectures, simply because Mr Hale is in them and Mr Hale is a failure. (He is the inevitably Victorian tribute to the tedious pathos of self-pity.) But there is one passage of discussion which strikes the eye nowadays because of its curious modern echo. Thornton is answering the liberal intellectual Platonist from Oxford:

'Remember we are of a different race from the Greeks . . . I belong to Teutonic blood; it is little mingled in this part of England to what it is in others; we retain much of their language; we retain more of their spirit; we do not look upon life as a time of enjoyment, but as a time for action and exertion.'

(He would certainly get that in marrying Mildred.) The don cuts him short when Thornton declares for tribal independence:

[100]

'In short you would like the Heptarchy back again. You are regular worshippers of Thor.'

Rosenberg in Yorkshire! Is it an inevitable phase in the development of new communities which are feeling their strength? The discussion ends in the air, indeed it is cut short by a more familiar Mrs Gaskell who has the art of introducing a distrait remark which will also indicate a fresh touch to the development of a situation. Her sister writes from Corfu (Margaret suddenly interjects), that calico is cheaper and better there! Just a small, trite remark apropros of nothing and yet, what has the author done? She has shown that Margaret is beginning to get interested in the vulgar textile trade – a sign favourable for Mr Thornton – and that before long Mr Thornton will have to keep his eye on foreign competition. It would be foolish to make much of a point of such a detail, but Mrs Gaskell's work was built out of thousands of small, light, truthful touches. The parish visitor sees what is in a room, though she may not grasp the forces that have made that room what it is. In the long domestic gossip of that visit, Mrs Gaskell is one of the quickest pairs of eyes, one of the frankest tongues.

The Proximity of Wine

The desire for settlement comes with peculiar force to stockbrokers; but the wish of Mr Crotchet, the retired City man of Weybridge, is common to us all:

'The sentimental against the rational,' said Mr. Crotchet, 'the intuitive against the inductive, the ornamental against the useful, the intense against the tranquil, the romantic against the classical: these are the great and interesting controversies which I should like, before I die, to see satisfactorily settled.'

Even those of us who have not the disputatious, metaphysical Scottish blood which Peacock had slyly infused into the veins of Mr Crotchet may join in his unhopeful sigh. What is the good of inviting intellectuals down for the week end unless they settle matters like these once and for all? Alas, the habit of the intellectual is to be unsettling and in both senses of the word. There is a chronic Mr Firedamp in every *posse* of the brainy; even when final order seems to have been achieved, there is always one bat left in the belfries:

'There is another great question,' said Mr. Firedamp, 'greater than those, seeing that it is necessary to be alive in order to settle any question and this is the question of water against human woe. Wherever there is water, there is *malaria*, and wherever there is malaria there are the elements of death. The great object of a wise man should be to live on a gravelly hill, without so much as a duckpond within 10 miles of him, eschewing cisterns and water butts . . .'

Dr Folliott, a Tory and a practical man, had at any rate the answer in his cellar. 'The proximity of wine', he said, was of more importance 'than the longinquity of water.' After sufficient Burgundy the endless and cantankerous algebra of life appears lucid and limited. Wine has the triple merit of enriching the vocabulary, cheering the heart, and narrowing the mind, and the sooner one cuts the cackle of the intellectuals with some good food and drink the sooner comes peace on earth.

The food and drink question is fundamental in Peacock. On Samuel Butler's theory that all Radicals have had digestions, it is clear that from the wine and food test Peacock comes out true-blue Tory. There is no stab of that sublimated belly-ache which drives the rest of us into progressive politics. Of course we know that Peacock called himself a Liberal and wrote for the Liberal reviews; but the enemies of the Utilitarians considered him a joke and Hazlitt teased him for 'warbling' on the wrong side of the fence.

The game Peacock played was a dangerous one, and in a man less original and gifted it would have been disastrous. Peacock's virtue was that he had no political opinions in a very political age; or rather, that he had all the opinions, as a dog has fleas in order to keep his mind off being a dog. Peacock's mind kept open house and ruled the table; too often that leads, in literary circles, to banging the table. One can see this in the Rev. Dr Folliott. A great character, perhaps the greatest of the Peacock characters, but how close the guzzling clergyman comes to being one of those vinous boors, one of those bottled, no-nonsense dogmatists who tyrannise the table and bully the world of letters with comic bluster about their common sense:

> MR. MACQUEDY. Then, sir, I presume you set no value on the right principles of rent, profit, wages and currency.
>
> REVD. DR. FOLLIOTT. My principles, sir, in these things are to take as much as I can get and to pay no more than I can help. These are everyman's principles, whether they be the right principles or no. There, sir, is political economy in a nutshell.

There is too great a finality in the well-fed; and though Dr Folliott redresses a balance and is a brilliant and mature device for winding the theorists back to the earth – very necessary in the novel of ideas – one's mind does wander to 'poor Mrs. Folliott' who, having combed her husband's wig, is firmly left at home. One remembers other poor Mrs Folliotts pecking a timid and hen-like way behind their boozy, commonsensical cockalorums. And while we have still got political economy in a nutshell it is interesting to note how strong a respect for money is ingrained in the crackling, phlegmatic temper of our satirical writers. It is strong in Iago, it is strong in Swift (the Drapier letters), Shaw is an enthusiastic accountant and Peacock's principles regarding paper money amount to mania. On that subject he was a Firedamp. We may imagine his reactions when, having invited Shelley to live in Marlow, he heard that the poet was giving away his clothes and his money to the indigent inhabitants. It is always surprising when poetic justice is benevolent, and most critics have gasped with incredulous satisfaction at Peacock's luck in hooking a job worth £2,000 a year or more out of the East India Company; what is significant and even more poetically fitting is that Peacock was a success at the job. He it was who organised the building and dispatch of the flat-bottomed gunboats used by the company in the East. There blossomed the Utilitarian. One doubts whether Wordsworth was as efficient at the Excise.

The life of Peacock covers a period of enormous differences. One of Peacock's modern critics, Mr John Mair, has pointed out how fantastic is the range of his life.

> He lived through the French Revolution and the Great Exhibition; he could have read his first books to Nelson and his last to Bernard Shaw [who would not have understood it], Dr. Johnson died a year before his birth and Yeats was born a year before his death. He both preceded and survived Byron, Shelley, Keats and Macaulay; he was contemporary with Rowlandson and with Landseer.

For a satirical mind this was the perfect feast; history at its most conflicting and indigestible. For a temperament liable to be infected by all schools of thought in turn and unable to resist cocking snooks at them, here was wealth. Peacock dined off his disabilities and one can almost hear his unholy highbrow cackle when he finds himself not only pre-dating but surviving his victims. Some annoyance has been felt because he became a kind of reactionary by default; you ought not to pull the leg of your own party. But could there have been a more delightful occupation for one whose baptismal water had a drop of the acid of perversity in it? A Grub Street hack in his time, and one who (according to Hazlitt anyway) overpraised as wildly as any of our commercial reviewers, he sneers at the puffs of Grub Street. A hater of Scotsmen, he was a theoretical Scotsman for, as Professor Saintsbury discovered, Peacock was baptised at the Scottish kirk. He scarifies Miss Philomel Poppyseed for saying true love is impossible on less than £1,000 a year but is as acute about the marriage settlements of his own characters as Jane Austen herself. Everywhere the satirist is reacting against his own wishes and disappointments. There is little doubt that an erratic education fostered his originality as it also failed to provide some strong stamp which would have made up his mind; there would have been no Peacock if he had gone to the University. But those sneers at the University which always crop up in his books are prolonged; and when the debates between the deteriorationists, the progressives, the transcendentalists and rational economists bore us, we cannot reject the suspicion that Peacock spent a good deal of his literary life training to be an undergraduate.

If Peacock's mind was not made up, if he snapped at his opponents and his friends, it would be a mistake to think of him as a complete *farceur*. When the effervescence has died down there is a deposit of belief which is not party belief but is rather his century's habit of mind. The eighteenth century had formed him; he belonged to that middleman and professional class which did not share – at least, did not directly share – in the rewards of the industrial revolution. When Mr Escot speaks against the mills in *Headlong Hall*, he is not putting a party view; he is pleading like a merchant philosopher for the content of living in a world that was violently altering its form in the optimistic delusion that the content would look after itself. If Mr Peacock-Escot is a reactionary, then one can only reply that it is the rôle of reactionaries, once they have given up obstruction, to remind us that the Sabbath was made for man. Their function is to preserve amenities and that private humanity which revolutionaries care for so little. Here is Mr Escot with his everything-is-as-bad-as-it-can-be-in-the-worst-of-possible-worlds:

> You present to me a complicated picture of artificial life, and require me to admire it. Seas covered with vessels; every one of which contains two or three tyrants, and from fifty to a thousand slaves, ignorant, gross, perverted and active only in mischief. Ports resounding with life: in other words with noise and drunkenness, the mingled din of avarice, intemperance and prostitution. Profound researches, scientific

inventions: to what end? To contract the sum of human wants? to teach the art of living on a little? to disseminate independence, liberty and health? No; to multiply factitious desires, to stimulate depraved appetites, to invent irrational wants, to heap up incense on the shrine of luxury, and accumulate expedients of selfish and ruinous profusion.

He goes on to a description of children in the cotton mills, a true piece of Dickensian phantasmagoria – 'observe their pale and ghastly features, more ghastly in that baleful and malignant light, and tell me if you do not fancy yourself on the threshold of Virgil's Hell. . . .' Did that passage have any effect on the more ruthless of Peacock's readers? One doubts it. The voice of the Age of Reason was reactionary and decadent from the point of view of the nineteenth-century liberals, and most of us were born into the nineteenth century's belief that a period is decadent which has arrived at the civilised stillness of detached self-criticism. Peacock said the wise thing in the wrong way, i.e. the detached way. It was the attached people, more vulgar, more sentimental, more theatrically subject to the illusions of the new period, who could and did attack child labour and the mills with some effect.

For a man as mercurial and unseizable as Peacock was, what really counted was the farce. Detached, isolated, hiding caution behind a fantasticating brain, silent about the private urges of his heart, unimaginative, timid of 'acrimonious dispute' (as the scathing so often are), he enjoyed the irresponsibilities of an intellect which cannot define its responsibilities. His cruelty to his victims is merely the brain's. There he can display an extravagance which elsewhere a prudent nature denies him. His satire was not resented, as far as one knows, by the victims. Shelley laughed at Scythrop in *Nightmare Abbey*. No doubt Shelley's own irresponsibility responded to Peacock's distorted picture of him torn between Harriet and Mary Godwin, 'like a shuttlecock between two battledores, changing its direction as rapidly as the oscillations of a pendulum receiving many a hard knock on the cork' – the cork! – 'of a sensitive heart and flying from point to point in the feathers of a super-sublimated head'.

As they come fragmentarily into focus, the Peacock novels have the farcical dream-atmosphere of the surrealists' dreams. Their slapstick and their unexpected transitions, their burlesque discussions, and their fancy

[106]

lead through *Alice in Wonderland* to the present. It is amusing to find present parallels for the deteriorationist and the rational economist. Peacock chose permanent types; but without the knock-about and the romance, that amusement would soon become bookish and musty. Scythrop concealing his lady in the tower and lying about the movable bookcase, Mr Toobad jumping out of the window at the sight of the 'ghost' and being fished out of the moat by the dreary scientists who are down there with their nets fishing for mermaids, Squire Headlong's experiments with explosives, Dr Folliott's adventures with the highwaymen – this picaresque horseplay is the true stuff of the English comic tradition from Sterne and Fielding, a new gloss on the doings of the Pickwick Club. And Peacock can alternate the perfunctory with the heroic manner, which our tradition especially requires. Gradually, as he perfected his genre, progressing from the Hall to the Abbey, from the Abbey to the Castle, Peacock balanced his extremes. Romantic love plays its part, not the wild meadowy stuff of course, but a romance which secretes an artificial sweetness, the *faux naturel* of the eighteenth century, which at once suggests the formal and untutored. In this heady world the women alone – if one excepts the highbrow Poppyseed and the awful Mrs Glowry – have the sense and sensibility. Peacock cuts short the sighs; marriages are arranged, not made in Heaven, dowries are not forgotten; but what a delightful convention (the India clerk reminds us) marriage is.

One might expect more broadness in so keen a reader of Rabelais, but Peacock (unless my memory is bad or my ear for *double entendre* dull) appears to share the primness of Dr Folliott, a primness one often finds among the drinkers. There is only one smoke-room remark in *Crotchet Castle* – and a very good one it is. It occurs after the cook has set her room on fire when she has fallen asleep over a treatise on hydrostatics in cookery:

> LORD BOSSNOWL.   But, sir, by the bye, how came your footman to be going into your cook's room? It was very providential, to be sure but . . .
>
> REVD. DR. FOLLIOTT.   Sir, as good came of it, I shut my eyes and ask no questions. I suppose he was going to study hydrostatics and he found himself under the necessity of practising hydraulics.

I suppose it should be argued that Dr Folliott's anger about the exhibition of an undraped female figure on the stockbroker's mantelpiece was grounded less in the prudery of the bibulous than in the general Peacockian dislike of popular education. He was against putting ideas into his footman's head. An act of benevolence, for no one knew so well as Peacock how funny a man with an idea in his head can be.

An Anatomy of Greatness

There are two books which are the perfect medicine for the present time: Voltaire's *Candide* and Fielding's *Jonathan Wild*. They deal with our kind of news but with this advantage over contemporary literature: the news is already absorbed, assumed and digested. We see our situation at a manageable remove. This is an important consolation and, on the whole, *Jonathan Wild* is the more specific because the narrower and more trenchant book. Who, if not ourselves, are the victims of what are called 'Great Men'? Who can better jump to the hint that the prig or cut-purse of Newgate and the swashbuckler of Berchtesgaden are the same kind of man and that Cæsar and Alexander were morally indistinguishable from the gang leaders, sharpers, murderers, pickpockets from whom Mr Justice Fielding, in later years, was to free the City of London? Europe has been in the hands of megalomaniacs for two decades. Tyranny abroad, corruption at home – that recurrent theme of the eighteenth-century satirists who were confronted by absolute monarchy and the hunt for places – is our own. Who are we but the good – with a small middle-class 'g' – and who are 'they' but the self-elected 'leaders' and 'the Great'? And *Jonathan Wild* has the attraction of a great *tour de force* which does not shatter us because it remains, for all its realism, on the intellectual plane. Where Swift, in contempt, sweeps us out of the very stables; where Voltaire advises us not to look beyond our allotments upon the wilderness humanity has left everywhere on a once festive earth, Fielding is ruthless only to the brain. Our heads are scalped by him but soul and body are left alive. He is arbitrary but not destructive. His argument that there is an incompatibility between greatness and goodness is an impossible one, but of the eighteenth-century three scourgers of mankind he is the least egotistical and the most moral. He has not destroyed the world; he has merely turned it upside down as a polished dramatist will force a play out of a paradox:

... contradicting the obsolete doctrines of a Set of Simple Fellows called, in Derision, Sages or Philosophers, who have endeavoured as much as possible to confound the Ideas of Greatness and Goodness, whereas no two Things can possibly be more distinct from each other. For Greatness consists in bringing all Manner of Mischief on Mankind, and Goodness in removing it from them.

Jonathan Wild is a paradox sustained with, perhaps the strain, but above all, with the decisiveness, flexibility and exhilaration of a scorching trumpet call which does not falter for one moment and even dares very decorative and difficult variations on the way to its assured conclusion. When we first read satire we are aware of reading against the whole current of our beliefs and wishes, and until we have learned that satire is anger laughing at its own futility, we find ourselves protesting and arguing silently against the author. This we do less, I think, in reading *Jonathan Wild* than with *Candide* or *Gulliver*. If there is any exhaustion in *Jonathan Wild* it does not come from the tussle of our morality with his. There is no moral weariness. If we tire it is because of the intellectual effort of reversing the words 'great' and 'good' as the eye goes over the page. Otherwise it is a young man's book, very vain of its assumptions and driven on with masterly nonchalance.

To the rigidity of his idea Fielding brought not only the liveliness of picaresque literature but, more important, his experience as a playwright. Of its nature satire deals in types and artifices and needs the schooling of the dramatist, who can sweep a scene off the moment the point is made and who can keep his nimble fingers on a complicated plot. Being concerned with types, satire is in continual need of intrigue and movement; it needs tricks up the sleeve and expertness in surprise. We are distracted in *Jonathan Wild* between pleasure in his political references (the pointed one on the quarrels between the gangsters about the style of their hats for example, which Wild settles with the genius of a dictator), and the dexterity of the author. 'Great men are lonely': one of the best scenes in the book, one fit to stand beside Wild's wonderful quarrel with his wife Tishy when he calls her a bitch, is the superb comedy of Wild's soliloquy in the boat. Put adrift in an open boat by the Captain who has rescued Heartfree's wife from Wild's attempt at rape, Wild has his 'black Friday' and muses on the loneliness of 'the Great', their fear of death and their unhappiness. Since death is inevitable, Wild cries, why not die now? A man of action, for ever acting to an audience if only an imaginary one, he staggers us by at once throwing himself into the sea. Were we wrong? Was he courageous after all? We knew that a crook lives on gestures, that a show of toughness is all – but were we misreading him? Down comes the curtain, the chapter ends. Its dramatic effect is enormous, quite beyond the reach of the picaresque novelists who depend on the convolutions of intrigue alone. Among the satirists, only Voltaire, another writer for the stage, was capable of Fielding's scene; Swift was always willing to let a situation ease off into ironical discussion. And then, up goes Fielding's curtain again: Wild does not die. He is saved. He is in a boat once more. Saved by one of those disillusioning miracles of fiction? Not at all. He is back in his own boat. *He swam back to it.* Philosophy had told him to die, but Nature, whom he knew had designed him to be Great, told him not to be such a fool. That is a masterstroke.

Such cross-ruffing is the heart of farce and of the ordinary literature of roguery. But as Wild picks the pockets of his accomplices, double-crosses the card-sharping Count, swindles and is swindled in turn, each act shows a further aspect of his character and is a new chapter in the anatomy of Greatness. It has been said that Fielding's common sense and his low opinion that human beings were moved chiefly by self-interest restricted his imagination. This may be so, though the greater restriction was to his sensibility. In the light of our present painful knowledge of Great Men of action we are not likely to think the portrait of Wild unimaginative simply because Fielding takes an unpoetical view. There is the episode of the jewels. The Count, who, with Wild, has swindled Heartfree over the casket of jewels, has double-crossed his partner by substituting paste for the stolen treasure. Worse still, Tishy, whom Wild intends to seduce by the gift of the casket, has worked in a pawnbroker's and knows paste when she sees it. Wild is left to another soliloquy, to the sadness of Berchtesgaden or neo-Imperial Rome. 'They' are always sad:

How vain is human Greatness! . . . How unhappy is the state of Priggism! How impossible for Human Prudence to foresee and guard against each circumvention! . . . In this a Prig is more unhappy than any other: a cautious man may, in a crowd, preserve his own Pockets by keeping his hands in them; but while he employs his Hands in another's pockets, how shall he be able to defend his own? Where is his Greatness? I answer in his Mind: 'Tis the inward Glory, the secret Consciousness of doing great and wonderful Actions, which can alone support the truly Great Man, whether he be a Conqueror, a Tyrant, a Minister or a Prig. These must bear him up against the private Curse and public Imprecation, and while he is hated and detested by all Mankind, must make him inwardly satisfied with himself. For what but some such inward satisfaction as this could inspire Men possessed of Wealth, of Power, of every human Blessing, which Pride, Luxury, or Avarice could desire, to forsake their Homes, abandon Ease and Repose, and, at the Expense of Riches, Pleasures, at the Price of Labour and Hardship, and at the Hazard of all that Fortune hath liberally given them could send them at the Head of a Multitude of *Prigs* called an Army, to molest their Neighbours, to introduce Rape, Rapine, Bloodshed and every kind of Misery on their own Species? What but some such glorious Appetite of Mind . . .

Intoxicating stuff. The eighteenth century's attack on absolutism, its cry of Liberty, its plea for the rational, the measured, and even the conventional culminated – in what? Napoleon. And then democracy. It is painful to listen to the flying Prigs, to democracy's *Jonathan Wild*. Was the moral view of human nature mistaken? Is the Absolute People as destructive as the Absolute King? Is the evil not in the individual, but in society? We rally to the eighteenth-century cry of 'Liberty'; it is infectious, hotter indeed than it sounds today. We reflect that those good, settled, educated, middle-class men of the time of Queen Anne owed their emancipation to a Tyrant who burned half Ireland, killed his King and went in private hysterical dread of the Devil. Under that smooth prose, under that perfect deploying of abstractions, the men of the eighteenth century seem always to be hiding a number of frightening things that are neither smooth nor perfect. There is the madness of Swift, there is the torment of Wesley. Or was Fielding imagining the paradise of the anarchists where our natural goodness enables us to dispense with leaders? Sitting under the wings of the flying Prigs, we observe the common, indeed the commonplace, non-combatant man, behaving with a greatness which appears to require no leader but merely the prompting of sober and decent instincts.

Of course if the Great are wicked, the good are fools. Look at the Heartfrees! What a couple! But here again if you have made your head ache over Fielding's impossible theme, it is cured at once by the felicities to which the Heartfrees drive Fielding's invention. The letters which Heart-free gets from his impecunious or disingenuous debtors are a perfect collection; and Mrs Heartfree's sea adventures, in which there is hardly a moment between Holland and Africa when she is not on the point of losing her honour, are not so much padding but give a touch of spirit to her shopkeeping virtues and also serve the purpose of satirising the literature of travel. It is hard on Mrs Heartfree; perhaps Fielding was insensitive. Without that insensibility we should have missed the adventure with the monster who was 'as large as Windsor Castle', an episode which reminds us that the spirit of the nine o'clock news was already born in the 1700s:

> I take it to be the strangest Instance of that Intrepidity, so justly remarked in our Seamen, which can be found on Record. In a Wood then, one of our Mucketeers coming up to the Beast, as he lay on the Ground and with his Mouth wide open, marched directly down his Throat.

He had gone down to shoot the Monster in the heart. And we should have missed another entrancing sight. Mrs Heartfree perceived a fire in the desert and thought at first she was approaching human habitation.

> . . . but on nearer Approach, we perceived a very Beautiful Bird just expiring in the Flames. This was none other than the celebrated Phœnix.

The sailors threw it back into the Fire so that it 'might follow its own Method of propagating its Species'.

Yes, the Heartfrees would have a lot to talk about afterwards. There is a charm in the artlessness of Mrs Heartfree, if Heartfree is a bit of a stodge; one can understand why she introduced just a shade of suspense in the account of how she always managed to save her virtue at the last minute.

The Dean

T he world would be poor without the antics of clergymen. The Dean, for
example, wished he was a horse. A very Irish wish which a solid
Englishwoman very properly came down on; Lady Mary Wortley
Montagu was one of the few hostile critics of *Gulliver*:

> Great eloquence have (the authors) employed to prove themselves
> beasts and show such a veneration for horses, that, since the Essex
> Quaker, nobody has appeared so passionately devoted to that species;
> and to say truth they talk of a stable with so much warmth and affection I
> cannot help suspecting some very powerful motive at the bottom of it.

It *was* odd that a man as clean as the Dean should find solace among the
mangers; and there is a stable tip for psycho-analysts here. The function
which he loathed in Celia, and could never stop mentioning, had become
unnoticeable at last. Shades of the Freudian Cloacina imprison the growing boy, but are guiltlessly charmed away when, pail and shovel in hand,
we make our first, easy, hopeful acquaintance with the fragrant
Houyhnhnms.

Dr Johnson was also hostile. *Gulliver* was written 'in defiance of truth
and regularity'. Yet the Dean and the Doctor had much in common. They
were both sensible men in a century devoted to the flightiness of Reason.
What annoyed the Doctor was what enchanted the public; the *madness* of
Gulliver. Very irregular. We see now that the Augustan prose was a
madman's mask and that the Age of Reason was also the age of witchcraft,
hauntings, corruption and the first Gothic folly. History has confirmed Dr
Johnson's judgment first by numbing the satire – for who can be bothered
to look up the digs at Walpole, Newton and the rest? – and by giving the
book a totally different immortality. It is not an accident that *Gulliver* has
become a child's book; only a child could be so destructive, so irresponsible

and so cruel. Only a child has the animal's eye; only a child, or the mad clergyman, can manage that unhuman process of disassociation which is the beginning of all satire from Aristophanes onwards; only children (or the mad) have that monstrous and infantile egotism which assumes everything is meaningless and that, like children, we run the world on unenlightened self-interest like a wagon-load of monkeys. What a relief it is that the Dean's style is as lucid and plain as common water: it runs like water off a duck's back. If *Gulliver* had been written in the coloured prose of the Bible, bulging with the prophetic attitudinisings of the Jews, the book might have caused a revolution – there is some very revolutionary stuff in Lilliput – but a moderate church Tory like the Dean had no intention of doing that. There must have been satisfaction in reminding a Queen in the rational century that under her petticoat she was a Yahoo and savage satisfaction in knowing she liked the idea. In this she was a sensible woman; she had, like the rest of us, been charmed back to the minute and monstrous remembrances of childhood, she had been captivated by the plain, good and homely figure of Gulliver himself. She picked out the topical bits and when the Dean waded into his generalities about human nature, her eyes no doubt wandered off that almost too easy page and examined her finger-nails.

But there was a part of *Gulliver* which nobody liked or which most people thought inferior. Laputa missed the mark. Why? It was topical enough. The skit on science was a good shot at the young Royal Society and the wave of projects which obsessed the times. The highbrow is always fair game. Visually and satirically Laputa is the most delightful of the episodes. The magic island floats crystalline in the air, rising and falling to the whim of its ruler, and its absent-minded philosophers are only tickled into awareness by a fly-whisk. Laputa is the rationalist's daydream. Here is the unearthly paradise, an hydraulic and attainable heaven. True, the philosophers were fools and the scientists, with their attempts to get sunshine out of cucumbers, cloth from spiders, food from dirt and panic from astronomy, were ridiculous. The knowledge machine was grotesque. But what was the matter with the men of Newton's time that they could not appreciate Laputa? The Age of Reason enjoyed the infantile, the animal and irrational in Gulliver; it rejected the satire on knowledge.

The only answer can be that the Augustans had not had enough of science to know it was worth satirising. The Dean was before his time; and the world would have to wait a hundred and fifty years for *Bouvard and Pécuchet* to continue the unpopular game – the origins of *Bouvard* and *Gulliver* are, incidentally, identical and both Flaubert and Swift spent ten years on and off writing the books – and among ourselves, we have only Aldous Huxley's crib of Laputa, *Brave New World*. Yet Laputa is the only part of *Gulliver* which has not been eclipsed by subsequent writing. Voltaire, Wells, Verne – to take names at random – have all taken the freshness off Swift's idea; and what the Utopians have left out has been surpassed by science itself. The sinister functionalism of the termites, the pedestrian mysticism of the bee, the ribald melodramas of the aquarium and the Grand Guignol of the insect house, have all defeated human life and literature as material for the political satirist. These things have put the date on Lilliput, but Laputa is untouched. It stands among us, miraculously contemporary.

It is the surrealist island. At least Laputa is to Lilliput what *Alice in Wonderland* is to surrealism. The sportively clinical and sinister succeed to the human and extraordinary. One cannot love Laputa as one loves Lilliput, but one *recognises* Laputa. It is the clinic we have come to live in. It is the world of irresponsible intellect and irresponsible science which prepared the way for the present war. We enter at once into our inhumanity, into that glittering laboratory which is really a butcher's shop. What science does not dissect, it blows to pieces. The Dean, safe at the beginning of the period, did not foresee this – though he does note that, to crush rebellion, the King was in the habit of letting the island down bodily from the sky on the rebellious inhabitants.

We are also in the world of the cubist painters. The rhomboid joints, the triangular legs of mutton come out of Wyndham Lewis – has he illustrated Laputa? – those mathematicians take us to our Bertrand Russells. Among the astronomers, with their weakness for judicial astrology, does one not detect the philosophical speculations of Jeans and Eddington? Pure thought, moreover, led to a laxity of morals, for husbands devoted to the higher intellectual life were inclined either to be short-sighted or absent-minded, and the wives in Laputa found it necessary and simple to descend to coarser but more attentive lovers on the mainland below. In search perhaps of Gerald Heard's new mutation, the speculative despised sex or forgot about it; or having read their *Ends and Means*, thought of giving sex up. Yes, Laputa, the island of the non-attached, is topical.

Like all satirists, the Dean was, nevertheless, in a vulnerable position. By temperament and in style he is one of the earliest scientific writers in modern literature. He delights, with a genuine anticipation of scientific method, in those measurements of hoofs, heads and fingers, the calculated quantities of food, the inevitable observation of his bladder. One might be reading Malinowski or Dr Zuckermann. Yet when one puts the book down it is to realise that there is one more country in the story which is the counterblast to Laputa, Lilliput and the whole list. This is Gulliver himself. The world is mad, grotesque, a misanthropic Irishman's self-destructive fantasy; but Gulliver is not. Gulliver is sane. He is good, homely, friendly and decent. How he keeps himself to himself in his extraordinary adventures! No love affairs; Mrs Gulliver and family are waiting at home. Unlike the philosophers, he is not a cuckold. One is sure he isn't.

'I have ever hated all nations, professions and communities,' the Dean wrote to Pope; 'and all my love is towards individuals; for instance I hate the tribe of lawyers, but I love Councillor Such a One and Judge Such a One; principally I hate and detest that animal called man, although I heartily love John, Peter, Thomas and so forth.'

A religious mind, even one as moderate in its religion as Swift's, must, in the end, be indifferent to material welfare, progress and hopes. Gulliver is simply John, Peter or Thomas, the ordinary sensible man and he stands alone against the mad laboratories of the floating island. Gulliver could not know that people would one day make a knowledge machine or invent sunshine substitutes (but not out of cucumbers), but he does know that it is folly to let the world be run by these people. They will turn it (as the visit to Lagado showed, or, shall we say, to a blitzed town) into a wilderness. The world, the mad Dean says in the figure of Gulliver, must be run by John, Peter, Thomas, the sensible man.

The End of the Gael

The return of Synge from Paris to Ireland is a dramatic moment in Anglo-Irish literature. In significance that journey is equalled only by the one made in the other direction by Joyce when he broke with Dublin for ever and went angrily to the Continent. The thing which fired Synge seemed to Joyce to be tarnished by the vulgarity of Edwardian Dublin. Unhappily the dates do not quite fit, but nevertheless one has a picture of those two figures, most self-contained and priest-like in their attitude to literature, passing each other without signals of recognition on their opposition journeys across the Irish Sea. Each is going to what the other has left: Joyce is on his way to become something like the Irish pedant and æsthete abroad, moving to that dilettantism which always seems to catch the Irishman in exile, turning him into a kind of cold Tara brooch in the shirt-front of Western European culture; and Synge is on the way back to rub off some of the polish and to refertilise an imagination which culture had sterilised. Such migrations, exile and return, are a master rhythm in Irish life. And yet, when one thinks about these journeys in connection with the work of Synge and Joyce, their destinations are not effectively so different after all. Both writers are sedulous linguists and lovers of a phrase who sport like dolphins in the riotous oceans of an English language which has something of the fabulous air of a foreign tongue for them. In the beginning was the word – if that is not the subject of their work, it is the exciting principle. There would even be no difficulty in citing parallel passages. I have no copy of *Ulysses* or *Finnegan* to hand at the moment, but sentences from *The Playboy* like Christy's

'Ah, you'll have a gallous jaunt, I'm saying, coaching out through limbo with my father's ghost',

or,

'And I must go back into my torment is it, or run off like a vagabond straying through the unions with the dust of August making mudstains in the gullet of my throat; or the winds of March blowing on me till I'd take an oath I felt them making whistles of my ribs within',

are three parts on the way to *Anna Livia*. And this passion for the bamboozling and baroque of rhetoric leaves both Synge and Joyce with a common emotion: an exhausted feeling of the evanescence of outward things, which is philosophical in Synge and, in Joyce, the very description of human consciousness. The sense of a drunken interpenetration of myth or legend (or should we call it imagination and the inner life) with outer reality is common to them. Where modern Europeans analysed, Synge and Joyce, heirs of an earlier culture, substituted metaphor and image. Again and again, in almost any page you turn to in Joyce and Synge, the tragedy or comedy of life is felt to be the tragedy or comedy of memory and the imagination. It is their imagination which transforms Christy, Pegeen, Deirdre, and Nora in *The Shadow of the Glen*; but when 'the fine talk they have on them' is done, they are aware that time is writing on like a ledger clerk, that the beautiful girls will become old hags like the Widow Quin or Mrs Bloom grunting among her memories on the chamber-pot. Time dissolves the lonely legendary mind of man, killing the spells of the heart, draining the eloquence of the body – that seems to be not only the subject of Synge's *Deirdre* and all his plays, but the fundamental subject of Anglo-Irish literature.

Reading Synge again one feels all the old excitement of his genius. Nothing has faded. He reads as well as an Elizabethan. In his short creative period all Synge's qualities were brought to a high pitch of intensity and richness and his work stands inviolable in a world apart. It is unaffected by the passing of the fashion for peasant drama, for behind the peasant addict with his ear to the chink in the wall is the intellect of the European tradition, something of Jonson's grain and gusto. Synge was a master who came to his material at what is perhaps the ripest moment for an artist – the brink of decadence. The Gaelic world was sinking like a ship; and there was an enlightened desperation in the way the Anglo-Irish caught at that last moment, before their own extinction too. That, anyway, is how it looks now. The preoccupation with the solitude of man, with illusion and with the evanescence of life in Synge and Joyce is one of the signs that the old age of a culture has come, and Synge gives to the death of the Gaelic world the nobility and richness of a ritual. It is not, as in the Aran journal, a ritual of sparse sad words, but the festive blaze of life.

It is common in the eulogies of Synge to say that the unfinished *Deirdre of the Sorrows* hints at heights to which Synge's genius might have attained. For me *Deirdre* marks a dubious phase in his development. Even when I allow for the blind spot which English taste has in the matter of legendary or mythological subjects, I cannot help feeling that in attempting *Deirdre* Synge put himself into a literary straitjacket and went back on the sound opinions he gave in his prefaces to the plays and poems. No doubt anyone who knew Yeats at that time was simply ordered into the Celtic twilight and had to take his dose of it; but one hopes that Synge would have had the sanity to return to the doctrine he set out in the preface to *The Tinker's Wedding*:

> Of the things which nourish the imagination humour is one of the most useful, and it is dangerous to limit or destroy it.

More important:

> I have often thought that at the side of the poetic diction which everyone condemns, modern verse contains a great deal of poetic material, using poetry in the same special sense. The poetry of exaltation will be always the highest; but when men lose their poetic feelings for ordinary life and cannot write poetry of ordinary things, their exalted poetry is likely to lose its strength of exaltation, in the way men cease to build beautiful churches when they have lost happiness in building shops.

And more important still, these words from the introduction to his book of poems and translations:

> The drama is made serious – in the French sense of the word – not by the degree in which it is taken up with the problems that are serious in themselves, but by the degree in which it gives nourishment, not very easy to define, on which our imaginations live.

So *Riders to the Sea* seems to me genuinely tragic tragedy, but *Deirdre* to be simply poetic material for tragedy where Synge's genius moves stiffly.

Like the Russians in the Seventies, Synge 'returned to the people' when he went to Aran. Unlike the Russians he does not seem to have felt any mystical faith in doing this, and knew quite well that the heroic, primitive life of the West was doomed. There is always the sensation in Synge's work of being one of the last men on earth, the survivor of a dying family. One feels the loneliness of men and women in a lonely scene, and one is also made to feel the personal, inaccessible loneliness of Synge himself. At the back of the plays there is, for all his insistence on the necessity of joy and feasting in the theatre, a dark and rather *fin de siècle* shadow, and there is more than a hint, in the character of the Playboy, of the art-for-art's-sake artist of the Nineties who lives only in words and illusions. Joyce's legendary Dublin is, in a sense, the answer to Synge's legendary West. *Ulysses* is an assertion that modern urban man can have his myth and Joyce's 'ordinary men' are the sort of 'ordinary men' whom Synge would have found lifeless. Synge was too soon to see the enormous contribution of the American vernacular to popular culture in the towns, and too cut off from the knowledge of urban people to know what resources common urban speech had. Nowadays (and without mistaking courage for the Heroic pattern of living) we can discern the new heroic status of cities in their Æschylean devastation and their curious mass stoicism. Cities seem now to have become greater, in this sense, than individual men.

In one obvious way Synge does belong to an earlier world than ours, and that is in his humour. It is the strong, sculptured, corporeal and baroque humour of knavery, tricks and cunning. We have almost entirely lost the literature of roguery, the life of which has been prolonged in Ireland by the tradition of disrespect for foreign law. To his handling of roguery, Synge brought all the subtlety he had learned from Molière. This has, of course, often been said and it stands out a mile in his handling of the dramatist's use of continual contrast, whereby almost every speech creates a new situation or farcically reverses its predecessor. There is no falsity in his farces; one does not feel that the situation is an artificial one. How easily *The Playboy* could have become Aldwych knockabout; and yet how easily Synge makes us accept his preposterous idea, by trying it first upon the main character before our eyes. The texture of his drama is a continuous interweaving of challenge and riposte, a continuous changing of the threads in a single motif; so that we are involved in far more than a mere anecdote which has a jerk of astonishment in the beginning and a sting in the tail at the end. At the height of farce we may instantly, by a quick shift of focus, be faced by that sense of the evanescence of life which is Synge's especially, or we may be jogged by the sharp elbow of mortality. And as a piece of music will start on two or three plain notes before its theme is given a head, so these plays start in the simple household accents and come with the same domesticity to their end. The old man, having got rid of his wife, changes his tone and calls for the drink, the tinkers escape from the curse of the priest to their old life on the roads, Pegeen is left to clear up at the inn, the blind whom the saint has healed go back to their blindness. All are ordinary people once more, leaving us (as the comic genius does) to eye each other with new, unholy expectation, warming us with the love of human antics, fattening our thin wits, so that like Sir Mammon in *The Alchemist* we cry out as we put the book down, 'Oh, my voluptuous mind!'

The Steeple House Spires

One hesitates, since Freud, to admit to a strong personal feeling for church steeples, and yet who does not respond to the ring and vividness of that phrase which occurs again and again in George Fox's *Journal* and which puts the man and his book a key higher than the common chord of living:

> As I was walking in a close with several Friends, I lifted up my head and espied three steeple house spires and they struck at my life.

They do still strike at our lives, though with the stab of reminiscence rather than of faith, when we see them rising over the fields and elms of the English countryside. In the towns – and Fox, on this occasion was speaking of 'the bloody city of Lichfield' – the steeple commands the skyline no longer. Those words of Fox, more than any others of his, take us back to the seventeenth century. In the eighteenth century the steeple must still have denominated the towns to the arriving traveller, as it continues today to make our villages, but did the steeple strike at the eighteenth-century traveller's life? That is very doubtful. The decisiveness, the militance, the poignancy have gone out of English religious fervour. After the seventeenth century what religion has there been in England? There is only the revivalism of Wesley, a fruit of personal conflict, and Wesley side-tracked a revolution where the 'prophesyings' of the Puritans made one.

That is perhaps too great a simplification; Fox himself was a poor short-term revolutionary when one compares him with Cromwell's sectarian soldiers; the mysticism of the Quakers provided, *in their own time*, an alternative to the revolution, such as we see in the gospels of non-resistance, pacifism, non-attachment, etc., etc., today. If we continue that quotation from Fox's *Journal*, we cannot doubt that it contains a revolutionary emotion which is more dynamic than the feeling of Winstanley's peasant communists, for example, who, having taken the land, were content to keep the clergy and the gentry off by singing a song about 'conquering with love'.

> I asked [Fox goes on] what place that was and they said, Lichfield. Immediately the word of the Lord came to me that thither I must go . . . I stepped away, and went by my eye over hedge and ditch till I came within a mile of Lichfield, where in a great field, there were shepherds keeping their sheep. I was commanded of the Lord to untie my shoes and put them off.

And then, his feet burning like fire in the winter fields, he walked into the town where:

> the word of the Lord came to me again, to cry 'Woe unto the bloody city of Lichfield!' So I went up and down the streets, crying with a loud voice, 'Woe to the bloody city of Lichfield!' . . . And no one laid hands on me; but as I went thus crying through the streets, there seemed to me to be a channel of blood running down the streets, and the market place appeared like a pool of blood.

That is authentic and so is the characteristic English reaction: 'Alack George,' the inhabitants said, 'where are thy shoes?' The woe could take care of itself; what bothered the kindly, respectable, practical souls of Lichfield was the condition of George Fox's feet.

There is the attraction of Fox's *Journal* in a few lines. In his writing the personal fanatic cry of the visionary and the words of the homely are blended. The huge Leicestershire shepherd with his loud voice and his curling hair (which a disapproving Puritan lady in Wales tried to snip off with her scissors), with his horn of snuff and his leathern suit, has his feet on the soil, on the road of the seventeenth-century English wilderness and in the streets of the muddy towns. He has 'great openings'. He 'sees' this and that. The imps and devils are chained to his foot, the 'inner light' burns vividly in him and is easily distinguished from the 'false light' of other people's 'vain imaginings'; but he also knows the price of oats and how to obstruct magistrates. He can put off a pretentious theologian with the truly peasant remark that if the man thinks he is God, does he know if it is going to rain tomorrow? Unlike Bunyan's Christian traveller, Fox is a real man, travelling on real roads. He knows the inns, the houses of friends, the jails.

[124]

He was worn out on the Welsh hills, mired on the Yorkshire roads and saw the sea from the edge of Lancashire. From the age of twenty he was wandering all over England, from steeple to steeple, meeting the soldiers on the way to the Battle of Worcester, being beaten by the mobs, taken up by the sheriffs, arguing the Scriptures with Papists, Brownites, Independents, Ranters, 'rude jangling Baptists', and the 'hireling priests'. He was in Cumberland:

> Now were great threatenings given forth in Cumberland that if ever I came there again they would take away my life. When I heard it I was drawn to go into Cumberland . . .

If he feared any danger it was the danger of remaining in one place where long contact with people would blunt the edge of conscience and dull his ear for the word of the Lord. A man of little education, he is no great writer; his jogtrot Puritan prose ambles like his horse and cannot be compared with Bunyan's. But his own obstinate, innocent alarming character bursts through the repetitions. And the rest of his prose is made up of Biblical echoes, the sound of Hebraic incantation common to evangelical writings but in his time not yet mechanised and turned into cant.

A man of visions Fox lacks the introspective intellect. His mind, for all its exaltation, is even commonplace and he has frequently to fall back upon a dramatic muddle of Biblical metaphor when he is trying to describe his moments of darkness. There was a mysterious temptation, for example,

> that all was of nature, and the elements and storm came over me, so that I was in a manner quite clouded with it.

But the mood, whatever it may have been, passed and

> I was come up in spirit through the flaming sword into the paradise of God. All things were new.

Then the Leicestershire shepherd breaks at last into his own voice:

> All the creation gave another smell unto me than before, beyond what words can utter.

The virtues and vices of Quakerism lie in a startling mildness and literalness of mind. The other sects of the period were in ecstasies of

[125]

expectation or fear; they bore on their shoulders a back-breaking load of hopes of bliss and fears of damnation. The Quakers, those practical children of the Quietists and the non-attached, dissolved the coagulations of dogma and doctrine, and experienced their heaven and their hell in the present moment. They were in Abraham's bosom *now*. One sees the other Puritans fighting their way towards God as if towards an enemy; the Quakers purified themselves and waited for God to speak like a friend in their hearts. Unoppressed by dogma, unfettered by a programme, they were free to go on with their work or their philanthropy while the factions fought. They went on with their business – hence the jealousy of their wealth. Their affinity is, of course, with Santa Teresa, with her 'The Lord walks among the pots and pans' – a mysticism so tamed in their case that from the unreason of 'the inner light' sprang the necessity of Tolerance, the first break with the exorbitance of the age of revolution, the first glimmer of the Age of Reason, as Professor Trevelyan has pointed out in his book on the Stuarts.

But Fox, the founder, belongs to the dynamic age of Quakerism. We see the familiar human dilemma. Fox preached 'the inner light' by throwing many into the outer darkness. 'Drowned.' 'Had a miserable end' – how often one meets this comment on the fate of those who opposed him. A butcher put his tongue out at Fox; the tongue swelled up and would not go back. This is not said gloatingly, but with the fervour of fanaticism for its own logic. If a miraculous healing was impermanent, the patient had 'disobeyed the Lord'. Those who 'see' the truth are 'tender' or 'very tender'; those who reject it are 'rude' or 'light chaffy men'. Accused of witchcraft himself – when he was beaten Fox did not bleed, or bled very little, for there was a curious lack of blood in his huge frame – he is, of course, expert at discerning witchcraft in others. He speaks of seeing several women who were witches working in a field as he passed. One unhappy woman 'with an unclean spirit' had to be turned out of a meeting before he would speak. (His dramatic sense was enormous.) A pistol is fired point-blank at him; naturally it does not go off. And then there is the row about refusing to take the oath. One must sympathise with revolutionary authorities when they are faced by revolutionaries even more revolutionary than themselves. For Fox and his fellow quietists, apostles of non-violence, might turn the other cheek to physical violence but they provoked riots with their tongues. They marched into the steeple-houses crying 'Peace be unto you' and in the next breath were denouncing the preacher as a 'hireling', preaching him down in his own church, and then became indignant when the police or the soldiers had to come in to restore order. And they were even more indignant when asked to swear the oath of allegiance. Mysticism has always been recognised as a disintegrating force in society. That last thing successful revolutionaries can dispense with is loyalty.

It was an age of hatred and hats. One thinks of each century in terms of some article of fashion or clothing. In the nineteenth century the frock-coat symbolises the cult of political respectability; in the eighteenth century the wig is the emblem of political elegance. In the seventeenth century, there is the hat, the hat jammed down implacably on the brow and worn with a vehemence which has been equalled in the last decade of our own time by the feeling for the shirt. When the Quakers refused to raise their hats to their friends in the street, or in the courts, they were part of that anti-doffing movement to which Puritans in general subscribed as a protest against the long, feathery and sweeping bows of the Cavaliers. Lilbourne, when brought before the Council of State, had refused to remove his hat to people who had 'no more legal authority than myself'. It took the Quakers, with their obstinacy, their literalness of mind and their simple way of finding a precise moral justification in the Scriptures, to appeal beyond the courts to God. One cannot decide whether they were vexatious or remarkable in that wonderful judicial comedy which George Fox provoked at Launceston. He writes with pain, but surely with a sly peasant smile of private triumph:

When we were brought into the Court, we stood a pretty while with our hats on, and all was quiet; and I was moved to say, 'Peace be among you!' Judge Glynne, a Welchman, the Chief Justice of England, said to the jailer, 'What be these you have brought here into the Court?' 'Prisoners, my lord,' said he. 'Why do you not put off your hats?' said the judge to us; we said nothing. 'Put off your hats,' said the judge again. Still we said nothing. Then said the judge, 'The Court commands you to put off your hats.' Then I spoke and said 'Where did ever any magistrate, king or judge from Moses to Daniel, command any to put off their hats, when they came before them in their courts, either amongst the Jews, the people of God, or among the heathen? And if the law of England doth command any such thing, shew me that law either written or printed.' Then the judge grew angry and said 'I do not carry my law-books on my back . . . Take him away, prevaricator. I'll ferk him.'

Presently the judge cooled down and called the prisoner back:

'Come,' said he, 'where had they hats from Moses to Daniel? Come, answer me. I have you fast now.'

But George Fox knew the Scriptures.

'Thou mayest read,' he replied, 'in the 3rd of Daniel that the three children were cast into the fiery furnace by Nebuchadnezzar's command, with their coats, their hose and their hats on.' This plain instance stopped him so that not having anything else to say to the point, he cried again, 'Take them away, jailer.'

True anarchists, the Quakers would make a Star Chamber matter of a triviality. Yet their history shows them to have been both conservative and opportunist. They accepted Cromwell, they accepted Charles II; they would accept anybody. What they did not accept was the rule of bu-reaucracy in matters of belief; and it is interesting that neither Cromwell nor Charles persecuted Fox. Cromwell admired 'a people he could not buy', Charles was amused and indifferent. The persecution came from the underlings.

In two countries, Scotland and Ireland, the Leicestershire peasant was not at home. In Scotland he came up against pedants; Presbyterianism was an obdurate enemy of the Quakers. In Ireland, for the first time in the *Journal*, there is a suggestion of bewilderment, distaste and even fear; 'The earth smelt, me thought, of the corruption of the nation.' The smell, as in Lichfield, was of blood. In Lichfield, the blood shed by Diocletian; in Dublin the blood of the Popish massacres. Not, be it noted, of the Cromwellian massacres. In Cork he felt the peeping eyes at the windows; spies were everywhere; a description of him was sent on a hundred miles ahead in the manner of a sinister jungle message. 'A grim black fellow' – an evil spirit – appeared to be chained to his foot. He rode in fear of 'the

Tories' – gangs of disbanded soldiers – and was relieved to escape them. The voyage back to Liverpool was made in a tempest and in the end of the adventure so prosaically recorded, one sees one last sardonic thrust from the corrupt island. Fox was slanderously accused of having taken to drink.

No, Ireland, for all the 'tender' people there and the great meetings, was a nightmare. The Leicestershire shepherd was not made for the dark imaginations which bewitched that country. He was English. One sees him, the big man from a dull flat country, a peasant shrewd and, yet, in a massive way, naif; sober yet obstinate; gentle yet immovably blunt; a man who has made his mind up, who has the inordinate pride and yet the inordinate humility of the saints.

One of Our Founders

===

U p to the early nineteenth century who were the Puritan writers of autobiography? The names of Fox, Bunyan, Defoe, Cobbett and Franklin come to mind first of all. Not all wrote their life-story in a single piece, but the character of their writing is intensely autobiographical. They are plain and homely figures; there is no getting away from that, indeed, it is their boast. Sensibility, elegance, urbanity, imagination and culture are not notable in their natures or their work, the name of Franklin excepted. (The case for Bunyan's imagination fails, I think, because his imagination is a borrowed one, the dream of a mind gorged on the writings of the Hebrews.) If the Reformation turned us into a nation of shopkeepers, these are the men who keep the books. And here, I think, we should distinguish in our use of the words 'homely' and 'plain'. The sense of dull worth and stagnation which has accrued to these adjectives, came to them during the nineteenth century, when the domestic hearth was insulated from the world; but in the eighteenth century and earlier, the meaning had more of nature and less of complacency in it. Those times were nearer the dynamic period of Puritanism, times of revolution, colonisation and travel; and the reader must have noticed, with a smile, how little these prophets of the plain, domestic virtues stayed at home. In a man like Fox, the native restlessness of the virtuous Puritan is explicit: he feared to be corrupted if he stayed too long in one place. Bunyan is on the road or in prison and his Christian is on a journey. Defoe is on tour or in the stocks, and his Crusoe comes home only once every so often to beget a child. Cobbett is perpetually on horseback and Franklin is running away from his relations, crossing and recrossing the Atlantic. What a contrast there is between their precept and example! There they are warning us against the way of the world, but who is more in the world than they?

The answer is that whatever else the ideal of Puritanism may have been, its joint aim was always success. Preaching caution, moderation, industry

and sobriety to generations of shopkeepers, round whose necks they tie
their moral maxims like a sack of bricks, the great Puritan exemplars
pursue not the same course, but a parallel one which is livelier and more
extravagant. They live – it is why we read them – not in the family and the
shop, but in the world. They live to succeed extremely in the world. For
even Fox and Bunyan succeed: they inherit the heavenly riches. And why
should they not succeed? Remove the belief in success, material or
spiritual, from Puritanism and you remove its mainspring and its political
meaning. An unsuccessful Puritan is the disappointed sectary snapping
sourly at his neighbours because he is unable to get the better of them.

Still, at first sight, the great Puritan autobiographers are an unlovely
crowd. They have the vitality of weeds. We read them for their realism and
their eccentricity. But would we choose their company now? Only two
among those names might transplant into the twentieth century: Cobbett
because he might fit in with the Napoleonic pattern of our time, and the
other is Benjamin Franklin. Franklin is the only certain choice. One thinks
of him as the first of the civilised Puritans. With his urbanity, his humour,
his sagacity, his scientific adventurousness and his political vision, he can
easily be transplanted, though he would loll like some dog-eared and old-
fashioned compendium of good sense and information in our businesslike
world of isolated specialists. To entertain him would be like entertaining
one of our founders.

The Franklin literature is a large one. Among recent *Lives*, Carl Van
Doran's is the most thorough, sympathetic and readable. There is also an
intelligent study by a Frenchman done in 1929: *Benjamin Franklin, Bourgeois
d'Amérique*. But the reader should go first of all for the accent and flavour of
the subject and begin with Franklin's own story. The World's Classics
edition has the advantage of including a complete example from his famous
Almanac of Poor Richard, which was enjoyed by thousands in America and
which made D. H. Lawrence so angry. Lawrence's attack on Franklin in
his *Studies in Classical American Literature* ought to be read, but it is a typical
misfire. Lawrence, one supposes, could not forgive another Puritan for
knowing more about sex than he did, and before Franklin's irony, urbanity
and benevolence, Lawrence cuts an absurd figure, rather like that of a
Sunday School teacher who has gone to a social dressed up as a howling
dervish, when fancy dress was *not* requested. There is of course *something* in

Lawrence's diatribe; it is the criticism by the man whose life is all poetry of the man whose life is all prose.

The reader of Franklin's autobiography must be struck by the way the Puritans hang together. Defoe and Bunyan were Franklin's first instructors. Defoe and Franklin have also similar origins; they were both the sons of tallow chandlers, and Defoe's *Essay on Projects* was one of the books which had a lasting influence on Franklin's mind. The resemblances between their careers are simply resemblances of class. The chief difference between the two shopkeepers appears when we observe the benevolence of the American's mind, the flow of imagination that transforms the pawky philosophy of go-getting and self-interest. Defoe was a retailer to the end; Franklin was a wholesaler. His plans, his experiments, his political actions are not part of his career; they flow beyond himself upon society. We feel that with all its toughness, resource and courage Defoe's character was a narrow one and incapable of growth, and there is, in fact, his dubious middle phase as a spy. Franklin, on the other hand, expands. His life reminds one, as the life of Cobbett does, how good the American climate was for the English character at this period; for if Franklin got ideas from Defoe, his style from Addison, his irony from Socrates and the stimulus to his genius from France of the eighteenth century, he owed the enlargement of his nature to America. Without that he might still have been thought one of the greatest *savants* of his time, but he would not have been thought the most able or the most likeable.

As a life story the *Autobiography* is interesting for its events. It is far more interesting as a remarkable piece of amusing and considered self-portraiture. The best autobiographies are those which draw the writer's character full-face, and Franklin adds to this the capacity to describe the growth of his character. In one sense (the sense that D. H. Lawrence hated) the book is another success story, an early instalment of Samuel Smiles. How he sat up late to study, how he became a vegetarian to save money for books, how he watched his chances at the printers, twigged a trick or two from the Socratic method of innocent inquiry, bargained over an offer of marriage and at last earned enough money to eat his porridge out of a china bowl with a silver spoon, after years of earthenware and a wooden one – such stuff is apt to be despised by those who find themselves deeply interested by it against their wills. And if Franklin had left his narrative like that he would have been just one more successful mayor. But his belief in self-improvement, though deep, has an ironic inflection:

> It would not be altogether absurd if a man were to thank God for his vanity among the other comforts of life.

Such intimate and persuasive asides give a leisured shade to the blatant walls of Self-Help where, too often, one is asked to admire the placing of each unweathered brick. But there is more than the irony of an experienced old man looking back on his life in this story. We are shown the making of a mind, the formation of a temperament. The two qualities of Franklin are the variety of his interests and the originality of his intellect. He is always performing feats. There are the feats of brain, like the decision to learn the French, Spanish and Italian languages in middle age in order to prepare himself to learn Latin – and a very good short cut to Latin that is, too. There are the feats of citizenship: he started the first fire brigade, the first police force, the first system of street lighting in the American colonies, the earliest philosophical society and the earliest public library. His edition of *Pamela* was the first novel to be published there also. And there are the feats of invention which are famous, such as his investigation of dyes and his invention of a heating stove; an invention which pops up impishly between the great affair of the lightning rod and his theories about the paths of storms and earthquakes. And, all the time, this is the man who once swam from Chelsea to Blackfriars, working out a new system of swimming as he went, and was only saved by chance from setting up for life as a swimming instructor. Franklin's inventive faculty was directed even to working out a system, rather like book-keeping, for improving his moral character. He invented even new prayers.

Being a romantic, Lawrence imagined that Franklin's devotion to Use, Method and Order indicated the dreary objectives of his genius. They were its starting points, its immense stimulus. Against egotism – Lawrence's 'the self is a dark forest' – Franklin put the citizen and the *savant,* and the emotion generated by being a lively citizen in a new society released an exuberant creative capacity in Franklin which was certainly no less than the creative force which Lawrence and many others have thought to lie in sex alone. The jeers of Lawrence might have struck home had they been directed at estimable and lesser Self-Helpers, for the Self-Helper is usually a copyist only who ends by being all help and no self. Franklin was never a copyist. Least of all was he a copyist in sex – Lawrence's own speciality. Here (far from being the prudent shopkeeper) Franklin entered upon a marriage which was only 'a common law' marriage and which may have been bigamous, not out of self-interest, but because his moral sensibility demanded it. Franklin understood the dangers of repressing the moral sense. And then, lest one be deceived into thinking the considerate, the businesslike and the robust are incompatibles, there is his famous letter to a young man who is worried about women. Prudence directs (Franklin says) that if a young man must, for his health's sake, have a mistress, it is better that she shall be old, for she will be past child-bearing – and besides, the older a woman the more grateful she is! One would need to be very cynical indeed to think that remarkable advice wholly cynical. One may hardly blame the age of Reason and Order for being reasonable and orderly, or the first of the modern planners for believing that all plans should be practical and should produce concrete benefits for society – stoves for the draughty New England rooms, fire brigades for wooden cities, political union for threatened states, prayers that will guide us 'to our truest interest', and even discreet happiness for ladies past the prime of life.

The American Puritan

After reading Hemingway and Faulkner and speculating upon the breach of the American novel with its English tradition, we go back to the two decisive, indigenous Americans who opened the new vein – Mark Twain and Edgar Allan Poe. Everything really American, really non-English comes out of that pair of spiritual derelicts, those two scarecrow figures with their half-lynched minds. Both of them, but particularly Twain, represent the obverse side of Puritanism. We have never had this obverse in England, for the political power of Puritanism lasted for only a generation and has since always bowed if it has not succumbed to civilised orthodoxy. If an Englishman hated Puritanism, there was the rest of the elaborate English tradition to support him; but American Puritanism was totalitarian and if an American opposed it, he found himself alone in a wilderness with nothing but bottomless cynicism and humorous bitterness for his consolation. There has never been in English literature a cynicism to compare with the American; at any rate we have never had that, in some ways vital, but always sardonic or wretched, cynicism with its broken chopper edge and its ugly wound. We have also never had its by-product: the humorous philosophers; Franklin's Poor Richard, the Josh Billingses, the Artemus Wards, the Pudd'nhead Wilsons and Will Rogerses with their close-fisted proverbs:

'Training is everything. The peach was once a bitter almond: cauliflower is nothing but a cabbage with a college education.'

Or

'Consider well the proportion of things. It is better to be a young June bug than an old bird of Paradise.'

I say we have never had this kind of thing, but there is one exception to prove the rule and to prove it very well, for he also is an uprooted and, so to speak, colonial writer. Kipling with his 'A woman is always a woman, but a good cigar is a smoke' is our first American writer with a cynicism, a cigar-stained humour and a jungle book of beliefs which, I think, would be a characteristic of our literature if we become seriously totalitarian in the future. For English totalitarianism would create the boredom and bitterness of the spiritual wilderness, as surely as Puritanism did in America.

When Mark Twain turned upon the religion of his childhood because it was intolerable, he was unaware that it would destroy him by turning him into a money-grubber of the most disastrously Puritan kind. Fortunately the resources of the imagination are endless even when a fanatical philosophy wrecks human life, genius and happiness. Out of the mess which Twain made of his life, amid the awful pile of tripe which he wrote, there does rise one book which has the serenity of a thing of genius. *Huckleberry Finn* takes the breath away. Knowing his life, knowing the hell from which the book has ascended, one dreads as one turns from page to page the seemingly inevitable flop. How can so tortured and so angry a comedian refrain from blackguarding God, Man and Nature for the narrow boredom of his early life, and thus ruin the gurgling comedy and grinning horror of the story? But an imaginative writer appears to get one lucky break in his career; for a moment the conflicts are assimilated, the engine ceases to work against itself. The gears do not crash and *Huckleberry Finn* hums on without a jar. America gets its first and indisputable masterpiece. The boyhood of Huck Finn is the boyhood of a new culture and a new world.

The curious thing about *Huckleberry Finn* is that, although it is one of the funniest books in all literature and really astonishing in the variety of its farce and character, we are even more moved than we are amused by it. Why are we moved? Do we feel the sentiment of sympathy only? Are we sighing with some envy and self-pity? 'Alas, Huck Finn is just what I would have been in my boyhood if I had had half a chance.' Are we sorry for the vagrant, or are we moved by his rebellion? These minor feelings may play their part; but they are only sighs on the surface of the main stream of our emotion. Twain has brought to his subject far more than this personal longing; he has become the channel of the generic American emotion which floods all really American literature – nostalgia. In that brilliant, hit-or-miss book, *Studies in Classical American Literature*, which is either dead right or dead wrong, D. H. Lawrence called this feeling the longing of the rebel for a master. It may be simply the longing for a spiritual home, but it is as strong in Mark Twain as it is implicit in Hemingway. One finds this nostalgia in Anglo-Irish literature which is also colonial and, in a less lasting way, once again in the work of Kipling. The peculiar power of American nostalgia is that it is not only harking back to something lost in the past, but suggests also the tragedy of a lost future. As Huck Finn and old Jim drift down the Mississippi from one horrifying little town to the next and hear the voices of men quietly swearing at one another across the water about 'a chaw of tobacco'; as they pass the time of day with the scroungers, rogues, murderers, the lonely women, the frothing revivalists, the maundering boatmen and fantastic drunks, we see the human wastage that is left behind in the wake of a great effort of the human will, the hopes frustrated, the idealism which has been whittled down to eccentricity and mere animal cunning. These people are the price paid for building a new country. The human spectacle is there. It is not, once you have faced it – which Dickens did not do in *Martin Chuzzlewit*, obsessed as he was by the negative pathos of the immigrant – it is not a disheartening spectacle; for the value of a native humour like Twain's is that it records a profound reality in human nature: the ability of man to adjust himself to any circumstance and somehow to survive and make a life.

Movement is one of the great consolers of human woe; movement, a process of continual migration is the history of America. It is this factor which gives Twain's wonderful descriptions of the journey down the Mississippi its haunting overtone and which, naturally enough, awakens a sensibility in him which is shown nowhere else in his writings and which is indeed vulgarly repressed in them:

> . . . then we set down on the sandy bottom where the water was about knee-deep and watched the daylight come. Not a sound anywhere – perfectly still – just like the whole world was asleep, only sometimes the bull-frogs a-clattering may be. The first thing to see, looking away over the water, was a kind of dull line – that was on the woods on t'other side – you couldn't make nothing else out; then a pale place in the sky; then more paleness, spreading around; then the river softened up, away off, and wasn't black any more but grey; you could see little dark spots

drifting along, ever so far away – trading scows . . . and such things; and long black streaks – rafts; sometimes you could hear a sweep screaking; or jumbled-up voices, it was so still, and sounds come so far; and by-and-by you could see a streak on the water which you know by the look of the streak that there's a snag in the swift current which breaks on it and that streak looks that way; and you see the mist curl up off the water, and the east reddens up, and the river, and you make out a log cabin in the edge of the woods, away on the bank t'other side of the river, being a woodyard likely, and piled by them cheats so you can throw a dog through it anywheres . . .

And afterwards we would watch the lonesomeness of the river, and kind of lazy along and by-and-by, lazy off to sleep. Wake up, by-and-by, and look to see what done it, and may be see a steamboat, coughing along upstream, so far off towards the other side you couldn't tell nothing about her only whether she was sternwheel or side wheel; then for about an hour there wouldn't be nothing to hear nor nothing to see – just solid lonesomeness. Once there was a thick fog, and the rafts and things that went by was beating tin pans so the steam boats wouldn't run over them. A scow or a raft went by so close we could hear them talking and cussing and laughing – heard them plain; but we couldn't see no sign of them; it made you feel crawly, it was like spirits carrying on that way in the air. Jim said he believed it was spirits; but I says, 'No, spirits wouldn't say "dern this dem fog".'

(Note the word 'way' in this passage; it is a key nostalgic word in the American vocabulary, vaguely vernacular and burdened with the associations of the half-articulate. It is a favourite Hemingway word, of course: 'I feel *that way*' – not the how or what he feels of the educated man.)

The theme of *Huckleberry Finn* is the rebellion against civilisation and especially against its traditions:

I reckon I got to light out for the Territory ahead of the rest, because Aunt Sally she's going to adopt me and sivilize me and I can't stand it. I been there before.

Huck isn't interested in 'Moses and the Bulrushers' because Huck 'don't take no stock of dead people'. He garbles European history when he is discussing Kings with Jim, the Negro. Whether Huck is the kind of boy who will grow up to build a new civilisation is doubtful; Tom Sawyer obviously will because he is imaginative. Huck never imagines anything excepts fears. Huck is 'low down plain ornery', always in trouble because of the way he was brought up with 'Pap'. He is a natural anarchist and bum. He can live without civilisation, depending on shrewd affections and loyalty to friends. He is the first of those typical American portraits of the underdog, which have culminated in the poor white literature and in Charlie Chaplin – an underdog who gets along on horse sense, so to speak. Romanticism, ideas, ideals are repugnant to Huck; he 'reckons' he 'guesses', but he doesn't think. In this he is the opposite of his hero, Tom Sawyer. Tom had been telling 'stretchers' about Arabs, elephants and Aladdin's lamp. Huck goes at once 'into a brood'.

I thought all this over for two or three days, and then I reckoned I would see if there was anything in it. I got an old tin lamp and an irony ring and went out into the woods and rubbed it till I sweat like an Injun, calculating to build a palace and sell it; but it wasn't no use, none of the genies came. So then I judged that all that stuff was only just one of Tom Sawyer's lies. I reckoned he believed in the A-rabs and elephants, but as for me I think different. It has all the marks of a Sunday school.

That is, of American Puritan civilisation, the only civilisation he knew.

'Ornery', broody, superstitious, with a taste for horrors, ingenious, courageous without knowing it, natural, sound-hearted, philosophical in a homely way – those are the attributes of the gorgeous, garrulous Huck and they give a cruelly extravagant narrative its humanity. He obliges you to accept the boy as the devastating norm. Without him the violence of the book would be stark reporting of low life. For if *Huckleberry Finn* is a great comic book it is also a book of terror and brutality. Think of the scenes: Pap and d.t.'s chasing Huck round the cabin with a knife; Huck sitting up all night with a gun preparing to shoot the old man; Huck's early familiarity with corpses; the pig-killing scene; the sight of the frame house (evidently some sort of brothel) floating down the Mississippi with a murdered man in it; the fantastic events at the Southern house where two families shoot each other down in vendetta; the drunken Boggs who comes into town to pick a quarrel and is eventually coolly shot dead before the eyes of his screaming young daughter by the man he has insulted. The 'Duke' and the 'King', those cynical rascals whose adventures liven up the second half of the story, are sharpers, twisters and crooks of the lowest kind. Yet a child is relating all this with a child's detachment and with a touch of morbidity. Marvellous as the tale is, as a collection of picaresque episodes and as a description of the mess of frontier life, it is strong meat. Sometimes we wonder how Twain's public stomached such illusionless reporting. The farce and the important fact that in this one book Mark Twain never forced a point nor overwrote – in the Dickens way for example – are of course the transfiguring and beguiling qualities. His corpse and coffin humour is a dry wine which raises the animal spirits. Old Jim not only looked like a dead man after the 'King' had painted him blue, but like one 'who had been dead a considerable time'.

Judiciousness is carried to the comic limit. And then, Mark Twain is always getting the atmosphere, whether he picks up the exact words of loafers trying to borrow tobacco off one another or tells a tall story of an hysterical revival meeting.

Atmosphere is the decisive word. *Huckleberry Finn* reeks of its world. From a sensitive passage like:

> When I got there it was all still and Sunday-like, and hot and the hands was gone to the fields; and there was them kind faint dronings of bugs and flies that makes it seem so lonesome and like everybody's dead . . .

to descriptions of the silly, dying girl's ridiculous poetry, the sensibility draws a clear outline and is never blurred and turned into sentimentality. One is enormously moved by Huck's view of the world he sees. It is the world not of Eden, but of the 'old Adam', not the golden age of the past, but the earthly world of a reality which (we feel with regret) we have let slip through our fingers too carelessly. Huck is only a crude boy, but luckily he was drawn by a man whose own mind was arrested, with disastrous results in his other books, at the schoolboy stage; here it is perfect. And a thousand times better than the self-conscious adventures of Stevenson's *Treasure Island* and *Kidnapped*.

Is *Huckleberry Finn* one of the great works of picaresque literature? It is, granting the limits of a boy's mind in the hero and the author, a comic masterpiece; but this limitation is important. It is not a book which grows spiritually, if we compare it to *Quixote, Dead Souls* or even *Pickwick*; and it is lacking in that civilised quality which you are bound to lose when you throw over civilisation – the quality of pity. One is left with the cruelty of American humour, a cruelty which is softened by the shrewd moralisings of the humorous philosophers – the Josh Billingses, the Artemus Wards, and the Will Rogerses. And once Mark Twain passed this exquisite moment of his maturity, he went to bits in that morass of sentimentality, cynicism, melodrama and vulgarity which have damned him for the adult reader.

The Quaker Coquette

If there is not a novel in every man and woman we meet, there is at any rate a cautionary tale. 'That ridiculous and excellent person, Mrs Opie,' said Miss Mitford. 'What a miserable hash she has made of her existence.' Somewhere in the world – so we may console ourselves when we feel ignored and forgotten – there is bound to be a Miss Mitford holding us up as an awful warning, using us as a frightful example of what can happen to a human being when he or she strays from the Mitford path. We have, of course, our bad moments and it must be agreed that Miss Mitford had caught the widow of Opie, the painter, at that point in middle age where so many women are clumsy with their cues and seem not to know in what play they are acting. After a life of triumphant gaiety in London and Paris, after writing a number of gaudy, guilty and improper books, the tantalising and beautiful widow had suddenly rejoined the Quaker circle in Norwich where she had passed her youth. She had put on the Quaker gown and bonnet, she had started writing very boring, didactic tales and went about thee-ing and thou-ing her embarrassed acquaintances with all the gush of a convert and all the bounce of a reformed sinner. Norwich raised its eyebrows. The good may cry Hallelujah when the lost soul repents and returns to the fold, but there is often a touch of disappointment not to mention suspicion in the cry, for where would the good be if there were no sinners left to hearten them on their hard pilgrimage? At Earlham, the home of Elizabeth Fry and the Gurney family who thought they knew their Amelia so well, such doubts could not be concealed. A Quaker – but wasn't Mrs Opie still a friend of Lady Cork's? Hadn't she still got in her drawer the manuscript of an unfortunate novel? Could one credit the champion of Mary Wollstonecraft and Godwin with a change of heart? What prospect was there of 'the inner light' shining for long in a mind bedizened with the memories of fashionable society, of 'pink' parties for the gay and 'blue' parties for the highbrow? Wasn't Amelia Opie congenitally 'shallow'? Her conversation might even be a leg-pull, for she did seem to have what George Fox would have called (in the century before Quakerism became mellow) a 'light and chaffy' nature. But neither the Quakers nor Miss Mitford could take the severe view of Mrs Opie's vivacious character for long. They loved her too well to regard her finally as the awful warning against worldliness. And the truth is that Amelia Opie had not so much the awfulness of a warning as the piquancy of a recurrent type. Born in 1769 and dying in 1853 she had fed on ideologies. She had lived through a revolution and a European war, and then had repented. Today her kind of character and repentance has become common if not yet modish. Mrs Opie is a kind of heroine of our time.

What is the type? Amelia was a flirt, a highbrow flirt. She was the adored and adoring daughter of a Norwich doctor. Her mother had been an invalid for years and when she died the girl was still in her teens. She became her father's hostess. When one goes into the question of her coquetry one comes immediately upon that so common decision of nature that girls who have an inordinate devotion to their fathers shall deal coolly and in-decisively with other men or shall prefer those who are much younger or much older than themselves. Add to this the intellectual tastes of Amelia's father and one finds a young lady who coquettes with literature, politics and religion and calls them in to aid her in the more important business of catching men. Her susceptible nature – it was susceptible rather than passionate – made her into one of those women who, when they come into a room, shine with the certainty that they will succeed and the lightness of their feeling makes them do so. Later she was to harden into the vivacious snob and to fatten into the determined celebrity hunter who bosomed her way into the limelight with the infallible flair of the woman who knew her geniuses.

Being irresistible was not only an instinct but a business with Amelia Opie. She wrote frightful novels which made Sir Walter Scott weep, and awful verses which Sydney Smith quoted in his lectures – the bad taste of great men has a long history – but she had taken care, it might be observed, to get to know the great first. She asked Southey once to say a word to the reviewers. She was one of those women who, having addled a man's judgment by making herself physically desirable, like an ice on a hot day, then change about and insist on being admired for their minds. She was quite candid about this technique in her last novel. She was irresistible, she says, because she was herself unable to resist – at first; she began resisting only when, by flattering them, she had made others think they had become irresistible themselves. No grand passions for her, she said, no durable affections. 'My object is to amuse life away and *a little love*, just enough to give interest to scenes and places, is delightful . . . My attachments are like gentle squeezes of the hand.' A great passion would destroy her 'peace of mind'. No wonder the Norwich Quakers, plump, benevolent but trimly literal in matters of virtue, were a little dubious when the chatty best seller who knew all the celebrities of London and Paris put on the Quaker bonnet. Was the accomplished actress just putting on another act? Of course she was. And yet, of course, she was not. Amelia had some of that stupidity in her nature which some call ingenuousness. It is the price a woman has to pay for being vain of her unconventionality. But Amelia is a delightful argument for the charm of an ill-adjusted life, for the attraction of being a bit of a fraud and for a dash of the prude in the wanton female character.

During the many years of her mother's illness, Amelia's childhood had been one of solitude and constraint. She was shut away, silenced, ignored. Imagination awakened. She quickly picked up a love of the sensational, the guilty and the morbid. The effect of the death of her mother was to release Amelia suddenly from a world of dark, dramatic and lugubrious brooding into a world of sociability and light. The late eighteenth century was made for escapades of the mind, and many of the English provincial towns had the intellectual liveliness of little capitals. In Norwich, Crome was painting. Holcroft, Godwin and the Radical leaders dined with the doctor. The ideas of the French Revolution were in the air and, as she listened to her father's praise of Lafayette, the young hostess became a republican at a bound. Alone in her room, she began to write plays and poetry and when she had done a few pages she found that great men liked to be asked for their criticisms. At least, with young ingenuity, she *thought* that this was what interested them. Her mind (she was to tell Godwin and Holcroft as they looked with desire upon her person) was her chief preoccupation. It is a weakness of intellectuals to be interested in minds and Amelia's fervid talk about hers was the ideal bait; ideal because it hooked the listener and yet kept him thrashing away unavailingly at a safe distance, at the end of the line. With Godwin hooked, with Godwin jealous of her friends, begging her to rule her emotions by the light of Reason while he himself fell into an irrational condition because she would not kiss him, Amelia's technique was established. Now she could deal with anyone, indeed preferably with several at a time. She sat down to write an anonymous book called *The Dangers of Coquetry*.

In the meantime she had made another conquest, one which lasted her lifetime and which did not spring from her engaging vanity but was directed by a warmer need of her nature. As a child Amelia had not known the geniality of normal family life. She needed a family and she conquered one. The Gurneys of Earlham were Quakers, a large family of children younger than herself and glad to admire and love the literary belle with her poems and her song. Quakerism had softened; music, painting and dancing were permitted to the younger Gurneys who turned to Amelia with all the love which the prim feel for the worldly. The young Gurneys were in revolt against their tradition, its politics, its culture. Where was there not revolt in that generation? There were Corresponding Societies – the English equivalent of the Jacobin Clubs – in Norwich, respectable 'pinks' were being spied on and even tried for sedition, treason and revolutionary activity; even the religious faith of the younger Gurneys was lapsing. To Amelia, who was 'in the movement' and who had run into scandal because of her passion for Mary Wollstonecraft and her defence of Godwin's marriage, they turned as to a goddess. The fact that she was known by now to be in love with a married man brought even brighter confidence to the agony of the young atheists. They were to get their own back later when time brought their repentance, and Amelia, the converter, was to be reconverted by them. Elizabeth Fry was one of those children and Amelia, at her gayest and most 'worldly', in the midst of writing her 'immoral' novels about seduced heroines, mad fathers and women ruined by 'a false step', always responded uncomfortably to criticism from Earlham.

But this quaint fruit of Amelia's deep affection for the Gurneys was to ripen slowly. By the time she was 28 and still unmarried Norwich had begun to shake its head. It was all very well to be clever, beautiful, mysterious, the skilful heartbreaker (Norwich said), but the coquette who turns down one proposal too many ends on the shelf. And Amelia was in her first mess. 'Mr. B.', the married man, was only too well married and there was no way of getting him. It was a crisis of the heart; it was, even more, a crisis for her vanity with all Norwich watching, the Gurneys above all. The solution was – and how true to her type she was – to drown a scandal in a sensation. She did so. The elegant young provincial married Opie. Opie was a peasant with a strong Cornish accent, shocking table manners, a divorced wife. Amelia did not love him. But he was a fashionable painter and thoroughly in the limelight. His table manners made her hesitate – odd things made her hesitate in her life: after Opie's death she went all out for a peer with the idea of reforming him and turned him down in the end because 'they both had enough to live on' – but in the end she plunged. She married Opie. She pushed him into society, saw to it that he got commissions. Now it was that she wrote. When her husband's work went temporarily out of fashion she buckled to and wrote a best-seller. And when he died – for the marriage was a short interlude in her life – she fought to get him buried in St Paul's Cathedral and grieved so extravagantly, in so many poems, panegyrics, memoirs, and so loudly that her friends had to remind her that she was enjoying herself more than the onlookers.

The Gurneys were worried. They enjoyed being stirred up by the celebrity, though by this time Amelia's claim to have a mind was mocked by reviewers. The Gurneys were older. They had returned to respectable opinions and even to their old religion. A reconquest of the Gurneys was necessary, a new disturbing of their godliness. To this period belongs her characteristic affair with Joseph John Gurney, a strict young Quaker, and with Haydon, the elderly reprobate of Bognor, who had had a notorious *ménage à trois* with his wife and his servant. To Joseph John she talked and wrote about 'the world', a subject which shocked and fascinated him; to Haydon, she talked about religion, which shocked and fascinated *him*. Haydon was old, Joseph John was young. He listened, he reproved, he lectured. Amelia loved it. She was delighted that he did not despair of bringing her back into the fold. It would have dismayed her to know that the prudent Quaker would succeed in recapturing her for the Lord, but would be careful to marry someone else.

The second mess, 'the miserable hash' in fact, was the direct cause of her conversion. Sooner or later that amusing vanity, that too clever susceptibility, was certain to be snubbed. One does not suppose she loved Tom Alderson, her knowing young cousin, very deeply, but she was humiliated when he turned her down. The answer again was a new sensation: the Quaker bonnet. We need not agitate ourselves, as the Quakers did, about the sincerity of that conversion. At 60 when she broke out again and went to Paris on a celebrity hunt after Lafayette and to renew her revolutionary enthusiasms, D'Angers the sculptor called her a Janus, a two-faced siren who instinctively showed you the profile you did not ask for. Her misleading Puritanism, so perfectly chaste but with delusive promise of wantonness, delighted the Frenchman. But Miss Mitford cattily noted that Amelia ordered the silk for her Quaker gown from Paris; and Paris was astonished and enchanted by a celebrity who arrived in the disguise of the Meeting House. It was all in character. In her youth she had stood in court watching the trial of Holcroft for treason and had cried, Liberty in the streets; but she had insisted on meeting the aristocratic *émigrés* too.

And how misleading she is even in her portraits. The plump, soft, wistful wench with the murmuring eyes and sensual mouth, in Opie's painting, does not look like the dazzler of the great. The humorous, blunt-faced, double-chinned sexagenarian of D'Anger's medallion does not look like the spiritualised creature which his ecstatic letters describe. What was it that got them all? Was it the famous technique, the flattery of the perpetual promise? Or the most flattering of all flatteries, the most active and subtle of the social arts (as indeed the last of her 'unredeemed' novels suggested), the art of listening? For one cannot, one must not, believe that the title of the first book, written after her redemption, offers the clue. It was a didactic work entitled *Lying, In all its Branches*.

The Ancestor

When I was young and was reading too many novels the works of Fielding were regarded as one of the pleasant things in store for those about to reach the age of consent. He was the last novelist, as Thackeray said, to be allowed to describe a man, and there were book-soaked critics like Professor Saintsbury to expatiate over their wine upon Fielding's use of the privilege. It is true that Dr Johnson called Fielding a blockhead and that Richardson – who had reason to spit and squirm – dismissed him as an ostler; but on the whole the warm impression of his genius and character prevailed, the impression which was most frankly but tolerantly conveyed in one of the letters of Lady Mary Wortley Montagu:

> I am sorry for H. Fielding's death, not only as I shall read no more of his writings, but I believe he lost more than others, as no man enjoyed life more than he did, though few had less reason to do so, the highest of his preferment being raking in the lowest sinks of vice and misery. I should think it a nobler and less nauseous employment to be one of the staff-officers than conduct the nocturnal weddings. His happy constitution (even when he had, with great pains, half demolished it) made him forget everything when he was before a venison pasty, or over a flask of champagne, and I am persuaded he has known more happy moments than any prince upon the earth. His natural spirits gave him rapture with his cook-maid, and cheerfulness when he was fluxing in a garret. There was a great similitude between his character and that of Sir Richard Steele. He had the advantage both in learning and, in my opinion, genius; they both agreed in wanting money in spite of all their friends, and would have wanted it, if their hereditary lands had been as extensive as their imaginations; yet each of them was so formed for happiness, it is a pity he was not immortal.

Alas, the vogue of Fielding had passed by the time I grew up. The secret reading of the mid-Victorians, and late, had lost its spell. The muscular Christians who were privately addicted to his muscular impropriety had given place to a generation with a feminine preoccupation with sex and the fortune-telling science of psychology. If one was going to read the eighteenth-century novelists at all, Richardson was your man and the masculine tradition of Fielding was less congenial. It is typical of our taste that Proust was greatly influenced by Richardson; and that when we look back to the earliest realism, we prefer the ungarnished plate of Defoe to the stylish menu that is handed to us by the author of *Tom Jones* and *Joseph Andrews*. He is said to be altogether too hearty, towny and insensitive. He is said to be that most tiresome of bores, the man's man. He sets up as the shallowest of philosophers: the man of the world, whose world turns out to be a box of tricks. And what does the philosophy amount to beyond a number of small notions: that society is not what it seems, that self-love and self-interest are the beginning and end of human motive, and that the only real and virile view of human nature is the low one? His geniality laboured the offence.

One has to admit the force of such a criticism of Fielding, but I am far from thinking it fatal to his rank as a novelist. In the first place the criticism is really aroused by his style rather than by his matter. Fielding is out to cut a figure. When he sets up as a satirist, he believes in the robust satire of the man who lives, not in the more cruel satire of the weak-livered man who abstains and snarls. In their rebellion against the poetic hyperbole of the early romances which had been imitated from the French, the Augustans parodied the heroic style; they were not thereby mocking the noble view of human nature; they were insinuating the sensible one.

Yet, even when we have acquiesced in the brilliant assumptiveness of Fielding's style and have seen beyond his sardonic preoccupation with men of honour and women of discretion, there remains the difficulty that Fielding is the ancestor. In Fielding we are haunted by almost the whole of the English novel. Pages of Dickens, Thackeray, Meredith even, incongruously, of Kipling, Galsworthy and Wodehouse, become confused in the general panorama: Fielding has the disadvantage of being the 'onlie begetter'. Not only do we pick out the perennial characters of the main part of English fiction, but he has set many of its idiosyncrasies and limits.

[149]

Sociable man, social problems, middle-class humour, the didactic habit, the club culture, the horseplay, the gregarious rather than the single eye, the habit of treating country life as an opportunity for the exercise of the body or of the fancy, as though nature were a mixture of gymnasium and an open-air extension of the Established Church – these are some elements which have continued in the English novel and which date from Fielding. He expressed one kind of Englishness, so that many critics – Sir Hugh Walpole was one – seemed to think that conservative sociability or what is called 'the creation of character' contains the whole English tradition; that people who speak of the novel as something inspired by ideas or concerned with a sense of the real situation of society at any given time were importing tendentious and arid Continental ideas. If these critics had considered Fielding's work they could never have made such a wild statement. Fielding was an old Etonian, but he was one of Eton's recalcitrants, sneered at and, in the end, pursued because he let the side down. The fact is that, from the beginning, the English novel set out to protest and to teach. Its philanthropic campaigns in the nineteenth century are paralleled in the eighteenth century by its avowed desire to reform the brutal manners of the age.

The explanation is not necessarily that there has been an extra allowance of public spiritedness in our novelists; it is simply that the crucial problems of his own time provide a novelist with his richest material, whether he deals with it directly or by inference. The reform of manners was as vital in the eighteenth century as the reform of the Poor Law was in the nineteenth. From Elizabethan times, the Dutch, the French and the Spanish visitors had been appalled by the barbarity of English life. When Fielding and Richardson filled their novels with abducted heiresses, Tammany law, bribed judges, faked weddings, duels in Hyde Park, with squalid fights between half-naked women in Gin Alley or on the village commons; with scoundrelly nincompoops, bailiffs and middle-men from the Coffee House and the Court, they were not amusing themselves with the concoctions of artificial comedy. They were attacking the criminal violence and corruption that underlay the elegance of the time. There was a plea for the middle-class virtues at a time when the aristocracy had left the country for the Court and had abandoned its responsibilities in order to milk the Exchequer. Public societies for the Reform of Manners had existed in the early part of the century. Fielding spent his writing life fighting abuses and ended as an excellent Bow Street magistrate, trying to clean up the London streets. 'Great characters' there are in all his books, but they are inseparable from his social purpose.

In an essay on his own work Fielding always said that he drew from life. But like Cervantes, whom he hoped to copy, and whom he so much admired, Fielding had been trained as a writer in the theatre. The English novel was not a development from the reporting of Defoe, a way of writing which, of its nature, is prevented from imaginative development. In the end the reporter can do no more than cover more and more ground; his method gives him nothing to till the ground with. Fielding took his slice of life, his chains of picaresque episode which in *Joseph Andrews* had made a promising but inferior version of *Gil Blas*, and let the artifice of the theatre break them up and rebuild them. The English novel started in *Tom Jones*, because the stage taught Fielding how to break the monotony of flat, continuous narrative. The methods of the theatre are abstract and summary; there is an idea before there is a scene; and one of the fascinating things in *Tom Jones* is the use of the summary method to set the scene, explain the types of character, cover the preparatory ground quickly by a few oblique moralisings and antics so that all the realism is reserved for the main action. Is Tom Jones a loyal and honest man? Could he be the opposite if circumstances tempt him? No great paraphernalia of dialogue and literal detail has to be used in order to introduce such questions. Fielding puts them, then illustrates with action, and frames the whole in brief commentary. Scenes do not ramble on and melt into each other. They snap past, sharply divided, wittily contrasted, cunningly balanced. The pace of *Tom Jones* is as fast as farce, and indeed only a theatre man's expertness in the dramatic, the surprising, the situation capped and re-capped, could cover the packed intrigue of the narrative. The theatre taught Fielding economy. It taught him to treat episodes as subjects and not as simple slices of life. Thackeray, who is the only English novelist to have learned from *Tom Jones* – Dickens learned from the inferior middle-brow *Amelia*, which has much more of the drudging realism of the later English novel – developed this method of Fielding's in *Vanity Fair*, going backwards and forwards in time, as well as to and fro in moral commentary. The difference is that Thackeray was born in the time of the sermon, and Fielding in the time of the chorus and the stage aside.

Fielding's own ancestor is Ben Jonson. Coleridge compared the formal excellence of *Tom Jones* with that of *The Alchemist*. The satire in both writers is meaty and brainy, very packed and prolific in ridiculous situations. To every character life is surprising and Fortune perverse. In the love-chase of Sophia Western and Tom Jones, there is the familiar stage situation that when one is willing the other is not available. Tom is a healthy young rake who does not intend to be one, and he reads a severe lecture to Nightingale, the professional Lovelace, who is merely satisfying sexual vanity. In the picaresque novels there is growth or decline in fortune, and rarely is there growth in character; but in *Tom Jones*, Partridge grows once he has got rid of his wife. Sophia, in London, learns to tell a lie to her rival – for which one admires her as much as when she comes head first off the horse – and Tom himself passed from the loyal to the careless and, after the shock of being caught out in his infidelities at Upton, into Tom the frantic who will commit any folly. He is a young man in a mess by the time he is mixed up with Lady Bellaston. This intrigue is the one in which first her ladyship and then the lady's maid are hidden behind the curtain in Tom's room, a piece of turn and turn about which comes straight from the theatre; it *does* strike one as artificial, but Fielding brings the whole intrigue to earth by the brilliant short chapter which introduces Mrs Hunt. Many critics have objected to this chapter as a loose end; but the naïve proposal of marriage from someone to whom Tom has never spoken comes almost affectingly out of the blue. It is a *cri de cœur* among a lot of sharp practice, something beautifully silly in an ill-natured episode.

Joseph Andrews, Jonathan Wild and *Tom Jones* are the three important novels of Fielding, and *Jonathan Wild* is the diamond among them, the most dazzling piece of sustained satirical writing in our language. There remains *Amelia*: a hybrid that lies half-way between the Augustan and the Victorian novel. As a novelist Fielding was subject to two opposite influences which were to leave their mark on the English novel for a hundred years and to ensure that it had little resemblance to the French and Russian novels: he was trained in the rogue's tale which introduced untidiness and irresponsibility into the English novel; and, as I have said, he was trained in the theatre, which gave our novel its long obsession with elaborate plot.

Amelia is a compromise. By the time he came to write this novel, Fielding seems to have lost the heat of the theatre's inspiration. The first chapter describing the prison is in the old manner, but presently the narrative digresses and dawdles. The didactic intention comes out frankly and, alas, unadorned. There is white-faced indignation where before there was irony, and indignation is the weaker strain, for it interrupts, where irony undermines. I do not suggest that his old comic gift is dead; far from it. There is Colonel Bath's remarkable duel. And there is the devastating Miss Mathews, the would-be murderess, who is a development from the drawing of that hard old rip, Lady Bellaston, out of *Tom Jones*. Miss Mathews is a superb tart. One is delighted that the Colonel refuses to drop her; delighted, too, though Fielding does not seem to be, that she grows fat. She will so obviously enjoy growing fat. It is she who makes the celebrated remark about the English taste for prudish women: do they attract, enquires the ever-curious Miss Mathews, because they appear to promise to cool the heat of love? In *Amelia*, there is more psychological complexity than there was in *Tom Jones*; it is the book of an older man who has grown tired. If we contrast Tom Jones with Mr Booth of *Amelia*, we see that Tom commits his sins, repents in a moment and ingenuously forgets them. Mr Booth is far more complicated. He is a married man to start with; he sins with caution, is transfixed by remorse and then settles down to brood with growing misanthropy. The wages of sin is not death, but worry – middle-class worry. His case never improves, for we see the subtle influence of his affair with Miss Mathews on his relations with other people. Fielding's rising interest in psychology marks a break with his interest in moral types. It is a signal of the coming age. And if *Amelia* indicates a decline from the brilliant fusing of gifts that went to make his earlier books, it points the way the English novel would go when a new genius, the genius of Dickens, seized it.

Clarissa

The modern reader of Richardson's *Clarissa* emerges from his experience exhausted, exalted and bewildered. The book is, I fancy, the longest novel in the English language; it is the one most crowded with circumstantial detail; it is written in the most dilatory of narrative manners, i.e. in the form of letters. It is a tale perceived through a microscope; it is a monstrosity, a minute and inordinate act of prolonged procrastination. And the author himself is a monster. That a man like Samuel Richardson should write one of the great European novels is one of those humiliating frolics in the incidence of genius. The smug, juicy, pedestrian little printer from Derbyshire, more or less unlettered, sits down at the age of 50 and instructs young girls in the art of managing their virtue to the best advantage. Yet, ridiculous as *Pamela* is, her creator disarms criticism by a totally new ingredient in the novel: he knows how to make the reader weep. And, stung by the taunts of the educated writers of his time, Richardson calmly rises far above *Pamela* when he comes to the story of Clarissa Harlowe; he sets the whole continent weeping. Rousseau and even Goethe bow to him and take out their handkerchiefs; the vogue of sensibility, the first shoots of the Romantic movement, spring from the pool of Richardson's pious tears like the grateful and delicate trees of an oasis. Yet there he is, plump, prosaic, the most middling of middling men, and so domestically fussy that even his gift of weeping hardly guarantees that he will be a major figure. Is there not some other strain in this dull and prodigiously painstaking little man? There is. Samuel Richardson was mad.

I do not mean that Richardson was a lunatic. I do not mean he was mad as Swift was mad. At first sight, an immeasurable smugness, an endlessly pettifogging normality seem to be the outer skin of Richardson's character. We know, as I have already said, that from his youth he was an industrious and timid young man who was, for some reason or other, used by young women who wanted their love letters written. Profoundly sentimental, he sat like some pious old cook in her kitchen, giving advice to the kitchen maids, and when he came to write novels he was merely continuing this practical office. He lived vicariously like some sedentary lawyer who has to argue the disasters of other people's lives letter by letter, but who himself never partakes. Genteel, he is, nevertheless, knowing; prim and cosy, he is, nevertheless, the victim of that powerful cult of the will, duty and conscience by which Puritanism turned life and its human relations into an incessant war. There is no love in Puritanism; there is a struggle for power. Who will win the daily battle of scruple and conscience – Pamela or the young squire; Clarissa or Lovelace? And yet what is urging Richardson to this battle of wills? What is it that the Puritan cannot get out of his mind, so that it is a mania and obsession? It is sex. Richardson is mad about sex.

His is the madness of Paul Pry and Peeping Tom. I said just now that *Clarissa* is a novel written under the microscope; really it is a novel written about the world as one sees it through the keyhole. Prurient and obsessed by sex, the prim Richardson creeps on tip-toe nearer and nearer, inch by inch, to that vantage point; he beckons us on, pausing to make every kind of pious protestation, and then nearer and nearer he creeps again, delaying, arguing with us in whispers, working us up until we catch the obsession too. What are we going to see when we get there? The abdication, the seduction, the lawful deflowering of a virgin in marriage are not enough for him. Nothing short of the rape of Clarissa Harlowe by a man determined on destroying her can satisfy Richardson's phenomenal day-dream with its infinite delays.

The principle of procrastinated rape is said to be the ruling one in all the great best-sellers. It was in Richardson's genius that he was able to elevate the inner conflict of the passions and the will to an abstract level, so that the struggle of Clarissa and Lovelace becomes a universal battle-piece; and, in doing this, Richardson was able to paint it with the highly finished realism of the Dutch painters. At the beginning one might simply be reading yet another novel of intrigue, which just goes on and on; and but for the incredible suspense in the narrative I think many readers must have given up *Clarissa* by the end of the first volume. It is not until the third and fourth volumes are reached, when Richardson transposes his intrigue into the sustained and weeping music, the romantic tragedy of Clarissa's rape and long preparation for death, that we get his measure. She dies piously, yet like a Shakespearean conferring greatness upon all around her by the starkness of her defeat. At the beginning we are not prepared for this greatness in Clarissa; even in that last volume we are often uncertain of her real stature. It is not easy for virginity to become Virtue. Would she be anything without Lovelace? And yet, we know, she is the crown upon Lovelace's head. He too becomes tragic under her judgment as she becomes tragic by his act. These two reflect glory upon each other, like saint and devil. But in the first volume there is no difficulty about deciding who is the greater as a character or as an abstract conception. Lovelace has her beaten hands down. A practical and languid correspondence wakes up when he takes pen in hand. Anna Howe, the 'pert' friend, makes circles round her. Arabella, with her nose out of joint, is livelier comedy. The scheming brother, the gouty father with his paroxysms, the supplicating and fluttering mother, and the endearing uncles with their unendearing family solidarity, make a greater mark on our minds than the all-too-articulate Clarissa does. Our one hope is that witty Miss Howe is right when she teases Clarissa with maidenly self-deception. 'The frost piece,' as Lovelace called her, looks exactly like one of those fascinating prudes whose minds are an alphabet that must be read backwards. But no; though she will enchant us when she is rattled, with cries like 'Oh, my Nancy, what shall I do with this Lovelace?' her course and her motives are clear to her; and we begin the slow and painful discovery of a virtue which finds no exhilaration except in scruple. We face an inexhaustible determination, and this is exhausting to contemplate, for Clarissa is as interested in the organisation of human motives as Richardson himself; and he insinuates himself in her character so thoroughly, niggling away with his 'ifs' and his 'buts', that he overwhelms her, as Flaubert overwhelmed Madame Bovary.

Still this does not take from the drama of Clarissa's situation, and does, in fact, increase the suspense of it. If we skip – and of course we do, looking up the letters in the obliging synopsis – we do not, as in other novels, find ourselves caught out by an overlooked sub-plot; we are back in the main situation. Will the family relent? Will Lovelace abduct, marry, rape or reform? There's hardly a sub-plot worth mentioning in this huge novel. It follows the labyrinth of a single theme. And though we turn to Anna Howe for glimpses of common sense, and for a wit to enliven the glum belligerents of what Lovelace – always a psychologist and nearly a

Freudian – called 'the Harlowe dunghill' with its wills and deeds of settlement, we see in Clarissa's stand something more than a virtuous daughter bullied by her parents. She is a lawyer in family morals, and in Lovelace's too; but she is the first heroine in English fiction to stand against the family. Richardson called them 'the embattled phalanx', and in *Clarissa* he goes to the heart of the middle-class situation: money, accretion of estate, the rise in the world, the desire to found a family, in conflict with the individual soul. She and Lovelace complement each other here. She thinks her family ought not to do evil to her, yet takes their evil upon herself; she is not a rebel but is tricked and driven into becoming an outcast and at last a saint. Like Lovelace, she has asked too much, 'for people who allow nothing will be granted nothing; in other words, those who aim at carrying too many points will not be able to carry any'. Yes, and those who put up their price by the device of reluctance invite the violence of the robber. By setting such a price upon herself, Clarissa represents that extreme of puritanism which desires to be raped. Like Lovelace's, her sexuality is really violent, insatiable in its wish for destruction.

Lovelace is Richardson's extravagant triumph. How did such a burning and tormented human being come out of that tedious little printer's mind? In the English novel Lovelace is one of the few men of intellect who display an intellect which is their own and not patently an abstract of their author's intellectual interests. He is half-villain, half-god, a male drawn to the full, and he dominates English fiction. He is all the more male for the feminine strains in his character: his hatred of women, his love of intrigue, his personal vanity, his captiousness and lack of real humility. A very masculine novelist like Fielding is too much a moralist, and too confidently a man, to catch a strain like that. And how Lovelace can write! When Clarissa's letters drag, like sighing Sunday hymns, or nag at us in their blameless prose, like the Collect for the day, the letters of Lovelace crackle and blaze with both the fire and the inconsequence of life. His words fly back and forth, throwing out anecdotes and the characters of his friends, with wonderful transitions of mood. In one paragraph he is writing a set apostrophe to Clarissa, full of longing and half-way to repentance. He shakes the mood off like a man who is drunk with grief and throws off this description of his gouty old kinsman:

And here (pox of his fondness for me; it happens at a very bad time) he makes me sit hours together entertaining him with my rogueries (a pretty amusement for a sick man!) and yet, whenever he has the gout, he prays night and morning with his chaplain. But what must *his* notions of religion be, who, after he has nosed and mumbled over his responses, can give a sigh or groan of satisfaction, as if he thought he had made up with Heaven; and return with a new appetite to my stories? – encouraging them, by shaking his sides with laughing at them, and calling me a sad fellow, in such an accent as shows he takes no small delight in his kinsman.

The old peer has been a sinner in his day, and suffers for it now; a sneaking sinner, *sliding*, rather than *rushing* into vices, for fear of his reputation; or rather, for fear of detection, and positive proof; for this sort of fellow, Jack, has no real regard for reputation. Paying for what he never had, and never daring to rise to the joy of an enterprise at first hand, which bring him within view of a tilting or the honour of being considered as the principal man in a court of justice.

To see such a Trojan as this just dropping into the grave which I hoped ere this would have been dug, and filled up with him; crying out with pain and grunting with weakness; yet in the same moment crack his leathern face into a horrible laugh, and call a young sinner charming varlet, encoring him as formerly he used to do the Italian eunuchs; what a preposterous, what an unnatural adherence to old habits.

Or there is the awful description of that old procuress, Mrs Sinclair, a horror out of Rowlandson, who advances upon Clarissa on the night of the rape, when all Richardson's fascination with carnal horror breaks out. There is a double terror in it, because Lovelace himself is writing as if trying to drive evil out of his mind by a picture of evils still greater:

The old dragon straddled up to her, with her arms kemboed again, her eyebrows erect like the bristles upon a hog's back, and, scowling over her shortened nose, more than half hid her ferret eyes. Her mouth was distorted. She pouted out her blubber-lips, as if to bellow up wind and sputter into her horse-nostrils, and her chin was curdled, and more than usually prominent with passion.

[158]

The temperate, lawyer-like mind of Richardson does not prepare one for passages like this. When there is matter-of-factness in the eighteenth century, one expects it to be as regular as Pope's couplets were. But Richardson is not consistent. In the sheer variety of their styles the letters in this novel are astonishing. The bovine uncles, the teasing parenthetical Miss Howe, the admonitory Belford, the curt Colonel Morden, heading for his duel, the climbing neurotic brother whose descendants were no doubt in the British Union of Fascists, all have their styles, and they are as distinctive as Lovelace's or Clarissa's. Richardson is the least flat, the most stereoscopic novelist of an age which ran the plain or formal statement to death in the end. Another point: he is a writer of indirect narrative. We are shown scenes at second hand, for the epistolary method requires it so; and we become used to a sort of memoranda of talk and action which will tire our inward eye because our judgment is called upon at the same time. So there are many reported scenes which are relative failures, for example, the early and rather confusing ones between Clarissa and her mother. One has a muddled impression of two hens flying up in the air at each other and scattering their feathers. Yet even in this kind of scene Richardson can, at times, write talk which is direct and put action wonderfully under our eye. The scene of the rape is tremendous in this respect; and so is the awful picture of the brothel when Mrs Sinclair breaks her leg and the harridans come out in their night attire; and there is the comic, savage picture of Lovelace defeating the attempt of his family to try him. But where Richardson shook off the slavery of his own method is shown at its best, I think, in Belford's letter describing the prison scene where the two prostitutes offer to bail Clarissa out:

> 'We are surprised at your indifference, Miss Harlowe. Will you not write to any of your friends?'
> 'No.'
> 'Why, you don't think of tarrying *here* always.'
> 'I shall not live always.'

Even in those few lines one sees Richardson advancing his inner narrative and, if one continues this conversation, one also sees him patiently and unerringly preserving character. One might almost say that prolix as it was, his method was economical, given his chosen end. The slowness comes from an excess of examination, not an excess of words. No prose has fewer redundancies.

We come to the death scene. The torment of Lovelace pacing his horse past the gate of the house he dare not enter, though Clarissa lies dying within, is not rhetorical. It is defiant as fits a being so saturnine, it is in the mind as becomes a man of intellect, it is the changeable, imploring, ranging madness of a clever mind that has met its conqueror. Lovelace is a villain no man hates, because he is a man. He is candid, if he is vain. He can argue like Iago or debate like Hamlet, and in between send a purse of a few guineas to a rogue who has helped him to his present catastrophe. It is strange to think of him – the only Don Juan in English fiction and done to the last Freudian detail. Clarissa dies like a swan amid the formal melody of a prose into which Richardson fell without affectation.

> Her breath being very short, she desired another pillow. Having two before, this made her, in a manner, sit up in her bed; and she spoke then with more distinctness; and seeing us greatly concerned, forgot her own stutterings to comfort us; and a charming lecture she gave us, though a brief one, upon the happiness of a timely preparation, and upon the hazards of a late repentance, when the mind, as she observed, was so much weakened, as well as the body, as to render a poor soul hardly able to contend with its natural infirmities.

It is a strong test of the illusion that Richardson has cast upon us that we think of Lovelace like a shadow cast upon Clarissa as she dies; and of Clarissa rather than of Lovelace when *he* appears. These lives are known by their absences; they are inextricable, tangled in the thousands of words they have spoken about each other, and are swept away at last into other people's words.

The Shocking Surgeon

═══════════

The disappearance of illustrations from the English novel, and indeed the decline of the art of illustrating, is a loss to literary criticism. For one of the obligations of the critic is to possess himself of the eyes with which a novelist's contemporaries read him, and this the good illustrator helped him to do. Of course we never achieve this sight, but we can approach it. And how far off the mark we can be is shown by the shock that a good illustrator gives. Cruikshank, for example: he upsets all the weary pieties of realism that lie between us and a comprehension of Dickens; half the silly criticisms of Dickens need never have been written if Cruikshank had been studied as closely as the text. And Rowlandson: pick up an edition of Smollett that has Rowlandson's illustrations and see Smollett come into focus once more, so that his page is almost as fresh to us as it must have appeared to the eighteenth-century reader. It is true that outside this school of illustration the argument weakens; the wooden severity of late-Victorian realism was a lugubrious travesty of the text and one is glad that illustration has been dropped. The fact is that illustration was at its best when the English novel also was in its brash, vital, fantastic youth; when, though wigged in a judicious style, it had only a simple and crude concern with caricature, anecdote and the bad manners of society. Once the novel abandoned travel and developed plot and form, the English novel ceased to need the illustrator, or at any rate ceased to get the right one.

There are two pointers in the engravings which Rowlandson did for *Humphry Clinker*, pointers the reader of Smollett ought to follow. Look at the scrawny figure of that malign virgin Tabitha Bramble, as she comes accusing into the room where her philanthropical brother has been caught with a lady; look at Humphry in the gaol, moaning out his grotesque Methodism to the felons; look at her ladyship, gluttonous, diseased and warty, tearing out her friend's hair. They are not human beings. They are lumps of animal horror or stupidity. To Rowlandson the human race are cattle or swine, a reeking fat-stock done up in ribbons or breeches, which has got into coffee-houses, beds and drawing-rooms. He was nauseated by the domesticity and the grossness of the eighteenth century's new rich. In fact, every eighteenth-century artist and writer jibbed at the filth of domestic life, at some time or other. These pictures of Rowlandson's (of Hogarth's too) show how urgent was the task of the reform of manners which the writers of the eighteenth century had set themselves, from Addison onwards. (The movement had been revived by William III, who, when he came from Holland, was horrified by the brutality of English life. He encouraged Defoe, especially, to write in the cause of reform.) The second point is that Rowlandson's people are portraits of Swift's Yahoos. In these pictures we see the nightmare lying behind the Augustan manner. The nightmare of the pox, the scurvy, delirium tremens, of obesity and gout, the nightmare of the insanitary streets, of the stairway which was a dunghill, of the sedate Georgian window which was a place for the emptying of chamber pots; the nightmare of the suppurations that flowed into the waters at Bath, of the stenches that rose from the 'elegant' crowds at Assemblies; the nightmare of the lives of children flogged into stupidity – see the boyhood of *Peregrine Pickle* – so that, in Rowlandson and Hogarth, all the virtuous people look like lumps of suet; and, haunting this scene, the nightmare religion of Wesley. Smollett and Rowlandson run so closely together in the drawing of these things that one borrows from the other's brutality. Yet are they brutal? I do not know enough about Rowlandson to say, but I am pretty sure that Smollett, for all his obsession with the bladder and the backside, was not a brutal nor a filthy man. He enjoyed being the shocking surgeon who brings out horrors at the dinner-table; but because he was shocked himself. Smollett's sensibility is close to Swift's. There is enough proof of Smollett's intention in the reforms which followed his descriptions of the brutalities of naval life at his time in *Roderick Random*. And though there is a good deal of horseplay, battery and assault in his books, from the comic scene where Hawser Trunnion picks up a turkey from the table to beat an unwelcome visitor, to the one in *Roderick Random* where the hero and a friend tie up the schoolmaster and flog his naked backside with a rope, Smollett has strong views on the stupefying effects of flogging. These are clearly stated in *Peregrine Pickle*. It is true that Perry, after a period of beating, himself becomes the bully of the school, to

Hawser Trunnion's great delight, but Trunnion's views are always presented as further fantastic aspects of a fantastic and maimed character. We see more of what Smollett was like in the portrait of Dr Bramble in *Humphry Clinker*. Generosity and goodness of heart go together with an impetuous temper and a good touch of hypochondria. He has a morbid nose which smells out every stench that Bath, Edinburgh and Harrogate can provide; and Smollett's own nose, in his book of travels in France and Italy, was as fastidious. Smollett may have enjoyed the brutality he described, but his protests and his hypochondria suggest that he felt the pleasure and the agony of the man who has a skin too few. His coarseness, like that of Joyce, is the coarseness of one whose senses were unprotected and whose nerves were exposed. Something is arrested in the growth of his robust mind; as a novelist he remains the portrayer of the outside, rarely able to get away from physical externals or to develop from that starting-point into anything but physical caricature.

A course of Smollett is hard for the modern reader to digest. The theatre advised and animated Fielding and gave him form and discipline. Smollett might have remained a ship's surgeon – and would probably have been a happier man. (Smollett figures in the older Disraeli's gallery of literary calamities.) The difficulty of digestion is that he is raw and piquant meat; course follows course without abating, and one has a surfeit. One begins *Peregrine Pickle*, *Roderick Random*, *Humphry Clinker* or *Count Fathom*, exclaiming with pleasure at the physical zest and the racing speed of the narrative, but after a hundred and fifty pages one has had enough of the practical jokes, the heiresses and duellists, the cheats and the bawds. Our trouble is that the English novel changed direction after its early lessons with the French and Spanish picaresque writers. The novel of travel gave place to plot and developed character. The kind of thing that Smollett did in *Humphry Clinker* – which all the critics, except the unerring Hazlitt, over-praise – was turned into Young's *Tours* or Cobbett's *Rural Rides*.

One book of Smollett's can be recommended to the modern reader without reservations: the very original *Travels Through France and Italy*, the first ill-tempered, captious, disillusioned and vigorously personal travel book in modern literature. It is a tale of bad inns, illness, cheating customs officials, a thoroughly British book of grousings and manias – the aim of every Frenchman is to seduce your wife, or if not your wife, your sister, and if not your sister, your daughter, as a token of his esteem for you! – but packed with the irritable author and moments of fresh, unperturbed judgment. It annoyed Sterne and was meant to annoy him. Against Sterne's fancies stand Smollett's manias, and how well they stand. Elsewhere, in the novels, one thinks less of whole books than of scenes. *Peregrine Pickle* is not as vigorous in its strokes and movements as *Roderick Random*, but my favourite scenes come from the former book. Hawser Trunnion and his 'Garrison' are wonderful fantasies, which tumble upon the reader uproariously as if a party were going on upstairs and the ceiling had given way in the middle of it. Trunnion lying about his naval engagements, fooled by publicans, entrapped by women, and tacking across country to his wedding, is, as they say, 'a beauty and no mistake'. And his death – that is one of the great scenes of English literature, to be compared with that great death scene at the end of Dostoevsky's *The Possessed*. You can see, as you read, how Fielding's wittier and better-formed imagination would have improved this novel; though Smollett surpasses Fielding, I think, in female portraiture; his leading ladies have more spirit than Fielding's and can amuse themselves quite well without the help of the hero. *Roderick Random* is altogether more sardonic and violent; *Count Fathom* is more polished, an essay after the manner of *Jonathan Wild*. It contains two scenes which stand out – a robber scene, suggested, I suppose, by an early episode in *Gil Blas*, and an appalling chapter describing the Count's mother, who was a camp follower in Marlborough's wars and made a good living by cutting the throats of the wounded and robbing them. This is the kind of scene that reveals the exposed nerve in Smollett.

The physical realism of Smollett and his chamber-pot humour are one other link with Joyce and show how his mind may have had not dissimilar obsessions. Perhaps that is going rather far; but there is some hint of *Anna Livia* in the Welsh maid's letters in *Humphry Clinker*. Smollett extended the farce of punning and misspelling into new regions for his times:

> Last Sunday in the parish crutch, if my own ars may be trusted, the clerk called the banes of marridge betwist Opaniah Lashmeheygo and Tapitha Bramble, spinster; he mought as well have called her inkle weaver, for she never spun a hank of yarn in her life. Young Squire

Dollison and Miss Liddy make the second kipple and there might have been a turd, but times are changed for Mr. Clinker.

Or:

> Who would have thought that mistriss, after all the pains taken for the good of her prusias sole, would go for to throw away her poor body? that she would cast the heys of infection upon such a carrying crow as Lashmyhago, as old as Mathewsullin, as dry as a red herring, and as poor as a starved veezel . . . He's a profane scuffle, and as Mr. Clinker says, no better than an imp-fiddle, continually playing upon the pyebill and the new burth.

That's going farther than any Malaprop could go. It is more than the rollicking *double entendre* of Rowlandson's letterpress. It is a Scotsman making a Welsh woman play ducks and drakes with the English language. It is imaginative, festive and, like all Smollett's comedy, broad, bizarre and bold.

The Crank

If we are to define the spirit of the eighteenth century by its favourite word, I think the word 'man' or 'mankind', even more than words like 'order' or 'reason', is the one we ought to chose. Man dominates the minds and ultimately the hearts of the eighteenth-century writers, where God had dominated the mind of the seventeenth century. After the battles, the factions, the treasons, the private and partisan faiths of the religious wars, the men of the eighteenth century were concerned to impose an order on that chaos, to seek the common denominator, to reassemble the judgment of divided human nature. The warring consciences were to be fused once more into an amenable moral animal with all his greatness and all his folly. The lines of Pope proclaim him:

> Know then thyself, presume not God to scan,
> The proper study of Mankind is Man.
> Plac'd on this isthmus of a middle state,
> A Being darkly wise, and rudely great:
> With too much knowledge for the Sceptic side,
> With too much weakness for the stoic's pride,
> He hangs between; in doubt to act or rest;
> In doubt to deem himself a God, or Beast;
> In doubt his Mind or Body to prefer;
> Born but to die, and reas'ning but to err;
> Alike in ignorance, his reason such,
> Whether he thinks too little or too much:
> Chaos of Thought and Passion, all confus'd;
> Still by himself abus'd or disabus'd;
> Created half to rise, and half to fall;
> Great lord of all things, yet a prey to all;
> Sole judge of Truth, in endless Error hurl'd:
> The glory, jest, and riddle of the world!

And Man is not yet trapped in our later prefixes and qualifications. He is not yet industrial man, economic man, evolutionary man, civilised man, massman or man in transition. He is simply himself, a wonder ordained, like a tree watched in a garden. Inconstancy, levity, cruelty may be his habits; but so are generosity, the noble and the useful virtues. Even Swift declares that he loves plain John, Peter and Thomas. The name of Candide is itself a commendation. However ferocious the satire of the eighteenth century it is always balanced by a pleasure, sometimes trite and complacent, but always ingenuous and warm, in the habits of the new-discovered species; and we ourselves respond to such a fundamentally sanguine and well-found conception of human nature, even as we smile at the neat eighteenth-century labels. The Age of Reason was a revised, replanted and well-tended Eden; the serpent himself did obeisance to the great landscape gardener; and when we look back upon that world we cannot but suspect that half our present miseries date from the dissipation of the common feeling and philosophy that ensured the sanity of the age.

The notion of the sufficiency of man in himself encouraged the growth of peculiar character. The century enjoyed its fantastics. It allowed people to grow as they willed. One delighted in inventing more and more deformities and vices for one's enemies, more and more foibles and scandals for one's friends. The eccentrics of the age grew like cultivated blooms for all to admire; and its cranks could rely on the affection if not on the support of their circle. Misanthropy was especially respected, for among people who live well the melancholy man is slipped in by nature as a kind of sport and to restore the balance; and when the misanthropic man was a crank into the bargain, he was observed with that delighted eagerness which a naturalist feels for the smallest hint of a new mutation.

In this period, there is no more suggestive example than the author of *Sandford and Merton*. Mr Day is the modest and entrancing crank of the century. He is a crank who is the guide to all cranks, the pattern of the tribe. In their lives few earnest men have been more ridiculous. After his death, the growth of his influence indicated the crank's embarrassing usefulness: if he was ridiculous, we were dreadful; if he was to be laughed at, we were to be wept over. For the case of Mr Day perfectly illustrates the point that the crank is one of the growing points of society. He shows us not indeed what we shall become, but the direction we are likely to take. The special

madness of Mr Day was the belief that the errors of life were not due
to original sin, but to stupidity and the formation of bad habits. If we
could be caught young enough, in the age of natural innocence, we could
be trained to be wiser and better than our stupid fathers. It was the
madness of education. We shall see that when we come to *Sandford
and Merton*, but before we do so, a glance at Mr Day himself, as he is
drawn full length in the *Memoirs* of his friend Richard Edgeworth, is
indispensable.

Nature is malicious. She is likely to arrange that those who have
revolutionary ideas about the education of children shall have no children
of their own; and here we come upon the first flaw in Mr Day's private life.
He did not succeed in getting any children of his own; he was without the
recklessness of the philoprogenitive. An abnormal caution governed
the revolutionary life of Mr Day. He was unable for many years to master
the initial difficulty of getting a wife. Women surrounded him, but none
came up to his severe requirements. He believed, like any rationalist, in the
sufficiency of man; his cross was the insufficiency of woman. The heart of
the problem was that Mr Day was a perfectionist; he not only believed in
the perfectibility of man which is arguable, but he also believed in the
perfectibility of women, and women take unkindly to the notion that they
can be improved. The susceptible Mr Day – and he was very susceptible –
had either to take what he could get and like what he got, as the common
run of men have to do, or – the logic is unanswerable – construct his own
wife from blue prints in advance. Admirable mind of the eighteenth
century: Mr Day chose the second course.

What were the requirements of Mr Day? Like a planner, he wanted to
begin from the beginning, to make a fresh start. The whole invention called
woman was in error. First of all one had to persuade women of this
fundamental error in creation. Then one isolated them, cured them of
silliness, frivolity, caprice, love of clothes, love of flirtation, love of chatter,
flattery and society, the tendency to disobedience, lying and deception.
One cured them of their slavery to fashion. Into the resulting vacuum, one
poured modesty, decorum and the higher mental interests; the sex would
learn, not indeed to converse themselves, but to follow a man's conversation and to assimilate his opinions. And they would be the most advanced
opinions. Mr Day was sick of the silly women of the eighteenth century,

the creatures who were seduced, abducted and swindled, who giggled and fainted, danced and gambled and talked of nothing but clothes. The story is well known. Cautiously he obtained the two famous orphans – two because he realised there might be a failure. Lucretia and Sabrina were immured in the country, and Day waited for them to grow to the point where he could attend to their minds. Alas, the reformer who did not believe in original sin had not reckoned with invincible dullness! Lucretia turned out to be quarrelsome and trivial. She was married off quickly to a draper. For a time Sabrina seemed more hopeful. But it could not be concealed that she disliked reading. She could not bear science. She could not keep a secret. And she had no control over her emotions. Day established all these points by experiment. For example, to test her self-control he fired pistols close to her ears and her petticoats. She screamed. More serious – she was found secretly to be buying hats and putting lace on her dresses.

The experiment of Mr Day's is notorious. It caused the greatest astonishment in France where he took the two girls on an educational tour; but incredulous Frenchmen were at last convinced that Mr Day was genuinely engaged in an educational exercise, and retired from his party in terror. Mr Day was prepared to fight a duel with anyone who imperilled the curriculum. But the experiment is a mere episode in Mr Day's search for the right partner. He was only 21 when he undertook it.

At this point it is important to reveal the existence of another character who had been experimenting also, and who was the close witness and associate in some of Day's adventures. I refer to Richard Edgeworth. Here comedy fills out. Day is the initiator, but Richard Edgeworth is the foil. One man is the making of the other; and it is through the delightful memoirs of Maria Edgeworth's father that we see Mr Day drawn full length with all the century's love of strange human beings and with its special regard for friendship. The two men are examples of the dyspeptic and the eupeptic schools of experiment. They were both rich. They were both country gentlemen.

On the one hand there is the ingenious Mr Day, the exemplary Mr Day, the Mr Day who talked like a book, who neglected his appearance, who refused to dress like a man of fashion, who despised the polite conventions, who began his addresses to women by denouncing the sex. A clumsy man, greasy haired in the days of wigs, pock-marked and brilliant, Mr Day scowled cautiously all day over his scruples. At a time when a good masculine leg was admired he was painfully knock-kneed. On the other hand there was Richard Edgeworth, Irish, headstrong, handsome, generous, hot-tempered and gallant, the best dancer in Europe. Like Day he was a man with theories of education – he was bringing up his son on the lines laid down by Rousseau, to the astonishment of his neighbours and the despair of his lamenting wife – like Day he was a man of scruples. But his passions were always growing stronger and his scruples growing less.

And then Day was the theorist and Edgeworth was the man of practice. Day would a thousand times sooner read a book on housing than address a carpenter. His theories about women could be seen as a protective device. Edgeworth's character was the opposite. In the matter of education he got a son and tried his educational theories on him. In the matter of women – Edgeworth married four times, three times very happily. He was an incurable inventor of contraptions – one-wheeled coaches, patent turnip cutters, railway lines, interlocking carriages, telegraphs, patent tips and loading devices, a notable forerunner of the next century's engineers. One can see that a love of mischief was part of his ingenious temperament, and that it must have directed his affection for the prosaic Mr Day.

There is one remarkable episode in their friendship. It happened when Day had reached the point of desperation in his search for a wife. A delightful young woman called Elizabeth Sneyd who was Edgeworth's sister-in-law (years later she was to become Edgeworth's wife) agreed to consider Mr Day if he would improve his appearance and polish his manners. Not a simple decision for a man like Day; for him, polish was the Arch-Enemy, fashion the Pollution of life. To his drastic and puritan mind, the wearing of a wig meant the renunciation of his republican principles. But he was a desperate man. He agreed. He went off to France with Edgeworth, and, in his own mind, sold himself to the devil. Edgeworth describes how they got to Lyons where he had an enormous social success, while Day went through the pitiless school of a French dancing master. They cropped Day's lank Cromwellian locks. They piled a huge horsehair wig on his head. They dressed his ungainly body in the latest Parisian clothes. They taught him to bow and to dance. It was difficult for him to do this gracefully because of his knees and so soon they had him between boards which were screwed tight so that he could not move. Edgeworth had engineering projects of his own on the Saône, but he took a special and wicked interest in Mr Day's knee-straightening machine. It was no good. The knees still knocked. 'I could not help pitying my philosophic friend,' says Richard Edgeworth, 'pent up in durance vile for hours together, with his feet in the stocks, a book in his hand and contempt in his heart.' Day returned at last to England, but when Elizabeth Sneyd saw the Puritan Malvolio come bowing into the room, she collapsed with laughter, and that was the end of that.

Let us leave Mr Day standing with unbendable rectitude amid the debris of his personal comedy. He did find a wife in the end, exactly the wife he desired, who was delighted to abandon all her personal tastes, including her love of music – an art which distressed him – and to devote her ear to his endless conversation. It was usually about education, and education killed him in the end. Kindness to animals was one of his principles, and Day was killed trying out a new 'natural' method of educating an unbroken horse. The Age of Reason conceived wild nature and the noble savage to be tamer than they were.

When we read *Sandford and Merton* we feel that Day had this delusion about children. He had none of his own. Would they have broken him? Or would he have broken them? The father-prig, endlessly eloquent, mellifluously disposed to draw the ever-recurring moral, always pat with the tendentious anecdote, is a strain on his children. They relieve it at last by laughter. Perhaps Day would have become the ridiculous father as *Sandford and Merton* is the father's ridiculous book.

But not basically ridiculous. I have already suggested that *Sandford and Merton* is the fruit of the eighteenth century's humane belief in the sufficiency of man and the light of reason. The book is not merely a child's book with a purpose; it is a child's book with a coherent philosophy, and that humane philosophy seems to me to have made *Sandford and Merton* far superior to the religious literature prescribed for children up to and, indeed, after that time. In how many biographies do we read of children who were terrified by Foxe's *Book of Martyrs?* How many have been made to snivel in misery over *Sandford and Merton*'s pious rival of the nineteenth century, *The Fairchild Family?* Some undoubtedly enjoyed the terrors, and I am not sure that it is wise to prevent a child from transposing his inheritance of the guilt and crimes of human nature into the pages of imaginative literature. Throughout the nineteenth century Day's book was disliked because it was said to ignore religion. In fact it did not, for it contains a simple account of Christ's morality; but Day certainly was no friend to the idea of original sin, and he did not set out to take the growing mind from a consideration of its responsibilities to the outside world itself, by nagging it continually with morbid images of the world within. If he was going to talk about hell, it was the hell of poverty, the several hells which men make for their fellows, not the hell invented by sadistic servants. One of the important aims of Day – and also of Edgeworth, who has some claim to be called the father of modern education – was to free the children of the well-to-do from the corrupting influence of nurses, chambermaids and butlers. But Day's philosophy must be judged by the kind of interests it encouraged. No doubt, as Edgeworth at last came to see, we are not certain to choose virtue just because our reason tells us that vice leads to misery and unhappiness; no doubt authority and discipline are required. But what new fields the freedom of philosophy opened to the curious mind! While the fearful and pious child was sobbing over the catastrophes of sin and was enclosed in the dank cloisters of self-pity, the prim little rationalists of *Sandford and Merton* were seeing the world. They were exploring South America, studying elephants and tigers, conducting experiments with the sun and the moon, and learning about the society they lived in.

It is strange that such an uninspiring man as Day, a man so full of crotchets and so devoid of instinct, so poor in response to everything except a generality, should have written a book as limpid and alive as *Sandford and Merton*. He hits one or two tastes of children with nicety: the complacency of children, their priggish and fierce delight in codes of conduct and honour; their love of a crude argument in black and white; their cocky moments of discovery; their passion for being heroes. Day understands the elementary principle that children are human beings who are growing taller and more powerful every day. 'We are but little children strong' – not weak. It is true that the tears and the piety of the awful little Harry Sandford mark a stage in the 'too noble by half' tradition; but I imagine that the child reader identifies himself with the wilful Tommy Merton, and attends only to Harry Sandford's remarkable practical capa-

[172]

bilities – he knows how to deal with snakes, for example, and can take a thrashing without turning a hair – without being much perturbed by his virtues. Even the sentimentality about the honest poor, with its underhand appeal to childish pity, catches the child's love of showing off and making himself important. Old Mr Barlow, to do him justice, has an inkling of this.

But the important charm of *Sandford and Merton* is extraneous to these matters. Day succeeds because he has created a kind of travelling zoo, an elegant and orderly zoo whose head keeper maintains a lively and picaresque running commentary. Now he is telling the visitor about the elephant, about elephants he has seen, elephants in the wild, elephants he has tamed, how you ought to handle them, and what happened to a tailor who made the mistake of playing a trick on one. The jungle, the native village, the regal procession are thrown in; and the whole stream of pictures flows smoothly by. They flick away before boredom starts. We have the pleasure of listening to someone talking to himself. This musical and vivid manner comes straight out of Day's own character. He was a man who never stopped talking. The ladies found this suffocating. But a child would listen for ever, for Day was so delightfully unreal. 'Is not that the country, Sir, where the cruel animal, the crocodile, is found?' asks Harry Sandford, when Mr Barlow shows the human weakness of stopping for breath. The invitation is not to be resisted. 'It is an animal,' says the invincible Mr Barlow, off again for another couple of pages, 'that lives sometimes upon the land, sometimes in the water. It comes originally from an egg . . .' Little Harry Sandford, so liable to be infected by every germ of virtue blowing casually on the air, catches this manner in his talks with Tom Merton. Harry has just been thrashed by the wicked Squire for refusing to tell him which way the hare went, and Tom is sympathising:

> H.   Oh! it's nothing to what the young Spartans used to suffer.
> T.   Who were they?
> H.   Why, you must know they were a brave set of people that lived a great while ago; and as they were but few in numbers and were surrounded by enemies . . .

And so, by yet another happy dislocation of the narrative, the babbling stream of information resumes its cheerful flow.

Sandford and Merton is one of those books which are rich because they have taken a long time to mature and have out-grown their original plan. Day's first notion was to rewrite a number of well-known stories and fables for children; but he gradually saw that the stories could lead to Socratic dialogues and the arguments to still more stories.

Mr. B.   But when a person is not good to him, or endeavours to hurt him, it is natural for an animal to run away from him, is it not?

T.   Yes.

Mr. B.   And then you say he is wild, do you not?

T.   Yes, Sir.

Mr. B.   Why, then, it is probable that animals are only wild because they are afraid of being hurt, and that they only run away from the fear of danger. I believe you would do the same from a lion or a tiger.

T.   Indeed I would, Sir.

Mr. B.   And yet you do not call yourself a wild animal?

Tommy laughed heartily at this and said No. Therefore, said Mr. Barlow, if you want to tame animals, you must be good to them, and treat them kindly, and then they will no longer fear you, but come to you and love you. Indeed, said Harry, that is very true; for I knew a little boy that took a great fancy to a snake that lived in his father's garden; and, when he had milk for breakfast, he used to sit under a nut tree and whistle, and the snake would come to him, and eat out of his bowl.

T.   And did it not bite him?

H.   No; he sometimes used to give it a pat with his spoon if it ate too fast; but it never hurt him.

The aim of Day was to give a tendentious education. He loathed all that was meant by a man of fashion. He loathed everything that Lord Chester-field stood for, almost as much as Lord Chesterfield's son came to do. He loathed idleness, profligacy, the self-indulgence of the rich. He loathed the man of fashion's attitude to children. He was a plain Republican who believed that no one should eat who did not work. He was one of the earliest Abolitionists. All these views are directed at Tommy Merton, whose father is a rich slave-owner:

And what right have the people who sold the poor negroes to your father to sell them, or what right has your father to buy them? Here

Tommy seemed a good deal puzzled, but at length he said: They are brought from a country that is a great way off, in ships, and so become slaves. Then, said Mr. Barlow, if I take you to another country in a ship I shall have a right to sell you? – T. No, but you won't, Sir, because I was born a gentleman. – Mr. B. What do you mean by that, Tommy? – Why (said Tommy a little confounded) to have a fine house and fine clothes, and a coach, and a great deal of money, as my papa has. – Mr. B. Then if you were no longer to have a fine house, nor fine clothes, nor a great deal of money, somebody that had all these things might make you a slave, and use you ill, and beat you, and insult you, and do whatever he liked with you? – T. No, Sir, that would not be right, neither, that anybody should use me ill. – Mr. B. Then one person should not use another ill? – T. No, Sir. – Mr. B. To make a slave of anybody is to use him ill, is it not? – T. I think so. – Mr. B. Then no one ought to make a slave of you? – T. No, indeed, Sir. – Mr. B. But if no one should use another ill, and making a slave is using him ill, neither ought you to make a slave of anyone else. – T. Indeed, Sir, I think not.

If Day's instruction was tendentious and was written on the revolutionary impulse of the eighteenth century, his methods were also new. Lord Chesterfield's son was intended to be a miniature Lord Chesterfield, an awed and suitably diminished reflection of his father. Day's notion was that a child is a new and independent life. His education in fact and morality was to be gained in the course of living; he was not to inherit a convention. If father's gluttony leads to gout, if father's wealth leads to restlessness, cruelty and guilt, if mother's spoiling leads to ill-health, the child's ration faculty must be strengthened until he sees that other courses are better. Education is a guidance in the choice of good habits and the cultivation of a humane disposition.

This was revolutionary. So revolutionary that old Edgeworth was obliged to disinherit his own son who had taken the bit of freedom between his teeth. Reason, alas, could not control him; neither a parent's reason nor his own. Edgeworth hastened to warn parents that he and his friends had been labouring under an appalling error. This was years later; and there is no doubt that Tommy Merton was drawn from Edgeworth's dashing and wilful eldest son. And then there was another aspect to the revolution. The coddled manikin of the eighteenth-century portraits was given a healthier life. He was given lighter, freer clothes and was sent to harden himself to sun and cold. The Spartan ideal was established. But, excellent as a revolution and adventure, the Spartan ideal itself became a kind of grim, vested interest, a terrifying convention in the English public schools of the nineteenth century. The cult of nature became the cult of neglect. The gentleman of fashion was succeeded by the gentleman tough.

A Scottish Documentary

W hile Byron and Hobhouse were at Malta refusing to leave the ship until the Governor ordered the guns of the harbour to salute their arrival, there was another writer in the background. He was getting quiet pleasure out of the fact that the Governor had evidently no intention of wasting his honours on literature. This third person was John Galt, hitherto only a dull Scottish poet and young businessman, but later to become one of the most delightful humorous novelists of the Scottish hearth. Of his work, *The Annals of the Parish* is still entertaining, even for those who, like myself, never take kindly to the Scottish dialect and whose taste for glens, kirks, lochs and kailyards has suffered from an early excess of Scott, George Macdonald and Stevenson. With less pleasure one can also read Galt's *Ayrshire Legatees* and skip through his long novel *The Entail*. There is some well-tipped satire in both these books. Byron said that the Leddy Grippy of *The Entail* was the finest portrait of a woman in English literature since Shakespeare, but he was thinking, I am afraid, not of literature, but of the women who had annoyed him.

Of the three men who waited on board at Malta and who met several times later during Byron's Mediterranean travels, Galt was easily the most versatile, one almost had said the most original. At that time he was travelling with a scheme for capturing the Turkish trade and with an eye for any deal that came by the way. (He just missed buying the Elgin marbles as a speculation and was actually their nominal owner for a week or two while they were on the sea.) Galt showed the same sort of efficiency and enterprise in business which Peacock had, a capacity for large and problematical undertakings; and when one looks at the long list of plays, poems, hack biographies, pamphlets and novels which he wrote, it is a surprise to discover that the main business of his life was buying and selling, pushing plans for colonisation, or for damming great rivers like the Clyde and the St Lawrence, getting canal bills through Parliament and founding towns in Canada. The now thriving town of Guelph, in Ontario, was founded by him; he chose its site and planned its institutions; one other town in the same province bears his name.

Versatility, especially if this includes practical gifts, is a great danger to writers. To Galt, literature was always a sideline, a means of making a little extra, which he needed very badly. His work suffers accordingly. But there is always something sympathetic about the businessman novelist, the man who gets a little private amusement out of the Byrons, and himself never quite surrenders to the aberrations of the profession. Into the posing, frantic life of Grub Street, with its suggestion of the intellectual nudist colony, a man like Galt brings the mystery, indeed it amounts to the richness and romance of the conventional; he has the self-possession of one who does not earn his living by exposing his shame. *Tout se paie*, of course; Galt knew that he was a part-timer if not an amateur by temperament. But those writers whose main occupation keeps them on the outside of literary circles preserve a kind of innocence, a modest but all the more determined sense of their merits, and are less tempted to imitate and follow a school. Galt had such an individuality. He was brilliantly inventive by nature. He made a virtue of his inability to concoct plots and fables by writing documentary works, which, in his *Autobiography*, he calls 'theoretical histories'. And it is interesting to know that *The Annals of the Parish* was written long before *Waverley* – and was for twenty years without a publisher until Scott's work started the interest in Scottish subjects. Galt was indeed an innovator, and innovators do not generally reap fully where they have sown. Not many writers can say that they have founded a town, invented a new kind of book, and have given an important new word to the language: the word Utilitarian was taken by John Stuart Mill from the lips of the Rev. Mr Balwhidder of *The Annals of the Parish*.

Galt's inspiration for this book came from *The Vicar of Wakefield*. He set out to create a Scottish Dr Primrose. In fact, the Rev. Mr Balwhidder, timid, twittering, pious, cautious, decorous, yet possessed of a salty tolerance of nature, is very different. One is never quite certain whether the minister knows how comical he really is. And when I say that *The Annals* is an amusing book I am not addressing myself to the literary critic who can take his amusement spread very, very thin as long as he is sure he is dealing with a standard work. *The Annals* is brisk and diverting, and as succulent, within the bounds of clerical decorum, as local scandal itself. We see the life of the parish of Dailmailing year after year, growing, waning, growing again.

Smuggling seizes Dailmailing's fancy for a time, and along come the illegitimate babies; soldiering seizes it; revolutionary ideas get into its heads; the old laird gives place to a new order; a mill absorbs the free weavers. And on top of these main episodes there is the froth of gossip. Old ladies fly into tantrums, young girls elope, justices roar, and wicked old women conceal smuggled tea in their mattresses and go to bed on them, feigning illness when the Excise officer and his informer come round. If one is in any doubt about the character of this book the first page settles it at once. The minister of Dailmailing, whose prudence drove him to marry three wives in the course of his lifetime, belongs to the best dry vintage of Scottish humour, with its strange conflicting tangs of primness and animal spirits. He was put in by a patron over the heads of the angry villagers, and over their heads he had to go the Sunday he was 'placed' at the church. Pelted with mud and guarded by soldiers, he had to climb in at a window because the church door was locked, only to be greeted inside by one of the zealots with the appropriate scripture about those who enter 'not by the door of the sheepfold but by some other way'. And as the dismayed but long-suffering Mr Balwhidder kneeled at the induction ceremony a loud laugh went up from the congregation when the neighbouring minister gave him a tap on the head with a staff, and said, 'Timber to timber.' Having come in at the window, the minister was obliged to leave by it as well.

The inhabitants of Dailmailing, as can be seen, were people of spirit and with a turn for fantasy, but the quiet minister was soon their equal. A gamekeeper had seduced the Rev. Mr Balwhidder's parlourmaid, and the minister obliged the couple to stand in church. This happened after the death of the first Mrs Balwhidder and was a warning to the prudent minister that he had better get a second wife. Very different she was from the first, a managing woman with an 'overearnestness to gather gear'. She turned the meditative manse into a raucous farm, and worked day and night in the dairy, so that the minister was left in his study most evenings as lonely as a bachelor. He might have married a factory. But he outlived her, too, and the third one, married in his old age, was nearer his own nature. She was a professor's widow, and the minister's courtship of her is one of the most remarkable I ever remember in English comic literature. It is like something from Sterne, without the leer. One catches in this scene the frosty sparkle of Galt's comedy at its best:

On the Thursday the company was invited, came, and nothing extraordinary was seen; but in cutting up and helping a hen, Dr. Dinwiddie put one wing on Mrs. Nugent's plate, and the other wing on my plate, and said there have been greater miracles than these two wings flying together, which was a sharp joke, that caused no little merriment at the expense of Mrs. Nugent and me. I, however, to show that I was none daunted, laid a leg also on her plate, and took another on my own, saying, in the words of the reverend doctor, there have been greater miracles than that these two legs should lie in the same nest, which was thought a very clever come off; and at the same time I gave Mrs. Nugent a kindly nip in her sonsy arm, which was breaking the ice in as pleasant a way as could be.

The American war drains the minister's parish, and then the French revolution divides the village into Government men and Jacobins and the new cults of philosophy, philanthropy and utility grow among the weavers. One angry Tory JP, on being asked by an arrested weaver whether Christ was not a reformer, replied in a rage: 'And what the devil did He make of it? Was He not crucified?' Which, I should say, is a very accurate report of what Christians who are sitting pretty really think of Christ, without realising it.

The Annals is, besides comedy, a fascinating social history; and Galt succeeds, where so many artists fail, in showing how his place, his people and their interests grow and change. At the end the Rev. Mr Balwhidder is far from being the pious clown he was at the beginning. The zest of the narrative springs from its use of everyday speech. Here the dialect words are used sparsely but with vivid effect. Words like 'yellyhoo' and 'out-strapulous', full of sound and picture, are the hi-jinks of a vastly living vernacular. When we turn to the homely farce of *The Ayrshire Legatees* or the more complicated satire of Glasgow manners in *The Entail*, it is by these phrases and especially by the realism of Galt's dialogue that the eye is taken. A natural, stoical charm, a racy, nutty equanimity, unperturbed and unembittered by the shocks of the world, is in all Galt's books, and in his life too, which was filled with the disappointments that fall to a man who is more inventive than his fellows, as the reader of his *Autobiography* may see. The disappointments of affairs may indeed prepare a writer to take the dramas of the imagination less extremely and certainly rid him of the artist's temptation to pose. Galt, the part-timer, who reverenced the poet in Byron and wrote his life, was not in the least overawed by him nor deceived. So easily might Galt have sneered or, worse still, have become the prosaic toady; it is the mark of Galt's independence and talent that he kept his moderate Tory head. And in those times it was something to have a level head. When Godwin's works were banned for their Jacobinism in the Ayrshire library, Galt, who detested Godwin's opinions, fought to get the ban removed, and was successful.

Scott

===

'No one reads Scott now': how often one has heard these words! I have no doubt they are true, at any rate true of English readers. At some time in the last 30 years feeling against dialect and especially the Scottish dialect has hardened into a final dislike. It is troublesome to the eye, it is a language which nags and clatters; one would as soon read phonetics. And then dialect suggests the overweening conceit of local virtue, and if anything has died in the last 30 years, it is regionalism. Our society – why pretend? – has made war on regionalism and has destroyed it. We may question whether, under any disguise, it can be reborn in the modern world. That is the first difficulty when we look at the long brown row of the Waverley novels that have stood high out of reach on our shelves, unopened since our childhood. And here the second difficulty arises. We read Scott in our childhood and he is not suitable reading for children; few of the great novelists are. Why should a man, writing in his maturity, scarred by life, marked by the evils of the world, its passions and its experience in his blood, be consigned to the young who know nothing of themselves or the world? The fault is partly Scott's: this great man, the single Shakespearean talent of the English novel, drew far too often the heroes and heroines which have always appealed to the adolescent and gently reared reader – wooden idealisations, projections of our more refined, sixteen-year-old wishes. At sixteen we are in love with those sexless heroines with their awful school-mistressy speeches. We are in love with those stick-in-the-mud heroes whose disinterestedness and honour pervert the minds of boys with a tedious and delusive idealism. One grows up in the daydream that Scott has generated to discover it is a swindle; and one never forgives him.

Yet, if we except this serious criticism for the moment, and measure Scott in the light of the full noon of life, we see that he belongs to that very small group of our novelists – Fielding and Jane Austen are the chief of them – who face life squarely. They are grown up. They do not cry for the moon. I do not mean that to be grown up is the first requirement of genius. To be grown up may be fatal to it. But short of the great illuminating madness, there is a power to sustain, assure and enlarge us in those novelists who are not driven back by life, who are not shattered by the discovery that it is a thing bounded by unsought limits, by interests as well as by hopes, and that it ripens under restriction. Such writers accept. They think that acceptance is the duty of a man.

An error of our boyhood reading of Scott is, I fancy, the easy assumption that Scott is primarily an historical novelist. There is more reason to think of him as a comic writer. We would make a similar kind of error about Defoe, Fielding or Richardson if we took them at their word and believed that their only aim was to reform morals. The historical passion of Scott or the moral passion of these other novelists was the engine of their impulse. Where that engine took them is another matter. Hazlitt saw this when, in his too drastic way, he said that Scott was interested in half of life only: in the past of man and not in what he might become; and Hazlitt went to the length of thinking Godwin's *Falkland* fit to be compared with *Waverley*. But Scott's history meant simply his preoccupation with what is settled – and, after all, a great deal *is* settled for better or worse, in human life and character. One might even see in Scott's history the lame man's determination to impose and ennoble normality. The feuds of the clans are done with, the bloody wars of the Border are over, Jacobitism is a mere sentiment notable for its ironical inconsistencies as well as its heroic gestures. A period has ended and, for a novelist, there is no more favourable moment. Now he can survey. Scott gazes upon it all like a citizen who has dressed up. Now, vicariously, he can be physically heroic; but the real result of the historical impulse is not history but an immense collection of small *genre* pieces, a huge gallery of town and country faces in their inns, their kitchens, their hovels, their farms and their rambling houses. And the painting of them is as circumstantial, as middle-class – in the anti-romantic sense – and as non-aristocratic as anything of Hogarth's. Scott does not revive the past or escape into it; he assimilates it for his own time and for his own prejudices. He writes like a citizen. He asserts the normal man, the man who has learned to live with his evil; what his evil might have done with him if he had not learned to live with it can be guessed from the grotesque declamations of *The Black Dwarf*, the creature who cuts himself off from mankind.

The Black Dwarf is not a good novel. There are awkward lumps of unreality in it. The bad thing is the central drama, and this points to Scott's obvious fault as a novelist. He has an immense memory and the necessary taste for improving on memory. He has the power to present the outside of a character and to work from the outside to the inside. But once inside, he discovers only what is generic. That is the fault. He has, I would say, no power to work from the inside to the outer man. There is nothing feminine in him. So the black dwarf is excellent when he is seen as local recollection, a piece of Border hearsay, and no one could surpass Scott in portraying that tortured head, with its deep-sunken pin-point eyes, the almost legless and hairy little body with its huge feet and the enormous voice that issues from the abortion. But when we come to the mind of this tortured creature, when he speaks, what we get is not horror but a dreary, savage Calvinist lecture. The black dwarf's misanthropy is a mere exercise, a sermon turned inside out. There is a complete breakdown of the imagination: compare this story with Turgenev's *Lear of the Steppes*. I suspect that as we continue our rediscovery of Scott we shall often find that the chief drama of the novels breaks down in this way, for the great protagonists of fiction begin from the inside of a writer. One is inclined to divide the Scott characters into two classes: the secondary and minor ones who are real and are truly recollected, the children of his wonderful memory; and the major ones who are the awkward, stage figures of an imagination that is cut off from the sap of life. To go back to Hazlitt: Scott lacked a vital sense, the sense of what people may become. His history was not real history. It was the settled, the collectible, the antique.

I turn to *The Chronicles of the Canongate*, the tales of the second series, to see whether my last sentence is too sweeping. There is *The Highland Widow*. Here is real history – but you notice at once – history without costume. History in the rags of the people. The widow's husband has been a bandit, the Robin Hood of a clan that has almost died out. Her son perceives that times have changed; he enlists in the army which was once his father's enemy. The mother is appalled by the disgrace and plots to restore her son to a life of crime. The tragedy which is enacted springs from the clash of two orders of virtue, and the virtue of one age has become the vice of the age that succeeds it. There is no dialect in this story. It is heroic and not Hogarthian. It is the kind of thing that Mérimée and Pushkin took from Scott. And here, better than in his more elaborate compositions, we see the mark of Scott's genius as a story-teller. I say nothing of the suspense of which he is always a master; I am thinking of his power of suggesting the ominous, the footsteps of fate coming to meet one on the road. Frequently Scott used the supernatural and the hints of second sight to get this effect, and they are all the more effective for being explained as the domestic beliefs of his characters which the author himself hesitates to accept. But in *The Highland Widow* we come upon one of those real omens, one of those chance remarks made by a stranger which have another meaning to the one who hears. It is a device much used by Hardy. In Scott's story the young soldier has been drugged by his fanatical mother so that he shall not return to his regiment. The boy wakes up and rushes out to find what day of the week it is, for he fears more than anything else the degradation of his honour. The first person he meets is a minister, who replies: 'Had you been where you should have been yesterday, young man, you would have known that it was God's Sabbath.' The two meanings of those words mark the crisis of the tale, and after looking back upon it one realises how ingenious and masterly has been the construction of a simple story. The end we could foresee; the means we could not, and it is in the means that Scott always shows the power of a master.

It is less the business of the novelist to tell us what happened than to show how it happened. The best things in Scott arise out of the characters. He especially understands, as I said before, the generic differences between people. He understands the difference between the fisherman and the farmer, the shepherd and the drover, and so on. He understands, in other words, what all ordinary, simple, observant men know about one another: the marks of their trade, their town, their family. (His view of women is that of the simple man: he knows them by their habits in the house. In love he does not know them at all.) The tale called *The Two Drovers* is a fine example of Scott's watchfulness of male character. The honour of Robin, the Highland drover, seems to be quaint silliness to Wakefield, the stolid Yorkshireman; the sense and fair play of Wakefield, who cannot believe that enmity will survive a little amateur boxing, are meaningless to the Highlander. Each is reasonable – but in a different way. The clash when it comes is tragic; again two kinds of virtue are irreconcilable. The scene in the inn is wonderfully true to the men there, and the talk slips naturally off their clumsy tongues. Wakefield has challenged Robin to fight with his fists. Robin can't see how this will mend a quarrel.

Harry Wakefield dropped the hand of his friend or rather threw it from him.

'I did not think I had been keeping company for three years with a coward.'

'Coward pelongs to none of my name,' said Robin, whose eyes began to kindle, but keeping the command of his temper. 'It was no coward's legs or hands, Harry Waakfelt, that drew you out of the fords of Frew, when you was drifting ower the plack rock, and every eel in the river expected his share of you.'

'And that is true enough, too,' said the Englishman, struck by the appeal.

'Adzooks!' exclaimed the bailiff – 'sure Harry Wakefield, the nattiest lad at Whitson Tryste, Wooler Fair, Carlisle Sands, or Stagshaw Bank, is not going to show the white feather? Ah, this comes of living so long with kilts and bonnets – men forget the use of their daddles.'

'I may teach you, Master Fleecebumpkin, that I have not lost the use of mine,' said Wakefield, and then went on. 'This will never do, Robin. We must have a turn-up or we shall be the talk of the countryside. I'll be d___d if I hurt thee – I'll put on the gloves gin thou like. Come, stand forward like a man!'

'To be peaten like a dog,' said Robin, 'is there any reason in that? If you think I have done you wrong, I'll go before your shudge, though I neither know his law nor his language.'

A general cry of 'No, no – no law, no lawyer, a bellyful and be friends' was echoed by the bystanders.

'But,' continued Robin, 'if I am to fight, I have no skill to fight like a jackanapes, with hands and nails.'

And here once more the agent of tragedy is moving slowly down the road towards the two friends – the drover who is carrying Robin's dirk for him, to keep him out of trouble and to circumvent the fate that was foretold at the beginning of the story.

Except in the outbursts of *The Black Dwarf*, Scott appears to see evil as a fatality that ensues from the nature of the times. The civil wars have made men narrow and ruthless, and he writes at the end of an era, surveying the broken scene and pleading for tolerance. The crimes in *The Chronicles of the Canongate* are 'errors of the understanding', not examples of absolute wickedness. When we turn to *The Antiquary* we meet another side of his talent; his humour. I wonder how many of those who, like myself, had not read Scott since their schooldays will recall that Scott is one of the great comic writers? It is not purely Scottish humour, depending on the canniness of the speaker or on a continuous sly, nervous snigger, or on the grotesque and pawky asides of dialect. Scott's humour, like his best prose, is cross-bred with the English eighteenth century. Sterne and Fielding have put red blood into it. A character like Jonathan Oldbuck does not make thin jokes down his nose, but stands solidly and aglow beside all the well-found comics of our literature. The secret is that Scott's animal spirits are high, as Fielding's were. I have always enjoyed that strange scene in the early pages of *The Antiquary* in which Oldbuck supervises the rescue of the foolish, snobbish, bankrupt, treasure-hunting Sir Arthur, and his stick of a daughter, from the rising tide. Jonathan Oldbuck, who has only an hour before been snubbed by the angry baronet, now watches the men heave the scarcely conscious gentleman up the rock:

'Right, right, that's right, too – I should like to see the son of Sir Gamelyn de Guardover on dry land myself – I have a notion he would sign the abjuration oath, and the Ragman-roll to boot, and acknowledge Queen Mary to be nothing better than she should be, to get alongside my bottle of old port that he ran away from, and left scarce begun. But he's safe now, and here a' comes – (for the chair was again lowered, and Sir Arthur made fast in it, without much consciousness on his own part) – Here a' comes – bowse away, my boys! – canny wi' a tenpenny tow – the whole barony of Knockwinnock depends on three plies of hemp – respice finem, respice funem – look to your end – look to the rope's end.'

I can read about half of *The Antiquary* and enjoy the flavours of what I read. After that I skip through the preposterous plot and willingly leave the wooden Lovel and the disdainful Miss Wardour to the pleasure of talking like public statues to each other. In one respect it must be admitted they do surpass modern lovers. Severely regulated by their families and by circumstance, these antique couples are obliged to know their subject. The obstacles to love ensure that the lovers shall concentrate.

The criticism that Scott cannot draw a heroine has to be modified after we have read *The Heart of Midlothian*. To judge by this book Scott could not draw a hero. For neither the pious, pettifogging Butler nor the wicked George Staunton can be called human beings of anything but conventional interest. Effie and Jeanie Deans are quite another matter. They are peasants and Scott condescends to them with the gentlemanliness of his time, but they are alive as his peasants always are. Scott's inability to draw women life-size seems to be due to the fact that he can think of them only as creatures high above him, or safely below him; and the ones below are drawn better than the ones above. The maid is more interesting than the mistress. We owe this romantic and pedestalled conception of women partly to the lame man's feeling of inferiority. He idealised what he could not approach. But these idealisations also arise from that curious split in the puritan middle-class mind which had begun to unsex itself so that it might devote all its will to the adventure of getting on in the world of money or honour, leaving the warmer passions to the lower orders. But unlike the early Victorian novelists, Scott is not a prude. Miss Bellendon's maid, in *Old Mortality*, nudges, winks and uses all her enticements on the soldiery; speech is very free in the farms and the inns; only Miss Bellendon in her castle stands like a statue and talks like an epitaph. Once Scott is free of these inhibitions – and in the main they are fixed by considerations of class – Scott describes women as well as they can be described from the point of view of a man in the house; that is as scolding, fussing, gossiping, pestering, weeping, wilful and mercenary adjuncts of domestic life. They can always answer back. They never forgive a slight, they can always be persuaded to condone a crime. Expressed without satire but with sense and geniality this view has inspired many robust minor portraits of womanhood in Scott. The loveliness and attraction of Di Vernon in *Rob Roy* is due, I fancy, to the fact that she has a good deal of male in her. What is missing from all these portraits is the vitalising element: the sense a woman has of herself, the sense of what she may become – that sense of our fate which alone gives meaning to our character. And as I have said before, Scott's direct intuitive sense of that fate seems to have been weak; he grasps the importance of it only through the labours of the historian and the documentary artists. His researches, not his instinct, gave us his remarkable portrait of the passionate mother in *The Highland Widow*, and his researches also revealed to him, in the same way, the larger meaning of Jeanie Deans's character in *The Heart of Midlothian*.

A modern novelist who rewrote *The Heart of Midlothian* would certainly stress the unconscious jealousy which Jeanie must have felt towards her younger sister by her father's second marriage. We would say that Jeanie's refusal to tell the lie that would save Effie from the scaffold was not a stern moral act, but an animal retaliation; for psychology has altered for us the nature of many ethical dilemmas. Scott ignores the evident jealousy. And though Effie, in a remarkable prison scene, flies out at her sister, we are left with the impression that Jeanie is either too stupid or too conceited in her conscience to be endured. But Scott's strength in the handling of the situation between the two women comes from his knowledge of the effect of history upon them. They are children of history. And the one part of history Scott knew inside out was its effect upon the conscience. Jeanie's refusal to tell a lie had generations of Calvinistic quarrelling behind it, the vituperations of the sectaries who had changed the sword of the clan wars and the civil wars for the logic-chopping of theology. Instead of splitting skulls, they had taken to splitting hairs. The comedies, the tragedies, the fantastic eloquence and tedious reiteration of these scruples of conscience are always brilliantly described by Scott, who has them in his blood. And so Jeanie's refusal to lie and her journey to London on foot to seek her sister's pardon are not the result of conceit, heartlessness or even literalness of mind: they are the fruit of history.

And a history which produces not only plump, dumb, resolute figures like hers, but men of roystering violence like the bloody Porteous, tortured believers in predestination like Staunton, fanatics like old Deans, cranks like Saddlebright, lunatic harlots like Madge Wildfire, adventuresses like Effie, wonderful sea-lawyers of the criminal world of old Edinburgh, like Ratcliffe, the thief, and wonderful fools like the gaping old laird of Dumbiedikes. There is none of the sentimentality which Dickens spread like a bad fog over the suffocated bastards, baby-farmers, harlots and criminals of his novels; none of the melodrama. Scott's realism belongs to the time when gentlemen knew the mob because they were not yet afraid of the mob. There is only one false episode in *The Heart of Midlothian*; and that is the wildly improbable meeting between Jeanie and George Staunton at his father's vicarage in England, and we owe that to the influence of the theatre on the English novel. For that matter, none of the English scenes is really good and the final third of the novel is a failure. Here Jeanie is diminished as a character by the condescension of the author. But when she is in Scotland, we feel the force of her country and her fate in her, and these make her into a woman. One sees her even more clearly and fully late in the book when it is she, the rescuer, who has to pay tribute to Effie, the adventuress, who has, after all, got away with it. Scott was too much the man of the world to prevent Effie getting away with a good deal more than Dickens or even Thackeray were later on to allow their giddy-pated or wicked women. Scott recorded wilfulness in women with an appreciative eye; and an ear cocked for the back answer.

It has often been said that the decay of our interest in problems of conscience is a major cause of the feebleness of the modern novel; but there have been many poor novels stuffed tight with conscience. Might we not say more justly that the problems of conscience have changed? Our habit is to weigh man against society, civilisation against man or nature; individuals against groups. The greatness of *The Heart of Midlothian* arises, first of all, in the scope that the problem of conscience gave to Scott's imagination. He was not arguing in a void. His argument was creating real people and attracting real people to it. He made the story of Effie's murdered baby a national story. And then how wide his range is! The scenes in the Tolbooth are remarkable, and especially those that are built about the figure of Ratcliffe when the governor is working to turn him into an informer. Scott had the eighteenth-century taste for rogues, and their talk is straight from nature.

'Why, I suppose you know you are under sentence of death, Mr. Ratcliffe?' replied Mr. Sharpitlaw.

'Ay, so are a', as that worthy minister said in the Tolbooth Kirk the day Robertson wan off; but naebody kens when it will be executed. Gude faith, he had better reason to say than he dreamed of, before the play was played out that morning!'

[190]

'This Robertson,' said Sharpitlaw, in a lower and something like a confidential tone, 'd'ye ken, Rat – that is, can ye gie us ony onkling where he is to be heard tell o'?'

'Troth, Mr. Sharpitlaw, I'll be frank wi' ye: Robertson is rather a cut abune me – a wild deevil he was, and mony a daft prank he played; but except the Collector's job that Wilson led him into, and some tuilzies about run goods wi' the guagers and the waiters, he never did ony thing that came near our line o' business.'

'Umph! that's singular, considering the company he kept.'

'Fact, upon my honour and credit,' said Ratcliffe, gravely. 'He keepit out o' our little bits of affairs, and that's mair than Wilson did; I hae dune business wi' Wilson afore now. But the lad will come on in time; there's nae fear o' him; naebody will live the life he has led, but what he'll come to sooner or later.'

'Who or what is he, Ratcliffe? You know, I suppose?' said Sharpitlaw.

'He's better born, I judge, than he cares to let on; he's been a soldier, and he has been a playactor, and I watna what he has been or hasna been, for as young as he is, sae that it had daffing and nonsense about it.'

'Pretty pranks he has played in his time, I suppose?'

'Ye may say that,' said Ratcliffe, with a sardonic smile, 'and' (touching his nose) 'a deevil amang the lasses.'

'Like enough,' said Sharpitlaw. 'Weel, Ratcliffe, I'll no stand niffering wi' ye; ye ken the way that favour's gotten in my office; ye maun be usefu'.'

'Certainly, sir, to the best of my power – naething for naething – I ken the rule of the office,' said the exdepredator.

Then there is Scott's power of describing a crowded scene. I am thinking of the long narrative about the crowd's storming of the Tolbooth and the killing of Porteous. Scott has looked it all up, but his own version is so alive, so effortless, so fast moving. Every detail tells; the very pedantry of it is pedantry washed down by the rough wine of life. Everything is carried off with the authority of a robust and educated style, the style of a man fit to understand, master and govern, a man endlessly fair and excitingly patient in his taste for human nature. He understands popular clamour. He understands the mysteries of loyalty – all the diverse loyalties of a man's life and trade.

And after that Scott has the story-teller's ability to build a great scene and to make a natural use of it. I'm thinking of the search in the dark on Salisbury Crag when the police have persuaded Ratcliffe to help them catch Robertson, and Ratcliffe has brought Madge Wildfire with him to show them all the way. Madge is semi-lunatic, and Ratcliffe has to use all his guile to keep her to the job. He knows her mind is stuffed full of old wives' tales, and he reminds her of a notorious murder that was done on the Crag years before – a story the reader has already been prepared for: Scott's antiquarian asides ought never to be skipped – but Ratcliffe's cunning is turned against him at the moment of its success by the madness of the woman. She accuses him of being as bad as the murderer.

'I never shed blood,' he protested.
'But ye hae sauld it, Ratton – ye hae sauld blood mony a time.'

That chance shaft hits Ratcliffe's conscience and wrecks the expedition. In a short chapter Scott has ingeniously extracted every kind of surprise and apprehension; and without any frivolity or artifice. This adventure could have happened; indeed, we say, if we had had eyes at the back of our heads, we would have known that it *must* have happened so, fabulous as it is. Scott's knowledge gives a sense of necessity to his picture of life, and his freedom in mixing the comic with the serious, even at the most dramatic moments, adds to this pleasant sense. He is not overdriven by his imagination, whereas a writer like Dickens was. Scott, like Fielding, has both feet firmly on the ground.

Rob Roy is admired – but for one or two scenes only when we examine the matter, and it is really a poor novel. At first sight the claims of *Old Mortality* are less emphatic upon the reader's attention, and since Scott repeated himself so often one is tempted to neglect this novel. It should not be neglected. Into this book Scott put all his tolerance and civilisation, his hatred of fanaticism, and illuminated the subject of the religious wars in Scotland with all his irony, humour, all his wiriness of intellect and all his human sympathy. In Burley he drew the rise and the corruption of the fanatical character, and I do not know any other in Scott whose character grows and changes so convincingly. There is real movement here;

elsewhere the sense of movement in his characters is more the result of Scott's habit of dissertation than a real enacting of change. The portrait of Claverhouse is debonair, and the battle scene when the insurgents rout him is almost Tolstoyan; how much Scott owes to a sincere pleasure, even a joy, in the accoutrement of life. One can see how the Russians, like Tolstoy, Gogol and Pushkin first of all, must have been caught by Scott's wonderful pictures of the eccentric lairds. The miser in *Old Mortality*, or the ridiculous, gaping laird in *The Heart of Midlothian*, must have fathered many a landlord in *Dead Souls* and other Russian stories. Where the Russians were to succeed and where Scott failed was in conveying the sense of an abiding destiny going on beyond the characters described. For Scott life is a book that one closes; to the Russians it is a book that one opens. And although one feels his animal zest for life, one feels it as a delightful recollection of hours that are ended, not as the perturbation or languor of the hour which has still to go by on the clock as we read.

One looks up the critics. What did Scott add to the English novel? Is he just another Fielding, but planted in Scottish history? Has he simply added a change of scene and material? It looks like that at first glance: he is a writer from the outside looking in. But I think there is something else. I would like to argue that Scott is a complement to Richardson – an analytical and psychological novelist who describes to us the part of our motives formed by public events. He is certainly the first novelist to describe the political influence of religion and the peculiar significance of superstitions and legend in the mind; and he uses them to illustrate the promptings of unconscious guilt and fear. One sees this in the character of Ratcliffe in *The Heart of Midlothian* and in innumerable instances elsewhere; Scott does not use his apparitions and legends merely for the purpose of putting a shiver or a laugh in his story. They are there to convey hidden processes of mind. No English novelist has added to that sense of a general or public mind, and certainly no great novelist – Hardy is the atheistical exception – has used religion as Scott used it.

Our Half-Hogarth

The English humorists! Through a fog compounded of tobacco smoke, the stink of spirits and the breath of bailiffs, we see their melancholy faces. Look at Thomas Hood, his eyes swollen with the cardiac's solemnity, his mouth pouting after tears. There is a terrible account of his last days in Canon Ainger's *Memoir*, where we see the poet famous, forty-six, bankrupt and dying of heart disease, writing farewells to his friends and unable to stop making puns. They beset him like a St Vitus' dance. They come off his lips in an obsessional patter as if his tongue had become a cuckoo-clock and his mind a lunatic asylum of double meanings. And around him his doting family and his friends are weeping, 'Poor Tom Hood'. This is, alas, one of the too many crying-scenes of Victorian biography. It brims with that home-made beverage of laughter and tears which is handed round like a negus from the chiffonier of the lighter Victorian literature. The savage and vital indignation of the eighteenth century, its moral dogmatism, its body full of laughter and its roars of pain, have gone; melodrama replaces morality, a sprite-like pathos, all grace and weeping, and inked by fear of life, steps in where Caliban groaned and blubbered. I believe it was Charles Lamb who called Thomas Hood 'our half-Hogarth', and that is the measure of the difference between the two periods.

Hood marks the difference well. Only in Goldsmith do we find a tenderness comparable to his. We look at the eighteenth century and, when all is said, we can hardly deny that it had a coherent and integrated mind, a mind not deeply divided against itself. The proper study of mankind is man, who is very corrupt, but presently Divine Reason will teach him to cast off his chains and he will become a free child of nature. By the end of the century the chains are removed. And what is the result? Hood's early nineteenth century shows us. Man has not become free; he has vanished. Or rather, that humane abstraction called Man has been succeeded by two warring groups. Man has degenerated and has become the middle classes and the poor. No longer, like Swift, do the Victorians feel horror of mankind; on the contrary, looking at the little circle of mankind in which they live, they find the species has very much improved. At Clapham, at Wanstead Flats, even in Russell Square and Fleet Street, he is kindly, charitable and good. Their horror moves from man as a whole to a section of men. They are horrified, they are frightened – philanthropical and well policed though they are – by the poor. For generations now they will not stop talking about the poor. Did they pull down the Venetian blinds and turn to conceits and fancies because this fear is outside the window after dark? The feeling is that outside the sitting-room is an undefined world of wickedness, hunger, catastrophe and crime. Pick-pockets are nabbed, poachers are imprisoned, desperate labourers threaten arson, and children go to the mills and up the chimneys; the press gang and transportation are living memories, and sailors drown – oh, how many sailors drown! – in calamitous storms. These terrible things happen – to the poor. There we have Hood's background. There is his material. But writers are urged and taught to write not by society only but by other writers whose background and intention make them utterly different from their pupils. It is a strange fact that the England of Hood is not delineated by revolutionary realists, but has come down to us in the fantastic dress of German Gothic. The Cruikshank who frightens us; Mr Punch, with his pot-belly, his fairy legs and the arching nose like some cathedral fragment, who squats on Dicky Doyle's cover, are part of the Gothic colony that settle like a migration of gargoyles among the English chimneys and their myth-creating smoke.

Hood, who was a Cockney of Scottish parentage, writes very early in his career of 'doing something in the German manner'. In his serious verses he is a Romantic, with his eye on Shakespeare, Scott and Keats. But this is the less readable part of Hood. His serious verses, if one excepts pieces of singular purity like 'I remember, I remember', hardly amount to more than poetic dilutions for the family album, though contemporaries like Lamb, Southey and Byron had a higher opinion of them. Hood's best work is inflected, I suggest, by the basic early-Victorian fear and the fancies to which it led. He is on the side of the poor, of course, and wrote for the early, unsuccessful Radical *Punch*: but the Hood of *The Song of the Shirt* – which trebled the circulation of *Punch* – *The Lay of the Labourer* and *The Bridge of*

Sighs is the dying Hood who is touched by the indignation of the hungry Forties. The earlier Hood thinks the poor are quaint and that their crimes can be sardonically disinfected. The result is a vein of fanciful horror which fathered a whole school of ballad writing:

> The body-snatchers they have come,
> And made a snatch at me;
> It's very hard them kind of men
> Won't let a body be!
>
> You thought that I was buried deep
> Quite decent-like and chary,
> But from her grave in Mary-bone
> They've come and boned your Mary.

This is from *Mary's Ghost*. I could have quoted from *The Volunteer* or *Death's Ramble*. There is *The Careless Nurse Mayd*:

> I saw a Mayd sitte on a Bank
> Beguilded by Wooer fayne and fond;
> And whiles his flatteryinge Vowes she drank
> Her Nurselynge slipt within a Pond!
>
> All Even Tide they Talkde and Kist
> For She was Fayre and He was Kinde;
> The Sunne went down before she wist
> Another Sonne had sett behinde!

Or from *Sally Simpkin's Lament*:

> Oh! What is that comes gliding in
> And quite in middling haste?
> It is the picture of my Jones,
> And painted to the waist.
>
> Oh Sally dear, it is too true –
> The half that you remark
> Is come to say my other half
> Is bit off by a shark.

Gilbert, Lear, Carroll, Thackeray, the authors of *Struwwelpeter* and the cautionary tales continue this comic macabre tradition, which today appears to be exhausted. There is Mr Belloc, who digressed intellectually; and there are the sardonic ballads of Mr William Plomer. He has added brilliantly the horrors of vulgarity to the horrors of crime and accident.

Hood's special idiosyncrasy is to turn the screw of verbal conceit upon his subject. In *Eugene Aram* alone he cut out these tricks, even forbearing in the last verse when his temptation was always strongest. (How was it Hood failed to ruin what are, surely, the most frightening dramatic lines in English narrative verse?) But if Hood's puns are often disastrous, they do frequently show, as Walter Jerrold (his biographer) has said, a kind of second sight. They are like the cackle out of the grave in *Hamlet*. They add malice to the knife and give the macabre its own morbid whimsicalities. Take that terrible poem, *The Last Man*. The earth has been desolated by plague and only two men are left alive. They meet at a gallows and one, out of jealousy, decides to hang the other. He does so and is left, wracked by conscience, to lament that he cannot now hang himself:

> For there is not another man alive,
> In the world to pull my legs.

The wit in *Death's Ramble* shocks one first of all and then freezes the blood one degree colder. Death sees two duellists:

> He saw two duellists going to fight,
> In fear they could not smother;
> And he shot one through at once – for he knew
> They never would shoot each other.

And the comic funk of *The Volunteer* gets a grotesque double meaning. He hears the alarum:

> My jaws with utter dread, enclos'd
> The morsel I was munching,
> And terror lock'd them up too tight,
> My very teeth went crunching
> All through my bread and tongue at once
> Like sandwich made at lunching.

[197]

To the poor, Hood draws our attention by shuddering and laughing with them at the same time. His detachment, when he is writing about crime and catastrophe, is dropped when he is putting the case of the poor. Then he writes with something like the garrulous, flat statement of the broadsheets. These odes and poems lumber along. There is the washerwoman's attack on the new steam laundry which has taken her living. There is the chimney-boy's lament that the law against street cries forbids him to cry 'Sweep' in the streets. Drapers' assistants plead politely with people to shop early. These are pieces of topical journalism which time has blunted, and Hood's pen dipped deeply into that sentimentality which the philanthropical outlook of the period demanded. He was a prolific writer, and knew how to turn out his stuff. Like Dickens he was a sentimental Radical who hoped, as Dickens also hoped, that the problem of the poor could be solved by kindness; but the abiding note is that unpleasant one of Uriah Heep's: 'Me and mother is very humble.'

Hood prefers to let the poor or oppressed describe their lives uncouthly, rather than to attack the rich. The grotesque poem called *Miss Kilmansegg and her Precious Leg* is an exception. This poem startles because it is the first documented account of the upbringing of the perfect middle-class young lady whose parents are rising in the world. She is brought up to be a proud heiress, and the wonderful picture of arrogant surfeit recalls the awful overfed daughter of the mine-owner in Zola's *Germinal*. Money is the only subject of conversation. Then one day Miss Kilmansegg has an accident, her leg is amputated and is replaced by a golden one. A wooden one would not be good enough. Far from spoiling her chances, the golden leg doubles the number of her suitors. Her parents select the most plausible and least trustworthy one who is an alleged aristocrat. He turns out to be a bankrupt gambler who, very soon after the wedding night, gives a knowing look at the leg and

> The Countess heard in language low
> That her Precious leg was precious slow,
> A good 'un to look at, but bad to go
> And kept quite a sum lying idle.

She refuses to sell it. But unhappily she is in the habit of taking it off at night, and the Count sees his chance. Using the leg as a cudgel he bashes her brains out and absconds.

This long poem is like a grotesque novel, something of de la Mare's, perhaps, packed with realistic descriptions, and if its plot groans the lines scamper along as fast as Browning's dramatic narratives and are delighted with their own wit. And here the puns give the poem a kind of jeering muttered undertone. Hood had a great gift for domestic realism and the conversational phrase. In *Miss Kilmansegg* he is not half a Hogarth, but Hogarth whole. Or ought one to say, half a Hogarth and the other half that fanciful melodramatic sermoniser – as Dickens was in *The Christmas Carol* – which the nineteenth century loved? The poem is laboured but it is alive.

Hood's wit quietened and compassion melted him in his last years. *The Song of the Shirt* and *The Lay of the Labourer* last very well in their *genre*, because of their metrical brilliance and because they are taken directly from life. One would want to remove only two or three lines of self-parody from *The Bridge of Sighs*. Hood is as well-documented as the realistic novelists were to become. *The Lay of the Labourer* is based on a true incident. An agricultural labourer was convicted for threatening arson because he could not get work or food, and Hood kept the newspaper cutting about the event on his mantelpiece until he wrote the poem. The sentiment is bearable, the rant is bearable, because the facts cry out and are so tellingly reported. One must regret that his feeling for narrative, his instinct for the right tune to put it in and his kind of conscience too, died out of verse with the Victorians. In the higher regions where Hardy lived, as in the lower regions of the music-hall, the art of writing dramatic stories in verse seems to have gone for good.

Disraeli

'The leaders of the People are those whom the People trust,' said Sybil rather haughtily.

'And who may betray them,' said Egremont.

'Betray them!' said Sybil. 'And you can believe that my father . . . '

'No, no, you can feel, Sybil, though I cannot express, how much I honour your father. But he stands alone in the singleness and purity of his heart. Who surround him?'

'Those whom the People have chosen; and from a like confidence in their virtues and abilities. They are a senate supported by the sympathy of millions with only one object in view – the emancipation of their race. It is a sublime spectacle these delegates of labour advocating the sacred cause in a manner which might shame your haughty factions. What can resist a demonstration so truly national! What can withstand the supremacy of its moral power!'

So writes Disraeli of the rise of the Chartists in *Sybil* or *The Two Nations*. His people are speaking the language of opera; yet, after a hundred years, how exactly Disraeli has defined the English political situation. He is our only political novelist; I mean, the only one *saturated* in politics; the only one whose intellect feasts on polity. Strikes, riots, questions of social justice, elections and backstairs politics enliven the other Victorian novelists of the period frequently; but of Mrs Gaskell, George Eliot, Meredith, Trollope it cannot be said that politics are their blood. These writers do not convert us to this view or that; they are cautious; they do not inflame us; on the whole they leave us with the impression that political action is a disagreeable duty, distracting us from the major interests of human nature. Children of a competitive society, heirs of the Utilitarians, they see politics as the indispensable but tedious regulator. Politics are a method, a humane technique of adjustment; and, in general, it must be said that this has been the English view throughout the nineteenth century and after. To Disraeli, the Jew and alien, such a theory was pragmatic and despicable.

In his early years, at least, and especially in the trilogy of novels of which *Sybil* is the second volume, Disraeli brought to political thought the electric heat of the Jewish imagination and the order of its religious traditions. He demanded the glory of a dogma, the sensation of a re-birth, the emotion of a 'new era' – a phrase used for the first time at the accession of Queen Victoria. And when we pick up *Sybil* or *Coningsby*, with their captivating pictures of aristocratic life and their startling, documented pictures of the squalor of the industrial poor, we feel that here at last is a novelist who is impatient of immediate social issues and who has gone back dramatically to the historic core of the English situation. The tedium has gone. We may now be carried away by a faith, snared by passion. How precise is the diagnosis of the failure of his own party; they are not Conservatives but concessionaries, a party without beliefs. As we read *Sybil* and *Coningsby* we are swept along by a swift and exultant mind. It takes us, by a kind of cinematic magic, from the gold plate and languid peers of the Derby dinner to the delectable mansions and heavenly countenances of the exalted, and from them to the sunken faces of the starved and enslaved. We may find ourselves converted to a new medievalism, to those heady 'Young England' politics which read like a mixture of Marx, William Morris, Hall Caine and romantic fascism. Disraeli was wrong; wrong, that is to say, as things turned out. Young England came to nothing, and the English workers followed the solemn prophecies of Sybil and not the aristocratic theory of Egremont; but whether he was right or wrong is not the point. The secret of Disraeli's superiority as a political novelist is that he introduces imagination into politics; he introduces questions of law, faith and vision. He looked upon the English scene with the clear intellect of the alien who, as a Jew, identified himself with both the two English nations; with the race that was to be emancipated and with the aristocracy that ruled them. The romantic, Byronic pride of Disraeli – if we are to take the figure of Sidonia in *Coningsby* as a projection of himself, several times larger than life – is measureless. Under the ancient gaze of the hollow eye of Asia, the Norman family is as crude as a band of tourists standing before the ruin of Ozymandias, king of kings.

[201]

Disraeli's gift is for the superb and the operatic. And if there is more than a touch of the *de luxe* and meretricious in his understanding of the superb, that fits in with the political picture; politics is the world of façade and promises. Disraeli knew God and Mammon. So many political novels have known God, the party line, alone; and without Mammon the people fainteth. He was the romantic poet and yet the *rusé*, satiate, flattering and subtle man of the world. When we are exhausted by visions he can soothe us with scandal. No one, said Queen Victoria with delight when she read his letters, no one had ever told her *everything* before. The novels of Disraeli tell us everything. He not only plants the main spectacle, the house party of history; but he tells us the club gossip and the boudoir gossip – especially that – and speculates with malice on the dubious political career, on the unelevating comedies of political muddle and panic. He knows ambitious human nature. His eye is bright, his wit is continuous. His general surveys, notably those of the shams and disasters which overtook the regime of the Duke of Wellington, are wonderful destructive criticisms. No one describes a ball, or a house-party, or a dinner as well as Disraeli, for no one so quickly and neatly gives one the foibles and background of the guests. His family histories are masterpieces of irony; he knows the private cankers of grandeur, the long machinations that have produced a Lord Monmouth or a Lord Marney. (In our own time we can imagine the late Lord Curzon modelling himself on Disraeli's personages.) All his ladies are ravishing; nevertheless, though never losing his sympathy for the female character and never ceasing to flatter, he sets it out with the coolest impartiality. 'Although the best of wives and mothers she had some charity for her neighbours' – does that not 'get' the good woman precisely? Or take the portraits of Lucretia Colonna and her mother in *Coningsby*. They are social generalisations as all his characters are, and yet how definite too! I find it difficult to get the hard, grasping, silent and daring daughter out of my mind. Eighteen and a monster of imperiousness already; silent because ill-educated; how she will exploit the old peer who all his life has been exploiting others! Disraeli knows exactly how society has created the character of Lucretia; like Sidonia, he has flattered and observed her. The Lucretia episode in *Coningsby* is rich comedy; for it entangles the egregious Mr Rigby, Lord Monmouth's awful agent. There is nothing more amusing in this novel than the sight of Mr Rigby being sent off to subdue the emotions of the mother who has been jilted in favour of her secretive daughter. The vulgar Rigby is a master of tactics:

> He talked wildly of equipages, diamonds, shawls, opera boxes; and while her mind was bewildered with these dazzling objects he, with intrepid gravity, consulted as to the exact amount she would like apportioned independent of her general revenue for the purpose of charity.

Having flown at him like a tigress and poured out epithets – 'some of them true' – like a fish-wife, the Princess calms down, fanned by his promises, and ends with the faint, pouting complaint that Lord Monmouth 'might have broken the news himself'. The aristocrat is admired for doing what we would all like to do. Who would not pay a Mr Rigby to go down and break the brunt of the scenes that are being prepared for one? Still, we cannot call Rigby a great comic character. He is too rapidly generalised in his appearances. He is an essay on a comic character. Libellously drawn from the notorious Croker, he is a portrait, not a person. He is a rich and perennial political type; the yes-man. We add him to our collection of cads and buffoons. The summary of his character is exact:

> The world took him at his word because he was bold, acute and voluble; with no thought but a good deal of desultory information; and though destitute of all imagination and noble sentiment, he was blessed with a vigorous and mendacious fancy, fruitful in small expedients and never happier than when devising great men's scrapes.

Coningsby is a novel of static scenes. There is one that is rightly famous. This is where Coningsby, as a youth, goes to call on Lord Monmouth, his grandfather, for the first time and proceeds from stairway to stairway, apartment to apartment in the great house, until at last he comes into the presence. The emotion is too much for the sensibility of the shy youth, who bursts into tears; and the disgusted old peer, who cannot bear displays of feeling, dismisses him at once. This is one of the human scenes which stand out so movingly against the excess of artificial ones. Where *Coningsby* is still, *Sybil* moves. We pass from the sight of society to the pictures of working-class starvation and slavery. Disraeli investigated the conditions of the poor for himself, and his remarkable eye and ear collected a number of unforgettable notes and dialogues. There is nothing as terrifying in Dickens, for example, as Disraeli's picture of the slum town of locksmiths run by the toughest working men alone, a kind of frontier town without institutions. We see the knocker-up on his rounds, the starving weaver at his loom, the fever and the gloom of the rain-sodden houses, the new pubs and entertainment halls, the good factories and the bad ones. The conversation of the people is not falsified, but is indeed indigenous and racy. Disraeli drew miners, for example, very well and understood their lives. He could also draw the working-class girl. We have entered into a world already made familiar to us by the prophetic books of Blake. Blake-like cries come out of this darkness: 'I wish there was no such thing as coal in the land,' says the weaver's dying wife. 'And then the engines would not be able to work and we should have our rights again.' It is a cry from *The Daughters of Albion*.

Sybil is melodrama – it would make an excellent opera or film – it lacks the closely finished texture of *Coningsby* but is looser, bolder in argument, wildly romantic in scene. The satire at the expense of the Whig families, who are driving the cottagers off their land and selling out to the railway companies, is scathing: 'Sympathy is the solace of the Poor: but for the Rich there is compensation.'

The rioting and the attack on Mowbray Castle at the end is tremendous theatrical stuff, though – it must be remembered – Disraeli claimed that all his material about the Chartists was carefully documented. The unreality of certain characters, especially Sybil herself, is, of course, comical; but such characters are not unreal in their context. They are ideals walking and so romantic in their carriage that, in the end, one accepts them and their theatrical lamentations over their stolen heritage.

The *roman à thèse* is not commended as a rule by English critics; we read, as a rule, to be contented, and Disraeli's novels have caused a good deal of polite laughter. Such a world of superlatives invited ridicule. One can never be absolutely sure that Disraeli's imagination would distinguish between a great palace and a great Corner House; just as we can never be quite sure, as Lytton Strachey pointed out, that Disraeli was not himself carried away by the luxurious flatteries he poured into the ears of Queen Victoria.

Edwin Drood

When lately I was reading *The Mystery of Edwin Drood* I felt extremely the want of some sort of guidance on the Victorian fascination with violent crime. What explains the exorbitant preoccupation with murder, above all? In earlier periods, when life was cheaper, rape, seduction, incest were the crimes favoured by literature. If we look to literature rather than to life, it is certain the Victorian writers took over murder from the popular taste of the eighteenth century, and succeeded – against the outcry of the older critics – in making it respectable. But in the nineteenth century one detects, also, the rise of a feeling (so curiously expressed by a popular writer on the melodrama a few years ago, I have forgotten his name) that 'murder is cleaner than sex'. There is a clue there, I think. There is a clue, too, in the fact that organised police forces and systems of detection were not established until the Napoleonic wars – we are bound to become fascinated by the thing we punish – and another more sinister clue lies in the relative freedom from war after 1815. A peaceful age was horrified and fascinated, for example, by the ritual murders of the Indian thugs. Where else can we look? To the megalomania that was a natural field for the Romantic movement? To the guilt that is deposited in the mind after a ruthless exertion of the will, such as the Victorians made at the time of the Industrial Revolution? To the social chaos before the Fifties, when tens of thousands were uprooted, and if they did not rise with the rising tide were left to sink into the slums or to stand out alone in violent rebellion? The more one reads of the unrest and catastrophes of the nineteenth century, in social or in private life, the more one is appalled by the pressure which its revolution applied to human beings. And when we read again the rant of the melodramas, when we listen to the theatre organ of Bulwer-Lytton in *Eugene Aram*, and read the theatrical pages of Dickens, we feel, after the first shock of distaste, that these people are responding to a pressure which is not exerted upon us in the same degree. The violence of the scene suggests a hidden violence in the mind, and we begin to understand how assuaging it must have been, in novels like *Oliver Twist* or *The Mystery of Edwin Drood*, to see the murderer's conscience displayed in terms of nightmare and hysteria.

Assuaging to the Victorians, but not to us. We are not driven by the same dynamo. *Edwin Drood* stands at the parting of the ways between the early Victorian and the modern attitude to murder in literature, and also, I suspect, at the beginnings of a change in Dickens himself. The earlier murders of Dickens belong to the more turbulent decades of the nineteenth century. By the late Fifties a calm had been reached; the lid had been levered back on to the pot of society and its seething had become a prosperous simmer. When Wilkie Collins wrote *The Moonstone* and Dickens, not to be outdone, followed it with *Edwin Drood*, we begin the long career of murder for murder's sake, murder which illustrates nothing and is there only to stimulate our skill in detection and to distract us with mystery. The sense of guilt is so transformed that we do not seek to expiate it vicariously on the stage; we turn upon the murderer and hunt him down. Presently, in our time, the hunt degenerates into the conundrums of the detective novel which, by a supreme irony, distracts us from our part in the mass murders of two wars. One or two critics have suggested that the struggle with the unfamiliar technique of the hunt was too much for Dickens and that it killed him and his novel. We cannot know whether this is so; but both those who dismiss the book as the last leaden effort of a worn-out man, and those who observe that it is the most careful and private of Dickens's novels, are agreed that it is pitched in a key he has never struck before.

What is that key? Before I add my answer to the dozens that have been made, it seems important to define one's own attitude to Dickens. I am totally out of sympathy with the hostile criticism of Dickens which has been made during the last twenty years, which has ignored his huge vitality and imaginative range and has done no more than to say he lacked taste and that he sacrificed a profound view of human nature to the sentimentalities and falsities of self-dramatisation. To me it is a perversion of criticism to suggest that you can have the virtues of a writer without his vices, and the discovery of Dickens's failures does not make his achievement less. I swallow Dickens whole and put up with the indigestion. I confess I am not greatly interested in the literary criticism which tells me where he is good and where he is bad. I am glad to be instructed; but for us, at the present time, I think there is far more value in trying to appreciate the nature of his creative vitality and the experience that fed it – a vitality notably lacking in our own fiction. Now when we turn to *Edwin Drood* we do find some of the old Dickens. There is Mr Sapsea, for example, with his own account of his courtship, that beautiful shot plum in the middle of romantic love and Victorian marriage:

'Miss Brobity's Being, young man, was deeply imbued with homage to Mind. She revered Mind, when launched or, as I say, precipitated, on an extensive knowledge of the world. When I made my proposal, she did me the honour of being so over-shadowed with a species of Awe, as to be able to articulate only the two words "Oh Thou!" meaning myself. Her limpid blue eyes were fixed upon me, her semi-transparent hands were clasped together, pallor overspread her aquiline features, and, though encouraged to proceed, she never did proceed a word further . . . She never did and never could find a phrase satisfactory to her perhaps – too – favourable estimate of my intellect. To the very last (feeble action of the liver) she addressed me in the same unfinished terms.'

That is the old Dickens, but a shadow is upon Mr Sapsea. The tomb of Mrs Sapsea is, we are told, to be used by Jasper, the murderer, for his own purpose. Durdles, the drunken verger, tapping the walls of the cathedral for evidence of the 'old uns', is to be roped in. The muscular Christian, Mr Crisparkle, sparring before his mirror in the morning, is marked down by the plot; and that terrifying small boy, the Imp or Deputy, who is employed by Durdles to stone him homewards when he is drunk, will evidently be frog-marched into the witness box. Dickens is submitting to discipline, and how fantastically severe it was may be seen in Edmund Wilson's *The Wound and the Bow*. The background loses some of its fantasy, but the best things in *Edwin Drood* are the descriptions of the cathedral, the town and countryside of Rochester which are recorded with the attentive love one feels for things that are gracious and real. Chesterton thought that something of the mad, original Dickens was lost in this realism; other critics explain it as the influence of mid-Victorian settling down. Mr

Edmund Wilson seems to suggest that in *Edwin Drood* one finds the mellowness and the bitterness of the man who sets out with some confidence equipped to master his devil and to dominate his wound. I do not find a loss in this picture of Cloisterham:

Cloisterham is so bright and sunny in these summer days, that the cathedral and the monastery-ruin show as if their strong walls were transparent. A soft glow seems to shine from within them, rather than upon them from without, such is their mellowness as they look forth on the hot cornfields and the smoking roads that distantly wind among them. The Cloisterham gardens blush with ripening fruit. Time was when travel-stained pilgrims rode in clattering parties through the city's welcome shades; time is when wayfarers, leading a gypsy life between hay-making time and harvest, and looking as if they were just made of the dust of the earth, so very dusty are they, lounge about on cool doorsteps, trying to mend their unmendable shoes, or giving them to the city kennels as a hopeless job, and seeking others in the bundles that they carry, along with their yet unused sickles swathed in bands of straw. At all the more public pumps there is much cooling of the bare feet, together with much bubbling and gurgling of drinking with hand to spout on the part of these Bedouins; the Cloisterham police meanwhile looking askant from their beats with suspicion, and manifest impatience that the intruders should depart from within the civic bounds, and once more fry themselves on the simmering high roads.

The shocks in *Edwin Drood* come not from the sudden levelling of his fantasy and the appearance of realism. They occur when Dickens acts his realism – see the showdown between Jasper and Rosa – and we realise that it is really alien to Dickens's gift that his people should be made to talk to each other. When he attempts this he merely succeeds in making them talk *at* each other, like actors. His natural genius is for human soliloquy not human intercourse.

In criticism of the English novel and in appeals to what is called 'the English tradition', there has been a misunderstanding, I think, about this intrinsic quality of Dickens. One hears the word Dickensian on all sides. One hears of Dickens's influence on the English novel on the one hand, and of the failure of the English novel to produce a comparable genius.

While the word Dickensian lasts, the English novel will be suffocated. For the convivial and gregarious extravagance and the picaresque disorder which are supposedly Dickensian are not Dickens's especial contribution to the English novel. They are his inheritance from Sterne, Smollett and, on the sentimental side, from Richardson, an inheritance which may be traced back to the comedy of Jonson. What Dickens really contributed may be seen by a glance at the only novelists who have seriously developed his contribution – in Dostoevsky above all and, to a lesser degree, in Gogol. (There is more of Dickens, to my mind, in James Joyce's *Ulysses* than in books like *Kipps* or *Tono Bungay*.) For the distinguishing quality of Dickens's people is that they are solitaries. They are people caught living in a world of their own. They soliloquise in it. They do not talk to one another; they talk to themselves. The pressure of society has created fits of twitching in mind and speech, and fantasies in the soul. It has been said that Dickens creates merely external caricatures, but Mr Sapsea's musings on his 'somewhat extensive knowledge' and Mr Crisparkle's sparrings in front of his mirror are fragments of inner life. In how many of that famous congress of 'characters' – Micawber, Barkis, Moddles, Jingle, Mrs Gamp or Miss Twitteron: take them at random – and in how many of the straight personages, like Jasper and Neville Landless in *Edwin Drood*, are we chiefly made aware of the individual's obliviousness of any existence but his own? The whole of Dickens's emotional radicalism, his hatred of the utilitarians and philanthropists and all his attacks on institutions, are based on his strongest and fiercest sense: isolation. In every kind of way Dickens was isolated. Isolation was the foundation not only of his fantasy and his hysteria, but also – I am sure Mr Edmund Wilson is correct here – of the twin strains of rebel and criminal in his nature. The solitariness of people is paralleled by the solitariness of things. Fog operates as a separate presence, houses quietly rot or boisterously prosper on their own. The veneer of the Veneerings becomes almost tangible, whipped up by the repetitions. Cloisterham believes itself more important than the world at large, the Law sports like some stale and dilapidated circus across human lives. Philanthropy attacks people like a humour or an observable germ. The people and the things of Dickens are all out of touch and out of hearing of each other, each conducting its own inner monologue, grandiloquent or dismaying. By this dissociation Dickens brings to us something of the fright of childhood, and the kind of realism employed in *Edwin Drood* reads like an attempt to reconstruct and co-ordinate his world, like a preparation for a final confession of guilt.

George Eliot

═══════════

She looked unusually charming today from the very fact that she was not vividly conscious of anything but of having a mind near her that asked her to be something better than she actually was.

It is easy to guess which of the mid-Victorian novelists wrote these lines. The use of the word 'mind' for young man, the yearning for self-improvement in the heroine, and, lastly, the painful, reiterating English, all betray George Eliot. This description of Esther Lyon in *Felix Holt* might have been chipped out in stone for George Eliot's epitaph and, as we take down a novel of hers from the shelf, we feel we are about to lever off the heavy lid of some solid family tomb. Yet the epitaph is not hers alone. The unremitting ethic of self-improvement has been the sepulchre of all mid-Victorian fiction except *Wuthering Heights*. Today that ethic no longer claims the Esther Lyons of the English novel. The whole influence of psychology has turned our interest to what George Eliot would have called the downward path, to the failures of the will, the fulfilment of the heart, the vacillations of the sensibility, the perception of self-interest. We do not wish to be better than we are, but more fully what we are; and the wish is crossed by the vivid conflicts set up in our lives by the revolution that is going on in our society. The bottom has fallen out of our world and our Esthers are looking for a basis not for a ceiling to their lives.

But this does not mean that Esther Lyon is falsely drawn or that she is not a human being. Using our own jargon, all we have a right to say is that the objects of the super-ego have changed; and, in saying this, we should recall a minor point of importance. It is this. Not only English tradition from Fielding onwards, but no less a person than the author of the *Liaisons Dangereuses* delight in the delectable evasions of the prig and the reserve of the prude; and it would indeed be absurd to cut the aspirations to virtue out of characters and to leave only the virtue that is attained or is already there.

The critic needs only to be clear about the kind of aspiration that is presented to him; and here we perceive that what separates us from Esther Lyon and her creator is a matter of history. She is impelled by the competitive reforming ethic of an expanding society. One might generalise without great danger and say that in all the mid-Victorian novels the characters are either going up in the world, in which case they are good; or they are going down in the world, in which case they are bad. Whereas Goldsmith and Fielding revelled in the misadventures of the virtuous and in the vagaries of Fortune – that tutelary goddess of a society dominated by merchant-speculators – a novelist like George Eliot writes at a time when Fortune has been torn down, when the earned increment of industry (and not the accidental coup of the gambler) has taken Fortune's place; and when character is tested not by hazard but, like the funds, by a measurable tendency to rise and fall.

Once her ethic is seen as the driving force of George Eliot we cease to be intimidated by it, and she emerges, for all her lectures, as the most formidable of the Victorian novelists. We dismiss the late-Victorian reaction from her work; our fathers were bored by her because they were importuned by her mind; she was an idol with feet of clay and, what was worse, appeared to write with them. But it is precisely because she was a mind and because she was a good deal of the schoolmistress that she interests us now. Where the other Victorian novelists seem shapeless, confused and without direction, because of their melodramatic plots and subplots and the careless and rich diversity of their characters, George Eliot marks out an ordered world, and enunciates a constructed judgment. If we read a novel in order to clarify our minds about human character, in order to pass judgment on the effect of character on the world outside itself, and to estimate the ideas people have lived by, then George Eliot is one of the first to give such an intellectual direction to the English novel. She is the first of the rulers, one of the first to cut moral paths through the picturesque maze of human motive. It is the intimidating rôle of the schoolmistress. And yet when we read a few pages of any of her books now, we notice less the oppression of her lectures and more the spacious-ness of her method, the undeterred illumination which her habit of mind brings to human nature. We pass from the romantic shadows into an explicit, a prosaic but a relieving light.

Two of George Eliot's novels, it seems to me, will have a permanent place in English literature. As time goes by *Adam Bede* looks like our supreme novel of pastoral life; and I cannot see any novel of the nineteenth century that surpasses *Middlemarch* in range or construction. With *Adam Bede*, it is true, the modern reader experiences certain unconquerable irritations. We are faced by a sexual theme, and the Victorians were constitutionally unable to write about sexual love. In saying this we must agree that no English writer since the eighteenth century has been happy in this theme, for since that time we have lost our regard for the natural man and the equanimity required for writing about him. The most we have a right to say about the Victorians is that, like the ingenious people who bricked up the windows of their houses and painted false ones on the wall, in order to escape the window tax, the Victorian novelists always chose to brick up the bedroom first.

Now in *Adam Bede* we are shocked by two things: the treatment of Hetty Sorel and by the marriage of Dinah and Adam at the end. It is clear that George Eliot's attitude to Hetty is a false one. The drawing of Hetty is neither observation from life nor a true recasting of experience by the imagination; it is a personal fantasy of George Eliot's. George Eliot was punishing herself and Hetty has to suffer for the 'sins' George Eliot had committed, and for which, to her perhaps unconscious dismay, she herself was never punished. We rebel against the black-and-white view of life and when we compare *Adam Bede* with Scott's *Heart of Midlothian*, to which the former confessedly owes something of its plot, we are depressed by the decline of humanity that has set in since the eighteenth century. Humanity has become humanitarianism, uplift and, in the end, downright cruelty. The second quarrel we have with this book arises, as I have said, from the marriage of Adam and Dinah. There is no reason why a man who has suffered at the hands of a bad woman should not be rewarded and win the consolations of a good woman. If Adam Bede likes sermons, we say, better than infidelity let him have them: we all choose our own form of suffering. But George Eliot told lies about this marriage; or rather, she omitted a vital element from it. She left out the element of sexual jealousy or if she did not leave it out, she did not recognise it, because she could not admit natural passions in a virtuous character. In that scene where Hetty pushes Dinah away from her in her bedroom, where Hetty is dressing up and dreaming her Bovary-like dreams, the reader sees something that George Eliot appears not to see. He is supposed to see that Hetty is self-willed; and this may be true, but he sees as well that Hetty's instincts have warned her of her ultimate rival. The failure to record jealousy, and the attempt to transmute it so that it becomes the ambiguous if lofty repugnance to sin, spring from the deeper failure to face the nature of sexual passion.

This failure not only mars George Eliot's moral judgment but also represses her power as a story-teller. When Adam comes to Arthur Donnithorne's room at the Hermitage, Arthur stuffs Hetty's neckerchief into the wastepaper basket out of Adam's sight. The piece of silk is a powerful symbol. The reader's eye does not leave it. He waits for it to be found. But no, it simply lies there; its function is, as it were, to preach the risks of sin to the reader. Whereas in fact it ought to be made to disclose the inflammatory fact that the physical seduction took place in this very room. George Eliot refuses to make such a blatant disclosure not for æsthetic reasons, but for reasons of Victorian convention; and the result is that we have no real reason for believing Hetty *has* been seduced. Her baby appears inexplicably. The account of Hetty's flight is remarkable – it is far, far better than the corresponding episode in *The Heart of Midlothian* – but the whole business of the seduction and crime, from Adam's fight with Arthur Donnithorne in the woods to Hetty's journey to the scaffold, seems scarcely more than hearsay to the reader. And the reprieve of Hetty at the gallows adds a final unreality to the plot. It must also be said – a final cruelty.

Yet, such is George Eliot's quality as a novelist, none of these criticisms has any great importance. Like the tragedies of Hardy, *Adam Bede* is animated by the majestic sense of destiny which is fitting to novels of work and the soil. Majestic is perhaps the wrong word. George Eliot's sense of destiny was prosaic, not majestic; prosaic in the sense of unpoetical. One must judge a novel on its own terms; and from the beginning, in the lovely account of Dinah's preaching on the village green, George Eliot sets out the pieties which will enclose the drama that is to follow. Her handling of the Methodists and their faith is one of the memorable religious performances of English literature, for she neither adjures us not satirises them, but leaves a faithful and limpid picture of commonplace religion as a part of life. When she wrote of the peasants, the craftsmen, the yeomen, the clergy and squires of Warwickshire, George Eliot was writing out of childhood, from that part of her life which never betrayed her or any of the Victorians. The untutored sermons of Dinah have the same pastoral quality as the poutings of Hetty at the butter churn, the harangues of Mrs Poyser at her cooking, or the remonstrates of Adam Bede at his carpenter's bench. In the mid-Victorian England of the railway and the drift to the towns, George Eliot was harking back to the last of the yeomen, among whom she was born and who brought out the warmth, the humour, the strength of her nature. We seem to be looking at one of Morland's pictures, at any of those domestic or rustic paintings of the Dutch school, where every leaf on the elm trees or the limes is painted, every gnarl of the bark inscribed, every rut followed with fidelity. We follow the people out of the hedgerows and the lanes into the kitchen. We see the endless meals, the eternal cup of tea; and the dog rests his head on our boot or flies barking to the yard, while young children toddle in and out of the drama at the least convenient moments. Some critics have gibed at the dialect, and dialect is an obstacle; but when the great moments come, when Mrs Poyser has her 'say out' to the Squire who is going to evict her; or, better still, when Mrs Bede laments the drowning of her drunken husband, these people speak out of life:

'Let a-be, let a-be. There's no comfort for 'e no more,' she went on, the tears coming when she began to speak, 'now they poor feyther's gone, and I'n washed for and mended, an' got's victual for him for thirty 'ear, an' him allays so pleased wi' iverything I done for him, an' used to be so handy an' do the jobs for me when I war ill an' cambered wi' th' babby, an' made me the posset an' brought it upstairs as proud as could be, an' carried the lad as war as heavy as two children for five mile an' ne'er grumbled, all the way to Warson Wake, 'cause I wanted to go an' see my sister, as war dead an' gone the very next Christmas as e'er come. An' him to be drownded in the brook as we passed o'er the day we war married an' come home together, an' he'd made them lots o' shelves for me to put my plates an' things on, an' showed 'em me as proud as could be, 'case he know'd I should be pleased. An' he war to die an' me not to know, but to be a-sleepin' i' my bed, as if I caredna nought about it. Eh! an' me to live to see that! An' us as war young folks once, an' thought we should do rarely when we war married. Let a-be, lad, let a-be! I wonna ha' no tay; I carena if I ne'er ate nor drink no more. When one end o' th' bridge tumbles down, where's th' use o' th' other stannin'? I may's well die, an' foller my old man. There's no knowin' but he'll want me.'

Among these people Dinah's religion and their quarrels with her about it are perfectly at home; and George Eliot's rendering is faultless. English piety places a stress on conduct and the guidance of conscience; and George Eliot, with her peasant sense of the laws and repetitions of nature, easily converted this working theology into a universal statement about the life of man. Where others see the consequences of sin visited upon the soul, she, the Protestant, saw them appear in the event of a man's or woman's life and the lives of others. Sin is primarily a weakness of character leading to the act. To Arthur Donnithorne she would say, 'Your sin is that your will is weak. You are unstable. You depend on what others say. You are swayed by the latest opinion. You are greedy for approbation. Not lust, but a weak character is your malady. You even think that once you have confessed, your evil will turn out good. But it cannot, unless your character changes.' And to Hetty she says, 'Your real sin was vanity.' It is a bleak and unanswerable doctrine, if one is certain that some kinds of character are desirable and others undesirable; psychologically useful to the novelist because it cuts one kind of path deeply into human nature, and George Eliot knows each moral character like a map. If her moral judgment is narrow, it enlarges character by showing us not merely the idiosyncrasy of people but propounds their type. Hetty is all pretty kittenish girls; Arthur is all careless young men. And here George Eliot makes a large advance on the novelists who preceded her. People do not appear haphazard in her books. They are not eccentrics. They are all planned and placed. She is orderly in her ethics; she is orderly in her social observation. She knows the country hierarchy and how a squire is this kind of man, a yeoman another, a teacher, a publican, a doctor, a clergyman another. They are more than themselves; they are their group as well. In this they recall the characters of Balzac. You fit Dinah among the Methodists, you fit Methodism into the scheme of things, you fit Adam among the peasants. Behind the Poysers are all the yeomen. George Eliot's sense of law is a sense of kind. It's a sense of life which has been learned from the English village where every man and woman has his definition and role.

[216]

I doubt if any Victorian novelist has as much to teach the modern novelists as George Eliot; for although the English novel was established and became a constructed judgment on situations and people after she had written, it did not emulate her peasant sense of law. Hardy alone is her nearest parallel, but he differed from her in conceiving a fate outside the will of man and indifferent to him. And her picture of country life is really closer to the country we know than Hardy's is, because he leaves us little notion of what the components of country society are. The English peasant lived and still lives in a milder, flatter world than Hardy's; a world where conscience and self-interest keep down the passions, like a pair of gamekeepers. It is true that George Eliot is cut off from the Rabelaisian malice and merriment of the country; she hears the men talk as they talk in their homes, not as they talk in the public-houses and the barns. But behind the salty paganism of country life stands the daily haggle of what people 'ought' and 'didn't ought' to do; the ancient nagging of church and chapel. All this is a minor matter beside her main lesson. What the great schoolmistress teaches is the interest of massive writing, of placing people, of showing how even the minds of characters must be placed among other minds.

When we turn from *Adam Bede* to *Middlemarch* we find a novel in which her virtues as a novelist are established and assured; and where there is no sexual question to bedevil her judgment. No Victorian novel approaches *Middlemarch* in its width of reference, its intellectual power, or the imperturbable spaciousness of its narrative. It is sometimes argued by critics of contemporary literature that a return to Christianity is indispensable if we are to produce novels of the Victorian scale and authority, or indeed novels of any quality at all; but there are the novels of unbelievers like George Eliot and Hardy to discountenance them. The fact is that a wide and single purpose in the mind is the chief requirement outside of talent; a strong belief, a strong unbelief, even a strong egoism will produce works of the first order. If she had any religious leanings, George Eliot moved towards Judaism because of its stress on law; and if we think this preference purely intellectual and regard worry, that profoundly English habit of mind, as her philosophy, the point is that it was congenital, comprehensive worry. A forerunner of the psychologists, she promises no heaven and threatens no hell; the best and the worst we shall get is

[217]

Warwickshire. Her world is the world of will, the smithy of character, a place of knowledge and judgments. So, in the sense of worldly wisdom, is Miss Austen's. But what a difference there is. To repeat our earlier definition, if Miss Austen is the novelist of the ego and its platitudes, George Eliot is the novelist of the idolatries of the super-ego. We find in a book like *Middlemarch*, not character modified by circumstance only, but character first impelled and then modified by the beliefs, the ambitions, the spiritual objects which it assimilates. Lydgate's schemes for medical reform and his place in medical science are as much part of his character as is his way with the ladies. And George Eliot read up her medical history in order to get his position exactly right. Dorothea's yearning for a higher life of greater usefulness to mankind will stay with her all her days and will make her a remarkable but exasperating woman; a fool for all her cleverness. George Eliot gives equal weight to these important qualifications. Many Victorian novelists have lectured us on the careers and aspirations of their people; none, before George Eliot, showed us the unity of intellect, aspiration and nature in action. Her judgment on Lydgate as a doctor is a judgment on his fate as a man:

> He carried to his studies in London, Edinburgh and Paris the conviction that the medical profession as it might be was the finest in the world; presenting the most perfect interchange between science and art; offering the most direct alliance between intellectual conquest and the social good. Lydgate's nature demanded this combination: he was an emotional creature, with a flesh and blood sense of fellowship, which withstood all the abstractions of special study. He cared not only for 'Cases', but for John and Elizabeth, especially Elizabeth.

The Elizabeth who was not indeed to wreck Lydgate's life, but (with far more probability) to corrupt his ideas and turn him into the smart practitioner, was Rosamond, his wife. Yet, in its own way, Rosamond's super-ego had the most distinguished ideals. A provincial manufacturer's daughter, she too longed idealistically to rise; the desire was not vulgar until she supposed that freedom from crude middle-class notions of taste and bearing could only be obtained by marriage to the cousin of a baronet; and was not immoral until she made her husband's conscience pay for her ambitions. The fountain, George Eliot is always telling us, cannot rise higher than its source.

Such analyses of character have become commonplace to us. When one compares the respectable Rosamond Lydgate with, say, Becky Sharp, one sees that Rosamond is not unique. Where *Middlemarch* is unique in its time is in George Eliot's power of generalisation. The last thing one accuses her of is *unthinking* acceptance of convention. She seeks, in her morality, the positive foundation of natural law, a kind of Fate whose measures are as fundamental as the changes of the seasons in nature. Her intellect is sculptural. The clumsiness of style does not denote muddle, but an attempt to carve decisively. We feel the clarifying force of a powerful mind. Perhaps it is not naturally powerful. The power may have been acquired. There are two George Eliots: the mature, experienced, quiet-humoured Midlander who wrote the childhood pages of *The Mill on the Floss*; and the naïve, earnest and masterly intellectual with her half-dozen languages and her scholarship. But unlike the irony of our time, hers is at the expense not of belief, but of people. Behind them, awful but inescapable to the eye of conscience, loom the statues of what they ought to have been. Hers is a mind that has grown by making judgments – as Mr Gladstone's head was said to have grown by making speeches.

Middlemarch resumes the observation and experience of a lifetime. Until this book George Eliot often strains after things beyond her capacity, as Dorothea Casaubon strained after a spiritual power beyond her nature. But now in *Middlemarch* the novelist is reconciled to her experience. In Dr Casaubon George Eliot sees that tragedy may paralyse the very intellect which was to be Dorothea's emancipation. Much of herself (George Eliot said, when she was accused of portraying Mark Pattison) went into Casaubon, and I can think of no other English novel before or since which has so truthfully, so sympathetically and so intimately described the befogged and grandiose humiliations of the scholar, as he turns at bay before the vengeance of life. Casaubon's jealousy is unforgettable, because, poisonous though it is, it is not the screech of an elderly cuckold, but the voice of strangled nature calling for justice. And notice, here, something very characteristic; George Eliot's pity flows from her moral sense, from the very seat of justice, and not from a sentimental heart.

Middlemarch is the first of many novels about groups of people in provincial towns. They are differentiated from each other not by class or fortune only, but by their moral history, and this moral differentiation is not casual, it is planned and has its own inner hierarchy. Look at the groups. Dorothea, Casaubon and Ladislaw seek to enter the highest spiritual fields – not perhaps the highest, for us, because, as we have seen, the world of George Eliot's imagination was prosaic and not poetic – still, they desire, in their several ways, to influence the standards of mankind. There is Lydgate, who is devoted to science and expects to be rewarded by a career. He and his wife are practical people, who seek power. The pharisaical Bulstrode, the banker, expects to rise both spiritually and financially at once, until he sits on the right hand of God, the Father; a businessman with a bad conscience, he is the father of the Buchmanites and of all success-religions. The Garths, being country people and outside this urban world, believe simply in the virtue of work as a natural law and they are brought up against Fred Vincy, Rosamond's brother. He, as a horsey young man educated beyond his means, has a cheerful belief in irresponsible Style and in himself as a thing of pure male beauty with a riding crop. We may not accept George Eliot's standards, but we can see that they are not conventional, and that they do not make her one-sided. She is most intimately sympathetic to human beings and is never sloppy about them. When Vincy quarrels with Bulstrode about Fred's debts, when Casaubon's jealousy of Ladislaw secretes its first venom, when Lydgate tries vainly to talk about money to his wife or Fred goes to his erratic old uncle for a loan, vital human issues are raised. The great scenes of *Middlemarch* are exquisite, living transpositions of real moral dilemmas. Questions of principle are questions of battle; they point the weapons of the human comedy, and battle is not dull. In consequence, George Eliot's beliefs are rarely boring, because they are energies. They correspond to psychological and social realities, though more especially (on the large scale) to the functions of the will; they are boring only when, in the Victorian habit, she harangues the reader and pads out the book with brainy essays.

I see I have been writing about *Middlemarch* as though it was a piece of engineering. What about the life, the humour, the pleasure? There are failures: Dorothea and Ladislaw do not escape the fate of so many Victorian heroes and heroines who are frozen by their creator's high-mindedness. Has George Eliot forgotten how much these two difficult, sensitive and proud people will annoy each other by the stupidity which so frequently afflicts the intellectual? Such scruples, such play-acting! But Lydgate and Rosamond quarrelling about money; Rosamond quietly thwarting her husband's decisions, passing without conscience to love affairs with his friends and ending as a case-hardened widow who efficiently finds a second father for her family – these things are perfect. Mary Garth defying the old miser is admirable. But the most moving thing in the book – and I always think this is the real test of a novelist – is given to the least likeable people. Bulstrode's moral ruin and his inability to confess to his dull wife are portrayed in a picture of dumb human despondency which recalls a painting by Sickert. One hears the clock tick in the silence that attends the wearing down of two lives that can cling together but dare not speak.

The humour of George Eliot gains rather than loses by its mingling with her intellect. Here we feel the sound influence of her girlish reading of the eighteenth-century novelists who were above all men of education. This humour is seen at its best in scenes like the one where the relations of the miser come to his house, waiting to hear news of his will; and again in the sardonic description of the spreading of the scandal about Bulstrode and Lydgate. George Eliot followed causes down to their most scurrilous effects. She is good in scandal and public rumour. Her slow tempo is an advantage, and it becomes exciting to know that she will make her point in the minor scenes as surely as she will make it in the great ones. Mrs Dollop of The Tankard has her short paragraph of immortality:

> [She had] 'often to resist the shallow pragmatism of customers disposed to think their reports from the outer world were of equal force with what had "come up" in her mind'.

Mr Trumbull, the auctioneer, is another portrait, a longer one, smelling of the bar and the saleroom. Dickens would have caricatured this gift from heaven. George Eliot observes and savours. Characteristically she catches his intellectual pretensions and his offensive superiority. We see him scent the coming sale and walk over to Mary Garth's desk to read her copy of Scott's *Anne of Geierstein*, just to show that he knows a book when he sees one:

'The course of four centuries', he reads out unexpectedly, 'has well enough elapsed since the series of events which are related in the following chapters took place on the continent.'

That moment is one of the funniest in the English novel, one of those mad touches like the insertion of a dog stealing a bone, which Hogarth put into his pictures.

There is no real madness in George Eliot. Both heavy feet are on the ground. Outside of *Wuthering Heights* there is no madness in Victorian fiction. The Victorians were a histrionic people who measured themselves by the Elizabethans; and George Eliot, like Browning and Tennyson, was compared to Shakespeare by her contemporaries. The comparison failed, if only because madness is lacking. Hysteria, the effect of the exorbitant straining of their wills, the Victorians did, alas, too often achieve. George Eliot somehow escapes it. She is too level-headed. One pictures her, in life, moralising instead of making a scene. There is no hysteria in *Middlemarch*; perhaps there is no abyss because there is so much determination. But there is a humane breadth and resolution in this novel which offers neither hope nor despair to mankind but simply the necessity of fashioning the moral life. George Eliot's last words on her deathbed might, one irreverently feels, be placed on the title-page of her collected works: 'Tell them', she is reported to have said, 'the pain is on the left side.' Informative to the last and knowing better than the doctor, the self-made positivist dies.

An Irish Ghost

The leaves fly down, the rain spits and the clouds flow like a dirty thaw before the wind, which whines and mews in the window cracks and swings the wireless aerial with a dull tap against the sill; the House of Usher is falling, and between now and Hogmanay, as the draughts lift the carpets, as slates shift on the roof and mice patter behind the wainscot, the ghosts, the wronged suitors of our lives, gather in the ante-rooms of the mind. It is their moment. It is also the moment to read those ghosts of all ghosts, the minor novelists who write about the supernatural. Pushed into limbo by the great novelists with their grandiose and blatant passion for normality, these minor talents flicker about plaintively on the edges of fame, often excelling the masters in a phrase or a character, but never large enough to take the centre of the stage. Such a writer is J. Sheridan Le Fanu. In mid-Victorian literature Le Fanu is crowded out by Dickens and Thackeray, talked off the floor by Lever, that supreme raconteur, surpassed or (should one say?) by-passed on his own ground by Wilkie Collins: yet he has, within his limits, an individual accent and a flawless virtuosity. At least one of his books, a collection of tales republished sixteen years ago with Ardizzone's illustrations and entitled *In a Glass Darkly* is worth reading; it contains the well-known *Green Tea*. His other books show that, like so many talented Irishmen, he had gifts, but too many voices that raise too many echoes.

Le Fanu brought a limpid tributary to the Teutonic stream which had fed mysterious literature for so long. I do not mean that he married the Celtic banshee to the Teutonic poltergeist or the monster, in some Irish grave-yard; what he did was to bring an Irish lucidity and imagination to the turgid German flow. Le Fanu's ghosts are what I take to be the most disquieting of all: the ghosts that can be justified, blobs of the unconscious that have floated up to the surface of the mind, and which are not irresponsible and perambulatory figments of family history, mooning and clanking about in fancy dress. The evil of the justified ghosts is not sportive, wilful, involuntary or extravagant. In Le Fanu the fright is that effect follows cause. Guilt patters two-legged behind its victims in the street, retribution sits adding up its account night after night, the secret doubt scratches away with malignant patience in the guarded mind. We laugh at the headless coachman or the legendary heiress grizzling her way through the centuries in her nightgown; but we pause, when we recognise that those other hands on the wardrobe, those other eyes at the window, those other steps on the landing and those small shadows that slip into the room as we open the door, are our own. It is we who are the ghosts. Those are *our* own steps which follow us, it is *our* 'heavy body' which we hear falling in the attic above. We haunt ourselves. Let illness or strain weaken the catch which we keep fixed so tightly upon the unconscious, and out spring all the hags and animals of moral or Freudian symbolism, just as the 'Elemental' burns sharp as a diamond before our eyes when we lie relaxed and on the point of sleep.

Some such idea is behind most of Le Fanu's tales. They are presented as the cases of a psychiatrist called Dr Helvetius, whose precise theory appears to be that these fatal visitations come when the psyche is worn to rags and the interior spirit world can then make contact with the external through the holes. A touch of science, even bogus science, gives an edge to the superstitious tale. The coarse hanging judge is tracked down by the man whom he has unjustly hanged and is hanged in turn. The eupeptic sea captain on the point of marrying an Irish fortune is quietly terrorised into the grave by the sailor whom, years before, he had had flogged to death in Malta. The fashionable and handsome clergyman is driven to suicide by the persecutions of a phantom monkey who jumps into his Bible as he preaches, and waits for him at street corners, in carriages, in his very room. A very Freudian animal this. Dark and hairy with original sin and symbolism, he skips straight out of the unchaste jungle of a pious bachelor's unconscious. The vampire girl who preys on the daughter of an Austrian count appears to be displaying the now languid, now insatiate, sterility of Lesbos. I am not, however, advancing Le Fanu as an instance of the lucky moralist who finds a sermon in every spook, but as an artist in the dramatic use of the evil, the secret, and the fatal, an artist, indeed, in the domestic insinuation of the supernatural. With him it does not break the law, but extends the mysterious jurisdiction of nature.

Le Fanu might be described as the Simenon of the peculiar. There is the same limpid narrative. He is expert in screwing up tension little by little without strain, and an artist in surprise. The literature of the uncanny scores crudely by outraging our senses and our experience; but the masters stick to the simple, the *almost* natural, and let fall their more unnerving revelations as if they were all in the day's work. And they are. The clergyman in *Green Tea* is describing the course of his persecution, how it abates only to be renewed with a closer menace.

> 'I travelled in a chaise. I was in good spirits. I was more – I was happy and grateful. I was returning, as I thought, delivered from a dreadful hallucination, to the scene of duties which I longed to enter upon. It was a beautiful sunny evening, everything looked serene and cheerful and I was delighted. I remember looking out of the window to see the spire of my Church at Kenlis among the trees, at the point where one has the earliest view of it. It is exactly where the little stream that bounds the parish passes under the road by a culvert; and where it emerges at the roadside a stone with an old inscription is placed. As we passed this point I drew my head in and sat down, and in the corner of the chaise was the monkey.'

Again:

> 'It used to spring on a table, on the back of a chair, on the chimney piece, and slowly to swing itself from side to side, looking at me all the time. There is in its motion an indefinable power to dissipate thought, and to contract one's attention to that monotony, till the ideas shrink, as it were, to a point, and at last to nothing – and unless I had started up, and shook off the catalepsy, I have felt as if my mind were on the point of losing itself. There are other ways,' he sighed heavily, 'thus, for instance, while I pray with my eyes closed, it comes closer and closer, and I see it. I know it is not to be accounted for physically but I do actually see it, though my lids are closed, and so it rocks my mind, as it were, and overpowers me, and I am obliged to rise from my knees. If you had ever yourself known this, you would be acquainted with desperation.'

And then, after this crisis, the tortured clergyman confides once more to his doctor and makes his most startling revelation in the mere course of conversation. The doctor has suggested that candles shall be brought. The clergyman wearily replies:

> 'All lights are the same to me. Except when I read or write, I care not if night were perpetual. I am going to tell you what happened about a year ago. The thing began to speak to me.'

There is Henry James's *second* turn of the screw.

We progress indeed not into vagueness and atmosphere, but into greater and greater particularity; with every line the net grows tighter. Another sign of the master is Le Fanu's equable eye for the normal. There is a sociability about his stories, a love of pleasure, a delight in human happiness, a tolerance of folly and a real psychological perception. Only in terms of the vampire legend would the Victorians have permitted a portrayal of lesbian love, but how lightly, skilfully and justly it is told. Vigilance is a word Le Fanu often uses. We feel a vigilance of observation in all his character drawing, we are aware of a fluid and quick sensibility which responds only to the essential things in people and in the story. He is as detached as a *dompteur*, he caresses, he bribes, he laughs, he cracks the whip. It is a sinister but gracious performance.

One doesn't want to claim too much for Le Fanu. For most of his life he was a Dublin journalist and versatility got the better of him. He is known for two of his many novels: *Uncle Silas* and *The House by the Churchyard*. *Uncle Silas* has ingenious elements. Le Fanu saw the possibility of the mysterious in the beliefs and practices of the Swedenborgians, but the book goes downhill half-way through and becomes a crime puzzle. A good man dies and puts his daughter in his brother's care, knowing his brother is reputed to be a murderer. By this reckless act the good man hopes to clear his brother's name. On the contrary, it puts an idea into his head. This brother, Uncle Silas, had married beneath him, and the picture of his illiterate family has a painful rawness which is real enough; but such a sinister theme requires quiet treatment, and Le Fanu is too obviously sweating along in the footsteps of Dickens or Wilkie Collins. Lever is another echo. It is his voice, the voice of the stage Irishman which romps rather too nuttily about *The House by the Churchyard*, into which Le Fanu seems to have thrown every possible side of his talent without discrimination. There are ghosts you shrink from, ghosts you laugh at, cold murder is set beside comic duels, wicked characters become ridiculous, ridiculous ones become solemn and we are supposed to respect them. It is all a very strange mixture, and Sterne and Thackeray, as well as Lever, seem to be adding their hand. A good deal is farcical satire of the military society in eighteenth-century Dublin, and Le Fanu is dashing and gaudy with a broad brush:

> Of late Mrs. Macnamara had lost all her pluck and half her colour, and some even of her fat. She was like one of those portly dowagers in Nubernip's select society of metamorphosed turnips, who suddenly exhibited sympathetic symptoms of failure, grew yellow, flabby and wrinkled, as the parent bulb withered and went out of season.

His comic subalterns, scheming land agents and quarrelling doctors, his snoring generals and shrill army wives, are drawn close up, so close up that it is rather bewildering until you are used to the jumpy and awkward angles of his camera. One gets a confused, life-size impression, something like the impression made by a crowded picture of Rowlandson's, where so much is obviously happening that one can't be sure exactly what it is and where to begin. Le Fanu was spreading himself as Lever had done, but was too soaked in the journalist's restless habits to know how to define his narrative. He became garrulous where Lever was the raconteur. He rambles on like some rumbustious reporter who will drop into a graceful sketch of trout fishing on the Liffey or into fragments of rustic idyll and legend, and then return to his duels, his hell-fire oaths and his claret. I can see that this book has a flavour, but I could never get through it. The truth is that Le Fanu, the journalist, could not be trusted to *accumulate* a novel. You can see in *Uncle Silas* how the process bored him, and how that book is really a good short story that has unhappily got itself into the family way. His was a talent for brevity, the poetic sharpness and discipline of the short tale, for the subtleties and symbolism of the uncanny. In this form Le Fanu is a good deal more than a ghost among the ghosts.

A Victorian Son

The Way of All Flesh is one of the time-bombs of literature. One thinks of it lying in Butler's desk at Clifford's Inn for thirty years, waiting to blow up the Victorian family and with it the whole great pillared and balustraded edifice of the Victorian novel. The book Thackeray failed to write in *Pendennis* had at last been written. After Butler we look back upon a scene of devastation. A spiritual slum has been cleared, yet one is not entirely heartened. Was that the drawing-room where mamma daydreamed about marrying off her daughters to the school-friends of her sons? Was that the fireplace where papa warmed the seat of his trousers and worked up the power politics of godly inertia? Did guilty sons go up those stairs? Did catty sisters hiss from those landings and aunts conduct their warfare of headaches and slammed drawers in those upper rooms? Yes, says Samuel Butler, this was Heartbreak House. Yet not all of his very few admirers agreed with him. Butler writes to Miss Savage in 1883 when the book was circulating in manuscript:

> 'Mr. Heatherley said I had taken all the tenderest feelings of our nature and, having spread them carefully on the floor, stamped upon them till I had reduced them to an indistinguishable mass of filth, and then handed them round for inspection.'

I think it must be agreed that at least Butler spread them on the floor. Now that the floor has collapsed twice in a generation we begin to wonder whether it is still the best place for them; whether Norman Douglas was not right when he said, in *South Wind*, that Butler lacked the male attributes of humility, reverence and sense of proportion?

As Irish life runs to secret societies, so English life seems to run naturally to parricide movements. We are a nation of father-haters. *The Way of All Flesh* assuaged a thirst which, one supposes, began with the law of primogeniture and the disinheritance of younger sons. In the working class which gets little material start in life from its parents and which has to support them and house them in their old age, the obsession is noticeably rare. The normal human desire seems to be to bite the hand that feeds us, and not the hand we feed. But one has only to compare the quarrels of fathers and sons in, say, the eighteenth-century theatre, with Butler's development of the theme, to see a private struggle turning into a national disease. The thunder of the eighteenth-century father as he is helped out of the coach towards the trembling figure of a young scapegrace who has rejected one heiress in order to abduct another and prettier one, comes from a Jupiter engorged (by the generosity of nature) with biological authority and the gout. The eighteenth-century father is a pagan bursting a blood vessel in the ripeness of time; the nineteenth-century father is a Jehovah dictating an inexhaustible Deuteronomy. Money, as Butler saw, makes the difference; and money, in the nineteenth century, is very different from money in the eighteenth century. Fortune, the speculator's goddess – not money – pours out its plenty from the South Sea bubbles and the slave trade in the eighteenth century. Sacks of gold descend from heaven by fantastic parachute, and are stored in the gloating caves, and trade is still spacious and piratical. How different is the nineteenth century, when Economics appears as a regulated science. With the rise of industrialism, Fortune has given place to cash, cash has become Consols and debentures. Investment does not float down from on high. It seeps in, it is secreted, it accumulates. Its accumulation gives birth to new laws of property and these become moral laws and obtain divine sanction. Investment is a token of energy and a huge will to power, and the fathers who exerted this will expected their families to run like the machines that were making their money.

The Way of All Flesh struck this system at its most vulnerable points: its sentiment, its priesthood and their myth. Butler ignored questions of justice and went for the enfeeblement of religious life and the paralysis which crept upon the emotions. The Musical Banks of *Erewhon* pour out a useless coinage; and when Ernest Pontifex kneels in prayer he fails to save either the souls of the poor, who have no time for him, or his own investments. He is useless to God and Mammon, and to offend Mammon is as serious, for Butler, as to offend God, for Mammon is so much richer in vitality and meaning than the stuffed Anglican God. But what Butler really

[229]

opposed to Victorianism was not the sort of responsibility we would oppose to it; Butler opposed a system and its myth not with another system but with the claims of human personality. Against Victorianism he placed himself; himself with both feet on the ground, telescope to blind eye and in perverse self-possession, against people whose dreary will to power – and whose hold on spiritual and material property as well – had dried the sap of sense and life.

We cannot think of Butler without the Butleriana. We always come back to Butler as a man. We come back to the undigested slice of rebel egotism. Full of theories himself, he is constantly leaving the ranks of the specialists and joining the amateur ranks of the human beings. George Eliot may be all very fine, but he has bought a dictionary in order to read *Daniel Deronda* in the original! Now this is not nineteenth century at all. To start with, there is no ambition in it; and the more one thinks of him and his failure to fit in, the more one feels he is not a prophet, or at any rate not the prophet of Mr Shaw's invention. On the contrary, he is a sport or throwback. He looks more and more like a throwback to the eighteenth century. His science – with its affection for Buffoon – smacks of it. That science, one suspects, is a rather literary science. His literary antecedents suggest the eighteenth century, too. *The Way of All Flesh* by its egocentricity, its very flatness and discursiveness, calls to mind the autobiographies of the eighteenth century, things like the *Autobiography* of Gibbon.

The genius of that age was to display a man to the full and yet to contain him within some intellectual assumption. The worldliness, the curiosity, the plainness, the tolerance, the irony, the comeliness of the eighteenth century are qualities which *The Way of All Flesh* revives. Not wholly so, for he was kicking irritably against the pricks; but he leapfrogs over the backs of the Victorians to alight beside the author of *Jonathan Wild* and *Amelia* – those novels in which Fielding was especially concerned with the moral and financial illusions of the virtuous. Butler would be at home in the cudgelling matches of Johnson or in Swift's dry and incinerating indignations. *Erewhon* is a straight descendant of *Gulliver* – a poorer book because it lacks savagery and the sublime, plain figure of Gulliver himself – it is no fellow to a mild book like *News from Nowhere*. Where, but in Swift or Fielding, shall we find the suave parallel to this passage from *The Way of All Flesh*:

'It seems to me,' he continued, 'that the family is a survival of the principle which is more logically embodied in the compound animal – and the compound animal is a form of life which has been found incompatible with high development. I would do with the family among mankind what nature has done with the compound animal, and confine it to the lower and less progressive races. Certainly there is no inherent love for the family system on the part of nature herself. Poll the forms of life and you will find it in a ridiculously small minority. The fishes know it not and they get along quite nicely. The ants and the bees, who far outnumber man, sting their fathers to death as a matter of course, and are given to the atrocious mutilation of nine-tenths of the offspring committed to their care, yet where shall we find communities more universally respected? Take the cuckoo again – is there any bird which we like better?'

Shooting out his hatred and his contradictions, taking back his hatred with laughter, begging us, like Montaigne, to get our dying done as we go along, Butler is certainly an attempt at a rotund man, even though we know that the common-sense view of life is so often a refuge of the injured and the timid, and is neighbour to the conventional.

One's criticism is that the priggishness of Butler, rather than the roundness, gets into the characters of *The Way of All Flesh*. We must except Butler's working-class characters, those collector's pieces, like Mrs Jupp, the landladies, charladies and servants. A novelist picks those up as he goes along. It is the great weakness of *The Way of All Flesh* that the characters are dwarfed and burned dry by Butler's argument. They are often very tedious. He chose them for their mediocrity and then cursed them for it. They can't stand up to his tweakings. Here Miss Savage was a sound critic when she pointed out the dangers of his special pleading; and although one can feel the years ripening the book, one ends with the feeling that Ernest Pontifex does not amount to much. Why should he come into his fortune? Merely that the unrighteous should have their reward? One does not feel that Ernest has very deeply developed because of suffering or fortune. He has escaped only. And he seems rather lost without his enemy. The weakness is that Butler is doing all the talking. There is no contradictory principle. Ultimately the defence of orthodoxy, even an orthodoxy as dim as Theobald's, is the knowledge of human passions. The strange thing is that Ernest does not give us the impression of a man who enjoys himself; he sounds like a man whose hedonism is a prig's hygiene. He looks like becoming the average bachelor of the room marked Residents Only.

One would give anything to have met Butler. For Ernest, Butler's shadow, one cares very little. Unlike Butler he does not act; because of the necessities of the book he is acted upon. His indiscretions are passive. He has no sins; he has merely follies. Still, Butler made more of a hand of self-portraiture in this reminiscence than Thackeray made of Arthur Pendennis and Butler seems to have learned from Thackeray's disquisitional method. These two misfit novelists, born a hundred years too late, have many things in common. Christina is another Amelia from the latter pages of *Vanity Fair*, but filled out with richer comic truth. Her ruthless daydreams are wonderful, her play-acting diplomacy is observed with wicked affection. She is one of those mothers whose right breast never lets on what the left breast is feeling. We are given the great Jekyll and Hyde masquerade of the female bosom:

> As regards Ernest, the suspicions which had already crossed her mind were deepened, but she thought it better to leave the matter where it was. At present she was in a very strong position. Ernest's official purity was firmly established, but at the same time he had shown himself so susceptible that she was able to fuse two contradictory impressions concerning him into a single idea and consider him as a kind of Joseph and Don Juan in one. This was what she had wanted all along, but her vanity being gratified by the possession of such a son, there was an end of it; the son himself was naught.

'The matter' she was 'leaving', as the reader will remember, was a maternal plot to make him betray his friends. The paragraph goes on just as penetratingly into the male version of this kind of humbug:

> No doubt if John had not interfered Ernest would have had to expiate his offence with ache, penury and imprisonment. As it was the boy was 'to consider himself' as undergoing these punishments . . .

One is made to feel the pathos of human jealousies, hatreds and humbug. One is tricked into forgetting that they are inevitable. Butler believed that living, like money, should be in the foreground of human life and not an anxiety in its background. He hated the efficient mechanic doctrine, the mechanistic science and (as one sees in *Erewhon*) the machine with its stereotyped response. He pitied the conscious Ernest who toes the line and tried to inflame in Ernest the healthy sabotage of the unconscious. What, strangely enough, Butler failed to find, in this early introduction of the unconscious into English fiction, was the passion. It was odd going to the unconscious and finding there – what? That chronic perversity: common sense.

A Plymouth Brother

The reaction from puritanism has been so strong and general in the last forty years or more that we too easily assume the extreme forms of it are dying. I do not believe they are. One kind of puritanism goes, after a long battle, and a new one takes its place. In an irreligious age, puritanism simply becomes scientific or political. Or it becomes a severe, exclusive addiction to psychological method. We may suppose that the Plymouth Brethren are a declining sect; but their place is taken by new international sects like the Jehovah's Witnesses, and this group is manifestly on the increase. It is not difficult to see why. The attack on science, the attack on social and political effort, does not affect the educated alone; it is eagerly followed by the ignorant and powerless. And then there are more intimate attractions. Extreme puritanism gives purpose, drama and intensity to private life. One of the greatest mistakes which the genial critics of puritanism make is to suppose that puritanism seen from the outside is the same as puritanism seen from the inside. Outwardly the extreme puritan appears narrow, crabbed, fanatical, gloomy and dull; but from the inside – what a series of dramatic climaxes his life is, what a fascinating casuistry beguiles him, how he is bemused by the comedies of duplicity, sharpened by the ingenious puzzles of the conscience, and carried away by the eloquence of hypocrisy. He lives like a soldier, now in the flash of battle, now in the wrangling of camp and billet. However much he may bore others, he never suffers from boredom himself.

That distress eats into the lives of the children of the puritans. Puritanism burns up the air and leaves a vacuum for its descendants. When we read Edmund Gosse's *Father and Son* which describes the remarkable life of a family of Plymouth Brethren, we see that an insufferable ennui drove the son from his father's faith. Extreme peculiarity in a religious sect is exciting, even stimulating and enlarging to a child; it isolates him, and in doing so gives him a heady importance, an enormous lead (in some respects) over his more orthodox fellows. But the experience is too fierce. It creates that 'chaffiness' – so quickly burned out – which the early Quakers were always talking about. The real reason for the boredom to come lies in that war against the imagination which all puritan sects – the political and scientific it should be observed, as well as the religious – have undertaken. Sir Edmund Gosse's parents would not allow their child to read or hear stories. Fact, yes; but stories were not true, therefore they were lies. The young Gosse, whose father was a scientist, was familiar with birds, insects, the creatures of the sea, and with books of scientific travel; but he had never heard of Jack the Giant Killer or Little Red Riding Hood.

So far as my 'dedication' was concerned (he writes) I can but think that my parents were in error thus to exclude the imaginary from my outlook upon facts. They desired to make me truthful; the tendency was to make me positive and sceptical. Had they wrapped me in the soft folds of supernatural fancy my mind might have been longer content to follow their traditions in an unquestioning spirit.

Yet it would be hard to call the elder Gosse a totally unimaginative man. As a scientist he was unimaginative, and so nipped the promise of his own intellect and career; but as a religious man he was riotously imaginative. He lived in the Eastern imagery of the Bible; he believed in it literally; he apprehended the instant end of the world and prepared himself for a literal flight upwards into the air towards the arms of the angels. His was simply an intense and narrow imagination. And there is a comment by the son here which is very suggestive. We might assume that Gosse senior was a typical middle-class Victorian scientist and Nonconformist, presumably conditioned by his class and his age and bent on the general purpose of practical self-improvement; but, as the son points out, the father's religious life really sprang from a far earlier period. Gosse senior was not a nineteenth-century man; his Calvinism had survived, one might say intact, from the seventeenth century. Conduct, which meant everything to the nineteenth-century man, meant little to the elder Gosse; vision, the condition of grace, was everything. Later on, when the boy grew up and went to live in London, the father was worried very little by what the boy

[235]

did; but was in agony about what he might think or feel. Was he still a dedicated soul, had he fallen from grace? To such questions the elder Gosse might bring the exhausting and pettifogging enquiry of a lawyer, rather than the imaginative anxiety of the religious mystic; but the attitude, as the son says, is nearer Bunyan's or Jeremy Taylor's than it is to the nineteenth century's.

In our talk about environment we too easily assume that people living in the same time, in the same place, under the same conditions, are alike in their responses. We forget the time-lags, the overlaps, the sports and faults of history. It is surprising to find that American travellers to London in Victorian times saw an eighteenth-century city. We detect such lags and fixations in nations which are far enough away, in the Germans, the Spaniards, the Irish. We do not so easily detect them in private life. What was it that prolonged the seventeenth-century stamp upon the elder Gosse? A possible explanation is that, on both sides, the family was a genteel one of steadily declining fortune, and no family is more tenacious of the past, more prone to fixation than the declining family. We have only to compare Gosse's quarrel with Butler's to see the difference between two contemporaries. Gosse was fortunate; for Butler's nineteenth-century father had become a kind of practical Jehovah who thrashed prayer and Latin into his son indifferently. Gosse never hated his father. There was a break, a tragic and passionate break, not a clash of wills so much as a division of principles; and, since the breach was tragic, its agony was without resentment. Butler and his father, in their common hatred, were vituperative to the end; the Gosses gazed helplessly, emotionally across the gulf of history between them. Centuries separated them. The violence of the revolutionary nineteenth century did not possess them; and so it was the scorn, the satire and hatred of Butler and not the scrupulous, unavailing sympathy and impartial regret of Gosse that were to whip up the violent reaction against the Victorian family, and especially the Victorian father.

Gosse's attitude to his father is acquiescent and almost Gibbonian. If Gosse's imagination had been fed in childhood he might have used his father as a starting-point for one of those imaginative libels, like Dickens's portrait of Micawber, which are fatherhood's vicarious and unwilling gift to literature. But from Gosse, the ex-puritan and melodious prig, we get instead a positive, literal, sceptical document. What an incredible story the mere facts make. Nothing fixes the fantastic note like the episode of the moth. The naturalist, his wife and his child were at prayer one morning in 1855:

> . . . when through the open window a brown moth came sailing. My mother immediately interrupted the reading of the bible by saying to my father, 'Oh, Henry, do you think that can be *Boletobia*?' My father rose up from the sacred book, examined the insect, which had now perched, and replied 'No! It is only the common *Vapourer Orgyia antiqua*!' resuming his seat and the exposition of the Word, without any apology or embarrassment.

I said earlier that Gosse senior could not be called unimaginative, but as the son points out, he was certainly deficient in sympathetic imagination. In one sense his fanatical religion was scientific, an exhaustive classification and checking up. There was, for example, the question of Prophecy. The father said that no small element in his wedded happiness had been the fact that he and his wife were of one mind in the interpretation of Sacred Prophecy. They took to it as profane families take to cards or the piano. They played with the Book of Revelation as if it were Happy Families or Snap:

> When they read of seals broken and of vials poured forth, of the star which was called Wormwood that fell from Heaven, and of men whose hair was as the hair of women, and their teeth as the teeth of lions, they did not not admit for a moment that these vivid mental pictures were of a poetic character, but they regarded them as positive statements, in guarded language, describing events which were to happen, and could be recognised when they did happen. It was the explanation, the perfectly prosaic and positive explanation, of all these wonders which drew them to study the Habershons and the Newtons whose books they so much enjoyed. They were helped by these guides to recognise in wild Oriental visions direct statements regarding Napoleon III and Pope Pius IX, and the King of Piedmont, historic figures which they conceived as foreshadowed, in language which admitted of plain interpretation, under the names of denizens of Babylon and companions of the Wild Beast.

The conviction that the last days of the queenly arrogance of Rome had come so affected Gosse's mother that her husband wrote in his diary that it 'had irradiated her dying hours with an assurance that was like the light of the Morning Star'. As the years went slowly by – and how slowly they passed for the bored and ailing child who was expected to live at this pitch – it began to dawn on him that there was something incredibly trivial about such convictions. The elder Gosse could swallow one Eliot's stuff about prophecy and yet reject Darwin. He was an educated man, yet he could say that Shakespeare, Marlowe and Ben Jonson endangered the soul and that Dickens was preferable to Scott 'because Dickens showed love in a ridiculous light'. The child of such a man was obliged to develop two selves. One assented, got itself publicly baptised and dedicated at the age of ten, and confounded the wise with his theology and unction; the other quietly built up a very different mind – and as the sons of puritans will – an inveterate irony. This came out at the time when his father was thinking of marrying again. The father (the child sharply detected) was put, for once, in the position of the penitent. One was required, the child remembered, 'to testify in season and out of season'. Was the lady (he therefore asked) 'one of the Lord's children'? Had she, he pressed, 'taken up her cross in baptism'? The father had to admit that the lady had been brought up in the 'so-called Church of England'. 'Papa,' said the little prig, wagging his finger, 'don't tell me that she's a pedobaptist?'

Gosse was encouraged to draw this portrait by the revolt of the times. He was faced by the difficulty that at the moments when narrow or peculiar religion is behaving most ludicrously, it is also providing its adherents with emotions or intentions that one must respect. Nothing could have been more intellectually disgraceful and spiritually disastrous than the boy's public dedication; nothing more dingily farcical; or more humiliating when one considers that Gosse's father was, after all, an educated man. Yet one must respect the emotions that the participant felt. There is, as Gosse said, something comic and tragic, really tragic, in the theme. On a similar subject Mark Twain became savage; he was driven to a kind of insulting nihilism. Gosse, in the end, was rather more bored than outraged by his father, for he understood the defect of character that had caused the malady. He saw that the sin was the denial of the imagination and the pestering of the judgment. He saw that, at the time of the Darwin crisis, his father had really sold his intellect and perhaps his soul. The flight to Devonshire was a flight from the society of his equals, who would challenge his faith every day, into a society of rustics who could be guaranteed to swallow everything he said. We smile with amusement and irony at the two figures; the father examining his insects under the naturalist's microscope, the son applying the lens of the biographer and producing one of the most brilliant specimens of his century.

The Scientific Romances

A cloud of dust travels down the flinty road and chokes the glossy Kentish greenery. From the middle of the moving cloud come the ejaculations of an unhandy driver; the clopper of horses' hooves, the rumble of a wagonette or trap. One catches the flash of a top-hat or a boater. One smells horse manure and beer. And one hears that peculiar English spoken by the lower middle class, a language in which the syllable '-ing' either becomes '-ink' or loses its final 'g', and which is enlivened by cries of 'Crikey' and 'Golly'. The accent is despairing, narrow-vowelled yet truculent, with something of the cheap-jack and Sunday League in it, and it is broken by a voice, not quite so common, which says things like, 'We're not the finished thing. We're jest one of Nature's experiments, see. We're jest the beginning.' And then – I don't quite know why – there is a crash. Over goes the wagonette, the party inside hit out with their fists, noses bleed, eyes are blackened. Most surprising, a nearby house catches fire. Do not be alarmed. The time is the late Nineties and you have simply been watching the outing of a group of early H. G. Wells characters who have become suddenly aware that science is radically changing the human environment. No Frenchified or Russianised fiction this, but plain, cheerful, vulgar, stoic, stupid and hopelessly romantic English. It is as English as the hoardings.

There are always fist-fights and fires in the early Wells. Above all, there are fires. They occur, as far as I remember, in all the scientific romances except *The Island of Dr. Moreau* – a very pessimistic book – and are an ingredient of the Wellsian optimism, an optimism whose other name, I fear, is ruthlessness. I have lately read all those scientific books from *The Time Machine* to *The War in the Air* and it has been a refreshing experience. There was a time, one realises, when science was fun. For the food of the gods is more entertaining than the prosaic efficacy of vitamins; the tripods of the Martians are more engaging than tanks. And then, here you have

Wells at his best, eagerly displaying the inventive imagination, first with the news and at play, with an artist's innocence. Here you see his intoxicated response – a response that was lacking in his contemporaries – to the front-page situation of his time, and here you meet his mastery of the art of story-telling, the bounce and resource of it. Above all, in these early books, you catch Wells in the act, his very characteristic act, of breaking down mean barriers and setting you free. He has burst out himself and he wants everyone else to do the same. 'Why', cries the engineer in *The Food of the Gods* – the poorest of these books – 'Why don't we do what we want to do?'

For that matter, I have never read any book by H. G. Wells, early or late, which did not start off by giving me an exhilarating sense of personal freedom. Every inhibition I ever had faded from me as I read. Of course, after such a high, hard bounce one comes down again. The answer to the engineer's question is that we do not do what we want to do because we want to do opposite things at the same time. Yet that infectious Wellsian sense of freedom was not all anarchy, romantic ebullience or Utopian uplift. That freedom was a new fact in our environment; one pays for everything – that is all. I do not know what date is given to the second scientific revolution, but one had to go back to the great centuries of geographical discovery for a comparable enlargement of our world; and it is a suggestive fact that we had to go back to Swift, the Swift of Lilliput and Laputa, before we found another English novelist going to science for his data and material as Wells had done. (The influence of science, in the 150 years that lie between those two writers, is philosophical, not factual.) Wells's eager recognition of the new environment is one of the sources of the sense of freedom we got from him. I make no comparison of the merits of Wells and Swift – though the Beast-Men of *The Island of Dr. Moreau* are derivatives of the Yahoos and are observed with Swift's care for biological detail – but in his best narratives Wells does go back to the literary traditions of the early eighteenth century, the highest traditions of our narrative literature. The ascendancy of Swift is a question of imaginative range and style; above all it is due to a humanity which is denied to Wells because he arrived at the beginning, the crude beginning, of a new enlargement, whereas Swift arrived towards the end of one. None of Wells's narrators, whether they are South Kensington scientists or people, like the awful Bert, who appear to be suffering from an emotional and linguistic toothache, is capable of the philosophical simplicity and sanity of Gulliver; for Wells has only just spotted this new world of agitating chemicals, peculiar glands, and obliterating machines. The sense of wonder has not grown far beyond a sense of copy. He is topical and unstable, swept by eagerness yet visited by nauseas sudden and horrifying. Suppose we evolve into futility or revert to the beast from which we have arisen? Such speculations are alien to the orthodox eyes which were set in Swift's mad head; he had no eye to the future; the eighteenth century believed in a static world. The things Swift sees *have happened*. To Wells – and how typical of an expanding age – the things he sees have *not* happened. They are possibilities. In these scientific romances one catches occasionally the humane and settled note: in *The Time Machine*, in *The Island of Dr. Moreau* and in *The War of the Worlds*, which are the most imaginative stories of the group and are free of the comic Edwardian horseplay. The practical experiment has been detached from the practical joke; the idea is untainted by the wheeze. The opening sentence of *The War of the Worlds* suggests a settled view of humanity, besides being an excellent example of Wells's mastery of the art of bouncing us into belief in anything he likes to tell us:

> No one would have believed in the last years of the nineteenth century that human affairs were being watched keenly and closely by intelligences greater than man's and yet as mortal as his own.

It is not surprising that the passages of low comedy, which elsewhere are Wells's excellence, should be a failure in the scientific romances. Naturally they break the spell of the illusion with their clumsy realism. And if love is born, Wells is Walt Disney at his worst. The love scenes between the giants in *The Food of the Gods* are the most embarrassing in English fiction, and one wonders that the picture of the awful Princess, goggling in enormous close-up and fanning herself with half a chestnut tree, did not destroy the feminist movement. But except for faint squirms of idyllic petting in *The Time Machine*, none of these aberrations misdirects the narratives of the three books I have mentioned. I cannot include *The War in the Air* among the best; it *is* an astonishing piece of short-term prophecy and judgment. One remembers the bombing of battleships and the note on the untroubled minds of those who bomb one another's cities; but the book is below Wells's highest level. So, too, is *The Invisible Man*, which is a good thriller, but it develops jerkily and is held up by horseplay and low comedy. Without question *The Time Machine* is the best piece of writing. It will take its place among the great stories of our language. Like all excellent works it has meanings within its meaning and no one who has read the story will forget the dramatic effect of the change of scene in the middle of the book, when the story alters its key, and the Time Traveller reveals the foundation of slime and horror on which the pretty life of his Arcadians is precariously and fearfully resting. I think it is fair to accuse the later Wells of escaping into a dream world of plans, of using science as a magic staircase out of essential social problems. I think the best Wells is the destructive, ruthless, black-eye-dealing and house-burning Wells who foresaw the violence and not the order of our time. However this may be, the early Wells of *The Time Machine* did not escape. The Arcadians had become as pretty as flowers in their pursuit of personal happiness. They had dwindled and would be devoured because of that. Their happiness itself was haunted. Here Wells's images of horror are curious. The slimy, the viscous, the foetal reappear; one sees the sticky, shapeless messes of pond life, preposterous in instinct and frighteningly without mind. One would like to hear a psychologist on these shapes which recall certain surrealist paintings; but perhaps the biologist fishing among the algæ, and not the unconscious, is responsible for them. In *The Time Machine* – and also in the other two books – Wells is aware of pain. None of his investigators returns without wounds and bruises to the mind as well as the body, and Dr Moreau is, of course, a sadist. *The Island* is hard on the nerves and displays a horror more definite and calculated than anything in Wells's other books. Where *The Time Machine* relieves us by its poetic social allegory, *The Island of Dr. Moreau* takes us into an abyss of human nature. We are left naked at the end of the shocking report, looking with apprehension at the bodies of our friends, imagining the tell-tale short legs, the eyes that shine green in the dark, the reversion to the wolf, the hyena, the monkey and the dog. This book is a superb piece of story-telling from our first sight of the unpleasant ship and its stinking, mangy menagerie, to the last malign episode where the narrator is left alone on the island with the Beast-Men. Neither Dr Moreau nor his drunken assistant is a lay figure and, in that last episode, the Beast-Men become creatures of Swiftian malignance:

> The Monkey Man bored me, however. He assumed, on the strength of his five digits, that he was my equal, and was forever jabbering at me, jabbering the most arrant nonsense. One thing about him entertained me a little: he had a fantastic trick of coining new words. He had an idea, I believe, that to gabble about names that meant nothing was the proper use of speech. He called it 'big thinks', to distinguish it from 'little thinks' – the sane everyday interests of life. If ever I made a remark he did not understand, he would praise it very much, ask me to say it again, learn it by heart, and go off repeating it, with a word wrong here and there, to all the wilder of the Beast People. He thought nothing of what was plain and comprehensible. I invented some very curious 'big thinks' for his especial use.

The description of the gradual break in the morale of the Beast-Men is a wonderful piece of documented guesswork. It is easy enough to be sensational. It is quite another matter to domesticate the sensational. One notices, too, how Wells's idea comes full circle in his best thrillers. There is the optimistic outward journey, there is the chastened return.

It would be interesting to know more about the origins of *The Island of Dr. Moreau*, for they must instruct us on the pessimism and the anarchy which lie at the heart of Wells's ebullient nature. This is the book of a wounded man who has had a sight of sadism and death. The novelist who believed in the cheerful necessity of evolution is halted by the thought of its disasters and losses. Perhaps man is unteachable. It is exciting and emancipating to believe we are one of nature's latest experiments, but what if the experiment is unsuccessful? What if it is unsurmountably unpleasant? Suppose the monkey drives the machine, the gullible, mischievous, riotous and irresponsible monkey? It is an interesting fact that none of Wells's optimistic contemporaries considered such a possibility. Shaw certainly did not. Evil, in Shaw, is curable. He believes in the Protestant effort. He believes that men *argue* their way along the path of evolution, and that the life force is always on the side of the cleverest mind and the liveliest conscience. When he reflects on the original monkey, Shaw cannot resist the thought that the monkey was a shrewd animal going up in the world, and Shaw feels a patronising pride in him which the self-made man may feel about the humble ancestor who gave him his start in life. There is certainly no suggestion that he will ever lose his capital, which is civilisation, and revert. There is no thought, in this quintessential Irish Protestant, that the original monkey may be original sin. Nor could there be: the doctrine of original sin is a device of the emotions, and about our emotions Shaw knows absolutely nothing at all. But to the emotional Wells, the possibility of original sin in the form of the original monkey is always present. The price of progress may be perversion and horror, and Wells is honest enough to accept that. Shaw appears to think we can evade all painful issues by a joke, just as Chesterton, the Catholic optimist of his generation, resolved serious questions by a series of puns.

Wells can be wounded. It is one of his virtues. One is reminded of Kipling, another wounded writer – was Wells satirising Kipling in that chapter of *The Island of Dr. Moreau* where the Beast-Men are seen mumbling their pathetic Law? – and Kipling and Wells are obviously divergent branches of the same tree. Wells and Utopian, Kipling the patriot – they represent the daydreams of the lower middle class which will either turn to socialism or fascism. Opposed in tendency, Wells and Kipling both have the vision of artists; they foresee the conditions of our time. They both foretell the violence with a certain appetite. Crudity appeals to them. They are indifferent or bad-hearted, in human relations. They understand only personal independence which, from time to time, in their work is swallowed up in mass relationships. In the final count, Kipling – like Wells's man in the sewer in *The War of the Worlds* – falls back on animal cunning. It is the knowing, tricky, crafty animal that survives by lying low and saying nothing. Kipling, for all his admiration of power, believes in the neurotic, the morbid and defeated mind. This strain is in Wells also, but he has more private stoicism than Kipling has, a stoicism which blossoms from time to time into a belief in miracles and huge strokes of luck. Impatient of detail, mysteriously reticent about the immediate practical steps we must take to ensure any of his policies, Wells believes – like Kipling – in magic: a magic induced by impudence or rebellion. Wells and Kipling – these two are light and shadow to each other.

Wells's achievement was that he installed the paraphernalia of our new environment in our imagination; and life does not become visible or tolerable to us until artists have assimilated it. We do not need to read beyond these early scientific works of his to realise what he left out. The last war, whose conditions he so spryly foresaw, has made that deficiency clear. When we read those prophetic accounts of mechanised warfare and especially of air bombardment, we must be struck by one stupendous misreading of the future. It occurs where we should expect it to occur: in the field of *morale*. Wells imagined cities destroyed and the inhabitants flying in terror. He imagined the soldiers called out to keep order and the conditions of martial law and total anarchy. He imagined mass terror and riot. He did not reckon with the nature, the moral resources, the habits of civilised man. Irresponsible himself, he did not attribute anything but an obstructive value to human responsibility. That is a serious deficiency, for it indicates an ignorance of the rooted, inner life of men and women, a jejune belief that we live by events and programmes; but how, in the heyday of a great enlargement of the human environment, could he believe otherwise? We turn back to our Swift and there we see a mad world also; but it is a mad world dominated by the sober figure of the great Gulliver, that plain, humane figure. Not a man of exquisite nor adventurous spirituality; not a great soul; not a man straining all his higher faculties to produce some new mutation; not a man trying to blow himself out like the frog of the fable to the importunate dimensions of his programme; but, quite simply, a man. Endowed with curiosity, indeed, but empowered by reserve. Anarchists like Wells, Kipling, Shaw and the pseudo-orthodox Chesterton had no conception of such a creature. They were too fascinated by their own bombs.

The Five Towns

It is a long time now since the earth seemed solid under the feet to our novelists, since caprice, prophecy, brains and vividness meant less than the solid substance of time and place. And Arnold Bennett, in books like *The Old Wives' Tale* and *The Clayhanger Family*, seems to be the last of the novel's four-square gospellers. I return to him often and always, once I get into him, with satisfaction. A book like *The Clayhanger Family* has the sobriety as well as the tedium of a detailed engraving; and there is, oddly, enough of the connoisseur in Bennett to induce a modern taste. He is not a dilettante in the ego's peculiarities and he is without interest in elegance; he is the connoisseur of normality, of the ordinary, the awkward, an heir – one might say – of the makers of the Staffordshire figures who thought Moody and Sankey as good a subject as equestrian princes of the blood. We speak of the disciplines of belief, of art, of the spirit; Bennett speaks of the discipline of life itself, reveres its frustrations, does not rebel against them; kneels like some pious behaviourist to the drab sight of reflexes in process of being conditioned. He catches the intolerable passing of time in our lives, a passing which blurs our distinctiveness and quietly establishes our anonymity; until our final impression of him is a kind of estate agent's valuer walking with perfunctory step through the rooms of our lives, ticking his inventory and treating us as if we were long deceased. He cannot begin – and I think this is his inheritance from the French naturalists – until we are dead, until we and our furniture have become indistinguishable evidence. I find this very restful. Frustration – *pace* H. G. Wells – is one of the normal conditions of life, and calming is the novelist who does not kick against the pricks.

Fidelity and sincerity are the words one puts first to Arnold Bennett's work. Some years ago there appeared an anthology called *The English in Love*, containing love passages from the English novelists, and I was much struck by the superiority of Bennett's contribution to the work of specialists like Meredith and D. H. Lawrence. Bennett was not describing passion; but against his quiet exactitude and sincerity, the lyricists looked forced and trite. The very matter-of-factness of Bennett made him one of the best portrayers of women we have had. The vices of romanticism or of misogynist satire passed him by in his best work completely. What other words come to mind when we think of him? They are his own words: 'detracting' is one, 'chicane' – a great favourite – is another; but there is a sentence in the early pages of *The Clayhanger Family* which contains a volume of criticism on him. He is writing of young Edwin Clayhanger coming home from his last day at school in the Five Towns: 'It seemed rather a shame,' Bennett says of Edwin, 'it seemed even tragic, that this naïve, simple creature, immaculate of worldly experience, must soon be transformed into a man wary, incredulous and detracting.' The essence of Bennett's mind is packed into that awkward sentence with its crick in the neck at the feeble beginning and the give-away of its three final words. Bennett had borrowed the manner and methods of the French naturalists without being seriously formed by the scientific, political and philosophical ideas which made them naturalists and gave them their driving force. Timidity rather than conviction is behind the brevity of his address. The result is that the apostle of will, efficiency and success appears to us hesitant and uncertain; he is between two stools; he cannot make up his mind whether life is 'rather a shame' or 'tragic'. And when you compare *The Clayhanger Family* with the contemporary French *Les Thibaults* – which, like *Clayhanger*, contains a prolonged study in fatal illness and is also concerned with the relation of father and son – you feel at once, though you recognise the conscious artist, Bennett's lack of imaginative stamina and resilience. What Bennett observes will be truthfully, almost litigiously, observed. Hazard will set the points wrongly in the lives of humdrum people and push them off the rails. Time will get its teeth into them more deeply year by year. We shall feel, as Edwin felt, that we must 'brace ourselves to the exquisite burden of life'. We shall feel we are interpenetrated 'by the disastrous yet beautiful infelicity of things'. What we shall miss is the sense that life is conceived of as anything in particular, whether it be the force that makes the Five Towns or forms the bleak impetuosity of Hilda Lessways. We shall not feel that life is much more than a random collection of *things*.

[248]

Admitting the absence of a frame, allowing for some lagging of narrative which the modern novelist would speed up, everything else in *Clayhanger* is good. Bennett, as I have said, was the connoisseur of the normal, the ordinary and the banal. Where other novelists add, he – as he said – detracted. For example, how easy for the novelist to identify himself with the sixteen-year-old Edwin and to exaggerate that sense of being alone with the universe which the boy had when he sat in his room alone at night. Bennett collects that emotion, astutely yet compassionately – but he collects it, labels it – it becomes part of the collection of human samples which make up Edwin Clayhanger's life. Bennett's pursuit of the normal is even better illustrated by his treatment of the character of the hard, impulsive, passionate figure of Hilda Lessways. Here he uses a characteristic device: he makes two full-length portraits of her from two different points of view, a method which gives a remarkable suspense to the story. The first portrait of Hilda is romantic and mysterious outline. In the second, with enormous dramatic effect, he fills in the plain reality of her life. That second appearance of hers, as she cleans the house and quarrels with her mother about money, is a remarkable portrayal of the relationship of two women. As spectators of Hilda's character we might easily exaggerate, romanticise and misread her disaster; but Bennett's gift as a novelist is to abolish the rôle of spectator. He almost painfully domesticates the reader, puts him in the slow muddle, murmur and diurnal perturbation of a character's life, so that the reader knows no more than Hilda knows, where she is going or why she is going there. Where most novelists live by a sort of instinct for imaginative scandal, Bennett – by some defect of imagination which he is able to turn to advantage – clings like a cautious puritan to sober likelihood. He doesn't bet: 'It's a mug's game.' The result, in the portrait of Hilda, is a staggering probability. There is a passage when she discovers her husband is a bigamist and a crook, that the child she is expecting is illegitimate, and that she will be left penniless in their boarding-house at the mercy of bailiffs. She is faced by ruin. How do people face ruin? Variously, unexpectedly; they traipse, protected by conviction, through their melodramas. Bennett seems to reply:

Hilda in a curious way grew proud of him. With an extraordinary inconsequence she dwelt upon the fact that was grand – even as a caterer, he had caused to be printed at the foot of the menu forms which he had instituted the words: 'A second helping of all or any of the dishes will willingly be served if so desired.' And in the general havoc of the shock she began to be proud also of herself because it was the mysterious power of her individuality that had originated her disaster.

The determination to avoid the dramatic has led to something far more dramatic: revelation, a new light on character, the unexpected vistas in ordinary life.

Bennett's characters have three dimensions; the slow but adroit changing of the light that is thrown upon them makes them stereoscopic and gives them movement. And this movement is not the swift agitation of the passions but the dilatory adjustment to circumstance.

One of the reasons why bad novels are bad is not that the characters do not live, but they do not live with one another. They read one another's minds through the author. In *Clayhanger*, we feel at once that the characters are living together because, quite without prompting and entirely in the course of nature, they misunderstand one another. Edwin never understands his father because he does not know his father's past. The father cannot understand the son because the father's whole attitude to life is that his rise from barbarous poverty is a primitive miracle. He is primitive, the son is rational. Each one bumps awkwardly along in the wonder of his own nature. When the father is stricken by fatal illness the son becomes the tyrant. Their emotions about each other are strong; but the two men do not feel these emotions for each other at the same time. The fierceness of the father's battle for life in the long, grey death scene startles the son – and yet he feels how strange it is that a dying man should be strong enough to return again and again to the struggle, whereas he, the son and slave, should be at the point of collapse. A writer with little poetic feeling, Bennett thinks of our awkwardness with each other, of the unbridgeable gaps of time, experience and faculty which separate us, and not of our ultimate isolation. That is why he is a pathetic and not a tragic writer; one who feels uncertainly that 'it is rather a shame' that we have to bear time's burden of 'beautiful infelicity'.

Bennett's collector's passion for ordinariness is a kind of poor relation of Meredith's passion for the fantastic. It is amusing to make an irreverent comparison between Meredith's chapter *On an Aged and Great Wine* with Bennett's fervent hymn to building materials and plumbing in *Clayhanger*. This tedious literalness of Bennett's culminated in that nightmare of deified gadgets, *Imperial Palace*. But the virtues of Bennett lie in his patient and humane consideration of the normal factors of our lives: money, marriage, illness as we have to deal with them. Life, he seems to say, is an occupation which is forced upon us, not a journey we have chosen, nor a plunge we have taken. Such a view may at times depress us, but it may toughen us. Bennett really wrote out of the congenital tiredness of the lower middle class, as Wells wrote out of its gambling spirit and gift for fantasy; and in the end, I think, Bennett's picture, with its blank acceptance of the Sunday School pageants, the Jubilees, the Band of Hope, the fear of the workers, the half-baked attempts at culture, is the more lasting one. It is history. History presented – when we glance back at Bennett's French masters – with the dilettante's and collector's indifference to any theory of what history may be about.

Sons and Lovers

What of the writers who came out of World War II? D. H. Lawrence – can he tell us anything; how does he seem now? A great influence, like Wells was, on ordinary conduct; a whole generation dropped the puritan tradition and made love after the fashion of Lawrence's new puritanism. The cult of sex was also a protest against the ignoble atmosphere of city life. Wells supplied the blueprint for free-love; Lawrence replied with the content. It was a new content for marriage. Free-love awakens Lawrence's irony; he admires the restlessness of it but sees that it is governed by the law of diminishing returns. Like Wells, too, Lawrence is one of the journalist-novelists. He writes a novel a year about his travels and the mistakes of his friends, a religious journalist where Wells is political. Has Lawrence had any influence on contemporary writers? Yes, he is responsible for the fact that no living writer has any idea of how to write about sexual love. Lawrence's phallic cult was a disaster to descriptive writing. The ecstasies of sexual sensation are no more to be described than the ecstasies of music which they resemble. The realism of the Chinese *Golden Lotus*, for example, makes Lawrence look silly. But above all, it was fatal for imitators of Lawrence to pick up his contagious manner and leave the beliefs that did so much to create the manner; on the other hand, no one could possibly believe what Lawrence believed, and Lawrence hated people if they tried, because he believed in the inviolable, personal contradictions. One day when Lawrence and Frieda were out riding in Mexico, Frieda cried out, 'Oh, it's wonderful, wonderful to feel his great thighs moving, to feel his powerful legs!' 'Rubbish, Frieda,' Lawrence shouted back. 'Don't talk like that. You have been reading my books. You don't feel anything of the sort.' Quite rightly and consistently Lawrence allowed no one to believe what he believed. All the same, Frieda persisted; she did feel like that! Certainly she *wanted* to feel like that. Lawrence's teachings are interesting because they are a compendium of what a whole generation wanted to feel, until Hitler arose, just after Lawrence's death, and they saw where the dark unconsciousness was leading them. Seen in this light, Lawrence represented the last phase of the Romantic movement: random, irresponsible egotism, power for power's sake, the blood cult of Rosenberg. And Lawrence was representative, because tens of thousands of people in England and Europe were uprooted people, like himself.

Still, that was only one of the lights in which Lawrence could be read. The man of genius is a melting-pot and everything that came to the surface in the English soul between 1910 and 1940 can be found in Lawrence. We are interested now not in what he taught – if it *was* teaching – but in his disposition: and that is vivid the moment we pick up any of his writings. First of all, *the whole of England*, before and after the last war, acted upon Lawrence's imagination. His angry paganism of demi-gods released a repressed religious imagination in English literature. He reintroduced the direct apprehension of experience. He wrote from within – from inside the man, the woman, the tree, the fox, the mine. His people and his scene, whether it is a German road, a Nottingham kitchen or a Mexican village, are no longer fingered with one hand in the manner of naturalistic writers; they are grasped with both hands, with mind and senses. The impersonal novelist, the god with the fountain pen, has gone; the people, the trees, the mines, the fields, the kitchens come physically upon the page. And although Lawrence is the most personal of novelists, quite as personal as Thackeray or Meredith was, yet he does not continually obtrude. At his best, he puts the reader instantly in the scene; instead of drawing it up neatly to be considered with all the feeling left out.

He saw the whitish muddy tracks and deep scores in the road where part of the regiment had retired. Now all was still. Sounds that came, came from the outside. The place where he stood was still, silent, chill, serene; the white church among the trees beyond seemed like a thought only.

To you, who are not a writer, the white church *would* have been exactly that: a thought, a mark on the skin of your mind. Or:

He, in his semi-conscious sleep was vaguely aware of the clatter of the iron on the iron stand, of the faint thud, thud on the ironing board.

Once roused, he opened his eyes to see his mother standing on the hearth rug with the hot iron near her cheeks, listening, as it were, to the heat. Her still face with the mouth closed tight from suffering and disillusion and self-denial, and her nose the smallest bit on one side and her blue eyes so young, quick and warm, made his heart contract with love. When she was quiet so, she looked brave and rich with life, but as if she had been done out of her rights.

'Listening to the heat'; 'done out of her rights' – those are instantaneous, intimate, non-literary observations. They are natural, personal and not considered. Personal to Lawrence, they become personal to us. The greater part of our observation of the world has no conscious purpose; from the point of view of the good life, society, our work and so on, it is refractory. It feeds the unorganisable soul. And the soul cannot be ordered about and cannot compromise: see the miner in *Jimmy and the Desperate Woman*:

'I'm nothing but made use of,' he said now talking hard and final to himself, and staring into space. 'Down the pit I'm made use of, and they give me a wage, such as it is. At the house I'm made use of, and my wife sets the dinner on the table as if I was a customer in a shop.'

'But what do you *expect*?' cried Jimmy, writhing in his chair.

'Me? What do I expect? I expect nothing. But I tell you what . . .' he turned and looked straight and hard into Jimmy's eyes. – 'I'm not going to put up with anything either . . . If I give in to the coalface and go down the mine every day to eight hours' slavery more or less, somebody's got to give in to me.'

He is an impossibilist: one of the stock comic characters or simply the obstinate brute; but he is a piece of nature and it is useless to argue with him. Lawrence writes of that part of our nature with which it is useless to argue. He shows us things carelessly, as they cannot help being:

A flat, shallow, utterly desolate valley, wide as a bowl under the sky, with rock-slopes and grey stone slides and precipices all around, and the zig-zag of snow-stripes and ice-roots descending, and thin rivers, streams and rivers rushing from many points downwards, down in waterfalls and cascades and threads, down into the wide, shallow bed of

[254]

the valley, strewn with rocks and stones innumerable, and not a tree, not a visible bush.

It is interesting to contrast a very consciously made novel like Bennett's *Old Wives' Tale* with Lawrence's *Sons and Lovers*. Both novels cover a lifetime of family life and untruthfully recreate English sentiment. Bennett feels from the outside. He puts down what he has known. He sympathises, pities and invents. And he condescends. In the mind's eye the characters of any novel can be measured for height, and Bennett's characters always seem to me small people, miniatures seen from a height as Bennett looks down upon them on the writing-table. The characters of *Sons and Lovers* are less complete in their detail, there is a blur in many of them so that we are not always sure of the focus; but they are life-size. They are as big as Lawrence is. He has got inside them until they have grown to normal size. We *follow* Constance in *The Old Wives' Tale*; we walk *with* Mrs Morel in *Sons and Lovers*. We are as uncertain as she is, from day to day. The very muddle of the narrative in this book with its puzzling time sequences, its sudden jumps backwards and forwards, gives us a sensation that is familiar and real; the sensation that life sprawls, spreads sideways, is made up of reminders and recapitulations, and sags loosely between one point of definition and the next. The Russian novelists had this interest in the loose texture of life whose crises begin so far away from their overt moment, and sometimes clean off the track of the expected drama. Not only that, they and Lawrence see that what we call a crisis in human relationships is a collection of crises, a rumbling and grumbling, a gabble and to-ing and fro-ing of human intercourse. Rarely does a crisis come to its final decisive outburst; nothing is final; we do not boil over, we leak away. Lawrence's sense of the life-size of people is his gift; it is also his weakness; but if we are to look for the virtues of a novelist we shall find them in those places where he is wriggling his way round his weaknesses. Lawrence is a muddling narrator, totally unskilled in construction; all right, he seems to say, let the living people drag on as best they can. They will move and compel because they live, because he will make us share their life in the collier's cottage, in the factory where Paul Morel works, on the farm where he spends his holidays. Instantaneously we shall breathe with them. And it is this power to make the reader's chest rise and fall, as it were, with the breathing of the characters in all the off moments, the lost hours, the indecipherable days of their life, that gives *Sons and Lovers* its overwhelming intimacy. There is no novel in English literature which comes so close to the skin of life of working-class people, for it records their feelings in their own terms. The description of the older son's death, the many scenes describing the father's halting resentment or remorse, little moments of daily life when the children hang round the father's chair, are beautifully done. Common English life wears the habit of things gone wrong, of awkwardness and frustration, and Lawrence touches this quality with faithful hands. To the fidelity and the submissive spirit of the early part of *Sons and Lovers*, he returned in only a handful of short stories of which the *Odour of Chrysanthemums* seems to me the most impressive. He wrote unanswerably well – and this is true of so many English novelists – only of the environment of his childhood.

Sons and Lovers goes wrong when Lawrence begins telling lies, that is to say when he starts arguing, as in the Miriam episode which is often boring and obscure. English novelists are afraid and ashamed of adolescence because, later in life, to be serious about oneself is considered priggish and conceited. The young prig is taken at his own valuation in French literature – see Stendhal and Flaubert's *Sentimental Education* – and is generally admired because the French respect the gradual formation of the mature nature. They are also interested in the formation of artists. But Lawrence grew up in a community and indeed in a country where the biography of an imagination embarrasses and is despised. I have always liked the Clara Dawes episode in *Sons and Lovers*, partly because it begins well, and partly for the grotesque scene where Clara's mother sits up belligerently determined to prevent the lovers from going to bed together. There is a guilty hang-dog humour and great truth of observation in this episode, although the character of Clara Dawes is overglorified by her sexual attraction to the author. Certainly *Sons and Lovers* is patchy – it was much rewritten – and English novelists who write autobiographical novels seem to plunge in and have no idea where to bring their life story to an end. Lawrence cheats about the story of his adolescence; the spirit of rebellion brought with it a shame not only of his shames but of his happiness. The suppressed secret is that the pressure of Paul's environment made him a snob. He half admits it, but only in discussion. It is never enacted.

Imagine Stendhal, the supreme portrayer of very young men in European literature, missing that.

To the English novel as a farm Lawrence made one or two important contributions. He brought in new subject matter. He put the reader more or less in the position of writing the novel for himself, by giving him instantaneous observation and by slackening the strings that move the puppets. Like the Russians, he made the days of his characters' lives more important than the plot. From Meredith he developed the notion that people are not individual characters, but psychic types, flames lit by the imagination. They do not (after *Sons and Lovers*) develop, but leap higher and higher until they strike their certain fate. This conception of character was used in another sense by Marxist satirical writers who followed him. Lawrence gave novels a subject instead of a plot. Especially in his short stories, Lawrence used a summary, stand-still description of character, so that the whole story (see *The Prussian Officer*) is a series of dramatic assertions and reiterations about two men, culminating in the tragedy. This tense and even frenzied method was made tolerable by the colloquial sound of his own voice, i.e. the reader believes he is instantly saying it all himself. This manner arises because Lawrence is often clumsy and commonplace in straight narrative and because he is too egotistical and lacking in humility to know what people are really like; it accounts for much that is boring incantation. But to the short story, which can support the *tour de force*, these dramatic summaries are an excellent addition, though we must allow, as in Meredith, for a certain air of theatre. Like Meredith (and Hall Caine) Lawrence writes at the top of his voice and is railing against his subject. Only his extraordinary sense of physical life and his lapses into accidental nature save these rhetorical stories. In the end, the mining stories, things like *The Fox* and the rich irony of pieces like *The Rocking Horse Winner*, survive whole. For the rest, we must dip for his descriptions. Once he was uprooted from the Midlands and his class he ceased to be a novelist; he was a traveller, a remarkable letter writer, brilliant in discoveries which he buried under pulpit loads of nonsense about people and a life he could not tolerate.

A Pole in the Far East

A good deal of our culture as well as our capital is locked up in the Far East. Looking at those investments again, one fingers the scrip with the last-minute love of a nervous shareholder. They have acquired an unreasonable personal value, even though the bottom may have fallen out of the market. Stevenson, Conrad, Maugham – we read them in the bleak perspective that opens in the dirty wake of the Pacific war. Literature has followed the flag. What sort of literature? The answer is – hopelessly romantic literature, that is to say romantic literature without hope, literature filled with guilt.

What about Conrad? I have been reading some of the Malayan novels again, after a lapse of twenty years – books like *Almayer's Folly*, *The Outcast of the Island*, *The Rescue*, *Lord Jim* and shorter pieces like *Youth*, *The Secret Sharer* and *Freya of the Seven Isles*. What struck me was how vague and even falsified these books were in my memory. The atmosphere one remembered, of course. But even stories like *Almayer's Folly* were muddled in my mind like the memory of a dream. They *are* dreams, these books. Their colour, their unreal major characters, their insectile minor ones, their tortuous action, live in the compelled twilight of a hypnotic dream, a dream that slows down to the intense heat of nightmare. Here and there the temperature becomes colder and, as in the yacht episode of *The Rescue*, you touch that *Tatler*-like actuality of the Maugham subject; but it is only for a moment. The half-light comes down, the shadow and the sun-shot fog of Conrad's ruminations cloud the obvious issue, and the dream thickens in the head. Afterwards it will be difficult to say once more what *was* the issue Conrad had in his tentative, evasive, suspicious and rather exasperated imagination.

This is not true of Conrad's best work. *Youth*, for example, is one of those stories where elaboration did not get to work. It is a story of sunrise and not sunset in the East; and I think all Conrad's best work is in what may be called his straightforward daytime manner. *Youth* has little of the famous Conrad atmosphere and mystification. It is not written in sackcloth and ashes. In *Youth* one is led only to the frontiers of that fog which possess so many of the writings whole. (I put *The Secret Sharer, The Nigger of the Narcissus* and *Typhoon* in the *Youth* class.) That *Youth* leads you to the edge and does not engulf you is, of course, Conrad's intention. It is a story of travel, not of arrival. The capture of a first marvelling glance of the longed-for East, the song of an immaculate delusion is all its object. The wrecked sailors have arrived exhausted at Bangkok:

Further out old Mahon's face was upturned to the sky, with the long white beard spread out on his breast, as though he had been shot where he sat at the tiller; and a man, all in a heap in the bows of the boat, slept with both arms embracing the stem-head and with his cheek laid on the gunwale. The East looked at them without a sound.

I have known its fascination since [Conrad never knew when to stop, but as the next passage foreshadows the rest of his Malayan work, it needs to be quoted]. I have seen the mysterious shores, the still water, the lands of brown nations, where a stealthy Nemesis lies in wait, pursues, overtakes, so many of the conquering race, who are proud of their wisdom, of their knowledge, of their strength. But for me all the East is contained in that vision of my youth. It is all in that moment when I opened my young eyes on it.

Destiny, Nemesis, those dirty inquisitorial familiars who turn up on the deck lifting their hierophantic palms behind the backs of Conrad's simple Devonshire sailors or half-cracked traders in the jungle of the archipelago, do not appear until the last page of *Youth*. I often wish it could have been the same in books like *The Outcast* or *The Rescue*. For though Destiny is a laconic conception, it is one which encourages wordiness in novelists; and the reader of Conrad feels a baffled irritation, as if he were a commercial traveller getting heavy admonitions every day from an importunate head office. One ought not to feel like this, and I am convinced that one would not do so in Conrad if one felt that Conrad's Destiny was endowed with the sublime and indispensable gift of inevitability. Conrad's Destiny seems to be an idea poisoned by exile, dwarfed by a bad temper and embittered by a failure to meet great men worth destroying. To characters like Willems, in *The Outcast*, or Almayer, Destiny can only be nasty, as the police are nasty to tramps.

The valuable side of Conrad's conception of Destiny is that it is a sense of history – a sense of history which the Slavonic imagination has made theatrical. Conrad seems to have turned the Polish exile's natural preoccupation with nationality, history, defeat and unavailing struggle, from his own country to these Eastern island. The natives are a defeated people. They remember massacre. They live under the Dutch and English overlords, swindled by the Arab traders, with eyes and hearts in the past. They turn, as the conquered must, to intrigue, which is relieved on rare occasions by sudden ecstatic, despairing loyalties. They turn from corruption to nostalgia for the sublime virtues. Babalatchi, the one-eyed scoundrel, diplomat and philosopher who wrecks the outcast, and shakes but does not break the fortunes of Lingard, is one aspect of the temperament of the defeated; Hasim, its aspect of fierce hope, poetic loyalty and timeless experience of evil. It has been said that Conrad does not draw the Malay as he really is, and that his Malays are idealisations. They are really transplantations from Polish history. They are an exile's interpretation of the bloody history of the islands, and of the historical situation at the time he was writing. And knowing the situation, he knows the intrigue – how it is something which goes far deeper than human idiosyncrasy and private jealousy or ambition, but is the ferment of a defeated society itself. Conrad's gift for handling intrigue in his novels is at its best when it has real intrigue to work on – such as can be seen in *Almayer*, *The Outcast* or even in the stodgier *Rescue*; when this gift of his is turned from society to psychology, that is to say, to a man's intrigue with himself, as in *Lord Jim*, then Conrad is less successful. The sense of intrigue grinds down human motive too fine.

I say 'less' and then hesitate. As Conrad exhausted his early material, his imagination naturally turned to improvisation. He who had been, in the sense of my earlier use of the word, an historical novelist, now became a prophetic one. What is a prophetic novelist? He is hard to define, but I should say he is one to whom human beings are timeless; they are souls and not persons, and good and evil and fate fight for the possession of their future. This element had always been in Conrad's work and gave his realism the distorting stamp of a spiritual vision. But, on the whole, in

[260]

England we reject the prophets; it is so obvious that they are disappointed men. We find this in D. H. Lawrence, whose affinity with Conrad is very close. Lawrence is angry about sex; Conrad is angry about honour. They are both inordinately conscious of failure, the one of the failures of sex, the other of the failures of loyalty. An undertone of guilt runs through their writing. When we consider Lawrence's diatribes about sexual failure we answer that there are a lot of other things to do besides going to bed; and when we consider Lord Jim, running away from job after job, on the waterfront, because of his treachery to himself, or Tom Lingard confused by the crassness of human nature, we feel that human nature has quite enough on its hands without crying because it isn't perfect. The soul may be marred by the evils it commits, but it is far more commonly marred by the failure *to admit* that it has committed evil, or by the mania of admitting too much. Conrad's problems are esoteric. Lord Jim was not a good man gone wrong, but, like the outcast, a compulsive neurotic. The charge of morbidity originally brought against Conrad must be sustained; his morbidity was in fact the irritant which created the Conrad fog.

The excellences of Conrad do not lie, in my opinion, in that dubious Romantic over-world, but in his real observation, in his feeling for real life. In the big elaborated books he is always avoiding his climaxes, and on principle – when he doesn't, you get the impossible dialogue between Lingard and Aissa at the crisis of *The Outcast* – in the daylit stuff he is never worried by these false climaxes. They are mixed in with the stream of life: the captain going into his bathroom in *The Secret Sharer*; the 'old man' admitting the existence of the fire in *Youth*. The normal portraiture is astonishing. Conrad's eye for the soul, before the soul ran away with him, is tremendous. Here is the first glance at a City man; not Conrad's best at all, but how percipient he is:

> His clear pale face had under its commonplace refinement that slight tinge of overbearing brutality which is given by the possession of only partly difficult accomplishments; by excelling in a game, or in the art of making money; by the easy mastery over animals and over needy men.

Or the portrait of the 'old man' in *Youth*:

> He was 60 if a day; a little man, with a broad, not very straight back, with bowed shoulders and one leg more bandy than the other, he had

that queer twisted-about appearance you see so often in men who work in the fields. He had a nut-cracker face – chin and nose trying to come together over a sunken mouth – and it was framed in iron-grey fluffy hair, that looked like a chin-strap of cotton wool sprinkled with coal dust. And he had blue eyes in that old face of his, which were amazingly like a boy's, with that candid expression some quite common men preserve to the end of their days by a rare internal gift of simplicity of heart and rectitude of soul.

The genius of Conrad was directed to intensifying the life of a man or a woman and to contrasting that intensity with the slacker, ragged commentary of their real circumstances. His characters live on the edge of a great anxiety, an unbearable exasperation, a threatened loss. They are faced by the sardonic refusal of life to play up. He got this last effect even in his picture of native life. Take this scene from *The Outcast*, in the native compound where Babalatchi has been talking about the tragedy of his race. He is sitting among the domestic noises:

> From under the house the thumping of wooden pestles husking the rice started with unexpected abruptness. The weak but clear voice in the yard again urged, 'Blow up the embers, O brother!' Another voice answered, drawling in modulated, thin sing-song, 'Do it yourself, O shivering pig!' and the drawl of the last words stopped short as if the man had fallen into a deep hole.

That slackening of the tension, that anticlimax is typical Conrad. It is the grimace of the bear with the sore head; but, when it is done in terms of real life, it is dramatically perfect.

The Irish R.M.

――――

'Did you ever eat my grandmother's curry?' said Flurry to me, later, as we watched Bernard Shute trying to back his motor into the coach house.

I said I had not.

'Well, you'd take a splint off a horse with it,' said Mrs. Knox's grandson.

The Aussolas woods were full of birds that day. Birds bursting out of holly bushes like corks out of soda-water bottles . . .

Yes, there is no doubt about it: the *Experiences of an Irish R.M.* are your grandmother's curry. They are a light literature which takes the skin off your tongue, the breath out of your lungs and – to quote a favourite phrase of the authors – 'puts your eyes on sticks'. And then, even those sentences I have quoted have a horse in them. There are horses on nearly every page of this book, malicious and heroic creatures of deep character which seem to be out on a perpetual hunt. It is indeed hard to know which are the people and which are the horses. Perhaps they are all horses. Flurry Knox would willingly have become one. So would his grandmother. Most of the Somerville and Ross women, with their rain-fiercened complexions, their long heads and box-like bodies, their sprained ankles and strained shoulders and their frightful high spirits, are unimaginable without their chestnuts and greys. Their pace is spanking, their talk flies out like froth. It was not a freak of satire that in the beginning of Anglo-Irish literature, Swift drew the Houyhnhnms as the master race; he was simply recording the national religion.

With a malice and madness that match the Somerville and Ross characters, the Irish climate acts as a mirror to their antics. The frost is crisp on the fallen leaves in the bare woods, the woodcock rise out of the trees or the snipe zip away over the frozen bogs into a sky of Neapolitan enamel;

but within an hour rain is spouting off the hat brims of the sportsmen, and days of mugginess or downpour jail the mind and drive it to thoughts of the whiskey bottle, the long meditated intrigues of tribal life, the treacheries and despondencies of the lonely colonial wits. A world that was on the verge of becoming Turgenev's turns into a jumble of Surtees, Tom Moore and *The Fall of the House of Usher*; and half the farce lies not in the horse-play, but in the ingredients themselves. We begin to laugh before we start reading and that is apt to mean that we stop laughing before the end, and wonder why the authors dare not be quiet for a moment. What would happen if they were quiet? What did the Major do when he was trying not to keep pace with Flurry Knox's mare or (far more complex) follow Flurry's mind? There were mornings, we are told, when he spent the time in the gentlemanly task of writing letters. What was he writing? Or what was old Mrs Knox thinking as she sat with her stockinged feet in the fireplace, oblivious of the good feed for poultry which always lay under the Louis Quinze chairs on her drawing-room floor at Aussolas, and lulled by the pompous cooing of the doves which flew into the room and perched on the picture frames of the smoke-kippered portraits of her ancestors? Unless there is an answer to these questions there is force in the criticism of Somerville and Ross that used to be made in the sour, wan yellow dawn of the Irish revival, when it was a crime for anyone to laugh in Ireland, unless they laughed for the right party; the criticism that these ladies were simply purveying the stage Irishman to English magazines and winding up the old parish hurdy-gurdy of Irish farce.

And, of course, they were. The tradition of Irish farce is permanent. The stage Irishman is permanent. He is as permanent as the Irish narrative gift and the use of words as an intoxicant. The puritanism of Maynooth and Merrion Square cannot put its gooseflesh on the warm native fancy. But there is more than one Somerville and Ross. An early novel, written before the *R.M.* made them popular, does attempt to say what the Anglo-Irish were like between one View Hallo or one petty sessions and the next. That book is *The Real Charlotte*. I don't want to be a spoil-sport, especially now the *R.M.* has been canonised by *Everyman*, and I write as a foreigner, but *The Real Charlotte* did something which had not, up to the Nineties, been done in Irish literature. It portrayed the Anglo-Irish with the awful, protracted mercy of the artist. It 'placed' them as no novelist had thought of 'placing' them before; as surely, for example, as Mrs Gaskell knew how to place her world in *Wives and Daughters*. I do not mean that *The Real Charlotte* is as sound or as accomplished a novel as Mrs Gaskell's. It was a first novel, awkwardly built and, like so many Anglo-Irish writers, the authors never got rid of an amateur, almost a juvenile streak; but *The Real Charlotte* was a beginning of great promise. One went to Ireland looking for the characters of the Irish R.M.; one found oneself, thirty years after it was written, surrounded by the disquieting people of this one serious novel.

The scene is Galway and the long loch beyond it. There is the big estate on the lake. There is the agent's modest place near by. There are one or two absurd houses. And then, back in Dublin or the worst end of Bray, there is the genteel squalor of Francie Fitzpatrick's life. In England Francie would be a lower-middle-class beauty on the make; in the Ireland of the Nineties she is a beautiful hoyden, a tomboy and a flirt, coarse-grained yet childishly unaffected. If she ceases to be prim she will be a mess; a noise without innocence. She goes to Galway to hook a husband, preferably a mindless young officer who will mend her family fortunes. Too ingenuous to be called an adventuress, too beguiling to be thought entirely vulgar in her man-hunt or her manners, Francie will never find her place.

In England, the class system would provide repose for Francie's soul; in Ireland the tribe system, with its withering snobberies, punishes her at every point of her social climb. She is doomed to be second-rate, to attract second-rate behaviour. And though *The Real Charlotte* is a novel about jealousy and the never-ceasing intrigue and treachery of Irish life, its main stuff is this snobbery. Not a plain, excluding snobbery that tells us where we may go and where we may not, but a snobbery that is in the blood. Not a snobbery versed in distinguished ancestors only, but a snobbery be-devilling the character with the pretensions of second cousins and the mildewed memories of better times. It is a snobbery that has become the meaning of life. It permeates everything: good sense, idealism, hatred, tenderness, religion – even pity. We must allow something for the fact that this book is written in the Nineties; and when the Dysarts wince because Francie keeps her gloves on at tea, we are charmed by the comedy of the manners of a period. Anglo-Irish snobbery was pretty genial about such quaintnesses. But underneath this were the inturned passions of a small, defensive and decaying colonial society: Francie is a social casualty in the everlasting skirmish with the other Ireland. Only by exaggerating their exclusiveness and creating low comedy around them can the Ascendants keep their ascendancy.

Of course, we may read in the Dysarts a devotion to manners, sensibility and excellence; but the devotion is so defensive that it becomes negative. It has become a mania like Lady Dysart's acrostics. And the mania spreads downwards. So Lambert, the land agent, wishes to impress as much as the Dysarts do, and his desire turns to self-destructive hatred of them. He ends by trying to cheat them. Francie's cousin Charlotte, who is half peasant and whose clumsy mind can yet devise labyrinthine schemes, bids too high on Francie's behalf, hopes to capture a Dysart for her, and is betrayed by the girl. In a curious passage, the young Christopher Dysart feels a mingled envy and pity for Francie's vital but ill-judged insouciance; and Francie, to whom he is incomprehensible because he is too far above her, rubs her low breeding into him in order to cause him pain and, by causing pain, to bring him nearer to her understanding. Again, Lambert enjoys making a fool of Charlotte by arousing her feelings in order to exploit her purse and cut a figure. Snobbery creates victims to pity, and all these characters discover the strange pleasure of forgiving the people they have injured. If they all only knew it, the logical end of their mania was the sensitive, tedious ineffectuality of Christopher Dysart. In him there is a masterly portrait of the lifeless, hopelessly neutral, decent young aristocrat of the period.

Cousin Charlotte has been compared to Cousin Bette and, allowing for the change to the raw Irish scene, there is something in the comparison. The money motives, the class structure, are there. To these elements one must add a peculiar psychological quickness to catch the perversity of human feeling and the cross-ruffing of Fate: for example, in her jealous plottings Charlotte cannot bear not to give herself away. Feeling presents itself as intrigue. Francie is not the only flirt; they are all flirting with every dream and issue. They cross one another and double-cross themselves. Pity becomes hatred, hatred turns into tenderness, tenderness into cruelty. We watch with fascination while the dull, irritable land agent with his debts, his horses and his ailing wife, ingeniously plots his own downfall.

All this must be visualised against an animated scene which is broken by some of the *R.M.* comedy that was to come. The absurd pleasure launch on the lake, tooting away at the least convenient moment, and its inane comment on the people is a delightful invention. The awful English officer and Don Juan is an excellent cad. The middle-class carpet dance is a fearful romp. A hundred small touches keep this small world in a continual ripple and change of colour. On the other hand, the chorus from peasant life is boring. Fifty years of politics lie between us and these skirling *commères*, with their high-pitched domestic life and the loquacity of displaced Elizabethans. But the narrative writing has the Irish visual gift, so bold in its metaphors, so athletic in its speed, as if tongue and eye were racing against each other. There is the native animism:

> Tall brick houses, browbeating each other in gloomy respectability across the street.

The shrewd is punched home by the baroque:

> She was losing hold of herself; her gestures were of the sort that she usually reserved for her inferiors, and the corners of her mouth bubbled like a snail.

And then, though there is hardly a breath of Irish politics in the story, they are there by implication. For the characters are exclusively the Irish Protestants and their isolation gives a strength to the strokes in which they are drawn.

The faults of *The Real Charlotte* are obvious. The national malady of not 'letting on' what you are up to enables the novelist to catch the changeableness of human character; but towards the end the elusive becomes the frantic. It is unforgivable that Francie is killed out riding; especially as her death, one is pretty sure, is due to the profound snobbery of the authors. There is no way of making a lady of her, so she has to be killed. But after one has removed the old-fashioned trappings, the irony, the insight and portraiture of this novel, show that Anglo-Irish society might have got its Mrs Gaskell, if the amateur tastes of the discursive colonial had not breezily ridden the chance off the page.

An East End Novelist

'And the effect is as of stables.' My eye has been often baffled by lack of the words which would define the poor streets of the East End, as they used to be before the war; and here in Arthur Morrison's *Tales of Mean Streets*, which were written in 1894, I find it. Those acres of two-storey houses which lay below the level of the railway arches of Bethnal Green, and which stood like an alien stretch of unfeatured ploughing beyond the Commercial Road, are particularised at last. The mind has won a foothold in a foreign city.

For, east of Aldgate, another city begins. London flattens and sinks into its clay. Over those lower dwellings the London sky, always like a dirty window, is larger; the eyes and hands of people are quicker, the skins yellower, the voices are as sharp as scissors. Every part of London has its smell, and this region smells of rabid little ships, bloated factories, sub-let workrooms and warehouse floors; there is also the smell of slums, a smell of poverty, racy but oftener sour; and mingling with these working odours, there arises an exhalation of the dirty river which, somewhere behind these streets and warehouses and dock walls, is oozing towards the flats of the Thames estuary like a worm. The senses and the imagination of the stranger are so pricked by this neighbourhood that he quickly gets a fevered impression of it; it will seem dingier or more exotic than it really is. And when we turn to literature for guidance, we are even less sure of what we see. For the literature of the East End is very largely a stranger's literature. It lies under the melodramatic murk and the smear of sentimental pathos, which, in the nineteenth century, were generated by the guilty conscience of the middle classes. They were terrified of the poor who seethed in an abyss just beyond their back door. The awful Gothic spectacle of hunger, squalor and crime was tolerable only as nightmare and fantasy – such as Dickens provided – and the visiting foreigner alone could observe the English slums with the curiosity of the traveller or the countenance of the anthropologist. And there was another difficulty. Philanthropy, for all its humbug, did slowly have its effect on the public conscience in every generation, so that it was genuinely possible to say 'things have changed'. The Ratcliffe Highway went. Limehouse had been purged, and there arose a romantic literature of the East End, based on a riotous evocation of the bad old times. The stranger's literature was the literature of a time which first strengthened morale by giving the reader a fright, and then went on to make the fright pious, sentimental and picturesque.

But what of the literature written from within the East End, the really saturated literature which has been lived before it has been written? For many years now, in accounts of the realism which came into fashion at the time of Gissing, I had noticed a recurring title: *Tales of Mean Streets*, by Arthur Morrison, and lately I have been put on to *The Hole in the Wall* and *A Child of the Jago* by the same author. They are written from the inside and they have extraordinary merit; *The Hole in the Wall* strikes me as being one of the minor masterpieces of the last sixty years. It has the kind of fidelity to scene that the modern documentary writers have sought, yet is never flattened, as their work is, by concern for conditions; let us not allow 'conditions' to deflate the imagination or argue away the novelist's chief delight and greatest difficulty: the art of constructing and telling a story complete in itself. For unless he learns this art, a novelist neutralises his power of observation, his power to observe more than one thing at a time, his power of writing on different planes and varying perspectives, and discriminating among the accumulated incrustations of fact that clog an impressionable mind. Arthur Morrison had this power. 'Conditions' were in his bones; his books stand apart from the worthy and static pathos of Gissing, from the character albums of the writers of low comedy, from the picturesque and the nightmare schools. Mr Morrison's early novels and sketches are often modest in their art, like the work of someone learning to write, but they have an anthropological drama of their own, and, at any rate, are not more awkward than Bennett's *Tales of the Five Towns*. What is missing from these novels is the modern novelist's sardonic exposure of the economic rackets which make the poor man poor; the brutality of poverty is subject enough for Mr Morrison. A book like *A Child of the Jago*, the story of a young thief in Bethnal Green, shows a sharp-eyed and intimate knowledge of how East End society used to behave as a society, of how it used to deploy its cunning and uphold its customs. Injustice is done and the President of the Immortals has already abandoned the hopeless scene to the human instinct of self-preservation when Mr Morrison comes in to record it. Out comes the cosh, the street wars begin, the half-naked harpies run at each other with broken bottles, the pimps and fences step over the bodies of the drunks who lie, pockets turned inside out, in the gutters. It's a world of sullen days in backrooms with the baby lying half dead on the bed and the hungry women gaping listlessly at the empty cupboards, while the men go out in search of loot and drink and come back with their eyes blackened and their belts ready to flay the undeserving family. I have picked out the seamier side of *A Child of the Jago* not to gloat over the horrors but to indicate the material. Such incidents are not raked into the book without discrimination; these novels are not pools of self-pity in the Gissing manner; nor are they worked up with that sadistic touch of angry ecstasy which Dickens brought to his pictures of poverty. In Mr Morrison's book slum life is the accepted life, a dirty but not a turgid stream. In their position, you say – as one ought to say of all human beings – these people have lived, they've kept their heads above water for a spell. Man is the animal who adapts himself.

A Child of the Jago describes the brutal, drunken, murderous London of the late nineteenth century which used to shatter the visiting foreigner and send him home marvelling at English violence and English hypocrisy. Its picture of the street wars is unique. *The Hole in the Wall* raises this material to a far higher plane of narrative. Here is a thriller set in Dockland, where the filthy river, its fogs and its crimes, stain the mind as they did in *Our Mutual Friend*. Every gas-lit alley leads abruptly to some dubious business. The average thriller takes us step by step away from probability. It strains away from likelihood. *The Hole in the Wall* belongs to the higher and more satisfying kind, which conducts us from one unsuspected probability to the next. Mr Morrison has employed what is, I suppose, the classical method of writing this kind of book; he shows us the story mainly through the eye of a young boy. The child goes to live with his grandfather who keeps a pub at Wapping and there he gradually discovers that his heroic grandfather is really a receiver of stolen goods. The old man comes by a wallet containing £800 which has been robbed from a defaulting shipowner – who has been murdered – and the plot is made out of the attempts of various criminal characters to get this money back. The merit of the book lies in its simple but careful reconstruction of the scene – the pubs and gin-shops of the Old Ratcliffe Highway, the locks and swing bridges, the alleys and gateways of Dockland with their police notices, the riverside jetties and their lighters, the way over the marshes to the lime kilns. I take it to be a mark of the highest skill in this kind of novel that nothing is mentioned which will not have, eventually, an importance to the tale; and that the motives for action arise in the characters and are not imposed on them by the need of working up a mystery and creating suspense. We do not know what their next step will be, because these people are still ruminating upon it themselves. Marr, the absconding shipowner, disguises himself as a sailor, but forgets that he will blab if he gets drunk; Dan Ogle, who merely intends to take his watch, gradually sees that murder will be necessary if the £800 is to be taken; the blind fiddler, who does not mind very much being double crossed, thinks otherwise when he is assaulted and ridiculed as well as cheated. And Mr Morrison succeeds with them because he shows them to us, first of all as ordinary shady characters muddling along the path of shifty illegality, and then suddenly faced by a new, a more terrible temptation and jumping at it.

The Hole in the Wall moves calmly from one major scene to the next; there is no sagging of the narrative. We see Marr, stunned and tottering, led like a broken marionette between his murderers. They are bawling at the tops of their voices so that, in the night, passers-by will think they are drunken sailors helping a pal, instead of murderers, dragging an almost lifeless body to the river. We see the body fished out – and what a remarkable piece of description that is. It 'tells' – as Henry James used to say – because of the very homeliness of the boy's narrative. (There is a lesson to the modern tough writers here. They lose their effect because they are tough all the time. They do not allow us to have the homely, frightened, law-abiding emotions. They do not allow us the manly fear, and they lose the interest of moral conflict.) And then there is the tremendous scene where the blind fiddler takes his revenge on Ogle, the murderer. He is hiding in a lime-quarry. At night the fiddler gropes across the marshes to the shed where Ogle is sleeping:

[271]

He had been gone no more than a few seconds, when the snore stopped. It stopped with a thump and a gasp, and a sudden buffeting of legs and arms; and in the midst arose a cry; a cry of so hideous an agony that Grimes the wharf-keeper, snug in his first sleep fifty yards away, sprang erect and staring in bed, and so sat motionless for half a minute ere he remembered his legs and thrust them out to carry him to the window. And the dog on the wharf leapt the length of its chain, answering the cry with a torrent of wild barks.

Floundering and tumbling against the frail boards of the shed the two men came out at the door in a struggling knot; Ogle wrestling and striking at random, while the other, cunning with a life's blindness, kept his own head safe and hung as a dog hangs to a bull. His hands gripped his victim by ear and hair, while the thumbs still drove at the eyes the mess of smoking lime that clung and dripped about Ogle's head. It trickled burning through his hair and it blistered lips and tongue, as he yelled and yelled again in the extremity of his anguish.

The blind man had blinded his persecutor.

One puts the book down looking back on the ground it has covered, seeing how economically it implanted that sinister Dockland of the Eighties on the mind, with a simple warmth and precision; how it mocked the little criminals, and then, suddenly, struck out into the squalor behind the drink in the snug bar and the bawling songs in the upper room; and how finally it pierced out with human fear and horror, without once cutting adrift from probability and an identifiable daily life. It is a masterly course, sustained, calm and never exaggerated. The style is a little old-fashioned, but it never scuttles away for safety into period dress. There was a London like this – we are convinced – mean, clumsy and hungry, murderous and sentimental. Those shrieks were heard. There were those even more disturbing silences in the night. Dockland, where the police used to go in threes, has its commemoration.

An Amateur

The businessman who is a novelist in his spare time, an occasional and amateur novelist, is a character who must always be envied by professionals. For here is a man who has avoided the treadmill of talent and the catastrophes which lie in the path of genius. The businessman who is a novelist is able to drop in on literature and feel no suicidal loss of esteem if the lady is not at home, and he can spend his life preparing without fuss for the awful interview. There need be no last-minute slapdash *à la* Dostoevsky; no years of painful groping among the hallucinations of the intellect, such as Flaubert suffered; no spiritual crises which will split a masterpiece in two; no flagging hackwork to patch the interval between one work and another. The amateur can afford to be thorough, and he usually is thorough precisely in those places where the professional slurs, skimps, and hopes for the best. But there is yet another advantage to be envied. I am not thinking of the solid income of the businessman whose leisure really *is* leisure and not a haunted escape from contracts and creditors; I am thinking of the businessman's solid character. To have that and yet also to have the gift, to know that the gift can never play the devil with his life – those seem to be outrageous advantages.

The novels of J. Meade Falkner, an almost forgotten writer of the late Nineties, bring such reflections to the mind. Falkner was not a businessman novelist of the Italo Svevo size; but he has his small place. *The Nebuly Coat* and *The Lost Stradivarius* are mystery stories tinctured by scholarship and are now, I think, too slow and unmysterious for our taste – the last war hurried the pace of these things – but in *Moonfleet* he wrote a story of adventure that will have a permanent place among the minor *genre* pieces of our literature. A word about Falkner, first of all. He was a most remarkable man. By taste and education a scholar whose researches in archaeology, folklore, palaeography, architecture, church music and medieval history earned him a papal medal and many honours at the

[273]

Universities, Falkner spent all his life in Armstrong Whitworth's, whose chairman he was during and after the last war. He was a brilliant diplomatist and negotiator with foreign Governments. He travelled all over the world for his firm. He said that he owed his versatility to his medieval mind, and in her preface to the abridged Penguin edition of *The Nebuly Coat*, Lady Longford says that he applied the same minute care to his reports for Armstrong Whitworth and his researches in the Vatican library. In the Civil Service the various mind has been common; in the bustle of industry it is rare. And during his packed career, Falkner wrote works of learning and these three novels.

The Nebuly Coat and *The Lost Stradivarius* recall the books of Sheridan Le Fanu, but they are not on the level of the Irish master. Falkner lacked Le Fanu's psychological curiosity and the uneasiness of his imagination. Where Le Fanu was skilled in disturbing the mind, Falkner, with the habits of research, spoiled things by setting our minds at rest. It is true that the character of Westray, the young architect in *The Nebuly Coat*, is peculiar, and that he is distressed about the morality of shielding an impostor who is possibly a murderer; but the episode is so obscure that I cannot help suspecting Westray's real motive was snobbery. He thought it blasphemy to expose a lord or to throw doubt upon the records of Somerset House and the College of Heralds. Again, in *The Lost Stradivarius*, there is a suggestion of wicked practices in the occult. Le Fanu would never have descended to anything so gentlemanly and so scholarly as the suggestion that the habits of Medmenham Abbey had had a secret revival. When Le Fanu's characters are haunted by guilt, the guilt is guilt, not a connoisseur's lucky historical find. If either of these two novels of Falkner's are attractive light reading, it is because of their antiquarianism and because of the precision of their setting. We are at the beginning of that passion for antiques which started in the nineteen-hundreds, I suppose, and which so oddly foreshadowed the genteel auctioning off of heirlooms which swept Britain and Europe after the last war. *The Nebuly Coat* is an antique in itself. With wonderful verisimilitude, Falkner invented a cathedral town and worked out a carefully documented and imaginary catalogue of its family stains and historical dilapidations, and he hinged his plot on no less a matter than the technical delicacies of architectural restoration. There is also some heraldry in this book and, in *The Lost Stradivarius*, a good deal of musical scholarship. This material, and his use of it to create an atmosphere, interest us a little now, for he wrote with clarity; but Falkner showed up to this point small sense of character or narrative. This is a mark, so often observed, of the diligent amateur. No professional would document his work so well; but no professional would throw it all away on uninteresting people.

Moonfleet is another matter altogether. Here is a novel which has the sustained excitement, if not the richness of character, of the best work of Stevenson. It is a brilliant *pastiche* of eighteenth-century adventure, limpid, tender and running over the complicated score of its great detail without ever striking a wrong note or a superfluous one. How true the note always is. Pedantry has vanished. Now when Falkner is describing the history of the wicked Mohunes and the legends of their wickedness and burial in the church beside the sea; when he describes how the tides flood the crypt and the evils that come from it; and later on, when he troubles us with an account of the disused marble quarries of Dorset and the habits of the quarrymen, he pours these things into a story which flows more swiftly on, because of them, to fresh eddies of excitement. The elements of detection and mystery are multiplied. We want to know about those quarries as badly as we want to know about the escaping smugglers who have gone to earth in them. A whole coast with its cliffs, its marshes and its shingle roaring in the storms, has become urgent to us, such is the life which Falkner can impart to topography. These descriptions cannot be skipped, for Falkner achieved here, with an apparent ease, the art of gradual revelation. It was the eighteenth century's great lesson to narrators who had not yet been disorganised by the cult of nature, and who therefore did not throw in a ton of scenery for emotion's sake. Nature was used and useful, and the gradual disclosure of its usefulness was an invaluable accompaniment to the voice of narrative. This is apparent in writers as widely different as the circumstantial Defoe and the melodious Abbé Prévost. There is something of the latter's tone in Falkner's writing, a modest candour, which sets the young hero a little apart from the too stalwart ranks of boy heroes, and gives a tenderness to the circumspect descriptions. Here is Falkner's picture of the country into which the boy and the smuggler escaped after their climb up the cliff face. They are on the edge of the abandoned quarries:

We had left the stony tillage fields, and the face of the country was covered once more with the closest sward, which was just putting on the bright green of the spring. This turf was not smooth, but hummocky, for under it lay heaps of worthless stone and marble drawn out of the quarries ages ago, which the green vestment had covered for the most part, though it left sometimes a little patch of broken rubble peering out at the top of a mound. There were many tumbledown walls and low gables left of the cottages of the old quarrymen; grass-covered ridges worked out of the little garden-folds, and here and there still stood a forlorn gooseberry bush or a stunted plum or apple tree with its branches all swept eastward by the up-channel gales. As for the quarry shafts themselves, they too were covered round the tips with the green turf, and down them led a narrow flight of steep-cut steps, with a slide of soap-stone at the side, on which the marble blocks were once hauled up by wooden winches. Down these steps no feet ever walked now, for not only were suffocating gases said to beset the bottom of the shafts, but men would have it that in the narrow passages below lurked evil spirits and demons . . . We waited a few minutes and then he took me in his arms and began to descend the steps, back first, as one goes down a hatchway.

That is a fairly static description, a breathing space in the action of the story. Yet how it moves, how it flows and coils like the water receding along the snaky course of one of those southern estuaries that Falkner liked to write about. And the same, simple, inevitable movement is in the passages of action. This is the scene at the end where Elzevir loses his life in trying to rescue the boy on the terrible Chesil Beach.

I saw the string of men lashed together and, reaching down as far as man might, to save any that came through the surf, and heard them shout to cheer us, and marked a coil of rope flung out. Elzevir was by my side and saw it too, and we both kept our feet and plunged forward through the quivering slack water; but then there came an awful thunder behind, the crash of the sea over the wreck, and we knew that another mountain wave was on our heels. It came in with a swishing roar, a rush and rise of furious water that swept us like corks up the beach, till we were within touch of the rope's end, and the men shouted again to hearten us as they flung it out. Elzevir seized it with his left hand and reached out his right to me. Our fingers touched, and in that very moment the wave fell instantly, with an awful suck, and I was swept down the beach again. Yet the undertow took me not back to sea, for amid the floating wreckage floated the shattered maintop and in the track of that great spar I caught, and so was left with it upon the beach thirty paces from the men and Elzevir. Then he left his own assured salvation, namely the rope, and strode down again into the very jaws of death to catch me by the hand and set me on my feet.

But the secret of the success of *Moonfleet* does not lie first of all in its ingenious and masterly unveiling of an adventure; nor even in the naturalness of it all. The secret, I think, is that Falkner makes us feel for the church and village of Moonfleet something of that touching emotion which we have had for a place we have lived in and unaccountably loved in its smallest particular. He has hit upon our love for place and on the feeling that, in such a place, great happenings may start as innocently, but as irreparably, as spring water bubbles up from the earth to start a river. And once he had struck this note he sustained it. Not once does it falter. It grows clearer and stronger like a rising wind, like the high note of *Treasure Island*, which never loses its eagerness, or the grave and ominous accent of *The Fall of the House of Usher*.

I do not rank *Moonfleet* with these tales, for it has not their scope. Falkner was no great maker of characters. The boy-narrator and Elzevir the smuggler, who slowly adopts him in place of his dead son, are simple beings; not wooden, not lay figures indeed, but simple. They grow a little, experience makes them, and the dumb growth of their affection into an austere and self-sacrificing love is a moving undertone to the story. Theirs is not the conventional relationship of partners in adventure. One sees the passage of time reversing, or at least modifying, their attitude to each other. But outside of these two there is nobody. In this book, Falkner does not attempt what he could not do excellently; and like one of those small academic paintings in which we detect the flash of a minor master, *Moonfleet* arrests the mind because it has satisfied the eye. We have seen something that is small, perhaps, but exquisitely, affectingly well done.

Two Writers and Modern War

And so good-bye to the war. I know not how it may have been or may be to others – to me the main interest I found (and still in recollection find) in the rank and file of the armies, both sides, and in those specimens amid the hospitals and even the dead on the field.

This passage comes from *Specimen Days*, from those pages where Whitman described his work in the hospitals during the American Civil War. The interest of Whitman's pages about this war lies in the fact that he is the first to reveal a modern attitude. He stands at the breaking point with the past.

The American Civil War was the first modern war. It is true that the Crimean War, some eight years earlier, has resemblances with the American conflict. There is the awakening of public concern for the care of casualties, a concern which had grown with medical knowledge. But the Crimean War was fought in a small area. It was fought by professional soldiers – the British commander-in-chief directed operations from his private yacht to which he returned to dine and sleep every night – and the casualties, though heavy, were less than half of those suffered in America, where a million men died in the field, the hospitals and the prison camps. The Civil War involved everyone, the armies became conscript armies almost at once. The professional soldiers were put to the task of training the man in the street. Similar conditions, it will be said, existed in the Napoleonic wars – for Napoleon was the first to use conscription on a great scale. But the Napoleonic army was the Grande Armée. The conscript was transformed by the professional and national notions of Glory and the impulse of the Revolution. He was, in a sense, a party man and not a citizen in military dress. And then, when we read the memoirs of those wars, in English or in French, we notice that they are the work of men bent on the military career. They have the professional officer's outlook. Gleig – a

[278]

subaltern of Wellington's – who wrote an account of his adventures in the Peninsula, is typical of them. One can imagine Gleig reborn in the Sixties and exclaiming at the moral deterioration of his profession, once it is overweighted by every Tom, Dick and Harry. There is a loss of style and manner, both in action and in the narratives written afterwards. The precise horrors of war are sometimes mentioned in the classical records but, generally, rhetorical clichés are preferred: carnage, slaughter and so on.

If Gleig were to return and read Whitman's notes, he would first be struck by the importance given to the casualties and the hospitals; and then by the unprotected nakedness of human feeling. The classical manner was not inhumane; but it put military dignity and professional virtue first. It was the manner of leaders. War, the most lawless of activities, was given a frame of decorum; you might not always fight by the code of honour, but a code of honour existed and, above all, you spoke and wrote in accord with it. The British troops sacked San Sebastian and fired at the officers who tried to stop them; but Gleig in *The Subaltern* speaks in the voice of a gentleman when he describes and deplores the event. There is no suggestion that war is a human tragedy. This suggestion is not made until the civilian fights. He cannot shrug his shoulders and say, 'C'est la guerre.' He is stunned by his own fears, stupefied by his own atrocities, amazed at his happiness, incredulous at the point of death. When all people are at war, no code, no manner, can contain the experience. The nearest writers to Whitman are Tolstoy and Erckmann-Chatrian – it is interesting to note that they were all writing about war at the same time – but Tolstoy's ironical pacifism and Erckmann-Chatrian's mildness and peaceableness are a branch of the main stream of popular feeling. They are not, like Whitman, the stream itself. The *Histoire d'un Conscrit de 1813* was written in 1864. It has been called *l'Iliade de la peur* and it portrays the pathos of the conscript's situation. The tragedy of the conscript is a passive one: that a quiet, peaceable man like himself should be killed. But in Whitman – as in Wilfred Owen – the tragedy is not passive; it lies not only in what is done to a man but in what he himself does and in what happens to him inside. When we compare these things with the sentiment of Erckmann-Chatrian we see that these authors are propagandists concerned with society. The freshness of their document is deceptive. They describe the Napoleonic wars with wonderful verisimilitude; but the wars are not taken direct from life. These writers have digested the moving simplicities of old men's hearsay. They are propagandists with an uncommonly delicate ear. They write to warn opinion in the fond domestic parlour behind the little shop.

Compared with them, Whitman does not know his mind. He is all over the place. He is the public. It is typical of *Specimen Days* that its first picture of the war is of the news spreading in the streets at night. The emotion of the street catches him. He is not intoxicated with patriotism but he does not deny the message of the pennants and the flags in the street. He is the man in the parlour who goes out into the street and loses his head. He feels the herd instinct. Two great wars have made us guarded, and when we read *Specimen Days* and especially the poems called *Drum Taps*, we resist that old-fashioned war. The sun has faded the defiant and theatrical photograph, and paled the headlines to a weak-tea brown. The uniforms are shabby. We suspect Whitman's idea that out of this a nation is born; it sounds like the cracked bugle and slack drum of propaganda. And yesterday's propaganda puts no one in a flurry. Yet, in all this, the loquacious Whitman is right. It is the bewildering thing in all his work, that this dressed-up egotist with all the air of a ham actor is always half-right when he is most dubious. He is the newspaper man who reflects the ambiguous quality of public feeling. His virtue is that he begins on the pavement and that, like the streets, he has no shame and no style. Excitement and incantation take the place of it. The soldiers straggle into Washington after the defeat at Bull Run:

> The men appear, at first sparsely and shame-faced enough, then thicker, in the streets of Washington – appear in Pennyslvania avenue, and on the steps and basement entrances. They come along, in disorderly mobs, some in squads, stragglers, companies. Occasionally, a rare regiment, in perfect order, with its officers (some gaps, dead, the true braves), marching in silence, with lowering faces, stern, weary to sinking, all black and dirty, but every man with his musket, and stepping alive; but these are the exceptions. Side-walks of Pennsylvania avenue, Fourteenth street, etc., crowded, jamm'd with citizens, darkies, clerks, everybody, lookers-on; women in the windows, curious expressions from faces, as those swarms of dirt-cover'd return'd soldiers there (will

they never end?) move by; but nothing said, no comments . . . Amid the deep excitement, crowds and motion, and desperate eagerness, it seems strange to see many, very many, of the soldiers sleeping – in the midst of all, sleeping sound. They drop down anywhere, on the steps of houses, up close by the basements or fences, on the sidewalks, aside on some vacant lot, and deeply sleep. A poor seventeen- or eighteen-year-old boy lies there, on the stoop of a grand house; he sleeps so calmly, so profoundly. Some clutch their muskets firmly even in sleep. Some in squads; comrades, brothers, close together – and on them, as they lay, sulkily, drips the rain.

All that effort to produce one last remarkable phrase – that is Whitman.

After this the reality begins. And the reality, as the first modern war drags on, is the casualty list. In the classical narratives men are merely shot. Sometimes they are blown up. The aftermath was not minutely described. 'Bloodshed', 'carnage', generalise it. Whitman, too, uses those words but with all his voice. And he went round the hospitals and saw the gangrene, the amputations, the unspeakable wounds. He smelt the ether. Saw the tiptoe walking. The screens put round. He saw the stretcher cases lying out in the rain and glad to be cooled by it. He knew men crawled under bushes to die by inches. He took down the last words and wrote letters for men too weak to write. The men were not sorry for themselves. They talked very little. They had become detached and incredulous. Thousands, he knew, died and were never identified. It struck him, when he saw the burial trenches, that the typical soldier of this first modern war was 'unknown'.

That discovery marks the beginning of the modern attitude to war. We write as followers, not leaders. And though Whitman likes the heroic act, the message in the leader's eye, enjoys seeing the President ride past with his escort of cavalry and feels the public emotion of the 'great convulsive drums', he writes more surely when he goes back to the rank and file, when he recovers his sense of anonymity. (Odd that this huge and often so flaccid egotist should be able to puff himself large enough until he is identified with all the people and lost in them: it is his paradox.) It is his paradox, too, that doggerel and the real thing traipse along together like the blind leading the blind, unable to see, unable to stop. In avoiding literary jargon, he easily wallowed in the tear-jerking stuff of small town In

Memoriam notices – to emerge from the bathos with perhaps one line or
two worth writing:

'Grieve not so, dear mother' (the just-grown daughter speaks
    through her sobs,
The little sisters huddle around speechless and dismay'd)
'See, dearest mother, the letter says Pete will soon be better.'

Alas, poor boy, he will never be better (nor may-be needs to be
    better that brave and simple soul),
While they stand at home at the door he is dead already,
The only son is dead.

But the mother needs to be better,
She with thin form presently drest in black,
By day her meals untouch'd, then at night fitfully sleeping, often
    waking,

In the midnight waking, weeping, longing with one deep longing,
O that she might withdraw unnoticed, silent from life escape and
    withdraw,
To follow, to seek, to be with her dear dead son.

Blake could be simple, but he was never maudlin.
And there are the curious parallels with the poetry of the last war, the
same mixing of the romantic note with the realism. We turn from Wilfred
Owen's

    I am the enemy you killed, my friend,
    I knew you in this death.

to Whitman's

Word over all, beautiful as the sky,
Beautiful that war and all its deeds of carnage must in time be utterly
    lost,
That the hands of the sisters Death and Night incessantly softly wash
    again, and ever again, this soil'd world:
For my enemy is dead, a man divine as myself is dead,
I look where he lies white-faced and still in the coffin – I draw near,

Bend down and touch lightly with my lips the white face in the
   coffin.

Well, there it is. The set-piece has gone, the full-bottomed formal
patriotism of the eighteenth century, the episodic poetry of the early
nineteenth. The sense of occasion has gone. There are no more 'incidents
from the French camp', there is no loss of the *Revenge*, no *Charge of the Light
Brigade*, no *Burial of Sir John Moore*. The serving soldier has been outnum-
bered and swamped by the civilian soldier. The profession has been
drowned in the classes. Nor can we attribute the change to a decay of the
love of country – as critics tried to do at the beginning of the last war – for
Whitman was a bombinating patriot, yet he wrote no pieces of occasion of
that kind. *Drum Taps* describes the general scene, what the unknown and
anonymous man did and saw and how filthily he died. Patriotism has not
decayed; but the human being has emerged. He emerged first of all, it is
interesting to observe, in a civil war, a war of ideas; and in the country
which, to so many people, had seemed the Promised Land, where no
formal tradition of war existed. Whitman himself observed, in his confused
groping way, that a new way of warfare was necessary to America. A new
way of writing about war certainly emerged; perhaps that is what he was
trying to say.

It is worth while turning at this point to an American novelist who is the
child of the Tolstoy-Whitman movement, the child of the Crimea and Bull
Run. I am thinking of Stephen Crane and his book *The Red Badge of Courage*
which was published in the Nineties. The achievement of Crane was
individual and high, but in placing it we must now confess that it came in
on the Tolstoy wave; and that but for Tolstoy, it would never have been
written. There is an important difference of experience between Tolstoy
and Crane. In writing respectively about the Napoleonic and the American
Civil Wars, both writers were reconstructing wars they had not seen; but
Tolstoy *had* seen the Crimea, he had been a soldier, whereas Crane had
read Tolstoy but had never seen war at all when he wrote his famous book,
just as Defoe's *Journal of the Plague Year* was done by a writer who had
never seen the Plague. Crane became a war correspondent *after* his book
was written. It is in fact a romance or fable, subjective in impulse in the
tradition of Poe, Hawthorne, Melville and James. An American critic has

[283]

suggested that it was the fruit of a conflict of religious conscience and, indeed, the battle is compared with a mad religion and, at times, with a war of sectaries. The writer has been committed to fighting 'the good fight', is frightened by the open clash and then has to reassemble his self-respect out of doubt and lies and learn to live with his experience. This may or may not be true of the origins of the book; what matters is that, Tolstoy and war memoirs aiding, Crane has completely transposed himself into an imaginary eye-witness. One curious common emotion nevertheless unites the master and the disciple. They reject the formal, the professional and rhetorical attitude to war; they reject the illusions of the profession and the traditional litanies of patriotism; but they cannot quite conceal a certain sadness at the passing of these things. In Tolstoy one so often suspects the secret longing of the repentant, the too-repentant soldier.

The Red Badge of Courage is a *tour de force*. Crane starts a bugle call and sustains it without a falter to the end of the book. The scene is a single battlefield in the American Civil War, and the purpose of the novel is to show the phases by which a green young recruit loses his romantic illusions and his innocence in battle, and acquires a new identity, a hardened virtue. War has ceased to be a bewraying and befogging dream in his mind; it has become his world and he derives virtue from his unity with it. There is a second element in the story. To Crane a battlefield is like a wounded animal. The convulsions of its body, its shudders, its cries and its occasional repose, are the spasmodic movements and dumb respites of the groups of soldiers. There is not only the individual mind in the battlefield, but there is the mass mind also. Crane watches the merging of the individual with the herd. There is no plot in this book; it is a collection of episodes. We do not know which battle is being described or what are its objects. The rights and wrongs of the war itself are not discussed. No civilian and hardly a sight of the work of man, like a house or a cultivated field, comes into the picture. Few of the characters are named; the central figure is known simply as 'the young man'. The enemy are just the enemy, something fabulous and generally invisible in the blue smoke line of the engagement, terrifying and dragon-like at the worst, and at the best a singularity to be mistrusted. Who wins or loses is obscure. The whole thing is almost as anonymous as a poem or a piece of music and has the same kind of tension and suspense. For we are not specially interested in the mortal fate of the boy. We do not specially fear that he will be killed, nor do we privately hope he will cover himself with glory. Our eyes are fixed on something different in him; on each adjustment in his character as it comes along. At the end of this book, we say to ourselves, we too shall know how we shall behave when we discard our illusions about war and meet the reality. Romantically we fear or hope for battle as a way of singling ourselves out and dying; but underneath this daydream is the awe of knowing that battle is a way of living before it is a way of dying, and one in which we cannot calculate our behaviour in advance. It was one of the discoveries of the unrhetorical attitude to war in literature that even the men on the right side and in the just cause are afraid; and to Crane – an adventurous man who died young from the effects of going to see trouble all over the earth – the deep fear of fear was a personal subject.

This comes out in the first chapter of *The Red Badge of Courage*, where the young man is seen in the camp listening to the rumours and torturing himself with questions. He feels courageous but will courage stand? Will he stay or will he run in panic? These are overmastering questions. The first dead do not scare him, nor does the early uproar. He can stand the first attack and face the fear hidden in the wall of forest where the enemy lie, and after the frenzy of the first onslaught he lies for a few moments in the trench overcome by a sense of fellowship with his companions and experiencing with astonishment 'the joy of a man who at last finds leisure'. But, fixed on their intense personal problem, his heart and mind have not yet understood that while the imagination expects decisive and single answers, reality does not deal in such simplicities. The attack, to everyone's despair, is renewed. The second phase has begun. It is too much. The youth throws down his rifle and runs. Here Crane shows his power as a novelist, for in this part of the story he writes those dramatic scenes and draws those portraits which have given the book its place in the literature of war. This is where the dying soldier, walking white and erect like a rejected prince among his broken court, goes stiffly towards his grave. Crane was an observer of the ways of dying, but this death is one of the most terrible, for it is a progress to death:

> The spectral soldier was at his side like a stalking reproach. The man's eyes were still fixed in a stare into the unknown. His grey, appalling face

had attracted attention in the crowd, and men, slowing to his dreary pace, were walking with him. They were discussing his plight, questioning and giving him advice. In a dogged way he repelled them, signing to them to go on and leave him alone. The shadows of his face were deepening and his tight lips seemed holding in check the moan of great despair. There could be seen a certain stiffness in the movement of his body, as if he were taking infinite care not to arouse the passion of his wounds. As he went on he seemed always looking for a place like one who goes to choose a grave. Something in the gesture of the man as he waved the bloody and pitying soldiers away made the youth start as if bitten. He yelled in horror. Tottering forward he laid a quivering hand upon the man's arm. As the latter slowly turned his wax-like features toward him the youth screamed:

'Gawd! Jim Conklin!'

The tall soldier made a little commonplace smile.

'Hello, Henry,' he said.

If the boy's horror and quivering seem conventionally over-emphatic in that passage, the rest is not. Writers are always faced by two sets of words before they write; those which will draw a literary curtain over reality, and those which will raise the veil in our minds and lead us to see for the first time. Crane's gift for raising the veil is clear. The presence of 'spectre' and 'commonplace smile' in that portrait is imaginative observation at its best.

The book is filled with observation of this kind. Some is placed there by poetic intuition:

The sun spread disclosing rays, and, one by one, regiments burst into view like armed men just born of the earth. The youth perceived that the time had come. He was about to be measured. For a moment he felt in the face of his great trial like a babe, and the flesh over his heart seemed but thin. He seized time to look about him calculatingly.

But he instantly saw that it would be impossible for him to escape from the regiment. It enclosed him. There were iron laws of tradition and law on four sides. He was in a moving box.

This inner sensation of the experience is matched by wonderful, small phrases of verisimilitude: 'His *forgotten feet* were constantly knocking

[286]

against stones or getting entangled in briars.' Or there is this picture – how common it has become in modern realism, which Crane anticipates by thirty or forty years:

> Once the line encountered the body of a dead soldier. He lay upon his back staring at the sky. He was dressed in an awkward suit of yellowish brown. The youth could see that the soles of his shoes had been worn to the thinness of writing paper, and from a great rent in one the dead foot projected piteously. And it was as if fate had betrayed the soldier. In death it exposed to his enemies that poverty which in life he had perhaps concealed from his friends.

The only word a modern reporter would not have written in that passage is the word 'piteously'.

Toughness, that is to say fear of facing the whole subject, as Crane faced it, has intervened to make the modern writer's picture purely visual and inhumane – one remembers the turned-out pockets of the dead in Hemingway and his bravado about writing a natural history of the dead. The pathetic fallacy abounds in Crane's prose and we hear of 'the remonstrance' and 'arguments' of the guns; but for all the artiness – which belongs to the Nineties – there is pity, there is human feeling. There is a background of value and not a backdrop gaudy with attitudes. There is a quest for virtue – what else is the meaning of the young boy's innocent odyssey among his fears, his rages and his shames? – and not as one sees in Kipling, the search for a gesture or some dramatic personal stand which avoids the issue and saves the face. Crane ignores the actor in human beings, the creature with the name on the personal playbill; he goes – at any rate in *The Red Badge of Courage* – for the anonymous voice in the heart.

Cavalleria Rusticana

Growling still, he went off at an ambling pace of his mule, under the burning sun; a sun which split the stones now, and made the stubble crackle as if it was catching fire. At the gully between the two mountains he seemed to enter into a furnace; and the village on top of the height hanging above the precipices, scattered between enormous rocks, mined with caverns which made it seem suspended in that air, blackish, rusted, appeared abandoned, without a shadow, with all the windows open in the heat, like so many black holes, the crosses of the church towers trembling in the sun-dark air.

This is a description of the country north of Catania in the summer. I have taken the paragraph from one of the few descriptive passages in Giovanni Verga's Sicilian novel *Maestro Don Gesualdo*. Readers who have been in that heat-hammered island will appreciate the exactitude of Verga's eyes and perhaps the jolting of D. H. Lawrence's translation. The critic will observe how the phrases which do not directly describe heat most intensely convey the sensation of it. 'Furnace' is, of course, direct enough, and if you have looked down an industrial furnace, one of those long, ochreous, silent and unsurpassably intent corridors of short flame, the word will not be simply a conventional literary metaphor. Furnace is indeed the only word for a mountain gully under a vertical sun. But the thought of summer in Sicily brings back to my memory those black holes in the stone houses and the darkening, smoked-glass effect of tyrannical light. The sun is an enemy; earth and sun are at war with each other, and the candour of the Mediterranean scene is not disclosed until the evening when the battle has its sudden southern end or in the early morning, before it has begun.

Those are the hours when we can think of Theocritus and the Greeks.

But in the middle hours of the day images of violence come into our minds. We think of earthquakes, the *mafia*, the bombs and shots of the factions and all those tales of boiling jealousy, the Judas kiss of the duellists and the long knife lying in the flat of the hand. It was, after all, upon Verga's story, *Cavalleria Rusticana*, that Mascagni built his opera. The story was not romantic, southern hyperbole. We saw Sicilian violence transplanted in Chicago a few years after Verga's death, a violence still naïve, spontaneous and quite outside the range of our moral judgments. It belonged to an earlier culture than ours, and strangely enough to that pastoral world of the delightful Theocritus. The sweet notes of the reed were drawn from the lips of men enjoined to kill in certain psychological situations. But what went on behind the violence? What was life like in the broken streets of the mountain towns and villages? Verga, who had been born near Catania in the Seventies, came back from Naples when he was about forty to find out. His journey was one of those returns to the source which are commonly fruitful in the lives of artists. He was tired of writing novels about leisured people who make love to one another's wives and who go on chewing over the really not very astonishing sensations which they have detached from the meat of living. He had nothing new and certainly nothing brilliant to say about the subject. He came to Sicily to get back to something more important, which was going to be stark in the manner of Zola. And, first of all, Verga was very stark. *Cavalleria Rusticana* is an admirable, naked story, ruthlessly economical and as plain a piece of surgery on the passions as you could ask for. It is more than surgery; the more terrible Sicilian knife is at work. *La Lupa*, the story of a man-devouring peasant woman who has to be killed by her son-in-law, is another of the same kind. There is something superb, an excess which amounts to the poetry of pride, about these acts of transcendent psychological justice among people who are blinded by the rage of honour, amid starvation, crippling toil and rags.

Unlike Mérimée who looked at the violent and idyllic remnant of pastoral culture in the Mediterranean with the eyes of a connoisseur, Verga was committed. The Sicilians were his own people. He got back inside them. There was not much inside them, in our sense anyway, for they were southerners without introspection, black and white in their souls, like their light; but as a society they had a great deal. Verga planned to write five novels, each one to deal with a class in Sicilian society. The first dealt with the poor. (An American translation exists.) The second dealt with the people who are just above the masses; and this one, *Maestro Don Gesualdo,* was translated by D. H. Lawrence, who was just the man to feel an idiom. In this book we find what it is that lies behind the Sicilian violence. The answer, according to Verga, is more violence. Violence of tongue, violence of will, greed, push, scramble, gossip, the awful ruthless, comic, bitter, incorrigible barnyard belligerence of family life; fights for money, fights for food, fights for possession. Misery is the basis of it, the misery of poor land, the misery of the isolated towns where the nail-scratches of scandal and contempt are scrawled over everyone's life. The beautiful are the humble and submissive who refuse to join the fight; worse luck for them, they are kicked out and trodden on and their poor-spiritedness is a byword. So we should describe the people in Verga's novel and yet they do not distress us. Only the suburban townsman idealises the countryman and is shocked by the malignance of country life and its poisoned solitudes. Only the suburban townsman conveniently forgets that the countryman must fight for money and property like the rest of the world. Far from distressing us, Verga's people gradually take possession of our minds, seize us with their grasping hands, harangue us about their case until we are forced to see the point of it, and to see that here, in this ludicrous family screeching about pride, money, marriages, and ownership, something elemental is taking place. His people are able to convince us of this not merely because it is true but because Verga is a very considerable novelist. He has a rich range of mood, a pungency of metaphor; something in him is equal to the clamour of the heart; he has a comprehensive grasp of scene; and without being naturalistic he seems to be able to pull up people by the roots straight out of nature and put them, rife as they are, upon the page. They come out with such vocal, physical emphasis that at first one is stunned and deafened. Verga depends on the crackle of his dialogue and on an allusive atmosphere which each sentence creates. You have to watch that and keep your senses keen or you will miss his transitions. And then these Sicilians think and feel at the tops of their voices. Their bellies are 'full of poison', their mouths 'spit bile' – a vast amount of bile is spat in this book; Lawrence must have loved the anger of it – and in a few pages you will see people compared to vipers, wolves, hounds, tigers, wasps, pigs, cows, donkeys, scorpions and vampires, a whole menagerie. All this makes the early chapters trying until you acquire a kind of sardonic animal grin yourself; then things go splendidly.

You notice that Verga is not a regional novelist in the provincial sense of the word. *Maestro Don Gesualdo* is no more regional in this rather derogatory meaning than Turgenev was in *A Lear of the Steppe*. No, Verga is European and modern. His visual power, which is heightened by his constant use of peasant metaphor and his identification with the peasant mind, is very modern. This visual quality is one which literature has developed in order to fill the place previously taken by traditional, moral and religious generalisations; the traditional Catholic novel, for example, about Sicily had no need of this physical vividness. Verga, no doubt like Cézanne, supposed he was being scientific. Now the visual, oral style becomes monotonous, unless the human heat of the book grows until it becomes convulsive and momentous. And Verga's story does grow. We see Maestro Don Gesualdo, a common worker on the roads, in his first rise in the world. First his fight against his own family over their petty trade; then his marriage and the fight against his wife's aristocratic relations – they are a scarecrow lot of decayed aristocrats but not too grand to smell the main chance a long way off – then his fight against the town's jealousy of his wealth. And finally his fight against his daughter and her husband who is a duke. In that last fight Don Gesualdo attains the rigor of spiritual agony. The struggle begins when the cholera has driven his patriarchal family to the mountains. It develops when revolutionaries from Palermo incite the peasants to get back the common lands which he has taken. It gets the better of him when he has to fight for command not merely of his property but of his wife and daughter. He defeats his daughter but loses the wife who has never loved him. The whole world rises against him. They see his weakness. He is not a monster but, searching for power, he has forgotten he is capable of sorrow; and meaner people spring upon the shoulders of this man whose will has been exorbitant. There, it occurs to me, is the Sicilian subject as one sees it in Verga; exorbitance. A man must carry his passions to the extreme, and Fate, like a counter logic, will come down the road to meet and defeat him, not with one clean blow but a long, slow bludgeoning, beating him to his knees and then down into the dust of the greedy generations from which he sprung.

The intensity of Verga is achieved by dense detail. He is totally without rhetoric. Of a suspicious man he writes: 'Don Ferdinando, always after them, sewed to their heels, silent . . .' Of the Duke's servants in Palermo in the wonderful final scene when Gesualdo lies dying among the idle footmen in his daughter's grand house: 'An army of lazy rascals, lackeys and chambermen, yawning with their mouths shut, walking on tip-toe and serving you without saying a word . . .' Those phrases take one back to Browning's *Ring and the Book*. But thinking about this intensity has led me to forget Verga's comic gift. Verga saw the fantastic comedy of the family struggle. He saw the sardonic farce of Sicilian politics, and how much they depended upon local personality. The intruding priest, for example, who gets the men of property on to the revolutionary side so that they can save their property, is a real, slippery beauty. Who has not met that busy little ferret? Then there is the young Baron seducing the awful touring actress by sending her food to guzzle from his mean mother's larder; and there is the christening scene where all the relations get in their digs at the right point. They all hate Don Gesualdo, and very likely, they point out, the child is not his. An important point to notice in Verga's dialogue is that people do not always talk to one another. They declaim out of themselves.

Don Gesualdo kept on chatting with Cousin Zacco, each of them with his heart in his hand, oh so friendly! Then the baroness spat out the question that was boiling inside her:

'Is it true that your husband lends him money – on the quiet? – Have you seen him come here to him? Tell me, what do you know?'

'Certainly, certainly,' replied Don Gesualdo at that moment. 'You must take children as they come.'

To confirm this Zacco pointed to his own girls ranged in a row like so many organ pipes, modest and pleasing.

'Look you. I have five girls, and I'm fond of them all alike.'

'Why, of course,' replied Limoli. 'That's why you don't want to marry any of them off.'

Donna Lavinia, the eldest, threw an ugly look behind her. 'Ah, are you there?' said the baron. 'You are always ready, like the devil, in the litany, you are!'

All at once down in the square below there exploded the deuce of a noise of crackers . . . It was Santo, Don Gesualdo's brother, celebrating the baptism of his niece in that fashion, in his short sleeves, on all fours down there below, with a lighted fuse. Don Gesualdo opened the window to pour out a sackful of abuse.

'Fool! You'd have to be doing something! Fool!' The friends calmed him.

'Poor chap! Let him alone! It's one way of showing his pleasure.'

A novelist is tested by his power of sustaining long scenes and large groups of people and by his power of continual dramatisation. It is his duty to break a marriage, a birth, a death, or some enterprise into living fragments. This gift of fragmentation is given only to the greatest novelist; lacking it, the glib, second-rate ones are perhaps more quickly read. They are certainly quickly forgotten. But Verga is one of the great in this novel, a Balzacian. He sees a society, and that society working in men and women. Perhaps, like the Sicilian sun, he hammers his words too pitilessly on our heads and batters us with the theme of self-interest; but he has the space of the masters. I would say to any young novelist who wanted to shake himself into a fresh consideration of the art of the novel, to get hold of Verga quickly. When Italians boasted about him in Paris before the war they were not far wrong.

Poor Relations

The small house on the cliff of Passy, hanging like a cage between an upper and lower street, so that by a trick of relativity, the top floor of the Rue Berton is the ground floor of the Rue Raynouard, has often been taken as a symbol of the life of Balzac. The custodian of the house – now a Balzac museum with the novelist's eternal coffee-pot, his dictionary of universal knowledge and with his appalling proof sheets framed on the wall – shows one the trap-door by which Balzac escaped to the lower floor in the Rue Berton. Down it the fat breathless novelist of 41 went stumbling and blurting, like his own prose, to the Seine. Two houses in one, a life with two front doors, dream and reality; the novelist, naïve and yet shrewd, not troubling to distinguish between one and the other. Symbol of Balzac's life, the house is a symbol of the frontier life, the trap-door life of the great artists, who have always lived between two worlds. There Balzac wrote his letters to Madame Hanska in Poland, the almost too comprehensive, explanatory and eloquent letters of a famous and experienced writer who has the art, indeed the habit, of self-projection at his finger-tips; there, when the letters were posted, he went to bed with the docile housekeeper who was finally to turn round and blackmail him, and so provide him with the horrifying last chapters of *Le Cousin Pons*. At this house in the worst year of his life, the least blessed with that calm which is – quite erroneously – supposed to be essential to the novelist, Balzac wrote this book and *La Cousine Bette*, respectively the best constructed and the most fluent and subtle of his novels.

A new Life of Balzac was published in Paris in 1944. It is called simply *Vie de Balzac* and is by André Billy. This biography contains nothing new, but it gathers all the immense biographical material in a couple of volumes. Its detail is as lively and exhaustive as a Balzac novel; the manner is warm but sceptical, thorough but not dry. Very rightly, M. Billy looks twice and three times at everything Balzac said about his life, for he is dealing with

[294]

the hallucinations of the most extraordinary egotist in the history of literature. One can imagine a less diffuse biography; one in which the picture of his time played a greater part and where every detail of a chaotic Bohemian career was not played up to the same pitch. But given the gluttony of Balzac's egotism and the fertility of his comedy, one is not inclined to complain.

Like the tons of bronze and antiques – Balzac estimated the weight and value of himself with the care of an auctioneer's valuer – with which he darkened the house he finally took for Madame Hanska when he had got his hands on some of her fortune, the novels of Balzac weigh upon the memory. The reader is as exhausted as the novelist by the sheer weight of collection. One is tempted to see him as the stolid bulldozer of documentation, the quarrying and expatiating realist, sharpening his tools on some hard view of his own time. He seems to be stuck in his task. Yet this impression is a false one, as we find whenever we open a novel of his again. Balzac is certainly the novelist who most completely exemplifies the 'our time' novelist, but not by his judgments on his society. He simply *is* his time. He is identified with it, by all the greedy innocence of genius. The society of rich peasants brought to power by revolution and dictatorship, pushing into business and speculation, buying up houses and antiques, founding families, grabbing at money and pleasure, haunted by their tradition of parsimony and hard work, and with the peasant's black and white ideas about everything, and above all their weakness for fixed ideas, is Balzac himself. He shares their illusions. Like them he was humble when he was poor, arrogant when he was rich. As with them, his extravagance was one side of the coin; on the other was the face of the peasant miser. The cynic lived in a world of romantic optimism. We see the dramatic phase of a century's illusions, before they have been assimilated and trodden down into the familiar hypocrisies. To us Balzac's preoccupation with money appears first to be the searching, scientific and prosaic interest of the documentary artist. On the contrary, for him money was romantic; it was hope and ideal. It was despair and evil. It was not the dreary background, but the animating and theatrical spirit.

Balzac learned about money, as M. Billy says, at his printing works in the Rue du Marais. He expected to find that fallen aristocrat, the goddess Fortune of the eighteenth century; instead he found that in the nineteenth century the goddess had become a bourgeois book-keeper. His laundry bills, his tailor's bill, his jeweller's bills were mixed with the printing accounts. The imagination of the businessman is always governable; Balzac's was not. Financially speaking, Balzac was out of date. Like his father, who also was willing to work hard enough, he sought for Fortune not for Profit; far from being an example of Balzac's realism, his attitude to money is really the earliest example of his Romantic spirit. Balzac's attitude to money was that of a man who did not understand money, who could not keep it in his hands, the plagued spendthrift and natural bankrupt. His promissory notes were a kind of poetry in his early years; later on they became articles of moral indignation; in the end – to quote M. Billy's delightful euphemism, he lost all 'pudeur morale'. The creation of debts began as exuberance; it became an appetite, one of those dominant passions which he thought occurred in all natures, but which really occur only among the most monstrous egotists. Madame Hanska's fortune did not calm him. He went on buying here and there, incurring more debts, scheming without check. And the last people he thought of paying were his wretched relations and especially his mother. To her, he behaved with the hypocrisy and meanness of a miser and the worse he treated her the more he attacked her.

At this point it is interesting to compare Balzac with Scott whom he admired and consciously imitated. Madame Hanska's estate in Poland was for many years his visionary Abbotsford; the passion for antiques, the debts, and the crushing labour, the days and nights of writing without sleep, were Abbotsford too. Balzac saw himself as an aristocrat; Scott saw himself as a laird: they are by no means the first or last writers to provide themselves with distinguished ancestors. He went to the length of travelling to Vienna as a Marquis, with coronets on his luggage; it was ruinous, he discovered, in tips. But the honourable Scott was broken by debts; they drove him to work as a duty; they wore out his imagination. Balzac, on the contrary, was certainly not ruined as a writer by his debts. His debts were a natural expression of a voracious imagination. One may doubt whether any of his mistresses moved his inspiration – though clearly their maternal sympathy was necessary – but one can be certain that Balzac's imagination was ignited by the romance of purchase, by the mere sensual possession of things. The moving impulse in his life was, as he said, the discovery of the 'material of civilisation', the literal materials; and although he considered this a scientific discovery, it was really a mysticism of things. Every object he bought, from the famous walking-stick to the museum pieces, represented an act of self-intoxication that released the capacity – so vital to the creative artist – to become unreal.

It is easy, as M. Billy says, a hundred years after, to blame Madame Hanska for delaying her marriage with Balzac and for adding the afflictions of reluctance and jealousy to his life of appalling labour, but obviously he was possessed by a kind of madness, and he would have stripped her of all her property. One understands her hesitation after reading his later and maniacal letters about money and things.

> Je suis sûr qu'au poids il y aura, dans notre maison, trois mille kilogrammes de cuivres et bronzes dorés. C'est effrayant, le bronze! Cette maison est, comme je te le disais, une mine de cuivre doré, car mon ébéniste me disait qu'il y en a mille kilogrammes. À huit francs le kilo, à vendre aux chaudronniers, c'est trente-deux mille francs de valeur réelle. Juge de la valeur, en y ajoutant le valeur d'art.

Ruinous. There was no 'valeur d'art'. His brain gave way under the strain of his schemes and combinations. Yet, *Le Cousin Pons* and *La Cousine Bette* were written in that year; and when Pons makes the fortune of his persecutors with his collection of antiques which they had despised, one sees Balzac avenging himself for the complaints of his mistress. No; he was not weighed down by debts, in the sense of having his talent ruined by them. His extravagances floated him on the vital stream of unreality. He was the Micawber for whom things were only too continuously 'turning up', a Micawber who worked. Balzac and Micawber are, it is interesting to note, contemporary financiers of the period.

The ox-like groans, the animal straining and lamentation of Balzac, his boasting, his bosom-beating letters to women like Madame Carraud, before whom he parades in the rôle of the indomitable martyr of circumstance, have created an imaginary Balzac. One sees – his own phrase – 'the galley slave of fame'. A rather different impression was formed by his contemporaries. Once he had put his pen down he was childishly gay:

> Naïveté, puérilité, bonté, ces trois mots reviennent sous la plume de tous les contemporains. Le portrait de Balzac que nous a laissé le poète

des *Meditations* se trouve confirmé en tous points par celui qu'a tracé George Sand: puéril et puissant, toujours envieux d'un bibelot et jamais jaloux d'une gloire, sincère jusqu'à la modestie, vantard jusqu'à la hâblerie, confiant en lui-même et dans les autres, très expansif, très bon et très fou, avec un sanctuaire de raison intérieure où il rentrait pour tout dominer dans son œuvre, cynique dans la chasteté, ivre en buvant de l'eau, intémpérant de travail et sobre d'autres passions, positif et romanesque avec un égal excès, crédule et sceptique, plein de contrastes et de mystères . . .

Some indeed found him grubby, ill-kempt and uncouth. Hans Andersen hardly recognised the dandy of the evening party in the touselled Bohemian of the following day. There was a Rue Raynouard and a Rue Berton in his appearance and in his nature.

Instant in his admirations and schemes, Balzac was like a child for whom everything happens *now* and in a *now* that is connected with no future. Certainly with no future of incurred obligations. The burden of Balzac's life is not apparent until one sees him at work; and then we see that not debt but his method of writing was the fatal aggravation.

In a sense Balzac is a made, or rather re-made writer. There were times when he rushed down to the printers at 11 o'clock at night and they took the chapter of his novel page by page as he wrote it. But such moments of inspired exhibitionism were rare. In general Balzac strikes one as being the gifted talker whose mind congests when he sits down to write what he has just spoken. No doubt he could have turned out the cheap thrillers of his early period as easily as he spoke; but with his other books the process was agonising. There would be several versions of the text, each one smothered with erasures and additions; chapters were put into different places, more chapters were sandwiched in between. Pages and pages scrapped, more pages added. The historian of the contemporary scene had only to go out of his door to see a new thing to squeeze somewhere into the text. And this was not the end of the confusion and the struggle. Once the printers had sorted out the manuscript and had produced their galleys, the ungovernable author began a hardly less drastic process of destruction and reconstruction. Night after night, from midnight until seven – and these were merely regular hours. There were days and nights of almost continuous labour without sleep. Il ne savait pas sa langue, said Gautier. The time spent and the printers' costs would have eaten seriously into earnings not already mortgaged by extravagance.

Let us return to the double house in the Rue Raynouard and look once more at the two great novels Balzac wrote in that small room above the trap-door, when his brain was already breaking under the appetites he imposed upon it. Open *Le Cousin Pons*. There is the expected chapter, that roughly and in a domineering way generalises and clears a space for the characters in the Parisian scene. And then, like a blow in the face, comes the brutal sentence: 'On n'a jamais peint les exigences de la gueule.' One stops dead. What on earth has poor Pons done that his fastidious habit of dining at the expense of his better-off relations should become a treatise on the trough? Comically treated, of course; Balzac examined the dossier of human nature with the quizzical detachment of some nail-biting, cigar-stained Chief of Police who is going rapidly up in the world; who has seen so many cases; who thanks heaven that he does not make the moral law and that a worldly Church stands between himself and the Almighty. Passion, even when it is a passion for the best food, always becomes – in the experience of the Chief of Police – a transaction; Pons trades the little errands he runs on behalf of the family for the indispensable surprises of the gourmet. In the pursuit of that appetite he is prepared to ruin himself where other men, more voluptuously equipped by nature, will wreck themselves in the capture and establishment of courtesans. Sex or food, money or penury, envy or ambition – Balzac knows all the roads to ruin. If only men and women were content with their habits instead of craving the sublimity of their appetites.

But *Pons* is a type. He is a poor relation. In that isolation of a type, one detects the main difference between the French and English novels. The English novel has never lived down its early association with the theatre, and has always had to wrestle with a picaresque or artificial plot. But even if this had not been so, we could never have been a nation of moralists. Our instinct is to act; our interest in morals is a practical interest in results. The French novel – and how obvious this is in Balzac – is dominated on the contrary by a sense of law. Behind the individual lies the type, behind the act lies a law governing the act. The French novelists are the lawyers of the passions; they proceed from the prototype to the particular and then carry it back for comparison. Subtle and litigious in tactic, they conclude that human experience, however bizarre, however affecting, can never escape the deep inscription of its category or evade the ordinance of some general idea.

To an English taste there must always be something arbitrary in such a structure. Natural Protestants, we resist a determinism so Roman and so Catholic. But we must be abashed by the double reference in which French fiction is so rich. Look at the delightful Pons. His character has so many departments. He is an old man, an ugly man, an outmoded but respected musician, a dandy survived from an earlier period, a collector of antiques, a poor man, a careful man, a simple man who is not quite so simple – see his valuable collection of pictures and bric-à-brac cunningly picked up for next to nothing – a sexless man, a gourmet, a hanger-on, shrewd in his own world, lost in the society into which he has grown up. Pons is the kind of character who, inevitably, becomes fantastic in the English novel simply because no general laws pin him down. He would become a static 'character'. Instead Balzac takes all these aspects of Pons and mounts each one, so that Pons is constructed before our eyes. We have a double interest: the story or plot, which is excellent in suspense, drama and form – this is one of Balzac's well-constructed novels, as it is also one of the most moving – and the exact completion, brick by brick, of Pons and his circle. There are the historical Pons – he is an *incroyable* left-over from the Directoire – the artistic Pons, the financial Pons, the sociable Pons, the moral Pons, and in the end Pons dying, plundered, defiant, a man awakened from his simplicity and fighting back, the exquisitely humble artist turned proud, sovereign and dangerous in his debacle. Pons is a faceted stone, and part of the drama is the relation of each facet with the others. Thus his fantastic dress is related, via dandyism, to his small, esteemed, but out-of-date position in the world of art. That adjoins his love of good living – picked up in smarter days – which links up with the solitariness and social spryness of the bachelor, his timidity and his sexual innocence. We have the portrait of a man who in every trait suggests some aspect of the society in which he lives. The history of his time is explicit in him. Yet he is not a period piece. A period piece is incapable of moral development and the development of a moral theme is everything in the novels of Balzac, who facilitates it by giving every character not merely a time and place, but also an obsession. Among English novelists only Henry James, George Eliot and, on occasions, Meredith, move their drama not from incident to incident, but from one moral situation or statement to the next. (In Meredith's *The Egoist* one recalls the tension, tightening page by page, that precedes the accusation: 'You are an egoist.') So it is with the story of Pons. He is snubbed by his ignorant relations who do not realise even the financial value of his collection of antiques and pictures. In consequence, rather than be dropped or ridiculed, he gives up his beautiful dinners and retires to taste the blessings of the concierge's motherly cooking and pure friendship with the delightful Schmucke, a man even more simple than himself. At that point an English novelist might have given up. The lesson was clear. But Balzac, like Henry James, saw that drama lies in the fact that there is no end to moral issues. For him – recomplication, further research. And so, just as Pons is getting a little tired of his landlady's cooking, society tempts him again. His relations apologise, and Pons is one of those good men who cannot bear other people to say they are in the wrong. He conceives a grandiose scheme for returning good for evil. He will find a husband for the unmarriageable daughter. He will announce the enormous value of his collection and leave it to her in his will. Result, gratitude? Not a bit of it. The family is longing to wipe out the memory of their humiliating apology by vengeance, and when the marriage scheme collapses, they finish with Pons. Once more we have come to a natural end of the novel. But once more Balzac recomplicates. Pons falls into the grip of his concierge, who has suddenly become covetous now that she has two harmless, childless, womanless old men in her power; and his downfall is ensured by the very innocence of Schmucke, who cannot believe evil of anyone.

Balzac is the novelist of our appetites, obsessions and our *idées fixes*, but his great gift – it seems to me – is his sense of the complexity of the human situation. He had both perceptions, one supposes, from his peasant origins, for among peasants, as he was fond of saying, the *idée fixe* is easily started; and their sense of circumstance overpowers all other consideration in their lives. A character in Balzac is so variously situated in history, in money, in family, class and in his type to begin with; but on top of this Balzac's genius was richly inventive in the field least exploited by the mass of novelists: the field of probability. It is very hard to invent probabilities. This simply means that Balzac knew his people as few novelists ever know their characters. The marriage scene in *Le Cousin Pons* for example: there we have the rich German all set to marry the daughter of the family. The awful facts of the 'régime dotal' – a phrase repeated in pious chorus by the family with the unction usually reserved for statesmen like 'God is Love' – have been accepted by him. He has merely to say the word. At this tense moment the German electrifies everyone by asking the unexpected question: Is the girl an only child? Yes, she is. Then he must withdraw. A man of 40 is an idiot who marries a girl who has been spoiled in her childhood. She will use the fact that he is so much older than herself to prove she is always right. That way lies hell. The respectability of the institution of marriage is in itself no satisfaction.

But *Le Cousin Pons* moves from one surprising probability to the next, backed by the massed ranks of human circumstance. The change in the character of the charming, motherly landlady of Pons who suddenly takes on the general professional character of the concierges of her district creates another powerful situation – powerful because so isolated are we, so obsessed with possibility and hope, that the probable is unperceived by us. The last thing we care to believe is that we are governed by type and environment. Balzac believed nothing else.

I do not know that I would put anything in *Le Cousin Pons* above the first part of *La Cousine Bette*, though I like Pons better as a whole. Pons is the old bachelor. Bette is the old maid. The growth of her malevolence is less subtly presented than the course of Pons's disillusion, because Balzac had the genuis to show Pons living with a man even simpler than himself. One sees two degrees of simplicity, one lighting the other, whereas Bette stands alone; indeed, it may be complained that she is gradually swamped by the other characters. She is best in her obscurity, the despised poor relation, the sullen peasant, masculine, counting her humiliations and her economies like a miser, startling people with her bizarre reflections. They laugh at her and do not conceive the monstrous fantasies of her painful virginity. And we are moved by her in these early pages when she is hiding her Polish artist, shutting him in his room like a son, driving him to work; or, later, when Madame Marneffe gives Bette the shabby furniture. Bette is a wronged soul; and when her passion does break it is, as Balzac says, sublime and terrifying. Her advance to sheer wickedness and vengeance is less convincing, or, rather, less engrossing. It is a good point that she is the eager handmaid and not the igniting cause of ruin; but one draws back, incredulously, before some of her plots and lies. Acceptable when they are naïve, they are unacceptable when they fit too efficiently the melodramatic intrigue of the second part of the book. But the genius for character and situation is here again. La Marneffe, rooted in love's new middle-class hypocrisy and growing into a sanctimonious courtesan, is nicely contrasted with the besotted Baron who had grown up in an earlier period – 'between the wars' in fact – when the fashion of love was brisker and more candid. That situation alone is a comic one. The diplomatic farce of La Marneffe's supposed pregnancy is brilliant. The lies and short repentances of the sexagenarian Baron are perfect. Only Adeline does not, to my mind, come off in this novel; and here we come upon Balzac's rather dubious advocacy of marital fidelity. He sounds as little convinced as a public speaker haranguing his way to conviction. Adeline's pathetic attempt to sell herself, in order to save her husband's fortunes, is embarrassing to read; are we to admire virtue because it is stupid? Balzac protests too much.

No one has surpassed Balzac in revealing the great part played by money in middle-class life; nor has anyone excelled him in the portraits of the parvenu. Henry James alone, coming at the zenith of middle-class power, perceived the moral corruption caused by money; but money had ripened. It glowed like a peach that is just about to fall. Balzac arrived when the new money, the new finance of the post-Napoleonic world, was starting on its violent course; when money was an obsession and was putting down a foundation for middle-class morals. In these two novels about the poor relation, he made his most palatable, his least acrid and most human statements about this grotesque period of middle-class history.

The Bohemian

The English visitor to the Continent is always surprised by the part played by students in society and in politics. They have even become the subjects of music and literature by a sort of natural right which, I believe, has never existed in England since the time of Chaucer. The drinking songs and the tales of Heidelberg, a book like Murger's *Scènes de la Vie de Bohême*, have no parallel in England; and the explanation seems to be that the English universities preserved the monasticism of the Middle Ages but cut themselves off from the medieval spirit. A student tradition, one that goes back to Abélard and Villon, is not nurtured in seclusion; it depends upon poverty and mingling with the ferment of the town. This has not been in the character of any of our older universities; for us the student does not exist. We have never idolised youth. Our idol, oddly enough, has been the public school boy, and when a Frenchman asks us for the parallel to Murger's book, we are forced to hush up the fact that *Charley's Aunt* is the only play about an undergraduate, and to divert his attention to the enormous importance of *Tom Brown's Schooldays*. Among the Anglo-Saxons it was the unsecluded Americans, rather than ourselves, who took to the Quartier Latin as ducks to water before the last war.

Like many English readers, when I was young I owed my first notions of the Quartier Latin to the sentimental and watered-down works of Thackeray, Du Maurier and W. J. Locke. These fanciful imitators of Murger were said to be harmless; while the sentiment, the tears and the picaresque farce of Murger were condemned as misleading. A Bohemia like his had never existed. Or, if it had, it certainly existed no more. Only lately I have read his *Scènes de la Vie de Bohême*, and I regret, as usual, that I did not go to the fountainhead before. Some of it is tedious, but the sketches have very amusing moments. Murger has that acute Parisian sense of comic pose, a kind of wit of situation as well as a wit of words and ideas, that crisply feathers the surface of life as he skims along. But the interesting thing about *La Vie de Bohême* is less the story than its success. Not entirely does Murger owe that to the accident of Puccini's opera. Murger had already made a very successful play of the book before Puccini took it up. A suggestive light is thrown by a remark of the Goncourts which they put down in their *Journal* in 1856:

> 'When Murger wrote La Vie de Bohême,' they said, 'he had no notion that he was writing the history of a social world which was to become a power within five or six years, yet that is the fact today.'

The Bohemians, they say, bar the way to the well born who are damned as amateurs. 'The advent of Bohemia means the domination of socialism in literature.' They should have written 'the domination of that new uprooted class "the intelligentsia"'.

If socialism does owe something to Bohemia, what Bohemia really did to artists and writers in the long run was, of course, to isolate them from society. Not socialism, but art for art's sake came out of that fruitful myth and produced in figures like Gauguin, Verlaine and Modigliani an isolation more haggard and stark than anything the frittering Murger and his little circle ever knew. Murger went to seed among the obliging tears of a small Parisian clique. The Goncourts maliciously note his first tailcoat, and his official break with the hungry past when he set up at the Café Riche. He became a journalistic slave, and in the words of his own Rudolphe honestly said, as we all have:

> 'Je veux bien consenter à regarder le passé, mais ce sera au travers d'une bouteille de vrai vin, et assis dans un bon fauteuil. Qu'est-ce-que tu veux? – je suis un corrompu. Je n'aime plus que ce qui est bon.'

He had, the Goncourts remarked, one of the largest funeral processions of his time, and among the mourners of the poet of hunger was Théophile Gautier, who talked, not very suitably, of the influence of cattle-cake on the flavour of steak, all the way to the cemetery.

Where the Goncourts' sharp nose for tendency was right was in detecting the enormous potential of publicity in the early idea of Bohemia. Murger, who was half-German, had given a halo to romantic disorder and, by the end of the century, Puccini and English best-sellers like Du Maurier and W. J. Locke had carried the idea triumphantly into every vicarage and suburban villa. If you sat on the floor or boiled an egg unassisted you became a Bohemian. The romance of the Fifties had become the myth of the century. The English Bohemians of Du Maurier and Locke are no longer poor students. They are the sons of rich parents. The famous Trilby is a model, but she comes from a distinguished Irish family! Du Maurier's Laird – the only agreeable character in a dreadfully coy book – has his Broadwood and his furniture sent over from England to the Quartier Latin; and Locke's heroes always belong to the best county families and are tired of their clubs. The strange thing is that we are shown the lives of poor artists no more, but the lives of people whose ambition is to throw up everything and become poor in order to be artists or to live near them. Middle-class society is kicking over the traces. It is in conflict with itself. Yet the conflict is, so far, not very profound. The illusion of the new Bohemia was that it could preserve the middle-class amenities while throwing over the irksome conventions that protected them. And by the Twenties we had arrived at a paradoxical situation which would have soured the faces of Murger's circle at the Café Riche: the bourgeois had been converted to art. All the world was bent upon becoming artistic. The Quartier Latin and Montparnasse had become the quarters of the rich. I remember my own early bewilderment in Paris. Brought up to believe that my intellectual emancipation depended on my finding a cheap room to live in on the left bank of the Seine, and that damnation awaited those who dwelt on the right, I gloomily remember I could not afford to be a Bohemian. Life was cheaper in Passy; one went to Montparnasse or the Rue de Seine to borrow money and to wonder what spirit of perversity and masochism had possessed the sons of rentiers that they must put on fancy dress and live among the worst drains of Europe. The Goncourts were right – Bohemia had become a racket, a greater racket than they could have guessed.

No doubt I exaggerate. My nose, insufficiently Bohemian, has many times led me out of the pensions of the Mont St Geneviève and so has closed a world to me except as a spectator. I recognise my own facial expressions in Murger's picture of the bourgeois who used to go night after night to the café to watch with a craving he dreaded to reveal. There is, and will always be, the temporary Bohemianism like that of Murger's

Rudolphe; and always, no doubt, what Murger called the Bohemianism of the *impasse*. That gaunt man with the Christ-like face and the invalid's straggling beard, who sat all day over his cup of coffee and who looked as if he were starving, was a one-time silk salesman despite his 'artistic' appearance. But he was in fact starving, God knows why, and they picked him up half dead in the street. The Bohemians of the *impasse* were, as Murger said, chronically unproductive and garrulous. If I wish to visualise a Bohemian of this kind I always think of a middle-aged man who, as an alleged fashion journalist, spent his days with the mannequins of the Rue de la Paix and played the harmonium on Sundays at a Methodist chapel. Murger knew his subject. It was his only subject. He knew and illustrated in his own life and work the drift into finicking which the life of the clique encourages. The frenzied hunt for the *pièce de cent sous*, the strangling estimate of whether the next meal lies north, south, east or west as you leave the door, are not the only enemies of the Bohemian; nor the hospital its final dread. The dreaded enemy is self-discovery. The inner terror which Murger described in another of his books is the fear not that the talent for which one suffers is insufficient, but that it simply is not there at all.

Socialists – the most respectable of men – have come to attack Bohemia for its disorder and its philosophy of isolation; but I wonder whether those who do so really attack it from a rival Bohemia of their own, the equally ancient Bohemia of the exile and refugee. Political Bohemia, from the time of Herzen and through the life of Marx, offers a story no less wretched and picaresque than the lives of students and artists. If the Bohemia of the artist had been taken over wholesale by middle-class society in 1931, and had gone, its place was taken by this revived Bohemia of the refugee. Colourless and despondent, watchful and suspicious, whispering in groups over the backs of chairs at the Coupole or the Dôme, the exiles sat waiting for news from home, where the gaudy and gregarious figures of the earlier decade hoped they'd heard the last of it. And perhaps that is a portent. Mr E. M. Forster has lately recommended a return to Bohemia for writers; but tomorrow independent political thought, not art, may be one of the seven deadly and unremunerative sins. Du Maurier's Little Billee turned 'deathly pale' when he saw Trilby, a lady of one of the best Irish families, posing in 'the altogether'; his grandson may crumple up if he catches her indecently exposing the charms of a majority mind to oblige a few friends.

I have said very little about Murger's sketches themselves. They have a boulevard wit and when, later on in life, Murger decided to give up the fastidiousness of art and to go after money in the theatre, he made the right decision. He was not a natural highbrow. His melancholy temperament was that of the clown, not of the poet; he was a born writer of farce, and his young men have that too eternal youth of the theatre. His student wit is exact. And his sense of *blague* never fails him. The youth who paints a luxurious room on screens in lieu of furniture, the expert borrower who has noted down where he can get a free meal for every day of the week and, going out for it, discovers his host has left and is on his way to see the borrower on the same mission – these are the brainwaves of the theatre. The light sentiment, the conventional Parisian irony, punctuated by an occasional real phrase taken from life, are agreeable enough in short snatches. And the Mimi of the book, whose life with Rudolphe is frankly, if rather cosily, described as a hell of jealousy and injudicious expense – hats and boots were Mimi's weakness – is a good deal livelier than the Mimi of the play or the opera. The ornately facetious style is not the journalese of the comic writers, though I don't know that makes it any better. Really, there is no serious reproach which can be fairly made against Murger. He is simply a little writer, a brilliant dabbler in unreality, high spirits and sadness, whose very melancholy, as it ripples along, reveals a fundamental lack of seriousness. His letters, with their outcry against hunger and their hard tale of work, describe with bitter dignity a Vie de Bohême which he glossed over with a phrase or two in the sketches. His own horrible death – his flesh was decaying; shortly before he died his lip fell off when he was shaving – and the death of the real Mimi were the end of a story very different from his light elegy of lost youth.

The English Frenchman

> He counted on a certain repugnance in those who most admired him, as men of his disposition count on the help of a certain instinctive dislike in those of whom they are most anxious to make themselves masters.

So wrote Arthur Symons in an acute preface to a collection of Prosper Mérimée's stories. Repugnance certainly disturbs our admiration of them; indeed, between Mérimée and the reader one might say that repugnances are exchanged like the names of seconds in a duel. We open *Colomba* or *Mateo Falcone* with the feeling that it is sunrise, that presently our infinitely accomplished adversary will come coolly through the woods and in a couple of minutes put a bullet through our lungs. We shall have died for God knows what, though Mérimée himself will suggest that our fate was no more than the icy flash of a diamond on the dark finger of death. For Mérimée a life is a campaign.

For us who have two wars in our blood such a writer has a peculiar interest. He can count on our repugnance and our attraction still. As a writer of *nouvelles* he is, without question, a master; and in the construction of stories of action or, perhaps one should say, in stories of the consciously active man, he is inhumanly exact. 'I have spent my nights lately writing for posterity,' he wrote in the *Lettres à une Inconnue*. It is true. As bodies are preserved endlessly in ice, or the fly for ever printed flawlessly in amber, so his stories appear new to the minds of every generation, and we cannot imagine a time when *Carmen* is forgotten or *Colomba* unreadable. It is an effort to approach and read many of the overwhelming figures of literature. But Mérimée remains crystalline, exact, apparent; he can be approached at once. The interesting thing is his refusal to be great; I mean his refusal to be a great man in the histrionic manner of the nineteenth century. Where his contemporaries in France and England seem to have gone to the

wig-makers to dress for the character-part of prophet, thinker and visionary, and to prepare the long oration of their careers, Mérimée steps back.
Where they are positive and aggressive, he is negative and critical. They,
in the manner of the century, are going to be great men. Their rôle and
their audience will be everything to them. But when we look at Mérimée it
appears to us that the sight of so many vibrant egotisms, warming up their
engines and preparing to take off with a roar, must have produced in him a
perverse decision, a decision without modesty, to stay isolated on the
ground. And we know that it was his aim – a singular one for a writer – not
to be a great man, but to obtain regard as a scholar and a gentleman; an
English gentleman, of all things, as romantic Frenchmen conceive that
character to be. In this, Mérimée was just as much an actor, just as much an
heir of the Romantics and just as much a prophet as the rest of his
contemporaries. He was simply the reverse of the medal. Like Stendhal, he
discloses that the other side of Romanticism is the quest for personal
power and for a primitive justification of it. He is not an aristocrat who
inherits power in some sense as a trust; he is the intellectual, the clerk or
servant of aristocrats, who becomes the libertine of the will to power,
pursuing it, inciting it, probing it, and in the story of *Colomba*, exalting it.
The themes of *Carmen*, of *Tamango*, of his superb historical novel, the
Chronicle of Charles IX, of *Mateo Falcone*, and even of that ironical little
comedy of manners, *L'Abbé Aubain*, are all alike in this respect: they
indicate ruthless private wars; his people are goaded by pride or vanity to
seek dominion. And when one side or the other has won, or when both
have destroyed each other – what is left? Mérimée is too honest an artist
and too clear-minded to suggest that anything can be left for people like
this but the emptiness of conquest. War in the heart and mind destroys as
infallibly as war on a continent. It is an absolute evil. A shocking laugh
there may be, like Colomba's derision when she sits back well fed by her
revenge; but in general Mérimée leaves us abruptly and we see an empty
stage where pity cannot tread. For pity has not been born.

In this attitude of mind Mérimée was prophetic. He foreshadowed one
kind of writer who would succeed the prophets. His critical intelligence,
the hard rapier-like sound of an intellect without heart, evokes an echo in
ourselves. He is the scholar, the artist, the poet of insensibility. He is – one
hardly likes to breathe the suggestion – tough. We have often thought that

the visions, the sentiment, the complacencies of the nineteenth century deluded us; we turn for respite to Mérimée who encases his heart, prepares to repel by a skilled display of strategy and marksmanship, and declares that the aim of man must be a self-control so established, a mistrust so masked, that he can never be duped. That decision of his, 'not to be duped', is famous. The word recalls a fashionable contemporary word: disabused.

And yet how refreshing Mérimée is! What brilliant uses may be made of an arrested development! The shock does not come, after all, until the ends of his stories: when Tamango's broken glory fades into a Governor's anecdote, or when Carmen's death is merely a gloss on the customs of the gypsies. And that final shock is wiped out by the memory of the first shock we get when we begin a new story; the shock of pleasure and exhilaration in something new and strange. Mérimée is never boring. He writes like a gifted raconteur who is nonchalant, entirely at ease, but always alert in the presence of his circle. A bore has been defined as a man who tells us everything, and Mérimée never falls into the trap. He rewrote *Colomba* sixteen times to be sure of avoiding it. His economy of narrative is native to his guarded and scholarly mind. One may resent a curtness which was the fruit of mistrust, and one may add that the man who is not duped does not live to the full – 'life is time's fool' – but if Mérimée is curt, he also has the rare gift of order, which I take to be the first essential of good narrative. Mérimée's gift of order enables him to place his scenes, as Turgenev and Pushkin placed theirs, briefly but infallibly before our eyes; to know, in *Colomba*, for example, how much of Corsica to describe, how far to dilate on local custom, how far to build up his anecdotes about the vendetta until the main vendetta of the story looms over like an iron cloud, impassable and momentous on a mountain road. A great part of the pleasure of reading his stories comes from our awareness of their construction. At each phase we are conscious of being set free from the irrelevancies by which other writers mystify the reader, and of being directed by a mind that knows how to eliminate. One of the many difficulties the novelist has is to discern the situation clearly and many greater writers than Mérimée fail to do this; whatever Mérimée may lose by his gift of isolating certain elements of character, he gains by the clarification of issues. So that we are able in *Colomba* simultaneously to hold in the mind many contrary things. We watch Colomba's will to revenge working on her brother's mind, but we do not lose sight of the civilisation he has, or the difficult nervous English girl he has left in Ajaccio. Even at the crisis of the book, when Colomba's conspiracy breaks and murder, somehow and somewhere, is inevitable, we never lose sight of the sunlight and the fog on the maquis and of the chattering Colonel and his daughter ambling cheerfully towards the awful hour when – as the bandit says – there will be fresh meat for sale in the town. Mérimée, of course, gets his effect by a lucid prose style which deliberately lowered the emotional temperature in order to heighten the intellectual excitement. He excels in his skill at rendering the depths by keeping to the surface, by attending to the beguiling and untrustworthy smile of life. His own emotions abstain from the narrative and, as I said before, we are free – that sense of freedom is the great gift of the Romantic tradition. With him we are free, also, of the Romantic burden. And even at the end, when the shock comes, as it always does in Mérimée, when we see him going too far and Colomba jeering at the broken father whose sons have been murdered, we are left reluctantly admiring the wicked perfection of the scene, the injurious irony. In the same way the end of *Tamango* is perfect.

In their dissociation of power and energy and pride from the rest of life, Stendhal and Mérimée are prophetic of an aspect of fascism. And Mérimée added a predilection for primitive types. He is saved from the complete accusation by his scholarship and by his detachment. Mérimée does not desire to return to the primitive or to a world without mercy. He declined to have an organic conception of history. He was an anthropologist, not a mystic. Even his Byronism was moderated to the temper of what became a gentleman with the spleen. He has a little in common with Pushkin, whom he translated, a harder, frozen Pushkin always on guard. His mind was sceptical. There is a clear statement of his scepticism in his historical novel, *The Chronicle of Charles IX*, where he extracts the utmost irony out of the religious wars and the massacres of St Bartholomew and detaches himself from the tale half-way through in order to explain his method of writing history to the reader. 'This is not the last time brothers will kill each other in France,' says the dying convert to his Huguenot brother; and Mérimée excels in describing the ambiguities of conscience in an age when professions of faith do violence to the soul. This novel set out to undermine the laden and stolid histories of Sir Walter Scott, and it reads as if it were written, not in the first half of the nineteenth century, but in the last twenty years. There is a succession of incomparable scenes, and there is no dead wood. Again, our pleasure is a double one; we are watching the building of the characters and the story while we are borne along by it. And again we are struck by another aspect of Mérimée which brings him close to us: what he passes off as his belief in anecdote is really his perfunctory name for documentation. Unfeeling he may be, but he can reconstruct an environment, a period, the corner of a battlefield, a gaming table, a Corsican hut or a house of rendezvous in Seville, with a fidelity to their normal condition which many a more profuse writer, and more humane, has failed to achieve. He has the patience, the grace, the exactitude if he has also the perfunctoriness of the amateur. A writer might learn his art from him and dread the perfection he had learned.

The Centenary of Anatole France

Anatole France was born on April 16th, 1844. He ripened with the century and died (over-ripe, the critics said) in 1924. His centenary comes too soon, for it has caught his reputation floating indeterminately in the trough that always follows a wave of fame. We find it hard to face the elders whom we admired when we were young and who dominated our scene, for they contain too much of our discarded life. Reading them again we find them mocking us with our own image, like a parent or a brother who is ourselves yet not ourselves. And yet it is not hard to disentangle oneself from Anatole France. Despite his artifice, his epicureanism, his air of ripeness and scepticism, he is at heart an adolescent writer. His world – as he says towards the end of his last autobiographical book, *The Bloom of Life* – is the world of desire and illusion. His way is the primrose path of nostalgia, sensual pessimism and self-love. The famous irony is the artful weapon of the bookish man who never grows up, who tastes life and history. They are a gourmet's dish, sweetened by the senses, salted by horror. He observes, but does not experience; and, beginning as a dreamer, a writer of historical *pastiche*, a faun-like comedian of the museums and the libraries, he ends in moral nihilism. One is reminded of his own phrase about Van Dongen's portrait in his old age: 'It makes me look like a Camembert that is running.'

The notes of tenderness and the naïve which appear in both the sentimental and the savage writings of Anatole France led many critics to feel that, if he was appalled by human nature, he also pitied it. But now one begins to doubt. One does not pity men until one understands their dignity. As one reads his life and rereads his books one builds a picture of Anatole France shut up in a daydream world, protected by all the authority of a superb culture, tortured by self-pity and not by pity for mankind. His reminiscences of childhood and youth, his essays in the archaic improprieties of history, and his two or three realistic novels reveal a man who chooses to exploit the pleasure, the terrors and the final anarchy of a personal solitude. He became a kind of Gibbon who has lost the love of liberty in the love and hatred of himself and who, tactfully withdrawing from the battle of history, contents himself with the footnotes. It is the course of the bookish man, the man who has tippled the illusions of the library and whose irony scarcely conceals the complacency of the non-combatant. One might suppose, after reading his novel about the Terror, *The Gods are Athirst*, that the French Revolution was an idle piece of human sadism caused by boredom or some northern incursion of the sirocco, and that the forces of history are really nothing but the agglomerated aberrations of human character. The complacency of this view is as shocking as the Terror. It is not a cold complacency; it is the complacency of the day-dream and self-love.

To this passive and cunning view of life, Anatole France brought the genial resources of his unorganised reading, the power to crystallise it in anecdote and to link the anecdotes together, with the subtlety and wit of the French tradition. One is rummaging in a second-hand bookshop – and, of course, he was the son of a famous bookseller – and each volume has its human habit and voice. As a novelist Anatole France was less a creator of characters than a compressor of them. He squeezed them out of books, as wine drips out of the press. His naïve priests and his fanatics, his trenchermen and his sluts, his always beddable girls, his politicians gulled by their own corruption are the fantasies of the library, jocosely or morbidly removed from the treadmill of life. There is scathing diagnosis – see his handling of the Dreyfus case in *Penguin Island* – there is art. But a heavy price is paid for the intellectual high-colouring of France's characters: we cannot take them seriously. They have wine instead of blood; sex but not vitality. The Terror in *The Gods are Athirst* does not terrorise except as a theory about the Terror. We are engaged by the sensational notion that hundreds offered themselves voluntarily to the guillotine, that the Moscow confessions were anticipated, that a woman would cling to her lover with a wilder ardour and attain an even more powerful satisfaction when she knew he had that morning condemned innocent men peremptorily to death. For we know that some women do offer themselves to murderers with special zeal. And yet, in the end, we put down this novel which was to blast the puritan out of us and to replace him by the mellow

and stoical reader of Lucretius – we put it down with the feeling that we
have been tricked. Surely, we say, huge scenes have been left out. Surely it
is perverse to personify the Revolution in a narrow prig like Gamelin and
to treat the Terror as an outburst of self-righteousness or to isolate it as a
clinical instance of insanity. Is it enough to regard the Terror merely as one
of the frenzies of human nature? Was it not inevitable and therefore tragic?
Is it not an insult to those cartloads of human beings jolting towards the
guillotine, to give them the pathos of marionettes, to treat them as a cat
treats a mouse, to use them as a psychiatrist's anecdote? The sadism and
pity of Anatole France are certainly powerful and unrelenting in this book;
but, in the end, one comes to regard it as a piece of erotica, while its
judgment – that after revolutions have done their worst, life eventually
goes on exactly as before – relies on an obvious confusion of ideas.

I see nothing humane in this book. On the contrary, it seems to me a plea
for human isolation, and it has paid the price of such pleas; it has missed the
sight of human dignity. Irony has made horror trivial. One sees it through
a keyhole. Anatole France professed to recover something of the eighteenth century, but the humanity of the eighteenth century was not the fruit
of a philosophy of contemplation. Gibbon recorded the crimes and follies
of mankind, but his History was imbued with a hatred of tyranny; and
Voltaire, that 'chaos of clear ideas' – was driven by the same passion. The
humanity of the eighteenth century was an active faith, enlarged by the
variety, not desiccated by the absurdity of human nature; and men like
Gibbon and Voltaire did not suppose themselves to be standing on some
magically stationary point in history. A mystic like Blake did not think of
the Terror as chiefly an example of the savour of human cruelty.

The purely literary critic would say that the talent of Anatole France was
the talent of annotation. He was, like so many of his characters, a collector
of bric-à-brac, a *bouquiniste* of the quays, a conversationalist. He arranges
his material. He does not build with it. The pleasure we get from a book
like *At the Sign of the Reine Pedauque* springs from grotesque contrasts. The
salacious is followed by the lyrical, the philosophical by the picaresque.
The patchwork manuscripts of Anatole France, posted into ledger-like
notebooks from diverse rewritings, show the care with which he placed
each sentence and each episode. No one could have arranged *bibelots* on a
table more maliciously. But the failure to rise to the fullness of a great

theme is curious in a brain and taste so greatly gifted. One is tempted to turn away from literary criticism and to explain the failure, as Mr Edmund Wilson has done, as the result of the lack of some comprehensive and energising philosophy of life. Bourgeois culture has become static and self-contained. Anatole France has written enough about himself – and very honestly, too – to show that he was essentially a timid and egoistical writer; and one can understand how the First World War must have scattered his learned dreams by showing him history out on the hunt and with a purpose in its eye. But a writer cannot have a comprehensive philosophy of life just for the asking. And if there is no comprehensive view about mankind in Anatole France beyond the notion that we are going round in circles, there is a pretty constant view about one subject in his books – that is, the Church. There his scepticism could bite because it had something for his teeth to bite on. The fame and influence of Anatole France with the large public were due, one suspects, to his response to the religious crisis of the late nineteenth century. After all the sneers, the comedies and the satire at the expense of the Church there remains a nostalgia, like his own nostalgia for his childhood, which was typical of the minds of those caught in this religious conflict. And, especially in England, his sophisticated and Rabelaisian manner, alternating with the pretty manner of the folktale, soothed the struggles of our over-strenuous consciences. For at least a generation no English writer offered the same irreverent consolations.

My own taste is divided between the autobiographical books about childhood and the one or two realistic novels. *Le Petit Pierre* and *Pierre Nozière* are studied, but they are graceful and convey the dogged smallness and anxiety of childhood. They evoke, as *The Crime of Sylvestre Bonnard* does also, the life of the narrow streets of the Quartier Latin and of the Quais, so that one seems to be treading again the shadows of the plane trees and seeing the severe ripples of the Seine. The quality of meditation is filled with Latin sentiment; the fairy-tale charm is of the period. (That it may be a little fake is part of the charm.) The Bohemianism is harsh and native. It belongs to an entirely French society, unpolluted by the raucous Bohemia of Montparnasse. The tragedy of Anatole France was that he drifted from this fanciful world into the more violent world of religion, political and historical fable. The realism of books like *The Elm Tree on the*

Mall or *The Red Lily* has a smaller scope, but its note is truer. One cannot call a book like *The Red Lily* a great novel about jealousy, but in its severe frame it reflects a few things perfectly and with supreme economy. Formal and quite unspeculative, it makes its comment on 'mœurs' with a clarity that is worth all the juicy Abbés, the tavern sluts and tedious scholars of the epicurean novels. These are good for a page, or good for a chapter, but they have the tedium of marginalia. They are a connoisseur's collection, a professor's conundrum, a bookseller's whisper. The great foot of Rabelais comes down upon the pretty pickle and leaves it looking flat.

The Russian Day

What is it that attracts us to the Russian novelists of the nineteenth century? The aristocratic culture made more vivid by its twilight? The feeling, so readily understood by English readers, for *ennui*? No. The real attraction of that censored literature is its freedom – the freedom from our kind of didacticism and our plots. The characters of our novels, from Fielding to Forster, get up in the morning, wash, dress and are then drilled for their rôles. They are propelled to some practical issue in morality, psychology or Fortune before the book is done. In nineteenth-century Russia, under the simpler feudal division of society, there is more room to breathe, to let the will drift, and the disparate impulses have their ancient solitary reign. In all those Russian novels we seem to hear a voice saying: 'The meaning of life? One day that will be revealed to us – probably on a Thursday.' And the day, not the insistence of the plot or purpose, is the melodic bar. We see life again, as we indeed know it, as something written in days; its dramas not directed by the superior foreknowledge of the writer, but seeming to ebb and flow among the climaxes, the anticlimaxes, the yawnings of the hours. Turgenev, who knew English literature well, used to say that he envied the English novelists their power to make plots; but, of course, he really disdained it. The surprises of life, the sudden shudders of its skin, are fresher and more astonishing than the imposed surprises of literary convention or the teacher's lesson. And in seeing people in terms of their anonymous days, the Russians achieved, by a paradox, a sense of timelessness in their books. Gogol, for example, seems to date far less than Dickens. In the Russians there is a humility before the important fact of human inertia, the half-heartedness of its wish to move and grow, its habit of returning into itself. This is true of Turgenev; obviously true of Chekhov, and I think also of Dostoevsky. His dynamism and complex narratives are the threshings and confusions of a writer who –

if we consult his notebooks and letters – could never bind his mind to a settled subject or a fixed plot.

Yet the use of the eventless day could not alone give the Russian novel its curious power; indeed, it can be its weakness. No novelists are easier to parody than the Russians. Those people picking their noses at the windows or trying on their boots while they go through passion and remorse! The day is a convention like any other. What gives those novels their power, and these persons their gift of moving us, is something which comes from a profound sense of a presence haunting the day. There lies on those persons, even on the most trivial, the shadow of a fate more richly definitive than the fate of any individual human being. Their feet stand in time and in history. Their fate is corporate. It is the fate of Russia itself, a fate so often adjured with eloquence and nostalgia, oftener still with that medieval humility which has been unknown to us since the Renaissance, and which the Russians sometimes mystically identify with the fate of humanity itself.

I have been reading Turgenev again and dipping occasionally into Avraham Yarmolinsky's thorough and discerning evaluation of him. It was a great advantage to the Russian novelists that they were obliged to react to the Russian question; a great advantage, too, that the Russian question was to become a universal one: the question of the rise of the masses. The consequence is that Turgenev's political novels – especially *Rudin* and even *Fathers and Sons* – are less dated outside of Russia than they are inside it, for we can afford to ignore the detail of their historical context. I first read *Rudin* during the Spanish Civil War and, when he died on his foreign barricade, Rudin seemed to me (and still does seem) one of 'the heroes of our own time'. At the end of all Turgenev's political stories one may detect the invisible words 'And yet . . .' left there by his hesitant and tentative genius. He is so close to the ripple of life's process of becoming that at the very moments of decision, departure, farewell, he seems to revise and rejuvenate. The leaf falls, but the new bud is disclosed beneath the broken stalk.

Turgenev solved the Russian problem for himself, as he solved his personal question by an ingenious psychological trick. It is rather irritating, it is a little comic when we see it in the light of his personal character, but it was serious and successful. It was the trick of assuming a premature old age. Now this device was a legacy of Byronism. One can see how it must have infuriated his younger contemporaries to hear him declare that at 35 his life was finished; and then to have him live another thirty years in full possession of his gracious and pertinent faculties. The trick was a kind of alibi. For behind the mist of regret, that autumnal resignation, the tenderness and the wave of the scented handkerchief in a good-bye that was never quite good-bye, there was a marksman's eye. Yarmolinsky speaks of him stalking his characters as he stalked his grouse on the steppe of Orel or Kaluga. Every time he picks off his man and notes, as he does so, his place in the Russian fauna. Look at this from *A Nest of Gentlefolk*:

> I want above all to know what you are like, what are your views and convictions, what you have become, what life has taught. (Mihalevitch still preserved the phraseology of 1830.)

The comic side of this adroit sense of time – so precise, so poetic and moving in his writing – comes out in Turgenev's private life. His autumnal disguise enabled him to give his large number of love affairs a protective fragility. The autumn is the hunting season.

A Sportsman's Sketches, *A Nest of Gentlefolk*, *Fathers and Sons* – those are the perfect books. Turgenev is the poet of spring who eludes the exhausting decisions and fulfilments of summer and finds in the autumn a second and safer spring. He is the novelist of the moments after meetings and of the moments before partings. He watches the young heart rise the first time. He watches it fall, winged, to the common distorted lot. The young and the old are his fullest characters: the homecoming and death of Bazarov and the mourning of his parents are among the truest and most moving things in literature. To this tenderness, this capacity to observe the growth of characters and the changes of the heart, as the slow days of the steppe change into the years that rattle by in Petersburg or Baden, there is, as I have said, a shrewd, hard-headed counterpart, the experienced shot:

> In the general the good-nature innate in all Russians was intensified by that special kind of geniality which is peculiar to all people who have done something disgraceful.

Or:

Of his wife there is scarcely anything to be said. Her name was Kalliopa Karlovna. There was always a tear in her left eye, on the strength of which Kalliopa Karlovna (she was, one must add, of German extraction) considered herself a woman of great sensibility.

Or:

Panshin's father, a retired cavalry officer and a notorious gambler, was a man of insinuating eyes, a battered countenance, and a nervous twitch about the mouth.

Looking back over the novels, one cannot remember any falsified character. One is taken from the dusty carriage to the great house, one meets the landowners and the servants, and then one watches life produce its surprises as the day goes by. Turgenev has the perfect discretion. He refrains from knowing in advance. In *Rudin* we are impressed by the bellows of the local Dr Johnson; enter Rudin, and the brilliant young man demolishes the doctor, like a young Shelley; only himself to suffer exposure as the next day shows us more of his character. His people expose themselves, as in life people expose themselves, fitfully and with contradiction. The art is directed by a sense which the English novel has never had – unless Jane Austen had something of it – the sense of a man's character and life being divisible into subjects. Career, love, religion, money, politics, illness and the phases of the years are in turn isolated in a spirit which is both poetic and scientific. There is no muddle in Turgenev. Romantic as he may be, there is always clarity, order and economy. He writes novels as if he were not a story-teller, but a biographer.

It was Edward Garnett who, in defending the disputed portrait of Bazarov, pointed out that Bazarov ought to have been judged as the portrait not of a political type, but of the scientific temperament. (There is nothing wrong with Bazarov really, except that Turgenev showed him in the country, where he was a fish out of water, instead of in the city.) This temperament was Turgenev's, and because of it one easily discounts the inevitable sad diminuendo of his tales, the languid dying away which is the shadow of his own wish in his work. The rest stands clearly and without date. But the method has one serious weakness. It almost certainly involved drawing directly from life, and especially it meant that Turgenev was (or thought he was) stimulated to write by an interest in living persons for their own sakes. Turgenev knew his own lack of invention, his reliance on personal experience, and he studied character with the zeal of a botanist watching a flower; but, in fact, the study of character, for a novelist, means the selection or abstraction of character. What is selected is inevitably less than what is there, and since Turgenev was (as he said) governed by the actual life story which he saw, he does not add to or transform his people. They have the clarity of something a little less than life. What is missing from them is that from which he personally recoiled – fulfilment. There are spring and autumn – there is no summer. If success is described, it is by hearsay. Marriage, for Turgenev, is either scandal or rather embarrassing domesticity, something for a fond, indulgent smile, but a quick get-away. Strangely enough, it is his objectivity which leads to his limpness.

There are two qualifications to add to this criticism. One is suggested by *A Sportsman's Sketches*. His people derive a certain fullness from their part in the scene of the steppe, which none described better than he. In this book, his scrupulous habit or necessity of stopping short at what he saw and heard gave his portraits a laconic power and a terrible beauty. There the Russian day brings people to life in their random moments. The shapelessness of these pieces is the powerful shapelessness of time itself. The other qualification is the one I have indicated at the beginning of this essay. If his people lack the power to realise themselves because Turgenev himself lacked it in his own life, they have their roots in the fate of Russia. You localise them in a destiny which is beyond their own – tragic, comic, whatever they are – in the destiny of their society. They may fail, Russia goes on. One remembers that startling chapter at the end of *A Nest of Gentlefolk*, where, after the bitter end of Liza's love, the novelist returns to the house. One expects the last obligatory chords of romantic sorrow, but instead, there is the cruel perennial shock of spring:

Marfa Dmitrievna's house seemed to have grown younger; its freshly painted walls gave a bright welcome; and the panes of its open windows were crimson, shining in the setting sun; from these windows the light merry sound of ringing young voices and continual laughter floated into the street.

[323]

The new generation had grown up. It is the most tragic moment of his writing, the one most burdened with the mystery of time as it flows through the empty light of our daily life.

The Hypocrite

====

We walk down a street in the dead hours of the afternoon, looking at the windows of the villas as we pass by. They are glass cases; they are the domestic aquarium, and what our idle eye is seeking is a sight of the human fish within. And presently we are taken by surprise. We see a face in one of those rooms. Agape, bemused, suspended like some torpid trout, a man or woman is standing alone there, doing nothing, and sunk in the formidable pathos of human inertia, isolation and *ennui*. It is always a surprising sight and, to a novelist, always a disturbing one. We are used to the actions of human beings, not to their stillness. We are taken back suddenly to our childhood, when time went by so slowly, and when we, too, were shut in a room with some grown-up who was occupied entirely by the mysterious, enormous process of sitting. How they could sit! And sit alone! And how their figures grew larger and larger in our eyes, until their solitude and silence seemed to burst the room. It was, I think, one of the first intimations of mortality in early childhood.

The Russian novelists of the nineteenth century owe everything to their response to the man or woman sitting alone in his room, to the isolation, inertia, the off-beat in human character. They are naturally aware of what André Malraux has called, in a recent book, 'the crevasse that separates us from universal life'. The chief subject of the Russian novelists – the monotonous life of the country house which is scores of miles from its neighbours – draws this response from them. And as they stand alone in the room, drumming their fingers on the window and looking out at the slow, cumbrous changes of cloud in the Russian sky over the steppe, the characters of the Russian novel fill out with the unoccupied hours of life. Loneliness intensifies character. The great personages of literature have so often been the solitary natures who overflow into the void that surrounds them, who transcend their personal lives and expand until they become prototypes. The Russian novel abounds in such figures. Oblomov is an example. Stefan Trofimovitch in *The Possessed* is another. Iudushka of *The Golovlyov Family* belongs to this category. One is tempted to say novels are important only when they create these abnormal, comprehensive people. But in saying this it is important to note one difference between the Russian figures and those of the West. Those strong-minded, bossy, tyrannical Varvara Petrovnas and Arina Petrovnas who honk their way through Russian life like so many vehement geese; those quietly mad, stagnant, frittering men who spend their time dodging these masterful women, are different from the English eccentrics. Our eccentricity or excess is a protest against the pressure of society; the Russian excessives of the nineteenth century were the normal product of a world which was so lax that it exercised no pressure at all. 'We Russians,' Shchedrin wrote, 'are not drilled, we are not trained to be champions and propagandists of this or that set of moral principles, but are simply allowed to grow as nettles grow by a fence.' Iudushka and Oblomov are natural weeds of a neglected soil. They grow by running rife and they derive their force not from private fantasy alone, as Pecksniff or Micawber do, but from the Russian situation. They are puffed out by the sluggish, forgotten hours and days of the steppe. For in the empty hours and the blank distances which separate them from their neighbours, all the fate, the history, the significance of Russia itself, is gazing back at their gaping eyes.

After reading Shchedrin's *The Golovlyov Family* one sees why a character like Iudushka, the liar and humbug, is greater than Pecksniff who is, I suppose, the nearest English parallel. Iudushka is greater, firstly, because he has Russia inside him, and, secondly, because he is encumbered with the dead weight of human dullness and vulgarity. He is greater because he is a bore. I do not mean that Iudushka is boring to read about. I mean that Dickens had no notion that Pecksniff was a boring and vulgar man; Dickens's mind was interested only in the dramatic and absurd exterior of the whited sepulchre. Shchedrin did not stop at the farce of human hypocrisy, for the tricks of hypocrisy are really too crude and blatant. Shchedrin went on collecting the evidence with the patience of one of those static realists like Richardson; and he presently came upon the really terrible thing in Iudushka's character. We can laugh (Shchedrin seems to say) at the obvious hypocrisies of Iudushka and, like his neighbours, we can grin at his eye-rolling, his genuflexions and his slimy whimsicalities;

but there is something more serious. The real evil is the moral stagnation in Iudushka's character. The real evil is the muddle, the tangle of evasions, words, intrigues by which he instinctively seeks to dodge reality. We forgive his sins; what eludes forgiveness is the fact that his nature has gone bad; so that he himself does not know the difference between good and evil. He is a ghastly example of self-preservation at any price. In middle age he is befuddled by daydreams. He will pass a morning working out fantastic conundrums such as, how much money he would make out of milk if all the cows in the neighbourhood died except his own. He works out the most detailed but essentially ridiculous systems of bookkeeping, and imagines that he is working. Less and less is he able to face any decision, however small. He is a hive buzzing with activity – but it is the buzz of procrastination. I do not ever remember seeing such a picture of our character in any English novel; yet the humbug's art of evading an issue by confusing it is a universal one. There is one remarkable picture of Iudushka's evasion in the account of his behaviour to the servant girl whom he has got with child. Iudushka manages never to admit that the child is his, but allows everyone around to say it is. His own reaction is to groan and to say 'This is unbearable' – subtly conveying that his sufferings, not his act, are the unbearable thing. Iudushka reaches the sublimity of self-deception here. He has achieved detachment and isolation from his own actions. And the strange thing is that we begin to pity him at this point. He feels an agony and we wince with him. We share with him the agony of being driven back step by step against the wall and being brought face to face with an intolerable fact.

There is nothing notably remote from our experience in *The Golovlyov Family*. Neither the emancipation of the serfs which stupefies Arina Petrovna, nor the fact that one is reading about a remote, semi-feudal estate, makes the book seem exotic or alien to us. Our own Arina Petrovnas do not starve their sons to death, but they have driven some to alcoholism; our own Iudushkas do not publicly drive their sons to suicide. But, in the main, we must be struck by the essential closeness of Shchedrin's novel to the life of the successful middle class in England. Iudushka's prayers for guidance have a sinister echo. Walter Bagehot, I believe, said that the mind of the businessman lived in a kind of twilight, and the character of Iudushka is a remarkable example of a man whose cunning requires an atmosphere of vagueness and meaningless moral maxims. He has the stupidity of the slippery. In the end, is it not so much his wickedness that shocks his nieces, as the fact that he has become such a talker, such a vulgar babbler and bore. Cucumbers, pickles and the mercy of God indiscriminately mix in his mind. He bores one of the girls out of the house; and one of the most terrible chapters in the book is that one towards the end when the girl comes back to his house to die and wonders whether she can bear to spend her last weeks in the house of a man who never stops drivelling on and on about trivialities. She can tolerate him only by persecuting him. This picture of the triviality of Iudushka's mind is Shchedrin's master-stroke.

The Golovlyov Family has been described as the gloomiest of the Russian novels. Certainly the characters are all wretched or unpleasant, and the reader of novels who professes that strange but common English attitude to literature: 'Would I like to meet these people?' must leave the book alone. Yet Shchedrin's book is not gloomy; it is powerful. It communicates power. It places an enormous experience in our hands. How many of the realists simply indulge in an orgy of determinism and seek only the evidence that indicates damnation. Shchedrin does this up to a point, but he is not looking for quick moral returns. His method is exhaustive and not summary. Old Arina Petrovna is a tyrant; but her lonely old age has its peculiar rewards. She enjoys guzzling with Iudushka, she adores his boring conversation; she is delighted to queer his pitch when he seduces the servant-girl. The compensations of life are not moral; they are simply more life of a different kind. Here are the last years of her life:

She spent the greater part of the day dozing. She would sit down in her armchair in front of a table on which smelly cards were spread out, and doze. Then she would wake up with a start, glance at the window, and without any conscious thought in her mind gaze for hours at the wide expanse of fields, stretching into the distance as far as the eye could see. Pogorelka was a sad-looking place . . . But as Arina Petrovna had lived all her life in the country, hardly ever leaving it, this poor scenery did not seem dismal to her, it touched her heart, stirring the remains of feeling that still smouldered in it. The best part of her being lived in those bare, boundless fields, and her eyes instinctively turned to them at

[328]

every moment. She looked intently into the distance, gazing at the villages soaked with rain that showed like black specks on the horizon, at the white churches of the countryside, at the patches of shadow cast by the wandering clouds on the sunlit plain, at the peasant walking between the furrows, and it seemed to her that he never moved at all. But she did not think of anything or, rather, her thoughts were so disconnected that they could dwell on nothing for any length of time. She merely gazed and gazed until the drowsiness of old age began to ring in her ears, covering with a mist the fields, the churches, the villages, and the peasant walking far away.

No, Shchedrin is not gloomy because he does not soften. He undertakes to scald us with the evidence; he does not pretend that it will make vulgarity romantic or ignorance pretty. He is powerful because he remains severe. And so, at the end, when Iudushka and his niece, after their awful drunken quarrels, suddenly admit their despair to each other, and Iudushka makes the one truly heartrending cry of his life, we are moved beyond description. 'Where are they all?' he cries, thinking of the mother, the brothers, the sons he has tricked and bedevilled into the very grave. He has felt the clammy coldness of a hand touching him – and the hand is his own. His cry is like Lear's. And it is all the more appalling that he utters this cry when his broken niece is still with him; if he had cried out when he was alone we would not believe. One had indeed not grasped it until then – the total disappearance of a family, the total disappearance of all that suffering and hatred. And the force of the book is all the greater because we do not look back upon a number of dramatic intrigues capped by their scenes, but we see Russia in our mind's eye, the steppe, the little-changing sky, the distance of people from each other, and the empty hours of all those lives. The English novel of family life inevitably turns from such a pessimism, but not, I think, because the English family is or was any nicer than the Golovlyovs were. The middle class, up to now, have lived in an expanding economy, which has enabled people to be independent where they could not be indulgent. If that economy becomes static or if it is put on the defensive, then a different tale will appear. The story of our money and of our religion has yet to be written.

The Great Absentee

If literature were to follow the excellent custom of the Catholic Church which adds a new saint to the calendar in every generation, and with more than half an eye on the needs of the time, it is easy to see which character in fiction is now ripe for canonisation. Not the propaganding figure of Don Quixote; not the innocent Pickwick; certainly not Robinson Crusoe, that too industrious town-planner knocking up a new society. The function of the saints is to assuage the wishes of the unconscious, to appeal to that part of a man which is least apparent to himself, and today we must turn away from the heroic, the energetic, expansive and productive characters. Falstaff the coward, Oblomov the sublime sluggard and absentee, seem to me our natural candidates. Oblomov above all. In a world of planners he plans himself to sleep. In a world of action he discovers the poetry of procrastination. In a world of passion he discovers the delicacies of reluctance. And when we reject his passivity he bears our secret desire for it like a martyr. For us he sleeps, for us he lies in bed daydreaming, for us his mind goes back to the Arcadia of childhood, drinking the opiate of memory. For our sakes who live in clean rooms and who jump out of bed when the alarm clock goes, Oblomov lies among his cobwebs and his fleas, his books unread, his ink dry in the bottle, his letters unanswered. While we prosper, he is cheated. And at the end of our racketing day we see his face – the moon-like face of the obese and the slack, and with that wry kink of fret and faint madness which the moon sometimes has on it – we see his face looking upon us with the penetrating, disturbing criticism of the incurable, the mysterious reproach of the man who is in the wrong. Slowly, guiltily, his foot comes out of the bedclothes and dangles furtively above the slipper on the floor and then, with a tremor of modesty before the implications of an act so obscenely decisive, the foot is withdrawn. Who knows what valuable grains of sensibility are lost to the soul when man is persuaded to stand upright?

In all the great mad literature of nineteenth-century Russia, Goncharov's novel is, to my mind, the gentlest and most sympathetic in its feeling. Like so many great books, *Oblomov* grew beyond its author's intention. Goncharov was one of the new realists and reformers. He wrote to satirise the sluggishness of the old-fashioned landowner. The industrialisation of Russia was beginning, and he wrote to praise the virtues of the new businessman. *Oblomov* is an excellent example of the ambiguous value of propagandist purpose to a novelist: in a great novelist this will stimulate the talent until it swallows the purpose. Without genius Goncharov might have written a tract. Having genius, he has created one of the sublime comedies of all literature. After we have read this book we do not hate idleness, escapism, daydreaming: we love Oblomov. We have discovered a man, a new man whose existence we had never suspected; a ludicrous Russian nobleman who, we realise, has dwelt for a long time not in Russia but in ourselves. And, so deceptive is the relation of moral purpose and literature, we are not in the least impressed by Stolz, the busy, cheerful man of affairs, who is held up for our admiration. It is easy and natural to admire *him*; we take *him* in our stride; our sense of justice, our humanity and our sense of adventure, demand more delicate and difficult tasks. Oblomov loses Olga, Stolz marries her; but, like Olga, after her years of happy and successful marriage, we have an intuition that something was lost when Oblomov was cast away. As Goncharov wrote – and he spent many years on this book – he began to see beyond the comedy of Oblomov's condition and discern the value of it. Propaganda does not become art until it has the grace and the courage to welcome the apparent defeat of its purpose.

There is reason to regret – though such regrets are really irrelevant to criticism – that Goncharov did have a purpose, and that he took it seriously enough to create the character of the virtuous Stolz. I do not mean that Stolz is a failure as a character. Goncharov had the gift of original observation, and he was incapable of palming off on us a wooden or sentimental idealisation in the manner of our Victorian novelists. He has the kind of closeness to fact which Trollope had. One's criticism of Stolz is simply that he exists at all. The book could get on quite as well, indeed it might have taken a more startling and imaginative turn, without him. And this is not pure conjecture. We now know enough about Goncharov to see that he was not merely a pedestrian realist; Russian critics have pointed out that *Oblomov* is a much more subjective book than it appears to be at first sight. There is more than one hint in the drawing of Oblomov's character. That he should pay for his torpor by being filthy and getting swindled we easily see. What other price is there? Ill-health, of course. But there is something more. A faint furrow comes sometimes between those bland and mooning brows; a perceptible dryness gives, once in a while, an unguarded edge to his voice. Oblomov has the horrors. Under that passivity lies a possible madness, a frantic, abysmal, screaming despair. Now, that element is neglected by the book. Goncharov's preoccupation with Stolz took his mind from it. And so, once Oblomov has retreated from his affair with Olga with all the faultless strategic skill of the neurotic, he slumps to a comfortable, though pilfered, life in the arms of his landlady. He is ill. She mothers him. She recognises in him an innocent. This is a shock to a moral man like Stolz, who believes in self-mastery, self-knowledge, the muscular development of human character; to Stolz, Oblomov is like a man who has gone native. But benign to the end, ineffectual, happy and blessed by Fate, Oblomov dies in his sleep, protected from his enemies and wept by the few who love him.

Nothing could be more assuring. There is a transcendent gentleness, an ineffable prosaic delicacy, in the book. But we can't get away from it; the second part, although benign and moral, is dull. Suppose, for one moment, that Goncharov had not kept up his guard. Suppose that, undirected by Stolz and moral purpose, he had told much more of the truth. For Goncharov was, of course, a potential Oblomov – the fat man with the phlegmatic and malicious tongue, they called him. And Goncharov did have the horrors; he knew what they were. His life is one of those tales of mania that shadow literature, as we are said to be shadowed all our lives by our agonies at birth. Goncharov's minutely observant disposition concealed a nature eaten up by malice and jealousy. A slow, vegetating writer who wrote little, he could never forgive Turgenev for his adroitness, his skill and his success. He conceived the notion that Turgenev had stolen one of his plots and some of his characters, and even a humiliating public arbitration on the matter did not cure him. As the years went by and Turgenev's fame grew, Goncharov built up a fantastic dossier of Turgenev's supposed plagiarisms. Jealousy grew, as it will, into persecution mania. That is the drama which is missing: Oblomov's hatred of Stolz. Alternatively Oblomov's hatred of himself. Dostoevsky would have seen that; but, thank heaven, Dostoevsky did not seize the character of Oblomov. He would have made him one more Russian Christ.

Looking back on that paragraph, I begin to wonder if I have not strayed into a too strenuous conception of Oblomov's character and have forgotten his humility and its complement: his immense and passive conceit. No one can say that Oblomov is a divided man, he is as perfectly integrated as a blancmange. Oblomov's relation with the swindling Zahar, his servant, is like that of wife and husband; and the master rises to feminine heights in the wonderful quarrel which takes place in the early pages. Like some inured husband Zahar watches with resignation the familiar sight of Ilya Ilyitch Oblomov building up an emotional scene:

'Then why did you talk of moving?' said Oblomov. 'Why, no man can stand it!'

'I merely thought other people are no worse than us, and if they move we can,' Zahar said.

'What? What?' Ilya Ilyitch asked in surprise. 'What did you say?'

Zahar was confused, not knowing what he could have said to cause his master's dramatic gesture and question. He was silent.

'Other people are no worse!' Ilya Ilyitch repeated with horror. 'This is what you have come to! I shall know now that I am the same as "other people" to you!'

Oblomov bowed to Zahar ironically, looking deeply insulted.

'But Ilya Ilyitch, I've never said you were the same as anyone else . . .'

'Out of my sight!' Oblomov commanded, pointing to the door. 'I can't bear to look at you. Ah, "other people"! Very well!'

The scene goes on. Oblomov calls for kvass, and begins again on an ominously quiet note:

'Well, how do you feel?' Ilya Ilyitch asked gently. 'You aren't happy, are you? Do you repent your transgression?'

'Whatever is this?' Zahar wondered bitterly. 'Something heartrending, I expect; one is bound to cry if he goes for one like this. How have I grieved you, Ilya Ilyitch?'

'How?' Oblomov repeated. 'Why have you considered what *other people* are? Comparing me to "other people",' Oblomov said. 'Why do I rush about or work? Don't I eat enough? Do I look thin and wretched? Do I go short of things? I should hope I have someone to wait on me and do things for me. Thank heaven I've never in my life put on my stockings myself. As though I would trouble! Why should I?'

And so he goes, pulling out all the stops, to the final words of this sublime quarrel, until Zahar is sobbing with contrition which – experience has taught him – is a necessary part of the play:

'And you,' Oblomov went on, not listening to him, 'you should be ashamed to say such things! That's the snake I've warmed in my bosom.'

'Snake!' Zahar cried, clasping his hands and setting up such a howl that it sounded exactly as though two dozen bumble-bees had flown into the room and started buzzing. 'When have I mentioned a snake?' he said amidst his sobs. 'I never even dream of the cursed thing.'

Both had ceased to understand each other and now no longer understood themselves.

Goncharov had all the comic gifts. He had the art of capping one absurdity with another yet more absurd. He is fantastic in this scene; but in the beautiful chapter which describes Oblomov's childhood and youth, he is also the master of the quieter humour of real record. The talk about the evenings drawing in, in the Oblomov drawing-room, is a perfect fragment of satirical observation. Again his purely descriptive drollery is superb. There is the hour of the siesta when, the family and servants having guzzled in their plump and sunny Arcadia, all are asleep. It is a folk picture, a scene from the *Sleeping Beauty*, a fairty-tale – to those scenes Russian humour owes a profound debt:

The gardener stretched himself out under a bush in the garden beside his mattock, and the coachman was asleep in the stables. Ilya Ilyitch peeped into the servants' hall; everyone was lying down on the benches, on the floor, and in the entry; the children, left to their devices, were crawling about the yard and rummaging in the sand. The dogs retreated into the depths of their kennels, since there was no one to bark at. One could walk straight through the house and not meet anyone; one could steal everything that was about and cart it away unhindered – but there were no thieves in these parts. It was an overwhelming irresistible sleep, a true semblance of death. There was no life anywhere: only sounds of snoring of various pitch and quality came from every corner. Occasionally some sleeper would raise his head, look in senseless surprise about him and turn over or spit without opening his eyes, and munching with his lips or muttering under his breath, drop asleep once more. Another would suddenly, without any preliminaries, jump off his couch as though afraid of losing precious moments, seize the jug of kvass, blow the flies that floated in it, causing them to move violently in the hope of improving their position, take a drink, and again fall on the bed as though shot dead.

The undertone of dream and fairy-tale runs through the book like the murmur of a stream, so that to call Goncharov a realist is misleading. Oblomov himself becomes one of those transfigured characters which have grown over a long period of writing, which exist on several planes, and which go on growing in the mind after the book is put down. Now he seems to symbolise the soul, now he is the folly of idleness, now he is the accuser of success. He is an enormous character.

One other character ought to be mentioned: Olga. She is a direct descendant of Pushkin's Tatiana. In drawing her Goncharov achieved something unusual. Ever observant, he set about describing the birth and growth of a girl's personality; and especially he set out to describe what most novelists – always too much in love with their heroines – omit: the growth of their will. Goncharov showed that the apparently incalculable Olga was really quite calculable. You could show how much she would change from week to week. It is an oddly cool psychological analysis of 'the young person' and something I do not remember seeing as clearly done anywhere outside of Henry James. Much might be written about her, and much more still about a comic masterpiece which does not agitate the mind as some comedies do, but which seems to become grafted into it.

The Minor Dostoevsky

I have been reading the shorter novels of Dostoevsky. It is natural to pause before doing so for one last glance at the exalted glaciers of the major works. We stand in the sun on the modest contours of the foothills, looking up at the haggard and fog-hung precipices of Mounts Karamazov, Myshkin, Stavrogin and Raskolnikov, rather awed to think we have been up there, shuddering at the memory of it, impelled to go again, but glad of an excuse not to try it this time. We have been so lost on those heights; laughter at the wrong moments was so apt to cap the ecstasy of our expeditions. We would have periods of asking, with Tolstoy and Turgenev, whether our leader need be so shameless; and our Western natures rebelled at the notion of returning with the hangdog air of pretty criminals. We conceived society to be our neighbours and their works; not a spawn of souls, half-born and without even an hour's civilisation. And then, in the Twenties, too heady a tradition of salvation was hung around those peaks, and it was the wrong kind of salvation. The world is not saved by novelists; and the unreason of the psychological mystics of the Twenties seems to us now, I think, a rather shady attempt to get to God by the stage door. One thing scientific culture has done for us is to give us a desire for order and for intellectual propriety, and I hope we are beginning to see again that egging readers on to personal conversion is not one of the functions of the novel. In any case, the kind of salvation which Dostoevsky appeared to urge was not as private as it seemed to his adorers of twenty years ago; he did not offer a personal salvation in the form of a semi-religious pyscho-analysis. The people of Dostoevsky's novels are notable not for their isolation but for their gregariousness. The infection is common. They run in crowds. If they plan to suicide or murder they tell everyone. They are missionaries in mass-morbidity, mass-guilt, and mass-confession. Even when alone they are not absolutely alone; they have at least two selves. One hears not the private groan but the public lamentation. I can well imagine that the next time I read the great works of Dostoevsky – and we are growing nearer and nearer to his temper – I shall find he has everything to say to a Europe which is becoming a morass of broken pride, vengeance, humiliation and remorse. As a political journalist he will have a great deal to say about Christianity and Socialism, about Germany and Russia, about the criminality of Europe; as a novelist he will seem to show a profound instinct for the character of groups of people, their ideas and the common hungers that bind them.

The irrational is no longer the novelty it was, and we are consequently less struck by the madness of Dostoevsky than we used to be. A sensationalist he was; but now, whenever I open a novel of his, my first impression is one of realism and sanity. He knows the world from behind the scenes. The accent is decisive. The voice bristles with satire and expands with a capacious humour. Dostoevsky at his best writes like a hunted man who, for the moment, has fooled the bloodhounds and has time to confess and to laugh before the baying drives him on again. He is laughing hotly from the midst of experience. He is not laughing in order to forget it. The shorter novels of Dostoevsky – and in shorter works like *The Eternal Husband, An Unpleasant Predicament* and *Uncle's Dream*, we see the ground plan of all his greater works – are festive with experience of human society. Dostoevsky could see the terrors of our double natures, the fever in which our inner ghosts encounter each other, but he saw the raw comedy of this conjunction. It is frightful that we have so many selves and that the unconscious may wreck us; on the other hand there is something bizarre, something comic, something pitiable, in this squabbling assembly that has somehow got into one unpleasant pair of trousers. Look at *Uncle's Dream* for a moment. It is a farce; a masterful provincial lady in a scandal-mongering clique attempts to marry off her beautiful daughter to a decrepit prince. One can picture the whole story as a very funny and quite unreal piece of theatre. But even this mechanical piece of fooling lives on several planes. One moment the Prince, with his wig, his false beard and his derelict body, is a horror; the next moment he is ridiculous. Then, suddenly, he appears delightful. We long for him to appear again as we long for Stefan Trofimovitch in *The Possessed*. The Prince even attains a rickety dignity, and from dignity, he dwindles to a thing of pity. After all, we say, he did not really lie when he said his proposal of marriage was a dream. The conventional comic writer draws his characters to a single pattern of wit or makes the world a convenience for his joke. Dostoevsky does not do this. He is one of the great comic writers because, however satirically he may begin, he always grows into humour, and the humour is not imposed on life but arises out of it. He is aware of the collisions that take place in our natures. Somewhere – I forget where – Dostoevsky said he merely pushed things to extremes where other people went only half-way. And yet when we compare Dickens's *A Christmas Carol* with Dostoevsky's *An Unpleasant Predicament*, it is Dickens who seems to be the unreal and exaggerating artist. For Dickens exaggerated in seeing only one side of his characters. (Tony Weller's life is reduced to a reaction to widders, Barkis is merely 'willin'', and so on.) Dostoevsky explored the whole, and the thing that is comic on one page may become tragic on the next. The profoundly humorous writers are humorous because they are responsive to the hopeless, uncouth concatenations of life.

In *An Unpleasant Predicament* we have the simple story of a pompous official who, in an excess of philanthropical conceit, goes uninvited to his clerk's wedding celebrations, just to show that all men are brothers and that he is above social prejudice. Far from having a good effect, the visit ends in his total disgrace and almost succeeds in wrecking the marriage. The stages of Ivan Ilyitch's downfall, until he is carried dead drunk to the bridal bed and breaks up the wedding, are brilliantly described, and Dostoevsky, who, like all the nineteenth-century romantics, excelled in describing the moods of crowds, keeps us in uncertainty until the end. Exploring all the possibilities, that is to say raising all the mystifying issues which can be raised, as if he were writing a long novel and not a short story, he ends with justice to all. Ivan Ilyitch is not alone to blame. The poor clerk, with his pride and his private quarrels with his wife, is in a muddle as well. We cannot be made responsible for the unnerving manners of our friends. No one is malignant, but everyone is to blame. It is all very well to talk about humanity and brotherhood, but be careful that in doing so you are not forgetting your own pride when you contemplate the pride of other people. Each man and woman, I warn you (says Dostoevsky, the incurable novelist), is capable of becoming a novel in himself, a novel by Dostoevsky, moreover. I warn you it is impossible to do anything whatever with any human being, unless you are fully willing to take the tumultuous consequences of his being human.

As I said before, it is odd that Dostoevsky should ever have been regarded as the novelist of the isolated soul. I can only suppose that very few readers read these comedies and do not know *The House of the Dead*, that wonderful documentary mine in which Dostoevsky describes his Siberian experiences, without hysteria or ideological puffing. In the great novels he is so blatantly the writer of spiritual headlines; in *The House of the Dead* he was content with the laconic news. No one who has read it can say that he ignored the problems of society. Like Balzac, on the contrary, he plunders society. He is acutely aware of class differences. So gregarious and populated is the unconscious that in the typical dreams of his characters crowds of people will appear. There are, for example, the dramatic dreams in *The Eternal Husband*, Dostoevsky's most purely intellectual and accomplished comic novel. The sinister gangs of dream figures stamp up Veltchaninov's stairs and point at him with horror as he lies asleep in his guilt. In this novel it has been said that Dostoevsky parodied himself – it was written after *The Idiot* and *Crime and Punishment* – and certainly all his ideas are here: the double, the unconscious, the fantasies, dreams, persecutions, suspicions, shames and exchanges of personality. Even a child is tortured. But surely this comic masterpiece, a comedy which (as always in Dostoevsky) carries its own underworld along with it, stands completely on its own feet. In the first place the growth of Veltchaninov's sense of guilt from a vague irritation to mind and health into definite consciousness is described with wonderful objectivity and suspense. The value of psychological analysis to the novel lay, for Dostoevsky, in its latent dramatic quality. Psychology was dramatic; for us it becomes more and more a metaphor or explanation. The farcical duel between Veltchaninov and 'the eternal husband' whom he has cuckolded has an undertone of imaginative gravity which makes the farce more dangerous. Dostoevsky, once more, is pushing things to extremes because at the end of the extreme is the pity of human nature. Half-way – where other writers leave this kind of story – lie the conventions of melodrama and intellectual comedy; and, mad though the story is, it is full of the madness we all know about in the lives of people. The madness is the madness of life, not the madness of the mind. No one will ever accuse

Dostoevsky of failing to complicate a situation, and this book is a succession of superb complications. The very last one, in which 'the eternal husband' is being bullied by his new wife, and has silently to beg Veltchaninov not to cuckold him again, is one of the funniest and most moving in comic literature. The unconscious, Dostoevsky discovered, gave probability to the most bizarre situations and turned coincidence into fate. And, it is interesting to note, in the middle of this comic novel there occurs one of the very few pictures of normal, happy, family life to be found in his work.

The Eternal Husband is no doubt so refreshingly precise in its psychology, so well composed and economically written, so brilliant in its commentary because – for the time being – Dostoevsky had exhausted his anxiety for salvation. This is his one Western novel. It came from that part of him that liked to cut a social figure and was written during a rare period of equipoise and untroubled self-satisfaction. It has the genial air of a successful presumption, and it might easily have been written in our century, not his. And yet it could not have been. For the effect of psychological intuitions and discoveries upon our novel is to make it reminiscent, autobiographical, plotless; whereas in Dostoevsky's hands the novel became inventive, dramatic and far richer in plot than the rest of Russian fiction. How rich *The Eternal Husband* is in episodes; the absurd house-watching scene, the dramatic interviews, the discovery that the husband is torturing his child, the scandal at the brothel, the visit to the country, the nights which husband and lover spend together, where the husband first poses as his wife's ghost and later attempts murder! When one compares the realism of Chekhov with the romantic realism of Dostoevsky one sees how much was thrown away when novelists threw out plot. When plot went, the isolation of characters began; and though, by Dostoevsky's time, plots were stale, he showed that even the most hackneyed and novelette-like plot became rich and new when it was replenished by a new view of human nature.

A Russian Cinderella

And what happened after the glass slipper fitted and Cinderella married the beautiful Prince? Marriage changes the character of women; what kind of woman did Cinderella become? Going back through the story and looking for those experiences which must have marked Cinderella's life, we cannot but be alarmed by the probabilities. How humiliation must have intensified her emotional and imaginative life! What a crowd of impulses will fly up, fierce and disparate in their flight, like birds suddenly set free, when the years and years of repression come to an end! What an appetite for life, for pre-eminence, for power, for perpetuating the glittering success, will come to the down-trodden and humiliated one. Heaven protect us (we say aloud, as we glance at the history of society) from the tongue, the will, the parading ego, the unstable moods of the slave set free! And how did Cinderella escape – if she did escape it – the worst evil that can puddle the eyes and slur the lips of a beautiful woman: the vice of touchiness?

I know of no book that presents this case with more imagination and percipience than Aksakov's *A Russian Gentleman*. Sofya Nicolayevna, in that most limpid of the Russian autobiographies, is a portrait of Aksakov's mother. For years she had been outrageously treated by a stepmother. Then had followed a time of extravagant social success. At the time of her marriage, when she came as a guarded and resolute stranger into the patriarchal family of pioneers who had settled in the swollen and luscious region of Ufa, the old Abrahamic grandfather of the family judged her character:

'Well, now, friend Ivan, what say you of the daughter-in-law? As a man you are a better judge of the point than women are.' Karatayeff, disregarding a signal from his wife, burst out with enthusiasm: 'I do assure you, batyushka, that such another dazzler' – he always used this

[341]

phrase of a beautiful woman – 'as brother Alexyei has bagged is not to be found in the whole world. A look from her is as good as a shilling. And her cleverness! It's past all telling. But there's one thing, batyushka: she's proud: she can't stand a joke. When you try to have a little fun with her, she gives you a look that makes you bite off the end of your tongue.'

And Aksakov himself says of the mother he adored and who adored him with all the violence of her heart, 'Reluctantly,' he says, 'I must confess that love of power was one of her ruling passions; and the germs of this passion, now that she had been released from the cruel oppression of her stepmother, were sprouting actively at this time.' Much, evidently, would depend upon the Prince. But power-loving women who are the belles of local society have a surprising tendency to fall for nonentities. They do not marry Princes. They look for slaves.

In Aksakov's father, Sofya Nicolayevna found a man whose deference, obedience and humility made him the perfect, the passionate slave. She would rule him, raise him up, mould him to the shape of her brilliant, town-bred ideas. She would scare him into wakefulness, blow him up in scene after scene till she had made him into another being. It was a bad beginning. But strong characters are often convinced that there is virtue not for themselves alone but for everyone else in violent purges of self-expression; and Sofya Nicolayevna was too young and too blindly herself to discern that violent outbursts appalled her husband, paralysed him and drove him into the consuming daydreams of disillusion and resentment. She won her victory – but what a victory! It was empty. For she had begun by destroying his power of candour. Like many weak people, Alexyei had learned under the despotism of his father to develop a capacity for strategic retreat and adjustment. The weak – and how it maddens the strong! – have their own resources. The strong – and how it surprises the weak! – are so subject to sudden collapse, hysterical dependence, remorse and despair. Aksakov's father had his moments of pre-eminence. And in any case there are always compensations in life. He would leave the tumultuous bedroom to sit by the deep river which tumbled past the house, watching the sight which – Aksakov says – no Russian can resist: the sight of moving water. There was superb, Homeric fishing at Ufa; and the end of a scene (Sofya Nicolayevna would observe in despair) was often a fishing expedition, when the perch came out of the river by the dozen and – engrossed now by an unhuman antagonist – her husband would be seen in his boat, playing an heroic bream. Flustered by human nature, he could slip away from the incomprehensible campaigns of love into a passion no less solacing or primitive; the passion of the chase. In the crystalline air of the steppe and among the evening fogs of the water meadows and birch woods he would wait for the rising quail which had been decoyed by the peasant's flute, and shout, undeterred, at the hare bolting for cover.

The real Prince was Sofya Nicolayevna's father-in-law, the stupendous grandfather whose portrait dominates the book and whose wise, patriarchal mind and arbitrary nature seem to reign over every page. In this old despot, with his terrifying rages, his implacable regard for truth, godlike in the solemnity of his habits, so that every eccentricity from chopping his shirts up on the doorstep, dragging his wife about by the hair, or standing more or less naked in the farmyard every morning to watch the sun rise, had the weight of something like the whole Mosaic Law behind it – in this tribal hero Sofya Nicolayevna recognised a force more powerful than her own and an indispensable ally among the jealousies of the family. Here she came upon her match in love and found her quality justly estimated and admired. The love of this old man for his daughter-in-law, in a family rat-ridden with that fear and that jealousy which natures too strong always create around them, is incomparably moving. In this first volume of his recollections, when Aksakov was describing the early life of his grandfather and his parents, he was an imaginative artist of the highest order.

In the second volume of his recollections, called *A Russian Schoolboy*, Aksakov reveals the second great passion of Sofya Nicolayevna. It was for himself. Intense in all her passions, she directed her whole life upon the ailing boy and he depended utterly on her. Their separations brought them both to fevers, fits and the brink of suicide. One must suppose that the fixity and joy of this overpowering and constant emotion must have been the cause of Aksakov's minute and exalted memory of his childhood, a memory that is hardly surpassed by Proust's. To Aksakov, childhood was the Golden Age. Not a bird song, not the flight of a butterfly or flash of a fish was forgotten. They were embalmed in the stillness of an unhesitating recollection. Like Goncharov's recollections of his childhood in *Oblomov*,

[343]

Aksakov's have the warmth of some tale of the folk, where the sun always shines and where even the wickedness of man or the savagery of nature charms us as legends do, illuminating our lives without overpowering them. Aksakov's recollections are a retrospect without remorse. We are endeared by the permanence of human types and the profit and loss of living. The turbulent emotion of Aksakov's adoration of his mother has calmed into one of those deep and now untroubled feelings so beneficent to works of art. No other Russian writer, not even Tolstoy, has achieved the extraordinary stillness and ecstasy of Aksakov's picture of family life. No other Russian writer has held the mirror up to life so steadily, so that we see how the hours pass at Ufa in all their enchanting detail, without a tremor of the glass. In Proust, the act of remembering, the search for the past, the sensibility of the seeker, are important, perhaps the most important elements, in the task of memory; in Aksakov's mirror the agitation and flaws of such a brilliant egoism are not there to distract. Aksakov is not speculative. He is simple, tender, comic, delicate and factual.

The dinner passed off in the usual fashion. The young pair sat side by side between the old couple; there were a great many courses, one richer and more indigestible than another; the cook, Stepan, had been lavish with his spice, cloves and pepper, and especially with his butter. The bride ate the dainties pressed upon her by Stepan Mihailovitch, and prayed that she might not die in the night. There was little talking, partly because every mouth was occupied and also because the party were not good at conversation. Indeed, they were all uncomfortable in their own ways. Yerlykin in his sober intervals drank nothing but water, and hardly spoke at all at such times, which gained him a reputation for exceptional intelligence; and Karatayeff dared not open his mouth in the presence of Stepan Mihailovitch except to answer a question, and went no farther than repeating the last words of other people's remarks. If they said 'The hay crop will be good if we get no rain' or 'The rye made a good start till the sudden frost came' – Karatayeff came in like an echo 'if we get no rain', 'till the frost came'; and his repetitions were sometimes ill-timed . . . Mazan with long boots smelling of tar on his feet, and wearing a long coat which made him look like a bear dressed up in sacking, handed round the loving cup . . .

How is it that so still, so conservative a memory nevertheless conveys to us an impression of animation, excitement and suspense? For nothing like the airless gleam of a Dutch interior halts the descriptions of the scene. The answer must be that Aksakov's memory conceals the act of remembering, that his imagination works in hiding; he holds the mirror so still that we see not the writer but the movement of life itself, as the hunter or watcher of birds does when he sits in the fields unmoving for hours until life has the courage to resume its business. We watch with Aksakov and observe the huge suspense that hangs upon every detail of life from minute to minute.

Aksakov was a Slavophil and a conservative. No hint of the political problems that were to disturb Turgenev and his successors comes into his work. To him the life of the country house in Russia – at least as he knew it – was as sound as an apple. It is true there may be sadistic and drunken landowners, who beat and even murder their serfs. It is true that his grandfather was a violent man who expected to be obeyed on the spot and gave summary punishment. But such things are in the order of nature. His grandfather prospered. His people or tribe prospered. To be relieved of evil we must all pray to God. One cannot say that Aksakov was indifferent or complacent. He was simply under a spell.

It was the spell of private life; that life which goes on whether there is justice or injustice, war or peace, struggle or inertia, the web we spin. One reads Aksakov now with a natural nostalgia – not indeed for the past, nor for the delectable life of landed prosperity; not even for the abundance of food and drink – for what is the story of family life but the story of the hours spent between one meal and the next? – but for the fixed state of living, some settled condition of judgment. Aksakov's grandfather sat watching the happy young couple, Sofya Nicolayevna and her husband:

> His happiness had a shade of fear and of disbelief in the solidity and permanence of a state of things in itself so charming. He would have liked to speak his mind on the subject, to give them some hints or some useful advice; but whenever he began, he could not find the right words for thoughts and feelings which he could not make clear even to himself; and he went no farther than those trivial commonplaces, which, for all their triviality, have been bequeathed to us by the practical wisdom of past generations and are verified by our own experience.

[345]

What is it we admire about these words? We admire their closeness to a simple mind. But above all we admire the spaciousness of the experience from which they come. To that sense of space, in the Russian novels of the nineteenth century, we return eagerly again and again.

A Russian Outsider

The great Russian novels of the nineteenth century so dominate their scene that we forget they stand on the shoulders of minor figures who would impress the reader in any less fertile literature. One of these minor figures is Nicolai Leskov. I am not sure whether, considered as a writer of short stories, Leskov can justly be called minor. In England, translation of Aksakov came very late in the day, when his contemporaries like Turgenev and Dostoevsky were already established with us. There has been a great delay in translating Leskov. A small collection of his tales called *The Sentry* was translated by A. E. Charnot and given to us by Edward Garnett in 1922; then in 1926 Gorky introduced us to *The Enchanted Wanderer*; and since then there has been one more volume: *The Musk Ox*, translated by Mr L. Norman. Those who read *The Sentry* will remember Leskov's quality in that powerful story of squalid murder called *The Lady Macbeth of the Mzinsk District* and in the bishop's dramatic tale of his mission to Siberia, called *On the Edge of the World*.

Nicolai Leskov was born in 1831 and died in 1895. He was born of mixed class – clergy, merchants and the gentry were his forebears – and this puts his range of observation closer to Dostoevsky's than to the landowner writers'. His origins are not very different from Dostoevsky's. For a long period of his life Leskov worked for an Englishman who was managing one of the great estates – the Englishman is amusingly drawn in the tale called *The Stinger* in Mr Norman's translation – and he travelled all over Russia. When Leskov came to write he had a wide, travelling experience of Russian life and custom to draw on, an experience which had been formed without literary intent. He 'went to the people' not as a self-conscious intellectual, but as a practical man of affairs. One can see how this worked both advantageously and disadvantageously on Leskov's talent. He is, we are told, one of the 'unplaced' writers of the nineteenth century, very popular with the public but regarded with caution by the critics; and this caution comes from the suspicion that many of Leskov's stories are ready made. They come too unevenly, too amateurishly and only partly digested out of life. They smack sometimes of the reminiscences of a District Commissioner. It seems to be a fact that a writer of the highest class must be driven by the instinct of the artist to strike a balance between life and literature very early; then only will he have time and place in his mind for the hourly discipline of imagination and sensibility which is essential to the well-being of a talent. The sight of the self-conscious artist 'going to the people', or doing the opposite and shrinking from external experience, is a subject for satire and, nowadays, for sociological attack; but the artist is in the right of it. The greatest artists have always rationed themselves. In the life of Leskov one can see that he paid for the rich experience which enabled him, among other things, to form an astonishing ear for the real speaking habits of people by beginning to write too late in life. One has only to compare his manner of narration with Turgenev's. Both Leskov and Turgenev used what is now considered the old-fashioned device of setting a story within a story. The Baron puts down his glass after dinner and is reminded of an extraordinary man or woman he met years before. Or he retells something he heard when he was a student, or when he was out shooting. Now in Turgenev the convention is graceful, because we feel that he has invented the setting. There never was such a Baron with his glass of wine, nor such a student. The device convinces because it is an artifice. In Leskov one has no similar illusion. We feel that his beginnings, his containing stories are muddled up with real life and, by the great paradox of art, they are distracting and unconvincing just because they are probably true.

Another reason for the uncertainty about Leskov's talent and the neglect of it in Russia is said to be political. A practical and experienced man, Leskov attacked the Left, especially the nihilists, and was boycotted by the Liberal papers and critics for the rest of his life. He was also especially interested in the religious subject, and was accused of being a debased clerical writer fond of mixing lewdness and religion. He deserted the impressive ranks of Russian pessimism for a gentler, more tolerant and warmer view of life. I can only say that I do not believe Leskov's position was seriously affected by these sins. Dostoevsky did far worse in *The Possessed*, and Turgenev went almost as far in *Fathers and Sons* and *Virgin*

Soil, and both survived the anger of the political fanatics. Aksakov was a Conservative of the Conservatives. If Leskov's position was unsatisfactory to the critics the reason is plain. He brought the independence, the originality of the man who has put his own life and experience before his political and religious views. Revolutionaries, Liberals and Conservatives both disliked him; and perhaps they had some right on their side, perhaps there is no special merit in refusing to be labelled. That kind of independence is frequently egotistical and unstable.

There are eight stories in *The Musk Ox,* and many of them stop at the point where Dostoevsky would have begun to inflate them. Leskov is in many respects a Dostoevsky without the epileptic fits. The tale called *The Musk Ox* is about an uncouth and vagabondish fellow who is deeply religious and is training to be a priest. But he cannot get on with people. He is dirty, he is difficult, he has no pliancy. He becomes a tutor and finds the family he is with are corrupt, and goes scowling away at a moment's notice to tramp the roads. Everyone, according to him, is tainted. There are fewer and fewer people worth seeing or talking to, and so, tramplike and morose, refusing to work, demanding his bread at any door, he loses himself in the depths of society, looking for signs of the resurrection of the human spirit among the outcasts and disinherited. In the end, he finds a reformed estate run by a hard and thriving businessman who recognises his originality and lets him hang around. The businessman knows that 'the musk ox' will try and upset his workers by preaching his peculiar Gospel Hall revolution to them; but the businessman also knows that the workers will regard the tramp not as a messiah but as a comedian. And so it turns out. They love 'the musk ox' and humour him. Everyone loves and humours him, and this is too much. 'The musk ox' has depended on getting on badly with people; humoured, he goes and hangs himself.

Like many of Leskov's stories, this one is slow in starting. He is best in describing the unexpected reactions of peasant people and in recording their devious or stone-walling conversation. And he is especially attractive because of his sympathy. Leskov had a particular gift for leading one, step by step, into the quiet obstinacies of sainthood, and for creating the awkward, the almost humdrum saint, the very ordinary man who has become isolated from the beliefs of his fellows by the force of experience. Where other writers interest us in ordinary people by giving them some bizarre habit of life or mind, or by turning them into eccentrics, Leskov sticks closer to his observation. The King Charles's head is not an amusing decoration in these people's lives; it is very often the main, clumsy, immovable piece of furniture. In one of his tales, the mournful chair-mender, who is made to change his name by an erratic nobleman, lives with the new name all his life, as if it were a sofa or a sideboard he was keeping for someone. He lives with it religiously, without comprehension; there is nothing eccentric in this. For the new name is his luck. Too perturbing to be thought ludicrous, too useful to be inquired into. Again and again in Leskov's stories, something comes into the lives of the people and settles there immovably like an animal. There is the sensation of a thing or a presence mysteriously 'in occupation', a sensation one has also in stories of Kafka's. When the Lady Macbeth of the Mzinsk district commits adultery, we detect at once a change in the character of her husband's house. She herself walks about like an empress giving orders, quieting the whispers about her adultery with gifts, until the servants say, 'That's all. It's her affair – she will have to answer for it.' When she goes from adultery to murder, we see guilt living in the house. In a remarkable passage Leskov actually gives a form to this presence – there is a symbol in all his stories – without deviating into fantasy, but indeed by adding to psychological truth. After her first murder when she is lying down on her husband's bed dreaming of her lover, Katerina Lvovna sees a cat come on to the bed and she strokes it. She is puzzled because there is no cat belonging to the house. She does not realise that she is dreaming the cat.

In this dreadful story, in all of Leskov's best work, every sentence adds and tells, and Katerina moves towards her doom trammelled by her crimes, and only death can set her free of them. Circumstance, we feel, has moved into her life like the hostile figures of a dream, and has ousted her will. Her drama is impelled. And because of the laconic simplicity of the writing and the awkward garnishment of plain but real dialogue, her lot seems to us unanswerable and cuts speculation short.

Leskov's powers as a writer were brought out most strongly in his religious stories; but unlike most religious writers he was capable of many moods. He comes closest, I suppose, to the one or two Irish writers who are sometimes pious, sometimes sceptical, sometimes even ribald; and while he satirised the clergy or described religious failure, he also described the search for pure religion. And he did this, as a novelist should, without being didactic. His mind was saturated with the religious folk-lore of the peasants. Leskov seems to have a more genuinely religious nature than 'the great sinner', as we can see in the story called *On the Edge of the World*. Here the mystery of faith and the question of the nature of Christ are described as a search, and indeed, paradoxically, as a gradual shedding of what is formally thought to be Christian. A young bishop is obliged to put his life in the hands of a pagan tribesman during a Siberian blizzard; they exist together on an animal level, and at every turn the dull, ignorant peasant who refuses to be baptised and whose simple mind argues in a maddening and small circle, obliges the bishop to shed one certainty of dogma after another. The setting is unforgettable. In some ways the religious mystery has moved into the bishop's life in the shape of the stinking, stoical, immovable tribesman. And the bishop is not presented as an obtuse or conventional figure of satire; he is sensitive, educated, courageous and altogether a delightful human being. There is a wonderful scene at the height of the blizzard when the peasant covers the bishop with a reeking reindeer skin and then crawls underneath with him, puts his nose against him and snorts his bad warm breath into the bishop's nose in order to keep him alive.

The Musk Ox is not as good a selection of Leskov's stories as *The Sentry* is, nor is it as well translated. The translator of Leskov has a cardinal difficulty. Leskov excelled as a writer of common speech and wrote many of his stories as they would be spoken in a kind of vernacular, which he sometimes stylised. This must have given his work a quality which escapes translation.

The Poet of Tourism

The Holy Door in St Peter's is closed; the Holy Year is over. What impressions of Rome have the pilgrims taken back with them, those labelled train-loads, those families of peasants, the pious socialites and those big, bruising American priests? I turn back to what has always seemed to me the best evocation of the tourist's Rome, indeed of the tourist himself – the *Amours de Voyage* of Arthur Hugh Clough written a hundred years ago:

> Is it illusion or not that attracteth the pilgrim transalpine
> Brings him a dullard and dunce hither to pry and to stare?
> Is it illusion or not that allures the barbarian stranger,
> Brings him with gold to the shrine, brings him in arms to the gate?

Like Bagehot, Clough is one of the few Victorians who seem to belong to our time rather than their own. The lack of the histrionic air, the lack of that invoked and obligatory sense of greatness, so characteristic of the chief and, no doubt, excelling writers of the age, makes these two writers at once accessible to us. Clough, for example, makes no bones about calling himself a tourist in Italy; and although all the English writers who went to Italy from the time of the Romantic movement were tourists, part of that great check and tartan exodus which was one of the strange sights of the time to continental observers, Clough is the only one to confess and expound the role. It was he who perceived the tourist as a subject and suggested him as a symbolical figure. Uncommitted, detached, languid, Clough does not strain, as Browning does, to pass himself off as an Italian; there is no effort to 'get to know the people' or to be 'off the beaten track.' As so often happens, the sceptic who is unable to make up his mind about ultimate things drifts doggedly into the conventional and it has been said that Clough's weakness as a poet comes from shortness of imagination, from the logician's determination not to see beyond his subject. But if in isolating a theme, we drain the overflowing spirit from it, there are the advantages of freshness, truthfulness and exactitude. And to these qualities Clough added one of his own: a naturalness which is a relief, almost a revelation, after the usual manner of the Victorian stage. Not until the novels of E. M. Forster do we meet anything like Clough; and not until Forster, either, do we meet with the distinguishing portrait of the English tourist in our literature.

What is a tourist? A comic character, of course, for he is a fish out of his proper waters. A watered-down Hamlet, perhaps: will-less, unadapted and consumed by that self-consciousness which is the cruel psychological price exacted by regulated travel. There is a three-cornered relation: between one's countrymen, the foreigner and the base, disconnected self, haunted more than ever when it is abroad, by the vague, ghostly specification of what it might have been. The loneliness of the evenings! Stendhal exclaimed in Rome. The mild, doubting face of every tourist is haunted by the murder he ought, sometime in his life, to have committed. If only I could have brought myself to do it, the face seems to be murmuring, I should not be here alone, when the lights come up, with my dreadful dilemma.

Clough, as we know, from his life and his poetry, was the poet of dilemma. In an age of professional trumpets, he engaged the dubious, the personal, the inquiring, the definite but conversational flute:

> Rome disappoints me much: I hardly as yet understand, but
> *Rubbishy* seems the word that most exactly would suit it.

It is the voice of the Common Room:

> However, one can live in Rome as also in London.
> It is a blessing, no doubt, to be rid of, at least for a time, of
> All one's friends and relations – yourself (forgive me!) included –
> All the *assujettisement* of having been what one has been,
> What one thinks one is, or thinks what others suppose one;
> Yet, in spite of all, we turn like fools to the English.

The lines open *Amours de Voyage* and Hamlet, with his guide-book, stands worried in the Eternal City which he had imagined to be marble and had found 'instead brickwork.' This is the opening despair of the tourist as he turns from the comfort of the lovely, grave, blank-minded domesticity of the Italians to the grim, cultural work that waits him. Not a street in the golden, rusted city but will ask him to take sides in the struggles of a dozen civilisations; not a building without murder, art, religion in its doors. There are the Greeks to deal with, the Romans, the endless underpinning of Western civilisation. There are the Goths and the decadence. There are the Christian question and the question of the unlikeableness of the early Christians. The Renaissance blocks the way, not as an idea only, but in solid instances of stone and acres of painted canvas. There are the beguiling and ambiguous corridors of the Vatican and St Peter's, the tremendous railway terminal from which we set out on our ornate journeys to death. There are centuries of the Christian Party Line. There is Truth, but then there is also Beauty. There is Beauty, but there is also Art. And then – but that is enough for today. The tired don gives up as the domestic crowds watch the crimson Roman sunset from the Pincio, and comes back to his Victorian hotel to talk to the English to whom 'like fools' we always turn when Art has become too much.

The English: *Amours de Voyage* is an epistolary novel in hexameters. Claude, the intellectual, writes to Eustace his friend. It is 1849. The English are the Trevellyns 'with the seven and seventy boxes, Courier, Papa and Mamma, the children, and Mary and Susan'. George is there too with moustachioes, as grossly bent on marriage as Claude is refined in evading it. But Claude is vulnerable. Alas, for the effect of days passed in the contemplation of statuary and in considering the highest questions – 'the Coliseum is large; but is this an idea?' – one is inclined to sink into self-indulgence. One is likely to sink to the Trevellyns, who, like all the English met by the tourist abroad, are not out of the top drawer. Socially speaking they are prone to a sort of indecent exposure, and indeed this inability to conceal that they are not 'quite quite' is a kind of secondary sexual characteristic of the English race. Claude is not quite unspeakable; tourism has simply encouraged afflicting introspection. He hangs round Mary Trevellyn – the chattering Georgina is too spry: no dons for her – snubs her, charms her, coolly relies on a mixture of *laissez faire* and *laissez aller*, or on not having his cake and not eating it, and at last, lets her go. Then, of course, he wakes up to what he has lost and chases her all the way to Como in vain and returns wretchedly to 'the great massy strengths of abstraction' once more in Pisa, in time for the awful Italian rains. One more love affair without a bang in it has ended without a whimper.

That is not all there is to say about the tourist in Clough's light opera. While Claude is denouncing Ignatius and repeopling the niches of the Pantheon with forms of 'an older, austerer worship', while he is writing

> Death may
> Sometimes be noble; but life at the best will appear an illusion
> While the great pain is upon us, it is great; when it is over,
> Why, it is over. The smoke of the sacrifice rises to heaven,
> Of a sweet savour, no doubt, to Somebody; but on the altar,
> Lo, there is nothing remaining but ashes and dust and ill odour –

while he thinks and philanders, the still landscape starts to rumble and to move. From the Pincio one can see distant smoke. There is rifle fire. There are riots in the street. The French have broken their truce with Mazzini and their troops are storming in from Civita Vecchia. The tourist takes on a torture familiar to our generation. Is he going to escape to the Embassy, become a reporter or even commit himself to the incitement of a patriotic war for liberty? Claude becomes a figure of the 1930s; the doubts and impulses of our wars become his. Clough had been in Paris in 1848, and now Claude, begging Eustace 'not to whisper it in thy courts, Oh Christ Church!' dreams of great angers and a sword. But not to defend the ladies:

> Now supposing the French or the Neapolitan soldier
> Should by some evil chance come exploring the Maison Serny
> (Where the family English are all to assemble for safety)
> Am I prepared to lay down my life for the British female?
> Really, who knows? One has bowed and talked, till, little by little,
> All the natural heat has escaped of the chivalrous spirit.
> Oh, one conformed, of course; but one doesn't die for good manners,
> Stab or shoot, or be shot, by way of graceful attention.
> No, if it should be at all, it should be on the barricades there;
> Should I encarnadine ever this inky pacifical finger,
> Sooner far should it be for this vapour of Italy's freedom,
> Sooner far by the side of the d . . . d and dirty plebeians,
> Ah, for a child, in the street I could strike; for the full-blown lady –
> Somehow, Eustace, alas! I have not felt the vocation.

Claude does not fight, of course. But he is excitedly out for the news. Brilliantly Clough's eye for reality – the gift of a mind so fatally adroit at changing its position – captures the absurd, tragic, confused scene in the streets; the comic flicker of the tourists, the reactionary cries of the dear, bourgeois girls who spread wild tales about Garibaldi's Negro. And the episode has the perfect tourist ending; he has not killed, he has not been killed but he has *seen* someone killed:

> . . . the swords are
> Many and bare in the air. In the air? They descend; they are smiting,
> Hewing, chopping – At what? In the air once more upstretched? –
>   And
> Is it blood that's on them . . .
> Passing away from the place with Murray under my arm, and
> Stooping, I saw through the legs of the people the legs of a body.

The critics of Clough used to be severe. He was not a great poet but (more serious for his reputation in Victorian times) he had not 'the vocation', as he might have said, for importing greatness into his subjects. Lytton Strachey made fun of his continual doubts and his weak ankles. In fact, Clough was a champion athlete and his doubts suggest not vacillation but modesty, hardness of mind, the strength of integrity and candour, the point of naturalness. It will be noticed in the portrait of Claude (which is not, however, a self-portrait) how the moments of weakness are the admissions of an honest character and immediately lead to strength. The famous 'Say not the struggle nought availeth' is the work of a courageous man. Clough was really in advance of his time; his unofficial manner, his truthfulness about personal feeling, his nonchalance, his curiosity, even his bitterness and his use of anticlimax, are closer to the poets of the Thirties than they were to his contemporaries. His line is clean. His lack of pretence is austere. The account of Rome is a wonderful evocation of the Rome that is in our minds, mixed up with our private life and business, our incapacity to answer the numberless questions that come from the city that has more of human fate in each of its stones than any city on earth.

Cellini

For 180 years the autobiography of Benvenuto Cellini has diverted a large number of English readers in every generation. Indeed, the English, perhaps because of their taste for eccentrics and for ripe and unabashed human portraiture in the 18th century, were the first to translate him from the Italian; and when the French and Germans followed, the fame of the book caught the Romantic movement at the flow. That is to say when, with faith in nature, love of energy and the sense of human beings as pieces of autonomous, emotional tumult, the long Romantic rule began. A second Renaissance looked back upon the first, and Cellini (as Mr John Pope-Hennessy says in a thoughtful and instructive introduction to the Phaidon Press edition) is seen fermenting to the life in the historical novels of Scott and Dumas as if he were still clattering, with temper alert for affront, over the changeless cobbles of Rome.

It is easy to see what the Romantics got out of Cellini, but what about ourselves? Romanticism is discredited; the 16th century is far away and the Renaissance is frowned upon by those of religious and political mind who like to point out how individualism has come to no good in the end. Is the autobiography to become for us one of those classics whose vitality and vividness make them irresistible but of no moment? Shall we regard Cellini as part of the forgotten childhood of modern Europe, stamping, yelling, biting till the blood comes, and uncontrollable? Will he suggest to us the natural bombast of dubious genius in a gangster state? Or shall we continue (if we are humanists) to find some lasting human substance in his refractory figure, to toughen and feed our abused faith? If the arts are to survive in a society grown hostile to them, the portrait of Cellini ought to be read, for it is one of the elementary statements of one kind of artist's mind, above all of the power, range and detail of its sustained hallucinations. Cellini was a pestilentially dedicated figure.

Mr John Pope-Hennessy's introduction does one important service to

his subject. I am not qualified to criticise his view, but he does rehabilitate
Cellini as an artist and especially as a sculptor; and he does seem to dispose
of the general notion that he was a second-rate artist who happened to
write a book of genius in order to inflate the value of his own works. No
one would deny Cellini's capacity to go in for something as shameless and
cunning as this; but his exorbitant self-praise is in itself so natural to him
that it amounts, by a paradox, to modesty. And he defers always to his
masters.

> In common with other artists [Mr Pope-Hennessy writes] who were
> brought up like himself under the shadow of the Battle of Cascina of
> Michelangelo and who gravitated to the Rome of the Sistine ceiling
> and Raphael's *Galatea*, Cellini reacted against the classicism of the
> Renaissance. But the sophisticated and eclectic forms which he and his
> contemporaries evolved were not, as Symonds and the 19th century
> supposed, an aberration from an aesthetic norm, but an autonomous
> independent style.

It was fostered by the climate of autocratic Courts. For the ordinary
reader that judgment has the importance of taking Cellini out of the class of
entrancing but ill-founded liars, who are covered, in Mr Pope-Hennessy's
words, by the ambiguous term 'artistic personality'. Behind him is the
single conviction of his kind of truth.

In the Renaissance, the individual broke bonds and silence and in his
own right came alive. If Montaigne gives birth to the self, that stoic and
questioning invalid, with the first sad, luminous and broken eyes; if before
him Rabelais has discharged upon us the chaotic imagination of the
creature and the sensualities it feeds upon, a figure like Cellini's is of the
same exemplary kind. He parades for the first time – and, remember, he is
contemporary with Rabelais and not with Montaigne – a nature, a libido
which has never known the censor unless it is there in the mask of that
surprising melancholy of temperament to which he lays claim. It is, no
doubt, the melancholy of the serious artist and the face in the portrait
certainly suggests the naïve and morbid sadness of some miracle-working
friar. Despite the worm, or because of it, Cellini jumps from art to
homicide, from the complacencies of intrigue and the ironies of persecution mania to the animal transfigurations of *le rage*. He can be held by no

inner constraints, only by the unrestricted libidos of the other animals who gang up against him. His life is a vendetta. But even then, when his crimes have put him into the power of his enemies and he is left to waste his body in the squalor of a medieval dungeon, his pride is unconquered. For he strikes out into that famous vision in which, longing to see the light in his dungeon, he prays to see the sun and is at once led within sight of heaven. Led by his dream-guide, 'a young man whose beard is just growing, with a face of indescribable beauty, but austere, not wanton', he ascends by huge stairs until there is the sun before him:

> Albeit your rays may blind me, I do not wish to look on anything again but this. So I stayed with my eyes fixed steadily on him; and after a brief space I beheld in one moment the whole might of those great burning rays fling themselves upon the left side of the sun; so that the orb remained quite clear without its rays, and I was able to contemplate it with vast delight.

As always with Cellini, who understands the laws of narrative, he goes from strength to strength, from one important success to the next. Out of the sun bulges the figure of the Christ; another bulge and out comes the Madonna; and then, with his back turned, who should be there but St Peter 'pleading my cause, for the shame he felt that such foul wrongs should be done to Christians in his own house.' And to cap that, as if God could never do enough, he finds that his forehead had been 'meddled with'. A halo has been affixed. He thoroughly understands lying as a fine art:

> This is visible to every sort of men to whom I have chosen to point it out, but those have been very few. This halo can be observed above my shadow in the morning from the rising of the sun for about two hours, and far better when the grass is drenched with dew.

It could also be seen at sunset and better in France than in Italy where the mists annulled the effect.

To this absolute pride which is carried away, so sympathetically, into condescending mania, there is only one response: his death or our deafness. The Popes, the Medici, can do nothing with an animal of such resources; and, as surely as when, turning his corners wide, he walked up the street that leads to the Palazzo Farnese and found the Corsican murderer waiting for him in the middle of it, it is our life or his. The autobiography might be said to commemorate the discovery of that part of the human self which declares there is no room for two.

Always the most 'honest' man in any collection; always quarrelling, wounding and occasionally killing in the heat of the blood, but never (as witnesses can be brought to prove) in an unrighteous cause; always persecuted by the jealous, always getting the better of his enemies and avenging himself of real or imagined wrongs on every page of his book, Cellini is the libido at its most naïve. He alone saves Rome. It is *he* who shoots the Constable of Bourbon from that crenellated beer barrel, the fortress of San Angelo. We have laughed at his boasts but they are not empty stories, like the tales of Münchhausen or the American frontier. They are (and this is their fascination) packed with people, the life of the palaces and streets, closely and vividly reasoned. They are, in the true sense, creative, for they spring out of the interminable activity of Cellini's extraordinary egotism. He shoots fatter pigeons than anyone else, but then excellence is his aim; and he goes on shooting to relax so that he may return to his fanatical and single concern in life: his art. If he kills a man, takes a girl or conspires with friends, his art is at the bottom of it. He is not merely a boaster; he is a maniac of consuming ingenuity. And this ingenuity convinces us that we have to deal with not an extravagant but a total man. He portrays, without knowing it, a complete character, for the lie on one page is shamelessly given away a page or two later.

Goethe said that a whole century comes to life in the autobiography of Cellini and that one learns more from him than from the historians. Stendhal said that he contained the Italian character. Violence goes with an unresting curiosity, cunning with a capacity for naïve surprise: one remembers his astonishment when his model (whom he had beaten up) came back for more, became his mistress and was the best of models as long as he had the energy to beat her once a day. Vanity and indignation led him to go, with tremendous zest, into the charges of homosexuality that were brought against him; he does not notice that it is perfectly clear he is homosexual. He cannot resist being the centre of any story: the heroic or the squalid. If he gets 'the French disease' it leads to astonishing anecdote. When an attempt is made to kill him with powdered diamonds, he discovers in a few lines a plot which could come straight from Boccaccio; for the man who had been given the diamond to crush had cheated his employer:

> poverty induced him to keep this for himself, and to pound for me a greenish beryl of the value of two carlines thinking, perhaps, because it was also a stone, that it would work the same effect as the diamond.

When there is a row at the inn it is Cellini who stays behind at the inn to avenge himself on the landlord by ripping the bedding to ribbons; when a lover seduces one of his mistresses he forces the man to marry her; and then takes her on as a mistress, in order to make her commit the greater sin of adultery. Never was a man more determined to extract the extra drop from the art of success. It may not be 'life' that he is recounting, but it unquestionably makes a book.

We see before us, indeed, a many-sided man, released, fulfilled in all his powers to the full length of Freudian expectation. First, the one continuously the artist, utterly wedded to the point of pettifogging frenzy with his work, blind to the existence of anything else, humble only before his master, Michelangelo. Then the natural man, incited by the awakened scientific curiosity of his time – for what is the dream of looking full into the sun but a scientific experiment, inspired by the same spirit which moved him to the great labour of the casting of the famous horse – and finally the story-teller trained in all the fine points of the art. Ourselves, like the fourteen-year-old boy to whom, in middle age, he dictated his life in the Florentine dialect, must be agog as we listen to the pouring, exterminating voice which creates an age only for the purpose of portraying a man.

An Italian Classic

====

I Promessi Sposi (in English, *The Betrothed*) is often said to be the only Italian novel. It is certainly the only Italian novel that can be compared with the great European novels of the 19th century. It was begun in 1821 when Scott dominated European taste and when Balzac had not emerged from the writing of shockers, and it was revised many times before the final edition of 1840. The last rewriting is said to have taken twelve years and the result is that we have a compendious Romantic work in a state of real digestibility which neither Balzac nor Scott troubled to attain. *The Betrothed* was Manzoni's only novel. It contained the fullness of his mind, his sensibility and creative power and (as Mr Colquhoun, a new translator, says in a very informative preface to a new edition) seems to represent the culmination of an experience to which life could add no more. In Italy this novel is a kind of Bible; long passages are known by heart; its reflections are quoted in the political debates that have taken place in Italy since the war. But in England, possibly because the chief translation was done over a hundred years ago – and not very well, by a clergyman who disapproved of its theology – the book has been but mildly regarded. The English had already the novels of Scott, with their energetic romance, their bourgeois valuation of life, their alternating choice of the highly coloured and the domestic. Scott was a Tory and, though a generous man, he drew in his horns before the outcome of the Enlightenment, whereas Manzoni had exposed his mind to it in his youth. Our critical ancestors preferred a safer, unreal Italy and, later on, the libertarian, anti-clerical Italy of the Risorgimento. Among the mass of Victorian readers we must remember those who were drawn towards Manzoni by the Oxford movement; but in matters of piety the critics seem to have preferred their own Protestant vigour and sentiment to Manzoni's obedient, passive, Catholic gravity, and it is a good indication of Victorian feeling that the clergyman who translated Manzoni said that he wished the name of Christ could be substituted for that of the Virgin throughout.

Manzoni's reformed Catholicism – that old desire to do without the Jesuits and the temporal power – is a greater obstacle to Protestants, one seems to notice, than the ultra-montane. Manzoni's religion is, in tendency, liberal and democratic, but it is also melancholy and pessimistic. In *The Betrothed* our ancestors would miss what they so much admired in the English novel – the high-minded woodenness of the exemplary characters. The chief victims of tyranny and evil in the story – the two peasant lovers who are forcibly separated by the lawless Don Rodrigo – are passive sufferers who do little to help themselves and are, in fact, finally rescued not by their own efforts but through the aid of a remarkable priest and the sudden conversion of the chief villain. There is no Protestant suggestion of an aggressive worth or a self-reliance that depends on direct access to God; on the contrary there is an ironical recognition of the mysterious drama of Fate and of the painful need for selfless love. It is true that the wicked are destroyed by the plague which comes to Milan at the end of the book – this is a magnificent episode – and that the good lovers are quietly rewarded; but the lasting impressions are not of righteous success but of moral good fortune, and of luck in catching the mysterious eye of the Almighty. One is reading a benign, spacious and melancholy fable of the most tender moral sensibility, an epic of understatement; whereas the English novelist of the 19th century – and the 18th century, too – commonly provided his reader with a number of obvious statues to socially estimable Virtue and the reader admired them because he hoped, if only in his own eyes, to become a statue himself.

Changed times and a translation which is closer to our idiom make *The Betrothed* immediately sympathetic to the contemporary reader, once he allows for old-fashioned methods of narration and apostrophe. We turn with recognition of other times of chaos, as Manzoni himself transposed the upheaval of the French Revolution into the material of the religious wars of the 17th century. Manzoni is the novelist of those who expose themselves but cannot take sides. They belong, where humanity abides, to the spiritual third force. His personal history was of the kind that makes the psychologist, the man whose thought and feeling are finely meshed; an aristocrat, a Voltarian and militant anti-Catholic, he married a Protestant woman and was reconverted by the Capucines to a profound if ambiguous faith. He writes with the gentleness, the irony, the anxiety and love of one who has passed through a deep personal crisis. His texture is rich, his variety is great; we enter a world of innumerable meanings and contrasts. Beside the account of the plague, which recalls the curious realistic precision of Defoe, must be put very different things, like an abduction to a brigand's castle or a flight to a convent. In contrast again with these, there are comic scenes like the famous one where the peasant lovers try to trick the timid priest into marrying them, which is at the height of Italian buffoonery; the portraits of politicians have the flowering malice of Proust; the historical reflections are wise, subtle and dyed with experience, and in every episode there are psychological perceptions that have the fineness of the French novelists without their often wounding vanity in their own effects. Manzoni was devoid of the intellectual's self-admiration. His grave manner removes the sickliness from piety and restores to it the refinement of nature.

I will quote two examples of Manzoni's kind of perception to which the reader of Proust will at once respond.

One is taken from the colloquy between the neurotic and tragic nun and the peasant girl who has found sanctuary with her.

> [The peasant] also tried to avoid replying to Gertrude's inquisitive questions about her story before her engagement. But here the reason was not prudence. It was because to the poor innocent girl this story seemed a thornier and more difficult one to describe than anything which she had heard or thought she was likely to hear from the Signora. Those dealt with tyranny, treachery and suffering – ugly, painful things, yet things which could be expressed but hers was pervaded by a feeling, a word, which she felt she could not possibly pronounce, and for which she would never be able to find a substitute that would not seem shameless – the word love.

Put this beside a very different situation, an innkeeper putting his drunken guest to bed. He covers the snoring drunk and

> Then, drawn by the kind of attraction that sometimes makes us regard an object of our dislike as attentively as an object of our love, and which is only the desire to know what it is that affects our sensibility so

strongly, he paused a moment to gaze at this irksome guest, raising the lamp over his face, and shading it with his hand so that the light fell on him, almost in the attitude in which Psyche was painted as she gazed stealthily at the features of her unknown spouse.

In all the meetings of his characters, in the strong situations and in the neutral, there is this watchful, instinctive, animal awareness of the other person, a seeking of the meaning of their relationship. To compare the innkeeper to a spouse is not grotesque: the drunk man has already involved the innkeeper with the secret police, there is the marriage of two fears. Fear and love are, in fact, Manzoni's subjects.

The story of *The Betrothed* is a strong one. The hired bravoes hold up the cowardly priest. There is murder on the road. There are bread riots in Milan – Manzoni is an excellent narrative writer unencumbered by picturesque baggage – there are flights and pursuits, tremendous confrontations of the tyrannous and the good. The immunity of the priests gives them boldness. There are political intrigue, invasion and looting by foreign armies, the plague. Manzoni is as brilliant as a diplomat in recomplicating the moral issues; the brigand's sudden conversion, for example, frees the girl from her dangers and seems to guarantee her happiness but, perversely and in her terror, she now vows herself to the Virgin! To the obstacle of wickedness is added the obstacle of faith. That delicate tangle of faith and desire and pride has to be undone. The characters are not thrown on in crude, romantic strokes but are put together precisely by a writer who has understood their pattern and the point at which they will behave unexpectedly or feel the insinuations of time, Fate and mood. There is not a stock character anywhere; nor can a too gifted author be seen bursting through these figures. The skill in the change of mood or in anti-climax is wonderful.

When Manzoni described how the notion of writing *The Betrothed* came to him – I quote from Mr Colquhoun – he said:

The memoirs of that period [the Counter Reformation] show a very extraordinary state of society; the most arbitrary government combined with feudal and popular anarchy; legislation that is amazing in the way it exposes a profound, ferocious, pretentious ignorance; classes with opposed interests and maxims; some little-known anecdotes, preserved

[365]

in trustworthy documents; finally a plague which gives full rein to the most consummate and shameful excesses, to the most absurd prejudices, and to the most touching virtues.

With this stuff he did fill his book. The contemporary reader must reflect that this is exactly the kind of material which has, in our time, become degenerate in the novel. The great, even the extensive subjects, have fallen into inferior hands. They have become the fodder of the middle-brow novelist. Is it really true that this kind of material can no longer attract the best minds in the novel? Has it exhausted itself? Clearly Manzoni, like Scott and Balzac, had the excitement of doing something new and they had the tremendous intellectual and emotional force of the Romantic movement behind them. But they were more than capable inventors, copyists, historians or story-tellers who comfortably relied on a commonly accepted language and values. Indeed, although it is generally said that our lack of these common symbols is the central difficulty for contemporary artists, I wonder whether Manzoni's situation was as different from ours as it seems to be. He is a singular example of the artist, who, finding no common basis for himself and a disjointed society, sets laboriously to make one. His religion was uncharacteristic for a man of advanced ideas; as far as its elusive quality can be discerned, it seems to have connected the ideas of Pascal with those of liberalism and this profound change of spirit led him to seek an equally important change of language. He wished to find a language in which all men communicate with one another and to abandon literary language. Problems of belief raise at once problems of style: in both Manzoni was revolutionary. His case somewhat resembles Tolstoy's though, with Manzoni, conversion was not a mutilation of the artist but his fulfilment. He succeeded (where the English Protestant novelists on the whole failed) in creating characters who were positively good, yet his 'message' that love above all, self-sacrifice, courage, long-suffering and charity are the only, and not necessarily successful answers to tyranny and injustice, is not introduced as a sort of pious starch into the narrative, but is native to it. One is undermined rather than incited by this teaching, as in one or two of the Russian writers; and the very pessimism of Manzoni, by which he continually moves the rewards of the righteous just a little beyond their finger-tips with a gentle scepticism, is like that of Cervantes.

Verga

I talian critics tell us that Verga is one of the greatest Italian novelists and, until recent years, the undisputed second to Manzoni; even so he is a neglected writer in Italy, though I have heard Victorini speak well of him. When D. H. Lawrence made his excellent translation of *Maestro Don Gesualdo*, Verga was known to us only by the stories in *Cavalleria Rusticana*; an earlier American translation of *I Malavoglia*, his greatest novel, was out of print. This translation was good, although it inclined to be mild and smooth, where Verga was evidently elliptical, hard and pungent. Eric Mosbacher's new version is harder; it retains the old title of *The House by the Medlar Tree*: Malavoglia is a surname meaning the Ill-willed. Destiny shows ill will to this family and they were to have been part of a trilogy grimly called *The Defeated*. It was to be divided into a study of the very poor, the non-manual workers or Dons of Sicilian life and the upper classes. The last book was never finished.

These novels came from a revelation which, Verga says, he had in the Eighties. He had left Catania where he was born, and had become an adept writer of novels about 'elegance and adultery' in Milan and Florence in the current Italian style. I quote Verga's words from D. H. Lawrence's biographical note on his translation of *Don Gesualdo*:

> One day, I don't know how, there came into my hand a sort of broadside, a halfpenny sheet sufficiently ungrammatical and disconnected, in which a sea Captain succinctly related all the vicissitudes through which his sailing ship passed. Seaman's language, short, without any unnecessary phrase. It struck me, and I read it again; it was what I was looking for, without definitely knowing it. Sometimes, you know, just a sign, an indication is enough.

Verga set out on one of those returns to original and despised sources which have often been fruitful to novelists.

His first step from sophistication was effected by the naturalism of Zola. In *Cavalleria Rusticana* Verga became stark. Here he is a kind of Mérimée without the velvet glove. We notice that the pride and violence of the Sicilians is hyperbolical, sublime and close upon us; whereas Mérimée sees his Corsicans and Spaniards at one remove. They are the exotic if excellent anecdotes of a civilised connoisseur of primitive manners and passions. Corsican honour, too, is calculating; the Spanish, tragic. The wound in Mérimée's nature gave him the aesthete's curious admiration of power and turned him outward to the primitive. Verga has the advantage of turning inward, of going home and is filled with instinctive knowledge. He is not a mystic, either, about 'the people'.

I Malavoglia indicates the second phase, the rapid arrival at the source. He is no longer the teller of frightening dramatic episodes which isolate the passions of people from the conditions of their life. The high passions, the murderous traditions of honour, have survived (we suspect) not only because of natural inheritance, but because old habits of feeling are preserved longest by the downtrodden and wretched. The upper classes evolve more rapidly and are more sensitive to change than the poor whose humane virtues emerge only every so often when civilisation cracks. Verga found himself inside the thoughts, words and interests of the poor Sicilian fishermen. He did not stand with one foot safely in the picturesque, as most of us do; but went into their life, found it complete, and took it, almost, at its own valuation. From the moment we open *I Malavoglia* we are pitched into the squabble of village life, straight among the talk of the misers, the spies, the honourable, the wasters, the modest, the hypocrites, the officials, the skirling village shrews. Their voices deafen us, their quarrels confuse our ears, their calamities catch us, and we are subject also to those strange truces in the rancour of a community when, for a day, a disaster will quieten it with a common emotion. Verga's aim was to write as closely as he could in the language of the people, for talk is the interminable litany of the poor. Especially he makes wonderful use of their metaphors and their vivid proverbs, and although the polished reader may wince at memories of books written by only too knowing outsiders in this manner, he will find that Verga has invented a style which carries these images and sayings naturally, and without the effect of tuition, on the one hand, or artificial colouring on the other:

During the squall all the big fish, even the stupid ones, stayed under water without showing themselves, leaving Silkworm, the mayor, gazing skywards as though he were looking for a leaf to nibble.

or

I bet he was going to wander about in the lava field behind St. Agatha's garden. You cannot ask more than to love the girl next door, for courting by the fence saves both trouble and expense.

or

Piedipapera found Uncle Crocifisso only too ready to talk about that little matter which was dragging on and on, with no end in sight. Long things turn into snakes, as the saying is.

The matter of *I Malavoglia* is less a story than a stream of rabid country talk, built around the changes of fortune in an honourable family losing the boat on which they depend, getting into the hands of a moneylender, recovering the boat and after heart-breaking work, losing their house and the unity of the family altogether. 'Ntoni, the grandfather, is the dominant character, a figure of patriarchal passion, energy and rugged wisdom, a wonderful, powerful portrait of an honest man. His son, corrupted by military service, half showy, half good, is excellent too, on the downward path. In ten years one sees a family and a village change before the eyes in their fixed frame. There are three or four good set scenes: a funeral, a betrothal, an escape from shipwreck, a smugglers' affray and these – so hackneyed a part of picturesque literature – have a very different aspect in Verga. To begin with they are more raw; then, they are economically dealt with, not with a novelist's colour print in view, but to catch human beings in the act of living.

That is Verga's great virtue. He is closer to contemporary writers than to the writers of the 19th century, with their landscape, their explanations, their expatiations and their theories. One small incident, which is at first incomprehensible to the sophisticated reader, shows how thoroughly Verga knew the minds of his people. Mena's pretty sister Lia has become the mistress of the gendarme; and Mena, because of this shame, refuses the lover she hoped to marry. The family honour has been injured; she must pay the price of the injury. She points out to her lover that the village tongues will never let a Malavoglia woman alone after this, and that her husband would live surrounded by scandal and backbiting. The lover recognises the truth of this and agrees that her argument is unsurmountable. Their deep love for each other is thus thrown away on a point of honour, which is communal virtue in disguise. The basic thing in the lives, in the culture of these people, is the role. Each one has a role in the community which he acts every day, elaborates and lives by. In a fixed community it is the reason for life. The cheat must cheat, the hypocrite must practise hypocrisy, the scold must scold, the humble man and the good must preserve their characters; everything is simple and public. Change will bring inner conflict and self-inflicted evils. The tongue rules the Mediterranean like a lash and its aim is to prevent change, to preserve the unity of the group which is greater in value than the life of any individual.

I have probably conveyed that *I Malavoglia* is a book about the darker side of anchovy fishing. That is not the impression. Though it is generally described as a tragedy, it is rather a pungent, spluttering vivid picture of life, often comic and sometimes lyrical; it is a rich description of circumstance. There are one or two long passages of rest in the middle of the book describing days on the sea, 'green as grass' under the doubtful clouds, or those hard times when the Malavoglia, always anxious to pay off their debt, risked their damaged boat for the sake of a few fish:

But when the weather was bad, and a nor' wester blew and the corks bobbed up and down on the water all day long as though someone were playing the fiddle for them to dance, and the sea was as white as milk or seethed as though it were boiling, and the rain poured down on their backs all day long and they got soaked to the skin, because no coat could possibly keep it out, and the waves leapt all round them like fish in a frying pan, then it was different . . . and 'Ntoni with his coat collar buttoned up to his nose had no desire to sing, and he had to keep bailing the *Provvidenza* the whole time, and his grandfather kept saying that a 'White sea means a sirocco' or 'a choppy sea means fresh wind', as though they were here to learn proverbs.

And at dark, when the *Provvidenza* came in with her belly full of the grace of God and her sail billowing like Donna Rosolina's skirt and with the lights in the houses winking to one another behind the black Fariglioni rocks as though they were signalling, Master 'Ntoni would point out to the beautiful fire blazing in La Longa's kitchen . . . 'What did I tell you?' the old man would exclaim with delight. 'Just look at the fire that La Longa has made for us.'

In *Maestro Don Gesualdo* the scene was more violent. In the class above the very poor, there was a larger field for pride and for private war; there was the possibility of the great bourgeois madness, megalomania; Don Gesualdo had all the superb force of a rising man. He was a Lear tortured by the daughter who had married into the aristocracy. He was hoodwinked into violent political schemes. *I Malavoglia* is a quieter book. Its metaphors are less electric, its feeling is more pitiful. I do not find novels about foreign peasants of a hundred years ago tolerable unless they are done with economy. Verga, like Mérimée, though in a very different mode, stripped his narrative to the bone. He is one of the few novelists still readable in his genre and very close to the tone of our own day.

The Early Svevo

The last thirty years have been one of the great ages of the English translators. Scott Moncrieff's Proust, Arthur Waley's Chinese Poems, the Powys Mather's version of Mardrus's *Arabian Nights*, Madame Bussy's work on Gide, the work of Constance Garnett on the Russians, and many other translations of high talent or genius have transformed our knowledge of foreign authors. One has only to look at the muddy translations of two generations back, or to compare them with the mass of unfelt American work, to see how English translators have reached an extraordinary supremacy; and if we turn to a precise example like Miss Beryl de Zoete's admirable rendering of Italo Svevo, a most difficult author, we realise how fatally easy it would have been to ruin a delicate writer for us and to have shut him off for years. Italo Svevo's *As a Man Grows Older* (in Italian, *Senilità*) first appeared fifty years ago and, after its complete failure with the critics and the public, Svevo turned to his business in Trieste, became a rich man, and was persuaded to write again twenty-three years later only by the interest of James Joyce. To that persuasion we owe Svevo's comic masterpiece *The Confessions of Zeno*, which has been compared to the work of Joyce and Proust, and has called up the ghosts of Freud and Otto Weininger. The prosperous businessman, we are told, enjoyed his astonishing fame with the innocent wonder of the amateur: did it not, indeed, justify his passive philosophy that all positive intentions blunder and that our success, our happiness, our virtue itself, settle in us by chance, though not by indolence and indifference? As Renato Poggioli's acute introduction to *Zeno* pointed out, Svevo's novels are about people in their empty, off-time or leisure, the hours they have been longing for as they watched the crawl of the hands of the office clock; yet they strike us by a driven and unceasing busyness. Svevo's mind wears itself out like the grasshopper, sings endlessly like the needle of a machine.

Nearly half of Svevo's not very long life lies between *As a Man Grows*

Older and *The Confessions of Zeno*, and all the difference between failure and success. Self-improvement is the obsession of his unlucky heroes, and, as Svevo's life went on, they do improve. Their anxious analysing of motives, their eagerness for illusion, their inevitable failures, and their anxiety to understand and to arrive at a sane attitude to life gives them the pathetic air of miming clowns: they talk so much that it creates, by a paradox, the pathos of dumbness. But they become as wise, gentle, restful in their indetermination as the Chinese and walk with the fullness of the super-annuated. It has been their curious fate to learn the lesson of life backwards, becoming younger and more apt for life as they grow older; so that if they were to look back upon their youth, and even their middle age, these would seem to them like a puzzling sleep from which, little by little, they have been permitted to awake.

As a Man Grows Older can be considered as a half-awakening from Svevo's grim, earlier novel *Una Vita*. *Una Vita* is the story of a bank clerk's fatally insincere love affair which ends in suicide: the lovers have destroyed the meaning of their lives. An austere smile appears between the lines of the next book: the exactions of conscience are severe, but it is perhaps comical that they are self-inflicted. Brentani, a clerk in an insurance office, is too poor to marry and indeed has to support his plain and delicate sister. He is literary, dreamy, a victim of that disease of the sentiments which is called Bovaryisme, which Paul Bourget defined as 'le mal d'avoir connu l'image de la realité avant la realité' and which, tinctured by puritanism and snobbery in English literature, produced certain heroines of Scott and Dickens. Brentani has never had a love affair, for he evidently satisfies himself in dreams and repents in analysis; and when he at last decides to fall in love, he makes the worst possible choice in a young, beautiful, hopelessly deceitful working-class girl. The cynicism of the affair owes something to the curious social customs of middle-class life in Trieste at the turn of the century – in general they resemble those of the Mediterranean, where the demi-monde has a precise defined economic status – but Brentani absurdly encumbers his own path with hallucinations about the girl, unpredictable jealousies and the cruelties of his conscience. A love affair that would not have wrecked his extroverted friend Balli is fatal to the introverted Brentani; and the effects of the affair are not merely to exalt him or drive him to despair, but to create the desire for love in his sister. A shaded and faltering creature, she conceives a sincere passion which is unrequited; she is taken ill and dies and Brentani is made to see that his impossible behaviour has been the cause. Or rather – for the egoism of Svevo's characters is unfailing and is the source of their comedy – Brentani chooses to think he is the cause; and marrying the delicate image of his sister to the passionate one of his now discarded mistress (who has run off with a bank thief), he has now a new 'image of reality' to dream about, console himself with, and no doubt to impose with results just as devastating, on the next adventure, if he ever has sufficient strength or wilfulness to undertake one.

When I first read *As a Man Grows Older*, some years ago, it seemed to me one more trite little tale about the 'little mistress', a grey and listless exercise in Viennese subtlety. I had been carried away by the comic Italian dazzle of *Zeno*; and the only virtue I saw in his earlier book was Svevo's gift for writing innumerable short epitaphs on the nuances of human feeling. I was wrong. In the first place the story of *As a Man Grows Older* has the emotional fullness which is the reward of perfect form and internal balance. How discreetly the cold mists, the sudden rains, the rough seas of the Adriatic port, the glimpses of the city – its business quarter where beautiful women are stared at if they should happen to pass, its empty walks by the sea, its hard-faced flats lit by candles and oil in the poorer quarters, its café meetings – are made to break into Brentani's unstable, never to be self-trusted, yet self-aware mind. In its way, this book is as complete a case-history as *Adolphe*, has the same lucidity, and its analysis the same ruthless serenity, but touched by the clear-headedness of the mad. Here is the passage where Emilio Brentani, in his jealousy, makes his friend Balli, the natural man, promise not to attract his girl who is already betraying him:

> 'I am sick with jealousy, nothing else but jealousy. I am jealous of the others too, but most of all of you. I have got accustomed to the umbrella maker, but I shall never get accustomed to you.' There was not the faintest touch of humour in his voice; he was trying to arouse pity so that he might the more easily get Balli to promise what he wanted. If he had refused Emilio had made up his mind to rush round to Angiolina at once. He did not want his friend to profit by a state of affairs for which he himself had been largely responsible.

Balli promises, out of pity. But a dreamy look in his eye betrays the natural hunter, tempted by the very fact of having given his word. Balli says he has long wanted to make a sketch of the girl 'because I thought you would like to have it.' Emilio sees through this at once. With ludicrous anxiety he cries out: 'You have promised me, you can't go back on it. Try to find your inspiration elsewhere.' And when Balli calms him, the base consequences of an apparently disinterested idealism are slyly shown:

> Emilio began lamenting his sad fate with an irony of self-analysis which removed from it every trace of the ridiculous. He said that he wanted all his friends to know how he looked at life. In theory he considered it to be without serious content, and he had in fact never believed in any of the forms of happiness which had been offered him; he had never believed in them and he could truly say that he had never pursued happiness. But how much less easy it was to escape suffering! In a life deprived of all serious content even Angiolina became serious and important.

Half the beauty of Svevo's work lies in his cunning gift of throwing away his lines. Were it not for his pain, Balli reflects, Emilio's situation would be ridiculous; and it is in the subtle balance of the delicacies of pain with the load of comedy that the excitement of the book lies.

The scenes of action are brilliant, freshly observed and as concrete as anything in *Madame Bovary* and a good deal better-natured. It is unforgettable when Amalia, the sister, puts Balli's cup back in the cupboard when she discovers her dream of love will not be realised. There is the long and really gripping account of her illness. Svevo's scenes of illness are among the most dramatic in any literature, for they observe the struggle of the mind with the body; is not life itself an illness, and sickness one of its more highly coloured, poetic and even thrilling acts? The love scenes with Angiolina are all excellent, for the Svevo heroes discover women as if they were a new species. These heroes are the kind of men at whose behaviour women smile. And when Angiolina pushes Brentani out of bed with the words 'Get out, my beauty,' she has said everything. Brentani for her is 'a beauty and no mistake.' Awed by a love quite beyond her and which would drive her out of her mind if she were to take it seriously, she quickly sets about deceiving him.

[375]

Social criticism has been at work on Italo Svevo and there is an interesting account of his work from this point of view by Edouard Roditi. But the weakness of this school of criticism is that, while it analyses the roots, it can only do so by disparaging the flower. And it falls into conventional judgments. It is no doubt true, as Roditi says, that Svevo and his heroes are 'culture-snobs' and that 'in a bourgeois society of culture-snobs illusions of intellectual grandeur thus compensate social or emotional maladjustment'. What of it? Don Quixote was a culture-snob. The type exists within and without the bourgeois order. Illusions of social grandeur compensate contemporary Russian writers for their spiritual failure. Renato Poggioli's introduction to *The Confessions of Zeno* is illuminating on the question of Svevo as a bourgeois. Here is an acute passage:

> Exactly because he does not judge the bourgeois spirit, Svevo amuses himself, tremendously and naïvely, by looking at it. A perfect bourgeois as a man, as a writer, he is almost alone in not looking like one. Instead of descending or condescending to the bourgeois spirit within his soul he raises it and uplifts it along with himself to the sphere of imagination, to a world of fancy and dreams, which is at the same time the world of reality itself. Once Stendhal asked for a literature written by bankers and industrialists able to understand, lucidly and cynically, the economy of life, the business of society, the value of man. Svevo was certainly a writer of this brand, and furthermore, endowed with such bourgeois honesty and common-sense as to refuse to transform his indulgent egoism into any set of theories, any 'egotism'. A kind of innocent wisdom was the real source of his greatness and originality.

Possibly Svevo's independence sprang from his Jewish background, from his plural personality – as Roditi shrewdly says – as an Austrian, an Italian and a Jew. When the 1914 war came Roditi says, Svevo 'treated the whole business as a sort of supreme Jewish joke in which all humanity is involved in the role of the unreasonable Gentile.' Svevo found 'normal' behaviour desirable but not reasonable. It was too easy. Like the blameless clown, he preferred the difficulty, the busyness of trying all the wrong roads first.

Galdós

The 19th century was the great age of the novel but, in Spain, Peréz Galdós is the only novelist who escapes to some extent from Spanish provincialism and can be compared with the European figures. He has a large range of scene and character; he has been beyond the Pyrenees; he is a social moralist. His masters were Balzac, Dickens and Cervantes and his huge output – he wrote forty-five historical narratives in addition to a number of ambitious novels, one of which is longer than *War and Peace* – composes a kind of Spanish *Comédie Humaine*. How is it that he is so little known outside of Spain, and so little translated? In the long and warm analysis of Galdós' work which Mr Gerald Brenan gives in his *Literature of the Spanish People*, he makes several points which suggest an explanation. The first is a 'lack of temperament' in Galdós. Then

> we look in vain in his portrait gallery for outstanding figures . . . One reason for this is that he never treats his characters in isolation, but always as members of a class or group or family. He is a social historian who aimed at giving the pattern of a society and, what is more, of a society which he regarded as corrupt and frivolous, rather than as an individualist.

Galdós was born in the Canaries and spent his long life in Madrid essentially as an observer, or as a kind of visiting doctor who comes in to diagnose an illness. In consequence, he keeps an objective eye on what he sees and his characters never exceed life-size: 'most of his characters' – I quote again from Mr Brenan – 'are mediocrities, some are almost painful in their lack of personality.' If, like the Russian novelists, Galdós gains in evocative power by testing his characters against 'the national predicament' he has not the Russian desire to magnify the key figures. He aimed, as he once wrote, at a special kind of naturalism which would be salted by Spanish irony, and though his psychological perception is fine, we have a

[377]

little the impression that his excellence depends for us on our feeling for the peculiarity of Spanish life in his time. In Spain, Galdós was greatly read, though there has always been some clerical opposition to his work and he has been very much forbidden. Under the present régime, I have been told, new editions of his work suffer from excisions by the censor. This is not surprising. Galdós was a liberal, an enemy of the ultramontanes. He made damaging fun of certain kinds of Spanish piety and of the perennial political corruption of the official classes.

The English reader has now the opportunity of starting on Galdós in Miss Gamel Wolsey's translation of *La de Bringas (The Spendthrifts)*. The characters of his novels reappear in other works, and this one follows *Tormento* and *El Doctor Centeno*, though it is quite independent of them. *The Spendthrifts* is a brilliant, well-constructed comic story, blooming absurdly out of the political realities of its time. The translation preserves the tone of the period and flows simply and naturally along. The immediate theme of the novel has the Balzacian mark of the theory of the dominant passion: a woman's passion for clothes. This is not a trivial subject. It leads Galdós to the heart of a society which has a mania for display at all costs. Indeed, the greater the poverty of the country, the greater the social and political corruption, the more important public display becomes. Refugio, the courtesan, who has tried her hand at dealing in dresses and hats smuggled through the customs, says towards the end of the tale:

> Here, except for half a dozen families, everyone is poor. Façade, nothing but façade. These people have no idea of comfort in their houses. They live in the streets; and so that they can dress well and go to the theatre, some families eat nothing but potato omelettes all the year round.

Where does the money come from? From bribes, sinecures, official swindles and an eternal tragi-comedy of cadging, sponging, borrowing and plain stealing – for half the people do not pay their bills. And the whole system has the lazy, generous, careless figure of the Queen at the top of the pyramid. Galdós has caught the comedy in the last year of Isabel's reign, and by the end of the book the *coup d'état* has occurred and the whole pack of cards comes down.

The Bringases are a modest but rising family in the upper official class.

The husband has a place in Court, the family lives in a wonderful menagerie of royal hangers-on, on the top floor of the Palace. Bringas has a horror of debt and has become a miser who watches every penny in the household accounts. He has succeeded in preventing his wife from entering society by keeping her without fashionable clothes. If clothes are her fantasy, Bringas too has a peculiar fantasy of his own. Like everyone else he owes his position and his son's advancement to 'influence', keeping important persons sweet, and tacit bribery. The boy has, for example, been given a government job at the age of sixteen, though in fact he is still at the university and only goes to the office to collect his salary. For this and other advantages Bringas wishes to show his gratitude to his benefactor in a spectacular way. He sets out to make a 'hair picture' as a memorial to his benefactor's dead daughter. The Spanish cult of death has never been so comically treated. Bringas' picture is a fretwork horror, a landscape of tombs, angels, willows, lakes and distant Gothic walls, set in an oval frame eighteen inches across; but it is woven from the tresses of the dead girl, with some help from the hair of her mother and her sister. The task is minute and monstrous; each thread of hair has to be picked up by tweezers, snipped by scissors into tiny pieces no larger than the smallest stroke of an etching, and is then gummed to the plate.

While Bringas sits half the day absorbed in this sepulchral folly his wife is gradually infected by a ridiculous friend with the mania for dresses. Soon she is caught up in debts and cheated by friends who borrow from her. When the crisis comes, a stroke of luck saves her: the minuteness of her husband's work has made him temporarily blind. She is able to sell candlesticks and tamper with his cash box without being seen. Eventually she finds herself helplessly drifting among a group of ruined and lying women, all borrowing from one another, and turns to take a lover for help. We see the gradual downfall of a nice, faithful wife, her humiliation at the hands of her lover, who politely evades helping her after his success and, finally, her total humiliation at the hands of a courtesan who claims to be a member of the family.

So far this is no more than a story by Maupassant, dry and ironical in its beginning, steely and inexorable in its end. But Galdós is far more interested in character and the density of human relations than he is in pure plot. His moral is never merely neat. There are two ways of looking at

Rosalia Bringas and her husband. We can see them as a good, devoted, pious married couple bringing up their children well; if Bringas is close with money, that is merely because he is determined not to live the silly life of pretence and debt around him, and the moment his sight goes Rosalia is the soul of care. They live clucking together like a couple of funny, anxious ducks on their little domestic island. Rosalia's passion for clothes is native, feminine and imaginative; her vanity is part of the ancient comedy of women's lives; her piety is appropriate. The dream of clothes is Don Quixote's dream in another idiom. But Galdós has prepared us, in *Tormento*, the earlier novel, for a Rosalia who has been poisoned by society. Envy, family pride, class pride are in her. She will stick at nothing in keeping up her social position; she will fight tooth and nail to keep the inferior woman out. Her religion is ignorant and vulgar hocus-pocus; it is also a financial drain. When her lover tricks her, when the courtesan – who claims to be a relation – makes her crawl for a loan and pours contempt on the respectable married woman and her 'superior' morality, Rosalia's Spanish violence comes out. She instantly thinks of murder. And far from being chastened, she reads her lesson otherwise. She hardens. For after the intolerable August in Madrid where she has been obliged to stay – and in this kind of atmosphere Galdós is admirable; he is the novelist of a city – the *coup d'état* comes, her reactionary husband is ruined, her safe place in the Palace has gone: and she gets a thrill of power as she realises that it is upon herself that the family will now depend. The lesson she has been taught is that it is important to go after the men with the big money; and she has learned how to do it. The tempted fool has turned into a formidable and spirited expert.

There are many good portraits in the book. Doña Milagros with the smart parties she cannot pay for, her self-deceit, her emotional lies, is at a stage more advanced than Rosalia. Doña Cándida, the simple, mad, harmless cheat, or Refugio, the courtesan, are at further stages. There is a delightful Proustian politician in Don Manuel Pez, the serene dandy and adept manager of formulae who expresses all his ideas in triplicate:

> 'It's impossible, it's very difficult, at least, it would be risky in fact to hazard an opinion. The revolution we have laughed at so much, joked about so often, jeered at so many times . . . '

And so on. Pez, the urbane centre of the bribery system, the system of influence and introductions on which the Spanish state was based – and still is – was soon back after the *coup d'état*. No committee, not even a revolutionary one, could work without him and his enormous army of friends and relations. How else could the system of free railway passes, wholesale smuggling from France, and jobs for the needy, be managed? In the minor portraits, the children are excellent: they play their part, indeed the compositions of Galdós are orderly, despite touches of Dickensian extravagance.

There is a mildness in Galdós, in spite of the vigour of his mind, which brings the reader back to Mr Brenan's remark on his lack of temperament. The historian broadens the note of the novelist who lacks the intellectual edge of the French novelists of the time or the English sense of theatre. There is a certain idleness in the Cervantesque irony, as if we were listening to the shrewd brain of a lazy mind. But to feel his full effect, it is necessary to see this novel in relation to others, to see it as a corner of his large, sad speculation on the Spanish predicament. There is no 'Spanish soul' to compare with the 'Russian soul', in the same kind of novel, nor does Galdós feel that he is making a natural history of human nature. Galdós is deep in Spanish egoism. But he was sufficiently a European to explore that; he wrote at the time of intellectual revival; he is free from that 'typical' regionalism which travels so poorly in literature. He has the certainty, sharpness and power of the novelist who is saturated in his subject. If, as they say, everything in Spain is personal, then Galdós is the novelist of this kind of society which destroys every idea and issue by the thickly involved personal concern. In Galdós one is deeply involved in 19th-century Spain, yet *The Spendthrifts* itself is one of his novels which seems to be about the present day.

A Portrait of T. E. Lawrence

What was the character of T. E. Lawrence? I have been reading a selection of his writings which Mr David Garnett has put together with the aim of making this character reveal itself. The book opens with a sardonically expert letter written when Lawrence was eighteen, goes on to his archaeological journeys in England, France and Syria; and then chronologically to the *Arab Bulletin* and *Seven Pillars of Wisdom*. It ends with extracts from *The Mint* and some of the final letters. Lawrence's Cairo reports were described by an official as 'observant, pungent in style and character' and these qualities made him a swift, singeing narrator, a sound and irreverent analyst of situations which were on the move. When situations do not move, when he is describing the static life of the Army and the RAF in peacetime, as in the passages from the unpublished *The Mint*, Lawrence strikes one as being deeply bored by his material. He tries to make it vivid by fixing it with his eye. In doing this he becomes mannered and bitterness gives his writing a thick and embossed effect, which is not the best side of a talent made for fluency and variety. We can judge, of course, from extracts only; the impression made by the whole of *The Mint* may be quite different. But since T. E. Lawrence's time there has been a good deal of documentary or disinterestedly observant writing about the airman's and soldier's life, and it has been soberer in tone, less egoistical in sensibility, less plagued than Lawrence's is by horror of the mass of men or, at any rate, instinctively forgives them. Lawrence felt cut off from them, especially – as he put it – from their carnality. Beside this writing – and I think of things like Alun Lewis's *Ward 03 (b)* – T. E. Lawrence sounds studied and precious. It is the end-result of the abstract and ascetic bias in Lawrence's mind, a gift he had learned to apply to men when he wished to use them in action.

Forgetting all one has read and heard of T. E. Lawrence, what portrait can one build up from his writings? He has the total, sanguine, efficiency of genius, of course. After that, the Anglo-Irish and Highland Scottish parentage makes a bold and distinctive general outline. Courage, militancy, imagination, clear separation of close-packed thought from withdrawn feeling, the ability to get 'inside the skin of the participants' in an action – which Sir Ernest Dowson noted – without losing oneself in the process, a dizzy sexless energy, irony – but that is the militant tradition – an instinct for mischief and intrigue, vanity and a core of diffidence, weakness, insecurity. History suggests that their insecurity as the lonely conquerors of a savage and treacherous country is a profound element in the general character of the Anglo-Irish and (as Lawrence's brother thought) the weakness provoked in T. E. Lawrence that transcendent will which is incessant in men and women of genius. Other Anglo-Irish traits are suggested by a comparison with Bernard Shaw. There are the continuous histrionic touch and the remorse that follows – an unavailing remorse because it, also, is theatrical. There is the merciless mental energy which pours out endlessly in words or action, and turns upon the character with humiliating self-criticism. There is the special kind of idealism: ascetic, bodiless, rational, unromantic, and it keeps a place for the inevitable cynicism of tactics. Unlike English idealism it is unsentimental and without hypocrisy. Lawrence's guilt about betraying the Arabs could not be dissolved by useful moral arguments; it was hard. An objective thinker cannot get rid of the objects he sees or deceive himself by turning them into something else. Lawrence's dislike of Imperialism was traditional; on the other hand, he was drawn irresistibly to the military fascination of Imperial power. Thus, to hold Alexandretta for ever is vital; to lose British soldiers for Mesopotamian oil is squalid and wicked. In this kind of judgment Lawrence may have been a strategist and not a political economist, but he was chiefly a kind of aesthete, plumping for abstract power which was, in some way, connected with honour. It had nothing to do with the squalid, practical interests of the oil trade. (His reading at this time is suggestive: Homer, the *Morte d'Arthur* and Blake; the epical, chivalrous and mystical.)

At any rate the attitude of Lawrence is not that of a 19th-century Romantic. Nor is there any Rupert Brooke in him. Of all those who wrote about the First World War, he is the only one to get into it with his eyes open. He had been studying castles, military science, the actual terrain of

his war and its people in his youth scientifically. The disillusion of the
other war writers of that generation arose because war was not what they
thought it would be; the strong ruling and military bent of the Anglo-Irish
seems to have preserved Lawrence from illusion. What he experienced
after the war was the disgust of success, the disgust following intoxication;
perhaps the affront that he was no longer a king-maker; and, of course, the
frustration of the guerrilla soldier's ideal of freedom for a race of soldiers.

I do not say this to whittle down the sincerity of his desire for Arab
Freedom, but to underline the importance of the idea of honour in his
character. It goes back to the Elizabethans in Ireland, not to the English
public schools; and his feeling for the Arabs – though there was always
some part of him that was the observer – seems to have been a natural
response to people who lived by honour, the corruption of honour by
eternal quarrels, and its ironies. It is an exquisite moment in *Seven Pillars of
Wisdom* when Feisal discreetly shows that he has guessed Lawrence is
doctoring the telegrams from Mecca; there is an Elizabethan taste for the
conceit, for the subtle arabesque of innuendo. When Feisal says to
Lawrence 'You always prefer my honour to your own,' the words have the
ambiguity of a verse cut by the diamond of a betrayed Tudor. For, as
Lawrence said many times in the *Arab Bulletin* and *Seven Pillars*, he *used* the
honour of the Arabs; he was stronger because he had a motive unknown to
them. He had the demon inside him, the will of the Allies; and he was
strong also because he had to make an enormous moral effort to live with
his own guilt:

> In compensation stood my energy of motive. Their less-taut wills
> flagged before mine flagged, and by comparison made mine seem tough
> and active.

The precocious Lawrence who, as a boy of five, could read a newspaper
upside down, who became a technician, an archaeologist and an historian
while he made himself into a deep and original military thinker, was a
'thought-riddled' man. He was the kind of man of action who did not value
what men of action valued. He was made to bear the Hamlet-like burden of
the double role; he became a legend, perhaps because he was a new and
prophetic prototype. The guerrillas of the 1939 war, the equipped indi-
vidualists, the educated men or the sensitive who had to stick out the

promiscuous living of the Nissen huts, were foreshadowed by him. He stands, rather flamboyantly guilty, at the beginning of a new age to which the conflicts of *Seven Pillars* were to become soberly familiar. In everything, from the hold-ups, the executions, the intrigue and the tortures to the final nihilism, he was the first guinea-pig of the underground. What a guilt-eaten book *Seven Pillars* is and how subtle. True to the feeling of his period (for the book is very much of the Twenties in its artifice, its mastery and egoism) and true to his own nature, it is theatrical; but it has to be so to make its corrosive mark as a new, progenitive kind of mind in war. *The Mint* was a good title for its successor, because it was Lawrence's place to stamp the hurt contemporary face on the new coin.

The theme of *Seven Pillars* seems to be ecstasy, guilt and suffering. In action, that means the satisfaction of the well-laid mine, the provision of timely loot, excitement and slaughter for the tribesmen; it means blood-guilt; and it means the martyrdom of leadership – having to shoot a man oneself in order to prevent a blood feud – and a curious moment like the one when, after a massacre, Lawrence went round and arranged the dead in more seemly positions. The self-questionings have the rhetorical touch – later Lawrence criticised the 'foppishness' of his mind – but the manner he adopted, one feels, was simply his device for screwing the last ounce out of sensibility, or a kind of flagellation:

> The practice of our revolt fortified the nihilist attitude in me. During it, we often saw men push themselves or be driven to a cruel extreme of endurance; yet never was there an intimation of physical break. Collapse rose always from a moral weakness eating into that body, which of itself, without traitors from within, had no power over the will. While we rode we were disbodied, unconscious of our flesh or feeling; and when at an interval this excitement faded and we did see our bodies, it was with some hostility, with a contemptuous sense that they reached their highest purpose, not as vehicles of the spirit, but when, dissolved, their elements served to manure the field . . .

Or:

> I seemed at last approaching the insensibility which had always been beyond my reach: but a delectable land: for one born so slug-tissued that nothing this side fainting would let his spirit free. Now I found myself

dividing into parts. There was one which went on riding wisely, sparing or helping every pace of the wearied camel. Another hovering above and to the right bent down curiously, and asked what the flesh was doing. The flesh gave no answer . . . a third garrulous one talked, wondered, critical of the body's self-inflicted labour . . . Telesius, taught by some such experience, split up the soul. Had he gone on, to the furthest limit of exhaustion, he would have seen his conceived regiment of thoughts and acts and feelings ranked round him as separate creatures; eyeing, like vultures, the passing in their midst the common thing that gave them life.

The pages on self-surrender, obedience and abasement are, in their way, religious and, indeed, were observed among believers in a warlike religion. The final desire is for physical solitude. Lawrence could not bear to be touched unless, one supposes, he was hurt.

And so one could go on about this strange actor whose aim – realised only among the Arabs – was to be notable for being unnoticeable, an actor both morally and physically. His self-analysis is not really the best part of *Seven Pillars*; what holds one is more than the story; it is the brain. Travellers have told before how they have stopped a quarrel by a well-turned tale, especially (one seems to remember) in the East, the home of convenient formulae; but Lawrence giving an impromptu parody of an Arab story-teller, at a bad moment, to an audience who (he tells us) had never heard parody before, is superb in assurance. Or again, Lawrence, dominating his illness by thinking out his campaign, shows us the will at work hour by hour. Throughout a swift, masterly narrative, packed with action, character and personal emotion, we have the extraordinary spectacle of a brain working the whole time. It is as if we could see the campaign thought by thought. The close texture of genius in action has rarely been so livingly done by an active man; it has been left, as a rule, to the self-watching invalids. And this density of thought was present from the beginning. If there had been no war in Arabia, and no epic to live, Lawrence would still have been a vivid, trenchant and sardonic historian. Hardly classical in manner (for that was 'out' in the Twenties and writers were looking for manners which would bring home their nervous singularity) *Seven Pillars* is the solitary classic of the self-conscious warrior, as Doughty is of the great self-conscious traveller.

The Notebooks of Henry James

The notebooks of the great authors are the idlest kind of reading as, for their writers, they have so often been the idlest kind of writing: in the forest of life they mark the trees to be felled. It is always a moment this, delicate and touch-and-go, when a piece of life is chipped off and is still neither life nor art, a fragment with the sap, the tang, the freshness still on it, to be picked up and considered. We are at a beginning, and there is a kind of pathos in knowing that presently this bright bit will be lost to life and become an anonymous, altered and perhaps undecipherable piece in the forbidding structure of a work of art. To some minds, and especially the critical, there will be a pleasure in tracing the history of that chip from the time when it flew off the axe until it found its present home in what Henry James called 'the real thing'; to lazier minds there is the pleasure of being there as the first stroke rings, even when it rings flat and untrue. 'A good deal might be done with Henry Pratt', wrote Henry James, recalling an evening with this friend of his in Venice. How one responds to that suddenly decisive and injudicious cry. Hurrah, the woodman has not spared the tree! Bring Henry Pratt in here. Let us *all* look him over. Let us keep him here, with the soil on his roots, while we make up our ingenious minds. That is one pleasure of notebooks: they are dramatic. A character, a scene, a smudge of scenery, half a dozen lines of talk, a few epigrams with no visible means of support, are caught in all their innocence. The other attraction is the strangeness of the workshop. Here are not only the acceptable ideas but the unacceptable, the discarded, the litter of a profession, the failures.

The Notebooks of Henry James belong to the working kind. Even the opening judgment on his first twelve years as a writer is done to clear the mind and not to indulge his memory. The great are monsters of efficiency, the mills work day and night. What strikes us is how much James's notes were used. Hawthorne's long notes, for example, seem to have been a studied alternative to his real subjects. Dostoevsky's – as far as we know them by quotation – generate fog rather than precision, though we may regard Dostoevsky as a note-writer whose object is to work up a fog of the right density. With James the matter is all literal: the American genius is technical and for production. The *Prefaces*, the anecdotes that have come down to us, show that nothing was lost: James was presentable and publishable in his very socks. His life was an arrangement in words, born to circulate.

These *Notebooks* of his were begun in Boston when he was thirty-eight and when he feared that he had let too many impressions slip by, and they cover thirty years. They confirm that the word was totally his form of life, as if sentences rather than blood ran in his veins. Outside of words lay the unspeakable:

> Meanwhile the soothing, the healing, the sacred and salutary refuge from all these vulgarities and pains is simply to lose myself in this quiet, this blessed and uninvaded workroom, in the inestimable effort and refreshment of art, in resolute and beneficent production. I come back to it with a treasure of experience, of wisdom, of acquired material, of (it seems to me) seasoned fortitude and augmented capacity. Purchased by disgust enough, it is at any rate, a boon that now I hold it, I feel I wouldn't, I oughtn't to have missed. Ah, the terrible law of the artist – the law of fructification, of fertilisation, the law by which everything is grist to his mill – the law in short of the acceptance of all experience, of all suffering, of *all* life, of *all* suggestion, sensation and illumination.

And again:

> To live *in* the world of creation – to get into it and stay in it . . .

This is a language, with its 'inestimables', its 'alls', its 'boons' and 'beneficences', which oddly recalls the otherworldly language (so blandly assuming solid rewards on earth) of his contemporaries, the American Transcendentalists: like them Henry James was turning in to a private Infinite which would give the painful American gregariousness a sense of privacy. His words to Logan Pearsall Smith who had described a desire to excel in literature (I quote from Simon Nowell Smith's *The Legend of the Master*) are the proper conclusion:

There is one word – let me impress upon you – which you must inscribe on your banner, and that word is Loneliness.

Loneliness, like a pair of empty eyes, stares between the lines of this volume. We see the empty silent room, the desk, the lost, blank face of the well-dressed writer. Already as he takes his pen, he is far away from the dinner party he has just left. He is caught by 'the terrible law.' As fast as Emerson he is turning matter into spirit. Nearly every note is made after a meeting with people whose words, or what he knows of their lives, have provided him with one of his 'germs', and at first sight, these pages might pass as the record of a vast sociability, a discreet mass of anonymous gossip. James himself, once attacked by Alphonse Daudet for frequenting people below his own intellectual level, might appear like another Thackeray ruined by dining out, or like the Major in *The Real Thing* with 'the blankness, the deep intellectual repose of twenty years of country-house visiting.' (The American editors of the *Notebook*, F. O. Mathiessen and Kenneth B. Murdock, point out that the French critic exaggerated: Henry James had a great many distinguished friends and some of the notes clearly are prompted by them. It is an illusion that a novelist needs high company continually, unless that happens to be his material; the conditions of the intellectual life are dangerously inclined to cut the novelist off from ordinary people who expose themselves less guardedly than the intellectuals do.) But examine a typical note carefully: the memoranda of Henry James are not jottings and reminders. They are written out, hundreds of them, at length. They are not snatched out of time, but time is in them; already the creative process has begun. A glance shows how much of James's life must have passed in the immense labour of almost continuous writing, and writing out in full detail, as if to fill the emptiness of the day with the succulence of its lost verbatim. The earliest reference to *What Maisie Knew* – a story which may be followed from behind James's shoulder in many entries in this volume – is not a hurried shorthand. It might be a minute passed from one civil servant to another:

Two days ago, at dinner at James Bryce's, Mrs. Ashton, Mrs. Bryce's sister, mentioned to me a situation that she had known of, of which it struck me immediately that something might be made in a tale. A child (boy or girl would do, but I see a girl, which would make it different

[389]

from *The Pupil*) was *divided* by its parents in consequence of their being divorced. The court, for some reason, didn't, as it might have done, give the child exclusively to either parent but decreed that it was to spend its time equally with each – that is alternately. Each parent married again and the child went to them a month, or three months about – finding with the one a new mother and the other a new father. Might not something be done with the idea of an odd and particular relation springing up . . .

James's method is uncommon among writers and explains why his *Notebooks* are more fertile than most others we have been allowed to see. A full, superfluous, self-communing phrase like, 'Might not something be done . . .' slows down the too bright idea, roots it in the mind, gives it soil. The slower the process of note-making the more likely it is to have sap and growth. James passing minutes to himself, James in colloquy, writing himself long and intimate letters: the note becomes one of those preliminary private outpourings, a 'voluminous effusion . . . so extremely familiar, confidential and intimate – in the form of an interminable garrulous letter addressed to my own fond fancy.' Not only is his material the subject: he himself is in it, adjured, egged on and cozened. Strange cries, like the whimper of hounds on the scent, comically, not without mockery – and yet touchingly and even alarmingly: 'I have only to let myself go' – break out. In life he is an outsider, but not in letters:

I have brought this little matter of Maisie to a point at which a really detailed scenario of the rest is indispensable for a straight and sure advance to the end. Let me not, just Heaven – not, God knows, that I *incline* to! – slacken in my deep observance of this strong and beneficent method – this intensely structural, intensely hinged and jointed preliminary frame . . .

The coverts are drawn:

What is this IX, then, the moment, the stage *of*? Well, of a more presented, a more visible cynisme, on the part of everybody. What *step* does the action take in it? *That of Sir C's* detachment from Ida –

[390]

Then comes the view:

> Ah this *divine* conception of one's little masses and periods in the
> scenic light – as rounded Acts; this patient, pious, nobly 'vindictive'
> (vindicating) application of the same philosophy and method – I feel as
> if it still (above *all*, Yet) had a great deal to give me, and might carry me
> as far as I dream! God knows how far – into the flushed, dying day – that
> is! *De part et d'autre* Maisie has become a bore to her parents – with Mrs.
> Wix to help to prove it.

> And so from field to field he runs, down to that kill, so protracted, so
> lovingly delayed lest one thrill of the chase be lost – 'Do I get anything out
> of Folkestone?' – where Mrs Wix at last '*dit son fait* to – or about.'

We could not ask for a more explicit statement of the compulsive quality
of the creative process; in fact, one could say that any other quality is
excluded from these notes. There is little that is casual or speculative.
'Writing maketh an exact man.' The conception is musical or mathematical. Method has become a divinity. There are few descriptions of places
though there is a warm evocation of what London meant to him in the
early and almost pathetically impersonal summing up of his life at the
beginning of the book. Our picture is continually of crowds of people, in
clubs or drawing rooms; but not of people seen – for they are not usually
described – but of people being useful to Henry James, in some way
working for him, wired in unknown to themselves and all unworthily to
his extraordinary system of secretive illumination. The lonely man lends
them his foreign mind. Abstract notions occasionally are flashed to him:
'What is there in the idea of Too Late?' – the idea of a passion or friendship
long desired? But, generally, the information is trite. Even where the
neatest plot is boxed, we see how the deliberate endeavour to heighten
consciousness, which contains the whole of Henry James's art, has transformed it at once (after, we can ask how much this very deliberateness lost
for him as a novelist). Situation, dilemma rather than character, except in a
very general way, mark the *Notebooks*; there is little portraiture and one
would not gather much of James's richness in this respect, a richness which
displaces for many heretical readers the metaphysical interest of the double
and triple turning of the screw upon them. How many readers, like hungry,
but well-provided spiders, run carelessly over that elaborate and

mathematical web, shimmering with knots and subtleties from one beautifully trussed fly to the next.

For other novelists the value of Henry James's *Notebooks* is immense and to brood over them a major experience. The glow of the great impresario is on the pages. They are unwearyingly readable and endlessly stimulating, often moving and are occasionally relieved by a drop of gossip. (It is amusing to see him playing with the plot of *Trilby* which was offered to him by Du Maurier.) Of no other stories and novels in the language have we been shown that crucial point where experience or hearsay has suddenly become workable and why it has. We see ideas taken too briskly; we see bad ideas and good ones, we see the solid mature and the greatest ventures, like *The Ambassadors*, spring from a casual sentence. The ability to think of plots and to see characters is common; the difficulty is that one plot kills the next, that character sticks in the mud, and the novelist is motionless from sheer ability to see and to invent too much. What made James a fertile writer was his brilliant use of what, as I have said before, can only be called a slowing-down process. His material begins to move when the right difficulty, the proper technical obstruction or moral load is placed on it. The habit of imposing himself, rather than the gift of a great impressionability, appears to have been his starting point; there was a conscious search by a consciousness that had been trained. For the kind of writer who stands outside life as James did, who indeed has no *life* in life, has to create himself before he can create others.

Butler's Notebooks

The period of excitement over *The Way of All Flesh* has passed. This novel anticipated the outburst of parricidal fury which was so strongly felt in England after the 1914 war; but there is an insensibility in Samuel Butler – the result of an injury to sensibility, really, – which is beginning to make him seem arid and even pedantic as the Victorian controversies fade. His *Notebooks* stand out as strongly as ever. They have the crankiness of nature, the stubbornness of personality. They store up Butler as a character, a minor of the Johnsonian school. They are the sketches of a mind and its habits, year in year out; and, taken together, they make an intimate portrait of a peculiarly English type of Worthy: the man who sets out to make recalcitrance respectable – even demure.

Behind those who make a cult of Common Sense we are usually, though not always, entitled to suspect the wounded heart. Benjamin Franklin, for example, was hardly an injured character; puritanism and self-interest fitted him like a glove and he had the urbanity of his period. But Butler, we know, was a hurt man. The love he must have proffered at one time to his father and which, on some stern conception of principle or duty, was rejected, rebounded and became the comic anger of satire. Feeling was cut short, pruned back in Butler and its full expression is rare; one remembers only the lines supposedly written about his love for Pauli and his remorse after the death of Miss Savage. But the latter was expressed with a defensive touch of brutality and our lasting impression of the emotional Butler is a wistful and misanthropic one. The ridiculous and ironical make their protective gestures. He is drily aware of a dull, edgy, armed neutrality in human relationships and he has the stubborn air of a man too sensitive to private pain. And so sensibility is shut off, the spirit of perversity wakes up, the comic eye aggressively winks, and if imagination is there – but there was more dialectic than imagination in him – it is soon nipped by the sobering eye for fact. Though fact itself (in Butler's kind of character) is liable to be turned into fantasy, caricature and the bizarre. The members of the parricide club have only one emotion and that is too original.

The amusement we get out of Butler comes from his stand for Common Sense, Equanimity, Worldliness and the Plain, and from comparing its downrightness with its underlying timidity; one sees the cult at work in his criticism of Bunyan:

> What a pity it is that Christian never met Mr. Common Sense with his daughter, Good Humour, and her affianced husband Mr. Hate Cant; but if he ever saw them in the distance he steered clear of them, probably as feeling that they would be more dangerous than Giant Despair, Vanity Fair and Apollyon all together – for they would have stuck to him if he had let them get in with him.

Like Shaw, Butler is without humbug. Possibly it was a form of humbug on Butler's part to pretend to be unrespectable and rebellious, when he was in fact a conservative and rather prim and tetchy character. He was a true Victorian – far more Victorian than a man like Bagehot who hardly belongs to his time at all, or Clough who seems to us now contemporary; and yet, having said that, we begin to doubt its truth, for Butler is not easy to catch. One thinks of him as a Victorian because he sallied into the great wars of religion in the 19th century but he turned them into private wars, fought with home-made weapons of his own invention. He attacked church religion with autobiography. He attacked it with his personality. Like a minor Johnson, he is pithy, downright and scathing. But where Johnson is orthodox, tragic and frontal in his declarations, Butler drops into the ill-wearing habit of paradox. He is out for dramatic effect and one often feels that when he has turned things upside down, it will only mean that someone is going to have the bother of turning them right way up again – and possibly that someone will be Butler himself:

> A drunkard would not give money to sober people. He said they would only eat it and buy clothes and send their children to school with it.
>
> An idiot is a person who thinks for himself instead of letting other people think for him.

[394]

Truth does not consist in never lying but in knowing when to lie and when not to do so.

Lord I do not believe, help thou my unbelief.

In Butler one sees the exasperation of the intelligence; in Johnson the baited bear, the growls that can become the roar of unanswerable moral rage or emotional agony. Then, one feels, Butler was unlucky in his time. He had, as it were, been forced into the Victorian age against his will; he seems to have been born to parcel out the Moral in the fashion of the 18th century, and not to gnash at its unsightly conversion into the conventional morality of the Victorians. And, in fact, their profession and their inherited wealth preserved the whole Butler family from any notion of what the Industrial Revolution did to England. He really wanted, one suspects, what the earlier century had had: a respectable cut-and-dried and formal God who, except for holidays with the Wesleyans, left the world alone.

Butler's science harked back to that humane period and his attitude to his interests has the versatility, the whim and the egocentric touch we see in the 18th-century amateurs; people like Maria Edgeworth's father, solid and yet crankish, who lapped up Rousseau, became practical philosophers, invented extraordinary mechanical and scientific devices. Butler broke into the fields of the specialists with the unholy joy of the independent nuisance, demolishing one kind of father-figure, eloquently erecting others, knocking down Aunt Sally and rigging up Aunt Handel; and he did this out of the love of the natural man which was his inheritance from the Enlightenment. Unlike the late-Victorian pessimists and agnostics, he is permeated by a discernible complacency, or rather, by a determination not to cry down his satisfactions; he has seen the devil who has told him that God is neither as black nor as white as he is painted, and is assured that the world is gradually becoming more sensible and more comely. Only one thing haunts the human comedy – the loneliness and the pathos of it, the price we have to pay for our good sense. There is a sad note on his half-wish for a son of his own to be hated by, which he turns off with a joke.

Butler's failure in his own lifetime does not seriously affect his spirits; it makes him more phlegmatic and a little touchy, that is all. The *Notebooks* suggest a packed life, the sword never back in the scabbard. Life in whatever *cul-de-sac* he gets himself into is so dense in its interest, so transformed by his personal curiosity and by his disagreement with it all, that he is more sorry for the bewilderment of the reader than perturbed by it. A parricide cannot fail to be fascinated by his own charmed life. Eccentrics gather round Butler. The upsets with his sisters are delightful in their tedium: the way they look twice at his cheques, get ill when their father gets better and recover when he gets worse! The family letters with the things that had better not be mentioned! They read like negotiations between governments. Around this family row, which Butler could never bear to leave alone, are the Cockney characters, the demi-monde of servant life with its ripe sayings:

> He is generally a little tight on a Saturday afternoon, he always speaks the truth, but then it comes pouring out more.
> Boss said that Mrs. Honor would drink everything she could stand upright and pay her money for.
> Boss said she wished the horn would blow for her and the worms take her that very night.

Alfred, the note-writing valet, is the strangest of this trite London chorus who, at times, seem to be the ageing Butler's only audience and public. One can think of no more charming scene from the peculiarity of London life than the one where Butler and Alfred are in the British Museum rubbing out the pencil marks the author had made on the letters of Dr Butler. The notes passed by Alfred were generally practical reminders about things like buying a hat, changing socks. There was once a request for a geranium; but as he worked beside his master in the British Museum Alfred slipped this to him: 'You cannot rub out half so nice as Alfred can.'

Butler's notes have a dry, almost scientific and specimen-like quality. Compressed, worked upon, shaped, made economical though not elegant, they are uttered without comment. It is the vanity of the aphorist. The good-and-evil, vice-and-virtue themes seem now the poorest, and to a contemporary taste the jokes about religion no longer shock and even require – what damns an epigram – an explanation. In an edition done by Geoffrey Keynes and Brian Hill, one or two new notes have been discovered. They are Butler's irritable accounts of collisions between rival vanities – a meeting with Augustine Birrel who is presented as an egotistical old bore; and a very wary note on Shaw. Butler's one-man war against the Victorian age led him to believe he was the only important writer in it. Of Shaw, he wrote:

> I have long been repelled by this man though at the time attracted by his coruscating power.

In their absurd meeting Shaw cried down Handel, praised the disgusting Ibsen, but agreed that the *Odyssey* was 'obviously' written by a woman –

> but I cannot forgive Bernard Shaw for sneering at Shakespeare as he has done this morning. If he means it there is no trusting his judgment – if he doesn't mean it I have no time to waste on such trifling. If Shaw embeds his plums in such cakes as this, they must stay there. I cannot trouble to pick it out.

Did the lowering, mistrustful old man apprehend that this sportive disciple was going to beat him at his own game and eclipse him? Worse – did he suspect that Shaw had that command of his own talent, that heaven-sent sense of proportion, which Butler could so rarely rely on having to hand? Where Butler lost himself in the craftsman's acrimonies, in the carpentering of belief, nailing down a joke or sawing off an outrage without an audience, Shaw was soon dancing to applause on the stage above. The fault of Butler is that he goes on arguing too long, that he chisels a joke until it vanishes.

Except in the *Notebooks*. In these he hit upon the form most congenial to him: a system of recording guesses about life. The great damage done to Butler in his childhood gave this able, virile and tender man of immensely original curiosity, a craving for the 'normal', and the normal could be surmised only by posing extreme statements and from their collision extracting the mean. His wisdom is a kind of practical guesswork and it has a power to move or convince when we feel the hourly puffing and blowing of his experience behind it.

> It is not by what a man has actually put down on his canvas, nor yet by the acts which he has set down so to speak on the canvas of his life that I will judge him, but by what he makes me feel that he felt and aimed at.

That is pure Butler: the doctrine of the conflict, the fantasy, the guess and the growing point.

A Victorian Child

After we have looked through the drawings of Cruikshank, we find ourselves haunted not by the gargoyle figures of the males, nor by the ethereal or comely silliness of most of the women; but by that other Victorian race, the pygmies in adult fancy dress, grave-eyed, elderly-headed, wraithlike, marked already by a Gothic intimation of delicacy and death: the children. They are, as we know, survivors who have escaped the large Victorian graveyard; and in their foreheads, we seem to detect, a knowledge – or is it an innocence? – beyond their years. In the violence of Victorian life these, and the poor, are the victims; and perhaps the attitude of the main body of Victorians to their children reflects an attitude to the appalling poverty upon which the fathers' prosperity was built. In the mellifluous and also blistering lecture Ruskin delivered in 1888 to a middle-class audience in the prosperous boscage of Tunbridge Wells he told them they were less attractive than the Borgias whose crimes, at any rate, had been crimes of sudden passion and not unknown to remorse. He was attacking the moral oppression of the deserving poor:

> Be assured, my good man – you say to him – that if you work steadily for ten hours a day all your life long, if you drink nothing but water, or the very mildest beer, and live on very plain food, and never lose your temper, and go to church every Sunday, and always remain content in the position in which Providence has placed you, and never grumble, nor swear; and always keep your clothes decent, and rise early, and use every opportunity of improving yourself, you will get on very well, and never come to the parish.

Is that very different from their injunctions to the deserving child?

The large untaxed profits of the middle class, the startling rise in their standard of living – at Herne Hill, in Ruskin's time, the rich shopkeepers kept powdered footmen and lived in enormous ostentation – was a violence which exacted a stringent virtue in the oppressed in order to balance the rapacity. The blessings of obedience, faith and peace, Ruskin said in *Praeterita*, were implanted in him in his childhood by his father, the sherry merchant who saved half his income every year and who, beginning without a penny, died worth £120,000. What was desired was the industrious apprentice, the obliging workman and the unchild-like child, as respectful and unperturbing as the trusted assistant of the counting house. The elder Ruskin (the son said) even chose a wife as he would choose a clerk.

In this the martyrdom of the rich child was as bad as the martyrdom of the poor, if not worse; better to be Oliver Twist than Paul Dombey. John Ruskin's life is an exemplary criticism of his time; and he knew it was. His education was forced by an ambitious mother who saw in him a future bishop. The family was isolated by her snobbery; she cooled off her humble relations and was too uncertain of herself and too proud to know those above her in station. In this delicate game the Ruskins never discovered any equals, from too much looking up or looking down. He was emasculated by her possessiveness and her fear for his innocence, and the whole scheme of his upbringing was calculated to enlarge the conceit and coolness of his nature if it did not create them. To this upbringing he traced his calamities in love and marriage; and it eventually provoked his savage attacks, culminating in madness, upon the society that had formed his parents and himself.

After the public disaster of his marriage, Ruskin understood his situation: the evil had lain in the perfection of his childhood and it was incurable. *Praeterita*, the autobiography which he wrote in the shortening intervals of sanity at the end of his life, is his final submission, the confession (as Sir Kenneth Clark says in a really admirable introduction to new edition of the work) of defeat. For here the struggle is given up. Only those things that are innocuous in memory are set down. His marriage is not even mentioned; there is only a passing reference to Rose la Touche; there is only a glance at his conversion to socialism, which was as dramatic and violent as Tolstoy's religious conversion and as tremendous a satisfaction of the ego. (Socialism was also a revenge: he had been derisively rejected by the daughter of his father's Spanish partner, Adèle Domecq, and when, later on, she made a fashionable marriage, he was stirred to condemn her indifference to the peasants in her father's vineyards.) In the last years, when reason flickered in his long-maned head and 'uninvited phantoms' came to disorder the slippery tongue of the eloquent old prophet, only the happy things were to be recalled.

What a bishop was lost in her son, Mrs Ruskin said. What a novelist was lost, said Miss Thackeray. *Praeterita* almost confirms her. The simple engagement of memory, the wandering precision of his picture of the sherry merchant's house at Herne Hill, the limpid, delightful portraits of cousins and friends, the ironical judgments, have no didactic nag; nor have they that too beguiling eloquence which brought tears to the eyes of his parents when he dutifully read his day's writing to them. Now Ruskin was no longer a middleman; he was an artist. Here is one of the Perth nephews:

A stumpily made, snub or rather knob-nosed, red-faced, bright-eyed, good-natured, simpleton; with the most curiously subtle shrewdness, and obstinate faculties, excrescent through his simplicity.

The occasional miniatures of this kind hang beside the grander studies of Papa and Mama. There is an evocation of the pleasures of suburban life which is droll, delicate and affectionate and astutely examined as they are brought up glittering in the net of time. We see again that fateful visit of the Domecq family, with their ravishing English-speaking daughters who flung him unprepared into 'the fiery furnace' of his first, sudden and unhappy passion. As he remembered it, what struck him was, characteristically, that 'nothing more tragic in the essence could have been invented by the skilfullest designer in any kind.' He thought, we note, of the pattern, the design. A galaxy of witty Andalusian beauties, in the brief excellence of their race, convent bred, in Paris clothes, tantalised a young man who was a combination of Mr Traddles, Mr Toots and Mr Winkle.

While my own shyness and unpresentableness were further stiffened, or rather sanded, by a patriotic and Protestant conceit, which was tempered neither by politeness nor sympathy; so that, while in company, I sate jealously miserable like a stockfish (in truth, I imagine, looking like nothing so much as a skate in an aquarium, trying to get up the glass) on any blessed occasion of tête-à-tête, I endeavoured to entertain my Spanish-born, Paris-bred and Catholic-hearted mistress with my own views upon the subjects of the Spanish Armada, the Battle of Waterloo and the doctrine of Trans-substantiation.

The character of Mrs Ruskin has so often been drawn by writers who, as Sir Kenneth Clark says, have gutted *Praeterita* and left no suspicion of Ruskin's mastery of the intricacy of portraiture. Unluckily she is the kind of Victorian who lends herself to caricature. We cannot help seeing Mrs Ruskin in black and white; the prudish and ambitious Protestant, managing and policing her house, mistrustful of her neighbours, shut up in an acquired intellectual pride. We see her taking her son six times through the Bible, settling him primly in the corner; after, Papa reads Shakespeare or Byron aloud for hours, whipping the boy when he falls downstairs to show him the folly of falling, allowing him nothing to play with but a bunch of keys and a box of bricks, commending his seven-year-old imitations of Pope. We see a cold and finicking Grundy who held up her marriage for ten years and even then, from prudence, would have delayed it. We cannot say that Ruskin's portraits of his parents are done with love for, as he himself says, he did not know what love was; nor even are they done with affection; but rather with that tranquillity of habit which might pass for affection. So that Mrs Ruskin is set down with the fidelity with which he would watch a stone, an irresistible view, a Venetian building or the formation of a tree. There is only the negative affection of forbearance in the portrait.

Sir Kenneth Clark suggests that the simple style of *Praeterita* is not the artlessness of an old man's writing, nor even is it to be interpreted as a final serenity and resignation; it is a conscious simplicity assumed by Ruskin to show the world that he had not lost his reason. And indeed, Ruskin was a master of pastiche. Here is a passage of near-Carlyle quoted by Collingwood in his *Life*:

All the fine ladies sitting so trimly, and looking so sweet, and doing the whole duty of woman – wearing their fine clothes gracefully; the pretty singer, white-throated, warbling 'Home Sweet Home' to them so morally and so melodiously? Here was yet to be our ideal of virtuous life, thought the *Graphic*! Surely we are safely back with our virtues in satin slippers or lace veils; and our Kingdom of Heaven is come again *with* observation, and crown diamonds of the dazzlingest. Cherubim and

[401]

Seraphim in toilettes of Paris (bleu-de-ciel, vert d'olivier de Noë, mauve de colombe-fusilée) dancing to Coote and Tinney's band; and vulgar hell shall be didactically portrayed accordingly (see page 17) wickedness going its way to its poor home, bitter sweet. Ouvrier and petroleuse, prisoners at last, glaring wild on their way to die.

Captivated as we are by the technical skill of his hands on the keys, we become restive when we realise that we are the instruments on which he is playing. We suspect the resourceful Celt. Where Shaw has the art of saying unpleasant things without making enemies, so Ruskin had the art of transporting unpleasant things into entrancing metaphors and flattering his readers and audiences by intoxicating their imaginations. In Tunbridge Wells they must have been delighted to be told that they had planted a poisoned asp in the bosom of society, especially when, in the previous sentence, they had been compared, in the most vivid colours, to the Borgias. Does he not make us feel, sometimes, in his political writing, not that injustice, wickedness and stupidity must be put down, but that indignation, anger, and the wrath of God's chosen, are themselves palatial and satisfying edifices to dwell in? When we compare the simple exactitude of Tolstoy, the other great convert, in similar writings, with Ruskin's, we see the difference between the saint and the saintly conjurer.

The Carlyles

The Universe, so far as sane conjecture can go, is one immeasurable swines' trough, consisting of solid and liquid, and other contrasts and kinds; – especially consisting of the attainable and unattainable, the latter in immensely greater quantities for most pigs.

Moral evil is unattainability of Pig's wash; moral good attainability of ditto.

We are back in the Animal Farm of the Victorian Age, among the Pig Propositions of Carlyle's *Later Day Pamphlets*. We are at the stage before Orwell, before the unattainable has been made attainable by revolution and has been distributed. So the Victorians haunt us for we are still not out of the mess they were in. But what a difference of tone lies between Orwell and Carlyle! A stoical bitterness has succeeded to the rage of frustration. There is all the distance that lies between the Calvinists' pulpit vision of disgust and doom and the betrayal in the trench. What was literature, vision, or exhortation to Carlyle, we have had to see with our own eyes. And history has been unkind to the preaching historian. We now pick up *Heroes & Hero Worship* gingerly: we have had to crush one or two dictator-heroes. Carlyle's ultimate contempt for the masses, his dream of an aristocracy of the wise, his call for a labour corps, take us back twenty years into Fascism. In England, where social injustice has been effectively attacked and constructively dealt with, the honour goes to the continuous, practical, rational efforts of the heirs of Bentham and Mill, and not to the mystics and supermen. Carlyle could describe the battlefields of the past, but he had no notion that war was the superman's chief export. He denied thinking might was right; but his statement that right is might 'in the long run' is comfortless; he certainly thought that might in the long run becomes right which was pleasant enough to believe in the long Victorian peace, but to our generation it seems to be one of those question-begging pieces of rhetoric which lead us straight to the concentration camp. It is not surprising that even at his most irascible and sadistic, Carlyle was pre-eminent among Victorian prophets: he embodied the energy and the pathos, the aggression and the guilt, of those who had exchanged belief in God for belief in themselves alone and, in many ways, Carlyle's attitude to religion is far more sympathetic than that of other apostates, for it was deeply tinctured by the tragic imagination and the sense of human pain. He never lost, as more optimistic or more accommodating figures did, the powerful morbidity of the Romantic movement into which, as a writer, he was born.

The Carlyle we have had in mind during the last thirty years or more is a very different character. We see a crabbed and complex person, a neurotic made for the problem-biography. Like Tolstoy, he is now almost more famous for the struggle of his married life than for his doctrine; he is one of the keys to Puritan marriage. Turning to his work we see that his pungency, his incomparable physical portraiture and power of image-making, might have made him a supreme satirist, a writer as great as Swift, if he had lived a hundred years earlier – or perhaps in some more solid period ahead of us. His literary fame lies, for us, in his *Reminiscences* and above all in his letters. Carlyle is one of the supreme English letter-writers, and there is something tragically fitting in that – for there he was a great artist because he was no longer kicking against the pricks and was perfectly assimilated to life and his material. We must add, I think, that *Sartor Resartus* is a masterpiece of the grotesque; the strain of sanity, like the strain of simple religion and pure poetry, never dried up in him, and they worked together to make him a wonderful comic writer, one of the great clowns who are subtle with self-irony and who are untainted (on the whole, in a book like *Sartor*) by the poisons of satire.

But are we entering a new period when the kind of portrait we have just been looking at will require modification? Professor Willey, in his *Nineteenth Century Studies*, has inquired with sensibility and sympathy into the question of Carlyle's religion; and in a new, deeply considerate biography Mr Julian Symons has patiently gone into those social and political prophesyings which, most of all, had horrified liberal and what may be called Fabian thought. He has put himself into Carlyle's shoes and

has related his life to his writings in a revealing and often delightful way –
for Carlyle's pitiless, unsparing, almost photographic memory of his own
life has preserved incomparable material for the biographer – and in
tracing the course from Chartism to contempt for the masses, he has
scrupulously looked at this from the point of view of Carlyle's own time.
This is, for a change, a non-theoretical book about Carlyle; I mean that
there are no dramatic theories about the notorious questions of his
dyspepsia, his sexual deficiency, and there is no *parti pris* on the marriage to
Jane Welsh. The human Carlyle is there in his incredible stoicism,
bearishness, tenderness, pathos, in his generosity, his rages and his
remorse; and to the intellect, when the exaggerations are washed away, are
restored the force of his remarkable insights.

The main insight, on which Carlyle was to build both sane and – in his
frustration – violent and sadistic conclusions, was into the power-basis of
human societies. Mr Symons writes:

> In a time when most thinkers believed that the world could be
> changed by good will, he understood the basis of force upon which all
> modern societies rest. In a time when political economists thought that
> the industrial revolution must bring automatically increase in prosperity
> he realised that it would involve the overturning of established society.
> In a time of continual abstract arguments about the amount of liberty
> that might reasonably be allowed to human beings, he saw that liberties
> are obtained by one social class at the expense of another and that they
> are not abstract ideas but concrete realities.

It is inevitable to argue that Carlyle's cult of the hero sprang from his own
pride, from the need to find a mystical father-surrogate and an alternative
to the lost Biblical God of his childhood. It is impossible not to see that the
individual who had been released from its classical chains by the Romantic
movement was moving, unchecked, towards megalomania. It is natural to
smile when, famous at last after years of grind, loneliness and suffering,
Carlyle began to believe in the wisdom of the aristocracy who had taken
him up and whom he had once nicknamed Gigmanity and Imposture. But
Mr Symons reminds us of the simplicity of Carlyle's character and the
major cause of his social frustration. Looking at the condition of Victorian
society he longed for action; looking at chaos he thought that it called for

decisive authority. Dangerous talk. At bottom, it is clan talk. Carlyle's mind was formed in a society which still lived in the mental climate of the 17th century. One more imaginative, fanatical, dogmatic Scot had failed to understand English compromise, or our unprepossessing, semi-religious veneration of inertia. That we prefer worry to drama.

Carlyle, says Mr Symons, was a great magician who rubbed the wrong lamps. I have a suspicion that even in his Chartist days, when his voice rings most truly, Carlyle's effect was not political in the sense that he added to the practical or theoretical thought of politics. He added, rather, to that part of the inner life of people, to the imagination above all, which may take them to religious or political action. His objection to Bentham and Mills was fundamentally the poet's or the preacher's: they had ignored the soul, they had ignored the individual's need for a vision of his own drama and significance. The most satisfactory of Carlyle's revolutionary acts was the creation of his enraging prose which, as Mr Symons says, was an act of genius: nothing more calculated to break the smooth classical reign than this Gothic and Gaelic confection. It takes us back to Sterne, Mr Symons says; but I think really it goes back to the language of another Puritan in whom the violent pressures of Puritanism had created an intense extravagance of fantasy: to the writing of Milton. I do not think Mr Symons makes enough of the Biblical strain. It is not the canting or whining of the dissenting tabernacles, or the uttering of magical passwords. It is a hybrid in which the Gaelic and Hebraic minds are joined. Energy, rather than the moral force of Milton, binds this writing which has all the Gaelic artifice, acting and love of decoration, all the intoxication of image with image, and the peculiar Gaelic cruelty. Carlyle was a Gaelic pagan with the Biblical rhythms thumping in his head and the German absurdities cavorting inside him 'in every conceivable sense.' Exhausting as we may find a style as consciously allusive as *Finnegans Wake* is, we cannot but feel our imagination enlarged. Humility vanishes, acceptance goes, egoism expands. We live no longer in the prose in which it has pleased God to call us, but suddenly have the rights of our wild poetic intuition. We recognise our genius. In other words, we become human souls. Was that not at the heart of the tragic struggle of the poor peasant Calvinist: the struggle to become not a citizen but a human being in an iron age.

[406]

And the marriage of the Carlyles? Because sex is the predilection of the 20th century, we have to turn to the late 18th century for the analysis of love, and to the Victorian Age for the specialists in marriage. We go, that is to say, to the professionals. For that is what the Tolstoys and the Carlyles are. No doubt enters their minds as to married monogamy being the only way and the most engrossing; their groans from the treadmill are part of their pleasure; they have the satisfaction of those who have chosen a fate. Like Fundamentalists they live by the Book. Deeply they suspect any attempt to ameliorate this or that condition of their married life. When Geraldine Jewsbury wrote a novel which argued for the 'right' of a woman for freedom to choose her love but within marriage, both the Carlyles were indignant at the 'indecency' of the notion. Were they any different, one must ask, from the lovers of the 18th century, the figures of the *Liaisons Dangereuses*, of *Manon Lescaut*, or *Adolphe*, who held on just as tenaciously to the pain of their free condition; or from ourselves who cling to the privileged wounds of sexual aberration. The professional knows that part of the satisfaction is in the struggle, in the price to be paid daily. If the Tolstoys paid with their reason, and the Carlyles with their health, that is the compulsion of extremists. Their tragic genius enables us to appreciate, at its full worth, the mere talent for marriage of, say, the Brownings; just as the strategy of the *Liaisons Dangereuses* illumines the talent for the naval warfare of love in Jane Austen; just as Lawrence is the turbulent prophet of the sexual bliss, which has become free for all at any clinic.

What was it that bound the Carlyles, the most touching of unhappy and clinging couples? Sincere love and long affection, admiration, too; but that says all and nothing. Getting her blow in first, as usual, Jane Welsh said that habit was stronger in her husband than the passions. And she herself had, or came to have, short patience with them in other people. The pitiful side of her story is well-known; its sexual misery is guessed at but not certainly known; but it has always been clear that she was not the down-trodden Victorian wife. The Carlyle marriage was a marriage between equals. On the negative side, difficulty must have been a bond between these arduous Scots; Scottishness, also, with its dry appreciation of the angers and humours of domestic recollection. The couple would be just a little tough about the miseries created by bad nerves, bad health, bad temper. On the positive side, the bond was surely their tongues; they had a common taste for satire, malice, exaggeration and everything that was singular, a zest for scorn and the damaging, picturesque images it could be expressed in. At their worst moments, in the absences brought about by their disagreements or their health, each could be tantalised by the thought that the other was seeing, saying, thinking or writing exaggerations of the most intimidating piquancy. Each would be feeling the hypnotic challenges of the other's wit.

There is a quality here that makes both of them arresting. Mrs Carlyle is one of the best letter-writers of the 19th century. He writes large and she writes small, but she rules her page, as certainly as he does his, like a circus master. Her exaggeration is conscious, too; it is not the helpless, personal hyperbole of a bosom too full. She was always fashioned to the subtle, disguising whalebone of common sense. She picks her subject and electrifies her brain. It is all irony. Why did she not, with her Jane Austenish tongue, become a novelist? Here, it is instructive to compare her with that disturbing gusher, Geraldine Jewsbury, of whom she said,

> her speech is so extremely insincere that I feel in our dialogues we are always acting in a play, and as we are not to get either money or praise for it, and not being an amateur of play-acting, I prefer good honest *silence* . . . she is as sharp as a meat axe – but as narrow.

With all her quick, fantastic interest in people, Mrs Carlyle did not become a novelist and the gusher did. Mrs Carlyle was too interested in hitting people off, and in keeping on top herself, for the novelist's life; she totally lacked that Messiah-producing and soulful inner glumness of the pregnant artist; or the inner silence which a Jane Austen had.

The good letter-writer has to be an egotist with a jumping mind. Even at nineteen Jane Welsh was the born boss of the notepad:

> Allons ma chère! – let us talk of the 'goosish' man, my quondam lover.
> He came; arrived at the George Inn at eleven o'clock at night, twelve hours after he received my answer to his letter; slept there 'the more soundly' according to his statement 'than was to have been expected, all the circumstances of the case being considered' and in the morning sent a few nonsensical lines to announce his nonsensical arrival . . . In a day or two after his return . . . there came a quantity of music from him.

(Pour parenthese, I shall send you a sheet of it, having another copy of *Home Sweet Home* beside.)

If Carlyle howled like a dervish, and went lamenting about his house like the Wandering Jew, when the cocks crowed or the dogs barked in the Chelsea gardens or the piano played next door, Mrs Carlyle had a tongue. It missed nothing. One evening, the impossible Mrs Leigh Hunt 'behaved smoothly, looked devilish and was drunkish.' Plain drunk would have been more amiable. When Mr Leigh Hunt, after the same party, went downstairs and gave a lady a couple of handsome smacks as he left and whispered 'God bless you, Miss Hunter,' Mrs Carlyle, with her 'wonted glegness', heard! Poor Mr Severn, so devoted to his wife, goes off to Italy alone with the sting that 'people who are so devoted to their wives are apt from mere habit, to get devoted to other people's'. What a power, 'beside a fund of vitality' Mr Sterling had of 'getting up a sentiment about anything or nothing'. And Geraldine, the never-spared, gets a letter with the immortal beginning: 'Dearest Geraldine, I am sending you two men.' The only way to get even with a lady as sharp as this was to use her own methods and make her laugh at herself; and this happily she could do. A young Charles Buller, who had been snubbed by her on the sound Annandale ground that he was an expert philanderer and unkind to his parents, was not going to be put down. For two days she held out against him without a smile – and her face with its fine but sullen brow, its full-orbed eyes and hard mouth could look formidable – until a brilliantly silly idea occurred to him. They were all standing in the hall watching the rain fall on the Norfolk garden when the young man exclaimed, 'I will shoot a hollyhock' and did so at once, bringing her the trophy with all the solemnity (the learned and topical lady writes) of Mr Petrucci in the character of Heraclitus. She was obliged to laugh, 'to the disgrace of her originality'. The immoral Mr Buller had subdued a fantastic satirist, by a fantastic act.

Mrs Carlyle was the most amusing woman in London. Everyone with any brains came to her house. She astonished Tennyson by allowing him to smoke; she gave Mazzini many a dressing-down. D'Orsay called twice: 'at first sight his beauty is that of the rather disgusting sort which seems to be like genius of no sex.' But he had wit and sense on the first occasion;

they had diminished by the second. No longer dressed like a humming-bird, he had cleverly subdued his finery to the recognition that five years had made a difference to his figure. She was quite aware, in spite of a flutter of pretence, that people liked seeing her as much as they liked seeing her husband; and when Carlyle was beguiled to Bath House by Lady Ashburton, there was a lively salon in Cheyne Row to put against it. And put against it it was. With the acid relish of inner loneliness, she was a great deal out and about observing the human comedy. The born letter-writer sees incident or absurdity in the smallest things and picks out what will divert the reader. This was written for the scornful preacher in Carlyle:

> A Mrs. Darbyshire, whom you saw once, came the night before last to stay while I stayed. She seems a sensible *gentlewoman* enough – a Unitarian *without the* Doctrines. But I could not comprehend at first why she had been brought, till at last Mrs. Paulet gave me to understand that she was there to use up Miss Newton. 'Not,' she said, 'that my sister is an illiberal person, though she believes in Christ, and *all that sort of thing*. She is quite easy to live with; but it will be pleasanter for herself as well as for us that she should have somebody to talk to of her own sort – a Catholic or Unitarian, she doesn't mind which.' After this initiation I could hardly look with gravity on these two shaking heads into one another's faces and bum-bumming away on *religious* topics, as they flatter themselves.

And she was capable of folly. There was the wonderful party when Dickens did his marvellous conjuring tricks, where the cracks went bang and the champagne flowed. She had been green, bilious and ill with her terrible nerves when she left Cheyne Row, but here in the uproar, she was suddenly cured. She talked mad nonsense to Thackeray; and at the climax Forster

> seized me *round the waist*, whirled me into the thick of it and *made* me dance!!! Like a person in the treadmill who must move forward or be crushed to death! Once I cried out, 'For the love of heaven let me go; you are going to dash my brains out against the folding doors!' to which he answered, 'Your brains! Who cares about their brains here? Let them go.'

[410]

There were other lettings-go of the brain. Obviously, taken in by Geraldine Jewsbury, she had left herself go too far for a moment or two. She was on the verge of a 'crush'. There was the Father Matthew episode, a pure case of hero worship, when she rushed to his meeting in the East End, and, climbing on to the platform, fell flat at the priest's feet. She gripped his hands, burst into tears and after a few choking words gave him a memento of herself, and went home sick and mad with exaltation. After her husband, the Father was 'the best man of modern times'. But here the ironist returned: 'Had you any idea your wife was such a fool?' And there was the sobering reflection that 'the Father got through the thing admirably'.

There must have been a good deal of 'getting through the thing' at Cheyne Row. It was, for all its ready sociability, a fort, with the old warrior upstairs, bloody and unbowed, and herself the sentinel below. They had, in this marriage, the belligerence and tenderness of soldiers. Her letters amuse like a novel because they catch the hour-to-hour life, the alarms and domesticity of this peculiar garrison. We are spared the hysteria of a Countess Tolstoy, for Jane Welsh and her husband were stoics; when the woe, the illness, the insomnia, the loneliness, the jealousy come through, and the wary hardness that followed their insoluble differences, it comes through a mind capable of some self-criticism. Strangely, it is not the *suffering* that moves one – only by an effort can one sympathise with neurotic or imaginary suffering, for one is always aware of how strong and relentless the neurotics are – rather, the happiness, the devotion, the love and the deep deposit of friendship that accumulate in a marriage, and the exquisite pain of the passage of time, that bring tears to the eyes. How quickly the early excitement goes; how warmly the devotion expands; how strong the ties between the contestants become. The Carlyle marriage becomes an archetype of the marriage of genius. We owe to Mrs Carlyle an intimate picture of a remarkable man caught, as in the Laocoön, by his own gifts; not once is there any attempt at that reckless, destructive criticism of his work, which animal jealousy and mania aroused in a woman like the Countess Tolstoy, unless the journals Mrs Carlyle destroyed contained such outbursts.

If both the Carlyles had a terrible power of speech – when one regards them from the Marriage Council point of view – they took a comic pride in the dramatic effect of their silences. Carlyle said hers was terrifying: and he would know, for he has given us a notion of his own when he speaks of resting on 'the iron pillar of silence and despair'. Mrs Carlyle denied she was a jealous woman when Geraldine Jewsbury was invited to stay, but the over-quickness of her denial, her clever turning of jealousy into what she could claim was ordinary worldly percipience about the effect of pushing young women on distinguished men, give her away. She was an exceedingly jealous woman. Carlyle, similarly, appears not to be a jealous man: she had far more men (and women) in varying states of passion for her than he had women. He never objected. *His* jealousy was directed outside the home, at other writers. We owe to him the most brilliant, destructive, ill-tempered portraits of the chief figures of his time: Lamb sodden with gin, Godwin vacuously playing cards, Emerson thin as a reed and with a head like a starved cockerel's. He could pretend that these caricatures were quintessences caught by an infallible artist in the godly or the grotesque, and not the jealousy of a tormented egotist. Her caprice must be matched by his manias; his determination to hold the floor, by her determination to manage the table. It was sufficient to give either of them a present or to offer money, to insult them. If he saw through every other writer she saw through every woman, especially every married woman, the moment they opened their mouths. If she made a dead set at the husband of every woman who came into the room, especially if he was famous, Carlyle, just as possessive as a prophet, took possession of every major aspect of the fate of England.

There was fire in both of them. There was also porridge – the curious, flat, short-tasting gift for finding nourishment in daily, domestic ironies which, when one looks back on the lame attempts to describe love in Scottish novels, appears to be its sentimental substitute. How the Carlyle marriage recalls those domestic scenes (so often placed in the sculleries, kitchens, and backyards) of the novels of Scott and Stevenson, where scolding, clatter, a gift of tongues, retort and counter-attack are the language of love, and raised from squalor by the wanton bellicosity of the Gaelic imagination.

The archetypal marriages – and the Carlyles' was the archetype of the wedding of wit and genius – owe their position to the outspokenness of the parties. The Tolstoy diaries! The Carlyle letters! Can human happiness survive so much forthrightness? The Carlyles were saved because they admired each other's wit. Their worst agonies seem not to have come from their common hypochondria, her jealousy or his monstrous selfishness, but from not getting letters from each other on the day they were expected when they were separated. It is the most moving thing about them: their craving for the other's voice. But behind her skill and humour, behind her simplicity, behind the habit of a certain obdurate competition with each other lay something one can only call primitive. Like some couple out of a novel by D. H. Lawrence – some anti-phallic couple one must say and Carlyle, oddly, uses the word – they had built, open-eyed, a contest of essences and prides.

Boswell's London

The discovery of cache after cache of Boswell's manuscripts, journals and letters at Malahide and Fettercairn between 1925 and 1948 is one of the truly extraordinary events in the history of English letters. It gave us the original journal of the *Tour to the Hebrides*, published in 1785, and now we have a totally new manuscript, appearing 180-odd years after it was written. This is the London journal which Boswell wrote in 1762 and 1763 when, twenty-three years old, he came to London to get a commission in the Guards, and, failing in that, met the man who was to be his god, his subject and his insurance of fame. What, we wonder, will be the state of our old editions of the *Life* of Johnson when the manuscripts yet to be seen are published? The *Life* has been a kind of lay scripture to the English, for it contains thought in our favourite, pragmatic form, that is to say, masticated by character. The book has been less a biography than a sort of parliamentary dialogue containing a thundering government and an adoring and obliging opposition. It will be strange if the proverbial and traditional characters are altered, though in the last generation the clownish Boswell has risen in esteem, and beyond Macaulay's derision. He has changed from the burr on the Doctor's coat-tails into an original blossom of the psychological hothouse.

Here we get on the dangerous ground of Plutarchian contrast. If Boswell created himself, we must never forget that Johnson made that possible. We lean to Boswell now because we have been bred on psychologists rather than philosophers, and love to see a man drowning in his own contradictions and self-exposures. The Doctor, who believed in Virtue, believed inevitably in repression, where we have been taught that it is immoral to hide anything. Boswell's very lack of foundation, his lack of judgment, are seen merely as the price he pays for the marvellous fluidity, transparency and curiosity of his nature. Dilapidation is his genius. Yet if Boswell is a genius we cannot forget that the Doctor is a saint, a man of richer and more sombre texture than his parasite. He is a father-figure, but not in the mechanical fashion of psychological definition; he is a father-figure enlarged by the religious attribute of tragedy. It was the tragic apprehension that was above all necessary for the steadying of Boswell's fluctuating spirit and for the sustaining of his sympathetic fancy.

The marvel is that at the age of twenty-three Boswell was already turning his gifts upon himself in the *Journal*. Professor Pottle, his lively American editor, thinks that his detachment is more complete than that of Pepys or Rousseau. Boswell's picture of himself has indeed the accidental and unforeseeable quality of life which better organised, more sapient or more eloquent natures lose the moment they put pen to paper. Boswell's detachment comes from naïveté and humility. He was emotionally surprised by himself. To one who had been knocked off his balance by a severe Presbyterian upbringing the world is bound to be a surprising place. To those who have lived under intense pressure, what happens afterwards is a miracle and release is an historical event. If the will has been destroyed by a parent like Lord Auchinleck, it may be replaced by a shiftless melancholy, an abeyance of spirits, and, from that bewilderment, all life afterwards will seem an hallucination, when a high-blooded young man engages ingenuously with it.

There is an obscure period in Boswell's youth when he joined the Roman Catholic Church. We do not know whether passion, giddiness, his irrational fears, or his tendency to melancholy, moved him to this step. But native canniness got him out of the scrape which socially and materially would have been a disaster in that age, and we can be grateful that the confessional did not assuage what Puritan diarising has preserved. For that confession contains more than an account of his sins; it contains his sillinesses, his vanities, moods, snobberies, the varying temperatures of his aspirations. 'I have a genius for Physick,' he says. For what did he not think he had genius? If only he could find out how to develop it! No symptom was too small when he studied the extraordinary illness, the remarkable fever, the very illusion of being a Self, James Boswell.

Exhibitionism? Vanity? The *Journal* was not private. It was posted every week to a friend, one of the inevitable devotions of the hero-worshipper. It is amazing that a young man should be an ass with such art, that judgment should not sprout anywhere. How rare to see a fool persisting in folly to the point of wisdom. One of the earliest comedies in the book is his lamentable affair with the actress Louisa. Calculation is at the bottom of it. Meanness runs through it, yet it is an exquisitely defenceless tale. In time he hoped to have a mistress who was a woman of fashion, but social in-experience and poverty – he is wonderfully stingy, a real hungry Scot of the period – held him back. As an actress Louisa could *cheaply* create the illusion of the woman of fashion. All this is innocently revealed later by introspection; at the beginning he is all fine feeling. To emphasise the fineness of feeling, he astutely points out, in his first timid advances to Louisa, that love is above monetary considerations. Presently he begins to believe his own propaganda; he is in love and to the extent of lending the woman £2. In the seduction, his sexual powers at first disappoint and then suddenly surpass anything he (or Louisa) has ever heard of. The next time he has a shock. Love has vanished. He is an unstable character. Presently he discovers she has introduced him to the 'Signor Gonorrhœa.' Despair, rage, moral indignation – can he have left the path of Virtue? – hard bargainings with the surgeon, melancholy, the ridicule of friends, nothing to do but to stay at home and read Hume's *History*. Philosophy calms him until the surgeon sends his bill. (In the matter of cash, the dissolving selves of Boswell always come together with certainty.) He writes to Louisa, points out what she has cost him, and asks for his £2 back, and says he is being generous. The doctor's bill was £5:

> Thus ended my intrigue with the fair Louisa which I flattered myself so much with and from which I expected at least a winter's safe copulation.

To be so transparent, thinking neither of the impression he makes upon himself nor of the figure he will cut before his friend, is possibly to be fatuous. But Boswell's fatuousness, which seems to arise from a lack of will or centre in his life, is inspired. Instead of will, Boswell had that mysterious ingredient of the soul, so admired in the age of sensibility: 'my genius', or, as we would say, his 'id'. On that point only is his *amour propre* unyielding. Drowning in midstream, unable to reach the shore of Virtue and swept back into Vice and Folly, he clings to the straw of his 'genius' and spins round and round until, what is he but a frantic work of art?

'How well I write!' he exclaims, after flattering a peer in six lines of doggerel. How wonderfully 'facetious' he is with the Earl, how wonderful are 'the sallies of my luxuriant imagination.'

> How easily and cleverly do I write just now! I am really pleased with myself, words come skipping to me like lambs upon Moffat Hill; and I turn my periods smoothly and imperceptibly like a skilful wheelwright turning tops in a turning loom. There's a fancy! There's a simile.

Sheridan punctures him brutally, but Garrick comes along:

> 'Sir,' said he, 'you will be a great man. And when you are so, remember the year 1763. I want to contribute my part towards saving you. And pray, will you fix a day when I shall have the pleasure of treating you with tea.' I fixed the next day. 'Then Sir,' said he, 'the cups shall dance and the saucers skip.'

Like Moffat lambs, no doubt; fancy has been at work on Garrick's talk. Boswell continues innocently:

> What he meant by my being a great man I can understand. For really, to speak seriously, I think there is a blossom about me of something more distinguished than the generality of mankind.

If only it can be left to grow, instead of being chilled by 'my melancholy temper' and dishevelled by 'my imbecility of mind.' The extraordinary thing is that a man so asinine should be so right.

The words of a man fuddled by middle-age? No, we have to remind ourselves, they are the words of a coxcomb of twenty-three. Hypochondria, as well as the prose manner of the time, has doubled his age. 'Taking care of oneself is amusing,' he says, filling his spoon with medicine. Life is an illness we must enjoy. In goes the thermometer at every instance. How is the genius for greatness? How is the fever for getting into the Guards, for chasing after English peers and avoiding the Scottish – if their accents are still bad – the fever for the theatre, for planning one's life, for wrecking the plan by the pursuit of 'monstrous' whores or by fanciful fornication on Westminster Bridge; the fever for wit; for being like Mr Addison; for a trip down the river; for lashings of beef; for cutting down his expenses and for freedom from error and infidelity in the eyes of Providence? Boswell goes round London with his biography

[417]

hanging out of his mouth like the tongue of a panting dog, until the great climax comes. 'I am glad we have met,' says the Doctor, and the dog with the genius beneath the skin has found its master.

Boswell's picture of life in London drawing-rooms, coffee-houses, taverns and streets is wonderful. It is done by a man much alone – and such make the best observers – to whom every word heard is precious. Listening to the plays, listening to the ordinary talk at Child's, he makes his first experiment in that dramatic dialogue which later was to give the *Life* its crowning quality. His ear is humble as Child's:

1st citizen: Pray, doctor, what became of that patient of yours? Was not her skull fractured?
Physician: Yes, To pieces. However, I got her cured.
2nd citizen: Good Lord!

Transparency is his gift of nature; affectability turns it into art; his industry, above all, fashions it. For Boswell stumbled soon upon the vital discovery that experience is three parts hallucination, when he made up his diary, not drily on the spot but three or four days late. He had, as his present American editor shrewdly points out, a *little* foreknowledge His 'genius' taught him to prepare the way for surprises which the reader could not know. It is one of his cunning strokes – he was not a regular theatre-goer for nothing – to repeat to Louisa, at the calamitous end of the affair, the words she had primly used at the beginning of it: 'Where there is no confidence, there is no bond.' And he is plotting, too, for that moment – surely handed to him by his Genius and not by Life – when she will send his £2 back in a plain envelope without a word. To illustrate, no doubt, his genius for stinginess. By the end, when the Doctor comes, the *Journal* overlaps the *Life*, but until then this is new Boswell, disordered and unbosomed.

Swift to Stella

━━━

The literature of common sense is a gift of the early 18th century; it derives from the citizens' view of life. Hence, after reading, say, Swift's *Letter to a Very Young Lady* our pleasure and our restlessness. What excellent advice and yet, what a slaughter of the innocents – the innocent instincts and emotions – has been committed before the advice could be uttered. In Swift, at any rate, common sense has been arrived at, only by a lifelong pruning of the random buds, a ruthless cutting back; in the end we have the impression of reading epitaphs on human hope, and what is displayed as the sensible view of life disturbs us with an underlying suggestion of anger, mutilation and misanthropy. There is a double sense in everything Swift wrote that imposes a strain upon our reading of him; we feel the rod of an over-ruling will and it is only at those times when we ourselves are capable of rancour, passion and the spleen that the iron touch in his simple, deceptive writing can really be endured for long. Swift's words arrive on the page with the regular tap of a day's rain, mono-tonously clear, and positive in its sting; but they shut us into our own house, and it is not until we, too, have reached this point of bitter claustrophobia, it is not until we think of all that we have lost by having to sit inside, that the spell begins to work.

Once we are shut in and can gaze at the foolish world from which we are cut off by contempt, Swift can affect us; but before that happens his habit of reducing everything to the plain terms of personal business makes the *Drapier Letters* a labour to read and *The Tale of a Tub* sound like a tedious piece of fantastic personal litigation, an old case flogged by a rasping and pedantic lawyer who cannot bear a hatred to die or an old folly to be forgotten. The very plainness is the argument of Swift's innate madness; so that even when his imagination is at its most savage or its most freakish, in *Gulliver* or in *A Modest Proposal*, he distracts us by the smallness and homeliness of his means. Is this the new minute method of science or the pestering of the local archaeologist? Is he putting on the knowing humdrum of the careerist politician who knows how to hammer the homeliest instances into the thick, self-infested head of the plain man? Or is it the humanism of the century?

Questions like these must harass the inquiring reader as he listens to the dry Dean cracking his facts and his arguments, as the busy Franklin dished out his endless proverbs or the plain Defoe put his draper's yardstick on human circumstance. But after reading a Defoe or a Franklin, nothing happens to us; after Swift, also, for a little while; and then, old wounds begin to burn, old sores to open, and old infirmities awaken under our skins. He has revived in us our personal hatreds, he has revived and exacerbated angers that we thought we had forgotten; out of his local instances he has raised the universal pain. And with such undermining violence does his simple method work that our pain is, as it were, reflected back upon his own character and his legend: the Swift legend walks again, haunting and terrible. Like him, when this power of his falls upon us, we cry 'I am a fool' and will our money to the madhouse. He has retaught us our personal megalomania.

When the Dean's legend begins to walk in our thoughts, the exact impression of him vanishes. Any lie, any anecdotal invention, any imaginative guess about a legendary figure seems more acceptable and revealing than what the strict evidence will concede. This is especially true of Swift. He was a careerist and a secretive man. Now it is true that secretive men are often without interesting secrets and that careerists are surrounded by enemies only too eager to suggest that they have; but even the least suspicious of biographers would have to concede that certain mysteries of Swift's life make him unaccountable.

Was he impotent? Was he the bastard of Temple? Was he Stella's half-brother? Was he married to Stella, as early biographers believed? Did Vanessa challenge Stella with this story in that dramatic scene which Scott has described? Was Vanessa his mistress? Can the little language be so interpreted as to mean, in two direct references, that he thought of Stella as his wife; and are the very blots and evasions in the manuscripts part of a double secrecy in their code? Such questions go to Baconian lengths of fantasy; we have to reject them as fabrications and tittle-tattle, as Mr Bernard Acworth does in his latest study. And yet we do so with reluctance because they would give us a Swift less inhuman than the monster who rises from the strict evidence; they would soften an egotism or a pride which are appallingly self-contained.

Mr Acworth's interest is to discover in Swift the Christian and the moralist. Swift's relation with Stella is presented as a perhaps presumptuous but, at any rate, a noble attempt to advance the minds of women to a higher plane; but Mr Acworth might also have pointed out that Swift's great power over women may have been due to his profession and his rudeness to them. The book is readable but it has the weakness of Christian urgency and I cannot believe that Mr Acworth has taken the most revealing approach to Swift's genius. The scholarly discretion of Mr Harold Williams in his new, meticulous and exhaustive edition of the *Journal to Stella* is more rewarding. With him the legends vanish at once; what cannot be proved he will not have. We are not likely, for example, loosely to accuse Swift of changing his party for reasons of power or favour, before weighing this against Swift's purpose in coming to England; on the other hand, even after reading Mr Williams's defence, the character of Swift himself strides into our minds. Had he no appetite for power, the man who would make the great Harley come half-way to meet him? He hated faction, but why? He was an intolerant High Churchman; was faction a vice because it interfered with his friendships or because it thwarted his despotic nature?

The cool-headedness of Mr Williams's summing up is a severe preparation for a book so intimate, so revealing and yet so unbetraying as the *Journal* – unbetraying in the sense that it keeps the shell of Swift hard and can be quoted like Scripture, for and against. The *Journal* is the complete picture of a man managing himself, managing the full team of his affairs with the rein in hand – career, friends, love and health all trot together; none can get out of his hard and playful grip:

> Morning. I am going this morning to see Prior who dines with me at Mr. Harley's; so I cant stay fiddling and talking with dear little brats in a morning, and tis still terribly cold – I wish my cold hand was in the warmest place about you, young women, I'd give ten guineas upon that account with all my heart, faith; oh, it starves my thigh; so I'll rise, and bid you good-morrow, my ladies both, good morrow. Come stand

away, let me rise: Patrick, take away the candle. Is there a good fire? So –
up a dazzy. At Night. My Harley did not sit down till six, and I staid till
eleven; henceforth I will chuse to visit him in the evenings, and dine with
him no more if I can help it. It breaks all my measures, and hurts my
health; my head is disorderly, but not ill and I hope it will mend.

And money is there too – how often money trots with the successful team.
Are we to think him avaricious? Mr Williams thinks not; is it then an aspect
of the exhausting matter-of-factness of his nature?

Lord Halifax is always teazing me to go down to his country house,
which will cost me a guinea to his servants and twelve shillings coach
hire; and he shall be hanged first . . .

or something else to be cunning about:

I dined with Mr. Lewis of the Secretary's office at his lodgings: the
chairmen that carried me squeezed a great fellow against a wall, who
wisely turned his back, and broke one of the side glasses in a thousand
pieces. I fell a scolding, pretended I was like to be cut to pieces, and made
them set down the chair in the Park, while they pickt out the bits of
glasses: and when I paid them, I quarrelled still, so they dared not
grumble, and I came off for my fare; but I was plaguily afraid they would
have said, God bless your honour, wont you give us something for our
glass? Lewis and I were forming a project how I might get three or four
hundred pounds which I suppose may come to nothing.

The portrait that we build up from this prattle is not of the madman or the
terrible Dean; nor indeed of the man who had flayed the soul of Varina
with his words:

I shall be blessed to have you in my arms, without regarding whether
your person be beautiful or your fortune large: cleanliness in the first,
and competency in the other, is all I look for.

but of a man, without mysteries in his life, spryly attending to his business.
The childishness of the little language:

[422]

Well, well, we'll have day-light shortly, spight of her teeth; and zoo must cly Lele and Hele and Hele aden. Must loo mimitate pdfr, pay? Iss, and so la shall. And so leles fol ee reetle. Dood Mollow.

comes as expertly to him as the way to handle a Prime Minister or terrorise a Duke.

Why do we read on and on through these 700 pages? Their events are reduced to shorthand. Compared with the letters to Pope or the great array of lords and bishops (letters more polished, far richer in judgment or comedy, even in masculine affection) the *Journal to Stella* is a ragbag of jottings about people we do not know. We are in the candlesmoke of the great world, but we have to rack our memories of history to place the quarrel of St John and Harley, to fit in the orgiastic figure of Marlborough and to remember which European war they were arguing about. Who are all these supplicants at the Court, why is this Duchess less important than that? One looks to Mr Harold Williams's notes: they are as mysterious as Debrett is to the uninstructed. And yet, one does read on. What is the fascination? It is, I think, the fascination of the magnifying glass. Swift puts it into our hands and, behold, everything is out of proportion; a corner of a room becomes larger than the room itself, an hour at the coffee house fills a day: the entrancing, minute glimpses of London life in the 18th century crowd out the generalities of history; we are given the intensely distorting glass of private life into our hands. The boredom we have felt has not been the boredom of dull writing, but the charming ennui of the busy life itself. The lackey is drunk again. Have I strained my thumb, or is it the gout? It rains, it snows, it blows. Now the sun shines. Here is a bit of gossip only you will understand. Guess who is thinking of whom now. I dreamed that I was in Ireland without my clothes: 'Oh, that we were at Laracor this fine day! The willows begin to peep and the quicks to bud.'

So the trivialities enlarge under the glass of this extraordinary egotism: they are the threads of an ambition, the iridescence of a success. Here rather than in the diplomatic bag of Swift's correspondence with his contemporaries – correspondence which was measured and cut to the fine fashion of the period – will be found the affray of his genius; for here he is in Lilliput itself, now large and hard with power, now small as Tom Thumb acting his part. Here, too, in the very objectivity of the writing, its

[423]

sudden jump not from thought to thought but from thing to thing, we see the mark of his isolation: all things, for the egotist, the madman of tomorrow, are related to one another only through him. Only he knows; only he controls; only he has the sense, the clarity of mind, the sanity. But, when we turn from the *Journal* to some other piece of his writing, we feel the temper rising as the clear prose rains down in its regular drops, and our legend making begins: for only Swift knows the price of that appalling pride and in what mysterious transactions of his life he paid it.

The Unhappy Traveller

There is one in every boat train that leaves Victoria, in every liner that leaves New York, in every bar of every hotel all over the world: the unhappy traveller. He is travelling not for pleasure but for pain, not to broaden the mind but, if possible, to narrow it; to release the buried terrors and hatreds of a lifetime; or, if these have already had a good airing at home, to open up colonies of rage abroad. We listen to these martyrs, quarrelling with hotel keepers, insulting cooks, torturing waiters and porters, the scourges of the reserved seat and viragos of the sleeping car. And when they return from their mortifications it is to insult the people and the places they have visited, to fight the battle over the bill or the central heating, again and again, with a zest so sore that we conclude that travel for them is a continuation of domestic misery by other means.

Character that provokes fuss or incident is valuable to the writer of travel books, and it is surprising that this liverish nature, so continuously provocative, has rarely been presented. I do not forget the hostile travellers who, after being cosseted by the best hotels, turn round and pull their hosts to pieces, but to those who travel because they hate travelling itself. Of these Smollett is the only good example I can think of, and after 180 years his rage still rings out. Why is he still readable? Literature is made out of the misfortunes of others. A large number of travel books fail simply because of the intolerable, monotonous good luck of their authors. Then, it is a pleasure to be the spectator and not the victim of bad temper. Again, Smollett satisfies a traditional and secret rancour of the English reader: our native dislike of the French even when we are Francophile; and recalls to us the old blisters of travel, the times *we* have been cheated, the times *we* threatened to call the police, the times when *we* could not face the food or the bedroom. But these are minor reasons for Smollett's readableness. We could, if we wanted to do so, let out a louder scream ourselves. Smollett is readable because he is a lucid author – as the maddened often are – writing, as Sir Osbert Sitwell says in his well-packed preface to a new edition, 'in a beautifully clear, easy, ordered, but subtle English, a style partly the result of nature, and partly of many years of effort.' It is the sane, impartial style which makes his pot-boiling *History of England* still worth dipping into and *Humphry Clinker* nutritious to the end.

There is one more explanation of his instant readability. There is an ambiguity, always irresistible, in books of travel if in some way the unguarded character of the author travels with him like a shadow on the road. Smollett draws his own dour, stoical, irascible character perfectly. It is vital, too, that the author should have an interesting mind. Smollett has. He is not a gentleman on tour, but a doctor, and he carries the rash habit of diagnosis with him. His observations, like his quarrels, are built up with light but patient documentation. His passions are not gouty explosions, but come because his sense of fact, order and agreement has been in some minor particular outraged. It is laughable, but before the end we feel a touch of pity. If (it had slowly been borne in on him by the time his journey was done) he had been content to be cheated a little, to pay a trifle extra, to forget the letter of his bargains, if he had not bothered about the odd sous, he would have travelled faster in comfort and happiness. Alas, it was impossible. The one-time ship's surgeon who had made his own way in the world on little education, whose sense of inferiority had not been reduced either by a rich marriage nor by great monetary success in his profession, who had been thrown into prison (and very rightly) for libel after an outrageous attack on his admiral, and had sought out gratuitous quarrels with every English writer of his time, was not the man to allow others any latitude. The quarrel was what he wanted. Since the author of *Tom Jones* was not on the Continent Smollett took it out of the innkeepers.

It began on the Dover Road where

> the chambers are in general cold and comfortless, the bed paltry, the cooking execrable, the wine poison, the attendance bad, the publicans insolent; there is not a tolerable drop of malt liquor to be had from London to Dover.

It continues in Boulogne where the people are filthy, lazy, 'incompetent in the mechanical arts', priest-ridden, immoral, their wine bad – he drank no good wine in France – and their cooking worse. Smollett, who was travelling with his wife and servants, five persons in all, preferred to buy and prepare his own food, such were his British, albeit Scottish, suspicions of the French *ragoût*. As for the French character, vanity is 'the great and universal mover of all varieties and degrees'. A Frenchman will think he owes it to his self-esteem to seduce your wife, daughter, niece and even your grandmother; if he fails he deplores their poor taste; if you reproach him, he will reply that he could not give higher proof of his regard for your family:

> You know Madam [Smollett writes to an imaginary correspondent], we are naturally taciturn, soon tired of impertinence, and much subject to fits of disgust. Your French friend intrudes upon you at all hours: he stuns you with his loquacity: he teases you with impertinent questions about your domestic and private affairs; he attempts to meddle in your concerns; and forces his advice upon you with unwearied importunity; he asks the price of everything you wear and, so sure as you tell him, undervalues it, without hesitation: he affirms it is bad taste, ill-contrived, ill-made; that you have been imposed upon both with respect to fashion and the price . . .

Has this race of egotists and *petits-maîtres* any virtues? They have 'natural capacities' (it appears) but ruined by giddiness and levity and the education of the Jesuits. It is, however, unfair to describe them as insincere and mean:

> High flown professions of friendship and attachment constitute the language of common compliment in this country, and are never supposed to be understood in the literal acceptation of the words; and if their acts of generosity are rare, we ought to ascribe that rarity not so much to a deficiency of generous sentiments, as to their vanity and ostentation, which, engrossing all their funds, utterly disable them from exerting the virtues of beneficence.

No, there is nothing to be said for the French. Their towns are often better than their inhabitants and in the descriptions of places we see Smollett's virtue as a writer. Clearly, like some architectural draughtsman, ingeniously contriving his perspectives, he has the power to place a town, its streets, its industries, its revenues and even its water supply, before us like a marvellous scale model. We get a far clearer notion of what a French town was like in the 1760s than we can form for ourselves of an English town today. Smollett was a sick man on this journey, he was travelling in search of health, and he brings to what he sees the same diagnostic care that he brought to the illnesses of others or his own; but he had grown up under the matter-of-fact and orderly direction of his time. Even when one of his inevitable rows begins – he swears he has been given bad horses, bad servants, bad meals, made to wait beyond his turn at the coaching stations and so on – they are conducted with all the sense of orderly manœuvre which he must have observed in his life at sea. We know exactly where he sat and where the innkeeper stood when the row began, and how often the doctor banged up the window of the coach and – one can see his ugly, peevish, stone-yellow face, for in a fit of repentance he describes it – refused to budge until the bargain was fulfilled to the letter. The astonishing thing is that he is always defeated; but petulance has no authority. Here is a typical upset at Brignolles – it was followed by worse at Luc: there the whole town turned out to see the defeat of the Doctor:

> At Brignolles, where we dined, I was obliged to quarrel with the landlady, and threatened to leave her house, before she would indulge us with any sort of fresh meat. It was meagre day, and she had made her provision accordingly. She even hinted some dissatisfaction at having heretics in the house; but I was not disposed to eat stinking fish, with ragouts of eggs in onions . . . Next day when we set out in the morning from Luc, it blew a north-westerly wind so extremely cold and biting that even a flannel wrapper could not keep me warm in the coach. Whether the cold had put our coachman in a bad humour, or he had some other cause of resentment against himself, I know not; but when we had gone about a quarter of a mile, he drove the carriage full against the corner of a garden wall and broke the axle tree.

'Resentment against himself!' Smollett would understand that. It is the antidote to Sterne.

A useful and detailed *Life* of Smollett has just been written by a conscientious American scholar, Mr Lewis Mansfield Knapp. One sees that Smollett, caught between Grub Street and the gentleman writers, a commercially popular professional who made enough money to employ ghosts and hacks, was a man of hyper-sensitive, jealous yet remorseful temper, ardent and generous, yet easily stung and quick to sting. His sensibility has led to the suggestion that the passages of grossness and brutality, his chamber-pot humour, are not the broad comedy of a man who liked a dirty joke and the writing on the lavatory wall, but disclose a horror of the flesh, the wincing of the man with a skin too few. Like many doctors, he jokes brutally about the body because it shocks him. Up to a point this seems to me certainly true: to deny it is to deny the double mind of many eighteenth-century writers who were not less moved to reform manners because it happened to pay them to be gross and licentious in presenting the case. Smollett in his *Travels* is a fastidious man; he has the doctor's dislike of filth and the eighteenth century (as we see again in the case of Swift) saw the beginning of a hatred of filth in the person and the home. The bad temper of Smollett, though it was aggravated by ill-health, became, to some extent, a protest against the squalor, incompetence and cruelty which impeded the sensible desires of the civilised man. He liked decorum. He hated the raffish, the Bohemian and the wild. He was, in short, one of the earliest respectable men, when respectability was a weapon of reform; when it meant that you were jeered at for objecting to capital punishment, flogging, the public exposure of bodies broken on the wheel by the roadside, and the maddening disorderliness of a system of travel which belonged to the Middle Ages and not to 1763. Smollett's temper was, in some respects, a new, frost-bitten bud of civilisation, of which sick, divided and impossible men are frequently the growing point.

Maupassant

When, as a young man, Maupassant sat in the talkative company of writers and was asked why he was silent, he used to say, 'I am learning my trade'; and that is what the hostile criticism of his work comes down to in the end. That he learned, and some better writers never have. He is one of the dead-sure geniuses, a hunter without a blank in his magazine. What one means by Maupassant's genius – for he was very limited in his range and depth of subject – is hard to say. The opening chapters of *Une Vie*, and many of the Seine stories, are Tolstoyan: there is the same limpid, timeless animal eye, alert without innocence to every movement, to every blink of light and shallow. There is the same crisp lick of the feathered surface by the perfect sculler. The difference is that Tolstoy is a man and Maupassant is a male; that Tolstoy is a man who can repent, Maupassant a machine that can only wear out. Or we might say, as Henry James did, that Maupassant is unable to reflect and that the existence of an inner life astonished him and struck him as being a surprising pathos. Conrad said, 'Such is the greatness of his talent that all his high qualities appear in the very things of which he speaks, as if they had been altogether independent of his presentation.' Life itself seems to be writing his best stories, to have inked itself upon the page; the only thing that makes one wish to qualify such a statement is that Maupassant was fly enough to say something of the kind himself in one of his letters which is quoted in the *Louis Conard* edition of his works. He is too consciously the successful writer to be trusted:

> No, my spirit is not decadent. I am quite unable to look inside myself; I am dominated by the unceasing, involuntary effort of penetrating the souls of others. Really it is not I who make the effort: what is around me penetrates and possesses *me*. I am impregnated by it, I give myself to it, I drown in the flow of my surroundings.

A feminine and passive analogy. It was learned from Flaubert and many writers have since professed it. One has noticed that the writers who train themselves to *be* life in this way become, in fact, less than life; and when Maupassant says he is unable to look inside, that is to say to record the human wish to enlarge life (as Chekhov did), one suspects he means he is unwilling to succeed: one must limit one's objectives. There, possibly, we have the hint that Maupassant's genius was not inclusive, like Tolstoy's, but selective and taught.

Like pretty well all Maupassant's work, *Une Vie* is a story from a life very close to his own. The book is his first novel. It arises from Maupassant's strongest emotion: his feeling for his mother. Jeanne, transposed into a Flaubertian key, is Laure Maupassant. Jeanne is a Madame Bovary who is not drawn to adultery by reading romances, but who is made obstinately innocent of the world by them. She receives one brutal shock after another in a life of virtue which seems touching but obtuse.

Laure Maupassant was a woman of more nerve and brain than Jeanne, who is at heart the conventional upper-class bride of the period; but Jeanne's story is Laure's in essentials. In the first place Jeanne is given a family rather more distinguished than Laure's. On both sides, the Maupassants came of moneyed mercantile families. It was Maupassant's father who quietly interposed the aristocratic *de* with its touch of the Trade Market. Jeanne's father is, however, noticeably not a parvenu when Maupassant tells *her* story. He is the agreeable, spendthrift country gentleman whose fortunes are dissolved by the impulses of eighteenth-century philosophy. The Maupassants who moved into the chateau in Normandy were climbers who overspent on the way up; they were hard as the rich bourgeois are; they were committed to success, and were drily scornful of the aristocracy of the old regime who creaked like marionettes taken out of the cupboards of their damp and solitary houses. Maupassant, who was trained by his mother to hate his womanising father, hated him far more for giving him no money and making him work as a poor clerk in a government office. The clerking injured Maupassant's pride, and it irked the sense of efficiency which is the strongest instinct of the self-made rich.

It is impossible to know what hardens the heart, what checks the impulse to 'look inside'. In a general way we can surmise that the broken home of the Maupassants had fixed the detachment, the watchfulness, the habit of *surveillance* in the child; hardness of heart comes, perhaps, from being forced by one's imperilled situation to be continually on the look out. When Laure left Maupassant's father, the son stepped into his place in the home, and there are instances of iron-willed impudence in his childhood which show that he was precociously aware of his powerful position as the supplanting male. Again and again (as Mr Steegmuller, an American biographer, has pointed out) his stories are of humiliated women and cuckolded men. There must have been precise scenes that remained in his memory all his life; perhaps that scene in *Garçon! Un Bock!* where a man recalls how, as a frightened child, he secretly witnessed a violent quarrel between his father and mother in which the mother is struck to the ground. Such scenes awake double emotions in a child, and they are not a pleasure to recall. They certainly fix in the child's mind a precocious, ungraduated and crude conviction that human relations are to be reduced at once to a question of animal dominance. To see life naked too young is never to observe, later on, that, characteristically, life is dressed. The animal watchfulness of Maupassant is the watchfulness of a childhood not outgrown; his cynicism is the recognition that he is like the father whom he can never cease to hate. And why should he 'look inside', in any case? Evil, the child has seen, comes from the outside. It is the outside that must be watched and, towards the end of his life, the very title of *Le Horla* – 'what is outside' – shows that the horrors come from an outside world that cannot be trusted. In the last stages of syphilis, this was Maupassant's terror: that the world would crash inwards upon a nature which, for all its assiduity, could not make itself hard, efficient, drastic, sealed off and settled enough.

Time is the subject of *Une Vie*. It is the pervasive theme of a large number of his stories. The early destruction of his moral sense – which was replaced only by an acceptance of the conventional moral sense of his class – led Maupassant to see the teeth of time eating up everything. It is disgusting of the Vicomte to betray Jeanne, but as time goes by Jeanne's virtue becomes something like stupidity. Live and let live; life will turn out to be neither as good nor as bad as we think. If we live long enough we shall see things turn into their opposites. So strong and harsh are these passive sentiments in Maupassant that it is strange that time is bungled in *Une Vie*; after the miraculous clear and truthful picture of a girl's awaken-ing to love, at first painful and then mature, after the shock, the novel scrambles hurriedly over the years, in too great a haste to point the moral and turn the irony. There is evidence that Maupassant altered and corrected the plot many times; he was at home only in the disconnected episode. His nervous nature needed to work in a limited field; his intense feeling for time is a feeling for its minutes which became, as it were, concrete. The more slowly his narrative moves, watching dream change to love and love to desire, the more certain is he to put his finger upon the exact shiver of change. Out of this is born his wonderful awareness of the feelings of women who are more sensitive to the climatic changes of feeling than men are. Few chapters in any love story can equal Maupassant's descriptions of the marriage night and the honeymoon of Jeanne; for it is the sense of change in sexual experience, the sense of the hours or the days going by, which enables him to write of sexual experience explicitly. In his preoccupation with the sexual act in every conceivable circumstance from the brutal and the comic to the ecstatic, there is always an unruffled observation of the changes of mood that make the act possible and the changes that are part of it. To those who value sexual conquest, the stages are as important as the conquest, and Maupassant, who is often hypocritically reproached for this excellence, may be compared with those sportsmen who love the creatures they kill. He has a natural sexual curiosity and he is, in consequence, freed from that obscuring zeal for personal and vicarious participation in the coupling of his characters that ruins the descriptions of inhibited writers. There is not a woman in the sexual episodes of Maupassant's stories who does not come to life because of them.

Maupassant's open vanity in his submission to life is softened by his patient sense of time. The launch of a boat, a drink in a café, an empty afternoon anywhere, the preparations for a shoot, the inquiring hours when lovers sit side by side unable to speak, are not matters to be hurried over. He is so slow that the minutes become dramatic. Every word is an event. The most banal thoughts can be so placed that ecstatic happiness is conveyed by them: 'It seemed to her that there were only three beautiful things in the whole of creation: light, space and water.' Or again – 'They felt happy – each thinking of the other.' Time breathes in such simple sentences; they have the turning of the earth in them. Just as they have in innumerable minor observations in this novel. Everyone grows old in *Une*

Vie, yet each in a distinctive way. The day itself and not some constructing, self-imposing author might have written a passage like this:

> In the morning Jeanne would set out to meet him, with Aunt Lison and the Baron, who was gradually growing bent and who walked like a little old man with hands clasped behind his back as if to prevent himself from falling flat on his face. They went very slowly along the road, sometimes sitting down at the edge of the ditch and staring into the distance to see if the rider were not yet in sight. As soon as he appeared, a black dot on the white line, the three of them waved their hand-kerchiefs. Then he would break into a gallop and arrive like a hurricane, which always made Jeanne and Lison shudder with alarm and produced an enthusiastic 'Bravo' from the grandfather who cheered with all the enthusiasm of one whose active days are over.

Only one or two Russians, Tolstoy above all, have surpassed Maupassant in describing happiness, the delicious sensation of simply being alive; and it is done by fidelity to what is passing, by making concrete the sense of evanescence in ordinary things.

I have possibly been too summary in my comments on Maupassant's character and have also tended to move too speculatively between the man and his work. Let us look, as much as possible, at the work alone. What are his chief interests? Sex, animal delight, of course; more important, I think, the effect of poverty and circumstance on character. Life is made endurable by sexual love and by usage; only these relieve the meaningless and unremitting irony of circumstance. It is interesting, here, to compare Maupassant's novel *Une Vie* with Arnold Bennett's *Old Wives' Tale*, which, one recalls, was prompted by Maupassant's book and which patiently attempts the same attitude of mind. Immediately one is struck by a strain of dry triviality and perfunctoriness in Bennett's masterpiece, a connoisseur's diffidence which keeps his people at a certain distance, whereas in *Une Vie* one is struck by the nearness of Maupassant to his Jeanne, the unguarded and sincere intimacy of his observation of her as a character. He is sexually aware of her. And his picture of her sexual reserve and of how, unexpectedly, it dissolves and she becomes a woman is the mark of Maupassant's superiority to Bennett as an intuitive artist. Jeanne is an obscure woman, but she is never trivial. The pessimism of Maupassant is pitying, sympathetic and humane.

Listening to the criticisms of his stories that have been made chiefly since the rise of Chekhov, one is given the impression that he was simply a brilliant conjuror or special pleader. He has been held up as the arch-exponent of the trick plot, the cynical moral and the surprise ending. Nothing could be less true of his best work. Where is the trick in *La Maison Tellier* or in *Une Fille de Ferme*? The test of the artificial story is its end. Do you, at the end of a story, feel that the lives of the people have ended with the drama of their situation? Do you feel that their lives were, in fact, not lives, but an idea? That is the artificial story. All short-story writers produce stories like this, for, like the sonnet, the short story is liable to become a brilliant conceit. But a large number of Maupassant's tales, and especially those which deal with the lives of the Normandy peasants, do not belong to this group. The ends of these tales are, so to speak, open. The characters go on living. They are beginning to live their way into a new situation. Rosa, in *La Maison Tellier*, will not be quite the same woman after she has taken the child into her bed. The *fille de ferme* is at the beginning of a new story when she tells her husband about her illegitimate child. The triumph of custom – the custom of avarice – justifies the girl in *L'Aveu*, who sleeps with the carrier in order to save her fare, and you see her at the story's end, grown into the cramped, terrifying world of peasant poverty. It is a growth, not an end. It is true that in all these stories the characters are dominated by a strong, dramatic situation; but to call this method arbitrary, when one compares it with Chekhov's, is a mistake. Chekhov's subject was life, life breaking and running like a chain of raindrops upon the window. Now the drops run and pool together, presently they part, slide off on their own and momentarily catch the light in some new, fragile and vanishing pattern. There are meetings and partings, crises and respites. For Chekhov life is an arpeggio of moments. But when Maupassant looks at the life of one of his characters he is a moralist thinking of the custom of their life. One has the sensation of seeing not merely the crises in *Boule de Suif*, but all of the lives of the people in that story. We come back to Maupassant's French respect for usage. The peasant comes out in him. There is a negative virtue in our acceptance of Fate. There are certain permanent things, he seems to say: poverty, hard work, the obligations of work, the begetting of one's kind, the scheme in which a life has been set. And into this circle the heart brings its untidy animal fire, often trodden down, but never quite extinguished. Moments are a reality in that life – the *fille de ferme* will never forget the moment when, dazed by the sunlight, she lay down on the straw in the barn and woke to strike the farm hand who crept up to touch her; nor will Jeanne, in *Une Vie*, forget that time, long after her marriage, when her miserly young husband suddenly, inexplicably, became desirable to her – but these moments are part of the grave and fatal pattern of their respective lives. There is indeed an appetite for life, a robust reaching out to life in Maupassant, and especially a love of animal life, innocent and lazy in the country scene. Suppose, for a minute, that *La Maison Tellier* is a joke. I mean, suppose Maupassant did not originally intend to go beyond the farce suggested by the notice on the door of the brothel. And now look at the story again. How quickly he leaves the farce of the original ideal behind. His animal spirits warm up, his heart expands; how quickly the idea ripens and becomes life itself. The description of the carriage ride through the dusty, dazzling countryside flashes with poetry; but it is an earthy poetry, written out of the heart and not twanged and tweaked on the nerves:

> Une lumière folle emplissait les champs, une lumière miroitant aux yeux; et les roues soulevaient deux sillons de poussière qui voltigeaient longtemps derrière la voiture sur la grande route.

La Maison Tellier dazzles one like a May morning; but in the harder story, *Une Fille de Ferme*, one also sees the same pagan love of nature. When the girl runs away from the farm before dawn, thinking to drown herself, one sees the strange, mad aspect of the countryside before sunrise. The moon appears at its unexpected and crazy slope in the sky, and the fields lie in a yellowish light, and only the warm smell of the earth in the odorous Normandy morning and the play of the leverets in the furrows remind the girl that man may be mad but the earth is not. Maupassant's feeling for nature, a feeling that went back to his childhood, is the assurance of his sanity and his heart. And nature for him is the nature of a man close to the work of the land, close to the hunter – there he reminds one of Turgenev –

and close to use. How simply, too, this nature distracts and heals the human sufferers for a while: the little boy who runs away from the boys who are jeering at him, and forgets his shame in playing with a frog. And, as I said before, I think it is from his closeness to the peasant's knowledge of nature that Maupassant got his sense of the pattern of fate or necessity in life.

The morbidity, the mere ingenuity and sentimentality of Maupassant have been explained as the bad wages of the doctrine of art for art's sake, but that criticism is not very valuable. Writers write badly when they write too much; possibly Maupassant's physical disease ensured that he would write with a frenzied facility. At his second best he is still enjoyable simply because he has that gift which no theory can explain – original talent; and that quality which cannot be obtained by taking thought – sincerity, which I take to be clarity and singleness of mind. Whatever the idea of the moment, however poor or flippant, Maupassant gives himself up to it. I think this is true of a mechanical story such as the one where the man blows his brains out because he is afraid to show his fear of fighting a duel, or in that cynical story of the prostitute who attracts her customers in the cemetery by weeping at the grave of an imaginary husband. Maupassant has a wide range of character-anecdote, if not a very wide range of character or situation, because of his curiosity. And 'art for art's sake', plus curiosity, is a formidable combination. Usually, when this useful doctrine is attacked, the critic forgets that Flaubert, who was Maupassant's master, insisted that great curiosity was indispensable. The weakness of Maupassant's mind is that its atheism was cynical. It was a personal despair unsupported by any great intellectual structure – a quality in him which, oddly enough, as Mr Desmond MacCarthy has reminded me, attracted Tolstoy: 'What is truth if a man dies?' This atheism was not damaging to Maupassant when he was writing about the pagan Normandy of his childhood, but outside of that world, cynicism left him isolated and he was reduced to seeing small, ironic, moral conundrums everywhere. There are accidental resemblances to Turgenev, who was also an atheist, in Maupassant; but he has neither the feeling of the sensitive aristocrat for his people nor anything to correspond with the mystical Russian cult of the humble. And he made no political judgments about his country, as Turgenev did. Maupassant was a child of the disaster of Sedan, and that line from the opening of *Boule de Suif*: 'L'angoisse de l'attente faisait désirer la venue de l'ennemi,' reads like his epitaph, the inscription of an isolated and haunted man.

A Love Affair

========

It seems to be true that the love affair is not a subject which, for its own sake, can engage the exclusive interest of the English novelist. We have little or nothing in our literature to compare with books like *Adolphe* or *Dominique*, with Daudet's *Sappho* or Colette's *Chéri*, or with a novel like Svevo's *As a Man Grows Older*. I do not think this is entirely due to the puritan tradition and, in any case, many contemporary writers who are free from this tradition have attempted the subject and yet have failed to convey immersion in it. The inability to transplant this admired continental genre arises, I think, from a permanent habit of mind. We tacitly refuse to abstract or isolate a subject or to work within severe limits. The love affair, with us, is regarded as a chance to illustrate something more than itself: to lead to some kind of action, to cause manifestos (D. H. Lawrence), to make religious, social or satirical pronouncements, to provide opportunity for our special taste in the comic, the romantic or the bizarre. It appears to be impossible for the English writer to treat love as an idea in itself, to confine himself to the meteorology of the emotion, to believe that it can be thought of as a climate in itself to which every other consideration must be, for the time being, subservient; for departmentalisation is a method which a northerner is bound to resist. A native instinct warns him that he could learn more than it is good for him to know. He could learn, for example, final fatalism and acceptance; whereas the last card the northerner always relies on is something very different: it is action, eccentricity, extravagance, even personal tastelessness and the absurd. There is an ageing English cocotte in Daudet's *Sappho* whose case illustrates the point. Where her French companions have compounded with their fate and have turned into tyrants, gossips or melancholy alcoholics, the Englishwoman rails at the *injustice* of being rejected by a lover because her face is ugly while her body is still beautiful. Something ought to be *done* about it! It is enough to drive one, she says – vulgarly undoing her dress – to walking naked in the

[439]

street; it is a pity that convention prevents one from doing that. The awful probability – we reflect – is, that one of these days, the sense of injustice will in fact drive her to just this exhibition, and one more English eccentric, lonely, hard-bitten, naïve and unassuaged, will be born.

For the English reader Daudet's *Sappho* is an easy introduction to the genre. It is not too abstract, nor too exacting, and it is a story busy with Daudet's invention. 'Fineness' was above all Daudet's quality – it was he who rebuked Henry James for living among people who were 'moins fins' than himself. But, as Mr Hodge says in his introduction to a new edition, we admire not the invention alone, but the grace with which Daudet's powers are used and the ease with which he passes from comedy through irony to tragedy. Perhaps tragedy is too strong a word for a writer who strikes one as being a weather prophet of the climate of passion rather than a native and victim of it, but it is true that Daudet moves as quickly as the mood itself. He is one of the magicians of the surface of life, one of the masters of the moments of the heart. He has also a genius for selecting the small Dickensian *milieux* of petit bourgeois society: the absurd picnic, the vulgar boating party, the boarding house where the droll boarders are more respectable than the retired demi-mondaines who run it, the holiday shack on the outskirts of Paris, the gay and idiotic fancy dress 'do'. Yet all these distractions are here to extend our knowledge of the love affair which is the only subject of the tale, to establish not only the changes it goes through in the course of five years, but how these are conditioned by something we hardly ever see mentioned in English fiction: the *kind* of love affair it is.

Sappho, or rather Fanny Legrand, is the Bohemian mistress, the model who is 'educated' by a number of distinguished lovers who have been artists or writers, who has the reputation of being a clinger, but who does not expect to marry. She is given many of the bourgeois virtues, she is gay, kind, intelligent; but she is sexually accomplished and, therefore, she is a damned soul. When she takes up with Gaussin, she has quietened a little, she has lost her first youth, and he is the first lover to be a great deal younger than herself. In a rather alarmingly cosy state of mind, she prepares for a peaceful, if temporary, liaison, until the time comes for him to pass into the Quai d'Orsay, marry and go abroad. We must note, here, the conventions of Daudet's period. Since this is an irregular union its nature must be lust. Daudet's philosophy is that of 'the romantic agony' reduced to the prosaic; love is known only in marriage to a girl of one's own class. Sexual talent will move inevitably to jealousy about previous lovers; and, after the first quarrels, from physical modesty to unbounded physical indulgence and perversion. The greater the physical pleasure, the less respect for the person; the body infects the soul. Here, the confused reader may well blink and wonder if he is not reading Tolstoy's account of regular, conjugal love in *The Kreutzer Sonata*. But the acceptance of a convention does not, in any way, injure Daudet's practical sensibility to every moment of the affair, or the subtlety of his psychological judgments. Jean Gaussin is a homely version of Adolphe. He is less of a moralist and more the fearing, bewildered, entangled young man at the mercy of his youthful generosity, his hatred of scenes and his dislike of causing pain. Fanny's desire to hold him begins when he changes from an impulsive youth into a guilty, worried and complicated young man like the rest. She loves and he does not, and guilt as usual takes on the clothes of jealousy. Within a few months his jealousy has become the real bond between them, for it releases their unreasonableness. From that moment he has the right to suffer and to accuse and she has the right to let fly all she has learned in her life. She can become a slut, a howling termagant, screaming out obscenities and then collapsing into remorse. There is an excellent scene – which Mr Hodge rightly points to – in which Jean obliges her to burn all the letters she has kept from her previous lovers. But with the desire of jealousy to add to its own tortures, he insists on reading each one before it is thrown into the fire, and interrogating her line by line. Her reticence pleases him no more than her candour. There is such a letter-burning that night that the chimney catches fire, the fire brigade is called, and the wretched lovers find their misery turned into farce, and then back into the ferocity of reconciliation. But they have gone too far, and temporarily the lovers part.

Daudet shows wonderful skill in this story, by pausing to take breath before each stage of the affair. In these pauses lies the happiness of the lovers. What is their happiness? Daudet has a natural and continuous delight in the detail of life and he does not find it impossible to describe happiness nor is he embarrassed in the description of desire. His method is, so to say, to filter the longing and the physical passion of his characters through the commonest events of their lives. The love is in the eating, the shopping, the furnishing, the sitting apart in a room, the looking out of the window into the noisy streets by the Gare de l'Est, as well as in the scattered clothes of the bedroom. It is an obsession with things; to things it has given an inescapable part of evocation. When Jean leaves Fanny to visit his parents in Provence and hopes that the sight of the good life will appease and cure him, Daudet writes with simple truth:

> The seductive image of her loomed before him whenever he went out; it walked with him, it echoed in the sound of his steps on the wide, lofty staircase. It was to the rhythm of Sappho's name that the pendulum of the old grandfather clock swung to and fro, her name that the mind whispered in the big stone-paved, chilly passages of this summer dwelling, her name that he found in all the books he opened in his country house library, old worn volumes with red edges and binding out of which crumbs fell, crumbs he had dropped there as a child nibbling cake. And her obsessive memory pursued him even into his mother's bedroom, where Divonne was doing the sick woman's hair, drawing the beautiful white tresses back from a face that was still rosy and peaceful in expression in spite of the unceasing pain that racked all parts of her body.
>
> 'Ah, here is our Jean,' his mother would say.
>
> But with her neck bare, her little coif, her sleeves turned up to do those things that only she could do for the invalid, his aunt reminded him of other awakenings, other mornings, called to his mind yet once again how his mistress used to spring out of bed in a cloud of smoke from her first cigarette.

Daudet is the master of the inner juxtapositions of love, as he is also of life's devilish yet apparently innocent supply of warning or ironical contrasts. There is Dechelette, Jean's idea of what a cool-headed lover ought to be, who suddenly loses his head over a mere chit. Dechelette has left dozens of women, knows the art of separating – but this time he blunders. The chit throws herself out of his window. Then there is the grotesque example of the bourgeois Hettémas. Amorous, gluttonous, lazy, sordid, endlessly amiable, continually eating and drinking, the Hettémases are the picture of bovine contentment. But that is the awful thing: the good, gross, motherly woman is a reformed prostitute and Hettémas is a fool. He does one brilliant thing, however. Tired of the quarrels of Jean and Fanny he buys a trumpet to drown the noise. At Rosa's pension – Rosa is a cocotte who has retired from the circus – where Fanny goes to help during one of the breaks in the affair with Jean, there is the same sort of disturbing insinuation in the comedy. Fanny is being pure and respectable; but it soon occurs to Jean that Fanny is not called Sappho for nothing and he notes her dread of the old courtesan. Not only that, he sees in Rosa's elderly lover who cannot escape from her, though he hates her, a glimpse of his own future. The end of the book is tremendous. For when at last Jean steels himself for the appalling scene he dreads so much and goes through with it, he enters into a false freedom. Daudet has the rare capacity to describe grief and loss, and it is a master stroke that Jean goes back when he hears that an old lover of Fanny's has returned. Jean strikes her in his rage and it is her triumph; he loves her at last. The time for her to break with him has come.

How cleverly Daudet turns the struggles of pride, of wills, of jealousies, of vanities, into life; how continually he converts insight into incident, and how astonishingly – and a moved and alert astonishment is the continual feeling we have in the book – he frees his people from the oppression of his own criticisms of their passion. If Fanny is such a disastrous woman, how delightful she is made to appear; the tricks and cheapness and slyness in her are part of her attraction; her honesty is complete and one is satisfied by a complete portrait and one that has not been marred by 'good trouper' sentiment or by the rather turgid melancholy which French romantic guilt was inclined to apply thickly to the demi-monde. Here, indeed, is Baudelaire without tears. If Daudet is apt to settle the difference between love and lust rather too neatly, his sense of physical love was not accompanied by the automatic disgust which many novelists have taken out as a kind of insurance policy. He is warm and disinterested in his candour and gaiety, he bows – the accomplished anecdotalist – to life alone. He is one of the small, fine superficial masters whose touch is quick and perfect within the undisturbing limits in which they work.

Zola

The novel seeks whom it may devour. It reaches out to more and more people, greedily assimilates them to the likeness of the writer, and when a Flaubert truthfully or half-truthfully says '*Madame Bovary* – c'est moi' we bow obsequiously to our ruling monster. We are the natural fodder and we have the pride of slaves. Only when the novelist openly writes of himself do we begin to eye him with suspicion, for then he subtracts something of himself, and if he should turn to his fellows in the other arts suspicion is likely to become protest. A monster is inclined to be overfond and professionally soft when he turns to his own kind. He has ceased to be at one remove from his material. The pretensions of the novelist are too great, the seductive impurities of literature are too easy; too fluently will he assume that other arts can be described in his loquacious terms and will pompously forget that all arts directly describe themselves.

It was Cézanne's opinion that his paintings were their own description. He had suffered enough from journalists; he believed his personal life to lack importance. But, more secretive than the journalist, the novelist hunted him. He was to come under the industrious, hammering pen of Émile Zola. The solitary was to be auctioned off by the great auctioneer who drew his breath from crowds; the visionary was to be weighed by the constructor; the 'failure' was to be judged by the 'success'; the friend of a lifetime publicly exposed to affection, understanding, pity. God protect us from those who praise us! We know, of course, from Zola's own notes on *L'Oeuvre* that Cézanne was not the only model for Claude Lantier. We are assured by research that the portrait of Claude was not the cause of the breach in a profound friendship, which had lasted since Zola and Cézanne were schoolboys in Aix; though one critic, John Rewald, has made the point that Cézanne must have been wounded by the pity Zola displayed. Zola had never written articles about him, as he had of the Impressionists: now he saw why – Zola had not thought him important enough! But the two had quarrelled many times and Zola, on his way to ever vaster and more rhetorical panoramas and notorieties, ascending to apotheosis in his frock coat, was already distant from the painter who stared at nature in a solitude which could never be too intense, and where the difficulties could never be too great. It was less and less likely that the writer whose needs drew him to the orgies of the public stage and the painter who had been ridiculed, ruined and persecuted in them would have anything to say to each other. There was nothing to bind them but the strongest tie – the passionate memories of their young days together – and, as the successful years go by, nothing snaps like a strong bond. The irony of Zola's novel remains all the deeper. It is the irony of an irrelevance.

What Cézanne may have felt, we can suspect, is what painters have commonly felt about literature: a sardonic anger at being, as it were, swallowed alive by another art. It is true that what is swallowed is usually a dummy. But, even by proxy to have swelled the maw of that Romantic glutton, to see paterfamilias (rather brilliantly) fattening himself so that *you* become *him*! To see him, above all, disposing of his private doubts by transferring them to yourself! For that Zola very curiously did in his portrait of Claude Lantier. 'The struggles of the artist with nature' – we hear the novelist chugging out his notes like a great puff-puff – 'the effort of creation', 'blood and tears.' He is going to 'give his flesh.' There are to be battlings with truth, wrestlings with the angel. 'In a word', Zola explodes, 'I shall recount my own intimate life as a creative artist, the ever-lasting pains of childbirth.' What an appalling thing the thought of intimacy with Zola is. It suggests the dreadful intimacy of a prosperous laundry greedy for one's dirty linen. Why, then, pick upon poor Claude Lantier? Zola has already planned his own portrait in Paul Sandoz, the slave of the pen, suffering from all the morbidities of success. If Claude is still required, why must he be after the same kind of thing as Sandoz-Zola – 'the wish to execute huge modern decorative works, frescoes giving a complete survey of our day and age . . . At bottom he is a Romantic, a constructor.' Why must Lantier-Cézanne paint novels by Zola? Why must Claude fail where Paul succeeds? It is true that until then Cézanne had in fact failed, and was still, as far as Zola could see, a pitiable Bohemian, without the talent for extracting his own genius. Zola, even though duped by his romantic notions about greatness, had some grounds for his judgment. But there is evidently a deeper reason.

There is a very pertinent comment on the plot of *L'Oeuvre* in a new English translation of the novel done by Mr Thomas Walton, and it reminds us that although a novelist may require this kind of plot or that as an urgent personal need, he will be inclined to take what is still fashionable or conventional in the wardrobe of literature. It is a paradox that the more 'realistic' a novelist is with his right hand, the more, with his left, he reaches for the well-worn garments. Mr Walton points out that

> the failure of the pseudo-genius, the 'conquest' of Paris by the younger generation, the fatal attraction of the Capital, and the rivalry between Woman and Art, had been part of the stock-in-trade of French novelists at least since Balzac.

Why, we may pause to ask, did this subject become so suddenly obsessional in the 19th century? There must always have been pseudo-geniuses, there must always have been the desire for fame and its corruption, there must always have been some conflict between the interests of the artist and the woman. The answer seems to lie in the momentous changes that had taken place in French society after the revolution. The Court and the idea of classical authority had gone. The individual had been 'set free', and once he is free he deifies himself. There is, theoretically, no limit to the rights and potentialities of men and women, and they become known by their dominant passion to which no restriction from the classical moral or fatal order can be applied. Before each individual lies an ultimate goal: fulfilment or success, and the new morality denies that these are subject to the gods or that 'absolute power corrupts.' We are at the beginning, in French literature, of the morality of a commercial society – to put the matter at its lowest; but, to take a loftier view, the Artist is felt to be the only really free man in an ugly commercial world, and has replaced the ruler or the great man as the highest subject of spiritual drama. And, in any case, after Napoleon the individual can only be conceived of in Napoleonic terms. In individualistic societies all individuals are at war. The individual is not corrupted by himself, but by other individuals and Woman inevitably corrupts Man; yet, underlying this doctrine one detects in the theatrical view of Woman, an excessive protest.

It looks like a guilt felt towards the discarded classical order; the opposite of success is mere failure and, compared with classical Comedy or Tragedy, failure has the indignity of a personal domestic mess. The theme of *L'Oeuvre* is matched by Balzac's *Le Chef d'Oeuvre Inconnu*. Claude Lantier has to bear the burden of Zola's own dread of his own Romantic tendencies and the guilt that eats at old friendships. Zola-Sandoz marries because marriage ensures order, peace and freedom from Woman for the artist; yet marriage rather disturbingly contains Woman, and who knows when She will not arise and manifest Her traditional jealousy of art, her hatred of a passion stronger than anything she can evoke? By transference, this evil can be place upon Lantier who can also be made to bear another nightmare of Zola's, indeed of any writer's life: the fear of creative impotence. For Zola the passion for art is sexual. Chaste in life we are potent in art. And in this book, as in so many of his novels, the sexual motif and its symbols are blatant and orgiastic. They are also signs of deep neurosis. In *Germinal* we saw the broken engine of the mine raise its lever and fall in the last stroke of the sexual act, a stroke that indicates its death. In *L'Oeuvre*, Claude is raped by his wife, made to renounce his picture, and then goes off in remorse at his betrayal and hangs himself before it. Its central figure, characteristically academic and promisingly shocking in the Zola fashion, is an ornate, splendidly indecent and luxurious female idol. And this (we hardly need a psychologist to tell us) was the loved and hated mother-figure which dominated Zola's sexual life, first in his own mother and then in his mother-wife.

Nothing is impossible, as we soon discover when we find our way into the secret lives of people. Suicides have been known to go in for an erotic decor. An obscure painter, who had killed himself because he was rejected by the Salon, is said to have put this final scene into Zola's head. There are jealous women who wreck pictures, tear up manuscripts, and head men off to the office. What displeases is the inevitable operatic note in Zola's story: the painter is obliged to fail at the top of his voice. He lives with visions which are well argued but which, upon reflection, look like poster advertisements. Yet, in the midst of it all, the one acceptable artist – and he is very convincing – is Paul Sandoz, working like a factory, faithful to his wife, charitable to his friends, worrying to death about his reputation, unable to believe or disbelieve in it, cozening the public, buying antiques, going respectfully to funerals and regularly to meals. How Zola's own death was to fail the theatrical formula! And yet, since he was working off the dread (as Mr Walton says) of his unconquerable Romanticism, how gratifying to the Naturalist to be scientifically asphyxiated by the fumes of his stove! But Sandoz is a writer, and the writers must have a square deal. The good portraits of painters are the brief glum sketches of Bongrand (who is Manet) hating his early work because he fears he has been unable to surpass it; and the minor fry of cunning imitators. They are not burdened with a mystique which Zola, as his critical articles on Impressionism had shown, did not understand and was impatient of because it showed no signs of producing a 'great' man – a fresco painter.

Zola is the novelist of simplification, inflation, drama, the large, slack, crowd-catching line. He seeks the pictorial. The weakness of L'Oeuvre as a novel is that the content of one character is divided among two. We know it is beside the point – for Cézanne was still a failure, a ridiculed, persecuted painter, and easily presented as one of the ratés of a Murger-like Bohemia, incompetent in life as in art – but suppose Cézanne had, by this time, succeeded? Would this have persuaded Zola to stick to the facts of Cézanne's life? Or was failure romantically necessary to the novelist? What ham theatre, what Hollywood stuff it is when Claude 'fights' his canvas, gazes at Notre Dame (of all places), watches his child die without concern! Or rather, how trivial it seems beside Cézanne's strange, busy, silent life: the efficient separations from his wife – he adroitly got her another room in Aix when she came back – his dependence on his mother and sister, his adoration of his son, his secretiveness with his rich father, the quiet cunning of his Catholicism. The drama of Cézanne's life is in the simplicity of his passions, the secrecy of an intense life that uses naïveté to veil the path of single-mindedness.

The Romantic dogma of death, failure and the hidden taint is responsible for the false twists in Zola's realism. Yet L'Oeuvre, of course, does not fail to display his great gifts as a novelist. He is a master of large scenes. The crowded account of the Salons is brilliant; if the studio talk is unbearably jaunty and slangy, the general essay on the preoccupations of the artist's life is touching, tolerant and true. Claude's wife is well-drawn, especially when she is a modest young girl, and Zola modest and domestic is always superior to Zola repelling himself in scenes of physical passion, when he presents reality as if he hated it. There are reasons, indeed, to suspect his sexual capacity; the most convincing and pleasing sexual descriptions in literature appear in the comic writers in whom sensuality has the hunter's delicacy and the easy grace of appetite. There are dozens of small, tenderly observant touches in the portrait of Claude's wife, especially in the record of her changes of opinion about her husband and his work; these things go to the heart. Zola knew married life. He can convey sadness without sentimentality, resignation without the poison of an injected pessimism. *L'Oeuvre* is a bad novel except in those passages where it is moved by that sad and universal music which stirs when we look back upon our youth and the friends of that time and see the changes that have been brought to hope, the transformations grotesque, beneficient or ineluctable, that experience has forced upon our desires. It is a novel about the injustice of time itself; and everything springing from that knowledge in it is truthful and good. Claude himself, in those moments, is a friend, and friendship itself appears as a passion.

Yet – back to the novel factory at Medan. Art has been polished off in *L'Oeuvre*. Science must be dealt with in *Dr. Pascal*. Back to the hell of success which, to be habitable, depends on the comforting knowledge that failure abounds. Back, indeed, to work for work's sake, despite the dismal suspicion that even the virtue of the treadmill is dubious, for posterity will not care a damn about these terrible personal conflicts. One goes out in an ugly scene at a cemetery with a random train-whistle going off. The terrible temptation towards one more operatic scene, one more orgy of sexual symbolism, visits the labouring Naturalist; he has covered the families, the professions, the industries, the passions. Megalomania points to the cities; perhaps if he enlarges enough, the weary rationalist will find a meaning to life.

L'Assommoir (*The Dram-Shop*) was the first novel of Zola's to have enormous popular success and notoriety. Henry James, who crept very gingerly round the subject and who said one or two final things about it, put *L'Assommoir* beside *Germinal* and *La Débâcle* at the top of Zola's productions. It seems to me superior to *Germinal*, because it is not theatrical. Compare the famous mine engine of this book with the distiller's engine of *The Dram-Shop*: the former is a theatrical sexual symbol and throughout the book there is an obsessional preoccupation with sex, which comes dangerously near the ludicrous. The distiller's engine is merely a fascinating machine, perhaps a witch's cauldron, throbbing, bubbling and dripping its poison, which infects the life of the slum around it. That is no more than the plain truth: the delusions, the corruption, the diseases, the tempers, the fights, the murders and final madness of alcoholism are not fancies. And then the crowds which Zola excelled in describing are not poster-work. In *Germinal* one remembers the crowds described as if they were panicking and slavering cattle, as gluttonous and hungry maws; in *The Dram-Shop* there is nothing herd-like or anonymous in the hordes of the Paris slums; they are particularised with a delicacy which is unexpected in this coarse-grained novelist. For Zola had been wretchedly poor in his own youth and he understood that poverty individualises like a frost; it etches upon human beings lines and traits as refined in their way as those of happier sensibility. Coupeau the plumber, Lantier the hatter and Gervaise the laundress are not mere documentations for the purpose of illustrating the life of the industrial poor at that time; they are subtle, variable, extraordinary human beings. They are not more than life size, but we see more and more in them as we turn each page.

The Dram-Shop is a novel without a plot. We see the rise of Coupeau and Gervaise from abject poverty to the condition of prospering working people, enjoying the decencies of life. They work hard; they save; but they do not become miserly and oppressive. Then Coupeau has an accident. It ruins his character, for he discovers the pleasures of idleness, the ease of living on his admirable wife; and after an idyllic period this corrupts him. He gradually tipples, takes to idleness on principle, invents every kind of rationalisation and drifts gradually into alcoholism. He takes his wife's former lover as a boon companion; between them they exploit her and bring her ruin, for the sweetness and goodness of her nature have rested on an element of acquiescence; and prosperity has corrupted her. No more than any other human beings are the poor freed from the seductions of success; poor Gervaise lets herself go and is soon whirled bewildered into sluttishness, laziness, blurred amiability, drunkenness. Coupeau dies of DTs; Gervaise, a tippler rather than an alcoholic, dies of starvation, and Lantier, her former lover, moves on to exploit another couple, an absurd gendarme and his wife. This is not a plot, in the usual sense of the word; it is a moralisation which must be slowly disentangled from the driftings and confusions of everyday life. If Zola is an indiscriminate writer, if he is mainly an appetite for life, people and conditions, this has an important compensation: any plot we care to see in *The Dram-Shop* arises out of daily life as his people knew it and is not imposed with the *parti pris* of the story-teller. It could be complained that we are too much submerged in daily life in this book, in all the goings on of the tenements, the interminable small quarrels, envies and chatter of the neighbours, of the bars, of Gervaise's steaming laundry; but out of this Zola produces two or three wonderful long and dilatory episodes.

There is the fight between Gervaise and another woman in the wash house, a terrible and heroic affair of animal fury and comedy. Far better, there is the wedding party of Coupeau and Gervaise, a superb piece of comic rambling: in which the climax is reached when the party fill in time before dinner by going up the column in the Place Vendôme in wild good humour, start quarrelling at the top and come down in silence:

They all of them made their way to the top. The twelve members of the party had to climb the narrow stairway in single file, and this they did with much stumbling on the worn steps, keeping close to the wall for safety. The interior soon became pitch dark, and there was a great deal of loud laughter. The ladies uttered little screams, because the men started tickling them and pinching their legs. But they weren't so silly as to protest, thinking it better to pretend that what they felt were mice. Anyway, it wasn't worth making a fuss about, because the practical jokers, they were convinced, wouldn't go too far. Boche produced a witticism which they all took up. Everyone started calling down to Madame Gaudron, pretending to believe that she had got stuck. Was there enough room, they asked, for her belly? A nice thing it would be if she got 'took', and not able to go up or down! She'd be jammed in the fairway, and none of them would be able to get out! The belly of the pregnant woman gave rise to such hoots of laughter that the whole column shook. Boche, flushed by the success of his sally, was now well launched. They'd be in this chimney-stack, he said, for the rest of their lives! Wasn't there no end to it? – short of the sky? He tried to frighten the ladies by declaring that he could feel it move. All this while, Coupeau said nothing. He was just behind Gervaise, holding her by the waist. He could feel her leaning on him. He was just about to kiss the back of her neck when, suddenly, they found themselves in the open air. 'A nice thing, I must say!' observed Madame Lorilleux with an air of outraged propriety. 'Oh, don't mind us!'

Bibi-la-Grillade appeared to be thoroughly put out. 'You all made such a damned row,' he grumbled, 'that I couldn't even count the steps!'

Like Balzac, Zola is the novelist of our appetites, especially of their excess in satisfaction or nausea, but he lacks Balzac's irony and subtlety. He is less civilised and less instinctively refined by the comic spirit. He excels until he exceeds, in atmosphere: the laundry of Gervaise is worked up until the point of sensual disgust is reached and we long to get out of that hot, damp room reeking of female sweat, filthy garments and dirty jokes. On the other hand, when he is not on his obsessive themes, he finely observes human nature. Goujet, the good workman who tries hard to keep Coupeau straight, who has a serious political conscience, and understands the situation of the industrial worker, is not presented as the perfect man. Zola understood the wounds of human beings: Goujet is under the thumb of an excellent but stern mother and is paralysed in matters of decision in his private life. The variety of character in this novel is large, but even larger is the variety of mood and passion within the characters. Zola did not believe in the sacred working class; and, no doubt, this was the reason for the attacks on the book for being a travesty of French working-class life. Quite clearly, now, it was not: it simply contained everything; in it the poor ceased to be purely and simply the poor. They became individuals.

There are only two seriously false scenes in *The Dram-Shop*, and they occur towards the end, at the point where a novelist becomes over-heated by his own world and attempts to force the logic of events. The first occurs when Gervaise is told by her husband that she might just as well go on the streets. Gervaise sets out, starving, ragged, gross-looking and begs un-availingly in an awful night tour of the streets of Paris. At one point she runs into another starving being whom she has once befriended: this is excellent – starvation looks into starvation's eyes. But when she finally accosts the noble Goujet who had once loved her, the melodramatic cliché is too much. It is true that Zola's humane realism puts the episode right in the end, but it has been a strain on our trust. The second episode follows close on this one. Rejected by Goujet Gervaise throws herself at her neighbour in the next room, the drunken undertaker who is known as the Ladies' Comforter: not the comforter of the reader – he is an embarrassing symbol of the motif of Love-and-Death. Unlike the rich episodes of the wedding and the party, these incidents belong to the false, theatrical world of plot.

The argument for plot of that kind in the novel is, at its highest, the argument for meaning and value: but meaning and value in Zola lie in the rendering of life itself. It was necessary, one might say, to write novels of this kind because the 19th century saw the dehumanisation of man. Christianity had become meaningless. It was necessary to write about conditions simply because the dominant class were trying to live without knowing what their life was based on. The marvel is that Zola came so close to the skin of his people. He was able to do so perhaps because of his peculiar vice: the idealisation of the ugly. His obsessive taste for the revolting, the dreary, the bestial was an energy, and put him completely at one with the dreadful spirit of the times; he was as ugly, disfiguring and, also, almost as ludicrous in his puffing and blowing as the early steam engines. But there is another reason for his success. Henry James gives us a clue to it when he reports, with a shock, Zola's decision to conduct research into popular speech, slang and foul language: Zola saw that this was not a barrier but the card of admission into the slum world. If he knew its language he would know its soul. A great deal of *The Dram-Shop* is written in an attempted vernacular – which Mr Gerard Hopkins has tackled heroically in his translation with a very passable measure of success – and though Zola is far from contemporary feeling for common speech, he does make the first bold approaches. He succeeds chiefly where it is macabre and comical, especially when it is gross. It is a wonderful moment, for example, when Gervaise goes to the asylum to see Coupeau and finds him, temporarily cured, and squatting on the lavatory pan making jokes which are indeed lewd but are also very moving in their effect. Zola's following of bad words has led him, paradoxically, to the profoundest human feelings; and his own search for disgust and hatred is not proof against the surprising insinuations of the love that is mixed with the revolting – may even arise because of it. Finally, *The Dram-Shop* is free of that set Puritan piety which makes the moralising of Hogarth on Gin Alley or the Rake intolerable in the end. Human beings have the right to their tragedy; they have the right to be incurable. Zola's sense of corruption was, no doubt, based on specious scientific theories; but it was a larger, more humane sense than the Puritan moralist's trite preaching of domestic virtue and the merits of the savings bank.

A Political Novel

Lucien Leuwen is a political novel, a novel about the effects of the class war upon manners and sensibility, about 'the grand dispute which saddens the 19th century – the rage of rank against merit'; and, one might add, the rage of merit against mediocrity. It is a novel which startles by its frequent contemporary note, and a first English translation by H. L. R. Edwards under the title of *The Green Huntsman* is welcome. The book was begun in 1834 and written very fast at Civita Vecchia when the weather was not too hot. Stendhal was French consul. He was fifty-one, a hard-working official, bored and disillusioned. He put the novel aside in 1836 and for one reason and another never finished or revised it. He withheld it from publication because it contained contemptuous criticism of the regime that employed him. He could not afford to quarrel with his bread and butter and ironically foresaw the stupidity of the censorship. The present translation, though a shade Gallic here and there, is admirable; it crisply transmutes the hard, clear, nonchalant prose of Stendhal with its faint smell of gunpowder – the duellist's pistol has just gone off. The hardness is more noticeable in this novel than in his others because, as he said, it is still 'an ossature'; revision would have cut the excess of detail; the flesh and the smile, as he said, would have been put on the skeleton. The book breaks naturally into two parts and Mr Edwards calls the second half *The Telegraph*. The first has Lucien's life in the garrison at Nancy, his love affair with Madame Chastellar and ends with the grotesque episode which broke the affair and sent Lucien galloping back to his mother in Paris. The second part takes the reader inside the cynical French political machine under Louis Philippe and the farce of a provincial election under the new democratic system.

'Character of this work: exact chemistry: I describe with exactitude what others indicate with a vague and eloquent phrase.' So in his notes Stendhal described the method of *Lucien Leuwen*. The poetry was to be in the chemistry. Science and *logique* – and *logique* was surely petulance in disguise, as it so often is in men whose good sense really comes out of the pain of an old wound – ought to define what a man's attitude to the world was and to propound what it ought to be. This central preoccupation of Stendhal's is personal and egotistical: uprooted from his own class, gifted, ambitious but without means or rank, bearing the scars of father-hatred in his nature, Stendhal begins from an imaginary blank sheet to find out what 'a superior man' can make of himself in a world hostile to high feeling. And so all his novels have the critical tone of experiments in autobiography. They are, more watchfully than in other novelists, the lives of possible selves. Detached writers are often more truly sensitive to the spirit of their time than the committed: revolution, war and *coup d'état* left Stendhal energetically disgusted. He became indifferent. What did persist with him was the sense of campaign: his psychology is generalship.

There have been a great many novels about what politics are about, but their writers have had little knowledge of politics in themselves. Mrs Gaskell, George Eliot, Dickens, Zola, show us the social dramas; to Stendhal the social drama is chiefly the nourishment of politicians and, like some zoological keeper, he shows them to us at their feeding time. The soldiers, who had once fought with Napoleon, are reduced to the political trough, too. It is true that in *Lucien Leuwen* we are shown all this through the eyes of a young man who has the innocence of the very rich and that Stendhal's object is to give us a young man learning his lesson, not about politics, but about life. But it will not be the kind of lesson that young radicals were taught by the English novelists of the 19th century: Lucien will not end by acquiring 'sound' political beliefs. His one abiding political belief is the love of liberty; but the only concrete notion is negative: to turn the army upon the workers is a degradation and a crime. Still, the working classes have hardly come into the political picture and, for all his hatred of tyranny, Stendhal is in a very similar situation to Voltaire's and he hated Voltaire. Lucien will end by giving up politics altogether. If he retains a kind of sneaking affection for one or two Republicans it is because personally they are energetic and mad; America, their promised land – the Russia of our time – will seem to him a sink of mediocrity and human indecency. What, then, will Lucien learn? That the highest life is beyond politics. It lies even beyond personal relationships – as Mr Martin Turnell pointed out in his study of *La Chartreuse de Parme*. It is revealed at the height of love, in reverie and contemplation.

Lucien Leuwen is, as Mr Edwards says, a milder figure than the working-class Julien Sorel or the aristocratic Fabrice. Lucien's amiable father has been too civilised, too sagacious and too good at business and politics. He is a figure of the 18th century; the son is at sea before such an admirable parent who can unobtrusively arrange everything from a box full of opera girls to an under-secretaryship. The 19th-century son requires difficulty, duty, conscience, Puritan energy; he wants, above all, to keep his hands clean. His fatal disadvantage is wealth; it will take years, Stendhal points out, for Lucien to live that down. Lucien is a charming but conceited young prig, a hopeless mixture of ingenuousness and arrogance, prema-ture worldliness and tongue-tied inexperience; absurd calculation and self-consciousness are combined with sudden affectability and spirit. In short he is a masterly model of the Young Man, in the drawing of whom Stendhal, to my mind, surpasses all novelists. Lucien, prickly with vanity and throwing his weight about as a young lieutenant in Nancy, practising irony, hauteur and frigidity in the mess, is engaging because he is almost unbearable. He is a charming, impossible puppy. We see him heroically giving up his money and deciding on exile: very fine, very spirited – but will he bring it off, we wonder, and in any case what precisely does he want to bring off? Here, the scientific observations of Stendhal come in: Lucien is not a hero, he is the complete, intelligent wealthy young man of the period: and no doubt a daydream of imaginary autobiography. 'Suppose I had loved my father and had been rich: how then would I have dealt with the fundamental issue of life – freedom!' So one can imagine Stendhal's thought.

The brilliant part of the book is the statement of the political situation in Nancy and of the plight of an unpopular army in a society that snubs them or hates them. Each character is planted in his political pot. When the rich young officer of the new army comes into the drawing-rooms of the 'ultra' aristocracy, the young ex-officers of the old regime hang round, drooping and posing with airs of aggressive and calculated futility. When the Prefect sells a horse we see a young man just shot up into office by the new regime, arrogant, timid, and still learning what face to put on while one is feathering one's nest. The older soldiers, who have seen the great campaigns

[457]

and who have known what *la gloire* is, are wonderful artistic onions; peel off the top skin of political caution, peel off the next skin of military anecdote, and the next to find the man who will accept a tip or a case of liqueurs – and underneath one finds, at last, the puzzled, rancorous, bewildered human being. All these portraits are rich and marked by Stendhalian minuteness – 'a face already crinkled with envy.' The aristocrats, carefully listed, are not all of a piece; Stendhal has caught the moves of a coterie isolated and drying up in a futile class-hatred of the government.

He is equally pointed in his observation of the bourgeoisie. Class-hatred had insulted the classes in Nancy and their outline is therefore clearer. The bourgeois who shouts his opinions almost verbatim from his newspaper is excellent, and so is Mlle Sylvanie, the shopkeeper's daughter and bourgeois beauty:

> A statue of Juno, copied from the antique by a modern artist: both subtlety and simplicity are lacking; the lines are massive, but it's a Germanic freshness. Big hands, big feet, very regular features and plenty of coyness, all of which conceals a too obvious pride. And these people are put off by the pride of ladies in good Society! Lucien was especially struck by her backward tosses of the head, which were full of vulgar nobility and were evidently meant to recall the dowry of a hundred thousand crowns.

This is a portrait done with irony, but without hatred; there is bitter envy in Stendhal, a good deal of it, but it is the envy of the outsider, of the observer, for the planted human being. Lucien may be snobbish about Mlle Sylvanie, but that other passionate, warmer part of Stendhal knows that she is life.

The most interesting portrait is of Dr du Poirier, the brilliant intriguing demagogue of humble parentage, the non-stop talker and political agent who has got the aristocracy in the palm of his hands. Here talent and vulgarity, quickness and naïveté, intelligence and a touch of careerism are wonderfully mixed. Vanity makes him think he can turn Lucien into an 'ultra'; Lucien plays with him – a shade too maturely, I think, for a young man – and then, when du Poirier sees it, he brings his profound roguery to bear. Du Poirier is responsible for Lucien's disaster and for the most

[458]

improbable scene which causes him to break with Madame Chastellar. It is said that Stendhal was nervous about this grotesque episode. It seems to me that novelists who are as detached as Stendhal was run two major risks: dryness and a failure of judgment when they come to the grotesque and bizarre. Only a wild and minor Elizabethan dramatist – or perhaps a Richardson – could have brought off this scene, where the lady is falsely supposed to be in childbirth and a dummy child is brought in.

The loves of Lucien and Madame Chastellar are a mild but not wooden business. Stendhal is an expert in the hesitations, the misunderstandings, the trembling moments, the sudden meltings, freezings of love and – most baffling of all – its complete disappearance at the height of a love affair; but while we must recognise the master's hand, we must also be surprised by his refusal to give the lovers their heads and make them more interesting. Truthfulness has, of course, won, as it usually does with him; we are witnessing, I suppose, a classical case of love conceived in vanity or self-interest and which, owing to the inexperience of the parties, is likely to side-slip into confusion. Because he has the absurd incident of the false childbirth up his sleeve, Stendhal's 'humour' – one suspects he called it 'English humour' – holds him back. We cannot, however, judge the affair as a whole, for the novel was never completed; we can only say that in a dozen small moments the touch and the comedy of the lovers' conversations are exquisite. For Lucien the affair is one more terrible political test. Stendhal mocks at his first response.

> The suspicion that he was in love had filled him with shame; he felt degraded.

He feels not only that initial fear which is the sign of love (since conscience is everything in this young man) but another dread:

> 'What a disgrace,' suddenly exclaimed the opposite side of love. 'What a disgrace for a man who has worshipped duty and his country with a devotion which he could call sincere! Now he has eyes for nothing but a little provincial legitimist, furnished with a soul which basely prefers the private interests of her caste, to those of all France. Soon, no doubt, following her example, I shall place the happiness of two hundred thousand nobles . . . before that of the other 30 million

Frenchmen. My chief reason will be that these privileged two hundred thousand have more elegant drawing rooms . . . in a word, drawing rooms that are useful for my private happiness.'

This double context in which Lucien's feelings are placed is characteristic of Stendhal's genius. There is always, in his novels, the extra dimension. This is Stendhal's version of the sense of general law upon which all the great French novelists have built, and which distinguishes them from those of other countries. They are the lawyers of the passions. Dry Stendhal often is, but his clear experiments in human chemistry give us the illusion that we have, for a glittering moment, seen what life is composed of before it becomes our daily bewilderment.

André Gide

'I do not like your lips,' Oscar Wilde said to Gide, when he first met the young Protestant with the Nazarene beard in Paris, 'they are quite straight, like the lips of one who has never told a lie.' In old age Gide's lips were still like a long truthful line ruled across a face to which experience had given that look of dominance and seduction sometimes found in the saint, the confessor and the actor. The penitents of this confessor were those who had committed the sin with which he himself had at times either struggled or ironically philandered: what he regarded as the sin of faith. He was, in the Socratic sense, a corrupter, one who liberated only to impose an infinitely arduous pursuit of virtue, and this made him a hard moralist as all the puritans are. For most of the moralists – Goethe and Montaigne are the exceptions who come to mind – have the attraction of working in a fixed climate from which there is no escape; they write us into an algebra which is a pleasure in itself, and gives us at least the relief of a sort of fatalism. But Gide's climate is changeable; the spring is defeated but the spring returns; the moral frontier, like the year, is open, exposed and dangerous. This calls for courage, the loveliest of the virtues; but, alas, also for diligence, the grimmest of them.

But, fortunately, the pastor in Gide is there to exacerbate Gide rather than torture the reader. We are not, unless we are theologians, involved in the religious issue as it presented itself to him, for its own sake, any more than we can now be involved in the historical state of Montaigne's faith. The issues of religion are universal; literature interests us by what they have imaginatively provoked; in Gide (as in Montaigne) the obsession has given us the psychologist and moralist, a spirit now lyrical, now scientific. We respond to Gide's luminous curiosity about himself, which is less melancholy than Montaigne's, indeed not melancholy at all, for it extends beyond what he is at a given moment to what he is becoming. Here is, in fact, the trait which holds the secret of his extraordinary resilience and

[461]

youthfulness; and when, after reading a translation of the last volume of his *Journals*, we notice his serenity, it is really youth prolonged. For he is always expectant. Like Stendhal (another master of his) he makes us feel more intelligent, more honest than we are without him, for he brings more into the light of day. He conserves the bite and gaiety of the intelligence; all that he says, even when he is bewildered, despairing or tragic, is on the side of life, for (he conveys to us) the pride of life revives, the intellect lasts.

The fourth volume of the *Journals* begins with the war in 1939 and ends ten years later. Mauriac has spoken of his 'aggressive serenity', and if the radiant agitation of the earlier years is not here and Gide is inclined to be above his enemies where before he hit back, there is an astonishing vitality; and very little testiness. If he is more studied, more aware of his role, his power of ecstasy and joy is not lost; he still has those moments of being 'born again' in the reading of a book, perhaps, or before some sight of nature. The intensity is now, naturally, of reflection rather than of action and feeling. Comparing, page by page, the younger *Journals* with this volume, we find in the earlier ones a sharper zest, a more cutting pain, a greater animation; but the new volume adds the indispensable and grave finale and its range is wide. Mr Justin O'Brien's edition is well-edited and his introduction is very good; the translation is far from impeccable, though it serves. At the beginning of the war, Gide felt, as he had felt in 1914, that the duty of the writer was to be silent; he learned German and read Goethe. Presently, the disaster, the question of its causes, the moral situation of France preoccupied him and, if nothing else, the *Journal* is a remarkable record of an open civilised mind in agitation, trapped in political defeat. But I do not think this is the most interesting part of this book, and it is, in any case, for Frenchmen to argue about. Gide belonged to an essentially non-political generation. If he had fallen into 'the trap of the social problem' (he said) he would have written nothing, and he wrote (he also said, with vanity perhaps but also with prescience) for 'the next generation, not this.' That seems to me true: the issues of freedom and authority, truthfulness and propaganda, are the only issues for Western people. Their drama moves from the outer to the inner life. What is interesting to a generation younger than Gide's is his fascination with authority and his obliquity in dealing with it. Gide was a resistance

[462]

movement in himself, and the lasting impression one has of him is of a man who is working at a technique for freedom: it will be needed.

> I am reproached for my oblique gait – but who does not know that when the wind is contrary, one is obliged to tack? It is easy to criticise for you who let yourselves be carried by the wind. I take my bearing on the rudder.

Tacking is always Gide's method, for he is most alive when there is an opposing force and he draws as close to it as he can. The charge of vacillation was never just.

But Gide's true work is to paint the self-portrait of a free man determined on freedom and yet checking it, as if what he most wanted was intensity. The portrait itself is formidable and amusing. The old man afraid to waste a day; the old Protestant torn by the problem of idleness: is it worse to do bad work than none? He translates Virgil, he translates *Hamlet*, he reads Corneille, Koestler, Shaw, Browning, Johnson, Goethe, Pearl Buck, hundreds of writers good and bad, studies radioactivity, sea animals, a history of Moslem customs – reads and writes on what he reads. (He has always done so: he has gone to other writers continuously – for sympathy.) The judgments are very sharp: no patience with Conrad's *Romance*, a shrewd verdict on Johnson. Of a performance of *King Lear*: 'It ceases to be human; it becomes enormous. Hugo himself never imagined anything more gigantically artificial and more false.' And there is the sharp-eyed note: 'Strange part played in that drama by papers and missives, presented, stolen, falsified; up to seven times, if I counted aright.' (The device of the diary in *Les Faux-Monnayeurs*.) But reading, which has played a larger part in his life than it does in the lives of most imaginative writers, is for this puritan artist 'the unpunished vice.'

> By reading I seek to distract myself from myself, and whereas it would be essential to commune with myself, it seems that, almost without choice, I welcome everything that may help me to forget myself . . . it would be better to give (my mind) a total holiday than constantly to interpose a screen between it and God. I must learn to know solitude all over again. What I must take walking with me henceforth is not a book, but this notebook.

Conscience is the instrument he works and lives by; and the hypnotic effect of the *Journals* perhaps comes from the feeling we have of watching not a free man but a technician or tester of freedom.

The portraits in North Africa are fewer than in the earlier volume, though there are touching sallies into scenes of the past. One grotesque living figure stands out, during the time of the siege of Tunis: the awful boy Victor, a son of the family in whose house Gide was staying. The situation is piquant. The greatest living French writer is driven to the point of illness and flight by the tortures of this truly horrible adolescent. Victor has contempt for the master. Victor bosses the house, is rude, surly, silent, scornful, grabs the best fruit, eats his food with his hands like an Arab, sucks his fingers, lies with arrogance. He is hoarding bullets to sell as war souvenirs, has a secret cache of chocolate and gold coins to be sold at profit, and has just joined the Communists. He is filthy in the lavatory. Several days a week he runs a gambling den for his school friends, where poker and baccarat are played from two till six p.m. 'In principle' (he says) he doesn't smoke, but only in principle. This sudden appearance of a character from *Les Faux-Monnayeurs* hits Gide like a plague; and through the account of the bombardment the nasty comedy weaves its coarse human thread. A progressive child, Victor devours Rousseau, Diderot, Voltaire and seems to be heading for success as a gangster. It is, the more one reflects upon it, a terrible Jamesian story; almost, the enemies of Gide might say, a sardonic retribution; and, at one point, where the tortured sage is afflicted, as usual, by conscience and asks whether he himself is not to blame because he has not been able – nor ever has all his life – to suppress his instinct to reform others, one is on the point of tears. For Gide's irony, under the strain of the heavy air raids and illness, has left him for the moment.

The episode is short. We are back among the aphorisms, the ecstasies, the delightful quotations, the memories and the fine points once more. But we appreciate all the more, by the accident of this raw interruption, the enlarging intimacy we have been privileged to share with a mind that has observed its experience with more method and surgical curiosity than any other of its time, except Proust's.

Like *Ulysses*, that other novel to end all novels, Gide's *Les Faux-Monnayeurs*, has settled peaceably into literature; it is a criticism of the novel as it was, rather than an indication of what the novel might become.

The generation of experiment has been followed by figures more harassed by life and less constrained by the metaphysical delicacies of literary form. Or perhaps we should say that the formal experiments of novelists like Sartre and Camus have not led to a question of how much more should be left out, but to the difficulty of getting much more in. When we look back now on Gide's notion of a novel about a novelist writing a novel, and engaged in reconnaisance along the frontiers between literature and life, appearance and reality, we recall the tourism of the untroubled decades before the wars of the Thirties. The problem for later novelists has been another, more dangerous frontier: the torn, sometimes secretive, sometimes blatant boundaries of private and public life, what could still be fermented into art and what would run out raw into journalism. When Gide was writing that man must play out his hand, it was forgivable to think that the Boulevard St Germain would be always there to play it in; it was not imagined that the new trick might be the destruction of civilised man altogether. And so the fine experimental works, like the intrepid experimental living of that period, recede into isolation rather than show any strong influence on what has followed. Unless, in a general way, one says that the important novels of the last twenty years have been dominantly intellectual and critical in spirit, the daring defiance of the gods having been replaced by the habit of doing without either the gods or the stimulus of defying them. A dull and worthy lot has followed the brilliant rebels.

At the end of his introduction to *Oedipus* and *Theseus* Mr John Russell catches the evasive genius of Gide for an instant in a good phrase: 'it is only just to acclaim him, as he acclaimed Goethe, as "the finest example, at once grave and smiling, of what man can wrest from himself without the help of Grace."' That deftly defines a volatile yet methodical temperament. He is the good and the bad conscience of those who had thought to dispose of Grace; the most subtle and dangerous of the Calvinists who know – as his Theseus knew – that they are of the Elect. Gide has been compared to Rousseau and to Montaigne also, and his closeness to the latter is obvious, in the cast of his genius and in his historical situation: he is a Montaigne for whom a Protestant pastor replaces the melancholy of the stone and who has always stood his mind in the sun. But when we recover from the giddiness of making great comparisons, we cannot but feel we ought to be modest about our contemporaries. Like Montaigne's, Gide's work is an immense collection of scientific footnotes; but in Gide's the main text is missing. We cannot look above to the militant, passionate text of the Faith, as yet unmutilated by the natural ageing of Western civilisation.

Les Faux-Monnayeurs (*The Counterfeiters*) is manifestly a novel of footnotes, the text of life as it has been written by the novelists is assumed to be in our hands. We no longer ask whether the book is a novel or not; it is an egoist's enquiry, and yet it has the suspense of a narration. The shocking use of coincidence is brilliantly brought off, within the artifice of the book. The fatal reappearance of Boris's talisman, for example, which wrecks the security a careless psychoanalyst has given to the boy, was complained of in the past, but one might just as well complain of the story of Oedipus. In any case Edouard, the novelist, has made plain his taste for fables. The critic of Gide has the difficulty, when he makes objections, that he is dealing with one of the most clear-headed, the most alert, elusive and subtle of divided minds, who has usually guarded his main pieces. I agree with the French lecturer Hytier, who finds in the demon who clinches the fall of Vincent, and the angel with whom Bernard wrestles, the two small misty and unsatisfactory patches in the design. The devil and the angels rarely seem to be more than useful rhetorical arguments to the Protestant mind, and there is an insincere click of the lantern slide when they are mentioned. These two pieces are certainly open. Another point on which I am not sure is the character of Passavant. He is Edouard in reverse, a kind of double. What they have in common is disconcerting: amusement. Why can we be assured that Passavant's amusement is corrupting and Edouard's is not? In fact there are times when Edouard's amusement is shocking, for although we may trust him as a high-minded writer, are we sure we can trust him as a man? Perhaps we can, but as hostile critics of the novel have pointed out – those who have regarded Gide as a kind of Satan – *The Counterfeiters* indicates what a good thing it is to steal people's suitcases, take their money and read their private papers in the certainty of finding something to one's advantage. The evil of Passavant is that he is a short-term man, buying and selling fast on the moral market; the virtue of Edouard seems to lie in little more than a longer view. He has the working security of those who can always fall back, when in difficulties, upon the moral respectability of their personal conflicts. But an unlucky visitor might fall clean through that wide-open mind.

[466]

The stories of all Gide's young Julian Sorels are still affecting but they are not to be compared with the portrait of La Perouse, where the realism Gide despises is brought to a high pitch; or with the stories of Laure and Douvier, of little Boris and the anxieties of the pastor's school. As usually happens in the novel, the characters that are not the author's desired and predilection are the best observed: 'I lean with a fearful attraction over the depths of each creature's possibilities and weep for all that lies atrophied under the heavy lid of custom and morality.' The true element of surprise in this novel is Gide's unveiling of these awkward characters who so dramatically expound the theme of the debased spiritual coin: Armand, desiccated by a harsh clowning that he owes to his puritan upbringing; the pastor deceiving himself with his energy; Rachel, who will have sacrificed herself in vain for a family which has been inevitably ruined by its narrow religion. The novel is a triumph of the critical spirit, for one dreads the extension of these people. One does not want to know more about Douvier than the crucial fact that he will not be loved, and that, however low his wife may fall, his desire to regard her as one above himself will make him abase himself still further. Gide's diagnoses are not, however, theoretical, too avid or simply arbitrary. There is always a recognition of the surprising in human nature: it is brilliant that Douvier's theatrical determination to find out the name of his wife's seducer exhausts itself in the mere excitement of making a journey. (*Amour propre*: it is the key subject, one is inclined to say, of half French literature!)

The *Oedipus* and *Theseus* (the latter written in 1944) have been put together at Gide's suggestion. They interlock and they are fables growing out of the main division in his mind. Oedipus, the enlightened, godless man, who reaches forward to all that promises extra inches to his mind, is brought down by the gross intrigue of original sin. Even so he is not destroyed and he is certainly not reconciled to official religion.

> Is that what you wanted, Tiresias? In your jealousy of my light, did you seek to drag me into your darkness? I, too, gaze now upon the celestial dark. I have punished these eyes for their failure to guide me thither. No more can you overwhelm me with the superiority of the blind.

[467]

And when he is reproached for leaving Thebes to become an outcast and traveller among strangers, he replies:

> Whoever they may be, they are men. I shall be glad to bring them happiness at the price of my sufferings.

That is the Oedipus of 1930.

When he reappears in 1944 at the end of the story of Theseus his understanding of his disaster has become almost, but not quite, orthodox:

> I believe that an original stain of some sort afflicts the whole human race, in such a way that even the best bear its stripe, and are vowed to evil and perdition; from all this man can never break free without divine aid of some sort . . . perhaps I dimly foresaw the grandeur of suffering and its power to redeem; that is why the true hero is ashamed to turn away from it. I think that is the crowning proof of his greatness; and that he is never worthier than when he falls a victim; then does he exact the gratitude of heaven and disarm the vengeance of the gods.

Not quite orthodox, because Oedipus is allowed to be a spectator of himself: he has experienced, one would say, the spectator's catharsis, not the victim's ruin itself. It is the great point in Gide that that particular hard core of human pride shall never be broken. The reply to Oedipus comes frankly from Theseus, a reply noble but worldly, not without a touch of the happy incurable cunning of the human creature:

> 'Dear Oedipus,' I said, when it was plain that he had finished speaking, 'I can only congratulate you on the kind of superhuman wisdom which you profess. But my thoughts can never march with yours along that road, I remain a child of this world, and I believe that man, be he what he may, and with what blemishes you judge him to be stained, is in duty bound to play out his hand to the end. No doubt you have learned to make good use of your misfortunes, and through them have drawn nearer to what you call the divine world. I can well believe, too, that a sort of benediction now attaches to your person, and that it will presently be laid, as the oracles have said, upon the land in which you will take your everlasting rest.'
>
> I did not add that what mattered to me was that this blessing should be laid upon Attica.

The mystic and the active man are unreconciled, but at least sit side by side united in their loneliness. The hostile moralists take the evening sun and have sacrificed to benignity some of their earlier edge. But the adventure of Theseus and the Minotaur has the clear, sensual joy, the laconic boldness, the sudden exhilarating refusals of the obvious turn of the story, or the received view of it, which Gide has always had at the height of his powers. The Minotaur is not a gross monster: the shock is that he is beautiful, drowsing, intoxicated, beguiled and witless in the delights of his labyrinth. The struggle is not against evil but against pleasure. There can be pleasure when Greece is free. The Theseus (of 1944) hesitates before he kills such a creature in such a divine place, in order to free his country. But the instinct that makes the hero choose freedom at whatever cost puts upon him the obligation to rid mankind of monsters. The application of the fable spreads like ripples from its first, obvious point.

The Act of Believing

═══════

I have worked but I put aside my chief production. I need more peace of mind. I jokingly began a comedy and jokingly conjured up so many comical circumstances, so many comical figures, and grew to like my hero so much that I abandoned the form of comedy, despite the fact that it succeeded, for my own proper satisfaction, in order that I might further follow the adventures of my new hero and laugh over him myself. This hero is somewhat like me.

So Dostoevsky, after he had been released from prison in Siberia and when, with his customary air of a stage conspirator uttering deadly secrets out loud, he was planning his way back to political favour and literary recognition. The comic book was *A Friend of the Family*.

All Dostoevsky's geese were swans. The tale does not succeed like its immediate predecessor, the exquisite *Uncle's Dream* which he despised; and is in many respects inferior to the novel *Nyetochka Nyezvanov* which was cut short by his arrest and imprisonment. A feeling of effusive insincerity and misguided over-confidence is occasionally and disturbingly purveyed by his writing; there is a kind of double-facedness which we may suppose comes from the anxiety that was fundamental in his life. Over the wagging pavement of that anxiety he sways like some suspicious, spiritual drunk. *A Friend of the Family* is a careless, exaggerated, complacent book, with a good deal of crude Gogol in its picture of provincial society. We know so well, by now, those masterful Russian widows, those 'phantasmagorical' spinsters, those dull scheming young men and their half-baked conversations. The very smell of provinciality hangs about them all. Yet, the vitality of a master, spluttering, but in some passages irresistible, is there. Pride and humiliation – a point André Gide elaborated in his celebrated study – are Dostoevsky's 'subject' and *A Friend of the Family* is written out of the cocksureness rather than the humility of the comic spirit.

The smallest works of Dostoevsky cast long shadows. The hero who is 'somewhat like me': who is he? Is he Rostanev, the old Colonel of the Hussars? A man

> peaceable and ready to agree to anything. If by some caprice he had been gravely asked to carry someone for a couple of miles on his shoulders he would perhaps have done so.

The Colonel foreshadows the Meek figures of Dostoevsky, for he can speak evil of no one and submits, with remorse, to every injustice. He has the morbid sympathy of the hero of the *Notes from Underground* who, seeing a gentleman thrown out of a window during a fight in a billiard room, 'envied him so much that I even went into the tavern and into the billiard room. "Perhaps", I thought, "I'll have a fight, too, and they'll throw me out of the window."' With a shrewd native touch of the real Dostoevsky he later reflected that he was 'not even equal to being thrown out of the window and went away without having any fight.' The characters of Dostoevsky – and their huge garrulousness – are fantasies tried out, half-realised. Hence the confusion they at once create on the page. Rostanev has not the enticing slyness of the masochist, or of the great Meek figures. He has what is rare, we begin to suspect, in Dostoevsky's characters (for most of them have a dual nature), the quality of innocence. He is one of the few figures who does not know his own character and might pass for a Pickwickian Englishman in blameless deliquescence.

The other possibility is that Dostoevsky conceived himself to be the ludicrous and tiresome Foma Fomitch. Here Dostoevsky may have dipped his pen into the ink of his suffering in prison. Foma Fomitch is a Double. This grizzled and insignificant pedant with a wart on his chin, a hook nose, a sneering, imperious little head sticking out of his open-necked shirt – how brilliant are Dostoevsky's physical descriptions – has the arrogance of the slave turned master. (He is said to have been drawn, with Dostoevsky's usual malicious jealousy of other writers, from the Gogol of the mad period.) A bad writer turned toady, Foma had been the buffoon in the family of a general who played all kinds of torturing tricks upon him. Foma used even to be made to crawl round the drawing room on all fours. But now the General is dead and Foma, who had the sympathy of the General's wife and the other ladies in his humiliation, dominates the

[471]

household, ruling it like a martinet, terrifying everyone by his tongue and reigning by his stinging exploitation of human weakness. He has become the casuist of abasement. There is a wonderfully comic scene, when Foma turns the tables on Rostanev who is the master of the house and has been trying to get rid of him. Foma soon has Rostanev begging for forgiveness; and, relentlessly sure of himself, goes on to bully the master into giving him the title Your Excellency.

'Well, if I am worthy of it, why will you not say "Your Excellency" to me?'

'Foma, I will, perhaps.'

'But I insist. I see how hard it is for you, that is why I insist. That sacrifice on your side will be the first step in your moral victory; for – don't forget it – you will have to gain a series of moral victories to be on a level with me: you must conquer yourself, and only then I shall feel certain of your sincerity.'

'Tomorrow then I will call you "Your Excellency" Foma.'

'Not tomorrow, Colonel, tomorrow can take care of itself. I insist that you now at once address me as "Your Excellency".'

'Certainly, Foma, I am ready; only what do you mean by "at once" Foma?'

'Why not at once or are you ashamed? That's an insult to me if you are ashamed.'

'Oh well, if you like Foma. I am ready . . . I am proud to do so, indeed; only it's queer Foma, apropos of nothing. "Good day, Your Excellency." You see, one can't.'

Until, arguing word by word, winning inch by inch, Foma has the Colonel apologising, blushing, bowing and uttering the words. Having succeeded, Foma doesn't want the success. He merely wants to demonstrate his power.

Foma is a little monster. He tortures the serfs by educating them, which they hate, but he educates only for the pleasure of seeing simple people tie themselves into knots. He finds out their secrets and then bullies them. One pretty young boy who has become the lapdog of the General's widow is a special victim. Foma discovers that the boy has only one dream: he always dreams of a white bull. No day is complete until Foma works up a scene about the feeble-mindedness of those who have only one dream. And yet, at the end of the book, when Foma is defeated and exposed, he is still triumphant. For after all, since everyone is happy now they are free of his tyranny, isn't he, in some way, the creator of their happiness? If he hadn't slandered the lovers, how would they have pulled themselves together and declared themselves? And so everyone cries out 'Hurrah for Foma'; even the lovers he has nearly ruined; and Foma, with delighted vanity, leads the cheering.

The richness of Dostoevsky as a writer arises from the fertile uncertainty of his moods. A comic theme may become serious and then, transformed, become comic once more. The tragic theme may produce its comic undercurrent. As André Gide says, the schizophrenic has two contrasting personalities which operate at different times; but the double roles in Dostoevsky's characters operate simultaneously: love and hate, pride and abasement, cruelty and tenderness are not mingled but appear dramatically, incongruously side by side. Foma's defeat is an ecstasy. The effect is, of course, the notorious note of self-parody in Dostoevsky's writing, and yet those very parodies break off and assume a serious artistic life. We shall see Foma become, perhaps, Smerdyakov; in the meek Shatov we shall find a successor of the comic Colonel. The hysteric can laugh and weep at will. This inconsequence of mood has been an overwhelming advantage to Dostoevsky as a didactic writer, for it has taken the deadweight out of his teaching and has launched it on the confusing, chopping and changing currents of individual human life. Where other novelists state beliefs, put down the thing believed, Dostoevsky breaks belief down into its phases, as though the act of believing were a fate, an unsought suffering that has been thrust on us. Dostoevsky is able to catch the *process* of believing as it first stirs the entrails, as it breaks down the unity of personality: for his characters have all this dramatic propensity for turning into the opposite of themselves. One believes in their believing because, like the comic characters of Dickens, they live in the manias of the human solitude. The maniacal inner solitariness is all the more convincing because of the gregariousness of his people. A new character enters with his soul on his sleeve, but he brings all his quarrelling relations, his picaresque family history with him, and can be almost heard blatantly proposing a new novel. All the books are packed with short biographies and each dives with shameless irrelevance into the past. How important it is that Dostoevsky's psychological interests should be pathological and obsessed – as they are if we compare them with Balzac's – for without obsession, there would be no way through the hundreds of human lives that come on us in all their physical explicitness, suddenly, over-poweringly, like figures appearing dramatically out of a fog with the rime upon them.

The second tale, *Nyetochka Nyezvanov*, which appears in the same volume as *A Friend of the Family*, in Constance Garnett's translation, was left unfinished. It has two things which have the mark of Dostoevsky's genius. The first is the portrait of a drunken cornet player, who is tortured by the delusion that he is a great violinist, and who is driven to drink and the ruin of his wife and child, by his failure as an artist. Not only is this incomparably solid, raw and touching, but it is frightening too: Dos-toevsky knew the artist's nightmare dread of failure, his fanatical isolation. But the richness comes from the knowledge of souls. The story is told as a reminiscence of childhood by a young girl and the wrong judgment of a child's mind gives dimension, the sense of the ceaselessness and insolubility of human illusions. In Dostoevsky there is no time: time is simply the catalogue of illusion. For the child the tragedy is that she hates the wrong parent, and the tragedy of the father's life becomes more terrible when she realises she was deceived by him. The second and very astonishing distinction of this tale is the story of this child's passionate, sensual love for a nobleman's child of the same age, a love affair inflected by all those sensuous desires for suffering, those agonising entreaties, those wars of pride in the heart and those lyrical ecstasies, which are seen in Dosto-evsky's descriptions of adult love, and which seem more fitted to the mute, watchful, remorseless lives of children.

Putting these stories down, glancing afterwards at the great works, we cannot help wondering whether a good deal of our talk about the necessity of form and so on in the novel is not, after all, nonsense. Dostoevsky is a force, ignorant of all the rules. He switches from the first person to long second-hand passages, written without change of voice. He pants back and forth just as he likes; he appears never to eliminate. He is far too garrulous and can never resist confusion. He relies on the dramatic urgency of what he has to say; he enormously relies on character and 'characters'; yet he never misses or mauls the finest effect of a great scene, because the whole thing is never finished in his own mind, and it is certainly not preconceived – except in the vaguest sense. Exhausting and exasperating as this may be, it brings to us the sense that life is overpowering, full of a darkness which only he, at that time, can illumine; that we live on the point of Judgment Day and dissolution. As a novelist he is like some face on the screen which gets larger and larger, coming closer and closer to us, until frightened, exalted and perhaps a little disgusted, we are engulfed by the spongy, unhealthy face, laugh when it laughs and are submerged in its nightmares which shortly come to seem our own.

Tolstoy

===

Of all the Russian novelists Tolstoy has been the easiest to naturalise and domesticate in England; and he himself suggested there were affinities between the Russian and English characters. Whether he was remarking upon anything more than the character of the country gentleman in each country we cannot say; there is certainly a very English lack of intellectuality in Tolstoy, and he is nearer to us, if only because of his extroversion and energy, than either Dostoevsky or Turgenev is. He is a gentleman of the family-loving kind, a farmer, a soldier and a sportsman. He is a Puritan and an anarchist; a creature sanguine, class-conscious and egocentric and he has our particular Protestant madness: the madness of practical morality. The problem of evil is solved, quite simply, when we are drastically pure in private life. His genius for rendering the surface of life recalls to us the gifts of Scott and Jane Austen in their very much smaller scale, though in Tolstoy this genius springs from the classical tradition of Pushkin and from a primitive animality no English writer has ever had. We may even conceive the wild idea that a late novel like *Resurrection*, written when he was over seventy and enormously popular in England when his teachings were at their highest point of influence – was the last of our Victorian novels, the Victorian novel we failed to write but which some unblinkered Ruskin might have written.

Once again in *Resurrection* we can be deluded by Tolstoy's 'Englishness' and imagine Tolstoy's Puritanism to be our own. But a great many Russian novels have come our way since 1905 when *Resurrection* was first translated. Now when Nekhlúdov begins his conversion and his long task of retrieving from penal servitude the woman he has seduced, our first thought is that, unknown to Tolstoy, he is mad; that the moral shock he suffers when he sees Máslova in the dock, a condemned prostitute, is something which the trite process of social reformation is unadequate to deal with. Here, we feel, after Dostoevsky, is a problem that has been stated without intensity, and has not been solved except by over-simplification. If Nekhlúdov is Tolstoy, he is Tolstoy without the spiritual pride and the love of his own lusts: Tolstoy as the Countess never saw him.

Nekhlúdov and Máslova are still left with their natures and their lives, and what they really are has never been spiritually or imaginatively grasped by the drastic old puritan who believed in simplifying life by chopping off its limbs. It is, of course, presumptuous to speak of a failure of imagination in a novelist as great as Tolstoy is; but we know that he depended on living models and actual events, and in *Resurrection* he had no model for Máslova beyond a recollection of the servant girl he himself had seduced when he was a youth. Tolstoy's imagination was not of the kind that adds to life in the sense of fusing something new and blinding with it; his imagination was a luminary which lit up and brought back the living detail of experience as the moon in midsummer will miraculously turn a dark landscape to the sparkle of its lost daytime life. What Tolstoy recovers is the motion of time in the events themselves, the continuous approach, young-eyed and innocent, towards the death he feared so much. In that all-searching light of his, life is seen with clarity, understood with awe and watched with compassion; for it moves upon a scene we shall soon leave and which is recreated with the desire of the animal to preserve the goodness of its brief moment.

And then, another point that is bound to strike us: what an advantage the prophet has over the preacher, the bad Christian over the good Christian, the Dostoevskian over the Tolstoyan when they come to writing religious novels. The preacher is forced to prove his point. Sinners *are* reformed, we all know; men and women *do* undergo conversions; they *can* be made better; they may even be none the worse for being made better; and not, as in Dostoevsky, all the better for being worse. But the life of no man or woman can be mapped so neatly into black and white: the value of a life, imaginatively, is in all of a life. What is interesting is that *Resurrection* is written on that socially Messianic impulse which informed nearly all the Russian novels of the 19th century; and that it stands at the beginning of the deterioration of the impulse towards precise ends. *Resurrection* may be said to be the first of the Soviet novels of immediate propaganda for visible objectives. When he was young Tolstoy had dreamed, characteristically, of a religion that was not otherworldly, but which would create heaven on earth, and it is not surprising that many of the Soviet novelists are Tolstoys watered down who have added nothing to his realism. How natural to choose him for a model. No subtler master of the didactic – if we leave allegorists like Bunyan or satirists like Swift aside – has ever written. His is close to the method of Swift, but Swift enlarged from the reign of island hatreds and the dryness of the 18th century.

For Tolstoy is one of the preachers, at least while he is preaching, who does really convert, where others build up in the audience an obstinate resistance. Tolstoy really does most cunningly persuade. We are glad that Nekhlúdov's life is changed when he sees his guilt; we recognise one by one all his feelings; we applaud his honesty, for we are, in some corner of our souls, honest too. Our Protestant heritage makes us glad that he acts. We are glad, too, that Máslova is recalcitrant, angry and bewildered at first; that she can exactly estimate, in her detached and feminine way, what there is of opaque self-exaltation left in him and what there is of transparent repentance. Her sense that repentance is unnecessary makes her real as woman (if not as a character, for she is a shadow) and when, at the crisis of her relationship with him in the prison, she resists what she regards as an attempt to rape her spiritually as she was raped physically, our deepest sense of justice is called out. 'The old man', as Tolstoy touchingly said of another tale of his, 'wrote well.'

How has Tolstoy managed to persuade us while he writes? Not by any special light which came to him after his conversion; not because, except in a purely literary sense, he was imbued by the spirit of the Gospels. He persuades us, as all the epic writers do, by his native possession of the sense of simple inevitability, and he has this sense from his profound affinity with the peasants with whom, as a feudal nobleman, he was in natural communion. He believes, as a peasant might do, in a lost golden age when all was good. 'If each man believes in the Spirit that is within him,' says the saintly old tramp as he crosses the river with Nekhlúdov, 'we shall all be united. Each man will be himself and all will be as one.' Each man wakes up in the morning and sees the sky: Tolstoy's religion is like the primitive response to night and day. His simplicity is harsh and unjust enough where he is proud and scornful; and yet it moves us because it springs from a universal feeling that the simple is possible. But his simplicity is not all of a piece; it is not mere tenderness. It is cunning also.

Gorky has recorded in his wonderful portrait of Tolstoy how the old man conveyed an impression of knowing all there is to know and of having made his mind up about everything; how he would suddenly bark out harsh, bitter, and coarse sayings and chuckle with malice, grinning like some animal before the horrors of life. He seemed, Gorky said, sometimes not like a human being but a stone; a piece of nature mindlessly contemplating itself and not wishing (we may suppose Gorky to mean) to escape from nature by adding to it in the sociable fashion of other men. What Tolstoy saw, in his egotism, his solitude, his strong animal passion, was the simple physical fact, and he puts this down as if, in the naïveté of love and the satisfaction of ever-watching eyes, he were discovering it for the first time. So, for example, in his picture of the early love of Nekhlúdov and Máslova he sets down things so plain and so true that we are struck by their boldness:

> Katúsha, too, was under the same spell. And this was dominant whether they were together or away from one another. The mere knowledge that there was a Nekhlúdov and a Katúsha seemed to be a great joy to them.

In the wonderful scene of the Easter service it is the same: how serene and always limpidly in movement the tale is, as if life were a brook rippling away through the grave course of time itself:

> Mária Ivánovna's pastry-cook, a very old man with a shaking head, stopped Nekhlúdov and gave him the Easter kiss while his wife, an old woman whose silken kerchief did not hide the Adam's apple in her withered throat, drew a saffron-coloured egg from her pocket handkerchief and gave it to him. A stalwart young peasant in a new sleeveless coat with a green sash came up to him.
>
> 'Christ is risen,' he said, with smiling eyes, and as he drew nearer Nekhlúdov could perceive the peculiar, agreeably peasant odour; then tickling him with his curly beard, the youth kissed him squarely on the mouth with his firm fresh lips.

Again:

> He noticed, too, that Princess Sóphia Vassílyevna, even during the

conversation, was all the while casting uneasy glances at the window, through which a slanting sunbeam was moving towards her, a betrayer which might shed too bright a light on her wrinkled face.

'Please lower the curtain, Philip,' she said, with a glance at the window hangings as the handsome footman entered the room in answer to the bell. 'No I cannot agree with you, I shall always insist that he has a great deal of mysticism and poetry cannot exist without mysticism.' Angrily one of her black eyes was following the man's movements as he adjusted the curtain. 'Mysticism without poetry is superstition, and poetry without mysticism is prose,' she said, with a sad smile, her eyes still fixed on the footman and the curtains. 'Philip, that's not the one I meant; it's the one in the large window,' she exclaimed.

Tolstoy persuades because he is always bringing his next word to our lips, gently unveiling what we shall all recognise when we see it.

Persuades but, of course, does not convince. The philosophy of Tolstoy is atavistic; it is a retreat into the collective common mind of the peasant. In one way, though hating Marxism and keeping apart from revolutionary politics, he prescribes a similar ideal. His Puritanism is revolting; his egotism is monstrous. It is interesting that gluttony had been one of his vices; he had enjoyed his lusts with the ferocity of a Tartar. And in *Resurrection*, though Nekhlúdov is sympathetic throughout, we find the prison chapters dreary, the criminal histories as boring as a chaplain's memoirs when we compare them with the rich and intense portraits of Dostoevsky's *The House of the Dead*. Compare them: which writer has enlarged our knowledge of the human spirit? Not the preacher. The good things in *Resurrection* are the account of the early love of Nekhlúdov, the brilliant, ironical, immensely wily and experienced descriptions of fashionable life and the back ways of the law. We can smell the wine on the breath of those torpid judges; we catch the officials in the very act of improving their careers. And how charming – for Tolstoy was unable to resist the sense of a man's delight in women's beauty, wit and experience – are those civilised parties which we are asked, in vain, to regard as the hollow haunts of vanity and hypocrisy. It is this rounding against his own instinct and his own civilisation which is unbearable in Tolstoy, as all self-mutilation is, and which strike us as dishonest. Gluttonously he has swallowed pleasure and now there is no more. And yet, we cannot say that his Puritanism with its self-display has the aridity, the meanness, the smugness, the bent for the hypocrisies of success or the lapses into sentimentality, the cult of the possible, which our kind of Puritanism has commonly had. At least Tolstoy preached the impossible.

The Art of Koestler

Between imaginative writing and journalism the distinction is easy to make; but in some periods the critic is not required to refine on it. In the 19th century the readers of Dickens or Dostoevsky could see the journalism of these writers at a glance, and could without difficulty snip an editorial on the Poor Law, or a feature article on the Russian soul and its need to occupy Constantinople, from the imaginative pages. The readers of great European journalists like Herzen, Engels and, in our own time, Trotsky, were in no danger of mistaking these writers for artists in an important sense, for great artists towered above them. Today the relation has changed. It is generally agreed that the last decade has been unpropitious for the imaginative writer and that the distinguished work of our years has been fragmentary and small in compass; and as the imaginative writer has receded, so the journalist has advanced. It is he who has towered and glowered, the obstreperous, overgrown child of events; and it becomes necessary once more to mark his difference from the creative writer. The task is delicate because the distinction may be thought invidious. It is not, for many imaginative writers have been journalists in the last decade and with every advantage to the range of their interests and their talent. The digestive process of journalism is coarser than that of art, and we have lived through a period when a coarse digestion became indispensable. The journalist has had the task of accommodating violence to the private stomach and of domesticating the religious, revolutionary and national wars in the private conscience. He has been the intermediary between our private and public selves and, in doing this office, has become a hybrid and representative figure, the vacillating and tortured Hamlet expressing our common disinclinations and our private guilt. For it is typical of the contemporary journalist that his case-history goes with him. Like Hamlet, he travels with his court of private disasters, his ghosts, his Ophelias, even his Rosencrantz and Guildenstern; and though we may often think the sight ridiculous, we must give him the credit for attempting the creation of a new kind of first person singular, a new hero, who can 'take' the assaults of decivilisation, who has invented a certain style which enables him to face the spectacle of mass suffering and official medievalism, with passion, stoicism and humanity. To him the style is as important as the humanity; and eventually we may be sure that artists will collect his vestiges, as once they eagerly collected the sacred relics of Byronism.

To the journalism and the reporting of the higher kind the work of Arthur Koestler is a copious guide. He is not at the level of Malraux or Silone, for he lacks the hard self-control of the Frenchman, the brain and luminous sensibility of the Italian. Koestler's gift is bold and fresh, but it is theatrical. He is the declaiming and compelling actor. No one has known better than he when to drop what he is doing and rush to document the latest convulsion. In this fashion, he has run through the political infections of our generation; through Marxism, Leninism, anti-Stalinism; and practice has accompanied theory. He has known and documented the political prisons and torture houses. He has belonged to the class described in his book *The Scum of the Earth*, the human wreckage of the Left which Fascism scattered over Europe. How much in his writing is personal experience and how much is an intense imaginative identification with the people he describes is not important; or rather, only the identification is important. It is passionate because it is moral; it is complex because it is at once theatrical and aware of itself. There are other qualities: Koestler is more than a simple reporter. He is intellectually volatile; it is second nature for him to generalise about events; he is politically trained, and likes to be politically bespattered. It is the business of the journalist to interview everything and Koestler is able to interview philosophy, science, economics, history, and to come back with a notebook full of general ideas which are put to dramatic use. For the rest, the traits of the profession are emphasised in him by his lack of roots. He was born a displaced person; half-Hungarian, half-Jew, he was educated in Vienna, worked in Germany and Palestine, lived in France. He has been created to wander without mundane allegiances. His allegiances were always with the world of ideas or myth; and when these failed, to the world of random physical events. Guilt and self-pity have been the price. With some exceptions – Strindberg is one – imaginative writers appear to allay their neuroses in works of art; but the neuroses of the journalist are exacerbated by his special opportunities for seeing life.

Yet definitions like these do not bring Koestler into the intimate scope of the English critic. He is separated from us by the education and the politics of the Continent, by the vast difference between the large, stable middle-class in England and the small, precarious middle-class of Central Europe. He can easily dazzle us because we have no café conversation and no café writers. We have no skill in playing poker with ideas. We are not trained to pretend that things which are entirely different may (for the pleasure of effect) be assumed to be opposites. We have no eternal students. We have no intelligentsia. These differences have led Koestler himself to as complete and conventional a misreading of English life as any that have been done by Continental writers. (See *The Yogi and the Commissar*.) We must assume that our judgment of him will suffer from similar difficulties of contact.

We come nearest to him in *Scum of the Earth*. This is partly because the book is a personal record of the events at the fall of France where, at last, English experience came close to the experience of the Continent. A second reason is that here Koestler has cleaned his slate and is putting down just what he saw and heard and, with emotion, is pulling down the curtain on a period. This report is alive; it is packed with human beings; it is resilient and almost buoyant. He is in his natural element, or rather in one of his natural elements: anarchy and disillusion. His eyes are skinned for every incident as, sombre and sardonic – but not with detachment – he notes down the fates of his friends. This book (and *The Gladiators*) contains his least opaque writing.

But we first heard of Koestler in *The Spanish Testament* and here a play is beginning, not coming to an end. We see the sullen sky over Vigo harbour glowing 'under an evil spell.' It is the Koestler spell. We are in for melodrama. 'The constriction in the throat that affects a whole town, a whole population, like an epidemic'; as in the theatre, generalisations, simplifications. The characters wear the make-up of revolution. This writer does not appear to know Spanish history, but he knows current Marxism. He is briefed. He is in control, and can switch on and off when effects are needed. Sardonic anger, raw humour and the punctures of anthropological inquiry let the wind out of his hysterical passages at the right moment. All this is good journalism, but compared, say, with Brenan or Borkenau on Spain, it is slapdash. Koestler was a smatterer, and the only thing of value that emerged was personal: *The Dialogue with Death*. There have been finer, more sensitive, more humane and more objective accounts of life in Spanish prisons than Koestler's, for Koestler had to be the leading actor, and he writes with one wall of the prison down; but the attempt at a personal revelation is intellectually impressive, and precisely in the study of hysteria which elsewhere in his writing is his least attractive quality. In the end, when the curtain comes down in *The Spanish Testament* we are not entirely convinced or convicted. Perhaps because we have been overconvinced. The impression remains after other books by Koestler. Against ourselves must be put his strongest card; he has had to combat the English unwillingness to face the appalling facts of medieval atrocity on the Continent.

Yet this may not be the explanation of our uneasiness. The source may be literary; Koestler has a voice, an urgent voice, vital, voluble and lively, above all never boring – a voice, but an arid and mechanical style. On the face of it this is an unkind criticism to make of a displaced writer who is not writing in his own tongue, who has to make shift to write our own and has mastered it. But we suspect that no language is an inconvenience to him; language is a machine; not even in his own language, we feel, has he any love of words or any sense of their precision and grace. Here is a passage from *The Yogi and the Commissar*, and I think the manner itself forbids belief in the argument, and leaves us with the sensation that Koestler himself would only half-believe in it if he could express it simply, for it is only half-true:

> The law of the novel-perspective prescribes that it is not enough for the author to create 'real life', he must also locate its geometrical place in the co-ordinate system, the axes of which are represented by the dominating facts, ideas and tendencies of his time; he must fix its position in an N-dimensional space-time continuum. The real Sylvia spins around the centre of a narrow family-vortex of conditioning factors, whereas the author, in promoting her to novel life, places her in the centre of a vortex formed by the great trade winds, typhoons,

depressions, and hurricanes of her time. Of course he need not describe or even mention them. But implicitly they must be there.

Koestler uses words as thought-saving gadgets from the ironmongery counter, and draws especially on the vocabulary of science and economics which is paralysed by patents. Like the Latin tag, they may appeal to the vanity; and the Central European mind appears to be susceptible to technical coagulations, but neither exactitude nor illumination issues from them. The love of jargon suggests the lack of an instinct or a sense, and suggests a deaf and arbitrary nature.

The deficiency is more damaging to Koestler's reporting than to his earliest novels. Shaky as some passages in *The Gladiators* are – it was his first 'English' novel, and, presumably, a translation – they are pretty free of vices of style. The jargon of Marx, Freud, Einstein, would have been grotesque in a story of ancient Rome and the Spartacus revolt. We are captured at once in this novel by the sardonic vivacity of the author, the raciness of his reporting, his light mastery of the novelist's and historian's material, even by his boyish humour. We also feel a quality which is rare in the melodramas that come after: the sense of the human tragedy and a pity that is truly pitched and moving. That feeling for tragedy is never recovered, and in my opinion *The Gladiators* is his most impressive book. No personal hatred, no extraneous obsession with persecution or guilt, clutters the running of the narrative, or impedes the growth of the argument: for though the matter of the Trotsky-Stalin conflict is present in the chapter on 'the law of detours' and is implicit in the main crisis of the book, Koestler has not yet projected himself into the Moscow trials. Success destroys: the revolutions that fail preserve their myth; and to Koestler faith and myth are everything. Another reason for Koestler's excellence in this book is that it has a settled subject, set in the remote past, and history has agreed on it. By gift a reporter, he is a hundred times better in recording what is given than in contriving imaginatively what is not; with him, controversy simply brings out the 'old soldier' of the clinics.

The subject of *The Gladiators* is the rising of the slaves under Spartacus, their race to triumph; the tragic split with Crixus, and the final defeat. On the one hand the laxity and shamelessness, the experience and corruption of Rome are comically and diversely rendered with a ribaldry and a talker's scholarship that recall the early Aldous Huxley. These Roman portraits are plump and impudent medallions, cheerfully unclassical; they are the foot-notes of Gibbon turned into agreeable and scabrous cartoons. On the other hand is the raw, rushing, high-voiced rebellion, tearing down the roads, laughing, shouting, guzzling, raping, killing. The wings of the traditional humane ideal raise riot above its own lusts; the brotherhood of the camp makes the spirit flesh. There is a pity for the mindless hopes and follies of simple people: this is the only book of Koestler's to show us the lowly material of revolution in the mass, the simple man who, even in his excess, does not wish to die, and whose last look, as he falls, is of surprise. (In the later books, the dying of the revolutionary leaders has lost all human quality; it has become a transaction of policy.) The masses in *The Gladiators* are incapable of salvation, and between the Gadarene downrush which Crixus will lead, and the slow, painful political course for which the mind of Spartacus is pathetically groping, they choose the former. He who cannot stand the screams of his own prisoners is overwhelmed by the necessity of being a tyrant. He parts company with half his horde; 'objectively' he ought to have killed them.

We feel the earth under our feet in this book, and whether or not it has the developed qualities of a novel is not important. In fact, it is a collection of brilliantly placed episodes, linked by a commentary; and growing characters are not required. (This is fortunate, because it turns out in his later work that Koestler has little power to create or sustain large characters.) All that is required in this book is that his pictures of people shall have instantaneous physical reality – Spartacus himself needs very little to fix him in our mind's eye – and that the atmosphere and the feeling shall be actual like the news. The best of Koestler is in a passage like the following one on the fate of the Praetor; and the end of the passage indicates where Koestler goes wrong:

On foot – for his horse had been left with the robbers – the bald-headed Praetor Clodius Glaber climbed down into the plain. He had been separated from his fleeing soldiers, and walked through the night, alone. He strayed from the trodden path, stumbled over the crooked, stony edge of a vineyard, looked around. The vineyard, studded with pointed stakes, looked like a graveyard by the stars' light. It was very quiet; bandits and Vesuvius dimmed to unreality, Rome and Senate were blotted out; yet one more deed asked to be done. He opened his cloak, felt the place with his fingers, gently pressed the sword-point to it.

The deed asked to be done, but it was only now he understood its full meaning. Little by little the point must be driven home; little by little it must tear through the tissue, cut tendons and muscles, splinter the ribs. Not till then the lung is reached, tender, mucuous, thinly veined; it must be ripped asunder. Now a slimy shell, and now the heart itself, a bulbous bag of blood – its touch beyond imagination. Had ever a man accomplished this? Well he might, with a sudden thrust, perhaps. But once you knew of the process and every one of its stages, you would never be able to do it.

'Death', up to now a word like any other, seemed removed into unattainable distance. All the relatives of Death, such as Honour, Shame and Duty, exist for him only who has no ken of reality. For reality, mucuous, unspeakably delicate, with its mesh of thin veins, is not made to be torn to bits by some pointed object. And now Praetor Clodius Glaber knows that dying is unutterably stupid – more stupid still than life itself.

He realizes that his shoes are full of pebbles. He sits down on a stone and empties the shoes; he observes that the pebbly discomfort had been a responsible element of his despair. As compared to the ignominious defeat of his army, the sharp little pebbles – seven in all – admittedly shrink into ridiculous insignificance. But how can you sift the important from the unimportant if both speak to your senses with equal vehemence? His tongue and palate are still covered with the stale taste of interrupted sleep; a few forgotten grapes lurk between the vines. He plucks a few, looks around; only the stars are witnessing the curious sequence of his actions, and their sight is no rebuke to him.

He feels ashamed and yet he must admit that his actions are no way senseless; no amount of philosophy can alter the fact that grapes were made to be eaten. Besides, he has never before enjoyed grapes so much. He sips their juice together with the tears of an unexplained emotion. He smacks his lips with defiance and shame.

And night with the lights of its indifferent stars gave as a further

[488]

knowledge unto Praetor Clodius Glaber: all pleasure, not only defined versions of it, and Life itself, are based on age-old, secret shamelessness.

Why can't these Central Europeans learn when to stop? The myth of 'age-old, secret shamelessness'! Not *another* myth, we exclaim, not a new thesis, a new antithesis, a new synthesis!

The real core of Koestler's thought in *The Gladiators* – it is taken up again in a moving passage towards the end of a later book *Thieves in the Night* – is in the words of the Essene to Spartacus:

> 'Prophecies are never worth anything,' said the Essene. 'I explained that before, but in the meantime you've been asleep. Prophecies do not count; he who receives them counts.'
>
> Spartacus lay in thought, his eyes open.
>
> 'He who receives them will see evil days,' he said after a while.
>
> 'Aye,' said the Essene. 'He'll have a pretty rotten time.'
>
> 'He who receives them,' said Spartacus, 'will have to run and run, on and on, until he foams at the mouth and until he has destroyed everything in his way with his great wrath. He'll run and run, the Sign won't let go of him, and the demon of wrath will tear through his entrails.'

Spartacus listens to the Essene through the night, until the sky lightens: 'The black shadows in his eye sockets had, as it were, evaporated . . . Spartacus looked again at the glowing East and at the mountain whose everyday shape gradually broke the spell of its nightly distortion.'

Night, dawn, noon, the spell: the symbols are theatrical.

Spartacus fails, but now the dawn has come; we are moving towards the success at Noon, the darkness at Noon which is the corruption of success. This is an ancient and haunting Jewish theme. The Race, by numberless pronouncements of Jehovah, has been fated to be destroyed in success, to be searching for ever.

Darkness at Noon is a *tour de force*, a book terrifying and claustrophobic, an intellectual thriller. The efficiency, the speed, the smooth order of the narrative as it runs fast to its end, are extraordinary. Here is the story of a man arguing his way (or being argued) towards the confession of crimes he has not committed, an interpretation of the Moscow trials, a dramatised examination of the problem of ends and means. As a novelist, Koestler has a superb gift for the handling of argument in a living way; he knows when to break off, when to slip into the personal or the small incident, when to digress into the minor character, where to tighten the screw. Rubashov, the accused, makes the pace all through the story; he is an alert, intelligent man, a brain where Spartacus was passive. And occasionally, like a sudden fragment of sunlight in this grey and horrifying book, horrifying in its grim pistol-barrel logic, glimmers of human illumination occur in Rubashov. They are moving. But when all praise is given, *Darkness at Noon* remains a melodrama. Rubashov and Gletkin are a sad pair of Jesuits consumed and dulled as human beings by their casuistry. The Communists have taken over the doctrine of original sin from the Roman Catholic Church, and have tacked the Calvinist doctrine of Predestination on to it; but they have dispelled the visionary and emotional quality of these dogmas, with the dull acrimony of the makers of company by-laws. An irredeemable dreariness surrounds the lives of Rubashov and Gletkin. They are not 'great'; they are merely committee men or chess players.

The book is not tragedy. Yet to be destroyed by your own Church or by your own beliefs ought to be tragedy. It is surely tragic for the young to destroy the old. There were (if Koestler had not been so gifted in the art of making a case) tragic springs in Rubashov's history. Somewhere in the tale, Ivanov (one of the Inquisitors who is drugging himself with drink) remarks that the murders of Raskolnikov were trivial because they served, or failed to serve, private ends; had they served the ends of the collective morality, they would have been significant. But in *Darkness at Noon* the official killing of Rubashov to serve the collective end fails to reach this high standard. It is a police act, not a tragedy, the end of a case. Koestler could reply that the casuistry of Gletkin & Co. has destroyed the concept of tragedy on the collective plane; but the casuistry is, after all, Koestler's. Rubashov, who has betrayed so many people in the name of 'objectivity', has destroyed himself in advance, and is simply getting what is coming to him. By inference, the same will happen to Gletkin. The two rascals are agreed. Wolf, as the tsarist officer says, eats wolf. Great ideas are in conflict, but in this book they are not embodied in great men.

We have to turn to the greatest of all novels about the revolutionary, Dostoevsky's *The Possessed*, to see that *Darkness at Noon* is a powerful book, but not an imaginative work of the highest kind. It has the intensity of obsession, the interest of surgery, but no largeness. It is a document, pulled up by the roots from a native soil. The revolutionaries of *The Possessed* are living people with biographies, and they are set among other living people. Russia breathes in Dostoevsky's novel, its landscape, its towns, its climate, its history, and grants them the pardon of time and place. For it is evident, from our post-war contacts with them, that the Russians are as Dostoevsky drew them: a people living by wont in a natural atmosphere of suspicion and mistrust, and consumed by fantasies. *The Possessed* is soaked in its own people, grows out of Russian soil. It is felt.

Compared with *The Possessed*, *Darkness at Noon* grows out of nowhere. It is Central European allegory. Yet even the Party is not the same in all countries, and the problem of ends and means is decided not by moralists, but by temperament, feeling, tradition. The objection to *Darkness at Noon* is not that it has overstated its case, but that it has stated only a case; the book understates its field of human, psychological and historical reference. Koestler's own mind is like a prison, with its logical corridors, its dazzling but monotonous lighting, the ingenious disposition of its control towers, its traverses and walls. And there are also the judas slots through which we are led to observe the sudden, shocking, physical revelation; those cells where the dingy human being stands in his day dream; and, outside, the courtyard where the man circles, dragging his shame in his scraping feet. No selfless emotion, no love above all, can be felt there, but only the self-love and self-hatred of the prisoner. And Koestler, who occupies this prison, is like some new and enterprising prison governor, humane enough, but more and more attached to the place and infected with the growing belief that the guilty are ourselves, the free, the people outside. This is a position he shares with the Communist intellectuals of his generation. Their habit of hypnotising and magnetising a subject by the incantations of repetitive argument, so that it becomes rigid, is his. *Darkness at Noon* might be called a major act of literary hypnosis. And the argument is so successful and complete that we begin ceasing to believe in its human application the moment we put the book down.

After *Darkness at Noon* there is a decline. The tight organisation of Koestler's gifts goes slack. Disillusion brought his power to a climax; and since then he has descended to nihilism. *Arrival and Departure* is an attack upon belief itself, due to an enterprising encounter with psycho-analysis:

> If one wanted to explain why Peter had behaved as he did, one had to discard from the beginning his so-called convictions and ethical beliefs. They were mere pretexts of the mind, phantoms of a more intimate reality. It did not matter whether he was a hero of the Proletariat or a martyr of the Catholic Church; the real clue was this suspect craving for martyrdom.

More accurately, this book is Koestler's attack upon himself as a member of the small middle-class intelligentsia of the Continent, and it ends by justifying isolation. The Cause has been thrown over and humanity goes with it. Koestler appears to have had a theatrical view of faith; it was a vision, not a bond. By a really crass misreading of Freud the neuroses of the revolutionaries are made to cancel the traditions of humanism, indeed any strivings of the mind. The civilised, the believing and creating mind is dismissed. Peter solves his conflicts by refusing to recognise one side of them, and after he has exploded his beliefs goes off to fight nevertheless because 'reasons do not matter.' Intellectually a poor book, it has all the old skill in story-telling, the old lack of acceptable characters; an incapacity to describe love – love equals lust, etc. – but a terrifying power to describe torture. The effect is overpowering. One could do with the old framework of good and evil to hold this picture in, and the framework existed if Koestler had cared to recognise it. The despised liberal English and Americans of the ordinary kind were impelled to fight and destroy the nation which committed these atrocities. Koestler's atrocities appear to have been taken out of the moral scheme and to have become pornographic. He is like Ivanov in *Darkness at Noon*, who said that ever since the invention of the steam engine, there has been no normality, only war. A remark that is deeply untrue. There is always normality. *Arrival and Departure* shows those vices of style – the use of jargon – which have marked his essays, and the psycho-analysis is too schematic for words.

With *Thieves in the Night* Koestler returns to something nearer the mood of *The Gladiators*, and his ambivalent attitude to violence – and to ends and means – is almost decided. He has come full circle, i.e. he is *very nearly* prepared to justify violence; or rather he has quite decided to throw out justification. He is among the people whom he really envies and admires, the violent people, the people with grenades in their lorries. This is an old legacy from Communism; one can see it in Malraux also. If anything, Koestler is more depressed by the Zionists' capacity as colonists than by their readiness for killing; practical capacity has no Byronism. We have the suspicion that the Neanderthalers of *Darkness at Noon* are being reproduced in the Promised Land. Can it be that the inhabitants of Utopias are always dull and muttonish:

> I have watched them ever since they arrived – these stumpy, dumpy girls with their rather coarse features, big buttocks and heavy breasts, physically precocious, mentally retarded, over-ripe and immature at the same time; and these raw arse-slapping youngsters, callow, dumb and heavy, with their aggressive laughter and unmodulated voices, without traditions, manners, form, style . . .
>
> Their parents were the most cosmopolitan race of the earth – they are provincial and chauvinistic. Their parents were sensitive bundles of nerves with awkward bodies – *their* nerves are whipcords and their bodies those of a horde of Hebrew Tarzans roaming in the hills of Galilee. Their parents were intense, intent, overstrung, over-spiced – they are tasteless, spiceless, unleavened and tough. Their parents were notoriously polyglot – they have been brought up in one language which had been hibernating for twenty centuries before being brought artificially back to life . . .

But the Joseph of *Thieves in the Night* has found what Peter of *Arrival and Departure* had defined as a psychological aberration: a Cause. More than a Cause: something that none of the Koestler characters has ever had – the lack is their fatal weakness in debate, a nutritional deficiency of Marxist teaching – a country. It is the embryo country, the almost theoretical country of Zionism, but still a country. In his youth, Koestler had lived for a time in the Jewish communities of Palestine, but had, for some reason, tired of them and left; now, once violence has arisen, his personal interest and his alert journalist eye for the topical story have been stirred. The truth is, of course, that he is cosmopolitan and European; that is his real virtue politically; he sees the interaction and unity of European events, and this rational attitude is clearly in conflict with his new Faith, and so much so that scepticism, detachment, the yearning not to be so committed is the impression that still survives the rifle shots and the Hallelujahs. Such a conflict makes an excellent basis for Koestler's best vein: his talk, and this book has some readable passages.

Joseph looked round the terrace and sighed. The khamsin lay on people's faces like a spasm. The women were plump, heavy-chested, badly and expensively dressed. The men sat with sloping shoulders and hollow chests, thinking of their ulcers. Each couple looked as if they were carrying on a quarrel under cover of the *Merry Widow*.

'I can't blame the gentiles if they dislike us,' he said.

'That proves you are a patriot,' said Matthews. 'Since the days of your prophets, self-hatred has been the Jewish form of patriotism.'

Joseph wiped his face. The khamsin was telling on him. He felt sick of it all: Judaism, Hebraism, the whole cramped effort to make something revive which had been dead for two thousand years.

'It is all very well for you to talk as a benevolent outsider,' he said. 'The fact is, we are a sick race. Tradition, form, style, have all gone overboard. We are a people with a history but no background . . . Look around you, and you'll see the heritage of the ghetto. It is there in the wheedling lilt of the women's voices, and in the way the men hold themselves, with that frozen shrug about their shoulders.'

'I guess that shrug was their only defence. Otherwise the whole race would have gone crackers.'

The possibility that the terrorists are really Fascist or copying Fascist methods raises the old bugbear about ends and means, and these discussions are boring.

The central figure, narrator and diarist of this report is now, for the first time, English, an English half-Jew. A naïve snobbery is disclosed here; he belongs to that romantic idol of the Continent, the English country gentry. It is the Disraeli touch. When this character goes to Palestine, he has a low social opinion of those members of the British ruling class who do not come out of the top drawer. One lady – imagine it – has an official position and yet is only the wife of a sergeant! The only real 'lady' is an agreeable sketch, but women have always to be punished in Koestler's novels, and she is made to go through a boring official dinner when afflicted by her periods. Koestler's attitude to sex has always been neurotic – least in *The*

Gladiators – and, in one of his articles, he threatens to raise the question of the menarche, no doubt as a new myth in the space-time continuum.

Bedevilled by his journalistic habit of treating differences as opposites – it makes a brighter page – Koestler can only draw the Jewish colonists with ironical sympathy and vigour, by covering the Arabs and the English with ridicule.

As we ourselves – see *Passage to India*, George Orwell, etc. – have a robust tradition of satire at the expense of our own people, Koestler's looks thin and conventional; the attack on the Arabs, since it is rarely done in English, is fresher, but historically silly. All the same, the bias of the book works to its advantage as a piece of reporting, but only in the first half, that is, say, up to the rape of the girl Dina. The narrative is brisk and dramatic, the picture of the colony is in full colour, the description of its way of living tolerant and moving. We see an Old Testament world; but debated of course, and enlivened by Koestler's short, snorting, schoolboy humour. After the rape – and rape or lust without love is a special interest of Koestler's; down to fundamentals; strip the pretences, debunk, be honest, away from liberal and *petit bourgeois* prevarications in the bedroom – after the rape, suspiciously enough, the novel disintegrates, wanders around, Koestler's doubts appear. The story ends in 1939, which is very lucky for the Anglo-Jewish hero who, in any case, is going to be violent, not with bombs after all, but with a wireless station.

One new quality appears in *Thieves in the Night*: an interest in landscape. The descriptions of Galilee are imaginative. Koestler's talent has always been for the hard, surprising, physical image that stamps a person, a crowd, a place on the mind; and now he is extending this poetic interest to places. It brings an amenity up to now uncommon in his work. We welcome it for in his intense and strung-up work there have been no points of rest; the vice of the 'dynamic' conception of life is that it does not record the consolations of inertia, and never contemplates a beautiful thing. His attempts consciously to inject beauty have ended in the sentimental.

Thieves in the Night is an improvement on *Arrival and Departure*, but it represents the coarsening and mechanisation of a talent. One looks back upon his novels. What is the final impression? They are not novels; they are reports, documentaries, briefs, clinical statements, animated cartoons of a pilgrim's regress from revolution. They are material, formative

[495]

material: their opponents, as well as their disciples, are formed by them. The effect is hypnotic. It is a paradox that these lively and fast moving books, at a second glance, have no motion at all, Koestler has fixed them, made them static; it is he with his 'case' who is on the move; the story and the people do not move of themselves. Our eye is following *him* and not them. The result is that, underlying the superficial excitement, a bored sensation of unbelief is built up – why read about people who merely illustrate an argument and are foils for the author? Quickly the people recede before the inevitable half-truths of a magnetising talker with a good conceit of himself; and while he rarely makes a dull remark, he also rarely makes one that common experience does not flatly contradict. And yet the confidence with which Koestler grasps important themes makes the continued privacy of the English novel look eccentric. It commonly has been eccentric, but at any rate, except for Orwell we have no novelist of the social or public conscience who has Koestler's scope or force – no journalist or reporter either. It is the price we pay for our lack of interest in general ideas for their own sake: empiricism is not dramatic. General ideas become, however, an infatuation; for example, it may be that the Soviet runs a police state, forced labour camps, etc., because Russia has always had these things, and not because of a recent ethical lapse. It may be that Koestler has imposed a Central European efficiency upon the Russian scene in *Darkness at Noon*. Perhaps the English novelist is wise to avoid general ideas and to stick to life as it is presented to himself, and to leave what he doesn't know to the newspapers and the Blue books. For the novels of Koestler are skeletal. They are like the steel frameworks of modern buildings before the bricks go in; and up there, shaking all over with the vibration of the thing, is Koestler furiously concentrating on his pneumatic riveter. A guilty figure: he can't get over an old wish that it was a machine gun and the principle is maddeningly similar. So guilty does he feel that presently he stops work, harangues the crowd below, and the building is never completed. It remains, a stimulus, an incitement to others, a theatrical outline against the sky.

Tristram Shandy

A little of Sterne goes a long way – as long as nearly 200 years, for his flavour never dies in the English novel. It is true we cannot live on tears, fancy cakes and curry. But, take him out of the English tradition; point out that George Eliot, D. H. Lawrence, Conrad – the assembled moral genius of the English novel – ignore him; explain that he is not Henry James; despise him because he created 'characters', a form of dramatic person out of fashion for a generation or more – and still his insinuating touch of nature comes through. He is obvious in figures as different as Thackeray and Firbank; and *Ulysses* is sometimes thought of as the *Tristram Shandy* of our century. We see the releasing hand of Sterne in those instances where the English comic genius leaves the usual moral territory of satire or the physical world of knockabout, and finds a third region which is neither pure intellect, pure fantasy nor pure imagination and which is indeed an evasion of all three. To call this the eccentric strain explains nothing; it is well known that the English are eccentric. Sterne – it is better to say – is mad, using the word as we commonly do in England to avoid facing and judging people who themselves are engaged in not facing what they are really up to. Eccentricity is, in fact, practical madness. It is resorted to, Henry Adams said in his severe and shrewd New England way, by those who are up to something shameful or stupid or muddle-headed. And, in England, most of us are.

It is possible that the comedy, half artifice and half nature, which we extract from our 'madness' is fundamentally stupid; there is an excessive and stupid streak in Ben Jonson where this comedy abounds. All the same we have sometimes raised stupidity to the level of a fine art. The 'madness' of Sterne, the hostile critic might say, is a practical device for foisting upon the reader a brilliant but shameless egotism, an inexhaustible selfishness and a clever smirking insincerity. Compare his shamelessness with Boswell's: the Scotsman is wanton, transparent and artless, haunted by

[497]

fear of the Presbyterian devil, whereas we can be sure the devil himself was afraid that the half-Irish Sterne would drag him into bad company. Boswell calculated nothing or, at any rate, nothing right, except his money. Sterne calculated eloquently. Constantly he reckoned up how much he was going to feel before he felt it; even calculated his words so subtly that he made a point of not ending half his sentences and preferred an innuendo to a fact. He relied on the reader's imagination. I notice that in the sympathetic and unprejudiced inquiry that Mr Peter Quennell made into Sterne's character in *Four Portraits* – and this contains the most illuminating study of Sterne that I know of – there is the suggestion that he was the first to use the word 'sentiment' in our imaginative literature and to found the modern meaning of the sentimental. I do not know whether this is so, but it ought to be. For Sterne was a sentimentalist, because his imagination was morbidly quick to impose the idea of a thing, its image-provoking words and its *ambiance* long before the feeling was evoked. He could talk his heart into beating. He could talk tears into his eyes. Or so we feel as we read him; never sure whether this sociable, good-natured, too impressionable man is sincere or not.

One can see Sterne's temperament at work in the account of the beginnings of the Widow Wadman's love of Uncle Toby. The widow's passion was not born until she had seen him among her things in her own house:

There is nothing in it out of doors and in broad daylight, where a woman has a power, physically speaking, of viewing a man in more lights than one – but here, for her soul, she can see him in no light without mixing something of her own goods and chattels along with him – till by reiterated acts of such combinations he gets foisted into her inventory –

This may be a universal truth about love, but down to the last *double entendre* – and, above all, because of it – the fancy encases the feeling as it did in the parallel circumstances of Sterne's courtship of his wife. His passion warmed when she let her lodgings to him in her absence.

'One solitary plate,' he wrote,

one knife, one fork, one glass! I gave a thousand pensive penetrating looks at the chair thou hadst so often graced, in those quiet and sentimental repasts – then laid down my knife and fork, and took out my handkerchief, and clapped it across my face, and wept like a child.

Obviously one who felt so strongly for a chair could live very well alone in the comforts of his own imagination.

Alone: it is that word which rises at last to the mind after it has been dragged for miles at the heels of the bolting, gasping fancies and verbosities of *Tristram Shandy*. The gregarious, egotistical Sterne is alone; garrulously, festively and finally alone. If there is one thing he likes better – again, in literature as in life – than the accident of meeting, it is the agreement to part. One can put this down, at a guess, to his severance from his detested mother. In *Tristram Shandy* it is notable and important that all the characters are solitaries. Mr Shandy and his wife, Dr Slop, Uncle Toby and the Corporal live shut up in the madhouse of their own imaginations, oysters itching voluptuously upon the pearl within. Mr Shandy silences his brother with his philosophical systems and his cross-references, never sees a fact but he recedes from it into abstraction, and is determined that the palaverings of the search for Truth shall have one end only: that he gets his own way in his own home. The blameless Uncle Toby sits in his innocence, conducting his imaginary campaigns, short of speech and blinking at the world. Mrs Shandy hurriedly agrees with her husband; nobody knows what is on *her* mind. Dr Slop is shut up in the horror of his pendulous belly and Corporal Trim does what he's told, loves his master, but lives by his memories of his poor brother Tom in Lisbon. Habit rather than communication keeps them all happily together. They are bound by ennui, grey days and indolence. But, read the dialogue: it is a collection of monologues. True, Uncle Toby and the Corporal have occasional awkward interchanges, but the general impression is that no one answers serious questions and that they know one another far too well to listen. In family life there is nothing to do about the hard core of the human ego, but to accept it. The indecencies and the double meanings of Sterne, if anything, intensify the solitude; they provoke private reflection and erect barriers of silent lecherous satisfaction. How can the Widow discover where Uncle Toby was wounded, when he can only answer: 'In the siege of Namur.' Sterne displays the egotist's universe: life is a personal dream.

[499]

Those who deny Sterne talent of the highest order and think of him as outside our tradition must strip away half our tradition and character first. Sterne's discovery of the soliloquising man, the life lived in fantasy, is the source of what is called the 'great character' in the English novel, a kind which only Russian fiction, with its own feeling for 'madness' in the 19th century, has enjoyed. *Tristram Shandy* is the inspiration of the solitaries of Dickens, the idea-ridden people in Peacock and many others in our literature; they are not literary theories but comic abstractions from a faculty of life. It must be admitted that Mr Shandy and Uncle Toby are both very stupid men; they are funny because Sterne is so much cleverer than either. He plays tunes on them. They are also bores – always the richest game for the comic instinct. If we compare them with other great bores, like Bouvard and Pécuchet, the Shandys have the advantage of not riding their hobby-horses to any purpose. They prove nothing either to us or to themselves, but illustrate rather the vegetable inertia of the fanciful life and display the inhabiting of one's temperament as the most sensible thing to be engaged in. Every dog to his basket. Even in the torpor of their domesticity, the imagination can beguile.

The bother was that Sterne was a bore himself, as boring in his way as Mr Shandy is. That Irish loquacity which he got from his mother and his early years in Tipperary had deluded him. He had that terrible, professional, non-stop streak of the Irish. One feels, sometimes, that one has been cornered by some brilliant Irish drunk, one whose mind is incurably suggestible. Although we have a hypnotised picture of Uncle Toby's dubious fortifications they take on, in our minds after an hour or two, the heavy appearance of those surly battlements one sees during a migraine. *Tristram Shandy* must be the most put-down book in English literature. One can respond, of course, to the elaborate cunning of its counter-point; there is method in the anarchy. But the book is a collection of fragments in which every fragment sticks: Mr Shandy fallen geometrically with grief in his bed; Uncle Toby dazed by the fire; the pipe stem snapping as the child is born upstairs; the ludicrous discussion about the landboat, with its foreshadowing of Peacock; Bridget putting Mrs Wadman to bed; Mr and Mrs Shandy on the 'bed of justice' with the inevitable chamber pot sticking out from under the vallance while they talk of putting young Tristram into breeches; the pretty picture of Brother Tom going into his sausage shop in Lisbon where there was a Negress driving off fleas with a feather.

Sterne has a genius for mosaic; for being any self he has decided to be; for living in the effervescence of his nature. The sentimentalist is a cynic, naturally:

> Love, you see, is not so much a Sentiment as a Situation, into which a man enters, as my brother Toby would do, in a *corps* – no matter whether he loves the service or no – being once in it, he acts as he did . . .

Many have wondered at the feverish receptivity of his eye and some have seen the dread of death – for he was a consumptive – in his determination to look at each event through a microscope as if enlarging it would slow the course of time. That Sterne's sensibility to the passage of time was unusual is certain; he seemed to see each minute as it passed, and to be eager to hold it with a word. But others – of whom Mr Quennell is one – see in his minuteness the training of the painter. Every sight, every thought was a physical model. There can be no doubt that he broke into the stream of consciousness and was the first to splash about there – in rather shallow water; there can also be no doubt that he was never going to commit himself to anything deeper. It was enough that one thing led to another and that the sensibility was ready for the change. It was Sterne's wife, a woman heavily committed to housework and a bad temper, who, for a time, went out of her mind.

The Roots of Detection

W hat is the lineage of the detective story? It begins, presumably, with the first detective: Vidocq. After that important invention, Hoffmann's *Mlle de Scudéri* seems to be next in the succession and here the moral and technical basis are properly laid down. We are on the side of virtue and justice against evil conspiracy and plausible accusation, and the latter have to be exposed step by step. Poe's *The Murders in the Rue Morgue* grew out of *Mlle de Scudéri*, but in Poe the stress is on the horror of crime and evil, rather than on detection. I have never read the Frenchman, Gaboriau, to whom Wilkie Collins is said to owe a debt, but Wilkie Collins is, at any rate, the first properly uniformed and impressive detective novelist in English literature. The pure conundrum, intricate, sufficient to itself and an exercise of the faculties, has at last been extracted from the double meanings, the symbolism, allegories, crimes and hauntings of the Germanic or the Gothic tales, by the pragmatic English genius. When young Franklin Blake in *The Moonstone* is finally shown to have taken the moonstone without knowing it, the explanation is that he has been doped with laudanum, and not that he has a second self, or a higher and lower nature; he is allowed no more than an accessible and God-fearing Unconscious. In short, Wilkie Collins is as British as they are made.

Two new editions of the *Tales of Hoffmann* and *The Moonstone* have been published. Tenuously united, at some point, in the roots of their art, the two authors are suggestive in their fundamental divergence. The Hoffmann, which retains many of Gavarni's excellent illustrations, is well-edited and contains *The Golden Pot* (which Carlyle translated), *The Sandman*, *The Deed of Entail*, *The Story of Krespel* and *Mlle de Scudéri*. I will begin by quoting from Mr J. M. Cohen's acute analysis of Hoffmann which has explained to me why (when it comes to the test) I prefer Hoffmann's kind of tale, a book like Hogg's *Confessions of a Justified Sinner*, or (with reservations) *Jekyll and Hyde* to nearly all works of detective fiction. 'There are

[502]

for Hoffmann three realms,' says Mr Cohen, 'a comfortable Philistia – comically drawn in *The Golden Pot* – a borderland of dangers and hidden significances, and a third region of spiritual power and serenity.' In Collins and his descendants there is Philistia alone: the detective novel is the art-for-art's sake of our yawning Philistinism, the classic example of a specialised form of art removed from contact with the life it pretends to build on. It is an abstract reduced to the level of harmless puzzle and pastime. It provides a pleasant way of not-reading, sharpening the instruments of the intelligence, but giving us nothing to use them on. We could go on – if we were attacking detective fiction – to say, as people used to in the old Marxist days, that it exemplified the spirit of self-regarding isolation in middle-class culture, and that, in its way, it was as precious as Pater. Or, in its defence, that it represents a core of private sanity, a tenacious belief in the effectiveness of intelligence and reason, which still survives in us despite the conditions of our age.

Hoffmann's world, on the contrary, is the underworld or overworld of Romance, the world of Good and Evil, not of Right and Wrong. We shall meet the flesh and the devil, wickedness and virtue, imagination and the world. A tale like *The Golden Pot* is a charmed allegory of the life of the artist. Those who find German fantasy repugnant, who groan before its archaic paraphernalia and see in its magic, its alchemy, its vision, its hypnotic dreams and trances, its ghosts and its diabolism, all the disordered tedium of the literary antique shop, will find Hoffmann more engaging, more concrete, and cleverer than he seems at first sight. He is a wonderful story-teller, his humour is gracious, he is circumstantial and his invention is always witty. In *The Golden Pot*, for example, where the artist takes to drink, he is represented not as a drunkard but as a little creature imprisoned in a bottle. *The Entail* is a vivid and satisfying *nouvelle* and the management of the two sleep-walking scenes is the work of a master of ingenuity. And if his world is Romance, then it defines what Romance ought to be: not extravagance, but life reflected perfectly in a mirror or a lake, true in detail, but mysteriously ideal. Mr Cohen says:

> The most important events in Hoffmann's life were fantasies; his early love of Cora Hatt and his later love for Julia More had no basis in reality – the ladies were not as he imagined them; on the other hand the

Napoleonic wars, which he affected to disregard, were the very real background to a great deal of his life. Dream and reality had changed places for him.

(And here Hoffmann became the forerunner of those characteristic modern Romances: the imaginative case-histories of Rilke and Kafka.)

But greater authority was given to his dream visions by the decay of religious myth in the age immediately preceding his. Robbed of the immediacy of miracle stories, which had been part of Christianity's millennial heritage, the 18th century was forced to look for evidence of the supernatural elsewhere, in order to satisfy man's instinctive belief in events not subject to material law. Following Swedenborg's lead, they looked to mesmerism, spiritualism and psychic phenomena, for the proof of God's existence; the artist's frenzy and the madman's alike provided evidence of possession by forces superior to man's; dreams rendered everyone familiar with a world outside the closed kingdom of cause and effect.

And, I suppose, the late survival of medieval life and of folklore in Germany must be partly due to the destructive effect of the Hundred Years War, on culture. War and revolution *do* give a meaning to life, but the heart and the sensibility feel that meaning to be of a low order and even spurious. Hoffmann is a sweet dessert wine, but he has that extra clear-headedness in a restricted field which is often noticeable in the fuddled; he was a startlingly complete artist, though in miniature. He had grasped the lesson of folklore; that the extraordinary, the unheard of, must be made minutely, physically real, and the pleasure he gives is that of exactitude and recognition.

Like Hoffmann, Collins, of the divergent branch of Romance, was a lawyer. Collins takes a practical view of the cranky new material and makes a fine art of not seeing beyond the end of his nose. How thoroughly, exhaustively and yet memorably one has the whole story of the moonstone at one's finger-tips. I find it hard to remember nearly all plots, but I can remember every detail of *The Moonstone*, though the plot must be one of the most elaborate in literature. The explanation lies in his skill and his perfect balance. He never goes too far, and is very particular; he also understands the reader's anxiety to follow, whereas Dickens in *Edwin Drood* had no mercy and counted every confusion in the reader's mind as a victory. As Hoffmann was at heart, Collins is a rational man. There is, of course, no fantasy or mystery-mongering in Collins. The Hindus in *The Moonstone* use a boy medium, but (to our relief) Collins knows all about mediums. He uses the character of an opium addict, but not – we thank heaven, again – for exploring opium dreams, but as one of the perfectly working pistons of the plot-machine. Delirium comes in and we approach the alarms of free-association and psycho-analysis but Collins is interested only in the *utility* of the mysterious. The doctor's free associations are there – to be taken down in shorthand. There are many high moments in the book, but the best is fittingly at the climax: the scene where Franklin Blake, drugged once more with laudanum, re-enacts his part in taking the moonstone from Miss Rachel's cabinet; and here Collins displays his mastery of one of the great principles of story-telling, which is to appear to do the same thing twice, but on the second occasion to make a significant alteration. The moment where Blake drops the stone which the onlookers expect him to hide is wonderful. The art of the story-teller lies, of course, in surprise; but the art of surprise must come from the continuous knowledge that the reader, in his anxiety, is always playing for safety. It is the story-teller's business to make the path of safety into a path of change and danger. There is a parallel scene in the sleep-walking scene in Hoffmann's *The Entail*. The first time the guilty servant walks in his sleep the observer realises that silence is essential. The second time he forgets to tell a second observer to be quiet. The man shouts and the tragedy comes down with a crash.

Sergeant Cuff, Collins's detective, has been much admired. He is well characterised, as all Collins's people are; he is something like a real detective – Holmes owes many details to him – and is never in danger of becoming a legend. His withdrawal from the middle of the tale which is beyond his professional competence, and the fact that he is wrong, are excellent moves. Only the suicide of Rosa Spearman jars, and here one suspects a superlatively clever writer is taking on too much stage-property. There is said to have been a film company which liked a scene from a moving stairway in all its films because the company owned a piece of moving stairway. Having exuberantly introduced some quicksands – a favourite Victorian property – into his tale, Collins had to use them. There are complaints, too, about the excessive characterisation of the narrators. This does, indeed, delay the narrative; but with one character, the pious, tract-distributing Miss Clack, Collins hit upon a wonderful type; and though he piles on her follies where the genius of Dickens would have cut them until she was a comic fantasy, Miss Clack is a startling break with the slightly sententious habit of the other narrators. Smugness was thought to be the defect of Collins's character, but it was the engaging smugness of the most fertile example of efficiency in the English novel. Never was there such a specialist. *The Moonstone* is the first and the last of the detective novels, and I would like to ask the addicts what more has really been added to the genre since his time.

The Poe Centenary

A hundred years after his death what are we to make of Poe? He is a writer into whom large, inexact things may be read and from whom many things important to literature have been taken; a second-class writer, yet a fertilising exclaimer. The paradox is that his genius was merely probable and narrow and yet his influence was wide. Read those poems again which Baudelaire compared to crystals: it is a strange comparison for verses so slack in their simplicity, so mechanical in their devices. And yet we are haunted by overtones of an exceptional experience. It is no ordinary tomb on which Poe weeps; there is more than loss in those tears. There is guilt and dismay. Afterwards, the mourner will be haunted not by the dead but by himself. When we turn to stories like *The Pit and the Pendulum*, *The Murders in the Rue Morgue*, *Ligeia*, or *The Fall of the House of Usher*, the accent is self-assured, but we are not, after two wars, bounced or interested by the rhetoric of suffering and sadism. D. H. Lawrence found the material conventional, meretricious and vulgar. The voice of incantation appears to be disguising the experience, is slurred and constructs the conventional nightmare of the drug addict or the facile alcoholic:

> Not hear it; – yes, I hear it, and have heard it. Long – long – long – many minutes, many hours, many days, I have heard it – yet I dared not – oh, pity me, miserable wretch that I am! I dared not, *dared* not speak. *We have put her living in the tomb!* Said I not that my senses were acute? I *now* tell you that I heard her first feeble movements in the hollow coffin. I heard them – many, many days ago – and yet I dared not – *I dared not speak*! And now – to-night – Ethelred – ha! ha! – the breaking of the hermit's door, and the death cry of the dragon, and the clangour of the shield! – say, rather the rending of her coffin, and the grating of the iron hinges of her prison, and her struggles within the coppered archway of the vault.

Efficient, silly and yet its harangue can overpower. It is theatrical and yet not pure theatre. If we set aside the skill of narration – and we ought not really to do so because part of Poe's gift to literature is his teaching and example of the conscious artist – there is more than the expert tale of mystery or horror; there is the sustained enacting in conditions amounting to claustrophobia, of a universal human pain. The redeeming thing is Poe's gift of generalising morbid experience.

Poe's parents (it is well known) were actors; and one is obliged to see him as an actor-writer. Perhaps his technical genius in creating new literary forms came from the application of the actor's temperament to a medium that was alien to it. He comes on to the stage, among his grotesque properties – the pit of the Inquisitor, the rotting ancestral mansion, the luxurious Disraelian palace or the jewelled valley – and with the first oratorical words and the first hypnotic gesture, he has created an at-mosphere. An atmosphere, the hostile must say, that one could cut with a knife. We suspect the old trouper and there is no doubt that his prose comes out of the catalogue; he goes from one cliché of Romance to the next; the names of his characters, the Lady Madeleine, Ligeia, Berenice, Lenore, are shamelessly stagy; and like the notorious 'Nevermore' are made for the parodist. But what grips the reader is that Poe is evidently not acting an *alien* part; the story is *his* story, this is his pain, enlarged and generalised as poetry is, and it can suck us into its whirlpool just as, irresistibly, the death ship of *The MS. Found in a Bottle* was drawn down into the ocean. Suffering and guilt are his subjects: to magnify is his method.

There is a point at which the magnifying glass makes the object too large, when the close-up loses nature; and that is the point of vulgarity in Poe. But I do not believe there is a story in this assiduously inventive writer which is not taken from his own state. He was the first writer of any importance in English to take, possibly from Hoffmann and Vidocq, the notion of the tale of detection. He must have been one of the first writers of scientific romance. These are remarkable inventions. It is not merely by lucky chance that he saw the interest of these forms of writing, for both his extraordinary flair for literary genre and the peculiarity of his temperament predisposed him to them. They seem, when we speculate upon it, to be the natural interest of his divided nature and the fruit of personal guilt which has been turned to literary advantage. We can see the clever mind of the expert neurotic observing its own sensibility and its terrifying private fantasies. The mysterious, he sees, can be chemically split; explanation can be, he perceives, as exciting, sensationally, as the mysterious thing. In the tales of the dying woman prematurely buried, in the story of Ligeia rising from the dead to poison and annihilate her rival, we can see Poe dreading the death of his Virginia, wishing for it and willingly incurring remorse and punishment. One understands what such themes could suggest to Baudelaire and Dostoevsky; moreover, the writings reflect a life that seems itself to be a direct expression of Poe's own theory of 'the unity of effect'. His character is, in a sense, to be read at a sitting; it was constructed, we feel, from the end first; it was a suicide, the deliberate seeking of a pre-conceived fate. For Poe is steeped in pride; allowing for D. H. Lawrence's manias, his criticism that Poe blasphemed against the Holy Ghost within him is a true one.

Poe the alcoholic, Poe the incestuous, Poe the unconscious homosexual, Poe the Irishman, the Southerner, the derelict, Poe isolated in American life and ruined by the *odeur de magazine* – these versions are familiar. They have their share of truth. In a quietly provocative introduction to *The Centenary Poe*, Mr Montagu Slater reminds us of the part played by simple financial misery in Poe's life. He got £2 for *The Raven*. It seems doubtful whether writing for magazines ruined him: he was a magazine-man. He was a brilliant lecturer. He was not a physical weakling: he had been a regimental sergeant-major and a fine swimmer. Mr Slater goes on to a vague argument of the kind that might be useful if it could be fully documented – and I do not see how it can be – that art for art's sake began with Poe, and has remained dominant in Western literature ever since. He links the doctrine with solipsism and with Poe's own doctrine, expressed in characteristic tones of incantation in *Eureka*: that the soul is a particle of God that must return, annihilated, into His Oneness. Poe's famous proposal of the short poem, that long poems are merely short ones connected by prose, that works of art must be grasped at a sitting and that there must be unity of effect, is made to support Mr Slater's argument. But to say that intensity and the love of beauty above all else have any special connection with art for art's sake is to force argument. Poe's doctrine of the instantaneous has, indeed, been realised, as Mr Slater says, in many important forms of modern art; but that is far from meaning that copious works are more diverse, or that intense works are incapable of deep humanity. The personal voice and experience of Poe underlie his artificialities, and we now understand that what used to be called morbid experience is universal and has a direct bearing on spiritual life.

One great difference in kind between Poe and Sartre, Camus and Graham Greene, whom Mr Slater regards as the latest if not the last of Poe's aesthetic line, is one of energy. In the sense that he carries within him the feeling of power which was felt in the early 19th century, Poe is electric: a positive neurotic, a wilful madman, an aggressive suicide. His terrors, his pains, his guilt, his punishment, his melancholy itself, are represented as inflations and energies of the soul. They are not presented as maladies to be cured and he does not wish to lose them. He feels, romantically, all the larger and more powerful because of them as if they were a gift and privilege. The Romantics felt all the greater for their cult of death and pain, whereas psychology has taught us to regard our sickness as mutilation or a misleading of our powers. Poe is perfectly able to live his derelict and isolated life regardless of the community. A loquacious and throbbing pride enables him to do so; his sorrow runs a pipeline to the eternal. The later writers lack this aggressiveness. Pain is inflicted upon them. They are ciphers of passivity – as, indeed, the ordinary man is among the political horrors and farces, the double-faced institutions of our time, where persecutors and persecuted change places with the nullity of papers in a file. Though they attempt to dignify themselves with the belief that they are drifting to annihilation in the One, the Nothing, the Historical, or the Nevermore, they bob up and down on their way over Niagara with the feebleness of corks. Long ago they lost their bottles. They do not die: they black out. Destruction is taken out of their own hands. They just run into it absurdly. Poe on the contrary did not believe life was a fraud; he believed it was an orchestrated tragedy; he had the Romantic afflatus. Loss and death were inevitable; pain was an action felt or done. It is pure speculation but, if he could be reborn, one imagines him writing his stories not about the victims of the Inquisition, but about the great repressed subject of our day: the morbid psychology of the Inquisitor and torturer and their guilt; simply because that is now the dominant, positive and energetic aspect of contemporary pain. The Inquisitor has had his romantic wish for power: what has *he* paid for it?

[510]

It is usually said that Poe is an un-American and cosmopolitan writer, and Baudelaire declared that America was Poe's prison. But Poe was a natural prisoner. It seems to me he was very American and especially so of his time; intellectually aggressive and provincial, formed by journalism, a practical and exacting technician and critic – see his analyses of novels by Dickens and Hawthorne – as cranky in his way as Thoreau, Emerson and Hawthorne, for example, of rather wild personal independence in opinion. Above all, he is American in the capital hold that nostalgia has on his emotions. It is the melancholy, lonely dominant note in the feeling of American literature: from the Mark Twain of *Huckleberry Finn* to T. S. Eliot. It is indeed this feeling which encloses even the slack poems, that seemed to us sentimental or merely pathetic; it is on a general and native longing that he is able with all his power of rhetoric to play. The melody that runs through his writing, impure but sweeping and haunting, the loneliness of his incantations, themselves seem to be designed to deploy that simple feeling; and the dream world which is not really a dream world owes its effect to the fear and the longing it is meant to convey. We feel that a nation of lonely people is projecting his fantastic palaces or is considering his unlikely dungeons; for in a new and rapidly successful country, part of the human personality is a casualty, and in that injury is the desire that cannot be realised.

Oliver Twist

==========

*O*liver *Twist* is the second novel of Charles Dickens. It was begun before *Pickwick* was finished when he was twenty-six and in the full conceit and harassing of sudden fame; and *Barnaby Rudge* was started before he got Nancy murdered and before Bill Sikes slipped by accident off the wall on Jacob's Island into his own noose. It is a novel speckled with good London observation, but the critics agree that the book which gave the word Bumbledom to the language is a gloomy and inferior work, stretched out on an incredible plot, blatant with false characters and false speech and wrecked by that staginess which Dickens was never long to resist. The story is a film scenario full of tears and 'ham', an efficacious splurge of Cockney self-pity. On the other hand, the reader must protest that all this is no drawback to his excitement. The popular thriller is generally based on the abstraction of sinister human wishes from the common reality of life; and, willingly suspending disbelief, we can eagerly accept Fagin, even Bill Sikes and Mr Brownlow, even Nancy and Rose Maylie, as permitted fantasies. Is it because of the hypnotic fame of Dickens or because he is completely responsive to the popular taste for uninspected myth that all his characters stay in the mind? Only the neurotic Monks and the creaking, sceptical Grimwig have one false foot in the world of our experience.

A new edition of *Oliver Twist* has the advantage of a really brilliant, melancholy and subtle appreciation by Mr Graham Greene, himself a thorough initiate in the art of writing thrillers. It is one of those uncommon prefaces that expertly test the technical merits of a book and enlarge its suggestion. Before turning to his main points, there are two obvious yet easily forgotten virtues in *Oliver Twist* which put what might have been a total failure on its feet. For there is no doubt that *Oliver Twist* 'comes off.' In the first place it is a literary novel, nourished by Dickens's early reading. The echoes from Monk Lewis, the touches from *Jonathan Wild* in the framing of the portraits of Mr Bumble or the Artful Dodger, the preface which curiously boasts that at last we are to be given real criminals – except in the matter of bad language – and not romantic ones, are all touching and agreeable glances from a spruce young author towards his tradition. (And, as Mr Greene shows, we certainly get real thieves' kitchens and the sour poverty of criminal life, the background but not the foreground.) In the second place, the book is given a kind of authority by the frank copying of Fielding's mock heroic and disquisitional moralising. By this Fielding displayed the assurance of his sensible morality, and it is true that Dickens debases the manner by turning it into something journalistic, sprightly and even facetious; nevertheless, the manner enabled him to assume a central place in the tale, from which he could exploit, without confusion, the variety of its moods.

It was Mr Edmund Wilson who first saw the biographical importance of the melodramatic and criminal episodes in Dickens's work. They are for the most part the least successful as literature. They are commonly over-acted and, indeed, too much stress on these and the didactic side of Dickens, is likely to take us away from his greatness. It is all very well for modern critics to neglect the comic Dickens for there, as a writer, he was completely realised. On the other hand, the impurity of Dickens as a creator is an important fact; in his confusions and concealings, strange psychological shapes are disclosed. His relation was with the public which he bowed to and upon whose not always reputable feelings he played. Upon them, as upon an analyst, he enacted a transference. Mr Graham Greene's main point is, in a sense, an extension of Mr Edmund Wilson's into the field of religion. He suggests the religious cast of Dickens's imagination:

How can we really believe that these inadequate ghosts of goodness [Mr. Brownlow and Rose Maylie] can triumph over Fagin, Monks and Sikes? And the answer is, of course, that they never could have triumphed without the elaborate machinery of the plot disclosed in the last pages. The world of Dickens is a world without God; and as a substitute for the power and the glory of the omnipotent and omniscient are a few sentimental references to heaven, angels, the sweet faces of the dead, and Oliver saying, 'Heaven is a long way off, and they are too happy there to come down to the bedside of a poor boy!' In this

[513]

Manichaean world we can believe in evil-doing but goodness melts into philanthropy and kindness . . .

And Mr Greene ends with this paragraph:

> . . . Is it too fantastic to imagine that in this novel, as in many of his later books, creeps in, unrecognised by the author, the eternal and alluring taint of the Manichee, with its simple and terrible explanation of our plight, how the world was made by Satan and not by God, lulling us with the music of despair?

That is too fantastic, of course, as a description even of Dickens's demonic imagination, of his unconscious as distinct from his conscious, orthodox religion. The terror of *Oliver Twist* is the acted terror inherited from literature and married to personal hysteria. The Manichee is good theatre. But the suggestion is an interesting one and if we follow its lead, we must be struck by the flashes of contact between *Oliver Twist* and the Manichaean myth. The child of light is lost in the world of darkness – the terrors of childhood are the primitive terrors of the dark – from which the far-away Elect will save him. When he is saved, the end of the world of darkness is brought about – Nancy is murdered, Sikes and Fagin are hanged. We might grope farther along the strange tunnels of the Manichaean allegory and discover there a suggestion upon which the Freudian analyst of the tale of ghosts or terror will immediately pounce. These tales are now held to be artistic transpositions of the fear of castration and when one turns (as an ignorant reviewer so often must) to the authority of the *Encyclopaedia Britannica*, one indeed finds that the thriller writers have pious if tainted progenitors in the fourth century. In their belief 'primal man descends into the abyss and prevents the further increase of the generations of darkness by cutting off their roots.' What is notable (one reflects) is that the enormous preoccupation of Victorian literature for murderous melodrama – and we remember the horrifying success of Dickens in his public readings of murderous scenes – goes with an extreme sexual prudery in literature. Murder – as the saying is – is 'cleaner' than sex. We seem to see a violent age seeking a compensation for its losses.

Whether or not the imaginative world of *Oliver Twist* is without God in the Christian sense we must leave to the theologians; the interest of Mr Greene's suggestion is the inevitable implication that the emissaries of light, the Elect, are the middle classes. It is Mr Brownlow and Miss Maylie who come down, to the tune of the ineffable music of the Three Per Cents. Only by sitting at the throne of Grace could they face the abyss of darkness in which the industrial poor, the everlastingly guilty were damned and lived waiting for their doom. Only by making Rose Maylie an angel could the existence of Nancy be assimilated; only by making kindness old-fashioned and respectable could Sikes be faced as a modern, sullen and temperamental brute. It does not follow, as Mr Graham Greene suggests, that the evil represented is stronger than the good, in the imaginative effect; the balance between these cardboard unrealities is perfect and a thieves' kitchen always sounds more dramatic and 'strong' than a drawing-room. And so, too, on a more reputable plane: against the half-dreamed figures of Monk and Fagin at the window that seemed like the imprint of a primitive memory, must be placed those other half-waking intimations Oliver had of some happiness in a far-away past never known. What we are convinced of, even though by the long arm of coincidence, is the long arm of humanity and justice.

Oliver Twist is a literary novel. Magnificent juvenilia is Mr Graham Greene's just phrase. The plots of Dickens were to improve and one does not know whether to put down their tedious elaboration to Mr Chesterton's belief that they were an attempt to set out 'something less terrible than the truth.' That looks like a Chestertonian attempt to put down something more eccentric than a fact. Perhaps Dickens in his exhibitionism wanted to put down something *more* terrible than the truth. Either explanation sharply applies to the disastrous passion for plot general to the Victorian novel. It is a fact that Dickens had the greatest difficulty in inventing probabilities and that may be related to the fantastic turn of his mind.

All the main strains of his genius are crudely foreshadowed in *Oliver Twist*. There is the wonderful clean snap of scene and episode; nearly everything is 'realised'. Mr Greene has perceived one of those reflective passages, memory evoking or regarding its own act, which Proust admired, and there are occasional phrases – the absurd servant's face 'pale and *polite* with fear' – or touches of detail that show the hand of the master.

[515]

We recall things like the wisp of human hair on Sikes's club, that sizzled for a second when he threw it in the fire; the notices in the country village warning vagrants to keep out. Sikes's speech is ludicrous – '"Wolves tear your throats," muttered Sikes' – but his death is wonderful; one remembers the boy at the window taken by surprise when the hanged body drops and shuts off his view and how he pushes it aside. The crude London scenes have the rattle of the streets in them; it is a novel of street journeys.

Mr Bumble's proposal of marriage and all the sour and tippling termagants which foretell Dickens's long gallery of patchy and disgruntled women have the incalculable quality of nature. Dickens (and Forster supported him) believed Oliver to be real; and indeed he sometimes is. He is hardly the evacuee of our time; a hundred years had to pass before the happy English middle classes were to discover what a child from the industrial slums could be like. Oliver is simply 'one of Lord Shaftesbury's little victims'. But the misery and the fear of Oliver are very real, his leaning to virtue (now so unfashionable) profoundly convincing. Why should we complain if Vice is over-exposed and Virtue over-exalted; the convention has the authority of Hogarth, and belongs to the 18th century, the morality of pre-industrial England. Hence – we may be tempted to think – not the absence of God or the taint of the Manichee, but the author's lingering assumption that the belief in justice, the knowledge of retribution and of the passion of mercy are self-evident in human nature, and that a good dose of terror and a long tangled plot of ill-chance and malignance will bring them out. Dickens was not the first or the last novelist to find virtue more difficult to portray than the wish for it.

Meredith

'He put a laurel on my head and then gave me a buffet in the stomach,' Meredith said when he read Henley's appreciation of his work. And when we turn to what Henley really did say we find this: 'Meredith is a sun that has broken out into innumerable spots . . . He writes with the pen of a great artist in one hand and the razor of a spiritual suicide in the other.' There is also the judgment of Henry James. 'Poor old Meredith,' Henry James is reported to have said. 'He writes these mysterious nonsenses and heaven knows what they all mean.' To which Meredith replied: 'Poor old James. He sets down on paper these mysterious rumblings of his bowels – but who can be expected to understand them?' Later on, Henry James expanded his thoughts to Edith Wharton. The central weakness of Meredith's art was unconscious insincerity. He was a sentimental rhetor- ician 'whose natural indolence or congenital insufficiency, or both, made him in life, as in art, shirk every climax, dodge around it and veil its absence in a fog of eloquence.' But when Meredith died, James relented. He said, 'He did the best things best.'

The bother – it must seem to a contemporary eye – is that Meredith so *strained* after the best things. He lived off the hyperbolical. Even the worst, dullest, the flattest things had to be cooked in hyperbole. To our restricted stomachs he is high feeding. To read him is like living on a daily diet of lobster; a kind of brain fever follows it. Half-way through *The Egoist* or *Harry Richmond*, through *Evan Harrington, Beauchamp's Career* or *The Ordeal of Richard Feverel*, we have had a surfeit not of the matter but of the manner and the mayonnaise. We know we are confronted by the vitality of genius, but we are uncomfortably convinced that we are also faced by one of those calamities of genius, which the English 19th century occasionally pro- vides. It is a calamity comparable with the disaster of Carlyle. What is the explanation? Is it that the eloquence of the Celts – the Welsh, the Irish and the Scots – outruns what they have to say, and leaves behind it brilliant but broken and unfinished works of art? Is it that they are brilliant beginners only? It is, we must feel, the virtue of Meredith that every sentence *is* a new beginning; but his vice that almost no sentence is a continuation from what has already been said. He is a man fixed gyrating to the spot.

In a forbearing and rather idle Life of Meredith, written a few years ago, Mr Siegfried Sassoon made the sound point that Meredith was a young man's novelist. He brims with the earliest, sun-dazed sensations we have at the age of twenty, before experience has taught us that the senses and the heart itself, are our gaolers. He is bursting with the young man's pleasure in the exaggerated and fantastic, the bombastic and consequent. What back-slapping, what mysterious private jokes go on in his suburban walking tours! In youth our judgments are driven off the track by our natural energy and this part of Meredith we acquiesce in with some nostalgia. But, sooner or later, Romance collides with reality, what goes on inside the Meredithian figures seems to have only a perfunctory relation with what they do and then – perhaps because of the pride of Meredith's imagination has been too strong for them – they become vulgar and ugly without Meredith being aware of the fact. The early love scene in *Richard Feverel*, to take an example, has been much admired, but the end of the affair is an over-furnished bathos, and sets the early lyricism in a new and dubious light. Richard had been just as much in love with the Thames Valley as with a young lady, and Meredith did not know it.

The lumpish inequalities of the Victorian novel have been put down to the fact that the Victorians so persistently wrote beyond their range and often seemed to have had little idea of what their true range was. They seem to have been – as I believe Lord David Cecil has written – sure of themselves only in what they knew from their childhood. After that their growing up was uncertain. It was their energy that drove them beyond their artistic means; and energy is indeed the fundamental subject of the 19th century, provoking questions that are never answered because, in the end, the Victorians considered energy was its own justification for it led inevitably to progress. The discovery of German idealism confirmed the cult of energy. Carlyle took from Germany that Gothic halo of the hero and put it – though intending the very opposite – on the head of the rosy, humdrum cult of effort in commerce and manufacture. In copying

[518]

Carlyle's style and going to school with Carlyle's German masters, Meredith carried the new heroism on to the end of the century.

It is bad (one is inclined to say) when the Scots are educated in Germany; when the Welsh go there, and add their taste for local giants to the Teuton's infatuation with the leader-hero, the result is grotesque. Meredith brings the Victorian novel to a close with a panegyric of power and that, as Irving Babbitt pointed out years ago, is the penultimate act of the Romantic movement. The last act we have seen, in our own time: its suicide and annihilation. Henley was perceptive when he made his remark about the razor of the spiritual suicide in Meredith's hand.

Energy is always Meredith's subject. It draws out his full powers in *The Egoist*. This brain-vexing novel has all Meredith's vices as a novelist but turns them into something like virtues. These virtues belong to the original English tradition of the 18th century which is built on the diffuse, the sense of theatre, on the comedy of moral types and a general reference of all moral issues to 'the opinion of the world.' Educated, well-bred, instructed and experienced people subscribe to a polite opinion, and what they lose thereby in private sensibility, they gain in the assurance of summary judgment. They are certainly unable to go to the lengths Proust went to or to the edge of that abyss where behaviour ends and the soul is exposed and alone. But the 18th-century writers had considerable curiosity about human beings and Meredith has very little. He has taken the types. Would we recognise Colonel de Crayl or Mrs Mountstuart if we met them? Only after a process of de-cerebration: two women are compared to yachts. Bursting with himself Meredith knows people only as they stimulate his vanity, only so far as they help him to cut a figure in uttering 'the opinion of the world', and to dominate the brilliant dinner party. Meredith himself, transfigured and universalised into a general ogre as Sir Willoughby Patterne, is the only 'character' in the book, but we know him also as the theatrical projection of a moral category. One of the really colossal acts of Meredith's energy as an egoist is performed at the end of this novel when, having exhausted the egoism of Sir Willoughby, Meredith turns in search of fresh prey and discovers Laetitia (of all people) to be an egoist too. No doubt she is in her way. So are we all egoists. But to generalise the theory like this makes character meaningless. If all the characters in the book are Meredith, they become nothing. By going on to the stage with his puppets,

Thackeray at least gave them a minute but individual life; but Meredith goes on to the stage and drives the people off by acting all their parts for them.

The method kills an ordinary problem novel like *One of Our Conquerors* by sheer effusiveness and insensibility. The exhibitionist metaphors reduce a novel, which has a well-stated social theme, to the clownish:

'We cry to women: Land Ho!' he shouts in the middle of a passably affecting scene in this book. 'A land of palms after storms at sea; and at once they inundate as with a deluge of eye-water.

'Half a minute, dear Victor, no longer,' Nataby said, weeping, near on laughing over his look of wanton abandonment to despair at sight of her tears. 'Don't remind me. I'm rather like Fenellan's laundress, the tearful woman whose professional apparatus was her soft heart and a cake of soap.'

Or there is that awful, prolonged comparison of the clouds over London with Rubens's *Rape of the Sabine Women*.

But in *The Egoist*, and if we except the opening chapter, passages of exuberance are toned down. He continues the course set by *Jonathan Wild* and, even in the subject – self-love, isolated from all other human passions and set supremely among them – there is a typical 18th-century simplification. There are two over-riding qualities, it seems to me, that give this tiring novel, with its impossible dialogue, an important breadth and authority. The first is the total power of Meredith's own egoism and self-knowledge; egoism is his subject, unashamedly understood in maturity, and seen (since he could not be tragic about it) on the highest comic plane. The second quality lies in the constant implication that Sir Willoughby is more than himself, more even than a general moral analysis of egoism: he has the spread and weight of England behind him. His character is a portrait of the dominant English temper of the time; in the high noon of its self-confidence Sir Willoughby and the presumptuous, over-fed English scene play into each other's hands.

Meredith's capacity for putting England into his characters – once again at the opening of *One of Our Conquerors* or in *Beauchamp's Career* – enriches his novels with a temporal emotion. What other novelist, before Kipling, has so explicitly done this? Only another exotic – for there is something very exotic in the Welsh Meredith – the Jew, Disraeli. The rest of the English novelists always take England for granted.

The duality and depth of the main theme of *The Egoist* eclipse the tedium of its minor scenes. Sir Willoughby's egoism was more than conceit; it has the conscious zest of the man-hunt. He was

> quaintly incapable of jealousy of individuals – his enemy was the world, the mass which confounds us in a lump . . . the pleasure of the world is to bowl down our soldierly letter 'I.'

or again

> Consider him indulgently: the Egoist is the Son of himself. He is likewise the Father. And the son loves the father, the father the son . . . Are you, without much offending, sacrificed by them, it is on the altar of their mutual love, to filial piety or paternal tenderness.

Self-torture itself is indulged to feed this ravenous pride. In this book there is no doubt about it: Meredith had the razor in his hand.

We know why it was in his hand. Exuberance exhausts itself, the theatrical Celt is spent. And there are those three or four lines in *Richard Feverel*:

> Well! All wisdom is mournful. Tis, therefore, coz, that the wise do love the Comic Muse. Their own high food would kill them. You shall find great poets, rare philosophers, night after night on the broad grin before a row of yellow lights and mouthing monks. Why? Because all's dark at home.

Horrible writing. It is the Stratford-on-Avon style, Romance decaying into the language of advertisement. Peacock's daughter had just left Meredith when he wrote these self-pitying words but 'all was dark at home' in Meredith's life long before that and long after. His, we may surmise, was the darkness of loss and self-love. It is generally said that Meredith was a great snob and that he was ashamed of his humble origins 'in trade', but once the natural period of snobbery in youth was passed, there is no evidence of unusual social snobbery in Meredith. He enjoyed his gifted and ridiculous ancestors. But snobbery as a form of romanticism does certainly pervade Meredith's novels, and that was passed down from father to son in his family. The Victorian novel derives half of its subject and most of its comedy from this social and spiritual delicacy. Book after book deals with it: if a man looks like a gentleman, dresses like a gentleman, how is it that he is still, quite patently, not one? This was a fundamental question in the Meredith family. They were handsome tailors who could easily make the clothes and the money and were gifted actors who could live the part they dressed for. In them, we feel that everything that has been said about 'being in trade' (in the words of the 19th century) has been concentrated and has become even transcendental. They know all the victories, all the defeats, and are ripe with the comedy of their own situation; they are acting, with a self-knowledge that is both Romantic and comic, a role which the rest of England is taking with either mundane or godly seriousness. When, indeed, Meredith talks of England in his foreign and detached way, he is seeing a real England which the English are too solemnly involved in to see themselves. No other writer has so richly and so ironically conveyed the sheer pleasure the Victorians had in social position.

We can see how the fundamental question in the history of the Meredith family gave Meredith his subject. Old Mel of *Evan Harrington*, courtly, arch and amusing, had simply bounced into the county. His son, Meredith's father, who was crippled financially by the old man's sallies into the great world, was cured of the ambition but not of the preoccupation with it. When we get to Meredith himself the impulse has reached its platonic stage. An only child who had grown up without a mother, Meredith inhabited the solitude of clever boys and lived like a prince, secretly, in it. In him romantic snobbery reappeared in its highest incarnation, as the love of the rare and superb, as the belief in epithet and refusal of reality unless it was highly inflected.

And there is a terrifying will in Meredith's dreaming childhood. It is interesting to compare his case with Hawthorne's. The proud solitude of Hawthorne in New England had the same preoccupation with the ancestor; but whereas Hawthorne really was, within the prim New England limits, a kind of aristocrat, Meredith was not. He had to be his own ancestors and the success of his family had made him an optimist. How vastly he would have been improved as a novelist if, like Hawthorne, he had felt the worm in the bud; but, not being an aristocrat, he had no worm in the bud; he blossomed wilfully, fully, and was too sanguine. We are alarmed by this precocious Hampshire child who, seeing his own superiority as an intellect, briskly takes his education into his own hands and goes off to school in Germany without consulting his elders, alone. His will, though it is the will of a spoiled, handsome boy, is astonishing. The disciple of Darwin – with Hardy he is the only English novelist to make use of Darwin's ideas aesthetically – was seeing to it that the excellent shall survive.

And that is what Meredith's snobbery is: the will to excellence. Of all the Victorian novelists he presents the subject with most profundity. He knows snobbery at all levels and he knows the price that has to be paid for it: coldness of heart, egoism, artificiality, self-sufficiency and meanness are the price to be made for the richly imagined role. The accomplished snob must be impenetrable. Evan Harrington is openly warned of this. The young snob, the secret prince and dreamer, who is lost in the glitter of his vision of honour and his own talent, runs the danger of becoming an actor for life and, in any crisis, his lost sense of reality will make him evasive, lonely, perhaps cowardly and without trust in life. There will be wounds – the defection of Meredith's wife – which will never be forgiven. And insincerity, an emotional over-dressing will haunt every rhapsodic sense of the better and enchanted thing.

The best things in Meredith lie in his general perceptions of character, for he has the great novelist's gift of generalisation. By that he moves with a brilliance that catches the breath and excites the mind. The social utterances in *Beauchamp's Career* are resounding in their comedy and penetration. And then he excels in plain comedy and the purveying of minor characters. They abound, a little crudely – but the crudity is very English – in that novel. There is Mr Tripehallow letting Beauchamp 'twig' – there is a good deal of vulgar 'twigging' in Meredith – that he has heard all about his French mistress:

'You young nobs capering over our heads – I nail you down to your morals. Politics secondary. A-dew, as the dying spirit remarked to weeping friend.'

There is the interchange between bland Mr Oggler, who runs adverbs in pairs, a forerunner of the disciples of the success-religions of our time, with his 'honestly and sincerely.'

[523]

'I really and truly don't know what it is not to know happiness.'

'Then you don't know God,' said Carpendike, like a voice from a cave.

Then the candidate's sordid friends at the election:

'I repeat, my dear sir, the infant candidate delights in his honesty, like the babe in its nakedness, the beautiful virgin in her innocence. So he does: but he discovers it's time for him to wear clothes in a contested election. And what's that but to preserve the outlines pretty correctly, whilst he doesn't shock and horrify the optics. A dash of conventionalism makes the whole civilised world kin.'

And there are the epigrams:

'He is no true Radical. He is a philosopher – one of the flirts and butterflies of politics.'

For in his unique fiction of overfed England, Meredith did not restrict his comedy to personal relationships. These, indeed, were incomplete to him, unless what he would call the comedy of the ideologies were fixed round them like a frame. His people were hatted in what they believed.

Mr Sassoon believes that the three-volume novel was the ruin of Meredith. That convention may have led a careless technician to throw his plots together and rely on brilliant presentability to fill the gaps. But we cannot have the virtues of a writer without his vices: the fact is that Meredith's virtues are all in his personal mobility, his aplomb and his presumption. His stories do not progress; they are waltzed with violence from line to line, and chapter to chapter. The unremitting footwork of Meredith may give us the first chapters of *Richard Feverel*, may take us to that comical scene in the solicitor's office where young Ripton is caught reading a book about Woman under his desk. Or to the wonderful set portrait of Adrian 'the wise youth' who 'caused himself to be required by people who could serve him'; to the death of Old Mel, the unveiling of Sir Willoughby, or to one of those artificial scenes – excellent devices and a development from Fielding – like the temptation of Sir Austin. The staginess of Meredith is in the 18th-century tradition and is an effective method of linking the main action by witty discursions before the curtain.

[524]

But the same method perverts narrative. It is a kind of snobbery raised to the *n*th, that hopes to pass off a plain sight of gambling at the table as everything except what it is:

> He compared the creatures dabbling over the board to summer flies on butcher's meat, periodically scared by a cloth. More in the abstract they were snatching at a snapdragon bowl. It struck him that the gamblers had thronged in on an invitation to drink the round of seed time and harvest in a gulp. Again they were desperate gleaners, hopping, skipping, bleeding, amid a whiz of scythe blades, for small wisps of booty. Nor was it long before the presidency of an ancient hoary Goat-Satan might be perceived, with skew-eyes and mouth, nursing a hoof on a tree.

A snobbery, or poetry curdled and gone wrong. There is too much labour in that passage for good poetry; there is too much exhibitionism in it for it to be tolerable prose.

'All is dark at home': the comic writers are injured poets. Meredith is our most foreign novelist, and in some ways this foreignness brings him near to us today. He is pagan, too. He has the aptitude for a provoking generalisation. He has reacted to science. He has a gambling intellect. He saw, better than his more sensible contemporaries, some of the outlines of our world. No doubt, the poetic approach can be called a new form of the Old Victorian humbug, but it enabled him to sharpen his psychological eye: Richard Feverel's seduction after the champagne dinner is a vulgar piece of writing but at least it is true to life in the essentials. (What distresses us is that Meredith does not know when he is vulgar.) The notion that Sir Austin Feverel's System was a means of unconscious revenge is as rare a perception as anything in Henry James. And *Modern Love* is not only one of the finest sonnet sequences of the language: it is also a recognisable, an unabashed and almost contemporary *Huis Clos*. Meredith appears, in England, at the first break of the intellectual with society, and that in itself brings him closer to us. Just as Thackeray held that he was born several generations too late, perhaps Meredith's difficulty was that he was born at least two generations too soon, and so, like Thackeray, he ends by satisfying nobody. That air of experience is specious because it is heartless: that thumping sense of the world is too thumping: he has gone to the intellect and its pride to seal off the wounds of life, as a young man will before he learns that the brain will do nothing for us. That last sight of Meredith, so often reported, of an old man with a loud voice shut off by deafness from his friends, muttering his fantastications, bitter and still straining for more brilliance in a final defiance of reality, is a parting allegory.

Poor Gissing

═══════

About Gissing I once heard H. G. Wells throw off this remark some years ago: 'Poor Gissing,' he said, 'he thought there was a difference between a woman and a lady. There is no difference, as we all know.' On second thoughts we know nothing of the kind. Thinking for the third time and reading again that drastic yet moving cartoon of Gissing's life which Wells drew in his *Autobiography*, we suspect that in his life and in his work, Gissing was not a deluded romantic but a man born out of his time. It was an accident – though a very likely one – that the literature of social conscience should bounce along the ebullient, flashing and practical course laid down by the optimism of Shaw and Wells; the still expanding economy of England guaranteed that those members of the lower middle class who had impatience, clear-headedness and energy could get out of it; but the story might have been different if England had not continued to get richer. The social conscience might have been pessimistic. The stress might have been placed on the spiritual casualties of the class struggle, as it was in Gissing, and not on the material hopes.

When Gissing's novel *A Life's Morning* was published again a few years ago, it contained a thoughtful introduction by William Plomer. Some words of his seem to hint at the observation I have just made. He says:

> It is hardly to be wondered at that Mr. Wells, who was a good friend to Gissing, thought him 'horribly mis-educated' while Gissing thought Mr. Wells (so Mr. Wells says) 'absolutely illiterate.' It was not that Gissing looked forward and Mr. Wells looked backward; it was that when Gissing looked forward and Mr. Wells looked backward neither liked what he saw. What worried Mr. Wells was that Gissing was 'not scientific' and had had a classical education.

When Wells wrote of those members of the lower middle class who had the gift of creating good luck, who could invent a fire, and fight for their lives like Mr Polly, Gissing wrote of the trapped, who were too weak, who too often felt (as he said with bitter penetration) the final impulse of self-pitying egoism 'towards the fierce plunge into ruin.' To these the struggle presented itself as an attempt to grasp with failing hands the spiritual content of life.

To this point the contemporary social reformer has belatedly arrived, after a generation of successful revolution. The crises of the unclassed, the poor women, shop girls, teachers, dressmakers and governesses of Gissing's novels are always spiritual as well as economic: 'It was her terrible misfortune' (Mr Plomer quotes from *Demos*) 'to have feelings too refined for the position in which fate had placed her.' We feel for Emma Vine but we also smile expectantly at this judgment on her; Emma is a stock comic character who was been made serious. Gissing, who had the sensibility and tastes of a cultivated man, himself tired eventually of creatures so stolid, so maimed and so frustrated in the fulfilment of either their own or his ideal. Emma is one more Victorian 'lady' who forgets she is a woman; one more victim of the comedy of gentility. All the same, we take the point because it is, for all the unconscious comedy, a real point. The heroines of George Eliot had similar aspirations; and thrived on them because they were better off. That class-ache was and is profoundly true to the inner English life.

Among the more spirited and sociable figures of the late Victorian novelists Gissing is the one who brings the accusing, self-consuming face of failure, the lordly silence of the lonely man. His failure is the source of his persistent fame; he is one of those novelists who are neither discarded nor made immortal, but whose reputation drags its heavy-footed way in a kind of perpetual purgatory. His lack of humour, his lack of fantasy – that essence of the English novel – leave him worrying unattended on the pavement of his anxieties and his scholar's dreams. Take books of his at random: *Thyrza, Eve's Ransom, Denzil Quarrier, Odd Women, The Unclassed* – they are well, but stiffly written, without individuality, but as Mr Plomer says, in the sound conventional prose of the scholar; their psychological passages are acutely argued but the words never fly, never leave the ground. The dialogue is stilted, though the reported speech of the slums is alive. Their plots groan. Their characters (if we except Dickensian shapes like the Irish schoolmaster in Tootle's Academy in *The Unclassed*) are weighed down by self-pity or moan under an excess of good intention, and only when we break through this encasement do we find how real they are. There is – how right Wells was in this respect – a fundamental sentimentality and more than a touch of conceit and pretence. Gissing was a novelist in error, for he lacked the gift of melting life and pouring it into the mould of artifice. Life and artifice stand side by side in his novels like some ill-assorted couple.

If these very grave criticisms are true why do we read Gissing? The answer is that at certain points in nearly all his novels, he speaks seriously about matters which no other novelist has taken so seriously. Instructed by his reading of the French and Russian novelists he is bleakly aware of the situation of his time. Snobbery, priggishness have been subjects for wit and gregarious laughter to the other English novelists. Injustice has aroused passion, but these novelists end by coming round to the sociable view. Gissing conserves the lonely, the private personal opinion. He is a thinking person thinking for himself; and his contribution as a novelist – as Virginia Woolf suggested – is the thinking of ordinary people who so far had not been credited with thought. No more than the French or Russians is Gissing afraid of prigs and dreamers. He sets out to find them; he can be relied upon to discover them in the seamstresses of *The Unclassed*, in a villain like the manufacturer in *A Life's Morning*, a character who comes to life when the desire for refinement stings him like a gadfly. Or in that tired clerk Mr Hood who had all his life desired to see Holborn Viaduct – a comic character, there, and how austerely refused! This discovery that in all character there sits a mind, and that the mind of the dullest is not dull because, at its very lowest, it will at least reflect the social dilemma into which it was born, is arresting.

Where the discovery is most fruitful is in Gissing's portraits of women. Women were known to have feelings. They were known to be shrewd. But who supposed them to have thoughts beyond themselves! The fact is that Gissing realised women were ladies, and now that the modern novel since D. H. Lawrence has presented them as sexual combatants and aggressors, it is refreshing to discover again their thoughts about their social condition. This is one of the best points in Mr Plomer's valuable and sympathetic introduction: and I would go further and say that no English novelist of the realistic kind has drawn women so variously and so intimately. In this sense Gissing's feminist novel, *Odd Women*, is one of his most interesting. It is a picture of loneliness in urban life. Once one has broken the back of the first chapter or two, one's impatience with Gissing's old-fashioned methods of narrative goes. Life show its teeth. The lonely rooms of London, the lonely pedestrians, the real population, one is inclined to say, of this seedy and disconsolate place take possession. We see the three daughters of an improvident doctor thrown on the world, untrained, almost penniless, hardly educated and terrified of losing caste. They are contrasted with a fierce and vivacious young feminist, Rhoda Nunn. Gissing analyses the fanatical Rhoda Nunn and he prepares for her the most delicate psychological drama. (One understands, after this portrait, the admiration Henry James had for Gissing's work.) He finds for Rhoda Nunn a man of the world whom she converts to her feminism, and having done so, she is made to realise that vanity not love has impelled them. Her brain has deceived her; she is obliged to behave unjustly and irrationally like any 'silly' woman; and wrecking her own happiness, returns to loneliness and feminism again. She has passed through the strict spiritual test to which Gissing put all his women – for that, he felt, is what the minds of so many women fear and desire – and is left matured by the test but, of course, unhappy. Gissing despised happiness. He had the masochistic imagination of the adolescent.

In life and in literature Gissing's method was severely to criticise women in order to be gratified all the more by the discovery of their graces. This led, of course, to being over-gratified and to self-deception in life, but it led to balance in literature where he could be ironical and urbane. This is Mrs Rossall of *A Life's Morning*:

This lady had just completed her thirty-second year; her girls were in their tenth. She was comely and knew it, but a constitutional indolence had preserved her from becoming a woman of fashion, and had nurtured in her a reflective mood, which, if it led to no marked originality of thought, at all events contributed to an appearance of culture. At the time of her husband's death, she was at the point where graceful inactivity so often degenerates into slovenliness. Mrs. Rossall's home-keeping tendencies and the growing childhood of her twins tended to persuade her that her youth was gone; even the new spring fashions stirred her to but languid interest, and her music, in which she had some attainments, was all but laid aside. With widowhood began a new phase of her life. Her mourning was unaffected; it led her to pietism; she spent her days in religious observance, and her nights in the study of the gravest literature. She would have entered the Roman Church but for her brother's interposition. The end of this third year of discipline was bringing about another change, perhaps less obvious to herself than to those who marked her course with interest, as several people did. Her reading became less ascetic, she passed to George Herbert and the 'Christian Year' and by way of the decoration of altars proceeded to thought for her personal adornment.

The attempt to revive Gissing is desirable, for we are less likely to be depressed by his novels and to misjudge him than his contemporaries were. By a long detour through the wilderness of literary reputation he arrives at our door. But this revival will confirm, I am afraid, his substantial failure as a novelist. The shadow of Ryecroftism (as Mr Plomer says) is often dank upon his work; in short he lacks the quality of self-disregard which is essential to novelists. It has been complained justly that his novels have the very amateur fault of being without focus or central plot. Precisely: Ryecroft's shadow takes its place. That unshaped ego is blobbed over his tales. But Gissing is a store-house for novelists. One of his books, the study of Dickens, is a translucent piece of criticism. For the rest, he foreshadows a type which has become commoner: the uprooted intellectual of a later generation, cut off by education from his own class and by economic and social conditions from any other place in society. From this point of view Gissing's novels are less dated than those of the early Wells; despite our wars and our large social changes, the forgotten neighbourhoods of large English cities are still packed with Gissing characters, even though the material conditions of their lives may have improved. Their essential spiritual problem, the problem of industrial society, remains untouched:

Natural men, revolting against the softness and sweetness of civilisation; men all over the world; hardly knowing what they want and what they don't want; and here comes one who speaks for them – speaks with a vengeance . . . The brute savagery of it! The very lingo – how

appropriate it is! . . . Mankind won't stand it much longer, this encroach-
ment of the human spirit . . . We may reasonably hope, old man, to see
our boys blown into small bits by the explosive that hasn't got its name
yet.

Those words, spoken by a Gissing character in *The Whirlpool* and
discussing the newly published *Barrack-Room Ballads*, still stand.

An Émigré

T he daily evil of the émigré is his isolation. He has lost the main ground of the moral life: that we do not live until we live in others. The temptations that face him are embittering to any man capable of reflection: he can live in the past; he can become an uprooted dilettante; he can cultivate, in the words of Heyst in Joseph Conrad's *Victory*, that 'form of contempt called pity' which comes easily to the isolated man; he can regard anarchy as the ruling spirit in the world. Crime may come nearer to his fingers and, with less obstruction, to his imagination than it does to rooted people. In a world like our own, the solicitations of the police, the secret agent, the revolutionary, the traitor, are very likely, under one guise or another, to come his way. No doubt these extreme enticements are evaded by most émigrés, who alleviate the sense of persecution by living in the past and keep their nostalgias and their rancours indoors; but, mild or extreme, they unite to force upon the isolated man his main addiction. He becomes pre-eminently a conscience.

Isolation and conscience are the dominant motifs in the novels of Joseph Conrad and, two of them especially, *The Secret Agent* and *Under Western Eyes*, become more and more suggestive to the contemporary reader. They attract because they are free from that sudden fogginess, that enlarged bad temper which Conrad called Destiny, and from the melodrama or rhetoric which plays tricks with the lighting and climate of many of his ambitious works. They have the compactness, the efficiency of that peculiarly modern form of writing, the thriller with a bitter moral flavour. And they put a central modern question to ourselves – what is our attitude to treachery and other moral consequences of a belief in revolution?

Conrad's terms are out of date, of course, though not as seriously as might be thought. Anarchists do not throw bombs in London; in Russia, the tyrant is not assassinated. But the essentials of European history have not changed since the Eighties of last century; what was talked about has simply come true. The revolutionary thug who has the fine art of bursting Razumov's ear drums in *Under Western Eyes* is an anthropoid forerunner of thousands who have gone one better than that in the police states. Conrad is a reactionary; for him the old despotism and the new Utopianism are complementary forms of moral anarchy. Their end is cynicism, more despotism, more destruction and to that opinion some have now reluctantly come. But Conrad was a fixed reactionary; he had never tried to tack across the revolutionary tide; he hated the Russian revolution as a Pole who was already a generation away from the hatred of his time; his hatred was glued into the past. The positive contribution of his political views is that they double the precision of our dilemmas of conscience by presenting them in reverse. The weakness – let us get it over at once. Conrad's judgment is true and untrue, but what he said of Heyst in *Victory* points out the weakness:

> The young man learned to reflect, which is a destructive process, a reckoning of the cost. It is not the clear-sighted who lead the world. Great achievements are accomplished in a blessed warm mental fog.

Conrad is an exile. He is not committed except to pessimism. He is, for private and public reasons, tortured by the danger of becoming a moral dilettante. Because he is so excruciatingly aware of all the half shades of that case, he has his authority.

Razumov in *Under Western Eyes* is a sympathetic character. He is the recurring 'lonely' being in Conrad's novels. Another Conradian theme, perhaps Slavonic and certainly Romantic: he has a 'double' in Haldin, the student assassin. 'In times of mental and political unrest,' the Razumovs of the world keep

> an instinctive hold on normal, practical everyday life. He was aware of the emotional tension of his time; he even responded to it in an indefinite way. But his main concern was with his work, his studies and with his own future.

Not a prig, not a careerist, not dull; he is intelligent and sensitive. His worst fault is a bad temper which comes from one of Stendhal's definitions of misfortune: 'Not having the evils of his age' – if we can use the word 'age' in a double sense. The irrational driving force in him comes from insecurity and loneliness; he is a bastard. Just when Razumov's good resolutions are ripe, Haldin the terrorist hides in his room and, by the very contact, dooms Razumov to eternal political suspicion. There follows a scene in which Conrad's highest dramatic gifts as a novelist are brought, uncorrupted, into play: the picture of the student's room, Razumov's despairing journey through the snow at night to the inn to fetch the cab driver who will enable the exalted assassin to escape, Razumov's discovery that the man is dead drunk; and then the journey back in which, having failed, Razumov revolts against his unjust situation and his own quietism, changes his mind and betrays Haldin to the police. The scene is a very long one and also exposes Conrad's weakness – the creaking sentence, the rumble of stage scenery and some staginess of dialogue.

Conrad wrote *Under Western Eyes* perhaps to bring a harder Western focus upon a theme of Dostoevsky. There is an evident Polish contempt for the lack of fixed positions in the Russian mind; or, at any rate, an ironical wonder at its readiness for cynicism. With brilliant ingenuity he caps scene after scene with its opposite. The exalted assassin is plainly sensitive about the 'greatness' of his action. Razumov has acted from a sense of right and discovers even *that* will not be its own reward; exile alone is possible. Guilt (as always in Conrad) marks the drifter. Yet even exile is poisoned, though not by remorse; it is poisoned because the authorities can now force Razumov to become a spy on the revolutionaries as the price of concealing his act. Razumov is obliged to take on the mind of a guilty man when, by his morality, he is virtuous; in doing so, and by contact with Haldin's young sister in Geneva, he comes to see the innocent and honourable illusions that precede conversion to revolutionary action. The inevitable Russian confession follows, not because Razumov has changed his mind, but because he longs for moral freedom.

What is contemporary in this book is the response to seediness, treachery, slackness and corruption. This response is the direct product of the last words of Heyst in *Victory*:

> Woe to the man whose heart has not learned while young to hope, to love – and to put his trust in life.

Conrad himself found a strong if not lasting interest in the order and discipline of life at sea, and his scorn is softened in *Under Western Eyes* by the attempt of one kind of Slav to understand another. In *The Secret Agent* there is no such emotional entanglement; his scorn, unrestrained, now becomes almost overpoweringly rich and pungent and his irony leaves nothing standing.

The masters of Conrad's day were Meredith and Stevenson, and Conrad's book about the lazy *agent provocateur* who gets his feeble-minded brother-in-law killed by mistake shows the strong influence of these writers. *The Secret Agent* is a thriller, a very artificial form of writing which realism rarely redeems from its fundamental fantasy. No thriller can be believed and even when meaning and psychological ingredients are put into it, its people and events cannot really bear the weight. *The Secret Agent* begins with the incredible character of Vladimir, the absurd, highly stylised intellectual plotter, and the artifice is at odds with the truly real and powerful elements in the book: the descriptions of London, the portraits of those perfect if intellectually diagnosed Londoners, Mrs Verloc, her mother and Steve. Outside of this warm, human centre Conrad is dangerously exhibitionist. Here conscience has its sardonic comedies and he seems superbly to be showing off his obsession with the dirtiness, the shabbiness of foolish or dishonoured minds:

> His descent into the street was like the descent into a slimy aquarium from which the water has been run off.

A detail like that – and Conrad is a master of image – describes a London street and defines the book. Verloc's birth control shop takes one down and down to the grubbiness of London's back streets and the pathetic vulgarities of cheap civilisation.

Conrad's genius was for picturesque discussion rather than for narrative – he was tortured, one is told, by the difficulties of invention – and what always impresses is his rummaging about, back and forth, in the lives of his characters. Verloc, the agent, is wonderful in his laziness, his dull humour, his amorousness, his commonplaceness and his injured vanity. It was a master-stroke to make this destroyer respectable and to pounce upon the isolation – once more, the Conrad theme – in which this foolish member of the French letter trade lived. Towards the end, when the idiot Steve has been killed through Verloc's irresponsibility, it is wonderful that Verloc quite unblinkingly expects the tragedy to make no difference to his relations with his wife. After all, she has got *him*! The murder is not well done. It is, in fact, too cleverly done, with an eye for all the effects and shows Conrad at his most self-conscious. The crime is in keeping with the contrived tone of the book, the general unsavoury sapience; but the author's irony is too much with us. Mrs Verloc is as wonderful as the husband she kills. She is a simple, reserved woman, governed by the desire for security, living on two or three strong and usually concealed feelings. Her words, in the London way, rarely reveal what these are; in fact the way in which she talks off the beat of her feelings the whole time is well-observed. But when she discovers that her husband is a monster, that he is a worse monster because he does not realise it or does not see why *that* should upset his domestic bliss; when she realises he is a moral idiot and that his reply to grief is 'Let her have her cry. I'll go to bed with her, that'll put her right,' a terrifying woman rises up with a carving knife in her hand. Afterwards, it is perfect that she relapses into the simple resource of a feminine guile, so pathetically vain, that a crude crook can do her down as easy as winking.

Head, the police superintendent, is another sound portrait. His Assistant Commissioner belongs to the dubious higher moral reaches which thriller writers have a perennial fancy for: contact with crime and the police sows in them the desire to have everything taped: God comes to Scotland Yard. The Assistant Commissioner, one notices, has the now professional 'sense of loneliness, of evil freedom', but this is, at the last moment, made real to us by one of those sardonic afterthoughts by which Conrad saves himself from sentimentality. The Assistant Commissioner, we are told, finds 'the sense of loneliness and evil freedom *rather pleasant*'. This is indeed why he is an Assistant Commissioner: he is a hunter. (It is always, in Conrad, the small additional comment that puts on the rounding and convincing touch.)

Conrad, the exile, the isolated man, was the master of any atmosphere. That gift comes at once to the sensibility of the émigré. Like the French novelists, like Meredith and Henry James, he moves in narrative from idea to idea, to the change in moral climate rather than from event to event. The first part of *Under Western Eyes* comes beautifully to a close on Councillor Milukin's short inquiry when Razumov says he is going to retire: 'Where to?' Obviously there is nowhere. Conrad's novels are marked by such crucial sentences, which change a whole view of life, and his dramas are the dramas of the change of view. Conrad, the dilettante, takes the soul or the conscience, and tries them now in this position, now that; a new Good means a new guilt. Heyst in *Victory* knows the reason: the son of a brilliant man who has seen through all human values, Heyst is a born exile in a world that shocks. His aim must be to avoid committal. But like the Captain in *The Secret Sharer* who has the runaway hidden in his cabin, Conrad also has the committed 'double' in his life. This dichotomy provides the drama and the rich substance of his books.

The Octopus

═══

It was like a visit to the theatre or the waxworks. One walked into the
Langham Hotel out of the London daylight and was shown, at last, into a
large, darkened apartment twinkling with candles. Heavy black velvet
curtains were drawn over the windows; masses of exotic flowers were
banked against them and, enthroned in an enormous bed in the midst of all
this, sat the genius: a small, ugly, dank-eyed woman with her hair down
her back, scratching away fast with a quill pen on large sheets of violet-
tinted paper and throwing each sheet on to the floor when it was done with.
A large dog guarded the morning's work from the visitor's touch. One had
gone to have one's head bitten off either by Ouida or her dog.

Ouida would be under thirty at this time, a woman with her father's
excessive nose and a rude grating voice. Already conceit, indeed megalomania, had settled on a theatrical character. She is not the first novelist to
have delusions of grandeur – Scott had his Abbotsford, Balzac had coronets
put on his luggage – for when one is dealing in fantasy, it is not unnatural
to help oneself. In the secret room of Ouida's life, where the shames of her
childhood in Bury St Edmunds were hidden, there must have been a
shrewd, hard, frightened being which stiffened its chin and told her that she
had earned the right to folly and exorbitance. She had become the most
famous novelist then living in the world when she was hardly out of her
teens; she had slaved as only the bestsellers can; she had raised her
unhappy mother from poverty to wealth; she had proved that the 'realities'
so meanly admired in a gossiping provincial town were despicable. She
was original. The daydreams of an adolescent girl had been imposed
successfully upon herself; they were triumphantly imposed upon the
world. How was it done? At the end of her life when she lay dead of neglect
in a wretched Italian tenement, her maid reverently placed two of her
mistress's quill pens on the table at the foot of the bed. The quill which had
flamed over the violet paper in the gloom of the Langham, which had

[539]

tossed ahead of the sprawling cavalry charge of Ouida's prose, had once more proved itself mightier than the reviewer's bitter pen.

Firbank, as Miss Bigland, a new biographer, and other critics have pointed out, had read his Ouida. The daydreams of Bury St Edmunds where her plausible French father came to fill her head with nature lessons, tall stories of international plots and the dazzling intrigues of European courts, were the daydreams of the whole of middle-class England and America. Liberal democracy was bored with its routine. The aristocracy and idle rich with their Turkish tobacco and their tremendous sins – how these haunted the heads of Victorian wives and their hard-working husbands. It did not matter that Ouida was ignorant of the fashionable world; all the better could she describe what the fashionable *ought* to look and sound like. The fashionable world itself, so childishly romantic and sentimental underneath its brisk airs and its levity, rather wished it like that, too. Her novels were the fantasies of the outsider, of those who have to keep their station in life, of those who, obeying all the rules and calculating all the main chances, keep one corner in their minds for visions of an insouciant and gorgeous race which performs such non-interest-bearing acts as wrecking a career 'to save a woman's name from the breath of slander', and lives with heroic and insolvent melancholy in recklessly furnished rooms. 'Beauty', the guardsman,

> had the drawing-room floor of a house in Kensington Gore, well-furnished and further crowded with crowds of things of his own, from Persian carpets bought on his travels to the last new rifle sent home only the day before . . .
>
> A setter, a retriever and a couple of Skyes

(Ouida was always crowded with crowds of dogs) –

> were on the hearthrug (veritable tiger skin). Breakfast in dainty Sèvres silver stood on one table sending up an aroma of coffee, omelettes and devils; the morning papers lay on the floor, a smoking cap was hung on a Parian Venus; a parrot, who apparently considered himself master of the place, was perched irreverently on a bronze Milton, and pipes, whips, pistols and cards were thrown down on a Louis Quinze couch, that Louise de Kérouaille or Sophie Arnould might have graced. From the

inner room came the rapid clash of small-swords, while 'Touché, touché, touché! Riposte! Holà!' was shouted, in a silvery voice, from a man who, lying back in a rocking chair in the bay window of the front room, was looking on at a bout with the foils that was taking place beyond the folding doors.

Snobbery is often a form of romanticism; it is the chastity of the perfectionist. But on Ouida's level romance is not romance until it is snobbish; and not, we may say, as we look back upon the Victorian novel, on her level alone. One of the better rumours about Ouida's novels was that they were the secret work of the not very nice George Eliot; and do not George Eliot's heroines unfailingly go up in the world as they become more refined by moral struggle? Are there not pages of Tennyson that look like Debrett put into verse? And are there not, indeed, modern novels in which souls are brought humbly to the Faith by the glamorous sight of an earl on his deathbed? The material luxury of Ouida's early novels, with their crammed marble halls and their general air of being expensive bazaars of history, is the expression of an expansive society becoming every year richer on colonies and luxurious colonial wars. And is it far-fetched to see in the hysterical dialogue of her books something of the repressed emotional violence of Victorian society? Why else this taste for melodrama and the smell of sulphur:

'Your lips were mine,' she cried, laughing still in that mocking mirth, 'their kisses must poison hers. Your hand slew him! its touch must pollute hers. Oh, lover, who lived on my smile! Did you not know the dead love would rise and curse the new?'

There can be no doubt when one has read Miss Bigland's account of Ouida's painful and ludicrous love affair with the Marchese della Stufa in Florence that she herself felt in phrases of this operatic violence. And underlying it is her curious, rather seductive melancholy, the fervid not unintelligent Byronism which her French father must have brought over to Bury St Edmunds from the Continent. (What happened to him? 'Only the Emperor knows.') It was a sadness all the more romantic for being decked out with shrugs, floods of ungrammatical French and Bohemian cynicism; and it was also the inevitable undertone of the daydreamer's life as, exhausted, she wakes up from her drug.

[541]

Miss Bigland's new life of Ouida is fuller than the memoirs already in existence. There are still many mysteries, but it is a just book and cannot help being entertaining. It is marred, however, by a prose that is stiffened with clichés which are a good deal duller than Ouida's. What takes one's breath in nearly every detail of Ouida's life is her boldness, her huge guzzling confidence in her powers, her ability to impose her life, as if she herself were a work of the imagination and not a human being. One is aware of a gusher. There is an appalling vitality which is undistracted by self-criticism or unstayed by the existence of any other person. She plays up shamelessly to the men. She had, for the purposes of her work, an extraordinary speed of assimilation, a greed for more facts to be turned into more dreams. Her so-called immorality – Miss Bigland has no difficulty in showing that Ouida was a prudish woman whose sensual desires had been sweepingly sublimated – enabled her to break conventions and, for example, to give dinners 'for Guardsmen only' which were very useful in supplying her with local colour as well as giving her the best kind of publicity: the scandalous. A word or two about the Foreign Legion, a skirmish, an Arab café, and men who wish 'to forget', would soon be transfigured by her reckless imagination. She saw the thoroughbreds crushing the skulls of the enemy; she threw in an abduction. Her tragedy (some thought) was that she was a *grande amoureuse* who was too ugly to find a lover. One suspects that her only 'lover' had been that elusive refugee, her father. Though she may be said to have been continually in love all her life with one man after another, there are no signs that her love was anything more than a terrifying and possessive hallucination and often known to herself alone; if disclosed, it drove every man to horrified flight. He had seen the octopus and it wore white satin.

Ouida was an actress who never settled to her role. Now she was a foreign aristocrat, now the great political figure, now the humanitarian defending the virtuous poor against the wicked rich, now the cynic as wilful as her one remarkable creation, the Cigarette of *Under Two Flags*; now the misunderstood artist, who will not sell her soul to a public of hucksters. They were the leading roles of an internal drama.

Her financial recklessness, which ultimately ruined her, was another egotistical refusal to face reality. One need not go into her endless quarrels with her friends, her appalling rudeness, her idiotic lawsuits which made her a byword. And yet, as many intelligent and sensitive people thought, the impossible woman had some talent. Her conversation was often worth hearing. The kind of tragic dignity of the battered dreamer attends her end. A total independence of human kind – they imposed reality – was her desire. Her unassuaged personal emotions were unloaded upon her swarms of dogs; for them she fought her friends, quarrelled with the Italian authorities and indeed, in the end, starved and neglected herself.

There are some apologists for the novels of Ouida. She is said to have been an influence, though it is surely unkind to see it extending to Lawrence, as Miss Bigland does. We must agree, however, that she raises an early peacock wail of passion in the Victorian novel. *Pascarel* (which is admired) seems to me watery and unreadable stuff. The studies of the lives of the Italian poor are more interesting; they indicate a break with the earlier English preoccupation with Italy and, indeed, Ouida with a social conscience is a sentimental but bold writer. As Miss Bigland justly says, the reviewers who brought academic guns to bear on her fiction were themselves a little ridiculous in their solemnity. I have read only two or three of her novels and of these I prefer the unredeemed like *Under Two Flags* and *Strathmore* to the more respectable ones; the cigars, the passionate riding crops, the Rhenish of her country houses, the shooting women of her Algerian camps and the overproof Cognac of her Parisian Avernus, to the trite Italian works of her reformed period. I confess, I have not read *In Maremma* which is praised for its landscape. Shockingly repetitive as she was, wild in her skiddings across drawing-rooms and deserts, she was not without shrewdness. She had an eye for raffish character. One responds to the tidal wave of her awful vitality, the terrific swamping of her prose. One would have given anything to go to her parties in Florence. Mr E. M. Forster has told us that it is the novelist's duty to 'bounce' us. Ouida does that with all her might; so hard, indeed, that her novels bounce high out of sight into that luscious upper air – somewhere between Mayfair and the moon – where the super-ego practises its incredible scales and beats its frightful bosom. In its way, her stuff is more honest than the worst of Disraeli or Bulwer Lytton from which it derives; and more genial than the Barclay and Corelli for whom she prepared the way.

[543]

Firbank

Fun in English literature is as regular as muffins; the honest bell rings in the sad fog of the London Sunday and we stir ingenuously between one indigestion and the next, in our drowsy chairs. Poke the fire, bring in the tea, and soon, if we cannot be gay, we shall be cheery. But folly is rare. High-voiced, light-headed, dangerous and abashing, it flocks in its own mad air, just beyond the reach of our hands. Congreve, Peacock have it now and then, Hood has a little, Lear, Lewis Carroll, Wilde and Beerbohm play with this brilliant and tragic froth. It is for the few writers with missing hearts, whose clown eyes and enlarged ears live for themselves alone; the comfort and normality of fun are alien to it. Like wit, folly is the child of the collision, the smash-up; its laugh is heard just as the last pane of glass goes out of the window and the first groans are heard. Something fatally damaged has to be feverishly replaced; an intolerable vacuum must be filled; a gag must plug the awful abeyance. We feel this at the ballet, the most lyrical and cruel of the arts; maimed in the power of speech and ordinary sense, human beings are transposed into impulse and movement, to what can go on without heart, to the cold poetry of self-parody.

To the ballet the reader's eye strays when he is reading the wild satires and fairy tales of Ronald Firbank – *Valmouth, The Flower Beneath the Foot, Prancing Nigger, The Eccentricities of Cardinal Pirelli, The Artificial Princess.* They are antics in a void left by life, elegies on burst bubbles. They celebrate the unworldliness of the rich, the childishness of aristocracy, the ubiquity of priests, the vim of the sensual life, the venom and the languor of taste and pleasure. They commemorate the comi-tragedy of the superlatives and fashions in which the heart thrills and dies a hundred times a day. There are anecdotes in Sir Osbert Sitwell's very funny, very touching and very acute portrait of Ronald Firbank, in the introduction to these novels; in one, it is said that Firbank once sold a Welsh cemetery. In another there is a tremendous purchase of orchids. In another he eats a single pea for lunch. Between the laughter of the macabre and the tears of extravagance, his hair-raising talent wanders, an unattached faculty in a world of its own. In their inexplicable way aesthetes like Firbank – but there have been none, of course, *like* him, for none has his wailing, brain-splitting, peacock laugh – transpose the smash-up of their time more clearly than many a writer whose earnest ear is to the ground. And it is a simple fact that technically Firbank cleared dead wood out of the English novel, in one or two convulsive laughs; laid down the pattern for contemporary dialogue twenty or thirty years ago and discovered the fact of hysterical private humour – the jokes the mind makes and does not communicate. If narrative and speech have speeded up, if we can swing out of one episode into another, without an awful grinding of literary gears, if we can safely let characters speak for themselves and then fail to keep up a conversation, if we can create an emotion by describing something else, it is in part due to Firbank's frantic driving.

Let us grant that Firbank's baroque paradises, his jazz-band kingdoms, his over-heated and flower-stuffed conservatories would have been intolerable if he had been a larger writer, and had not the skids and evasions of startling economy by nature. *Valmouth* is very pretty, but the beautiful note of weariness which has been carefully sounded becomes wearisome itself. The Negress and masseuse is, in action, a boring symbol of a virile culture and has the strictly limited speciality of a homosexual joke. Firbank is an on-and-off writer. One inhales him and it is important not to take too much at a time. Even so, he is tricky; for as one turns the page for the next hilarious breath, the story is over and one is caught with an empty nose. It is not easy to say what the novels are about, though we shall remember surgical sentences and wounding paragraphs by heart. *Prancing Nigger*, the most felt of his books, and one which was originally intended as a kind of documentary study on the unhappy condition of Haiti, can be defined, perhaps, more closely than the rest. Mr Mouth, the evangelical Negro, and his simple pushing wife with a passion for society, are clearly going to their ruin, unaware that urban, industrialised Haiti is going to wring their hearts out of them; and there is in this book a rumble of indignation which replaces the stylish horror he lets fall in his satires on fashion and chic. A not very happy moral note is in this tale, and there is a rather gummy sentence or two about the evils of rootlessness, which are heavy on the tongue of a dandy; one cannot go in for both the stylish and the moral. But *Prancing Nigger* is made by its warmth and its lyrical pathos; and although Firbank may have made his Negroes sing hymns like

> Time like an ever-rolling stream
> Bears all its sons away

for the lark of it, the sentiment was close to his own sensibility to the transient in life. Time is his subject. He is a poet of the surface of life and the writers who can feather a surface are rare. The comedy is in the inconsequence; the poetry in the evanescence; the tragedy in the chill of loneliness and desolation which will suddenly strike in a random word. The element common to all these novels is melancholy: a girl's heart is broken, another's soon will be, fidelity is cut short by a shark and time cheats all these farded ladies who have spent their afternoons pleasantly cheating themselves and others. One follows these untrustworthy Royal Families and randy Princesses from the throne to the barouche, from the assignation to the confessional, through terraces and nunneries, embassies and balconies, lavatories and coronations, simply out of malice, to see egos as lethargic as *foie gras* ('Whenever I go out,' the King complained, 'I get an impression of raised hats'). Dissociation – we may guess – was the private smash of Firbank's stricken personality. His comic genius rises from the fatality of rarely seeing life steadily and never seeing it whole. It is in bits.

His art is to make stained glass out of the unlikely bits. The famous jokes come from that: 'How one's face unbends in a garden.' At a death bed: 'Her spirit soars: her thoughts are in the Champs-Elysées.' Of a woman putting her long head out of a box at the opera: 'She ought to hatch.'

The search for the *mot juste* disclosed to him the wild territories of the *mot injuste*. A man's kiss has an 'unsavoury aroma of tobacco and charcuterie.' 'Poor Princess! Has anyone the right to look so dying.' Or

> Nevertheless some late sirens were only arriving. Conspicuous among these was Catherine (the ideal-questing, God-groping, and insouciant), Countess of Constantine, the aristocratic heroine of the capital, looking half-charmed to be naked and live. Possessing but indifferent powers of conversation – at Tertulias and dinners she seldom shone – it was yet she who had coined that felicitous phrase: *Some men's eyes are sweet to rest in.*

[546]

But the word is not always unjust. The satirist of the mannequins turns into the poet, and this line on a broken heart might have come from the affecting Murasaki (perhaps it did: Firbank was a talented collector):

> Such love-blank, and aching void! Like some desolate and empty cave, filled with clouds, so her heart.

The 'new' slang: 'love-blank'; the dead cliché: 'aching void' are not accidents in that sentence. Firbank (one imagines) had the gift of shutting his eyes and testing society with his ears, so that the dead patter which was its soul, and the breathlessness which was its life, came over minutely, in crotchets and quavers and absurd chords to him like the whine of a tired dance band two floors below. He must have been the first disinterested, clinical listener to the lunacy of conversation, one of the first to notice the date of its sentences, and to telescope the rest.

It is pleasant to have five Firbank novels in one volume, but by the end one has had a surfeit. *The Eccentricities of Cardinal Pirelli* has a cloying and faded corruption and naughtiness. In general, the brilliant indecencies of Firbank (so wonderfully timed and without the tedium of lascivious lingering) are best when he is not being naughty about the nuns and priests. This kind of joke is wearying, a sort of Catholic convert smut which Firbank (who was a convert) did not escape. The best religious jokes are those in which the religious orders are treated as if they were so many *couturières*. The sisters of the Flaming Hood are always welcome. For myself, *The Flower Beneath the Foot*, with its wild account of an African visit to a European court, is the most successful of the satires. It is a sharp salad; and it contains the superb death-bed scene of the mad Archduchess. At the bedside the Princess is already writing the telegrams announcing the coming death:

> 'Poor Lizzie has ceased articulating,' she did not think she could improve on that and indeed had written it several times in her most temperamental hand, when the Archduchess had started suddenly cackling about Vienna.
>
> 'Sssh Lizzee – I never can write when people talk' – *Ultra* feminine, she disliked that another – even *in extremis* should absorb all the limelight.

That must be the highest point reached by Firbank's ecstatic love-hate of the elements of excess and rapacity in female character.

It is a surprise that so much of Firbank has survived from the Twenties, but as he is totally unreal and Fashion is eternal, he is dateless, though one can see that his freakishness may be despised and its décor become a bore. There is a force of feeling, scattered in his works, which recalls the ambiguous emotions we meet in John Betjeman's poems, and which gives his absurd world a vitality and determination of its own. His absolute originality, as well as his technical brilliance, seem to make his survival as a minor treasure inevitable. A virtuoso, he is the natural victim of mode; flimsier than Carroll, he does not create a memorable character except, possibly, Mr Mouth. Firbank's survival will be, one would say, like his work, on and off. It is the strength of detail that counts in writers like this; the taste – if that can outlast a generation – for a certain tone of voice, breathless, snobbish, frightening and full of malice. Unlike Max Beerbohm he is the incumbent of a fundamental literary innocence. In life, a hermit almost speechless, helplessly gesticulating, a bizarre and feather-headed traveller unable to communicate, Firbank would be found sitting among the silliest illustrated papers, 'getting ideas' from them, and seeing life – by some alarming but beneficent deprivation – flat and without perspective. Of our contemporary satirists he alone has the traditional quality of total artifice.

W. W. Jacobs

The scarcity of comic writing in the last thirty years or so is often remarked. It has vanished (some will say) with our happiness. It has gone with sanity and civilisation. The comic writer, who is above all a man of sense, has no place in our world. Certainly the attack on Zoschenko in Russia has indicated how unsympathetic official cultures are to the comic writer; and as far back as 1910 we had seen our own Wells abandon the cheerful greenery and sly alleys of comedy for the straight asphalt paths of propaganda. The apostasy seems inevitable when we consider the two wars. The break-up of the small patterns of living, the levelling of local life and its absorption into larger patterns, have turned characters into citizens. Mr Polly and Kipps break out of their cages now; they need submit no more to the local pressure that cramped their style and made them comical. For it is the pressure of set circumstances that helps to form and encrust the comic character and the only pressure one can see nowadays in our fluid society is of the kind that comes from inside a character rather than from his environment. I am thinking of the weight of personal mania; the English comic characters of our generation – the characters of Waugh, Wyndham Lewis, Firbank – are noticeably mad. They are without attachments, but like human snails they carry a house of private madness on their backs. How different the new comic is from the fixed characters of our tradition may be seen by going back to the last of the old school, to the stories and novels of W. W. Jacobs.

Jacobs had the fortune to grasp a small, fixed world at its moment of ripeness and decline, a time always propitious to the artist. A Thames-side clerk, Jacobs knew the wharves where the small costing ships and land-hugging barge fleets tied up on their rounds between London and the wizened, rosy little towns of the Essex estuaries. This was a fading traffic: the cement, the flour, the bricks, the road flints, were more and more being diverted to the railway; the small mills and shippers were being devoured by the larger firms; the little towns with their raucous taverns and fighting inhabitants had already quietened; and unemployable and unspeakable old men sat on the posts of the empty quays, refining upon their memories of a past, spicy in its double dealing, prone to horseplay and cheered by the marital misfortunes of others:

'Love?' said the nightwatchman, as he watched in an abstracted fashion the efforts of a skipper to reach a brother skipper on a passing barge with a boathook. 'Don't talk to me about love, because I have suffered enough through it. There ought to be teetotallers for love the same as wot there is for drink, and they ought to wear a piece of ribbon to show it, the same as teetotallers do . . . Sailormen give way to it most; they see so little o' wimmen that they naturally have a high opinion of 'em. Wait till they become nightwatchmen, and having to be at 'ome all day, see the other side of 'em. If people only started life as nightwatchmen there wouldn't be one arf the falling in love that there is now.'

To these rosy and high-tempered seaports whose lattice windows flashed with the light of the silver estuary mud, no stranger ever came, unless it was a gentleman-painter who disgusted the patriots by painting only the ruins; the yachtsmen, holidaymakers and estate agents of a later day had not yet appeared, to dissolve the nightwatchmen in free drinks and to develop in the young an even more ferocious financial cunning than their fathers had. In other words, Jacobs found a world unstained by change, its inhabitants contentedly absorbed in the eternal human problem of how to get the better of one another, a fruit mellow and ready to fall into the comic artist's hands. The coachmen of Dickens, the landowners of the Russians, the booby squires of Sheridan and Fielding had been in their time precisely at this point of ripeness. The talent of Jacobs is a small one, when he is compared with the masters, but like theirs, his type are not chosen until they are already dated; like theirs his humour is fantastic and artificial. No notions of realism or social purpose, as Mr Henry Reed rightly says in an introduction to *Dialstone Lane*, cross his mind: he writes, so to say, from the ivory fo'c'sle. He recognises that in his nightwatchmen, his decisive widows, his sailormen, he is dealing with an advanced and sophisticated culture which has become firmly barnacled on the coarse surface of common life; and that the elegance, the speed, the riposte and the intricate plotting of something like Restoration comedy, can alone do justice to his highly developed people. Any page of his many short stories will illustrate this; indeed, only in his macabre stories, like *The Monkey's Paw*, or, as Mr Reed points out, in the ambitious *Master of Craft*, will one find anything like realism. I take this from *Dialstone Lane*:

'I've got her,' said Mrs. Chalk triumphantly.

'Oh!' said Mr. Chalk.

'She didn't want to come at first,' said Mrs. Chalk. 'She'd half promised to go to Mrs. Morris. Mrs. Morris had heard of her through Harris the grocer and he only knew she was out of a place by accident. He . . .'

Her words fell on deaf ears. Mr. Chalk, gazing through the window, heard, without comprehending, a long account of the capture of a housemaid which, slightly altered as to name and place, would have passed muster as an exciting contest between a skilled angler and a particularly sulky salmon.

Mrs. Chalk, noticing his inattention at last, pulled up sharply.

'You're not listening!' she cried.

'Yes, I am; go on, my dear,' said Mr. Chalk.

'What did I say she left her last place for, then?' demanded the lady. Mr. Chalk started. He had been conscious of his wife's voice and that was all. 'You said you were not surprised at her leaving,' he replied slowly, 'the only wonder to you was that a decent girl should have stayed there so long.'

Mrs. Chalk started and bit her lip. 'Yes,' she said slowly. 'Go on. Anything else?'

'You said the house wanted cleaning from top to bottom,' said the painstaking Mr. Chalk.

'Go on,' said his wife in a smothered voice. 'What else did I say?'

'Said you pitied the husband,' continued Mr. Chalk thoughtfully.

I have quoted only the overture to the gruelling hazards of Mr Chalk's relations with his wife; Jacobs has something like Fielding's gift, which came from the stage, for capping situation with situation, for never letting sleeping dogs lie. Two things will strike us about that passage: first, the lack of conventional facetiousness. Facetiousness gets shriller and lighter;

humour sinks deeper and deeper into its ribald and wicked boots. The other point is that the extreme elaboration of Jacob's wit, the relentlessness of his innuendo, are applied to the traditional subjects of the English music-hall: the mother-in-law, the knowing widow, the fulminating wife and the henpecked husband, the man who can't pass a pub. Fighting, black eyes, man-handling, horseplay, stealing of people's clothes, assuming disguises, changing names, spreading lying rumours, the persecution of one man by his mates for a lark, are the common coin. A man in love is fair game. Bad language is never given verbatim, but it is never let pass. (The old jokes about swearing are given a new polish. Mr Henry Reed quotes this jewel: 'The langwidge 'e see fit to use was a'most as much as I could answer.' Only Mark Twain's Mississippi boatmen could equal that.) The laziness of the working-man is another stock joke which, in spite of political pressure, has not yet died; indeed only the false teeth joke is missing. The feminine side of the mixture is conventional music-hall too. There is no sex. There is no hint of illicit love. With this goes a low opinion of married love. Young girls are pretty, tidy, heartless and always deceptively grave. They flirt. They terrorise with their caprices like any Millamant. They outwit everyone. It is their brief moment. Presently they will become mothers of ten squalling kids; and their husbands will be beating them; or they will become strong-willed monsters, the scolds of the kitchen, the touchy and jealous Grundys of the parlour.

Material of this kind dates when it is used realistically and it would be simple to show that Jacobs draws the working-class and the lower middle-class as they were before even the Nineties; and treats them as comics for reasons that are, unconsciously, political. It is certain that Polly and Kipps, for example, are greater characters than the Nightwatchman or thick-headed knockabouts like Ginger Dick, simply because Wells relates them to something larger than themselves. That is to attribute no artistic falsity to Jacobs's characters; they are merely limited and within those limits they are perfect. Jacobs's general impression of the poor is sound; the psychology of sailors, shopkeepers and so on is exact. And one important aspect of working-class character, or at any rate of male character when very ordinary men are thrown together, is strongly brought out and justifies his intricate plots from Nature; I refer to the observation that the rapid, oblique leg-pulling talk, with its lies and bland assertions which no

[552]

one believes, is part of the fine male art of cutting a figure and keeping your end up. The plots in Jacobs are the breath of the fantasticating life of men. They are superior to the plots of a writer like O. Henry. They spring naturally from the wits of the characters as trickery comes naturally to cardsharpers; they seem to pour off the tongue.

The flavour and the skill of Jacobs are of course all in the handling of the talk. At first sight the talk looks like something merely funny in itself; but Jacobs had the art of adding the obstacle of character to narrative:

'Come here,' said the mate sternly.

The boy came towards him.

'What were you saying about the skipper?' demanded the other.

'I said it wasn't cargo he was after,' said Henry.

'Oh, a lot you know about it!' said the mate.

Henry scratched his leg but said nothing.

'A lot you know about it!' repeated the mate in rather a disappointed tone. Henry scratched the other leg.

'Don't let me hear you talking about your superior officer's affairs again,' said the mate sharply. 'Mind that!'

'No sir,' said the boy humbly. 'It ain't my business, of course.'

'What ain't your business?' said the mate carelessly.

'His,' said Henry.

There is no doubt that Jacobs is one of the supreme craftsmen of the short story. It is extraordinary that he should have brought such pellucid economy to material that was, on the face of it, stuff for schoolboys, or the Halls; but in doing so, he transformed it. The comic spirit was perhaps his thwarted poetry. He knew his limits. The only carelessness or rather the only indifference in his work appears in his novels. Of these *A Master of Craft* suggests a partial attempt at the Mean Street realism of the period; and a desire to go beyond his range; it contains a lady-killing skipper – instead of the usual skipper-killing lady – and he is, for Jacobs, an ugly character. Jacobs shows his wounds a little in this book; but, for some reason, he slips back into his shell. I think we may be glad he decided to remain in the ivory fo'c'sle. The artificial, the almost pastoral Jacobs of *Dialstone Lane* is more satisfying. The spring sunlight of pure malice and self-possessed sentiment gleams on this story about three gullible townsmen who dream of going to sea; and the story has two immortally awful wives in it: the oppressed and the oppressor. But it is a major error in the plot that the dream voyage actually takes place. Jacobs would never have been so slapdash in a short story.

The Hill-Billies

The vogue of Faulkner in France at the present time is easily understand-able. Writing after 1918 about a society which had not recovered from the Civil War and which was to be marked by the demoralisation of the period of Prohibition and the gangsters, Faulkner anticipated some of the circum-stances of the lawless life which rose in France under the Occupation and in the Resistance. Society was paddling in general crime, publicly selling the law at every street corner, and the college boy and his girl in *Sanctuary* were vicious replicas of the adolescents who had first appeared in Gide, and who, in the last war, moved beyond civilised judgment. The only comment possible came from the Negroes – the verse occurs in *Sartoris*:

> Sinner riz frum de moaner's bench,
> Sinner jump to de penance bench;
> When de preacher ax 'im whut de reason why,
> Say, 'Preacher got de women, jes' de same ez I.'
> Oh, Lawd, oh Lawd.
> Dat's whut de matter with de church to-day.

And the women had got the moonshine whisky.

Faulkner's obscure and rankling genius began to work at the point when, failing to find a place from which to make a judgment, he set to writing about people from the whirlpool inside them, floating along with experience as it came out. His confusing, difficult, punch-drunk novels are in fact elaborately patterned and, as time has gone by, they have become (I think, ingeniously) didactic; but they fill the demand made by some Existentialists for a novel without a centre and which works outwards from the narrator in all directions at once. They exploit 'the absurd', the cruel meaninglessness of existence and they hope, by making every instant of any character's consciousness a life and death matter, to collect at the end a small alluvial deposit of humanism.

Faulkner is an affected but seminal writer for those who are in situations similar to his. In England, because the situation does not exist or because our overwhelmingly strong social instinct can still fairly successfully cover up and deal with disintegration at the same time, Faulkner's vogue has passed. He was admired for his devices and as a romantic and exotic; he seemed to have opened rhetorical or poetic avenues into popular life and speech and to have caught a kind of Elizabethan dramatic spirit. In the end, Southern misery and his mannerisms palled. We had heard enough of hill-billies for a lifetime and he seemed to be an obsessed provincial stewing too long in his own juice.

Soldier's Pay is Faulkner's earliest work in prose. Reading it again, one sees immediately, it is much fresher than the later, ruminating and didactic Faulkner. It has the lyrical hardness, the mark of experiment, the crispness of design which were to be found in *Light in August* and *The Sound and the Fury*, and is written before Faulkner became so deedily engrossed in his own complexity. He belongs to the period of difficult writing, obliquity, the self-propagating image that grows like a brilliant fungus all over his prose. And when this Southern dandyishness is given up, he is apt to convey the agony of the South in an agonising prose which appears to be chewed like tobacco and occasionally squirted out, instead of being written. The total effect is, however, hypnotic. After being trained for a generation since Joyce on difficult, associative writing, we ought not to be set back, and I can only suppose the English reader lacks the necessary links with the Southern Negro and poor white cultures. But there *is* more than that to the difficulty of Faulkner: it is not that he is allusive or perpetually putting fresh obstacles in the way of his vision, but that he gives all his allusions and obstacles the same value. I will quote a long passage from a late book, *Intruder in the Dust*, which describes the capture of a fugitive who has jumped into a river. In isolation it is excellent -- but, remember, a whole book has been written in this eye-blinding, mind-stunning incantation:

> . . . he saw the old man jump feet first off the bank and with no splash, no disturbance of any sort, continue right on not through the bland surface but past it as if he had jumped not into anything but past the edge of a cliff or a window-sill and then stopping, half-disappeared as

suddenly with no shock or jolt; just fixed and immobile as if his legs had been cut off at the loins by one swing of a scythe, leaving his trunk sitting upright on the bland, depthless milklike sand.

'All right, boys,' old Gowrie cried, brisk and carrying: 'Here he is. I'm standing on him.'

And one twin got the rope bridle from the mule and the leather one and the saddle girth from the mare, and using the shovels like axes the Negroes hacked willow branches while the rest of them dragged up other brush and poles and whatever else they could reach or find or free and now both twins and the two Negroes, their empty shoes sitting on the bank, were down in the sand too and steadily there came down from the hills the ceaseless strong murmur of the pines but no other sound yet although he strained his ears listening in both directions along the road, not for the dignity of death because death has no dignity, but at least for the decorum of it: some little at least of that decorum which should be every man's helpless right until the carrion he leaves can be hidden from the ridicule and the shame, the body coming out now feet first, gallowsed up and out of the inscrutable suck to the heave of the crude tackle then free of the sand with a faint smacking plop like the sound of lips perhaps in sleep and in the bland surface nothing: a faint wimple wrinkled already fading then gone like the end of a faint secret fading smile, and then on the bank now while they stood about and over it and he was listening harder than ever now with something of the murderer's own frantic urgency both ways along the road though there was still nothing . . .

Faulkner clutches at every sight and suggestion with the avidity of suspicion and even mania, and all manias create monotony. This is true even of the mania for domestic realism in Defoe. But in that passage Faulkner is simultaneously conveying the effect of the event on a boy's mind – for the story is seen through the eyes of a boy. Faulkner's ambition is visually poetic and he is attempting the instantaneous delivery of a total experience. In all his novels, he is trying to give each instant of experience in depth, to put not only physical life as it is seen directly on the page, but all the historical and imaginative allusions of a culture at the same time. And to the eye alone. If the reader is stunned by the slow deliberate blow, that is precisely the effect Faulkner is seeking, for we do, in fact, live stunned and stupefied by the totality of our experience and our present position in our own life story is simply the little clearing we have cut and the devious fading path we have left behind us, in the jungle. Order, or at any rate pattern, is that which comes *afterwards* to this romantic novelist who begins in the middle of the mind. He is a man outside the imposed, clarifying authority of some established system of values. We do not really know the beginning of Faulkner's stories until we have reached the end, till we have worked our way out of the jungle.

Faulkner's method of story-telling requires no justification: ·it has the conundrum quality of a pattern, and intricate patterns are as interesting as elaborate plots. He is a superb creator of episode – the opening train scene in *Soldier's Pay*, the comic brothel scenes in *Sanctuary*, the account of the raid on the Federal breakfast table in the opening chapters of *Sartoris* – and when he creates passing character, the awful politician Snopes for example, the ink bites. But the true justification of the method is that it creates the South in depth as, I think, no other part of America has been created by a novelist since the time of *Huckleberry Finn*. American novelists have composed reports, records, chronicles of other regions, but the impression is of life in some passing, cynical, littered encampment; Faulkner, on the other hand, seems to be engaged in a compulsive task, as if he had undertaken awkwardly the building of a culture out of its ruins, as a one-man mission. And perhaps, because of its social tragedy, its knowledge of ruin and decadence, the guilt felt because of its crimes against the Negro, the South is America's richest artistic soil.

Faulkner has the ubiquity of the reporter who knows the corruption of a town or a region inside out. He has also the moodiness of the man of letters. His capacity to catch mood is apparent in *Soldier's Pay* when he placed a dying, speechless, returned soldier in the midst of his story and played the reviving post-war world of 1918 around him, as it moved into jazz and bootlegging. His lyrical power in that book is mannered, but his mannerisms represent a passionate attempt to burn the scene into our senses for ever. He is excellent at crowded scenes; in social life, in dances, court house gatherings, riots, train journeys, Saturday night streets, where a sinister action winds separately in and out among the wanderings of people. He is a novelist of journeys. He is no great hand, indeed he is painfully stiff, in describing the inner life of sensitive people; and he is too concerned with the visual scene for the crucial business of creating large characters. Even his distinctive people are minor figures, and this suggests sterility of imagination. But he is remarkable in grasping the essential fragment, the live coal which keeps a life going, so that we are aware of living among the unconscious motives of people and of knowing how they will act. His men are rarely friends, his women nearly always enemies except for idealised creatures like Mrs Powers in *Soldier's Pay*. He is especially good at shallow young women, whom he hates and exposes, but whose points and vanity attract him. His weakest characters are the rhetorical cynics whose Shakespearean tone adds a vague oratorical fog to the tale; but this strange mixture of artifice and realism is his native mixture. In all his people, except the figures of pure evil like Popeye, he is sifting until he comes down to the infinitesimal deposit of humanity. His brutality is frightening because it is sardonic and always has a theatrical twist – one thinks of the man, running with a petrol can at a lynching, who gets himself blown up by mistake.

Faulkner's sense of human pain and the damage done to people, their blank cruelties and the disguised suffering which they have accepted as part of the furniture of life, comes from a maturity rare in American novels; and he has shown here the power to grow out of the bitterness and cynicism and bragging sentimentalities which Hemingway never advanced from. In the didactic novels of his later period there is no uplift. He inculcates the rudiments of humanity, by cunning and the correcting of observation. If the boy in *Intruder in the Dust* is likely to side with the accused Negro, it is because he has learned to test his experience and to listen to his sensibility. He will always remember what the smell of the Negro really is after being wrapped in the old Negress's quilt in her cabin: it is the smell of poverty.

I do not know whether these merits could have made Faulkner a great novelist, but they make him a source. Rancorous and obsessive, he has carried his quarrel with his region very wide, like some preacher chased out of town. And, what subjects – the English novelist will sigh – he has to hand. What advantages a lawless society brings to the writer.

The Eye-Man

Art was the religion of the Twenties; originality was its attempt to invent rituals. It was a time of calculated disorientation, of the impertinent even perverse occupation of new sites, a time of disconnection and energy in the arts. What would a total reconsideration of everything, from the word upwards, reveal? The result – as we glance back over the works of the period – was a good deal of physical glitter and exhibition and some pomposity; but, now time has ebbed away, some of the carefully constructed ruins of the time remain impressive – in their strange way, like paralysed and abandoned machines, the works of Wyndham Lewis most curious of all. They do not rust or decay, no ivy grows about them, they cannot be used and have never been assimilated into the landscape; old block-busting guns and tanks skewed on the abandoned field, they stand still, fantastic without their thunder. Their interest lies in their massive detail, for their purpose has become academic; we wonder why such rage was worked up in *The Apes of God*, why such electric flashes were sent out by *The Childermass*; until it dawns on us that these peculiar objects were machines for destructive laughter, whose target was really less interesting or, at any rate, harder to pinpoint than the glorious noise they made.

I do not mean that Mr Wyndham Lewis's thought-war was useless; apart from anything else it was provocative, and its attempt to recondition classicism was interesting, though it led to political folly. But every artist understands himself. Mr Wyndham Lewis wrote of his character Tarr that the 'curse of humour was on him, anchoring him at one end of the see-saw whose movement and contradiction was life,' and that he was 'a sort of quixotic dreamer of inverse illusions' who, unlike Quixote, 'instead of having conceived the world as more chivalrous and marvellous than it was, had conceived it as emptied of all dignity, sense and generosity.' It is the laughter that has remained and the curse has been removed from it. After twenty or thirty years *Tarr* is still an exposure of sentimental German romanticism – and ought to have warned Mr Lewis and ourselves of the silly nastiness of fascism – but it has become a considerable comic novel, a masterpiece of the period. It hangs round the company of Nashe, the Butler of *Hudibras*, the professional butchery of Smollett. Though it intellectualises in the cosmopolitan manner of the period, and does its best to look like a foreign book – and I suppose it might be called a piece of Welsh exhibitionism – it is restrained by the fundamental good sense, the lack of final intellectual cruelty, in our tradition.

The new note in *Tarr* was the notion of human relationships as mere fodder for a new master-race, the artists, those distorted Martians, all eye and brain and the will to power. This brought back the physical grotesque to our comic writing. *Tarr* is theatrical in the Celtic way; it is the savage comedy of small things made large – hence the proper comparison with Swift. But when one critic in the Twenties called the portrait of Otto Kreisler 'almost Dostoevskian' there was an unconscious exactness about the description, for we are reminded of the comic Dostoevsky in his short, Westernised, civilised and expatriate phase, when he wrote *The Eternal Husband*. In a sense, Mr Wyndham Lewis has always been an expatriate and that condition enormously stimulates the brain at the expense of feeling; yet perhaps the tendency to continual over-stimulus in his writing was only a new version of the Welsh obsession with fantastic verbal image and the behaviour of giants. We can even imagine a thesis on his debt to Meredith. The common dangerous Germanic ingredients are obvious.

The early success of *Tarr* was partly due to its shrewd penetration of the German character at the right moment, after the first world war. The raw, beastly, foolish, mad and simple cry-baby Otto Kreisler, the eternal hysterical student, is almost a tragic character. Lack of feeling on the author's part, Mr Wyndham Lewis's high suggestibility, hold Kreisler back from the tragic apotheosis: he is ludicrous, detestable, pathetic. He comes, interestingly enough, very close to the character of the husband in Dostoevsky's Western novel. The memory of the second world war revives the accidental interest of *Tarr*, but Otto Kreisler and Montparnasse are so far away by now that they begin to have the picturesque, sentimental charm of an old-fashioned Bohemianism, rather than a disturbing psychological point. I would not undervalue the nostalgic quality *Tarr* has acquired in the course of a generation; but what strikes one still is that its originality in description, episode and attitude of character is more than innovation. It is an enlargement of the novelist's means; a new territory has been subdued: the *terrasse*.

Mr Wyndham Lewis's originality lies in his use of a non-literary eye, the eye of the painter. He does not judge by experience, association, feeling or cogitation, before he has first considered all the physical implications of what he has physically seen. An eye, promoted in this way to an uncommon, even perverse position of power, becomes inevitably sardonic, expert in false, freakish, intuitive juxtapositions. It is almost certain to be brutally funny; it will sometimes hit upon important general truths. And so we get his gift for fresh generalisation:

> 'Well then, well then, Alan Hobson – you scarecrow of an advanced fool farm –'
> 'What is that?'
> 'You voice-culture practitioner –'
> 'I? My voice? But that's absurd! If my speech . . .'
> Hobson was up in arms about his voice although it was not his.
> Tarr needed a grimacing, tumultuous mask for the face he had to cover. He had compared his clowning with Hobson's pierrotesque vanity; but Hobson, he considered, was a crowd. You could not say he was an individual, he was in fact a set. He sat there, a cultivated audience, with the aplomb and absence of self-consciousness of numbers . . .
> A distinguished absence of personality was Hobson's most personal characteristic.

The descriptions can be more precise, the more they are picturesque. Kreisler is shaving:

> His face, wearing, it is true, like a uniform the frowning fixity of the Prussian warrior, had a neglected look. The true Bismarckian Prussian would seek every day, by little act of boorishness to keep fresh this trenchant attitude; like the German student with his weekly routine of duels which regimen is to keep courage simmering in times of peace . . .

A dancer:

> a rather congested, flushed and bespectacled young woman, her features

set in a spasm of duty. It was a hungry sex in charge of a flustered automaton.

And, in action, the figures become as grotesque as clowns in a circus, enlarged by the coarse fancy of a child's eye:

> She crossed her legs. The cold grape-bloom mauve silk stockings ended in a dark slash each against her two snowy stallion thighs which they bisected, visible, one above the other, in naked expanses of tempting undercut, issuing from a dead-white foam of central lace worthy of the Can-Can exhibitionists of the tourist resorts of Paris-by-night.
>
> Tarr grinned with brisk appreciation of the big full-fledged baby's coquetry pointing the swinish moral under the rose and mock-modesty below stairs, and he blinked and blinked as if partly dazzled, his mohammedan eye did not refuse the conventional bait.

The descriptions of people, of places and scenes are often surpassed for gritty vividness in *The Childermass* and *The Apes of God*; but in those books they are so piled on in the monotony of a morbid glitter that they eventually kill their effect. *The Apes of God* can be read for one or two fine broad scenes of libel – the dinner party with the Finnish poet bawling his French verse – and for its general blood bath in the literary society of the Twenties. Its fatal limitation is triviality of subject; it was topical to attack the cult of art, but there is a whiff of provinciality about the odd man out. Exciting sentence by sentence, image by image, it is all too much page by page. The note of sanity is excellent, but sanity that protests too much becomes itself a kind of madness. *The Childermass*, a brilliant idea, stands still and stuttering. The fact is that the influence of Joyce, the determination to be *avant garde*, was ruinous to Wyndham Lewis as he went on. To blow up Bloomsbury was an excellent idea: to sit out the long persecution mania of a cold war was too much.

But *Tarr* is a perfectly shaped and classical work. The characters are tried by the traditional and always rewarding test of their love affairs; and these are subjected to the scornful criticising of the brain. Like some repressed and arrogant savage, the brain is brought forward to make fun of the sogginess of human sentiment. Tarr does not apologise for being a two-girl man; he does not moralise, he does not torture himself, he is not even cynical. Human beings are enjoyed as the dangerous animals who are determined – whatever fairy tales they may tell themselves or others – to have their cake and eat it. They are dangerous because they dream, and dreams create an inflated physical world. Human nature is disgraceful; the only thing to be said for it is that it may produce a little, a very little, Art.

Mr Wyndham Lewis's genius lies in his strange capacity for reducing mind to matter: 'her lips were long hard bubbles . . . grown forward with ape-like intensity, they refused no emotion noisy egress if it got so far.' Women for Kreisler are 'vast dumping grounds for sorrow and affliction', huge pawnshops in which he deposits himself in exchange for 'the gold of the human heart or any other gold that happened to be lying about.' Anything in life which becomes unmanageable – i.e., his failure as an artist – becomes converted into love. The pleasure of *Tarr* is that it wallows in the nature of the physical world: the butcher's shop provides many an analogy, not always coarse, indeed often comically delicate. The body is not respected; it is frequently insulted, especially if it is female, but the happiest love is where the laughter is loudest; on the other hand, it is recognised that we need a relief from the happiest love. We need – or at any rate Tarr in his sardonic way, and Kreisler in his suicidal way, need – something different from what we had before. The tail (when we become his character, the eye men) is invariably wagging the dog. There lies the virtue and the strain of his hard-hearted genius; he carries the burden of his laughter which has tipped the scale against life. But in Kreisler cadging, scrounging, loving, fighting, crawling back, breaking up parties and ending in murder and suicide, he has created a permanent character. (The fact is he created Hitler.) It is a strange experience to put down a masterpiece in which one has had the impression of not only knowing the characters but of giving them a pinch all over to see if they were ready for the comic pot of life on earth.

Fordie

════════

'I once told Fordie that if he were placed naked and alone in a room without furniture, I would come back in an hour and find total confusion.' Ezra Pound's joke about Ford Madox Ford hits the mark. Confusion was the mainspring of his art as a novelist. He confused to make clear. As an editor, as a source of literary reminiscence, he attracts because he is always sketching his way from inaccuracy to inaccuracy in order to arrive at some personal, translucent truth. His unreliability may have annoyed, but it is inspired.

As a novelist – and he wrote some thirty novels, nearly all forgotten – he is one of those whose main obstacle is his own talent. A Conrad cannot invent; a Lawrence cannot narrate: such deficiencies are fortunate. They force a novelist to compensate, with all his resources, so that we shall hardly be aware of what is lacking and shall, in any case, think it unimportant. Ford is obstructed less by his defects than by the effusiveness of total ability. He has been called brilliant, garrulous and trivial, but what really happened was that, with the exception of *The Good Soldier*, parts of the Tietjens trilogy and most of *The Fifth Queen*, he never sank into the determined stupor out of which greater novelists work. It is comforting to think that the unduly brilliant may eventually have their stroke of luck: *The Good Soldier* is a small masterpiece.

Interest in Ford's work is now reviving in England and in the United States, where technicians are studied with a useful if exhausting piety. Mr Richard Cassell has got in early with a handy, basic investigation, *Ford Madox Ford*. He is alert to the peculiar effects of the Pre-Raphaelites on Ford, the French influence on the English novel of the period, and so on, but does not discuss the curious romanticising of the idea of 'the gentleman' which has made Ford seem tiresome and false to the modern reader. The dilemma of 'the gentleman' preoccupied Shaw, James, Conrad, Galsworthy, and has even been revived in the latest novels of Evelyn

Waugh. It was once a burning topic – one that Forster, with his marvellous aversion to burning topics, ignored. But there are overtones in Ford's writing on the subject which recall his own criticism of what the Pre-Raphaelities felt about love – they swooned. Swooning about love was a way of not knowing the facts. Ford swooned about the country gentry, and nothing dates so much as fashion in love.

Still, *The Good Soldier* survives the swooning over the character of Colonel Ashburnham and does so because, for once, Ford had his excessive gifts under control. For once he remembered that if he was to be an Impressionist writer, he had better not confuse writing with painting. The confusion of memory need not be coloured; indeed, in writing, if the parts are too prismatically brilliant, the whole will become grey instead of luminous. As this novel shows, Ford was equipped by intelligence and by grief to be a moralist once he could be freed from the paint-box and, above all, from High Art. Conrad must have been a very bad influence on a man who had already too much vagueness in him; Henry James can have only been harmful to one with already so much consciousness. To them Art did nothing but good; the idea is excellent in itself; but it is dangerous to a man of talent who only very seldom in a laborious literary life hits upon a subject that draws out all his experience.

The Good Soldier and *The Fifth Queen* succeed. The former has the compact and singeing quality of a French novel; it is a ruthless and yet compassionate study in the wretchedness of conventional assumptions and society's war upon the heart. The latter is a historical romance and tells the story of Henry VIII and Katharine Howard; it suffers a little from Ford's chronic allusiveness, but a great issue is at stake and the ambiguities in it awaken all his interest in intrigue. His mind was one that hated conclusions, not because it was a sceptical mind but because it wanted to be put to one more test. From this spring his ingenuity as a story-teller – a gift so rare that it is often scorned – and his constant concern with technique. Critics have usually praised this technical capacity, but have said that this was all he had; yet it is – and one ought not to have to say so – a capacity of enormous importance. (Imagine that Jane Austen had left *Sense and Sensibility* in its epistolatory draft!) One can see that to a mind as given to confusion and to posture as Ford's was, technical capacity was his one reality. He asks nothing better than to be seen making difficulties work for

[566]

him. The famous device of the 'time-shift', which was a mania with him, enabled him to begin his scene in the middle and yet arrive with a whole tale of suspense that was thick with suggestion and memories caught on the way ashore.

In *The Good Soldier* the time-shift enabled him to effect those dramatic revaluations of people which give his novels their point. We had supposed, for example, that Leonora was vulgarly jealous when she slapped Mrs Maidan's face; but in a page or two we dart back in time to discover that there was another and stronger motive, one that exposes a hidden part of Leonora's nature: her shocked frigidity, her greed for money. When that is threatened, her passion for appearances collapses. In choosing for the narrator a dull and unemotional man who fumbles his way through a tale of passion which leads to death and madness, Ford has found someone who will perfectly put together the case of the heart versus conventional society, for he is a mild American Quaker perpetually astonished by Catholic puritanism. Meanwhile his own do-gooding wife is, unknown to him, a destroyer and nymphomaniac. Ford is often accused, by the hospital nurses, of criticism, of triviality, but in this book the trivia are sharp and enhance the awful dull force of the tragedy.

Rewrite *The Good Soldier* in straightforward narrative and Ford's vision of life as a minutely operating process of corrosion vanishes, and with that, of course, his particular Catholic outlook. Corrosion, as it is presented in this novel, means that we have more parts to our lives than one and that they work fatally upon each other. One has a quite extraordinary sense in the book of the minds of people perpetually thinking away their heart-beats.

Ford's preoccupation with technique – point of view, time-shift, *progression d'effet*, rendering and so on – was both a godsend and a curse, for he was constitutionally distracted, impatient and shy of coming to terms. By concentrating on the *means* of creating an impression he seems to have hoped, in some of his novels, to find that the means would suggest an end darker, more inscrutable and mysterious, than anything in the author's mind at the outset. Life was an intrigue that was never resolved, a meaningless experiment. This approach might lead, as it does in the works of Conrad, to fogginess; in Ford it could lead only to an excessive high-lighting of detail and to staginess. The secret, Romantic Ford leans too much on the ominous and sardonic outsider, the shadow figure breathing heavily down the neck of the reader, Art pretending to be Destiny. But when Ford is at one with his subject, as he is in *The Fifth Queen*, he stages well. His delight in playing fast and loose with time, in beginning a scene in the middle of a broken sentence, dropping it and picking it up again until the crisis is built up, his whole patterning and puzzling, are vividly justified.

He succeeds, more often than not, in his ingenious system of getting at the inside of things by looking intensely at the surface alone. This, of course, he inherited from the painters. He may see more than we can in the way people's hands lie in their laps, or how their legs look when they are kneeling, or how much of Henry VIII appeared as he went upstairs; but in the larger pictorial actions – Tom Culpepper rushing up drunk from Greenwich to Smithfield eager to see some martyrs at the stake because he'd never seen a burning before – the sense of daily life dancing by in a man's mind is wonderfully conveyed. Ford was a master of episode. If he is stagey, he does not ham. We notice, for example, that Tom Culpepper doesn't in fact see the actual burning because he gets into an absurd brawl. As a story-teller Ford recognised life when he saw complication and chance. His brutal scenes are benevolently comic; his women are originals; wherever there's human naïveté and deviousness he is as happy as Kipling was, but with compassion. And throughout there is no detail that fails to bear on the religious quarrel which is his central subject. He responded very much in all his work to the margin men and women leave in their minds, to their long-headedness; and one can see that he found a parallel between the corruption of the Reformation and that of the Edwardian world which had killed the heart, he would have said, by reducing virtue and honour to the condition of masks.

No doubt *The Fifth Queen* is too close to the eye in a cinematic way to have the spacious historical sense of a great historical novel like *Old Mortality*; it hasn't the coolness of Mérimée's superb short novel, the *Chronicle of Charles IX*; but it makes most of our historical fiction up to 1914 look like the work of interior decorators. Literature for Ford was a passion; its rituals were sacred. But there is no doubt about his moral seriousness or the cumulative effect of the main story. How, by what stages, will Katharine bring the King to the point of making his submission to Rome? How will the King procrastinate? What lies will trap the Queen? Will the

King, for once, be able to escape from his changeable and fatally political nature? What belongs to Caesar, what to God – and what to Good Learning? There is nothing allusive in the handling of this massive central conflict and it is brought to its climax without melodrama. One thing Impressionism could do was to catch the day as it passed through the minds of the actors in it. It could record confusion by a scrupulous and ingenious use of the means of art. Allowing for Ford's pleasant vanity in the imposture, this bravura piece – as Graham Greene calls it in his introduction to the Bodley Head collection of Ford's stories – is rather fine.

Half-English, half-German and, by fancy, French, Ford Madox Ford was nature's expatriate. His only country, he said, was literature. To be precise, it was 'the Novel'. He simply lived for it. Consider him as an incurable and dedicated work of fiction, one of the most diverting yet serious and instructive of 'living lies', and he becomes comprehensible. As a brilliant human being he was self-dispersing, moving from one hallucination to another, dumping his luggage in the hotel room of two or three cultures; he reassembled himself, for a while, in words and stories and in them he believed with an industrious and short-lived intensity. He succeeded in only three remarkable stories – *The Good Soldier*, the *Fifth Queen* trilogy and *Parade's End*. They vindicate his happy yet tortured incapacity to go straight from a starting-point, for he had none. They put his lack of self-confidence, his shortness of spiritual breath, his indolence, to use. They brought out and exploited with full resource the price he had to pay for his extraordinary cleverness: the emotion of anguish. One is tempted to say 'passion' also – but one has to hesitate here. The writers who convey passion also convey the terrible calm of its purgation and aftermath and Ford is too full of his own skill and ironical humour to allow that. But he does leave us with an indignant sense of unforgettable pain. One always finds that at the bottom of the baggage Ford left about the world.

Some pain is self-sought – the pain, for example, of our choice of impossible incarnations. It is hard, here, to separate the factitious from the inevitable. When he became incarnate as Tietjens in *Parade's End*, Ford could not obliterate Ford. One does not want him to do so, for Tietjens is Ford's anguished hallucination. No novelist can completely become another character; in Tietjens Ford constructed an English gentleman as only something like German romanticism or idealism could see him. Ford was

[569]

no gentleman; he was a fine artist. He seems minutely to have observed the type, and at the same time to have loaded him with history and an inhuman willingness to suffer everything for the sake of suffering. So often one has seen expatriates find their home in a past that has not existed: Ford's plain feudal Yorkshire squire, with his love of the pre-industrial way of life, his scorn of the vulgar modern world, his dislike of ambition, his irritable abstention, his martyred sense of decency, looks today like a romancing not about a man but a code.

When Ford created Tietjens the dilemma of the gentleman was very much the fashion, as I have said. These talented agrarians existed. The coarse businessmen, speculators and careerists were breaking in on them, the press had turned yellow, the conventions were shocking when they worked and even more shocking when they did not. If Tietjens and his scruples about sex and society seem odd now, they did not fifty years ago. Rock-like before the unanswered slanders of his bankers, his military friends, his father, his cold, promiscuous wife who tricked him over the paternity of his child, Tietjens was exactly the figure to expose by his silence and his suffering the rottenness of Edwardian society. Further, he was not a Roman Catholic but his wife was, and the curse on the Tietjens family is thought to go back to the Reformation and the thieving of Roman Catholic lands. This adds to Tietjens's martyrdom a touch of destiny which is pretty gamey stuff. That old row has been hung too long to be digestible. One is rather exasperated by Tietjens's stubborn determination to collect all the slings and arrows going; after all, where does the family get its millions from? From the sacred soil of a great estate? Hardly. Towards the end of the novel there is a hint that the family controls a lot of industry in Middlesbrough. Tietjens is just as much a child of the industrial revolution as anybody else. He may not like the men of the new order who were coming in just before 1914: not being gentlemen they were certain to cheat. But isn't he simply an idealiser of convention? One has a sneaking sympathy for his wife, who at one moment complains that her husband is trying to be Jesus Christ as well as the misunderstood son of a great landowner. Her cruelties are an attempt to turn a martyr into a man.

In creating Tietjens, Ford chose a character utterly unlike himself and did the detail admirably. He caught the obtuse pride of the social masochist. He caught the spleen of the gentleman because this accorded well with the ironic spleen that Ford himself felt as an artist, even when it was a pose. The gregarious, voluble, intelligent nature of Ford could not be prevented from mingling with the Yorkshire squire; what one does not accept in Tietjens is the romantic German aura. Any German can do a better job of being an English gentleman and Tietjens is just a Germanised squire. He is even a classical scholar.

Two more able American critics, John Meixner* and Paul Wiley†, have written studies that will stimulate the Ford addict, and both agree that *Some Do Not* is the best of the Tietjens novels. It is a complete 'Affair'; the famous time-shifts are well-patterned. And both understand that Ford, being an indolent man with little self-confidence and an observer before everything else, was best at beginnings. Any paragraph is better than a page. All the good things, large or small, are beginnings. The boredom we experience in Ford comes, indeed, from the strain of reading innumerable beginnings on every page. So these critics find that Tietjens does not grow. His wife turns melodramatically wicked as the book goes on. I don't entirely agree with the first part of the verdict: Tietjens may be better done in the earliest volume but he becomes more representative and important as a human being in the account of the war in France, and especially because his puzzling private life is in abeyance.

Ford's response to the war brought out his highest quality: his historical sense and his exactitude. He surveyed with sardonic relish the chaos of the staff officer's labours: the numbering and allotting, the terrible paper-work in a war no one understood. The Canadians are going up the line, but where are they? They have been held up somewhere by a train smash. What is to happen to the men they are supposed to relieve? Ah, now the Canadians have been found! And now we've got them, the orders have been countermanded. The intrigue and the rot at the base produce a natural defensive reaction: the chaos is intended by the politicians, the *embusqués* at home. And who are they? The new men, of course, the climbers and careerists. (This certainly was the legend of the period.)

The general picture of a whole society floundering is done with a wonderful precision and not in the form of easy diatribe. Tietjens is just the

* Ford Madox Ford's Novels, University of Minnesota Press, 1963.
†*Novelist of Three Worlds*, Syracuse University Press, 1962.

right kind of numbed Homeric figure to record the sudden killing of a man in the staff dugout, a man to whom he had refused leave; or the explosion of a mine and the rescuing of the buried. As a character Tietjens escapes from the cliché of almost all the war novels of that time in which the hero conveys that the whole war has been declared against him personally. Tietjens knows that a civilisation, or at any rate a class, is sinking. Responsible and capable, Ford-Tietjens has an unselfed and almost classical sub-Olympian view of the experience. Although he was self-consciously an impressionist, Ford has some inner sense of a moral order. Or, if not that, a moral indignation at the lack of it. Or, if not that, a taste for the moral consolations of defeat. He brings not only an eye but a judgment to what he sees.

There is something odd but also – from a novelist's point of view – tolerant about this judgment. A craftsman, through and through, in everything, Ford is interested in the way things are done. Even corruption has its curious status. What are gunners like, what are their interests, their follies, what is the *virtu* of the trade? He is deeply interested in the idle detail of human nature and his own lazy aloofness enabled him to catch the detail perfectly. A variety of scenes comes to mind: the death of O Nine Morgan or the astonishing scene where a gunner chases a solitary German with shells.

His antics had afforded these gunners infinite amusement. It afforded them almost more when all the German artillery on that front, imagining that God knew what was the matter, had awakened and plastered heaven and earth and everything between them for a quarter of an hour with every imaginable kind of missile. And had then abruptly shut up.

And it had all happened merely because Tietjens had lightly told a gunner that any Italian peasant with a steam-plough could pulverise a field at a cost of thirty shillings, which was cheaper than the cost of high explosives. As a craftsman the gunner was put on his mettle.

That incident is anecdotal, but Ford could create the people who lived the anecdotes. His art – particularly the theory of the time-shift – was in part based on an analysis of talk, the way it plunges and works back and forth. The method was perfected in *The Good Soldier*; in the later, Tietjens novel, it does not succeed so well. It often becomes a device for refusing to face a major scene. One has only a confused notion of what went on in the hotel bedroom when the drunken General broke in on Tietjens and his wife at a crucial point in their sado-masochistic relationship, when it is important that we should know all. Ford's view seems to have been that no one ever quite knows what goes on at the crucial moments of life. His craftsmanship becomes obscurely crafty at such moments, as though, with tiresome cleverness, he had decided that it was the business of art to impose chaos on order. At his worst, he turns never saying Yes and never saying No into an aesthetic neurosis.

Where do we place Ford in relation to the contemporaries he admired – James and Conrad? For Mr Meixner Ford was 'locked in the prison of his own theories' and lacked 'the personal audacity, the conquering boldness', required by a masterpiece. He was a penetrating historian, a man of fundamental insights, but he did little with them; his ingenuity made him intellectually thin. *The Good Soldier* succeeds because it is done in the first person, which allows him to rid himself of the stiff aloofness and impersonality he thought he was copying from the French – by a paradox this is his unmistakably French novel. He has not the range of a James or a Conrad, nor the mass of good work; but Conrad's characters are 'static and inert', despite the subtlety and penetration of his analysis; and Ford (for Mr Meixner) surpasses Conrad in *The Good Soldier* and *Some Do Not* because Ford's people have great inner life, are more various, more real, more fluid and more pleasing and more moving. I would have thought Conrad's sceptical moral sense, as a *déplacé*, was richer than Ford's. Compared with James, Ford goes deeper (for Mr Meixner) into the range of spiritual terror and anguish. If, after a lot of wrangling, one came to agree with this last point, one would have to qualify it by saying that the very nature of Ford's methods made these depths brief and rare; and that they came as a result of calculated shock. We feel the shock felt by Tietjens when O Nine Morgan is killed before his eyes; we are startled by the picture of Tietjens trying to recover his memory when his brain has been affected by bombardment – but these episodes remain superb fragments.

Mr Wiley is good at showing the consistency of Ford's career as a novelist and as theorist of the novel and pays a lot of attention to the forgotten works. Although the discussion of Ford's methods, in his last novel, *Vive le roy*, is interesting, it does not succeed in making this maddening work more readable. Like a first-class teacher Ford gives his ideas the force of his personal life. But, except in his two best books, he had so many ideas that he was exhausted by the time he got to the page. He had not the breath. He creates the spell of someone always on the move; the pen itself was expatriate. His theories, in the end, become devices for postponing the novelist's task: which is to settle and confront. Impressionism – and with it a desire to impress – becomes an unconscious journalism. One sees him, and his characters also, wearing themselves out by continually changing trains.

The Forsytes

Galsworthy? A City toff, decent fellow, fond of the Turf. Good shot. A bit damp-eyed. Some trouble with a woman. Gave up shooting birds, took to novel-writing and shooting his own class – rich lawyers, company directors – until the Germans unsportingly cleared the covers. In the end, wrote telegraphese like this and forgave all. 'The rum thing to me,' said Gilbert Murray who admired *The Forsyte Saga*, 'is that I don't feel that I know in the least what a Forsyte is like and I am not conscious of having seen one.' This is not Oxford snobbery: after forty-odd years one feels exactly that. Galsworthy's imagination was lukewarm: thin, partial, thumb-nail sketches of people, poor invention, jog-trot realism, blur when there is a question of feeling, embarrassment or jauntiness when there should be thought.

On the other hand, D. H. Lawrence *did* jump at Forsyteism as a social illness and even respected the satirical force of *A Man of Property*. It opens well and has an idea. Before the family history drifted into genteel soap opera, thousands of readers recognised their relatives; on the Continent and in America, the *Saga* became the standard guide to the English character. Even today, especially on the other side of the Iron Curtain, 'the great Galsworthy' is brought out like a trump card when one is playing a hand or two with foreign intellectuals. The world has a hunger for the single, simple explanation and Galsworthy explained where the Victorians had put on a complex, congested, preaching face.

For him property was the English passion; convention disposed of the inconvenient emotions. You bought everything – from houses, pretty country, works of art, to women and children. Every human feeling had to pass through a more or less brutalising shareholders' meeting; it had somehow to pay and, if you had your losses, you put a soothing cream of sentiment over them. The foreigner brought up on Victorian impenetrability was ready for Galsworthy's inside view. It explained that peculiar foreign fantasy: the well-off, buttoned up, blue-eyed, blank-faced Englishman who was a sort of gun dog to a master called the Right Thing and trained to love life only when it was decently dead. In short, the Forsytes are 'rum' because they are a theory. The theory works in *The Man of Property* because Galsworthy's anger is roused; once that dies, the *Saga* becomes a family charade and a hymn to crustiness.

A man of property himself, Galsworthy was a rebel against his own class for reasons of chivalry rather than of deep principle. His private story is very relevant – too relevant. It has long been known and Mr Dudley Barker has written a mild, tactful and, occasionally, sceptical account of it in a biographical study, *The Man of Principle*. A young man with a handsome allowance and pleasant expectations, Galsworthy amused himself with horse-racing and not much more at Oxford; came down to idle at the Law; was sent round the world to get over a mild, unsuitable love affair; returned to discover religious doubt, guilt about the condition of the poor, and to slip into a liaison with his cousin's wife. In the mercantile euphemism for describing sexual unhappiness, the couple were not 'on terms': even worse, she played Chopin and he preferred the Yeomanry. The fear of scandal, the certainty of ostracism and the danger of hurting his father and, possibly, losing his income kept the liaison fairly secret for ten years. Then the affair blew up. The central theme of *A Man of Property* – the indecency of property rights in love – was provided. Try to own Beauty and it vanishes.

But once the scandal died down and the divorce was over and the ostracism of Ada Galsworthy came to an end, Galsworthy's rebellion ended too. He continued all his life to be indignant about cruelty and social injustice, but within the system. He became a very likeable kind of English crank and this crankiness found an effective outlet in his plays; but as a novelist he sank back into an ironical apologia for the class he represented. Soames, the villain, the only character of any account in *The Forsyte Saga*, becomes Soames the stoic, bearing the weight of his own dull, tragic compulsion to possessive love. That development is commendable. Galsworthy has at least seen that possessive men who put a money value to everything are not thereby cut off from tragic or, at any rate, pathetic experience: if Soames is mean, he is also emotional and, in stoicism, he gains a pitiable strength. But gradually Soames becomes Galsworthy's mouthpiece and that is a betrayal of the meaning of the first volume of the *Saga*. Galsworthy has not the talent, the vitality, the conviction to deepen an idea.

One realises that Galsworthy is not going to face everything out when one sees his handling of the Soames-Irene-Bosinney situation. All that is said conveys nothing about Irene and everything of the Narcissism of those who admire her: they are caressing their own feelings. She is a sentimental mystery – an erotic dream. If she were not, Galsworthy would have to come out with the plain fact that she is a real female, as ruthless as Soames and indeed a bitch in all the crises of the story. Defending his study of erotic passion in an earlier book, *The Dark Flower*, Galsworthy said too much had been written about the physical realities of erotic passion, too little of its spirit; the truth is that he goes straight into sentimentality by a high-minded evasion of the facts. The famous passivity of Irene is a fantasy: she must be seen as the victim. We must be prevented from seeing that Beauty is making victims of her two husbands and her son. For there is a Galsworthian theory that irresistible Passion comes uncalled for in our lives, transfiguring, destroying, vanishing. So it may, but at least we know what and who hits us. The novelist who does not know will be guilty of one of those moral tergiversations that are fatal to his quality as a writer and even to his craftsmanship. Galsworthy is so bemused by Irene that he cannot even get the woman to speak except in lines that sound like bits of a breathless telegram. And she is, more often than not, sitting by an open window near flowers! Clever woman!

After this central failure, Galsworthy is left to exercise the skill of a gentleman amateur on the surface of social life. Here and there he practises a port-wine irony in his little sketches of testy old men and foolish aunts. There are embarrassing pictures of un-Forsyte-like artists. There are one or two good boardroom scenes, for Galsworthy had observed company meetings when he was idling at the Law. There is some expert comedy: Soames, in Paris, mistaken by a detective for his wife's lover. Or the break-up of horse-racing Montague Dartie's rickety marriage, where the manœuvres intended to separate the couple only succeed in re-uniting them. Galsworthy's lapses into the raffish are good.

The interesting thing about him is that he was a taught writer: his wife above all, then Edward Garnett, Conrad, a whole committee, worked on his manuscripts in a manner that would have been intolerable to a less determinedly masochistic figure. He slaved away, like a Forsyte at the office, until he attained a non-stop facility which was his personal triumph and, in the end, his downfall. What no one detected was that his weaknesses fitted him for the stage: his simple sentimental view of the class situation, his feeling for moral melodrama, his eye for the short scene, his topical sense of justice and a reformist temper made acceptable by dialogue done in offhand remarks. He could knock off a play in a few weeks without help from the committee; and actors gave life to what, in his novels, was really lifeless.

It is fashionable to think him crude as a dramatist; and his situations are really head-on collisions in unlikely circumstances. But he got the admiration of Shaw, and even Wells, who was no admirer of the novels, was won over. The fact is that Galsworthy was an ingenious craftsman. The sudden entrance of the exquisitely serpentine Jew in gorgeous dressing-gown, among a group of the squirearchy struggling into their boiled shirts in the country-house scene of *Loyalties*, 'tells' symbolically and theatrically in an instant. Galsworthy also hit the taste of a decade in which – as Mr Barker says – the Welfare State began to kick in the womb. Plays like *The Silver Spoon, Strife* or *The Skin Game* had much the same effect on its first audiences as *Look Back in Anger* has had in our own time. He had hit upon that mysterious thing – the idiom of a period. The theatre was just the place for those black-and-white notions of Decency and Vice, Property and Poverty, Truth and Pharisaism which were buried in the confusions of his mind. His novels, he once said, were not social criticism, they were 'spiritual examinations', conversations between two halves of himself.

As a man Galsworthy was the gentlest of toffs, and a moral toff to the end. Guilty about his inherited wealth, he scrupulously gave away large sums of money to the needy, to hangers-on, to causes, and still managed to leave £98,000. He was a soft touch for ex-convicts. He was whimsical about the enormous list of good causes he supported. They ranged from prison and divorce reform, the establishment of a minimum wage in sweated industries, woman's suffrage, slum clearance, down to the protection of prostitutes and animals and the improvement of slaughterhouses. His generosity to servants and tenants infuriated his neighbours. Yet he remained very much 'the man at the club window' – a phrase of Edward

Garnett's that rankled – in the sense that he found it hard to make real contact with people outside his own class. As Mr Barker says, he had no notion that the poor had their own life. He was always the district visitor, solemn, formal and modest.

Galsworthy's character appears most clearly in his relations with Ada Galsworthy. She was the daughter of an eccentric doctor who spent many years building an elaborate mausoleum for himself and used to sit in Norwich cemetery gazing at it with pleasure and thinking of little touches to add to it: an apt progenitor for the original of the mysterious, passive, silent Irene. As a muse – a model from whom the novelist was rarely separated – she was, not surprisingly, exigent. She became a hypochondriac and he was her continual nurse. He said that he had found a talent for nursing. In a sense, he wanted to nurse England. He also said, with a sort of helpless pleasure, that Ada paralysed him. That is a Forsyte story that was never written.

The Knightsbridge Kennels

W hy do the novels of Ada Leverson survive? How is it that these water ices of the Edwardian drawing-room have kept their crispness and have not melted away? One can put it down to the Wilde revival; one can regard it as a side effect of the present turdish taste for chichi; or as a passing nostalgia for the tritenesses of a small, safe, set, satiny world of tea-cups and little dinners, where the gravest dangers are things like being seen riding in a hansom with a wan Bohemian girl from the wrong side of the Park. Ada Leverson's urban males are vulnerable to pity for ill-provided females through whose designs any well-appointed woman can see. We are offered a life lived according to 'the rules', which smoothly prevent the emotions from becoming more than inconvenient. To cover the inevitable boredom there are always the bitchings and counter-bitchings of the Knightsbridge kennels. Thus, a rather too jolly Mr Mitchell will be 'almost any age between 60 and 65'; a Sir Charles is 'distinguished to the very verge of absurdity'. All this is pleasant enough, but – I agree with Colin MacInnes who writes an ardent preface to Ada Leverson's best-known trilogy *The Little Ottleys* – it has little to do with her merits. The only unconvincing touches that occur in her last novel are those that are closest to the modern world: they record one or two glimpses of the outbreak of the 1914 war. It is natural that they should be unconvincing, for that war killed the comedy of manners. She survives because she is an original and considerable artist.

A writer can be a considerable artist without being more than a minor novelist. If they are to last, the minor novelists depend on sparkle, a freshness of view and a perfection of means; if they are comedians, on the gift of living in a perennial present. Economy and distinction of style and – in Miss Leverson's case – skill in construction are indispensable. They must delight in their limits if we are to delight in them: they must always refuse – and how few middling novelists do make this refusal! – to borrow the courage of other people's convictions. Miss Leverson understood this. It is possible that the pleasure she gives owes a lot to a clever adaptation of the methods of the theatre: the two-dimensional tale passes as quickly as an expert charade. A scene never lasts too long; it is as sharp as repartee. She is careful, even when moralising, to keep to the surface of life and it is often when she appears to be most trivial that she is life-enhancing and most serious.

To the somewhat extravagant praise given by Mr MacInnes, I would add the warning that she has not the range of, say, an Edith Wharton; and although it is true that, in a general way, she writes in the tradition of Congreve, she dilutes with the very different comedy of *The Diary of a Nobody*, the Ottleys being the Pooters, but younger and smarter and moved from Finchley to Knightsbridge. They are little Somebodies. This is the comedy of 'life's little ironies' which came in during her lifetime. When the clownish Bruce Ottley and his wife chase from one Hamilton Place to another in London looking for where they are supposed to be dining and find they have got the week wrong; above all, in Bruce Ottley's querulous time as an amateur actor, we have pure Grossmith:

> 'I told Mitchell what I thought of him in very plain terms. I went so far as to threaten to throw up my part, and he said, "Well, all right, if you don't like it you can give it up any time." I said "Who else could you get at the last minute to play a footman's part?" and he said "Our footman."'

The other strain in her comedy is her concern for integrity. She rejoices in the banality of her characters; but in her heroine, Edith Ottley, she has created a young wife who clings to the conservative conventions of her world yet is disturbed to find that she may in her marriage be sacrificing herself to them when she supposes she is doing something sensitive and fine. In other words, Miss Leverson introduces the question of personal truth into her comedy. There is a point at which Edith, despite her coquettishness, is in danger of becoming as tiresome as Thackeray's Amelia; it is no great credit to Edith's probity that she is rescued from having to solve her dilemma by her husband's inane flight with the chief comic character of the book and, ultimately, by the breakdown of the standards of Knightsbridge in the war. I find Edith a shade calculating. Her asinine husband is at his shamefaced worst when the marriage collapses and, in a wonderful scene, comes out with the one honest remark of his life, a ridiculous, fierce *cri de cœur* that punctures the basic assumption of her ethic and her comedy:

'No, Edith. I can't endure married life any longer. It doesn't suit me.'

This cry from a prime domestic fusspot who is always carrying on about being master in his own house is marvellously funny, but it has a wildness about it suggesting that the Ottleys, like the rest of this Edwardian world, had somehow begotten two children without having done more than meet socially.

It is sometimes said that artificial comedy in English suffers from a lack of brain. It really celebrates the English genius for hardening off, refusing to face issues and creating an ennui which will be the great guarantor of social, moral and emotional eventlessness. The most boring and self-centred of men, Bruce Ottley thrives on boredom and develops in consequence a character so eccentric that it never ceases to fascinate his friends. Our comedy, like our way of life, depends on the evasion of ideas or knowledge and on the creation of character. Edith is about to marry a fine fellow at the end of the novel, but as far as comedy is concerned he is a dead loss: he bores us with his £5,000 a year and his undoubted enlightenment. And it is an odd conjunction of life and art that, after she wrote this novel in 1916, Miss Leverson wrote no more.

But she had by then created a comic character far more original than the lunatic Bruce – Madame Frabelle. This portrait is satisfying because it is not caricature. It is the truth about Madame Frabelle that is so funny; and the fact that she is a likeable monster makes her funnier. She is the Life Force gone dowdy, shady and kind, but never dormant. Indeed, advancing years make her phoneyness redoubtable. It is she who runs off with Bruce in the end – one can imagine her picking him up like a puppy in her teeth and wobbling off with him – and anyone who is interested in skill in writing must admire the cleverness with which Miss Leverson insinuates the stages that lead to this dénouement. The splendid thing about Madame Frabelle is that she is absurd, false, but sympathetic – this comes from Miss Leverson's truthfulness:

Madame Frabelle (of course) was dressed in black, *décolletée* and with a good deal of jet. A black aigrette, like a lightning conductor, stood up

defiantly in her hair. Though it did not harmonise well with the
somewhat square and *bourgeoise* shape of her head and face, and
appeared to have dropped on her by accident, yet as a symbol of
smartness it gave her a kind of distinction. It appeared to have fallen
from the skies; it was put on in the wrong place, and it did not nestle, as it
should do, and appear to grow out of her hair, since that glory of
womanhood, in her case of a dull brown going slightly grey, was
smooth, scarce and plainly parted. Madame Frabrelle really would have
looked her best in a cap of the fashion of the Sixties. But she could carry
off anything; and some people said that she did.

Madame Frabelle's great gift is that of being wrong about everything.
She is a monument to the failures of feminine intuition. She is an exciting
store of inaccurate facts and false conjectures. She is the queen of
nonsensical law-giving, masterfully inhabiting a very heaven of self-
deception, as dotty as a horoscope. But people are charmed – again Miss
Leverson's truthfulness – because Madame Frabelle is helplessly charmed
by them. When she carries off Bruce, no one really minds. Two absurdities
will have fulfilled themselves. Edith's excellences bored Bruce: he needed
the dramatic companionship of a fellow self-deceiver.

Miss Leverson's admired males are too psychologically decorative: they
are 'connoisseurs of human nature', 'urbane observers', 'collectors of
experience'. They call Edith '*impayable*' when, frankly, she is really a moral
coquette. But Miss Leverson's wit and perceptions are original. There are
Lady Cannon's florid and massive clothes which, like her furniture,
'express a violent, almost ominous conventionality, without the slightest
touch of austerity to tone it down'. Edith Ottley's appearance has 'the
rather insidious charm of somehow recalling the past while suggesting
something undiscovered in the future'. The random dialogue of parties
turns, with hardly a pause, from the disturbing perception – 'something in
his suave manner of taking everything for granted seemed to make them
know each other almost too quickly, and gave her an odd sort of self-
consciousness' – to the hilariously vapid:

Captain Willis lowered his voice to a confidential tone and said:
   'D'you know what I always say is – live and let live and let it go at
that: what?'

'That's a dark saying.'

'Have a burnt almond,' said Captain Willis inconsequently as though it would help her to understand.

Writers of comedy have to bear as best they can the charge of triviality, in spite of the fact that their eye for detail and their instinct of selection give them an exceptional power to render the surface of life. How rarely do realists catch that surface. The other charge that they are evasive or, of all things, not 'serious' is even more stupid, for they above all convey by their laughter the sense of danger that is inseparable from delight in the moment. In artificial comedy and the comedy of manners this sense of danger is intense. Miss Leverson lives by this. But the quality that has helped most to keep so much of her work in the perennial present is, quite simply, her feminine appetite for news:

All women love news of whatever kind; even bad news gives them merely a feeling of pleasurable excitement . . .

Heavier novelists die off in a decade or two from a surfeit of information.

An Irish Oblomov

<hr>

There is a terrifying sentence in James Stephens's account of his meeting with Joyce in Dublin that unfortunately came to my mind when I was struggling with Samuel Beckett's trilogy, *Molloy*; *Malone Dies*; *The Unnamable* – 'I looked at him,' says Stephens, 'without a word in my mouth except vocabulary.' Will someone not chart the vivid but interminable ocean of Irish garrulity for us, point out the shallows and the depths, tell us where the words are vocabulary only and where they connote ideas or things, where they are propitiatory magic, where egomania filling in time and place? Where is language used for language's sake, and where is it used as a gabble-gabble ritual to make tolerable the meaninglessness of life? It would be of practical help to know whether a writer was drowning well within his own depth or out of it; and when it would be decent to leave him to it – possibly coming back later, after a smoke, to see how he was getting on.

One does this with *Tristram Shandy*. One does it with *Finnegans Wake*. Pending necromantic guidance, with Beckett's novels, one does the same. They are lawsuits that never end, vexations, litigations joined with the tedium, the greyness, the grief, the fear, the rage, the clownishness, the physical miseries of old age where life is on the ebb, and nature stands by smiling idiotically. Why was I born, get me out of this, let me live on less and less, get me to the grave, the womb, the last door, dragging this ludicrous, feeble, windy broken old bag of pipes with me. Find me a hole. Give me deafness and blindness; chop off the gangrened leg; somewhere on this rubbish dump where I crawl there must be some final dustbin, where I can dribble, laugh, cry and maunder on the this and the that of the general mystery and occasionally give a toothless grin over an obscene word or a farcical sexual memory.

Flight, old age, and the wrangle about personal identity, these are Samuel Beckett's themes. A man is a vestige left to hop around in wearying argy-bargy after his invisible master: punishment, for the old, unremembered sin. Life is the *belle dame* with the mindless smirk and she hardly troubles to look at the victim who has been reduced to the total lethargy of compulsive speech. That is the joke: the mutilated thing can *talk*. In the first volume the man is Molloy, the tramp with crutches, a mixture of simplicity, hurt and lunatic energy. He can still spit with contempt at society:

> One of us at last! Green with anguish. A real little terrestrial! Choking in the chlorophyll. Hugging the slaughterhouse walls! Paltry priests of the irrepressible ephemeral!

He bashes along on his bicycle, through the town, trying to get to his mother. He runs over a dog –

> an ineptness all the more unpardonable as the dog, duly leashed, was not out on the road, but in on the pavement, docile at his mistress's heels. Precautions are like resolutions, to be taken with precaution. The lady must have thought she had left nothing to chance, so far as the safety of her dog was concerned, whereas in reality she was setting the whole system of nature at naught, no less surely than I myself with my insane demands for more light. But instead of grovelling in my turn, invoking my great age and infirmities, I made things worse by trying to run away. I was soon overtaken by a bloodthirsty mob of both sexes and all ages, for I caught a glimpse of white beards and little angel faces, and they were preparing to tear me to pieces.

– but the lady stopped them, saying she was taking the dog to the vet to be put down, in any case, and he had saved her a painful task.

This volume has all Beckett's headlong comic gift. Molloy is in the clownish state of senility, his disqualified life has the spirit either of a fairy tale or inverted idyll; and in his pestiferous search for 'more light' on everything and nothing – mostly the latter – there is a grin half of mockery and half of frenzy on his scabby face. His sexual memories are funny because they are few, take him by surprise, and they are a mixture of the grotesque and touching, the dirty and the modest. He has dragged his body around all his life, and it follows him like some ignorant valet. There is far more to compare with *Tristram Shandy* in the caprices of this volume and its exploits in self-contradiction in order to hold the floor than there is with Joyce.

In the second volume, *Malone Dies*, we move from the freedom of rebellion to loneliness. Malone, by the way, may be another aspect of Molloy; he doesn't know who he is. As far as I can make out the scene of the novel is a madhouse or infirmary for the old, and Beckett becomes the grammarian of solitude. The senses are dying. How does Malone know where the veils of air end and the prison walls begin? The body turns in smaller and smaller circles; the mind conjugates trifles. Here Beckett intervenes with some satirical observation of normal people, a trite couple and their favourite son, a piece which might have come out of Sartre's *Nausée*, or Nathalie Sarraute, and we are reminded that Beckett writes his novels first in French.

But we return to endless hair-splitting, metaphysical speculation sliding from association to association, and these convey that as age increases the tedium of life, so the unwearying little talker in the brain, with his lawsuit against life, bosses every half minute of it. Grief and pity hang between his words; but the book unexpectedly ends in wholesale murder, when the feeble-minded inmates of the infirmary are taken out on a picnic.

In the third volume, Molloy, Malone, Mahood, Murphy – whatever the name now is – is a lump, almost sightless, stone deaf, always weeping, mutilated, immovable, the helpless centre of a world that he can be conscious of very rarely. He is about to become Worm, all human identity gone. The archaeological kind of critic who can recover a novel from its ruins may be able to make something of this volume. I find it unreadable, in the sense that I cannot move from paragraph to paragraph, from page to page. It is all significance and no content.

The stream of consciousness, so lively and going dramatically from image to image in Joyce, is here a stream of imageless verbosity occasionally broken by a jab of obscene anger, but grey, grey, and it goes monotonously along in phrases usually about seven words long, like some regularly bumping old tram. This is, of course, not so much the stream of consciousness as the stream of solitude and provides the comedy of overhearing a man talking to himself – Bloom, one recalls, rarely talked; things 'came up' in his mind. He was in the midst of drama – a comedy that is genuine enough certainly, but not of boundless interest.

[587]

Why is Beckett interesting as a writer? As a contemporary phenomenon, he is one more negative protest against the world going to the
slaughterhouse, one more protest on behalf of privacy, a voice for myopia.
He is a modern Oblomov, fretful and apathetic, enclosed in private fantasy,
dropping off into words instead of sleep. They are eloquent, cunning,
unremitting words.

He is far from feeble, for there is a devil-like slyness in the half grin on
the faces of his old men who can hit out with their crutches. What tedium!
they exclaim – speaking not only of existence and human solitude – but, we
suspect, of ourselves. His imagination has the Irish cruelty and self-
destructiveness that Yeats once spoke of. Beckett's anti-novels, like all
anti-novels, have to deal with small areas of experience because their
pretension is to evoke the whole of life, i.e. life unfixed by art; the result is
that these verbose books are like long ironical, stinging footnotes in small
print to some theme not formulated. But there is a flash of deep insight in
the madness he evokes: it is strange that in a generation which has put all
its stress on youth and achievement, he alone should have written about
old age, loneliness and decrepitude, a subject which arouses perhaps our
deepest repressed guilt and fears. He is the product of a civilisation which
has become suddenly old. He is a considerable, muttering, comic writer,
and although he conveys unbearable pain, he also conveys the element of
sardonic tenacity and danger that lies at the heart of the comic gift.

Alexandrian Hothouse

In France, Germany and in the United States, we are told, Mr Lawrence Durrell is now the most admired of British novelists. For ourselves, he is a mixture of traveller, poet and the brilliant raconteur in depth, of non-stop loquacity. Our literature grows blooms like this in the expatriate and Imperial hot-houses – Mr Durrell was planted in the Middle East and the Mediterranean – a Ouida as well as a Kipling, a Norman Douglas as well as a D. H. Lawrence; a Byron, but also a Disraeli and a Hichens.

Where our exotics excel is in a matchless sense of place which, I believe, is not approached by any literature in the world. Mr Durrell's evocation of Alexandria, in *Justine*, *Balthazar* and *Mountolive*, and now in *Clea*, is one of the finer mirages in our writing. It is an astonishing collection of fragments, a self-perpetuating generation of vivid pictorial illusions, obsessive, poetic, curious, scholarly, and headily at the mercy of mood and memory. This writing of his is splendid, even when the pedal is down, because the poetic image is the image of precision; and arresting, because contemporary English prose has either – in one of Durrell's phrases – got a hot potato in its mouth or has been nibbled close by the bleak teeth of modern criticism. In either case, it looks like rain. The writer whose subject is illusion – Mr Durrell's – is entitled to colour, image and fantasy and it is no good complaining that, on the subject of cities, he does not write like Smollett, who succeeded fearfully in a different way. Fragments stick:

> Streets that run back from the docks with their tattered, rotten super-cargo of houses, breathing into each other's mouths, keeling over . . .

> the early spring dawn with its dense dew, sketched upon the silence that engulfs a whole city before the birds awaken it . . . the sweet voice of the blind muezzin hanging like a hair in the palm-cooled upper airs . . .

> in the summer the sea-damp lightly varnished the air. Everything lay under a coat of gum.

And there are the set pieces, like the sight of the desert at the meeting of the Copts or the duck-shoot in the delta. Or those long interiors: the cellar in which the child prostitutes come out by candlelight like a cloud of bats, or the Minister of the Interior's appalling reception-room, with the old, sugared and slothful spider pillowing his stomach on the divan.

But as a novelist? A novel can be anything; but, struggle as Mr Durrell does with his conviction that he is conducting an experiment in 'the novel of sliding panels', or creating a mosaic of plot and symbol in layers and depths, he is really a raconteur, a master of the episode. He cannot stop. *Clea* appears to round off the Justine series, but in it he is clearly hankering after new twists and densities. In *Justine* he was all surface; in *Balthazar* he showed us it was a false surface; in *Mountolive*, the political novel which really rooted his characters, he got depth at last. I think this volume is the making of the quartet. But in *Clea*, invention and ingenuity have become a habit. The difficulty is that the war has come, the spell of old Alexandria and the decadent elation that sustained it have gone. There is no artifice to believe in. Pursewarden, who began to shape in *Mountolive*, lectures us for hours about sex, literature and the North in the only too-well-known voice of Norman Douglas. This is not the earlier, difficult Pursewarden of scandalous sexual misbehaviour, fighting the Foreign Office, and dumb-founding and seducing that honking, hysteric lesbian, Justine; breaking the lock-jaw of her desire for martyrdom by making her laugh at herself for the first time in her life. In *Clea* poor Pursewarden, who has had to bear much from Mr Durrell, is given a guilty secret; he has committed incest. It is as solemn as the committal to the deep. It is made to sound like one of the seven deadly virtues. His smut is below standard, too.

And then, in *Clea*, those letters, diaries and mimicries which Mr Durrell has skilfully used to give a change of view to the earlier books, swamp the narrative. There is still good farce, which, after place, is one of Mr Durrell's strong gifts. The saga of Scobie, the Catholic Police Chief with 'tendencies' (Eonism), gets broader after his death. This sinning and Cockney prowler, with a bad accent, is canonised as a Moslem saint by accident because of local popularity. His tomb contains his bath tub – no body available – and works miracles. There is Dr Amaril's romance with a girl for whom he makes an artificial nose, a charming tale; and more dreadful, the tale of Dr Balthazar's last love affair. In a panic because he is obliged to take to false teeth, and sees in this a sign of declining powers, the philosophical old dabbler in the Cabbala falls in love with a beastly young actor, and is driven to the most extravagant and pitiable humiliations of homosexual jealousy. He ends by attempting to cut off his own hands. (Hand symbols and hand-cutting occur more than once in Mr Durrell's quartet, for as he annotates the course of European sexual practice and fantasy from Rabelais to Sade, Sade gets most of the cheers. As a gesture to Home, there are two cheers for D. H. Lawrence.)

Mr Durrell's ingenious method of sliding the panel and showing us many episodes again with new and unexpected shadows is dramatic and absorbing; it cannot disguise the fact that his leading people are not people at all. They are vehicles of events; they are a poet's notes; they are fables, subjects of one another's conversation and, in the case of the women, are seen only in the light of desire. It is Mr Durrell's point as an artist that they are fervid aspects of the city, created by its moments. They build up, of course, as time passes. Justine, the nymphomaniac, the banker's wife, the narrator's mistress, is shown first as a figure of mystery, then as a raucous hysteric and finally we get a real insight into her nature when we discover that she is diverting her desire to suffer into serious political plotting. Politics calm her sexually. She is the perpetual *intrigante* with a rage for power. When the plot fails she turns upon her husband and becomes not the mysterious holy whore, but the true married scold. So Justine acquires character – but only through the say-so of her lovers who observe her. She is less a woman than a gossip. We see the rest of Mr Durrell's characters as we might see them in Casanova, almost only in their relation to some peculiarities of sexuality, its pleasures, pains, dissimulations, ironies and unpredictable turns.

Mr Durrell and his people are continually talking. They talk well and wittily, with instructed scepticism and an immense amount of quotation, including quite a few old intellectual gags, like Mommsen's about the Celts destroying civilisations and creating none of their own. It indeed often seems that loquacity has been substituted for sex. And *are* they talking about love? Not really; only about Narcissism and desire. Sterile, they are talking about its perversity, its sadness, its anecdotage, its variety, its passing. Their sexual love is easy, but after the sexual act there is still unsatisfied desire. Exhausted romantics, they are looking over the sleeping lover's shoulder. Love – and Mr Durrell as a good Mediterranean prides himself on his knowledge of its variety – rarely grows beyond that first stage in his novels. He speaks in Stendhalian phrase of *amour passion*, but does not give us an example of it. No one is possessed.

Here and there, there is a *glimpse* of love – and we have to grant that he sets out to be a novelist of fragmentation – as when, for example, in a very fine scene, an old man cries for his mistress on his death-bed in hospital. He is an old dealer, she is a cabaret dancer with many customers who has long ago left him. He wants her now, not for comfort, not to expose a broken heart, but to confess to her that he once or twice robbed her and cheated her. He wants to clear his conscience. Surely, love is the bloodstream of the moral nature; Mr Durrell sees human beings as thinned-out spirits off on some kind of erotic hunt who live only in the eyes and the senses, on the nerves, in expert pleasure and in terror. We accept this because he tells us we are in Alexandria, the androgynous, where people are 'wounded in their sex'; but it knocks the bottom out of old Pursewarden as a sage. It is noticeable indeed that Mr Durrell's people acquire character when they are seen outside of love, especially the men. Narouz, the rich Copt and farmer, for example, who murders and is murdered, is far more real than his brother, the mysterious Nessim, the banker who is caught in Justine's affairs. Nessim becomes real only when we see him plotting to run arms into Palestine. Mountolive, the ambassador, becomes real when he is shocked out of his long day-dream of desire for Nessim's mother, is caught by political intrigue, and goes through the shocking and terrifying scene in the child's brothel.

If mutability and illusion are the subjects of this novelist who is afloat on fine words and an avidity for art and ideas, his means are shock, boldness and a mastery of intrigue, patterning and story-telling. His experiment in repeated rewritings succeeds to a great extent because the shift has some of the abruptness of the theatre in it. In all things he is an artist; even when he bores, he bores us as an artist by striking too many attitudes. When the shift fails it is because he relies excessively on long-winded narrators who are supposed to be new voices, but who are in fact as clever in the same way as he is. The influence of Norman Douglas and the desire to out-Juan *Don Juan* have been baneful. It produces Ouida. But one does not forget the absurdities of Scobie, the love life of Pombal, the French diplomat. One

admires the caricature, the murder of Narouz, the scene in which Pursewarden fails to make love to Melissa, succeeds when he has confessed a secret to her, and drops her suddenly when she accidentally reveals a trivial yet deadly secret to him; one does not forget Scobie's death, the horror of the brothel – or anything which springs from intrigue. For intrigue buzzes out of Mr Durrell's tremendous power of observation and invention. His eyes are forever watching; his ears forever hearing. The Decadent palls, the compulsive talker goes on and on, but again and again the romantic inventor breaks through like a bursting flower. He is unlike any novelist we now have.

Kipling's Short Stories

After Dickens, Kipling is the only very considerable English writer of fiction to have been popular in the most popular sense and to excite the claim to genius. He might dabble in popular myth-making and put on the swank that goes with journalistic writing, but impurity had to be reckoned as in the nature of his bristling and generous gift. By 1910, the critical esteem had begun to go; for anyone who grew up in the Twenties it had gone; when one looked at a page or two of Kipling in the Thirties, he looked like a progenitor of The Thing we all hated. It was easy to tie his politics round his neck and sink him. Long after that, it was a shock (when we opened one of his books) to discover that his politics might not have been as important as we had made out; that his real themes were anterior and that he had an independent gaiety and authority in his sentences suggesting a much darker experience than the political. One was faced by a variable but continuous exhibition of musketry over an enormous terrain, which alerted the mind so long as he never allowed his own feelings, or those of his characters, to come out into the open, but left them to be guessed. He was, in any case, better at what was choked and strangled and, puritanically, admired pain. But, of course, he did not always leave us guessing; blatancy, emphasis, the breezy sentences beginning with a relative came back and, being sensitive, we put the book down and resumed our ignorance, preferring those writers who had grown up and who were not ashamed of the heart.

It is in this mixed state of prejudice, ignorance and unwillingness to go back to old topicality that I approach a subtle and partial critical study by Miss J. M. S. Tompkins, *The Art of Rudyard Kipling*. She invites one to enter a labyrinth and to trace the course of a genius she believes to be undeniable and which went on painfully growing until, in his later, complex and allusive work, it was purified and at its fullest. It is a little embarrassing, when one looks from her book into Kipling's tales, to find she is more

sensitive than her subject was. The study does not claim to be comprehensive; startlingly but firmly, she leaves his politics out altogether. ('I was a child of the British Empire, as I am a subject of the British Commonwealth, and I have never found either position embarrassing. I regret that I shall not live long enough to see our humanly imperfect but undeniably great achievement of Empire fairly assessed in the long view of history.') This decision is not as damaging as it might sound, for she is not a biographer, nor a critic who runs the writer and the man together at every point. She is concerned only with the writer and, even there, most of all with the short stories. It is by these, she conveys, that what he did must be judged. To say that Kipling is the greatest English writer of short stories is to astonish oneself. He is – because no others before him made it expressly their *métier*.

Kipling's choice and aptitude are un-English; they are a little French; they are very American. If one were to raise political questions, one would say that Englishness was thrashed into him, that it was imposed. He invented myths for the sahibs, full of moral words, tribal signs and masonic grips, but the matter of his stories has often more in common with that of American predecessors like Twain, and successors like Hemingway and Faulkner, than it has with anything English writers have done. *Mary Postgate* is a foreigner's searching portrait of an English spinster. We cover that sort of thing up. The fantasy of *The Man Who Would Be King* is a frontier story, a natural for Mark Twain – see the King and Duke episode in *Huckleberry Finn* – and the preoccupation with toughness, cunning and shrewdness, and above all with the testing of personality, is not restrained by our sociability, dignified by our severity of satire or confined to studies of character seen in its security. In fact, the common opinion is that Kipling failed precisely in character-drawing where traditional English novelists have succeeded. I do not think he felt much need to draw character; from his Anglo-Indian point of view he thought the islanders too set, smug and narrow. This would have to be the starting point of any discussion of his politics; he became an English patriot in a most un-English way – except for the sentimentality – not by rebellion from within but from a sense of grandeur from without, and from that sense of colonial superiority which always made Anglo-Indians an annoyance and a joke. But the theory of a crypto-American Kipling is mine; it is not Miss Tompkins's. Indeed, far from it. For her he is an Elizabethan:

. . . a traditional writer with a traditional and recurrent cast of English temperament . . . he delighted in the Elizabethan dramatists. Man in a state of strong excitement stretched beyond his normal stature on the rack of anguish, passion, or his own will, was as much his theme as theirs though in him the will is stretched to service rather than to self-assertion. In Kipling, as in his elder brothers, the moral and sensational go hand in hand. Strain, the oppression and horror of melancholy throw up for him, as for them, eccentricities of behaviour which he observes with curiosity, and open up tracks of mental experience, of which he seeks to convey the strangeness . . . Like the Elizabethans he had an original and unembarrassed love of eloquence . . . his danger, like theirs, was excess, the premature outbreak of the imagination into extravagant emphasis and unsupported hyperbole.

Kipling loved pattern, craftsmanship and the science of all trades. Yet the novel he could not master. Perhaps he had learned brevity too young; perhaps it was due to his facility as a poet; perhaps he burned up himself and his material too quickly or – as Mr Edmund Wilson suggested in *The Wound and the Bow* – failed to confront himself. Miss Tompkins thinks Kipling mastered the novel by relinquishing its form and became our unique short-story writer, and one of the greatest in all literatures, by straining into the short form the intense, highly charged essences of the longer one. He sought complexity as he sought discipline. The greater the material – *Mrs Bathurst*, for example, which covers the affections of a lifetime, trails across a continent and ends in passion and horror – the more the essentials are reduced to a line or two, the quicker and more cunning the dodging among events and time. He proceeds, as a novelist does, less by narrative than by changing structure. We have seen Hardy reduce a novel to a dozen lines of verse. Kipling's dramatic cutting is more like Browning's, and the art of both writers lies in making us supply the missing scenes and often the most important one. Time is no difficulty for him. The setting he always gives us vehemently – after that, it is all fencing as if he were outmatching us, driving us into a corner, until we give in, and it is we who tell him, not he who tells us, what happened.

Kipling is not one of those short-story writers who settle on a mere aspect of a subject, a mood, an emotion or a life. He takes the whole subject and reduces it, in form, to the dramatic skeleton. Important issues are left obscure as if the author himself did not know what had happened or was trying to trade on mystery, and we often have to read back to see where we went wrong; yet the effect is of extent, panorama and crowded life. One explanation lies in Kipling's genius for conveying place and physical presence; the more important one is his triumph over what, as a novelist, would have been his failing: his incapacity to write of character in detail. What he tells us about people, what by a paradox makes them vivid, is that they belong to the common run; they are ordinary engineers, seamen, soldiers, housemaids, reliable villagers, conventional youths, Indians anonymous within their sects, occupations or races. They have no character; they have, simply, a fate; and it is this that evokes the presence of hundreds like them. Kipling is able to suggest that he has no life of his own but has lived by knowing all about such lives. He may be – he often is – too much of a know-all, swaggering shrewdly in and out with the low, the mean or the extravagant view, but this basic losing of himself and knowing is a powerful gift.

Miss Tompkins is aware that Kipling presents difficult problems of taste. The exaggeration, the sentimentality, the horseplay, are dealt with as best she can. I doubt whether his sentimentality can be discussed as a question of fashion: sentimentality – as distinct from sentiment – arises when we impose an idea upon a feeling in order to obscure it. Kipling is sentimental about duty, when he wishes to conceal his ambiguous feelings about suffering and cruelty. *Mary Postgate* is an unsentimental story because it does not evade the terrible fact that old Miss Postgate looked beautiful, attractive and satisfied when she had experienced a sadistic revenge. The most displeasing sentimentalities in Kipling relate to his guess-work magic and mysticism and they lead to mistakes in craftsmanship – the letter-box which sticks out like a gadget in the superb story of *The Wish House*. But in sketching out the map of Kipling's pilgrim's progress, from the period of brashness and hurt into the arenas of revenge, anger, healing, pity and the terror of illness, breakdown and the abyss, Miss Tompkins shows us a Kipling who is far less a trickster and far more a man deeply caught by injury, pain, hatred and the craving for purgation, and who uses every ounce of his experience. He had been born in the Methodist tradition and knew the burden is on the individual soul. It is also one of the splendid characteristics of Kipling as an artist that he can consider this burden disrespectfully, in jeering and fantastic terms, as well as in terms of mercy, pity, horror and resignation.

To make her point about the density of Kipling's art, Miss Tompkins makes a long and ingenious analysis of the baffling *Dayspring Mishandled*. Like many of the late stories it requires minute attention from the reader, but although it has all the marks of a master of building and technique, and although the theme of the emptiness and irrelevance that waits on a life-long scheme of revenge is a good one, the story seems to me an example of Kipling's vice of attitudinising in order to avoid the explicit. Miss Tompkins suggests it may be a story about the dangers of his own imaginative obsession with revenge and, in this sense, the tale has the interest of a piece of ingenious self-criticism. As a tale it is dim and esoteric; who and what poisoned whom with what? we ask. The later Kipling was a conjuror, not a mystifier like the later Henry James.

Mr Edmund Wilson has said that Kipling lacked faith in the artist's vocation and put the doers, makers and rulers of the day before the artist in esteem. This is true when we consider Kipling as a propagandist, and Miss Tompkins has purposely avoided that aspect of his work. At his best – *On Greenhow Hill, The Wish House, Love-Women, The Gardener, The Man Who Would Be King* or *The Bull that Thought* – the criticism misses. In this last tale, indeed, the artist is the explicit conqueror, and *The Man who would be King* can be read as farcical and deadly satire on the British in India. Kipling had the gaiety of the word in his veins and he saw himself as an artist through and through. What Mr Wilson may be getting at is Kipling's often showy and evasive pose of common sense, in which the average comes out on top; or that hard, no-nonsense grin on his face which flatters average human insensibility by calling it experience. Pain is over and over again his subject; so much so that he cannot evoke simple feeling without encasing it in bandages or see the fullness of love except in the perspective of its dire consequences.

He is indeed afraid of deep feeling in the foreground and the fear – perhaps because of his enormous gifts – leads him into stretches of middling vulgarity. But, in fact, Kipling grew out of clever journalism to have the strongest feeling for the means of art and all the artist's deference to difficulty. He can even be said to have had this feeling exorbitantly; but given the man he was and his populous mind, it is what made him our prolific and unique writer of short stories. The art thrives on personal limitations.

El Cid

Until fifty years ago our interest in the great epic heroes was literary and nothing else. Figures like Arthur, Roland, the Cid and many others, had been revived by the Romantic movement and were charged by its taste for hero-worship and history. So slight was their relationship with anything going on in the world in the nineteenth century that the interest in them looks like an attempt to escape from a grey mercantile present into a glamorous past. It was not entirely that; there were the psychological sympathies of the power-lovers, the hankerings after the superman in the Victorian age, the desire to reduce the hero to the outstanding bourgeois. And there were occasional emotional rebounds as well. Southey's superb translation of *The Chronicles of the Cid* may have owed something to emotions stirred by the citizens of the Revolution or the figure of Napoleon, as well as to the dramatic personal contact with Spain. Yet all these responses remain literary and even antiquarian, and some readers must have felt, as I very often have, that the epic heroes were epic bores of featureless and exhausting simplicity.

Times have changed. The conditions out of which a living epic literature might arise have appeared in many parts of the world. Not in the West, perhaps, but certainly in continents where there has been continuous war, and where new orders are forming themselves. We have seen popular movements give a legendary character to their leaders. We have seen leaders looking about them for useful myths. Myth-like figures bob up continually in popular culture. They do not last, for one eclipses another. But the myth-making faculty has generally revived, is no longer derided, is eagerly studied and is made to serve the ends of government – political, religious and psychological. We are back at a moment when a magic, like the discovery of the bones of St James at Compostela, is firmly exploited. In this climate the epic heroes come closer to us and we can see their roots in life. A book like Mr W. S. Merwin's translation of the *Poem of the Cid* has now an extra dimension, and since Southey wrote, the Cid has been liberated by that great Spanish scholar Ramón Menéndez Pidal. The Champion now stands clearly and firmly on the dusty soil of Castile and we can know for what solid reasons he became the legendary national hero, and why one of the impulses behind the writing of the poem was what we would now call propaganda. We can see a myth being used, and why it was used.

Rodrigo Diaz, the Cid or Lord, as the Moors called him, the Champion as he was called by the Castilians, was born in 1045 in the village of Vivar in the cornlands near Burgos. He died fifty-six years later in Valencia and the *Poem* of his real or fantastic feats was written forty years after his death by a Mozarábe (i.e., a Christian born under Moorish rule) who may have known him. Many who knew him must have still been alive. Vivar was a frontier town. As a boy the Cid fought in the frontier wars of Navarre, and he was brought up at court. He could write. He came of noble stock, though not of the highest nobility, a matter of great importance and strong resentment in his life. The effect of the endless wars had been to increase the number of lesser nobility, the men who had horsemen and vassals, and the Cid belonged to this group. In Navarre whole populations became armigerous. They had their property in land and mills. (The Cid was mocked for his mills.) Their road to great wealth was to obtain the spoils of war and here the Cid enormously succeeded. His 'ill-shod outcasts' told the court of Barcelona: 'We keep alive by taking from you and others.' The prodigious loot obtained by him from his enemies turned him into a type of self-made millionaire whose daughters are sought for their money by the high nobility, but who, like their father, are socially despised. The *Poem* brings out strongly the private pride in something like a democratic attitude to life which was the great strength of the spirit of Castile, and which made that kingdom, and not feudal Leon, the leader in the wars of Reconquest and the most powerful of the Spanish states. The *Poem* is, in this sense, the voice of an unconscious wartime revolution.

The Cid has often been described as a freebooter, a soldier of fortune who sold himself to Moors and Christians, according to where the profit lay. This is not at all what he would have seemed to his contemporaries. At his birth, Christian Spain lay in the north, Moslem Spain in the south and east; but the majority of Spanish Moslems were, after three hundred years, of Ibero-Roman or Gothic stock. There was a mingling of races which had been made possible by Islamic rationalism. The people were bi-lingual. The Cid appears at the moment when a Moorish dynasty was weakening and becoming more penetrable by guerrillas who could capture castles if they could not gain territory, and when many Moors had become vassals of the Christian north. In the eleventh century it was not astonishing that a Moorish king should entrust the government of his land to the Cid, nor that the Cid should fight for the Moorish Emir of Saragossa against the Count of Barcelona, nor that he should at other times extend Moorish lands at the expense of Aragon and Castile. The strange thing is that his loyalty to his own king, who had banished him and wronged him out of personal envy and perhaps because of the intrigue of the great landowners and high nobility of Burgos, was constant.

Slaughter and booty are the trades of the Cid. One of the famous moments of the poem occurs after the siege of Valencia where he takes his frightened wife up to the top of a tower so that she can watch the battle and 'see how they earn their bread'. In its terse, plain, homely, always concrete fashion, the poem sets out the labours of an astute fighting man's life, in the sense that he is earning his living and doing what he wishes with his own. Religion is there, but hardly more than formally recognised. There is little of the ideological crusader in him. He is a generous conqueror. There is frequent stress on his legal rights. He insists at the court on every tittle of them but always bows to the law himself. The amusing and well-known episode of borrowing money from the Jews on a false security – the boxes of sand said to be boxes of gold – indicates that the writer of the poem was aware of the economics of guerrilla warfare and knew all about calling on bankers and arranging for commission. This plainness about the ordinary things of a country dealer's life, and the charming small touches – the little girl of nine who explains to the Cid that her family cannot allow a banished man into the house – set the hero in a recognisable world that he loves, and as a man to be esteemed. His pain at parting from his wife is not written up, but is thought of as an excruciating physical pain, in the traditional manner of Spanish realism:

> 'now we part; God knows
>   when we shall come together'
> Weeping from his eyes

> you have never seen such grief
> Thus parted the one from the others
> as the nail from the flesh.

He is a real man among real things even when his exploits are fantastic:

> There the rout began
> as it pleased God.
> My Cid and his Knights
> rode in pursuit;
> You would have seen so many tent cords
> snapped, and the poles down,
> And so many embroidered tents lying on the
> ground.

And in the court brawl where the Cid storms at the rich nobles who have married his daughters and then left them stripped and beaten in a wood because they are not good enough socially, the scene has the roughness of nature. Here, above all, one sees the Cid quietly affirming the law. He is not a lawless man.

This plain, bare, directness of the *Poem*, its lack of hyperbole and of elaborate message, are in themselves delightful, but there is another aspect in which we see the myth-making faculty at work. Brenan discusses this in his *Literature of the Spanish People* and it can be followed in more detail in Pidal. The *Poem of the Cid* was written directly under the influence of the *Chanson de Roland*, which commemorated the greatness of Charlemagne three hundred years after his death, whereas the *Poem of the Cid* was almost contemporary. The *Chanson* has a quality, Brenan says, peculiar to French art but never found in Spanish. It does not stop at telling a story, 'it sets up a universal pattern or example. Already in this period we can see the French mind at work, consciously and deliberately creating ideas and values.' It is a work animated by the crusading spirit and fortified by national and religious propaganda; for it was the French, and especially the Benedictines of Cluny, the intellectual commissars of Europe, who had established the figure of St James of Compostela as a symbol of the Christian drive against Islam, and who had established the pilgrimage route across the Pyrenees to the shrine as a sort of political duty. The famous battle at

Roncesvalles occurs on the pilgrims' road over the Pyrenees and is an incident in ideological warfare.

But as the Spaniards fought back against a real occupation of their country, they began to resist the centralising sophisticated ambitions of a remote French Europe. The Spanish peasant disliked the new feudal tenures the Cluniac monks sought to impose. There was strong opposition to the introduction of the Roman rite. The Cid's handwriting itself is in the old script, not the new standard script being introduced by the planners of the new Europe. The *Poem of the Cid* is, in short, the assertion of the Spanishness of the struggle. The Cid is more than a great fighter, he represents the appearance of a Spanish view, opposed to the spirit of the French propagandists. Brenan says there is nothing in French literature of the twelfth century to compare with the assured and responsible political feeling of the *Poem of the Cid* and that one of the reasons for this was that the Spaniards were not taken up with the international question of the relations of the Church to the civil authorities. There was no ideological right and wrong for the Spaniards; on the contrary, from the simple view of the ordinary free man, the tone is set by that famous line: 'God, what a good vassal, if only he had a good lord.' If we are to look for a contemporary parallel – admittedly a dangerous amusement – we see the Spanish relation to the new monolithic system of France and Rome as something like, say, the relation of Yugoslavs to Russians. The situation is as primitive. The other point is that heroes may rise spontaneously, but they are not heroes unless they arise out of fundamental situations in their age – they are not merely courageous, fortunate men or splendidly tragic men – and that no myth crystallises about these popular figures except through the means of an acceptable propaganda. The French genius had to suggest an idea; the Spanish genius, to be effective politically, had to turn to a man and to convey that Islam was conquered and Europe saved, not by a complex organisation and an ideology, but by a banished man of just instincts, well-set in his own land.

Mr Forster's Birthday

―――――

'May I never resemble M. de Lesseps', E. M. Forster wrote when he considered the famous statue by the Suez Canal on one of his journeys to India. 'May no achievement upon an imposing scale be mine.' He has indeed been a haunting absence in the English novel, but on the occasion of his eightieth birthday, we can allow ourselves to dress up our prose in the boater and blazer of 1905 and think of his silence, since *Passage to India*, as 'a rotten business', without a moral – like Harold's dropping of the oars and dying, in *The Point of It* – and of Forster's survival in our literature as a 'cert'. How does one survive if one does not impose? Forster has survived so far by interposing. Where his elders, Shaw, Wells, Kipling, imposed by sheer efficiency and manpower, Forster has interposed and influenced by a misleading slackness, by the refusal to speak in a public voice. This has given the personal a startling strength. He has had, one guesses, more influence on the educated middle classes than any other English writer in the last thirty or forty years; for it is he who has taught them to disengage themselves from their inherited official, not to say imperial, personality. The Empire Kipling celebrated, Forster destroyed, and by a handful of out-of-date novels – for it was his fate to have a great deal of his material pulled from under his feet by the 1914 war. In saying his say against imperialism, he exhausted in advance what he could have said, as a novelist, against totalitarianism. He was kind enough to write articles.

One can rely on English life to produce these personal voices: a Samuel Butler, a Mary Kingsley, a Forster; in our own generation, a George Orwell. Their voices are direct, natural, distinct and disengaged, malignly flat. The machine stops when they start talking. We are so used to various sorts of 'side' in English life that we are startled and pleased by the note of authority from nature. Outside of our poetry we find that voice hard to hit on. Forster's gift has been just that: the private voice, carrying without effort, in the public place. The refusal to be great; the attack on the will and the bad heart; the two cheers instead of the usual three for democracy, the third being reserved for 'love the Beloved Republic, which feeds upon Freedom and lives'; the belief in personal relationships – 'the heart signs no document' – and an aristocracy of 'the sensitives, the considerate and the plucky'; the debating-point plea for a 'period of apathy, inertia and uninventiveness' – these are not withdrawals. Some are principled assertions of the supreme value of individual life; some are there to redress a balance. None is a brilliant paradox put down by a consuming brain. The apologist for softness is intellectually hard; the liberal who has been flounced out of economic *laisser faire* and who believes that, nevertheless, *laisser faire* is the only doctrine that 'pays' – a favourite ironic word – in the world of the spirit, is not proposing to let us do what we like. No one is let off in Forster's novels; like Jane Austen, he is a moral realist. Leonard Bast, the prototype of the angry young man, will get a rap on the knuckles for being a crushed soul. Having a chip – a maiden aunt seems to say – is no excuse for hysteria and making messes. Mr Wilcox catches it for being a soul-crusher. No tears, I seem to remember, are shed in Forster's novels. The sins of the heart, the failure to 'connect', don't pay: they end in emptiness and panic. Those are better words than the jargon we have learned to use since the nervous breakdown, if only because they imply the moral imperative which is necessarily lacking in scientific studies of the mind.

There is the voice of the decided moralist in Forster; fortunately for the English novel, it has been transposed into the accents of the brusque and off-hand sanity which is in the central tradition of our comedy. Like Shaw's – though in the private interest, being more concerned with intimate feeling than with justice – Forster's is a comedy of ideas, and the danger there was that it would be expressed in a comedy of types or that he would have chosen people possessed of too great a skill in debate. He escaped this danger by his brilliant use of people who had been thoroughly unfitted to deal with their situations; like so many of Henry James's characters they are null or dull. Looking again at the early short stories which try out the themes to be taken up by *Where Angels Fear to Tread* or *Howards End* one is, at first, shaken by their pedestrian characters. How faded the people are now; they were born faded. Everyone outside Cambridge, one suspects, had to bear that accusation. Pompous, shabby, fussy suburbans they are, a collection of dim windows, daughters genteel or bossy, sons emasculated or emotionally congested. There are the mild, mechanical soldiers and all are liable to the blood-pressure, the wilfulness or the frostbite of a class-consciousness that has passed out of our knowledge. Formidable to deal with, these injured families are in danger of suffering (as Gissing's characters do) from an initial social pathos which is unforgivable in works of art. (Class theories play the part of the famous pathetic fallacy.) But, at second glance, the pathos goes. For these unlikely dullards are suddenly shaken by issues that had never occurred to them as existing; they are tripped up by melodrama, and their dullness makes their situation more arresting. They are made to skip and look lively. Mr Forster's beliefs are gentle, but he has no sentimental indulgence for weakness, and we remember that behind the fineness of his spiritual scrutiny lie the scrupulous traditions of the Clapham Sect; working in him is a spirited agnosticism and he does not see why the moral stakes for these muddled gamblers should not be put very high or why the upper middle classes should not have to risk all. In a way, he treats the English as if they were foreigners – a good idea considering how anti-foreign we have always been. His people swing between two states of mind – the disinterested and the benighted; and they fall into four foreign groups: the Teutonic, heading towards suicide in a sea of general ideas; his Latins – vulgar, avaricious but redeemable because they have not been castrated by good taste, are in the sink-or-swim of the instinctive life, and are liable to racial memories of Mediterranean paganism; the Oriental – passive, touchy and affronted; and the inhabitants of Tonbridge. Where have we seen the Forster situations before? In the novel-poems of the poet Clough, but whereas Clough is torn in half and is half-guilty, half-aggressive about his passivity and his escape into abstract thought, Forster presents the picture of a united personality who knows his mind. He knows what he is committed to.

It is not like the committal of Shaw or Butler – with whom he has, however, some affinity – nor any of the other committals of those who attacked the official late Victorian or Edwardian personality. His comedy is not freakish; it is not accommodating; there is no comfort in his scepticism. He is not scabrous and not at all the satirist, even if he caricatures; he is without the orgiastic sense of the full comic writers who revel in meaninglessness. He is not very sociable. His comedy is positive and spiritual; it has one most alarming trait: assurance. It is lonely. It has courage. He has always got his deadliest effect from a pretence of soppiness, from a casual, slangy disregard of the spirit of composure, or from a piece of parenthetical bathos. That opening argument about the cow in *The Longest Journey* is an example. If he is casually disrespectful, he is also casually abrupt about matters of life and death: the echo in the cave, Gino's outbreak of physical cruelty at the crux of sorrow in his child's death, young Wilcox getting three years for hitting someone with an old sword, Leonard dying perfunctorily because a bookcase falls on him, the baby falling out of the carriage, and those brief, dismissed sudden deaths in boats, playing fields and at the level-crossing. The intellectual must face causality; but he had better remember casualty and the inexplicable. None of these famous incidents will 'do' in a realistic novel; the shock is too great and one might attack them as pointers to a suspicion that Mr Forster has exaggerated the device of not belonging to the world, and even that he grew up so quickly because he refused to join it. But these incidents, of course, succeed in romance where the writer has the licence to load his dice as he wishes. He has, also, a hankering after the pagan acceptance of mercilessness and the absence of tears.

Since his time, anyone in the nature of a personage has vanished from the English and American novel. The official has gone. The conversational, the vernacular voice has come in, but only in the interests of naturalism. It is common now to read novels in which physical life is rendered so clearly that we have the impression of seeing it before our eyes like the pebbles of a clear running stream. That impression can be had from Mr Forster's novels also – but with an important difference. It is the moral life that has the pebble-like clarity in *his* writing; he has made it tangible and visible. He has, so to say, speeded up the process of contemplation by making it clear what, in his view, needed to be contemplated. The plain conversational style is truly conversational in the sense that we feel several people are talking and trying to find out; in spite of James's influence, there is no sense of monologue. Forster's talk, like all good talk, has the quality of surprise.

It is easy enough to demonstrate that Forster represents the end of something. He has almost said so himself, though not quite: civilisations are a string of intermissions in the anger of time. He speaks at the end of liberal culture and, since there is no other, there is no implicit accusation. He agrees that this firm attachment owes something to privilege and we all know the dogma that, in its penultimate phase, a culture sees spiritual order in art alone; in its ultimate post-Forsterian phase it crumbles into a sort of Byzantine pedantry.

Forster's contribution to our present collective society is the reminder that it will be an arid and destroying desert if we remove the oasis of private life. But he is a dangerous master. All very well for him to refuse to be great: he had to fight the portentous. Educated and inured by the powerful, he was free to develop apathy and softness as an unexpectedly useful muscle. He had something pretty unscrupulous to disbelieve in. Does he feel, now, the burden peculiar to famous old age, that an age has caught up with him? Does he feel that, in England at any rate, a younger generation is carrying the cult of privacy and personal relationships to the lengths of whimsicality and eccentricity? It often strikes one that far too large a portion of educated energy is going into running England as a kind of private joke, an ingenious personal crossword. We are more gentle with one another, but we spend an inordinate amount of time being gentle; we are bathed to the point of sleep in tolerance and understanding. Forsterian teaching has been taken on without our recognising that it had the virility of a reaction. It is very pleasant to relax, as he taught us, and to believe (for example) in his notion that the bucket drops down into the unconscious and brings up the substance of the work of art. It is true. But isn't it Mr Forster's old enemy, the will, that has turned the handle and let the bucket down? It is a mistake to take this infertile and original writer literally. Thus his 'apathy' really means 'integrity'. One other writer of his generation, Boris Pasternak, has it, and has demonstrated its phenomenal spiritual strength. Like him, Forster hands back the ticket, bored by the verbosity of the strong-willed, knowing that there is a creative force in the secrets of life. He is fresh because he is unable to conceive of a life without free choice; perhaps we would think him more than courageous, and actually great, if his novels had conveyed the other half of the argument: that we have to choose for others and that choice is made by others for us. But this is to ask for an inrush of ungoverned emotion beyond the scope of comedy.

[609]

Pain and William Golding

═══════════

The essence of the novelist's art – especially the English novelist's – is the quotidian. From the moment Crusoe domesticates and diarises his desert island, the novel reflects the confidence the individual derives from the society he lives in. The risks of romance are gone: he is safe in the realist's nest: Selkirk was lonely, but Crusoe is the least lonely man in the world. This confidence has lasted in our tradition. But when we look up from our books into the life around us today, we wonder how the prosaic observer in realistic fiction can be so certain of himself. The quotidian art goes on describing and describing and, as far as externals are concerned, we cannot complain that the modern realist fails to describe the features of a changing, violent or collapsing society. But he is the spectator, in some lucky way insured and untouched; rarely does the novelist find the point at which we are involved or committed; rarely does he touch the quick, so that for once the modern alibi – 'it is beyond the power of the imagination to grasp, etc., etc.' – does not work. The imagination will never grasp until it is awakened; and facts will not awaken it. They merely strengthen opinion; and there is nothing so apt to shut us off from the world as the correct opinion about it. The imagination can be awakened only by the imagination, by the artist who has the power to break us down until the point of secret complicity is reached. It was this point which the writer of romance, undeterred by the day's events, and lost in his world of dramatic wishes, once knew how to reach.

Mr William Golding is an artist of this kind. His first three books, *Lord of the Flies* (1954), *The Inheritors* (1955) and *Pincher Martin* (1956) are romance in the austere sense of the term. They take the leap from the probable to the possible. *Lord of the Flies* has a strong pedigree: island literature from Crusoe to *Coral Island*, *Orphan Island* and *High Wind in Jamaica*. All romance breaks with the realistic novelist's certainties and exposes the characters to transcendent and testing dangers. But Golding does more than break; he

[610]

bashes, by the power of his overwhelming sense of the detail of the physical world. He is the most original of our contemporaries. Many writers have been concerned, as a matter of argument, with what is rhetorically called 'the dilemma of modern man', and have given us, as it were, lantern slide lectures on the anarchy of a poisoned future; they are really essayists sitting in comfort. Golding, on the contrary, scarcely uses an argument or issues a warning. He simply shakes us until we feel in our bones the perennial agony of our species. By their nature, his subjects – prep-school boys on a desert island in a world war, the calvary of a sailor who gave the right order but whose half-conscious body is being washed about the gullies of an Atlantic rock, the conflicts of a handful of Neanderthalers – could easily become the pasteboard jigsaw of allegory, pleasing our taste for satire and ingenuity; but the pressure of feeling drives allegory out of the foreground of his stories. He is a writer of intense visual gift, with an overpowering sense of nature and an extraordinary perception of man as a physical being in a physical world, torn between a primitive inheritance and the glimmer of an evolving mind. A dramatic writer and familiar with the strong emotions that go with the instinct of self-preservation – blind love for his kind, hatred, fear and elation – he is without hysteria. He is not cooking up freakish and exotic incident; he is not making large proclamations about man against nature, God, destiny and so on; he is seriously and in precise, individual instances gripped – as if against his will – by the sight of the slow and agonising accretion of a mind and a civilised will in one or two men, struggling against their tendency to slip back, through passion or folly, and lose their skills in panic. And there is pity for the pain they feel.

Pain is the essence of Mr Golding's subject. In *The Inheritors* it is the obscure pain of a baffled and dying group of ape men who see themselves supplanted by the more skilful new being called Man. The ape man experiences the pain of the grunt, of trying to communicate from one poor mind to another – 'I have a picture. Can you see my picture?' – and also the pain of trying to distinguish, for a moment, what is inside from what is outside himself. From his tree he sees Man who is not afraid of water, as he is, who gets drunk on honey, who has invented love-play; he sees with a kind of grieving as an animal might grieve. In *Pincher Martin,* the tale of a modern sailor whose broken body is washed about the Atlantic rock, who eats limpets, is poisoned by his store of food and who eventually goes mad and dies, the pain is in the fight against physical hurt and loss of consciousness, in the struggle to put his educated will against his terrors. It is also in the Job-like protest against a defeat which wrongs everything he has believed in. In *Lord of the Flies* – the first and, I think, the best of these books – a group of schoolboys re-enact the *Coral Island* story and the pain is in the struggle between the boys who revert through fear to the primitive and turn into savage hunters, and those who are trying vainly to preserve foresight and order. In the end, the boys are rescued, but not before they have lived through the modern political nightmare.

Mr Golding's sensibility to pain is the spring of his imagination and if, in all three stories, the heroes are smashed up, he is by no means a morbid or sadistic writer. The chest of the creature, running in terror from its enemies, scorches, the calves cramp, the skin tears, the body has to endure what animal panic lets it in for. Pain is simply the whole condition of man; it is the sign that he is awake and struggling with his nature, and especially with the terror which so suddenly scatters the mind. *Lord of the Flies* contains one episode of great horror. The rotting body of a dead parachutist is blown across the island in the night, almost stepping on the trees and the beaches, until it is taken out to sea. The sight is the final and clinching argument to the very young boys that a devouring Beast has really been among them; and one might conclude that this is a decisive symbol of human defeat and the meaninglessness of the struggle. The idea is irrelevant. Mr Golding's imagination is heroic. Against the flies that buzz round the dangling scarecrow must be put the elation of the adventure, the love of natural life, the curiosity of the eye, that run through the writing. And the compassion.

It is natural to compare *Lord of the Flies* with *Coral Island* – and then with *High Wind in Jamaica*. In *Coral Island* we see the safe community. A century without war and with a settled sense of human personality has produced it. In Richard Hughes's book, we saw the first sign of disintegration: the psychologists have discovered that children are not small fanciful adults, but are a cut-off, savage race. In *Lord of the Flies* we understand that the children are not cut off; anthropology, the science of how people live together, not separately, reflects the concern of the modern world which has seen its communities destroyed. The children in *Lord of the Flies* simply re-enact the adult, communal drama and, by their easy access to the primitive, show how adult communities can break up. Of course, Mr Golding's improbable romances remain improbable; they are narrow and possible. The modern romancer has the uncluttered chance of going straight to the alienation of the individual and to the personal solitude that is one of the forgotten subjects. In our world, which is so closely organised, we are hardly aware of what we are privately up to. We use large words like calamity, disaster, racial suicide, devastation; they are meaningless to us until an artist appears who is gifted enough to identify himself with a precise body being washed up against a precise collection of rocks, a precise being sniffing the night air for his enemy or feeling the full force of a particular blow. Until then, we are muffled in our alibi: 'the imagination cannot grasp'.

Lord of the Flies is the most accomplished of Mr Golding's novels. Its portraits of the shipwrecked boys and its understanding of them are touching and delightful and he is master of a rich range of scene and action. In this book his spirit and his serenity are classical. *Pincher Martin* is more chock-a-block, but it has fine descriptions of the roaring, sucking deafening sea scene on the rock which we know stone by stone. He is a modern writer here in that his eyes are pressed close to the object, so that each thing is enormously magnified. We see how much a man is enclosed by his own eyes. The important quality of all Golding's descriptions is that they are descriptions of movement and continuous change and are marked by brilliant epithets. (One remembers: 'three prudish anemones'.) There is this picture of the swimming sailor, almost at the rock:

> Ropes held him, slipped and let him go. He saw light, got a mouthful of air and foam. He glimpsed a riven rock face with trees of spray growing up it and the sight of this rock floating in mid-Atlantic was so dreadful that he wasted his air by screaming as if it had been a wild beast. He went under in a green calm, then up and was thrust sideways. The sea no longer played with him. It stayed its wild movement and held him gently, carried him with delicate and careful motion like a retriever with a bird. Hard things touched him about the feet and knees. The sea laid him down gently and retreated. There were hard things touching his face and chest, the side of his forehead. The sea came back and fawned

round his face, licked him. He thought movements that did not happen. The sea came back and he thought the movements again and this time they happened because the sea took most of his weight. They moved him forward over the hard things. Each wave and each movement moved him forward. He felt the sea run down to smell at his feet then come back and nuzzle under his arm.

But this book succeeds less when it takes us into the sailor's chaotic recollections of his life. It contains some flashes back to scenes of jealousy and rivalry which are hard to grasp. It may be that Golding's sense of theatre – often strong in writers of romance – has overcome him here. (He is the author of a witty satirical play, *The Brass Butterfly*, which is excellent reading.) But in making us feel in the current in the modern world, instead of being stranded and deadened by it; in providing us with secret parables; in unveiling important parts of the contemporary anguish and making them heroic, knowable and imaginable, he is unique.

Grub Street

'Gissing: the English Gorky with a butterfly collar,' says Mr G. W. Stonier in his introduction to *New Grub Street*. Moscow, transmuted, becomes Camberwell and is lamed. It is as well to remember the Russian quality of our very suburban novelist for, like Meredith and Disraeli, Gissing brings an alien's or exile's unconventional insight into English society. They are all self-created foreigners: Disraeli, the Jew; Meredith with his German education and his Welsh illusions; Gissing living abroad in dreams of Renaissance man and the Greek classics while he listens to the Museum cough in the Reading Room of Great Russell Street. (A scholar, Gissing must be one of our few novelists who is also a linguist; he spoke French perfectly, read German and Italian easily, beside the classical tongues. He knew some Spanish and attempted Russian.) One sees what moods and material the English novel has lost in being written by Englishmen; that is to say, by those Englishmen who, in Mr Stonier's good phrase, could 'only dramatise their own self-satisfactions'. And we recall that the great Russian novels of the nineteenth century arose from the failure of a class, whereas the English sprang out of its success.

Gissing's failure and his exile are the cause of his fame. We are driven back, as always with imperfect artists, to the entanglement of the person and his work. As Mr Walter Allen has pointedly said in *The English Novel* the fiction of Gissing is 'too personal, the powerful expression of a grudge'. No other English novelist until then had had a chip the size of Gissing's; self-pitying, spiritless, resentful, humourless, his lucid bleat drags down his characters and his words. There is a disturbing complacency in him as he stands at the sink and tells us that life is wretched and defeating, and many an indignant reader must have felt that Gissing was myopic. Like the young Jasper Milvain in *New Grub Street* he seems to raise his chin and talk to the upper air when talking about himself. And then, like many men whose life is shut in by unbelievable domestic wretchedness, Gissing was self-centred and did not recognise that, if one is going in for this sort of thing, one had better open one's eyes and recognise that life is not merely dreary and miserable; it is savagely cruel and utterly appalling. Gissing wrote less of the horror he knew than of the apathy which it engendered. He writes as if he were a mere effect. To return to Mr Stonier:

> One need only lose oneself in London or in the similar streets of any large town, to experience the monotony of anguish uppermost in Gissing. He respects the low affront, not hurrying, in imagination, to overpaint it with bright colours; the life behind windows does not grow comic or enormous; distance lends no enchantment, and no music steals up the gutters to transform what is into what is not. He lacks the fairy or imp of entertainment; but as the bias of fiction-writing goes, that is not such a disadvantage. He cannot help seeing plain, being faithful, taking the bad tooth into account.

Gissing is very Russian in his overpowering sense of the stale and unoccupied hours we have to lug around with us and this is his peculiar importation into the English novel.

Today, Mr Walter Allen's suggestion of the grudge is more interesting. In some ways the grudge of several of our young novelists resembles Gissing's, as if Gissing were their perverse prophet and progenitor. There are hints of it in all his work and it is particularly strong in *New Grub Street*. The grudge is concerned with education and opportunity. It has two aspects. Why pass an Education Act, giving clever Board School boys the chance to become cultivated men, when they will only find themselves in stultifying and unseemly surroundings and without the means to live in some accord with their minds; and why educate ordinary boys so that they can become the customers for everything that is vulgar and trivial in popular, commercial culture? When Gissing wrote *New Grub Street*, the new journalism with its obsession with things like 'What the Queen Eats' was showing its first signs. Now, it is easy to show that either the competitive instinct or the reforming spirit of social conscience – both of which Gissing lacked – were required of the clever Board School boy in return for his privilege. Gissing resented that only the rich could join the Past. For the unclever, Gissing had somehow got the idea (as Mr Walter

Allen says) that the aim of education was merely to teach people to read books. He was the scornful scholarship winner. (He appears to make one exception in his dislike of the new journalism; in its higher forms of popularisation it educates women. One recognises there the man who suffered from the tongues of ignorant viragos.)

The grudge of Gissing is the grudge of the outsider. He shows the psychological characteristics in his attitude to the prostitute and the servant girl he married. The violence in these vicious women is really matched, not by the passivity of his temperament, but by what one suspects to be the isolation and ruthlessness of his own mind. Morley Roberts, in his disguised biography of Gissing, *The Private Life of Henry Maitland*, happily reissued in 1958 with a key, by Richards Press, believed that Gissing simply desired the whole sex and, in his self-imposed loneliness and incapable of love, thought anyone would do. One has the horrible suspicion that he felt punishment justified him and so set him free. But – to get on more certain ground – Gissing was an outsider in rejecting modern society altogether because it did not provide a place for the recalcitrant scholar and the pure artist who was poor. The theme of *New Grub Street* is the tragedy of the intellectual worker. The book is a full conspectus of the literary situation done with Gissing's grey exactitude and clarity. The vulgar comic view of writers as a collection of eccentrics is dropped; he catches their fundamental dignity, anxiety and egotism. It is bad enough to be an artist, with its appalling gift of self-knowledge, without being obliged to kill the love of your wife, slave till you are blind, and end ill, half-starved and counting the pennies, behind the tightly drawn curtains of lower-middle-class respectability. The portrait of the wretched, gifted and only moderately saleable Reardon in this book is masterly, for Gissing is unremitting in observation. Without money, a James or a Shaw would just as certainly go down to the smell of last night's dinner in the seedy back room. Gissing's simple description of the writer's day as he sits at his desk is exact, touching and terrifying; one feels half-elated, half-sickened at the end of it. For, allowing for one deficiency in Reardon's character, the morbid lack of will, the portrait would serve for any novelist.

Those who have the grudge nowadays have, of course, no interest in Gissing's concept of the artist or in his belief in the culture he belongs to. All the same the conditions of literary society have not changed much since

Gissing's times. Journalism, with its short-term shots of success, its weekly injection, still offers its therapy to the writer who can stand the ulcers and suicidal depressions of creative writing no more. Inflation and high taxation have wiped out the rewards of the successful and have reduced the less successful to the role of commentators frantic for a new slant. Our society will reward highly any writer who agrees to compound on his gifts and abandon them. A creative writer must have time. In Gissing's day he had time but little money and, after the first successful start, the lack of money ate into the time. Still, the little money Gissing had was his and he lived in a low-cost society. In our high-cost society we have money, but a large portion of it goes back to the State and we may not invest in our talent. In consequence, we have no time.

Morley Roberts, who was an intimate of Gissing, thought that he shared with most English novelists the ability to create situation and the inability to develop it owing to the national *mauvaise honte* and dread of feeling. But Gissing excelled, as many have, in irony. Each character is solid in *New Grub Street* and if the dialogue is still and the action is slow, there is nothing wooden in the people. Their temperature is, indeed, low. In their varying ways, they are all afflicted, of course, with Gissing's chronic passivity; but in two instances, in the characters of Peardon's wife Amy, and the young, climbing, versatile journalist, Jasper Milvain, he introduces us to two new and disturbing developments of the passive character. Milvain is not passive in his profession; he climbs boldly, cleverly, even engagingly; it is his conscience that is passive. He practises an ingenious technique of self-deception: i.e. he believes that if he is frank about his motives, if he tells the truth, this will clear him of moral obligations. He has the insincerity of the detached. Amy's passivity is feminine, and realistic. She has no will but she drifts with skill. Gissing is unusual among English male novelists in discerning the mental life of his women. Living in an ideal world himself he understood their ideal world. It did not shock him that Amy should resent her husband's failure; and that her love would not stand up to it. It was natural to wish to marry a great man, but it was also natural that, under his influence, she would develop into a creature alien to him and with an intellect of her own. She marries the conscienceless Milvain with her eyes open and with a delicate lack of scruple. Easy enough to make fun of her as a female climber; Gissing sees the comedy but he is detached enough to see

[618]

she has a right to drift with her self-esteem. She will become genteel. Poverty is over.

When we wince at Gissing's uncritical acceptance of the lower-middle-class dream of gentility and respectability, and at its emblem, the butterfly collar; when we shudder at the tepid, timid ideal world he obtained from classical scholarship, we ought also to point out that he saw people in two troubled phases: as they are and as they would wish to become. To him the individual dream was or could become a serious extension of their emotional range as characters. Indeed, it is out of the soured homes, where dreams have gone bad, or have become ludicrous or catastrophic, that the vitality of this class has sprung. To most English novelists, invigorated but narrowed by class consciousness, one class has always seemed comical to another; that is where Gissing is so un-English, a foreigner or an exile. He sees nothing comic in class. He writes as if it exists chiefly as a pathos or a frustration, a limitation of the human keyboard.

Miss Lonelyhearts

Nathanael West is one of the novelists of the breakdown of the American dream in the Thirties. His real name was Nathan Weinstein, he moved in fashionable literary society, became a script writer in Hollywood after the success of *Miss Lonelyhearts* and was killed in a motor accident at the age of forty. Two of his novels, *Miss Lonelyhearts* – which is very well known – and *The Day of the Locust*, show that a very original talent was cut short. He was preoccupied with hysteria as the price paid for accepting the sentimentalities of the national dream. He feared hysteria in himself, he was morbidly conscious of it in his people; he was attracted and repelled by its false dreams as one might be by a more poisonous way of mixing gin. West did not feel that life was tragic, for the sense of tragedy was lost in the moral collapse of the period he lived in. Like Chekhov – but only in this respect – he was appalled by the banality of city civilisation. Instead of being tragic, life was terrible, meaningless and without dignity. Mr Alan Ross, in a warm, if sometimes difficult, introduction to a volume containing all four of West's novels, makes this point and suggests that while the English writers of the Thirties reached their conclusion 'through a series of well-bred intellectual convictions', Americans like West were thrown helplessly among the brute economic facts. For them the experience was emotional and even theatrically so, because hysterical violence is very near the surface in American life.

West's resources were Art – he learned from the surrealists – and compassion. Except in his satire, *A Cool Million*, which is an American *Candide* done in the manner of a parody too obvious and prolonged, he was not a political writer in the literal sense. He explored the illness behind the political situation. Human beings have always fought misery with dreams, Miss Lonelyhearts observes; the dream and its ignoble deceits, the panic, anger and frustration these deceits expose, gave him his material. In *The Day of the Locust*, his mature novel, it is the boredom exposed by the failure of the Californian dream of an earthly Paradise that puts an expression of hate and destructiveness on the faces of the weary middle-aged population who have retired to Los Angeles. As they pour in to gape at the stars arriving for some world première, they have the look of lynchers. Lynch, in fact, they do, and for no reason.

This does not convey that West is a comic writer. He has freakishness, wit and a taste for the absurd from the surrealists, also their sophistication in parody and styles, but moved quickly away from their gratuitous and perverse humour. He became comic and humane. *Miss Lonelyhearts* is a potent and orderly distillation of all the attitudes to human suffering. Miss Lonelyhearts himself is the drunken writer of an Advice Column in a newspaper, who begins running it as a joke, a sort of sobbing *Americana*, and ends by becoming overwhelmed by the weight of human misery and by his inability to do anything about it. The office gambits sicken him. Christ, Art, the Karamazov line, the Value of Suffering, back to Nature, on to Hedonism and so on have been taped long ago by Shrike, the editor with the deadpan face, an expert in 'how to play it'. Shrike is one of West's many attacks on the dream-generators of the mass-media – an attack in the sense of being one of those unholy recognitions that lie at the centre of the comic view of life:

'I am a great saint,' Shrike cried. 'I can walk on my own water. Haven't you heard of Shrike's passion in the Luncheonette, or the Agony in the Soda Fountain? Then I compared the wounds in Christ's body to the mouths of a miraculous purse in which we deposit the small change of our sins. It is an excellent conceit. But now let us consider the holes in our own bodies and into what these congenital wounds open. Under the skin of a man is a wondrous jungle where veins like lush tropical growths hang along overripe organs and weed-like entrails writhe in squirming tangles of red and yellow. In this jungle, flitting from rock grey lungs to golden intestines, from liver to lights and back to liver again, lives a bird called the soul.'

In the vulgar, exhausted way of the mass-media, deadpan Shrike is an aesthete. His jaunty little face looks like a paralysed scream of fright. His remarks are pictorial, but without relation to any meaning. Miss Lonely-hearts is muddled by Shrike's cleverness. He would like to be able to believe in the efficacy of Christ, but the name for him has become another word for hysteria, 'a snake whose scales are tiny mirrors in which the dead world takes on a semblance of life'. He plowters through a series of alcoholic bouts, tries to seduce Shrike's cold and salacious wife, gets into fights in speakeasies, terrorises and tries to torture an old man in a public lavatory; for Miss Lonelyhearts has strong sadistic fantasies, his pity has a strain of cruelty in it and he has begun to hate the sufferers who have the tempting horror of freaks. He is seduced by the nymphomaniac wife of a cripple, tries illness, love on a farm. These struggles are fuddled but heroic; he feels his 'great heart' is a bomb that 'will wreck the world without rocking it'. In the end he has a vision of the love of Christ and rushes to tell his friend the cripple about it; but the cripple shoots him in a fit of jealousy. Christ may not be hysteria, but he is a tale told by an idiot.

This might have been a slushy book, the derelict lot behind James Barrie's hoardings. It is, instead, a selection of hard, diamond-fine miniatures, a true American fable. West writes very much by the eye and his use of poetic images has a precision which consciously sustains his preoccupation with the human being's infatuation with his dream and inner story. (All his people are spiders living in the webs they spin out of their minds.) Leaves on trees are like thousands of little shields, a woman's breasts are like 'pink-tipped thumbs', a thrush sings like a 'flute choked with saliva', a cripple limps along 'making waste motions, like those of a partially destroyed insect'. If we call *Miss Lonelyhearts* a minor star it is because we feel that the Art is stronger than the passion; that, indeed, Miss Lonelyhearts himself is capable only of pathos. His advice to the nymphomaniac who is torturing her husband, to 'let him win once', is just wise old owlishness; her happiness is to accuse and torture, his to drag his loaded foot. West has not considered that human beings overwhelmingly prefer suffering to happiness and that their sobbing letters are part of the sense of the role or drama that keeps them going. Still, as a performance, *Miss Lonelyhearts* is very nearly faultless.

The Day of the Locust is an advance from fable and from fragments of people, to the courageous full statement of the novel. I say 'courageous' because in this kind of transition the writer has to risk showing the weakness of his hand. The artificial lights of the freak show are off in this book and we see human absurdity as something normal. This is a novel

about Hollywood. West worked in the hum of the American dream
generators and he chose those people who have done more for American
culture than their coevals in Europe have done for theirs: the casualties, the
wrecks, the failures, the seedy and the fakes. They are the people to whom
the leisureless yea-sayers have said 'No'. The observer is a painter from the
East who is dreaming up what sounds like a very bad picture, a sort of
Belshazzar's Feast. (He is a vestige of West, the aesthete.) He has fallen for
Faye, a daydreaming creature who secretly earns money as a call-girl for a
'cultured' brothel, and who hopes, like others in the novel, to get into
pictures. She lives among a ramshackle group which includes old stage
hangers-on, a ferocious dwarf, a woman who is grooming her son to be a
wonder-child of the screen, an absurd, fairly genuine cowboy extra and a
pathetic hotel clerk from the Middle West. Faye is carefully observed. She
is the complete daydreamer, insulated to such an extent by the faculty that
it acts as an effective alternative to innocence; she is sexually provoking,
cold, little-minded and cruel, but puts gaiety into the roles she takes on and
has the survival power of a cork in a storm. If Los Angeles were destroyed
by fire she would easily survive, not because she is hard but because she is
flimsy. Already, in *Miss Lonelyhearts*, West had been a delicate student of
the American bitch.

This Hollywood novel is mature because the compassion has no
theatrical pressure; because now West is blocking in a sizeable society, and
because his gift for inventing extraordinary scenes had expanded. The
novel is dramatised – in Henry James's sense of the word – in every detail,
so that each line adds a new glint to the action. His sadistic streak comes
out in an astonishing description of an illegal cockfight in a desert lot. His
comic powers fill out in the scenes with the angry dwarf and in the pages
where the hero gets lost in a film Battle of Waterloo. The psychological
entangling is brought to an appalling climax when Faye leaves her
exhausted hotel clerk for a Mexican and this leads on to the great final
staging of the world première, where riot and lynching are sparked off by
the wonder boy of the screen and the hate behind the Californian myth
comes out:

Once there, they discover that sunshine is not enough. They get tired
of oranges, even of avocado pears and passion fruit. Nothing happens.

They haven't the mental equipment for leisure, the money nor the physical equipment for pleasure . . . Their boredom becomes more and more terrible. They realise that they have been tricked and burn with resentment. Every day of their lives they read the newspapers and go to the movies. Both feed them on lynchings, murder, sex crimes, explosions, wrecks, love nests, fires, miracles, revolutions, war. This daily diet makes sophisticates of them. The sun is a joke. Oranges can't titillate their jaded palates. Nothing can be violent enough to make taut their slack minds and bodies.

It was a warning against fascism; it makes the witch-hunt understandable; by extension, it is a statement about the nearness of the violence in American life.

The Day of the Locust has the defect of insufficient ambition. It calls for a larger treatment and we have a slight suspicion that the painter-observer is slumming. But West had not the breath for full-length works. Script-writing snaps up the clever. His important contribution to the American novel was his polished comedy, which he displayed with the variety of a master and on many levels. If his talent was not sufficiently appreciated in the moral Thirties, it was because comedy as a world in itself and as a firm rejection of the respected was not understood. West had something of Europe in him, where it is no crime to know too much.

Henri de Montherlant

Henri de Montherlant was born in 1896. He belongs to the brilliant generation of rebels on whom the label Recalcitrant and Unseizable can be fixed. 'There have been three passions in my life: independence, indifference and physical delight', he has written; the words were sharpened in the trenches of the First World War to which we can trace his anti-romanticism and the determination to strip away the disguises of experience and to present only the 'authentic'. In *La Rose de Sable* (*Desert Love*) he wrote: 'For we should all be most suspicious of any venture of spirit or conscience which we knew had begun by being merely one of the heart.' His hostile studies of women, more particularly bourgeois women, in the pre-war novels, sprang from this mistrust of the duplicity of the heart: their speciality. Desire revitalises; love corrupts because it is corrupt in itself. In an interesting introduction Mr Quennell reminds us that the ruthless Montherlant hero used to be compared with Renaissance man. Well! Well! Nowadays he looks simply like one more writer; tough indeed, but evasively bent on self-preservation. In a long account of how he set out to make his life in his *Selected Essays*, he describes how he broke his ties with France after the First World War and went off to live anonymously and alone, in complete freedom in Algeria. He had ceased to be a Catholic; he was attracted to Spanish mysticism. Spanish critics found in him that intellectual excess which they always dislike in French culture when it seeks an exotic, foreign trellis. The essays are the work of man of changeable and restless temper and the ones he wrote during the Thirties when Hitler was rising are egotistical and, on the whole, silly. Where he impressed, as Mr Quennell says, is as a descriptive writer. In this volume, Montherlant's account of his irritable, defensive acquaintanceship with a Jewish soldier during the First World War is worth the rest of the book. It is at once a portrait and an exact, cold estimate of his own prejudices as a stupid young man.

[625]

Since the Second World War, Montherlant has emerged as a fine playwright. His novels seem less important. His attitude to life is interesting now only as it contributes to his descriptive power. Montherlant's descriptions are drained of personal excess and present a scene as if it were the residue left when dozens of conflicting eyes and minds have moved away from it. There is one novel which, because it lies outside his usual belligerence, begins to look like lasting. This is *The Bachelors* (*Les Célibataires*) published in 1934 and translated by Mr Terence Kilmartin. It is one of those carefully framed, precise and acid studies on a small canvas in which French writers again and again excel. The small becomes vast. Cosiness vanishes from cosy corners. Eccentricity is seen to be tragic. Two absurd old men cease to be only absurd; their comedy is dreadful. Their tale contains one of the repressed subjects of our time, one of the subjects that has in fact been secreted while our society has been devoting itself to 'independence, indifference and physical delight', for Montherlant's three passions were not peculiar to him; they are principles that, by now, have taken possession of two generations. The subject is old age.

The two bachelors are an elderly uncle and his nephew, the survivors of a family of the Breton nobility, who share a little house in filth and poverty in the Boulevard Arago. We meet the older one standing outside a lighted shop window reading a newspaper with the help of a stamp collector's magnifying glass. He looks like a tramp. His clothes date back to the fashions of 1885; his overcoat and all his clothes are fastened by safety pins, his boots are tied with string. His pockets contain an old crust of bread, two lumps of sugar, bits of tobacco, solid bread pellets and a beautiful gold watch with his coat of arms on it. He is Elie de Coëtquidan, a baron. At home, he sleeps in a filthy bed. He is hysterically devoted to cats. He is a keen remover of stamps from envelopes. He has fits of writing scandalous anonymous letters, for he delights in causing trouble. He is avaricious and dishonest. The only secret in his life is that he is a virgin; but since his principle is to frighten his other surviving relation, a rich banker, he pretends that a Jewish lady, to whom he takes a few sausages or cakes every Saturday, has been his mistress for thirty years or more and may make claims on the family. He is maliciously trading on the family's latent anti-Semitism.

The nephew, Léon de Coantrés, goes about in workman's clothes. After a promising beginning – he excelled at Latin verse, played the piano, invented a photographic enlarger – he sank into neurotic sloth. His natural direction was downhill. He loathes Society and his ideal is to be an odd-job man or labourer, fetching coal, sweeping up, polishing floors – anything that requires no thought and no worry. He has by now cut himself off from women of his own class; in any case, his love affairs had been with servants and prostitutes; the sudden disappearance of one of these, for whom he had a tenderness, had given him a powerful shock. For twenty-five years he has dreamed of her and never spoken to a woman. He washes once a fortnight. His whole life is based on a resentment of his aristocratic birth; and he suffers from the public scorn given to the French aristocracy. A clue to his neurotic condition is that his father had ruined the family and that he, the son, is being stripped, little by little, by newly discovered creditors of the family. With bewilderment he sees his tiny income vanishing. When the novel opens we see him trying to make his uncle face up to the terrible fact that they will have to sell up and separate. The loneliness of old age is about to set in.

And here the familiar French drama of avarice and hypocrisy begins. Uncle and nephew visit lawyers and their rich relative Octave, a banker – a beautifully drawn study in the evasions of a man who covers up his dishonesties by convincing himself of his own charitableness. He insures himself by openly deceiving himself. For example, when he realises that he is about to be touched by the old gentleman, he at once gives a largish sum to an orphanage so that he will be able to say 'in all honesty' that he has 'so many claims'. His other motive is that he is being sued by a tenant for charging an illegal rent, and the charity is a sop to his conscience. The gift is secret, yet in his idiotic way, he feels it will help his lawsuit morally!

Of the two supplicants, the malign elder is more successful. In a splendid scene he bluntly blackmails the banker with the totally unreal threat that he will go and live with his Jewish 'mistress'. He gets an allowance at once and then sits in the banker's splendid office and refuses to go, getting the utmost out of Octave's humiliation.

Being fundamentally innocent, Léon does worse. He is down to his last few francs and still the banker shuffles and evades. The household is broken up and then, suddenly, the baron reluctantly lets him live in the lodge of his summer château. The last evening of the two old men together is nearly wrecked by a small incident. The old one is rolling up a filthy bread pellet as he chatters and suddenly he stops and a wild look comes into his eyes.

'What is it, Uncle?' asked Léon anxiously.

'I've lost my pellet,' said the old man with a look of desperation. Léon got down on his hands and knees and searched with him. When he saw it, he hesitated; then he remembered that it was his last evening with his uncle and, in the name of the past, the family and his mother's memory, he picked up the ignoble object and gave it to him.

We come to the final scene where Léon goes enthusiastically to the little place of his own in the country. He will be 'away from Society', in the 'bosom of nature', 'living the life of the common people'. (Montherlant is mordant about class masochism.) He eats with the labourers at the inn who call him Monsieur le Comte for a day or two, but stop at once in terrible silence when he tells them he is poor. The minuteness of Montherlant's descriptions of a sick old man's empty days is terrible. One can count the hours. He can't think of anything to do, so he lies in bed; but once he is in bed, a log rolls off the fire or the chimney smokes and he has to get out. He begins to feel dizzy and ill.

Like a drowning man searching desperately for something to cling on to, he wanted to concentrate on some action or other, so he snatched up a pair of nail clippers and cut his nails . . . He went to look at himself in the mirror, convinced that it must show in his face that he was a sick man. But he could see nothing abnormal in his face. He simply found it ludicrous.

Outside he can see the formations of wild geese flying away over the dunes in their autumn migration. The lines might come out of a Russian novel.

Montherlant's picture of old age is searing in its intimacy and the effect is all the more keen because he has a searching comic gift. The snobbish, negligent and dirty country doctor to whom Léon goes is a comic figure; and, back in the Paris pages, there is a brilliant short sketch of an aristocratic lady who finds Léon and pretends not to notice he is looking like a tramp, and shouts with ecstasy about his 'simple life' and how 'ravishing' it is. She would (Montherlant observes) have called *The Critique of Pure Reason* ravishing. Montherlant never skims the surface; he knows the habits of life, mind and speech of the different social classes, and especially of the aristocracy; and without labouring his points, can exactly place any word or act in its context. His sense of *milieu* is exact. His epigrams do not wear so well – it was clever in the Thirties for a novelist to make a mocking intervention; it was a dig at literature. But his irony devastates. After Léon's death, the innkeeper sends to Octave the banker a heavy bill for drinks the wretched Léon has never had; and Octave pays up willingly. He can now quieten his own conscience with the happy delusion that Léon's total failure as a human being was due to alcohol. The key to Montherlant's outlook on life is contained in an armed sentence: 'People do not do us all the harm they are capable of.' One lives in danger, on the edge of things. Montherlant's distinction is that he writes a prose that catches perfectly this sense that the course of life is perilous and unexpected.

Algeria, the romantic and patriotic cult of the Sahara: Montherlant's *Desert Love* is a novelist's response to 'the colonial situation' and the private dilemma of the conqueror. The introduction to the English translation by Alec Brown is not clear about this book. It has been drastically cut. The translation is from the French edition of 1955 and this is an extract from a much longer manuscript written in 1932. I am not sure whether this has ever been published; the suppressed portion is political. Why suppressed? Out of date, perhaps; or the author has changed his mind. We ought to be told and we are not. The book is evidently an attack on the conventional, upper-class European, nature's Second-in-Command. His class has dulled him. The present story contains the love story only of the original manuscript, and this is complete in itself. Love is M. de Montherlant's speciality: women are pitiable or contemptible instruments, men are exasperated executants. The curse upon man is the worship of maturity. Love is regarded as a delusive transaction between technicians who have engaged in it out of *amour propre* and are surprised by emptiness, hypocrisy, suffering and loneliness. Passivity predominates in his characters; from this they go on to cruelty and pity. They are hurt and hurting. Aiming at exactitude (which is not possible without heart) Montherlant's view is fundamentally perverse, but it has edge and clarity. He lacks the faculty and humility of human blindness.

[629]

Desert Love is one more of his examinations of the insulted and the injured. By the influence of his patriotic and socially influential mother, Lieutenant Auligny is posted to a remote station in the Sahara. She wants the glamour of a son 'out there'. He, too, is willing to believe in it. Lacking intellect, he is a passive passenger of contemporary rhetoric. He is ready to believe in the Sahara myth and when this illusion is quickly killed he falls back on the grumpy chauvinism of small things. This is good: upper-class chauvinism has become petty. Auligny is good, upright, kind, without military ambition, and stupid. He is also morbidly sensitive. If we compare him with his English opposite number, the nice or decent fellow, Auligny probably lacks the group or social instinct which is second nature to the English and is their conventional hideout when in personal difficulties. Auligny tries to think consistently; his opposite number would grope his way through an undergrowth of sentiment and worry. Auligny finds that the Sahara post is hell on earth. Heat, squalor, boredom, have driven the older hands to near-madness, drink and squalid nights with the one local prostitute. Auligny decides that he can keep his sanity if he finds an Arab girl companion. There must be some human tenderness which will give him security of spirit. A girl is quite easily contracted for; she is hardly more than an inarticulate, illiterate and obedient child. It upsets Auligny that he has had to rent her; it fusses him that the contract requires that she shall remain virgin – a conflict here between honour and personal vanity.

Auligny is a man without self-confidence. He invites a friend (the familiar artist-Casanova of French fiction whom one never really believes in) to share the girl. Guiscart-Casanova foresees the worst; a connoisseur of bizarre sexual situations, he refuses at the last minute. The effect on Auligny is excessive. The girl yields to him suddenly and he is in love with her. He is not only mentally entangled now; he becomes pro-Arab.

> Nobody even suspects the business of carnal love at the root of this or that action of ours which today seems so disinterested. And presumably this is all to the good. For we should all be most suspicious of any venture of spirit or conscience which we knew had begun by being merely one of the heart.

The last sentence there is more interesting than the first: as a minor La Rochefoucauld, Montherlant is apt to fire only on one cylinder.

A parallel sympathy for the French is not, as we can see, aroused in the sandy, illiterate and passive girl. Goodness knows – Montherlant doesn't – what sex does for her. She is well-drawn and is certainly not sentimentalised. Once awakened she quickly tires; in any case, Auligny is a man who watches. He does not give. Neither she nor her father sees in him anything but the conqueror who commands and pays. Their desperate hunger is not sexual. The soft-hearted Auligny wishes to get more out of sex alone than can be bought, or is even there to buy. He is rejected. She and the one or two Arabs are silent when he makes pro-Arab remarks – a characteristic situation of the Thirties.

They do not hate him. They find him laughable. The reason seems to be that they are secure through living with their race; he is insecure, like a child whose pride is to pretend to be alone. There is the passing gaiety of the flesh. What else is there? (Auligny asks.) He calls the girl 'the sand rose' because 'she resembled those little petrifications in being as charming as their petals on the surface, but underneath as cold and inert as the stone of which they are formed'.

Montherlant is a tender and exact analyst of the pagan processes of lust and his descriptions of carnal love are intimate without coarseness. He is not one of those erotic novelists who describe in order to excite themselves. Even in a brutal or squalid scene he keeps his head. His success here springs from the fact that he is more interested in the mind as the body affects it. His chief curiosity is for the character of Auligny, in pulling to pieces a character who combines stupidity and sensibility. Above all Montherlant is interested in the worry and pathos of human inconsistency. In 'the colonial situation', indeed in any human situation, there is no such thing as a fixed type. Montherlant's other novels have left an impression of emotional immaturity, but this works to his advantage in describing the abortive love of transaction. And if there is something intrinsically mean in the scale and people of the episode, his strong physical feeling for the desert gives a large impression of loneliness, desuetude and the grinding-down of life:

> For he was now wide awake, in the centre of the bivouac, drowned in the pungency of the troop's leather, and staring into starless sky. With strident whinnies, just like so many women laughing, some of the

horses struggled and stamped their hooves, trying to get free from their hobbles. A man went across to tighten the knots. At last there was quiet. Auligny rolled over on the other side. Under the ash, the fire seemed to be out, but every now and then a little flame leapt up to illuminate the *shesh*-enwrapped head of one of the men, a shadowy bundle on the ground . . . All around him his men lay asleep, their faces completely covered or with the *shesh* concealing their mouths. They sprawled like children, some so covered and bundled up that one would not have suspected they were human beings at all, others the opposite stretched out in the naivest postures. Some forearms were stretched up stiff in the air. There were lovely rings on the fingers of some of the uncouth soldiers. Their knuckles gleamed.

Were they human, was the Berber girl human? The conqueror's mind was tortured. He had the vanity of his principles, the burden of his backslidings. The sandstorm reduced one to frantic animal restlessness. It blew up the stench of smoke, turned the air to glue and rustled maddeningly on the dunes. In the heat one could have been lying under the furnace of a locomotive. A knife could have been stuck fast in the dense air. They told Auligny to keep cool by singing: 'Lah, lah, lah, lah.'

The portrait of Auligny is dispassionate and exhaustive. He is the well-brought-up young man, uprooted and lost. His difficulty is his inadequacy for the role of conqueror; very few can naturally fill it – those who know and those who do not ask. Auligny even lacks the desire for military distinction. His sensibility is really self-regarding and, when out of his depth, he is either brutal or wounded. His 'case' – if he has one – is that he has never really moved out of Paris and in any very serious novel about the colonial situation, he is really not strong enough to be fully in it. He never really finds out about the Arabs, indeed in his humiliation, he cries out against the High Command for sending inexperienced men who do not know the language to the country. He is taken aback when he observes a 'human' reaction in the Arabs – if he sees tears or some 'unreasonable' behaviour. He is crushed when the girl he has bought does not love him and tells lies.

What has all this to do with Algeria? Isn't it a good deal just the dear old French theme of the bought little mistress, something neat about the disappointments of too-neat an idea? It is not Montherlant's fault that the Auligny situation is now out of date. He has done what he set out to do – to reduce the exotic Sahara myth to the experience of one of its nonentities. Implicit in this is also the exposure of nonentity love: the love that fears to meet an equal. In its erotic pages French literature has colonised wildly since the Romantic movement. That is now put right. Auligny rides off with his dream in his head, like any other sad officer in French fiction, but 'trampled underfoot'. It is 'a closed dream'. The road back is barred by ridicule. He has not even the consolation of remorse. It is as if the young ladies in Chekhov had had no intention ever of going to Moscow. There is not even Goodbye. End of the European myth of the departing garrison.

The Tin-Openers

One of the nice things about foreigners is their faithful regard for English light humour. When we disclaim it, when we snobbishly indicate that this fanciful persiflage goes out of date very quickly, they reproach us. If we explain that the speciality had become sententious at the turn of the century and was in decline after 1914, when wit, impatience, cruelty and vivid scorn returned to our comic writing, the foreign reader persists that our gracious light humour was civilisation itself. Victorian civilisation, we may reply; but millions have read a book like Jerome K. Jerome's *Three Men in a Boat*, and in all the languages of Europe and Asia. One would hardly have thought that this modest little tale of the misadventures of three tin-opening suburban clerks on the Thames would stand up to American connoisseurs of Mark Twain's Mississippi, but it did. Pirated at once, the book conquered America as it amused the students of Bombay, Peking and Valparaiso.

The gag-book, of course, follows the flag. It is now American. The American response to Jerome arose possibly because he had the episodic, digressing, garrulous quality of their vernacular writers. He is close to the Twain of *The Jumping Frog*. But Jerome, like the authors of *The Diary of a Nobody*, and like W. W. Jacobs, belongs to a secure, small Arcadia where the comic disasters of life are the neater for being low. Jerome's humour is a response of the emerging lower middle class to the inconvenience of their situation. Their dreams have left a legacy of small comic defeat. Overworked, they regard idleness as a joke. They have to do everything in penn'orths and ha'porths. Genteel, they have to repress their hilarious envy-disapproval of any burst of bad language on the part of the undeserving poor. The humour of life's little troubles was called the 'too real', the joke lying in deadly and misleading accounts of humiliating trivia. One might take Jerome as the signal that, in 1889, holidays for this overworked and masochistic class became possible. It is 'too real' that the tin-opener (new emancipating gadget of democracy) has been forgotten. It is 'too real' that George and Harris have to share the same bed; that the bed is two foot six wide and that they have to tie themselves together with the sheets in order to keep themselves from falling out. It is 'too real', i.e., only too likely, that the dog will bring a rat to drop into the terrible stew they are making. It is 'too real' that a worn-out child will drop a half-eaten bun in the maze at Hampton Court. The packing, the rain, the clubbing together to hire a cab, the mockery of small boys, the troubles with towropes, laundry, butter, the belief that the banjo is a lovely instrument and that 'Two Lovely Black Eyes' is a beautiful song are the vulgarities of life. There is nothing surreal about the 'too real'; it is the chronic. We know little about the inner lives of Jerome's characters. It is true that Harris has a comic nightmare, but this is merely the traditional joke about strong drink. The odd thing is that the 'too real' could be appreciated in Bombay. Is the tale of Uncle Podger a universal domestic myth? Would Arabs laugh at it? The appeal of Jerome lies in his gentleness and irony, in his power of digression, his gift of capping his comic moments with a final extravagant act that outbids life altogether. Above all, his book is an idyll. Jerome himself, astonished by the book's success, guilefully argued that it could not be due to its vulgarity alone. The absence of women gives us a clue – there is one, but she is a mere body that floats by, drowned: *Three Men in a Boat* has the absurdity of a male pipe dream. *Huckleberry Finn* is basically this also; but the tobacco is stronger and indeed, generally, chewed.

The idyll is the stream on which the vulgar, bickering, banjo-playing boat-load floats lightly along. Not lightly, of course; sculling blisters and half kills them. The joke lies in the modesty of the incident; bumping the bank, getting someone else's shirt wet, eating the horrible camping food, annoying fishermen and motor launches, singing with self-confidence and out of tune, drifting unawares towards the weir, getting the tent up for the night. A lot of it is stock comedy. We know the tent will fall down; the question that awakens the ingenuity of the masters is, how will it fall down? At Cookham these suburbans will imagine themselves in the 'wild heart of nature'. They are not mugs; they have to match their bounce against the primeval cunning of landladies and the pensive malice of innkeepers, anglers and boatmen. Skilfully Jerome plays everything down. He relies on misleading moral commentary and on that understatement which runs like a rheumatism through English humour. Certain jokes date. Bad language is no longer a joke since swearing came in after the First World War. Idleness is no longer a joke – we have moved into an age that says it believes in leisure. And we find nothing piquant in the silliness of girls. The silly girl in light humour was soon replaced by Wodehouse's pretty power stations. (The light humorists of Jerome's period were obliged to avoid sex; they became experts in femininity.) But the dating of a joke does not matter; the laughter in Jerome is caused less by any fact than by the false conclusions drawn from it. He will mildly note that bargees are sometimes 'rude' to one another and use language 'which, no doubt, in their calmer moments, they regret'. Again the work-joke has the intricacy of a conceit in Jerome's skilful hands.

> It always seems to me that I am doing much more work than I should do . . . But though I crave for work I still like to be fair. I do not ask for more than my fair share. But I get it without asking for it – so at least it seems to me and this worries me. George says that he does not think that I need trouble myself on the subject. He thinks it is only my over-scrupulous nature that makes me fear I am having more than my due; and that, as a matter of fact, I don't have as much as I ought. But I expect he says this only to comfort me.

The son of a preacher, Jerome saw that one of the funniest things about a human being is his conscience.

The light humorists get too much pleasure out of educated periphrasis and self-congratulatory club wit. These lead inevitably to heavy prose. Jerome, like W. W. Jacobs, escaped the danger. His prose is clear and simple. It muses on like some quiet, ironical tune played on a malicious whistle. He is free from the journalistic vice of exhibitionism and frantic juggling with bright ideas. He sits by himself on the river bank and drifts on from tune to tune, happily and regardless. He is a very economical writer. In anecdote, he is a master of leading the reader on quietly and then of rushing in a line that suddenly makes the joke take to the air and go mad. The tale of Uncle Podger hanging the picture is a notable piece of technical virtuosity. The packing of the trunk begins as a joke but ends in the complexity of French farce or Restoration comedy. The good light humorist is not a careless fellow with one or two brainwaves and surprises

[636]

only; he is a needy lover of the detail that delays the action until the pressure has reached the proper bursting point. There are some conventional phrases in Jerome's famous account of opening the tin of pineapple, but it is a model. They had tried the penknife, a pair of scissors and a hitcher: the tin merely rolled over, broke a tea cup and fell into the river. George and Harris were no more than a little cut about the face:

> Then we all got mad. We took that tin out on the bank and Harris went up into a field and got a big sharp stone and I went back into the boat and brought out the mast, and George held the tin and Harris held the sharp end of his stone against the top of it and I took the mast and poised it high in the air and gathered all my strength and brought it down.
>
> It was George's straw hat that saved his life that day . . . Harris got off with a flesh wound.
>
> After that I took the tin off myself and hammered at it with the mast till I was worn out and sick at heart whereupon Harris took it in hand.
>
> We beat it out flat; we beat it back square; we battered it into every form known to geometry. Then George went at it and knocked it into a shape so strange, so weird, so unearthly in its wild hideousness that he got frightened and threw away the mast. Then we all three sat down on the grass and looked at it.
>
> There was one great dent across the top that had the appearance of a mocking grin, and it drove us furious, so that Harris rushed at the thing and caught it up and flung it into the middle of the river, and as it sank we hurled our curses at it and we got into the boat and rowed away from the spot and never paused until we reached Maidenhead.

This is pure music hall, of course; much of Jerome is quiet comic patter. He was, in fact, something of an actor. But the idyll frames it all. And peacefully transforms it. A collection of light articles becomes a complete mirage. A world is never created on any level, without the secret structure of conflict. Jerome's case was like that of Dickens in the *Pickwick Papers*. He was commissioned to write an historical guide to the Thames and bits of that survive in the book. He was also a meditative man with a religious background. One or two little sermons are embedded in the text. To us they are incongruous, but late-Victorian farce was not hostile to sentiment. These pieties give an engaging wash of pure sentimental purple to

Jerome's water colour. He was always saved by his lightness of touch. He succeeds less with history. Jokes about Queen Elizabeth and Magna Carta are heavy going. It takes a schoolmaster or a Mark Twain to get the best out of them. Nonconformists like Jerome are apt to be too fervently conventional about history. As for the landscape, it is agreeably kept in its place. The glitter of the main stream, the rankness of the shadows, the gushing of the locks and the streaming of the weirs at night are done with a pleasant subdued versifying. These sights do not overwhelm his true business – that row of elderly anglers (for example) sitting on their chairs in a punt, who are suddenly knocked off, fall into the bottom of the boat and are left – in sublime phrase – 'picking fish off each other'.

Mr D. C. Browning, who writes an introduction to the Everyman Edition of the book, which contains also *Three Men on the Bummel*, tries to persuade us that the latter is as good. What the German tour does is to point to the reason for the superiority of the book about the Thames. It is an idyll of youth. In the German book the heroes are older. They are married. They have lost the happy, impartial rudeness of unattached young men. This time they have to be informative. They will sparkle, but the lark has turned into a tour. Jerome was very shrewd about the Germans and these, sedulously trying to penetrate the mystery of English fancy, used *Three Men on the Bummel* as a textbook in German schools.

The Brutal Chivalry

───────────

Robert Surtees is a sport, in both senses of the term, who flashes in and out of the English novel, excites hope and reduces the critical factions to silence. He has all the dash, all the partiality and all the prospect of an amateur. There is a rush of air, a shower of rain drops from the branches, a burst of thundering mud, a crashing of hazel, the sight of a pink coat and, as far as the English novel is concerned, he has gone. In that brief appearance he has made the genial suggestion that all the other English novelists have been mistaken; they have missed the basic fact in English life – that we are religious, that our religion is violent sport. The unwritten life of a large proportion of the characters in English fiction is passed in playing or watching games in the open air; nature is being worshipped with the senses and the muscles. We are either bemused by fresh air or are daydreaming of some lazy, cunning and exhausting animal life in the open. In that condition, our hourly and sedentary habit of worry as a substitute for thought vanishes and we become people in love. It takes an amateur, like Surtees, to see an obvious thing like this and to exaggerate so that the part becomes the whole of English life. He was a north-country squire, an excellent sporting journalist, but handsomely innocent of the future of hunting in England. He really thought that the Industrial Revolution would make the sport democratic. His assumption is that English violence can be appeased only by the horse. He is the final authority on our horse civilisation, and Jorrocks is a sort of Don Quixote of the last phase of a brutal chivalry. *Après moi* (he might have said) *le garage.*

It is natural that hunting people should admire Surtees. It is not surprising that serious literary critics should admire him also. He creates a complete world. It is the world which Fielding's and Thackeray's people knew in their off-stage lives. It has no relation with the feeble sub-culture of horse-lovers, pony-worshippers, or with the gentility of the jodhpur that spread over England as the coach gave way to the railway, provoking the cult of the New Forest pony. The natural democrats of England live in the north and, though Surtees was a Tory squire, he sincerely believed that the horse was an insurance against the new, snobbish exclusiveness of the shot-up Victorian middle class. He imagined, as so many have done before, that class revolutions will not become snobbish and exclusive. Happy pastoral delusion! Surtees did not foresee either the hardness or the sentimentality of the coming urban England. Or, perhaps, he half guessed it. For the point about Jorrocks is that he is (1) not a horse-lover but a fox-lover, (2) that he rides, buys and sells horses, (3) that he has not an aitch to his name. He is, boldly, incontrovertibly, aggressively, in mid-nineteenth century – a grocer. His fame is that he is not merely a sportsman, but a Cockney sportsman. He has all the trading sharpness and romanticism of a man who sells tea. Surtees is content (purposefully content) with this reality. Jorrocks is as vulgar as Keats; and, as a northerner and a gentleman, Surtees refuses to accept the improved accents of the new-rich in the south. He exploits the rewards our class system offers to our literature. We are continually supplying a number of vulgar geniuses who stand out against the new snobberies which the Puritan streak in us is liable to create; and, in the case of Surtees, there is the anomaly that a Tory squire provides the vulgar protest. The heir of Jorrocks is Mr Polly. Both are native protests against the mean and successful revolutions that deny the instincts of genial, sincere and natural men.

Surtees owes a lot to the low side of Thackeray and does seamy society a good deal better. His dialogue is as quick and true as the master's. He extends a robust and native tradition: the masculine strain of English comic writing. This comedy is broad and extroverted. It grins at the pleasures and pains of the human animal – if it is male – and has little time for the female. Occasionally Surtees sees a tolerable female, but very rarely. We need not suppose that he agreed with Jorrocks that a man ought to kick his wife out of bed three times a month, but we suspect this was only because he regarded the act wistfully as an ideal unfortunately unattainable. The fact is that our comic extroverts are like Mr Sponge and bring a horse-dealer's eye to the consideration of women – 'fifteen two and a half is plenty of height' for them. In its male world, the comic tradition likes the misfortunes of the body, the bruises, the black eyes, the drinking sessions, the gorging at table; prefers the low to the refined, the masterful and unreasonable to the sensitive and considerate. There is a strong regard for the impossible element in human character, for the eccentric and the obsessed. The brutes have their engaging moments. (They give the right kind of girl half a dozen smacking kisses.) But their transcendent emotions emerge in another direction. Jorrocks will quarrel with his huntsman, Pigg, but be reconciled, to the point of embracing him, at the kill. These people are dedicated. They will suffer anything, from drowning upwards, for their sport. They will experience an ecstasy which goes beyond the animal into the poetic. And, in the meantime, they will rollick. Thoroughly non-Puritan, they understand that the life of animal pleasure is the life of animal dismay and they accept it. What these writers in the masculine comic tradition dwell on is the variety of human character. They know that action brings this out, and with a kind of mercy, they will forgive anything so long as action, not introspection, has revealed it.

Mr Aubrey Noakes has written a good brief appreciation of Surtees*. It does not add to earlier studies, but it does bring out the importance of his experience with the law and his adventures in politics. Mr Noakes also goes into the interesting reluctance of the Victorians to take to him until Leech illustrated his novels. On the one hand, Surtees was a man of the eighteenth century – hence Thackeray's understanding of him; on the other, he was an amateur who dealt almost entirely with background figures, the great Jorrocks excepted. He was deeply knowing about English sporting life, the squirearchy and the law, but he did not construct the melodramas and elaborate plots of the other Victorian novelists, nor did he issue their moralisings. He often excelled them in the recording of ordinary speech and day-to-day incident. He is fresher than the masters, but he is artless. A good deal of his humour is the humour of shrewd sayings which, later on, we find in Kipling. His original contribution is in the field of invective. Surtees has a truly Elizabethan power of denunciation. Here is Jorrocks loosing off to his servant:

'Come hup, you snivellin', drivellin' son of a lucifer-match maker,' he roars out to Ben who is coming lagging along in his master's wake. 'Come on,' roars he, waving his arm frantically, as, on reaching

Horses, Hounds and Humans, Oldbourne Press, 1957.

Ravenswing Scar, he sees the hounds swinging down, like a bundle of clock pendulums into the valley below. 'Come hup, I say, ye miserable, road-ridin', dish-lickin' cub! And give me that quad, for you're a disgrace to a saddle, and only fit to toast muffins for a young ladies' boarding school. Come hup, you preter-pluperfect tense of 'umbugs . . . Come on, ye miserable, useless son of a lily-livered besom-maker. Rot ye, I'll bind ye 'prentice to a salmon-pickler.'

This is all the more splendid because Jorrocks keeps to the ' 'ard road' as much as possible, and can't bear taking a fence. He is eloquent, perhaps because he is as cowardly as Falstaff and yet as sincere in his passion. He knows what he wants to be. His is the eloquence of romance. And this is where we come to the Dickensian aspect of Surtees, too. Dickens has several degrees of comic observation. There is the rudimentary Dickens of caricature, of the single trait or phrase turned into the whole man. And there is the Dickens where this is elaborated into soliloquy, in which the character is represented by his fantasy life. Like the rudimentary Dickens, Surtees has the feeling for caricature. *Handley Cross*, *Facey Romford's Hounds* and *Mr Sponge's Tours* are packed with minor eccentrics of the field, the fancy and the law; but in Jorrocks, Surtees enters upon the more complex study of people who live out the comic orgy. 'By 'eavens, it's sublime,' says Jorrocks, watching the hounds stream over a hundred acres of pasture below him. ' 'Ow they go, screechin' and towlin' along just like a pocketful o' marbles . . . 'Ow I wish I was a heagle.' A 'heagle' he is, in that moment; sublimity is his condition. He has shrewdly built up his pack, he has given his uproarious lectures, he has had his vulgar adventures in country-houses; he has got the better of his betters and has outdone the new rich in vulgarity – making among other things that immortal remark about mince: 'I like to chew my own meat' – he has disgraced Mrs Jorrocks, but he has pursued an obsession utterly, so that it has no more to teach him, beyond the fact that it has damaged his credit among the unimaginative in the City. Fortunately, Surtees has given him power of speech. Jorrocks is never at a loss for repartee or for metaphor. He is remarkable in his duels with Pigg, and the only pity is that Pigg's dialect is nearly incomprehensible. But Pigg and his master are well-matched. They battle like theologians about the true business of life: the pursuit of foxes.

Surtees is a specialist. But he is, to an important extent, outside his speciality. He had strong views about sport. He hated the drunkenness of sporting society and the old squirearchy. He hoped the new age would bring in something better. He was hostile to the literary conventions. His parodies of *Nimrod* show him as an opponent of literary snobbery. He disliked the obsequious regime of servants and the rogueries of the stable, the auctions and the law. It is odd that one so saturated in his world should have seen it all with so fresh an eye. Perhaps he had that morbidity of eye which is given to some men at the end of a period, when they can see things with the detachment which considerable art demands. He was too much the gentleman and amateur to construct a great novel; but he was independent enough and sufficiently instructed by obsession to create in Jorrocks a huge character who could go off and live an episodic life of his own. The Victorians were shy of Surtees's honesty. They were moving away from the notion that there was a level on which all Englishmen could be united. They were building the split-culture of our time. Surtees was trying to save England on the acres of Handley Cross.

The Performing Lynx

'I'm living so far beyond my income,' says one of the characters in Saki's *The Unbearable Bassington*, 'that we may almost be said to be living apart.' That is a pointer to Saki's case: it is the fate of wits to live beyond the means of their feeling. They live by dislocation and extravagance. They talk and tire in the hard light of brilliance and are left frightened and alone among the empty wine-glasses and tumbled napkins of the wrecked dinner-table. Saki was more than a wit. There was silence in him as well. In that silence one sees a freak of the travelling show of story-tellers, perhaps a gifted performing animal, and it is wild. God knows what terrors and cajoleries have gone on behind the scenes to produce this gifted lynx so contemptuously consenting to be half-human. But one sees the hankering after one last ferocious act in the cause of a nature abused. The peculiar character called Keriway who crops up unexplained in the middle of the Bassington novel tells the story of a 'tame, crippled crane'. 'It was lame,' Keriway says, 'that is why it was tame.'

What lamed and what tamed Saki? The hate, passion, loneliness that closed the hearts of the children of the Empire-builders? Like Thackeray, Kipling and Orwell, Saki was one of the children sent 'home' from India and Burma to what seemed to them loveless care. Saki did not suffer as Kipling suffered, but we hear of an aunt whom his sister described as a woman of 'ungovernable temper, of fierce likes and dislikes, imperious, a moral coward, possessing no brains worth speaking of and a primitive disposition'. A Baroness Turgenev, in short. She is thought to be the detested woman in *Sredni Vashtar*, one of Saki's handful of masterpieces, the tale of the boy who plotted and prayed that she should be killed by a ferret. Boy and ferret were satisfied. But something less pat and fashionably morbid than a cruel aunt at Barnstaple must lie behind Saki's peculiarity, though she may go some way to explain his understanding of children. We are made by forces much older than ourselves. Saki was a

Highland Scot and of a race that was wild and gay in its tribal angers. Laughter sharpens the steel. He belonged – and this is more important – to an order more spirited, melancholy, debonair and wanton than the pudding Anglo-Saxon world south of the Border, with its middle-class wealth, its worry and its conventions. He could not resist joining it, but he joined to annoy. *The Unbearable Bassington* is a neat piece of taxidermy, a cheerful exposure of the glass case and contents of Edwardian society, a footnote to *The Spoils of Poynton*. In a way, Saki has been tamed by this society, too. Clovis likes the cork-pop of an easy epigram, the schoolboy hilarity of the practical joke and the fizz of instant success – 'The art of public life consists to a great extent of knowing exactly where to stop and going a bit further' and so on – he is the slave of the teacup and dates with every new word. His is the pathos of the bubble. But Saki has strong resources: he is moved by the inescapable nature of the weariness and emptiness of the socialite life, though unable to catch, like Firbank, the minor poetry of fashion. Francesca is too shallow to know tragedy, but she will know the misery of not being able to forget what she did to her son, all her life. She is going to be quietly more humiliated every year. And then, Saki's other resource is to let the animals in with imprudent cruelty. The leopard eats the goat in the Bishop's bathroom, the cat rips a house-party to pieces, the hounds find not a fox but a hyena and it comfortably eats a child; the two trapped enemies in the Carpathian forest make up their feud and prepare to astonish their rescuers with the godly news but the rescuers are wolves. Irony and polish are meant to lull us into amused, false comfort. Saki writes like an enemy. Society has bored him to the point of murder. Our laughter is only a note or two short of a scream of fear.

Saki belongs to the early period of the sadistic revival in English comic and satirical writing – the movement suggested by Stevenson, Wilde, Beerbohm, Firbank and Evelyn Waugh – the early period when the chief target was the cult of convention. Among these he is the teaser of hostesses, the shocker of dowagers, the mocker of female crises, the man in the incredible waistcoat who throws a spanner into the teacup; but irreverence and impudence ought not to be cultivated. They should occur. Otherwise writers are on the slippery slope of the light article. Saki is on it too often. There is the puzzling half-redeeming touch of the amateur about him, that recalls Maurice Baring's remark that he made the mistake of thinking life more important than art. But the awkwardness, the jumpiness in some of these sketches, the disproportion between discursion and incident or clever idea has something to do with the journalism of the period – Mr Evelyn Waugh's suggestion – and, I would add, some connection with the decadence of club culture. The great period of that culture was in the mid-nineteenth century: by the early 1900s it had run into the taste for the thin, the urbane and the facetious; and to sententious clichés: Lady Bastable is 'wont to retire in state to the morning-room'; Clovis makes a 'belated appearance at the breakfast-table'; people 'fare no better' and are 'singularly' this or that. The cinema, if nothing else, has burned this educated shrubbery out of our comic prose. But Saki's club prose changes when he is writing descriptions of nature (in which he is a minor master), when he describes animals and children or draws his sharp new portraits. His people are chiefly the stupid from the country, the natterers of the drawing-room and the classical English bores, and though they are done in cyanide, the deed is touched by a child's sympathy for the vulnerable areas of the large mammals. He collected especially the petty foibles and practical vanities of women (unperturbed by sexual disturbance on his part), and so presented them as persons, just as he presented cats as cats and dogs as dogs.

> Eleanor hated boys and she would have liked to have whipped this one long and often. It was perhaps the yearning of a woman who had no children of her own.

Or there is the scene between the pleasant Elaine who, having just become engaged to be married, decides to increase her pleasure by scoring off her aunt and her country cousin who has also just got engaged. Saki is clear that Elaine is a thoroughly nice girl:

> 'There is as much difference between a horseman and a horsy man as there is between a well-dressed man and a dressy one,' said Elaine judicially, 'and you have noticed how seldom a dressy woman really knows how to dress. An old lady of my acquaintance observed the other day, some people are born with a sense of how to clothe themselves, others acquire it, others look as if their clothes had been thrust upon them.'

[646]

A stale joke? Beware of Saki's claws; he goes on in the next sentence:

> She gave Lady Caroline her due quotation marks, but the sudden tactfulness with which she looked away from her cousin's frock was entirely her own idea.

Saki's male bores and male gossips are remarkable in our comic literature, for he does not take the usual English escape of presenting them as eccentrics. Bores are bores, classifiable, enjoyable like anacondas or the lung-fish. There is Henry Creech with 'the prominent, penetrating eyes of a man who can do no listening in the ordinary way and whose eyes have to perform the functions of listening for him'. And bores have lives. When Stringham made a witty remark for the first time in his life in the House of Commons one evening, remarking indeed that 'the people of Crete unfortunately make more history than they can consume locally', his wife grasped that some clever woman had got hold of him and took poison.

E. V. Knox's edition of Saki's tales (published by Collins) is a pleasant one, but it inexplicably omits all the stories from *Beasts and Superbeasts* in which Saki was at his best. I do not much care for Saki's supernatural stories, though I like the supernatural touch: the dog, for example, in *The Unbearable Bassington*, at the ghastly last dinner-party. His best things are always ingenious: the drama of incurring another's fate in *The Hounds of Fate*, the shattering absurdity of *Louis*, the artificial dog; and the hilarious tale of the tattooed Dutch commercial traveller who is confined to Italy because he is officially an unexportable work of art. The joke, for Saki, is in the kill. On the whole, it is the heart that is aimed at. He is always richly informed in the vanities of political life and does it in a manner that recalls Disraeli. Except for novels by Belloc, there has been none of this political writing since. Artificial writers of his kind depend, of course, on the dangerous trick-logic of contrivance. Success here is a gamble. For morality he substitutes the child's logic of instinct and idea.

The Unbearable Bassington is one of the lasting trifles. Its very surprising quality is the delicate apprehension of pleasure and misery. Saki was short of pity. He was an egoist and had no soothing word for pain. He knew that certain kinds of pain cannot be forgotten. Self-dramatisation, self-pity, none of the usual drugs, can take that stone from the heart. He is thoughtful but will offer nothing. In this frivolous novel Saki begins to mature. His next novel, *The Coming of William*, written in 1912 and warning lazy and corrupt Society of the German menace, was good propaganda. He imagined an England annexed to Germany and it makes uncomfortable reading; for silly Society turns instantly to collaboration. There is a more serious discomfort here; a disagreeable anti-Semitism shows more plainly in this book and one detects, in this soldierly sado-masochist, a desire for the 'discipline' of authoritarian punishment. He is festive and enjoyable as the wild scourge; but the danger obviously was that this performing lynx, in the demi-monde between journalism and a minor art, might have turned serious and started lecturing and reforming his trainer. In earlier and more spontaneous days, he would have eaten him.

Hugo's Impersonations

'Hugo began life as a mature man and is only now entering on adolescence.' The words of Vigny's referred to Hugo's life when he was twenty-seven, not to his work, but they come back when we read *Notre-Dame de Paris* and *Les Misérables*. There are dreams we dream no longer, powerful frescoes without intimacy. They belong to the volcanic periods of life – so apt to return – when the unconscious erupts, when the super-ego pronounces, when the monstrous and the ideal hog or transfigure our natures, when the self is still molten and has not been hardened into unproductive habit. In Hugo, it never became hardened. He spread into journalism and epic. Content to impersonate medieval history in *Notre-Dame de Paris*, Hugo became universal history, man, justice, natural and spiritual law, the Infinite by the time he came to the 2900 pages of *Les Misérables*. It has been said that, like Balzac, he had too much confidence in his own genius. So had all the Romantics. The criticism is useless: take away excess from Hugo and the genius vanishes. One has to agree with M. André Maurois's comment that Hugo had by nature the gift of portraying the gigantic, the excessive, the theatrical and the panoramic, and is justified by the truth and nobility of his feelings. Our difficulty is that we can nowadays recognise, by general psychological aid and the torture chambers of contemporary history, the monstrous side of a book like *Notre-Dame de Paris*, but have disconnected it from the ideal. We can re-cognise horror and grotesque, and even respond to the rhetoric of darkness; we are unable to credit the rhetoric of light. We are too absorbed in the rediscovery of evil. For Hugo, the black and white artist, one could not exist without the other. He was a primitive in that respect – or a commercial.

In *Notre-Dame de Paris* Hugo's dreams are magnified in outline, micro-scopic in detail. They are true but are made magical by the enlargement of pictorial close-up, not by grandiloquent fading. Compare the treatment of the theme of the love that survives death in this book with the not dissimilar theme in *Wuthering Heights*. Catherine and Heathcliff are eternal as the wretched wind that whines at the northern casement. They are impalpable and bound in their eternal pursuit. A more terrible and more precise fate is given by Hugo to Quasimodo after death. The hunchback's skeleton is found clasping the skeleton of the gypsy girl in the charnel house. We see it with our eyes. And his skeleton falls into dust when it is touched, in that marvellous last line of the novel. Where love is lost, it is lost even beyond the grave. The reader is made to see this finality with his own eyes. If we object that Hugo's world is rhetorical, his scepticism, irony and wit give the rhetoric earth to stand on. Quasimodo is put to the torture in a ferocious scene, but it follows a trial which is based on the stock sardonic comedy of deaf prisoner at odds with deaf judge. The novel is a romance, but its parts exist in equilibrium. Interwoven with the tragedians – Quasimodo, the girl, the lusting priest – is the pedestrian Gringoire who has been quick to make his peace with the world, like some Shakespearean clown. He grows before our eyes, as all the characters grow. Beginning as a bore, he becomes the nervous smile on the face of that practical pusillanimity which we call the common experience and the instinct to survive. (We live by our genius for hope; we survive by our talent for dispensing with it. Turning to M. Maurois's *Life* and recognising that part of Hugo's greatness lay in his efficiency in using every item of his life, we wonder if Gringoire was some malicious version of a Sainte-Beuve, for he has married the Muse platonically. He will be a critic.) 'What makes you so attached to your life?' the haunted archdeacon asks him. Gringoire makes the gracious Pyrrhonian reply about the sun, flowers, birds and books and adds the sublime sentence: 'And then I have the happiness of spending every day, from morning to night, in the company of a man of genius, myself. It is very pleasant.'

Hugo was the impresario of a split personality. Out of the depths came the monsters created by chastity: lust, cruelty, jealousy, violence, maiming, murder, in pursuit of the innocent, the loving and the merciful. The black and white view is relieved by the courage of the priest's feckless brother and the scepticism of Gringoire, the whole is made workable by poetic and pictorial instinct. It has often been pointed out that Hugo had the eye that sees for itself. Where Balzac described things out of descriptive gluttony, so that parts of his novels are an undiscriminating buyer's catalogue; where Scott describes out of antiquarian zeal, Hugo brings things to life by implicating them with persons in the action in rapid 'takes'. In this sense, *Notre-Dame de Paris* was the perfect film script. Every stone plays its part. We can be sure the bells of Notre-Dame are not there merely to ring; they will act upon a life; and, in fact, they deafen Quasimodo and that deafness ruins him in the courts, saves him and ruins him in love. In *Les Misérables* we can be sure Hugo does not describe, say, the inn sign at the Thénaudiers' out of sheer love of describing inn signs; a volume later Thénaudier turns up with it, in another setting, trying to palm it off as a picture by David. Once we have caught on to this clinching habit of Hugo's, every scene springs to action. We are waiting for the magic to work. Sometimes the trick is too obvious: we know the dancing girl will find her mother by matching her shoe. 'The reader will have guessed' – a ham phrase often repeated, but therein lies half the pleasure. We *have* guessed, as we guess in magic.

More important than this, for the critic, is the fact that Hugo's simplifications of the inner life are required by a superb sense of the theatre. He works entirely within its terms. One can see where he was trained. He works by stage scenes. The scene before Notre-Dame is a stage set. He has the art of placing a situation, opposing an obstacle, creating a new situation, reversing it, doubling and redoubling. Rushing in the dark to save the gypsy in the tower of the cathedral from her attacker, Quasimodo triumphs in his strength, but when he discovers the attacker is his master, the priest, all his will and strength collapse. Yet if the priest wins that round he loses it because of the new situation; it is he, the master, who has the bitterness of being enslaved. Not merely by lust for the girl, but by the new thing – jealousy of his hunchback servant. Hugo was popular but not necessarily false because he put the obsessive and strong situations in simple theatrical terms. He is rich in dramatic irony. There is a purely stage scene where Louis IX inspects at length the construction of a wooden cage in which a prisoner is wailing for mercy. The king does not notice the prisoner because, in his avarice, he is too interested in the cost of the wood. Yet when another prisoner appeals for mercy the king lets him off out of whim. Fate rules us all, the Wheel of Fortune is a trickster. Hugo's whole method as a novelist is contained in these dramatic ironies and reversals, but he applies it in such a variety of ways and at so many levels that we do not notice the mechanics of it. In story-telling the method has the immense advantage of a delaying tactic: see the manner in which the dreadful Thénaudier in *Les Misérables* is made to reveal his adroitness, chance by chance. And if we ask ourselves whether Hugo's characters live outside the theatre, Thénaudier provides one answer. Hugo has to see them in that spotlight in order to see them truthfully at all. A typical passage of Ciceronian oratory on Thénaudier's wickedness ends with the typical epigram which contains a truth: in this wicked man there was 'quelque chose qui était hideux comme le mal et poignant comme le vrai'. The ideal world is a world of opposites; in the rhetorical evocation of it, it is the last short sentence of the harangue that makes the dramatic point and clinches the scene. Hugo never fails with that sentence. The old dying Jacobin denounces the Church like an orator for pages on end and, for reply, the saintly Abbé simply kneels and says: 'Give me your blessing.' That is good theatre, for it does not make the priest theatrical; it convinces us that he is alive. One has to admit that Hugo can overdo it. In the very next line, the old Jacobin falls back dead. That is too much. The critics who warned Hugo of his excess of originality, and of his weakness for doubling his metaphors and his points, were right; at a deeper level there is the objection that a love of paradox is likely to turn into the high-flown belief that everything equals everything in the end. (Which one is pursuer, which pursued: Javert or Valjean?) But the highest moment of an art so ingeniously staged in its particulars is not metaphysics but spectacle. The attack on Notre-Dame by the army of beggars; the preparations for the execution of the gypsy girl and her escape; the scenario of Waterloo – these are all crises on the grand scale and classical operative instances of the mass scene.

The fact that Hugo's characters are larger than life as individuals and are only life-size when they are part of a crowd – judges, soldiers, beggars, populace – does not mean, of course, that they are not individual and recognisable, or even that they are either allegorical or caricature. There are no unconvincing or sentimentalised characters in *Notre-Dame* or *Les Misérables*, as there are in Scott. (The two novelists are not really comparable; it would be more sensible to call Hugo 'incurious Dostoevsky' rather than 'inferior Scott'. Hugo was simply too extroverted to know how morbid the sources of some of his ideas were; he merely knew that they drove his brother mad, not himself.) If *Les Misérables* is a lesser and more ambitious work than *Notre-Dame*, this is partly because it is humourless and has little comedy. But Hugo's genius was for the creation of simple and recognisable myth. The huge success of *Les Misérables* as a didactic work on behalf of the poor and oppressed is due to its poetic and myth-enlarged view of human nature – intermingled with that fundamental regard for human cunning which a popular culture seems to call for. Hugo himself called this novel 'a religious work'; and it has indeed the necessary air of having been written by God in one of his more accessible and saleable moods. Myth and theatre, rather than fact and dogma, are what have made Quasimodo, Valjean, Javert universal in popular esteem. It is remarkable that the eight hundred superfluous pages of digression did not wreck the book.

Trollope Was Right

The comfort we get from Trollope's novels is the sedative of gossip. It is not cynical gossip, for Trollope himself is the honest check on the self-deceptions of his characters, on their malicious lies or interested half-truths about each other. It is he, a workaday surrogate of God, sincere, sturdy, shrewd and unhopeful, who has the key. Trollope does not go with us into the dangerous region that lies just outside our affairs and from which we draw our will to live; rather, he settles lazily into that part of our lives which is a substitute, the part which avoids loneliness by living vicariously in other people. If it is a true generalisation – as some say – that the English, being unimaginative, are able to live without hope but not without the pleasure of thinking they are better than their neighbours, Trollope's are the most English of our novels. But the generalisation is not true. Trollope himself – as Mr Cockshut says in a very intelligent study – is saved by eccentricity. There is something fervent, even extreme, in his admiration of endurance. He was a man whose temper could flare up. His preoccupation with what is normal is the intense one of a man who has had to gain acquaintance with normality from an abnormal situation outside it. His special eccentricities are his mania for work and his passion for spending energy. From his point of view, novel-writing was obsessional. It convinced him that he, the outsider in a society of powerful groups of people, was justified in being alive. Even his most contented novels leave an aftertaste of flatness and sadness. He has succeeded in his assertions, to the point of conveying a personal satiety.

The plots of Trollope and Henry James have much in common. But if we compare a novel like *The Eustace Diamonds*, one of the most ingenious of Trollope's conundrums, with, say, Henry James's *The Spoils of Poynton*, we see the difference between a pragmatic gossip and an artist of richer sensibility. Sense, not sensibility, governs Trollope; it is fine good sense and, though he lumbers along, most notable for the subtlety of its timing.

He is an excellent administrator and politician of private life. But whereas James saw how the magnificent spoils of the Poynton family could corrupt by their very beauty, Trollope did not envisage anything morally ambiguous in the imbroglio of the Eustace diamonds. The 'spoils' were treasure; the 'diamonds' are property. The former are made for the moral law; the latter for the courts. It is true, as Mr Cockshut says, that the brilliantly delayed climax where Dove, the lawyer, points out the stones are worthless has its overtones. But to Trollope's imagination the diamonds are ultimately meaningless; one might defend the wicked Lady Eustace and say that she alone gave them a symbolical meaning. They at least stand for her will. But Trollope in fact dislikes her childish will as much as her propensity for lying; her poetic side is shown to be false. One wonders if he could have portrayed it if it had been genuine. She is a perjurer, a bitch and a coquette and, quite rightly, ends up as a bore; but in a novel filled with irritable and spiritless people, she is the one figure of spirit. Trollope merely knows that she is wrong.

With all his mastery, Trollope is interested only in what people are like, not in what they are for. The limitation comes out most clearly in his political novels when we see how politics work and never for what purpose, beyond those of personal career. Some critics have put down this fundamental concern of Trollope to his good-natured and sensible acceptance of mid-Victorian society, and would say that he accepted his world just as Jane Austen accepted hers. Others – and I think Mr Cockshut would be among them – point to his constitutional melancholy. It has the effect of devitalising his characters. I do not mean that old harridans like Lady Linlithgow, the delightful self-willed Lady Glencora, or Lord George in *The Eustace Diamonds* lack personal vitality; the deficiency is in artistic vitality. If we compare the portrait of Lady Eustace with Thackeray's Becky Sharp it is interesting to see how much passivity there is in Lady Eustace and how much greater is the adventuress than the stubborn fool. Lady Eustace drifts. Her wickednesses are many, but they are small. She is little more than a tedious *intrigante* who relies on chance. She, of course, succeeds with us because of her obstinacy, her wit, her courage, her seductiveness and her beauty and because her wickedness is that of a child. Indeed Lord George, the 'corsair', pats her on the head and treats her as such. Becky is a more positive and interesting figure of evil because she is grown up.

In *The Eustace Diamonds*, there are only two moments when Trollope breaks through his melancholy to write out of strong feeling. The first is an unpleasant outbreak: the anti-Semitism of his portrait of Mr Emilius, 'the greasy Jew'. Trollope, honest observer that he is, notes that Lady Eustace is far from being physically repelled by the preacher who is said to be repulsive. The female masochist – as Mr Cockshut says – has recognised a master, the coquette her master-hypocrite. The second outbreak occurs in describing the brutal, forced engagement of Lucinda Roanoke to Sir Griffin, and the violence with which the Amazon repels him when he tries to take her on his knee. Here the revulsion is physical. These are two disconcerting glimpses into the Trollopian alcove and both are blatant. Trollope with his blood up is better seen on the hunting field; he will be kinder there to the women who are to be humiliated.

Mr Cockshut has read the whole of Trollope and I have not. His book provides an able analysis of the novels and a fresh approach to Trollope himself. The critic might have said, with advantage, more about Trollope's curious life; Mr Cockshut is more detailed than other critics have been about Trollope's response to mid-Victorianism; he is fascinated by the moral issues which Trollope propounded, but he is apt to digress. As a critic he depends on paraphrase which is always suggestive and enjoyable though it also runs into the danger of crediting a novelist with ideas he may only dimly have discerned. Is it true, for example, that masochism is Lady Eustace's central characteristic? Surely it is a lack of interest in truth. Mr Cockshut's main point is that there are three phases in Trollope's pro-digious output: the daydream stage; the genial middle period when he accepts the world; and the final one, beginning with *He Knew He Was Right*, when he is bitterly disillusioned about the society which he has affirmed his right to. Mr Cockshut cannot think of any special reason for the change. Perhaps Trollope's leaving the Post Office and failing to get into Parliament had something to do with it. Leisure depressed, indeed terrified him and, perhaps, what Mr Cockshut calls his 'belated understanding of the changes that were coming over Victorian England' became unpleasantly observable with leisure. We need not think that hard work exhausted him, but men who are hard on themselves become harder on other people as time goes by. 'He knew he was right' could have been his device, the rightness not lying especially in his opinion, but in his choice of what might be called 'practical hallucination' as a way of living. He was perhaps reverting in late middle age to the misanthropy of his early, unhappy youth. The cycle is common enough. Dickens, too, became harsh and, to present-day taste, the harsh or obsessional phase of novelists happens to have become attractive.

He Knew He Was Right and *The Eustace Diamonds* are not genial books. There is something savage in them. The values of society are rotten, the people are fools, brutes or lunatics. Lady Eustace may be bad; but what are we to say of the virtuous Mrs Hittaway, the social climber, who does not scruple in the name of virtue to employ Lady Eustace's servants to spy upon her and who is so morally exalted by her own slanders that she does not even want to consider the evidence for them? These people are a nasty, grubbing lot, no better than they should be. Their story is redeemed and 'placed' by Trollope's smiling remark that the scandal managed to keep the old Duke of Omnium alive for three months and gave everybody in London something to talk about at dinner. Trollope may be pessimistic, but he was too alert a comedian to be misled into rancour. His good nature was truthful if it grew less and less hopeful. Himself morbidly subject to loneliness and boredom and capable of portraying characters who were destroyed by these evils, he never fell into exaggeration – nor indeed rose to it.

The Eustace Diamonds is a triumph of ingenious construction and of story-telling. Trollope is a master of that dramatic art which the English novel seems to have inherited from its early roots in the theatre; the art of putting the right in the wrong and the wrong in the right. He also understands Society and the difference between the weary meaningless-ness of the conventional and the vicious aimlessness of the unconven-tional. The fast set and Grundys such as Mrs Hittaway are opposite sides of the same coin. Yet if, as Mr Cockshut's analysis patiently shows, the gossip is morally organised, it is not schematic. The characters are various in themselves. A dull man like Lord Fawn becomes fascinating. We see the figure of Frank Greystock in all the colours of a merely moderate honesty. Each character is brought to its own dramatic head. Will Greystock jilt the governess and marry Lady Eustace? Trollope is not content to stop at answering that question, but goes one better and shows Greystock falling asleep in the train, bored stiff by a flirt who had captivated him. Trollope's observation can make even a Commissioner of Police interesting. Nor does the comedy remain on one level. The love affair of Lucinda and Sir Griffin approaches the grotesque and the horrible and the sharp financial deals and recriminations of Lady Eustace and Mrs Carbuncle are as savage as anything in *Jonathan Wild*. Trollope is a remorseless exploiter of fine points. If he had been a mere plotmaker he would have been satisfied to expose the perjuries of Lady Eustace in the court scene, but he squeezes more than that out of it. He sees to it that a sadistic counsel, powerless to be other than cruel, makes the liar tell the truth a dozen times over, unnecessarily. And when the bogus preacher proposes, Lady Eustace doubts if he is bogus enough.

The critic must admire these skills. He must admire Trollope's knowledge of the groups in the social hierarchy. He must notice how fertilising was Trollope's own dilemma: that he was a man of liberal mind crossed by strong conservative feeling. There remain the serious limitations that his manner is slovenly, repetitive and pedestrian, that his scene has no vividness, that – as Mr Cockshut says – the upper steps of his moral stairway are missing, that he lacks fantasy. There will be sin but no sanctity. It is, after all, Lady Eustace's crime that she was not the average woman and it is supposed to be Mrs Hittaway's justification that she is. And so, when we emerge from Trollope's world, we, at first, define him as one of the masters who enable us to recognise average life for what it is. On second thoughts, we change the phrase: we recognise that he has drawn life as people say it is when they are not speaking about themselves.

One of the chronicler's 'failures' – *The Prime Minister* – was the penultimate volume of what Trollope considered his best work: the series which begins with *Can You Forgive Her?* and runs on to the Phineas novels. As Mr Amery says in his introduction to the attractive Oxford Crown edition, it raises the question of politics in the novel. The failure of *The Prime Minister* is, of course, relative; no novel containing Lady Glencora could be called dull. But this one has no personable young hero like the frank and susceptible Phineas Finn and Emily Wharton is a bit of a stick as the meek but obstinate young bride in love. On the other hand, Lopez, the speculator and fortune-hunter, is a genuine figure of the age; drama is created by his shifty fingers, he is bold and credible. The only bother with Lopez is that he is made the vehicle of Trollope's peculiar dislike of 'outsiders' and foreigners – he loathed Disraeli really because he was a Jew – and a hostile lecturing tone comes into Trollope's voice when he writes of him, which is absent from the portrait of that other rapscallion, Burgo Fitzgerald. Yet Trollope tries very hard to be fair to Lopez, who is presented with objective care and is never all of a piece. He has courage, for example, and one notices that he does not lie until he is kicked when he is down. Only his suicide, at the end, is out of character, for obviously a man like Lopez will always start again from the bottom. He perfectly illustrates what a novelist like Galsworthy would have made a lot of moral fuss about: that in a rich oligarchic society, the Lopezes will always be sacrificed when their heads are turned or when it is a question of class-solidarity and self-defence. Trollope is very accurate as a psychologist of the uncomprehending rogue; a little cynical as he shows how mad it is to think of succeeding in England if you use your imagination and disobey the rules. It is a tremendous moment when Lopez attempts to blackmail the Duke of Omnium and the best kind of surprise: the brilliant Lopez has lost his head. We had forgotten how stupid cleverness can be. Finally, in the major conflict between the lofty-minded Prime Minister and his wife, Lady Glencora, whose whole idea is to exploit her husband's political eminence socially, there is wit, and drama too.

Where is the specific failure, then? I do not mean the general criticism of Trollope that he is commonplace, that reading him is like walking down endless corridors of carpet, restful to walk on, but in the end enervating. What is the failure within Trollope's own honest terms? The reader is bound to agree with the experienced opinion of the politician who introduces the book: as Mr Amery says, it was possible for Trollope to write about the Church without engaging in religious controversy, because this is only fitful in religion and, anyway, is only one aspect of it. But controversy is the living breath of politics, and Trollope leaves it out altogether. He purposely makes the Duke of Omnium Prime Minister of a Coalition, in which controversy is momentarily quiet. The fact is that Trollope the civil servant despised politicians and the Duke of Omnium is really a Treasury official, plus an immense sense of rank and a vast income. And so, though we hear in detail of the machinery of Parliament, the intrigues for safe seats, the machinations of the drawing-rooms and have an excellent picture of political comedy and humbug, we have no notion of politics as anything more than a career disputed between the 'ins' and the 'outs'.

It infuriated Trollope to see that Disraeli's political novels were more highly thought of than his own. He wrote of them:

> Through it all there is a feeling of stage properties, a smell of hair-oil, an aspect of buhl, a remembrance of tailors, and that pricking of the conscience which must be the general accompaniment of paste diamonds.

Even so, Disraeli's *Sybil* and *Coningsby* are far more convincing as political novels. They burn with the passions of the day and if there is falsity in the lighting, that is an essential political quality. Disraeli presents politics as prophetic dogma; he understands that politics grow out of beliefs, interests and conditions, though they degenerate into expedients. The working class are not excluded as Trollope excludes them; and though Trollope lived in a quieter political period, it can hardly be said that the workers were without voice. Disraeli's vision of politics in his novels was exotic and perhaps no purely English novelist is capable of this, any more than he has been capable of the dialectical fantasies of Shaw; to write well about politics one has got to believe in them in the abstract and to regard them as a possible imaginative world. Trollope hated the idea of such a thing, and in consequence, though he gets the surface brilliantly, he misses the reason for its existence.

Character is the whole interest of Trollope and if his portrait of the Prime Minister, the Duke of Omnium, is meant to be a picture of the perfect gentleman and statesman, it is neither idealised nor forced. The Duke's skin is too thin, he has scruples, he is moody, morose and capable of ducal temper. Though he is in conflict with his wife, who gives a fantastic house party – 40 guests a night for six weeks, and none to stay more than 48 hours; think, says the housekeeper at Gatherum Castle, as if she had Arnold Bennett at her elbow, of the towels and the sheets! – the Duke clearly understands that if she is a woman with no scruples, she is kept straight by her feelings and convictions. And Trollope is expert in crossing the intentions of his people with the accidents of life. The climber

Lopez might have got his safe seat, if only the bumptious Major Pountney – 'a middle-aged young man' – had not annoyed the Duke on another matter. But we get, I think, a better idea of the political entanglement in the earlier book, *Phineas Finn*. Phineas is not an outsider, and therefore Trollope is in a better temper. He is the ingenious, penniless, handsome young fellow, going into politics against the author's affectionate advice, and we are led with him step by step into his career. There are even glances at the Irish Question. We see Phineas funking his first opportunity to speak and making a mess of it when he does get up, full of indignation, on another occasion.

There are shrewd portraits of the Whips – but there is nothing to equal Disraeli's wonderful libellous sketch of Croker – and Trollope knows how to grade his politicians according to the condition of their careers. There is a hostile portrait of John Bright. He is Turnbull, who is contrasted with Monk, an imaginary Radical 'ever doubting of himself, and never doubting himself so much as when he had been most violent and also most effective, in debate'. But Turnbull-Bright has no doubts:

> I think that when once he had learned the art of arranging his words as he stood on his legs, and had so mastered his voice as to have obtained the ear of the House, the work of his life was not difficult. Having nothing to construct he could always deal with generalities. Being free from responsibility, he was not called upon either to study details or to master even great facts. It was his business to inveigh against existing evils, and perhaps there is no easier business . . . It was his work to cut down forest trees, and he had nothing to do with the subsequent cultivation of the land. Mr Monk had once told Phineas Finn how great were the charms of that inaccuracy which was permitted to the opposition.

That is all very well, but the very irony at the expense of politicians shows the failure to rise to the imaginative opportunity. As Mr Amery says, Disraeli would have plunged for the excitements of foreign policy. He would have risked.

Indeed, although *Phineas Finn* is an amusing guide to Parliamentary life as it then was, it interests us really for things like the famous portraits of the violent red-eyed Lord Chiltern – this plunging , dangerous man would be the hero of a contemporary novel, not a minor character – the superb Mr Kennedy, so gloomy, so evangelical, who adroitly lengthens family prayers when he is jealous of his wife's lover:

[He] was a man who had very little temptation to do anything wrong. He was possessed of over a million and a half of money, which he was mistaken enough to suppose he had made himself . . . He never spoke much to anyone, although he was constantly in society. He rarely did anything, though he had the means of doing everything. He had seldom been on his legs in the House of Commons, though he had been there ten years. He was seen about everywhere, sometimes with one acquaintance, sometimes with another – but it may doubted whether he had any friend . . . though he would not lend money, he gave a great deal – and he would give it for almost every object. 'Mr Rbt. Kennedy, M.P., £105' appeared on almost every charitable list that was advertised. No one ever spoke to him as to this expenditure, nor did he ever speak to anyone. Circulars came to him and the cheques were returned. The duty was an easy one to him and he performed it willingly. Had any moment of inquiry been necessary it is possible the labour would have been too much for him.

That is a close study of something not often observed: the neutrality, the nonentity of rich men. And then there are the women of the book who all talk so well and who are very well distinguished from each other. The stress on sex in the modern novel has meant that women have lost their distinctiveness as persons. Trollope excels in making the distinctions clear.

Trollope is a detailed, rather cynical observer of a satisfied world. Honest, assertive, sensible, shrewd, good-humoured, he is content. As Henry James said, he gives us the pleasure of recognition. But content is, so to speak, a summit that he has attained, not a torpor into which he has fallen. He grew worldliness like a second skin over the raw wounds of his youth, and the reason why he describes what is normally observable about people as well is that he longed merely for the normal. He had been too insecure to want anything more than that security, and it was by a triumph of personal character that he attained it. Trollope might excusably have become a neurotic – and without talent. It is maddening to see the themes of Henry James taken back to the platitude of their starting point and left there; strange to have to recognise that what are called 'things as they are' can be soothing. It is dangerous to marry for money, but it is also dangerous to marry for love; it is dangerous to commit adultery for society will drop you, yet society is greedy and hypocritical. It is bad to borrow; it is mean not to lend. One is listening to human nature muddling along on its old rules of thumb. The only pattern we can discern is that made by the struggle of the individual within his group: politics, the law, the Church. It is not a passionate struggle. It is mainly a question of faintly enlightened self-interest. We feel about his people what we feel about our relatives: the curiosity that distracts us from a fundamental apathy. The sense of danger and extremity which alerts us in the war-like compositions of Jane Austen is dulled. His novels are social history, without the movements of history; life as we see it without having to think about it. It has no significance beyond itself; it is as pleasant, dull and restful as an afternoon in an armchair. The footpads in the London parks, the frightened family of the crooked bankrupt, the suicide on the suburban line, are there, not to frighten us unduly, but to give further assurance to normal people that normality is stronger than ever. Can we wonder, in these times, at the Trollope revival?

Ross at the Depot

W ithheld from the public in the Twenties when it was written, T. E. Lawrence's *The Mint* is one of those time-bombs of literature which fail to go off when the hour comes. Its mystery, kept alive by a leak here and there, a single copy circulating somewhere or other, and by people 'privileged to see', had been artificial; and the habit of building up expectation of 'revelations' in his work was maintained even on publication, 1955, by issuing an unexpurgated edition in leather at extra cost. It is an odd comment on our manners that we have contrived to make the short list of four-letter words, on which an army moves, into the nuggets of a publisher's gold-mine. Lawrence was, of course, writing when the revival of the rights of blasphemy and bad language was regarded as an ethical duty; but, for a later generation, military service and war have not been a novelty, linguistically or otherwise, and I doubt whether anyone under forty will want to pay to read exactly what the soldier said so often. No scandal, no sex, no sodomy. *The Mint* is simply an earnest documentary work. It was noted down night after night in the Nissen huts of the RAF Depot, records what went on in the huts and on the square and what it felt like to have one's spirit broken and to be turned into 352087 A/c Ross. This experience has become a commonplace to the majority of living males and dozens of documentaries have described the process. In waiting till 1955 the book has waited too long and discloses nothing much about Lawrence himself.

All the same, there is a curious period interest in *The Mint*. It is an arty book: Lawrence's own injured romanticism and his self-pity see to that. One sees now a pathos in the stilted originality which was worked into so much of the more ardent prose of the time and which I take to be a hangover from Meredith.

So the appellant moon easily conjures me outside . . .

On the western slope swelled the strident activity of red-and-chocolate footballers.

Lawrence's prose attempts to attract attention to its airs and merits; he is a word prig. Occasionally, in a portrait, an eventual touch of fantasy justifies him:

China . . . is a stocky Camberwell costermonger, with the accent of a stage Cockney. Since childhood he has fought for himself and taken many knocks, but no care about them. He is sure that safety means to be rough among the town's roughs. His deathly white face is smooth as if waxed, the bulging pale eyes seem lidless like a snake's, and out of their fixedness he stares balefully . . . China has said, 'F———' so often, inlaying it monotonously after every second word of his speech with so immense an aspirated 'f', that his lips have pouted to it in a curve which sneers across his face like the sound-hole of a fiddle's belly.

It must be said that *The Mint* is more laboured in its first painful 165 pages, which are based on notes taken certainly too close to the object; the remaining forty pages, based on letters, are both happier in themselves and are more freely written. (This part of the book contains an excellent description of speeding on a motor bike.) Lawrence wrote spiritedly about action. Another virtue of *The Mint* lies in its honest effort to get to the bottom of his subject. At first the impression is that what is unique experience for him in his egocentric way is commonplace for his fellows, but presently he notices that it will not be commonplace for them either. In 1923, with a million and a half unemployed in England, enlistment meant the open acknowledgment of defeat by life. Having lost their souls, men glumly hesitated as they handed over their last possession: their bodies.

We include 'lads' and their shady equivalent, the hard case. Also the soft and the silly: the vain: the old soldier who is lost without the nails of service: the fallen officer sharply contemptuous of our new company, yet trying to be well-fellow and not proud. Such a novice dips too willingly at the dirty jobs, while the experienced wage-slave stands by, grumbling.

The dressy artisans, alternately allured and repelled by our unlimited profession, dawdle for days over their trade-tests, hoping some accident will make up their minds. Our Glasgow blacksmith given only bread and tea one day in dining hall, cried, 'Aam gaen whame,' muddled his trial job and was instantly turned down. That last afternoon he spent spluttering crazy, non-intelligible confidences at every one of us. A dumpy lad he was, with tear-stained fat cheeks, and so glad to have failed. 'Dry bread,' he would quiver half-hourly with a sob in his throat. Simple-minded, like a child, but stiff-minded, too, and dirty; very Scotch.

Lawrence himself joined the RAF under the name of Ross at a time of physical and spiritual exhaustion in his life when (he said) he was capable of only negative decisions. He wanted, he says, to get back to human kind and, half-way through the book, he thinks the plan has failed. It probably did fail: it was loveless and despairing. The malicious and the knowing have described Lawrence's enlistment as an example of his chronic play-acting, but human motives are rarely simple; even if he were play-acting, this is as serious and complex a compulsion as its opposite, and not less 'real' or 'sincere'. Self-dramatisation is common among gifted men and provides its own experience. At the Air Force medical, the doctor noted, Lawrence says (no doubt with some self-infatuation), that he looked as though he had been going short of food for months. If he had, there was no need for him to have done, and he may have half-starved in a sulking desire to show he had not received sufficient attention. That does not alter the fact that a hungry man was abasing himself before the doctor. The theme of abasement already occurs in *The Seven Pillars of Wisdom*; in *The Mint* one is struck by the analogy with religious conversion. The book might indeed be a histrionic footnote to Alfred de Vigny's elaborate comparison of the religious and military vocations. The world is abandoned, and the gates close on the recruit. As private possessions, the body and the mind are systematically destroyed, the will is thrown away, the subject is in a condition as abject as that of Saint Ignatius when he stood in rags at Montserrat; only after abasement can obedience become an instinct and the old man give place to the new man, the required automaton, fulfilled in corporate pride and corporate wholeness. That is the ultimate reward; in the interim, he sinks restfully and unresponsibly into the dull, kind, corrupt world of the closed community, where promiscuousness kills the desire for intimacy, where sex is a dirty word, and the last feeble ghosts of private life escape in groans and babblings from the lips in sleep at night. That is purgatory. It is a loss that Lawrence had to leave the RAF: the will to describe the experiences of the technician's heaven vanished.

To his companions, as far as so impersonal a writer can disclose it, Lawrence was an oddity. He could not swear. They were considerate about his age – he was eight years older than most and was physically exhausted more quickly than they. They admired his use of long words, they borrowed a little money. They must have seen him wince at the sight of their bullocky animality. He let them down in one respect: every man has some small advantage he can exploit; why, as a 'toff', did he not exploit the fact? There was no masochism in the men, there was no point in being a 'mug'. This complaint came to a head in the conflict with a sergeant who was one of two or three sadists who made his life hell at the Depot in those days. This sergeant was a killer. One day, when he had reduced his squad to a helpless, gasping collection of sweating and frightened animals, he made a short inspection to finish them off, stopped in front of Lawrence and said: '"When did you have a bath? Open your collar," thrust his hand roughly inside against my wet breast. "Christ, the bloody man's lousy . . . March the filthy———out to the wash-house and scrub the———out of him properly."' Lawrence was marched off by Sailor, who had a great command of picturesque obscenity. The blanks lengthen in Sailor's dialogue: 'God if that long———streak of———pokes his head in here after us, I'll knock seven different sorts of———out of him. But, mate, you let the flight down, when he takes the mike out of you every time. Give the ignorant———bag a———great gob of your toffology.'

Pain is the subject of *The Mint* and it is not pain quietly borne. It is relieved by rough kindness. When Lawrence, who slept badly, went for a walk at night he was treated with sympathy, wonder and pity by the sentries. He observed their new character growing up in the men. Once the hell of drill was over and they got to the machines, they found the unconscious solace of mass men: the machines belonged to them, not to the silly fools who flew them and messed them up. Lawrence was moved by this, and the puritan in him responded to the dull self-righteousness of unexceptional people. Since he was exceptional himself he must have been divided in mind. It is pretty evident that he knew he had no place there and that the cure – that old, mystical, muddled notion of 'going back to the people' – was, stunt, or no stunt, a failure. The affair of the motor bicycle suggests the trouble was one that could not be solved by immolation in the corporate life. And there *The Mint* leaves us. It is, in point of writing, one of the first documentaries, tortuous and self-conscious, vivid and affected, powerful and yet weakened by shrillness and mannered introspection. Writing was not his medium. Or, rather, to be his medium it had to have the great, cruel, false, personal, romantic subject, with Carlyle's 'dark curtains' coming down on it in the end. The Royal Air Force was precisely not that in 1923 and, in seeing the commonest men only in relation to their failure in civilian life and their military training, he showed his distance from them. Those writers who have succeeded in portraying common men have not made them the acolytes of the writer's own personal rituals. One is left, at the end of *The Mint*, moved by the writer's pain and nagged by the peculiarity of his case. One is not left with very much more.

The Military Necessity

——

It has taken nearly one hundred and twenty years for Alfred de Vigny's apologia for the military life to come once more into its own. It has had to wait for the tide of peace to turn and for the birth of two war generations. Like some writers of our own Twenties, Vigny had imagined that negotiation was bound to succeed war in the diplomacy of nations and that science would eventually bring in the world state and make war impossible. He did not see that it would make war more alluring and interesting. Yet his accent is persuasive when he expresses this feeling, for he had the art of keeping rational hope faint but alive and of surrounding it with compassion for its insignificance. A lesson to propagandists: the pessimism which addresses itself to the last feeble spark of reason in our minds has a longer life than the bullying good will which slaps and pushes us along. From our point of view Vigny's personal aloofness and melancholy hit the mark. Mr Humphrey Hare, who has made an excellent translation, says that Vigny was never temperamentally at home in the circumstances of his life which were, indeed, generally dejecting, and that the crisis of the Revolution seemed to be 'perpetually alive in him'. He was not born until 1797 but his mind was formed by the eighteenth century, his parents were aristocrats whose property was sequestered, and although he was brought up to the idea of military glory, he was also taught that Bonaparte was an impostor. His coldness and remoteness were the formal mask of the man who finds himself between two worlds, but they were not the Byronic mask of a 'doomed' or 'lost' generation, for Vigny was a natural stoic who understood abnegation and pity. He had little egoism. He astonished and amused people like Dumas and Hugo by his fastidiousness – his mistress said she had only once seen him eat, and then only a carrot; as a soldier, he treated the army stiffly, as a 'nomad monastery', a place for order, solitude, contemplation and self-effacement. Sainte-Beuve mocked him for being a Trappist and Vigny himself put down his failure in the army to having brought a passive and reflective mind to an active avocation. Vocation it certainly was not.

Vigny had an aristocratic dignity, the sense that Duty is Fate. This gave him a backbone which is lacking in the other disillusioned Romantics. When he occasionally falls into their inflated manner he writes poorly. 'In the universal foundering of creeds', which was felt in his time, as it has been in ours, he believed in the aristocratic and 'earthly religion' of honour: 'the virtue of the life of this world'. The argument and the stories that make up *The Military Necessity* are based on this sense, and it enabled him to define the moral essence of a soldier's life and the tragic mutilation of the individual, humane soul by the corporate spirit. The key to his thought lies in his account of the explosion at Vincennes when the kindly over-zealous quartermaster is blown to pieces.

> Like a stone from a sling his head and torso had been hurled sixty feet up against the chapel wall, and the powder, impregnating this appalling bust, had cut its outline deeply on the wall at whose foot he had fallen back. Although we gazed at it for a long time, no one uttered a word of pity. Possibly because to have pitied him would have been to have pitied ourselves for having run the self-same danger.

Any society requires the inhibition of feeling in its members and Vigny's point is that this is inevitable, and perhaps desirable. But he also indicates the price that has to be paid: a loss of heart and above all a loss of compassion. We should feel most compassionate of all to the soldier who sacrifices himself to society's requirement that he shall have no compassion:

> The army is blind and dumb, strikes down unquestioningly those to whom it is opposed, desires nothing for itself and acts under compulsion. It is a great machine wound up to kill; but it is, too, a machine capable of suffering.

For Vigny the modern army is a 'body divorced from the great body of the nation'. It is the scapegoat. In his long time of service he was painfully sensitive to these definitions, because he himself saw no active service against a foreign enemy: the most he had to do was to help quell a riot of liberal citizens in the town of Pau. It was bad enough to be the licensed murderer abroad; but to have the role in one's own country was pathetic and false. (This is the situation Stendhal angrily described in *Lucien Leuwen*.) What Vigny is commemorating is the frustration of the old Napoleonic sense of glory – Napoleon appears unsympathetically in one of the stories in this book – the loss of romance.

Does the modern soldier still feel himself to be in a false position, in Vigny's sense? By 1914–18 he certainly did, but has the feeling continued in the conscripted, peace-time armies? Some have felt military service to be a happy return to their schooldays; but for most men the experience is that of the guinea-pig who is made to suffer the effects of a major psychological operation. Like the novice, he submits to mutilation in order to obtain a special kind of soul. Like the soldier of Vigny's time he is a man 'thrown, changed, recast, shaped for ever to a common pattern. The man is lost in the soldier' – as he is lost in the monk. Routine, the check on the intelligence, reserve, obedience to artificial authority, bring out the melancholy and coarseness of boredom in military life; the gain, Vigny says, is abnegation and sacrifice:

> This utter abnegation of which I have been speaking, together with the constant and careless expectation of death, the complete renunciation of all liberty of thought and action, the delays, suffered by a limited ambition and the impossibility of acquiring riches, all produce virtues which are much rarer among those classes of men who remain free and independent.

A monastery, a prison, the chains gladly accepted – such are Vigny's metaphors. A stoical doctrine, yet if it is wisdom and even freedom to submit to Fate and to obey, this submission is as corrupting as the pride of the man who believes he is free. Vigny wrote as a soldier of the peace-time bodyguard and garrison; he did not know the passion of action except by hearsay and he was austerely, humourlessly unaware of the corruption of the bored camp. He himself wasted a large part of his life in a profession to which he was unsuited – except that it gave him this book.

As a personal document, in which the self is disciplined to the point of anonymity, *The Military Necessity* is a classically clear and direct piece of writing. It is originally conceived. Vigny is an artist-philosopher. He sets out his theme a little at a time and then breaks off to tell at leisure a story that illustrates it. The military argument is a frame, as Turgenev's after-dinner conversations were or Mérimée's reflections on travel and custom, for three dramatic stories of character and action. This method of writing a short story will always attract the aspirant because it seems to be the easiest, for it gives the writer points of rest and provides him with the easy opportunity of stating an argument or a moral. The reader is deceived: for the requirement of this art is that one shall state a case without appearing to do so. Mr Humphrey Hare quotes Sainte-Beuve's praise of Vigny's poetry:

> He never . . . produces his tears as tears; he transforms them . . . If he wishes to give vent to the anguish of genius or to the loneliness of a poet's heart, he does not do so directly as would M. de Lamartine, with a lyrical effusion, instead he takes the indirect method.

Vigny is always concrete. He is various and resilient in feeling and in portraiture. The poor quartermaster is blown up at Vincennes but the tragic irony of this perfunctory death is effective because we had seen the old man in his youth, in his fairy-tale love affair, his love of homely music, in his fussing care and his fantastic life-long luck. Vigny has taken care to move us; his very arguments about the military life are feelings purged of personal rancour. His second virtue is that of surprise. When we meet the broken officer who is trailing through the mud of Flanders, with a mad girl in the cart behind him, we expect some tale of the misery of war, but it turns out to be far worse, an affair of political execution and the sea. The soldier has been ordered to shoot the girl's lover and he has saddled himself with his guilt. The officer with the malacca cane in the next story is similarly engaged in expiation. By doing their duty all his soldiers isolate themselves from humanity and accept a guilt which they cannot forget, and which is not 'their fault'. They are the martyrs of society. The event which causes this, in every case, is always astonishing, sudden and fearful.

Vigny has an exquisite sensibility to atmosphere and place. One will not easily forget the Flanders road, the attack on the Château at Reims, the simple barrack scenes at Vincennes or the long, dull, noiseless night in Paris deserted on the eve of the Revolution; such scenes have the supreme deceptive and allaying effect found only in the great story-tellers. What are those fires? The shopkeepers are merely burning down the trees that have darkened their shops; so does a revolution begin. It is on the day when nothing happens that everything happens. Then, at the critical moment of action, this quiet and reflective writer breaks into unforgettable physical detail. It is detail, uniquely of the occasion, which a writer of stories must always seek – the muddle of the execution at sea and when the girl is put by mistake in full view of her lover's death; the terrible moment in 'The Malacca Cane', when Captain Renaud, afraid of being afraid, runs his sword into a body during the night-scrimmage at the Château:

> an elderly officer, a big strong man, though his hair was grey, rose like a ghost, uttered a fearful cry at the sight.of what I had done, and thrusting violently at my face with a sword, fell instantly beneath the bayonets. I, too, fell to a sitting position beside him, stunned by a blow between the eyes, and I heard near me the dying voice of a child saying, 'Papa.'

Thus we know that Captain Renaud has killed a child, not a man, before its father's eyes. Or there is the dramatic eavesdropping on the meeting of Napoleon and the Pope. These crises are burned into all their special detail upon the reader's mind, as the outline of the quartermaster's body was printed by blast on the wall. One never forgets the physical scene which has been exactly caught from the chaos of feeling by a cool artist.

The admirable thing in *The Military Necessity* is the novel and unobtrusive interweaving of story and argument. Again and again, when we think we are about to be fobbed off with an anecdote or a memory, we find Vigny going much further. Though the story of the malacca cane culminates in the episode at the Château, it has taken us through the life of Admiral Collingwood, through a consideration of the character of Bonaparte and the seductions and errors of the idea of glory. It has discussed whether we shall serve men or principles; it has discussed the dehumanisation of man; the acceptance of retribution; the fact that ultimately life will deny us justice. We are always in deeper than we expect; we retrieve the idea of 'the military necessity', just at the moment when it seemed forgotten and when false freedom seemed to be breaking in. The book does set up against the amorphous literature of our day the dramatic blessings of an original and ingenious sense of form, the value of a decisive sense not merely of material but of fundamental subject. The latter is what we lack today. Vigny's life suggests that subjects are best found by writers who submit themselves to an intolerable spiritual pressure.

The Major's Daughter

He was greatly mourned at the Curragh where his cattle were well-known; and all who had taken up his bets were particularly inconsolable for his loss to society.

The quotation does not come from *The Irish R.M.*, but from the mother, or should one say the aunt, of the Anglo-Irish novel – Maria Edgeworth. The eighteenth-century note is unmistakable but so, even without the word Curragh, is the Irishness. One will never quite get to the bottom of that sentence out of *Castle Rackrent*. On the surface it is felt and good-natured. 'Poor' Sir Kit, after hitting a toothpick out of his adversary's finger in a duel, received a ball in a vital part, and 'was brought home in little better than an hour after the affair, speechless on a hand-barrow to my lady'. A sad business; but landlords come and go; we know them by their debts; only cattle are eternal. Irish irony has been sharpened to a fine edge; it is more drastic than the corresponding irony of the English writers of the time. Sententious, secure in the collective, educated self-regard of their class, the English ironists regard folly from the strong point of cultivated applause and moral platitude, whereas an Irishwoman, like Maria Edgeworth, has uncertainty underfoot. The folly of the death of Sir Kit is only equalled by the absurdity of the mourning; beyond both lies the hopeless disaster of the state of 'the unfortunate country'.

Behind an ironist like Fielding is assurance, courage and complacency; behind Maria Edgeworth, and Irish irony, lie indignation, despair, the political conscience. The rights and wrongs of Irish politics come into her works by implication. We see the absentees, the rackrenters, the bought politicians, and English, Jewish, Scottish heiresses brought in to save colonial insolvency. We see the buffoon priests and the double-minded retainers. We do not see the rebellion, the boys hiding in the potato fields,

[674]

but we do catch the tension. The clever, wise daughter of an enlightened father, a woman always ready to moralise about cause and effect in the neat eighteenth-century way, Maria Edgeworth was Irish enough to enjoy without shame the unreasonable climate of human temper and self-will, Irish enough to be generous about the genius for self-destruction. She was a good woman, ardent but – as Sir Walter Scott said – formidably observant, probably cool, perhaps not strong in sensibility; but she was not sentimental. Her irony – and surely this is Irish from Swift to Shaw – is the exploitation of folly by a reckless gaiety.

Castle Rackrent is the only novel of Maria Edgeworth's which can be read with sustained pleasure by the reader of today. Its verve and vivacity are as sharp as a fiddle's. It catches on like a jig; if it belongs to the artless time of the English novel, it is not clogged up by old-fashioned usage. I have never read *The Absentee*, which is often praised, but I have tried *Belinda*, a picture of the London smart set, and *Ormonde*. They, too, are vivacious, but there is not much point in finding time for them. They have a minor place in the history of the novel. One can only say that she has an original observation of men and women, an unspoiled eye for types; her moralisings are at any rate free from Victorian sentimentality, but are not in themselves interesting. Is it better for affection to follow esteem, or for esteem to follow affection? How are we to keep the peace between sensitiveness and sensibility, between the natural and the frivolous heart? How do we distinguish the line where generosity becomes self-indulgence? All this is good training, no doubt; but Maria Edgeworth was at her best when she was not being explicit about it. Character for its own sake, as the work of so many women novelists has shown, was the strong subject of this kind, clear-headed, irreverent woman, who never disturbs but also rarely comes to the foregone conclusion.

Belinda is a sharp-eyed tour of the London marriage market. No woman is less deceived by other women than this unsoured spinster who adored her father, wrote handbooks on education with him, managed his estate, 'got on' with his four wives and looked after his twenty-one children. The Edgeworths were a nation in themselves. She could draw an old rip like Lady Delacour, a matchmaker like Mrs Stanhope pushing her débutantes, and a dangerous 'metaphysical' woman like Lady Millicent in *Ormonde* with 'the sweet persuasive voice and eloquent eyes – hers was a kind of exalted sentimental morality, referring everything to feeling, and to the notion of *sacrifice* . . . but to describe her notions she was very nearly unintelligible'. Maria Edgeworth was the Major's daughter; the unintelligible was the unforgivable. It was very plain to her that the Lady Millicents of this world are so exalted that they do not know right from wrong. The men are as firmly drawn as the women. *Ormonde* contains a rich portrait of one of those hospitable, sociable, gallant, warm-hearted Irishmen, the souls of courtesy, whose imagination leads them into difficulties and ends by corrupting them, until the warm heart goes stone cold and they become the familiar Irish politician who will sell himself and anybody. Such a portrait might be done flat in bitterness and satire; Miss Edgeworth works in depth, engages our sympathy for the man, makes him captivate us – as he would in life – and gradually undeceives us without melodrama or ill-nature. None of these are great characters, but they are faithful observations of character. They are a truthful gallery, as capricious as life, of the figures of a class and an age. Such – we can be certain – was the life she knew.

Her other gift as a novelist is for writing spirited dialogue. The talk of *Belinda* or *Ormonde* is always light, engaging and natural. It is that 'modern' talk which goes on from generation to generation – one meets it in Jane Austen; then, after the Regency, it died out, until the modern novel revived it – and which has not been written in, like sub-headings, into the story. Maria Edgeworth owed her gift to her indifference to plot, that great torture-rack of talk in the English novel. Plot was forced on her by her father, the brilliant Major, who suffered from a rather delightful excess of confidence in his own powers; but, like Scott at the beginning of his career, Miss Edgeworth was interested only in sketching the people around her, and that is how the true gift for dialogue arises. Yet she owed something even of this to the Major, for it was he who, determined to out-Rousseau Rousseau, made his daughter write down the dialogue of his twenty-one children in order that it could be examined afterwards in his moral and linguistic laboratory.

Of course, she had the Irish ear for Irish expressiveness. In *Ormonde*, King Corny cries out with the gout:

'Pray now,' said he to Harry who stood beside his bed – 'Now that I've a moment's ease – did you ever hear of the stoics that the bookmen

[676]

talk of, and can you tell me what good any one of them got by making it a point to make no noise when they'd be punished and racked with pains of body or mind? Why I tell you all they got – all they got was no pity – who would give them pity, that did not require it? I could bleed to death in a bath, as well as the best of them, if I chose it; or chew a bullet, if I set my teeth to it, with any man in a regiment – but where's the use? Nature knows best, and she says *roar!*'

In a subtler way, she is as good in her plain passages, notably in her scenes between men and women. She hardly can be said to try a love affair, indeed one might say that she has noticed men and women pursue one another but is not sure why they do so. What she likes best is caprice, misunderstanding, the off-days of married life, flirtation: that side of love which, in short, supplies repartee and comedy, sociability or its opposite. Her people are always being interrupted and, though this shows some incompetence on the novelist's part, it also allows that crisp animation or restlessness which gives her stories their unaffected drift.

There are no interruptions in *Castle Rackrent*. Thady the steward tells the tale in his plain words and with his devious mind, and he rattles off the decline and fall of the riotous Rackrents over the generations, in a hundred pages. Drink, company, debt and recalcitrant foreign wives ruined these roisterers and Thady's own son, turned lawyer, quietly collected the remnant and indirectly made it his own. At the funeral of one Rackrent, the body was nearly seized for debt:

But the heir who attended the funeral was against that, for fear of consequences, seeing that those villains who came to serve acted under the disguise of the law; so, to be sure, the law must take its course and little gain had the creditors for their pains. First and foremost, they had the curses of the country and Sir Murtagh Rackrent, the new heir, in the next place, on account of this affront to the body refused to pay a shilling of the debts, in which he was countenanced by all best gentlemen of property and others of his acquaintance, Sir Murtagh alleging in all companies that he all along meant to pay his father's debts of honour, but the moment the law was taken from him, there was the end of the honour to be sure. It was whispered (but none but the enemies of the family believe it) that this was all a sham seizure to get quit of the debts, which he had bound himself to pay in honour. It's a long time ago, there's no saying how it was . . .

That is Defoe, but with whiskey added.

Major Edgeworth did not touch *Castle Rackrent*. He is known to have had a didactic hand in the other works and some have thought he stiffened them. Possibly. Yet his daughter owed her subsequent inspiration to the excitable, inventive, genial mind of the masterful eccentric and amateur. *Castle Rackrent* was the first attempt to present the history of a family over several generations as a subject in itself. It marks a small step in the expansion of the novel. Where the Major's influence is most felt is in the remarkable range of his daughter's work. Ireland is only one of her scenes. English society, Parisian society are done with the same natural touch. Her work was a triumph for the Major's revolutionary system of free education. Not a patch on Fanny Burney or Jane Austen, no doubt; the minds of father and daughter were too much dispersed by practical and inventive attention to the good, rational life. Scott thought Edgeworthstown a domestic paradise and possibly noted it was an Abbotsford one hundred and fifty years old without the worry and the expense. Abbotsford meant absurdity, obsession, and imagination; Edgeworthstown meant enlightenment. In the last count, the good life does not produce the great novelists.

The Young Gorky

The lasting work of Gorky is to be found in the three volumes of autobiography which he wrote between 1913 and 1924 and in the famous portraits of Tolstoy and Andreyev. Most foreign readers have been appalled by the scenes of squalor and gloom which Gorky set down from his life. The opening pages of *Childhood* are characteristic; Gorky's young and merry father lies dead in the room, the grandmother and the pregnant wife are lamenting, the police are at the door to hurry the funeral, and grief suddenly brings on the wretched mother's labour pains. The child has a terrifying vision of death and birth and there is the inevitable Russian touch of farce: frogs jump on top of the father's coffin as it is lowered into the muddy grave and are buried there. We foresee that Gorky's mother is one of those austere, sensitive, fine women doomed to be destroyed by the brutality and hopelessness of life; and so it turns out, when she takes the child to her father's house. Grandpa has a small dyeworks and is a man of substance. But he has an uncontrollable temper; in his sadistic bouts and partly on pious principle, he beats up the women and children of his family and also his employees. He is surrounded by drunken, quarrelling, vindictive and covetous relatives all whining for his money. Uncle Mike crowns everything by setting the family dyeworks on fire and, in general, one can only say that the cruelty of nature and the viciousness of the social system are outmatched by the natural animal malice of one human being to another in this book. There *are* scattered moments of goodness and quiet, but the general gloom is relieved by one figure alone: Gorky's grandmother. This captivating old lady is the soul of love and pagan sweetness and a story-teller of genius; there is a strange mixture of mysticism, poetry and stoicism in her nature, and she seems to be a throwback to some earlier, Arcadian phase of the Russian folk. It is because of her influence, as we read on, that our disgust declines. We find we are being seduced by the expressiveness of all Gorky's people, by their self-abandon and by what, later on, Gorky is to call their capacity for turning their sorrows into carnival. Fatalism does not always degrade: it often enlarges.

Gorky does not snarl; he neither maunders nor does he coarsely glut a secret appetite. He is totally free of that hysterical connivance which we get from Zola; he is never prolonging a private orgy. He is not a sensationalist wallowing in the sins of society; nor is he a smug social realist congratulating himself, like some Victorian reformer, that he at any rate has the right social and political views. We are elated because in these books Gorky has the heroic eye, a sort of giant-creating eye; because he has the strongest compassion and practises an almost saintly exclusion of himself from his own life. What matters to him is the strange spectacle of humanity. The boy grows, but the world grows too; everything is in physical movement. Gorky has a memory, we say, that allows the world to have existed to the full, without first having to ask a tacit moral or intellectual permission from himself. He has his standards, of course, he has his fastidiousness and there *is* a judgment, but none of these distorts his emotions or robs his extraordinary eye of his pity and its liberty.

Some critics have pointed out that Gorky's realism is a revolt against the puritanism of earlier Russian writers; if this is so, we notice that it takes a puritan to revolt, though many puritans relapse instead and go to seed. Gorky retains the puritan core, the puritan energy and tenacity; he is moved by what he mixes in with – the orgy at Petrovsky's in *My Universities*, for example – he is marked by it, yet he retains his integrity and he is not corrupted. An interesting reflection on his pessimism is made by Mirsky in his *History of Russian Literature*.

> Gorky [he says] is not a pessimist and if he is, his pessimism has nothing to do with his representation of Russian life, but rather with the chaotic state of his philosophical views, which he has never succeeded in making serve his optimism, in spite of all his efforts in that direction. As it is Gorky's autobiographical series represents the world as ugly but not unrelieved – the redeeming points which may and must save humanity, are enlightenment, beauty and sympathy.

This is the optimism native to all artists which is always more important than what they *think* they believe and is frequently at complete variance with it. In the course of his sometimes portentous self-education, Gorky was never able to tame his extraordinary eye. It remained autonomous and unweakened, a kind of person in itself like one of those boys that lead the blind. Indeed that is how Gorky often seems to us: a powerful, blind man being led by a voracious, all-seeing child.

To an astonishing extent all Russian literature is led blindly on by the inconsequence of the eye. Russian fantasy, the effect of the naïve and childish, the sudden dislocations which make the Russian novel so loose and life-like, above all the sense of the grotesque, owe everything to it. To some extent this use of the eye – and also the habit of describing violently contradictory feelings almost in the same breath – have stereotyped Russian literature for the foreign reader who is, perforce, unable to see differences of style. But one has only to compare Tolstoy's superb use of the eye with Gorky's to see there *are* differences and that this is not a national manner alone. Tolstoy watches life unblinkingly, like some subtle, impartial animal whose many-faceted lenses reflect all without effort. He lies still and natural life is imprinted on him line by line. Gorky, on the other hand, is like a hundred-eyed man who goes aggressively into life catching detail at every blink and who amazes us by forgetting nothing. Where he looks something is always happening. If a foolish soldier has turned to face his tormentors, Gorky sees him tuck his shirt in; if half a dozen chickens are being chased on a boat, he will see three fly overboard; he will remember how many times his grandmother told him to get from under her feet when the dyeworks caught fire, and afterwards see her blow on her scorched fingers as she talks; he will remember thousands of faces and gestures, every change of mood, every word spoken in his grandpa's tormented family, in the shops, ships and sheds where he worked, or on the roads where he tramped. The seeing and hearing are consuming. If the whole is invented memory, it is invented down to the most casual acts and finest shades and in a manner seemingly effortless. As far as I can define it the art seems to lie in combining contrasting things; in his accounts of people he first describes their appearance or their life from the outside and then catches something unexpected which reveals a part of the inner life that is bubbling away inside them. This is what human beings look like (he seems to say) – violent, vindictive, malicious, foolish, innocent, unfortunate, rascally or good – but what is on their minds all day, how do they get through the hours? So much fighting, scheming, quarrelling, hoping,

[681]

suffering – but what is deposited by it all for their empty moments, what is their particular form of the human bewilderment? So, for example, when the boy is left with the temper of his uncontrollable grandfather:

I lost all interest in grandpa's talk which grew duller, more nagging, more self-pitying, day by day. It had practically become a habit with him to quarrel with grandma and forbid her the house, and then she stayed at Uncle Mike's or Uncle Jake's. Once she was away for a number of days and grandpa cooked for us. He burned his fingers, yelled, cursed, smashed dishes; and he became noticeably gluttonous. Coming to my little hut, now and then, he would take his ease on my turf bench and, after watching me for a time would suddenly ask: 'Why so quiet?'

'Because I prefer it. Why?'

And that would precipitate a picture. 'We're not upper crust. No one bothers about our education. We have to learn by ourselves. For them books are written and schools are built; but no time is thrown away on us. We have to get along by ourselves.' And he lapsed into a pre-occupied silence; he made me feel uncomfortable and tense, as he sat there inert and oblivious.

The next moment the pious, diddling old savage is turning his old wife out of the house, saying that he has fed her long enough. But whereas a pitiless satirist like Shchedrin portrayed such a man in the storming and whining hypocrite Iudushka, Gorky sees people as victims of forces they do not understand and not as souls wicked in themselves. Grandpa is horrible, but he is also absurd, touching and not without a queer, half-frightened dignity.

Gorky's judgments are instinctive, not intellectual. He is torn between compassion and an aggressive resentment, himself as contradictory as the characters he draws. As he reflects upon the murderous quarrels in the home where he was brought up, he says:

In time I came to understand that out of the misery and murk of their lives the Russian people had learned to make sorrow a diversion, to play with it like a child's toy; seldom are they diffident about showing their unhappiness. And so through the tedious weekdays, they make a carnival of grief; a fire is entertainment, and on a vacant face a bruise becomes an adornment.

A carnival, these three volumes of autobiography are, a carnival that wanders all over the Russia that existed before the beginning of this century, steadied here and there by one or two serious people of good will and illuminated by the gracious old figure of the grandmother, the pagan saint and story-teller. This old woman is beaten from time to time, like everyone else in the book, but she takes that with a guileless and humble laugh, goes on with her stories and her simple pantheism. She has the civilisation and humanity of a poet. What Gorky understood as an artist he must have learned from her. She chanted her tales:

> When she had finished I begged for another, and this is an example of what I got. 'Now an old goblin lives in the stove. Once he ran a splinter into his paw. As he rocked back and forth with the pain, he whined "I can't bear it, little mice, it hurts so much."'
>
> And she lifted her own foot in her hands and rocked it comically, screwing up her face as if she actually felt the pain.
>
> The bearded, good-natured sailors would listen, too, and applauding the stories would urge: 'Give us another, grandma.' And in reward they would invite us to supper with them. There they plied her with vodka and me with watermelon. This was done in secret, for there was a man patrolling the boat, dressed like an official, who forbade the eating of fruit, confiscating whatever he found and throwing it overboard. Everybody kept out of the way of this man who, besides, was perpetually drunk.

The story and Gorky's epilogue have the same turn of inconsequence, the same immediate candour and acceptance of life.

Gorky is a writer strong as cheese and raw as onion. It is strange to think of him reading Fielding and praising the trim English as the originators and matters of realism, for his vision is heroic. He had a primitive directness of apprehension, a sensibility unspoiled by civilisation. That he was idolised by the people was just; like them he was growing; like them he drew his imaginative forces from the past. He was really a life rather than a novelist, a learned and circumspect vagrant who became, for one period, as Mirsky says, the only alternative government in Russia. What he lived and saw, not what he constructed, contained his importance. Often intellectually indigestible as a writer he is always a blind, moving force.

New York, 1900

A novel by Mrs Wharton in her best period is a correcting experience, a pain when the correction seems to be directed at ourselves, a pleasure when it is being handed out to other people. She is – so many of the important women novelists have been this – a mother-figure, determined, pragmatic, critical and alarming. How inevitable not to come up to her moral, intellectual, above all her social standards. Once we get out of the room where we have been sitting alone with the formidable lady, we foresee that we shall break out or go downhill once more. We know she is no fool; she can startle us by her range of observation; but we shall suspect that what she calls discipline is really first cousin to puritanism and fear, and that what she calls the Eumenides are really projections of the aunts who run the conventions and man the barricades of the taboos. The acerbity of a novelist like Mrs Wharton is *mondain* before it is intellectual; it denotes a positive pleasure in the fact that worldly error has to be heavily paid for spiritually. Her sense of tragedy is linked to a terrifying sense of propriety. It is steely and has the hard efficiency of the property market into which she was born. When, in *The House of Mirth*, Lily Bart is told that she will have to choose between the values of the smart set in New York and the 'republic of the spirit', we are not absolutely convinced that this republic is not a new kind of puritan snobbery. The men who belong to this republic signally fail to rush the women off their feet into this excellent world, and Mrs Wharton is drily aware of their failure. In its first decades the rise of American Big Business created an upper class whose sensitive men cut themselves off from a crude society that shocked them and which was dominated by women. She noted this in her autobiography and it is plain in all her books. Her own interesting situation is that there is an emotional force held back in her, which resents the things her mind approves of and it is this dilemma that gives her mind its cutting edge – at

[684]

any rate in the books she wrote before she found personal happiness. That happiness, it now seems, dulled her talent.

There is, of course, more than all this to Mrs Wharton, both as person and novelist. She elaborated the balance sheet of renunciation and became the accountant-historian of a rich society, and nothing passed her merciless eye. She wrote best when the pressure had been hardest to bear, even though that pressure may have frozen the imaginative and enhanced the critical character of her talent. Her prose has a presentable cold pomp: 'The cushioned chairs, disposed expectantly under the wide awning, showed no signs of recent occupancy.' Under great bitterness and frustration we have learned to expect outbursts of sentimentality – as a far greater writer, like Mauriac, has shown us – and when she drags the Eumenides into three or four melodramatic pages of her best novel, *The House of Mirth*, we are embarrassed. But it is exceptional for her control to go. Her study of rich New York in the early 1900s in that book will pass for smart sets anywhere and at any time, for even in our day, when most conventions have gone, when people no longer behave like 'deaf mutes in an asylum', the cheerless figure of the socialite remains. The smart set is the quintessential dust bowl. In a later comment on this novel Mrs Wharton wrote 'that a frivolous society can acquire dramatic significance only through what its frivolity destroys. Its tragic implication lies in its power of debasing people and ideals.' The idea is Jamesian and if the execution of it lacks the poetry, the heightened recitative of Henry James, we do get from Mrs Wharton the hard, unpitying moralist who will forgive but not forget, and the derisive critic of social architecture.

Indignation about the sins of another social class is, of course, easy money, and does not, of itself, get a novelist very far. One slightly suspects that Mrs Wharton did not like new people getting rich. But she did examine her subject with scientific efficiency, and in Lily Bart she created the most rewarding kind of socialite: one who was morally a cut above the rest of her circle, but who had been fatally conditioned from the first. Lily Bart is a beautiful and very intelligent girl, delightful company and really too clever for any of the men her society was likely to offer. On the lowest level, she is hopeless about money, about pushing her way in first, about intrigue, about using people, about the main chance. Her own view is that she behaves as she does because she has no money. It is Becky Sharp's cry:

virtue on five thousand a year. But this is only half her case. She is a superb artist in the business of being in the swim, a brilliant contriver of success; she has a wonderful sense of timing – when to be in the spotlight and when not. Her startling weakness is that she sows but she does not reap. At the last moment she is wrecked by the sudden boredom and carelessness of the very clever. On the day of victory she oversleeps. Her self-confidence is such that she does not bother to play her ace; and she imagines her gift for dispensing with success at the last minute will make her impervious to her enemies. It does not. Selden, who wants to marry her, imagines that her last-minute failures are signs of grace, impulses from the unconscious. They make her very likeable, but they must be considered as opportunities for further displays of courage and sang-froid rather than happy, non-social back-slidings into 'the republic of the spirit'. Her courage is half vanity. So low are the standards of her set that she is encouraged thereby to mistake thrilled nerve for an access of intelligence:

> She . . . listened to Ned Silverton reading Theocritus by moonlight, as the yacht rounded the Sicilian promontories, with a thrill of the nerves that confirmed her belief in her intellectual superiority.

Theocritus is, in short, the right poet, at the right moment, among the right people, at the height of the season. A venial folly; after all, are we quite sure that the enlightened Selden is any better for cutting himself off from the life of his country and reading La Bruyère?

Lily Bart has the beauty and vanity which George Eliot thought so wicked in women, but Lily's attractions are energy, an occasional capacity for honesty and innocence. She is not ashamed of her cunning in getting money out of a married man like Gus Trenor, for she has used her brains; what really shocks her is the price demanded. Her match is Rosedale, the rich rising Jew who reads her character perfectly, who puts his price up as hers goes down and, in the end, out of sheer admiration for her abilities, is willing to behave disinterestedly. But he is defeated by her gift for last-minute failure: she refuses to silence the women who have ruined her. Pride or a sense of virtue? Neither, I think – and here Mrs Wharton is very penetrating: those who believe in their star believe also in despair. Lily Bart is a gambler. One enjoys her as one enjoys the electric shocks of roulette, as one enjoys the incorrigible and the plunger. And one enjoys her also because Mrs Wharton turns her inside out:

> Moral complications existed for her only in the environment that had produced them: she did not mean to slight or ignore them, but they lost their reality when they changed their background.

Or, when it is a matter of getting a financial 'tip' out of Trenor:

> She was always scrupulous about keeping up appearances to herself. Her personal fastidiousness had a moral equivalent and when she made a tour of inspection in her own mind there were certain closed doors she did not open.

The only element missing from Lily Bart's character is her obvious sexual coldness to which, when the novel was written, Mrs Wharton could hardly have referred even if – to suppose the impossible – she had desired to do so.

New York's social scene is expertly set down in *The House of Mirth* with an anthropologist's thoroughness and the novel is remarkable for its skilful visits from one smart set to the smart set on the stair below. These tours are conducted with all Mrs Wharton's superlative snobbery.

> Mrs Bry, to Mrs Fisher's despair, had not progressed beyond the point of weighing her social advantages in public.

There was smart hotel society:

> Through this atmosphere of torrid splendour moved wan beings as richly upholstered as the furniture, beings without definite pursuits or permanent relations, who drifted on a languid tide of curiosity from restaurant to concert hall, from palm-garden to music-room.

Here reigned Mrs Hatch, the simple lady who, surrounded by beauty specialists, wished to soar socially; the Bovary of the gossip columns, who wanted to do what was 'nice' and to be taught how to be 'lovely'.

Mrs Wharton hated the smart set she had been brought up in and she is good in this novel no doubt because she is anatomising the monster whose stupidities and provincialities might have crushed her. But the making of her as a novelist is her power to create incident and to conduct great scenes.

Strangely enough her ironical power and gift of surprise often recall those of an utterly different novelist – Thomas Hardy. She has – usually under iron control – a persistent sense of fate, a skill in entangling her characters before striking them down. The scene at Gus Trenor's when this magnate turns nasty and looks like going to the point of sexual assault is wonderfully handled and Lily is marvellous in it; every cliché in this well-known situation is avoided, every truth in it discerned and the end is perfect. And Bertha Dorset's revenge on Lily: that is as brilliant a *volte-face* and surprise as one can remember in any plot in social comedy. Mrs Wharton did not touch these heights afterwards, though even in her weaker novels, there is the same astringency, the same readiness of invention.

Again and again we find that novelists who have attacked the conventions because they stultify the spirit, who attack the group for its cruelty to individuals, will end by pointing out the virtues of submission. Mrs Wharton may have hated old New York, but she hated the new New York even more. She disliked the prison of silent hypocrisy, but she drew in her skirts when candour came in. Especially after her long life, *en grand luxe*, in Europe. What indignation denounces creeps back in the name of sentiment. *The Age of Innocence* shows a man giving in, loyally marrying the conventional girl he does not love, throwing over the Europeanised woman who is his natural equal. It is the surrender to the established bourgeois standard. No great harms come of it; only dullness and disappointment. The sweet young girl he was engaged to was slyer than he thought. She became like her mother-in-law to whose face 'a lifelong mastery over trifles had given factitious authority'. Perhaps, after all, her husband reflects, that old New York which would not 'know' a divorced woman was rather charming and quite right. Better renunciation than a hole-in-corner affair. Mrs Wharton always believed in the sterner condition; but her brain resented it. Not even snobbery and respect for 'factitious authority' could get her into the Catholic Church at the end of her life. The old Puritan worldling stood out firmly for patching, for facing unpleasantness, making the second best of things, refusing accommodations. Worry, culture and character were the thing. One imagines God wondering if he dared leave a card. The strange thing is that we mistrust her at once when, late in life, she becomes benign.

A Viennese

Robert Musil's *The Man Without Qualities* is an immense unfinished novel, which this Czech-Austrian began writing in the Twenties and was still working on when he died an exile in Geneva in 1942. It is a wonderful and prolonged firework display, a well-peopled comedy of ideas, on the one hand; on the other, an infiltration into the base areas of what we call 'the contemporary predicament'. There is the pleasure of a cleverness which is not stupid about life: 'Even mistrust of oneself and one's destiny here assumed the character of profound self-certainty,' Musil wrote – not altogether ironically – of the Austrian character and these words suggest the conflict which keeps the book going at its cracking speed. Of course, Musil's kind of egoism had a long run in the first twenty years of the century and he has been – the translators tell us – written down by the standard German literary histories. Musil's tongue does indeed run away with him; but it is stupid to denigrate him. Proust and Joyce, with whom he has been exaggeratedly compared, approached the self by way of the aesthetic imagination; Musil reconstructs egos intellectually. What ideas do our sensations suggest? What processes are we involved in? If Musil has come to us regrettably late, if he sticks for his subject matter to the old pre-1914 Vienna and has some of that period flavour, he is not stranded there. The revival of Henry James has taught us that writers who live passively within history may be more deeply aware of what is really going on than those who turn up in every spot where the news is breaking.

The nearest parallel to Musil is not Proust but Italo Svevo in *The Confessions of Zeno*. Musil is very much an intellectual of that strain. The two writers represent opposite sides of the same Viennese school. They are restless, headlong psychologists and sceptical talkers, to some extent café writers. Like Zeno, the Ulrich of *The Man Without Qualities* is a gifted and self-consuming man. He burns up his experience. But whereas Zeno is a hypochondriac, a man of endless self-doubt, the clown of the imagination

and the heart, whose great comic effect is obtained by the pursuit of folly
with passionate seriousness, Ulrich is a healthy, athletic, extroverted and
worldly character whose inquiring brain captivates and disturbs men of
action. He is a mind before he is a sensibility. He has only to appear for
others to behave absurdly; his irony muddles them; his perception alarms.
Musil's achievement is to make this formidable character tolerable and
engaging. Ulrich is endlessly, perhaps pitilessly patient; he has learned that
humility of the intellect which comes of continuous use and which is
necessary to those who look into other people for what may be useful to
their own imaginative and intellectual search. Like Zeno he can never resist
a theory; but whereas Zeno's love for other people is really a kind of
remorse for having had so many ideas about himself, the love of Ulrich is a
feeling of gratitude to others for suggesting so many ideas that he has been
free of them personally. His attraction and power come from an imagination which transposes. Here is a comment on one of his comic characters,
a cabaret singer, a Juno of refinement who has a passion for eating. After a
good meal she would feel obliged to repay her lover:

> She would stand up and tranquilly, but full throatedly, lift up her
> voice in song. For her protector such evenings were like pages torn out
> of an album, animated by all sorts of inspirations and ideas, but
> mummified, as everything becomes when it is torn out of its context,
> loaded with the tyrannical spell of all that will now remain eternally the
> way it is, the thing that is the uncanny fascination of *tableaux vivants*
> when it is as though life had suddenly been given a sleeping draught;
> and now there it stands, rigid, perfectly correlated within it itself, clearly
> outlined in its immense futility against the background of the world.

One can see, after this, why Musil has been compared with Proust –
though, if the translation is to be relied upon, he does not write as well –
yet, where Proust seeks to crystallise a past, Musil is always pushing
through that strange undergrowth to find out, if possible, where he is,
where life is tending, and what is the explanation. His book is a crab-wise
search for a future, for what has not yet been given the sleeping draught.

In the first half of Part One of the novel the time and scene are the
Vienna of the Austrian Empire. The main episodes are Ulrich's love affairs
with the guzzling singer and with a rueful nymphomaniac; his friendship

with a gifted but unstable girl and with a superb bourgeois lady, notorious for mind, whom he calls Diotima, and who goes in for the True, the Good, the Beautiful on the grand scale. Diotima is a monument, an outsize schoolgirl. But the larger themes are political and social. Before long we have, by brilliant implication, an amusing but moving picture of a complete society whose intentions become nobler the nearer it is to destruction. Nobler and more absurd. For Musil has invented a wonderful farce called the Collateral Campaign. This vague political movement is meant somehow and simultaneously to celebrate the Emperor's birthday, boost Austrian culture – with a meaning glance at the Germans – preserve the stagnant existing order and yet arise spontaneously from the hearts of the common people and bring new spiritual life to the greatest minds desiccated by scepticism, intellectualism, etc. In short it is an all-purpose piece of uplift which is touchingly sincere and hopelessly muddled. It is very fond of the word 'true' – not patriotism but 'true' patriotism, not values but 'true' values. The comic beauty of the Collateral Campaign is that it can never settle on its precise form; it swells into committees, exhausts all the clichés, and turns into its opposite: a movement for chauvinism and rearmament. Really it is a midwife of fascism. Nothing is more certain of comic reward than Musil's sympathy. It is tender and deadly.

The people of the Collateral Campaign are 'good'. They are responsible. They represent 'the best elements'. They can choose. They choose ridiculously. But what of the bad, the irresponsible who cannot choose – a man like the homicidal maniac Moosbrugger who may or may not be executed? (He wants to be executed because he has an almost pettifogging regard for the law.) The Moosbrugger case puts its shadow on all the characters in the book and one of Musil's feats as a novelist is to show us exactly how Moosbrugger seeps into every mind in some way or other. If society is tending towards progress what is it going to do about this Caliban? Ulrich reflects: 'If mankind could dream collectively it would dream Moosbrugger.' If we do not know by what absolute standards to settle the Moosbrugger case, then a great social catastrophe is inevitable. Writing in the Twenties Musil could hardly have been more prophetic.

There is an interesting account of Musil's life in the very good introduction to the Wilkins and Kaiser translation of his novel. He came, we are told, of a gifted family. He was educated for the Army, fought in the 1914 war, became a civil engineer, a distinguished inventor, a mathematician, a psychologist, and was about to teach philosophy at Munich before he turned to writing. Musil brought to his writing not only the capacity for seeing but also the habit of hypothesis. Ulrich is, in many ways, Musil translated. In his several attempts to define what he means by 'the man without qualities', he notes,

> He will perform actions that mean something different to him from what they mean to others, but is reassured about everything as soon as it can be summed up in an extraordinary idea.

Or again, the translators give us these lines from the page he was adding to the last volume of his novel on the day he died:

> Of course it was clear to him that the two kinds of human being . . . could mean nothing else than a man without qualities and, in contrast, the man with all the qualities that anyone could manage to display. And the one might be called a nihilist, dreaming of God's dreams – in contrast to the activist who is, however, with his impatient way of acting, a kind of God's dreamer too, and anything but a realist, who goes about being worldly clear and worldly active.

Consciousness was Musil's real subject, not the 'stream' but the architecture, the process of building, stylising and demolishing that goes on in the mind. How does an idea like the Collateral Campaign grow in various minds? How, sensuously, does it breed? At what point does sensation become idea? How does reality look after that intoxication? These things bring out Musil's alacrity and focusing power as a novelist; for though he never stops talking he always enacts what he sees. He has a poetic yet practical ability for showing an idea coming to someone – a slow-minded and simple aristocrat, a blackamoor servant, a woman beginning to feel indignation and remorse in love, any transition in fact from one state of consciousness to another. He has the merit of loving people for their essence. There is, to take one example, a striking study of that special bourgeois protégé, the failed artist who takes to blaming his failure on the collapse of culture. From a hero he has turned into a petty domestic tyrant and rules his wife, who has ceased to love him, by making her play duets on the piano. Their marriage is sustained by a neurotic frenzy of piano-playing:

> The next moment Clarisse and Walter shot away like two railway engines racing side by side. The music that they were playing came flying towards their eyes like the glittering rails, then vanished under the thundering engine and spread out behind them, as a chiming, resonant, miraculously permanent landscape . . . Precise to a fraction of a second, gaiety, sadness, anger, fear, love and hatred, longing and weariness went flying through Walter and Clarisse. It was a union like in a great panic. But it was not the same mindless, overwhelming force that life has . . .

The more music sublimely unites them, the more they are separated in life, each thinking his way away from the other. Walter, the rejected husband, fearing failure and impotence, begins to slip into thoughts comfortably too large for him, and ends by playing Wagner for erotic reassurance. Here he begins to strike wrong notes. Clarisse's mind jumps from image to image and to questions becoming more and more savage: does civilised life yearn for brutality? Does peacefulness call for cruelty? For there is an empty room in Clarisse where 'something tore at the chains'. At the end of this volume we get a glimpse of that empty room.

In making raids like this into Musil's novel one risks making it sound thin or melodramatic in the heavy Central European way; a pound of realism to a ton of essay-writing. He is, on the contrary, subtle, light, liquid, serious. He is, no doubt, a bit over-fond of himself, perhaps a bit too tolerant to the 'I' who is never brought up against anything stronger than itself; a bit too much on the spot, especially in the love affairs. What the novel does show is that the habit of intellectual analysis is not stultifying to drama, movement or invention, but enhances them. It is a delightful insight that a movement like the Collateral Campaign, which has no distinctive idea, will inevitably attract all those people in the Austrian Empire who have only one idea; it is perfect that Ulrich shall be put in charge of sorting out these cranks. His theories, the whole apparatus of the book, are the forgiveness of the artist, not the examination papers of the master. Consciousness is, for him, a pardonable folly. Some critics have discerned what they believe to be a mythological foundation to this novel, in the manner of *Ulysses*; the density, suggestiveness and range could support the view. For it is cunningly engineered. The second volume of *The Man Without Qualities* sustains the impression of a major writer of comedy in the Viennese manner, and of an original imagination.

A French friend of Musil's, M. Bernard Guillemin, suggests that what Musil meant by 'a man without qualities' (*Mann ohne Eigenschaften*) was 'a man completely disengaged and uncommitted or a man in quest of non-accidental attributes and responsibilities self-chosen – the German counterpart of Gide's "homme disponible" though there is nothing of Gide in Musil's work'. In the later volumes, it is said to have worried Musil himself that a character as disengaged as Ulrich is will eventually become isolated and by-passed by life. The sense of adventure which exhilarates the early volumes becomes paralysed in the later ones, where the intellectually liberated man is not able to take the next step into 'right action'. It is significant that Musil's novel was never finished. He had spun a brilliant web of perceptions round himself and was imprisoned by them.

In this second volume, the absurd Collateral Campaign is still going on in Austria, Diotima, the lofty-minded Egeria, who runs the social side, discovers the 'soul' just as she is getting tired of her husband, a high government official. She has risen out of the middle classes into aristocratic society, and she plants this idea of the soul in an international financier and arms manufacturer, a German called Arnheim. There are generals who come in because 'the Army must keep an eye on things'; Diotima's social rivals appear to keep an eye on her, and so on. There is a wonderfully complete picture of a society at the edge of the precipice of 1914. The novelist's comic sense of character is speculative, and is strengthened by his penetration into the kinds of consciousness current at the time, into how private ideas become public, and public ideas affect the emotions of private life.

In the meantime, the Moosbrugger case – Moosbrugger is the homicidal sex maniac awaiting execution – underlies the social picture and makes its own disturbing footnotes. What about the law's attitude to insanity in murder; what about violence in the state, in personal life? At the most unexpected moments, Moosbrugger – who is merely a name in the papers to most of the characters – raises his idiot head and poses his devastating questions. 'Ordinary life,' Ulrich concludes, 'is an intermediate state made up of all our possible crimes.' So Musil dresses a platitude in epigrammatic form; he becomes rather free with epigrams; but his gift is to enact epigrams imaginatively.

In this volume the analysis of character is done at much greater length than in the introductory volume and so there is more discussion and less action. Of the portraits, Arnheim's and the absurd yet subtle General's are the most impressive, but we must not omit the girl Gerda and her lover who are moving towards an early form of fascism. Musil's Arnheim is by far the most cogent and exhaustive study of a millionaire magnate's mind that I have ever read. The irony is exact and continuous. Arnheim, for example, had 'the gift of being a paragon':

> Through his understanding of this delicate interlocking of all forms of life, which only the blind arrogance of the ideologist can forget, Arnheim came to see the prince of commerce as the synthesis of revolution and permanence, of armed power and bourgeois civilisation, of reasoned audacity and honest to goodness knowledge, but essentially as a symbolic prefiguration of the kind of democracy that was about to come into existence . . . he hoped to meet the new age half-way.

Under the influence of his love for Diotima, Arnheim seeks to bring about the 'fusion of interests between Business and the Soul'. His craving for power leads him to writing books: 'with positively spectral prolixity' his pen began to pour out reflections on 'the need of this fusion' and 'it is equally certain that his ambition to master all there was to be known . . . found in the soul a means of devaluing everything that his intellect could not master'. Arnheim is morally devastated by his love for Diotima, for she is monumentally high-minded; and Musil has the pleasure of showing us a sumptuous, high-minded *femme du monde* reduced to the frantic conditions of a woman forced to the bed of a testy, cynical husband, and a magnate paradoxically reverting to his native instincts the more his 'soul' is elevated. All roads leave from the soul, Musil reflects, but none lead back to it: Arnheim is no more than a magnate after all and, once Diotima can be his, he falls back on the old maxim that in love, as in business, one had better spend only the interest, not the capital. Arnheim's character reminds one of Walter Bagehot's dictum that a kind of intellectual twilight, with all its vagueness, is necessary to the man of business and, towards the end of this volume, Musil reveals what Arnheim is really after in the ideological mists of the Collateral Campaign and the higher life of Diotima: he is after control of the Galician oilfields.

Ulrich, the man without qualities, is the natural enemy of Arnheim; his natural foil is the comic General. An air of unworldliness in civilian life is an obligatory mask of the military profession; all 'a poor soldier man' may permit himself to point out is that, if the military have a virtue, it is their sense of order. There is a farcical scene of discussion when this soldier describes his visit to the National Library where he approaches the whole task of improving his mind in the spirit of the strategist. The General is a wit in his way. Even after a carefully worked-out campaign of reading, in which he allows for substantial casualties, he discovers it will still take him 10,000 years to read what is necessary. 'There must be something wrong about that,' he says, raising his glass of brandy.

Musil writes with the heightened sensibility of a man in love; that is to say, under the influence of the unrest of seeking harmony and completion in things. The Collateral Campaign itself is a kind of communal love affair. In the description of love affairs and especially in the portraits of women in love, Musil is truly original; in managing scenes of physical love, he has not been approached by any writer of the last fifty years. What has been missing, in those accounts, has been Musil's transcendent subject: the sense of the changing architecture of consciousness. He brings the effect of the imagination into the fears and desires of these women, their sense of living out an idea which may indeed well be a love fantasy about quite a different lover from the one in whose bed they lie. He is sensitive to the power of 'erotic distraction'. Of Rachel, the maid who goes to bed with a fellow servant because she has been stirred by the touch of a guest's hand, he writes:

The object of this yearning was actually Ulrich, and Solimon was cast in the role of the man whom one does not love and to whom one will nevertheless abandon oneself – a point on which Rachel was in no sort of doubt whatsoever. For the fact that she was not allowed to be with him, that for some time past they had hardly ever spoken to each other except in a whisper, and that the displeasure of those in authority over them had descended upon them both, had much the effect on her as a night full of uncertainty, uncanny happenings, and sighs has on anyone in love; it all concentrated her smouldering fancies like a burning glass, the beam of which is felt less as an agreeable warmth than as something one will not be able to stand much longer.

The high-minded love affair, the violently neurotic, the absurd one, the desperate affair carried on against the will, the one crossed by other lives; from all these Musil extracts the essence with dignity and gaiety, the comi-tragedy of human loss and incompleteness. The history of love is the history of absence, of arrival and departure. He is able to do what no contemporary ever does: to move from the imaginative and emotional to the physical without change of voice; even the naked fight on the bed or the brazen or terrified undressings are not marred by the worst fault of our erotic realism: its unconscious grotesque. The tenderness, subtlety and disinterestedness of Musil's intelligence enable him to do this; and the almost conversational style. Critics tell us that, whatever the awkwardness of translation may be, he has in German a style that is as lucid as that of Anatole France and less florid than Proust's. One cannot judge this, though the translation of the second volume seems to me an improvement on the first. (The whole difficulty has been to avoid translating German abstractions into the kind of technical or administrative super-jargon which these become in English.) Musil is an addiction. The most irrelevant criticism made of him by some Germans and Austrians is that his kind of café sensibility is out of date. It may certainly be familiar in Schnitzler and Svevo, but Musil's whole scheme prophetically describes the bureaucratic condition of our world, and what can only be called the awful, deadly serious and self-deceptive love affair of one committee for another. And he detects the violence underneath it all. In only one sense is he out of date: he can conceive of a future, of civilised consciousness flowing on and not turning back sick and doomed upon itself.

Quixote's *Translators*

====

Don Quixote has been called the novel that killed a country by knocking the heart out of it and extinguishing its belief in itself for ever. The argument might really be the other way on. *Don Quixote* was written by the poor soldier and broken tax-collector with the hand maimed in his country's battles because the Spanish dream of Christian chivalry and total power had passed the crisis of success. The price of an illusion was already being paid and Cervantes marked it down. When Don Quixote recovered his sanity, his soul lost its forces, and he died. What must strike the foreign reader is the difference between the book as it appears to Spaniards and as it appears to the world outside of Spain. The difference is that in Spain *Don Quixote* had a basis in contemporary fact; outside Spain it is morality, metaphysics, fable. The romances of chivalry were read during the Counter-Reformation and specifically moved two of the Spanish saints to action – St Teresa and St Ignatius de Loyola. Longing for the freedom of a man as her brothers went off to the New World, St Teresa read these books with excitement, and Loyola's famous vigil at Manresa was made consciously in imitation of Amadis, and might be a chapter of *Don Quixote*.

Outside Spain, the novel began a new life in countries where the idea of chivalry had no tradition of national awakening and power, where the tragic core was missing. To the English and French translators who got to work a few years after the book was published, *Don Quixote* was simply the greatest of the picaresque novels, indeed the only great one in a genre which elsewhere kept strictly to exaggeration, meaninglessness and popular anarchy. The book became farce – though the contemporary Shelton sins far less than Motteux who translated the book at the beginning of the eighteenth century – a string of adventures and scenes of horseplay tied up with ironical conversations about the noble disadvantages of idealism and its conflict with proverbial self-interest. If we turn to the English novelists who, in the early eighteenth century, were deeply influenced by the tale, we can see how they altered the characters of Don Quixote and Sancho to suit the new middle-class morality. Don Quixote, especially, the violent and subtle madman with his visions of the lost Golden Age, becomes in England a mere eccentric, an unaccountable squire, a hilarious Scot in Smollett, an unworldly but rough-and-tumble clergyman in Fielding. Figures like Parson Adams are misfits, cranks, clowns, often enlightened but always simple and without authority; whereas Don Quixote's mind is darkened and dignified by the counsels of his madness. He has the endless resource of the neurotic; he has pride and the habits of pride and command. In England, the ingenious gentleman is opposed by the worthy forces of self-interest, so much admired in Cheapside. The question is practical: idealism or realism? The answer always sentimental: failure is lovable and what is lovable is commercial. These imitators in the sensible eighteenth century delight in freaks because they love individuality; but they do not enter, as Cervantes in his great mercy did, into that universal region of the human spirit where the imagination reigns like an ungovernable and fretful exile in a court of shadows.

The late Samuel Putnam translated *Don Quixote* and three of the *Exemplary Novels*. They were published in handsome volumes printed on a fine large page – a great advantage – and contain a critical account of many earlier translations and a very large collection of valuable notes; altogether a scholarly piece of work by an American amateur. He had translated a good deal of Brazilian literature. Mr Putnam believed *Don Quixote* to be one of the dying classics and thought an accurate and contemporary translation might revive it. Compared with Shelton, the abominated Motteux – the one guessed and the other added colour – with Ormsby, Jervas and even the Penguin done efficaciously (especially in the dialogue) by J. M. Cohen, Putnam's translation is toned down. This means that the fine shading of the irony of Cervantes becomes clear and Mr Putnam has taken great trouble with the difficult proverbs. A few contemporary colloquialisms, mainly American, surprise but do not seem out of place; there is often a mildness in Mr Putnam which leads him to choose a weak word or phrase where the Castilian is strong, terse and concrete; and in straining after accuracy he has missed sometimes the note of repartee or satirical echo in the conversations of Don Quixote and Sancho. In the scene at the inn with Maritornes and the muleteer, and in the chapter following, Motteux, Jervas and Cohen – to take only three – are superior in vigour to Mr Putnam, whose colloquial phrases have a citified smoothness from easy over-use. To give an example: Don Quixote is about to reveal that the daughter of the supposed Castilian had come to him in the night, but stops to make Sancho swear that he will tell no one about this until after the Knight is dead, for he will not allow anyone's honour to be damaged. Sancho replies, without tact, that he swears, but hopes that he will be free to reveal the secret tomorrow, on the grounds that: 'It's just that I am opposed to keeping things too long – I don't like them to spoil on my hands.'

Both Motteux and Cohen stick closer to the more vigorous original image. The Spanish word is 'go mouldy' or even 'rot', and not 'spoil'. Literally 'go mouldy on me'. In the earlier chapter one can catch Motteux adding direct, eighteenth-century animal coarseness where Cervantes is not coarse at all; in fact, *Don Quixote* is unique in picaresque literature in its virtual freedom from obscenity, except in some of the oaths. When Maritornes rushes to Sancho's bed to hide there from her angry master, Motteux writes:

> The wench . . . fled for shelter to Sancho's sty, where he lay snoring to some tune; there she pigged in and lay snug as an egg.

This is picturesque, but it has arisen from the mistranslation of two words in the text. Possibly it is an improvement on Cervantes who wrote merely that 'she went to Sancho's bed and curled up in a ball'. Mr Putnam's pedantry spoils his accuracy here for, instead of 'ball', he writes, 'ball of yarn'. The objection to Motteux is that in making Cervantes picturesque and giving him Saxon robustness, he endangers the elegance and the finely drawn out subtleties of the original. Motteux was half-way to Smollet, which is a long way from Cervantes. The picturesque and pungent in Cervantes lie wholly in Sancho's proverbs, where Mr Putnam excels. When Doña Rodriguez says that she can see 'the advantage which a maiden duenna has over a widow, but he who clipped us kept the scissors', Sancho comes out strong and to the life:

> 'For all of that,' Sancho said, 'when it comes to duennas there's so much to be clipped, according to what my barber tells me, that it would be better not to stir the rice even though it sticks.'

Don Quixote begins as the description of a shy, timid, simple, eccentric provincial gentleman who, after the first clash with reality, develops an always growing complexity of mind that is the satisfying and diverting substance of the book. For as he goes deeper into delusion, so he is dogged by a dreadful doubt and self-knowledge. At the end, when Sancho returns home leading his master, with their roles reversed – for it is he, the realist, who has triumphed, having governed an island and having even rescued maidens in distress – Don Quixote is said to have failed in all, but to have known glory and to have won the supreme victory: victory over himself. The novel is a powerful example of the process of the growth of a work of art in a writer's mind, and of the luck of writing. For at the end of the first part, which Cervantes at one time regarded as the end of the book, one can see the idea in crisis and at the point of breaking down. Some critics have thought that the irrelevant stories stuffed into the end of the First Part show a fear that the reader will be bored by the colloquies of two characters only: and that he also wished to show that he was not a mere popular writer, but could write a polished, psychological short story in the best manner of the time. (He, indeed, succeeded in the story of Don Fernando and Dorothea and, in the latter, drew a delightful analytical portrait of cleverness in women.) But in the long interval between the two parts, the idea matured and became richer in fantasy, invention and intellectual body; the range of character became wider and success – so bitterly delayed in Cervantes's life – released confident powers that delight us because they delight in themselves. Not only does Don Quixote's own case branch into its full intricacy; not only are we now taken into all the casuistries of the imaginative life; by a master-stroke, Sancho is infected. The peasant gets his dream of material power, like some homely Trade Unionist, to put against the gentleman's dream of glory. Realism turns out to be as contagious to fantasy as idealism is. *Don Quixote* begins as a province, turns into Spain and ends as a universe, and far from becoming vaguer as it becomes more suggestive, it becomes earthier, more concrete, more certain in real speech and physical action. *Don Quixote* does not collapse, as the Second Part of Gogol's *Dead Souls* does, because Cervantes is not mad. He remains pragmatic, sceptical and merciful; whereas Gogol got the Russian Messianic bit between his teeth and went off his head. Spanish fantasy goes step by step with Spanish sanity. Nor, if we read *Don Quixote* truly, can it be described as a work of disillusion, if we mean by that the spiritual exhaustion which follows a great expense of spirit. The Spanish crack-up had begun, but it had only just begun. The force of that national passion was still felt. Though Cervantes was the broken soldier, though he was imprisoned, hauled before the Inquisition, and knew all the misery and confusion that the Spanish expansion abroad had left behind at home, he was not the enemy of the Spanish idea. He valued arms more than literature, as he explicitly said – incidentally in the character of Cardenio he drew an excellent portrait of a coward. What *Don Quixote* does is to enact the tragedy of experience as something still passionate though commingled with reflection: experience now more deeply felt. The comic spirit of the book is not satirical or tired, but is vital, fully engaged and positive. The wisdom runs with the events, not after them. It is stoical, not epicurean; sunlit, not eupeptic; civilised, not merely robust. *Don Quixote* bridges the gulf between two cultures, not by an inhuman cult of the people, but by excellence of intellect; by the passion a writer has for his means; by irony and love.

The Bored Barbarians

In the Fifties Mr Anthony Powell was the first to revive the masculine traditions of English social comedy. He retrieved it on behalf of the upper classes. The joke that he is a Proust Englished by Wodehouse has something in it; in fact, the big influence was Aubrey, but where Aubrey had an almost fretful appetite for scandal and oddity, this was dignified, in Mr Powell's generation, as the belief in personal relationships. Other values, in the Twenties and Thirties, were in flux; one could become an anthropologist, a Malinowski of Mayfair, Bloomsbury and country-house life, and try to establish a culture pattern. I confess that I have got more out of Mr Powell's novels, as each one of them stands, than I have out of his ambition to fill out the social panorama during his period. I am not convinced that any pattern is emerging. It is enough that *A Question of Upbringing*, *The Acceptance World* and *A Buyer's Market* introduced a new kind of nerve, comic effrontery and invention. They caught and played with that ineradicable core of boredom that has been the resource as well as the blight of upper-class English life, a boredom produced by the inherited genius for ironing our feelings, and doggedly covering the loss with bouts of dottiness, alcohol, adultery and class-consciousness. Mr Powell's English are punishing and punished. Their comedy has no silken threads; the threads are tweed.

What are the characteristics of this masculine tradition in our comedy? It is intelligent rather than sensitive; it is prosaic rather than poetic; it is sane rather than extravagant. It is egocentric and not a little bullying. It has manner, and that manner is ruthless and unkind. To stand up to the best manners of English society one has to be rude, exclusive and tough. One must be interested in behaviour, not in emotions; in the degree to which people hold their forts – and how much money the forts cost – not in what human beings are. The tradition begins with Fielding; it is there, minus the animal spirits, in Jane Austen. Its values are bound to the social class the writer belongs to – in Wells, for example, to the lower middle class. Hard-headed, often gifted, snobbish – for the most part – appreciative of other people's disasters and evasive about their own, self-oppressed and taking it out in horseplay and libertinage, Mr Powell's characters are a sort of club. They can listen unexhausted to gossip about each other, but their faces become suddenly masked if an outsider comes up. Their privacy is phenomenal. Widmerpool, the go-getter and man of will – a considerable comic creation – is damned because people affect not to remember whether he comes from Northamptonshire, or is it Derby? Mr Powell's narrator really hounds him. Yet, of course, Widmerpool also hounds himself.

The world Mr Powell is describing is dull, incurious and barbarous, judged from the outside, but very funny to read about. It certainly defeats foreigners. But the people of high comedy *are* generally dull. (The characters of Henry James's *Portrait of a Lady*, for example, are barely conversable.) The question is, What has Mr Powell done with them?

The early novels like *Afternoon Men* and *Venusberg* and *From a View to a Death* shared a sharp, electric, almost lyrical, performance. One of the earliest writers to expose people, and even more their way of life, by the follies of their dialogue, Mr Powell took a number of specimens of the Jazz Age and drily left little commentary. *Afternoon Men* gave one a stiff shot of party life; *Venusberg*, romantic yet lapidary, commemorated the love affair abroad; *From a View to a Death*, that social return-match: the undesirable artist among the speechless fox-hunters. Here Mr Powell's Stendhalian dryness began to warm and a deadly moralist appeared. For this is the novel of Major Fosdick, a very rare bird indeed in the English Tweedery, and one of ingenious complication. A tendency to overdress, so that even 'the skin of his face was covered by small diagonal lines similar in pattern to that of his coat', was not to be attributed to any shortness of genealogy in Major Fosdick; he was far from being a stockbroker. The deep boredom and privacy of English country life had brought out something cross-gartered in his nature. He would lock himself in his dressing-room, when the fit was on, and would dress himself in a woman's evening dress and picture hat and then, taking out an exercise book, write poetry. What we so anxiously hope for indeed happens: he is caught by an enemy squire and neighbour in this rig-out and, wits not moving fast in those acres, he might have been able to palm himself off as his own wife. A moustache betrayed him.

A scene of this kind is, of course, a stock one in farce and it is funny enough as it stands. But everything lies in the handling and here we see the first signs of Mr Powell's coming maturity. He is never satisfied with a mere joke. The encounter has two beauties: first that Fosdick compromises. He takes off the picture hat and swings it absurdly as he talks; second, neither man mentions his astonishment or horror, but treats the whole episode *à l'anglaise*, as a test of character and upbringing. Fosdick knows he will have now to surrender in the long row over his pheasants. He retires, stiff in the upper lip, to a nursing home in the proper way. Mr Passenger, the squire, will go home and, as is proper, forbid his daughters the house, but he too recognises moral defeat. He had considered himself a man of independent genius whose luck was always out, a potential superman who had never had his chance. His tragedy is that:

> In this moment of emergency he had been thrown back on the old props of tradition and education and when he might have enjoyed a substantial revenge he had behaved with all the restraint in the world.

The characters in *From a View to a Death* are perennial in the classical English comedy of country life and the national mixture is there, even to the mad cynicism of the cautionary tale. I am thinking of the barrel organ players who appealed for charity on the grounds that they were orphans.

> The postulation rested wholly on the handicap of loss of parents, which because the youngest of the orphans must have been at least forty years of age, was in their case presumed to have persisted into early middle life.

But if the characters are the same, the observation is revised. They are done in new colours. Mr Powell is, as I have said, devoted to Aubrey's *Lives* and his comedy has behind it a stolid native melancholy that is terrifyingly full-blooded. He has wit, but it is not rapier-play; rather it leaves a skilful boxer's marks upon the body of the enemy. The characters retired bruised, not nicked, from the ring. And then an unusual dimension is added to his people: they are reconsidered. They are not only figures of fun and

[705]

amusement; they have a serious relation to their own experience or to the author's, so that we are shown the comedy of social history.

In a world in which standards and values have vanished, to what do we turn? To the attempt to find out a personal pattern – that favourite word of unbelieving anthropologists – to the sober technical question as to where we were accurate and where (through immaturity) off the mark in the consideration of ourselves, our friends and our world. We become the pedants of the cult of personal relationships.

This pedantry is the basis of Mr Powell's new comedies. *A Buyer's Market* reconsiders the characters of *A Question of Upbringing* and both books fill in at length the social scene that was left out in *Afternoon Men*. So we have a finely painted, detailed picture of the last year at Eton, the London Season, the first ventures in society, the first stages of a career; and in the background the upper classes start on that peculiar course of chasing after artists, drifting into Bohemia, the demi-monde and the business rackets, which has been typical of our age. *A Buyer's Market* contains three absurd figures from this time: Mr Deacon the ageing bad painter, Uncle Giles the shady rebel, and the superb Widmerpool whom we had first seen at Eton – wronged, earnest, narrowed and ambitious. Widmerpool is a wonderful portrait of the go-getting young man – he is Fielding's Blifil, but now in business – whose pursuit of the main chance has given a growing squint to his life. He talks like a Pep book, he calculates absurdly aloud, he is prone to social disasters of the first magnitude. He is not debagged by the young oafs at the debs' ball, but he does get covered with castor sugar; it is he who is made to pay for the Free Love girl's abortion; it is he who drives his car into the ornamental urn at the magnate's castle and who makes a ludicrous appearance behind the bars in the dungeon there. Widmerpool never comes up smiling; muttered indignation attends his injuries. He becomes the victim one cannot love, crouching round the ashes of his private shames, but he has his own private laugh. For his pursuit of private respectability and the windy justifications of the yes-man is always successful.

The farce of Widmerpool gains from the sententious, slow motion manner of Mr Powell's writing. The deb sprinkles Widmerpool lightly with the sugar pot:

More from surprise than because she wished additionally to torment him, Barbara did not remove her hand before the whole contents of the vessel – which voided itself in an instant of time – had descended upon his head and shoulders, covering him with sugar more completely than might have been thought possible in so brief a space. Widmerpool's rather sparse hair had been liberally greased with a dressing – the sweetish smell of which I remembered as somewhat disagreeable when applied in France – this lubricant retaining the grains of sugar, which, as they adhered thickly to his skull, gave him the appearance of having turned white with shock at a single stroke, which judging by what could be seen of his expression, he might very well in reality have done underneath the glittering incrustations that enveloped his head and shoulders. He had writhed sideways to avoid the downpour, and a cataract of sugar had entered the space between neck and collar; yet another jet streaming between eyes and spectacles.

Mr Powell is excellent with the raffish. Some critics have objected to his sententious manner; but even if it is true that this is what happens to Proust if one drains off sensibility and makes him appropriate to clubs, I think the sententious irony succeeds. It is, after all, native and part of the tradition. It adds a very English flavour either of comic tautology or deflation.

'Shall we leave the gentlemen to their port?' said Mrs Widmerpool, when finally the subject had been picked bone dry.
She mouthed the words 'gentlemen' and 'port' as if they might be facetiously disputable as strictly literal descriptions in either case.

That final 'in either case' is the devastating torpedo. Mr Powell may have got overfond of phrases like 'in his case' and all those 'unquestionablys', 'alternativelys', 'undoubtedlys' and 'if anythings', but in their forensic malice, they rub the salt in hard. (The narrator's desire to pass as the impartial norm conceals a fierce melancholy which I suppose to be Mr Powell's energising wound as an artist.) The habit of labouring a point may also at last add the macabre to the grotesque:

A direct hit had excised even the ground floor, so that the basement was revealed as a sunken garden, or site of archaeological excavations long abandoned, where great sprays of willowherb and ragwort flowered through the paving stones; only a few broken milk bottles and a laceless boot recalling contemporary life.

And the deliberate intellectualisation of an absurdity may become disturbing:

> The name Casanova's Chinese Restaurant offered one of those unequivocal blendings of disparate elements of the imagination which suggest a whole new state of mind or way of life.

These words come from *Casanova's Chinese Restaurant*. The story has two musicians, three writers, a painter, a biography-writing peeress, a left-wing peer turning intellectual; we may find ourselves in a country house like Dogdene, a discarded first or second wife may drag us down to Earl's Court or Pimlico.

The aim of Mr Powell's sententiousness is to appal by the judicious: in a sense, his comedy is hysterical. There are several references, in this novel, to a ghost train the narrator and his friends used to go on when they were young; and it is implied that their lives, in the Bohemian period he is describing, have been like this absurd and finally ghastly journey.

But these novels constitute a *roman fleuve*. The same characters reappear, with new wives, husbands, careers, fortunes and fates; they are connected intimately in their social set. They live in a whispering gallery, in a mocking music of echoes from the past. They astonish one another by their unpredictable actions and their new chummings-up. Who would have thought, in *At Lady Molly's*, that Widmerpool would fall for that brassy ex-VAD, Mrs Haycock? Or, in *Casanova's Chinese Restaurant*, that the grand Mrs Fox would take up with a ballet dancer and shower him with presents? Here a difficulty arises. After the deep state of their early flow, such novels run into shallows. What began as a panorama begins to sound like a gossip column. One noticed this in *At Lady Molly's*; in *Casanova's Chinese Restaurant*, the habit of gossip has really set in and the central interest – the examination of two marriages – is not strong enough to stop it. One has the irritating impression that Jenkins, the narrator, has no other profession but to run about collecting the news; his stability has become fitful. The characters exchange too much hearsay. This is the danger with the *roman fleuve* when it lacks a strongly sustaining idea beyond the convenience of its own existence. I am not sure that the idea of the decadence of a class anecdotally viewed is strong enough. I think Mr Powell has now to guard against the risk that his characters will be so familiar and real to him that he will cease to make them important to us; that they will lose their true strength, i.e. that they are obsessive fictions. The constant difficulty of the novelist is to avoid the engaging demi-monde that lies between art and life. Hearsay enfeebles, if Aubrey's brief emblematic lives become Aubrey's long ones.

Against this natural drift Mr Powell puts his set comic scenes and uses, of course, his notable organising powers. But, in *Casanova's Chinese Restaurant*, there is only one of these comic set pieces strong enough to stand against the current. It must be said that this particular one is as good as any he has done; it is the scene in which the drunken Stringham mocks the nagging out of the tragic Maclintick's terrible wife, and is himself finally carried off by his old governess. It is marvellously observed and the tragic sequel is all the more forceful for it; one notices here how brilliantly Mr Powell arranges material that has become immense. He is very accomplished in pulling things up out of the past and planting them massively before us. I put this scene beside the earlier one in *At Lady Molly's* where the General, newly come to psychological studies, makes his absurd, slow-motion diagnosis of Widmerpool's sexual misfortune. Mr Powell is a master of such refracted comedy and that is where the sheer intelligence of the masculine school counts. Such things are far superior to his social commentary.

In praising Mr Powell for his hard-headed comedy, his mastery of burlesque and farce, I do not undervalue his serious reflections. He is not diffused by urbanity. He is misanthropic, sane, experienced; there is no cynicism. His epigrams are withering but they do not utterly demolish. Their balance is as formidable as their wit:

> He also lacked that subjective, ruthless love of presiding over other people's affairs which often makes basically heartless people adept at offering effective consolation.

He has a sense of proportion, yet he also has edge. It is an uncommon pair of gifts. When one speaks of his melancholy one is not describing a passive condition; one is speaking of a driving force. His almost geological utterances suggest that even Mayfair and Pimlico have their Egdon Heaths:

> Love had received one of those shattering jolts to which it is peculiarly vulnerable from extraneous circumstances.

A sentence like that could go on the title-page of *Casanova's Chinese Restaurant*. It contains, down to the very word 'peculiarly', the undertones and overtones of this novelist, in whose work the human comedy is grimly engrained.

Meredith's Brainstuff

Does anyone know what to think of Meredith's novels now? I think not. The lack of sympathy is complete. Difficult to read in his own time, he is almost impenetrable to ourselves. 'Full of good brainstuff', Gissing said of *Diana of the Crossways*, and added joyfully that the true flavour of this book came out only after three readings! It was Meredith's brain that annoyed his early critics; today we suspect his heart. Insincerity and freakishness are held against him. Yet, we ought to feel some contact, for he is the first modern highbrow novelist in the sense of being the first to write for the minority and to be affected, even if unconsciously, by the split in our culture. George Eliot, his rival intellectual, was not so affected.

Those who visited the chalet at Box Hill in the period of Meredith's old age and fame were astonished by the mass of French novels there. He set out, as the French do, to facet life so that it became as hard as a diamond, to shape it by Idea. (At the time of the death of his second wife, he wrote: 'I see all round me how much Idea governs', and Idea was 'the parent of life as opposed to that of perishable blood'.) The notion sometimes gave an intellectual dignity to his creations, but just as often dignity was merely stance. For Meredith's imagination housed the most ill-assorted ideas: there was dandyism, there was the oracular Romance of his claim to be a Celt, there was the taste for German fantasy, the feeling for supermen and women and the heroic role of the fittest. If we follow his own habit of metaphorical association, we find ourselves saying that the descendant of two generations of naval and military tailors in Portsmouth was born to the art of dressing-up. In fact, his grandfather, and his father before him, had been as fantastic in their lives as he was in his novels; the son was able to survive his own self-deceptions by the aid of wit. The difficulty of Meredith does not lie in his thought, but in its conceits, in the flowered waistcoats of his intellectual wardrobe. Gosse used to object to this passage from the description of a scene at the gaming table:

[711]

He compared the creatures dabbling over the board to summer flies on butcher's meat, periodically scared by a cloth. More in the abstract, they were snatching at a snapdragon bowl. It struck him that the gamblers had thronged on an invitation to drink the round of seed-time and harvest in a gulp. Again they were desperate gleaners, hopping, skipping, bleeding, amid a whizz of scythe blades, for small wisps of booty. Nor was it long before the presidency of an ancient hoary Goat-Satan might be perceived with skew-eyes and pucker-mouth, nursing a hoof on a tree. Our medieval Enemy sat symbolical in his deformities, as in old Italian and Dutch thick-line engravings of him. He rolled a ball for souls, excited like kittens, to catch it tumbling into the dozens of vacant pits.

Brainstuff, indeed. For our welfare (Meredith warned us) Life was always trying to pull us away from consciousness and brainstuff. On the other hand, 'Matter that is not nourishing to brains can help to constitute nothing but the bodies that are pitched on rubbish heaps.' Human felicity is always trying (he said in a letter) to kill consciousness. There is often an extraordinary violence in Meredith's neo-pagan metaphors.

Meredith, like Browning, had too many ideas. And, as in his novels, so in his life, the brilliant egoist appeared to be an artificial construction. An American biographer, Professor Lionel Stevenson, notes in *The Ordeal of George Meredith* that by the time he was fifty, Meredith 'had completely molded himself in a dramatic personality'. He had become the Comic Spirit in person and if there was overstrain, it was for clear personal reasons: 'The components had been collected with a kind of genius. Impenetrably screened behind it lurked the Portsmouth tailor shop, the bankrupt father, and the dreadful decade of his first marriage.' The price was that he did not inspire intimacy:

> It was not that he seemed either aloof or insincere; but he created the effect of a perpetual and consummate theatrical performance and the pilgrims to Box Hill were not so much consorting with a friend as they were appreciating a unique work of art.

It would be misleading to continue to press a comparison between Meredith's life and his work as a novelist. Professor Stevenson is concerned with the writing life and very little with literary criticism. He comments on the novels, as they come along, but does not examine them in much detail. He notes (what Henry James deplored) Meredith's evasion of the *scène à faire*; for example, it is the point of all Meredith's novels, as Professor Stevenson admirably says, that the chief characters shall be tried by ordeal. They are burned in the fire of their own tragic or comic illusions and emerge from self-deception into self-knowledge. Yet, in *Diana of the Crossways*, the scene where Diana commits the folly of letting a political secret out of the bag is skipped. Is she an hysterical egoist? Is she as immoral as she appears? Has she merely lost her head? Only a direct account of the scene at the newspaper office, where she hands over the secret, can tell us. Meredith was no story-teller – a fatal defect, above all in the days of the three-volume novel. He is a novelist who gesticulates about a story that is implicitly already told. The cage of character is his interest. The rest of Professor Stevenson's criticism is appreciative but not considerable. I find only one point of disagreement. He says that Meredith was the first to introduce something close to natural dialogue in the English novel. Certainly Meredith breaks the convention in which dialogue had been written up to this time; the result is not natural speech. Meredith simply applied his own allusiveness to dialogue, and allusiveness happens to be a characteristic of ordinary speech anyway; he was too full of himself to see the characters or speech of other people, except in so far as they could be elaborated as 'idea' and in stylised form. Meredith's dialogue is simply Meredith cutting a figure in his own society.

As a biography Professor Stevenson's *Life* tells a well-known story competently. A writer has not much time for living and Meredith's life is one more variant on the theme of the calamities of authorship. There is the aloof, handsome, snobbish youth making that first break with his environment by sheer pride of obsession. There is the unhappy marriage to Peacock's daughter and the hardening of the heart – yet Meredith's heart must have hardened in childhood. And then the literary grind follows. *The Ordeal of Richard Feverel* is a failure, so is *Evan Harrington*. *Harry Richmond* gets a few admirers. His integrity was untouched by neglect; he worked without a public until he was fifty, and by that time, his health went to pieces. The tall, eagle-faced man, the non-stop wit, talker and laugher, with his bouts of 'manly' boisterousness and back-slapping, had always been a dyspeptic. Now he suddenly became deaf. He presently had the symptoms of locomotor ataxia. To keep his family he had ground away for years as a publisher's reader and wrote three articles a week for a provincial newspaper. For years also he made a small annual sum by reading to an old lady once a week. His letters are full of the groans of laborious authorship. At fifty he had had enough, but he was fated to live into his eighties, unable to hear speech or music; unable to walk, which had been his chief pleasure in life. He was drawn about in a donkey chair. He was sixty before he became famous; the relative comfort of his old age was only in part due to his success – he inherited a little money from an aunt. In his personal life, he had seen the death of his two wives and the son whom he had once adored, but who had become estranged from him after his second marriage. A psychologist might say that Meredith's life is an ironical illustration of the theory that we get what we are conditioned to desire. The death of his mother in very early childhood, and the pride and fecklessness of his father, had formed Meredith for self-sufficiency and loneliness: the brain rapidly filled in the hollows left by affections which had been denied. His own affections certainly became intellectual; his love letters are clearly of the kind that exhaust the feeling in an excessive flow of lyrical expression. He grieved over the death of his wife, but he *had* compared her to a mud fort! Friends found an annoying disconnection between brain and heart. There was one reward. It seems frequently to come to the egoistic temperament: the exciting, if heartless, power of living in the present. He tore up old letters and, in old age, is said to have scorned the common consolation of that time: living in the past. The torrential talker, the magician, was in short a picturesque monster, relishing his scars. One whimsical young American admirer – mentioned by Professor Stevenson – made the shrewd, even Meredithean remark, that he would probably have been happier and better organised if he had been a woman.

To return to the unreadableness of Meredith. He is not unreadable; he exists a page at a time; he is quotable, to be skipped through. The large characters like Sir Willoughby Patterne or Richmond Roy are myths. Meredith is tedious only in his detail; when he intends to be preposterous he is wonderful, as he is in that scene in *Harry Richmond*, where Richmond Roy poses publicly as an equestrian statue. Meredithean irony is excessive, as all the brainstuff is, but it is excellent when the character or the scene is fantastic enough for him. He is impossible until one submits to his conception of Romance; after that he is only hard work. He is a rhapsodist who writes about people who are really souls moving impatiently out of their present into their future, towards destruction or self-knowledge. They are pagan souls in the poetic sense, not characters in the moralistic sense; giants of the Celtic tradition, grotesques in the German; all their geese are swans. Their lives are portrayed as heightened exercises in their integrity and their sense of honour. Professor Stevenson remarks that Meredith was attacked with ridicule until he was fifty, not only because he was a pagan who could not tell a story and at odds with popular realism, but because Romance was out. His fame began when Romance came in. Stevenson and Conrad contain strange echoes. Chesterton's suburban romance owes a lot to him. D. H. Lawrence was the last to be influenced by him. Another element in making his fame was the rise of feminism. It is very hard for ourselves to imagine another revival in Romance. What a future generation of novelists may find stimulating in him is that preoccupation of his with what he called 'the idea'. He enlarged the novel with a brilliant power of generalisation. It was spoiled, as so much English fiction has been, by the obsession with romantic class-consciousness, but in *Beauchamp's Career*, or even in a clumsy novel like *One of Our Conquerors*, he has an ability to generalise about society as living history. And his presentation of character – Diana Merion, for example, in *Diana of the Crossways* – as idea and person at once, is a fertile addition to the old English tradition of character types, removed from our moralising habit. The pile of French novels at the chalet, the attempt to turn Molière into English, had their point.

Harry Richmond contains fewer difficulties of style than most of his work, chiefly because it is written in the first person. Meredith was a poetic or rhapsodic novelist, and *Harry Richmond* is a romance about the serious deceits and comedies of romance. Several of the characters are more than life-size, or speak and live in the heightened language of an imagination which is sometimes fine, at other times wooden or uncertain of its level; but there is no doubt that Meredith creates a complete world. Critics have often said that Meredith's taste for the chivalrous and high-sounding takes him clean out of the nineteenth century and sends his novels floating away in clouds of non-existent history. They have said that we can never pin him

[715]

down to time and place, and that he is intellectually Ruritanian. This is only superficially true. We must take into consideration a novelist's temperament before we judge like that. Because Meredith's mind was microscopic, because his subject again and again is people's imaginative, ideal, future-consuming view of themselves and of their environment, this does not mean that they have no known place in a recognisable world. Nothing could be more thoroughly Victorian in imagination than *Harry Richmond*; if the neo-medieval colouring is precisely that, this novel reads as if it were an attempt to glamorise Victorian life out of recognition. This is a well-known habit among the poets of the nineteenth century. The cult of the picturesque history can be described as an escape from the grim squalor of the industrial revolution; but we can also think of it as a confident and imperial enterprise of colonisation. The Victorians were high-feeders on what is felt to be foreign in time or place. *Harry Richmond* is cast in the imperial frame of mind, and if Meredith can be justly accused of being merely Ruritanian, he did not fall into the ludicrous which so often imperils (shall we say?) Tennyson's historical or legendary poems. The very pretences of Harry Richmond's fantastic father to the throne of England and to royal blood expresses the rising, exuberant side of the situation in England at that time when people were very liable to be plethoric about the greatness of their history. The plot and many details of narration are also true to the period. It was a time of violent changes of fortune in private life, of tremendous claims to estates and titles. Meredith is known to have got the idea for Richmond Roy's wild claim from the fact that William the Fourth had many children by an Irish actress, and also from the marriage of George IV to Mrs Fitzherbert. Meredith's remoteness has been greatly exaggerated by critics brought up on realism.

The spell of *Harry Richmond* – for to read it is to pass into trance – exists because of the brilliant handling of an impossible subject. If Meredith had confronted Richmond Roy's claim squarely and realistically he would have been lost. His art lies in building up the character of the father as the romantic and charming figure seen by his child, and then in gradually disclosing that he is first an adventurer, living in state one minute and in a debtor's prison the next; at last, by evasive insinuation, comes the royal claim. Richmond Roy grows larger and larger, richer in resource and effrontery, more and more triumphant for every setback, but skating on thinner and thinner ice the farther he goes. Meredith learned from French novelists the method of working up to the key phrase. The moment the farmers on whom Harry Richmond is boarded when he is a child start deferring to him, and are heard at last to whisper superstitiously 'Blood rile', the thrill is aesthetic. It has exactly the effect of the words 'You are an egoist' when they are spoken to Sir Willoughby Patterne and when they transform the tension and tighten the focus of that book. Richmond Roy has been too obviously compared with Micawber; he is far more complex than that; his follies and dreams have genius. He is not a windbag; he is a fine actor. He is nearer to Falstaff. Richmond Roy alarms. He alarms when he brazenly orders scarlet liveries, permitted only to the Royal Family, for his postilions. He alarms by his knowledge of our weaknesses. He can bounce his way into buying a château or a yacht. He can spellbind a foreign court and rout the hostess of Bath. Notoriety he thrives on. His impudence when he poses as an equestrian statue at the German court is splendid. These imaginative episodes set off the scurvy ones; the father's nasty relationships with the press, his unscrupulous robbery of his adoring son, his caddish exploitation of the young man's love for the German princess, his cold-hearted swindling of his sister-in-law. He pretends that the money came from personages who are anxious to keep him quiet. He is a mountebank, and if we are glad in the end that Squire Beltham exposes him in good Squire Western style, it is not really because we like to see vice punished, but because the rogue has got too maddening and has reached an hysterical and pathetic stage where he will become a figure too farcical to bear his real weight as a symbol; hence his tragedy. Meredith works up to that proper conclusion but, like a great artist, explores all the other possibilities first. He has the piling-on instinct of the story-teller. We are delighted towards the end when Richmond Roy is confronted with another false claimant, a so-called Dauphin who claims to have marks on his body which prove his heredity. Meredith is clever enough to give this episode twice; in two different kinds of gossip, one showing Richmond Roy the master of an insulting situation, the other through Squire Beltham's hilarious British scorn. Meredith's mastery of comedy does not exclude the low and, indeed, in the low he is not tempted to his vice of over-polishing. When the ladies retire from the dinner table – a nice touch that – the squire lets go:

They got the two together, William. Who are you? I'm a Dauphin; who are you? I'm Ik Dine, bar sinister. Oh, says the other; then I take precedence of you! Devil a bit, says the other; I've got more spots than you. Proof, says one. You first, t'other. Count, one cries. T'other sings out. Measles. Better than a dying Dauphin, roars t'other; and swore both of 'em 'twas nothing but port wine stains and pimples. Ha! Ha! And, William, will you believe it? – the couple went round begging the company to count spots to prove their big birth. Oh Lord, I'd ha' paid a penny to be there! A Jack of Bedlam Ik Dine damned idiot! – makes the name o' Richmond stink.

It has been said that Meredith is not a story-teller – but a story need not depend very much on plot; it can and does in Meredith depend on pattern and the disclosure of character through events. The weakness is that the fantastic father engrosses the great part of the interesting incident; when he is off-stage our interest flags. Meredith's narrative is not a straight line; it is a meandering back and forth in time, a blending of events and commentary and this Meredith must have gone for instinctively, because he is wooden in straightforward narration. We follow an imagination that cannot bear precision. He depends on funking scenes, on an increasing uncertainty about how exactly events did occur. There is a refusal to credit reality with importance until it has been parcelled out between two or three minds and his own reflections on it. Even in the duel scene in Germany, the excellence is due to the ironical telescoping of the event; we are hearing Meredith on the duel, telling us what to look at and what not to bother about. The effect is of jumping from one standstill scene to another. Life is not life, for him, until it is over; until it is history. (One sees this method in the novels of William Faulkner.) The movement is not from event to event, but from situation to situation, and in each situation there is a kernel of surprising incident. In realism he is tedious. One can almost hear him labouring at what he does not believe in and depending on purely descriptive skill.

The love scenes in *Harry Richmond* present a double difficulty to ourselves. The mixture of realism and high romance is awkward; we are made to feel the sensuality of lovers in a way remarkable to mid-Victorian novels; their words appear to be a highfalutin way of taking the reader's mind off it and, in this respect, Meredith's pagan idealism is no more satisfactory than the conventional Christian idealism of other novelists. Like Scott, Meredith is always better at the minor lovers than the major ones. His common sense, touched by a half-sympathetic scorn, is truer than his desire, which is too radiantly egocentric. In Meredith's personal life, his strongest and spontaneous feelings of love were those of a son and a father, and this is, of course, the theme of *Harry Richmond.* That is why, more than any of his other works, this one appears to be rooted in a truth about the human heart. In erotic love, Meredith never outgrew his early youth and the fact over-exhilarates and vulgarises him by turns.

Harry Richmond is thought to be less encumbered than Meredith's other novels because it is written in the first person. Unfortunately, as Mr Percy Lubbock pointed out some years ago in *The Craft of Fiction,* the first person has to be both narrator and actor in his own story, and in consequence stands in his own light. I do not believe that this is a serious fault in *Harry Richmond* as a story, for what carries us forward is Meredith's remarkable feeling for the generosity, impulsiveness and courage of youth and its splendid blindness to the meaning of its troubles. Harry is blinded by romantic love for his father and the German princess; he is weak in not facing the defects of the former and in not being 'great' enough for the latter; but both these sets of behaviour are honourable and have our sympathy. With his father he shares a propensity for illusion and romance and is cured of them. Since he is the narrator we have only his word for it, and one is far from convinced that Harry Richmond has been cured or even examined. Put the story in Henry James's hands and one sees at once that the whole question of illusion or romance would have been gone into far more deeply. It is the old Meredithean trouble; he is an egoistical writer, fitted out with the egoistical accomplishments, and one who can never be sufficiently unselfed to go far into the natures of others. His portraits start from him, not from them, and the result is that he is only picturesque, a master of ear and eye, a witty judge of the world, a man a good deal cutting a figure in his own society; we are given brilliant views of the human heart, but we do not penetrate it. He has no sense of the calamitous, no sense of the broken or naked soul, and – fatally – no sense of evil. More than any other novelist of his age, he has the Victorian confidence and in a manner so dazzling and profuse that it is natural they called him Shakespearean. In the effusive Victorian sense, he was; but Shakespearean merely linguistically, glamorously, at second hand, without any notion of human life as passion or of suffering as more than disappointment. He is a very literary novelist indeed.

Conrad

Conrad exists in English literature, but he is a harsh exotic who can never quite be assimilated to our modes. No English novelist has his peculiar accent in psychological and moral curiosity; it is like the knowing accent of Kipling, a foreigner's acquired slang, but expressing a far more elevated sensibility than Kipling had; only Henry James, another alien, with his pursuit of fine consciousness, approaches Conrad's fencing with extremes. Yet here all Conrad's critics have been dissatisfied. They have felt, as Forster did, that he was following extremes into a fog of argument or rhetoric; or they have been obliged to agree with the comment of Dr Leavis – the most substantial of Conrad's critics – on the inequalities of *Heart of Darkness* and that

> he is intent on making a virtue out of not knowing what he means. The vague and unrealisable, he asserts with a strained impressiveness, is the profoundly and tremendously significant.

Even in *Nostromo*, where Conrad's powers of concretion were married to a great subject, we shall not exactly know where we stand. We are always liable in his work to lapse from the certainties of art into the restless brilliance of opinion, to find the matter in hand being explored with the cleverness of the café writer and the moral dilettante. We shall be haunted by the special and tragic brilliance of the exile who, as he exhibits himself and plays his role, is never unconscious of the fact. As Mr Douglas Hewitt says in *Conrad: A Reassessment*, his novels are not tragedies – they *resemble* tragedies. They are, generally speaking, one must add, inhibited from tragic fullness by his famous, defensive and histrionic irony. He is, at bottom, a rather sadistic and sardonic writer. His irony is ultimately perverse – or, as earlier critics used to say, morbid – because it is a personal irony and does not always lie in the nature of the events he describes. Is *Nostromo* a great classical novel or a brilliant commentary? That is to say,

[721]

superb as it is, does it not strike one as being a commentary on the kind of novel or dramatic work that could, at some time, be written on its subject?

Nostromo is the most strikingly modern of Conrad's novels. It might have been written in 1954 and not, as it was, in 1904. All the issues of the economic exploitation of a backward country are here; the politics of Costaguana over two or three generations are telescoped in depth without losing the focus on the present. We see both the ideal and fraud in colonial exploitation, in the fight for liberalism, progress, reform, the bent to revolution and the advent of a foreign power. Even the rise of two of the now dominant forces in his kind of situation is clearly noted: the desire of America to take over everything in the world and, against or with that, the rise of the masses. Conrad did not set these things down in a political or historical essay, nor in a novel of propaganda, but in the impure detail of a large sceptical and imaginative work. Every moment is physically realised not by a right-minded and insensitive political reporter with a mind hardened-off (or softened) by his programme, but by an artist dealing, as art must, in the waste, the elusive, the incalculable. It is one of the prophetic felicities of this work that it is pervaded by a profound, even morbid sense of insecurity which is the very spirit of our age, and that sense is (as it must always be) personal. Before anyone else – though we may pause to give Mr E. M. Forster his due – Conrad the exile foresaw that in half a century we should all become exiles, in a sense.

One or two reflections follow from our astonishment with *Nostromo*. The first is a general reflection on the social soil in which the modern English novel is planted. The great English subject – one is inclined to say – and at any rate the great subject which includes a picture of society, lies outside England, simply because English life itself has for long been parasitic on life abroad and does not wish to recognise the fact. 'Abroad' is where English institutions have been put to the test and not in South Wales, Tyneside, Birmingham or Surrey. As I say, apart from Conrad, only E. M. Forster seems to have known this; possibly Lawrence, too, in a book like *Kangaroo*. The second reflection is one that throws a light on some of Conrad's defects as a novelist. He suffers from being before his proper time. It is a freak of time that he is a Romantic. Even in small yet not unimportant matters like the use of dialogue, Conrad was unlucky. If he could be writing *The Secret Agent* or the bandit pages of *Victory* now, he would certainly not write the wooden Cockney or the ludicrous melo-drama of his gangster's dialogue; the intellectual energies of the refugee would not have been spent on acquiring literary English, but the English of speech.

Conrad is a man in what we may call the post-1940 situation, but who is obliged to conceal the fact under a dramatic fog of rhetoric. He loved rhetoric, of course, and became – as Mr Hewitt says – more prone to it when his talent went to pieces from *Chance* onwards; vaguely emotive words like 'unspeakable', 'nameless', 'inscrutable', 'horror', 'pure evil', 'mystery', 'Woman' are the well-known pedals of the Romantic organ. Behind them lay things which, a generation or so after, he could have named, and as an incipient nihilist he would have been bound to name them. He would have been obliged to live or set down in precise physical detail the nihilism which he feared so much in his nature. It would have been drawn out by a nihilist age. The case of Kurtz in *Heart of Darkness*, the case of Heyst in *Victory*, or Decoud in *Nostromo*, is contemporary, but now the full glare of the interrogator's lamp is on their faces. Conrad would have been drawn out of the grandiloquent shadows that exasperate us and which seem to exasperate him; he would have found less to opine upon and more, cruelly, to state. The morbidity of which early critics complained – quite rightly; before 1914 certain values seemed impregnable – would not strike one in our imaginary Conrad who had been drawn out by times that would fit his temperament like a glove. Betrayal, guilt, isolation, the double self, corruption, the undisguised sadism that has appeared in our life, the anarchy, are not matters of speculation and pious lament. They are contemporary facts.

Mr Hewitt is of the opinion that the decline of Conrad's work which began with *Chance* comes from a failure to see any secure or positive values which could counter the force of his negative criticism. The alternative was to plump for popular Romance and an unreal, black and white world of wholly good or wholly evil people. These later books are simply the early rhetoric expanded. Mr Hewitt's book is a short one which sticks to the text of a few of the novels and is concerned with the specific moral health of Conrad's genius at different times; it is far from com-prehensive and though its main points are excellent, one misses a sen-sibility to detail. Gould and his wife, for example, are hardly realised

[723]

characters in *Nostromo*: they are states of mind, like the Dukes who hold the Court in a Shakespearean drama. Why in comparison does Mr Hewitt find Heyst's conversations with the girl on the island less acceptable than Mrs Gould's conversations with Decoud in *Nostromo*? The dialogue is wooden in both instances but the matter is allusive and subtle. Is not the difference between Gould and Heyst simply that one is a practical and obsessed solitary scheming for his mine, whereas Heyst is a passive solitary? Mr Hewitt warns us of the danger of paraphrasing Conrad, but Conrad paraphrases himself in characters like Gould, Heyst and Decoud. They are attitudes, not people, though they are attitudes lit up here and there by the novelist's power to given them flashes of individual life. The fact is that Conrad was a writer of restless and changeable conceptions, but he was poor in invention. His imaginative eye did not easily move; it was fixed upon brilliant detail so that the sound of a thing like the clank of railway trucks, with its suggestion of prisoner's fetters, becomes so powerful as an image that it is more real to us than the people who have to be explained or 'talked on' in brilliant but ultimately elusive colloquies. He is a jumpy, attitudinising, artificial writer, bedevilled by his eye. The selection of the isolated subject is, in part, the expression of his maddened desire for a subject that can be made to stand still so that it can be forcibly elaborated. The pattern of *Nostromo* is wonderful. It is like some grim brocade; yet was it necessary to be so elaborate in order to get the utmost out of the subject? And did Conrad get the utmost? On the level of a great tragic conception, I think, it must at last be thought he did not. We are overburdened by detail, by a too constant intensity. We are hypnotised. We 'come to', but there has been no purgation.

The Secret Sharer, in Mr Hewitt's opinion, marks the deciding crisis in Conrad's life as a novelist. In this excellent tale he thinks Conrad exorcised his personal devil and thereafter turned away from the central conflict which had fertilised his art. Leggatt, the man who takes refuge in the young Captain's cabin, has killed a man in some squabble, and he plays the part of the Dostoevskian 'double' as Gentleman Brown had done to Lord Jim. Leggatt is the hidden transgressor in the unconscious, an embodiment of the fear 'that there are parts of himself which he has not yet brought into the light of day' and which may interfere 'with the ideal conception of one's own personality every man sets up for himself secretly'. The Captain is put to a strain leading almost to madness by his secret partnership and actually risks his ship; but having pushed the pact to the limit, he conquers and sails off, free at last, where Kurtz, Gentleman Brown of *Nostromo* and Lord Jim represent failures in this struggle with the unconscious. It is a shrewd point of Mr Hewitt's that *Chance*, with its optimism of black-and-white Romance and reliance on the sailor's simple code immediately follows these histories of failure. Conrad's pessimism, his lack of a positive scheme of spiritual values, clearly left him, as a Romantic artist, in an intolerable situation.

Exile, the fact of being uncommitted, is at the bottom of Conrad's triumphs and his failures. He is a writer of great vanity. One has the impression of a writer more suited to the theatre than to the novel. The wonderful faceting of *Nostromo* is essentially theatrical in effect; self-consciousness, artifice, the sense of his rôle which every Conrad character feels, including Marlow himself, strengthen our impression. Of course, he was no more a dramatist than Henry James was, but there is this straining towards the drama. It is, indeed, the self-dramatising, evasive, speculative quality in his own comments on his work which make him an unusually unreliable guide to his achievement.

Two things strike us about Conrad. The first is that despite his life of action, his true heritage was political and literary. He took to the sea, as a writer might, if he had a good stomach, out of a romantic passion for travel and geography. He was not a born seaman who eventually takes to writing as another form of extroversion. Conrad's father was a well-known if minor literary figure in Poland, a dilettante of reckless political nerve, and the son's decision to go to sea was a violent break with the formative influences of his upbringing. It was a protest, an adventure, could almost be thought an aberration, and was likely to recoil. Secondly, we must note the immense importance of politics and especially of political defeat in his life. He saw defeat lived out in tragedy, in the death of his father and mother after their exile in Russia. He was with them there; he nearly died there. He learned exile as a child. The 'gloom' of Conrad was not the broad, passive gloom of the Russians which seems to arise from the dull excess of space; he disliked being called a Slav. He was a Westerner who despised the Dostoevskian Russian. Conrad's 'gloom' – as his biographer says – began with his early schooling in sorrow. It grew, later on, into something hard and sardonic. It is the bitter irony of the active man of strong imagination who sees, with personal indignation, the relativeness of experience. The exile has the illusion of moral freedom and becomes a connoisseur of the ironies of his situation.

There is some parallel in the lives of Conrad and his father. The dangerous political gestures of the father were patriotic, noble, passionate and romantic, but they were carried on in the futile void created by an all-powerful tyranny. There was a total lack of prospect. It was oceanic. In the life of the son the conception of tyranny that wastes life has changed into the embittering notion of Destiny. There is something odd about Conrad's idea of Destiny; so often it is merely exasperating, when it should surely be dreadful; perverse when it should be impassive. The men of the generation of Conrad's father knew evil by direct experience. The police rapped on the door. The arrest was made. The lies were told. The trial took place and the protests. The sentence to Siberia, which was really a sentence to fatal illness and the loss of everything valued in life, was a fact – to Conrad's father. To the son, when he grew up, evil was a bad dream, a sinister memory, a dark rhetorical suggestion. Again and again in his work, the evil thing becomes diffused and generalised into an indefinable reek of corruption. Indeed Conrad's special contribution to the English novel is to have insinuated into it the sense of an atmosphere of evil which is notoriously lacking; but as Dr Leavis has fairly said: 'he is intent on making a virtue out of not knowing what he means. The vague and unrealisable, he asserts with a strained impressiveness, is the profoundly and tremendously significant.' On the other hand, we have to note that Conrad is better at the evil fact – the cannibal helmsman lying dead in the wheelhouse in *Heart of Darkness*; the crew disappointed that they cannot eat the body – than he is at evil in the general sense. There are times when the belief in original sin sounds either histrionic or professional; and in *Heart of Darkness* far too much play is made with words like 'inscrutable', 'unfathomable', 'impalpable', 'mysterious', 'inconceivable' in a manner that suggests an attempt to create a system or dogma of evil by sheer rhetoric. Conrad's description of the Congo is unforgettable, but his moral reflections look like stage-drawings or temporary constructions. I think the exile's temperament gave Conrad his obsession with the allusive. He could never resist a symbol; and his images tend to submerge his people at their crisis, as if they were evasions. Even so, such a concern for texture does not really explain why

'Mistah Kurtz', the whole focus of *Heart of Darkness*, is a ghost or figment. His extreme lusts – what are they? What unnameable things did he do? Was he a cannibal? He murdered, we suppose. It is curious that when Marlow actually sees the heads on the poles outside the hut, he sees them not by the defenceless naked eye but by the magnifying intervention of binoculars. At the very crisis of the story we do not directly face the fact; we are given the distortion.

Kurtz is, of course, made into an ubiquitous, diffused, romantic symbol in this manner and is the symbol of two kinds of corruption: the primordial, and the disgusting aspect of colonial exploitation in its first greedy rush. The whites have gone mad with greed. Kurtz has simply been logical. He has gone over the borderline into 'complete freedom'. He has accepted the union of 'desire and hate'; he has split into the prim hypocrite citizen and the savage lunatic. In love (we are led to conclude) he found 'horror'. All this is psychologically absorbing, for Conrad means it to apply as a potential to all of us; but it is mere hearsay in the novel. The novelist does not show us an instance of it in action.

Conrad was concerned with fear, guilt, remorse and the tincture of corruption in good things. He is preoccupied by betrayal. It is the rootless who betray. His greatness lies in the handling of a large range of moral types who suffer these evils each in a different way, so that we feel he understands a universal condition. The preoccupation stirred up certain Polish critics years ago. What crime or betrayal had Conrad on his conscience? Why did he write *Lord Jim*? What about *The Secret Agent*? His work is close to personal experience – did he commit some fault at sea? It seems certain that he did not. He may have felt, as a foreigner, the morbid anxiety that he might not come up to codes of the nation he had made his own. The Poles suggested that Conrad felt the guilt of the *émigré*, a guilt all the sharper because he was the son of a man who had been a national martyr. Conrad did not evade the criticism and answered it very sensibly. He was especially unlucky, because he reached forward prophetically to a time when exile has become, to our sense, a general experience.

Lewis Carroll's Inkpot

Even among the prolific letter-writing Victorian authors, Lewis Carroll is a phenomenon. He said that a third of his life seemed to go in receiving letters and the other two-thirds in replying to them – 'wheelbarrows full, almost'. He got about two thousand replies done every year but, even so, was often seventy or eighty names in arrears. The teacher of Euclid and mathematics, the ordained clergyman and Curator of the Senior Common Room at Christ Church, Oxford, was not only compulsively scribacious; he was also a systematic keeper of his postal records. From the age of twenty-nine until his death, he kept a précis of every scrap he wrote, and also a register. The recorded number of letters runs to over ninety-eight thousand, and this does not include letters concerned with college business. So fascinated was he by his addiction that he once did a kind of time-and-motion study of his flow. He wrote, he said, twenty words a minute, and took seven and a half minutes to do a page of a hundred and fifty words; an original draft of twelve pages took two and a half hours and a fair copy one and a half hours more. The learned bachelor was married to his inkpot and a harem of ingenious pens of his own invention, which included an 'electric pen' that he used for writing under the covers when at last he got into bed in the small hours of the morning. He even wrote letters that could be read only in a looking glass. He was far from solemn about his eccentricity:

> I hardly know which is me and which is the inkstand . . . The confusion in one's mind doesn't so much matter – but when it comes to putting bread-and-butter, and orange marmalade, into the *inkstand* and then dipping pens into *oneself* and filling *oneself* up with ink, you know, it's horrid.

A breakfast in Wonderland! One thing to note is that if he is obsessional he is not one of the educated indecipherables who write entirely out of self-infatuation: he wrote in a clear hand in purple ink. He was determined, on principle, to give pleasure to others.

From the tens of thousands in Carroll's 'wheelbarrow', Professor Morton N. Cohen – aided by Roger Lancelyn Green, who edited Carroll's diaries twenty-five years ago – has selected thirteen hundred letters, which have been published by Oxford in a handsome and scholarly two-volume edition. The annotation is profuse, and Carroll's photographs and drawings are diverting. The selection includes a very large number of his nonsense letters to children and many letters on his love of the theatre, the arts, and literature, on his pioneering skills as a photographer, on his interest in science and medicine; it also reflects his fastidious religious orthodoxy as he considers the manners and doubts of Victorian family practice. We are led once more to speculate on the private springs of the genius that created *Alice in Wonderland.* Carroll was a man who carried his childhood within him as a privacy all his life. It is simple to see him as the timid, pernickety don – all brain but emotionally arrested, for reasons we can only guess at. He hated publicity. He preferred to fill a monastic loneliness with fuss, puzzles, parodies, and fancies – a 'case', as so many humorists have been.

But before we try this tunnel there is the second letter in this edition to consider. It is from Carroll's father, Charles Dodgson, written to the boy when he was seven. The boy had asked for a present. The father writes:

As soon as I get to Leeds I shall scream out in the street *Ironmongers*, *Ironmongers.* Six hundred men will rush out of their shops in a moment – fly, fly, in all directions, ring the bells, call the constables, set the town on fire. I will have a file and a screw driver and a ring and if they are not brought directly in 40 seconds, I will leave nothing but one small cat alive in the whole Town of Leeds, and I shall only leave that because I'm afraid I shall not have time to kill it. Then what a bawling and a tearing of hair there will be! Pigs and babies, camels and butterflies, rolling in the gutter together – old women rushing up chimneys and cows after them, ducks hiding themselves in coffee cups and fat geese trying to squeeze themselves into pencil cases.

A High Churchman, from a long line of churchmen, a scholar, and a man of dominant, driving character, the father was Archdeacon of Richmond, and had his own wanton relation to the inkpot. The son's resort to fantasy is inherited. Other factors favoured its growth. He was the oldest son in a precocious family of eleven children – four boys and seven girls – living in an isolated country rectory. To see a cart pass down the road was a startling event. At home, there was the Victorian stress on brainwork. There was the lifelong stammer that afflicted Carroll and his sisters and that brought too many words to the tongue at once. There was the very conscious need for the self-control necessary to conquer whatever blocked utterance; perhaps the minds of the clever children skidded into absurdity as they paused before they hit the right word. (It is known that the character of the Dodo came from Carroll's real name, which was apt to come out of his mouth as 'Do-do-dodgson'.) If the stammer is a minor matter, it is surely important that Lewis Carroll was the eldest son in a family of many sisters, and the leader in the story-telling, the parodies, the charades, puppet shows, puns, conundrums, and other pranks of the brain that made for wit in a jolly family life in which privilege was assured and serious studies were exacted. The Archdeacon had been a double first in his time and had translated Tertullian: a first was confidently expected of Carroll, a born examinee, and of course he got it. If he was a mother's boy and a swot, indifferent to sport, he was neither namby-pamby nor a prig: he quietly held his own in the roughhouse of Tom Brown's Rugby. He worshipped Tennyson. He had a taste for poetry, though his own talent for serious poetry was wan, and he turned, as the too clever will, to parody; he ground away at mathematics and logic and amused himself, like many a Victorian polymath, with scientific gadgets. Here he was influenced by an adored Uncle Skeffington, of whom he wrote:

He has, as usual, got a great number of new oddities, including a lathe, telescope stand, crest stamp (see the top of this notesheet), a beautiful little pocket instrument for measuring distances on a map, refrigerator, etc. etc. We had an observation of the moon and Jupiter last night and afterwards of live animalcula in his large microscope: this is a most interesting sight, as the creatures are most conveniently transparent; and you see all kinds of organs jumping about like a complicated piece of machinery, and even the circulation of the blood. Everything goes on at railway speed, so I suppose they must be some of those insects that only live a day or two and try to make the most of it.

[730]

The young man has an intellect that will make the most of the detail in everything, whether he writes an exact report of a dogfight in Oxford or – inevitably – turns to mastering that new fashionable gadget the camera. Much has been made, quite naturally, of the possible unconscious sources of his genius for nonsense; but what strikes one is that he displays an extreme, perhaps obliterating consciousness. He lives for figures, words, and propositions – as a game, even a career. His fantasy has none of the melancholy of the autobiographical Edward Lear, his great predecessor, who was half in love with failure. Carroll's is a surplus of efficient, inventive intellectual energy, the positive energy of a busy child. One has to be content with attributing his fondness for little girls (he hated little boys) to the natural continuation of his love for his sisters, and his lack of emotional interest in adult love to the shock of his mother's death, when he was eighteen. He could never, after that, connect sex with love. After girls reached the age of eleven, they lost interest in him and he in them. He had only a sort of register of them in his albums of photographs. Many wrote to him when the 'Alice' books appeared – but often confessed in later life that they could not remember much about him except that he was fun.

Nothing in his diaries or his letters suggests that his interest in the scores of little girls he told stories to, played with at the seaside, and loved to take very formally to the theatre, when mothers allowed this, was other than innocent. The clergyman was strict in his religion and in the acceptance of the sexual taboos and social conventions of his time, though he did complain of Mrs Grundy. He never breaks into the rhapsodic language of a fellow-lover of girl children, the now famous and equally innocent Reverend Francis Kilvert, whom he knew. Carroll plays but he never worships. His well-known references to the torment of his 'pillow thoughts' may, of course, indicate deep sexual miseries, but one notes that the man whose overworked brain may have killed natural feeling suffered all his life from insomnia. Kilvert speaks of the 'wild passionate hearts' of his little friends; Carroll of their evanescent love – and, indeed, feeling, for him, takes the form of a nostalgia for childhood itself. Really, he is delighting in the behaviour of a species; he catches what Kilvert misses – the child's puzzled sense of growing. A superior person himself, he does not condescend but listens, knowing that children feel themselves to be superior, too, and grow by playing: they love rules, they are little bosses in behaviour. Carroll had the attraction of a conspirator in the libertinage of his grotesque theatrical invention. As he listened, he studied faces and physical peculiarities very much as children do, and then turned his observations of eyes, noses, heads, and legs into mad fancies. His manners were as proper as any child could desire. A pedant himself, he satisfied the pedant in the child. He carefully avoided the moral. Let nannies and mummies indulge in that; he would not.

Carroll's letters are packed with hidden quotations and disguised nursery verses. Having told little Agnes Hughes a satisfactorily violent story of how he knocked three cats down with a rolling pin, he adds in the next letter an appeasing dramatic sequel:

> Of course I didn't leave them lying flat on the ground like dried flowers: no, I picked them up, and I was as kind as I could be to them. I lent them the portfolio for a bed – they wouldn't have been comfortable in a real bed, you know: they were too thin, but they were *quite* happy between the sheets of blotting paper . . . Well then . . . I lent them the three dinner bells to ring if they wanted anything in the night.
>
> You know I have *three* dinner bells – the first (which is the largest) is rung when dinner is *nearly* ready; the second (which is rather larger) is rung when it is quite ready; and the third (which is as large as the other two put together) is rung all the time I am at dinner . . . In the morning I gave them some rat-tail jelly and buttered mice for breakfast and they were as discontented as they could be. They wanted some boiled pelican, but of course I knew it wouldn't be good for them. So all I said was 'Go to Number Two Finborough Road and ask for Agnes Hughes, and if it is really good for you, she'll give you some.' Then I shook hands with them all . . . and drove them up the chimney. They seemed very sorry to go and they took the bells and the portfolio with them. I didn't find this out until after they had gone, and then I was sorry too and wished for them back again. What do I mean by 'them'? Never mind.

There it is – a drama that ends pawkily in a grammatical poser. The detail of the drama is masterly in the little world in which it is enacted. It is a riotous distraction from the boredom of manners at upper-class family meals and eating what is set before you – an attack on Nanny.

Lewis Carroll was much opposed to allowing servants to bring up children. He was also critical of the absurd overdressing of children that became a form of conspicuous waste in the latter half of the century, especially at the seaside. And here we come to his troubles as a photographer of little girls: he wanted them to be as near to innocent nature as possible. The ideal, he tries to convince mothers, was to take pictures of the girls naked or as near naked as possible. There was, indeed, a Victorian cult of the idealised, sexless naked child. Painters and illustrators of fairy tales were allowed the subject. Why not the photographer? Parents were divided about this. Carroll's negotiations were elaborately tentative and polite yet also persistent. He was reassuring. No girl over the age of eleven. If necessary, he would take two girls at a time – if possible without their mothers, so that the children would be natural. It was, of course, a principle, for him (he said), never to take a frontal picture. The movement against Mrs Grundy had begun; often he got his way, but often there was a break with old friends, and eventually, in later life, he gave up photography in despair of the age he lived in. He was indignant at the questioning of his motives – *that* he never forgave. My own impression is that Carroll's pictures of the solemn, overdressed child are better than his semi-nudes, which he hoped would embellish the walls of the parents' drawing-rooms. The overdressed girls are simply bursting with will and repressed emotion. One has the suspicion that nowadays, when the silence about sex has been broken and no one believes in the innocence of either children or adults, the opposition would be stronger. The cult of the idealised child has gone. Carroll had his own reservations. He would never have boys at these scenes in his studio; they would be too enterprisingly curious. Any form of sexual curiosity or marital misbehaviour shocked him. He refused to meet Ellen Terry – whom he had loved deeply when she was a child – when she left her husband for another man; many years passed before he would agree to meet her. It has been said that he'd wished to marry her.

In his biography of Carroll, published in 1954, Derek Hudson wrote that the surface life of this self-controlled man 'disguised a precarious balance. He was at once selfish and unselfish.' Perhaps the dominant will of the Archdeacon had been unnerving. The son was noted 'for statements no sooner made than they were nervously reversed'. The stammerer was a waverer. And so in the main his few letters on public and business matters are full of assertions nervously made and then half withdrawn. In religion, he could not be sure whether he was as High as his father; in his disputes with agnostics, he was the winning logician who escaped apologetically into the argument for faith, in a gentlemanly way. He was a touchy grammarian in dispute. This comes out early, in a rather telling youthful quarrel with Tennyson. Carroll had been given a copy of an unpublished poem of Tennyson's, and he felt it would be wrong not to reveal this to the poet. Tennyson was angry and called Carroll's request to circulate the poem ungentlemanly. The proud young Carroll demanded an apology and got one – but it was grumpy and half-hearted, and he let the great man know it:

> Nevertheless I accept what you say, as being in substance, what it certainly is not in form, a retractation (though without a shadow of apology or expression of regret) of all dishonourable charges against me, and an admission that you had made them on insufficient grounds.

At Christ Church, he was noted for such donnish precisions about elections, architecture, and the college wine. There came a time when the crustiness became strained. He was the loneliest of busy men.

The Con-Man's Shadow

Humorists have a hard life. As a matter of habit the reader comes round to saying, 'I don't think he's funny any more', the point being that life is so unfunny that the pace gets hotter with every joke. There is the inborn feeling that the humorist is a temporary fellow. A jester must not be allowed to approach the norm. He has to divert you from the intolerable or make you digest it. The difficulty is that while stomach-ache becomes funnier the worse it gets, the stomach-ache genre becomes standardised. In her introduction to *The Most of S. J. Perelman* Dorothy Parker says of humorists in general that they find a little formula and 'milk it till it moos with pain'. Her list is rather more American than European: 'the tyrannical offspring, the illiterate business associate (American), the whooping devil-may-care spinster, the man trying to do a bit of carpentry and the virtuous criticisms of the little wife, mainly European.' The virtuous wife in America is outsize: she arrives home grandiose, in mink, to take hell out of the husband who has burned the dinner. As S. J. Perelman, or rather his stand-in Prebbleman, remarks of his Xanthippe, she has the classical, martyred look of someone who would be 'a wow as St Joan at a Little Theatre'.

The one or two English humorists I have met have been sad men, anxious of eye, hag-ridden by efficiency of mind, mechanically ulcerated and teetering on the edge of religious conversion or the hospital. Their writings have usually contradicted this impression. The English thin man has a fat man inside him, a creature dilatory, sedentary and nourishing his joke, often over-nourishing it. Our humorists have mostly been juicy men dwelling in the belly of society; or, if this was not possible for them, have become mad cherubs like Carroll or Lear. The one general characteristic of the English humorists, good or bad, is that they are at home, dreaming private follies or shut up under lock and key in the attic, but still in the family. There is a profound satisfaction in the perils of the public face. Even

[735]

if the family rejects, the pubs and clubs accept. The clubs, alas, in the older generation, have been a disaster for English humour; there it falls into persiflage. The best Americans escape this. Homelessness and the nomadic – as Miss Constance Rourke instructed us in her classic work on *American Humour* – are basic to the American tradition. So is overstatement, that Elizabethan gift which we carelessly exported lock, stock and barrel to America. So is the monologue which has been left, by us, to the Irish – see Beckett and Joyce. Our humorists – even Saki and Anstey – have had good digestions, the joke with them being that they knew that they bloody well *had* to digest what was given to them and put a peculiar face on it. Less subjected to the pressures of a dense society, Americans have had the freedom to send up howls of enjoyable pain at the raw muck set before them and instead of being digressive they have put a poker face on their duodenums. The elongated joke has been important to both traditions, but this has worked to the advantage of the American humorist who relies so much on monologue; the European cult of conversation may inspire refinement in comedy but is likely to comb all the nits out of the hair. The American monologue leaves the nits in. It can also dip into myth and, to be endurable, this has to be enlivened by image and pungency of language. In England, since the decline of the joke of middle-class periphrasis, we are only just beginning to explore exaggeration again; and at the very moment when American humour shows some signs of becoming middle-class, the sick joke being fundamentally suburban.

The huge advantage of American humour, as one sees it in S. J. Perelman, is in the punishment of character and the use of language. Unlike Thurber who has been much admired by us, Perelman is not an understater who suddenly throws out an almost spiritual blossom. He drops ash into the dessert. Perelman either grew up with burlesque or soon got caught up in it. Immediate action is his need. An idea has to seize him. His very best things have come out of grotesque experiences in Hollywood; or when, not having enough time to read Palgrave's *Golden Treasury*, he has had to feed on the advertising columns of glossy papers. One gets the impression that English humorists snub the commercials, whereas an American like Perelman regards them as part of the general awful meal that makes us what we don't want other people to be. Having acquired a stomach of zinc, he knows it's his duty to swallow the poison,

The Con-Man's Shadow

like someone who feels it a duty to see what cyanide does to the system. As a character, he is a harassed detective, stuck in some lobby, chain-smoking, pedantic, always in disguise, with the air of one about to follow footprints and tracking something down. He is Groucho Marx's more sensitive alter ego, the con-man's shadow. What one owes to the other, apart from cigars, may be conjectured from Groucho's letters – especially those to Kurnitz – which are very funny about Hollywood. The T. S. Eliot letters suffer, on both sides, from the paralysis which occurs when a highest common factor meets a lowest common denominator and both are awed. On the evidence, Perelman's life has been passed in film studios, dressing rooms, cigar stores, hotels, tailor's, barber's, steak grottoes and in bad journeys on inferior shipping lines to the phoney Orient. He will be caught – trying to hide behind *Time* or *Harper's Bazaar* – by acquaintances with names like Spontoon, Henbane, Follansbee and Crump who, spotting his lonely but springy figure, have treated him like flypaper and have buzzed in an ear made for higher things. He has been the sort of man who having, for the moment, to identify himself with a No. 1 Stripteaseuse who has married a young Maharajah, can say that 'although she had little need of paper work in her line of business', she is obliged to be 'the only ecdysiast on record with a Zoroastrian amanuensis'. The phrase is her agent's. She breaks it down into the following:

> A skinny little man with a big bugle on which one flange has a diamond the size of your pinkie welded into it. He has a shift embroidered with rubies and around his neck five strands of pearls like Mary Garden or Schumann-Heink in the Victor Book of Opera.

Flustered by the pass he makes at her after this aesthetic impression, she asks what about his family in Cawnpore. 'Don't you,' she asks, 'have any wives?' It is at the centre of this tradition of American humour to build up a rococo fantasy and then slap its face with a wet towel. Mr Perelman has that art. Many a gorgeous balloon goes 'pop' at the touch of his cigar tip. Occasionally, under the name of Prebbleman, he is at home, usually minding something in the oven and waiting for his Joan of Arc to come back, rather late, in something new and blinding, and full of complaint. He defends himself: 'I haven't the faintest clue to what you're foompheting about.' Wherever else he may fail it is not in adding a valuable word to the

gag book. And he is soon off to a sentimental reunion of the old alumni of Dropsical High. There the old folk are 'acquiring a skinful' wearing paper hats, clutching phials of adrenalin, nitroglycerin and other restoratives.

Again the puncturing anticlimax: 'I give them a wide berth because they may topple on to me during a seizure and wrinkle my suit.' The noise is deafening. In it one hears 'the clash of bridge work and the drum fire crackle of arteries snapping like pipe stems'; the chief speaker, recovering from his third stroke, has a voice that 'ripples from his tongue as if strained across an entire creek of gravel'.

Perelman's speciality, like O. Henry's and Mark Twain's, is Fraud. He looks at the landscape and it is gashed and bill-boarded with the poetic news that here someone made a killing and cleared out quickly. The inner life of a grey Puritan culture is dramatic, gaudy and violent; fraud, in the sense of the double-think, double appearance or fact and the image that palms them off, is basic. The tall story, wearisome in Europe, so that a Münchausen is a bore and a meaningless liar who wastes your time, has a more nourishing role in the American tradition. Fantasy – in English comics – has a different part to play. The distinction is suggested by comparing the extravagances of, say, Dickens with those of the O. Henry, Twain and Perelman school. The speeches of Mrs Gamp or Mr Pecksniff are, in essence, soliloquies that fountain out of their inner lives. They tell us less about the scene in which they live than about the privacies of their minds and of their history. The flights of a Carroll, a Lear, a Beerbohm, an Anstey or a Wodehouse reject the oppressive scene around them and assert the rights of private vision in a culture which has generally been obsessed – as John Stuart Mill said – with the necessity of a social discipline. The exaggerations of the American humorists have a different impulse. If you look at their greedy use of the grotesque, you see that they are guzzling impedimenta and nameable products. You hardly see the people there but you see American paraphernalia; their metaphors take you on to the joints or to what is happening semi-legally on the sidewalk. Chicken Inspector No. 23 Perelman of the Fraud Squad surveys the field of conspicuous waste, the biggest fraud of the lot, with a buyer's hypnotised eye. He is the un-innocent abroad; at his best in the subjects of showbiz, he is a tangy raconteur, though I find him less speedy when he turns his idea into a script with dialogue. This is odd since he has been one of the finest

script writers in the funny business; indeed, remembering the Marx Brothers, a genius. He is above all a voice, a brisk and cigary voice, that keeps up with his feet as he scampers, head-down, upon the trail; in his own words 'button-cute, rapier-keen and pauper poor' and having 'one of those rare mouths in which butter has never melted'. He has a nose for non-news. For a long time the English humorists have suffered from having achieved the funny man's dream; they have either gone straight for the information or have succumbed to the prosaic beauty of their own utterance. They are 'facetious' without being Boswell. Mr Perelman is not entirely free of the English vice. I have caught him adding an unnecessary 'I said with hauteur' or 'I said with dignity'. This weakness he may have picked up on his annual visits to those fake cathedral closes of ours in Savile Row. (The metaphor is his.) But he does not wear thin. There are four or five narky things in the present book which are as good as anything in *Crazy Like a Fox*.

La Cousine Bette

Those who admired the careful dramatisation of Balzac's *Cousin Bette* must have noted that television is always at home with the novels of the nineteenth century. These novels are bold and orderly in structure; the descriptive passages, often boring to the reader, are valuable to producers; the moral drama can be gutted. Easy to do Balzac and Henry James; impossible to handle *To the Lighthouse* without upsetting sacred technical habits. There was a repressed dramatist in most of the nineteenth-century novelists whose theatrical impulses had to be steam-rolled into narrative prose because the novel had replaced theatre as the dominant literary form. So, given taste and tact, the script-writer has found it simple to extract the drama without seriously gutting the book. But if we assume that only a few of the viewers have read or will ever read *Cousin Bette* the question is: what will they have missed?

The voice of the author, of course, and in Balzac's work this is a tremendous loss. It was – as many of his contemporaries thought – a rather loud, pushing, incessant voice; though others found that its powers of story-telling, wit and fantasy, and its energy, imposed an irresistible spell. The voice of Balzac performs. It changes like an actor's. It is sanguine, sceptical, sensible in a blunt way, ready with the rash generalisation, the journalistic caricature; it easily contorts the larynx in passages of lurid melodrama and absurd hyperbole, and yet passes without a blush to asides that may be caustic, shameless or tender. It is a voice bursting with a non-stop interest in whatever his eye catches and the guesses of his own genius. Above all it is personally intrusive: Balzac bustles in among his characters and stops the action to explain to their faces that they are specimens taken out of a natural history of society; and performs the double feat of classifying their social type and of allegorising their inner lives. Balzac, without his 'Voici pourquoi . . .' – the famous explanatory phrase that comes out at all turning points of his story – would lose all *his* point.

Cousin Bette and its companion piece *Cousin Pons* stand a little outside the planned scheme of the *Comédie Humaine*. They represent an astonishing renewal of his genius, at the penultimate crisis of his life. His mortal illness had begun to get its grip on him; the hopes of marriage to Madame Hanska had been set back once more; he had plunged maniacally into larger debts as he speculated with her money in railway shares; with something like insanity, he was spending fortunes on antiques – the subject of *Cousin Pons*. He felt the competition of Eugène Sue as a rising popular novelist, and he suddenly found the energy to break new ground. Or rather, the energy to go back to unfinished work and to see it in the light of a new vision. In three years, at the age of fifty-one, he would be dead. These two novels represent what every artist hopes to achieve: a revival and crowning of the imagination. One can believe they contain a personal assertion. *Cousin Bette* is the study of a poor relation's jealousy turning into a will to revenge that seeks to destroy a whole family. To achieve this Bette has to see that the elderly Baron Hulot – her rich cousin's husband – is put in the way of ruining himself and the family by pouring out his fortune and indeed robbing government funds, in order to keep a courtesan. The ruin is accomplished. A virtuous wife is reduced to misery. Bette, the 'monstrous virgin', is triumphant. Certainly, before the end of the story, the family is reunited, at any rate until the last page but one. The courtesan dies a horrible death, Bette dies, the wife herself dies; but the Baron, senile but still sexually insatiable, lives on. A villain? No; deplorable, out of control, a victim of history, always engaging, almost decent, but one endowed – if that is the word – with an animality he cannot contain. The Baron is far from being Balzac, but he does seem to be a Balzacian protest on behalf of the revived life-force in Balzac, a protest against approaching extinction.

There is another, less speculative point to make when we consider the expansion of Balzac's creative ingenuity in his novel: he moved his story forward and nearer than had been his habit to the time of writing. In 'modernising' – that is to say in moving further away from the Napoleonic shadow and figures of the Regency except to mock them – and turning to the domestic complacencies of the reign of Louis Philippe, he refreshed himself. Adeline is the Baron's virtuous Catholic wife, but her virtue is timorous, Crevel is the parvenu shopkeeper who had once worked for Birotteau, the perfumer who wrecked himself by speculation in property.

Crevel is too cunning for that. He suddenly wants to be a gentleman. He accepts that, at his age, love costs 30,000 francs a year. He plunges for Madame Marneffe because he imagines she is 'a lady' and can teach him fashionable manners. So she can, but maliciously: he wants to be 'Regency' and she well knows that is out of date. He also wants a revenge at Hulot's expense because Hulot is a Baron. Madame Marneffe knows that the new early-Victorian morality requires moral, indeed remorseful religious airs from its courtesans; and Crevel justifies keeping her by telling himself that, as a widower, he is still respectable because of his passionate affection for his daughter. When he is desperate for money, Hulot turns to the new colonial booty in Algeria – another morally topical theme. Hulot had been a good husband when he was a Napoleonic soldier, but after Napoleon's fall he is without serious occupation beyond a nominal job in the bureaucracy. He has lost the dignity of a profession. Idleness, in short, leads him to the pursuit of women. So the disquisitional Balzac who hands out shrewd, journalistic statements on the servant problem, the need for married women to keep their husbands by becoming the wife-mistress, the difference between artists and would-be artists, creates the new age of domesticity and corruption. The descriptions of furniture, which have caused many groans among Balzac's readers, now become malign and interesting. The furniture of Crevel has failed to climb as fast as its owner:

> The candelabra, the fire-dogs, the fender, the chandelier, the clock, were all in the most unmeaning style of scroll-work; the round table, a fixture in the middle of the room, was a mosaic of fragments of Italian and antique marble, brought from Rome where these dissected maps are made of mineralogical specimens – for all the world like tailor's patterns . . . The bedroom, smart with chintz, also opened out of the drawing room. Mahogany in all its glory infested the dining room, and Swiss views, gorgeously framed, graced the panels. Crevel, who hoped to travel in Switzerland, had set his heart on possessing the scenery in painting until the time should come when he might see it in reality . . . Everything was as spick and span as the beetles in an entomological case.

The differences between the furnishings at Madame Marneffe's love-nest and at Josépha's – the opera singer – are sharply marked; also the cost, of course. When Adeline calls nervously on Josépha to see if his ex-mistress knows where the Baron has fled after his downfall, the scene is masterly, for although genuinely moved by Adeline's misery, the actress cannot resist playing contribution and kindness as a new role with the skill of an artist:

> Like those worthy folk who take men of genius to be a sort of monster, eating and drinking, walking unlike other people, the Baroness had hoped to see Josépha the opera singer, the witch, the amorous and amusing courtesan: she was a calm and well-mannered woman, with dignity of talent, the simplicity of an actress who knows herself to be at night a queen, and also, better than all, a woman of the town whose eyes, attitude and demeanour paid full and ungrudging homage to the virtuous wife, the *mater dolorosa* of the sacred hymn . . .

She made a charming bouquet for her 'as the Madonna is crowned in Italy'. Yet this respectable Josépha had thrown Hulot out noisily for a richer lover years before, and had called him an 'old popgun' when he crawled back to her for help. And when she heard the enormity of his behaviour she had cried out: 'Well, I admire that. It's a general flare-up! It is Sardanapalus! Splendid, thoroughly complete . . . I tell you I like a spendthrift, like you, crazy over a woman . . .' for, she says, *he* has ruined only those who belonged to him whereas the calculating bankers, speculating in railways, are ruining hundreds of families every day. We see, after such scenes, the pathetic inadequacy of Adeline's cry to her husband when he comes home to confess: 'Let me try to be an amusement to you'. The cry is all the more heart-rending for being ridiculous: the passive, mundane characters have not the imagination to grasp the force or the artistry of the obsessed.

With his rather endearing pretentiousness Balzac thought of his story as a tragedy in the manner of Racine. He certainly overdoes the 'sulphurous' and 'infernal' when he describes Bette's diabolical jealousy. He is even absurd about it in his melodramatic way: virgins are monsters in their desire for power and vengeance. The only acceptable virgin is the Virgin Mary and, for a moment, it looks as though he is going to dash off a sermonette on the subject. If he did he, luckily, cut it. (He was getting his own back – it is thought – on Madame Hanska's Aunt Rosalie, who was succeeding only too well in delaying his marriage.) He half convinces us that jealousy so long repressed will certainly be appalling when it turns to action; what is hard to believe is that it will be consistent and continuous in its plotting. But Cousin Bette is a peasant and, as he says, the passions of peasants last for life; they are ruled by a single idea. And Balzac – often blamed for not being subtle as a psychologist – was surely brilliant in one respect: he perceived that plotters like Bette will work in secret through a third party, like Madame Marneffe, and all the more passionately because the relationship is a good deal erotic.

Balzac can be relied on to rescue himself from total melodrama by his curiosity about the recesses of human nature: the impartial doctor supplants the declamatory actor. The story is indeed no tragedy by Racine. It contains several comedies that flow from one to the other and set one another off. The relationship of Hulot and Crevel makes a farce by Molière, as Balzac well knew. There is an ostensible moral lesson, but in fact no one is shown to be perfect – not even, as he said, the virtuous. His texture is rich if coarse in the weaving because he is an endless questioner, insensitive but hurrying to the next turn of the screw so that we forget to question him. One gets attached to his comic pretensions, as when he shows off about painting and sculpture and furniture or about literature – Bette, he says, could have been an Iago or even Richard III – not to mention his entomology, phrenology, his animal magnetism, his weakness for a word like 'sublime' – a cant word of the period – and for phrases like 'incredible perfection'. Balzac was a greedy man. As he revised his proofs a dozen times, throwing in more and more, he could not resist swelling his invention and yet also refining it. But when he wrote *Cousin Bette* and its companion *Cousin Pons* he was able to rise above the disastrous confusion of his private desires and attain a kind of serenity as a gourmand artist. He often spoke of the artist's right to revenge. In this effusive pessimist the idea of vengeance was obsessional. *Cousin Bette* is about nothing else.

Goya

The Spanish Civil War was felt to offer both a prophetic meaning to the art of Goya and an irresistible chance to Marxist critics. The most remarkable of these was Francis Klingender, whose *Goya in the Democratic Tradition* (1948) is still important. Klingender was a sociologist but, as the son of a painter and sculptor, had a spontaneous feeling for the diffused responses of art. His subject was the effect of society and history on the artist. For example, Goya's mysterious breakdown in 1792–3, at the age of forty-six, which left him stone-deaf for the rest of his life, was seen as a reaction to a personal conflict in which he was caught: between the need for conformity and the instinct of revolt. Later criticism suggests that Goya's social attitudes as a man and an artist who had grown up in the Enlightenment were more ambiguous and ultimately more pessimistic than Klingender thought. Thirty years on, in *Goya: The Origins of the Modern Temper in Art*, the art historian Fred Licht is rather less tendentious in his approach. Although Licht shares much with Klingender, he is closer to the autonomy of the artist's imagination; he sees Goya as a precursor of the development of painting in the 'modern epoch', until the present day, and one who has a special meaning for us in our disorientation in the continuing wars, revolutions, and atrocious persecutions of our time. (After 1790, the long classical tradition – and its market – collapsed.) For myself – whose approach to Spanish art, society, and history is that of the addicted amateur – Licht's book is a refreshing corrective. His erudition is rich and allusive. He looks minutely at the pictures, his argument is arresting, and the many illustrations – although they are in black-and-white, and most are small in size – are placed at exactly the pages in the text where his interpretations can be tested. One ought not to go to the Prado without him.

The son of a gilder, of modest family, Goya was a canny man of the people, with a keen business eye for the right patron; he rose fast to be a court painter. He had the art of survival in dangerous times and all his life was skilful in covering his political moves and his troubles with the Inquisition by holding a plausible alibi in reserve. He was adroit with money and was blessed with the extraordinary Spanish gift of prolific, and even inchoate, invention. He survived the collapse of Habsburg feudalism, the savagery of invasion, and the corruption of the Bourbon succession. A liberal, and no friend of clericalism, he managed to keep his supremacy by, as it were, 'living inside the whale'. Mr Licht says:

> Owing partly to his own character, owing perhaps also to his deeply rooted Spanish bias, he was the only artist to absorb the very principle of revolution and anarchy into his art . . . Goya was willing and able to express revolution in revolutionary terms. Living in a time that he perceived to be basically anarchic, he invented a language that conveyed the very principle of anarchy. Our baffled attitude towards a universe that grows more alien the more scientific data we accrue about its nature was already presaged in the images he created.

He goes on:

> Rejecting with equal force the faith in God of his ancestors and the faith in history and progress of his contemporaries, he set about to construct a new world built of the pieces and fragments of his knowledge, his intuition, and his invincible pride in being a man – no matter how reduced in stature.

Licht's point is that Goya is 'modern' because, with the collapse of Christian and aesthetic values, he was left staring out of vacancy at the plain facts before him, unembellished by mystical or traditional consolation. His death scenes, for example, are final. The body loses dignity. In sickness and in death, the soul dissolves among the shadows of animal terror and is then extinct. The sick are in misery; the dead are alone and unblessed. The blacks and greys in the backgrounds of his maturing work suggest meaningless space. The person, the thing can exist only for its own sake. Spanish painters, like Spanish writers, have always been drawn to a realism that is carnal, unflinching, and harsh. Spanish individualism finds it natural to 'set figures as it were against each other'. There is a hostility to

[746]

Italian ornament and bravura. If there are scenes of butchery and hangings, hackings-to-death in war, we are not given emotions by Goya: the detached rendering of the sight evokes the scream inside us, rouses our own fantasies, and makes us recognise that brutalities rise from our own fears and the unseating of our reason. And here, indeed, with a growing pessimism and detachment – perhaps, too, with Goya's haunted intuition of his own pathology, as some psychologists have suggested – Goya makes his famous utterance: that monsters arise in our minds when our reason sleeps (i.e., is forgotten or abandoned); we are then at the mercy of common superstitions or primitive fantasies, which may even become embodied.

Mr Licht follows Goya's growth as he passed the early neoclassical influences to the satirical 'Caprichos', the early portraits that have his undismayed eye for weakness of character, and the 'Disasters of War' (for some unknown reason unpublished until well after his death), and is arresting, because he shows the artist impelled by his inner nature. In the 'Caprichos', Goya does not attempt to reform society, as the bourgeois Hogarth does; nor is he a Gillray, who distorts as he rages. Where I find Licht at his best is in things like the detailed discussion of that famous, insulting picture 'The Family of Carlos IV'. Even though we know of the decline of the passion for splendour as Spanish decadence moved toward its nadir, even if we recognise that Spanish individualism can assume an easy and proud indifference to shabbiness, and could do so especially in the nineteenth century, it is hard to imagine a royal family consenting to be portrayed in such homely disarray. Were they pretending – as Louis Philippe was to do in France – to be an ill-assorted bourgeois family? How did Goya nerve himself, as the court painter, to this performance? As Licht says, Goya may have been an impetuous man, tolerated as a 'character', but as a painter he was strictly disciplined, and careful in the preparation of his subject and its design. Velázquez and Rembrandt were his masters. He was immensely knowledgeable in European painting. So Licht turns for his explanation to the Velázquez of 'Las Meninas'. There are many portraits and drawings that show Goya's preoccupation with the double effect of mirrors and with what one may call the mirror's freezing or suspending a moment of life and splitting the personality. Goya's royal family were not standing before the painter in the manner of actors taking a curtain call; he was behind the straggling group and shows them standing slack yet bemused by themselves, in a mirror we cannot see. They have slowly slumped, as if entranced with themselves to the point of apathy: Goya 'has presented them as they saw themselves'. The only aspect of royalty on which they may be congratulating themselves is that they are human and need not appear to be royal. This, of course, suits Goya's love of experiment and the secretiveness of his insight. Here, by the trick of the mirror, is 'the thing itself'.

And here Licht turns back to the historical argument of his book. Goya is not caricaturing. He is looking at a group of shabby bodies that have lost faith in their rôle. History has made a king who cannot bear himself as a king: 'He doesn't know how to be himself because he doesn't know who he is.' The picture is 'a tragic comment on a condition of human life that is essentially modern'. It expresses man's lack of 'a higher ideal of himself, man's doubt in the significance of his destiny and in the guiding hand of an all-powerful divinity'. Once more: Goya 'presents us with a painting that no longer attempts to transcend or artfully simulate nature and that has no pretences beyond that of being an impassive reflection of *what is*'. That, Licht says, is the position of the artist in the 'modern epoch'. And he neatly quotes the well-known exchange of courtesies between a German official and Picasso in Paris during the Occupation. Seeing a reproduction of Picasso's 'Guernica', the officer asked, 'Vous avez fait ça, n'est-ce pas?' To which Picasso replied, 'Non, monsieur, c'était vous.' The artist cannot be anything but a medium who signals 'recognitions of the world without being able to testify to their meaning'. The painter knows he has finished a work when he has 'painted himself out of it'. For Licht, the hermetic quality so frequent in modern painting dates from this picture.

The discussion of Goya's 'Third of May' takes an unexpected turn. We had been persuaded that as a painter, if not as a man, Goya was detached from the classical or religious statement of man's case, that he was neither a consoling nor an adjuring artist – he saw that he was alone, 'alienated', without an availing ethic. But here Goya 'for the last time . . . paints a picture that still bears a full didactic charge.' Licht adds, 'For the last time he tries to wake us from "the sleep of reason".' The figure who is screaming, his arms raised, before the firing squad as he stands among the dead bodies has what may be called a lay-Christliness, even the stigmata, but whereas in the pictures of Christian martyrdom the light of Heaven shines on the martyr, here the light comes from the utilitarian lamp on the ground which enables the firing squad to do its night work. '"The Third of May" is the first altar to the anonymous millions whose death is irrelevant,' Mr Licht writes. 'Anonymity becomes a condition of modern man.' And in his continuing examination of the structure of the picture Licht also notes that there is no space for the spectator in the picture except behind the French executioners: 'To survive is to be guilty of complicity' with them. For Licht, 'the heart-rending quality' of the defiance or the terror in the young man about to be shot 'lies partly in its being addressed not in the oratorical manner to a neutral audience or to God, but in the urgent and heedless intimacy that exists between the murderer and the murdered.' The word 'heedless' is striking, for it can be felt in a great number of Goya's paintings and groups of figures, even among the graceful. There is no other painter, I would say, who so completely gives one a clue to the anarchic egotism of his countrymen at the crisis of passion before that passion suddenly collapses into indifference or resignation. But let this literary generalisation pass. Goya does not deal in generalities. We make them. He does not.

Many important pages of this book are given to Goya's curious position in society and his intuitions about the new social condition of man. Mr Licht says – quite rightly, it seems to me – that it is a mistake to think of Goya as a partisan of any given system of political doctrine. On this matter, he shows how profoundly Goya differs from his French contemporary David:

> David's great strength lay in his ardent desire to teach, in his passionate will to place art and the artist in an efficient, practical position within a rationally established governmental system. The painter must be in equal parts artist and responsible member of the body politic. Goya's position was far more equivocal. He, too, often wished to teach. But he taught a subject that he had apprehended either intuitively or by means of bitter personal experience . . . Goya teaches by arousing our sympathy and our curiosity . . . David the regicide, David the sincere republican was an enlightened, militant member of the middle classes.

Whereas Goya was closer to the worker and the artisan:

> Men doing a job and doing it well, the dignity of workers caught in the performance of tasks that require mastery – these were the true themes of much of Goya's best later work.

In his etchings of the bullfight, the bullfighter is the 'artisan of courage'; like the artist, he finds 'the only fulfilment there is in modern life: the consolation of work freely accepted and perfectly done'. Here there is a very intelligent comparison of Wright of Derby's 'Iron Forge' and Goya's 'The Forge' – both powerful examples of physical action caught at its climax:

> It was in work that [Goya] found the strongest intimation of the survival of man's dignity . . . It is his only painting that is an integral whole rather than a meaningful fragment torn out of an inscrutable context.

And then we come to portraits of working women, such as 'La Aguadora' – the water carrier, who was until very recent times a perennial Spanish figure. These women are more composed than the pretty figures of Murillo, the sentimentalist. More satisfying, to my mind, are Goya's late portraits of mature and sensuous women, and, indeed, of men. As he aged in politically risky times (if Licht is right), Goya became more attached to his few close Anglophile friends, and evaded the passing celebrities of aristocratic life.

A dozen suggestions have jumped to scholarly minds when faced by the almost inexplicable 'Black Paintings', which the seventy-five-year-old man painted on the walls of his little house outside Madrid. These paintings may be the expressions of a deep melancholia or of schizophrenia, but when Licht reminds us of Fuseli and of Frankenstein and the Gothic frenzy, and talks of them in relation to nightmares – such as the legend of the Witches' Sabbath – and then takes a leap forward to contemporary consciousness, we are ready to believe that the 'Black Paintings' may be concerned with 'the infectious nature of evil', the preoccupation with monstrosity, or the sense in which we may feel that the chaos of the unconscious is not an 'intruder' but the real, subverting inhabitant of the scene. What is most striking in these paintings is Goya's concern for the massive – perhaps because of fading sight. The pictures are 'primitive', but at the same time they evoke a particular sensation of horror about the future as an epic aroused by a past that has not been outgrown. There is also the possibility that they spring from private sources: the self-mockery of melancholic old age, the malicious jeering at dying faculties. It is said that the horrifying image of Saturn devouring one of his children was painted on the walls of Goya's dining room. When one recalls the bloody Crucifixions of classical Spanish painting, especially those in which the subject is plainly treated as a divinely permitted murder, one realises that the 'Black Paintings' may belong to a tradition that events had revived. The sense of menace is like the menace of nightmare, which in real life is brief but here is spelled out as if the suspended moment had become flatly eternal. Unlike the Spaniards, other Europeans had to wait for the theatrical props of the Romantic movement – the hideous ravine, the abandoned monastery, the House of Usher – before they could face the nihilism that Goya seemed to be able to evoke at random in his fantasies, from whatever dark sources they came. It is only Licht's stimulating gift for eager cross-reference as a man soaked in his subject which prevents me (as an amateur Spanish hand) from pressing some evidently literary suggestions. He takes us back to the art gallery and brings the pictures into the double light of Goya's time and our own.

Turgenev in Baden

In 1861 Turgenev's great novel *Fathers and Sons* was published in St Petersburg. He was forty-three; the book was his masterpiece but it brought violent abuse upon him in Russia both from the conservatives and the young radicals who considered that they had been caricatured in the portrait of Bazarov, the nihilist doctor. The abuse was wounding, for until then Turgenev had been able to think of himself as the liberating voice of the young. From this moment his life as an expatriate began: he left Russia in disgust and anger.

The attacks were not the sole cause of his decision to leave. There was an emotional reason of deep importance. Ever since he was thirty, indeed earlier, he had been in love with Pauline Viardot, the famous Spanish opera singer. At one time they were possibly lovers, living out the drama of *A Month in the Country*, but it seems that the feeling was stronger on his side than on hers and that she put her art, her career, her marriage, and her children first and kept Turgenev at a distance.

But in 1861 there was a change: the feeling or the need for Turgenev revived on her side. Her famous voice was failing although she was scarcely forty; she withdrew from the great opera houses of Europe, and she and her husband settled at the immensely fashionable spa and little court of Baden on the Rhine, where she could hold a salon, give concerts, and take a few pupils for enormous fees. Now she beckoned to Turgenev once more. He was rich. He could build a small theatre for her, help her publish her musical albums, and he was an enormous social asset at her salons. The slavery (as he called it) of his old love for her revived, their affections were close. What Russians resented was that from this time until his death his home was Europe and close to the Viardots: to his estate in Russia he certainly went from time to time, but as one whose ties were elsewhere.

It is clear from his letters to his friends in the Baden period that he feared expatriation would injure his talent. More and more, he feared he would drift into mere reminiscence and lose his knowledge of contemporary Russia. He began to defend himself and to ask what was wrong with non-contemporary characters, what was wrong with the past. In 1870 – which turned out to be the end of his Baden period because of the outbreak of the Franco-Prussian war – we find him writing to a correspondent that a 'Russian writer who has settled in Baden by that very fact condemns his writing to an early end. I have no illusions on that score, but since everything else is impossible, there is no point in talking about it . . . But are you really so submerged in what is "contemporary" that you will not tolerate any non-contemporary characters?' Such people, Turgenev says, have lived and have a right to be portrayed. 'I admit no other immortality: and this immortality of human life (in the eyes of art and history) is the basis of my whole world.'

What is one to think of Turgenev's writing in the Baden period? The most important book to come out of it was the novel *Smoke* (1867), and although the Russian critics attacked it violently for political and patriotic reasons, it is a very able book. His occasional visits to Russia had not been wasted: he had another long book in mind – *Virgin Soil* – but he was not ready for it and, after *Smoke*, his Baden period is remarkable for his long short stories in which he rarely failed. He was simply, he said, 'too full of subjects'.

In his early fifties he wrote two reminiscent stories – one of them the horrifying tale 'The Brigadier', based on an incident in the life of his Lutvinov grandmother who had committed murder. A very old and senile brigadier, 'of the age of Catherine', is seen fishing, accompanied by a bullying servant who ridicules him. The brigadier has become a ruined and childish simpleton, reduced to poverty and ostracism because in middle years he had loved and lived with a terrifying young widow who, in a rage, had killed her page. Out of love and in a fit of honour the brigadier assumed guilt for her crime and was tried for it, but his sentence had been short. The widow and (after her death) her sister bleed him of all his money until he is destitute. Yet once a week he visits the widow's grave with adoration. At last he knows he is going to die. He knows because of a dream.

[753]

I, as maybe you know, often see Agrippina Ivanov [as he now calls her] in my dreams – heaven's peace be with her – and never can I catch her: I am always running after her but cannot catch her. But last night I dreamed she was standing, as it were, before me, half turned away and laughing . . . I ran up to her at once and caught her . . . and she seemed to turn round quite and said to me 'Well, Vassinka, now you have caught me . . .' It has come to me that we shall be together again.

The tale is told in the old-fashioned way of picking up the story by hearsay in the manner of a folk tale, but in the servant's mockery there is something of the mockery of Shakespeare's cynical comics and Turgenev has made it powerful. The hearsay, the careful reader will notice, is not flat in its convenience but is subtly varied as changes of scene and voice are made to carry it. The theme is, of course, familiar in his writings: a man dominated and enduring abasement and suffering in love. He will give everything to the monster but he lives by his honour, which is a kind of exultation. The dream of death as a woman is also a common theme and so is the myth of bewitchment offered as a psychological fact.

The theme of honour as the real test in love and indeed in all crucial circumstances is of great importance in Turgenev's writing and it must not be taken as a romanticisation of an old-fashioned or picturesque idea common enough in the historical novels of the nineteenth century. If the brigadier's honour is not to be questioned, this is for reasons of Russian history. Turgenev believed that Russia was uncivilised in the Western sense because there had been no experience of an age of chivalry in its culture. And if we look beyond this story to his own life, it would seem that his own Quixote-like concept of love in his feelings for Pauline Viardot is a chivalrous vow which once uttered must never be betrayed; in that sense his love of her was not a weakness or an obsession. It was an anachronism – the lifelong vigil. It was not even romantic, but a spiritual law, an article of the aristocratic faith.

'The Brigadier' is not only an important story, but a very revealing one in another connection. In his own life, Turgenev felt he owed it to himself as a duty of chivalrous principle to give money secretly to revolutionaries like Bakunin and others – the Populist leader, for example – even though he hated violence and terrorism and feared the loss of his property.

The idea of honour abused is at the heart of 'An Unhappy Girl', a story drawn from his student days. The girl is half-Jewish, one of the maltreated 'orphans' handed on: the Jewish aspect of her beauty is ancient, ennobled by race and aristocratic instinct. She is helplessly trapped in a coarse German family. Her tale is remarkable for its scenes of vulgar lower-class life, its gambling episodes, and a drunken funeral meal which follows the funeral of the tormented girl who has been driven to suicide. Unfortunately there is an element of plot: it is suggested that the girl may have been poisoned so that her small inheritance would then pass to the awful Germans if she died unmarried. Plot-making was outside Turgenev's competence. The girl's wretched state is well done but Dostoevsky with his dynamic power of dramatising the inner life of the 'insulted and injured' would have made more of her, for Dostoevsky believed in free will whereas the art of Turgenev, the determinist, is in this sense static: people live under fate. Or rather time flows through them: they do not drive blindly forward through time.

In 'The Story of Lieutenant Erguynov' a young naval officer is stripped of his money by a sly, amusing, fascinating girl who is a decoy used by thieves. Again the plot is awkward but there are some brilliant things in the tale, particularly in the account of Erguynov's state of hallucination when, his drink being doped, he sails out of consciousness to the sound of the balalaika, is robbed, knocked on the head, and dumped with his skull split on the roadside. And we get pleasure from the fact that, in old age, the simple lieutenant loves telling the whole story again and again, and loves to dwell on his hallucination so that the company knows the tale by heart. For what we are shown is an innocent young sailor growing into a knowing old fellow, enlarging himself as he talks. He makes us feel that he is telling us something that is now more completely 'true' than it was when it was scattered in the fragmentary experience of real life.

The point of honour crops up at the end, but comically. The thieves escape and so does the girl, but much later she writes to the sailor begging him to believe she herself was not responsible for the attempt to murder him. She had no idea they would go *that* far, and she would like to see him and convince him that although she did deceive him she is not a criminal. The sailor – an honourable fellow – is rather taken by the idea, but he puts it off and does nothing. The fact that he does nothing makes the story rest delightfully in suspense – which is an aspect of life.

None of these stories approaches the power of 'A Lear of the Steppe'. This is a major work. The Lear is Martin Petrovich Harlov, a hulking, rough, bearlike figure who farms 800 acres and owns serfs but who, though claiming to come of noble Russian stock 'as old as Vassilievitch the Dark', is a hard-driving peasant farmer, a stern, shouting, but honest man. He lives in what he calls his 'mansion', a ramshackle homestead he has built with his own hands, a small manor with courtyard and a tumbledown thatched lodge. His own room in the house is unplastered. His riding whips, his horse collar hang from nails on the wall. There is a wooden settle with a rug, flies swarm on the ceiling, and the place smells, as he himself does, of the forest. In the house live his two daughters: Anna, who is married to the whining and greedy son of a petty official, and Evlampia, who is being courted by a battered and broken major. Both girls are beauties.

The narrator is fifteen when the events begin, the son of a wealthy landowning widow. The story has, but only superficially, the tone of *A Sportsman's Sketches*, but it will go much deeper. The widow has always been Harlov's friend and adviser, so that we see Harlov through the eyes of an awed boy, as it might be Turgenev himself as a boy living with his mother at Spasskoye. If Harlov is a primitive giant he seems all the more gigantic to a boy's wondering eyes. Turgenev is careful to convey the physical force of Harlov's person with metaphors that evoke the man and the working scenes of his life. The voice that came out of a small mouth was strong and resonant:

> Its sound recalled the clank of iron bars carried in a cart over a badly paved road; and when Harlov spoke it was as though someone were shouting in a high wind across a wide ravine . . . his shoulders were like millstones . . . his ears were like twists of bread . . . he breathed like a bull but walked without a sound.

It is important to the story that the boy's mother had found a wife for Harlov, a frail girl who lasted only long enough to give him two daughters, and saw to it that they had a superior education. Times are changing: we

shall see the result of this kindness. The daughters will eventually turn their father out of his own house and drive him to frenzy and death.

The wonder is that this confident, dominant, and roaring man who frightens everyone – 'the wood demon' as people call him – will bring about his own downfall by an act of Lear-like weakness. He is liable to fits of melancholy during which he shuts himself up in his room and starts to hum 'like a swarm of bees'. The hours of humming end in singing meaningless words. He recovers. It is after one of these fits that he comes to his friend the widow and announces that Death has appeared to him in a dream in the form of a black colt that rushes into the house, dances about, and finally gives him a kick in the arm. He wakes up aching in every bone. It is this terror that has driven him to a bid for power which is exorbitant and, indeed, a sign of folly: he is going to divide his property between his daughters now; willing it to them is not enough for he wants to see their gratitude. He wants to establish his absolute rule after death now and before his eyes. Nothing will persuade him that this is foolish.

The story now expands. We are in the Russia of *A Sportsman's Sketches*. A crowd of characters come in, the lawyers, the police officials, the grasping son-in-law, and a spiteful jeering figure called Souvenir, an orphan, the brother of Harlov's dead wife who is a hanger-on in the landowner's house. Souvenir has a mawkish laugh that sounds like the rinsing of a bottle, and whenever Harlov calls at the house he goes swaggering after him and saying, 'What made you kill my sister?' Souvenir has a goading diabolical role to play. The deed of gift is signed and Souvenir tells the old man with delight that now his daughters will turn him out.

Turgenev always understands how to insert points of rest in which a story can grow of itself. The boy narrator goes away for the summer. In the autumn he goes out shooting snipe and sees a stranger riding Harlov's horse. It is the first sign of the truth of Souvenir's prophecy. Horse and carriage have been taken from Harlov by Anna and Sletkin, her husband. Harlov is being starved and stripped of everything. The two sisters are at odds. Evlampia has turned the major down and is having an affair with Sletkin – the boy catches them in the woods – and when he hears of this Harlov rushes in a state of madness to the big house. In his bid for power, Harlov has exhausted his great will. He has lost his terrifying force and has become helpless, acquiescent, and meek. This is Souvenir's moment. He

mocks the old man for his fall, jeering without pity. Suddenly the old man rises to the taunts, recovers his old violence, and rushes back to his manor, and in a terrible scene climbs to the roof and starts tearing down what he has built with his own hands. The peasants cannot stop him as he rips away the rafters and knocks down chimneys. In a final triumph of strength he wrenches a gable and a crossbeam off and is crushed when he falls with them to the ground.

One does not expect such a scene of violence from Turgenev. It succeeds because it is made to seem likely among the people of the steppe. The two daughters have been skilfully kept in the background where, by one small touch or another, they have aroused our apprehension. We have seen Anna's cold smile; we have seen Evlampia, silent as stone, a still, sensual beauty with a store of power in her. Of Anna, the boy remarks in a disturbing Turgenevian reflection:

> In spite of the negligence of her attire and her irritable humour, she struck me as before, as attractive and I should have been delighted to kiss the narrow hand which looked malignant too, as she twice irritably pushed back her loose tresses.

The tragedy is over and the story is restored little by little to the norms of peasant life.

In studying the peasants as a group, Turgenev has gone beyond the scope of *A Sportsman's Sketches*, though the luminous quality of that early work gives the scene perspective and truth. At first the peasants stand aloof from Anna, but for Evlampia there was a kind of sympathy, except from an old man who said: 'You wronged him; on your soul lies the sin.' At the funeral the faces of the crowd condemn the family, but the condemnation has become impersonal. That is the next stage.

> It seemed as though all those people felt that the sin into which the Harlov family had fallen – this great sin – had gone now before the presence of one righteous Judge and for that reason there was no need now for them to trouble themselves and be indignant. They prayed devoutly for the soul of the dead man whom in life they had not especially liked, whom they feared indeed.

Anna's voice, we remember, was 'very pleasant, resonant and rather

plaintive . . . like the note of a bird of prey,' but she says nothing. Evlampia, fierce, monumental – 'a free bird of the Cossack breed' – fierce in the glance of her dark blue eyes, was silent too. Sletkin tries to get a word out of her, but she treats him as she has treated the absurd major who wanted to marry her.

In a day or two she has sold her interest to her sister and has vanished. Years later the narrator sees her again, driving in a smart pony trap, splendidly dressed. She has become the founder, the dominant mother of a dissenting Order of Flagellant Sisters who live without priests. Whether this is a genuine order is uncertain: is her house a place of rendezvous? For the peasants wink and say the police captain does well out of the Order. It is she who inherits the primitive spirit of her father, maybe is honest – but maybe not: the spirit of an extremist.

Sletkin, Anna's scheming husband, has died – the peasants say, probably untruthfully, that she poisoned him – and she is now an excellent farmer, better than her father was, clever in the legal negotiations that have followed the change in the land laws after the Emancipation. The great landlords and officials respect her judgment.

In other words, after tragedy and indeed crime, a new generation rises and forgets, as Turgenev always likes to show when the present grows out of the past. Human life is short.

There is little of love in this tale, but one notices Turgenev's skill in suggesting there has been an act of sexual love. The boy comes across Sletkin and Evlampia in the woods.

> [Sletkin] was lying on his back with both hands under his head and with a smile of contentment gazing upwards at the sky, swinging his left leg which was crossed over his right knee . . . A few yards from him Evlampia was walking up and down the little glade, with downcast eyes. It seemed as though she were looking for something in the grass, mushrooms perhaps: now and then she stretched out her hand. She was singing in a low voice. An old ballad.

> *Hither, hither threatening storm cloud*
> *Slay for me the father-in-law*
> *Strike for me the mother-in-law*
> *The young wife I will kill myself.*

Louder and louder she sings while Sletkin laughs to himself as she moves round and round him.

'The things that come into some people's heads,' Sletkin said.
'What?' said Evlampia.
'What were those words you were singing?'
'You can't leave the words out of a song,' said Evlampia.

And then they see the boy, cry out, and rush away in opposite directions.

The scene tells us all, even to the fierceness of an act of lust and what hidden fantasies it releases in the mind.

'A Lear of the Steppe' is, no doubt, a drama seen from the outside, but it shows Turgenev's mature power of suggesting the inside of his people and of concealing its documentation. The kind of documentation that obtrudes, say, in Zola's *La Terre*, or indeed in most stories of peasant life done by writers who are not peasants, is mercifully absent. In the manner of the greatest artists, he contrives to make us feel that people should be seen as justifying themselves. The choice of a growing boy as the narrator, with some character of his own, makes this possible and evades the smoothing-over effect of hearsay.

Unsafe Conduct

━━━━━

The suppression of *Dr Zhivago* in 1957 exposed the obsequious proceedings of the Union of Soviet Writers to international ridicule and contempt. We know now that after publishing a portion of autobiography, *Safe Conduct*, in 1931, Pasternak had published no original work under the Stalinist repression between 1932 and 1943 and that was silenced by the absurd gauleiter Zhdanov from 1946 to 1954. Cautiously Pasternak planned a collection of poems to introduce an *Essay in Autobiography*, his natural mode, which would have prepared the way for a fuller understanding of the novelist's idiosyncrasy and imagination, and the changes they passed through since *Safe Conduct* was written.

The *Essay* was translated by Manya Harari in 1959. It is short enough to give some idea, Pasternak says, 'of how in my individual case, life became converted into art and art was born of life and experience'. It is a reminiscence touched upon tactfully and confined within the narrator's intimate circle. To take the story further and describe a 'world, unique and not to be compared with any other', a writer would have to write 'in such a way as to make the hair rise and the heart falter'. So the book is a reticent sketch, but does draw at least an outline. As Edward Crankshaw says in his warm introduction, Pasternak's battle has been with himself. Is there any other battle for an artist? His achievement is to have upheld the fact of the artist's conscience in a time when committees, programme makers, administrators and so on, thought literature had obligations to *them*! 'I dislike my style before 1940,' Pasternak says, 'just as I quarrel with half of Mayakovsky's writing and some of Yesenin's. I dislike the disintegrating forms, the impoverished thought and the littered, uneven language of those days. It is more important in life to lose than to acquire. Unless the seed dies it bears no fruit.' *Safe Conduct* – the earlier autobiography – dies: *Dr Zhivago* is born. *Safe Conduct* is a congested poetic embryo.

Part of Pasternak's tenacity comes from his upbringing and an inherited, strong yet evasive gaiety of spirit. The *Essay* sketches a family and circle of like-minded friends dedicated to the arts. The father, a painter, was a friend of Tolstoy; the mother, a distinguished pianist. Scriabin came to the house and the young Pasternak decided to become a composer and pianist. The portraits are less reminiscent than active, for Pasternak's prose, even in translation, has the present clarity of notes struck on the keys of a piano. The preoccupation with the ideas of resurrection and rebirth must have, I think, a link with the re-creating effect of music which never embalms a past. Scriabin and the elder Pasternak went for walks:

> Scriabin liked to take a run and then go on skipping along the road like a stone skimming the water, as if at any moment, he might leave the ground and glide on air. In general, he had trained himself in various kinds of sublime lightness and unburdened movement verging on flight.

He defended Nietzsche, and we find in Pasternak's comment the traditional Russian feeling for the limitless. It was also Dostoevsky's:

> Scriabin's defence of the superman was an expression of his native Russian craving from the superlative. Indeed, it is not only true that music needs to be more than itself if it is to mean anything, but that everything in the world must surpass itself in order to be itself. There must be something limitless in a human being and in his activity for either to have definition and character.

The elder Pasternak had to make a drawing of Tolstoy on his deathbed at the station of Astapovo; the son went with him. In the corner of the room lay

> a wrinkled old man, one of the dozens of old men invented by Tolstoy and scattered through his books. The place bristled with fir saplings which stood round the bed, their outlines sharpened by the setting sun. Four slanting sheaves of light reached across the room and threw over the corner where the body lay the sign of the big shadow of the crosspiece of the window and the small childish crosses of the shadows of the firs.

Outside the world press 'brayed' and waiters at the station restaurant were galloping about with plates of 'underdone beef steaks. Beer flowed like a river'. The word 'underdone' evokes the whole of journalism in one of its raw and macabre news-gathering fiestas.

Pasternak gave up music because he found he lacked perfect pitch. He was sent to Germany for his education, travelled to Venice. He was the equipped intellectual. He felt the excitement of that iconoclasm which was to provoke the last glories of art in Europe. The poets Mayakovsky, Yesenin, Marina Tsvetayeva and Paolo Yashili come in. There is excitement and argument and then the aftermath; the tragic list of suicides – Mayakovsky killing himself (out of pride); Yesenin (without thinking it out) carelessly; Marina Tsvetayeva because she could not put her work between herself and the reality of daily life any longer; Yashili bewitched by the purges. There is compassion for the wretched Fadaev, the novelist who sold out:

> And it seems to me that Fadaev, still with the apologetic smile which had somehow stayed with him through all the crafty ins and outs of politics, told himself just before he pulled the trigger: 'Well, now it's all over. Good-bye, Sasha'.

Fadaev once told me that the decline in the drawing of grotesque characters in the Soviet novel was due to the fact that, under Communism, people were better integrated!

To go back 28 years to *Safe Conduct* is to meet the affected Pasternak. His self-criticism is just. Edited by Stefan Schimanski, it was first published abroad in 1945 and has been reissued with an introduction by J. M. Cohen. The translation is by Beatrice Scott. Robert Payne has done the stories, which include *Aerial Ways* and *The Childhood of Luvers*. Mr Cohen translates the poems. Another version of *Safe Conduct*, the stories and poems, comes from Alec Brown and Lydia Pasternak-Slater. I prefer the Beatrice Scott translation: Mr Alec Brown is heroically literal when dealing with the images, but he is conventional and commonplace in the straightforward writing. It is not surprising that translators differ and that they should drop sentences in the dazzle they have to face. Here are two versions of the firework scene in Venice. From Beatrice Scott:

> Under the open sky the faces of the audience glowed with a clarity which is characteristic of the baths, as in a covered wonderfully

[763]

illuminated hall. Suddenly from the ceiling of this imaginary ballroom fell a slight shower. But hardly had it begun when the rain ceased. The reflection of the illuminations shimmered above the square in a coloured dimness. The bell tower of St Mark's cut like a red marble rocket into the rose mist in wreaths halfway up to its summit. A little farther off dark-olive steams circled, and as in a fairy tale the five-headed shell of the Cathedral hid within them.

Mr Alec Brown's version is rhetorical. It begins:

The outdoor audience was drenched in a bathhouse froth of brilliance, as if in a magnificently illuminated ballroom. All at once a fictitious ceiling began gently sprinkling it as if the assembled audience were a seminal square of the far north. Scarcely had a shower of another sort begun than it suddenly ceased.

In what way can a square be seminal? Mr Brown has 'whorls of dark purple vapour' for Miss Scott's 'dark-olive steams'. Miss Scott's renderings of Pasternak's reflections on the fertilising conflicts in European culture are far clearer than Mr Brown's and the two translators have a serious difference of meaning in the passage on the roles of the genius, iconoclast and rebel. In Pasternak, the stress on tradition is strong; without it, he says, the rebellious are 'empty-handed'.

Safe Conduct is a longer, richer, denser autobiographical work than the *Essay* is. It contains a throbbing account of the poet's relationship with Mayakovsky and of the wild scene of grief at his death. Simplicity and the sense of the limitless favour the Russians in the expression of extreme emotions. The Western reader toils to impose order as he reads. One sees this again in the story of Pasternak's short love duel with his pretty cousin in Marburg in his student days. Each moment of this experience – and of all others – is so sensuously active that we have the characteristic Pasternak vision of chaotic sense impressions, all spring and the effervescence of the blood, yet enclosed as by a serene medallion. The affectations of style and the teasing out of the thought have their difficulty, which is a torture for translators who cannot catch the tone of a poet whose mind has been formed by music and, to some extent, by painting. One has one's doubts, in prose at any rate, about the value of putting one art to the service of another. In the story *Childhood of Luvers*, the beauty of the tale and the deep perception into a girl's life take time to emerge from the orchestration.

Pasternak never looks from society to the individual. Society is some formless thing, a general fate or flux of circumstance which, in his lifetime, has been riven by events that are like inexplicable storms and lightning – a symphony of which he does not know the score, but he does know that it cannot exist without him. Only, much later on, in the far future, will it be possible to understand what happened and what the symphony was. There, once more, is the traditional Russian nostalgia for the future. It is a faith in distance. Pasternak is not a closed and accomplished egoist. His feeling for the autobiographical comes from a capacity for living and re-living and putting passion into it. His continual reflections on memory are those of one who thinks of memory not as a fixed picture, but as a force in motion, perhaps like a storm that has passed, but is still banked up and reverberating. The present has its *élan* because it is always on the edge of the unknown and one misunderstands the past unless one remembers that his unknown was once part of its nature. For this reason Pasternak is able to raid the past and carry off people and places from it with the gleam of their own passion and bewilderment still on them. Such a view of life is poetic in the absolute sense. It is as hostile to the academic attitude to literature – Pushkin's feelings for his wife are more important than Pushkinism – as it is to the -isms of religion, politics, history and economics. It is the role of the poet to look at what is happening in the world and to know that quite other things are happening.

Those who expect some kind of counter-revolutionary or anti-Soviet journalism from *Dr Zhivago* will be disappointed. It is not, in that sense, a political novel at all, although it is entirely about the effects of the revolution of 1905, the First World War, the 1917 revolution and the last war, upon a group of families of the upper-class intelligentsia and others. Pasternak is apolitical. His temper is Christian; Marxism is dismissed scornfully as half-baked folly and pomposity. The ground is cleared for an account of what really happens to people in catastrophe and the human, moral and spiritual loss. Pasternak has written a confession of anguish. We see it largely in the experiences of Dr Zhivago, a young doctor and poet who is neither for nor against the regime, but who suffers and endures. The son of an alcoholic, wild millionaire whose suicide is unforgettably described in the opening chapter, Zhivago is a man torn in half by events.

He survives for a long time partly because he is a doctor. He sympathises with the revolutionary desire for social justice but many of his friends are on the White rather than the Red side. His chief idea is to save his wife and family and to get away from Moscow to some peaceful spot. He gets them, after an appalling journey, to Siberia. He is separated from them when he is taken prisoner by partisans who need a doctor, although he frankly tells them he is not of their party. When he escapes he finds his wife has got away to Paris. He is starving and pursued but – cool, indecisive, numbed in heart by suffering – he makes no attempt to join her; neither, at the end of his long and moving love-affair with a woman called Lara – whom we have met earlier as a seduced schoolgirl – does he stick to her and save himself. Wrecked in health and demoralised, he goes to pieces in Moscow, marries a peasant girl, deserts her and dies, eventually, of a heart attack while trying to open the window of a Moscow tram. He is the complete Soviet non-hero; yet at his death, his poems and diaries are treasured by the young generation. They recognise the integrity of the irreclaimable citizen who has only a grudging respect for the Soviet system.

As a novelist's just interpretation of the rights and wrongs of history and revolution, *Dr Zhivago* is useless. A political critic would say that it wilfully left out half the drama and argument. Pasternak would agree. He would add that people who are living history cannot know what history really is. Dr Zhivago himself is a passive and truthful character – a man out of E. M. Forster – and he survives, as long as he does, by submission to fate. This is a strength because he is inflexible in the sense of vocation. He reminds one of Chekhov.

The temper of Zhivago's mind can be judged best in a few passages. Back from the Front in the First World War and seeing the revolution, he finds his upper-class friends colourless:

The fooling, the right of idleness enjoyed by the few while the majority suffered, could itself create an illusion of genuine character and originality.

But how quickly, once the lower classes and the rich had lost their privileges, how these people faded! How effortlessly they had given up the habit of independent thought – which at this rate could never in fact have been genuinely theirs!

On the leap from peace to 'mass insanity and to the savagery of daily, hourly, legalised, rewarded slaughter', Zhivago says:

> It was then that falsehood came to our Russian land. The great misfortune, the root of all the evil to come, was the loss of faith in the value of personal opinions. People imagined that it was out of date to follow their moral sense, that they must all sing in chorus, and live by other people's notions, the notions that were being crammed down everybody's throat. And there arose the power of the glittering phrase, first tsarist and then revolutionary . . . Instead of being natural and spontaneous as we had always been we began to be idiotically pompous with each other.

He is sick of 'claptrap in praise of the revolution and the regime'. He can't accept that 'they' are all radiant heroes and he 'a mean little fellow'. A brilliant diagnostician, he is interested in mimesis in organisms. He gives a lecture, and there is a party outcry against his 'idealism, mysticism, neo-Schellingism'. The vulgarity of it disgusts him. Antipov – the husband of Lara, Zhivago's mistress – is a commissar whose star is beginning to fade. He is infected by obsessive self-criticism and the desire to confess:

> It was the disease, the revolutionary madness of the age; that in his heart everyone was utterly different from his words and the outward appearance he assumed. No-one had a clear conscience. Everyone had some reason to feel that he was guilty of everything, that he was an impostor, an undetected criminal. The slightest pretext was enough to launch an orgy of self-torture. People slandered and accused themselves, not only out of terror but of their own will, from a morbidly destructive impulse, in a state of metaphysical trance, carried away by that passion for self-condemnation, which cannot be checked once it has been given free rein.

Zhivago's perennial longing is to get away from the emptiness and dullness of human verbosity and to take refuge in nature, in sleep, in grinding labour or understanding 'rendered speechless by emotion'.

But Zhivago's musings are a small part of a book which has countless precise pictures of revolutionary happenings, as they appeared to the private eye of the characters. Some like the young Zhivago, the young

Lara, the young Pasha, the young Tonya, have grown up in quiet intellectual circles; but there are the railway workers, the peasants, individuals taken out of the Russian mass and soon to be scattered, martyrised or transformed. In twenty-odd years they became unrecognisable to one another. The shy Pasha will become the truculent commissar; Lara, the sensual, tormented girl who was seduced while still at school, will become the austere hospital nurse, the difficult wife and – after her sufferings – the tragic mistress. Fatal separations come sooner or later to all and destroy the heart.

From the point of realism, Pasternak's use of far-fetched coincidence to bring about meetings with his characters is absurd; but this book is really a romance in which the novelist is seeking the lineament or texture of a fate, not the detail of adventure or a construct of event and character. He jumps, without explanation, to new places and situations. How does Zhivago escape arrest after his unpopular lecture? How does he get to his hiding place in the forest? How did he intrigue? What happens to Lara when she is torn from Zhivago and goes off to degradation in China? These things are left out or are slurred over. The very slurring adds to our sense of the immeasurable quality of the general disaster. He conveys that cataclysms observably remove *meaning* from people's lives without leaving them futile.

Several large episodes stand out in the book, especially the long, quiet and unforgettable account of the Zhivago family's journey of escape by cattle-truck to Siberia. It takes them into the heart of the civil war, and yet (by a freak of war) into a village which is little touched by it and still living the old life. There are small episodes like the grotesque death of the revolutionary soldier Gintz who slips into a water-butt when he is making a speech. Simply because this happens suddenly and he looks so silly, a Cossack shoots him. Pasternak has an eye for the gratuitous actions of life; it deceives both in its fears and assurances. When the street fighting breaks out in Moscow, the Zhivago family is far more preoccupied with a fanatical attempt to make their stove work. Their child gets a sore throat and temperature and the guests they are sheltering bore them with ceaseless chatter. That is how revolution comes. Everywhere people are carrying their core of private life about with them. There is no cliché of invention in Pasternak; there is no eccentricity either. He has the eye of nature. Another

[768]

refreshing quality is the freedom from the Anglo-American obsession with sex. In love, he is concerned with the heart. It is hard to imagine an English, French or American novel on Pasternak's subject that would not be an orgy of rape or creeping sexuality.

Dr Zhivago is a great mound of minutely observed particulars and this particularity is, of course, expressive of his central attitude – his stand for private life and integrity. Even the look of the newspaper in which Zhivago reads the first news of the Revolution is described. He stands reading, overwhelmed, in the snow which 'covered the pages with a grey, rustling, snowy gruel'. There is a similar instantaneous detail in the lovely observations of nature. The snow melts, the forest comes to life in the smoking and steaming months of the thaw.

> Ancient pine trees, perched on dizzy heights, drank moisture almost from the clouds and it foamed and dried a rusty white at their roots like beer-foam on a moustache. The very sky, drunk with spring and giddy with its fumes, thickened with clouds. Low clouds, drooping at the edges like felt, sailed over the woods, and rain leapt from them, warm, smelling of soil and sweat, and washing the last of the armour-plating of ice from the earth.
>
> Yury woke up, stretched, raised himself on one elbow and looked and listened.

At another point, in a vermin-infested house, he writes of the rats, flopping down and squealing in their 'disgusting, pitiful, contralto voices'.

Dr Zhivago might be called an autobiography which breaks the rules and turns novel, reckless of form and restrictions of point of view. Pasternak never resists any hour of life that can be crystallised and fixed for ever, even if it is a digression. But we can guess, from Dr Zhivago's notes and especially from one which defends the 'seemingly incongruous jumble of things and ideas in the work of the Symbolists against the charge of stylistic fancy', that Pasternak's writing lives in the instant. The chief characters appear and then dive out of sight into time. Moving, urgent, vivid, they are suddenly swept away into nothingness. Zhivago's mistress vanishes into the street, was probably arrested (he says) and died in some labour camp 'as so many people did in those days'.

This does not make them seem futile. Zhivago's demoralisation has the effect of giving edge to his moral criticism. He is scornful when two of his friends, who are jailed and 're-educated', boast of their reformation: Dudorov taking the text-book orthodoxy of his sentiments as a sign of humanity. 'Men who are not free, he thought, idealize their bondage,' says Zhivago.

Health is ruined by the systemic duplicity forced on people if you say the opposite of what you feel, if you grovel before what you dislike and rejoice at what brings you nothing but misfortune. Your nervous system isn't a fiction, it's a fact of your physical body and your soul exists in space and is inside you like the teeth in your head. You can't keep isolating it with impunity. I found it painful to listen to you, Nicky, when you told how you were re-educated and grew up in jail. It was like listening to a circus horse describing how it broke itself in.

The doctor is the self-perfecting man and saint who goes downhill as a citizen. He refuses to be neutered by mediocre optimism. His story marks the return to the compassion of the great Russian tradition and repudiates the long, long reign of highly-coloured journalism and neo-Victorianism in Soviet writing.

The Gulag Circle

As a novelist Solzhenitsyn is very much in the powerful tradition of the nineteenth-century Russian novel as it appears in the prophet-preacher writings of Tolstoy and Dostoevsky, now one, now the other; as a polemical writer, in the tradition of Belinsky and Herzen. If history has altered his ground, another difference seems to me important. As far as one can judge he is far removed from the influences Western genius had upon his predecessors – for example, Shakespeare, Cervantes, Sterne, Dickens – his indoctrination as a young Komsomol was political and scientific. It is true that he was a poet, had read the poets of the revolutionary period and intended to be a novelist, but the tendencies of his youth drew him to the documentary and his unrest to a documentary which defied the Stalinist political monopoly of this mainly 'useful' form of writing. Since he is a passionate man, equipped with searing powers of irony, he was certain to find that man does not live by the record alone, but by the myths he creates, myths which contain his private thoughts and that sense of being 'elsewhere' when dogma becomes despotic. From Tolstoy and Dostoevsky, and as a man of imagination, he learned to hate contemporary materialism. There is a passage in the last of the Gulag volumes which makes the point:

> We don't mind having a fellow countryman called Lev Tolstoy. It's a good trade-mark. (Even makes a good postage stamp.) Foreigners can be taken on trips to Yasnaya Polyana . . . But my dear countryman, if someone takes Tolstoy seriously, if a real-life Tolstoyan springs up among us – hey, look out there! Mind you don't fall under our caterpillar tracks.

Not exactly the *style* of Tolstoy; it is closer to the crowd style of Dostoevsky.

[771]

Solzhenitsyn's reputation was made by the simple stark reporting of the horror and degradation of the labour camps, in *One Day in the Life of Ivan Denisovich*. The title phrase 'one day' is not only a clue to its immediacy, but far more to the tradition that the Russian novelists do not move by plot-time – which is an artifice – but by the felt hours of the day that run into each other. In its simplicity this 'story' is still the finest and most apprehensible thing he has written, for the prophet-preacher does not obtrude upon the simple character whose humble tale is told. He became a novelist in *Cancer Ward* and *First Circle*. Here documentary and the novel merge. The autobiographical element is strong but the symbols grow larger than the personal report of the author's own story. *Cancer Ward* is close to his own history. A twenty-six-year-old Captain of Artillery in East Prussia, with a university degree in mathematics and physics, he was sentenced to eight years of forced labour, for making derogatory remarks about Stalin. He was not freed until 1956. In exile in Kazakhstan where, in his time, Dostoevsky had also been sent – Solzhenitsyn was treated for a tumour and recovered. In this picaresque novel – the sick are the picaros of contemporary life – we get a day-by-day account of the life of an overcrowded cancer hospital, an exhaustive analysis of how cancer distorts the life stories of the patients and the doctors, and this is a way of describing what Russian life is really like outside. Hospital is like prison; it isolates. Every man and woman has his tale on his tongue; having cancer is a way of life. The people are all far from home, owing to the war or exile, and one sees the part played by distance, anarchy, and chance. The hospital is really an obscene Collective. Illness and overwork pretty well destroy private relationships; the irony is that the unanswerable punishments of Nature free one from the malice of the Secret Police and one has a brief liberty before one dies. The comedy is black: a philologist, for example, gets cancer of the larynx! No more languages for him. If you are a Party man, like the careerist Rusanov, you are astonished that your power has gone. His bed lies between the beds of two men condemned to exile:

If Pavel Nikolayevich were the same man he had been before he entered hospital, he would have gone and raised the question as a matter of principle – how could they put executive officials among dubious, socially harmful elements? But in the five weeks that the tumour had pulled him about as if he were a fish on a hook, Pavel Nikolayevich had either mellowed or become a simpler man.

Rusanov is quietly drawn as a Iudushka or hypocrite – see Shchedrin's classic portrait of the Russian Judas in *The Golovlyov Family* – a tedious, self-complacent, and exacting bureaucrat: he thinks he has the right to be the first to read the Party newspaper when it is brought to the ward; he is a glutton for all the boring articles about economics and politics. At first illness terrifies him, but as he recovers, his arrogance returns. Still, he has been a little mellowed until a new fear arises from the news that a new Presidium has been elected and that an investigation of the delinquencies of Stalinism will take place. He is calmed by his awful go-getting daughter who has written a few poems and has just intrigued her way into the Union of Soviet Writers. She tells her father that he need not worry; it's only a question of knowing the ropes and she has learned the tricks. He need not worry too much about that shameful intrigue by which he arranged to have someone sent to a labour camp in order to get the man's apartment.

The cancer ward is, of course, a symbol of Russia under Stalinism. The patients talk of their lives and their beliefs, and above all of the conflict between those who believe in power and those who rebelliously think of private happiness. Most accept the Communist society; it is daily life. But the experience of one or two has shown them what has been lost: the moral ideal of socialism. (The loss is like the loss of the American dream.) The ward is a sort of confessional. So far the limits of the novel are familiar; but halfway through there is a scene which shows Solzhenitsyn breaking new ground. He gives us that portrait of a happy family, the simple, ingenuous Kadims who, expecting nothing from the life of harsh exile, had found an absurd happiness with their dogs and cats: it recalls the idyllic pages of *Oblomov*. Solzhenitsyn is opening a window on a subject that has so far been obsessive and claustrophobic. In *First Circle*, he is quietly in command of powers that were scattered and now, like the great novelists, can control an orchestrated theme. The idea is taken from Dante. The first circle of Hell in Dante is the fate of the pre-Christian philosophers who are doomed to live there for eternity, and it is represented by the Mavrino Institute for scientific research on the outskirts of Moscow. The year is 1949, Stalin is ageing and becoming more ruthless. The Institute is staffed by scientists, engineers and academicians who have been taken out of the labour camps to do technical work under conditions only slightly less awful than the brutal conditions of the camps, for though they eat better, they are still cut off almost completely from their families. Most have been prisoners for ten years; at the end of it, their terms will probably be extended to twenty-five. They know they are there for eternity. With them, under the efficient police system, work a number of free workers from outside who go home at night and who act, together with some of the prisoners themselves, as informers. Eternal damnation could not be more certain. If their particular usefulness comes to an end, the prisoners will be returned to the savage camps and die at last in the prison hospital. It is exactly like the system applied to foreign workers by the Nazis during the war: feed them little, exhaust their muscles and brains, and let them die.

But eternal damnation is a kind of freedom, just as having cancer is. The prisoners of Mavrino have adapted themselves to their fate. Among them is the brilliantly drawn Rubin, a Jew and Party member, a philologist who was an organiser of sabotage in Germany during the war: then there are Nerzhin, a mathematician who has been a soldier; Pryanchikov, an engineer; Spiridon, a peasant and glass blower who has been taken on by mistake; Doronin, a young double agent; Sologdin, a designer, a re-calcitrant in for a twenty-five-year stretch. Their task is sinister: to design an apparatus for codifying speech patterns and tracing telephone calls – a machine that Stalin has specially asked for. It will lead to a huge increase in arrests and the novel indeed opens with a scene in which Innokenty Volodin, a diplomat, foolishly uses the telephone to warn a friend not to give a certain medicine to a foreign professor. By the end of the novel the completed apparatus traps him. It is typical of Solzhenitsyn that women play only a small part in the book. They are lost, touching, lonely figures and in only two or three chapters do they have any part. Incidentally, one characteristically Victorian aspect of the book is its scant interest in the perverting of sexual life in prison. Love is sorrow and sex is 'outside' and regarded as rather disgraceful. The idea owes something to Russian puritanism.

Within Solzhenitsyn's scheme, we see the curious nervous eagerness of life in prison, listen to the life stories, watch the effect of prison on character – on the guards and officials in charge. The prisoners are known as *zeks*:

> . . . One of those age-old prison arguments was in progress. When is it best to be imprisoned? The way the question was put presupposed that no one was ever destined to avoid prison. Prisoners were inclined to exaggerate the number of other prisoners. When, in fact, there were only 12 to 15 million human beings in captivity, the zeks believed there were 20 or even 30 million. They believed that hardly any males were still free. 'When is it best to be imprisoned?' simply meant was it better in one's youth or in one's declining years. Some zeks, usually the young ones, cheerfully insisted that it was better to be imprisoned in one's youth. Then one had a chance to learn what it meant to live, what really mattered and what was crap; then at the age of 35, having knocked off a ten year term, a man could build his life on intelligent foundations. A man who'd been imprisoned in old age could only suffer because he hadn't 'lived right', because his life had been a chain of mistakes, and because those mistakes could no longer be corrected. Others – usually these older men – would maintain no less optimistically that being imprisoned in old age is, on the contrary, like going on a modest pension into a monastery; one had already drawn everything from life in one's best years. (In a prisoner's vocabulary 'Everything' narrowed down to the possession of a female body, good clothes, good food and alcohol.) They went on to prove that in camp you couldn't take much hide off an old man, whereas you could wear down and cripple a young man, so that afterwards he 'wouldn't even want to get a woman'.

Rubin, the logical Jewish Communist, accepts prison, because 'the ways of Socialist truth are sometimes tortuous'. He has a violent row with Sologdin, the unrepentant designer, that goes to the heart of the novel. The row is about ends and means. An excellent distinction is made: Rubin's situation 'seemed to him tragic in the Aristotelian sense'. He had been

> dealt a blow by the hands of those he loved the most (the Party). He had been imprisoned by unfeeling bureaucrats because he loved the common cause to an improper degree. As a result of that tragic contradiction, in order to defend his dignity and that of his comrades, Rubin found

himself compelled to stand up daily against the prison officers and guards whose actions, according to his view of the world, were determined by a totally true, correct and progressive law.

The other ʒeks are against him and persecute him. The quarrels are wrecking the health of this clever, emotional man. Sologdin is his worst persecutor.

Sologdin knew very well that Rubin was not an informer and would never be one. But at the moment the temptation was great to lump him with the security officers . . .

Sologdin says:

'Since all of us have been imprisoned justly and you're the only exception, that means our jailers are in the right. Every year you write a petition asking for a pardon . . .'
'You lie! Not asking for a pardon, but for a review of my case.'
'What's the difference?'
'A very big difference indeed.'

As a Party member, though in disgrace, Rubin makes his Jesuitical point.
'They turn you down and you keep on begging,' Sologdin reports. And, Sologdin says, *he* would never demean himself by begging. (And in fact, he doesn't: Sologdin is a student of human weakness. He shrewdly waits till he has a brilliant idea about the encoding device and boldly plays one prison official off against another in a feat of blackmail which is the only thing officials are frightened of.)
And now we see Solzhenitsyn's mastery as a novelist: he is able to see the consoling contradictions of human nature and how they fertilise character. Rubin is not only the subtle and passionate Jewish Marxist and 'sea-lawyer': he is also the born Jewish comedian: he entertains the prisoners with a farcical historical parody of their own trials, filled with faked evidence from poetry, prison slang and innuendoes. And there is even more to this richly sympathetic man. His successes make him miserable and he becomes the practical Jewish mystic who is working on a plan for ritualising Communist life by introducing Civic Temples!
The density of Solzhenitsyn's texture owes everything to the ingenious

interlocking of incidents that are really short stories. This is the form in which he excels. His philosophical and political debates are always in this lively and purposive story form. He never fails to move forward. And the stories build up the central idea. The later tendentious Tolstoy is an obvious influence, more marked than Dostoevsky's in *The House of the Dead.* Our eye is on the most tragic character: Nerzhin, and his concern with what a man must do with his life. It is through his sorrow that we see that, bad as the lot of the prisoners is, the lot of their wives whom they can scarcely ever see or write to is a worse imprisonment in the open. They dare not easily admit that their husbands are political prisoners, for they will be shunned. Guilt by association is like plague: one is unclean. Nerzhin is a genuine stoic – in contrast to the endangered diplomat Volodin who is a genuine epicurean. Both men know they are doomed. In his early days as a Communist Nerzhin had noticed that educated or 'liberal' prisoners always let him down in a crisis; he turned idealistically to 'the People' in the labour camps and found they were worse.

> It turned out that the People had no homespun superiority . . . They were no more firm of spirit as they faced the stone walls of a ten-year term. They were no more far-sighted than he during the difficult moments of transport and body searches. They were blinder and more trusting about informers. They were more prone to believe the rude deception of the bosses . . .

With great tact Nerzhin nevertheless cultivates the peasant Spiridon who feels tragically the separation from his family, because in the family he saw the only meaning to life. He can never argue or think much but hits the nail on the head, peasant-fashion, with a proverb. His eventual reply to the question 'How can anyone on earth really tell who is right and who is wrong? Who can be sure?' is devastating:

> The wolfhound is right and the cannibal is wrong.

(Solzhenitsyn has read Hemingway and this scene reminds one of the only good thing in *For Whom the Bell Tolls* – the long talk with the Spanish peasant at the bridge in the Guadarrama.) Spiridon's view of life (Nerzhin sees) has an important and rare characteristic: it is his own. Nerzhin reflects:

[777]

What was lacking in most of them (the People) was that personal *point of view* which becomes more precious than life itself.

There was only one thing left for Nerzhin to do – to be himself . . . the People is not everyone who speaks our language, nor yet the elect marked by the fiery stamp of genius. Not by birth, not by the work of one's hands, not by the wings of education, is one elected into the people.

But by one's inner self.

Everyone forgets his inner self year after year. One must try to temper, to cut, to polish one's soul so as to become *a human being*.

And thereby become a tiny particle of one's people.

Nerzhin's integrity detaches him from the others; on matters of regulation and principle he risks everything with the officials and guards and insists on straight or cold ironic confrontations. They fear his powers of irony. Naturally – and he knows it – he will be sent back to the labour camp. He has understood the awful words 'For ever' as few of the others have; the words mean 'You have exhausted your power to hurt me'.

A passionate and agonised book like Dostoevsky's *The House of the Dead* owes much to the Romantic belief in the supreme value of suffering which is often said to be fundamental among Slavs. Prison has the monastic lure. Many of Solzhenitsyn's characters are haunted by this acceptance, but there is nothing mystical or romantic in him. He is quite clear that the Mavrino is not the Château d'If or Gorky's Siberia, that something has gone morally wrong and that courage in a changed attitude to the self is the important thing. He is, as I have said, more Tolstoyan than Dostoevskian.

The novel is not a sprawling, flat panorama, in spite of its range of scenes inside and outside prison. It has a serene command of space and time. It has architectural unity, and once the uneasy opening chapters are over, it is unshakeable. This beginning does contain, in my opinion, one weakness: the novelist has, with a daring which I find merely journalistic, introduced a live portrait of the ageing Stalin alone in his rooms. I simply do not believe the following words:

But reviewing in his mind the not-so-complex history of the world, Stalin knew that with time people would forgive everything bad, even forget it, even remember it as something good. Entire peoples were like

Lady Anne, the widow in Shakespeare's *Richard III*. Their wrath was short-lived, their will not steadfast, their memory weak – they would always be glad to surrender themselves to the victor.

A word about Solzhenitsyn's style: in these novels it is close to the vernacular and spiced with slang and proverbs and in two respects resembles the plain style of Swift: it sways between savage, educated irony and the speech of the people. Solzhenitsyn delights in exposing official prose and its deceits. There are two passages in *First Circle* which comment on the 'popular' or 'newspaper' style used by the poets when they addressed 'the People'.

Mayakovsky, for instance, considered it an honour to use a newspaper clipping as an epigraph for a poem. In other words he considered it an honour not to rise above the newspapers. But then why have literature at all?

For a good reason:

a great writer – forgive me, perhaps I shouldn't say this, I'll lower my voice – a great writer is so to speak a second government, that's why no regime anywhere has ever loved its great writers only its minor ones.

Whether Solzhenitsyn still intends to complete the historical trilogy he began in *August 1914* and continued in the fragment *Lenin in Zurich* is not clear. The influence of the Tolstoy of *War and Peace* is explicit. The subject of *August 1914* is the invasion of East Prussia and the military disaster of Tannenberg and that is the perfect Tolstoyan subject. It contains all the ironies: a General Staff corrupted by court favouritism and more con-cerned with seniority than battle; a muddled and ill-prepared campaign; yet a defeat which nevertheless did draw off so many German troops from the West that it enabled the French to save Paris at the Marne. There were two rival and out-of-date plans of campaign: drive into East Prussia with overwhelming manpower, cut off the East Prussian salient at the shoulder and encircle it; or force the way through to Berlin. If we check Solzhenit-syn's account with what the military historians have said, we find he is completely accurate. The actions of General Samsonov, the commander of the second Russian army that was destroyed, are set out correctly; the fact that the sad general was the victim of rival generals, and criminally ill-equipped and cut off from information, is set out in the history books, down to such details as the lack of wire for his field telephones and the neglect of signal codes, so that he had to send out all messages *en clair*.

The other figures in the High Command – Danilov, the master strategist, the Grand Duke Nicolas, Zhilinsky who cheated, the obsequious Yanushekevich who buried his incompetence in paperwork – are drawn to the life and, at the end of the book, there is a searching account of their behaviour at the conference table when the whitewashing of their responsibilities is completed. Solzhenitsyn has examined all the records. But until I read all this elsewhere I was often lost in his account of the confusion of the campaign: the great Tolstoy was a master of confusion in the field. He made the disposition of forces clear: one follows him easily without a map. To follow Solzhenitsyn without a map is very difficult. Still, in Vorotyntsev, the staff officer and fictional character who carries the moral burden of the narrative, we have the well-drawn portrait of both a feeling man and an intelligent professional soldier who can not only guide his remnant out of the mess, but who can guide us too.

Solzhenitsyn has Tolstoy's eye for the meaninglessness and the futilities of war – the town captured and then evacuated for no reason that is clear to the army; the loss of contact; the mystery of one's situation; the contradiction of orders; the jealousies of the officers; the baffled faces of the fatalistic troops; and when there is a question of action any given incident is vividly done and without journalistic rhetoric. One is struck, when Solzhenitsyn singles out an officer or a common soldier, by the fact that it is their particular type of mind that is thoroughly presented to us: they are thinking animals rather than the frightened, mad, simple, hysterical or violent men who appear in nearly all post-Tolstoyan books on war and in which war is turned into orgy. In the narrative the horror tends to be generalised, but here we notice an odd innovation. It seems that Solzhenitsyn either intended two kinds of war narrative, one to be read and the other to be filmed; or that a film director has inserted intervals of script-writing in which the physical horrors of war are set up for the exploiting cameraman. This insertion of film frankly destroys the illusion and if it is a new literary device it is a disaster and strikes one as cynical.

There are two exceptionally fine moments in the narrative. We have seen General Samsonov in all his moods but when the débâcle comes, he splits: half of him thinks he has an army still, the other wanders about with an innocent, mad smile on his face, raising his cap politely to his soldiers who themselves don't know whether they are soldiers any more. This and other passages are as good as anything in Vigny's *Servitude et grandeur militaires*. The other is a long episode describing the escape of Vorotyntsev and his remnant, through the forests and through the encircling German advance. They will succeed. We know from history what their lives are likely to become and by this hindsight it would have been easy for the author to show them with bitter irony as the marionettes of fate, but Solzhenitsyn rejects that; rather he speaks for them as the novelist should, feeling with the ignorance of each one in his different way and himself moving with their changes of feeling. This sensibility to change in the mind and heart is important to the book's intention, which is to show both the innocence and the ignorance of these men's involvement as they advance into their own and their country's future. He is clearly working up to a humane, sceptical exploratory conception of Russian history that will grow more and more at variance with official conclusions.

The war therefore is folly; when the son of one of the advanced families joins up patriotically he is regarded by his young friends as a traitor to an enlightened education. They are not part of the rootless intelligentsia; they are sincere, without being seriously deluded in their desire to get closer to the people. They, too, can't know their future and Solzhenitsyn has presented their innocence with the slow-moving care that he is to show in portraying the soldiers. One's picture of Russians of this kind in this period has been so stereotyped by Gorky and the melodramatic denigration of Marxists that one is astonished by the absence of the usual teeth-grinding doctrinal hatred and by the evidence of a free witness. Underlying the book is the criticism of the dogma that history can be rationally known or governed. History, says a teasing old professor to one of the ingenuous young students in the story, grows like a living tree.

Lenin in Zurich consists of a number of chapters which Solzhenitsyn cut out of *August 1914* because they ran too far ahead of the time scale of the huge historical chronicle he had in mind. These chapters have a natural intensity and unity, and something of the scenario for a film. We are plunged suddenly into Lenin's mind without preparation, as he stands with his wife and mother-in-law on an Austrian station platform staring at the engine of the train – frightening image of impersonal power – which will soon carry them to Cracow. The 1914 war has taken the logician by surprise. So deep in the tactics and mechanics of conspiracy is he that he simply has not expected the onset of a stupendous act of history and is utterly unprepared for its accidental element. Once more – as in 1905 – the conspirator finds real life has outpaced the tactician. When the train gets to Cracow his situation has again changed; he will have to make for neutral Switzerland. But at Cracow, where the first Polish wounded are arriving and the crowds of women are weeping over the stretchers, he has already been revived by an exultation that will keep him going:

> Piss-poor, slobbering pseudo-socialists with the petit-bourgeois worm in them would try to capture the masses by jabbering away 'for peace'. They must be hit first and fast. Which of them has the vision to see and the strength of mind to embrace the great decision ahead: not to try and stop the war, but to step it up? To transfer it – *to your own country.*
>
> 'Peace' is a slogan for fatheads and traitors! What is the point of a hollow peace that nobody needs, unless you can convert it immediately into *civil war with no quarter given?*

In the next three years Solzhenitsyn puts us inside Lenin's mind, crushes us against it, entangles us with it, takes us down into the pit of his rancours, the frustrations and the hatred that sustain him, as he keeps the political machine in his mind oiled and free of rust, while he is forced to live in limbo.

The thing was to be immediate on shifting ground. The war was a gift in itself to revolutionaries, but now – where would the revolution start? Russia was inaccessible. The one idea the war made plausible was the idea of permanent revolution, i.e., permanent civil war. Why could it not begin in neutral Switzerland? The idea came to nothing: the 'swinish' Swiss socialists were pusillanimous. They were in love with 100 years of petit-bourgeois neutrality; and were more interested – how could you believe it? – in defending their country! This failure made him furious with himself; why hadn't he seen that Stockholm was the place to set the world revolution going? In the end, the Germans were plotting to use him against the tsarists and he had the humiliation of hearing from others not condemned to inactivity (writing pamphlets in the Zurich library), and – in 1917 – he was once more taken by surprise and did not for a long time believe that the Revolution had begun in Russia.

Of course, this is a gross simplification of Solzhenitsyn's chronicle. *That* depends on his plausible if hostile estimate of Lenin's introspections, as they torment his mind and become minutely argued decisions. Solzhenitsyn says that the dialogue in the book is documented and close to the dreary language of the dialectic in which Lenin and his conspirators habitually chatted. One can be sure of that, and it is a relief to come upon two scenes in which Lenin is brought to life by rogues, the fantastic Parvus, the millionaire conspirator, and the brilliantly cynical Radek. This journalist is at his merriest when it comes to writing articles or letters of eager duplicity. The sight of shamelessness so happy and inspired is almost cheering. As for the fat Parvus who has made millions in Turkey and delights in getting funds for revolutionaries out of capitalist financiers – he is a sort of stage magician. He knows money is power and simply loves playing with it in order to buy women, châteaux and, in a most disinterested way, leaders. Thus he has been invaluable to the conspirators. The Red millionaire had no faith, we are told, in the Bolsheviks' organising ability. He attacked Lenin's concessions to the peasants. He ended by building himself an opulent house on the island of Schwanenberger in Germany and lived there to enjoy his orgies for the rest of his life.

A Doctor

The mark of genius is an incessant activity of mind. Genius is a spiritual greed. By the time of his death from tuberculosis when he was in his early forties, Chekhov had spent whatever breath he had, in every minute, not only in the writing of his hundreds of stories, his plays and his research on the convict island of Sakhalin – where he even took a census – but in exhausting work as a doctor, a founder of clinics and hospitals, schools and libraries, as the practical manager for many years of a small estate, as an indefatigable traveller in Russia, Europe and Asia.

From the age of nineteen he supported his family – a bankrupt despotic shop-keeping father, his fretful mother, a string of bickering relatives and hangers-on – mainly by his writing, under knockabout domestic conditions which were farcically at variance with what a serious artist is supposed to need. He appointed himself – even at nineteen – head of this tribe, who were 'depressed by the abnormality of living together' and who were people (he wrote in one of his letters) 'pasted together artificially'. They were touchy, lazy, talkative, noisy, pretentious and incurably hard up. Simply to listen to the noise they made drove him to despair and made him dizzy. To his brother he wrote (I quote from David Magarshack's *Anton Chekhov: A Life*):

> You know that I have a whole multitude of grown-up people living under the same roof with me. Because of some inexplicable set of circumstances we don't find it possible to separate: mother; sister; Michael who won't leave till he has finished his university course; Nicholas who is doing nothing and who has been jilted by his lady love and is always drunk and walking about in rags; auntie and Alexey who live with us rent free; Ivan who spends all his time here from three in the afternoon till late at night . . . and father. All of them extremely nice and cheerful people but vain and full of themselves, always talking, stamping their feet, and with never a penny in their pocket.

(He could lose his temper too.) They hung on to the precocious son and brother like leeches – and by mixing his pride with his comic sense, he hectored and coughed them into order. Although he was broad and strong as a young man, he was soon in bad health; he is the classic case of the doctor and consumptive who refuses to admit his case and neglects it.

On top of all this, Chekhov found time to write over 4,000 vivid letters, many of them merry, many of great literary importance, to critics, editors, novelists, friends and to women who were in love with him and whom he was evading. The notion of the melancholy, passive, defeated Chekhov vanishes when one considers these letters alone, and especially when one meets the candour, spontaneity, the humour sharp as horseradish and the intimacy of his correspondence. The man is alive to the tips of his fingernails and has the knack all good letter-writers have of springing in person before the reader's eyes. In letters a writer projects a large number of impromptu disguises, and, since he was often secretive in a self-preserving way, we do not get the whole of Chekhov – whatever that was – but we always see him in the hour he is living through.

A few of Chekhov's letters were published soon after his death. They were followed by a six-volume edition edited by his sister who adored him though she did make decorous cuts. There followed some of his letters to his wife, the actress Olga Knipper whom he married in the last years of his life. In 1948–1951 an official Soviet collection appeared and was revised and expanded in 1963–1964 to the number of 4,200 items. From this edition Avrahm Yarmolinsky has extracted some 500 of the 'most telling' – helped by the excellent translator Babette Deutsch. In another edition Michael Henry Heim and Simon Karlinsky have selected 185. Heim is the translator and Karlinsky gives a thorough critical commentary.

The editors of the two new volumes speak gratefully of the work of the Soviet scholars but cannot conceal their amusement or irritation with the well-known vagaries of Soviet censorship. The Russians have long been prudish about sex and the bodily functions, and in these matters Chekhov was often outspoken and sportive: after Pushkin (Simon Karlinsky points out), Russia became genteel as did the West, but the censorship in the Soviet Union has, uniquely, held on to nineteenth-century prudery. In a passage like:

There is no outdoor privy here. You have to answer the call in nature's very presence, in ravines and under bushes. My entire backside is covered with mosquito bites . . .

the word 'backside' has been deleted.

In matters of ideology, Chekhov's admiration of certain things in the West to the detriment of Russian efforts has been cut – yet not always in every edition. But here, when one considers how subversive Chekhov's ideas on artistic and personal freedom are, and how generally opposed to the tenets of official doctrine in the Soviet Union, the tolerance of the editors surprises. They pay their tribute to Caesar by cutting out what Chekhov said about the superiority of European actors to Russian actors, and other matters that offend Russian chauvinism, but the rest suffers little. The American editors have not found it difficult to put back much of what may have been tampered with.

The two selections of the letters now offered overlap, particularly in the important ones. Both volumes are well annotated. After a short and pleasant introduction the Yarmolinsky edition leaves Chekhov to speak for himself. There are more of his letters to his wife, Olga Knipper, than in the Heim and Karlinsky edition: they bring out more variously the harassed passion of the one powerful – and belated – love of Chekhov's life; and the letters written during the Sakhalin journey convince one of the revival of Chekhov's vigour. Both editors dismiss the notion that the journey to Sakhalin was undertaken because of a love affair with Lydia Avilov: they agree with Ernest Simmons that the lady imagined the affair when she wrote her book. (Chekhov would be the last man wholly to gratify the lady or indeed our curiosity on the point.)

The smaller Heim and Karlinsky selection is critical and informative and is framed in a general thesis. They group the letters in periods, each section preceded by an account of Chekhov's growth as a writer from phase to phase, so that the background is set out in some detail. This is invaluable. They are particularly concerned with his hostility to the long socio-political tradition of Russian criticism and the misapprehension this has caused. Where Yarmolinsky calls Chekhov 'the incomparable witness', they go deeper into the nature of his witness. They show that the precocious success of Chekhov at the age of twenty-eight annoyed the intelligentsia because he was held to be a man 'without principles' – which infuriated him: his belief in the freedom of the artist was a principle. They also show why, in the later years of fame, his opponents adroitly denigrated him by defining him as the moody, twilit poet of futility and despair. They were too partisan to see his truthfulness and grace.

Since then many Soviet critics have seen him as an incipient revolutionary and have even distorted his language to demonstrate this. Through either blindness or disingenuousness, they mistake the nature of the one or two apparently directly political stories – *The Anonymous Man* or *The Bride* for example – which are not dogmatic assertions. In a well-known letter Chekhov said that it was not the artist's business to solve questions, but to pose them correctly. Marxists do not allow the posing of the question: they state the answer first and then create the question. Chekhov wrote when he was twenty-eight:

> I am neither liberal nor conservative, nor monk, nor indifferentist. I would like to be a free artist and nothing else and I regret God has not given me the strength to be one . . . Pharisaism, dull-wittedness, and tyranny reign not only in merchants' houses and police stations . . . I see them in science and literature among the younger generation. I look upon tags and labels as prejudices. My holy of holies is the human body, health, intelligence, talent, inspiration, and the most absolute freedom imaginable, freedom from violence and lies, no matter what form the latter two take.

Or in a letter to Pleshcheyev about *The Name-Day Story*:

> It's not conservatism I'm balancing with liberalism – they are not at the heart of the matter as far as I am concerned – it's the lies of my heroes with their truths . . . You told me once my stories lack an element of protest and that they have neither sympathies or antipathies. But doesn't the story protest against lying from start to finish? Isn't that ideology?

And in defence of *Mire*:

> A writer is a man bound by contract to his duty and his conscience.

These replies are a defence against the accusations of the orthodox radicals who accused Chekhov of selling himself to the reactionary millionaire Suvorin and his paper. He was at once critical of Suvorin and his grateful friend.

Here we come to the continuous argument of the Heim and Karlinsky book: Chekhov was a subversive writer in the Russia of the Eighties and Nineties. He was exceptional in not belonging to the gentry class: he was one of the few writers – Leskov was another – whose elders had come from below. Although he was opposed to tsarism, his opposition had not been formed by the radical tradition of the literary intelligentsia, that is to say the tradition which, starting with the great Belinsky, demanded a didactic social content in literature and which was continued by Chernyshevsky, Pisarev and Dobrolyubov. (Lenin admired the last of these for turning a discussion into a 'battle cry, into a call for activism and revolutionary struggle'.) Chekhov believed that the radical utilitarians (with the exception of Belinsky) neither liked nor understood literature, and he was 'as subversive of the sociological presuppositions of a Russian Populist such as Mikhailovsky as of the Christian mysticism of Lev Shestov'. He was accordingly attacked for 'lack of social relevance', Karlinsky says, and the letters confirm him that

> . . . politically the most subversive aspect of Chekhov's thinking is his systematic demonstration of the illusory nature of all labels, categories and divisions of human beings into social groups and social classes, which are the starting point of all political theories of his time and ours.

The explanation is that Chekhov's intellect had been formed by the medical and biological sciences: his well-known practical work in hospitals, in building of schools, in the new local councils and in the clinics in the fight against cholera, brought him a great deal closer to the people and gave him a deeper knowledge of them than most writers of the time had. This has been awkward for some Soviet critics. In *The House with the Mezzanine*, the girl Lida (one of them complains) is doing exactly what Chekhov was doing in real life: dedicated social work. Yet Chekhov exposes her as an authoritarian and political fanatic who brutally wrecks her idle sister's life and he makes the reader admire the sweeter, weaker girl. In life Chekhov would no doubt have admired Lida's work. But, as Karlinsky says, he sees that Lida is a fanatic who will not tolerate opposition and indeed wishes to dominate the family. She will use any means to break those who oppose her beliefs. The story is not an attack on social concern but on the inhumanity and tendency of a particular humanitarian.

Chekhov's independent response to the pressure of the orthodox left-wing establishment is that of the working doctor: he is modestly self-accusing. He is bothered by abstract programmes and speculations. He wishes he were a 'great writer'. The best writers, he says,

> . . . are realistic and describe life as it is, but because each line is saturated with the consciousness of its goal, you feel life as it should be in addition to life as it is, and you are captivated by it. But what about us? We describe life as it is and stop dead right there. We wouldn't lift a hoof if you hit us with a whip . . . there is an emptiness in our souls. We have no politics, we don't believe in revolution . . . No one who wants nothing, hopes for nothing, can be an artist.

That Chekhov was influenced for a time by Tolstoy's teachings – especially by the idea of non-resistance to evil – is true: but he soon returned to his own nature. As an artist he exposed himself. His purpose as a man was practical and he admired the intelligentsia when they went out to the villages and fought the cholera epidemic. One has the impression that the power to believe – in the doctrinal sense – was destroyed in his childhood by the violence and tyranny of his father: 'What aristocratic writers take from nature gratis, the less privileged pay for with their youth' – though they have had the triumph of their liberation. Unprotected by radical doctrine, Chekhov nevertheless exposed himself as an artist to the full misery of Russian poverty in such stories as *The Ravine* or *The Peasants* which may have been prompted by his reading of Zola. (He read widely in European literature.)

The Peasants is less a story than a collection of incidents that convey what poverty is like, in the sense that it is a sub-culture of its own. Everything depends on the choice of the right detail and showing it as an aspect of living. A broken Moscow waiter decides to move back to the home where he was brought up in the country. His childhood memories have deceived him. How to describe the crucial shock of arrival? Chekhov describes him looking into a filthy hut, not a house, but a shed half-filled with a dirty stove, covered with soot and flies, on which a ragged girl is sitting. The parents are out in the fields and the child says nothing:

> A white cat rubbed itself against the fire irons on the floor. Sasha [the waiter's child] beckoned to it.
> 'Puss, puss. Come here pussy.'
> 'She can't hear,' said the little girl. 'Deaf.'
> 'Why?'
> 'Someone hit her.'

By a single line we are prepared for squalor, rancour, drunken fighting, the rabid greed of poverty, the blaspheming grandmother, the loose-living daughter who comes home stripped of her clothes. A neighbouring hut catches fire and no one knows how to put it out; the tax collector comes for arrears and takes the samovars from every hut. He is an obsessive collector of samovars and lines them up in his own place. One young girl can read and, in a conceited way, breaks into Gospel reading. Yet there is nothing Zola-like in Chekhov's descriptions of the vile: they are not rhetorically vile. The waiter dies and his wife and her child leave to beg on the road. The wife thinks:

> Yes, they were frightful people to live with. Still, they were men and women, they suffered and wept like men and women, and there was nothing in their lives for which an excuse could not be found . . . She now felt sick with pity for all these people and kept turning back to look at the huts.

What is striking about *The Peasants* is that Chekhov was able to catch every small drama in the lives of the community he describes in thirty pages.

One suspects that Chekhov's worry about 'purpose' had a good deal to do with his inability to write a long novel; he complained that he could not sustain a philosophic plan. The truth is that he lacked the novelist's vegetative temperament; he was avid for new beginnings and new 'good-byes'. His one serious attempt to write a long novel – it was scrapped after two or three years – collapsed from what he called 'fatigue' and because of the 'unreasoned' overcrowding of events, places, people, motives.

Oh if you knew what a wonderful subject for a novel sits in my noodle. What wonderful women, what weddings, what funerals! If I had money I would make off to the Crimea, seat myself under a cypress and complete a novel in two months . . . However, I am lying; if I had money in hand I would live it up.

Even in writing his stories he complained that he was a man of splendid beginnings who went flat from exhaustion in the middle and did not know how to go on. This self-criticism is of course absurd when one considers his very long stories *Ward No. 6, The Duel, Lady With a Dog* or *In the Ravine* in which he is certainly as great an artist as Tolstoy. Karlinsky quotes the hero of *Dr Zhivago*:

> Of things Russian, I love now most of all the childlike quality of Pushkin and Chekhov, their shy lack of concern over such momentous matters as the ultimate fate of mankind and their own salvation. They understand all that very well, but they were far too modest and considered such things above their rank and positions.

The letters indeed show that Chekhov did 'understand all that'. He attacked Suvorin, his friend and editor, on two crucial occasions: for the anti-Semitic articles Suvorin published at the time of the Dreyfus affair and the trial of Zola, and for Suvorin's attitude to the student riots of 1899:

> No one can pass judgment in print on the disturbances when all mention of the facts is prohibited. The state forbade you to write, it forbids the truth to be told, that is arbitrary rule . . . Right and justice are the same for the state as for any juridical person. If the state wrongly alienates a piece of my land I can bring an action against it and the court will re-establish my right to that land. Shouldn't the same rules apply when the state beats me with a riding crop?

About anti-Semitism at the time of Dreyfus:

> Little by little a messy kettle of fish began stewing, it was fuelled by anti-Semitism, a fuel that reeks of the slaughterhouse. When something is wrong we seek the cause from without and before long we find it: it was the French who messed things up, it was the Yids, it was Wilhelm . . .

Capitalism, the bogeyman, the Masons, the syndicate and the Jesuits are all phantoms, but how they ease our anxieties . . .

Even if Dreyfus were guilty,

> Zola is right, because the writer's job is not to accuse or persecute but to stand up even for the guilty once they have been condemned and are undergoing punishment. 'What about politics and the interests of the state?' people may ask. But major artists and writers should engage in politics only enough to protect themselves from politics.

As Karlinsky says, Chekhov's greatness does not lie in what he said about the culture of the time, indeed he often contradicts himself. It lies in his invention of 'dazzling literary forms' and particularly in finding a way of seizing the dramatic value in our very inability or unwillingness to communicate fully with each other. Rather pretentiously Karlinsky elaborates this as 'the semantic tragedy', and 'the changes in the texture of time's fabric which cause every attained goal to be different from what it was at the planning stage and which make a teleological approach to any undertaking or any personal relationship an absurdity'. What Chekhov saw in our failure to communicate was something positive and precious: the private silence in which we live, and which enables us to endure our own solitude. We live, as his characters do, beyond any tale we happen to enact. So, in the saddest as in the most sardonic of Chekhov's tales, we are conscious of the simple persistence of a person's power to live out his life; in this there is nothing futile. What one is most aware of is the glint of courage.

The letters do not say much about the making of this fabric. The most we learn is that his head was packed with people, that his early trash, as he rightly called it, was written by a very bright reporter and for money. Chekhov began by laughing at his stories. In 1883, in his 'trash' phase, he told his elder brother how to write a short story:

1) The shorter the better.
2) A bit of ideology and being up to date is most *à propos*.
3) Caricature is fine, but ignorance of court and service ranks and of the seasons is strictly prohibited.

A Doctor

In 1886, when the serious Chekhov first appeared, the instructions were drastic and in fact describe almost any good story he ever wrote:

1) absence of lengthy verbiage of political-social-economic nature.
2) total objectivity.
3) truthful descriptions of persons and objects.
4) extreme brevity.
5) audacity and originality: avoid the stereotype.
6) compassion.

He hated publicity and the pushing of his career. He was a self-perfecter and resented that he had to make money. He was an enormously responsible man who liked to pass as a reckless fellow. He was very susceptible to women and, indeed, said wine and women always set his imagination going. He wrote with more sympathy and understanding of women and was more their liberator than any other Russian writer except Turgenev. His many love stories are really woman stories in which the women are presented whole. If his own love affairs were generally short, his affection for the women concerned was lasting. Love did not turn into hatred. He was by nature too restless, too hard-working to be either a resounding romantic amorist or a compulsive seducer. He would marry, he often said, if he could be sure that the lady and he could arrange to live apart. Such love letters as survive are a mixture of fantasy, playfulness and farcical insults – 'There is a great crocodile ensconced within you, Lika' – and are really letters of friendship, in which his determination on his own independence is frank but unwounding.

One understands his curious, defensive insistence that the 'sad' plays are not only comedies but in fact farces. He is asserting that life is a fish that cannot be netted by mood or doctrine, but continually glides away between sun and shadow. And this feeling, his letters show, is at the bottom of the value he put on his freedom. Gorky reports that Chekhov did not like conversations about 'the deep questions with which our dear Russians assiduously comfort themselves'. And he certainly did not like the 'Chekhovians':

Once a plump, healthy, handsome well-dressed lady came to him and began to speak à la Chekhov. 'Life is so boring, Anton Pavlovitch.

[793]

Everything is so grey: the people, the sea, even the flowers seem to be grey . . . And I have no desires . . . my soul is in pain . . . it is like a disease.'

'It is a disease,' said Anton Pavlovitch with conviction. 'In Latin it is called *morbus fraudulentus*.'

Like a great many, perhaps all Russian writers of the nineteenth century, Chekhov caught people at the point of idleness and inertia in their undramatic moment when time is seen passing through them and the inner life exposes itself unguardedly in speech. He caught people in their solitude.

The comedy of Chekhov lies in the collisions of these solitudes. That is why, despite Stanislavsky and the Moscow Arts Theatre, Chekhov insisted that his plays were not dramas, not tragedies, but comedies and even farces. The tragedy, if there was one, lay in the very fact of farce: and the farce existed because it displayed people speaking innocently out of their own natures; the gigantic Pichchik believes he is descended from Caligula's horse; he calls out, astonished at himself, in the middle of a dance that he has had two strokes; he cries like a baby when he says goodbye to his friends. He is acting out his inner life. It is at once farcical and sad that a man has an inner life.

We shall misunderstand Chekhov if we do not grant him this starting point. Again and again his impulsive letters help to bring this out.

The Despot

T he life of Tolstoy is a novel that might have been written by Aksakov in its beginning, by Gogol in the middle and by Dostoevsky in the years following the conversion. He was not so much a man as a collection of double-men, each driven by enormous energy and, instinctively, to extremes. A difficulty for the biographer is that while we grin at the sardonic comedy of Tolstoy's contradictions and are stunned by his blind egotism, we are also likely to be infected by his exaltation: how is this exclamatory life to be brought to earth and to be distributed into its hours and days? And besides this there is the crucial Russian difficulty which the Russian novel revels in and which mystifies ourselves: there seems to be no such person as a Russian alone. Each one appears in a crowd of relations and friends, an extravagantly miscellaneous and declaiming tribal court. At Yasnaya Polyana the house was like an inn or caravanserai. There is the question of avoiding Tolstoy as a case or a collection of arguments. And the final affront to biography is the fact that Tolstoy exhaustively presented his life nakedly in his works.

One's first impression of Henri Troyat's remarkable Life is that we have read all this before and again and again, either in the novels or the family's inveterate diaries. So we have, but never with M. Troyat's management of all the intimacies in the wide range of Tolstoy's life. He was a man always physically on the move, even if it was only from room to room; even if it was simply gymnastic exercise, riding, hunting at Yasnaya Polyana. He is in Petersburg or Moscow, in the Caucasus, in Georgia, in Germany, England, France and Italy; and when he moves, his eyes are ceaselessly watching, his impulses are instantly acted on. His military career, his wild life, are packed with action and mind-searching. In sheer animality he outpaces everyone; in spirit and contradictions too. The amount of energetic complexity he could put into the normal search for a girl to marry outdoes anything that the most affectable sentimental novelist could conceive. Marriage, when it did come, was abnormal in its very domesticity. M. Troyat writes:

> Sonya was not sharing the destiny of one man but of ten or twenty, all sworn enemies of each other; aristocrat jealous of his prerogatives and people's friend in peasant garb; ardent Slavophil and Westernising pacifist; denouncer of private property and lord aggrandising his domains; hunter and protector of animals; hearty trencherman and vegetarian; peasant-style Orthodox believer and enraged demolisher of the church; artist and contemptuous scorner of art; sensualist and ascetic . . .

M. Troyat has managed to make this live with the glitter of the days on it. His book is a triumph of saturation. He has wisely absorbed many of Tolstoy's small descriptions of scene and incident and many of his phrases into the text. So when Tolstoy rushes off to one of his outrageous bullyings of his aunts in Moscow, we are at once back in a drawing room scene in *Resurrection*; and one can see M. Troyat going adroitly to the novels for exact moments of the life. He has learned the master's use of casual detail. He has learned his sense of mood and also of 'shading' the characters. He does not lose an instance of the ironic and even the ridiculous in Tolstoy's behaviour, but – and this is of the utmost importance – he keeps in mind the tortured necessity of Tolstoy's pursuit of suffering, and his knowledge of his situation. The conscience of the prophet often performs farcical moral antics, but fundamentally its compulsions are tragic. One can be angered by Tolstoy's hypocrisies, but also know that they agonised Tolstoy himself.

A test for the biographer is the exposition of Tolstoy's great quarrels. They are so absurdly jealous that the temptation must be to leave them in their absurdity. M. Troyat does better than this. The row with Turgenev, the breach and the reconciliation years later when Turgenev had become a garrulous old man, has never been so well-placed and made to live, as in this book. The comedy of the reconciliation brings laughter and tears to the eyes. There Tolstoy sits at the family table making enormous Christian efforts to repress his undying jealousy of the elegant and clever man who enraptures the family. Tolstoy grunts while Turgenev shows the girls how one dances the cancan in Paris. It is a farce that contains the sadness of the parting of irreconcilables; even more than that, for Turgenev is a dying man and does not fear death. He is interested in his disease and is sure that death is the end of all. The still vigorous Tolstoy is terrified of death; his flesh demands immortality. The search for God was really a return to childhood, an attempt at rejuvenation, but in Turgenev, Tolstoy was faced by a man who lived by an opposite principle. At thirty-five Turgenev had hit upon the infuriating device of attaining serenity by declaring his life was over, and then living on as a scandal until his sixties. One is present at a country house scene in a heart-rending play by Chekhov, where the elders are tortured and the young people laugh.

The story of Tolstoy's marriage is one of the most painful stories in the world; it is made excruciating by the insane diary-keeping of the parties. They exchanged hatreds, crossed them out, added more; from the very beginning the habit of confession was disastrous and brutal. Like the Lawrences and the Carlyles, the Tolstoys were the professionals of marriage; they knew they were not in it for their good or happiness, that the relationship was an appointed ordeal, an obsession undertaken by dedicated heavyweights. Now one, now the other, is in the ascendant. There is almost only one genial moment, one in which the Countess conquered with a disarming shrewdness that put her husband at a loss. It occurs when the compromise about the copyrights is reached. The Countess decides she will publish her share of his works herself and consults Dostoevsky's widow, who has been very business-like in a similar undertaking. The two ladies meet enjoyably and profitably; the Countess is soon making a lot of money, she is happy – to Tolstoy's annoyance. The art he had denounced was, as if by a trick, avenging itself on his conscience. He was made to look foolish and hypocritical. And yet, after all, they were short of money and his wife had proved she was right.

If there had been no struggle for power between the couple – and on both sides the feeling for power was violent – if there had been no struggle between the woman who put her children and property first and the man who put his visions before either; if there had been no jealousy or cruelty, there was enough in the sexual abnormality of both parties to wreck their happiness. Even though mere happiness was their interest for only a short period of their lives. She hated sexual intercourse and was consoled by the thought that by yielding to his 'maulings', she gained power; and he, whose notions of sexual love approached those of primitive rape, hated the act he could not resist. His sexuality tortured him. He hated any woman after he had slept with her. Conscious of being short and ugly, he was appalled that women were magnetised by him. Into this question – so alluring to psychologists – M. Troyat does not go very far; he simply puts down what is known and, of course, a great deal is known. It is an advantage, and in conformity with his method, that M. Troyat has not gone on the usual psychological search. He would far sooner follow Tolstoy in his daily life, tortured by lust or remorse, than dig into the unconscious. The fact is that Tolstoy seems to have known something nearer to love in his devotion to his aunts and to one or two elusive and distinguished older women.

About the Works M. Troyat has many interesting things to say. Because he was many men Tolstoy was able to get into the skins of many men, and the Countess understood that he was most fulfilled and made whole by the diversion of his protean energies into imaginative writing. On that she is unassailable; even his messianic passion produced religious fables of great purity and beauty; and in *Resurrection*, the recognition of the moral integrity of the prostitute is a triumph of Tolstoy's psychological perspicuity in a novel that does not promise it. Tolstoy's fear of death had a superb imaginative expression in *The Death of Ivan Ilich* – but, it is to be noted, this was not written in one of the passionate phases of his life, but in a period of coldness that was almost cynical. M. Troyat has a sentence which describes Tolstoy's love of quarrelling and his promise to reform, but only for the pleasure of going back on his promise, a sort of moral slyness, which contains a comment on his nature as an artist:

> Impenitent old Narcissus, eternally preoccupied with himself, he blew on his image in the water, for the sheer pleasure of seeing it come back when the ripples died away.

It is at the rippling stage, when he has dissolved himself, that he is an artist. And, of course, very conscious of what he is doing. He is watchful as an animal that sees every surface movement, he builds his people from innumerable small details of things seen. A misplaced button may tell all. He 'shades' – that is to say, he builds out of contradictory things: a cold dry character will be shown in a state of surprising emotion partly because this is true to nature, but also because that gives him an extra dimension that will surprise the reader. Tolstoy rewrites a scene again and again in order that the reader shall not know in the course of a conversation whose side he is on. He makes a great point of impartiality. Although *Anna Karenina* strikes the reader as a novel with a clear idea, set out in orderly manner and of miraculous transparency, the fact is that Tolstoy did not know what he was going to do when he started, and many times, in altered versions, changed the characters and the plot. He groped very much as Dostoevsky did, though not in a fog of suggestion, but rather among an immense collection of facts. The Countess and her daughters had to copy out many versions and the printers found on his pages a mass of rewriting which even Balzac cannot have equalled. One can see – and this is true of many artists – that the trivial idea from real life takes its final form only as the subject is finally assimilated to the self or experience of the author. He is edging towards a vicarious self-analysis.

It is fitting that this Life should have been done in Tolstoyan fashion with constant attention to the vivid and betraying surface. Not a single incident among the thousands of incidents fails in this respect. Yet the whole is not novelised. There is no imagined dialogue: it finds its place out of the immense documentation. The commentary is ironical, but a just sense of the passions involved is there: perhaps M. Troyat leans more to the side of the Countess but she is drawn as a woman, not as a cause, and we see her change, just as we see Tolstoy as an incalculable man. The complexity of the long final quarrel and the flight is made clear, and the narrative, at this dreadful point, is without hysteria. One can't forget such things as the old man sitting on a tree stump in the wood, secretly altering his will; or the Countess rushing out half-naked to pretend to drown herself in the pond. Then comes that awful train journey in the Third Class: the dim, inadequate figure of the worshipping doctor who went with Tolstoy; the whispers of the passengers who knew they had the great man with them; the bizarre scene at the station when the press arrived and were not allowed to take pictures of the station because it was illegal to photograph railway stations: the face of the demented Countess at the window as she looks at her dying husband to whom she is not allowed to speak – the whole scene is like the death of a modern Lear. As Isaiah Berlin wrote in *The Hedgehog and the Fox*, Tolstoy

> died in agony, oppressed by the burden of his intellectual infallibility and his sense of perpetual moral error: the greatest of those who can neither reconcile, nor leave unreconciled, the conflict of what there is with what there ought to be.

The Dream of a Censor

On the face of it, it is extraordinary that one of the great comic novels of the Russian nineteenth century should have come from the hand of the most pedestrian, industrious and conservative of state officials, Ivan Goncharov, a man outwardly devoid of fantasy and lacking inventive powers. From what leak in a mind so small and sealed did the unconscious drip out and produce the character of Oblomov, the sainted figure of non-productive sloth and inertia; one of those creatures who become larger and larger as we read?

The simple view – still held by some Soviet critics and encouraged by remarks of Goncharov himself – is that *Oblomov* was a solemn exposure of the laziness and ineffectiveness of the landowning class; but as it grew in the slow process of the writing (which took between ten and thirteen years) the novel became far more than that. Several contemporary critics have even suggested a prophetic kinship with Beckett and have noted the protest against the work ethic that has created a sense of emptiness and boredom in the modern world. Everyone exclaims at the influence of *Don Quixote*, to which Russian novelists so often responded; but, thinking of Goncharov's case, one could say that it is just as extraordinary that the Cervantes of the neat *Exemplary Novels* should also have burst the formal bonds of his period. All one can say is that literature has a double source: one in life, the other in literature itself, and if one is going in for the influence game, Goncharov's admiration for *Tristram Shandy* – the corresponding English comedy of domestic lethargy – may have helped to awaken his dilatory and very literary mind. From Sterne he learned to follow a half-forgotten tune in his head.

The interest of a new study of Goncharov by Milton Ehre lies in his close knowledge of Russian critical writing and his observation of the detail of Goncharov's impulses and methods as a novelist. *Oblomov* appears to be a work of objective realism as minute in this respect as a Flemish picture done from the outside, yet in fact it comes from the inner secret anxiety of an organised, even carefully dulled temperament. This anxiety arises from a haunting nostalgia for what has been lost, an edginess suggesting fear of a hidden 'abyss' that lies close to one who, torn between the ideal and the practical, has opted for the respectable golden mean.

There is, at times, an air of fret in Oblomov's nature that makes him seem on the brink of madness from which surrender to his sloth, perhaps, saved him. This madness came out in the form of paranoia in Goncharov himself towards the end of his life when he accused Turgenev and even Flaubert of stealing his ideas. Goncharov was State Censor and, maybe, the man who had such political power over the works of his contemporaries had been quietly boiling with the jealousies of the unconscious and the temptations of a right-thinking profession which hates the imagination. Censors go mad, just as prison governors come to feel, as prisoners do, that the only righteous people are those inside. The curious fact is that the unconscious of Goncharov, a lifelong bachelor, pushed him in old age into a fate like Oblomov's: will-less, drowsy, isolated, petulant, fond of food, he surrendered himself to the care of his manservant's widow, whom he called his 'nursemaid' and 'little mother', and he left his fortune to her and her children, whom he had virtually adopted.

Before making his closely analysed study of Goncharov the artist who wrote only three novels in his life, Professor Ehre points to the important wounds and compensations in the personal story. It is Gogol's, if it is less harrowing. It has some not dissimilar seeds of instability, and since Goncharov's writing was very autobiographical – and in this sense unimaginative – the real life is important. He came from a well-off family of the merchant class – and was the child of the second marriage of an elderly man and a girl of nineteen. The father died when the boy was seven, and a rich relation of the landowning class, an educated man of the world, took charge of the family. This Tregubov is one of the sources of the character of Oblomov. The boy had thus two fathers: the real one, a religious fanatic, dedicated to ritual and Byzantine formalism, and a melancholic; the other, an aristocrat, an intellectual, a humanist, a disciple of Voltaire and the Enlightenment, full of charm and totally indifferent, in the manner of the Russian landowners, to the practical demands of running his large estate at Simbirsk, a region often ridiculed for its sleepy and comic provinciality.

The place was an Oblomovka in itself and is precisely evoked in Oblomov's famous dream: one of the almost beautiful fantasies in Russian literature. As so often happens in countries where the males are denied a ruling political role, the women become the power figures: Goncharov adored his mother who was, however, one of those strict and practical Varvara Petrovnas who rule the Russian novel. She saw severely to his education, got him to Moscow University, and fitted him to become the efficient civil servant he eventually became. He was nevertheless uneasy in aristocratic company – rather jealous too – and among talented contemporaries like Belinsky, Herzen and Turgenev he was obliged to be only a spare-time writer. The truth is that his upbringing and temperament were as much to blame as his feeling of social inferiority for the neurotic indecisiveness which plagued and protracted his attempts to write. Indecisiveness also ensured that his one known love affair – the model for Oblomov's love of Olga – should fizzle out. There is a failure to adapt romantic idealism to natural feeling and action, to give up the pleasures of talk for the risk of the deed; the personality is split and, in the end, the deep boredom or ennui so familiar in Russian literature of the time becomes a sort of governing secret society in his nature.

Such maladies can be an enormous advantage to the man who can goad himself into the writing of a masterpiece. Cold, cold, cold, Chekhov complained of Goncharov; but knowing he had talent, susceptible if not inventive, turning self-mockery into play, frightened of the possibility of losing his talent, Goncharov dragged on year after year, forcing *Oblomov* to become a work of art. It is typical of the paralysing indecisiveness of his nature that he was working on another long novel, *The Precipice*, at about the same time and that while *Oblomov* was a study of stagnation almost without direct narrative and plot, *The Precipice* was sternly political and acted out with crude bad temper in dramatic episodes. This book was a failure.

But it would be wrong, as Professor Ehre shows, to think of Goncharov groping or blundering in his methods. The most revealing chapters of Ehre's study are those that follow in detail Goncharov's clear understanding of what he was doing, and the principles he stuck to and the value he

[803]

put upon the need to allow memory and the unconscious to ripen and form his work. He knew he was a conservative artist, that a form in which life stood still was indispensable; that he was dealing in types which would cease to be types and become symbols, that the more realistic his scenes were the more subjective must be the moving force.

In the chapter on the novelist's aesthetic views, Ehre quotes two passages from Goncharov's letters that show he had an exact notion of what he was doing and that Oblomov is not an oddity blown up to sprawling proportions:

> [The writer] should write not from the event but from its reflection in his creative imagination, that is, he should create a verisimilitude which would justify the event in his artistic composition. Reality is of little concern for him.

Art represents nature as a refracted image. Reality was too 'varied' and 'original' to be taken as a whole. He said much the same thing in a letter to Dostoevsky. If the Western calendared attitude to plot and precise action escaped him, he had on his side the Russian sense of the hours of the day running through his scenes and people like a stream or continuous present.

Since I do not know Russian I cannot comment on Goncharov's style and its rhythms, though I do see that plain or average styles such as his have to be consciously achieved. Writers who have no style are as obtuse as people who have no manners, either good or bad. Since Oblomov, like all extreme or outsize characters, is on the point of being mythical, I can, with some resistance, almost accept Ehre's references to Freud in his comments on Goncharov's relationship with his mother as suggesting the sun, warmth, a refuge from the Petersburg winters; and I can also see that if one looks back on childhood as an Arcadia one will have to recognise that one of the attractions of childhood is that it is lived under a system of magical rules whose chief use is that they give shelter to the imagination.

But we do not enact myths only in our lives. It is just as satisfying when thinking of Goncharov's difficulties in love to attribute these to the influences of Romanticism, in which it was natural even in split personalities both to idealise and fear 'ladies' as distinct from 'women'. Goncharov solved his difficulty by the ironic mockery of his feelings, i.e., by playing the game of being a man of the world. Oblomov, after all, is reluctant, not sexless but sly. In his early comedy of manners, *A Common Story*, Goncharov was content with the ironic reversals of idealism in love and to show, with some relish, the price of worldliness: the young hero becomes as cynical as his uncle – a Tregubov figure – and the uncle attempts disastrously to recover the follies of his youth and heart. But in *Oblomov*, the novelist broke out of his neat formula, with the result that the critics have been divided by the account of Oblomov's love of Olga and her marriage to Stolz; and Ehre is very suggestive.

At first reading Stolz is a virtuous stick and Olga is not much better; at later readings, Olga strikes one as being a remarkable portrait of an unformed sentimental girl acquiring the will of a real woman, and one can take the whole episode as a very penetrating study of the deceits of Romanticism in its watery mid-century form. When Oblomov falls into the arms of his servant and has children by her, Stolz feels the sluggard is lost and has taken the plunge into the 'abyss'. He has, so to say, gone native and Stolz breaks with him; but Olga begins to see him as one who, resisting the modern world's worship of will and activity, has preserved the quality called 'heart'. Perhaps Oblomov is self-indulgent; but Stolz remains stolid, and one understands, in theory, Olga's unrest in her sensible marriage to a responsible man.

If we accept this, it remains true that the Olga-Stolz episodes are unsatisfactory, but for another reason: one of style. How important that tune in the head is! The moment we get away from Oblomov himself the narrative becomes flat and toneless: as Ehre says, it becomes dry, argued, and conceptualised. One can even suspect here he had stolen from Turgenev a theme that was beyond his own sensibility.

Goncharov's unconscious had no living or literal material to offer when marriage or romantic love were the subjects. In his next novel, *The Precipice*, all the petulance and jealousy came out in the ageing censor. He could not use the tongue of the younger generation. His particular genius lay in the prolonged and loving farming of his only aristocratic estate: his private evil.

The Early Dostoevsky

W hen Dostoevsky was a cadet in the Academy of Engineers – the story runs – he designed a nearly perfect fortress, but forgot the windows and doors. A guide to the novels: the reader is dropped into the novelist's claustrophobia, and it must be said that the enormous amount of Dostoevsky criticism since 1880 makes the walls thicker. The task of tunnelling one's way out of his labyrinth is exhausting, and there is disappointment (if there is also relief) in discovering that the great artist was often, like Balzac and Dickens, also a journalist who skids into a phantasmagoria of 'the topical and *au courant*'.

This is a phrase of the Czech critic Václav Černý: all the critics have their phrases. We are helped for a moment and then we are forced to discard: the *âme slave* was the first to go; it was followed by Dostoevsky as 'the key' to the Russian character; we hesitate over the surely conventional theory of Dostoevsky as the product of medieval Russia in collision with capitalism. Too many 'ideas' occur to us. The root of the trouble is that the artist, the man in the act of writing, is lost – he was before anything else an improvising artist. As Mikhail Bakhtin put it in his well-known and difficult book, *Problems of Dostoevsky's Poetics*, which first appeared in Russian in 1929 and was expanded in 1963,

> The subject is not a *single* author-artist, but a whole series of philosophical statements made by *several* author-thinkers – Raskolnikov, Myshkin, Stavrogin, Ivan Karamazov, the Grand Inquisitor and others . . . The critics indulge in polemics with the heroes; they become their pupils, and they seek to develop their views into a completed system.

Such criticism is concerned with ideology alone and not with the evolving story-teller, at home in the slipshod but struggling against it, and auto-biographical to the point of apotheosis.

For the biographer who sticks for the moment to the early pre-Siberian Dostoevsky, as Joseph Frank does in *The Seeds of Revolt*, the ground is clearer. (There are three volumes still to come.) The great novels are not yet here to obscure the man whom Siberia enlarged and transformed. We are able to see the young man painfully growing. The story has gradually become well known, but it still contains its mysteries and Mr Frank's very long book can be called a work of detection and collation at its scrupulous best. Every detail is considered; evidence is weighed, and fortunately the author has a pleasant and lucid style, unleadened by the fashionable vice of fact-fetishism. He brings a clearer focus and perspective of things that have been often crudely dramatised, especially in Dostoevsky's childhood and youth, and we have a more balanced and subtler account of this period than we generally get.

There is no prophetic assumption, for example, that Dostoevsky's father was a rough, miserly, flogging, lecherous brute like the older Karamazov. The home itself could not be the source of Dostoevsky's knowledge of abandoned or lethargic poverty. Childhood was happy, if youth was not. The anxious father was ambitious, energetic, strict, but thought constantly of his children's piety, education, and future; the mother was deeply loving. The boy had his father's energy and determination and dash. Where was the flaw that made both father and son unstable, jealous, envious and instantly suspicious? When one looks at Dr Dostoevsky's past one sees how powerfully he was influenced by the dream of rank and advancement; even his narrow religion was the dreaming sort of dissident Puritanism which urges the family up the social ladder. This was very much a nineteenth-century dream. The worm in the heart of Dr Dostoevsky's success in achieving rank in the lowest grade of the Russian nobility was the knowledge that he had been merely admitted to the new service 'aristocracy' invented by Peter the Great and could never become part of the traditional gentry, in fact or in his attitudes.

The crowded Dostoevskys lived very much to themselves. They dwelled in the legend – perhaps it was a fact – that their forebears in the sixteenth century belonged to the old Lithuanian gentry class. Their history has a suggestive religious aspect. The ancient Dostoevskys were scattered and divided in nationality and creed.

The Orthodox Dostoevskys, falling on hard times, sank into the lowly class of the non-monastic clergy. Dostoevsky's paternal great-grandfather was a Uniat archpriest in the Ukrainian town of Bratislava; his grandfather was a priest of the same persuasion; and this is where his father was born. The Uniat denomination was a compromise worked out by the Jesuits as a means of proselytizing among the predominantly Orthodox peasantry of the region: Uniats continued to celebrate the Orthodox rites, but accepted the supreme authority of the Pope. Dostoevsky's horrified fascination with the Jesuits, whom he believed capable of any villainy to win power over men's souls, may perhaps first have been stimulated by some remark about the creed of his forebears.

The debate about reason and faith would have had an ancient edge and force to it if it ever occurred in the doctor's small apartment in his hospital. The Dostoevskys differed from the real gentry in a more important respect. The real gentry had become merely lax in religion and tended to be sceptical Voltaireans. Aristocrats like Tolstoy and Turgenev had had no religious education. But for Dostoevsky:

> The very first impressions that awakened the consciousness of the child were those embodying the Christian faith . . . Dostoevsky was to say that the problem of the existence of God had tormented him all his life – it was always emotionally impossible for him ever to accept a world which had no relation to a God of any kind . . .

If aristocrats like Turgenev's mother flogged their sons, the domineering doctor never once struck his children. Whether he flogged his serfs when his new status allowed him to own land and he bought a poor estate in the country is not really known; but he sent his elder sons to a private school in order to shelter them from brutality: until then he had been their strict schoolmaster. He saw they were taught Latin and the indispensable French well.

Yet if the childhood was happy, it lay under a lid: the strain of the father's anxiety for rank and success became hysterical after his wife's death. He had awakened a deep love of literature in his children, yet, still pursuing conventional status, sent Feodor to the Academy of Engineers against the boy's will. The Academy was a great drain on his pocket and the father was so beside himself that he had a stroke when Feodor failed to be promoted in his first year. Feodor became extravagant and wanted, in his turn, to cut a 'noble' figure, and we get the first signs of duplicity and guilt in the sanctimonious begging letters to the father.

At this point Mr Frank deals with Sigmund Freud's famous essay on the Oedipal nature of Dostoevsky's conflict with his father. Freud believed Feodor had become patricidal and, in fantasy, homosexual; and that his epilepsy now occurred as a discharge of the guilt he felt when his father, now deep in drink, was murdered by his serfs. (Dostoevsky's silence on this subject is extraordinary, and indeed the murder did not, in any case, become known until long after his death. It had, for respectability's sake, been hushed up.) Freud's case was easily demolished by E. H. Carr in his *Life* published in 1931. Mr Frank agrees with Carr and believes that Dostoevsky's disease did not appear until just before his imprisonment in Siberia or just after. If he was mentally ill in adolescence this is likely to have been so because, like his father, he had little control of his nerves and his temper.

In the ambivalence of Dostoevsky's relations with the father he resembled, and in his fluctuations between resentment and filial piety, Dostoevsky had his first glimpse of the psychological paradox. He came to seek 'self-transcendence, a sacrifice of the ego', and, says Mr Frank, 'whether one calls such a sacrifice moral masochism, like Freud, or more traditionally, moral self-conquest', is a matter of terms.

We move on to the early struggles of the writer and a far closer view of the literary scene than the foreign reader is usually given in other Lives. Russian culture in the 1830s was moving from German Romanticism and Idealism towards French Realism or Naturalism. The influence of George Sand, Balzac and Victor Hugo on young Dostoevsky was enormous (he translated *Eugénie Grandet*) and in Russian literature so were the influences of Pushkin and Gogol. We move on to the conflict with Belinsky who had praised *Poor Folk* and to the interminable debates on socialism with or without free will and Christian faith that lead us eventually to the Petrashevsky conspiracy, the climax of the trial at which Dostoevsky declared, 'Socialism is a science in ferment, a chaos, alchemy rather than chemistry, astrology rather than astronomy.' Mr Frank goes on to quote from the *Memoirs* of Alexander Milyukov, who suggests that there was a small Populist wing in the Petrashevsky group and that this is where Dostoevsky may possibly be placed.

The account of the Petrashevsky meeting is given at length, and if Mr Frank is not vivid – others *have* been – his account is gripping as a piece of detection among ideas. For 'What are your convictions? What are your ideas?' set the note of discussion in the many 'circles' – satirised at the time by Turgenev – that were characteristic of a society where there was no freedom of the press. Dostoevsky wandered in and out of these discussions, occasionally bursting out with emotional attacks on the tsarist bureaucracy, but in the main he simply floated giddily among the Radical speakers. Only one political question preoccupied him passionately: the emancipation of the serfs. The Tsar himself was hesitating in the matter.

There was a change in Dostoevsky when the extraordinary, dramatic figure of Speshnev appeared among the drab and circuitous intellectuals. A few years earlier in his life Dostoevsky had been bowled over by the perfect aristocrat: Turgenev ('I love him'). Speshnev, too, was an aristocrat; wealthy, cultivated, travelled, cold and strong. His melancholy feminine appearance fascinated (Semenov remarked that 'he could well have served as a model for the Saviour'). He was to become the model for Stavrogin in *The Devils*.

There is the report of Dostoevsky's doctor, who found the novelist irritable, touchy, ready to quarrel over trifles and complaining of giddiness. There was nothing organically wrong, the doctor said, and the trouble would pass. 'No, it will not,' Dostoevsky said, 'and it will torture me for a long time. I've taken money from Speshnev' – 500 rubles in fact – 'and now I am *with him* and *his*. I'll never be able to pay back such a sum, and he wouldn't take the money back; that's the kind of man he is. Now I have a Mephistopheles of my own.'

Speshnev was a sinister example of 'the double' who brings about catastrophe. The money, of course, was meaningless to Dostoevsky, the perpetual borrower, living the hard life of an unsuccessful writer; it was the will of Speshnev that was irresistible. It drew him towards what he abhorred – some form of evolutionary activity. What appalled him, Mr Frank argues, was that he had, in his unstable way, lost his moral freedom. Later in life he told his second wife that but for the *providential* accident of his arrest he would have gone mad! The strange thing is that living for

[810]

contradictory extremes, Dostoevsky was one of those neurotics who recover their health and even their serenity when disaster at last occurs.

Mr Frank's first volume stops with the arrest and trial. The last hundred pages deal with the novels and stories Dostoevsky had written up to this point. If we except *The Double* and *White Nights*, these belong to the Dostoevsky few people read, for although there are flashes of talent, they are derivative of Gogol, Hoffmann, Sand, clumsy in construction, garrulous and tedious. Mr Frank is conscientious in his hunt for signs of a developing moral insight, but I am afraid his exhaustive summaries of the stories and the examinations of the characters do not make the tedious less so. In one Hoffmannesque tale of incest and demonic possession, *The Landlady*, one does see (as Frank says) a new theme emerging: the crushing of the personality under traditional Russian despotism and, in the portrait of Katerina, there is his first study of masochism. (Katerina says, 'My shame and disgrace are dear to me . . . it is dear to my greedy heart to remember my sorrow as though it were joy and happiness: that is my grief, that there is no strength in it and no anger for my wrongs.')

When one tackles these stories, one has to admit there is a certain mastery and even a tenderness in evoking masochistic sensuality. But one also sees how this derives from literature. He had not read the Gothic novels in vain; he was a great borrower and already an expert in pastiche and parody. *Netotchka Nezvanova* is Russified George Sand and is for me, though not for Mr Frank, unreadable. It has the turgid air of obsessive conspiracy which certainly became a characteristic element of Dostoevsky's genius, but here the artist is cramming too much in. The one thing I miss in Mr Frank's reading is a real response to Dostoevsky's comic irony, although he does praise the brilliant hack's pastiches of the bedroom farces of Paul de Kock.

Dostoevsky was surely, from the beginning, a master of dialogue and situation, and one of the great comic wits. His morbid insight into psychological contradiction, his habit of seeing the conflict of inner and outer life, not only as a quest but an imbroglio, are constantly attended by the sardonic spirit when he reached the height of his powers. And it is in this, rather than in his religious or moral utterances, whether they are subtle or overweening, that one feels the iron quality of forgiveness which elsewhere is sentimental.

[811]

'Without art,' Dostoevsky once wrote, 'man might find his life on earth unlivable.' And, one must add, he might find the novelists and, above all, a certain kind of academic critic, hard labour. In Mikhail Bakhtin's *Problems of Dostoevsky's Poetics* the originality of this great Soviet scholar's work is obscured by a structuralist prose so opaque that one has to translate to oneself as one struggles on. An inventor of awful words in Russian – 'characteriology' for example – he has been a great trouble to his apologetic translators. But Bakhtin does understand that Dostoevsky is creating his own means as an artist. For him Dostoevsky is the inventor of a new genre, the polyphonic novel. His characters are not the author's voiceless slaves but rather 'free people who are capable of standing *beside* their creator, or disagreeing with him, and even of rebelling against him'. There is a plurality of voices inner and outer, and they retain 'their unmergedness'.

He goes on:

> Therefore the hero's word is here by no means limited to its usual functions of characterization and plot development . . . The hero's consciousness is given as a separate, a *foreign* consciousness . . .

The traditional European novel is 'monological', a thing of the past, and if Dostoevsky's novels seem a chaos compared, say, with *Madame Bovary*, so much the worse for the tradition. Man is not an object but another subject. As for Dostoevsky's ideas, they are

> artistic images of ideas: they become indissolubly combined with the images of people (Sonya, Myshkin, Zosima); they are freed from their monological isolation and finalization, becoming completely dialogized and enter into the great dialogue of the novel on completely equal terms with other idea-images (the ideas of Raskolnikov, Ivan Karamazov and others) . . .

Dostoevsky's principle as a novelist is simultaneity. There is no doubt that Bakhtin exactly describes the originality of Dostoevsky; one has indeed the impression of being among people whose inner lives are dangling at the ends of their tongues. The lasting defect is that so much self-dramatisation drives one into the ground. Not all tongues are equal. Polyphony suffers from the excess of voices. Only in *The Brothers*

[812]

Karamazov, where the effect is of theatre, has Dostoevsky really brought them to order. Where Bakhtin becomes most stimulating is in his remarks on Dostoevsky's shameless indulgence in literary genre: the detective novel, the story of adventure, parody, pastiche, boulevard farce, grotesque and melodrama. Dostoevsky has prolonged periods of seeing life as an enormous scandal or as a revival of the ancient folk traditions of Carnival in which the types are contemporary and not mythical.

At this point Bakhtin takes a long, effusive, learned flight into the history of the scandalous Carnival tradition and is immensely suggestive. It is delightful to see a scholar going too far. I am surprised to read that these scenes in which – to use Bakhtin's metaphor – the drawing room becomes a public square are thought by many critics to be artistically unjustified. Surely, no longer? They are at the height of his comic achievement. This kind of scene is organic, nothing invented in it (as Bakhtin says), though when he says such scenes really go back to the 'underworld naturalism' of the menippea of Petronius and Apuleius, I enjoy the scholarly trapeze act but I don't believe a word of it.

On the whole, European criticism of Dostoevsky has not paid much attention to him as a novelist at work; it has concentrated on his ideas. This is natural: the hunger for apocalypse has recurred, reviving, exhausting itself and reviving again, in every decade of this century as the human situation gets worse. One can see why Dostoevsky, the prophet and 'gambler who doesn't dare not to believe' is still the master; he moves forward with us as the sense of our own danger changes. We reject, as people fifty years ago did not, his preaching of the Russian Christ which so blandly overflowed into military chauvinism, for the notion of the man-God was Victorian and Dostoevsky's irrationalism offered us something unpleasantly close to the herd-God of fascism. But we were left with his insights into Russian history. When the West recovered from the catastrophe that he had accurately prophesied, there was still the great psychologist of the 'mystery of man'. And when that required counter-checking, we now find in him the authority on such strange elements in the Russian character as the communal personality and the morbid habit of confession. If anyone took up alienation as a profession it was he.

Yet we would not be reading him at all if he had not wrenched his great and his minor novels out of the chaos and contradictions of his own mind by a strictly artistic process. He was a novelist first and last. His very characters are story-tellers. It is the novelist who contains the prophet, the sensationalist, the rather smug hair-raising journalist and the often disingenuous mystic. To an exalted and agonised lady who thought he, above all, surely must know the synthesis that would heal the dualism tormenting her, he replied cheerfully that dualism has its delights as well, and that, for his part, he was lucky: he could always turn to writing. A wise remark, but one does have the impression that the gambler who played for the highest spiritual stakes had an unfair resource when he had lost all his money.

One turns therefore to a Russian critic for a sharper, native view of these matters. Professor Mochulsky died in Paris in 1948 and his admired book on Dostoevsky appeared in Paris the year before. A professor at Odessa and the Sorbonne, Mochulsky experienced a religious conversion and became a disciple of Berdyayev. For the reader who expects a new approach to Dostoevsky, this is ominous news. We have already had so much about Dostoevsky's spiritual struggles. Ernest J. Simmons, E. H. Carr and others had already used most of the immensely important notebooks, letters and journals which were available, and have made economical and skilful use of them; they caught also some of Dostoevsky's irony. And although Mochulsky does, in minute detail, show us the novelist struggling to arrive at his 'idea', changing and re-changing his plots and his characters until the idea becomes plausible life, we are far more aware, in the end, of the message than we are of the novel. It is no news that Dostoevsky's novels are dramas of conscience and belief; but they are great novels because he is able to translate this into specific acts and scenes of believing, and because he creates imbroglios of extraordinary physical vividness. He is a sculptor of molten figures.

Of course, it is important to see how the famous conflicts arose (the love-hate in the conflict with Belinsky, the utilitarians and the humanists; with the landowner tradition and the effect of being forced into the company of criminals) and he forged the contradictions of belief and nature into people; but there is far too much synopsis in Mochulsky's book, and far too little exposition of Dostoevsky's power of theatrical scene, of his gift of hallucination, his narrative whose strongest effects somehow arise from their disorder; and there is not enough about his humour and comedy.

[814]

A hurried but classically constructed novel like *The Eternal Husband* might be a conscious parody of the great tragedies; but it points to the barbed, sardonic laughter which makes his pages of exaltation, or tortured doubt and terror, finally human. The recurrence of the great scandal scenes – on which Mr Ronald Hingley was very good in *The Undiscovered Dostoevsky* – and indeed the fact that nearly all Dostoevsky's characters are seen in a scandalous light for his own purposes and even by compulsion, are matters which a less religious critic would have attended to. And there are questions like Dostoevsky's ability to put a whole houseful, a whole set of people, an officeful, on the page instantly. This is his *biographical* gift. Life stories of endless complexity hang shamelessly out of the mouths of his characters, like dogs' tongues, as they run by; the awful gregariousness of his people appears simultaneously with the claustrophobia and the manias of their solitude. Dostoevsky contrives always to select so that he is able to show everything happening at once, without freezing into dead statement, and without thereby exhausting his subjects at the outset. Dostoevsky's sense of time is a sense of bursting, continuous instants. A whole life, past and present, breaks open this minute and will go on bursting in every minute that follows.

Some of these things *are* implicit in Mochulsky's analyses of the books and he is properly aware that since Dostoevsky is a confessional writer, the links with his own dramatic life are important. He was experienced in finding enemies to whom he could glue himself, upon whom he could fawn, and with whom he could fight. Like the saints, he knew how to hit below the belt. Mochulsky knows that the novelist is theatrical – one can often grasp Dostoevsky far more easily on the stage than in the novels – that he is poetic, that his struggle to find a form for his work was part of the spiritual struggle; that he is, as he said, an expressive rather than a descriptive artist – one of the reasons for his attraction today. Mochulsky is good about his literariness, about Dostoevsky's growth out of literary forebears like Gogol, Hoffmann, Balzac, Hugo; the importance of Shakespeare, Cervantes and of Dickens. He was much swayed by foreign writers. He welcomed confusion. One sees him switching from an intended novel called *The Drunks* to *Crime and Punishment*, stopping to write *The Gambler* in a month and then putting *The Drunks* into *Crime and Punishment*. Raskolnikov was at first to be another Rastignac. The novel was to be a first person confession; this was abandoned for an outside narrator. Initially in *Crime and Punishment* the idea was to be that crime leads to moral rebirth and redemption. Suddenly Rastignac is replaced by Napoleon and we have Dostoevsky's involvement with the 'strong' character and the questions of pride, power and living beyond good and evil. At the end of the novel he looked for a compromise that would reconcile his conflicting ideas about Raskolnikov's fate:

> The 'vision of Christ' and his heroism at the fire had to be discarded; Svidrigailov and not Raskolnikov fell heir to the solution of suicide. An exterior dénouement still remained; his giving himself up to the authorities, the trial, his deportation to the penal colony; but this did not suffice for an interior spiritual development. Raskolnikov did not repent and did not 'rise' again to a new life. There is only a promise of his resurrection in the concluding words of the epilogue . . . 'the miracle-working force of life will sustain him'. . . . The murderer has not yet been saved, but he can be saved if he will completely give himself up to a spontaneous, irrational love of life.

The changes in the conception of the character of Prince Myshkin are even more extraordinary. At first he is quite the opposite of the final character: he is to be a powerful figure, a spiritual brother of Raskolnikov. (Dostoevsky swings giddily from one extreme to the other.) Myshkin is to be an epileptic. Then he is to be like Iago – another instance of a bookish choice – cold, envious, vindictive; after a glance at Turgenev, the enemy, he becomes 'a superfluous man', an idle power. Then he turns into a Stavrogin, a character whom we see trying to be born in other novels. After that he is the opposite, the 'holy fool'. Dostoevsky is really looking for the most dangerous solution. He finds it in 'a beautiful individual' – Christ, Don Quixote, Valjean – even Pickwick is considered. The idea was never certain for him until the fourth part of the novel and he was harassed by the feeling that the Prince ought to be, like Don Quixote, a comic character.

And, in fact, it is as a comic character that he almost succeeds. Dostoevsky's nearest approach to Quixote (though a more mundane one and untroubled by selflessness and the imagination; he is simply bullied and is an old liberal with out of date ideas) is the figure of Stepan Trofimovitch Verhovensky in *The Devils*. He is a reminder that there are periods of untheatrical tolerance and ripeness in Dostoevsky. There was a good deal of the sinful humanist left in the mystic; a good deal of slyness, of never quite letting the right hand know what the left was doing. It is here that prophet and novelist come together.

Mochulsky is clear that Dostoevsky is without landscape, is uninterested in nature, ignorant of peasant life – which makes nonsense of his mystical exaltation of the Russian people. Much to the taste of the Symbolists and some contemporary critics is the suggestion that he was seeking to enact basic human myths: 'the enchanted bride', 'the revolt against Mother Earth', 'the stranger'. He certainly portrayed the Man-God and the Covetous Knight. I find Mochulsky most informative about Dostoevsky's style: it is a talking style in which his own voice and the voices of all his characters are heard creating themselves, as if all were narrators without knowing it.

Founding Father

It is said that among foreigners only the Baltic Germans can see Pushkin's genius as a lyrical poet at once. The rest of us who have no Russian and read his poetry in English or French translation echo the remark made by Flaubert to Turgenev – 'Il est plat, votre poète'; it expresses our polite embarrassment before a mystery. To the dramatic poet-novelist in *Eugene Onegin*, to the prose tales and above all to his marvellous letters, we do respond. In the last we hear the natural voice of the man that goes leaping along beside the cooler voice of the conscious artist and we at once see why the Russians think him the greatest of their letter writers. He is there before us: 'In casual letters of confession/One thing inspired his breath, his heart/ And self-oblivion, was his art!/How soft his glance, or at discretion/How bold or bashful there, and here/How brilliant with his instant tear'. We learn to 'mourn for Russia's gloomy savour, Land where I learned to love and weep'. We see the courtier trapped by the Court; we see the rake who wears his nails long and who looks like a monkey, the aristocrat of two aristocracies: the Court and Art; the patriot who, like the Spanish Cid, is struggling with a false king. Pushkin had the art of appearing suddenly dishevelled or elegant, out of the very hour he was living. He is as concise as impulse itself. He is as clear as ice, as blinding as snow.

It is true that a lot of Pushkin's letters are mystifying – who are all these people? What is it all about? By now biographers have picked out the important ones, but it is still startling in the three-volume edition translated into English by an American scholar, J. Thomas Shaw, to find how all still have their instant upon them and bring out Pushkin's voice. It is a good idea to have a life of Pushkin handy when reading them; but Professor Shaw's exhaustive notes pin down a long list of minor writers, actresses, mistresses, social figures and officials, and point the detail of adventures, projects and scandals. A half-elegant, half-barbarous scene is there if one can piece the fragments together; and when this is too much for us,

Pushkin is there from youth to just before his death, never failing in accent or gesture. His mood, because it is so changeable, switching at every sentence, may seem careless at first. Looked at more closely almost all the letters are as certainly works of art as the letters of Byron are.

Pushkin has the appetite for life and, more important from a letter-writer's point of view, a genius for playing with it, for changing his tone, for leaving some things sardonically unsaid and others spoken bluntly. He is entranced by his laughing mastery of all kinds of style from the drily formal, the eloquent, the witty to the hotly argued and tenderly felt. He enjoyed rewriting. He was a keen tester of phrase. Each sentence rings like a true coin. For the moment he is all ours and we, on hearing him, are all his.

Here he is held up in quarantine because of the cholera and distracted because of the family quarrels concerning his marriage:

> All you say about society is just: all the more just are my fears that aunts and grandmothers and little sisters may start turning my young wife's head with folderol. She loves me, but look, Aleko Pletnov, how *the free moon goes its way.* Baratynsky says that only a fool is happy when he is a fiancé, but a thinking person is disturbed and agitated about the future. Up to now it has been I . . . but now it will be we. A joke! This is the reason I have been trying to hurry my mother-in-law along; but she, like a peasant woman of whom only the hair is long, did not understand me and was fussing around about a dowry; to hell with it! Now do you understand me? You do? Well, thank God! . . . I should like to send you my sermon for the local peasants on the cholera; you would die laughing, but you do not deserve this gift.

Pushkin is not one who, self-entranced, takes one underground into the labyrinth of introspection. He takes it for granted that he is known and that we know what it is to be a man. He is modest. He is expressive but neither tortuous nor exhibitionist. His stress is not on the egotist's 'I' because he is multifarious. He writes rather as the messenger or familiar of a human being called Pushkin who, though perpetually in some sort of scandal or trouble, is like a swimmer who knows how to survive in a storm of his own making and who will make no fuss if he sinks. The appetite for life is not simply a matter of extroversion; it is inseparable from the appetite for putting it into words. Yet he does not live in words alone. Once every three days he is in love with a new woman; he is quarrelling with the censorship, travelling on awful roads, drinking, gambling, listening to his old nurse, eagerly describing his poems, amusing himself in villages, flung into bouts of inspiration, driven forward by whim, never frosted with doubt and never green with guilt or remorse. These, he says, he never felt. He looks like a monkey and is as lithe and restless; and he has a touch of dangerousness too. He insists that he is an aristocrat. But he insists, too, that he writes to make money, for that frees one from the servilities of patronage.

Pushkin's biographers have all pointed to the powerful self-control he must have had and the letters show that he has reserves; but one thinks of him not so much as a man wrestling with his passions or in conflict with himself, but one who is in command of his experience. He is inhabited by a genius that guarantees his integrity; but his is not a mad genius: it is sane, orderly, generous, serene in feeling. It is impossible to imagine ourselves trusting the judgment or good sense of a Dostoevsky or a Tolstoy. Egotism distorts them. Pushkin one entirely trusts. He is so open. His follies expose the corruption of the society he lived in, rather than falsity in himself. Pushkin lived very much like other men of his class, very much in the world. The early letters are those of a brilliant, dissipated character living the loose life society willingly allowed to the young and well born.

> Everything is going as before; the champagne, thank God, is lasting – the actresses likewise – the former gets drunk up and the latter get f . . . Amen. Amen.

To women 'who have too much sense to be prudes', he writes with flattery and innuendo:

> I shall imitate a monkey, I shall slander, and I shall draw for you Mme de . . . in the 36 poses of Aretino.

(Professor Shaw, who belongs to the exhaustive tradition of American editing, does not forbear from telling us that Aretino's erotic work has 38.) To Mme Kern, one of his mistresses who wants to leave her husband, Pushkin writes:

My God, I'm not going to preach morals. But yet respect is due to a husband, else nobody would want to be one. Do not oppress the vocation too much, it is necessary in the world.

There is a more dangerous female who was to be with Pushkin all his life:

Give my greetings to the censorship, my ancient girl. I do not understand what in my elegiac fragments could have troubled her chastity . . . One may and must deceive the old woman for she is very stupid.

In obtaining the right to be censored only by the Tsar, who used the pretext of saving Pushkin from himself, the poet saw he was caught in a cruel comedy that was to be played out coldly to the end of his life.

They deprive me of the right to complain (not in poetry but in prose, a devil of a difference) and then they forbid me to be enraged . . . The right to complain exists in the nature of things.

At thirty young men of Pushkin's class were expected to marry and settle down. Obedient to convention Pushkin settled down. The rake turned with sudden tenderness to the 'necessary vocation' of being a husband and enjoyed the novel pleasures of family anxiety. He was captivated. But he was caught between a rancorous mother-in-law, a cunning Tsar and a coquettish wife. His marriage which mellowed him also destroyed him. That was tragic and yet, of course, both as a man and an artist, Pushkin got what was vivid and valuable in his life and work from venturing; not from change itself, but from the capacity to make it. His vitality jumps out in every sentence. For one who scattered his life in storms and comedies, he is astonishing for a fundamental seriousness. And what he read! Byron, Shakespeare, Corneille, Goethe, Scott and Voltaire, of course. Racine to quarrel with and Mme de Staël to defend. He hated German metaphysics. But he knew enough about Addison and Steele and the system of patronage in English literature. He could recall lines from the low characters of Fielding. He treats literature as a form of action.

Even when he picks an obscure friend's poem to pieces, he enhances as he criticises. His literary letters are entirely mixed in with the life of the moment:

[821]

The next day I ran across Nikolay Raevsky in a bookshop. '*Sacré chien,*' he said to me with tenderness, '*pourquoi n'êtes-vous pas venu me voir?*' '*Animal,*' I answered him with feeling, '*qu'avez-vous fait de mon manuscrit petit-russe?*' After this we set off together as if nothing had happened, with him holding me by the collar in plain sight of everybody, to keep me from jumping out of the calash.

This is from one of his letters to his wife, a touching correspondence beginning in awestruck devotion, going on to the tender, the possessive and playful and ending in the painful attempts to allay his dismay at her sexual coldness and her jealousy. It is a comedy in the French fashion, with a cold undertone and a dire end.

On one question that was to become crucial to later generations, the split between Westerners and Slavophils, he has a letter of great import-ance. The letter is a criticism of Chaadaev's famous pamphlet which argued that, having fallen into the hands of Greek Orthodoxy, Russia had had no real history, culture or tradition. Chaadaev was arrested and declared mad. Pushkin wrote to him, before this official persecution occurred, agreeing with Chaadaev's attack on Russian social life, but rejecting the religious argument:

We have taken the gospels and traditions from the Greeks, but not the spirit of puerility and controversy. The customs of Byzantium were never those of Kiev.

This is the characteristic view of the man of the world: the Russian clergy are backward because they wear beards and are not in good society; then patriotism is stirred:

What? Are the awakening of Russia, the development of its power, its march towards unity (Russian unity of course), the two Ivans, the drama that began at Uglich and concluded at the Ipatiev Monastery – is all this to be not history, but a pallid and half-forgotten dream? . . . Do you believe that (the future historian) will place us outside Europe?

Pushkin was deep in European literature. He was avid for the remodelling of literary forms; in a *Selection* of his literary letters, another editor, Tatiana Wolff, says:

[822]

When Pushkin wrote of his calling as a poet he did not write of afflatus: on the contrary he always wrote of himself as a craftsman. The Muse was his gossip and his mistress with whom he did not have to be on the best behaviour – powdered and in pumps. The letters came in spate, full of comments on the books he had read, requests for more books, praise, blame, vituperation, enthusiasm. He questioned, argued and swore . . . There was a note of increasing urgency in Pushkin's determination to replace the influence French literature had on Russian with that of German and English.

His letters are always dashing in their candour:

I sing as a baker bakes, as a tailor sews, as Kozlov writes, as a doctor kills – for money, for money, for money – such I am in my naked cynicism.

When we turn to Pushkin's prose tales, the common opinion is that he writes in frozen, formal, well-corseted style that seals the subjects from the outside air. In a very fine study, *Pushkin: A Comparative Commentary*, Mr John Bayley disposes of this view, gracefully and with learning. Pushkin was indeed so deep in English and French eighteenth-century writing that it is perhaps natural to see that classical style as having been transposed without change when, in fact, he was a pillager of styles. He was, as Mr Bayley says, fascinated by the way in which modern literature had imposed its stereotypes on the men and women of the period, a process particularly marked in Russia where the upper class tended to identify itself with a current European model. 'It made a contrast, sometimes a grotesque one with the solid ramifications of Russian life.' Pushkin is less a giant than Proteus, as Shakespeare was, presenting new forms with the laughing boldness of a Renaissance figure. Form is of the greatest importance and it is on this subject, particularly – to my taste – in his discussion of *Eugene Onegin* and the prose tales, that Mr Bayley is most penetrating. For there is a paradox here: the strictly formal artist is one who brings to Russian writing the sensation we have that the doors and windows of the closed house are open and that more than one person lives there to tell its tale. The watching writer can make no rigid claims because he himself is watched by other selves within himself or, maybe, only by the sky:

> *Eugene Onegin* and *The Bronze Horseman* . . . have a formal perfection and inevitability, combined in being provisional and open-ended, a paradox that has a parallel in the structure of the greatest Russian novels.

The carefully insured impersonality or evasiveness of the writing is warm: there is none of Flaubert's chill.

On the surface *The Queen of Spades* or *The Stationmaster* are no more than skilful anecdotes in an antique setting – which was one reason for Mérimée's regard for them. They emerge from 'old papers', hearsay or after-dinner talk, in the conventional manner, and a tale like *The Stationmaster* looks at first sight like a simple reversal of the Prodigal Son story, as it might be retold by Maupassant. On a second reading one sees that this is not so. At the end we do not give a shrewd grin at the expense of the poor stationmaster's mistaken belief that his daughter's 'fall' will be a moral disaster, when it has turned out to be a most respectable success. Indeed, the success is not the sort of paradox enjoyed by a man of the world, but is humanly moving. We see a life unexpectedly surviving the clever or stupid misunderstanding of experience, and compassion cuts the claws of irony. In the last lines of the flat ending, life, doubting life, assimilates not only father and daughter, but the narrator himself. The 'closed' end is really open. The same may be said of the far richer *Queen of Spades*, where the terse picture of a society and an obsession with meaningless luck can be read on several levels and where the curious Russian gift of exact portraiture-by-accident or devastating miniature puts an indelible glitter on the people. The story melts into the interests of other lives.

Pushkin was a constant literary collector, but he changed what he collected. He is an example of the writer who shocks old subjects into life by a gay and intelligent search for new means. It is interesting that the incident in *The Captain's Daughter* where the girl goes on a journey to the Empress to plead for the life of her betrothed was taken from the *Heart of Midlothian*, yet with what new dramatic ease or innocence of eye! The economy and the impudent bravura of these tales are shapely, but the sense of the open, passing hour is always there and it will pervade all the great Russian novels that follow.

The longest and most illuminating essay in Mr Bayley's commentary on Pushkin is the one on *Eugene Onegin*. To English ears the manner and the voice are Byron's and in the opening book Pushkin seems to be explicit. The young dandy is a fop, spending three hours before the looking glass, a pedant of fashion:

> Porcelain and bronzes on the table.
> With amber pipes from Tsaregrad;
> Such crystalled scents as best are able
> to drive the swooning senses mad,
> with combs, and steel utensils serving
> as files, and scissors straight and curving,
> brushes on thirty different scales;
> brushes for teeth, brushes for nails.

The loot of Paris and London. Then the sudden twist of irreverent comment:

> Rousseau (forgive a short distraction)
> could not conceive how solemn Grimm
> dared clean his nails in front of *him*,
> the brilliant crackpot: this reaction
> shows freedom's advocate, that strong
> champion of rights, as in the wrong.

He's off to Talon's, to hear the corks go flying up, as he sits before his bloody beef, his truffles

> and pâté, Strasbourg's deathless glory,
> sits with Limburg, vivacious cheese
> and *ananas*, the gold of trees.

He'll shout at the ballet, alarm the ballrooms. Don Juan is on the prowl. Soon he will be Childe Harold, 'glum, unpleasant, caught by the British *spleen* and the Russian *chondria*'. Who is he? Is he Pushkin himself, or is he being Byron out of sheer vivacity?

> I regularly take much pleasure
> in showing how to tell apart

> myself and Eugene, lest a reader
> of mocking turn, or else a breeder
> of calculated slander should
> spying my features, as he could,
> put back the libel on the table
> that, like proud Byron, I can draw
> self-portraits only – furthermore
> the charge that poets are unable
> to sing of others must imply
> the poet's only theme is 'I'.

This is Mr Bayley's moment. The autobiographical surgery of Constant's *Adolphe* is in the poem; but Pushkin is deep in *Clarissa*, in Fielding, Scott and above all in *Tristram Shandy*: he is parodying the novel of sentiment. For Mr Bayley this poetic novel is far more closely related to *Tristram Shandy* in form than to *Don Juan*. As in *Dead Souls*, *Don Juan*, *Finnegans Wake* or *The Waves* – Mr Bayley says –

> The impression is one of constant and brilliant improvisation, problems and contingencies recurring in endless permutations . . . under the guise of a dazzling helplessness . . . The author escapes at every moment into the new pattern of the structure that he is creating.

The poem is, so to say, one of the earliest anti-novels, and it is achieved by conscious art. Mr Bayley's great attraction is that he shows the pleasure of the poet at work and brings him closer to us by his asides. Pushkin shares with Joyce and Sterne

> an easy relationship with poetic facility and cliché. What Wordsworth and the romantic poets forget in their stricture on the poetic diction of their predecessors, was that the best poets who used it never took it very seriously, just as a great rhetorician does not take the rhetoric he makes use of very seriously.

The clichés of Pushkin are 'aware of their own obviousness and emphasise it with gusto'. Another good comment, which takes one back to the 'openness' conveyed in this stylised work, is that *Eugene Onegin* is not depressing – certainly not in the manner of the nineteenth-century realists.

The daily life of Russia in Petersburg and the country sparkle; and if ennui follows the frustration of love, recollection has its tenderness; there is a kindness in the acceptance of experience.

> The very incomprehension of one character by another, the abyss of distance between them, is as much an earnest of possible happiness as of deprivation. When Tatyana says 'yet happiness was so possible, so near . . .' her words have something more than the pathos of illusion . . . The perspective of 'life's humble journey' opens out from every point in *Eugene Onegin* where artifice, irony and the patterning of the novel of sentiment are most dazzling and triumphantly in control.

Possibly the changes of mind Pushkin went through during the years of writing the poem were a help. More important are the nonchalant changes of point of view in the narration. The elusive narrator-within-a-narrator gives the poem that circular, round-and-round view which was to become common in the Russian novel, so that the personages are at once 'we' and 'I'. The sentiments, the passions, are a dream; we are mocked but without ill will. We dream, we wake up. Time passes through us as we pass from youth to age. We are defined and redefined as the days melt and remake us.

A Bolting Horse

An intelligent edition of Strindberg's anti-feminist stories, *Getting Married*, has been done by Mary Sandbach. The commentary is detailed and valuable to those of us who have seen many of Strindberg's plays but who do not know him thoroughly as a prose writer and know even less about the tensions in Swedish life in the last half of the nineteenth century.

Among the Ancient Mariners who arrive to stop guests from getting into the wedding feasts of the European middle classes in that period, Strindberg has the most frenzied and unrelenting grip. The calms that lie between the bouts of paranoia are themselves dangerous. We can easily 'place' the sexual guilt in, say, *The Kreutzer Sonata*, for Tolstoy has immensely wider interests. But except, apparently, in his historical novels (which few people outside Sweden have read), Strindberg's personal obsession rarely ceases. He is the perpetual autobiographer who has at least three albatrosses – his three wives – hanging from his neck, and it is not long before he is telling us that the birds shot *him*. One of the surprising consolations of his life was that he liked going out into the country for a day's shooting, and it is a striking aspect of his lifelong paranoia in human relationships that he loved what he killed.

Strindberg's strange upbringing as the unwanted son of a successful businessman and a domestic servant, and as the victim of a stepmother; his poverty as a student; his quarrel with the Anabaptists and Pietists of a respectable society, who had him prosecuted for blasphemy because they hadn't the courage to bring him to court for his public campaign for sexual freedom; his flight from literature into experiments with sulphur that drifted into a half-insane obsession with something like alchemy; above all, his instability as a husband or lover – all these torments kept him at white heat. What astonishes is the lasting fertility – in his work – of these ingeniously exploited obsessions. I can think of no other writer with the possible exception of D. H. Lawrence who retold himself in so many impassioned ways.

One thought one had seen his case analysed and dramatised for good in *The Father* – where he is the sea captain, in fact the Ancient Mariner in person, who was driven mad by the cunning calculations of a respectable bourgeois wife – or in *Miss Julie*. Yet, in 1903, much later, the whole personal story is retold as a legend, folk tale or saga for children, in the droll story called 'Jubal the Selfless'. This tale appears to be serene, but its playfulness and resignation are deceptive. The title itself is misleading. Jubal's selflessness is not that of the saints. It is the selflessness of an opera singer who, in old age, realises that his ego or will has been systematically destroyed by a conspiracy between his father, his mother, and his wife (an actress who uses him in order to supersede him in his career). When he looks into his mirror – this is typical of Strindberg's brilliant theatrical imagination – he sees he is a body without a face. It is only when he finds his lost mother and puts his head in her lap that he recovers his ego – and, needless to say, dies!

The fable is a characteristic experiment with Strindberg's own history and it contains a truth about him as an artist and a person: the history and character are *disponible*. He is a model for the early nineteenth-century concept of Genius: the genius is free and without character but compelled to seek martyrdom. This is a matter for Strindberg's biographers. The work is far more important. Reading any story, particularly in the first section of *Getting Married*, one sees the link between the short story writer and the dramatist. He is a master in the use of overstatement; and one knows at once he is attacking a sententious and cliché-ridden society by the abrupt use of the offhand, natural voice:

They had been married for ten years. Happily? As happily as circumstances allowed.

or:

The couple met at dinner and at night, and it was a true marriage, a union of souls, and of two bodies into the bargain, but this they never mentioned, of course.

[829]

A young wife is fretting because she is not pregnant. The husband

> . . . had a confidential talk with his wife, and she went to see a doctor. Bang! Six weeks later the trick worked.

The word 'Bang' – used by many translators – seems to come, with a grin, from Strindberg the sportsman but it also shows his sense of theatre. A singer begins to get fat and to lose her audience – this is from 'The Tobacco Shed':

> She really began to get somewhat corpulent. She began so slowly and cautiously that she did not notice it herself until it was too late. Bang! You go downhill fast, and this descent took on a dizzying speed . . . the more she starved the fatter she got.
>   'It wasn't fat,' said the prompter. 'It was conceit.'

This devilish, grinning abruptness gives his stories a swinging elation. In play writing and story, the cutting from outside to inside the people has to be drastic and fast. There is no doubt of Strindberg's enormous talent; so that, in these stories, when he moves from one marriage to the next, one finds that as a realist with a message Strindberg is at ease in his mixture of the pugnacious, the pitying and the revealing.

Mary Sandbach says that Strindberg's misogyny has been overstressed; that he is as much concerned with the false values of a powerful upper merchant class which produces the unbending man and the cunning, idle female. His attack on 'Amazonian' women who wish to have careers or non-domestic interests is rooted in deep private jealousy of them – as in his first marriage – but he is talking of women who are 'idle' only because they have a huge supply of working-class girls as servants.

The message in the first series of the stories is that men *and* women must be liberated. In the second series, the excellent little scenes of life in town and country, the delight in the sea journeys and outings which bring out his high quality as an imaginative writer give way to arid, harsher analysis and polemic. But in the first part of one tale, 'The Payment', one gets that compelling and shrewd power of social analysis which D. H. Lawrence was to take further. The story is a full statement of Strindberg's case: the stifling of the sexual instincts leads women to use sex as a weapon, so that the men become the slaves while the women grasp occupational power outside the home. It must be read in the context of nineteenth-century life, but it approaches the Lawrence of 'St Mawr'.

Hélène, the young woman in the story, is the daughter of a general. In her home she sees the exaggerated artifices of respect paid to women and grows up to regard all males as inferiors.

> When she rode she was always accompanied by a groom. When it pleased her to stop to admire the view, he stopped too. He was like her shadow. She had no idea what he looked like, or whether he was young or old. If anyone had asked his sex she would not have been able to answer, for it never occurred to her that a shadow could have any sex.

One day she is out riding in the country alone – she in fact hates nature; it makes her 'feel small' – and when she gets off her mare the animal bolts off to mate with a stallion before her eyes. She is shocked and disgusted. In the next phase she takes to the out-of-date library in her father's house and becomes infatuated with Mme de Staël's *Corinne*, and this leads her

> . . . to live in an aristocratic dream world in which souls live without bodies . . . This brain-fever, which is called romanticism, is the gospel of the rich.

After the horse-riding episode, the analysis of the mind of a frigid, proud and ambitious girl as it grows degenerates into an essay, but it is nevertheless very thorough and alive. As Mary Sandbach says, 'For Payment' comes so close to the portrait of Hedda Gabler that many critics thought Ibsen must have read it. In the end Hélène marries in order to trade on her scholarly husband's political reputation and get herself into public life: she is a recognisable high-bourgeois female type.

I think Mary Sandbach is right in disagreeing with those critics who say it is incredible that Hélène's husband should submit to her rule even though, sexually, she has swindled him. This would be exactly in Strindberg's own character but – more important – there have been many observable and well-known instances of this armed frigidity since his day. Strindberg, the impossible, sincerely loved the recalcitrant woman, even if he reserved the right to take it out on her and then, with chronic masochism and double-mindedness, to crawl back for forgiveness. Strindberg's story fails not because it is false – emancipated groups, classes or individuals are often likely to be tyrannical and reactionary when they get power, as every revolution has shown – but simply because in the later part of this story the artist has been swallowed up by the crude polemical journalist. He has turned from life to the case book. Trust the tale, not the case history.

The original artist in Strindberg survives in his imaginative autobiographies, in the powerful and superbly objective and moving account of his breakdown in *Inferno*; in certain plays, and in the best of these stories. In many of these, a curious festive junketing, a love of good food and drink, a feeling for the small joys of Swedish life, and the spirit of northern carnival, break through. In 'Needs Must', the story of a bachelor schoolmaster who runs into a midsummer outing in the country and is eventually converted to a marriage which is very happy – 'no part of this story', says Strindberg drily – Strindberg suddenly flings himself into the jollities of the trippers. The schoolmaster listens to the accordion and 'it was as if his soul were seated in a swing that had been set in motion by his eyes and ears'. It is a story that contains one of his happiest 'Bangs':

> Then they began to play Forfeits, and they redeemed all their forfeits with kisses, real kisses bang on the mouth, so that he could hear the smack of them. And when the jolly bookkeeper had to 'stand in the well' and was made to kiss the big oak tree, he did so with comical lunacy, putting his arm round the thick trunk and patting it as one does a girl when no one is looking, that they all laughed uncontrollably, for they all knew what you do, though no one would have wanted to be caught doing it.

If there is elation in the black Strindberg it springs like music out of his sunny spells. One is always compelled by something vibrant and vital in him. He is a bolting horse whatever direction he takes; and, as Mary Sandbach says, he brought new life to Swedish prose by his natural voice and his lively images. He was, as some have said, a cantankerous Pietist or Anabaptist turned inside out. His lasting contribution was his liberation of the language. The reader feels zest of that at once.

Estranged

===

At the beginning of his 'Investigations of a Dog', Kafka wrote – in Willa and Edwin Muir's translation –

> When I think back and recall the time when I was still a member of the canine community, sharing in all its preoccupations, a dog among dogs, I find on closer examination that from the very beginning I sensed some discrepancy, some little maladjustment, causing a slight feeling of discomfort which not even the most decorous public functions could eliminate; more, that sometimes, no, not sometimes, but very often, the mere look of some fellow dog of my own circle that I was fond of, the mere look of him, as if I had just caught it for the first time, would fill me with helpless embarrassment and fear, even with despair.

The flat bureaucratic style strikes one as being a mask: Kafka notoriously did not know where he belonged. He was a Jew not quite in the Christian world; as a non-practising Jew – at the beginning anyway – he was not quite at home among Jews. The German critic Günther Anders, from whom I take these remarks, goes on:

> As a German-speaking Czech, [Kafka is] not quite among the Czechs; as a German-speaking Jew not quite among the Bohemian Germans. As a Bohemian he does not quite belong to Austria. As an official of a workers' insurance company, not quite to the middle class. Yet as the son of a middle-class family not quite to the working class.

In his family he wrote that he is 'more estranged than a stranger' and at the office he is alien because he is a writer. In love he is in conflict with literature. Because he was an extreme case which was exacerbated by fatally bad health, Kafka was able to enlarge, as by a microscope, the sense of exile which becomes visible as a characteristic of our experience in this century, its first martyr to 'alienation' which has become something of a cult.

When we turn from his books to his letters we have a series of self-portraits desperate and courageous, always eager and warm in feeling; the self is lit by fantasy and, of course, by drollery. His candour is of the kind that flies alongside him in the air. He was a marvellous letter writer. For these reasons alone the present translation of the *Briefe* first published in 1958 and collected by his great friend Max Brod is worth having. Richard and Clara Winston, the American translators, tell us that it is based on that volume and it is not clear to me whether 'based' means the whole or a selection from that volume – I fancy, the whole. (Other parts of Kafka's large correspondence have been translated, notably the important *Letters to Felice* by James Stern and Elisabeth Duckworth in 1973.) The present volume does contain now the full text of his long letter explaining his break with Julie Wohryzek to her sister, and the whole of the long letter to his parents a few days before he died in 1924 at the age of forty-one. There are also a few letters (of slight interest) to Martin Buber.

We hear the authentic Kafka when he is writing in a girl's album that words cannot carry memories because they are 'clumsy mountaineers and clumsy miners'; or to a fellow student when he is nineteen:

> When we talk together, the words are hard; we tread over them as if they were rough pavement. The most delicate things acquire awkward feet . . . When we come to things that are not exactly cobblestones or the *Kunstwart* [a cultural magazine, of Nietzschean tendency, edited by a nephew of Richard Wagner: another kind of paving], we suddenly see that we are in masquerade, acting with angular gestures (especially me, I admit), and then we suddenly become sad and bored . . . You see, we're afraid of each other, or I am.

Later on, letters are comparable to 'mere slashings of the waves on different shores: the waves do not reach one'. In 1916, quick to admit that his stories are painful, he adds proudly that he wants to be 'truly a man of his time'. In 1922 when his many illnesses have united to become the fatal tuberculosis of the larynx, he writes to Robert Klopstock, the young medical student who was often with him in his last years, that he wants no indissoluble bonds, beyond the tacit, with men or women:

[834]

Is there anything so strange about this anxiety? A Jew, and a German besides, and sick besides, and in difficult personal circumstances besides – those are the chemical forces with which I propose to straightaway transmute gold into gravel or your letter into mine, and while doing so remain in the right.

That may sound bitter, but he is really thinking about his role as a writer of fables who reverses the classic manner of fable in order to be truly that man of his time. Again:

The writer . . . is a scapegoat of mankind. He makes it possible for men to enjoy sin without guilt, almost without guilt.

He sways between assertion and qualification, between reaching out to the gold of friendship and retiring into defensive strategies. They are necessary, especially in his relations with women, in order to pursue literature and nothing else. Such manoeuvres have a sick man's pedantry, but in fact the self-irony, the kindness, the nimbleness, the fantasy, mask the pain. When it is certain that he is terribly ill he begs that this shall be kept from his parents and adds that his

earthly possessions have been on the one hand increased by the addition of tuberculosis, on the other hand somewhat diminished.

He imagines a battle of words going on between brain and lungs; talks of clinging to the disease like a child to the pleats of his mother's skirts. During a longish period at the house of his beloved sister Ottla at the village of Zürau he is plagued by country noises. A girl plays the piano across the street, children scream, men chop down trees, next comes the scream of the circular saw, then the loading of logs onto an ox wagon, the noise of the oxen, the shunting of the trains going away. A tinsmith starts hammering. Noise, he says, is the scaffolding within which he works; perhaps in the end, he says, noise is a fascinating narcotic. And then the house is alive with mice and the long half-farcical, half-obsessional drama continues for many letters. The creatures race round the room – he has the fancy that he can frighten them off by making his eyes glow like a cat's. He gets a cat in, the cat shits in his slippers; when the cat quietens the mice he still sits up half the night 'to take over a portion of the cat's assignment.'

Certainly this fear, like an insect phobia, is connected with the unexpected, uninvited, inescapable, more or less silent, persistent, secret aim of these creatures, with the sense that they have riddled the surrounding walls through and through with their tunnels and are lurking within, that the night is theirs . . . Their smallness especially, adds another dimension to the fear they inspire.

We see by his speculations about a Mouse Sanatorium that he is on the edge of one of his breakdowns and that soon he will once more find himself in hospital.

In love, Kafka sought perfection, knowing that it was an impossibility; knowing also the ideal served as a defence as ingenious as an insurance company's refusal to admit a claim. The most honest statement of this defence is in the long letter to Julie's sister, a confessional document of pitiless and subtle self-searching and, as always, frankly expressing his guilt – elsewhere he said that guilt so easily turned to nostalgia. The sincerity, and above all the sensibility to friendship, in letters to women, give them a spontaneous grace. The self he is preserving is in no way hard but clearly expatiated. Yet it glows under the friendship he receives and also offers.

As a sick man he is, one might say, negotiating a life which he knows is diminishing. He has the patient's ironical interest in the clinical state of his condition; and when he says, for example, that there is something fundamentally childlike in the Czechs of Prague, he describes a trait many foreigners have noted in the most tormented of all Europe cities, and a quality he shares. There is something of Italo Svevo, who was also partly Jewish, in his exploration of his condition: illness is a kind of second self that has cleverly moved in on him.

There is scarcely anything about the 1914–18 war – illness secluded Kafka – although he does have a few incidental lines about the shortage of food and, afterwards, some anxious joking about German inflation, especially in Berlin. He is even detached about anti-Semitism: this is interesting because it shows how active anti-Semitism was in the early Twenties in Germany; he makes a distinction between the Eastern European and the Western European Jews: the former were beginning to go to Palestine, to which he too was emotionally drawn and from which he withdrew: a spectator.

Kafka's most revealing things come most naturally in the letters to Max Brod, who is the strong, ever active, positive, generous and successful writer. Kafka reads Brod's latest works as they come out, comments on them with enthusiastic interest, and also takes over Brod's marital troubles in the manner of a brother exhaustive in advice. There is a letter to Brod in 1923, written from Berlin-Steglitz, which shows the continuous circling of Kafka's self-awareness:

> It is true that I do not write to you, but not because I have anything to conceal (except to the extent that concealment has been my life's vocation), nor because I would not long for an intimate hour with you, the kind of hour we have not had, it sometimes seems to me, since we were together at the north Italian lakes. (There is a certain point in my saying this, because at the time we had truly innocent innocence – perhaps that's not worth regretting – and the evil powers, whether on good or bad assignments, were only lightly fingering the entrances through which they were going to penetrate some day, an event to which they were already looking forward with unbearable rejoicing.) So if I do not write, that is due chiefly to 'strategic' reasons such as have become dominant for me in recent years. I do not trust words and letters, my words and letters; I want to share my heart with people but not with phantoms that play with the words and read the letters with slavering tongue. Especially I do not trust letters, and it is a strange belief that all one has to do is seal the envelope in order to have the letter reach the addressee safely. In this respect, by the way, the censorship of mail during the war years, years of particular boldness and ironic frankness on the part of the phantoms, has proved instructive.
>
> I forgot to add to my remark above: It sometimes seems to me that the nature of art in general, the existence of art, is explicable solely in terms of such 'strategic considerations', of making possible the exchange of truthful words from person to person.

Letters like this take one straight across the bridge from Kafka's private life into *The Castle* and *The Trial*, both of course unfinished and published after his death. There was a great deal of Swift (whom he read attentively) in Kafka's 'mad' imagination, above all in his habit of seeing people and sensations exactly, microscopically, as objects. He was much taken by

Swift's inflexible remarks on marriage and the bringing up of children. The letters to women have even something of Swift's advisory playfulness, and are all gentle to a degree one would have thought unlikely in a man so self-enclosed, alone, and perhaps even proud, with some delicacy of manner, of being incurable.

A Modern Nihilist

In the most literal sense of the phrase, Genet is a writer who has the courage of his convictions. Out of the lives of criminals, and following a tradition in French literature, he has built an erotic mystique, even a kind of metaphysic. Just as Zola was romantically stimulated by the idea of heredity as a fate, and by sex as a mindless habit of brutal instinct, so Genet is moved by an aspiration to the state of Absolute Evil. One thinks of him as a Vidocq without the gaiety, slipperiness and hypocrisy – a Vidocq who has read Dostoevsky; the autodidact of the jails.

Absolute Evil implies the existence of Absolute Good at the opposite extreme; but there is no sign of that in his writing. Absolute Evil is not the kingdom of hell. The inhabitants of hell are ourselves, i.e. those who pay our painful, embarrassing, humanistic dues to society and who are compromised by our intellectually dubious committal to virtue, which can be defined by the perpetual smear-word of French polemic: the bourgeois. (Bourgeois equals humanist.) This word has long been anathema in France where categories are part of the ruling notion of 'logique'. The word cannot be readily matched in England or America, and simply has associations of the grotesque in Germany. Although 'bourgeois' has a definite place in Marxist hagiography, it is hard to appoint a certain place for it in our empiricism. Some believe that its emotional force in France comes from the violent overthrow of the Commune in 1871. Possibly the self-love, the trim, pedantic obduracy of the French middle class, owes a great deal to its roots in the satisfactions of a successful peasantry. (They got what they wanted after the Revolution and, frugally, what they have they hold.)

Again, there seems to be a Manichaean overtone in discussions about the class: the conflict is between the children of light and the children of darkness. In Genet's novels, his criminals, traitors, male prostitutes, pimps, collaborators and Nazis are known by adjectives that convey light and brightness. Those of us who close his works in anger and disgust at his sacrilege live in the outer darkness of right thinking. Hell is not an extreme; it is in the middle.

Absolutists put their money on Being rather than Action: they are after our souls. If Genet can be said to have mystical claims they are in his interest in the 'dark night' – see the lives of the saints. Genet's murderers and cheats do not emerge. They live out of drama impenetrable to others. For Genet's experiences as a thief, a reformatory boy and burglar, and one who has seen murder (but is not a murderer) have taught him – because he is a gifted man, a sort of poet and rhetorician – that criminals are a stupid, dingy lot of short-sighted morons. Their 'dark night' is really a grey night. Having opted out of society, and narrowed by their monotonous hatreds, they find their momentarily experienced liberty is a wilderness: they long for punishment in the extremely complacent society of prison in which they spend most of their lives if they survive the treacheries of their friends. (Anyone who has had a passing acquaintance with the convicted knows that many consider the wicked are outside of jail.) Genet draws portraits brilliantly in detail with all the passion and *parti pris* of prison society: he admires what can be called the *virtu* of the profession like an aesthete. A good burglar may be self-condemned, but he has pride in his superstitions, his techniques and rituals. Reform is a loss of skill. To be incurable is both a fate and a vanity. He is unknown to loyalty, mercy, pity or charity (i.e., *bonté*).

How does it come about that Genet, a writer so committed to his theme, is able to be without illusions about the criminal? A Sade sees himself as a revolutionary energy; a Dostoevsky, who can so thoroughly abandon himself, for a time, in the idea of 'beyond good and evil,' sees Christ and Salvation. Genet sees nothing. He is a total nihilist, angered by *ennui*. In a really admirable exposition, Richard N. Coe describes him as a lucid schizophrenic and makes a very convincing (and anti-Sartre) case for Genet as one living between those disparate poles that at a touch create the electric spark of poetry. Philip Thody, in a cooler but equally searching work – written, I think, in 1968 – contains a little more biographical material, and suggests, if I read him aright, that Genet was a 'made' criminal and not a born one, relying on Genet's words that he became a thief because he was called a thief. It was the result of shock. And that he was able to 'cure' himself by a truly astonishing discovery of language; he entered not a moral world, but a world of words and images.

It is certainly true that his prose is very fine, and that his virtuosity as a writer is enormous: he proceeds from criminal ritual to the literary, without losing his innate interest in violence. He has a marked humour. The paradox and the ambiguity that floor the critic who tries to formulate Genet's thought are the sparks flying off from the brutal hammer-on-anvil of experience. He was born existential. His work is autobiographical but more forcefully so for anticipating the masks, the disguises, the involvement of the reader, assumed by later writers of the *nouveau roman*.

An important feature, also, is Genet's preoccupation with Things. Things exist, have a magnetism, and are as inciting as persons: the majority of his characters are homosexual, but it is the holster, the belt, the jackboot, the badge, the uniform of the male lover that allure: the picturesque argot of buggery, its unecstatic clinical detail, are themselves like objects in a 'black' museum at police headquarters. It is true there is a passing sexual tenderness and naïveté. Particularly in a book like *Funeral Rites* – which critics think to be a falling off and which shows an ambiguous and provocative attraction to Nazism – one seems to be in a collector's gallery. In defence of this book it must be said we have forgotten the seamy side of the Liberation in Paris.

The poetry of Genet's novels is fragmentary. This has a special force, because of the abrupt and necessarily fragmentary nature of the criminal's life: he never sees beyond his nose as he heads towards punishment or his own death. Genet's virtuosity lies in his management of rapid discursiveness and sudden clinching scenes, in the skill in moving back and forward in time, and in the convincing though arbitrary way in which the author takes himself with a sort of effrontery from the outside to the inside of character. The defects are sudden descents into a banal reflection and in overall pretentiousness. We are not all that far from the idealisation of the criminal. There is a theatrical suggestion – especially in the German references, the hatred of France, and so on – of 'the twilight of the Gods'.

And it is both the originality and the tedium of the writer that his impulse is one of personal revenge. (There are scarcely any women in Genet's novels and although this is due to his homosexuality, which is passive and feminine, it has an obvious root in his rage at being abandoned by his mother, who was a prostitute.) The hymn of hate springs from sterility, though it is relieved by a savage humour and by one or two remarkable big scenes. The locale is always deeply there: I think of the eerie seduction in the Tiergarten, or the horror of the hot stink of shooting, fear and rape in the long rooftop scene in the Paris street-fighting.

Genet is the natural production of an age of violence, a natural cult-figure for those who feel guilty because they have escaped martyrdom. He offers everything to the voyeur in ourselves. Sartre tried to push him into politics but except in his play *The Blacks* that has not borne results. I find the interest in the orgies of disgust in the novels, and the attempt to shock us by half-arguing for Hitler and the Nazis, monotonous as scandals. One gets in the novels something of the self-caressing dreariness and pettiness that date, I suppose, from a much better writer like Restif de la Bretonne. The lack of charity is an appalling defect and one rebels against the claustrophobia. His characteristic material is seen, to my mind, to far better effect in the theatre, simply because the theatre is drastic and has design. The scene in *Funeral Rites* where the drunken Nazi shoots at his Other Self in the mirror is pure theatre.

Genet's rather portentous conceit of the Self, the mirror Self and the Double, works well in the theatre and draws out his extraordinary technical skill. It emphasises the dream or nightmare frame in which his violence is set and which establishes him as an artist as well as a pornographer. *The Maids* is as good as anything in Strindberg's theatre.

Without the aid of commentators like Thody and of Coe I do not get far with the novels. Coe warns us not to stop at the fact that Genet's novels interpret criminal psychology; he tells us to see the symbolism. This puzzles me. Genet's paradoxes and contradictions seem to be native to the poet of violence and not to a thinker. It is a good argument that Genet is a taboo breaker rather than a law-breaker.

What I got from *Funeral Rites*, after its view of the hoodlum temperament and passive homosexuality, was his capacity to evoke a really frightening sadness, the *tristesse* of the incurable. It is a novel about hatred and sex, lived by people grieving in a void or limbo. The void is all the worse for being small, a place – if that is the word – where people exist only as bodies with sexual or bullet holes in them. Coe thinks that there are signs of something more than a factitious virility in Genet's later work. It would be striking to

[842]

see Genet achieving the masculine instinct for responsibility and a sense of proportion, but perhaps this would silence him as a writer. Inside his great vanity, a serious artist is clearly at grips with his conflicts.

Zola's Life

Zola stands in his time, the latter half of the French nineteenth century, when the energies of industrialism and social change throbbed, a time above all of awakened appetites for power. Zola, as we see him from the outside, is Appetite in person, a continuous consumer. Like some powerful locomotive, he eats up facts and lives as if they were so much coal, choking us with enormous clouds of smoke which were both dream and nightmare. This was what his public, on which he kept a close eye, looked for. Their lives were drab. They were looking for dramas of escape, the satisfactions of desires which had been repressed by the work ethic and, being the children of 'Get Rich' Guizot and his educational reforms, they were new to literacy and a little leisure. The scientific pretensions of Zola's Naturalism, his social concern and his half-poetic violence and melodrama, were exactly their meat.

Professor Hemmings's *Life* is the first biography in English for twenty-five years. He has collated the new material now available to scholars and his book is a thoughtful, inquiring and well-written book and commands a very necessary perspective. It puts the light and shade on a complex character whom we had seen only in black and white.

Professor Hemmings's first point is that Zola was a sensational artist in a century which had turned to the novel for its emotions and instruction very much in the way our own mass public turns to the cinema, television and radio. The novel was the medium. Like Dickens of an earlier generation, he went after his public. He was an excellent story-teller with a strong sense of fatality. The mills of Reason grind more dramatically than the mills of God: the fantasies of Zola depend on documentation and a deep concern for Truth and Justice. There *are* comic passages in Zola's novels, but our main impression is of the efficient pistons of the locomotive's seriousness. Yet, *L'Assommoir* (*The Dram Shop*), *La Terre* (*The Land*) and *Germinal* are probably great novels, and *Thérèse Raquin* is the work of an unflinching moralist. What can be held against him is that his subjects become vaguer as they become larger and larger at the end of his career.

Professor Hemmings is careful to see Zola's sensationalism against the background of his passionate liberal beliefs; Zola was no intellectual but he was the bitter enemy of authoritarianism, obscurantism and racial prejudice; he was the forceful man of reason who believed absolutely in the benefits of science; he can be called 'a true heir of the *encyclopédistes* of the eighteenth century . . . He sought to consolidate the achievements of the Enlightenment.' Truth and Justice are his slogans.

But unlike the immensely marketable believer, the man is not all of a piece. Like Balzac, his exemplar, he was an almost perpetual worker, mostly seen grinding at his desk, a fat, sedentary, myopic figure. Unlike Balzac he lacks magnetism; he is even dull, respectable, shy and personally humourless. He certainly makes no attempt to live out his fantasies as Balzac so ruinously did, though he did keep a considerable tonnage of absurd bric-à-brac in the famous house at Médan. Late in middle age, when he broke his long fidelity to his childless wife and took a peasant girl as his mistress, we do indeed see a repressed Zola appear; even so, there is something dogged and planned about the passion. Overeating had made him (and his wife) gross and hypochondriacal; when he was considering the possibility of love for a young girl, he saw he must prepare for the contingency by going on a diet. As thorough here in self-documentation as he was in his career, he undertook this.

What had Zola repressed? When we turn to the account of Zola's remarkable and far more attractive father, we can see what haunted the novelist. Zola *père* was a Venetian of distinguished family, a brilliant, amorous and adventurous mining engineer and a pioneer among the builders of European railways. Heads of governments listened to him. He was far-seeing and practical, but, at the last moment, men more gifted in raising capital either diddled him or took over his work. In early middle age, he died poor in Aix, where he had married a working-class French woman and thereby established his son's kinship with the common people. The son's emotional capital and capacity for living, one would say, had been exhausted by his gifted father, who left him, however, his respect for work and the imaginative intelligence. (One curious connection with his father's life and career as an engineer can be seen in the peculiar dream of tunnelling in *Germinal.*) Literature would be the young Zola's science and industry; his knowledge of working-class poverty and the desire to get out of it were the spur. His sexual temperature was low. His emotions would be absorbed by his simple mother first and then by the able and maternal mistress who became his wife. She also had had to make her own way as an illegitimate child and is thought to have been a florist.

It is a surprise to find that the vigorous, astute and apparently very masculine Zola was a frail and sickly, even rather feminine, young man shut in by anxieties. The violent interest in sex and the lusts of the flesh which give a carnal vividness to his novels was the fantasy of a shy man – it seems – of small performance. His continence in a free-living period was a popular joke among French cartoonists. His imagination was sensual to the point of being pornographic; his life was blameless. Men who have known hunger when they were young are likely to become gluttonous later on, and one can see why an imaginative greed and a dramatic sense of all human hungers appear in his novels: a greed for sex, fame, money and success, for huge novels that are like enormous highly spiced meals. In one of his famous crowd scenes in *Germinal*, the people are described in terms of their hungry mouths. In *L'Assommoir* the mouth is the drinker's mouth. In these scenes there is gaudy poetry which is also visionary.

The visions have – when we turn to his life – a double source. One can trace this first to his early childhood in Aix where he was a happy and intelligent boy until his spirited Italian father died; secondly to the serious, dreaming, hopeful friendship with the young Cézanne when they talked about their genius as they were swimming. (Zola was at this time a better painter than Cézanne.) After the father's death and the family's move to Paris, the struggle against extreme poverty began. The young Zola slaving in a bookshop felt the iron sense of responsibility for the family. This experience and the haunting friendship with Cézanne – their common feeling of the dream of art – formed him. Cézanne was determined on solitude; Zola was cut out for action and publicity. About the latter he was shameless and pushing; when he was savagely attacked he collected the libels as a sort of treasury or capital. The greater feeder chewed them over: they added to his energies.

Professor Hemmings is especially suggestive on the subject of Zola and the Impressionists. One can see how important they were to him, of course, from *L'Oeuvre*, in which Cézanne is one of his models and in the end theatrically dramatised. One can see what the attraction was; the Impressionists too practised a scientific Naturalism in their manner. They were also in revolt against authority; and Zola was the man for a cause. He was fighting for his career and their careers. He knew what poverty and obloquy were. When in middle life he turned against Cézanne it was because Cézanne had not succeeded. At the height of his own career Zola could only pity failure – and perhaps feared failure himself. All this is evident from the correspondence between the two men.

Far more interesting is another suggestion: Mr Hemmings ponders the question of Zola's bad eyesight. A curious personal vanity made him refuse to wear glasses until late in life, and the suggestion is that his poor vision may have prevented him from really *seeing* the pictures of the Impressionists; their prismatic light was created by the accumulation of immense detail which, to Zola, would appear as a vague general mist, dreamlike at first, ultimately muddy. Is this the reason for the vagueness in Zola's crowd scenes, his large-scale images and his poster-like symbolism? On the other hand, vagueness in these painters would come to suggest weakness of purpose and lack of social direction to which Zola the story-teller and social moralist was emphatically hostile. Except for its brilliant account of the crowd at the Salon, *L'Oeuvre* is a naïvely divided book in which Sandoz-Zola presents himself as the truly great artist – successful, responsible, toiling, suffering the agonies of creation: Lantier-Cézanne is the *raté*, who in a preposterous scene which perhaps discloses the hysteria buried in Zola's life is raped by his own wife, renounces his art, destroys his last picture and hangs himself.

It is common for writers, indeed all artists, to sink into depression when they have finished a work, but it is strange that Zola's pessimism at this time took the form of a fantasy of violence and self-destruction. When the man who scarcely left his desk began his liaison with the gentle seamstress his wife had taken into the bourgeois mansion, his guilt once more led to fears of violence. He was convinced that his wife would murder the girl and the two children she bore. Perhaps the idea was, as we would say, very Italian; his imagination perhaps craved the operatic. In prosaic fact, after frightful scenes, the wife refused divorce for she did not want to throw

[847]

away her status as the partner of a famous man, and was peaceably won over by the children. She had none of her own.

It is so much in character that Zola, the prophet of modernity and Naturalism, should have been taken by the craze for photography and, before the affair began, used the seamstress as his first model. His preparation via slimming now received the stimulus of a new form of documentation. Yet as Professor Hemmings says, the very nervousness and solicitude with which he approached the young girl were aspects of his solemn decency. His tenderness for human circumstance is the sign of a serious moral nature. If the theme of the guilty secret now appears in his later works, that simply shows that the great novelists have always used every bit of themselves. His guilt enhances his respectability and when we look between the excesses of his novels we see how moving and true he is about the consolations and responsibilities of everyday life in its work and its humble pleasures. When Madame Zola took an interest in his mistress's children, her husband wrote affectionate letters to her telling her what the children were doing and how once he had tested the little girl on her scripture lessons! Professor Hemmings writes:

> It is hard to decide which is stranger: that Zola should have kept his lawful wife informed about the activities of his children by another woman, or that this obdurate freethinker should have displayed such solicitude for their religious education. In a novel he would never have permitted himself such paradoxes . . .

His melodramas came from another self.

Zola's intervention in the Dreyfus affair – he did not meet Dreyfus until it was all over and found him dim and disappointing – might seem to have a theatrical and even self-publicising motive. In fact *J'Accuse* was the most disinterested act of Zola's life. It brought him great popular abuse and indeed exile. Stronger even than his hatred of anti-Semitism was his loathing of corrupt authority, the covering up by professional groups, the tricks of the High Command, the judges, the politicians and self-serving bureaucracy. Zola was unbendable in his stand for truth-telling and the principles of the law. His tenacity is amazing. He acted as a citizen, not as a novelist, and stood firm against the considerable mass of people who were opposed to him. There is a story that when years later he died of asphyxiation caused by the fumes from the stove in his study, an anti-Semitic workman confessed to having closed the ventilator in the chimney as an act of revenge. The tale has never been confirmed; it sounds too Zola-esque to be true, but it is certainly possible.

And Lélia

The spell imposed by George Sand on European and Russian readers and critics in the nineteenth century is understandable; her people and landscapes are silhouettes seen in streams of sheet lightning. For ourselves, what has been left is her notorious life story and the throbbing of her powerful temperament. Yet Balzac, Dostoevsky and – of all people – Matthew Arnold admired her as a novelist. Proust admired her sinuous and gliding prose and Flaubert her exotic imagination. There she was pouring out ink in her sixty novels, her enormous autobiography, her works of travel and her thousands of letters; a thinking bosom and one who overpowered her young lovers; all sibyl, teacher, a Romantic, and, in the end, a respectable Victorian moralist.

There were hostile voices of course. As Curtis Cate reminds us in his exhaustive biography published four years ago, Baudelaire burst out with an attack on what had most allured her admirers:

> She has always been a moralist. Only, previously she had indulged in anti-morality. She has thus never been an artist. She has the famous flowing style dear to the bourgeois. She is stupid, she is ponderous, she is long-winded: she has in moral judgments the same depth of judgment and the same delicacy of feeling as concierges and kept women.

(These last two words are wildly wrong: one thing she certainly was not was a pampered courtesan. She spent the large sums of money she earned extravagantly and a large part in charity.) Shuddering at her candour Henry James was closer to her in his judgment on her talents. Her novels, he said, had turned faint,

> as if the image projected, not intense, not absolutely concrete – failed to reach completely the mind's eye . . . The wonderful change of expression is not really a remedy for the lack of intensity, but rather an

aggravation of it through a sort of suffusion of the whole thing by the voice and speech of the author . . . [There is] a little too much of the feeling of going up in a balloon. We are borne by a fresh cool current and the car delightfully dangles, but as we peep over the sides we see things – as we usually know them – at a dreadful drop beneath.

The woman who was known for her gifts as a silent listener took to the upper air when she shut herself up at night and became garrulous in ink.

Now, it is evident, an attempt to draw the general reader back to George Sand is under way. The most obvious reason for this is opportunism of the women's liberation kind, where she is bound to be a disappointment to those who look for a guru. A disconcerting sibyl she may have been; as a priestess she hedged. The Saint-Simonians were discouraged when they tried to turn her into the Mrs Eddy of free love. A more interesting lure to contemporary taste is suggested by Diane Johnson in her introduction to the novelist's edifying Gothic romance, *Mauprat*, written in the 1830s. Mrs Johnson says that if George Sand's temperament was too strong for her writing, temperament was her subject as an artist:

> . . . readers have come to hold in new high regard the truths of the imagination, the romantic principle, the idea that the passionate artist had access to truths and secrets of human nature more interesting than mere dramas of social arrival.

Gothic melodrama is back with us, if in dank condition, 'for reasons best understood today in terms of psychology, but understood very well by George Sand in universal terms'. (The universal is the trouble.) It is true, at any rate, that the Romantics – especially those of the second wave, the *Hernani* generation – set the artist apart as the supreme seer in society; and that for all their extravagance of feeling and even because of it, they were excellent pre-Freudian psychologists. Their very violence is a prediction and their inflation of the ballooning self makes it dramatic and macroscopic. We have to add that she is shamelessly autobiographical. The love affair of the week, month or year, along with mysticism, socialism and The People, was transposed into the novel that promptly followed; she spoke of herself as 'the consumer' of men and women too, and the men often turned out to be projections of herself. The passions of her characters, their powerful jealousies, their alternations of exaltation and gloom, were her own. She was half Literature.

Her finer powers emerged when her fame as a novelist declined, above all in her *Histoire de ma vie*, in her lively travel writing and her letters. In her letters there is no need of Gothic castles or dreadful ravines: her mundane experience was extraordinary enough in itself. As a traveller she had eyes, ears and verve. The short pastoral novels *La mare au diable* (*The Haunted Pool*) or *François le Champi* (*The Country Waif*) are serene masterpieces drawn from her childhood and her love of nature, which awakened her senses as they awakened Colette's. She was close to the peasants of Nohant. The self is in these tales, but it is recollected or transposed in tranquillity – in her own early life she had known what it was to be a waif, albeit a very fortunate one. These works have never lost their quiet, simple, truth-telling power and we understand why Turgenev, Henry James, and, later, Malraux praised them.

George Sand was the child of one of Napoleon's well-born officers. He was a descendant of the great Maréchal de Saxe and therefore, on the wrong side of the blanket, of the King of Poland. Her mother was a plebeian woman, the hot-tempered daughter of a Paris innkeeper and bird fancier. The inner class conflict enriched both George Sand's exuberant imagination and those sympathies with the poor which took her into radical politics; strangely like Tolstoy – but without his guilt or torment – she turned to presenting the peasantry not as quaint folk or a gospel, but as sentient, expressive beings. She listened to the curious Berrichon dialect and translated it, without folkish affectations or condescensions, into a truthful expression of plain human feeling. She had the humility and concern to discard dramatic earnestness without losing her psychological acumen or her art as a story-teller who keeps her people in focus as the tradition of Pastoral does; very often her best work is a gloss on traditional forms.

In the feminist foreground of the present revival is *Lélia*, the confessional novel which she wrote at the age of twenty-nine in 1833 after the rebellion against her marriage, the break with Jules Sandeau, and the disastrous attempts to obtain sexual pleasure from an expert like Mérimée, or from any other man as far as we know. Chopin said she loved extremely but was incapable of making love. Partly because of its attacks on the

Church and the marriage system, the male hold on property and the double standard, partly because of its erotic revelation and the rumour of a lesbian attachment to the actress Marie Dorval, the book itself was attacked for outrageous and morbid candour. Lélia is intended to be a Romantic heroine, a doomed but indomitable soul, one pursuing a mystical quest for spiritual love. She is beautiful, intellectual, independent, yet tormented by a sensuality that is nevertheless incapable of sexual happiness. She cannot be a nun like Santa Teresa nor can she be a courtesan or married woman. The dreams of a poetically exalted adolescence have divorced the heart from the body. Literature has paralysed her. She says of a lover:

When I was near him I felt a sort of strange and delirious greed which, taking its source from the keenest powers of my intelligence, could not be satisfied by any carnal embrace. I felt my bosom devoured by an inextinguishable fire, and his kisses shed no relief. I pressed him in my arms with a superhuman force, and fell next to him exhausted, discouraged at having no possible way to convey to him my passion. With me desire was an ardour of the soul that paralysed the power of the senses before it awakened them. It was a savage fury that seized my brain and concentrated itself there exclusively. My blood froze, impotent and poor, before the immense soaring of my will . . .

When he was drowsy, satisfied, and at rest, I would lie motionless beside him. I passed many hours watching him sleep. He seemed so handsome to me! There was so much force and grandeur on his peaceful brow. Next to him my heart palpitated violently. Waves of blood mounted to my face. Then unbearable tremblings passed through my limbs. I seemed to experience again the excitation of physical love and the increasing turmoil of desire. I was violently tempted to awaken him, to hold him in my arms, and to ask for his caresses from which I hadn't yet known how to profit. But I resisted these deceiving entreaties of my suffering because I well knew it wasn't in his power to calm me.

The stone images of Catholic 'palaces of worship' give no comfort, for her imagination responds chiefly to the figurations of medieval nightmare: scaly serpents, hideous lizards, agonised chimeras and emblems of sin, illusion and suffering. Sublimation has two faces:

When the red rays of the setting sun played on their forms, I seemed to see their flanks swell, their spiny fins dilate, their faces contract into new tortures . . . While I contemplated these bodies engulfed in masses of stone, which the hand of neither man nor time had been able to dislodge, I identified myself with these images of eternal struggle between suffering and necessity, between rage and impotence.

The nightmares of the unconscious haunt the aspirant. And we are warned that when spring comes to stir the senses, all attempt to deny the calyx or the bud, by the study of botany, or to turn to science, will not annul the ferment of the imagination. As always in George Sand, poetic observation and imagery is rather fine: but the inevitable tutorial follows.

I take these passages from Maria Espinosa's translation. She has worked on the 1833 edition which George Sand toned down three years later. This early edition has not been done into English until now, and the version is remarkable for coming very close to the resonant vocabulary and its extraordinary physical images. If there is a loss it is because English easily droops into a near-evangelical tune; our language is not made for operatic precisions and we have a limited tradition of authorised hyperbole. Abstractions lose the intellectual formality that has an exact ring in French.

It is important to remember, also, that George Sand's prose feeds on a sensibility to music which dated from her childhood: she was alert to all sounds in nature and to all delicacies and sonorities of voice and instrument. (Her novels might be described as irresistible overtures to improbable operas which are – as they proceed – disordered by her didactic compulsion.) *Lélia*, I think, rises above this, because it is so personal and arbitrary in its succession of sounds and voices, and we are bounced into accepting the hyperbole as we would be if it were sung, though we may be secretly bored by the prolonging of the moans.

In *Lélia* we listen to five voices: there is the voice of Sténio, the young poet lover whom Lélia freezes with platonic love: she is an exalted *allumeuse*; there is Trenmor, the elderly penitent gambler and stoic – her analysis of the gambler's temperament is the best thing in the book: George Sand was at heart a gambler – there is Magnus, the fanatic priest who is made mad by the suppression of his sexual desires and who sees Lélia as a she-devil; there is Pulchérie, Lélia's sister, a genial courtesan living for sexual pleasure; and Lélia herself, defeated by her sexual coldness, horrified by the marriage bed, the mocker of a stagnant society, religion and the flesh. She is sick with self-love and her desires approach the incestuous: she seeks weak men who cannot master her, to whom she can be either a dominating mother, sister or nurse.

In chorus these voices sing out the arguments for and against spiritual love. As in opera, the plot is preposterous and scenes are extravagant and end without warning. Pulchérie introduces a pagan and worldly note and also – it must be said – the relief of more than a touch of nature. She reminds the miserable Lélia of a charming incident in their childhood when the beauty of Lélia troubled her as they lay sleeping on the mossy bank dear to Romantic fiction. Pulchérie says:

> Your thick, black hair clung to your face, and the close curls tightened as if a feeling of life had clenched them next to your neck, which was velvet with shadow and sweat. I passed my fingers through your hair. It seemed to squeeze and draw me toward you . . . In all your features, in your position, in your appearance, which was more rigid than mine, in the deeper tint of your complexion, and especially in that fierce, cold expression on your face as you slept, there was something masculine and strong which nearly prevented me from recognizing you. I found that you resembled the handsome young man with the black hair of whom I had just dreamed. Trembling, I kissed your arm. Then you opened your eyes, and your gaze penetrated me with shame . . . But, Lélia, no impure thought had even presented itself to me. How had it happened? I knew nothing. I received from nature and from God my first lesson in love, my first sensation of desire.

The scenes of Lélia's despair take place inevitably in an abandoned monastery, with its debris that suggest the horrors of death and the futility of existence. Lélia says:

> At times I tried to find release by crying out my suffering and anger. The birds of the night flew away terrified or answered me with savage wailings.

(Nature always responds to George Sand.)

[855]

The noise echoed from vault to vault, breaking against those shaky ruins; and the gravel that slid from the rooftops seemed to presage the fall of the edifice on my head.

That gravel, it must be said, is excellent observation. Her comment is typically orchestral:

Oh, I would have wished it were so! I redoubled my cries, and those walls echoed my voice with a more terrible and heart-rending sound. They [the ruins] seemed inhabited by legions of the damned, eager to respond and unite with me in blasphemy.

These terrible nights were followed by days of bleak stupor.

A scene of Oriental luxury was indispensable to the Romantics: the looting of Egypt was Napoleon's great gift to literature. There is the fantastic ball given by Prince Bambuccj in which lovers can disappear into boudoirs and artificial caves as busily as bees. The trumpets, one must say, acclaim the triumphs of fornication; they are gorgeously brazen in the lascivious scene; the perfumes are insidious. Pulchérie and Lélia are masked and Lélia plots to pass off Pulchérie as herself so that Sténio is deceived into thinking his cold mistress has relented. He awakens and is shattered by the deceit. He stands at the window of the palace and hears the voice of Lélia mocking him – in a somewhat classy way – from a pretty boat that floats by in the Asiatic lagoon. This is an operatic scene of a high order. Calamity, of course. Having tasted flesh, Sténio becomes a drunken debauchee and eventually commits suicide. If he starts, in real life, as the innocent Jules Sandeau, he ends as the drunken Musset. Magnus, the mad priest, is now sure that Lélia is possessed by a devil and strangles her. With a rosary, of course. One recalls that Lélia has had fantasies of strangulation.

Lélia is one of those self-dramatisations that break off as mood follows mood. She asks what God intended for men and women: whether he intended them to meet briefly and leave each other at once, for otherwise the sexes would destroy each other; whether the hypocrisy of a bourgeois society is the enemy; whether intellectual vision must be abnormal; whether poetry and religion corrupt. All the voices are George Sand herself – and very aware, as she frankly said, that she belonged to a generation which, for the moment, was consciously out to shock. What she did not expect was laughter. She had little sense of humour.

One can see how much of the book comes out of Hoffmann and even more precisely from Balzac's equally chaotic and melodramatic *La Peau de chagrin*. Lélia, it has often been noted, is the female Raphaël de Valentin. Both writers feel the expanding energies of the new century; both have the confident impulse towards the Absolute and to Omniscience; but hers is the kind of imagination and intellect that breaks off before suggesting a whole. Balzac and Sand were both absorbed by an imaginative greed; they worked themselves to the bone, partly because they were like that, partly because they created debts and openly sought a vast public. Their rhetoric was a nostalgia for the lost Napoleonic glory.

How thoroughly she toiled in her social-problem novels! The tedious *Compagnon du Tour de France* is a garrulous study of the early trade unions, a politically pious book, enlivened by her strong visual sense. In the far more sympathetic *Mauprat* she goes to the heart of her life-long debt to Rousseau: the young brutal Mauprat who belongs to the brigand and mafioso branch of an aristocratic family rescues the aristocratic heroine from his gang – but with the intention of raping her on the quiet. She frustrates the attempt and is shown redeeming her brute: to love he must pass through a long psychological re-education. This is achieved but not entirely in a sentimental way; both he and the women are hot-tempered, sulky and sensitive to points of honour.

George Sand herself did not think we should be punished for our sins or our grave faults of character, but that we were called upon to learn from them: they were – *grâce à* Rousseau – opportunities for interesting self-education and reform. She is not a doctrinaire like Gorky in his Communist phase. Her advantage as a woman is that she is a psychologist who gives hostilities their emotional due: they are indications of the individual's right to his temperament. She may have been a domineering, ruthless woman and very cunning and double-minded with it, but there is scarcely a book that is not redeemed by her perceptions, small though they may be.

She understands the rich very well – 'There are hours of impunity in château life' – and she thinks of the poor as individuals but flinches from them as a case. Two words recur continually in her works: 'delirium,' which may be ecstatic, bad, or, more interestingly, a psychological outlet;

[857]

and 'boredom' – energy and desire had been exhausted. One can see that she is woman but not Woman. The little fable of *François de Champi* shows that she used every minute of her life; for not only was she in a fortunate sense a waif, as I have said, but an enlightened waif; and we note that when François grows up he marries the widow who has been a mother to him. Most of George Sand's men were waifs in one way or another; the Higher Incest was to be their salvation. Women were the real power figures, whereas men were consumable. She liked to pilfer their brains.

She certainly sought only gifted men who were usually sick and with whom she could assume the more powerful role of mother and nurse. Chopin was her 'child'. Sandeau was her 'little brother'. What about Michel de Bourges, her proletarian lawyer and Christian Communist, who almost converted her to the need for violent revolution and the guillotine? Here was a virile man, and he could offer oratory, notoriety, and powerful embraces, but he was in bad health, too; she became frenzied – but was it the frenzy she desired? It may have been. She defiantly walked the streets of his native town in trousers and smoking her pipe, enjoyed the scandal, and caused scenes between him, his wife and his fat mistress. He was a tyrant, and one might think this was what she sought. Not at all. *She* could not dominate *him*; despite her passion for him, which drove her to ride for miles at night for a short, Chatterley-like tryst, he could not subdue the strongest thing in her – her intellect.

Michel de Bourges was responsible for her wordy novels of social revolt, but he could not break her opposition to the utilitarian view of art. Like all the Romantics, she believed in the vision of the artists as the unique and decisive spiritual force in society. He might dismiss all this as a self-regarding bourgeois delusion, but she would not yield. All the same, she wrote propaganda for the republican cause in '48, and when the reaction came she handed out money to the hunted proletarian poets and took advantage of acquaintance with Louis Napoleon to get her friends and fellow-writers out of jail. In Nohant, she was a scandal because of her lovers. The villagers imagined orgies when the young men came and went. After '48, she was a political scandal. The obsequious villagers touched their caps but sneered behind her back. This did not disturb her. She was a country girl at heart and knew that revolution was an urban industrial notion; in the countryside it meant nothing. And, in fact, the country crowd, particularly the women, took her side when the husband she had deserted made two savage and incompetent efforts in court to get Nohant from her.

This episode is thoroughly gone into by Mr Cate. It is important, for it brings out where she stood – or wobbled – on the crucial question of marriage and free love. The two court actions have the inevitable air of comedy: Michel de Bourges was her lover and her advocate, yet she had to appear respectable and demure. No trousers and no pipe now; she appeared in shawl and bonnet. An absurd but useful opportunity occurred for her to ascend astutely into the upper air when questions of adultery and free love were brought up. Those exalted ladies of the Saint-Simonian persuasion came to address her as a priestess. They invited her to become a 'mother' of the Saint-Simonian 'family', or phalanstery, and even sent a load of handmade presents, which included shoes, trousers, waistcoats, collars, one watercolour and a riding crop. In reply, she recommended them to practise the ancient morality of faithful marriage for 'being the most difficult, [it] is certainly the finest', though she would not blame those who shook themselves free of tyranny, which was the product of a false society. The fact is that for her, as for her fellow-Romantics, the just society already existed metaphysically, and that in this sense she was chaste. And she was no fool. She *was* temporarily chaste with her lawyer, but at home, at Nohant, she kept another pretender, whom she was maddening with the kisses of platonic affection. This was Charles Didier, a Genevan, and Mr Cate differs from André Maurois's judgment in his opinion of his character. How far they went, no one knows; to judge by his tortured 'Journal', Didier himself seems unsure. All he could report was hugs that seem maternal. It is nearly impossible to translate the language of the Romantics, but in reply to one of his injured letters George Sand is masterly. She could easily squash rancour:

You don't love, all I can do is love. Friendship for you is a contract with clauses for the well-combined advantage of both parties, for me it is sympathy, embrace, identity, it is the complete adoption of the qualities and faults of the person one feels to be one's friend . . . You attribute to me . . . a calculated dryness, how shall I put it? – something worse, a kind of prostitution of the heart, full of baseness, egotism, falseness, you

[859]

make me out to be a kind of platonic slut . . . My misfortune is to throw myself wholeheartedly at each fine soul I encounter . . . What I took for a noble soul is a gloomy, sickly suspicious soul that has lost the ability to believe and thus to love.

Honesty or sophistry? Goodness knows. Better to call it incantation. Didier was soon forgotten. The loss of Michel de Bourges looked fatal to her reason, but she was quickly, so to say, back in the saddle. An amusing actor arrived, and there was soon a troupe of young men, all hoping to be the favourite.

And, distributing her kisses, back to her room she went for her nightly five- or six-hour stint on the next novel. The blood – her own and that of others – was turned into ink. We remember the cold words of Solange, the daughter who was no less wilful than herself: 'It would take a shrewd fellow to unravel the character of my mother.'

The Quotidian

───────

Although marred by affectations of style, Professor Brombert's study of the themes and techniques of Flaubert's novels is a full and very suggestive scrutiny of Flaubert's love-hate of realism, as it is woven into the texture of his narratives. Flaubert's own ambiguities on the subject are clear. 'I abhor what has been called realism, although they make me out to be one of its high priests,' he wrote to George Sand. He hated reality. (Or rather it disgusted him; that is also an attraction.) Art held priority over life. If so much of his work is minutely drawn from everyday life, he forced himself to depict it (in Professor Brombert's words):

> partly out of self-imposed therapy to cure himself of his chronic idealism, partly also out of a strange and almost morbid fascination . . . Art for him was quite literally an escape . . . For hatred of reality . . . was intimately bound up with an inherent pessimism – and pessimism in turn was one of the prime conditions of his ceaseless quest for ideal forms.

In resilient moments he called himself an old 'romantique enragé': even, a *troubadour*.

All this is well known; we know an enormous amount about Flaubert and Professor Brombert brings all the important critics into his net. But, a good deal owing to Marxist and Christian criticism, the quite gratuitous notion has got about that Flaubert was not what he ought to have been. He ought not to have been 'an alienated bourgeois'; yet, surely, a vast number of great artists have been 'alienated' from their dispensation and especially in the nineteenth century. Alienation is a cant term for a necessary condition. The 'hatred' of Balzac, Stendhal, Zola, Flaubert or Proust are the characteristic engines of a century bemused by its own chaotic energies. The force of criticism from an outside position of Marxist, Christian or psychoanalytical neo-conformity is now fading and one is at least heartened to see Professor Brombert applying himself to 'the unique

[861]

temperament and vision that determine and characterize a novelist's work as we find them in the text'.

There can be two weaknesses in this kind of criticism; first it puritanically denies side glances at biography, social influences, etc., and rather hypocritically assumes that we have had these necessities privately at the back door. Professor Brombert is not too strict here; how could one leave out the effect of atheistic medical observation and the morgue on Flaubert's mind? Even Flaubert's obsession with style seems to have something of medical specialisation in it. Secondly, the critic may find too much in the text and build top-heavy theories on images and symbols, as one finds, for example, when this kind of criticism deals with Dickens: all that talk of baptismal water! (I have only one doubt about Professor Brombert's attention to key words: this is when he catalogues the symbols of liquefaction.)

In Flaubert the danger is usually small for he was the most conscious of artists; a most ardent collector of echoes and symbols. His documentary interest in *things* is also a concern with what they tell of the imagination. Things are corrupted or corrupting. He is tortured by the fact that the century has turned mind into matter, the ideal converted into ludicrous or detestable paraphernalia.

Take the matter of the Algerian scarves in *Madame Bovary*. They were coming into fashion with the beginning of French colonisation of North Africa: that is a comment both on bourgeois enterprise and greed, and on the absurdities of provincial taste. It is nearly a comment on the economy of the textile city of Rouen. The nineteenth century will colonise; so, in its fantasies, did the nineteenth-century soul. When Emma turns spendthrift and buys curtains, carpets and hangings from the draper, the information takes on something from the theme of the novel itself: the material is a symbol of the exotic, and the exotic feeds the Romantic appetite. It will lead to satiety, bankruptcy and eventually to nihilism and the final drive towards death and nothingness.

If anyone makes too much of his images, it will be Flaubert himself: for example, the snake, in the snake-like hiss of Madame Bovary's corset lace. It is a melodramatic excess, as one can tell by the eagerness with which the image was seized upon by the lurid and falsifying mind of the prosecuting lawyer when Flaubert was being charged with obscenity. The phrase could well have gone into the *Dictionnaire des idées reçues*. Flaubert's subject is the imagination and particularly of the orgiastic adolescent kind which he never outgrew and which received almost operatic support from an early reading of the Marquis de Sade and the early extremes of the Romantic movement.

How is it that – as it seems to us now – a whole century became adolescent? Is prolonged adolescence characteristic of a new class coming to power? This is not Professor Brombert's interest; but casting an eye on the ominous *Intimate Notebooks 1840–1841* – written when Flaubert was eighteen and already pretending to be twenty – and proceeding through the novels, Professor Brombert is able to show how, exhaustively and like an infected pathologist, Flaubert presented the hunger for the future, the course of ardent longings and violent desires that rise from the sensual, the horrible, and the sadistic. They turn into the virginal and mystical, only to become numbed by satiety. At this point pathological boredom leads to a final desire for death and nothingness – the Romantic syndrome. The *Notebooks* contain eager cries on behalf of adolescent bisexuality; moralise on the ecstatic yet soon-to-be ashy joys of narcissism; pass, without pause, into dreams of exotic travel:

> Often I am in India, in the shade of banana trees, sitting on mats: bayaderes are dancing, swans are fluffing out their feathers on blue lakes, nature throbs with love.

One is struck by the drunken accomplishment of the young diarist, particularly by the precision and clarity of his ingenious self-study at a time of life when one is most likely to be turgid and blind. The son of Dr Flaubert has made notes which a psychiatrist would find useful. How perceptive to write, at that age:

> Sensual pleasure is pleased with itself: it relishes itself, like melancholy – both of them solitary enjoyments . . .

The style has already the élan and excessive conviction which are the startling qualities of his first novel *November*, unpublished in his lifetime. Luckily it has in Frank Jellinek a translator who responded to the youthful yet (again) accomplished puerilities of the writer. This book, above all, contains the emotional source of *Madame Bovary*; it states the imaginative

condition of romantic love, underlines the onanism at the heart of the
fantasy of the virgin whore. The very absurdities of this first novel are
moving, not only because of the afflatus but because of the fidelity to the
course of an emotion that may be extravagant but is precisely recognisable.
What astonishes is Flaubert's understanding of his experience at that age.
Here he begins his career as the doctor who proceeds to diagnosis by
catching the patient's fever first.

We meet one or two of the famous Flaubert obsessions; 'There was one
word which seemed to me the most beautiful of all human words:
"adultery"'; his horror of begetting a child; and passages like:

> Since I did not use existence, existence used me: my dreams wearied me
> more than great labours. A whole creation, motionless, unrevealed to
> itself, lived mute below my life: I was a sleeping chaos of a thousand
> fertile elements which knew not how to manifest themselves nor what to
> be, still seeking their form and awaiting their mould.

As Professor Brombert says, *November* is indispensable to an understanding of *Madame Bovary*, where 'the thousand fertile elements' manifested themselves in the facts of Normandy life. Life is a dream, life is bad
art; only Art, the supreme reverie, can redeem it: Flaubert's pessimism is
clinical and absolute. Or is it? Keeping close to the text, Professor
Brombert tries to make a path through Flaubert's ingenuities, duplicities
and double meanings; and taking a tip from Flaubert's own phrase that it is
stupid to come to conclusions, he points out that Flaubert's pessimism is, at
any rate, resilient. Style may not save us but it is a force.

There are many good things in the discussion of *Madame Bovary*. It is a
novel as complex as the second part of *Don Quixote*: we shall never get to
the bottom of it. For example, there is the question of how Flaubert's
lyrical intention was to consort with the banal, especially in the matter of
speech. In fact Flaubert's impersonality was a fraud: he contrived – since
the book was a work of self-discovery and confession – all kinds of
intrusion. Often openly:

> . . . it is a grave mistake not to seek candour behind worn-out language,
> as though fullness of soul did not at times overflow in the emptiest
> metaphors.

And Professor Brombert comments:

> This feeling that human speech cannot possibly cope with our dreams
> and our grief goes a long way toward explaining why so often, in the
> work of Flaubert, the reader has the disconcerting impression that the
> language of banality is caricatured and at the same time transmuted into
> poetry.

(Yes: the comic is poetry inverted. The effect of pure comedy is poetic.)
Flaubert has the power of transmuting the trivial. He wrote:

> My book will have the ability to walk straight on a hair, suspended
> between the double abyss of lyricism and vulgarity.

As Professor Brombert says, one misses the charity, the 'imperceptible
human tremors' in Flaubert: there is a rift between the sophistication of the
author and the confusion of the characters: but it is the test of a great writer
that he can turn his dilemmas to effect. Flaubert disguises the rift by

> the telescoping of two unrelated perspectives which bestows upon the
> novel a unique beauty. A stereoscopic vision accounts in large part for
> the peculiar poetry and complexity of *Madame Bovary*.

On the subject of the death of Madame Bovary there have been
wearying differences of opinion. To some she has been hounded. To
others she is a silly and disreputable nonentity, her shame not worth the
expense of spirit. To D. H. Lawrence she was crushed by the intellectual
skill that had created her: to others no more than a cold exercise. Yet again,
she has been used by Flaubert to cure himself of his own disease. In fact, as
Professor Brombert shows, the theme and even something of the plot had
been known to Flaubert since his youth. There are no exercises in
literature. I was struck when I last read the novel – as Professor Brombert
was – by the extent of the sympathy with which she is treated. She has,
even when she is mocked, the honesty of an energy. Her periods of
depravity do not single her out as an exceptionally deplorable being, but
rather make her part of the general, glum strangeness of the people around
her. She belongs to Rouen: she is what belonging to a place or a culture
may mean. She is dignified by a real fate – not by the false word 'Fate', one

of the clichés Flaubert derided. Delusion itself dignifies her. The comparison with *Don Quixote* imposes itself: we see

> . . . her terrible isolation, her unquenchable aspiration for some unattainable ideal. Hers are dreams that destroy. But this destructive power is also their beauty, just as Emma's greatness (the word is inappropriate to literal-minded readers) is her ability to generate such dreams . . . at the moment of her complete defeat in the face of reality, she acquires dignity, and even majesty.

And despite the clinical attentions of Flaubert, her fellow adolescent, I can see no force in the criticism that, in drawing her, Flaubert tried to turn himself into a woman: it may be that in putting masculinity into her – as Baudelaire said – Flaubert made her perverse. But perversity is a normal sexual ingredient as well as an article in the Romantic canon. The Romantics were good psychologists.

Professor Brombert's final remarks are new. There is an apparent negation of tragic values in Flaubert! Does he suggest a new form of tragedy, the tragedy of the very absence of Tragedy, a condition familiar to contemporary writers? There is a link between him and ourselves.

> The oppressive heterogeneity of phenomena, the fragmented immediacy of experience, the constant fading or alteration of forms . . .

These are twentieth-century assumptions. Equally important, Flaubert diagnoses the crisis of language.

> The breakdown of language under the degrading impact of journalism, advertisement and political slogans parallels the breakdown of a culture over-inflated with assimilable data.

It leads to the incoherence of *Waiting for Godot*, the triumph of the rigmarole.

My only serious criticism of Professor Brombert concerns his own use of language. It is depressing to find so good a critic of Flaubert – of all people – scattering academic jargon and archaisms in his prose. The effect is pretentious and may, one hopes, be simply the result of thinking in French and writing in English; but it does match the present academic habit of turning literary criticism into technology. One really cannot write of

Flaubert's 'dilection for monstrous forms' or of 'vertiginous proliferation of forms and gestures'; 'dizzying dilation', or 'volitation'; 'lupanar' – when all one means is 'pertaining to a brothel'. Philosophers, psychologists and scientists may, I understand, write of 'fragmentations' that suggest 'a somnambulist and oneiric state'. But who uses the pretentious 'obnuvilate' when they mean 'dim' or 'darkened by cloud'? Imaginative writers know better than to put on this kind of learned dog. The duty of the critic is to literature, not to its surrogates. And if I were performing a textual criticism of this critic I would be tempted to build a whole theory on his compulsive repetition of the word 'velleities'. Words and phrases like these come from the ingenuous and fervent pens of *Bouvard and Pécuchet*

Literary criticism does not add to its status by opening an intellectual hardware store.

An Early Outsider

Stendhal was one of those gamblers for whom the wheel of Fortune turned too late. Ignored by almost everyone except Mérimée and Balzac who considered that *La Chartreuse de Parme* was the most important French novel of their time, he declared, without a trace of self-pity, indeed confident in his blistering vanity, that the wheel would turn 100 years after his death. In fact in forty years the great egotist was justified by Zola. For Zola he was: 'a man composed of soul alone . . . One always feels him there, coldly attentive to the working of his machine. Each of his characters is a psychologist's experiment which he ventures to try on man.' By the beginning of this century Henri Beyle – the figure hidden secretively behind more than 200 pseudonyms who had passed his life as a doubtfully combatant Napoleonic soldier in Italy and Russia, as a travelling and loitering journalist and plagiarising high-class hack, as a dilettante, petty Consul, ugly and coarse in drawing rooms, as a misfiring, theorising lover and a novelist poor in invention who left his great novels abruptly unfinished – had become a cosmopolitan cult.

One important reason for this is that he knew the lasting force of that clear, plain, dry and caustic prose style: and knew that something curt and preposterous in one's style as a person will have its hour. At certain periods of crisis in history and manners an intelligent man is forced to see that a change of style is being born. As a youth growing up in the French Revolution and with youth's need of a persona, he found himself divided between the eighteenth-century idea of 'the man of the world' and the first intimations of Romantic energy. One had to construct a new self. As an aspiring writer he was drawn to the art of his time: stage comedy – but he soon saw that this had become impossible. Stage comedy depended on a stable class system, fixed social values: these had gone with the Revolution and the post-Napoleonic world. He also saw that the novel was the new form to which the audience would respond but that it would impose a crude, impersonal omniscience and would be about 'other people' grouped in their acceptable categories: the novelist is drowned and effaced in other people, whereas he, Stendhal, secretive, addicted to masks and self-defence, was obsessed by his own intelligent private life, his need to begin constructing a Machiavellian and impervious self from the ground up-wards. The egotist lay awake at night, tortured by the question: 'Who am I?' Even more important: 'What shall I make of myself? What is my role? What are the correct tactics?' It is easy to understand why he is the precursor of Romanticism in *La Chartreuse de Parme* and why in *Le Rouge et le Noir* Julien Sorel foreshadows the large population of outsiders and the disaffected formed by the revolutions, wars, social crises, prisons and police states that have revived something of the climate and complacencies of the Napoleonic period. In a recent biography Joanna Richardson says that he was 'a provincial born outside the Establishment, enjoying none of the privileges of birth, wealth or education. His sense of inequality and grievance led him bitterly to make amends. He despised authority, he professed to scorn the nobility and yet – like Julien Sorel – he wanted to conquer the nobility. He ridiculed the dignitaries of the Tuileries, and yet, with monotonous persistence, he tried to ensure himself a barony . . . all his life he was conscious of status.' Yet, of course, the desire to be either Sorel or Fabrice was a deeply imaginative conspiracy that sailed far beyond social or political considerations. The egotist's pursuit of personal happiness – *la chasse du bonheur* – led him to the Romantic idealisation of solitude and reverie, the brief sublime moment.

The biographer of Stendhal is in competition with a perpetual auto-biography – Stendhal has no other subject, in his novels, his letters, his exhaustive *Journal*, in the *Souvenirs d'Egotisme* and *La Vie de Henri Brulard*. He saw himself as a conspiracy. He was given to minute research into the moral history of his attitudes, so the biographer is left chiefly with the problem of deciding where, if ever, the candour ceased to be fantasy or petulance, where calculation in love was coxcombry, and where they were signs of a fatally split nature. There is no doubt that his celebrated hatred of his father and his sensual passion for his mother, who died when he was seven, reiterated the old Oedipus story, but it was political as well. Stendhal despised his father for being a bourgeois lawyer and a supporter of the Bourbons; very early the boy convinced himself that he was a putative aristocrat and yet at the same time a child of the French Revolution. He also despised his father for being a shrewd Dauphinois and a speculator in property, despised him even more for being unsuccessful in this, and resented the loss of a good deal of his inheritance. Stendhal was even jealous of his widowed father's grief, and went on to imagine that, on the mother's side, the family were of Italian origin and that they combined passionate Italian traits with the pride he oddly loved to call *espagnolisme*. Here, rather than in social snobbery, was the root of his aristocratic idea: he felt he belonged to the élite of another age and another country. Yet his truculence covered deep timidity. His temperament was lazy, but he read and worked like a diligent bourgeois. Only those who work, he said, were equipped for the true end of living – the study of the arts and the pursuit of pleasure.

For one who thought himself born into the wrong class, Stendhal was lucky in 'the bastard', 'the Jesuit' (his father) who gave him a decent allowance and sent him to Paris to study. He was lucky also in family friends – the Darus, who took the conceited youth into their house. He refused to go to the École Polytechnique, and they got him a job in the Ministry of War. Stendhal thrived on influence. In a few months, at the age of seventeen, he was commissioned an officer in Napoleon's reserve army in Italy. Italy transfigured him. Italy was freedom; hearing opera for the first time – 'the Scala transformed me'. A lifelong dislike of France – indeed, the pretence that he was not really French – began. He fell in love with Angela Pietragrua, a married woman – older than himself – whom he was too timid to approach; she fulfilled his need for the remote goddess. There were untouched remote goddesses to follow; there was also syphilis, caught in the brothels of Milan, which affected his health for the rest of his life. The only woman he was really devoted to for many years was one of his sisters, and in his letters to her a tutorial figure appears and one begins to see that he is constructing his own system of self-education and behaviour. The outsider is studying and acting out a role, creating a self from scratch; it is defiant, touching and a good deal absurd. In his love affairs – he was determined on seduction – the tactics, the search for a style, the analysis of his amorous campaigns have the fidgetiness of artificial comedy; he spent half his youth putting obstacles in his own way, as Miss Richardson says. In the pursuit of these passions, he believed in the *coup de foudre*: when it occurred, he was paralysed and in tears; if he was encouraged, he fell into long storms of melancholy; if he was victorious, boredom arrived sooner or later, generally sooner. The perpetual cry of this adolescent, whether he is with Napoleon's army in Germany or Russia, whether he is back in Italy, is that he is bored to death. He is one of those who exhaust an experience before the experience occurs – the Romantic malady that becomes a pose and second nature. But if he did not succeed in creating an impenetrable new self and in becoming the superior man of sensibility, he had fitted himself to become a master of comedy in which scornful epigram and abrupt observation go off like rifle shots and leave the dry smell of gunpowder. Each sentence of his plain prose is a separate shock.

The later Romantics were too young for the Napoleonic glory, but in his harsh, sardonic way Stendhal had known it on the battlefield, though not as a fighting officer. From Smolensk he wrote in 1812, when he was twenty-nine:

> How man changes! My former thirst for seeing things is completely quenched, after seeing Milan and Italy, everything repels me by its coarseness . . . In this ocean of barbarity, there isn't a single sound that replies to my soul.

He was thinking of the music of Cimarosa and his love for Angela Pietragrua. When he watched Moscow burning, he had a toothache and read a few lines of *Virginie*, which revived him morally. He had taken the manuscript of his unfinished *Histoire de la Peinture en Italie* with him, read Mme du Deffand, pillaged a volume of Voltaire, whom he detested, and tried to think of the 'score of comedies' he would write 'between the ages of thirty-four and fifty-four' if only his father would die and leave him some money. He shows off to his correspondents, and rescues an early mistress who had married a Russian (she is very 'chilly'), but when the great fire starts he seems to keep his head and to display sang-froid – or so people reported. He was unconsciously collecting the material for the superb Waterloo chapter in *La Chartreuse de Parme*, and one catches its accent. (He was not at Waterloo.) Of the beginning of the retreat he wrote in his diary, as one seeing the scene *staged* for his benefit:

[871]

We broke through the lines, arguing with some of the King of Naples' carters. I later noticed that we were following the Tverskoï, or Tver Street. We left the city, illuminated by the finest fire in the world, which formed an immense pyramid which, like the prayers of the faithful, had its base on earth and its apex in heaven. [Very much like Stendhal's own nature.] The moon appeared above this atmosphere of flame and smoke. It was an imposing sight, but it would have been necessary to be alone or else surrounded by intelligent people in order to enjoy it. What has spoiled the Russian campaign for me is to have taken part in it with people who would have belittled the Colosseum or the Bay of Naples.

An aesthete's comment? Not entirely. It is an introspection we shall see transmuted when we find him examining the illusion of Napoleonic glory. Even before the grand scene the Stendhalian hero is a psychologist. History dished this outsider. He was the victim, he said, of the mediocrity that characterises an age of transition.

There have been two revivals of interest in Stendhal in this century. In the Twenties it was led by Francophiles who used it as a modish attack on the nineteenth century for its denigration of the eighteenth. Stendhal was useful, too, as a distant founder of the parricides' club which thrived after the 1914 war.

The hardness of his ego and his impudence were our admirations; and the 'enclosing reverie' no more than a charming Romantic nostalgia. Stendhal's curt, disabused and iconoclastic manner made the reader of Gide and Proust feel at home. But this movement fizzled out, though it persisted among Beylistes who had a delighted time taping Stendhal's mystifications, footnotes, vanishing tricks, love affairs and changes of address. In the Thirties left-wingers and Catholics were frosty about Stendhal's politics and withering about his atheism: he gleamed like an arid Sahara. When the wheel turned, in a second revival, we could feel ourselves to be in something like a Stendhalian situation. Existentialists found the self-inventing man sympathetic; practitioners of *le nouveau roman* looked to the novel without a centre.

In his *Stendhal: Notes on a Novelist*, Mr Robert Adams says:

Perhaps the most enchanting yet terrifying thing about the heroes of Stendhal is the sense that they define their own beings only provisionally and temporarily, in conflicts of thought and action, in negations; without enemies, they are almost without natures and wither away, like Fabrice, when deprived of danger. I think it is this vision of human nature which allies the novels of Stendhal with the great hollow, reverberant structures of Joyce, and the legerdemain card-houses of Gide; the fact that all systems of thought and feeling are tangential to the nature of their heroes is linked to the circumstances that their central natures are themselves a dark and hollow mystery. From this aspect there is no core or centre to the Stendhal fiction, as there is none to the fiction of Joyce: the more little anagrams and puzzles of correspondence one solves, the less one finds actually being asserted. What the novel means is its shape, its surface, its structure; the arcana of society, like those of thought, are simply emptiness which returns to the surface of life and the solitude of the cynical individual.

Another critic, Victor Brombert, writes in *Stendhal: Fiction and the Themes of Freedom*, that the self-inventing man is a lifelong pursuer of freedom:

Neither is it by coincidence that the greatest ecstasies of life take place behind austere and quasi-monastic walls. Ultimately it is freedom from all worldly ambitions, an almost spiritual elation, that Julien Sorel and Fabrice del Dongo achieve . . . Freedom remains a prisoner's dream, and man's vocation is solitude.

This conclusion certainly fits with Stendhal's view that our greatest happiness is in reverie. But it is important here to recall what he wrote about the purpose of *Lucien Leuwen*: it was to be 'exact chemistry: I describe with exactitude what others indicate with a vague and eloquent phrase'. The poetry is to be in the chemistry. Love is a consciously produced effervescence; it produces its transcendant, chemical moment of '*bonheur*'; then the beautiful experiment vanishes. One returns to contemplation until the next 'moment'. And it strikes one, especially when he abruptly creates his unbelievable and preposterous scenes – in this novel the affair of a faked childbirth before witnesses – that his model for the novel was opera, the failure to invent the plausible, or perhaps a success in rising above it.

Yet a political novel like *Lucien Leuwen* is saturated in the social material it offers. It is rich in people who have been 'placed' as astutely as any in

Balzac, but with more militancy. The unpopular garrison at Nancy is superbly done, for the minor characters have their own malicious concern for style and role also. They distress the hero. There are portraits of people who are drying up in futile class hatred. Stendhal is as cool – perhaps in his coolness lies the contemporary appeal – about the crude new middle class: he is exact but without the heavy hatred that is sometimes too black and white in Balzac. The following portrait of Mlle Sylvanie, the shopkeeper's daughter, is full yet compressed, poetic yet also ironically of this world. Here the chemistry is indeed exact:

> A statue of Juno, copied from the antique by a modern artist; both subtlety and simplicity are lacking; the lines are massive, but it is a Germanic freshness. Big hands, big feet, very regular features and plenty of coyness, all of which conceals a too obvious pride. And these people are put off by the pride of ladies in good Society! Lucien was particularly struck by her backward tosses of the head, which were full of vulgar nobility, and were evidently meant to recall the dowry of a hundred thousand crowns.

His young women have tenderness and verve: their capacity for growing into their passions is extraordinary. He is always beginning again with his characters for they too are 'making themselves'. And abruptly too. This abruptness is excellent in his portraits of young men; here no novelist in any literature or period has surpassed him, not even Tolstoy. No one has so defined and botanised the fervour, uncertainty, conceit, timidity and single-mindedness of young men, their dash, their shames, their calculation for tactics and gesture. They shed self after self and a date is put to their manners. Stendhal's sense of human beings living now yet transfixed, for an affecting moment, by their future, gives the doctrine of self-invention an ironical perspective which is not often noticeable in its practitioners today.

A Portuguese Diplomat

Eça de Queiroz (1845–1900) is the Portuguese classic of the nineteenth century – not an Iberian Balzac, like Galdos but, rather, a moistened Stendhal, altogether more tender, and despite his reformist opinions, without theories. He was a diplomat, something of a dandy and gourmet, whose career took him abroad in France, Britain, the Near East, Cuba and the United States, and he was responsive to the intellectual forces that were bringing the European novel to the height of its powers. The temptations of a light and elegant cosmopolitanism must have been strong, for he is above all a novelist of wit and style, and he was amused by the banalities of diplomatic conversation.

But the foreign experience usually serves to strengthen his roots in the Portuguese idiosyncrasy: under the lazy grace, there is the native bluntness and stoicism. A novel like *The Illustrious House of Ramires* is very rich, but it also contrives to be a positive and subtle unravelling of the Portuguese strand in the Iberian temperament. The soft, sensual yet violently alluring Atlantic light glides over his country and his writing, a light more variable and unpredictable than the Castilian; no one could be less 'Spanish' and more Western European, yet strong in his native character.

The fear that one is going to be stuck in the quaint, exhaustive pieties of the *folklorico* and regional novel with its tedious local colour, its customs and costumes, soon goes at the sound of his misleadingly simple and sceptical voice. The Portuguese love to pretend to be diminutive in order to surprise by their toughness. Portuguese modesty and nostalgia are national – and devastating. In an introduction to an early short story, 'The Mandarin', he wrote a typically deceptive apology to its French publishers, in which he puts his case. 'Reality, analysis, experimentation or objective certainty,' he said, plague and baffle the Portuguese, who are either lyricists or satirists:

We dearly love to paint everything blue; a fine sentence will always please me more than an exact notion; the fabled Melusine, who devours human hearts, will always charm our incorrigible imagination more than the very human Marneffe, and we will always consider fantasy and eloquence the only true signs of a superior man. Were we to read Stendhal in Portuguese, we should never be able to enjoy him; what is considered exactitude with him, we should consider sterility. Exact ideas, expressed soberly and in proper form, hardly interest us at all; what charms us is excessive emotion expressed with unabashed plasticity of language.

Eça de Queiroz, we can be certain, did not commit the folly of reading Stendhal in Portuguese. The most exact of novelists, he read him in French, and the comedy is that he was very much a romantic Stendhalian – he was even a Consul-General – and in exactitude a Naturalist. Under the irony and the grace, there are precision and sudden outbursts of ecstasy and of flamboyant pride in a prose that coils along and then suddenly vibrates furiously when emotion breaks through, or breaks into unashamed burlesque.

He was an incessant polisher of his style. The following passage, from *The City and the Mountains*, shows his extraordinary power of letting rip and yet keeping his militant sense of comedy in command. His hero has just been thrown over by a cocotte in Paris. His first reaction is to go and eat an expensive meal of lobster and duck washed down by champagne and Burgundy; the second is to rush back to the girl's house, punching the cushions of the cab as he goes, for in the cushions he sees, in his fury, 'the huge bush of yellow hair in which my soul was lost one evening, fluttered and struggled for two months, and soiled itself for ever'. He fights the driver and the servants at the house, and then he goes off home, drunk and maddened:

Stretched out on the ancestral bed of Dom 'Galleon', with my boots on my pillow and my hat over my eyes, I laughed a sad laugh at this burlesque world . . . Suddenly I felt a horrible anguish. It was She. It was Madame Colombe who appeared out of the flame of the candle, jumped on my bed, undid my waistcoat, sunk herself onto my breast, put her mouth to my heart, and began to suck my blood from it in long slow

[876]

gulps. Certain of death now, I began to scream for my Aunt Vicencia; I hung from the bed to try to sink into my sepulchre which I dimly discerned beneath me on the carpet, through the final fog of death – a little round sepulchre, glazed and made of porcelain, with a handle. And over my own sepulchre, which so irreverently chose to resemble a chamberpot, I vomited the lobster, the duck, the pimentos and the Burgundy. Then after a super-human effort, with the roar of a lion, feeling that not only my innards but my very soul were emptying themselves in the process, I vomited up Madame Colombe herself . . . I put my hat back over my eyes so as not to feel the rays of the sun. It was a new Sun, a spiritual Sun which was rising over my life. I slept like a child softly rocked in a cradle of wicker by my Guardian Angel.

This particular novel savages Paris as the height of city civilisation, a wealthy Utopia; it argues for the return to nature in the Portuguese valleys. Eça de Queiroz can still astonish us in this satire with his catalogue of mechanical conveniences. They are remarkably topical. (His theatre-telephone, for example, is our television or radio.) The idea of a machine civilisation that has drained off the value of human life recalls Forster's *The Machine Stops*. Maliciously Queiroz describes our childish delight in being ravished by a culture of affluence or surfeit. He was in at the birth of boredom and conspicuous waste. One brilliant fantasy of the hero is that he is living in a city where the men and women are simply made of newspaper, where the houses are made of books and pamphlets and the streets paved with them. Change printed-matter to the McLuhanite Muzak culture of today, and the satire is contemporary. The hero returns to the droll, bucolic kindness of life in Portugal, in chapters that have the absurd beauty of, say, Oblomov's dream.

The prose carries this novel along, but one has to admit there is a slightly faded *fin de siècle* air about it. *The Illustrious House of Ramires* is a much better rooted and more ambitious work. Obviously his suggestion that the Portuguese are not experimentalists is a Portuguese joke, for the book is a novel within a novel, a comedy of the relation of the unconscious with quotidian experience. One is tricked at first into thinking one is caught up in a rhetorical tale of chivalry *à la* Walter Scott; then one changes one's mind and treats its high-flown historical side as one of those Romances that addled the mind of Don Quixote; finally one recognises this element as an important part of psychological insight. What looks like old hat reveals its originality.

Ramires is an ineffectual and almost ruined aristocrat who is rewriting the history of his Visigothic ancestors in order to raise his own morale. It is an act of personal and political therapy. He is all for liberal reform, but joins the party of Regenerators or traditionalists whose idea is to bring back the days of Portugal's greatness. Ramires revels in the battles, sieges and slaughterings of his famous family and – while he is writing this vivid and bloody stuff – he is taking his mind off the humiliations of his own life. The heir of the Ramireses is a dreamer. He is a muddler and his word is never to be relied on. He shuffles until finally he gets himself in the wrong. This is because he is timid and without self-confidence: he deceives a decent peasant over a contract and then, losing his self-control when the peasant protests, has him sent to prison on the pretext that the man tried to assault him. Then rage abates and he hurriedly gets the man out of prison.

Ramires has a long feud with a local philandering politician of the opposite party, because this man has jilted his sister; yet, he makes it up with the politician in order to get elected as a deputy – only to see that the politician does this only to be sure of seducing the sister. The price of political triumph is his sister's honour and happiness. How can he live with himself after that? Trapped continually by his pusillanimity, he tries to recover by writing one more chapter of his novel of chivalry, fleeing to an ideal picture of himself. What saves him – and this is typical of the irony of Queiroz – is his liability to insensate physical rage, always misplaced. He half kills a couple of ruffians on the road by horsewhipping them and, incidentally, gives a fantastically exaggerated account of the incident; but the event and the lie give him self-confidence. He is a hero at last! He begins to behave with a comic mixture of cunning and dignity. He saves his sister, becomes famous as a novelist, long-headedly makes a rich marriage, and tells the King of Portugal that he is an upstart. Total triumph of luck, accident, pride, impulse in a helplessly devious but erratically generous character loved by everyone. Tortured by uncertainty, carried away by idealism and feeling, a curious mixture of the heroic and the shady, he has become welded into a man.

And who is this man? He is not simply Ramires, the aristocrat. He is –

[878]

Portugal itself: practical, stoical, shifty, its pride in its great past, its pride in pride itself raging inside like an unquenchable sadness. There is iron in the cosiness of Queiroz. He has the disguised militancy of the important comedians. His comic scenes are very fine, for there is always a serious or symbolic body to them. His sensuality is frank. His immense detail in the evocation of Portuguese life is always on the move; and the mixture of disingenuousness and genuine feeling in all his characters makes every incident piquant.

A match-making scene takes place in the boring yet macabre crypt where the ancestors of Ramires are buried. Ramires knows his ancestors would have killed his sister's lover; all *he* can do is to pray feverishly that her silly, jolly, cuckolded husband will never find out. Prudence and self-interest suggest caution; not mere caution but an anxious mixture of politeness, kindness, worldly-wisdom and a stern belief in dignity, if you can manage it, plus the reflection that even the most inexcusable adulteries may have a sad, precious core of feeling. Ramires is not a cynic; nor is Eça de Queiroz. He is saved from that by his lyrical love of life, his abandonment – for the moment – to the unpredictable side of his nature; in other words, by his candour and innocence. His people live by their imagination from minute to minute. They are constantly impressionable; yet they never lose their grasp of the practical demands of their lives – the interests of land, money, illness, politics.

In the historical pages of Ramires's historical novel, there is a double note, romantic yet sardonic. The scenes are barbarous and bloody – they express the unconscious of Ramires, the dreams that obsess him and his nation – but the incidental commentary is as dry as anything in Stendhal. During a siege:

> The bailiff waddled down the blackened, spiral stairway to the steps outside the keep. Two liegemen, their lances at their shoulders, returning from a round, were talking to the armourer who was painting the handles of new javelins yellow and scarlet and lining them up against the wall to dry.

Yet a few lines farther down, we shall see a father choose to see his son murdered, rather than surrender his honour. The violence of history bursts out in Ramires's own life in the horsewhipping scene I have mentioned earlier. The sensation – he finds – is sublime. But when Ramires gets home his surprise at the sight of real blood on his whip and clothes shatters him. He does not want to be as murderous as the knights of old. He is all for humanity and charity. He was simply trying to solve his psychological difficulty; that he had never, in anything until then, imposed his own will, but had yielded to the will of others who were simply corrupting him and leaving him to wake up to one more humiliation. It is a very contemporary theme.

The making of this novel, and indeed all the others, is the restless mingling of poetry, sharp realism and wit. Queiroz is untouched by the drastic hatred of life that underlies Naturalism: he is sad rather than indignant that every human being is compromised; indeed this enables him to present his characters from several points of view and to explore the unexpectedness of human nature. The elements of self-surprise and self-imagination are strong; and his excellent prose glides through real experience and private dream in a manner that is leading on towards the achievements of Proust. His translators have done their difficult task pretty well: Roy Campbell being outstanding.

A Spanish Balzac

================

Pérez Galdós is the supreme Spanish novelist of the 19th century. His scores of novels are rightly compared with the work of Balzac and Dickens who were his masters, and even with Tolstoy's. Why then has he been almost totally neglected by foreigners? One reason is that wherever Spanish city life had anything in common with Western European societies, it appeared to be out of date and a provincial parody; and where there was no resemblance it was interpreted by foreign collectors of the outlandish and picturesque. One of the anglicised characters in his longest novel *Fortunata and Jacinta* returns to England saying, bitterly, that all the British want from Spain is tourist junk – and this in 1873! One could read the great Russians without needing to go to Russia; their voice carried across the frontiers. To grasp Galdós – it was felt – one had to go to Spain and submit to Spanish formality, pride and claustrophobia. Few readers outside of academic life did so.

These objections no longer have the same force and it is more likely that the great achievement of Galdós can be recognised here today. A few years ago, his short novel *The Spendthrifts* (*La de Bringas*) was translated by Gerald Brenan and Gamel Woolsey and now we have Lester Clark's complete translation of the 1,100 pages of his most ambitious novel. It takes its place among those Victorian masterpieces that have presented the full-length portrait of a city.

The originality of Galdós springs, in part, from the fact that he was a silent outsider – he was brought up in the Canaries under English influences. In time he learned how to drift to the Spanish pace and then, following Balzacian prescription and energy, set out to become 'the secretary of history'. He is reported to have been a quiet and self-effacing man and this novel gets its inspiration from the years he spent listening to the voices of Madrid. His intimacy with every social group is never the sociologist's; it is the personal intimacy of the artist, indeed it can be said he

[881]

disappears as a person and *becomes* the people, streets and kitchens, cafés and churches. This total absorption has been held against him: the greatest novelists, in some way, impose – the inquirer does not. Yet this very passivity matches a quality in Spanish life; and anyway he is not the dry inquirer; his inquiry is directed by feeling and especially by tolerant worship of every motion of the heart, a tenderness for its contradictions and its dreams, for its everyday impulses and also for those that are vibrant, extreme – even insane. He is an excellent story-teller, he loves the inventiveness of life itself. Preaching nothing overtly, he is a delicate and patient psychologist. It is extraordinary to find a novel written in the 1880s that documents the changes in the cloth trade, the rise and fall of certain kinds of café, the habits of usurers, politicians and catholic charities but also probes the fantasies and dreams of the characters and follows their inner thoughts. Galdós is fascinated by the psychology of imitation and the primitive unconscious. He changes the 'point of view' without regard to the rules of the novelist's game. We are as sure of the likeness of each character as we are of the figures in a Dutch painting and yet they are never set or frozen, they are always moving in space in the Tolstoyan fashion. The secret of the gift of Galdós lies, I think, in his timing, his leisurely precision and above all in his ear for dialogue; his people live in speech, either to themselves or to each other. He was a born assimilator of speech of all kinds, from the rich skirling dialect of the slums or the baby-language of lovers, to the even more difficult speech of people who are trying to express or evade more complex thoughts.

The dramatic thread that runs through the panorama of life in Madrid in 1873 is the story of the love and destructive jealousy of two women. Fortunata is a beautiful and ignorant slum girl who is seduced by the idle son of rich shopkeepers before his marriage and bears him a son who dies. Jacinta becomes the young man's beautiful but pathetic wife, tormented less by her husband's love affairs than by the fact that she cannot bear children. The deserted Fortunata takes up a life of promiscuity from which a feeble and idealistic young chemist sets about rescuing her. She longs to be a respectable wife and is bullied into going into a convent for a time so that she can be reformed. But she cannot get over her love of her seducer and although she comes out of the convent and marries the chemist, she feels no affection for him. He is indeed impotent, and going from one philosophical or religious mania to another, ends by becoming insane and murderous in his jealousy of her first lover who has resumed the pursuit. It becomes a battle, therefore, between the bourgeois wife and the loose woman. Fortunata is a tragic figure of the people, a victim of her own sensual impulses who, in the end, has a second child by her seducer and regards herself as his true respectable wife because the other is barren. But her child is taken over by the rich and legitimate wife and Fortunata dies raging. The scene is overwhelming. The last time I wept over a novel was in reading *Tess* when I was 18. Fifty years later Fortunata has made me weep again. Not simply because of her death but because Galdós had portrayed a woman whole in all her moods. In our own 19th-century novels this situation would be melodramatic and morally overweighted – see George Eliot's treatment of Hetty Sorrel – but in Galdós there is no such excess. The bourgeois wife is in her limited way as attractive as Fortunata.

Among the large number of Fortunata's friends, enemies and neighbours, there are two or three portraits that are in their own way as powerful as hers. First there is Mauricia la Dura, an incorrigible, violent and drunken prostitute to whom Fortunata is drawn against her will in the convent. Mauricia attracts by the terror and melancholy of her face. She is a genuine Spanish primitive. There is a long and superb scene in which she manages to get hold of some brandy in the convent and passes from religious ecstasy to blasphemy, theft and violence. It is a mark of the great novelist that he can invent a fantastic scene like this and then, later on, take us into the mind of the violent girl after she has got over her mania. Galdós knows how to return to the norm:

'I was beside myself. I only remember I saw the Blessed Virgin and then I wanted to go into the church to get the Holy Sacrament. I dreamt I ate the Host – I've never had such a bad bout . . . The things that go through your mind when the devil goes to your head. Believe me because I'm telling you. When I came to my senses I was so ashamed . . . The only one I hated was that Chaplain. I'd have bitten chunks out of him. But not the nuns. I wanted to beg their forgiveness; but my dignity wouldn't let me. What upset me most was having thrown a bit of brick at Doña Guillermina, I'll never forget that – never – And I'm so afraid that when I see her coming along the street my face colours up and I go by on the other side so that she won't see me.'

Doña Guillermina, a rich woman who has given up everything for the rescue work, is another fine portrait of the practical good-humoured saint, a sort of Santa Teresa who – and this shows the acuteness of the novelist's observation – can be frightened, a shade automatic, and sometimes totally at a loss. Against her must be placed Doña Lupe, a lower-middle-class moneylender. She is a miser who shouts to her maid:

'Clean your feet on the next-door shoe-scraper . . . because the fewer people who use ours, the more we gain.'

But at the wedding of Fortunata to her nephew we recognise Doña Lupe as more than a grotesque. Galdós is superior to Balzac in not confining people to a single dominant passion:

Once back in the house, Doña Lupe seemed to have burst from her skin for she grew and multiplied remarkably . . . You would have thought there were three or four widow Jaurequis in the house, all functioning at the same time. Her mind was boiling at the possibility of the lunch not going well. But if it turned out well what a triumph! Her heart beat violently, pumping feverish heat all over her body, and even the ball of cottonwool at her breast [she had had one breast removed] seemed to be endowed with its share of life, being allowed to feel pain and worry.

The final large character is Max, the husband of Fortunata. She dislikes him, but he has 'saved' her. Puny and sexless, Max begins to seek relief in self-aggrandisement, first of all in prim and ingenuous idealism; when he realises his marriage is null and that his 'cure' of Fortunata is a failure, he turns to experimenting with pills and hopes to find a commercial cure-all. His efforts are incompetent and dangerous. The next stage is paranoia caused by sexual jealousy. He moves on to religious mania: thinks of murder and then invites his wife to join him in a suicide pact, in order to rid the world of sin. For a while he is mad and then, suddenly, he recovers and 'sees his true situation' – but recovery turns him into a blank non-being. Here we see Galdós' belief in imitative neurosis, for in a terrible scene poor Fortunata is infected with her husband's discarded belief in violence. She declares she will love him utterly, if only he will go and murder her libertine lover. But Max has fallen into complete passivity: he enters a monastery where he will become a solitary mystic – and he does not realise that the monastery he has chosen is, in fact, an asylum.

It is surprising to find this Dostoevskian study in Galdós but, of course, Spanish life can offer dozens of such figures. They are examples of what Spanish writers have often noted: the tendency of the self to be obdurately as it is and yet to project itself into some universal extreme, to think of itself mystically as God or the universe. But usually – as Galdós showed in his portrait of the ivory-carving civil servant in *The Spendthrifts* – such characters are simply bizarre and finicking melancholies. Around them stand the crowd of self-dramatisers in the old cafés, the pious church-going ladies, the various types of priest, the shouters of the slums. What is more important is his ability to mount excellent scenes, and in doing so, to follow the feelings of his people with a tolerant and warm detachment. He is never sentimental. There is one fine example of his originality and total dissimilarity from other European novelists in his long account of Jacinta's honeymoon. The happy girl cannot resist acting unwisely: little by little she tries to find out about her husband's early love affair, mainly to increase the excitement of her own love. No harm comes of this dangerous love game, but we realise that here is a novelist who can describe early married life without reserves and hit upon the piquancy that is its spell. I can think of no honeymoon in literature to match this one. The fact is that Galdós accepts human nature without resentment.

A Brazilian

Few English readers had heard of Machado de Assis before 1953. His novel *Braz Cubas* was translated in that year by William Grossman, under the title of *Epitaph for a Small Winner*, forty-five years after his death. There was also a very good translation published in 1955, by E. Percy Ellis. Since then we have been able to read *Dom Casmurro*, a collection of stories called *The Psychiatrist*, and *Esau and Jacob*, which has awkward inflections of truck-driver's American in the dialogue. Assis is spoken of as Brazil's greatest novelist. He was born in 1839 and his work comes out of the period marked by the fall of monarchy, the liberation of the slaves and the establishment of the Republic. He predates the later European immigration which was to change the great cities of Brazil completely and introduce new Mediterranean and Teutonic strains into the Brazilian character.

Assis said that his simple novels were written 'in the ink of mirth and melancholy'. The simplicity is limpid and delightful, but it is a deceptive distillation. One is always doubtful about how to interpret the symbolism and allegory that underlie his strange love stories and his impressions of a wealthy society. The picture of Rio could not be more precise, yet people and city seem to be both physically there and not there. The actual life he evokes has gone, but it is reillumined or revived by his habit of seeing people as souls fluttering like leaves blown away by time. In this he is very modern: his individuals have the force of anonymities. His aim, in all his books, seems to be to rescue a present moment just before it sinks into the past or reaches into its future. He is a mixture of comedian, lyrical poet, psychological realist and utterly pessimistic philosopher. We abruptly fall into dust and that is the end. But it would be quite wrong to identify him with the sated bankers, politicians, sentimental roués and bookish diplomats who appear in the novels. His tone is far removed from the bittersweet mockery and urbane scepticism of, say, Anatole France; and it is free of that addiction to rhetorical French romanticism which influenced all South American literature during the nineteenth century. He eventually became an Anglophile.

Epitaph for a Small Winner was a conscious break with France. It is a lover's account of an affair with a friend's wife. The affair is broken – perhaps luckily – by circumstance and the writer concludes that there was a small surplus of fortune in his life: 'I had no progeny, I transmitted to no one the legacy of our misery.' To get a closer idea of Assis, one must think chiefly of Sterne, Swift and Stendhal. He is an exact, original, economical writer, who pushes the machinery of plot into the background. His short chapters might be a moralist's notes. Like Sterne, he is obsessed with Time, eccentric, even whimsical; like Stendhal, accurate and yet passionate; like Swift, occasionally savage. But the substance is Brazilian. It is not a matter of background, though there is the pleasure of catching sight of corners of Rio and Petropolis – the little St Germain up in the mountains where Court society used to go to get out of the damp heat. Some of the spirit caught by Assis still survives in Rio: under the gaiety there is something grave; under the corruption something delicate; under the fever something passive and contemplative. The Portuguese *saudade* can be felt within the violence; and a preoccupation with evasive manoeuvre, as it occurs in games or elaborate artificial comedy, is a constant recourse and solace, in every department of life. Like the Portuguese before Salazar, the Brazilians attempted to circumvent their own violence by playing comedies.

Assis' career could be seen as a triumph of miscegenation. He was born in one of the *favelas* or shack slums that are dumped on the hills in the very centre of Rio, the son of a mulatto house-painter and a Portuguese woman. She died and he had no education beyond what he picked up in an aristocratic house where his stepmother worked as a cook. He learned French from the local baker, got a job as a typesetter and eventually turned journalist. It is not surprising that he was sickly, epileptic and industrious and that one of his interests was insanity. Like many other Latin American writers, he supported himself by working in the civil service; but in his spare time he wrote thirty miscellaneous volumes and became President of the Brazilian Academy.

It is said that he is even more admired in Brazil for his short stories than for his novels and from the small selection called *The Psychiatrist*, one can see why: here the dreamy monotone of his novels vanishes. From story to story the mood changes. He astonishes by passing from satire to artifice, from wit to the emotional weight of a tale like 'Midnight Mass' or to the terrible realism of 'Admiral's Night,' a story of slave-hunting which could have come out of Flaubert. In a way, all the novels of Assis are constructed by a short-story-teller's mind, for he is a vertical, condensing writer who slices through the upholstery of the realist novel into what is essential. He is a collector of the essences of whole lives and does not labour with chronology, jumping back or forward confidently in time as it pleases him. A man will be described simply as handsome or coarse, a woman as beautiful or plain; but he will plunge his hand into them and pull out the vitalising paradox of their inner lives, showing how they are themselves and the opposite of themselves and how they are in flux.

In *Esau and Jacob* there is a fine comic portrait of the pushing wife of a wobbly politician who has just lost his governorship. She is a woman who kisses her friends 'as if she wanted to eat them alive, to consume them, not with hate, to put them inside her, deep inside'. She revels in power and – a quality Assis admired in his women – is innocent of moral sense:

> It was so good to arrive in the province, all announced, the visits aboard ship, the landing, the investitures, the officials' greetings . . . Even the vilification by the opposition was agreeable. To hear her husband called tyrant, when she knew he had a pigeon's heart, did her soul good. The thirst for blood that they attributed to him, when he did not even drink wine, the mailed fist of a man that was a kid glove, his immorality, barefaced effrontery, lack of honour, all the unjust strong names, she loved to read as if they were eternal truths – where were they now?

The grotesque, Assis says in one of his epigrams, is simply ferocity in disguise: but here the beauty of the grotesque comes from tolerance. Sometimes people are absurd, sometimes wicked, sometimes good. Timidity may lead to virtue, deception to love; our virtues are married to our vices. The politician's wife gets to work on her husband and skilfully persuades him to change parties. He is morally ruined but this stimulates his self-esteem. The pair simply become absurd. This particular chapter of comedy is very Stendhalian – say, from *Lucien Leuwen*.

[888]

Esau and Jacob is, on the face of it, a political allegory, observed by an old diplomat. He has been the unsuccessful lover of Natividade, the wife of a rich banker, a lady given to a rather sadistic fidelity and to exaltation. She gives birth to identical twin boys and consults an old sorceress about their destiny. She is told they will become great men and will perpetually quarrel. And so they do. As they rise to greatness, one becomes a monarchist and defender of the old stable traditions, the other a republican and a believer in change and the future. They fall in love with the same girl, Flora, who can scarcely tell them apart and who, fatally unable to make up her mind about them, fades away and dies. (People die as inconsequently as they do in E. M. Forster.) The meaning of the allegory may be that Natividade is the old Brazil and that Flora is the girl of the new Brazil who cannot decide between the parties. But underlying this is another allegory. One young man looks to the Past, the other to the Future; the girl is the Present, puzzled by its own breathless evanescence, and doomed. All the people in Assis seem to be dissolving in time, directed by their Destiny – the old sorceress up in the *favela*.

The theme of *Esau and Jacob* is made for high-sounding dramatic treatment; but Assis disposes of that by his cool, almost disparaging tenderness as he watches reality and illusion change places. In *Dom Casmurro* we have another of his cheated lovers. A young seminarist has been vowed to the Church by his mother, but is released from his vow by a sophistry, so that he can marry a girl whom he adores and who patiently intrigues to get him. Their love affair and marriage are exquisitely described. But the shadow of the original sophistry is long. Dom Casmurro had made a friend at the seminary, and this friend becomes the father of the boy Dom Casmurro thinks his own. When the boy grows up, Dom Casmurro finds that he is haunted by this copy of his friend. All die, for the subject is illusion. The concern with exchanged identities and doubles – very much a theme of the Romantic movement – is not left on the level of irony or paradox: Assis follows it into our moral nature, into the double quality of our sensibility, and the uncertainty of what we are. We are the sport of nature, items in a game.

One sees how much Assis has in common with his contemporary, Pirandello. With the growth of agnosticism at the end of the nineteenth century, people played intellectually with the occult – one of the Assis bankers consults a spiritualist – and amused themselves with conundrums about illusion and reality, sanity and insanity. In *The Psychiatrist* a doctor puts the whole town into his asylum. But there is something heartless and brittle in Pirandello. The Brazilian is warmer, gentler. One does not feel about him, as about Pirandello, that intellect and feeling are separate. At his most airily speculative and oblique, Assis still contrives to give us the sense of a whole person, all of a love-affair, a marriage, an illness, a career and a society, by looking at their fragments. There is a curious moment in the *Epitaph for a Small Winner* when we are told that the poor, wronged, unhappy woman who is used by the clandestine lovers as a screen for their affair was perhaps born to have just that role and use in their lives: the reflection is good, for if it conveys the egoism of the lovers, it also conveys the sense of unconscious participation which is the chief intuition of Assis as an artist, and which makes his creatures momentarily solid.

The Myth Makers

It has often been said of the Spanish nature and – by extension – of those who have inherited Iberian influences in South America, that the ego is apt to leap across middle ground and see itself as a universe. The leap is to an All. The generalisation itself skips a great deal too, but it is a help towards beginning to understand the astonishing richness of the South American novelists of recent years. Their 'All' – and I think of Vargas Llosa and García Márquez among others – is fundamentally 'the people', not in the clichés of political rhetoric, but in the sense of millions of separate lives, no longer anonymous but physically visible, awash in historical memory and with identities.

After reading *Leaf Storm*, the novella written by Gabriel García Márquez when he was only nineteen, but not published until 1955, one sees what a distance lies between this effort and his masterpiece *One Hundred Years of Solitude*. The young author sows the seed of a concern with memory, myth and the nature of time which bursts into lovely shameless blossom in his later book. We get our first glimpse of the forgotten town of Macondo (obviously near Cartagena), a primitive place, once a naïve colonial Eden; then blasted by the 'leaf storm' of the invading foreign banana-companies, and finally a ghost town, its founders forgotten. Shut up in a room in one of its remaining family houses is an unpleasant doctor who 'lives on grass' – a vegetarian? – whom the town hates because he once refused to treat some men wounded after a civil rising. Now, secluded for goodness knows how many years, he has hanged himself, and the question is whether the town will riot and refuse to have him buried. The thing to notice is that, like so many South American novelists, García Márquez was even then drawn to the inordinate character – not necessarily a giant or saga-like hero, but someone who has exercised a right to extreme conduct or aberration. Such people fulfil a new country's need for legends. A human being is required to be a myth, his spiritual value lies in the inflating of his tale.

[891]

Far better than *Leaf Storm* are some of the short stories in the new collection, and one above all. 'The Handsomest Drowned Man in the World'. The story is an exemplary guide to the art of García Márquez, for it is a celebration of the myth-making process. Somewhere on the seashore children are found playing with the body of a drowned man, burying it, digging it up again, burying it. Fishermen take the corpse to the village, and while the men go off to inquire about missing people, the women are left to prepare the body for burial. They scrape off the crust of little shells and stones and weed and mess and coral in which the body is wrapped and then they see the man within:

> They noticed that he bore his death with pride for he did not have the lonely look of other drowned men who came out of the sea or that haggard needy look of men who drowned in rivers . . . he was the tallest, strongest, most virile and best built man they had ever seen . . . They thought if that magnificent man had lived in the village, his house would have had the widest doors, the highest ceiling, and the strongest floor, his bedstead would have been made from a midship frame held together by iron bolts and his wife would have been the happiest woman. They thought he would have had so much authority he could have drawn fish out of the sea simply by calling their names.

The women imagine him in their houses; they see that because he is tall, the doors and ceilings of their houses would have to be higher and they tell him affectionately to 'mind his head' and so on. The dead god has liberated so much fondness and wishing that when the body is at last formally buried at sea it is not weighed down by an anchor, for the women and the men too hope that the dead man will realise that he is welcome to come back at any time.

There is nothing arch or whimsical in the writing of this fable. The prose of García Márquez is plain, exact, subtle and springy and easily leaps into the comical and the exuberant, as we find in *One Hundred Years of Solitude*. In that book the history of the Buendía families and their women in three or four generations is written as a hearsay report on the growth of the little Colombian town; it comes to life because it is continuously leaping out of fact into the mythical and the myth is comic. One obvious analogy is with Rabelais. It is suggested, for example, that Aureliano Segundo's sexual orgies with his concubine are so enjoyable that his own livestock catch the fever. Animals and birds are unable to stand by and do nothing. The rancher's life is a grandiose scandal; the 'bonecrusher' in bed is a heroic glutton who attracts 'fabulous eaters' from all over the country. There is an eating duel with a lady known as 'The Elephant'. The duel lasted from a Saturday to a Tuesday, but it had its elegance:

> While Aureliano ate with great bites, overcome by the anxiety of victory, The Elephant was slicing her meat with the art of a surgeon and eating it unhurriedly and even with a certain pleasure. She was gigantic and sturdy, but over her colossal form a tenderness of femininity prevailed . . . later on when he saw her consume a side of veal without breaking a single rule of good table manners, he commented that this most delicate, fascinating and insatiable proboscidian was in a certain way the ideal woman.

The duel is beautifully described and with a dozen inventive touches, for once García Márquez gets going there is no controlling his fancy. But note the sign of the master: the story is always brought back to ordinary experience in the end. Aureliano was ready to eat to the death and indeed passes out. The scene has taken place at his concubine's house. He gasps out a request to be taken to his wife's house because he had promised not to die in his concubine's bed; and she, who knows how to behave, goes and shines up his patent leather boots that he had always planned to wear in his coffin. Fortunately he survives. It is very important to this often ruthless, licentious and primitive epic that there is a deep concern for propriety and manners.

As a fable or phantasmagoria *One Hundred Years of Solitude* succeeds because of its comic animality and its huge exaggerations which somehow are never gross and indeed add a certain delicacy. García Márquez seems to be sailing down the bloodstream of his people as they innocently build their town in the swamp, lose it in civil wars, go mad in the wild days of the American banana company and finally end up abandoned. The story is a social history but not as it is found in books but as it muddles its way forward or backward among the sins of family life and the accidents of trade. For example, one of the many Aurelianos has had the luck and intelligence to introduce ice to Macondo. To extend the ice business was impossible without getting the railroad in. This is how García Márquez introduces the railroad:

> Aureliano Centeno, overwhelmed by the abundance of the factory, had already begun to experiment in the production of ice with a base of fruit juices instead of water, and without knowing it or thinking about it, he conceived the essential fundamentals for the invention of sherbet. In that way he planned to diversify the production of an enterprise he considered his own, because his brother showed no signs of returning after the rains had passed and the whole summer had gone by with no news of him. At the start of another winter a woman who was washing clothes in the river during the hottest time of the day ran screaming down the main street in an alarming state of commotion.
>
> 'It's coming,' she finally explained. 'Something frightful like a kitchen dragging a village behind it.'

There are scores of rippling pages that catch the slippery comedies and tragedies of daily life, at the speed of life itself: the more entangled the subject the faster the pace. García Márquez is always ready to jump to extremes; it is not enough for a girl to invite two school friends to her family's house, she invites seventy horrible girls and the town has to be ransacked for seventy chamber pots. Crude or delicate an incident may be, but it is singular in the way ordinary things are. Almost every sentence is a surprise and the surprise is, in general, really an extension of our knowledge or feeling about life, and not simply a trick. Ursula, the grandmother of the Buendía tribe, the one stable character, is a repository of superstitious wisdom, i.e., superstition is a disguised psychological insight. In her old age, we see her revising her opinions, especially one about babies who 'weep in the womb'. She discusses this with her husband and he treats the idea as a joke. He says such children will become ventriloquists; she thinks that they will be prophets. But now, surveying the harsh career of her son who has grown up to be a proud and heartless fighter of civil wars, she says that 'only the unloving' weep in the womb. And those who cannot love are in need of more compassion than others. An insight? Yes, but also it brings back dozens of those talks one has had in Spain (and indeed in South America) where people kill the night by pursuing the bizarre or the extreme by-ways of human motive.

In no derogatory sense, one can regard this rapid manner of talk – non-stop, dry and yet fantastical – as characteristic of café culture: lives pouring away in long bouts of chatter. In North America its characteristic form is the droll monologue; in South America the fantasy is – in my limited reading – more agile and imaginative, richer in laughter and, of course, especially happy in its love of the outrageous antics of sexual life.

One Hundred Years of Solitude denies interpretation. One could say that a little Arcady was created but was ruined by the 'Promethean ideas' that came into the head of its daring founder. Or that little lost towns have their moment – as civilisations do – and are then obliterated. Perhaps the moral is, as García Márquez says, that 'races condemned to one hundred years of solitude do not get a second chance on earth'. The notion of 'the wind passeth over it and it is gone' is rubbed in; so also is the notion Borges has used, of a hundred years or even infinite time being totally discernible in a single minute. But what García Márquez retrieves from the history he has surveyed is a Homeric laughter.

Life is ephemeral but dignified by fatality: the word 'ephemeral' often crops up in *The Autumn of the Patriarch*, which has been well translated by Gregory Rabassa – the original would be beyond even those foreigners who read Spanish.

The Patriarch who gives the novel its moral theme is the elusive despot of a South American republic and we hear him in the scattered voices of his people and his own. As a young wild bull he is the traditional barefoot peasant leader; later he is the confident monster ruthlessly collecting the spoils of power, indifferent to murder and massacre, sustained by his simple peasant mother, surviving by cunning. Still later, in old age, he is a puppet manipulated by the succeeding juntas, who are selling off the country to exploiters, a Caliban cornered but tragic, with a terrifying primitive will to survive. His unnamed republic looks out on the Caribbean from a barren coast from which the sea has receded, so that he believes, as superstitiously as his people do, that foreigners have even stolen the sea.

By the time the novel opens he is a myth to his people. Those who think they have seen him have probably seen only his double, though they may have glimpsed his hand waving from a limousine. He himself lives among the remnants of his concubines and the lepers and beggars that infest the Presidential fort. His mother is dead. He stamps round on his huge feet and is mainly concerned with milking his cows in the dairy attached to his mansion. Power is in the hands of an untrusted Minister. The President no longer leaves the place but drowses as he reads of speeches he has never made, celebrations he has never attended, applause he has never heard, in the newspaper of which only one copy is printed and solely for himself. He is, in short, an untruth; a myth in the public mind, a dangerous animal decaying in 'the solitary vice' of despotic power, fearing one more attempt at assassination and, above all, the ultimate solitude of death.

At first sight the book is a capricious mosaic of multiple narrators. We slide from voice to voice in the narrative without warning, in the course of the long streaming sentences of consciousness. But the visual, animal realism is violent and forever changing: we are swept from still moments of domestic fact to vivid fantasy, back and forth in time from, say, the arrival of the first Dutch discoverers to the old man looking at television, in the drift of hearsay and memory.

The few settled characters are like unforgettable news flashes that disturb and disappear: the richness of the novel will not be grasped in a single reading. We can complain that it does not progress but returns upon itself in widening circles. The complaint is pointless: the spell lies in the immediate force of its language and the density of narrative. We can be lost in those interminable sentences and yet once one has got the hang of the transitions from one person to the next it is all as sharp as the passing moment because García Márquez is the master weaver of the real and the conjectured. His descriptive power astounds at once, in the first forty pages where the narrator is a naïve undefined 'we', i.e., the people. They break into the fortress of the tragic monster and find their Caliban dead among the cows that have long ago broken out of the dairy and graze off the carpets in the salons of the ruined Presidencia and even have appeared, lowing like speakers, on the balconies. This is from the opening scene:

> When the first vultures began to arrive, rising up from where they had dozed on the cornices of the charity hospital, they came from farther inland, they came in successive waves, out of the horizon of the sea of dust where the sea had been, for a whole day they flew in slow circles of the house of power until a king with bridal feathers and a crimson ruff gave a silent order and that breaking of glass began, that breeze of a

great man dead, that in and out of vultures through the windows imaginable only in a house which lacked authority, so we dared go in too and in the deserted sanctuary we found the rubble of grandeur, the body that had been pecked at, the smooth maiden hands with the ring of power on the bone of the third finger, and his whole body was sprouting tiny lichens and parasitic animals from the depths of the sea, especially in the armpits and the groin, and he had the canvas truss of his herniated testicle which was the only thing that had escaped the vultures in spite of its being the size of an ox kidney; but even then we did not dare believe in his death because it was the second time he had been found in that office, alone and dressed and dead seemingly of natural causes during his sleep, as had been announced a long time ago in the prophetic waters of soothsayers' basins.

Only his double had been able to show him his 'untruth': that useful ignoramus died of poison intended for his master. There had been a period when the President really was of the people, the easy joker who might easily get an upland bridegroom murdered so that he himself could possess the bride. The dictator's peasant mother who carried on in his mansion, sitting at her sewing machine as if she were still in her hut, was the only one aware of his tragedy. (Once when he was driving to a ceremonial parade she rushed after him with a basket of empties telling him to drop them at the shop when he passed. The violent book has many homely touches.) His brutal sexual assaults are not resented – he fucks with his boots and uniform on – but when very late he comes to feel love, he is at a loss. On a Beauty Queen of the slum called the Dog District, he pours gadgets and imported rubbish, even turns the neighbourhood into a smart suburb: she is immovable and he is almost mad.

He kidnaps a Jamaican novice nun and marries her, but two years pass before he dares go to bed with her. She spends her time bargaining for cheap toys in the market. She surrenders to him not out of love but out of pity and teaches him to read and sign his name. The market people hate her trading habits and her fox furs and set dogs on her and her children: they are torn to pieces and eaten. There is a frightful scene where his supposedly loyal Minister organises an insurrection. The old man's animal instinct detects a plot in the conspiracy. The Minister warns him: 'So things are in no shape for licking your fingers, general Sir, now we really are fucked up.' The wily President won't budge but sends down a cartload of milk for the rebels and when the orderly uncorks the first barrel there is a roar and they see the man

> floating on the ephemeral backwash of a dazzling explosion and they saw nothing else until the end of time in the volcanic heat of the mournful yellow mortar building in which no flower ever grew, whose ruins remained suspended in the air from the tremendous explosion of six barrels of dynamite. That's that, he sighed in the Presidential palace, shaken by the seismic wind that blew down four more houses around the barracks and broke the wedding crystal in cupboards all the way to the outskirts of the city.

The President turns to his dominoes and when he sees the double five turn up, he guesses that the traitor behind the rebellion is his old friend of a lifetime, the Minister. He is invited to a banquet and, at the stroke of twelve, 'the distinguished Mayor General Roderigo de Aguilar entered on a silver tray, stretched out, garnished with cauliflower and laurel, steeped with spices and oven brown – and, in all his medals, is served up roast'. The guests are forced to eat him.

García Márquez is the master of a spoken prose that passes unmoved from scenes of animal disgust and horror to the lyrical evocation, opening up vistas of imagined or real sights which may be gentle or barbarous. The portrait of the mother who eventually dies of a terrible cancer is extraordinary. He has tried to get the Papal Nuncio to canonise her and, when Rome refuses, the President makes her a civil saint and has her embalmed body carried round the country. Avidly the people make up miracles for her. Once more, in his extreme old age and feeble, there is another insurrection, plotted by a smooth aristocratic adviser. The President survives. In his last night alive he wanders round the ruined house, counting his cows, searching for lost ones in rooms and closets; and he has learned that because of his incapacity for love he has tried to 'compensate for that infamous fate with the burning cultivation of the solitary vice of power' which is a fiction. 'We (the multiple narrator concludes less tritely) knew who we were while he was left never knowing it for ever . . .' The 'All' is not an extent, it is a depth.

Medallions

<hr>

In one of his terse utterances about himself as an artist, Jorge Luis Borges says, 'I have always come to life after coming to books.' In a general sense this could be said by most story-tellers and poets, but in Borges the words have a peculiar overtone. He appears to speak of something anomalous with the dignity of one who has been marked by an honourable wound received in an ambush between literature and life. Like Cervantes, he would have preferred to be a soldier who had pride in his wounded arm and had been forced by singularity into turning to the conceits of the *Exemplary Novels* and the *Romances* out of which he made *Don Quixote*.

Among South American writers Borges is a collection of anomalies, exceptional in the first place in having been brought up on English rather than French models; towards the Spaniards outside of *Don Quixote* (English translation preferred) and Quevedo, he is condescending. He had an English grandmother and an Anglophile father who was himself a writer and who brought up his son on *Tom Brown's Schooldays*, Kipling, Wells, Stevenson, Chesterton and Emerson. The poetry of Swinburne, Tennyson and Browning was important in the Argentine family who, on the Spanish side, had been violently concerned in earlier generations in the savage South American civil wars. The boy was frail and too near-sighted to follow a military career. Father and son, both slowly going blind, went to Europe for cure and education, mainly in Geneva, Germany and Spain. They detested Paris and thought Madrid trivial. One would guess that the erudition of Browning and the abrupt images of his dramatic narratives made the deepest impression, though one sees no trace of this in Borges's own poetry. Returning to Buenos Aires where at first he could hardly leave his house, he eventually became a librarian in a small municipal library (from which he was dismissed for political reasons at the time of Perón), and later the Director of the National Library itself.

Borges has also spoken of how, after the age of thirty, when he began to

[899]

go blind, he has lived physically in a growing twilight in which the distinctions between visible reality, conjecture and an immense reading are blurred. He had to remember, and a memory, in which he is rarely at a loss for the exact words of a long poem, has become literary, and the library a printed yet metaphysical domain. It is not surprising that Berkeley and Schopenhauer are his philosophers, and no more than natural, to one so attached to English literature, that he should have read William Morris and De Quincey. In conversation with Borges one hears life emerging out of phrases and scenes from literature and this, one understands at once from his writing, is not a merely browsing habit of mind. The emergence is dramatic, a creative act, as new landscapes are imagined and populated.

Such a reader is a full man, too full for the novelist. He has said:

> I have read but few novels and, in most cases, only a sense of duty has enabled me to find my way to the last page. At the same time, I have always been a reader and re-reader of short stories – Stevenson, Kipling, Henry James, Conrad, Poe, Chesterton, the tales in Lane's translation of *The Arabian Nights*, and certain stories of Hawthorne have been a habit of mine since I can remember. The feeling that the great novels like *Don Quixote* and *Huckleberry Finn* are virtually shapeless, reinforced my taste for the short story form whose indispensable elements are economy and a clearly stated beginning, middle and end.

This sounds conventional enough. But in the writer of short stories as in the poet, a distinctive voice, unlike all others, must arrest us; in Borges the voice is laconic, precise yet rapt and unnerving; it is relieved by the speculations of the essayist and the disconnecting currents of memory. Even in a banal paragraph each word will create the sudden suspense made by a small move in chess. In the story of Emma Zung, a woman is shown getting a letter which tells her that her father, whom she has not seen for years, has committed suicide: I give the English translation in which the dry exactitude of the Spanish is weakened – but still it catches the effect he desires:

> Her first impression was of a weak feeling in her stomach and in her knees: then of blind guilt, of unreality, of coldness, of fear; then she wished that it were already the *next* day. Immediately afterwards she

realised that the wish was futile because the death of her father was the only thing that had happened in the world and it would go on happening endlessly.

Why did she wish it were the next day? Why should the death 'go on happening endlessly' in real life? Because she is intent on revenge. These phrases ring in the imagination like an alarm bell, and this alarm is at the heart of all Borges's writing. The endlessness, the timelessness of a precise human experience, is his constant subject. How to convey the sense of endlessness curtly – with a vividness that is, on the face of it, perfunctory – will again and again be his dramatic task.

Nearly all the stories of Borges, except the earliest ones, are either constructed conundrums or propositions. The early ones are trial glosses on the American gangster tale transferred to the low life of Buenos Aires. He moved on to the stories of the gaucho: he heard many of these from his grandmother. They begin deceptively as short, historical reminiscences and then, at the crisis, they burst into actuality out of the past; he is recovering a moment:

> Any life, no matter how long and complex it may be, is made up of a *single moment* – the moment in which a man finds out, once and for all, who he is.

In his stories of the gauchos, their violence will strike us as meaningless until Borges says:

> the gauchos, without realising it, forged a religion – the hard and blind religion of courage – and this faith (like all others) has its ethic, its mythology and its martyrs . . . they discovered in their own way the age-old cult of the gods of iron – no mere form of vanity, but an awareness that God may be found in any man.

The task of the writer in each story – it is usually a fight – is to find the testing crisis of *machismo*, as if he were chiselling it all out in hard, unfeeling stone. He is very careful to keep the tone of landscape or street low – he even refers to 'insipid streets' – in order to heighten the violence. The test may not be heroic, but will contain a dismissive irony. In *The Dead Man* a swaggering tough has been boasting to an able but ageing gang-leader.

The gangs are expert cattle stealers. To the young man's surprise the old leader of the gang lets him get the better of him and even sends him up-country in charge of the next job. The gang obey the new young leader admiringly: the young man has even had the impudence to take the old leader's girl. They obey and love the young man. Why? Because he is the supplanter and winner? Because they are naturally treacherous time-serving cowards? Or simply recklessly indifferent? None of these things. An ancient knowledge comes to them. They *love* the young man because he is virtually dead already. He must be loved for his moment. They are really waiting, with interest, for the time when the old leader will come up-country, take his rightful revenge and kill him.

Or again, in a superb tale *The Intruder*, there are two brothers. A girl servant looks after them. She becomes the mistress of one brother, but when he goes off on his work the other brother sleeps with her. Both brothers fear their jealousy, so in the end they put the girl in a brothel. This does not solve their problem, for both secretly visit her. What is to be done? The test of their love for each other has arrived. They take her off at night and kill her. Lust is dead and now their love for each other is secure. Or there is the tale of Cruz, a soldier with a savage career behind him, who has been sent off to capture an outlawed murderer. The outlaw is cornered by Cruz and his soldiers and fights back desperately. Borges writes:

Cruz while he fought in the dark (while his body fought) began to understand. He understood that one destiny is no better than another, but that every man must obey what is within him. He understood that his shoulder braid and his uniform were now in his way. He understood that his real destiny was as a lone wolf, not a gregarious dog. He understood the other man was himself.

So he turns against his own men and fights beside the outlaw. This is the story of the semi-mythical hero of the gauchos, Martin Fierro.

Because of the influence of the cinema, most reports or stories of violence are so pictorial that they lack content or meaning. The camera brings them to our eyes, but does not settle them in our minds, nor in time. Borges avoided this trap by stratifying his tales in subtle layers of flat history, hearsay and metaphysical speculation: he is not afraid of trailing off into a short essay, ending with an appendix, for the more settled a violent subject looks, the more we can be misled, the more frightening the drama. It will not only be seen to be true, but will have the sadness and dignity of a truth that our memories have trodden away. History, in Borges, is never picturesque or romantic. It is the past event coming back like a blow in the face.

When we turn to the fantasies of the poet in Borges we find him first of all at play with spoof learning. In one of his best-known works with the extraordinary title of *Tlön, Uqbar, Orbis Tertius*, the librarian puts on a learned, dry-as-dust air of research and slyly reveals how for generations a secret society of pedestrian scholars have slowly invented an imaginary planet, complete with civilisation and language derived from a faked edition of the *Encyclopaedia Britannica*, so that the non-existent has become established. Or in another tale he pretends to have discovered how the Idea of Luck gradually became rooted in the thought of a Compañía – a religious Order – who since ancient times have been inventing luck, little by little, by trial and error, until it pervades life and may be life itself. What they were really documenting was the monotony of life.

A more serious preoccupation comes close to nightmare. Our imaginations may be housed in intellectual constructions. The labyrinth is one. Or we may be enacting feelings, scenes or events that simply belong to 'an endless series' – a favourite phrase – over which we have no control. A fatalistic symbol of time or memory is a corridor with two mirrors facing each other: the infinitely repeated reflections are symbols of our consciousness of people, sensations and even things. Indeed things – a knife, a room, for example, and facts of landscape – have a threatening existence of their own and the dead force of inventory. In the story called *The Aleph* which contains his characteristic changes of voice, the narrator talks flatly of the death of a shallow society woman whom he had vainly loved:

> On the burning February morning Beatriz Viterbo died after an agony that never for one single moment gave way to self-pity or fear, I noticed that the billboards on the sidewalk round Constitution Plaza were advertising some new brand of American cigarette. The fact pained me for I realised that the wide, ceaseless universe was already slipping away from her and that this slight change was the first of an endless series.

The narrator who is a poet heightens his pain by going to visit another poet, a boring man called Carlos Argentino Daneri who was a cousin of Beatriz and probably her lover. Daneri is

> authoritarian and unimpressive. His mental activity was continuous, deeply felt, far-ranging and – all in all – meaningless.

Daneri is writing an enormous poem which will conscientiously describe 'modern man' and everything on modern man's earth. The attack on realism and fact-fetishism is obvious:

> Daneri had in mind to set to verse the entire face of the planet, and by 1941, had already despatched a number of acres of the State Queensland, nearly a mile of the course run by the River Ob, a gasworks to the north of Vera Cruz, the leading shops in the Conception quarter of Buenos Aires, the villa of Mariana Cambaceres de Alvear in the Belgrano section of the Argentine capital, and a Turkish baths establishment not far from the well known Brighton Aquarium.

In this curtly sarcastic comedy of jealousy over the grave of Beatriz Viterbo, Borges is leading us by the nose. He is preparing us for one of his eloquent imaginative leaps out of the dead world of things into a rhapsody on the tragedy of human loss. Daneri is annoyed that the narrator does not praise his poem and, knowing his man, says that embedded in the stairs of his cellar he possesses a great wonder which has inspired him and which will vanish tomorrow because the house is going to be pulled down. The wonder is a magic stone called the Aleph. The Aleph is the microcosm of the alchemists and Kabbalists, 'our true proverbial friend' (he calls it) 'the multum in parvo':

> Go down into the cellar, you can babble with all Beatriz Viterbo's images.

The narrator is locked in the cellar. He sees the stone which is only an inch wide:

> In that single gigantic instance I saw millions of acts both delightful and awful; not one of them amazed me more than the fact that all of them occupied the same point in space, without overlapping or transparency . . . I saw, close up, unending eyes watching themselves in me as in a

[904]

mirror; I saw all the mirrors on earth and none of them reflected me; I saw in a backyard of Soler Street the same tiles that thirty years before I'd seen in the entrance of a house in Fray Bentos; I saw bunches of grapes, snow, tobacco, lodes of metal, steam; I saw convex equatorial deserts and each one of their grains of sand; I saw a woman in Inverness whom I shall never forget; I saw her tangled hair, her tall figure; I saw the cancer in her breast; I saw a ring of baked mud in a sidewalk, where before there had been a tree . . . I saw in a closet in Alkmaar a terrestrial globe between two mirrors that multiplied it endlessly . . . I saw in the drawer of a writing table (and the handwriting made me tremble) unbelievable, obscene, detailed letters, which Beatriz had written to Carlos Argentino; I saw the circulation of my own dark blood; I saw the coupling of love and the modification of death . . .

The story ends in what is a typical Borges manner. There is a short discussion of the metaphysical theories about the Aleph which contains the malicious phrase 'Incredible as it may seem, I believe that the Aleph of Garay Street was a false Aleph':

Our minds are porous and forgetfulness seeps in. I myself am distorting and losing, under the wearing away of the years, the face of Beatriz Viterbo.

In the story the shock of jealousy, grief and loss is transposed into a reel of mechanical effects.

In the elaborate fable of *The Circular Ruins*, a grey and silent teacher takes refuge in a ruined temple. 'His guiding purpose, though it was super-natural, was not impossible. He wanted to dream a man; he wanted to dream him down to the last detail and project him into the world of reality'. He 'creates' this phantom, thinks of him as his son; and then remembers that Fire is the only creature in the world who would know he was a phantom. In the end Fire destroys the dreamer. What is the meaning of the fable? Is it a fable of the act of creation in art? A solipsist conceit? A missing chapter from the Book of Genesis? An experience of panic caused by insomnia or reading Berkeley? Borges says,

With relief, with humiliation, with terror, he understood that he too was a mere appearance dreamt by another.

[905]

One can argue that the later Borges is a learned pillager of metaphysical arguments: one who has made Chesterton rhapsodic, put blood into the diagrams of Euclid, or a knife into the hands of Schopenhauer, but the test of the artist is – Can he make his idea walk, can he place it in a street, a room, can he 'plant' the aftermath of the 'moment of truth'? Borges *does* pass this test. The poet is a master of the quotidian, of conveying a whole history in two or three lines that point to an exact past drama and intensify a future one.

To go back to the tale of Emma Zung. We see her preparing to avenge her father's death. To kill is a degrading act; first of all, therefore, she has to initiate herself into degradation by posing as a prostitute and sleeping with a sailor. She tears up the money he leaves her because to destroy money is impiety.

> Emma was able to leave without anyone seeing her; at the corner she got on a Lacroze streetcar heading west. She selected, in keeping with her plan, the seat farthest toward the front so that her face would not be seen. Perhaps it comforted her to verify in the insipid movement along the streets that what had happened had not contaminated things.

A small fact creates the impression of a link with some powerful surrounding emotion or some message from the imagination or myth. The very casualness of the sudden observation suggests the uncertainty by which our passions are surrounded.

Borges loves to borrow from other writers, either good or second-rate. He admires Poe who defined for all time what a short story intrinsically is. He certainly has been influenced by Kafka – he translated *The Castle* into Spanish – although he is far from being a social moralist. On the face of it he looks like one of the European cosmopolitans of the first thirty years of this century and, like them, very much a formalist. But on second thoughts one sees that his mind is not in the least European. The preoccupation with isolation, instant violence and the metaphysical journey of discovery or the quest for imagined treasure marks him as belonging to the American continents. His sadness is the colonial sadness, not the European.

A bookish comment occurs to me. A few years ago when I was reading Borges for the first time I read two of the very late stories of Prosper Mérimée: *Lokis* and *La Vénus d'Ille*. There is a vast difference between the

French Romantic and Borges, but they have one or two singular things in common. A short-story writer cannot help being struck by the similarities that, in the course of more than 100 years, have diverged. Both writers have the English coolness and *humeur*, the background of the linguistic, historical, archaeological and mystical erudition. Mérimée was very much the wounded man, cold and detached, conservative and rational, but he had the civilised Romantic's fascination with the primitive and the unbelievable. In these two late stories – possibly because of a personal crisis – he is suddenly concerned with dream and the unconscious. It is true that the polished and formal Mérimée plays with his metaphysical anxieties, and has no interest in the self-creating man or woman, but he shares with Borges a love of hoaxing pedantry and the common approach of the misleading essay. The terrible story *Lokis* affects to arise in the course of a serious study of the Lithuanian language. (Mérimée was a philologist, so is Borges.) Mérimée uses his learning to play down his subject for it will suddenly become a fantastic dream of the unconscious turned into gruesome reality. The same may be said of Mérimée's tale of Corsican vendetta and in the ghost story of *La Vénus d'Ille.*

A hundred and thirty years separate Mérimée and Borges. Where Mérimée's documentation is a closed study of folklore or custom, Borges takes a leap into space, into the uncertain, the mysterious and the cunning. The record has become memory feeding on memory, myth feeding on myth. Where Mérimée is the master of anecdote in which lives end when the artist decides, Borges has the poet's power to burst the anecdote open. He seems to say that the story must be open, because I, too, am like my characters, part of an endless series or repetitions of the same happenings. The risk is – and there are some signs of this already – that criticism of Borges will become an accretion that will force us to see his stories as conceits alone.

The Supreme Fairy Tale

_____

When a novelist takes to a bout of lecturing to university students he knows that for him it is sin to live by his mouth. He is throwing away his syntax and his prose; the charms of the impromptu will not work unless he has first gone through the drudgery of preparation. Without his habit of thorough preparation, his dash, his delight in mischief, prejudice, and the cheerfully perverse, Vladimir Nabokov's lectures would have been no more than pepper and salt. He was an extraordinary preparer. When he came to deliver his course on _Don Quixote_ at Harvard in 1951–2 he had, for example, gone to the length of writing a summary of the events in this enormous novel, chapter by chapter, so making an invaluable crib. He wrote and rewrote his script, and at once destroyed its virginal look by covering it with corrections, possible asides, alternative paragraphs and optional quotations. He arrived at the lectern with a mass of possibilities.

In collating these martyred pages his present editors have had what must have been an exasperating task; but, for the lecturer himself, the mess was a guarantee of clarity and natural utterance. (There is nothing like a clean typescript for arresting thought and destroying personality.) Nabokov had a special talent for quotation: he knew that students, even those who are keen enough to read, will not have heard the 'tune' or real voice of the author's sentences; that reading aloud tests a style. Then, as a linguist, he had strong views about the merits of Cervantes's translators. He was equipped also for skirmishes with the well-known Spanish and foreign critics. He found the terse intelligence of Madariaga good, but he loathed the mellifluousness of the learned Aubrey Bell.

Nabokov was amusing on minor disputes too: he was irritated by Joseph Wood Krutch's claim that Don Quixote was always defeated in his battles. He went to the trouble of reckoning the score of victories and defeats and was delighted to find the score even. And to be sure his students had some idea of what a book of chivalry was, he supplied them with pages of Malory and *Amadis of Gaul*. Most of us have taken these romances as read. In short, I strongly recommend this edition of Nabokov's lectures as a practical guide to all incipient lecturers.

Nabokov cleared the ground aggressively at once with his usual *de haut en bas*:

> We shall do our best to avoid the fatal error of looking for so-called 'real life' in novels. Let us not try and reconcile the fiction of facts with the facts of fiction . . . *Don Quixote* is a fairy tale, so is *Bleak House*, so is *Dead Souls. Madame Bovary* and *Anna Karenina* are supreme fairy tales. But without these fairy tales the world would not be real.

Don Quixote is seen as a fairy tale about a fairy tale. Not the greatest novel in the world but the supreme fairy tale. True, it is patchy in its narrative. Cervantes is patently improvising for a long time, without certainty of plan. On his dull days he is just filling in to keep the thing going. The stroke of genius is the invention of Don Quixote himself who imparts enormous and growing vitality to the book, so that his figure ends by looming 'wonderfully above the skyline of literature'; within twenty years of the publication of the first part, it started to fertilise other literatures, and went on doing so for centuries after it was written. Don Quixote became a universal myth. (And, one might add, has escaped the demise of, say, Don Juan, who has become suddenly unadaptable to our century.)

It is striking, Nabokov continues, that such a figure as Don Quixote should have risen serenely out of the knockabout roguery and low-life meanness of picaresque writing. (On the other hand, isn't there a gleam of light in *Lazarillo de Tormes?*) Distressed by his failure as a poet and playwright, Cervantes seems to have thrown himself on the mercy of an intuition which up until his fifties he neglected and despised. He seems to have been slow in seeing a plan; perhaps he intended no more than a short story. He was no good at landscape; he simply followed the painfully artificial tradition established by the Renaissance. Making landscape real and making it *work* for the story (Nabokov notes) did not appear until the nineteenth century.

What saved Cervantes was a gift that he may have learned as a playwright: the ingenious delight in all varieties of dialogue, high and low.

[909]

Sancho Panza's proverbs Nabokov finds boring – in translation – and one suspects he thinks the Russian peasant proverbs superior to the Spanish! The true spell of Cervantes is that he is a natural magician in pure story-telling. He has no mission, no particular social conscience. He is no fiery adversary of social evil. (However, what about those utterances in Part II, about the nature of plain justice and good government? Are we to take these as no more than the traditional Spanish complaint that 'good government' is impossible in his country, an impossible dream?) About the cult of chivalry:

> Cervantes . . . does not really give a hoot whether or not books of chivalry are popular in Spain; and, if popular, whether or not their influence is pernicious . . . Although Cervantes makes a great show of being morally concerned with these matters, the only thing about this chivalry or antichivalry affair that interests him is firstly its most convenient use as a literary device to propel, shift, and otherwise direct his story; and secondly its no less convenient use as a righteous attitude, a purpose, a flutter of indignation which in his pious, utilitarian, and dangerous day a writer had better take.

He had to keep a wary eye on the political and clerical authorities. Equally there is no reason for believing he was either for or against the great power of the Catholic Church. It seems that Nabokov would have no time for the theory that the fun at the expense of the romances of chivalry made *Don Quixote* the book that 'destroyed a nation'.

As for the book being humane or humorous, Nabokov thinks it a veritable encyclopaedia of shocking cruelty and brutality, one of the most barbarous books, in this respect, ever written. Its power to rouse belly laughs is vulgar and nauseating. Most popular humour is brutal and perhaps arises from an attempt to forget the pain. The tossing of Sancho in the blanket is unbearable – though is not Sancho's own comment on not knowing where he was as he was flung into the air an imaginative one? Even a comment on Quixotism? Of course Nabokov is indignant at the appalling acts of political cruelty of our own time. When his lecture moves on to Part II, in which the 'civilised' dukes and duchesses invent degrading torments for Don Quixote, Nabokov is as shocked as we are by sadism as an ingenious or fashionable amusement. But he goes on:

[910]

Art has a way of transcending the boundaries of reason . . . This novel would have died of the laughter its picaresque plot was meant to provoke had it not contained passages that gently usher or sweep the reader into the dream world of permanent and irrational art . . .

He is referring to the chapters in Part II when Don Quixote is alone after Sancho has got his promised island. Separated from each other they are unsustained by illusion, and a frightening element in their inner experiences emerges, above all for Don Quixote:

Don Quixote . . . is the maker of his own glory, the only begetter of these marvels; and within his soul he carries the most dread enemy of the visionary: the snake of doubt, the coiled consciousness that his quest is an illusion.

He experiences not 'the dark night of the soul' (as one might expect especially from a Spanish writer) but something far more delicate. We see him alone in his room, listening to the singing of the duchess's maid in the patio. It is that sometimes childlike singing of a *soledad*. Here Nabokov himself is very perceptive:

The inward hint, the veiled suspicion that Dulcinea may not exist at all, is now brought to light by contrast with a real melody . . . He is deeply moved because at that moment all the innumerable adventures of a like sort – barred windows, gardens, music, and love-making – all he has read of in those now strangely true books of chivalry – come back to him with a new impact, his dreams mingling with reality, his dreams fertilising reality . . . But his innate modesty, his purity, the glorious chastity of a true knight-errant, all this proves stronger than his manly senses – and after listening to the song in the garden he bangs the window shut, and now even more gloomy than before, 'as if,' says Cervantes, 'some dire misfortune had befallen him,' he goes to bed . . . This is an admirable scene . . . Back to the torture house.

What is Nabokov's final judgment? That the book is more important in its eccentric diffusion than in its own intrinsic value. Sancho is a bore, his proverbs lose their piquancy in English, but he is most interesting when he himself catches the infection of enchantment. The Don, on the other hand, undergoes a multiplication. He is enlarged by the ingenuity and subtlety of his madness. He embodies the mystery of reality and illusion. He is courageous to a degree.

We are confronted by an interesting phenomenon: a literary hero losing gradually contact with the book that bore him; leaving his creator's desk and roaming space after roaming Spain . . . We do not laugh at him any longer. His blazon is pity, his banner is beauty. He stands for everything that is gentle, forlorn, pure, unselfish, and gallant. The parody has become a paragon.

The students who listened to Nabokov used Samuel Putnam's careful, slightly bland translation but also J. M. Cohen's, which Nabokov often preferred. If they were able to turn to the Spanish the students would have discovered the sustained and luminous irony of the style, irony enhancing the subtlety of experience without any cruelty or dryness. From Nabokov they would have got stimulus. Fascinated by structure in his own work, he was very interesting on the growing ingenuity of the book. The introduction of the imaginary Arab author and of the notorious false version which stirred Cervantes to rise to the height of his powers in Part II were complexities very much up Nabokov's street. The only protest I have concerns his offhand comment on the redoubling of illusions in the grand scene at Montesinos's cave. That famous episode may have started as 'another twist that Cervantes gives to the Enchanted Dulcinea theme in order to keep the reader entertained and Don Quixote busy.' But what a powerful, critical, and dramatic elaboration of the theme of illusion it is. It amounts to a sight of imagination imagining itself.

Lord Byron's Letters

Byron's letters are among the most spirited in the English language, and are irresistible. They amount to an autobiography of the duelling kind. Byron is a good letter writer because whether he is scoffing, arguing, or even conducting his business affairs, he has a half-laughing eye on his correspondent; although he can turn icily formal, he has mainly a talking style of worldly elegance and is spontaneously the half self of the moment, for not only he but everyone else knew the duality of his nature. The whole person can be deduced from what he dashingly offers. His character is a springboard from which he takes a dive into what he has to say about himself for the moment, bringing other people to half-life in the splash. In saying that his style is conversational, one means that he was at his best when talking *tête-à-tête* – when he could be free with asides, sudden images, ironical glimpses of confession. He plays with his masks. He enjoyed scandal – not for its mean side but for its flashes of satirical fantasy and because it is 'a sort of cayenne to the mind'. In letters, as in talk, 'all subjects are good in their way providing they are sufficiently diversified'. As a passionate extremist and opponent, he easily dropped into the anticlimax of affectionate good humour. He was, as many have said, an opportunist where the passions were concerned; yet he had a plodding care in daily life for routine and regular habits. According to Lady Blessington, he said in one of their platonic chats, 'People take for gospel all I say, and go away continually with false impressions . . . Now, if I know myself, I should say, that I have no character at all . . . [This also was Balzac's view of himself and of artists in general.] I am so changeable, being every thing by turns and nothing long, – I am such a strange *mélange* of good and evil, that it would be difficult to describe me. There are but two sentiments to which I am constant, – a strong love of liberty, and a detestation of cant, and neither is calculated to gain me friends.'

The meetings with Lady Blessington occurred in 1823 in Genoa, where she arrived with her husband and her necessary dandy, the Count D'Orsay. Byron was well settled with the Countess Guiccioli and her father in their common exile in the nine months that preceded the poet's fatal departure for Greece. Leslie A. Marchand's *A Heart for Every Fate* is the tenth, and penultimate, volume of the excellent unexpurgated edition of all known Byron letters, and covers this period. The letters of the new volume are discernibly less vivacious than those in which Byron was seen, at the age of thirty-one, falling in love with the nineteen-year-old Countess and causing alarm among the Austrian Secret Police. After four years, the liaison is in the pleasant doldrums of something like a marriage. If, as Byron wrote, 'the great object of life is sensation – to feel that we exist', the sensational is now in abeyance. He is even dieting to keep down the threat of corpulence; there is no pursuit of other women, though the pretty Countess is often jealous. But there are signs of another restlessness: the political. The sight of the sea at Genoa – the port of so many adventurers – perhaps revived temptation. If there are signs of conjugal 'settling down', there are also rather secretive indications of 'clearing up' and putting his money affairs in order for a bolder purpose. He knows he is risking his life. There is a rush, canto by canto, to finish *Don Juan*, as if the poem were an investment; this leads to the quarrels with John Murray, his publisher, who is tiring of *Don Juan* and wants him to get back to the manner of *Childe Harold*. A canto of this period opens with a comic attack on the metaphysics of Berkeley. The poet says he has moved from the 'metaphysical' to the 'phthisical', because 'ever and anon comes Indigestion', not to mention inflammations and chilblains.

> I don't know what the reason is – the air
> Perhaps; but as I suffer from the shocks
> Of illness, I grow much more orthodox.

To the extent of going back to his early Old Testament Calvinist terrors and writing the play *Cain* in language that has lost its tune.

So his restless mind turns to Greece, in order to escape his buried despairs. He is happy with the Countess; nevertheless, he schemes to go, torn between guilt about her and his new desire. She fights back and wants to go with him – 'of course the idea is ridiculous'. She must be kept out of harm's way:

If she makes a scene – (and she has a turn that way) we shall have another romance – and tale of ill usage and abandonment – and Lady Caroling – and Lady Byroning – and Glenarvoning – all cut and dry; there never was a man who gave up so much to women – and all I have gained by it – has been the character of treating them harshly . . . When a man merely wishes to go on a great duty for a good cause – this selfishness on the part of the 'feminine' – is rather too much.

Before this, there is the professional annoyance: Murray delays publishing the new cantos of *Don Juan* and pretends to have mislaid the manuscripts. He gets many blasts from the poet, who eventually hands his work to Leigh Hunt's brother and the banker Kinnaird.
To Murray:

I have received and answered through Mr Kinnaird your enigma of a note to him – which riddle as expounded by Oedipus – means nothing more than an evasion to get out of what you thought perhaps a bad business – either for fear of the Parsondom – or your Admiralty patrons – or your Quarter*lyers* – or some other exquisite reason – but why not be sincere & manly for once – and say so? . . . The truth is that you never know your own mind – and what between this opinion and that – and sundry high & mighty notions of your own extreme importance in the planetary system – you act like the philosopher in Rasselas who took the direction of the Winds under his auspices – take care – that one of them don't blow you down some morning.

But he goes on to say that he believes, or at least hopes, that after all Murray 'may be a good fellow at bottom', and then makes a plea on behalf of one of Murray's authors, who is on her beam-ends, and who, instead of applying to the Bishop or Mr Wilberforce, 'hath recourse to that proscribed – Atheistical – syllogistical – phlogistical person – *mysen* – as they say in Notts'. The raillery and rancour often glide away like this, and turn into a half-Scottish peer's teasing of a Scottish tradesman. And there are other touchy domestic matters, such as Byron's famous loathing of Leigh Hunt's 'six little blackguards', who are 'dirtier and more mischievous than Yahoos' ('what they can't destroy with their filth they will with their fingers'). There is his charity to their father – Byron calls him 'a bore' but won't let this unworldly and childish man starve. After all, he *is* a combative liberal enemy of established society – a Radical – even though trying to help him 'is like pulling a man out of a river who directly throws himself in again'.

This comedy is very well known to literary history. There are tender, playful letters to his sister Augusta – letters that have a touch of the guilty 'little language' he and his sister had in common. He supposes that a Pimlico lady who has fallen in love with him for having written *Don Juan* is either mad or 'nau' (i.e., naughty), like Constantia, Echo, and La Swissesse – old loves Augusta will giggle about. There is a grotesque account of a flood in Genoa, where a preaching friar who prophesied the immediate date of the Day of Judgment had persuaded the population to send him 'presents' to avert it. The Genoese, true to their traditions, asked for their money back when the Judgment did not occur, and then had a fiesta. And there is news of new London scandals, such as the strange transformation of Lord Portsmouth after his marriage to a lawyer's daughter who horsewhipped him, seemingly because he was impotent and a lunatic, whereas he had appeared to be a man 'who had been allowed to walk about the world five and forty years as Compos – of voting – franking – marrying – convicting thieves on his own evidence – and similar pastimes which are the privileges of Sanity'. There is a pleasant friendship with a cousin of some sort, Lady Hardy, who is being pursued vainly by a coxcomb – 'now conceited into a knight (but of no order – a regular Address and City knight)' – who swears that his black wig is the 'flaxen poodle furniture with which Nature had decorated his head ten years ago'. Byron tries to make this ass return to his wife in Lausanne and utters the moral that lovers cannot be friends, 'because there must always be a spice of jealousy – and a something of Self in all their speculations'. Indeed, love is 'a sort of hostile transaction'. (He said the same of bargains in general, especially with Murray.) The reflection went into two lines of the continuing *Don Juan*. His own 'Love perils are – I believe pretty well over', he tells Lady Hardy, and hers, 'by all accounts are never to begin'. However, 'la mia Dama' (the Countess Guiccioli) was having 'a furious fit of Italian jealousy' because he went riding with Lady Blessington (of whom Lawrence had painted a portrait 'that set all London raving') and her supposed lover the Count D'Orsay. In later years, the Guiccioli said of one of Byron's own early

[916]

jealous letters to her that it had a 'jalousie magnifique – passionnée – sublime mais très injuste'. In another letter to his sister Augusta, he once said that the Countess was indeed pretty but 'a great Coquette – extremely vain – excessively affected – clever enough – without the smallest principle – with a good deal of imagination and some passion'. But a bore as an equestrian: 'Can't guide her horse – and . . . begins screaming.'

Byron admires the Count D'Orsay, because he

> penetrated *not* the *fact* – but the *mystery* of the English Ennui at two and twenty. – I was about the same age when I made the same discovery in almost precisely the same circles . . . but I never could have described it so well . . . He ought to have seen the Gentlemen after dinner – (on the hunting days) . . . and the women looking as if they have had [sic] hunted – or rather been hunted – too . . . [Dessert] was hardly on the table – when out of 12 of the masculine gender – I counted *five asleep*.

Byron admired D'Orsay's 'Journal' and showed it to Teresa Guiccioli, who found it gave her a much better notion of English society than 'all Madame de Stael's metaphysical dissertations'. We doubt if she had ever read those philosophical writings.

In all the 'clearing up' letters, in which he is obliged to look after the legal complications of his estate and his separation from 'Lady B' and is at pains to cause no trouble, one detects a desire to get rid of encumbrance for good and to make a bid for another romance – fame in the Greek cause. At the same time, one is struck by his skill in making the fuss of financial and organisational detail lively. As a libertine, he was a pedant. Byron was stirred by every intrigue, however mundane, that human nature is up to. The poet was very much a man of the world, the expatriate had a lot of time on his hands: the tedium had to be dispelled. He was more calculating than erratic. The play *Cain* brings his haunting private despair to the surface, but the letters contain nothing of it. The bravura is still there, and the amateur Satan's careless good nature is a kind of noblesse oblige.

A Rough English Diamond

O̲ne impression of ordinary English life from the mid-eighteenth century to the middle of the nineteenth is that it is thronged by an ever-increasing crowd of grotesque bodies, sprawling in their energetic vulgarity or skinny in their dramatic misery. The overwhelming impression is of a crowd bursting with involuntary imaginative and moral life, in the pathos, absurdity, and animality of the flesh. I refer not only to what we have had from novelists but, of course, to the caricaturists especially and masterly graphic artists, like Hogarth, Rowlandson, Gillray, and finally Cruikshank. In the last, the sense of the crowd becomes at times mythical and animistic; Napoleon is seen early in Cruikshank's career standing on a vast pyramid of crowded skulls; in the 'Hungry Forties' a giant mincer is seen turning thousands of sewing girls into the coins of the Capitalist's profits; as London expands crowds of steel spades looking like devilish Martians are tearing up the countryside without human aid; at the Great Exhibition, England pours its whole population – so that a city like Manchester is left empty – into Piccadilly; the tender triumph of Cupid packs the drawing with clouds of babies.

But after the Great Exhibition the free-for-all calms down, the country turns from its disaffections to self-satisfaction and gentility, and now Cruikshank's reign as the leading humorist and caricaturist of the time begins to decline. The middle-class respectability of *Punch*, for which he refused to draw, is established; low life is 'out' or is seen as 'a problem'. Cruikshank's *genius* did not decline, but he was less prolific, narrowed his field to propaganda against the evils of drink, and indeed changed his style.

Now Richard A. Vogler gives us a scholarly selection of 279 of Cruikshank's etchings and drawings taken from the five or six thousand he is known to have done. Each of them has a short and expert commentary and there is a long introduction expounding the techniques, changes of process, and other influences of his trade on his genius. There also is a serious defence of popular comic art, which has been neglected by art historians, and indeed of the essentially anarchic nature of comedy. Vogler protests against regarding Cruikshank in a belittling way purely as an illustrator of books.

Little is known about his daily life beyond the fact that he was a perpetual worker who liked jolly and Bohemian company and avoided High Society when he rapidly became famous. In person he was celebrated for the originality of his fantastically designed whiskers and for the ingenious pattern of his hairstyle: the strands were artfully held into place by concealed elastic bands. He could be said to have etched his hair.

Born in 1792 he was the son of a graphic artist who had migrated from Scotland to London and settled in the jungle of poor streets that lie between Pentonville and Camden Town – the deeply Dickensian maze. He and his brother and sister took up the father's craft, working for newspapers and booksellers, i.e. publishers, as caricaturists and illustrators. Cruikshank rarely left London or his district in the eighty-five years of his life though he once did a Cockney trip to Boulogne for a few days and (because he was something of a singer and actor) appeared in one of Dickens's amateur theatrical ventures in the north.

Ainsworth, Dickens, and others found him delightful company but distinctly quirky and stubborn in working arrangements. (In old age he claimed that these novelists owed many of their best touches to him, a matter which is hotly disputed: one trouble is that his work was copied and recopied without further pay from the booksellers and he strongly resented this.) Still, he did pretty well, married twice. Though it is thought he had no children, there is a suspicion that he had a secret family of nine or ten to whose mother he left a substantial legacy. Some of his impish illustrations for children's books suggest that he had strong philoprogenitive feelings.

There was one dramatic change in Cruikshank's life. It happened when he was forty-seven. The convivial fellow who had once begged Dickens to walk home with him because he feared what his wife would say about his unsteady condition suddenly gave up the bottle for good and now spent as much time speaking at temperance meetings as he did at his work. He became a fanatical propagandist and some critics, especially Ruskin, said this had a dulling effect on his work. Mr Vogler does not agree with this conventional view. Cruikshank gave up drink when he reached the age at which his father had died after a drinking bout: the conversion may owe something to superstition.

A more important argument surely is that hard drinking is incompatible with the minute and delicate demands of the etcher's art. Equally important was Cruikshank's long-frustrated ambition to equal the great Hogarth who was his master and to do a series of pictures that would bring Gin Alley up to date. Finally, Cruikshank was a man of strong will with an individualist's social conscience and a professional sense of the topical. The formidable temperance movement had begun.

In a well-known essay Thackeray called Cruikshank 'a fine rough English diamond' and 'diamond' is the sparkling word that sticks in the mind. Baudelaire wrote that his special merit lies 'in his inexhaustible abundance of grotesque. A verve such as his is unimaginable . . . The grotesque flows inevitably and incessantly from Cruikshank's etching needle, like pluperfect rhymes from the pen of a natural poet.'

The perceptions of the comic genius, even when they are directed to the vulgar or ordinary, are almost always poetic. Vogler speaks of 'the anarchic power of comedy': Cruikshank was neither a radical nor a conservative – he satirised universal suffrage; he did not agree with Dickens that the sole causes of the appalling evils of drink in the Victorian age were poverty and misery. There were others. His object was 'to cleanse by mirth' and strip away 'smugness'. And on his defence of Cruikshank as a popular artist, Vogler says,

> an artist like Cruikshank became the nineteenth-century exponent of a visual tradition in European religious and secular art which relates symbols and language in a unique way. Pictorial traditions tend to survive more pervasively in popular art forms like caricature than in almost any other kind of art . . . The recurrent use of a dunce's hat in Cruikshank goes back to the basic iconology available to artists from the time of the Renaissance. Cruikshank is a late but direct inheritor of a very complex visual language that has steadily lost its power over the modern world.

He is also very literary. These lines are written to stir the art historians. Let us look at Cruikshank's early graphics done during the Regency. One notices at once the bite and grace of ingeniously placed detail. Byron takes his romantic farewell to England in a boat full of luscious adoring ladies, but the comments of the vulgar seamen are rudely offhand; Napoleon's soldiers are not simply stuck in the Russian snow, they are up to their elegant cocked hats in it. The remnants of the Grande Armée are skeletons, their uniforms are in ridiculous rags. As for royalty at home – George IV is a balloon of flesh. A fat couple are stuck in a doorway of a crowded and fashionable drawing room. The appalled eyes, the pursed apologetic little mouth of the lordling who has trodden on a lady's trailing skirt are a subtle composite of the grimace and speechless abuse that will twitch on a polite face for a split second. Notice the man's clawed hand, notice also the young couple having a peaceful chat in this melée of colliding bellies.

In 'Villagers Shooting out the Rubbish' the coarse villagers are pushing out the bewigged clergyman and the gentry in wheelbarrows. In 'Effects of a Heavy Lurch on board an East Indiaman' the artist catches every bizarre angle into which arms and legs can fall, every shape of a shouting mouth, while an undisturbed seaman grunts, 'Hang on by your eyelids.' Note also the Hogarthian variety of detail, down to the upturned dog biting a passenger's leg; and, of course, a stout lady with her legs in the air as the centrepiece. She has just given a whack on the nose to a gentleman who is trying nervously to pull back her leg into decency. There are cracks at illness: gout and the colic are celebrated by gangs of devils – surfeit is a joke. There are the parades of monstrous fashions at Brighton. And if the Radical Reform has a death's head it is leading the scum of the prisons, the sword of constitutional Britannia has buckled and becomes putty. Cruikshank hated revolution; on the other hand, the English boroughmongers are seen pouring out bribes and sinecures from a water mill, while the poor lie dying under the pillars of Parliament.

It pays to use a magnifying glass on many of Cruikshank's smaller graphics and Vogler's notes are enlightening both on Cruikshank's fancy and on his topicality. So the *Sunday in London* series (1833) was undertaken as a humorous protest against an attempt to introduce a Bill in Parliament which would impose strict observation of the Sabbath – Dickens wrote an indignant pamphlet on the same subject. There was an attempt to close Sunday street-trading – a long-standing London liberty – during church services. The bill was an attack on the lower classes: the servants and delivery boys of the wealthy were exempted from restrictions! In 'The Pay Table', a drunken workman comes up for his wages, while a tavern-keeper stands by the employer in order to deduct the man's drinking debts from his pay. One sees the common crowd brawling cheerfully as they are being turned out of gin palaces, at church time, and the series ends with the high order sitting smugly in church. In contrast, in an illustration of Scott's *Heart of Midlothian*, Captain of Knockdunder is seen defying the preacher by smoking a foul pipe in church. Another sketch – an example of Cruikshank's jolly anthropomorphic fancy – shows a preacher in the shape of a weeping crocodile.

Vogler's book includes the pictures relating to 'The Loving Ballad of Lord Bateman' – a popular song which was one of Cruikshank's party turns. Bateman, the 'ruler' of Northumberland, travelled to Turkey, was imprisoned, but was set free by the Sultan's daughter to whom he promised marriage. He got away, was about to marry 'another', but the Turk's daughter rushed over to claim him – a delightful ballet, for Cruikshank was an incurable dancer.

Mr Vogler notes the use of language and punning symbols in his drawings. In 'The Fall of the Leaf' – in which half a dinner party is thrown to the ground when the leaf of the table collapses – there is a dim picture of Niagara Falls on the wall and on the floor there is a copy of Gibbon's *Decline and Fall of the Roman Empire*. Overdoing a joke? No. Echoes and repetitions extend the farce. Whether Cruikshank adds these glosses or is closely following 'things' that are tucked unannounced in a text he is illustrating, we see he is one artist complementing another. I go back to that overwhelming Victorian sense of the crowd: it is a crowd not only of people but of fantasies. They are like the charivari of gargoyles and imps on the Gothic cathedrals, a Gothic revival. Cruikshank's picture of himself in 'Reverie' shows him sitting smoking his pipe and puffing out thousands of passing delineations of people; in his 'Temptation of St Anthony' the saint is surrounded by a primitive bestiary most of which can be traced back to fantasies not unlike those of Bosch.

The best-known illustrations are those done for *Sketches by Boz* and *Oliver Twist*. To the last – except for Nancy – Cruikshank has been the classic guide. (So magical has been the picture of 'Oliver asking for more' and so strong the literary tradition among cartoonists, that an American cartoonist used it in connection with the request of Congress for more tapes in the Watergate scandal.) In the pictures of Fagin and Sikes it is noticeable that a preoccupation with strangulation and hanging slips in; the picture of Sikes's dog, faithfully following him to the roof from which Sikes jumps to hang himself by accident, is as chilling as it is in Dickens.

Yet Cruikshank could move with ease to the theatrical thunder and lightning of Ainsworth's histories. Some readers – and I was among them when I was a boy brought up on late-Victorian conventions – have felt that Cruikshank's fantasies were at disconcerting variance with the realistic images we imposed on the text; but this showed our blindness to the essence of the imagination of both artists. Also we had failed to accept the Gothic self-imagination of that escape from grim work into the dream-life of a riotously inventive and expansive age at grips with its conscience, its conviviality, its crimes, and the contrasts of rich and poor in the streets. Cruikshank was as prolific as the first half of the century was, his sense of so many public scenes being, at heart, a brawl or a fight, albeit caught with robust laughter or an irony as sharp as the etcher's acid, turning hard times into phantasmagoria.

His anti-drink drawings for *The Bottle* are plain, realistic confrontations: the sober become comely in their domestic virtue, the sinners go step by step downhill as in the plain moralising manner of Hogarth, dragging decency down into the unanswerable pathos of the home destroyed before us. The feverish care of the artist is still there; his wonderful command of details of people in their scene is unabated, though the crowd has gone, and the private moral life and the sinister figures who prey on individuals replace myth. Victorian drinking was indeed ruinous to the poor and Cruikshank's *The Bottle,* like Zola's *L'Assommoir*, was an inescapable social document.

The strange thing is that, in this austere period of his life, Cruikshank made a hero of the great legendary figure of Falstaff who is still a bursting wine-skin but who looks like a benign, rather cleaned up Henry VIII. In this portrait Cruikshank indeed standardised the Falstaff of theatrical productions for several generations. One can account for this only by Cruikshank's love of historical subjects and their clothing and the fantasies of the unreal world of the Victorian theatre. And that brings one back to an essential in his art – his constant, even theatrical eye for staging his scenes,

[923]

whether they are large or minute, tragic, pathetic, or comic, and for the hundreds of ways the dressed-up body can behave when taken unawares. Human beings are clothed doubles; they stand in a room or the street, yet in their minds they are also standing elsewhere in the passions of the moment. Standing? Not quite – something in them is on the move.

A Dandy

$=$

Among the masked dandies of Edwardian comedy, Max Beerbohm is the most happily armoured by a deep and almost innocent love of himself as a work of art. As the youngest child of a large and gifted family of real and step-brothers and sisters, he seems to have adroitly decided to be an adult Enigma from the cradle onwards and to be not merely an old man of the world as early as possible, but even to pass as ancient man, possibly on the principle that the last shall be first. If he could not be as tall as his eldest brother, the world-famous actor Beerbohm Tree, he could cultivate the special sparkle and artifices of the diminutive so that one now has the impression that he must have worn a top hat and a swallow-tail coat in his pram. One understands the point of Oscar Wilde's question: he asked a lady whether Max ever took off his face and revealed his mask. Max had no face; or if he did have one it was as *disponible*, as blank as an actor's is. If he had a secret it lay in his quite terrific will and the power to live as if he and the people he saw were farcical objects.

In his essay on *Dandies* Max Beerbohm asks whether a dandy's clothes can be seen responding to the emotion of the wearer. Needless to say, an instance of this sartorial melancholia is known to him:

> I saw with wonder Lord X's linen actually flush for a moment and then turn deadly pale. I looked again and saw that his boots had lost their lustre. Drawing nearer, I saw that grey hairs had begun to show themselves in his raven coat. It was very painful and yet, to me, very gratifying. In the cloakroom, when I went for my own hat and cane, there was the hat with broad brim and (lo!) over its iron-blue surface little furrows had been ploughed by Despair.

'Deadly pale', 'lost their lustre', 'gratifying': only such epithets from a dead usage could release the protest of fantasy that is alive. The art of Max in that passage is shown in a single word: the grey hairs appear 'in' the coat,

not 'on' it, as many a comic, careless of the full terror of his effect, would
have said.

Beerbohm's detachment must have owed something to the fact that his
father came of a distinguished Baltic German family. He had had two
English wives: one died, so he married her sister secretly in Switzerland – it
was illegal in Great Britain to marry a deceased wife's sister at that time.
The father was an amiably slack and cultivated man: the mother engagingly eccentric with a talent for erratic minor alterations in English
metaphors. She would say 'I feel as old as *any* hills' – to be old, seemingly,
was as important to her as it was to her youngest son. The foreign strain
was just the thing to give an edge to Max's talent and that of the family.
Expatriation allows one to drop a lot of unwanted moral luggage, lets
talent travel lightly and opens it to the histrionic. For his own talents Max
Beerbohm could not have chosen a better time. Putting aside, for the
moment, such matters as Dandyism, the Aesthetes, the Decadents, the
acquaintance of Oscar Wilde, Beardsley, the fading Pre-Raphaelites and
the last remorses of the Romantic Agony, no place could have been luckier
than London for the wits. The city had many clever newspapers and
reviews, the theatre had Shaw and Ibsen to deal with, Pinero and others to
insult. It was the time for the fancy of the essayist, for fantasy, the comedy
of manners, hoaxes, impersonations, caricature and for carrying on an
artist's war with England's fleshly Philistinism, led by a Prince of Wales
who looked like a licentious grocer, and for attacking the blustering side of
British imperialism, by exaggerating the size of Kipling's chin and the
bushiness of his eyebrows. Max's eyebrows were impeccable question
marks. The amount of theatre criticism and essay writing he did as a young
man, and the delightful trouble it stirred up among the respectable, is
remarkable.

The famous *Defence of Cosmetics* written when Max was still at Oxford,
and his closeness to the Wilde and Beardsley set, led some to suspect that
Max was on the then dangerous edge of homosexuality. In fact, Max was
horrified by the scandalous intimacies of the flesh; his sexual temperature
was low – perhaps, as Lord David Cecil suggests in *Max: A Biography*,
because he was the last child of elderly parents whose vitality had declined.
His temperament was narcissistic – as his innumerable caricatures of
himself show – and he seems not even to have attained the narcissism of

adolescence, but to have sat with the scrupulous prudence of the demure child in front of any mirror he could find, experimenting in poses and grimaces.

He lived by the eye and – as one can see by his drawings – discreetly beyond touch of hand. Two caretaking wives looked after him in middle and late life and – to all appearances – treated him tenderly if over-whelmingly, as a dangerous toy. And then – how typical this is of an intelligent and sensitive man who is without roots – he turned to literature and the arts for his nationality. Among other things, in the wide-eyed persona he invented, there is sadness. Was it the sadness of not being a genius on the great scale, like his admired Henry James? Possibly. Was it the sadness of knowing that his work must be perfect – as that of minor writers has to be – because fate made him a simulacrum? Or was he simply born sad?

And now to Beerbohm's centenary year in times that are so unsuited to him. Piously Rupert Hart-Davis has done a large catalogue of all Beerbohm's caricatures that have been framed or suitably reproduced, a volume useful to collectors. (It is amusing that Beerbohm's devastating caricatures of Edward VII and George V, done in his 'black' period, are among the treasures in Windsor Castle.) A selection of essays, *A Peep into the Past*, has also been made by Hart-Davis, and serves to show the development of the essayist. In later essays the charm has become benign and thin, but three of them are excellent: the remarkable spoof portrait of Wilde done when Beerbohm was still an undergraduate and suppressed after the trial, in which occur the well-known lines:

> As I was ushered into the little study, I fancied that I heard the quickly receding *frou-frou* of tweed trousers, but my host I found reclining, hale and hearty, though a little dishevelled upon the sofa.

The other, written on *De Profundis*, denies the comforting view of many English critics of the time that Wilde had undergone a spiritual change after his imprisonment. Beerbohm saw him as still an actor but with a new role.

> Yet lo! he was unchanged. He was still precisely himself. He was still playing with ideas, playing with emotions. 'There is only one thing left for me now,' he writes, 'absolute humility.' And about humility he

writes many beautiful and true things. And, doubtless, while he wrote them, he had the sensation of humility. Humble he was not.

And there is the hilarious pretence in another essay that a powerful bad poet of the period – Clement Shorter – had spent his life writing love poems not to a lady but to one of the awful British seaside resorts.

The best American essay on him, in my opinion, was by Edmund Wilson, dry and to the point. There was no mellifluous English nonsense about the 'inimitable' and 'incomparable'. I feared what would happen to Max if he was put through the American academic mangle. There seems to be a convention that this machine must begin by stunning its victim with the obvious, and when I found Mr Felstiner saying, in his study *The Lies of Art*, about the notorious essay on cosmetics that 'Cosmetics were a perfect choice to join the teachings of the moment, aestheticism and decadence', I understood what Max meant when he said that exhaustive accounts of the period 'would need far less brilliant pens than mine'. But, as I went on, I found Mr Felstiner a thorough, thoughtful, and independent analyst of Max as a caricaturist and parodist. He has good things to say about Beerbohm's phases as an artist in line and watercolour, about his absolute reliance on the eye. He is admirable on the parodies in which Max reached the complete fulfilment of his gifts, and his comments on *Zuleika Dobson* are the most searching I have ever read.

Beerbohm caricatured Americans, the working class and the bourgeoisie automatically as part of the impending degradation of civilisation and the arts . . . John Bull is the crucial figure throughout, shaming himself in Europe, vilely drunk or helpless in the face of British losses, and deeply Philistine. On the evidence of these cartoons, Shaw called Beerbohm, 'the most savage Radical caricaturist since Gillray'.

His Prince of Wales is a coarse, tweedy brute, imagining a nunnery is a brothel. His pictures of royalty were savage.

What angered Beerbohm during the Boer War was not Britain's damaged empire – he was indifferent to that: 'the only feeling that our Colonies inspire in me is a determination not to visit them.' It was the self-delusion and debasement of conduct at home, the slavish reliance on grandiose national myths.

But he was no Gillray nor was he a Grosz. He

> . . . enjoyed with an eye for what men are individually – for their
> conceits, contradictions, deadlocks, excesses. Beerbohm drew more for
> fun than in the hope of changing attitude or behaviour. In fact he
> depended as a man and artist on the survival of the context he satirised.

Edwardian literature has many, many sad stories, stories whose frivolity
half discloses the price a culture is paying for its manners and illusions.
Zuleika Dobson is one of the funniest and most lyrical and sad of these tales.
As in all Beerbohm's fantasies, literary cross references are graceful and
malign. Fantasy states what realism will obscure or bungle.

> Yet in comparison with previous jocular or sentimental treatments, he
> could claim to have given 'a truer picture of undergraduate life'. His
> book points to real elements of conformity and sexual repression . . . By
> chance the river itself has the name of Isis, Egypt's greatest goddess, all
> things to all men. So what emerges is an allegory of Youth forsaking
> Alma Mater, the Benign Mother, for the consummating love of woman.

Zuleika seems to have been modelled in part on the famous bareback rider
whom Swinburne knew, and she has a close connection with 'the Romantic
Agony'. She is a 'Volpone of a self-conceit: her mirror is the world', i.e. she
is the male dandy's opposite number. Mr Felstiner writes of her rapture
when she is spurned by the Duke:

> All the world's youth is prostrate with love but she can only love a man
> who will spurn her . . . 'I had longed for it, but I had never guessed how
> wonderfully wonderful it was. It came to me. I shuddered and wavered
> like a fountain in the wind' – sounds like the joys of flagellation. The
> Duke even finds himself wanting to 'flay' her with Juvenalian verses.
> 'He would make Woman (as he called Zuleika) writhe.'

The element of parody insures the tale: Beerbohm's excellence and his
safety as an artist are guaranteed because, unfailingly, he is writing
literature within literature. Parody, as Mr Felstiner again puts it, is a filter.
It drains both literature and life.

Beerbohm rarely drew from photographs. He drew from memory. The
recipe for caricature was 'The whole man must be melted down in a

crucible and then, from the solution, fashioned anew. Nothing will be lost but no particle will be as it was before'. So Balfour's sloping body becomes impossibly tall and sad in order to convey his 'uneasy Olympian attitudes'. Carson, who prosecuted Wilde, is a long curve like a tense whip, whereas Balfour is a question mark. Beerbohm thickened Kipling's neck and enlarged his jaw to stress the brutality he saw in him. Pinero's eyebrows had to be 'like the skins of some small mammal, just not large enough to be used as mats'. One difficulty, he noted in *How They Undo Me*, is that over the years a subject may change – the arrogant become humble, the generous mean, the slopping scrupulous. Yeats had once seemed like a 'mood in a vacuum' but the youthful aspect changed.

> I found it less easy to draw caricatures of him. He seemed to have become subtly less like him.

As Mr Felstiner adds, a shade unnecessarily,

> The truth is that he [Yeats] had become more like himself . . . An evolving discipline made his themes and his style more tough-minded, idiomatic, accountable.

Mr Felstiner has noticed that in Max's caricatures the eyes of the politicians are generally closed – public life has turned them into blank statues in their own life-time – but the eyes of the writers and artists are open. The eyes of James are wide open – sometimes in dread. Beerbohm wrote a sonnet to him: 'Your fine eyes, blurred like arc lamps in a mist'. Beerbohm's admiration for James and his closeness to his belief in the primacy of art are responsible for the excellence of his well-known parody in *The Christmas Garland*. It required an art equal – if for a moment only – to James's own to get so keenly under the skin; and, like all good things, it was not achieved without great trouble. Indeed, Max added to the famous Christmas story one more turn of the screw.

He constantly revisited his subjects. His parodies are indeed criticism and the silent skill with which nonsense is mellifluously introduced, without seeming to be there, is astonishing. James's manner has often been mimicked, but never with Beerbohm's gift for extending his subject by means of the logic of comedy. I do not share Mr Felstiner's admiration for the Kipling parody: Max was blind to Kipling's imagination though he was daring in suggesting there was something feminine in Kipling's tough masculine worship of obedience. Max here disclosed a violence on his own part. Kipling was as good an actor as he; had been brought up by a Pre-Raphaelite father and had as much regard for form and style as Beerbohm had. But, of course, like greater artists, the parodist celebrates his own blindnesses as well as his power to see.

He could even show open schoolboy coarseness in a way that is surprising in one of his circumlocutory habit. There are a few lines on Shaw, an old love-hate, in J. G. Riewald's edition of rhymes and parodies, *Max in Verse*:

> I strove with all, for all were worth my strife,
> Nature I loathed, and next to Nature, Art;
> I chilled both feet on the thin ice of Life,
> It broke and I emit a final fart.

This book has some of Beerbohm's best things: the parody of Hardy's Dynasts, the pseudo-Shakespeare of Savanarola Brown – only Max could have seen what could be done by splitting iambic pentameters into banal dialogue. The Shropshire Lad is told abruptly to go and drown himself, and for those puzzled about the origins and pronunciations of English place names like Cirencester, there is a gently malicious ballad. Thirty-four of these poems have not been published before, partly because Max was very tactful, at the proper time, about hurting people's feelings – he repressed the keyhole James until after James's death – and partly because he knew when his own juvenile phase had lasted too long.

Fairy Tales

The Edwardian period in English literature which runs, I suppose, from the 1880s until 1914 was prolific in light, satirical society novelists of remarkable urbanity and invention. The exclusive Meredith was one of the gods; the moment for high comedy had come. One can see why: an age of surfeit had arrived. The lives of the upper classes were both enlivened and desiccated by what seems to have been a continuous diet of lobster and champagne – a diet well suited in its after-effects to the stimulation of malice. The class system gave the ironies of snobbery their double edge. Society lived out its fairy-tale life, spent its time changing its extravagant clothes several times a day, and was entertained by the antics of social climbers. And whether they are writing about manners, high, middling, or low, the light novelists have a common quality: they are accomplished, they are even elegant.

For in this static period we must give society a small 's'. Each class felt itself to be exclusive, even the working class. They all stuck up for their manners and practised their own ripe exclusiveness and their peculiar formalities. This is as true of the fashionable like Oscar Wilde, Max Beerbohm, or Saki, who are in and out of drawing rooms all day, as it is of writers of minor classics almost unknown abroad, like the Grossmiths in their *Diary of a Nobody*, or the fairy tales of Wodehouse, the low but polished intrigues of Thames bargees in the tales of W. W. Jacobs, and even the farcical if indigent clerks in Jerome K. Jerome's *Three Men in a Boat*, which was translated into dozens of language. The worlds of these 'low' writers were as closed, sedate, and as given to their own euphemisms as the fashionable world was: the light novelists survive only if they write well, within their means. I have often thought that professors of English Lit. should take time off from the central glooms of genius and consider these lesser entertainers who are deeply suggestive; but perhaps it is as

well that the Academy winces at the idea for we would hate to see our fun damped down by explication.

One of the characteristics common to Edwardian comedy is that it is a fairy tale for adults – indeed in the double meaning of the word. Its characters are seen as sexless. We can put this down to convention rather than to Puritanism, but the artifice does not mean that the novelist does not know or cannot insinuate what is going on under the surface of manners. It may be the point in the *Lucia* comedies of E. F. Benson that his people are neutered and that they are exhilarated and liberated by taking part in a useful psychological fraud. His enormously popular *Lucia* novels, now published in one fat volume, may even be a comically insinuating diagnosis.

What does Lucia, his self-appointed Queen of Riseholme, want as she sits in her fake medieval house or her garden where only Shakespearean flowers are allowed to grow? Certainly not sex. Not even connubial sex; her ruling passions are for power and publicity; she wants the gossip columns to mention her. She wants to dish her rivals. What about her husband, Peppino, writing his privately printed and artily bound little poems? No sex there or, we can guess, elsewhere. The pair have sublimated, in dozens of little affectations, their happy marriage consolidated by the lies of baby talk and in snobbish snatches of Italian they have picked up from waiters in Italy. When an Italian singer comes to stay they can't understand a word he says.

And what about Georgie, Lucia's devoted *cicisbeo*, always on the go socially when she commands, playing his bits of Mozart to her, listening to her playing the first movement of 'dear Beethoven's' *Moonlight* Sonata – the second is too fast. Georgie keeps changing his clothes, sits in his doll's house, doing his embroidery, painting a little picture or two, and being 'busy at home' one day a week when he is having his toupee fixed and his hair dyed. Homosexual probably, but no boys in sight; certainly a Narcissus. There is no need to tell us: he gives himself away in his frenzied cult of youth, his fuss about his bibelots, his malicious pleasure in seeing through '*cara*' Lucia's snobbery, her frauds, and her lies instantly, enjoying horror of her as a sister figure he cannot do without. And then there are various loud masculine ladies of the clique in Riseholme: hearty hes in combat with Lucia's bitcheries; even the surrounding over-

weight wives with their sulking or choleric husbands are without children and exist in stertorous comic relief. The servants are faithful. The monstrous Lady Ambermere calls hers 'my people', as if she were an empress. The obsequious tradesmen of the town seem to be the only people engaged – but off the scene – in the vulgar task of begetting their kind.

Since it is not sex that makes this world go round, what does? Gossip above all, spying from windows, plotting about teas and dinner parties, a genteel greed for money and news, and above all matching wits against Lucia's ruthless gifts. Our culture hound, who poses at her windows, swots up in the Encyclopaedia before distinguished guests arrive, pretending to have read Nietzsche or Theophrastus, can't distinguish between Schumann and Schubert. She steals a guru from Daisy Quantock, hooks a medium – a fake Russian princess – and although these things lead to farcical disaster, she rises above it and is on to the next fad like a hawk. Her dishonesty is spectacular, her vitality endless; and if Riseholme tears her to pieces and is deeply hurt when she inherits a small fortune and takes a house in London to conquer society there with the same assurance, they long for her to return and, when she does, welcome her with joy. After all, Lucia may have made herself ridiculous but she has come back: she is Life.

Lucia's bids for power in London lead to disasters far beyond the mishaps of Riseholme; but her resilience in intrigue grips us. At the centre of the novels is Georgie – 'Georgino mio' – and their close relationship is based on fascination – she needs his spite, he needs her deceits. Each is the other's mirror. At one point a delightful opera singer almost snatches him because she can see Lucia as a joke; but this infidelity is nominal. When she shows signs of wanting to be cuddled in Le Touquet, he sheers off in terror and returns to Lucia, forgiven.

We see into the absurd shallows of Lucia's emotional life in two of central novels in the series. In Riseholme Lucia's social batt¹ provincial, her artiness is distinctly non-metropolitan, where the revival has become derisively passé and middle class: she had ' 'keep up'. If she is chasing titled notorieties and Prime Mir' drop the Daisy Quantocks who have only just got aro' and see what smart picture exhibitions, a top gossip wr' divorce case can teach her. The last is a revelation. ' through her silly mind:

Certainly, Babs Shyton, the lady whose husband wanted to get rid of her, had written very odd letters to Woof-dog, otherwise known as Lord Middlesex, and he to her . . . But as the trial went on, Lucia found herself growing warm with sympathy for Babs . . . Both Babs and he [Middlesex], in the extracts from the remarkable correspondence between them which were read out in court, alluded to Colonel Shyton as the S.P., which Babs (amid loud laughter) frankly confessed meant Stinkpot; and Babs had certainly written to Woof-dog to say that she was in bed and very sleepy and cross, but wished that Woof-dog was thumping his tail on the hearthrug . . . As for the row of crosses [at the end of her letter], she explained frankly that they indicated she was cross . . . Babs had produced an excellent impression, in fact; she had looked so pretty and had answered so gaily . . .

As for Woof-dog he was the strong silent Englishman, and when he was asked whether he had ever kissed Babs, replied:

'That's a lie' in such a loud fierce voice that you felt that the jury had better believe him unless they all wanted to be knocked down.

Always a positive thinker, Lucia draws the correct moral: it is no good, it is abhorrent, to take a real lover. Even in marriage her bedroom door is locked and her husband is content. The important thing is to have the *reputation* of having a lover: it gives a woman cachet. In the ensuing folly we see her pursuing a gossip writer who, when he tumbles to her plot, is determined not to be made a fool of like *that*! Gossip writers don't like gossip about themselves; it kills their trade and in any case he is a neuter not unlike 'Georgino mio'.

Like so many of her enterprises the London venture is a series of disasters from which she recovers fast. Her husband dies of general neglect and a rather despicable inability to keep up with her. She chucks Riseholme and moves to Tilling – which is in fact Henry James's Rye – to deal with a rival more formidable than Daisy Quantock and with lesbians tougher than the Riseholme set. The lady is Miss Mapp, a woman in her forties whose

. . . face was of high vivid colour and corrugated by chronic rage and curiosity; but these vivifying emotions had preserved to her an

[935]

astonishing activity of mind and body, which fully accounted for [her] comparative adolescence . . . Anger and the gravest suspicions about everybody had kept her young and on the boil.

As a spy on what is going on she can read the significance in every woman's shopping basket, every window lit or unlit, every motor that passes, what everyone eats, drinks, and thinks, what every woman has got on, on top and underneath. Every English village has its Miss Mapp. She intends to be mayoress of Tilling: Lucia has more hypocrisy and subtlety and beats her to it. And if admittedly this petticoat war is long drawn out it does lead to one splendid drama. Tilling (Rye), as everyone knows, is close to the sea marshes; it is liable to tidal floods. Miss Mapp is caught trying to steal a recipe in Lucia's kitchen just as the sea wall carelessly breaks its bank and she and Lucia are carried into the Channel on an upturned kitchen table and vanish into the sea fog for several weeks. They are presumed drowned. There is even a memorial service. Georgie has erected a cenotaph and a plaque recording their deaths – Miss Mapp's name is carved in smaller letters than Lucia's! Of course the two rivals turn up looking very healthy: they have been rescued by fishermen and have been fed on disgusting cod. Each gives unflattering accounts of the other's behaviour on the raft and with the seamen, and gives rival public lectures on the subject. Bitching is the permanent incentive to Benson's invention and his feline mind.

At the death of Lucia's husband and despite Georgie's total mistrust of Lucia, he marries her after an enthusiastic agreement that they will never go to bed together. They have that horror in common. It is noticeable that their affection declines at once, but their need for each other is increased. Miss Mapp marries the usual Colonel who, as she knows, is grossly after her money. But one must not be deceived into thinking that Benson hates the idiots he is writing about or suffers from *Schadenfreude*. Far from it, the sun of comedy shines on his pages; he adores his victims.

The period is surprisingly the post-1918 one, but that beastly war is not mentioned. Pockets of Edwardian manners survived long after that war, for inherited money is the great preserver of dead cultures. Many of his characters – notably minor ones like Lady Ambermere, a woman of slowly enunciated and grandiose rudeness – were in action fifty years ago. I can remember their accents and their syntax. And here lies part of Benson's absurd spell: his ear for the dialogue of cliques is quick and devastating, for he understands the baby talk of fairyland which, of course, sex and our four-letter words have destroyed. (Unless mass society's own nonstop chatter about 'fucking', 'screwing', and the boys 'having it off' is itself a new fairy-tale jargon.) The minor catchphrases preserve their cracked notes. 'How tarsome!' exclaims Georgie. 'Au reservoir' spreads like measles in place of 'au revoir'. There is a key to Benson's wicked mind in the following passage between Lucia and 'Georgino mio':

> '*I domestichi* are making *salone* ready.'
> '*Molto bene,*' she said.
> 'Everybody's tummin',' said Georgie, varying the cipher.
> 'Me so *nervosa!*' said Lucia. 'Fancy me doing Brunnhilde before singing Brunnhilde. Me can't bear it.'

The key word is 'cipher'. Benson knew the cipher of all his characters. His pleasure was in the idiotic gabble of life. Is he too tepid for export? Years ago Gilbert Seldes compared Benson with the Sinclair Lewis of *Main Street* but pointed out that Lewis spoiled his book by his violent fury. Benson was never furious when he killed an age. He believed that love lasts longest when it is unkind.

Still Riding

=====

Very rarely, when I was young, I seem to have had healthy tastes in literature. Mason, Weyman, Buchan, Rider Haggard passed me by. I was afflicted by a morbid interest in the adult and detested those sunny, athletic and strenuous leader-types who are supposed to be the schoolboy's natural heroes. It is only this week, when my duties have obliged me to read Mr Morton Cohen's careful and sympathetic life of Rider Haggard, that I have taken my first plunge into the choking verbiage of *King Solomon's Mines* and *She*, and I am past the age when I can bring to works of this kind the elation of a chaste and hero-worshipping sensibility. What ought to scare me simply makes me laugh. How can people who admire Stevenson, as I do, think anything of *King Solomon's Mines*?

An initiator of the revival of Romance in late Victorian times, his work deliriously received, Rider Haggard never understood why he did not rank with Stevenson, Meredith, Henry James and, shall we add?, Falkner, the author of *Moonfleet*, Kipling, who was his great friend, or Joseph Conrad. Today he would find his place among the gaudier historical or horror films or among the new school of science fiction writers. Like many popular best-sellers, he was a very sad and solemn man who took himself too seriously and his art not seriously enough. The fact is that he was a phenomenon before he was a novelist: other novelists are content to be simply themselves, Rider Haggard was his public.

To be identified with the public is the divine gift of the best-sellers in popular romance and, no doubt, in popular realism. E. M. Forster once spoke of the novelist sending down a bucket into the unconscious; the author of *She* installed a suction pump. He drained the whole reservoir of the public's secret desires. Critics speak of the reader suspending unbelief; the best-seller knows better; man is a believing animal. So, in the age of religious doubt, Rider Haggard tapped the mystical hankerings after reincarnation, immortality, eternal youth, psychic phenomena. He tracked down priestesses and gods. So, in a peaceful age, he drew on preoccupations with slaughter; and, in an empire-building age, on fantasies of absolute, spiritual rule in secret cities. His triumph – though it baffled him – was in the creation of *She*. The journey into mysterious Kor comes flawlessly out of the agonies of sexual anxiety; Ayesha herself is an identifiable myth or rather a clutter of myths: everything from Jung's Anima, the White Goddess, *la belle dame sans merci*, down to the New Woman or, as Henley said, 'the heroic Barmaid, the Waitress in Apotheosis'.

But the remarkable visions of Rider Haggard would have got him nowhere without three other qualities. One of these cannot be praised enough: he is a constantly inventive story-teller. The other two, paradoxically, support it: his stories are so tall that only bad grammar and slipshod and even vulgar writing can get him round the difficulty; and he dare not go in for more than pasteboard character. Anything in the nature of a human being would stand in the way. Look at Stevenson and one sees the enormous difference. Finally, Haggard has the enviable gift (common to many writers of popular romance) of pouring it all out in a great gush in a few weeks. He has the confessional form of genius. He never corrected a line.

Rider Haggard was one of the sons of an explosive and eccentric Norfolk squire who was feared by his family and 'awful to his tenantry'. The boy was backward and considered to be such a fool that he was given a poorer education than his brothers had had. He was subject to extreme fears. He was devoted for years to a doll. One of the odd traits that remained with him all his life was a childish mannerism of speech. He pronounced his 'r's' as 'w's' and always said 'v' for 'th'. A phrase like 'a very thorough rogue' (Mr Cohen says) would become 'a vewy fowough wogue'. But if he was the fool of the family, the family had a firm sense of its social privileges. The Squire got the youth on to Bulwer's staff when he was sent out to be Governor of Natal.

The experience transformed him. In a very short time, emancipation from his father, the shock of Africa and a taste of responsibility woke up the sleeping mind. He had arrived at the birth of an empire. It was he who 'planted the flag' in the Transvaal; it was he who worked with those who were putting order into the ramshackle legal system of the Boers. Above all he admired the Zulus and got to know them intimately. He hunted, he travelled and explored, and he listened to legends. He must certainly have heard of Zimbabwe, the prehistoric city of stone; and although later he denied that he had heard tales of the white woman ruler of the Lovedu tribe in the Transvaal, he travelled close to their country and the customs of the Lovedu closely resemble Ayesha's Armahaggers.

By this time Haggard had become a collector both of facts and of objects, a habit that led him, later on in life, to write an excellent documentary work on rural England. It also led him to turn his house in Norfolk into a grotesque and oppressive African museum. This collecting habit has an important bearing on his visions: they are a sort of dramatised ragbag. Nothing impresses so much – if we are spiritually at sea – as the spiritual furniture depository; it protects us from the pain of selecting and deciding. In Haggard's time, collecting offered the pleasures of colonising spiritually; his antiquarianism was a religion in itself.

Haggard's mind was almost totally serious. His humour, always uncertain, is clumsy and vulgar. Midway in his African adventure, he received an emotional shock from which he did not perhaps care to recover. He was jilted by a beautiful girl. *She* may have owed something to this disaster. And when he returned to England and married and, tragically, was to lose his son, one notices that Haggard is one of those men who harden over and do not recover from blows. Still later on in life he became explosive and irritable. The Haggards had loud voices; they were said in Norfolk to be able to 'chat across a field'. It is not a bad description of his manner as a novelist. He wrote to be heard a long way off.

So the impression one has is of a tall, handsome, bearded, wounded egotist, unable to stand criticism of any kind, who carries his secret sorrows rather histrionically. The tough man with the sorrow about which he will not speak is his characteristic narrator; and, once more, one recalls how much the creative impulse of the best-sellers depends upon self-pity. It is an emotion of great dramatic potential. He had a good deal of pride and he accepted its burdens. The result of the enormous success of the booby of the family was that he had to rescue his brothers or their families from the financial messes they had got into. They did not demean themselves by showing much gratitude for the extraordinary generosity of the man who had been dismissed by his father as 'a greengrocer' and a contemptible 'penny-a-liner'.

The blood lust and the moralisings are the worst things in the Haggard novels; the dramatic invention – the old witch crushed by the closing stone door in the cave, the sight of the mummified explorer in *King Solomon's Mines* – is marvellous and so also is the first vision of the mountains, although in description he is usually better in local detail than in the set piece. The sunbeam that lights the plank when Ayesha, Leo and the narrator are crossing the precipice in *She* is a brilliant stroke; and the account of the sinking of the dhow and the ride through the breakers in the same book is admirable. A collector in everything, Haggard had the art of piling it on. It is an art. His flow is molten, burning from one event to the next. And although we have to stress the triumphantly naïve part played by his unconscious we have to repeat that he was a voracious and intelligent observer. His two serious works, on English farming and the political issues in Africa, show him to be capable of the serious historical document. On one plane, the very great writers and the popular romancers of the lower order always meet. They use all of themselves, helplessly, unselectively. They are above the primness and good taste of declining to give themselves away.

Mr Cohen has many interesting critical comments on Haggard's work and especially on the celebrated problem of the significance of 'She-who-must-be-obeyed' and of the journey through swamps and down tunnels into Kor and the mystic presence. He follows the hint of Mario Praz and thinks Ayesha to be the type of exotic *femme fatale* who appears in Victorian literature with the decline of the hero: the heartless beauty, pitiless, cold, a close relation of Wilde's Salome – or Henley's terrifying barmaid. She is, in Haggard's account, more male than female: I am inclined to call her *He* but – as James Thurber once said about a grand piano – with breasts.

Ayesha is undoubtedly a disturbing figure and, I think, because she is a compendium. Soon after the book was published Haggard added to the confusion of her character by comments of his own. It is his misfortune that his compelling imagination could create a creature of primitive and overmastering passion and savage jealousy and yet, at the same time, apply the most trite Victorian moralisations to her case:

I saw him struggle – I saw him even turn to fly: but her eyes drew him more strongly than iron bands, and the magic of her beauty and

concentrated will and passion entered into him and overpowered him –
say, even there in the presence of the body of the woman who had loved
him well enough to die for him. It sounds horrible and wicked enough,
but he should not be too greatly blamed, and be sure his sins will find
him out.

And there is a curious suggestion, somewhat coarsely made, that if the
love of the temptress is evil, many men have found respectable marriage to
be hell. Haggard's rhetoric sounds like the kind that is clumsily covering
up.

One is led to speculate on the inner life of a generation that responded
eagerly to his allegory, to the fantasies of masochistic travel, to those
precipitous mountain walls, those caverns, tunnels, caves and tombs, and
all the bloodshed. And who liked to have it all dressed up in prose that is at
one moment all baccy and Norfolk tweed and, the next, Liberace's trousers.
Yet his African books represent a real response by a most suggestible man
to African legend, which – as we have seen recently in the works of Amos
Tutuola – is far bloodier than anything Haggard put down.

Mr Morton Cohen indeed argues that his books may find a place in an
African, as distinct from an English, tradition. He compares Haggard with
Fenimore Cooper, pointing out the distinction that Haggard was writing
for a people with a future. 'When they assert their independence and rule
once more in their native lands Haggard's Zulu saga may come into its
own. For he captures in it a clear, engaging picture of Zulu life and comes
to terms with the turbulent Zulu spirit.' He is writing especially of *Nada the
Lily*. I have not read it but if in that work he completely freed himself of
Norfolk, then I can see that the speculation is an interesting one. He had in
his impure imagination something powerfully accessible.

A Pre-Raphaelite's Son

The Strange Ride of Rudyard Kipling – the title of Angus Wilson's long-awaited exploration of Kipling's life and works is well chosen by an author who himself is a novelist, a searching critic, and an intelligent traveller who knows India and has his own early 'colonial' connection with South Africa. Kipling's 'ride' was indeed an exotic one, not only because of a childhood and youth passed between India and England, his sojourns in the United States, South Africa, and, later on, his habit of wintering in Cape Town and in France; but because of the restlessness of his eye and temper. As with many Victorian Englishmen change whistled by in his ears, his mind was the explorer's: in his middle years it also opened outposts in history, in Roman Britain and Christian Antioch, but also in his clinical studies of illness – illness itself being an inexorable country we are bound to know: its scenery was psychosomatic. Like many of the colonising kind he became more gaudily English than the English in the sense that Englishness became an extra conscience and a personal cause. That cause was Kim's, whose passionate cry 'Who is Kim?' indicates Kipling's similar search for an identity within a caste.

The main outline of Kipling's ride has been established with authority by Charles Carrington, and Angus Wilson acknowledges that debt. He has elaborated the story in lively detail by his own researches, interviews, an exhaustive reading of the works, and his own speculations. The result is a very full and clever book. It shows Kipling as he grows and changes through the phases of his life – Wilson really does succeed in the always difficult task of domesticating the man in the circumstances and fantasies of his daily life and times. If the manner is personal and diffuse, and the narrative circuitous as it moves forward and then goes back to reconsider, this is the habit of a gifted and serious talker. Mr Wilson is outspoken when he finds Kipling dropping into vulgarity, sentimentality, over-dramatising, or covering up; yet he confesses to a sneaking feeling for Kipling's philistinism even when he is most fervent in his admiration for the artist and craftsman. He puts Kipling's imperial afflatus in historical perspective, as he deplores the novelist's sneers at 'the long-haired liberal intellectuals'. Kipling was a hero-worshipper of men of action, especially common soldiers; but he could not match them.

His lasting attraction as a writer is his gift of conveying the magical. It springs from his childhood in Bombay and Lahore, and he never lost it entirely. Even the offensive belief in the supremacy of the white race is a form of projected moral magic, a boyish fantasy perverted by an adult. Kipling worshipped children, and easily and seriously abandoned himself to their private minds. For him, as Wilson says, children create a vast world of magical explorations within a small space as they make their maps of 'hazards and delights'. He saw childhood as the sacred age out of which it was painful and shocking to grow: until he was sent back from India to school in England, his own was blissful. The visual quality of Kipling's prose is not photographic but a perpetuation of the clarity and unquestioning response of the child's eye; it was this that gave him his unmatched sense of surfaces and place.

He had also the child's ear, the ear for magic in language, and it rarely turned into adult whimsy. In one of the Mowgli stories – which he wrote long after he had left India – the man-cub has to repeat 'the Master Words of the Jungle' he has learned from Baloo. 'Master-words for which People?' the seven-year-old Mowgli asks, delighted to show off his good memory of bear-talk, bird-talk, snake-talk. And boasts that one day he will have a tribe of his own. 'Now you have nothing to fear,' says Baloo. 'Except your own tribe,' mutters the panther under his breath. (We note that Mowgli has had these languages knocked into him by the clouts and blows, called 'love pats', from the panther. The boy deserves them because he is impertinent and swanks: he feels a sensual pleasure in the pains of discipline.)

There is much of Kipling as a man and writer in that talk from the fable of 'Kaa's Hunting'. He spoke Hindi before he spoke English; and the English he inherited was strongly marked by the Biblical cadences he had drawn from his Ulster Scottish and Yorkshire Methodist forebears, preachers uttering their didactic magic, softened though it was by the Pre-Raphaelite tone of his cultivated parents. He became the chameleon-like multilinguist who could enter the talk of common soldiers, engineers, workmen, and the Sussex peasants, or the rhetoric of the public speaker, changing his colour as he became for the moment one of them. The gift sprang from what he called his daemon – a very Pre-Raphaelite word – and the daemon was harnessed to Wesley's 'gospel of work'.

Here Mr Wilson raises a matter that will develop later on. Kipling had little interest in his own ancestry, which may seem strange in one 'for whom piety toward the past of mankind, whether historic or prehistoric, and toward his own childhood', was strong, but Wilson does not think this had anything to do with his dislike of a narrow religion. He writes:

> To lay emphasis upon personal heredity would be at once to assert the personal aspect of a man's identity rather than the group heredities of nation, race, caste and place which are man's true strengths and loyalties, and to lessen, by leaning upon genetic determination, a man's reliance upon himself, his absolute accountability . . .

When we ask why Kipling's sensitive father and intelligent if possessive mother sent him 'home' to England at the age of six with his three-year-old sister, to live for years with the awful family of 'Baa, Baa, Black Sheep', the Nonconformist belief in self-reliance and accountability must have played its part, though the Kiplings' own Methodist beliefs had lapsed. The Victorians had strong reason to believe that the Indian climate was dangerous to children: Mrs Kipling had just lost a baby when the children were sent off. And there was common talk of the precocious sexual habits of Indians – racial fears are commonly rooted in sexual obsession. Mr Wilson adds the important note that to be able to afford to send one's children back to England was also a sign of social status: the clever Mrs Kipling was out to push her shy husband's career. At 'The House of Desolation' in Southsea Captain Holloway and his wife seemed respectable: the captain was indeed a decent man and his wife's ferocious manner and Calvinism were not detected.

With his usual sympathy Mr Wilson does his best to be fair to Mrs Holloway and brings out more fully than any other account of the episode that I have read the real nature of the drama there. The Holloways were typical of that common Victorian category: the genteel family with the anxieties of people going downhill – poor relations. Mrs Holloway was jealous of young Kipling who was better connected than her own son and encouraged her son's bullying; and, like so many children sent home from overseas, the young Kipling was a swank, defiant and rebellious. In short the boy had to adjust himself to a new jungle – the English.

At this time his eyesight began to fail and his terrors doubled. Already he was a child who lived by sweeping metaphorical images, and he spoke of the dark coming into his head. And the dark, as Mr Wilson says, was suggested not only by failing eyesight and the violent punishment from Mrs Holloway but by his first experiences of death: his baby brother had died and presently the kind Captain Holloway dropped dead: the one mollifying influence at Southsea had gone.

Angus Wilson rejects Edmund Wilson's judgment on the lasting influence of the 'Baa, Baa, Black Sheep' experience as being schematic psychologically, and indeed I agree that Edmund Wilson's political hatred of imperialism distorted what was elsewhere a penetrating essay in *The Wound and the Bow*. The influence of Kipling's schooling at Westward Ho seems to me more important. Once again the parents made a choice that looked good and was within their means. Westward Ho was a minor public school which would not put the rubber stamp of the great English public schools on the gifted boy; but it was not the roughhouse of *Stalky & Co.* As so often happens in England the place flourished as an anomaly: intended to train boys for empire-building and the military life, it was run by a progressive crank and intellectual who shared the artistic tastes of the Pre-Raphaelites. His house was full of Rossetti drawings; he was devoted to William Morris and was even radical in politics; he was deep in English, French, and Russian literature. (In the school debating society he proposed the resolution that 'The advance of the Russians in Central Asia was not hostile to British power'. The young Kipling opposed it and got the militant schoolboy chauvinists to defeat it.)

Although Kipling was badly bullied in his first year, the perceptive headmaster allowed him the run of his excellent library. He soon spoke and read French rapidly and even tried Russian for a while; he read Pushkin and – above all – Lermontov, whose laconic manner made a lasting impression on him: all odd experiences in an empire-builder's school. As for the bullying, as we know from *Stalky & Co.*, he soon had his own élite gang or tribe, who were clever at running the traditional schoolboy secret society, outmanoeuvring the bullies and inventing the schoolboy guerrilla practice of cunning and crude practical jokes. Kipling never lost his taste for boring practical jokes as a comic form of vengeance: the story 'Dayspring Mishandled' is essentially this. The nasty thing was the cool and sadistic bullying of the 'baddies' by the 'goodies', who learned to take pleasure in the pain of others. This is common enough in human nature, but it has too much crude relish in some of Kipling's stories and (as in contemporary films of violence) has deplorable moral overtones which attract the philistine public. Kipling survived Westward Ho: his physical incapacity for games was an advantage and it also increased his double regard for duty relieved by cunning. Another point Mr Wilson makes is that at small country colleges boys succeeded easily in going out of bounds illegally among the people of the countryside. The place offered something of the day school's closer relation to everyday life outside.

Kipling is one more of those English novelists who did not go to the university. That might have taught him to think, but he was not by nature a thinker, he was an image maker. Not much is known about his night prowling in the London streets. Nor is enough known about his prowlings in Lahore when he returned to be a newspaper reporter at the age of seventeen, beyond what can be guessed from his stories. What, the modern biographer asks, was his part in the sexual half-world of London or India? He clearly observed it. Did he participate? No one knows, but one would guess that, at the last moment, a romantic with a strong imagination acting within a stoical discipline would not have done. There is more 'magic' in sin if it is not committed. Stories like 'Without Benefit of Clergy' may make us doubt; but Kipling was a born watcher and listener. He certainly opposed the closing of brothels to English troops, but that was because he took the part of the lonely British soldiers whom he knew well. His early, mild love affairs sound painfully platonic; and he was certainly mother's dutiful boy and continued to be so in his marriage. The most important experience in the rootless or gypsy part of his early life, Angus Wilson thinks, occurred when he went up to Peshawar and on to the no-man's land of Kabul:

From this border ride, Kipling's imagination must have carried remote and terrible sounds . . . The horrors came to him, I think, from the *visual* scene of the passes . . .

Here, at last, he was in the region talked of in Lahore bazaars, the lawless, treacherous land whence came Mahbub Ali, the horse-dealer, a real live disreputable acquaintance (as well as the ambiguous fictional protector of Kim). Here in an atmosphere of intrigue and vengeance, or power preserved by a brutal, irrevocably jesting justice like that of our Tudor Age, he found a terrible version of Stalkyism. Where the rough and ready practical joke may put things right in the simple, harsh world of boarding schools, torture and prolonged death agonies are authority's jest in Afghanistan where the slightest threat to the throne may shatter all rule and let loose tribal anarchy. From the bazaars of Peshawar and from talk with those in the Amir's entourage upon this 1885 assignment come, I think, the cruel teasing death of the blind mullah in 'The Head of the District,' and the deathly joke of 'The Amir's Homily,' and at least two powerful neglected poems – 'The Ballad of the King's Mercy' (1889) and 'The Ballad of the King's Jest' (1890). From these we see that those who suffer terrible punishment are not the open enemies of authority, but those who seek to please the King too much, or talk too much, or carry out too easily his cruel commands, or over-flatter him.

Angus Wilson believes that Kipling's stature rests on his fictional India, not only on *Kim* and the *Jungle Books*, but on *Naulakha*, *The Barrack Room Ballads*, and his Indian short stories. After he left India in 1889 he returned only once for a short time two years later. He had political squabbles with his paper and the authorities, but above all, it was under his mother's prompting that he left for fame in England and in America. There was an immense gain for the depth of his skills but, Mr Wilson thinks, at a cost to his poetic imagination. There is indeed a split and an increase in strains and tensions as the master craftsman takes over, as resourceful in his crude popular work as in the best of his compressed and intricate stories: it is a split which has some connection with being torn between his 'riding' life and his belief in the family square.

Mr Wilson's book is remarkable for its brief or extended comments on pretty well all the Kipling stories as he threads them through the life, and he thinks that modern critics overvalue the late stories, which are compressed psychological or emblematic dramas; he believes the present taste for the late Kipling arises out of literary fashion and our boredom with

India. I differ, to some extent, from Kipling's biographer and critic here. Kipling was hostile to Congress and the changing Indian situation. He was an artist whose India stops with the idyll of *Kim*. He was incapable of writing a novel, even on an English theme; his mastery would inevitably appear in the short story – a form which depends on intensifying the subject, stamping a climate on it, getting at the essence of it.

As they grow older, short-story writers tend to repeat themselves as Maupassant or Maugham did; Kipling escaped this by his variety and his boldness with usually intractable subjects and by increasing his difficulties. This last was well-suited to lifting the lid on his personal conflicts. I am with Mr Wilson in thinking that the terrifying story of 'Mary Postgate' is probably one of the finest stories in our language and becomes all the more impressive in our own terrible times. But I find 'Dayspring Mishandled' intolerably obscure and mannered, despite its apparent compassion. I think Mr Wilson has missed the significance of 'Mrs Bathurst', in which a rough lot of seamen and railway workers in Africa evoke the memory of a kindly woman who ran a bar they all knew and who came – it is suspected – to a ghastly end, seemingly with a lover no one can identify. Mr Wilson complains that Kipling never brings this woman on the scene and gives no clue to the identity of those cindered bodies on the railway line. It is, I agree, maddening not to be told. But the story is marvellously placed; Kipling is a master, even in his single-narrator stories, of making his narrator seem to be neighboured by other voices. In 'Mrs Bathurst' the several talkers are contributing from what they half know and half feel. They don't really know exactly what happened, but what they are revealing is themselves, and, in the end, what looks like a collective guilt – to what Mrs Bathurst of their own have they reasons to feel guilt and a horror of inexplicable fate?

The story stirs a collective fantasy which has its roots in some memory in their crude and inexpressive lives. Mrs Bathurst was apparently a decent woman but she was much more the *vision* of a decent woman. What have these men done in their time to a decent woman? A story which might have been one of sentimental remorse or a revelation of one disgusting man's sin, or even of her weakness, strikes a blow at each of them, all the more savage because it is gratuitous. That heap of cinders on the track is the common agglutination of a death – and Kipling feared death.

[949]

If we look at the change of note and intention in the voice, line by line, in the opening passages of 'Love-o'-Women', we see how fast he can announce a drama and intensify it line by line:

The horror, the confusion, and the separation of the murderer from his comrades were all over before I came. There remained only on the barrack-square the blood of man calling from the ground. The hot sun had dried it to a dusky goldbeater-skin film, cracked lozenge-wise by the heat; and as the wind rose each lozenge, rising a little, curled up at the edges as if it were a dumb tongue. Then a heavier gust blew all away down wind in grains of dark coloured dust. It was too hot to stand in the sunshine before breakfast. The men were all in barracks talking the matter over. A knot of soldiers' wives stood by one of the entrances to the married quarters, while inside a woman shrieked and raved with wicked filthy words.

The passage has sometimes been criticised because it is mannered; but line for line, it reveals his strange congregation of words. There is the classic desire to be as spare and drastic as a ballad, the temptation to sail off into what one imagines Henry Irving was like when he declaimed 'The Bells'. There is that unbearably exact photograph of drying blood – the lozenge. And then the aesthete's glance at the ancient craft of goldbeating, which – if one has ever watched goldbeating – precisely conveys the Biblical message that all flesh enters the process of becoming dust. In the last sentences, Kipling achieves his decisive and characteristic effect; he roots the story not in the 'I' or 'me' of the narrator but in 'our' common experience. Kipling's characters are always thickly neighboured: the story exists in the minds of all who were there.

The comments on these particular stories come in the middle of the book and are an example of Angus Wilson's disconcerting leaps out of chronology. Back to life then, and to the questions that have to be asked. The quarrel in Vermont was an unlucky family row with relations, perhaps stirred up by Kipling's half-American wife. There was a good deal of the severe French bourgeoise in her. Kipling was hot-headed, bursting with Britishness, and she lacked tact: Brattleboro thought the pair were snobs. Up until then he had loved America, except for the violence and the

American dislike of privacy – an old trouble between Americans and the British.

The odd thing is that his scapegrace brother-in-law, who was at the heart of the ridiculous trouble, was just the kind of character Kipling was more than half drawn to. But in his Vermont period he was naïvely amazed that Americans were cold about his suggestion of a Pax Anglo-Saxonica. The notion was muddled: it was essentially the ambiguous imperial creed, just as 'Recessional' is one of the hymns that can be sung in two voices, the patriotic or the repentant religious warning against bragging. Both voices, Mr Wilson says acutely, were surely addressed to himself; he knew that he must not be carried away by his popular skills; if he bragged, the powers of his daemon would depart. He was a very superstitious man:

> Of course, Kipling meant every word of his Imperial beliefs and gave most of his surface active life to them, but I am sure that the excess of the tensions they produced, his political frenzy in the years 1900–1914, can only be fully understood if one grasps that his fear of anarchy or foreign tryanny, his hopes of a sane, ordered Pax Britannica, a Pax Anglo-Saxonica, or, at last, a Pax Franco-Britannica were also a reflection of the deep inner struggle between the anarchic, romantic childlike force of his creative impulse and the ordered, complex, at times almost self-defeating pressure of the craft he imposed upon it.

On the question of Kipling's marriage and particularly on the criticisms of the character and behaviour of his formidable wife Carrie, Mr Wilson is very fair. She was certainly very domineering – and like many dominant people was liable to hysteria which her prisoner was called upon to calm. She was certainly, once more, a stern mother-figure. He was incompetent with money. She managed his financial affairs, his contracts, his correspondence. She is said to have opened all his letters and to have dictated the replies. Her daughter said she cut her husband off from stimulating intellectual company and indeed she was out of her depth in it. But she fiercely protected his privacy and stood between him and the plague of visitors who descend like vultures on famous men; if Kipling *was* cut off from his coevals, he was cut off chiefly by his wealth: his friends were the successful and important. She was suspicious by nature, particularly of women, and seems to have felt many people were really after his money.

But Kipling appeared to enjoy her rule, for he had been used to an excessive reliance on his parents, even in middle life. Visitors noticed that Rudyard and his Carrie shared the same harsh jokes.

She probably enjoyed hearing that the female of the species was more deadly than the male. Possibly he would not have married her *unless* he had loved her charming brother first and more spontaneously – he responded most to family affection – and one must remember that he and Carrie had the tragic bond of the loss of their two children and that she nursed her misogynist through his serious breakdowns and his hysterical, baseless, but harrowing dread of cancer. No; brought up in a tough school, Kipling found a tough wife. As for his restlessness – rich and comfortable, the pair who hated the English winter spent five months of the year abroad, especially in France, which he loved.

What is Mr Wilson's final judgment on him?

He was a gentle-violent man, a man of depressions and hilarity, holding his despairs in with an almost superhuman stoicism. Manic-depressive does no more than repeat this in big words. I prefer if I must a socio-historical description of long generations of Evangelical belief ending in post-Darwinian doubt.

He feared to know himself, but

[the critic] has to say that this persistent evasion of introspection, of further questioning of the source of the despair and anxiety and guilt that enmesh so many of his best characters in his best stories, does keep him out of the very first class of writing . . . *Kim*, I believe, is great in its own right; and, for the rest, he did so many, many things very well indeed that the greatest novelists never saw to do.

A Moralist of Exile

To the eminent father-figures – Galsworthy, Edward Garnett, Wells – who were in fact uncle-figures, as we shall see, and who nursed and praised him through the years when the great public ignored him, Joseph Conrad had the magnetism of a shaman risen from the ocean. In London literary circles he passed as the mysterious Romantic Slav – all the go at that time – a typical misrepresentation; there was nothing of the Russian *exalté* and deplorable Dostoevsky about him, as he firmly pointed out. Surely the British had realised that the Poles despised 'the Russian soul' and were Westerners to a man. Flatteringly he had gone through the British mill and become a British master mariner, had even read Marryat when he was a boy; it had been noticed that he was a shade stand-offish on the decks of clippers and avoided the crew when ashore. In a very thick and explosive accent, he would talk about Pater and Flaubert to the rare officer who had literary tastes.

These mischievous Edwardian impressions have their charm; once the ironic disparagement of Bloomsbury and Cambridge had passed by in the Thirties, later generations have understood that Conrad's genius was not merely descriptive; he was one of the great moralists of exile. And exile is not emigration, expatriation, etc., etc., but an imposing Destiny. He was marginal, even a drifter 'with prospects', until well into his thirties. In the course of an exhaustive psychological study of Conrad's three distinctive lives as a Pole, a British seaman, and a novelist, Professor Karl says:

> Conrad found in marginality itself a way of life, a form of existence, and a philosophy that added up to more than survival and well-being. In probing exile, dislocation of time and place, language disorientation, and shifting loyalties, he extended our view of the shadows of existence. Indeed, he suggested that the shadows were to be the main area of existence in the twentieth century.

So long as we do not take this to mean that Conrad was an early Existentialist or Outsider Professor Karl's words are acceptable. Marginality has its own tradition: Conrad thought of himself as a kind of Ulysses, when he was young. When one or two Polish critics accused Conrad of 'betraying' his country by leaving it to write in a foreign tongue – 'for money' one of them ludicrously said – they were as foolish as those who attack Henry James, T. S. Eliot, Joyce, Beckett and Auden for expatriation. The 'ground' to which the exile naturally belongs is bilingual, trilingual, language – not simply as syntax but as image, metaphor, and even conceit. A certain passivity and perhaps circulatory in-turnings of imagination may be the interesting price.

The last substantial biography of Conrad was done by Jocelyn Baines in 1961 and was discerning in a formal chronological way. Baines had a good deal to say about Conrad's Polish background; since that time a large number of unknown letters have come to light, and in the course of editing these Professor Karl has put together a richer Life that aims to get as close as possible to the complex interweaving of the novelist's real life and temperament as they were drawn into his work. Karl's ideal biography is George D. Painter's life of Proust, chiefly because he sees Proust and Conrad preoccupied with the imaginative retrieval of memory. He has sought to fit Conrad into Henry James's half-mocking sense of human experience. As James put it,

> Experience is never limited, and it is never complete; it's an immense sensibility, a kind of huge spider's web of the silken threads suspended in the chambers of consciousness and catching every airborne particle in its issue. It is the very atmosphere of the mind.

In consequence Professor Karl is a circuitous narrator, following Conrad's psychological threads back and forth. The reader may be maddened but must be patient as he treads and retreads old paths. For example: Conrad's so-called 'duel', which was really an attempt at suicide in Marseilles when he was twenty, is re-examined three times in sixty-two pages, but only in the last account does Professor Karl tell us what almost certainly happened and why, pointing out that there is an inordinate number of suicides in the works. Such a circling about incident is of course very Conradian; how long we have to wait when we read Lord Jim before we are allowed to know *what* the trial of Tuan Jim is about. So *Lord Jim* is to be thought of as almost completely an intrigue of memory – but in a double sense. The ostensible trouble we recognise at once:

> Based on an actual event, the entire novel is structured on various commentators recalling what occurred, or trying to make sense out of what has become for them part of a distant now dim past.

The other 'memory' spreads into guessing: *Lord Jim* and its ship the *Patna* are not simply a paradigm of Conrad's feelings about Poland 'but the expression of material lying deep within him'.

> The very country into which Conrad was born created divisiveness and was based as much on memory as on contemporary life . . . It was not only the country into which he was born that required constant artifice, it was the family also. Conrad's immediate family was itself split between idealistic and practical elements, with personal tragedy at its base and gloom, morbidity, and self-destructive obsessions as its routine experience.

The argument is interesting, though Professor Karl's prose does run into uneven patches. He hangs some heavy platitudinous quotations from other scholars on Henry James's slender spider's web. Since I have nothing but admiration for Professor Karl's command of the living detail necessary for an exhaustive biography of 1,000 pages, I hate to see him making solemn and obsequious gestures to the academy. Writing of Conrad's life as a seaman he drags in some words of Erik Erikson:

> Those twenty years at sea were not at all a waste but fell into what Erik Erikson, in a somewhat different context [i.e., writing of Gandhi], was to call the *epigenetic principle*. As he explains it, it is a principle derived from the uterine growth of an organism, although Erikson's use of it indicates that 'anything that grows has a ground plan, and that out of this ground plan the parts arise, each part having its time of special ascendancy, until all parts have arisen to form a functioning whole.'

Bully for the estimable Erikson. But we do not need Erikson or Gandhi to remind us that, in the case of Conrad, the sea years conditioned [him] to the disproportion of sea and land, to differing perspectives of time and space, and to the kind of tedious staring that becomes inertness and passivity in his work.

Conrad was doubly an exile, even before he left Poland at the age of seventeen: his country did not belong to him; it was not independent. It was divided between Russian and Austrian rule. Conrad's father, Apollo Korzeniowski, was of the gentry, a wildly improvident, gifted young man and a natural Don Quixote and plotter. The mother's family, the Bobrowskis, belonged to the stern Catholic aristocracy with large estates who had their rebellious past, but out of aristocratic self-interest had become accommodating to Russian rule and confined themselves to keeping what they held.

Both families had a deep contempt for commerce, though Conrad's uncle on his mother's side was a rationalist conservative who said that commerce at least had a moderating influence on Utopian ignorance of economic reality. Not so Apollo; two years after the Polish insurrection of 1861 he was still plotting. He was arrested and sent into exile with his wife and child. Their health was destroyed: the mother's sufferings brought her to an early death when the child was seven; the father was overcome with grief and remorse, turned mystical, and died when the boy was eleven. We see the child following his father's coffin through the streets of Cracow at a funeral that became an unforgettable political demonstration.

The romantic cause of Polish freedom had decimated both sides of Conrad's family: he had become dramatically orphaned. He had lost not only his parents but the influence of the ideology they represented. He was stranded in a spiritual wilderness. Some biographers have drawn a pitiable portrait of an ailing little boy who was thought to be epileptic and liable to become consumptive, sitting in silent misery with an extravagantly solitary and religious father, and stunned by the experience. Professor Karl rejects this view. In the first place the boy responded to his father's gifts as a distinguished poet, playwright, and translator: he was drawn to Shakespeare, Dickens, and, above all, Hugo's *Travailleurs de la Mer*, a book that must have had a powerful influence on Conrad's desire to travel or to go to sea.

In these influences Apollo was a really rewarding father, but in his political disaster and his Quixotism he represented the failure of faith, the loss of belief in solid ground. It was noted that the parentless boy would tend to run wild, to resemble his headstrong father and dream of escape and adventure; and that he would use his bad health and neurasthenia as weapons for getting his way. Far from being pitiable, the child became formidably difficult, recalcitrant in learning, obstinately determined to get out of his impossible, futureless country. He did get away – but as Professor Karl shows he took the dilemma of his relations with his loved and yet deplored father with him. It is Professor Karl's habit to shoot forward to the novels that twenty years ahead would still show Conrad struggling with the dilemma his father had left him in. In *Victory* we see the exploration of

> the most intimate of father-son relationships in [Conrad's] work; in the interplay between Axel and the older Heyst . . . he noted the ironic ambiguities of the relationship: portraying the father as if he were Apollo *after* his fall [i.e., after the insurrection], who, having finally seen the futility of all action, cautions silence, cunning, and withdrawal . . . By turning the relation into an ironic and a paradoxical one, Conrad relived the situation.

A surrogate father was, in fact, Conrad's salvation – up to a point: his mother's brother, Uncle Tadeusz Bobrowski, a wealthy and lonely widower who became the boy's guardian. Tadeusz was everything Apollo had not been: he became almost as much a mother as a father to the boy whose inherited recklessness was to plague him for years.

> Tadeusz Bobrowski was himself a man of many sides . . . As well as being a somewhat narrow moralist and positivist, he was a person of considerable intelligence and insight. He has unjustly been described as a right-wing conservative, even a reactionary force, thrusting upon Conrad a rationalistic, legalistic approach to life and its goals. Although some of this is correct – and should not be denied – Tadeusz deeply resented the Nałęcz [i.e., Apollo] strain of foolhardiness and self-destruction . . . He represented elements of balance and sanity.

In the correspondence with his nephew, which went on until Conrad's thirties, Tadeusz is a harassed and sometimes deceived Polonius advising the careless Laertes. He leaned toward the new scientific ideas but without much faith in the technological mind and certainly without optimism. (That would be a bond with his nephew, as was also his enormous reading in many languages.) It is an important point that Conrad's often reactionary views on politics and society did not outgrow his uncle's and those of his uncle's class: he certainly stuck to his uncle's hatred of revolution:

> We can assume that part of Conrad's withdrawal from the full political implications of his novels, or his caution in dealing with such matters, derives from lessons learned from Bobrowski: that the individual who joins movements, thinks politically, or tries rapid reform throws himself under the wheels of the juggernaut. Evolution, not revolution [Mr Karl leaps forward to *Under Western Eyes*], Razumov warns. Gradualism, for Bobrowski, was the sole hope, but even that modicum of optimism would not be acceptable to Conrad the writer.

Conrad came to believe that 'the individual intensifies his essential being and rides it to his doom', pitting himself against an absolute and implacable destiny. We recall, Karl says, Stein's injunction in *Lord Jim*: 'to immerse oneself in the destructive element' – an Apollo-like utterance, except that Stein adds, as Uncle Tadeusz may have done – 'and by the exertions of your hands and feet in the water, make the deep sea keep you up'.

The sea! We come back to the youth who, having read *Les Travailleurs de la Mer*, nags his uncle to let him become a seaman. One of the refractory devices becomes commoner: a skilful, perhaps hysterical use of bad health which eventually marked the whole of his life. (It is true that gout, rheumatism, and arthritis caught most seamen sooner or later.) But bad health gives freedom – freedom to read immensely, to avoid education and discipline. A large number of young men all over Europe who hated commercial society opted for the sea, travel, and adventure. The ports were crowded with them; there was a slump in shipping. For Conrad the sea would be a beneficent wilderness, above all for one who found he preferred the staring loneliness of the watch and the undoubted appeal of the beauties and terrors of fatalism. (Conrad also uttered some of his rhetorical words about the sea being a mother, delightful to Freudians, but a thoroughly second-rate generality, in an artist: I fear Mr Karl thinks it mythically ' significant'.)

Conrad was better when he spoke of the sea as a mirror. He had been staring at maps, longing to be tested by a new country. So Uncle Tadeusz gave in and let him go to France, the second home of gifted Polish émigrés, and, on a pleasant allowance, the young gentleman hung around in the port of Marseilles – a period he would late in life romanticise in *The Arrow of Gold*. One has the impression of Conrad being very much a dandy and poseur in his youth, perhaps inclined to play the aristocrat and man of honour, reckless with his money, sending home for more, and very Apollo-ish as a young wit and intellectual, playing at being Ulysses. Then comes the mysterious crisis: there are few berths on French ships, a lot of hanging about, angry letters from uncle, an urgent debt, and then, inviting the man who was his uncle's watchdog to tea, Conrad shoots himself, fortunately missing his heart: he will always overact. The French dream is over, a possible French novelist is done for – perhaps for the simple reason that the British merchant service had overwhelming prestige; more likely that the British were slack and unscrupulous and did not ask many questions; perhaps because he wanted to enter the new wilderness of a speech which he did not know, but whose literature he knew very well.

Professor Karl would like to think that Conrad had picked up some knowledge of the Symbolists in Marseilles. An attractive idea, but there is, he agrees, no evidence. The conjecture is pleasant and would be fitting. Really, Shakespeare and Dickens were more important, for they also brought with them a way of accepting the literary enthusiasms of a father whose political and philosophical life he rejected. To write in Polish would have meant the duplication of his father's disaster. His choice of the English language and métier amounted to a divorce. English also got him out of the landlocked Mediterranean and out to the East, to the casualties of colonial competition and exploitation, to the monstrous scandal of the Congo and the greed in *Nostromo*. It is strange and moving to see Conrad struggling with his own restlessness, submitting to discipline, trying to escape it, always secretive, not quite certain of what he is hoarding but hoarding because as a visionary artist he will need an immense amount of vivid detail to draw on.

Professor Karl is excellent on Conrad's strange marriage to a stoical but vocal girl of humble London family who had to struggle for a living, and though she was out of her depth intellectually, Conrad was devoted to her.

[959]

Perhaps there are glances at her depressing background in *The Secret Agent*: Galsworthy admired her and she certainly stood up to Ford Madox Ford.

During twenty years at sea Conrad had been a misogynist with a sailor's deep mistrust of women: the captain who takes his wife to sea is done for. The crew can't bear it. The only woman who seems to have matched Conrad intellectually was his novel-writing 'Aunt' in Brussels, but he eventually drifted away from all attachments once he had got what he wanted – which was not sex but moral support. The *femmes fatales* of his novels are the standard fantasies of the Romantic Decadents. Once he had settled in England as a story-teller his life was a hell of toil, muddle, the instant recognition of his talent by a few, his total rejection by the great public. They preferred the gaudier Kipling or Haggard to the morbid and elegant Pole, who thought of art as the transcendent reconciling illusion – like the sea, a mirror.

From his letters and from his conversation one would gather that Conrad was one of the most tormented of novelists whose agonies, blockages, and misfortunes can only be compared with Dostoevsky's. His health was wrecked by the time he reached his fifties; the *contretemps* of family life appeared to him as apocalyptic disasters. He was extravagant and was always in money difficulties which paralysed him. He became strangely commercial with collectors of his manuscripts.

It is odd that a novelist who had his enormous, vivid experience to draw on should have been stuck so often with nothing to say. Edward Garnett believed that he lacked invention. Memory, unless it is involuntary, is indeed static. As an expatriate Conrad was unable to draw on a body of experience common to his prospective readers. It is interesting to know that so much of his background material and so many of the episodes in his novels were suggested by reading, but, of course, the great novelists often owe their decisive power to their ability to turn their incapacities into qualities. If invention flagged, Conrad intensified his static scenes. When the realistic advancing of character beat him, he invented the garrulous and rather too clubbable Marlow as a narrator who could jump ahead; if a character did not move, Conrad used great ingenuity in labouring the character's moral uniqueness.

His people are morally and physically stamped like medallions, and he himself referred to his desire for an effect of sculpture. At his greatest he indeed achieved a sort of condensing and dramatic authority in vibrant and living stone; his seascapes are more alive than many of his people. He is careful to take his characters out of time into an isolated world very much in the manner of the dramatist – the ship, the small obsessional enclaves of conspiracy, the unget-at-able port in *Nostromo*, the captain's cabin in *The Secret Sharer* – so that the utmost can be got out of the closed moral dilemma. He was not among the great creators of character. He was an establisher of fates and situations. He wrote:

I have been called a writer of the sea, of the tropics, a descriptive writer, a romantic writer – and also a realist. But as a matter of fact all my concern has been with the 'ideal' value of things, events, and people. That and nothing else.

The world of ideal values becomes, so often, the exile's island in a world which has become doomed because he has no country. The connivance of Conrad's sense of these values with his own sense of isolation and catastrophe made him one of the most searching psychologists of that moral conflict in the European novel.

The Aesthete in War

Looking back on T. E. Lawrence and his legend after forty years one sees in him exactly the Hero called for by those who fought in the First World War and survived. It is perfect that he went into that war as the romantic happy warrior and emerged as the guilty Hamlet of his generation. In a far less theatrical way, so did others who fared worse: whatever singularity or genius *they* had was ground out of them on the Western Front where the 'real' war was being fought.

To them – and to the public trying to forget that mass slaughter – Lawrence's guerrilla war in the desert was war as they romantically dreamed it ought to be: terrible, but at least apprehensible like an exotic work of art, small yet visionary and having the epic quality of individual combat – known then only to flying men – in which the daring young leader leaps to privilege, gets his freedom to act alone, and wins by his courage and his cunning. And, as if this were not enough to dream of, the hero has the gift of enlarging his own legend so that it continues as he renounces his victory and abases himself. What, after forty years, has overtaken him? The Partisans and Resistance leaders, the guerrillas and underground fighters of the Second World War and after, have made clear that, at any rate, T. E. Lawrence was a sketch for a coming prototype. Or the reviver of an ancient one.

If heroes fulfil the unconscious wishes of others, their rank depends not only on a *virtu* that springs from their internal conflicts and their vision, but on their historical opportunity. Lawrence without British imperialism in its penultimate phase behind him would have had no driving force. Even the duplicity that haunts political visionaries would have failed him. And one cannot throw out the fact that, in mass societies like Britain and the United States, fame is made glamorous by the commercialised press and films, and by the hero's talent for staging himself and even for acting out the exceptional man's natural disgust with success. None of the reviewers of

Revolt in the Desert (the abridgment of *The Seven Pillars of Wisdom*), Lawrence wrote, has 'given me the credit for being a bag of tricks . . .' and he added with some vanity, 'too rich and full for them to control'. Inevitably the denigrators took the tip and looked into Lawrence's powers of mystification. The most extravagant in malice was Malcolm Muggeridge:

> [Lawrence] is superlatively the case of everything being true except the facts. Who more fitting to be a Hero of Our Time than this, our English Genet, our Sodomite-Saint with Lowell Thomas for his Sartre and Alec Guinness to say 'Amen'.

Bringing all the shallowness of the debunker and the meanness of the disappointed man, Richard Aldington added T. E. Lawrence to his 'exposures' of D. H. Lawrence and Norman Douglas. The most charitable comment one can make of Muggeridge and Aldington is that they were attacking the image created by the popular press and the films and ridding themselves of the post-war spleen at T. E. Lawrence's expense: he had tried to do it, more painfully, at his own.

But there *is* an obvious difficulty for biographers in dealing with Lawrence which John E. Mack points out in his long study *A Prince of Our Disorder*; the excellent title is a phrase of Irving Howe's. Dr Mack first approached the subject of the making and self-making of a hero as a psychologist but found himself in regions beyond the clinical. Dr Mack is no wit. He is a very repetitive writer; he has loaded and lengthened his book with worried platitudes. Lawrence, who was debonair and clear even when he was evasive in his own remarkable *Letters*, puts his own case better. Still, Dr Mack is thorough. He has searched and interviewed widely and feels even personal sympathy with his intractable subject. He says two things which are fundamental. The first could be more tersely expressed by saying that T. E. Lawrence was Irish in his taste for fantasy, as Shaw well understood:

> One of the purposes in writing [*The Seven Pillars of Wisdom*] was to invite the public to create with him a new and different self, a mythological Lawrence, larger than life, a self that would be immune to or beyond personal pain and conflict and that would replace the self he felt he had debased . . . The irony is that, objectively, the real Lawrence

corresponded in many ways to the ideal one he sought to create through his dramatising and embroidering. But from his inner psychological perspective that real self was debased by the war.

The second point is certainly exact whether one looks at Lawrence's upbringing, his education, above all at his prose style, or at the war and his career afterwards. He was a good deal the aesthete in war.

Lawrence is in many ways a transitional hero standing . . . between the neo-medieval romantic heroes of the nineteenth century and the moral realists of the twentieth.

If not a Hero, he exemplified what happened at a breaking point of European culture in 1914.

Lawrence's private story is the story of the wound and the bow. He had by birth the distinction (which passes as a fantasy through many children's heads for a time) of being illegitimate. His mother also had been an illegitimate child, the daughter of a journeyman shipwright in Durham, and farmed out on sternly religious Scottish families. She was sent at eighteen as a nurse to Ireland to look after the children of an unhappily married, hard-drinking, Anglo-Irish landowner called Chapman who passed his time hunting, shooting and fishing. They fell in love, he left his wife, changed his name and went to Wales, then to the south coast of England for the sailing and finally, since their four boys needed a good cheap secondary school, to Oxford. The new family had £300 a year left to live on, a respectable if modest private income in those days and representing the protective assurance of capital.

The two parents were devoted, the landowner accepted his decline in status and relative poverty happily: it could not have occurred to him to earn his living. He was by inheritance a rentier. The young Scots girl, of course, soon dominated him. She stopped him drinking and was the figure of power in their little villa. They were a deeply religious couple, an odd but determined pair of Puritans who disapproved of theatres, dances and shut themselves off from the curiosity of neighbours. Perhaps they were too discreet, for Lawrence senior went off at times to Ireland to see his sporting friends and to keep an eye on his estate: in Oxford a land agent would inexplicably arrive. It was not long before the Lawrence boys guessed the secret and although the indirect private effect on them was crucial, they benefited by their parents' serious care for their education: the secondary schools they were sent to had special opportunities for getting clever boys into Oxford.

The boys were stamped by the mother's Puritan religion which, Dr Mack thinks, she evidently saw as her redemption for the sin of taking a man away from his wife. I find this too simple; her religiosity was an assertion of pride. Lawrence's mother had charm and he inherited her strange, vacant, yet penetrating china-blue eyes and undoubtedly her will, which was powerful to a degree. She was a fanatical housekeeper, all for cleansing house, body and soul: the prudent austerity is common to Calvinist Scotland, northern England and indeed Germany and is far more the expression of superior virtue than of guilt. She did believe in discipline and physical punishment. She was determined to break the will of her mischievous second son by beating him on the backside and initiated him into the sensations of pleasure-pain: it is easy to argue that the mother (who was a remorseless questioner) was very conscious of her own guilt; if so she was close to being a Justified Sinner. This did not prevent her from enjoying the vanity of the humbly born in having carried off her grand landowner, in Lawrence's own words, as 'a trophy'.

The Victorians had resources in the subtleties of the class system: the one thing that must have protected the Lawrences was that the elder Lawrence was recognisably a gentleman; not only his self-effacing manner but the public respect for his mysterious private means guaranteed the view. But what was his influence? He was devalued, but on the mind and imagination of T. E. Lawrence his influence was enormous. The Anglo-Irish gentry were colonists who had been either Elizabethan or Cromwellian conquerors, soldiers all of them, rewarded with captured estates. They intermarried mainly with their kind and became tied up in hundreds of years of cousinage. It was a near enough assertion that one of the elder Lawrence's ancestors was closely related to Raleigh and, it was even claimed, he had Raleigh's looks. But the strongest element in the family was Cromwellian Roundhead and Dutch: it dulled the Elizabethan dash and brought in the Low Church Puritanism of Anglo-Ireland. The race traditionally bred soldiers but by the nineteenth century the soldiers, rakish or sedate, had become dull landlords who did little but talk correctly of horses, salmon, and snipe, though their brighter sons occasionally became Britain's best generals or outstanding servants of the Empire.

What Lawrence senior embodied for his famous son was a sense of history as an inheritance. What the self-isolated family of brothers gave to him was a lasting belief in the exclusive superiority of self-sufficient extroverted masculinity and brotherhood. This and the mother's power over her sons was enough to ensure – as Dr Mack suggests – Lawrence's chastity. He had no adolescence: he went straight from boyhood to manhood. It was part of the mother's plan of redemption that one at least of her boys should be a missionary in China: sexual purity was essential, marriage an obscenity.

The well-known avidity of the young Lawrence's studies in archaeology, his passion for medieval castles, the history of chivalry and the Crusades, and his curiosity about the Saracens were the perfect preparation for the desert war and the vision of Arab freedom. He was teaching and hardening himself. Like Doughty and other educated Englishmen who went as solitaries to the desert, he felt the pull of tribal life and the masculine cult of personal honour, long ago lost to Western life. (Honour and its concomitant knowledge of treachery had a battered meaning for the Anglo-Irish, and were perhaps a survival of Elizabethan influence, especially Raleigh's.) When Feisal discreetly showed that he had guessed Lawrence was doctoring the telegrams from Mecca and said drily: 'You always prefer my honour to your own', the words have the accent of an Elizabethan conceit, the ambiguity of words cut by the diamond of a betrayed Tudor on his window. Anti-imperialist as Lawrence was, he was drawn to the military fascination of imperial power. Oil was commerce and therefore contemptible, but Alexandretta must be 'held at all costs'.

In his political and military account of the war Dr Mack's eye is on Lawrence living an acquired legend. All has the fire of gifted youth until we get to the crises – what really happened when he was captured at Dera'a and what Dr Mack regards as the vengeance or the loss of self-control at the Turkish massacre of Tafas: here a hidden Lawrence appears. Which of the several versions in the rewriting of the rape at Dera'a is to be relied on? Is it, conceivably, a fantasy to cover some other act of sodomy? Research by Lawrence's sceptical or believing critics is not conclusive, as Dr Mack shows, but he is confident that an act of sodomy did occur and is certain there was a brutal beating; Lawrence's revisions are an attempt to tell the truth that shocked him, though 'the sequence of events is hard to follow'. There was an assault, Dr Mack concludes, 'and the element of sexual pleasure he experienced in the midst of such indignity, pain and degradation was particularly intolerable and shameful to him'. It has since become known that when Lawrence tried to hide in the ranks of the RAF after the Peace Conference and was in despair he hired a man to beat him brutally from time to time and concocted a grotesque fiction that would persuade a simple man to do it.

The difficulty of the biographer and especially one with wide – that is to say not simply clinical – psychological interests lies in avoiding the static summary of hindsight and showing a man as he changes. Here Dr Mack is good in portraiture and plausible in analysis. Lawrence's nature and his sexuality were not formed by a single cause. He was a mixture of the craftsman and aesthete in war. The literary tastes of his generation were very much directed by the Victorian cult of the medieval, a self-conversion to a heroic past which would disguise the defilement of the industrial revolution; the imaginations of the educated were filled with Chaucer, Malory, William Morris, Tennyson's *Idylls*, Jean Froissart, the *chansons de geste* and the ethic of courtly love. William Morris and Doughty wrote in a studiously mannered prose, so did Kipling the popular novelist.

This imagination was Lawrence's – he admitted to 'doing up small packets of words foppishly'. He swung between plain direct words and the imagery of masquerade. In the Twenties one finds him admiring Cabell's very dubious pseudo-medieval *Jurgen*, which is enough to show the split in his own mind. The rarefying, unsexing and idealising of women was borrowed from the neo-Romantics and the abhorrence of fleshly contact confirmed the message. Strangely this suited well with the demands of Empire which required men who could stand being alone and could live by self-discipline. Lawrence's mother would enter such a conspiracy without necessarily being driven by guilt: she would be asserting a faith and the fortifying of conscience. And one can add that sexual aberration is well known to be common among explorers and men of action who are fanatical, as Lawrence was, in hardening themselves to endure punishment.

Like pretty well all the men who came out of the 1914 war Lawrence had a badly damaged mind. At All Souls he was either sunk in deep depression or would suddenly tell wildly imaginary stories of his exploits. He both sought and hid from publicity. The visionary at the Peace Conference had the anger of an actor who is now in a political play he does not understand or rather understands too well. He hated the betrayal. He was forced to accept the moral consequences of the double role he had played in Arabia. Dr Mack writes of the exits and entrances in the drama frankly, though he is not writing as an historian. Shaw, who understood Lawrence as a fellow Irishman and who was an expert in what Lawrence called 'the solution of multiple personalities', told him that the limelight would follow him for the rest of his life; and one cannot say that Lawrence avoided it – at least not for many years.

The 'self-degradation' was dramatic as an act of conscience and punishment, even staged, yet clearly a genuine attempt to come to terms with himself. The RAF was a hard school, the Tank Corps was bestial. One has to read *The Mint* to see what he willed himself to go through. Most biographers, as I have said, have thought he inherited this will from his ruling mother, and yet in his exposed detachment one also sees the image of his father. The old landowner (who had become a baronet and had died by this time) must himself have been something of a spectator in his own family when in his time he had give up his status and, in the course of 'lawless' passion, had joined the common people. The fates of father and son have curious resemblances. We also have the not uncommon sight of passionate elders using up a family's erotic capital, leaving the children with little or none.

Lawrence was a Don Quixote before he became a Hamlet. What remains for us of the former? He was one of the first to see that after 1917 Asia itself was going to be a political force, even if he tried to see the Arabs as part of the then British Commonwealth – the imperial idea of Lionel Curtis. He imagined a natural coming together of the Jews and Arabs, too simply because he could not foretell what new imperialism might intervene. Arab commentators think he judged the situation badly. As Hamlet, he saw his career in the desert as a prostitution: his introspections, as Dr Mack shows, do reveal how 'unlovely the back of a commander's mind must be'. I do not think he was playing with conscience in the pedantic Irish way: he had his mother's earnestness.

[968]

How does his service in the ranks of the RAF and Tank Corps now strike us? Here he is tragically vivid in Dr Mack's portrait. The poor devil would slip out of the depot at night and was pitied by the sentries whom he silently passed. The service was intended as a therapy, but he was forced to live among common men who had become unwanted animals because they could not get other jobs: what most upset him, characteristically, was their obsessive lust. They were quite different from the conscripts of the Second World War who were politically-minded and, whether educated or uneducated, shared far more the common lot of a whole population. The therapy, if there was one, was public and not private. I think that Dr Mack's strongest compliment is that Lawrence was a born 'enabler'. He was a natural technician, a practical craftsman and teacher; he could get on with anybody and help people to help themselves. But his private philosophy of renunciation and a 'decent nihilism' did not save him from a deep boredom. Driving fast and dangerously on a motor bike to 'forget himself for a few minutes' was an escape into nihilist sensation. Not a suicide but a loss of will.

The Private Voice

===

It has often been said that the British venerate old age. The sins of the ancient are forgiven for they have become 'characters' – a national ideal. Even the talented survive their inevitable denigration: they have freed themselves from the national obsessions with social obligation and the virtue of worry. This is true of E. M. Forster who lived until he was ninety and who had become a kind of wayward holy man by the time he was seventy: a status he would hardly have achieved in France, for example, where old age is often publicly derided. Perhaps the British cult is simply Victorian, for the Victorians solemnly sought to get over youth as quickly as possible and assume elderly airs – children died like flies – and here one must note that the famous liberal, humanist, rationalist intellectuals seem to have had a gift for longevity. One can argue, of course, that they were all born whimsical and elderly; this was sometimes the impression given by Forster who was elderly when he was a boy and in many ways school-boyish to look at when he was old: the tweed cap too small, the sleeves of the shabby jacket too short, the shoes neglected as he skipped across to King's College chapel at Cambridge to hear the Sunday singing. He looked like a whim.

More decisive suggestions appear in Mr Furbank's biography which, while not ignoring Forster as the psychological and social 'case' or strange 'instance' he certainly was, recreates him and his succeeding circles of friends in close chronological detail and illuminates the intimate life that ran, often underground, with his public career as a novelist, critic, essayist, and figure of controversy. So much critical work has been done about him that it is a relief to see the man himself. He was at once comically drab and alarmingly alive, and so fresh in the offhand private voice speaking in the public place where it disconcerted because it dodged conventional utterance. The voice was the most important thing about him and his prose; it was unofficial, conversational, free of jargon, and dropped a dissident but carefully timed word or two of Edwardian slang into the solemn moments of argument. One or two of these malign words stick in the mind: certain kinds of thought and action did not 'pay'; or about his own kind of merit in which he liked to be that problematical racehorse, a possible 'cert'.

Mr Furbank's *Life* is long perhaps for a writer whose abstentions were long, but Forster's life was filled by seminal friendships with the eminent in literature, politics, the universities, and high administration; with Maharajahs, coolies, busmen, barbers, policemen, casuals, and soldiers and – it strikes one – perhaps the largest collection of female relatives any famous writer has ever had. The oddity is that this range of aunts, cousins, and connections came to a man who was shy and even timid, and yet drastic in moral courage, kind but tart when irritated, and who to many seemed old-maidish. Mr Furbank, a friend of a much younger generation, does not standardise his subject as a psychological case: he watches him live with perceptiveness and sympathy. He simply shows that Forster's dilemmas are deeply entangled with the privileges and manners of the class into which he was born, with emotional fatality and the rewards of a slow self-discovery.

There is so much detail in this book that the reviewer has to skip many piquant things. In 1879 when he was born, an only child, Forster was the odd product of interlocking families of the prolific and very mixed Victorian middle class. The important ladies came variously from the rich banking Evangelicals, known as the Clapham sect, who had in the past been eminent in the antislavery movement and had followed the traditions of philanthropical Puritanism and liberalism. From Northumberland appear clerics who became Anglo-Irish and, in the course of generations, returned to Britain to comfortable livings – Forster thought he owed his independence and his imaginative gifts to the Irish and also a Welsh connection. Another strain was from a penniless, rather Bohemian family once distinguished in marine painting who ended as modest teachers with occasional hushed-up scandals and embarrassing connections with 'trade'. There was present also a County connection led by a huntin' and shootin' uncle who was terrifying at the dinner table (his favourite battlefield), who had genially savage ideas about 'making a man' of his nephew and whose attitude to religion was 'If the house is religious, wear your trousers out and pray like blazes.' The uncle was exceptional.

But by 1879 Forster's relatives had become mainly part of the tame and snobbish semi-suburban class of independent means. They might be called the watered-down and villa-dwelling successors of the people in Jane Austen's novels, formidable at tea, but without the iron of the eighteenth century or the raffishness of the Regency in them. The working class and the poor were 'unthinkable'. Soon after Forster was born his young father died of consumption; a grandmother and aunts flocked to the rescue of the young mother who was proper, lively, capable, but in narrow circumstances. A duel was fought over the baby who was expected to be as frail as his father had been; he was therefore cosseted and spoiled and turned into a passionate and imperious child, a girlish mother's boy who played with dolls and was made precocious by adult company.

The inner 'sureness', the adult air Forster carried throughout his life, was established for good; but he was not being equipped to survive the horseplay and bullying and the gang life of English boys at private schools. They were quick to spot a 'muff'. E.M. were bad initials – he was very soon called 'Emmy'. A more serious and central situation developed between mother and son: they adored each other. He wanted to marry her, of course; and that delightful phase did not quickly fade. She refused – it is believed – to remarry because she doted on him, and his love for her embraced his long life. (She died when she was ninety and he was sixty-six and for a great deal of the time they occupied the same houses.) The hearty huntin' and shootin' uncle – and other uncles – complained of the boy's stumbling helplessness and incompetence – he couldn't even carry a tea tray without dropping it – and could see no future for him.

And then, there was the taboo subject of sex. When he was sent, rather late, to his first prep school, schoolboy smut puzzled him: at home his penis was known as his 'dirty' and he thought of it as some kind of punishment; well, children do perhaps still stick to peculiar ideas, but this one lasted. (In later life he said that it was not until he was thirty, and after he had written three distinguished novels about love and marriage, that he understood how sexual intercourse took place.)

But a sinister initiation into sexual practice was experienced when he was eleven years old. While walking on the Downs he fell in with a middle-aged gentleman in a deerstalker hat and knickerbockers who had stopped to have a pee. The man asked the boy to play with his penis. The young Forster was startled by the man's fierce-looking organ but politely did as he was told and was astonished by the result. The man also offered him a shilling which he refused. The boy ran back, frightened, to school and at once wrote home to his mother about it. She made him report the incident to a master at school, which he did. He was miserably embarrassed, the schoolmaster was inept. By now the boy was in a 'hard and important mood', enjoying the limelight there and at the local police station. He said boldly the man could easily be identified because his organ was 'diseased'. The curious thing is that he had before all this told his mother about the 'dirty trick' of masturbating. He was naïvely surprised by her distress and he decided he would never be frank again. 'So ended,' he said, 'my last chance of a confidant.' If he couldn't talk to the adored mother, to whom on earth could he ever talk?

Mr Furbank suggests that if the incident was forgotten it left a lasting pattern of panic and cross-purposes and that perhaps he returned to it in *Passage to India* where it became a model for Adela's vengeful and confused behaviour after she imagines she has been molested by Aziz. By this mid-teens Forster was no longer the imperious spoiled darling; he was a despised 'day boy' at Tonbridge School – the hellish Sawston of *The Longest Journey* – an enemy of the public school regard for leadership and the team spirit. He was already a prim, buttoned-up, and pedantic intellectual, widely read, demure, and a sharp judge of the character and snobberies of Tonbridge society. One or two clever boys thought he was certain to enter the Church and become a bishop. He left school and, since his father had been an architect, he was taken by his mother on a tour of French cathedrals in France, the first of many Continental journeys with her in the next years.

After the French cathedrals, freedom. A beloved great-aunt made a substantial trust on his behalf which would make him independent for life and in 1897 at the age of eighteen he went up to King's College, Cambridge. He was, Mr Furbank points out, no awestruck provincial: he would never have mistaken the famous gateway for medieval. If he fell in love with Cambridge, it would not be in the tragic fashion of those who were content to live ever afterward a scholar-gypsy life:

> For good or evil Cambridge gave a special stamp to the careers [of the sons of the professional middle classes], prolonging boyhood and

opening fresh vistas – of friendship, of intellectual self-fulfilment, of social climbing – at an age when for most of their contemporaries the choices had been made . . . Cambridge cushioned his existence ever afterwards.

There he started the process of 'finding himself' – a process which emotionally was to take an excessively long time, largely because of the possessiveness of his mother.

The main thing about Cambridge for him was that it was the place where things were valued for what they were in themselves and not for what use you could make of them. He was there in the G. E. Moore period and although, in Mr Furbank's view, too much has been made of Moore's influence (Forster never read *Principia Ethica*), the epigraph stuck in his mind as the 'idea of Cambridge "truth": "Everything is what it is, and not another thing".'

The received ideas of Tonbridge vanished. Forster cut a dim figure at first but he had influential friends in the enormously assured Darwin family. In his fourth year he was intellectually fit to be elected to the 'secret' society of the Apostles which after eighty sleepy years had woken up. Their arguments about 'states of mind' and 'what exactly do you mean?' bored him. ('Arguments,' he once said, showing that he was a novelist by nature, 'are only fascinating when they are of the nature of gestures and illustrate the people who produce them'.) The university also confirmed in him a prejudice which had been established in Britain early in the nineteenth century. It is one which still haunts British life and was an aspect of liberal thought: the prejudice that the scholars, civil servants, and the professional classes were the successors of the landed aristocracy and were the people who ran Britain – not the businessmen, or indeed their workers, who merely made the country rich. It is a theme which, in his sternly self-critical way, Forster dramatised in *Howards End*.

The Apostles who in 1901 exacted honesty in their debates spoke out about the taboo subject of homosexuality. Furbank thinks that by this time Forster must have known that his upbringing had made him homosexual by temperament. The 'love-affair' with his mother must have ruled out any possible attraction to other women. And

It would seem likely that, partly as a result of the traumatic experience at his prep school, the onset of puberty had brought with it very strong sexual inhibitions – so much so, that for much of his youth and early manhood, physical sex played very little part in his conscious thoughts; he did not have much in the way of erotic fantasies, or, if he did, they were infantile ones.

Even when he succeeded in breaking through his inhibitions, Forster does seem to have been a man of low temperature sexually. The homosexual affections he felt at Cambridge were platonic. The aftermath of the Oscar Wilde trial made gossip about homosexual practices secretive. Mr Furbank gives his portrait of him at the time when he had struck Lytton Strachey as being 'a taupe' [i.e. a mole]:

he was drab-coloured and unobtrusive and came up in odd places and unexpected circles. There was something flitting and discontinuous about him; one minute you were talking with him intimately, the next he had withdrawn or simply disappeared. He was freakish and demure, yet at times could be earnestly direct, as if vast issues hung upon simple truth-telling. And all the time there was something hapless or silly-simple about him; friends likened him to Henry VI . . . Yet there was a queer sureness about him, a super-quick sensing of immediate situations, and – in flashes – an extraordinary sweep of human understanding.

In the next ten years Forster lived the decorous life of the intellectual with his mother in their suburban villa. He had no particular career in mind, but he had begun to write. He satisfied his social conscience by teaching Latin in the well-known Working Men's College at Bloomsbury where many distinguished men had given their time, and he worried about the cultural snobbery of autodidacts like the Leonard Basts of pre-1914 Britain. At home the 'haze of females' appeared: he dropped tea trays but he was an excellent pianist. He visited relations. He was tutor for a while in Germany to the children of the hilariously devouring authoress of *Elizabeth and her German Garden*; and astonished a German tutor with his belief that telephone wires were hollow. And then – as was *de rigueur* in his circle – he went off with his mother on momentous cultural tours to Italy and Greece where he, like the ladies of these expeditions, was frugal with his tips and sharply cut them down if any porter or servant complained. (He lived frugally all his life but was wildly generous to his friends and to causes.) On these sentimental journeys in which the Edwardian tourists colonised the pensions and small hotels with their snobberies, moralisings, and their cultural bitching, he became expert in malice.

He, of course, had read up on everything, knew his painting and sculpture, his temples and palaces, and he was a vivid diarist. Pages of dialogue went into the notebooks from which *A Room with a View* and *Where Angels Fear to Tread* were written. But Italy played its ancient trick on him. At Cambridge he had easily shed the Christian religion. Italy confirmed the pagan. His imagination came to life. He experienced almost mystical visions or at any rate sensations of the presence of some primordial and universal beckonings and fatality. The stories of *The Celestial Omnibus* are slight but they relate the devastating effect of metamorphosis upon people dulled or mutilated by respectability. The characters of *Where Angels Fear to Tread* are forced to face pagan passion which is without mercy, and situations in which dull human nature is stripped of pretences and is or is not liberated by acts that shock the foundations of their merely sociable morality. Good and evil are interlaced.

Forster succeeded at once as a novelist. His originality as an observer of character and his daring as a moralist were recognised by the best judges. *Howards End* was a triumph. Here we meet Forster's fear of success, the fear of future sterility. Acclaim put him at a loss for a new subject. There was, he knew, a secret forbidden subject for the truth-teller: his scarcely achieved homosexual desires. All he could do was to console himself by writing erotic stories which he eventually tore up. He was determined to speak out, a good deal because D. H. Lawrence attacked him when they met. He made the disastrous decision to write *Maurice* – disastrous as a step forward in a novelist's life because the book would be unpublishable under British law at that time and would hang like a dead albatross round his neck; even more disastrous because his own experience was distinctly more wishfully sentimental than real. Yet he had to meet the self-accusation that he had been 'tea-tabling' about heterosexual love and marriage while being both a misogynist and an outsider. Lytton Strachey was among those who read the privately circulated manuscript and he saw much to admire. But he wrote:

I should be inclined to diagnose Maurice's state as simply lust and sentiment – a very wobbly affair; I should have prophesied a rupture after 6 months – chiefly as a result of lack of common interests and owing to class differences . . . and so your Sherwood Forest ending appears to me slightly mythical . . . I think he [Maurice] had still a great deal to learn, and that the très-très-noble Alec could never teach it to him. What was wanted was a brief honeymoon with that charming young Frenchman who would have shown Mr Eel that it was possible to take the divagations of a prick too seriously.

We know what followed: he turned to excellent literary criticism and politics. His liberal circles at Cambridge and in Fabian Bloomsbury were hostile to British imperialism in Egypt and India; he wrote for the *Independent Review* and the *New Statesman*; and at the core of his thought was his belief in the primacy of personal relationships: imperialism created the 'bad heart', the crude duty of shutting out intimacy with the ruled. He could afford to travel and, egged on by Masood, a genially fantastic, wilful, and mocking undergraduate who was the ward of the foremost Mohammedan in India in 1912, to soak himself in Indian sights and life.

In Mr Furbank's prolonged accounts of Forster's Indian experience, Forster's engaging letters to his mother enliven a narrative that might otherwise be mere record. One notes that his physical sexual liberation was not to occur until 1916 during the First World War, when he struck out again and worked for the Red Cross in Egypt. Alexandria was the scene of his bizarre, touching, astonishing affair with Mohammed, a miserably poor tram conductor. Strachey would no doubt have called it a 'divagation', but it was well documented by Forster's own notes and in them appears as the happy conflict of the two mocking yet feeling dignities – the dignities of the rich and the abysmally poor. (Rarely in biography do we hear what people really say to each other, but here Furbank can tell us.) Forster felt sexually released; and he had broken through the barriers of class and race. The story of his generous care for Mohammed and of his wife is strange and very moving. After the war was over and Forster had to leave, Mohammed died of illness brought on by the hopeless struggles of the Egyptian poor. Forster had to conceal his breakdown at the news of the death from his mother. One notices his own stern break with his own tears: 'a thing is what it is, and not another thing.'

Being away from his mother for three years and released from 'sexual apprenticeship', Forster returned to find himself under his mother's power once more. They agreed eventually that he might spend two nights away in London every week, but on each free day he sent her a chatty postcard! His dependence on her irked him less as he grew older and his fame as a writer was settled, but we notice the irony. With her, rather than with any man, he was making 'the longest journey' which had made the idea of marriage to a woman horrifying. When she died in 1945 at the age of ninety and he was sixty-six, he wrote to J. R. Ackerley, whose portrait is incidentally very good in this book:

> I wonder whether women are important to one's comfort and stability. I am inclined to think they may be. Although my mother has been intermittently tiresome for the last thirty years, has cramped and warped my genius, hindered my career and buggered up my house, and boycotted my beloved, I have to admit that she provides a sort of rich subsoil where I have been able to rest and grow. That, rather than sex or wifiness, seems to be women's special gift to men.

Still, if he dared not speak out to his mother, he did have one female confidante, the wife of a professor, who was eagerly sympathetic with his homosexual life, a harbinger of contemporary clear-headedness.

Piquant asides relieve the long chronicle. On the serious matter of Forster's second visit to India at the moment of political crisis in 1922 and the writing of *Passage to India* Mr Furbank is very discerning. He gives full attention to the situation in India and to the often angry protests made by distinguished Anglo-Indians, who fell upon Forster's mistakes. He admitted his errors. He agreed that he had only been in India eighteen months in all, but always argued that a novel cannot be judged by its 'fairness'. He wrote to Lowes Dickinson:

> Isn't 'fair-mindedness' dreary! A rare achievement, and a valuable one, you will tell me, but how sterile in one's own soul. I fall in love with Orientals, with Anglo-Indians – no: that is roughly my internal condition, and all the time I had to repress the consequences, or fail to hold

the scales. Where is truth? It makes me so sad that I could not give the beloved a better show. One's deepest emotions count for so little as soon as one tries to describe external life honestly, or even readably. Scarcely anyone has seen that I hoped Aziz would be charming . . .

An interesting point made by Furbank is that the influence of T. E. Lawrence is marked in the final chapters of the book. Forster admired Lawrence and feared a gang of right-wing people might get hold of him in time.

The diverting and richest aspect of the second visit is the account, drawn from Forster's letters, of his time as the secretary of the delightful, comic, and utterly incompetent Maharajah of Dewas, whose palace and kingdom were falling to pieces. The Maharajah hated catamites though his court was alive with their intrigues, jokes, and whisperings. In a panic Forster got up the courage to confess his tastes to the Maharajah and expected to be sacked. The Maharajah was surprised and felt sorry for him, and rather than encourage him to console himself with masturbation – a great evil because it was lonely – ingeniously arranged for him to have an affair with a court barber. Barbers could come and go without scandal. The comedy is picaresque and instructive.

Further comedies were to occur in Cockney London later on in Forster's life, in a strange local community in which the police had jolly private relations with a lot of minor crooks and others living cheerfully by their wits. This time the *British* class barrier was broken. It is not surprising that Forster regretted he had written *Maurice* before he really knew his subject. The comedy here was harmless. The pity is that it came too late for the novelist. He had become a natural teacher: it was noticed that one or two hefty and wild characters put on solemn cultural airs after their minds had been awakened by his puzzling company.

Forster's own judgment was that the affections were dominant in working men: they were easy about sex, but were not interested in the passion of love. This, one must say, is very sweeping. Yet in this time Forster did have his closest and lasting emotional friendship with Bob Buckingham, then a solid policeman, and his young wife. Just before Forster died Bob apparently denied that the friendship was homosexual and the matter is a mystery, for his wife assumed it was. A strange reversal

[979]

of the affections occurred in this relationship which has a bearing on Forster's outstanding characteristic – he was generous with money and considerate to a fault: his feeling for the delicacies of personal relationships was tender and endless – and it was the wife who understood him and cared for him when the husband seemed to be bored and cool. The only thing that irritated her was that Forster was untidy and had been used to being waited on by servants.

Why, after *Passage to India*, did Forster write no more novels? He wrote plays that have been lost and, of course, his important *Aspects of the Novel* and the famous *Two Cheers for Democracy*. He played a leading part in campaigns for civil liberties and for intellectual freedom in the Thirties and after. Furbank thinks that although he was a rationalist, Forster was superstitious about the dangers of success. Having been 'royally favoured' as a child he had magical feelings about his own life and would naturally 'have irrational fears at the realization of very deep wishes'. More practically, Forster himself saw that, being homosexual, he had grown bored with writing about love and marriage and the relations of men and women. He must also have felt that in *Maurice* he had written about a homosexual love affair as a substitute for having one. It is probable, Mr Furbank thinks, that he had, though not in the vulgar sense, 'only one novel in him' – 'I mean that he received his whole inspiration – a vision, a kind of plot, a message – all at once, in early manhood.'

Still more important, the social types which 'ruled his imagination' were those of his Edwardian youth – which had been made almost brutally out of date by the two wars which destroyed them. Changes move fast today for the novelist. The common idiom lasts scarcely more than a decade. Also, ruthless as Forster was a moralist, he had no great powers of invention. Perhaps also one must grant that although his private means did not make him idle, they encouraged his conscience to seek too many targets. Yet his strength as a teacher lay in the refusal to be 'great'. He had the almost magical, gnomic power of making himself inconspicuous while facing with pluck – another favourite word of his – the desperate state of our world.

Disloyalties

===

English novelists are not notable for their sense of evil. James Hogg of *The Confessions of a Justified Sinner* has it, and so, in a romantic way, has Stevenson, but both are Scots. Conrad, the Pole, has it; so has Henry James the American. Among ourselves it is hard to find. There are signs in *Clarissa*; in Dickens evil appears hysterically in the forms of staged melodrama. Only Emily Brontë fully exposes her imagination to the dark spirit and with a pagan or pantheistic exhilaration and pride which profoundly shocked her contemporaries. For Hardy evil is an aloof and alien polity. It can hardly be called more than mischance. The rest of the English novelists settle for a world which must be judged in terms of right and wrong.

Against this Protestant tradition the novels of Graham Greene are a rebellion or, rather, a series of guerrilla ambushes from a Roman Catholic point of view. He was once said to be a Jansenist and was certainly at variance with the accommodating Catholic tradition on the Continent. His religion – as we see it in his early novels – has the egocentricity, the scruple, the puritanism and aggression present in English nonconformity, though it finds more savour in failure than success. God is his misadventure and, for this reason, maybe he is a religious man, i.e. he does not expect to get anything but conflict and pain out of his religion. I must say this is a vast relief after the optimism of the success cults. To the spectator, it seems that Greene wishes to have an adulterer's, a gambler's or a spy's relation with his God and Church, finding more merit in despair than in the laborious conniving at the goodness the ordinary hypocrite goes in for. On the other hand, a man like Scobie, in *The Heart of the Matter*, can hardly rank with the great sinners; he lacks the pride. His muddles and illegalities rate official damnation but, as the priest suggests, there is still God's mercy. His portrait has some of that sentimentality which has come over the Channel from François Mauriac. I doubt if it is fair to Roman Catholic moralists to say that they believe the worst thing is to break the rules.

The light and serious novels of Graham Greene make their impression because of his phenomenal skill, his invention, and the edge and precision of his mind. He etches the conventional with the acid of the observable. His thrillers are not simply escapes from ordinary life, but are painful journeys into it: the agent, hunter or hunted, unveils. In *The Confidential Agent* the true subjects are pain and betrayal. He seeks the exact:

> She lay there stiff, clean and unnatural; people talked as if death were like sleep; it was like nothing but itself. He was reminded of a bird discovered at the bottom of a cage on its back, with the claws rigid as grape stalks: nothing could look more dead. He had seen people dead after an air raid; but they fell in curious humped positions – a lot of embryos in the womb. This was different – a unique position reserved for one occasion. Nobody in pain or asleep lay like this.

In one book at least, *The Power and the Glory*, he transcends his perverse and morbid tendencies and presents a whole and memorable human being; this wholeness is exceptional, for Greene is generally an impressionist, or rather a cutter of mosaics. We expect from incisive talents some kind of diagnosis, some instinctive knowledge of the human situation which we have not attended to; this Greene has had. His subjects are the contemporary loneliness, ugliness and transience. We disapprove of the ugliness of our civilisation without recognising that, for some reason, we *needed* to make it ugly. Greene makes great play with this in his novels; behind the ugliness is loneliness and betrayal. Very nearly all his characters are marked by the loneliness in our civilisation, and on the simplest level – Scobie's, for example – they are merely self-pitying. They fail to communicate. Scobie hates talking to his wife because of fear that she will make yet another scene; he knows that talking to his mistress will lead fatally to the re-enacting of the same stale dramas of jealousy. These people wish to be alone; yet when they are alone, the sad dialogues of nostalgia, conscience and betrayal begin in the mind; and presently each character breaks in two: the pursuer and pursued, the watcher and the watched, the hunter and the hunted. The relationship with God, if they are Catholics, is the same. One moment it is God who will have no mercy; next it is Scobie who is torturing

God. In *The End of the Affair* the narrator accuses himself of inability to do anything but hate; and Fowler in *The Quiet American* admits that he translates his personal hatred of Pyle and Pyle's dangerous political innocence into a fantastic hatred of the American continent. Loneliness, the failure to communicate in love, or rather to sustain communication, is the cause, and behind that is the first cause, the betrayal we are thought to have experienced in childhood when evil was revealed to us. This is a contemporary subject for, in Greene's rendering of the world, we are now anonymous. We are bleak, observable people in streets, on staircases, in boarding-houses, hotel rooms, cafeterias, Nissen huts, native villages, police stations – free, but disheartened and 'wanted'.

Greene's masterly power of evoking the shabby scene, whether it is Pimlico or Liberia, Mexico or Kent, is a matter of a vision true to its misanthropy and quickness of eye; but it owes something also to his sense of being an accomplice. We are guilty transients leaving our fakes and our litter. There is an odd and frequent suggestion that romantic literature misled us. China, Liberia, Mexico ought not to have looked like this. In the later books, particularly in *The Quiet American*, the mood has become rather too much the conventional habit of disillusion (assumed for self-protection) of the American school of reporting. In fact only one scene was real reporting, so I have since learned. Only the minor figures observed by the master reporter in the war scenes are individual; the rest have become types. Fowler is mere self-pity; Pyle is a flat profile. There is always a danger in Greene's novels that the stress on banality and anonymity will turn into type-casting and that he will forget that the loneliness of people, on whatever level, is only an aspect of them. In *The Heart of the Matter*, Scobie's scenes with young Mrs Rolt become typical and therefore forced. The sudden leap from pitiable youth to the jealousy of the trained virago on Mrs Rolt's part makes Greene's point of course, but is too pat. In his honesty he is too eager to see evil doing its stuff.

In *The Power and the Glory*, Greene succeeds above all the rest. In the other tales, by quickness of cinematic cutting, by turning everything he sees to the advantage of action, he makes circles round our doubts. The preposterous argument of *Brighton Rock* is lost in the excitement of the hunt. But in the Mexican novel no doubts arise. There is no overt resentment. There are no innuendos. There are no theological conundrums. It is actually an advantage that Greene hated Mexico and the tropical rot; he had worked the worst off in a vivid book, *The Lawless Roads*. Except for the portrait of the seedy Mr Tench, the dentist, at the beginning, and the account of the Catholic family reading their forbidden literature secretly, there is nothing to distract us from the portraits of the whisky-priest and the lieutenant, his pursuer. In this kind of drama, Mr Greene excels, but here there is meaning, not fear-fantasy; the priest is taken from depth to depth in physical suffering and spiritual humiliation. The climax is reached when he is disowned by his mistress and his child and this long scene is wonderful for the way in which the feeling is manipulated and reversed. The scene in the prison, into which he is thrown by mad misadventure, has to bear the moral burden of the story – that he is at peace with the criminals and outcasts from whom he need not hide his identity, and that he is in danger only from conventional piety. We should not forget that Greene trails his coat in order to provoke mercy and has a subtle and compassionate intelligence of unvoiced pain. As a novelist he is free of the vice of explanation in this book; we see a soul grow and recover its dignity. And the dialogue between the pursuing lieutenant and the priest at the end is a true dialogue; it is not a confrontation of views, but of two lives. The only weakness is in the transition to the Catholic family and the inter-cutting of scenes at the end. I do not know what the intention is. Is it to take us into the starchy world of Catholic piety, into that religious respectability which Greene detests and where, indeed, right and wrong take the place of good and evil? Or is it a return to Greene's boyish love of romantic literature? The child is 'believing' in a boy's heroic adventure in defence of the Faith, as Greene himself might have 'believed' in Rider Haggard. The misanthropy of Greene often reads as if it were a resentment of the deceit of books for boys and a rancour against the loss of the richly populated solitude of childhood.

In *The Comedians* Graham Greene returns to the reporter-novelising manner of *The Quiet American* and is in a better temper. This book has the usual self-indulgence, the usual zest in the sardonic view. A Greene character has a hard time of it. The couple whom Brown, the present narrator, saw copulating cheerfully in the hotel swimming-pool one night in Haiti could have no notion that he would make a sermon out of them later on, by placing the body of a politician with his wrists cut in the corner of the pool: later still, to ram home the text, the battered head of the same politician will confront yet another woman who kneels down in a garden to be had by a policeman. It is hard luck to be a figure in a parable of sado-masochism.

Another woman – a German whose burden is that her father had been executed for Nazi crimes and who is the mistress of the narrator – fights back against the 'dark brown world you live in'. There is danger, you see, even in Brown's name. Having got out of bed and sworn at her suspender, she gives him a lecture.

> To you nothing exists except in your own thoughts. Not me, not Jones. We're what you choose to make us. You're a Berkeleyan. My God, what a Berkeleyan . . . My dear, try to believe we exist when you aren't there. We're independent of you. None of us is like what you fancy we are. Perhaps it wouldn't matter much if your thoughts were not so dark, always so dark.

She is right. She has even accused him of being a novelist. And she is right again. In so many of his novels Graham Greene makes an overwhelming and literary intervention so that his people are reduced to things seen flat in the camera's eye and by the cleverest of living photographers. It is true that the author's mind is courageous, charitable and compassionate: no character can complain that he has not been enhanced in the very instant of being flattened or narrowed – and to say that is to say a great deal for Greene as an artist. If he piles it on, he does so with the inner gaiety of a great talent. But one often wishes that he were less of a contriver and would let the characters show for themselves what their meaning is. That passage about Berkeley is unlikely in the mouth of the German refugee wife of a diplomat in Haiti; it annuls her as an independent human being and breaks the novel's illusion. Not only that, one suspects the speech is there as an essayist's insurance against the suspicion that elsewhere, in the 'piled-on' incidents, Greene is parodying himself as a novelist. And perhaps as a conceit or a joke.

The theme of the novel is put by a priest preaching on the text: 'Let us go up to Jerusalem and die with him'. Indifference is to be condemned more harshly than violence. 'Violence can be the expression of love, indifference never. One is an imperfection of charity, the other the perfection of egoism'. The indifferent are the comedians, i.e. the egoists, in a tragic world. (It is odd to see indifference presented as the antithesis of violence; but I suppose we are back at that barbarous Manichean idea expressed in 'Because ye are neither hot nor cold' etc. etc.) The chief comedian is Brown himself, a lapsed Catholic speculator who has never known his father, was born in the no-man's-land of Monte Carlo and now runs a tourist hotel in Haiti. He has inherited it from his mother, a decent, now elderly tart found living with her black servant: she dies – need one say – after one last fling of intercourse. The black servant is so upset he hangs himself.

Brown had left Haiti, partly because of his possessive jealousy of his mistress, the diplomat's wife; now he returns to the disgusting police state and to the murdered politician. The horrible condition of this *triste tropique* is sharply evoked. No one so powerfully burns an exotic and seedy scene on the mind. Haiti is an island run by faceless Negro and mulatto crooks in sun-glasses. In Port-au-Prince arrives a farcical pair of American innocents, one-time freedom-riders, all for justice, who wish to persuade the government to open a vegetarian centre. The cranks are slow-motion slapstick, but they have their courage and dignity. They are also – in a business way – shrewd: this, and one or two adroit observations of their affectionate hypochondria, redeem them from pure caricature. They pass harmlessly from the scene – one can see that Brown's hotel had to have at least a couple of residents – to make way for a merry little spiv called Jones, self-styled hero of the Burma war, semi-secret agent, speculator, petty gambler, stoic, self-advertised Don Juan, and an instant friend of Papa Doc, the bloody dictator; selling out on him, however, he joins a Resistance group in the mountains.

Jones is a *comic* comedian – he is committed to making something out of the anarchy that the deeply comic are drawn into. It turns out that he has lied about everything – he is, in fact, wanted internationally for theft – but his lies catch up with him and he is forced to lead the guerrillas in the mountains because his bluff is called. Why do the Resistance people take him on? Because he is so irresistible. He makes people laugh. He has no real notion of what he is doing, beyond perhaps being a bit awestruck by people of principle. Eventually his feet let him down in the rough country. It is a surprising weakness that one has the death of Jones by hearsay; also that of Dr Magiot, the sad, upright Marxist who has managed to survive because Communists are useful political counters: they enable Papa Doc to blackmail the Americans.

In this context of secret shootings, beatings-up and dejected plotting, in which the Haitians have either the brutal or the dedicated parts, Brown and his mistress conduct their private sexual comedy, in momentary beddings in the backs of cars, and in a grave-like hollow under the trees. They are nervous of discovery; Brown thinks his mistress's child may be spying on them. It is an affair constantly on edge because of his possessive nagging jealousies – Greene is always on the *qui vive* for the ironies of impotence and desire. And of betrayal. Treachery has always been one of Greene's central preoccupations as a moralist. Brown betrays Jones because he is jealous, by working cynically on his vanity; and the irony is that Jones, the liar, is the better man. His life could be construed, Brown suddenly sees, as a series of delinquent approaches to virtue. Such paradoxes fit in admirably with Greene's gift for creating suspense.

Brown is cool enough in danger, but he is a born destroyer of his own and his mistress's happiness. It is he who is really the absurd figure because all his suspicions turn out to be untrue: he has so little perception of normal feelings. Jones, the shady liar, is capable of inspiring affection. Brown, the adulterer, is so tied-up that he inspires pity. But Brown *thinks* – it is noticeable how often the heroes of the reporter's novel are Hamlets, tortured by the guilt of being outside, of having kept an escape-route, as they knowingly rock their pink gin in the glass and misanthropically bitch their Ophelias – and guilt sharpens even while it perverts observation. He has one exciting episode – Greene at his best – in which he smuggles Jones out to his rendezvous. The moment in which the awful police chief – admirably called Concasseur – is shot and has his sun-glasses trodden on is very fine. That is the kind of detail that reconciles us to Greene when we are just about to cry parody again.

The end of *The Comedians* is, like the beginning, a sardonic essay. The vegetarian Americans are in San Domingo and, in their grateful and businesslike way, they get Brown a partnership in a funeral business where the drift of local politics offers growing prospects. This is a nasty but exact diagnosis; the speciousness lies in our feeling that the symbolism is being piled on and that the people are puppets in an animated disquisition. The effect is literary. We have been reading news and news leaves us with the sense of waste. But as San Domingo follows Haiti, as Nigeria distracts us from the Congo, Greene has obviously chosen an important subject; and though he is an outsider, there are moments in which he gets inside. The Voodoo scene in which we watch a sensitive man being turned by grotesque religious performance into a partisan catches a note of tropical excess.

> The priest came in from his inner room swinging a censer, but the censer which he swung in our faces was a trussed cock – the small stupid eyes peered into my eyes and the banner of St Lucy swayed after it. When he had completed the circle of the *tonelle* the *hougan* put the head of the cock in his mouth and crunched it cleanly off; the wings continued to flap while the head lay on the dirt-floor like part of a broken toy. Then he bent down and squeezed the neck like a tube of tooth-paste and added the rusty colour of blood to the ash-grey patterns on the floor.

But I think he overcrowds with the apparatus of horror; and especially in the sexual incident, one begins to grin and even to laugh.

Greene is laughing too, but we are at cross purposes; we are laughing at self-parody as we laugh at melodrama and he is laughing at his own pleasure in giving more and more turns to what, in both senses, is the screw. Brown is supposed to have lost his faith and to be adrift because he has found nothing to replace it. Yet in fact he *has* found something: the hotel-keeper has ostensibly written this remarkable book. That is an act of faith; certainly not an act of indifference. Or didn't Brown write the book? Is it all a game? All virtuosi are entitled to indulge their talents. But when Greene wrote *The Power and the Glory* he was not playing a game.

How many of his now huge audience know him in the very different role of the bookish man or as a literary critic and essayist? He has gone through the English mill. His *Collected Essays* contain a selection of these writings done mainly for the London weeklies or as introductions, during the last thirty years; there are also a traveller's portraits of two Popes, Philby, Ho Chi Minh, Castro and others. All display the well-known concerns which have given him originality and verve as a novelist; all – or nearly all – have the final sympathy which a real curiosity about human nature deposits in an observant mind.

In the manner of English periodical criticism where the writer has to get at an essence, show his wit and his hand, and make his decisive effect with alacrity in fewer than 2000 scrupulous words, Greene engages at once: 'A man must be judged by his enemies as well as by his friendships'. Himself he cannot resist the attractions of the enemy. He is before anything a novelist-critic, that is to say he writes to discover something for *his* purposes which might not be ours. His reviews are an artist's raids; he has the avid eye of the raider and will often pause before the corpse of his victim to note a quality or to ask what went wrong.

He has a cheerful, almost cannibal appetite for rationalists. For him, rationalists, figures like Samuel Butler and Havelock Ellis, are conceited and emotionally arid; then, among rhetoricians he cannot forgive Kipling; among sentimentalists, Barrie. Of the 'greatly gifted they are the two who have written with most falsity of human relationships'. Unresolved hatreds or infantile secrets have ruined them. Butler has the smugness of the Honest Man: 'Even Christianity would not be considered dispassionately because it is the history of a Father and a Son'. Herbert Read, who had hailed so many fashions in painting and literature, had himself supplied (in his grave books on childhood and his *Life* of Wordsworth) the 'standards of permanence by which these fashions will be condemned'. Whether they add or ruffle, Greene's opinions have an artist's necessity in them. Let the academics weigh up, be exhaustive, or build their superstructures – the artist lives as much by his pride in his own emphasis as by what he ignores; humility is a disgrace.

Greene has a marked loyalty to writers who have influenced him and to those who are out of fashion. He is free of the snobbery that pretends it has had no time for the juvenile or second rate. The books of boyhood – Ballantine, Hope, Mason, Weyman, Rider Haggard and the *Viper of Milan* – were decisive for him: two or three themes, central in Greene's own writing, expand from them. Exotic, thrilling adventure, the lost childhood and its betrayal, the warnings against success, the lure of perfect evil. In the *Viper of Milan* he thinks he saw

Perfect evil walking the world, where perfect good can never walk again, and only the pendulum ensures that after all in the end justice is done.

[989]

Life is not black and white; it is black and grey. After *The Power and the Glory*, *The Comedians*.

This theme was fulfilled when he confronted Henry James, Conrad – and equally important to him I would guess later on – Ford Madox Ford. Apart from anything else they are master craftsmen and, in all these reviews, we see Greene's concern with how things are done. He himself is, above all, skilled and eagerly interested in difficulty. But the importance of Henry James is the concern with supernatural evil, the nervous venture to the edge of religion; in the detection of the 'black and merciless things that lie behind great possessions'; in corruption and betrayal. This is far from being the whole of James, but the subject draws out the four most studied essays in the collection. In the Thirties, Greene was allured by the James who could conceive the damned soul and who might just have become a Catholic if his father had not exhausted the subject of an organised church. But, by the Fifties, looking at *Guy Domville*, he writes:

> To us today the story of Guy Domville seems . . . one more example of the not always fortunate fascination exercised on James by the Christian faith and by Catholicism.

Is there such a thing as agnostic prose? May not a rationalist be fully conscious of mental degradation or good and evil? Wasn't James?

The search for the seat of unease in his subject is Greene's point in a great many of these essays. There are eighty of them. Conrad Aiken, pushing the study of madness to its limits in *King Coffin*, 'is the most satisfying of living novelists'; in Walter de la Mare's stories – now absurdly underrated or forgotten – we meet the terrified eyes of a fellow passenger 'watching the sediment of an unspeakable obsession'; of Rolfe – whose *Hadrian the Seventh* is a work of genius – he writes: 'if he could not have Heaven he would have Hell and the last footprints seem to point to the Inferno'. The unease was not always gratefully acknowledged. One would have thought his delightful and affectionate essay on Beatrix Potter's tales written in 1933 would have pleased the authoress; we imagine she would have given a thunderstruck grin when Greene's King Charles's head popped up at the climax among the bunnies and the puddle-ducks:

> Looking back over the thirty years of Miss Potter's literary career, we see that the creation of Jemima Puddle-Duck marked the beginning of a

new period. At some time between 1907 and 1909 Miss Potter must have passed through an emotional ordeal which changed the character of her genius. It would be impertinent to enquire into the nature of the ordeal. Her case is curiously similar to that of Henry James. Something happened which shook their faith in appearance. From *The Portrait of a Lady* onwards, innocence deceived, the treachery of friends, became the theme of James's greatest stories. Mme Merle, Kate Croy, Mme de Vionnet, Charlotte Stant, these tortuous, treacherous women, are paralleled through the dark period of Miss Potter's art. 'A man can smile and be a villain', that, a little altered, was her recurrent message . . . with the publication of *Mr Tod* in 1912 Miss Potter's pessimism reached its climax.

An acid letter from Miss Potter – who had become a tough sheep-farmer in Westmorland – was the reward for this grand analysis. She was, she said, suffering from no emotional disturbance when she wrote *Mr Tod*: only the after effects of flu. She said she deprecated 'the Freudian school' of criticism. Perhaps the comparison with another artist annoyed the old lady. She was certainly cross when *Little Pig Robinson* was described by Mr Greene as being her *Tempest*: he called it her last tale when it was the first written, if not the first published. But as we know now, from Margaret Lane's *Life* and the published *Journals*, there had been two extreme crises in her life and an extraordinary change of personality. Graham Greene had been an expert detective.

The collection covers a reviewer's wide field. Anthony à Wood, some Oxford eccentrics, Evelyn, Charles Churchill, Darley, Fielding, Sterne are among his subjects and done with care and point. The novelist is botanising in human character; the traveller is absorbed by Parkman, Livingstone, Mungo Park; there is a fierce attack on J. B. Trend's book on Mexico, for though Trend was a conventional and timid Cambridge professor he was a violent anti-Catholic. (But he did write a very valuable if innocent book on Spain in the Twenties.) Greene's final essay on a sentimental return to Lagos, the Scobie country, in 1968, has the nostalgia for a lost innocence which encases much of his work, nostalgia for a lost innocence never quite as innocent as it looked. In Lagos, last year (in church, one gathers), the girl in front of me wore one of the surrealist Manchester cotton dresses which are rarely seen since the Japanese trade moved in. The word 'soupsweet' was printed over her shoulder, but I had to wait until she stood up before I could confirm another phrase: 'Fenella lak' good poke'. Father Mackie would have been amused, I thought, and what better description could there be of this poor lazy lovely coloured country than 'soupsweet'.

In all his moods, angry, serious or laughing, Greene has the patient precise eye of the connoisseur of 'brief lives'.

Club and Country

Many good writers live on their nerves and can turn to anything. Clever, they have only one self. This is not the case with Evelyn Waugh; he has many selves, deeply embedded, on which to draw. He might have settled down with Lady Metroland and tippled away at a mixture of the *Bab Ballads*, the cautionary tale and Firbank; but his real line was the prose, not the poetry, of outrage. The wild, feathered feminine scream of that last master was not for him. His temperament was sober. He moved to the hard-headed traditions of English satirical comedy; one glance at the English upper classes, imposing their private fantasies on whatever is going on, treating everything from war downwards as if it were all happening in one of their country houses, has been enough to provide comedians with material for a lifetime. Mr Waugh went on next to be inconvenienced by his Sir Galahad and St George complexes; but after *Brideshead Revisited* and a brief return to the outrageous in *The Loved One*, the gentleman moralist appeared, a clubbish writer assiduously polishing his malign sentences, daily persisting with the stings of mortifying circumlocution. His early books spring from the liberating notion that human beings are mad; the war trilogy, a work of maturity, draws on the meatier notion that the horrible thing about human beings is that they are sane.

For better or worse, there is a masculine vein in English comedy, a vein which is sociable and not intellectual, sensible rather than sensitive. It shows us willingly paying the price of misanthropy for the pleasure of making a go of life in clubs – day and night – parsonages, public schools, villas, furnished apartments and other privacies of the national masochism. It required a nerve on Mr Waugh's part to treat the war as something which could or could not be known socially in these terms. It also required the accomplishment of a lifetime to bring off those three volumes. It is true that they have the formal melancholy of a memoir, and that Sir Galahad strikes a few unattractive poses; but the comic invention is strong: and there is an advance towards a compassionate study of human nature. Crouchback's bad wife would once have been seen as a vile body; she is now discerned as a displaced person.

The melancholy note persists in the first volume of Mr Waugh's autobiography, *A Little Learning*. In his dire way he has done what he can to pass himself off as a fossil. Like his father – as he appears in this volume – the son is a considerable impersonator. His prose is set to the felicities of misleading. This book is of great importance to students of his novels – though he does not yet discuss them – for it shows how long-established his preoccupations as a man and writer have been. An outstanding quality of his work has been its care for cadence in English prose and his regard for craftsmanship as a moral duty; he comes of a line of clergy and doctors, some of whom were minor writers; his background is literary and unassumingly sedate. The youthful taste for working at medieval script is another sign of the craftsman to come and a sign too of that feeling for Romance which has been the less successfully manifested aspect of his work. (His father was also romantic; he would refer to the 'stout timbers' of the villa he built for himself as if it were some galleon anchored in the North End Road and never forgave the local authorities for incorporating his then rustic part of Hampstead into the ugly and socially ambiguous brashness of new Golders Green.)

As for religion, Mr Waugh was always interested in theology and never at all bored by church. There is nothing to suggest that his later conversion to Catholicism was Romantic; everything to suggest that theological ingenuity was an important appeal. A relative in the Bengal Lancers brought in the St George touch and the nostalgia for swords and regalias. The designs of the nursery wallpaper were medieval: it was a taste of the period. The boy's upbringing was quiet, instructed, entirely happy. No Oedipal struggles appear. There was nothing to provoke the later sense of outrage, nothing – apparently – to titillate the psychiatrist except the mildness of it all. Even at the end of the volume, when he plans to drown himself after coming down from Oxford, full of debts and depressed about lost fun, Mr Waugh takes the view that this was a normal adolescent gesture, abandoned at once when he swam into some jellyfish.

What provoked the taste for outrage? Mr Waugh is a thoughtful rather than an intimate autobiographer, in this volume. He keeps the lid on. His aim appears to be the desire to conform, no doubt ironically, to a carefully prepared conventional pattern and to repose, almost masochistically, upon a belief in the Unremarkable. Clearly this, in so dashing an imagination, suggests a conflict. His marvellous feel for the disreputable comes from a man with a family addiction to the neutral yet aspiring. But one thing *did* go wrong. There was no woodshed. But home was so happy that to leave it for school made him 'nastier' (on the general principle that all schoolboys are 'nasty'?). And then there was the despoiling of England.

As one who belongs to his generation, though coming from a very different background, I understand something of what Mr Waugh means when he writes of the shock caused by the ruin of rural England. It would seem all the worse to a literary suburban:

> This is part of the grim cyclorama of spoliation which surrounded all English experience in this century and my understanding of the immediate past (which presumably is the motive for reading a book such as this) must be incomplete unless this huge deprivation of the quiet pleasure of the eye is accepted as a dominant condition, sometimes making for impotent resentment, sometimes for mere sentimental apathy, sometimes poisoning love of country and of neighbours. To have been born into a world of beauty, to die amid ugliness, is the common fate of all us exiles.

The evil, then, was the sense of exile. Most, indeed I would say all, writers have this sense anyway. It was exacerbated for him, as for many schoolboys, by the frustration of 'being out of the war'. It was his brother Alec Waugh, not Evelyn, who would be the hero. One was reduced to dreamy, hungry, insubordinate futility. In some respects Mr Waugh's exile is snobbish. Mr Waugh senior was an industrious and kindly reviewer of the old school who hated the new thing in the best jocose tradition of elderly criticism; Mr Waugh junior turns rancorous: 'There are the State-trained professional critics with their harsh jargon and narrow tastes.' Mr Waugh senior has his jargon too. Of D. H. Lawrence's art he wrote: 'his fancy is half asleep upon a foetid hot-bed of moods.' But, as his son truly says, as a critic the elder Waugh was no snob. His limitation was the 'common enough inability to recognise the qualities he loved unless they were presented in familiar forms'. Mr Waugh's own 'State-trained' reveals a similar inability.

Prep school, public school, university: these now tedious influences standardise English autobiography, giving the educated Englishman the sad if fascinating appearance of a stuffed bird of sly and beady eye in some odd seaside museum. The fixation on school has become a class trait. It manifests itself as a mixture of incurious piety and parlour game. (Some of Mr Waugh's contemporaries are now writing or have written their autobiographies and are watching each other like chess-players. What was Rugby doing when Sherborne saw Waugh go to Lancing and did Eton care?)

Cautious, lonely, observant at first at Oxford, Mr Waugh eventually kicked out, did the right thing by drinking a lot and coming down deep in debt, and was ready for a far more interesting life than appears in this opening volume. One must hope that his feeling for impersonality will not become so subtle as to make the irony too sober. The best things in the present volume are those that recover the detail of a period. One recognises this room:

> The dining-room was dark and full of oil-paintings. The drawing-room was much cluttered with small tables, draperies, screens and ornaments on carved brackets. It contained two cabinets full of 'curiosities' – fans, snuff-boxes, carved nuts, old coins and medals; some of them unremarkable, such as, carefully wadded, encased and labelled, the charred tip of a walking stick with which some relation had climbed Mount Vesuvius and a lock [unauthenticated] of Wordsworth's hair.

There was even a phial containing a specimen of 'White Blood' from a patient dying of anaemia. Tourists' trophies had not yet become standardised.

Mr Waugh is a master also of the compressed portrait. There are three maiden aunts – an extinct genus now, as Mr Waugh points out:

> My Aunt Connie sat on the bench when women became eligible as magistrates and was much distressed by the iniquities there revealed to her. All three had the prudishness proper to maiden aunts, though Aunt Elsie in old age developed a tolerance of very slightly indelicate fiction.

The portrait is good, the prose embroidered here with the facetious parlance – is that the word? – of clubs. This is the trouble with club Mandarin – it becomes flunkeyish. Better write like Wooster than like Jeeves. The crisp manner used in describing W. W. Jacobs is preferable:

> In person he was wan, skinny, sharp-faced, with watery eyes. Like many humorists he gave scant evidence of humour in private inter-course. In losing the accents of Wapping he lost most of his voice and spoke through the side of his thin lips in furtive, almost criminal tones, disconcerting in a man of transcendent, indeed of tedious respectability. He was a secular puritan, one of those who 'have not got the Faith and will not have the fun' . . .

Except for the last sentence, the portrait is exact. The little man was skipping up and down, as merry as popcorn, when I once caught sight of him at a suburban 'hop'. It must be remembered that all humorists suffer from overwork.

The gentle portrait of the author's father is the longest in the book. It is interesting chiefly as an example of a quality that is generally overlooked by admirers of the son's comic originality. The wit, the hilarious transi-tions, the pace and savagery of his comedies, deceives us into seeing Mr Waugh as a writer who jumps with inspired carelessness from one fantasy to the next. The dialogue alone, his early forte, should undeceive us. Its quality is accuracy; in fact a grave exactitude has been the ground of his comic genius as it is of his serious writing in travel and biography. He can be accurate to the point of testiness. Indeed he is only bad when he is not accurate, that's to say when St George, panache etc. come in and make him slur.

Mr Waugh's eye for the fact enables him to catch the changing impressions so important to the faithful memorialist. Until he was sixteen he had supposed that his father was simple and prosaic; then a friend came down and said: 'Charming, entirely charming and acting all the time'. He was. Between bouts of coughing he would cheerfully call upon Death for release; declare in the middle of signing a cheque he was being driven to a pauper's grave. He talked aloud to imaginary people continuously. He assumed, without knowing it, Dickensian roles. Before the 'ingratitude' of his sons he became Lear. His sighs could be heard across a theatre. He had talent as an amateur actor and, on the evidence of his son's prose – on the confessions of Pinfold and the anecdotes that trickle down from the West Country about his histrionic mischief – one would guess that Evelyn Waugh's sobriety is a genuine impersonation. It is unsafe to trust the elegiac tone of this volume; he may also be trying out his own funeral in advance, to see what a literary demise could look like. Autobiography is a way of dressing up the past.

So far we have been reading about the unknown Evelyn Waugh. In the last chapter the frosts of youth vanish; the young sparkler appears. We see contemporaries who were later to become famous or notorious, among them Gerald Gardiner, Harold Acton, Robert Byron and Brian Howard. Of the last two we have striking, not to say pungent, preliminary sketches. Brian Howard, particularly, was one of those dangerous, destructive and seminal nuisances, a plaguing character of wasted talent who begins to barge about in the corridors of Mr Waugh's early fancy. Grimes turns up in Wales, an effusively homosexual schoolmaster. We have reached the verge of *Decline and Fall*, when Mr Waugh began to rise and shine.

With *Unconditional Surrender* Evelyn Waugh brought his wartime trilogy and Guy Crouchback's love affair with military servitude to a civil end. The infatuation had begun in *Men at Arms*. It was romantic, strenuous and hilarious, set in the glorious days of the Molotov-Ribbentrop treaty when Crouchback, a Catholic gentleman, no longer very young, was being taught to polish his sword and train for a St George-and-Dragon battle with the fundamental enemy: 'the Modern Age', i.e. everything between the days the family property went in the reign of Elizabeth I and the Nazi-Communist pact. He joined the Halberdiers, hung about Bellamy's Club. The comedies of military discipline and chicanery absorbed him; the tedium was relieved by minor campaigns, the war about Apthorpe's portable thunder box, his liability to bouts of 'Bechuana tummy'. Apthorpe was one of Waugh's richest comic creations.

The next phase – *Officers and Gentlemen* – was ambiguous. The Communists were on our side now and that rather muddled St George's objective. Also, a number of officers who were not gentlemen turned up – the shady and resourceful ex-hairdresser, Trimmer, for example. Bellamy's still stood but Turtle's, further down St James's, caught fire in the Blitz and the whisky poured down the street. Air Marshal Beech, not quite our class, was found over-staying an air raid under a billiard table. There were exercises on a Scottish island where the far-seeing Laird, choked by peat smoke in his Castle, was intriguing for supplies of gelignite for a private purpose. He had a daughter who was pro-Hitler and got Crouchback into prolonged trouble. Trimmer, in these rough days, was looking for a woman and picked up Guy Crouchback's ex-wife, a nymphomaniac, and, later on – being a ranker-officer – behaved with absurd cowardice on a Commando raid. For this he naturally became a national hero – the Press having been told to find one in order to impress our doubting Allies, the Americans. Later, in Crete, Crouchback experienced disaster. His *liaison dangereuse* with the military dragged on between farce, boredom, status quarrels, and ended in a few days of nightmare. He escaped from Crete in an open boat.

At the beginning of *Unconditional Surrender*, Crouchback's apathy is complete: but his capacity for pain has been noted by the gods. He persuades himself that it is his duty to remarry his ex-wife because she is going to have a child by the gaudy Trimmer who, punch-drunk with international publicity, has vanished. After a period of parachute training under another ranker, Ludovic, who – again, no gentleman – has murdered his CO in the flight from Crete, Crouchback is nagged by an ex-schoolmaster in Yugoslavia. On top of that there is the double-dealing of partisan warfare. He is obliged to watch helplessly the persecution of a party of homeless Jews and to see his discreet attempt to better the lot of two of them turn into the lunatic evidence that will send them to the People's Court and the firing squad. Crouchback's apathy breaks when he realises that a sense of the futility of life is not enough, for life has culminated in the monstrous. It is perhaps the final, mortifying irony of the book that Crouchback survives and prospers. He even has the pleasure of seeing Box-Bender, his extremely unlikeable Protestant brother-in-law, having trouble with his son. The boy talks of becoming a monk.

Evelyn Waugh has a genius for very specialised social effrontery and its delight in outrage. It required a nerve to treat the war as a sordid social jamboree of smart and semi-smart sets, who are mainly engaged in self-inflation and in climbing up the ladder, to present it as a collection of bankrupt sideshows. But Mr Waugh has more nerve than any of his

English contemporaries, and large portions of the last war were exactly as he describes them.

The war is not, of course, presented as anything more than heightened (or deflated) personal experience; the trilogy is a memoir rather than a novel. Other books about the war have gone straight for the conventional – the battle. He, too, can negligently turn out a battle, but his interest is, fundamentally, the moralist's. His eye is trained on the flat detail of human folly, vanity and hypocrisy; and although he can be rightly called a wounded Romantic, he is a most patient and accurate observer. His glances at London life during the period are laconic and just. The last war saw the birth of the organisation man and Mr Waugh was in, all eyes and ears, at the dreadful *accouchement*.

There are, we know, two Evelyn Waughs: the satirical blessing who wrote *The Loved One* and the appeasing, even tender comic moralist, the accomplished, testy, courteous, epigrammatic man of letters who wrote *A Handful of Dust*. (Crouchback characteristically takes Anstey's *Vice Versa* to read on his campaigns.) The trilogy is in his humane and perfectly finished manner. His scorn is modulated, his sentences are distillations. Most comic writers like to think they could play it straight if only their public would let them. Waugh is able to be grave without difficulty for he has always been comic for serious reasons. He has his own, almost romantic sense of propriety. His snobbery, when he is in this mood, is an amusing and acceptable mixture of High Romance, Puritan decorum and tartness, and has a professional sense of the rules of the English class game. To object to his snobbery is as futile as objecting to cricket, for every summer the damn game comes round again whether you like it or not.

Only one kind of snobbery is affronting in Mr Waugh: the violent. It is ugly, theatrical and falsely generalised. Even if we accept that ranker-officers are envious, calculating, unsure showmen and on the make, must we add cowardice, lack of nerve and – as in the case of the minutely observed Ludovic – crime? Is the envy of the lower classes any more likely to lead to dishonesty and cowardice than the conceit of the uppers? It is here that Mr Waugh's High Romance becomes vulgar sentimentality. In this book he throws Ludovic away as a recognisable human being and an original type rarely attempted: the solemn, climbing, half-sinister, half-hurt queer with shattering gifts as a bad writer. I do not deny that Mr

Waugh uses him with malign masochistic skill when he shows him writing a novel that falsifies a good deal of Crouchback's experience, for Ludovic has watched Crouchback like a cat.

Amid the antics of brigadiers, generals, politicians, socialites, partisans, wives and mistresses, the dry and stoical Crouchback is a frosty figure. His apathy makes him a perfect focus. He is given a nullity that, on the one hand, may represent the gentlemanly ideal: the whole of life will be vulgar to him. On the other hand, he is subtly endowed with the reticence and decency that suggest a life profoundly satisfied by the pains that have been inflicted on it, and by the one or two affections that remain.

Virginia, the faithless wife and good-time girl, is beautifully understood. The comedy of her conversation, full of four-letter words, with the almost virginal Uncle Peregrine is exquisite. He had never heard a lady use such language; it astounds rather than displeases; it also misleads, for he has the flattering illusion that she is making a pass at him and is piqued when he finds she is not. What she is after is re-marriage to her ex-husband who has come into money, for she is at the end of her tether. It is the measure of Mr Waugh's sympathy that he lets out no savage laugh at the cynical proposition and yet is not sentimental about it. The war has, at any rate, taught Crouchback to recognise a 'displaced person' when he sees one. He does not love her. She does not love Trimmer's child when it is born: she calls it 'that baby'. Crouchback does not weep when she is killed in an air raid, which lets him off some of the awkward consequences of playing so straight a bat in the sex test. And when, at the end of one novel, his awful brother-in-law complains that things have turned very conveniently for Guy, we muse happily on the richness of Mr Waugh's point. His comedy has always been hard, perverse and shocking; but that in no way prevents it from reproducing the human heart with delicacy, or at any rate, that portion of the heart that, however shallow, can still feel wrong and pain.

Only two episodes in this final volume strike me as being tame: the strange, dull set-piece when Ludovic files past the Sword of Stalingrad in Westminster Abbey. As symbolism, irony, fragment of war chronicle, whatever it is, this scene is in the way. Later on, Ludovic goes to a party given by the editor of a literary monthly whose grubby camel-hair coat and sharp Sultanic orders to the girls will bring back sentimental memories to knowing readers; but again, this is a tame jest. The vanities of the military

[1001]

and social servitudes are Mr Waugh's subject; it is good, of course, of Mr Waugh to call and all that on his Bohemian friends, but somehow the visit falls flat. No literary figure can compete with an Apthorpe, a Trimmer, an Uncle Peregrine or any of the huge list of exquisitely touched-in characters who fought the war with chits, passes and top secret reports, in Mr Waugh's terse *Who's Who* of the National Peril.

St George Crouchback ends by reassessing his views on the dragon. Mme Kanyi, a Hungarian Jewess, says to him:

'Is there any place that is free from evil? It is too simple to say that the Nazis wanted war. These Communists wanted it too. It was the only way in which they could come to power. Many of my people wanted it, to be revenged on the Germans, to hasten to the creation of the national state. It seems to me there was a will to war, a death wish, everywhere. Even good men thought their private honour would be satisfied by war. They could assert their manhood by killing and being killed. They would accept hardships in recompense for having been selfish and lazy. Danger justified privilege. I knew Italians – not very many perhaps – who felt this. Were there none in England?'

'God forgive me,' said Guy, 'I was one of them.' It was after being told, by an enthusiastic little bureaucrat, of her arrest, that Crouchback was tempted to strike an officer.

Going Downhill

$\blacksquare\blacksquare$

It is 'our life', says one of the characters in Angus Wilson's ambitious early novel *Anglo-Saxon Attitudes*, that lies between ourselves and reality. It is a novel about the conscience as it worries two generations of a middle-class family whose ample money comes out of steel and whose brains have gone into the academic world and popular politics. The title comes from Lewis Carroll who noticed – and who with better reason? – that the attitudes of the Anglo-Saxon were peculiar; they are formed by an incalculable mixture of going one's own gait and contorting oneself in the gymnasium of the English moral sense. Morally the English are liable to picturesque outbursts of self-deception: being intelligent, we are very conscious of this and if this is decadent it is also very interesting. When we say (as we have often said during the last thirty years), 'What right have we to judge him or her?', we know quite well that we are going to be led to awful questions, the conundrum of the greater or the lesser evil, the blandishments of the wider view, and so on. The countrymen of Lewis Carroll and George Eliot are born worriers; the relieving thing about them is that they are also an awkward squad, bad at drill, prone to brutal jokes, underhand tricks, romantic sensuality, poker-faced wangling and the smug exploitation of lucky accident. Show me a Puritan and I will (thank God) show you a rogue. At the back of the lives of Mr Angus Wilson's characters there is a dirty Anglo-Saxon trick – scabrous, silly, but rich in moral provocation. What more could we, who live on moral tension, desire?

As far as his novel is concerned, this angry practical joke is a useful device. It is full of symbolism which is a bore, but it has enabled Mr Wilson to begin with some excellent comedy about academic life among historians and archaeologists. As far as the general theme is concerned his joke is no more than a Gibbonian footnote. When the novel opens in the present day, the historians can still be set quarrelling about the discovery of a phallic object which was found in the coffin of the Saxon Bishop Eorpwald when he was dug up in 1912. It has not greatly disturbed the layman to suppose that Christians may have lapsed into paganism: after all, pagans had already lapsed into Christianity. But the Eorpwald discovery had sent one poor scholarly lady out of her mind: she connected it with Baltic trade and, thence, fatally, to the 'wider view'. There is more than a hint that the original discoverer, the eminent Lionel Stokesay, became very odd afterwards and certainly morally senile. He began to talk like Ramsay MacDonald. The probability is that people who take the wider view are covering up.

In the opening chapter of *Anglo-Saxon Attitudes* we are to understand that the Eorpwald row has died down and that it remains open only in the minds of cranks. On the other hand, the central character of the book, Gerald Middleton, a sixty-year-old historian who was Lionel Stokesay's disciple and his son's friend, becomes suspiciously irritable when the subject is reopened. For him, it reawakens what he is least inclined to examine: the errors of his life, the failure to go the full length of his talents, above all the failure of his will. He is a true Anglo-Saxon: he has a romantic sense of failure as well as a romantic sense of success. (I am not sure that Mr Angus Wilson is with us here.) At any rate, Middleton thinks – and so does Mr Wilson – that he has sacrificed reality or truth to 'his life'. For Middleton has the strongest reasons for suspecting that a serious fraud was committed by Stokesay's famous, destructive, sadistic and short-lived son at the time of the discovery. Middleton has kept silence in the interests of the old man's reputation. Moreover, Middleton's great love was for the younger Stokesay's wife. In these terms, Middleton's silence is a symptom of his general moral guilt and weakness, which make him accept a bad marriage instead of a difficult love; which force him to prolong the marriage for the sake of his children whom he nevertheless alienates and who are not going to respect him later; which drive his mistress to drink while he plumps for urbanity, compromise, rational marital arrangements, the limitation of his talents, intellectual indolence and picture-collecting – this last is unbecoming in a scientist and a scholar. (Puritanism will out: enjoyment of the arts by people with private means is morally suspect.) Middleton is saddled with money as well and has really bought his way out of his troubles – as many do who have *no* money – and now, at sixty, isolated by his habit of refusing life, he is left to look back upon the ruins of his life and to see his children infected by his mistakes. In the end, he gets a second chance. Or, rather, he makes it for himself. It is not a chance of reconciliation or of love – that is too late – but of acting with moral courage and of asserting his will to the full – when he's old enough to command with authority in any case.

The Gerald Middletons, the liberal humanists of the professional class, with their nineteenth-century inheritance, have been the victims of a good deal of sceptical inquiry since the Thirties. They have been made symbolic figures, sometimes satirically, sometimes tragically, of a fundamental error. Mr Wilson, I am glad to see, is more generous. He does not over-encumber Gerald Middleton with symbolism nor does he overload him with historical responsibility. Middleton is a good man with resources still to use. Good men have these resources. As far as the novel is concerned he is an excellent figure for conducting us through forty years of English life, and among a large number of characters, with perspicacity. And here lies the great originality of Mr Wilson as a novelist and the richness of his book. Its moral seriousness is matched by the comic explosions in our traditions. We are not Puritans: we are ironists. We can take a blow on the chin without hysteria. We see old Rose Lorimer boring a monkish academic audience with her well-known theories – she has gone off the rails of scholarship into the wilderness of the 'wider view' – we see the angry Professor Clun taking his academic disappointments out on his shrinking wife, with the sadism of a Casaubon. We see one of Middleton's sons, inheriting his mother's sentimentality, a self-deceived Radical with an act and a radio celebrity, in all the comedy of the sincerely insincere. We see his uneasy homosexual life, his awful young men. There is the sloppy yet generous Rammage who runs a boarding-house for these derelicts. There is Mrs Salad, Middleton's salacious and Dickensian housekeeper who is sentimental about his love nest. With sly, Cockney hypocrisy, she knows perfectly well what her son Vin and his boy friend, Larrie, are up to, and she lapses into a little shop-lifting herself – with plenty of tears when she is caught. And then, more respectable than these character parts and more subtle, there are Middleton's cloying and sentimental Danish wife, his raffish, twentyish mistress, Dolly, who is 'all on her ownio' and cannot keep off the bottle – she is cured by a gush of British Empire feeling in the Second World War and becomes deliciously prim in old age. In the younger generation there is her successor, the arty, hard-swearing Bohemian wench, Elvira – another hockey-playing Britannia gone wrong – full of candour but also full of gin; and, best of all, there is young Robin Middleton's French wife. Her grim conventionality, her avarice, her family egotism, her narrow mind and her dry resistance to moral inquiry are the answer to the Anglo-Saxon madness. For her, the whole trite meaning of existence is in the military certainties of family life, its boring seniorities, its day-dreams of successful lawsuits with in-laws. Her husband's (Anglo-Saxon) response is 'to use sincerity as his only protest against her existence'. By which matriarch shall we be ruled? By the knuckle-raps of a cynical French bourgeoise or by the fey and whimsical Dane, with her trolls, her gluttony and her humourless 'little mutter-ism'? Shall we be pickled in vinegar or suffocated by eiderdowns? Looking at her sons, the wife of the elusive English exogamist 'regarded their quarrels as a sort of tribute to her – with more truth than she realized'. She had the 'graciousness one expects of royalty and perhaps a little of their nullity'. She is a killer and a good cook. Young pansies love her and who knows that she does not know why?

Such a collection of characters is promising, especially when they are vividly realised and morally involved. Angus Wilson understands this and dives into their lives with alacrity and intelligence and sympathy. He is garrulous and epigrammatic but he moves quickly and at the right moment from person to person. The novel is closely patterned; indeed, one of its great pleasures is in its construction. But he is all effusive personality as a novelist, filling out his characters by opinionating and also, of course, taking from them some of their autonomy in so doing. In this he is like D. H. Lawrence and not like George Eliot, our great dutymonger. He has no great care for style, is more for English truculence than English urbanity. He is wicked in epigram though less sharp in his satire in this novel than he was in his short stories. He succeeds in the portrayal of character, is rather parsimonious of scenes (there is more opinionating reminiscence and talk). There are one or two very good scenes, of course. The ghastly party at the end of the book contains some delightful culture snobbery; the happy family dinner which is broken up when Dolly gets drunk is wonderful, surprising and rather moving. And any place where Larrie the Irish spiv turns up is packed with interest. Larrie and Vin are masterpieces of original observation and though I don't care for the melodramatic motor accident – a very odd fantasy to occur to a writer so on the spot as Mr Wilson – the whole business of Larrie's hysteria is absorbingly done.

In every generation one or two novelists revise the conventional picture of English character. Mr Wilson does this. There was morbidity, madness, even sourness in his stories – precisely qualities which our sociable tradition eschewed. They needed to be introduced by someone with humanity. We needed to recover our broadness without losing our moral sense. He has also bedded out in our rank social soil some of the hot-house blooms of our Dickensian tradition. Mrs Salad, for example, is a perennial London joy:

> 'Now the cyclermums is as delicate as my sister's skin. Her husband wouldn't have her wear a soiled garment not a day longer than was needed. Spurgins Tabernacle they was.'

This poetic old dear is nastier than Mrs Gamp, for she is close to crime and is thoroughly shady. She was – she is – a lavatory attendant and no shame to her; but that is a life, not a fantasy. Mr Wilson is subtle in conveying the social foundations of egocentricity. Mrs Salad is not a middle-class joke. He has given his people moral natures. He sees England with what looks like a foreign eye. That, for me, is an important virtue in a novel which, in any case, impresses by its range and its power of re-stating issues.

When we move on to a later novel, *No Laughing Matter*, we see what Mr Wilson owes to the histrionic tradition which goes back to Fielding and came to full bloom in Dickens. If Mr Wilson continues to be an anthropologist at work among the remnant of the upper middle class, he sees this class as people to whom performance is second nature. Whatever their virtues, their vices, their successes or their disasters, they carry them onto the stage, and can even be said to avoid self-knowledge by exposing themselves. One reviewer has correctly stated that Mr Wilson's perceptions here come from his gifts of mimicry and ventriloquism.

The period of *No Laughing Matter* lies between about 1911 and 1960 and we first see the whole Matthews family through the veil of their several daydreams. They are creating imaginary selves as they sit watching an early Wild West film. To only one of them, Great Aunt Rickard – known as Mouse – might the real Wild West conceivably have been known. The classic English spinster – she wanders about with a parrot on her shoulder and a sharp rat-a-tat-tat of sarcasms on her tongue – she has been a lonely, intrepid nomad. She has been at home in deserts, wild mountains, Indian and Asiatic plains. The rest of the family are sodden in unrealised fantasy. Billy Pop, the father – clever of Mr Wilson to hit upon the moment when Americanisms first came to England – is a failed writer of the Savoy and Strand period, a lazy, boozy philanderer living on the money of his wife's family. His jokes are terrible; his philosophisings evasive; he decays happily into shabby, Bohemian dandyism. The mother, mockingly known as the Countess by her bright and hostile children, is an Edwardian snob with a false accent – she says 'beautah' for 'beauty', 'meh' for 'me'. She lives in dreams of second-rate social grandeur, is capricious, petulant, very randy and rather unclean. Her taste in lovers is coarse. Her husband goes in for tarts. She can't afford the large Kensington house they all live in, on the grandparents' money, where all the cooking and cleaning is done by an old, fighting Cockney woman – who, in a pseudo-upper-class family, has a happy life as a knock-about comedian with a richly dirty mind. Her position gives her huge histrionic gifts a chance. Here she is, rolling home drunk:

Half past two. And down the road she comes. With a too ral, too ral, aye, does your ma know you're out? Swing, swing, how the bleeding pavements swing. Steady, me little cock sparrer. Hold on to the railing. Whoops, she goes! All to feed the fishes. Christ, what's that? There he comes, my own little Bobby, swinging his truncheon . . . What about it, cock, lend us the end of your finger? But they wouldn't lend you a sausage, not one of them, the bleeders. Not if your name *was* Henrietta Stoker, mother unknown, probably titled, six years with the Honourable Mrs Pitditch-Perkins, French cooking trained by Monser Jools what had been at the Savoy. Oh, Lord, up she comes. Oh, Jesus help me . . . Treated like dirt by the lot of them. Reagen do this, Reagen do that. Lend us a quid. Reagen. My name's Henrietta I'll thank you . . . Tradesmen owed everywhere, the guv'nor boozed every night and SHE can't keep her legs shut . . . Regular old cockney I am and one of the family. Make them laugh a caution sometimes. Oh, Ria she's a toff, darn't she look immensikoff, and they all shouted, waatch Ria!

The children of this quarrelling, sour-smelling setup are gifted and wretched. They see themselves as actors in a broken-down, stranded Rep company; and when things get bad they play what is called The Game. In this they act out a court scene in which the awful parents are on mock trial. Their satire is bitchy and disabused yet it is also compassionate. Why did whimsical Billy Pop call his wife the Countess? It's a nursery genteelism for Cuntess. Marcus, one of the sons, who will become a homosexual later in the chronicle, plays the part of his loved and hated mother:

'Do you remember, Billah,' she asked, 'when we bunnah hugged till dawn? Your breath smells Billah. Oh God! You've let yourself go to pieces.' 'Come to that,' says Billy Pop [played by Rupert who will eventually become a famous actor]. 'Come to that you stink like a whore's knocking shop.'

Quentin, the eldest son, home from the 1914 war, plays the judge all his life. He will eventually become a left-wing journalist, a trouble to the Communists and Socialists in the Spanish war. He will be beaten up by Irish Black Shirts, refuse to sign a manifesto in Moscow, and will end up as a well-known national broadcaster. He is never ridiculed, though he is often shouted down; if he acts it is in the real world and represents Mr Wilson's committal and conscience. (But public speaking is a form of acting.) Look at the others. Honest, clumsy Gladys, tennis player, first to know as a child what Cuntess means, and shamed by the semi-bankruptcy of the family, becomes a business girl and is eventually the secretive mistress of an obvious crook called Alf whose commercial affairs are sweaty-faced fraud. Naturally, he lands her in jail in order to save his own skin. The actress in Gladys emerges when she appears in court; she skilfully hides Alf's identity by behaving frivolously and impudently to the Judge. There is an important point of character here; it amounts to a social diagnosis too: the family has no respect for society. The hated family binds them. Gladys is a clumsy E. M. Forsterite who puts 'personal relationships' first, even bad ones. After four years in jail she settles down with an easy-going 'bloke' and breeds dogs.

Then there are Margaret and Sukey. Margaret will turn into a writer of integrity, waspish to begin with, softer and popular later on. We read bits of the novels she is writing and her progress is expertly and seriously shown. *Her* acting is seen in her compulsion to turn the family reality into the unreality of literature. Sukey, a headmaster's wife and practical mother, seems totally without inner life, but her energies go on to a stage where self-preservation and duty are in conflict. Easily settled: Sukey elects, *à l'anglaise*, for the great escape called Worry. Marcus, the youngest, whose schoolboy scenes with his brother are very well done, spits in the face of one of his mother's lovers, turns homosexual and, imitating mother, invites his boyfriends to the house. There is a very funny bedroom scene with a colonel who combines disciplinary moral lectures with seduction. Eventually Marcus finds the right man and goes in for lavish, theatrical parties in Hampstead and selling modern paintings. The thing to note is that all these children of the decadence are iron-willed. They have gone through a dreadful family mill; it has hardened their egos, and if they are emotionally disjointed they are not emotionally dead or deceived.

These are the people who have somehow to find their way through the Twenties and to react to the rise of Fascism, the Communist revival, the Second World War; to changes of fashion, to political and literary meetings. Quentin has to fight against being called a crank. Margaret, the novelist, has to defend herself against the charge that she is indifferent to the people she writes about – and indeed a lot of Mr Wilson's very witty book, which is full of malice as well as ideas, is a defence of the view that malice is not alien to the passions for truth, integrity, and the affections: a lot of blah and stupidity has to be cauterised. The picture of Margaret thinking her pernickety way from the real life character before her into the imaginary relations she is creating is good. In fact all the characters are sound in talk and action for – as one knows from his short stories – Mr Wilson is a master of the small iceberg that has much meaning beneath it. We see Rupert – who will be a success in Chekhov – studying this part seriously, and here the theatre scenes are excellent. The moment when Rupert gambles and astutely seduces a great actress is very good too. There are many such sharp instances within the cinematic commentary that carries the chronicle forward. And the characters are not static. They change with the years. Even the hopeless parents, Billy Pop and the

Countess, now supported by the family, become more tolerable as their joints stiffen. They have a cock-eyed dignity. Billy Pop's literary memoirs, recalling the good old days when he wrote that series on cricket for *Blackwoods*, are beautifully parodied.

Mr Wilson is a wit who repairs the damage he does by the natural overflow of his talent. He inclines to have too many ideas and in this novel his stress on The Game played by the family seems to me excessive. It is true that gamc-playing is a common escapist device in the lives of the people he is describing, but since all the characters in this novel are seen on their inner stage, it is overdoing the matter to repeat it in a family charade. Another difficulty is that the Matthewses are a special case: as Bohemians they are cut off from the rest of society, they are seen in almost picturesque isolation: we see remarkably little of their lovers and friends or the society from which these outsiders come. And finally, when a younger generation appears, they seem pale, unformed, even exhausted when compared with their shameless forebears. It is an occupational risk of the novelist who is writing a chronicle that he will tend, in the end, to become more intent on the years than on his characters.

In the Echo Chamber

Looking back on the novels of the late Twenties, a period when style and originality counted above all, I still think Henry Green showed a startling certainty of direction in his first novel. *Blindness* was written when he was about eighteen: superficially autobiographical, it was only very slightly derivative. The remarkable quality was the young author's accomplished sense of his 'line': he would sacrifice everything to seeing and hearing, not as a reporter, but as an artist feeling his way into the consciousness of others. Random calamity was to have a marked place in Henry Green's mature work and often echoes the accidental skids of our garrulous minds; but when, in this first book, the youthful writer is accidentally blinded for life, Green was not so much interested in blindness as a case for pity or stoicism but as a device for intensifying his sensibility and retrieving exact memory as a writer. Blindness was to be a journey into a country otherwise lost. The subject of all Henry Green's later novels is the inner language and landscape in which his characters lead their real lives. Under the spoken rigmarole they conceal their resourcefulness as human beings.

When he came to write his masterpieces, *Living*, *Caught* and *Loving*, his characters were for the most part ordinary workers on the factory floor, firemen, stunned soldiers, dull people in offices, servants and (occasionally) frantic upper-class people. The striking thing is that this distinctly upper-class artist is pretty well the first English novelist to have listened to working-class speech and to have understood its overtones and undertones, without being what, in the Thirties, one would have called politically committed. The 'committed' novelists did nothing like as well. He could, of course, have been playing a clever game; but he was not. The morbid, the comic, the lyrical and even the mannered aspects of his talent were not affected: fierce, fantastic and eccentric as it could be, his material came from the outside and mingled with his nature. He was not in the least sentimental: his eye was hard, his ear sharp. Some very fine artists impose

themselves, but Henry Green belonged to those who masochistically seek
to let their characters speak through them. In so speaking, they may expose
more than they know; but don't we all stubbornly feel that, for better or
worse, we are more than we know? There is a muddled justification for our
existence. We are encrusted in something like a private culture.

In *Blindness*, we are first shown the boy before his accident. Precocious,
scornfully determined to be a great writer, and with a quick, educated
mind, he is quite certain to be talented. He is also rich. His short diary about
friends and quarrels at a great public school is packed with swank and
tetchiness. Then the accident occurs. He is reduced at once to helplessness
in the family's grand country house, to be petted and pitied by the servants
and to arouse guilt in his stepmother, a hard-riding, capable ruler of the
estate and the village; she is struggling between her sense of emotional
inadequacy and her natural, ruthless worldliness. The boy's blindness – as
he coldly notes – has provided the household with an emotional orgy,
enlarging dramas of pity and bustling self-importance. In the stepmother's
chattering mind we see the beginnings of Henry Green's gift for drawing
on the inexhaustible wells of human egoism.

She leaves her dining room for the sitting room which looks out onto a
rose garden:

It ought to look well this year, not that he would see it, though. She had
lots of things to do this morning, she would not let the thing come up
and crush her. His was the sort of nature which needed to be left alone,
so it was no use going to see him. Plans must be made for when his new
life would begin, and some idea might emerge out of her work. Being
blind he could do work for the other blind and so not feel solitary, but get
the feeling of a Regiment. Meanwhile there was the Nursing Association. She must write to his friends, too, they ought to know that he was
blind. Would they really care? But, of course, anyone who knew John
must care. Then their letters would come in return, shy and halting, with
a whole flood of consolation from the neighbours, half of whom did not
care in the least. She would have to answer them: but no, she couldn't.
Then they would say that the blow had aged her, she had said that so
often herself. Their letters would be full of their own little griefs, a child
who had a cold, a husband worried by his Indian liver, one who had been

[1013]

cut publicly by Mrs So-and-So – but this wasn't fair. They would write rather of someone of theirs who had died recently or years and years ago. And she would answer suitably, for of course by now one knew what to say, but it was hateful people laying little private bits of themselves bare and she being expected to do likewise. Still, it would be all over some day.

She took up the Nursing Accounts.

A whole fox-hunting society, at a time when the big houses are beginning to go, comes to life, and is at a loss to know how to feel. For the boy, the new life means a proud angry battle with self-pity, an intensifying of the will to remember every detail of the country: exactly what the fields looked like, how the fish rose in the stream, where the grass and the nettles met, understanding sounds, listening to the inflexions of voices, wincing at too much oozing sentiment, discriminating between the notes of truth and untruth. The incipient ruthlessness of the artist is strengthened. There follows a halting friendship with the ragged daughter of the local, unfrocked, gin-soaking clergyman, a girl humiliated by her father's dilapidation. This episode is a shade too bizarre in a Powys-y rural manner, but the halting talk between the shy, rather cruel boy and the straightforward, kind girl is excellent and shows us the start of Green's remarkable talent for drawing simple young women. His gift lies in conveying the strangeness of the unspoken that underlies the spoken and for real dialogue which is a juxtaposition of voices that do not answer each other, but continue lives that will come nearer and will, in the end, be separate. Being young is a quest.

In the last stage of the boy's friendship with the girl, one sees Green's own mind made up as a writer. Country life is sinister, childish, futile. Towns and cities where real people work at their machines are to be his world, among people who have reserves of direction and skill, where humanity exists and love is grown-up. At the end of the book the out-of-date country house is sold. The boy and his stepmother go to London and there is new incitement to make what he can of life.

Like most first novels of talent, *Blindness* is a book of striking pages rather than a sound whole. The leap forward to the factory life of his next book, *Living*, is enormous. The study of blindness seems to express a strain of morbidity which was valuable to Green because it was not sentimental; it was, rather, a way of unselfing himself in order to enter the maze in which the minds and feelings and interests of ordinary people, totally foreign to himself, were going round and round in circles. He was not taking them up as a cause; he loved their mystery. He was a far closer and more feeling observer here than George Orwell was, for he had no polemic. Henry Green loved the obstinacy, the strangeness, the monotone of the deeply emotional culture which ran alongside his own cool one. Human repetitiousness was a sort of poetry for him. It also defined the inner territory of obscure rights, wrongs and blind stubbornness to which our devious self-interest or our waywardness cling like creeper. His people are new on top but old underneath. In spite of the mannerisms and a wild delight in calamity, Green seems to me to have been the most luminous novelist of the Thirties and Forties – as *Blindness* foretold – and truly seminal. For him people were echoing chambers. One has to pick out this voice or that before it turns into the general reverberation in which a society sinks its life.

Birth of a Hermaphrodite

W hen the second volume of Leon Edel's life of Henry James opens, the novelist is twenty-seven. He is forty by the end, a success, 'sufficiently great', but not yet the Master. The clever book-reviewer, the nimble writer of travel sketches, is at first seen worried and restive in Boston after his 'passionate pilgrimage' in Europe, fussed by the choice between American virtue and the beautiful European corruption. (In a hundred years how *that* international moral tale has changed!) He goes to his native New York and slaves for a while as a high-class hack. Travel writing once more releases him for Italy, France, Switzerland and Turgenev's Baden, but by the time he is thirty-three, his pleasant job as sentimental traveller for the *New York Tribune* is ending and he has run through the flimsy, seasonal acquaintance of his fellow expatriates in the spas and capitals. France has disappointed in the end for he has 'seen all round' Flaubert and Zola; French social life has turned out (it always does to the foreigner) to be impenetrable. He has been thrown upon the boulevards among a lot of third-rate tourists.

Sooner or later any travelling American swallows his love-hate for the British and is subdued by the convenience of the English tongue. The strain of linguistics gives place to the pleasure of even vulgar conversation. So James comes to London and finds what he needs – tradition, the back numbers of *Punch*, speaking likenesses of Dickens's people and Thackeray's everywhere, coal fires, draughts, and a home. Looking out of his window off Piccadilly he reflects that Becky Sharp once lived round the corner in Curzon Street and that – sublime contentment – Lord Ashburton's dirty brown brick wall is across the way. James was a Londoner at last, yet not quite smoked and kippered to our condition. He indeed fell back on French in his happiness: 'Je suis absolument comme chez moi.' The phrase preserves a nuance in his philandering relation to the city and the country he was, in the end, to adopt.

There was never anything flighty in Henry James's movements. He came to London with a prepared campaign and an inner calendar in his head. He steamed ponderously in like an engine, on time. If there is one thing that both Leon Edel's volumes have brought out it is that the Master was a major strategist as a writer and in his social life. There is – or was – no more highly-trained snob than the Boston snob; he got onto the right people at once and, that done, London was easy to penetrate, for the right people were not sticklers and asked only to be amused. Their deplorable lack of 'analytical intellect' assured that they would be pleasant. London was the chosen site, a 'regular basis of mundane existence', for James's next battle: after success, the organised achievement of Greatness.

Our usual picture of James comes from the later, old Pretender period when he seems to be genuflecting, somewhere in space, before the image of Art, mysteriously sustained by an invisible private income. The young James with the glossy beard is quite a different person: dashing, shrewd about ways and means, burning with energy. There is vast confidence in his malice and his ironic laughter. He is absolutely professional. He delights to earn his living; he is tough with editors; he is prompt and clever with his pot-boilers; he has an eye to serials and commissions. He was long-headed enough to know, within six months, when he would be able to switch to greatness. He arrived in London for the publication of a work of serious criticism and of his early novels, which were unknown here. A few rapid moves and he knew everyone. At first agog, but soon he was in the clubs – a 'member' in the full soporific sense. A word from Henry Adams – the supreme Yankee snob and expert at the game – and he was staying in the best houses. The lazy, genial Thackeray had been ruined by dining out; for James it was part of the plan. In his second winter, he had dined out 140 times and in the best society – 'behold me after dinner conversing affably with Mr Gladstone'. Not always, of course, in the best. There were flops. There were shabby, literary ladies. There were dreary Oxfordish parties, shoppish and local in their eternal gossip. If he was bowled over by the handsomeness of English men they had, he noticed, dirty hands.

Handsome himself, witty, attentive to women, especially to old ladies, James was enormously popular in mid-Victorian London. His talk was light yet serious. He pleased everyone, though he was careful not to speak his mind outright. The curse laid upon the British – it was the complaint of

Taine – was their lack of that analytical mind. He never really got to the heart of the English matter. Privileged travellers, like James, tend to see any society as obligingly static and displaying the end-products of character: to the forces that make a people what they are, James was blind. It is not the business of the novelist to do so, but the novels of Henry James tell us little about *English* life beyond the relations of the rich to their servants.

There are, all the same, two Henry Jameses: the novelist with his 'beautiful contrivances' and exquisite adumbrations who confines himself, with one or two exceptions, to upper-class life; and the traveller who slums with any company. He mooched in the London streets, swallowed the fog, looked at the gin-soaked squalor and so far unbuttoned as to go off with the crowd to the Derby. An unsuspected England showed itself – violent, jolly and uninhibited. He had, on the whole, a low opinion of the British female, though admittedly she did not run, after an early blossoming, to the American stringiness. The British female of the lower orders was alarming. She was 'too stout, too hot, too red, too thirsty, too boisterous, too strangely accoutred', yet (one was obliged to add) 'useful, robust and prolific'. Like Britannia, in short. In *The Princess Casamassima* he turned her to account in the fine picture of Millicent Henning, with her Cockney beauty, 'her bad grammar and good health . . . her shrewd perceptions and grotesque opinions'. (James could not bear it that English women were healthy.)

Once more in his second volume Leon Edel gracefully disposes of the notion that quiet lives, and especially the lives of writers, are uninteresting. James toiled. The hours of his life are filled up less with minutes than with words. They edge him out, phrase by phrase, from nearly all external experience except eating, flirting, walking alone at night and sleeping. The clues to the inner dramas are in his work. James's inner life – perhaps this is true of all novelists – is an affair of ghosts. The figures of father, mother and above all of William the brother and rival actively haunt him and provide their crises. No doubt all families are tyrannies of the affections, but the James family, withdrawn on principle from the contagion of participation in American life, conscientiously standing for 'being' rather than 'doing', was like some closed city state. The mother – 'too sacred' to be described by James – ruled it in what we now accept as the American habit. To think of breaking with it meant, in William's case and that of his sister, invoking the protection of illness. They are all held together by brilliance, irony, the private devices. William cannot manage to marry until he is thirty-six and is, strangely, in Europe when his child is born. Henry escapes because he is the spoiled boy, the second son, Angel as he was mockingly called, hiding his forbidding will to power and his egotism behind the mask of meekness. His deepest friendships are with elderly women, although there is one episode – his presumably platonic and prolonged and rather secret flirtation with Constance Fenimore Woolson – in which, meaning to be merely disturbing, he was himself disturbed and challenged. It led to headaches and, later, to the refinements of remorse. In art and the egotism of the artist James had found his safety and liberation.

But the ghosts could suddenly play a decisive part. They can be seen grouping and regrouping in the early stories where William and Henry grapple in disguise. When William got married the profound relation of Henry with his brother was shaken, and Mr Edel notes that one of his worst stories, *Confidence*, was written at this time: two young men fall for the same young woman who is called, of all things, Angela! The Angel has feminised himself. This might have been a fantasy of passing interest but the fraternal crisis coincided with the uproar in America about his study of Hawthorne: his deepest feelings were stirred.

Henry James, conquering London and its literary world, could be as assertive and powerful as Christopher Newman; but rejected like Newman – or pushed to the wall by his elder brother – told that he wasn't fit to play with rough boys or that his writing was full of knots and bows and ribbons, found himself reminded forcibly that he was a perpetual 'mere junior'.

Until now his novels had been about heroes. In the one seeming exception, *Daisy Miller*, the girl is seen through the eyes of a man. Henceforth they would be about heroines responding 'to their destinies in a world that jilted, denied and betrayed'. He would write *Washington Square* and *The Portrait of a Lady*. Was this a matter of imaginative dexterity, or did it come from his nature? A hermaphrodite – according to Mr Edel – discovered himself.

And in *The Portrait* Mr Edel directs us, with great perspicacity, to one of those inner dramas of compensation and confident self-extending that bring a writer's powers to maturity – if they come at the right time. Who is Osmond in *The Portrait*? He is, Mr Edel says,

> the hidden side of James himself, when his snobbery prevailed over his humanity and arrogance and egotism over his urbanity and his benign view of the human comedy . . . in creating him Henry put into him his highest ambition and drive to power – the grandiose way in which he confronted his destiny . . . In the hands of a limited being, like Osmond, the drive to power ended in dilettantism and petty rages. In Henry's hands the same drive had given him unbounded creativity.

If he closely watches the ghosts in James's life, Mr Edel is not tempted into those murkier areas of the psychological limbo which have been irresistible to the reckless school of biography. We are shown James living as we might have seen him. There he goes riding every morning in the Campagna with some lady he has charmed; there he goes out for his night walks in London; there he sits reading at the Reform; watching, very shocked, the great Turgenev playing with Pauline Viardot's children on the floor; obdurately working all the afternoon in Italy while William waits impatiently for him to finish. James lived in the extremes of solitude and sociability; his is one of the most peopled lives lived by a man of genius, for the genius depended on their chatter. To have got all these people back out of literature into James's life as Mr Edel has done is remarkable in itself, but the skill with which these things are made to build up James's own life as a man is more remarkable. The short chapters, each carefully pointed, take one with alacrity along the crowded peregrinations of James's mind and person, without a moment's boredom. Mr Edel has come close to the excited spontaneous sensibility and intelligence of a man who baffles us by being enormous and yet who, in a way almost enviable, has no life at all.

By the time the fourth volume of Leon Edel's rich and searching biography of Henry James opens, the Master has had to face the shattering fact of the suicide of Miss Woolson in Venice, and is about to receive another blow in the very sanctum of his so far invulnerable egotism: in his art. His plots for success in the theatre (and as an operator James was as exhaustive here as he was in his social stratagems), his hopes of the financial magnificence of the best-sellers at a moment when he was himself becoming noticeably less saleable, are to be brutally dashed by the booing of *Guy Domville*. He took the affair as if his person had been assaulted, as if he had been mugged. The strategist, in life and in art, the addict of military memoirs, has had a public defeat, and at a truly 'awkward age'. He is fifty; a younger irreverent generation of realists, who have no interest in High Romance, has burst open the door. He is called further to account by his first humiliating attack of gout.

The next five years, in Mr Edel's diagnosis, are a period of 'nervous breakdown', and he is to be shown slowly emerging from it by his invincible belief in the therapy of his art. At his age many artists turn to easier remedies, or slacken in their vigilance, for even art has its temptations; but James (perhaps because he was a solitary and a man of puritan energy) had always known that the important thing was to increase difficulty. In his case – and I would have said for all – the temptation is to thin oneself by looking forward: the difficult task is to reconstitute oneself by looking back. And so Mr Edel's purpose is to show James performing on himself 'what Freud was busily demonstrating' – the power to heal oneself of hardening wounds by retreat to earliest experience. The process is dramatically clear: it is not a question of curing himself by work, but of divining the right work. James found it in the treacherous five years, by writing his tales of children, ghosts and phantasmagoria: it is the period of *The Pupil*, *The Awkward Age*, *What Maisie Knew*, *The Turn of the Screw* and of that mystifying search for the heart of personality, *The Sacred Fount*, before the spacious final works are attempted.

For the comedy of Jamesian anecdote Professor Edel has little use. The adroit letters (he has said before) are either recklessly discharged smoke-screens or a collection of tactical feints. They are histrionically concealing. Professor Edel notes enough of James's familiar social life at Lamb House, his meetings with Kipling and Meredith, the devastating visits of Edith Wharton, the last journey to Italy, his bicycle rides and so on, to keep the spry, practical, restless 'character' alive and to preserve his engaging momentousness. But the cure is the thing and Professor Edel studies it, until it completes itself at the end of the book, with the tremendous sight of the Master shaving off his beard. But Professor Edel relies on James's clue: 'The artist is in every page of every book from which he sought so assiduously to eliminate himself.'

[1021]

The difficulty here is to avoid theory or dogmatic assertion about the meaning of echoes, symbols and images, and I don't know any writer who is so free of the vices psychology has offered to biography as Professor Edel is. He is pertinacious, but tactful, gracious and tender; indeed, this is the most moving of his four volumes. His suggestions, gathered from the novels, tend to build up a whole rather than a schematic figure, and he is aware that a writer may go far back into his past for a word or a crucial incident without consciously displaying an item of personal history. We can see Professor Edel's method at work in what he has to say about the melodramatic ending of *The Spoils of Poynton* and its possible relation to James's horrifying experience when he was booed off the stage after *Guy Domville*. Professor Edel notes that the book does not have one of James's traditional endings: why melodrama?

> Perhaps because he had himself been forced to the centre of the stage, in a bit of melodrama not of his own making. His imagery went further back however than the recent disaster in the St James's. In describing Mrs Gereth's departure from Poynton and her loss of her antiques, *her* work of art, James wrote 'the amputation had been performed. Her leg had come off – she had now begun to stump along with the lovely wooden substitute and would stump for life, and what her young friend was to come and admire was the beauty of her movement . . .' Thus James had recourse in this work to one of the most personal images out of his own childhood. It suggests how vivid for all his lifetime was the memory of his father's amputation and 'the noise . . . about the house'. The father had lost his leg in a stable fire and Henry subsequently had suffered a back injury while helping to fight a stable fire at Newport. Amputation and fire: these symbols out of the past now forced themselves into the story he was telling. Poynton and its 'spoils' had to be destroyed as *Guy Domville* was destroyed.

One practical result of the failure in the theatre was that he now turned to planning his stories as scenarios. This unluckily doubled their length. We are at the beginning of the period when over and over again his stories are too long for their subject. (This is true, for the contemporary reader, of masterpieces like *The Pupil*.) Before, he never revised; now he will revise interminably; and when he takes up dictation, the manner will take on the appearance of an intricate private reverie.

[1022]

So the cure has its price. But the gains are extraordinary in life and in literature. By taking his mind back to childhood, James was obliged to consider his femininity. His masculinity had been driven underground.

To be male was to risk [in the remote fantasy of childhood] such things as amputation like his father; . . . he could escape by thinking himself a little girl.

The rivalry with the older male, William, appears in tale after tale in many forms. Lack of male conviction was the weakness of *Guy Domville*. In retreating to Lamb House and brooding on his past, James was retreating into a simulacrum of his life in the James family; and hence the buried struggles of childhood come to the surface. The feelings that arose out of the past were a 'kind of conscious nightmare'. In *The Turn of the Screw* the ghosts are the ghosts of his boyhood. Little Miles's 'rude' battle with the governess, telling her he doesn't want to be cooped up with females, is a transference of James's own conflict. Miles is defeated, and it is important to see that, told in the first person by the governess, the story is a statement of female hysteria. The femininity of Henry James is speaking. Maisie is a study of himself in boyhood – she is, I remember noting years ago, facetiously addressed as 'my dear sir' by one of her guardians. Nanda of *The Awkward Age* would be a projection of the Henry of late adolescence. The little girls – and without writing a conscious series (as Professor Edel shows) James studies them at progressive ages – emerged 'out of the personal healing' which was going on under the surface of the practical, ambitious, successful man of the world.

Professor Edel's patient and careful method makes his point; for although one can say that any author's life is buried in his work in this way, James's distinction is that he knew what he was doing: his father's faith in compensations was part of family training. Only occasionally does the reliance on verbal echoes seem to me strained. When the governess feels her 'blow in the stomach' it seems merely ingenious to trace this back to the blow in the stomach James said he had had at the St James's Theatre. And when the child Effie is murdered by drowning, I think Professor Edel is pushing matters when he links this with what James called his 'subaqueous' feelings after *Guy Domville*.

The final chapters of the volume are as moving and perceptive as those that were given to the story of Miss Woolson in the earlier volume. There, a hardness of heart and a good deal of disingenuousness appeared in James's character. He certainly feared entanglement, but the part played by a distaste that looks secretive and snobbish seems plain. That by dying our friends extinguish part of ourselves is true enough, and it is characteristic of James's truth-telling and glacial egotism to show this as an affront. In *The Beast in the Jungle* he knows remorse. The present volume contains an account of James suffering as Miss Woolson suffered, in his extraordinary passion for the young, crude and climbing Norwegian sculptor Hendrik Andersen. They saw little of each other, but the separations were agonising and the letters are filled not only with ironical advice to the young god who was vulgarly on the make, but with physical longings. He wanted to touch the young man. He wanted to hug and embrace him: 'lean on me as a brother and a lover'. And 'I hold you close' and 'I feel my arms around you'. These expressions may be simply a well-known mode of Victorian emotionalism:

> Allowances must be made [Professor Edel says] for James's long puritan years, the confirmed habits of denial, the bachelor existence, in which erotic feeling had been channelled into hours of strenuous work and the wooing of *mon bon*. One also must remember that James had a fear of loss of masculinity . . . James was constitutionally incapable of belonging to the underworld of sex into which Oscar Wilde had drifted.

His feelings had been transferred to the intellect. His philanderings with his many women friends went to fanciful lengths, and were really utterances of High Romance. But clearly, this time, there was passion on James's part. He was still writing it at the age of seventy. He comes out of the affair with his reply to another young man who had asked him what port he had set out from as a novelist:

> The port from which I set out was, I think, that of the *essential loneliness of my life* – and it seems to me the port, in sooth, to which again finally my course directs itself. This loneliness (since I mention it!) – what is it still but the deepest thing about one? Deeper about me, at any rate, than anything else, deeper than my 'genius', deeper than my 'discipline',

deeper than any pride, deeper above all, than the deep counter-minings of art.

He wrote this while correcting the proofs of *The Sacred Fount* – that baffling and even trivial book which Professor Edel sees as the final therapeutic act that would mark his self-healing. Until now, as a novelist, he had never dealt with love in his novels, except as a 'force destructive of – or in competition with – power and aesthetic beauty'. He had now discovered that his egotism was vulnerable. Professor Edel's *Life* has not only scope and mastery of lively detail and argument; it goes with bold and yet controlled insight into the labyrinth of a great creative imagination. The man and the artist have been joined – a feat that biography so rarely succeeds in.

Henry James's *The American Scene* is still one of the very few excellent books of travel by an American about his own country. He is as exact and prophetic in his own restricted way as the extraordinary and very different Tocqueville was in his. The book is unique in a genre where – strangely enough, among a foot-loose people – American literature is very poor; for penetrating observation and evocation of the land and the cities we have to turn to novels and, above all, poetry. The remarkable thing about the book is that although it was written in 1905, and in spite of the huge changes that have occurred in America since that time, it presents (as Leon Edel says in a troubled introduction) an essential America that is still recognisable.

This ought not to surprise us: great artists are always farseeing. They easily avoid the big stumbling blocks of fact. They rely on their own simplicity and vision. It is fact-fetishism that has given us those scores and scores of American books on America, the works of sociologists, anthropologists, topical 'problem' hunters, working-parties and statisticians, which in the end leave us empty. Henry James succeeds because he rejects information. He was himself the only information he required.

It should be unfailingly proved against me that my opportunity found me incapable of imparting information, incapable alike of receiving and imparting it; for then, and then only, would it be clearly attested that I *had* cared and understood.

[1025]

He was looking for a personal relationship to the scene he had left twenty years before. In so many other books on the country the sense of a relation is lacking; indeed, they leave one with an impression of a lonely continent, uncontemplated, unloved, unfelt by a people who have got so much out of it, as they move on, that they see little in it and give or leave nothing of themselves to the scene. How else to explain that sensation of things, places, even people abandoned which is so painful in the American landscape! How often one has felt what James sensed about certain American scenes, especially in New England:

> And that was doubtless, for the story seeker, absolutely the story: the constituted blankness was the whole business, and one's opportunity was all, thereby, for a study of exquisite emptiness.

Or:

> Charming places, charming objects, languish all round, under designations that seem to leave on them the smudge of a great vulgar thumb – which is precisely what a part of the pleading land appears to hint to you when it murmurs, in autumn, its intelligent refrain. If it feels itself better than so many phases of its fate, so there are spots where you see it turn up at you, under some familiar tasteless inflections of this order, the plaintive eye of a creature wounded with a poisoned arrow.

Henry James knew what the poison was. It would eventually wreck the American cities – a process our planners, always out of date, are eager to imitate in England today.

James was a traveller, that is to say, a story seeker to the marrow. His novels themselves are conscious journeys into the interior. He had started by writing travel sketches of things in France, Italy and Germany and England when he was young; the 'vignettes' of a sentimental traveller, meant to tease the American fancy for the Atlantic trip. *The American Scene* is a totally different matter. Perhaps at the age of sixty the returning expatriate originally promised himself one more sentimental pilgrimage. But in twenty years American life had passed through a crucial change. It could either sink him or raise him by the challenge. He was roused. Half the pleasure of the book comes from the sight of a travelling mind reinvigorated. He met the challenge with a richer and revived analytical gift. He rejected the journalistic temptation. In the twenty years since 1883

[1026]

a huge immigrant invasion had changed the character of the cities; big business, the great industrial monopolies, had taken total power and had imposed the business ethos; the pursuit of money had become the engulfing and only justifying role. New York had been a rough, low-built sea port with pigs rooting in the streets of lower Manhattan when he left, Central Park was a farmland. He returned to find all Manhattan crammed, and the skyscrapers rising – 'simply the most piercing notes in that concert of the expensively provisional into which your supreme sense of New York resolves'.

James ignored the colossal news item. He saw that his subject was not shock and that he was not there to advertise or boost the obvious. His subject was how the consciousness of a half-repentant expatriate would be affected, and what inner meanings and sensibilities he could offer in return. Guilt there would be, but distaste: nostalgia for what was gone, but a feeling for the drama; he would have to be both personal and yet the analyst. He became the seeker. He would have to lay himself open to the full bewilderment of his situation. In his introduction to an earlier edition of this book, W. H. Auden described it as a prose poem; an excellent description. Generously evocative and labyrinthine in its tact, it also shows a man struggling with love and menace. The skyscrapers are a 'vocabulary of thrift' but there are 'uglier words' for that. With mild but deadly truth they evoke (he says)

> the consciousness of the finite, the menaced, the essentially *invented* state [that] twinkles ever, to my perception, in the thousand glassy eyes of those giants of the market.

Again and again, he remarks on the 'pathos' of a civilisation so exuberantly on the move, but bewildered in having to accept itself as temporary. Of the new rich he writes:

> What had it been their idea to *do*, the good people . . . do that is, in affirming their wealth with such innocent emphasis and yet not at the same time affirming anything else.

They live in houses that have

> the candid look of costing as much as they knew how. Unmistakably they all proclaimed it – they would have cost still more had the way but

been shown to them; and, meanwhile, they added, as with one voice, they would take a fresh start as soon as ever it should be. 'We are only instalments, symbols, stop-gaps', they practically admitted, and with no shade of embarrassment: 'expensive we are, we have nothing to do with continuity, responsibility, transmission, and don't in the least care what becomes of us after we have served our present purpose'.

And the governing motive:

To make so much money that you won't, that you don't 'mind' anything.

Not, as it has turned out, the awful sight of American cities. If you do 'mind' you can easily become an un-American activity.

For James, America was 'dancing on the thin crust of a volcano'. In personal relationships

the most that was as yet accomplished . . . was the air of unmitigated publicity, publicity as a condition, as a doom from which there could be no appeal.

There was the inability to communicate, which was not felt as a loss among the new immigrants, but rather as a gain; they had become American. James, the native, puts his finger on what often dismays the chatty European traveller in his casual contacts: the American chill.

To isolate James's hostile impressions as I have done or to quote his final denunciation of the reigning spirit of the time – a denunciation which did not appear in the first American edition – is to give a misleading impression of a book warm in feeling and rich in texture. Every page contains a picture or a phrase that will bring New York, Boston, the scrub forest of New Hampshire, to the eyes, but backed by his long loving knowledge of the places. He records such deeply American things as allowing the forest to come down to the edges of the innumerable lakes. The story seeker, as he calls himself, continually questions the landscape in relation to himself, and it is the self-questioning which is at the heart of his ability to create the scene in the superb chapter on New Hampshire. Why does it seem to be Arcadian? Why was he always brought back to the thought that the woods and rocks insist on referring themselves to the idyllic? Was it because they bore no burden of history? The thought charms him, but another thought makes him sceptical: perhaps he rhapsodised now, because in Europe he had been deprived

> to excess – that is for too long – of naturalism in quantity. Here it was in such quantity as one hadn't for years to deal with; and that might by itself be a luxury corrupting the judgment.

The irony is subtle; but hasn't James hit exactly upon what drifts through one's mind as one drives the scores of miles through the scrub, the brown rock and grey rock of New England, or stands by some clear cold pond in the woods – the lyrical and, at the same time, crushing quantity of Nature, stupefying the mind? How much the love of quantity, together with its inexorable, umbrageous detail, has meant to an American mind.

James spent about a year as a returned native. Business and immigration were the important themes, alien to him and to his natural nostalgias; no searching was needed as far as business was concerned. That hit one in the face. The immigrants were more difficult, but he took a lot of trouble to see what was happening on New York's Lower East Side.

There, as a writer, he was as excited as he was disturbed by what would happen to the language, and to character. How long would the melting take? Then he went south, and any romantic hopes he had were pinched by wretched weather and the general shabbiness. He is still good, but he is better on native ground. He discovered that Washington was the place where, for once, men ruled the conversation. Outside of known, friendly haunts, he had been starved of two things in America: conversation – all that was offered was talk – and privacy. He hated the open interior of the American club and house. But if, inevitably, he harks back to the times when a home was not a house, when locality existed and the tycoons were unknown, if he denounces the new age and sees it will lead to worse, he is soundly American in admiring the drama of the situation and in his feeling for the extravagant.

The search for the story, the inturned Jamesian story, is at once pertinacious and very touching. He creates an America because he creates himself in relation to it. The book is a true work of travel because it is a collaboration and with a living country that scatters a myriad unanswered questions about 'as some monstrous unnatural mother might leave a family of unfathered infants on door steps or in waiting rooms'.

[1029]

Towards Revolution

In 1972 Edmund Wilson's *To the Finland Station* was reissued with an introduction written by him about a year before. The book seems to me to have become crisper, in some mysterious way, in the long interval, to have moved away from the topical domestic hopes of his youth into the classic condition and to be Wilson's most enlarging work. I cannot think of any other American historical essay so fine in texture, in this century. What did Wilson himself think of it? He understood its roots in the agitations of the Thirties. Authors are usually their own exact critics:

> It is all too easy to idealize a social upheaval which takes place in some other country than one's own . . . The remoteness of Russia from the West evidently made it even easier for American socialists and liberals to imagine that the Russian Revolution was to get rid of an oppressive past, to scrap a commercial civilization, and to found, as Trotsky prophesied, the first really human society. We were very naïve about this. We did not foresee that the new Russia must contain a good deal of the old Russia: censorship, secret police, the entanglements of bureaucratic incompetence, an all-powerful and brutal autocracy. This book of mine assumes throughout that an important step in progress . . . had occurred, that nothing in our human history would ever be the same.

Now, with a changed mind, Wilson writes that the book is at least a basically reliable account of what reformers, revolutionary theorists and conspirators in Europe, and eventually in Russia, 'thought they were doing' in the nineteenth century in the interests of '"a better world"'. His precise criticisms are that he undoubtedly underrated the vigorous persistence of the French Socialist tradition and sinned in leaving out Jaurès and Zola, and that his dislike of the Abbé Coignard and *Le Petit Pierre* made him underrate Anatole France of the *Histoire Contemporaine* and *Les Dieux*

Ont Soif. I myself would have said that there is rather much of the gourmet in Anatole France's manner when he dwells on the sexual gratifications of massacre. A Goya saw terror as open nightmare: the fact that violence devours its children was neither a metaphor nor a psychological conceit to the Spaniard; in the indignation of Anatole France there is also a smell of tooled leather in the library. As for the charge that Wilson was too amiable to Lenin, Wilson admits that the critics have some grounds for saying this, but he had had, at the time, only the accounts authorised by the Soviet Government! With the truly Wilsonian appetite for new documents, he now adds several views of Lenin by people who knew him. He quotes a long passage from Pyotr Struve, a Russian contemporary, who said that in his attitude to his fellow-men Lenin 'breathed coldness, contempt, and cruelty'. This was bound up with his love of power. Another writer, recounting what he knew of the decision to kill the Tsar and his family, said:

> In the intellectual circles of the Party there probably were misgivings and shakings of heads. But the masses of workers and soldiers had not a minute's doubt. They would not have understood and would not have accepted any other decision. *This* Lenin sensed well. The ability to think and feel for and with the masses was characteristic of him to the highest degree, especially at the great political turning points.

Wilson's attentions to his critics are proper in their way, but not so very relevant; after all, the book ends with Lenin's dramatic arrival in Leningrad – a story told with all Wilson's glinting exactness – and says almost nothing about the Revolution itself. The originality of *To the Finland Station* lies not in its direct narrative or in its factuality but in its study of the writing and acting of history. The task Wilson sets himself is to follow the devious yet constantly renewed threads in the texture of conspiracy. His people and their actions are born when their minds make their act of discovery. So Vico, the modest Italian scholar who finds his academic career blocked because of his humble origins and because he is thought to be a crank, is driven into the wilderness where he discovers the subversive idea that society is organic: 'I speak of this incontestable truth: the social world is certainly the work of men'. This is in 1725. Then there is a leap to 1824, when Michelet, the son of a poor printer persecuted by Napoleon, finds Vico's name in a translator's note and – in brisk Wilsonian phrase – 'immediately set out to learn Italian'. History is born, and here, with Michelet as master, Wilson has half his method and strikes his subject. Michelet said that he dashed off his *Introduction to Universal History* when he was fresh from 'the burning pavements' of Paris and the workers' riots before Charles X abdicated, in 1830, and in the fervent chapters on Michelet's life and work one can see how much of Wilson's method was extracted and adapted from the historian. One main difference between Michelet's method and the method of the ordinary historian, Wilson says, is this:

> The ordinary historian knows what is going to happen in the course of his historical narrative because he knows what has really happened, but Michelet is able to put us back at upper stages of the stream of time, so that we grope with the people of the past themselves, share their heroic faiths, are dismayed by their unexpected catastrophes, feel, for all our knowledge of after-the-event, that we do *not* know precisely what is coming. Michelet responds with the sensitivity of a poet to every change of tempo, movement or scope and he develops an infinitely varied technique to register different phases . . . To give us a final symbol for the monarchy, Michelet has only to describe without comment the expense and the clumsy complication of the great waterworks at Marly which make the Versailles fountains play and which fill the air for miles around with their agonized creakings and groanings.

Wilson was no poet; he was a humane critic, but how closely his thinking method follows what in Michelet was learnedly emotional.

So, in Wilson's powerful essay, Michelet the historian is seen as a character playing a personal and creative part himself in history. He is a human continuation of it. Very early on in the book, we see him as both man and symbol. There he stands for us – the laborious and fervid son of a printer worshipping his father's printing press itself. It might be some allegorical object out of Balzac. The press represents enlightenment and liberty. When Napoleon's police took the whole family off to jail and put the seals on the machine 'the incident caused Jules such anguish that he afterwards made a stipulation in his will that his wife should not be obliged to seal his coffin'. When Wilson moves on to Renan, Taine, France and, briefly, to the Symbolists in order to show the ossification of the once Romantic impulse, the biographical detail links their thinking to their lives. And biography plays a major part as his grand examination of Babeuf, Marx, Engels, Bakunin, Lassalle, Lenin and Trotsky expands. It is amusingly typical of Wilson that he should turn to one of Meredith's novels for an oblique glance at Lassalle.

Wilson was not, in the academic sense, a scholar or historian. He was an enormous reader, one of those readers who are perpetually on the scent from book to book. He was the old-style man of letters, but galvanised and with the iron of purpose in him. He was proud of his journalistic alacrity and of the gift of combining symphonic effects with those of 'no comment'. One has read dozens of books about the development of Socialist thought; one's mind is a sort of photograph album of the riots, risings, and coups d'état: Wilson takes this for granted. He brings us something else: intimacy with the makers. He is a critic in whom history is broken up into minds. And despite the awkwardness of his prose, he is a coherent artist in the architecture of his subject. I mean that he is an artist – that is evident in so much of his writing – in the sense that he is a man possessed. Give him the subject and it fuses with his whole person as if something like Mesmer's famous magnetic fluid had flowed into him. The effect is all the stronger because he is not exalted; he is, indeed, phlegmatic, as if his whole idea were a matter of grasp. He is as penetrating and as summary as the lawyer or the doctor (there is a good deal of both in him): sceptical, pungent, even dry as he surveys the evidence. Then the artist blows and puts the glow of life into it and the critic sets the perspective. An egotist himself, he understands that the egotism of his conspirators is a passion and a fate.

This is what gives his long, argued portraits of Marx and Engels their supreme and moving place in the book. Here, in fact, are Michelet-like figures who do not know what will happen, and who had actually thought of Russia as a bugbear. Being Germans, Marx and Engels had a cultivated contempt for the Slavs. Marx had pinned his hopes on *Das Kapital*'s being published in English! It was not published in England in his lifetime yet from England he had drawn a huge part of his evidence, and when he heard of the Russian translation he complained that the Russians 'always run after the most extreme ideas that the West has to offer'. How tenderly, but without infatuation, Wilson follows the devotion of Engels to Marx's

[1033]

overwhelming labours. Marx felt that he was borne down by an incubus. Wilson's criticism is searching, but not destructive; it enlarges our sense of the intellectual and human drama of Marx's life; both his morbid personal hatreds *and* his idealising of necessity are organically part of a passion. Even the boils, the carbuncles, the rheumatism, the enlarged liver, the markedly sadistic metaphors of his prose, his guilt – all are part of the struggle. Marx groaned that he was a non-God-fearing Job. There is a background of myth and even of mysticism in the elusive and supposedly scientific idea of the Dialectic, the mystery of the Trinity reborn. Wilson goes on to write:

No: he is not so god-fearing. He sees himself also as 'Old Nick', the Goethean spirit that denies. Yet Old Nick is not the right symbol either: this Devil has been twisted and racked . . . It is Prometheus who remains his favourite hero; for Prometheus is a Satan who suffers, a Job who never assents; and, unlike either Job or Satan, he brings liberation to mankind. Prometheus turns up in *Das Kapital* (in Chapter 23) to represent the proletariat chained to capital. The Light-Bringer was tortured, we remember, by Zeus's eagle's tearing, precisely, his liver, as Karl Marx himself – who is said to have reread Aeschylus every year – was obsessed by the fear that his liver would be eaten, like his father's, by cancer. And yet, if it is a devouring bird which Father Zeus has sent against the rebel, it is also a devourer, a destroyer, fire, which Prometheus has brought to man. And in the meantime the deliverer is never delivered; the slayer never rises from the grave. The resurrection, although certain, is not yet; for the expropriators are yet to be expropriated.

But before Wilson goes on to inquire into the failure of Marx's drastic dogma when it meets the resilience of advanced industrial societies, he reminds us that the importance of a book depends on the depths from which it is drawn:

Only so sore and angry a spirit, so ill at ease in the world, could have recognized and seen into the causes of the wholesale mutilation of humanity, the grim collisions, the uncomprehended convulsions, to which that age of great profits was doomed.

Michelet, Wilson, says, had tried to relive the past as an artistic creation, an attempt that was to make a strong impression on Proust – and had seen history break the pattern. Would Lenin be able to impose not an artistic pattern but one of political direction? Of all the Marxists, Lenin was the least in love with prophetic visions. ('Theoretical classification doesn't matter now'.) And there, artistically, Wilson's symphony comes to an end, not with a crescendo or a crash of cymbals but, rather, leaving us to move out of biography, impression, the books, the conspiracy, to the frightful territory where history, like nature, is red in tooth and claw. The Wilson of 1940 thought that we must not be surprised if later events were not to be 'amenable' to the pattern either of the vision or of practice. In 1971 Wilson, the battered liberal, *is* surprised at the appearance of 'one of the most hideous tyrannies that the world had ever known'.

To the Finland Station is perhaps the only book on the grand scale to come out of the Thirties – in either England or America. It contains to a novel degree the human history of an argument, from its roots to its innumerable branches, domestic and emotional. It comes from a mind that is divided between something like an obsession with record for its own sake and the drastic habit of imposing a personal emotion. Yet, in the writing, simply because of the profound instinct of an imagination that has lived in the sun of art and is unrepentant, fed by the intuitions and idiosyncrasies of the artist, the book is lifted, with a thinking excitement, from the ground. Again and again its sudden queer asides, its touches of vernacular pugnacity, its minuteness and – for that matter – its shrewdness, piety and goodwill mark it as deeply American. Even in style it is democratic, in the sense that this distinguished man will not for long allow one phrase to be better than another; the whole argument, as in narrative, must be plain-spoken and cogent. The histories of conspiracy have often attracted the rival angers of the orthodox and the fanatic or the dismissive wit of irony; none of these authors, in my recollection, emphasises as Wilson does, that at the core of the history of the nineteenth century there is intellectual anguish, often ugly with the pain and vanity of human nature; if Europe was a brilliant assembly of courts and salons, with their commanding intellects, it was also – for the masses – half hospital, and in Russia almost all hospital. Wilson reminds us that Chekhov's *Ward No. 6* had a devastating effect on the mind of the young Lenin. It is because it never loses sight of the pain gnawing at the heart of the human conscience that Wilson's discursive record, untouched by rhetoric, achieves pages one can only call noble.

Jumbos

═══════════

Saul Bellow has the most effusive intelligence of living American
novelists. Even when he is only clever he has a kind of spirited intellectual
vanity that enables him to take on all the facts and theories about the
pathetic and comically exposed condition of civilised man and distribute
them like high-class corn so that the chickens come running to them. That
is the art of the novelist who can't resist an idea: to evoke, attract that
'pleasing, anxious being', the squawking, dusty, feverish human chicken.
Aldous Huxley could always throw the corn but nothing alive came
fluttering to it.

But immensely clever novelists have to beware of self-dispersal when
they run to great length. I enjoy Saul Bellow in his spreading carnivals and
wonder at his energy, but I still think he is finer in his shorter works. *The
Victim* was the best novel to come out of America – or England – for a
decade. *The Dangling Man* is good, but subdued; *Seize the Day* is a small grey
masterpiece. If one cuts out the end, *Henderson the Rain King* is at once
profound and richly diverting in its fantasy. These novels had form; their
economy drove their point home. By brevity Bellow enhanced our
experience. And, to a European reader – though this may be irrelevant – he
seems the only American of this generation to convey the feel and detail of
urban America, preserving especially what is going on at the times when
nothing is going on: the distinctive native ennui, which is the basic nutrient
of any national life.

It is when he turns to longer books, chasing the mirage of 'the great
American novel', that Bellow weakens as he becomes a traveller, spreading
the news and depending on the presence of a character who is something
like a human hold-all, less a recognisable individual than a fantastic piece
of bursting luggage. His labels, where he has been, whom he has met in his
collision with America are more suggestive than his banal personal story.
In *Herzog*, the hero or rather the grandiose victim, is a gifted Jewish

[1037]

professor and polymath with a rather solemn pretension to sexual prow-ess. He seems a promising exemplar of the human being exposed to everything without the support of a settled society or fixed points of belief or value. This theme has offered the American novelist a chance to show his vitality for a long time now and the Jewish novelists have done strikingly well with it, for as a group they have acutely felt the sense of a missing law or covenant.

What has happened to Moses Herzog, this restless dabbler in the ideas of four centuries? He is having a breakdown because his second wife has destroyed his sexual confidence. He sees himself – and Mr Bellow sees him – prancing through one marriage and several liaisons with success and then marrying the all-time bitch; exhibitionist, hysteric, looter of his brain, spender of his money, far-seeing in matters of law and property, adul-terous, glamorously second-rate but adroit with the castrating scissors. To add insult, not to mention symbolism, to injury, the man she goes off with is a one-legged radio phoney. The ruthless and learned Moses, a walking university, begins to look like a Jumboburger who has been told he has lost his mustard. His earlier women may say 'Serve him right', but neither they nor the reader are likely to think his sufferings of much importance when, in a ham ending, he solemnly shacks up with a tremendously international woman called Ramona – of all names – who is apt to come swaggering out of the bathroom with her hand on her hip like a dagger-carrying flamenco dancer, and wearing black frilly panties with saucy ribbons. Twice during the novel she clinches the entire deal by serving the gourmet the only dish, apparently, she knows how to cook: Shrimp Arnaud, washed down with a bottle of Pouilly Fuissé. His earlier ladies must have thought they had paid a high price. Why didn't they think of applying this particular nostrum to the exposed soul of modern man? One knows that the fantasy life of university professors is often surprisingly gaudy, that the minds of experts on seventeenth-century thought or the *condition humaine* often drift off to Hollywood in the evenings. If this is Mr Bellow's ironical realism it certainly describes the feeble state of contemporary erotic fancy: but I detect no irony. Yet irony and self-irony are usually Mr Bellow's strength. What is more, the one or two love affairs in the book suggest that Moses is looking for easily punishable women without his or Mr Bellow's knowing it. In a moment of insight Moses wonders if his obsession with sex and love

[1038]

isn't really feminine. The reader is likely to go further and ask whether Moses is not hermaphrodite.

Structurally and in content, the story of *Herzog* is unsustaining. But what Herzog sees, the accidental detail of his experience, is very impressive. Here he grows. He really has got a mind and it is hurt. It is a tribute to Mr Bellow's reserves of talent that the novel survives and over-grows its own weaknesses. The muddle Moses is in, his sense of victimisation, are valuable. His paranoia is put, by Mr Bellow, to excellent use. If the theme is lost, we have the American scene. Moses is not really exposed, but his New York and Chicago are. Mr Bellow has something like a genius for place. There is not a descriptive insinuator of what, say, a city like New York is like from minute to minute who comes anywhere near him. Some novelists stage it, others document it; he is breathing in it. He knows how to show us not only Moses but other people, moving from street to street, from room to room in their own circle of uncomprehending solitude. Grasping this essential of life in a big city he sees the place not as a confronted whole, but continually askance. His senses are especially alive to *things* and he catches the sensation that the *things* have created the people or permeated them. This was the achievement of *The Victim*, and it is repeated in *Herzog*. A wanderer, he succeeds with minor characters, the many small figures in the crowd who suggest millions more. The dialogue of a Puerto Rican taxi driver, a Chicago cop, a low lawyer, a Jewish family, people brash, shady or saddened by the need of survival and whose ripeness comes out of the dirty brick that has trapped them, is really wonderful. It is far superior to Hemingway's stylised naturalism: Bellow's talk carries the speakers' life along with it. Their talk makes them move. They involve Moses with themselves and show him living, as all human beings do, in a web spun by others as well as by himself.

The habit of seeing things askance or out of the corner of his eye has given Mr Bellow an even more important quality: it keeps alive a perpetual sense of comedy and feeds his originality. There is sometimes talk of a taste for elegance in his book; spoken of like that, as a sort of craving or innate possession, it sounds very nearly vulgar. But there is an implicit elegance of mind in his writing: it sharpens the comic edge and dares him to spirited invention. As far as the comedy is concerned it has all the fatality of Jewish comedy, that special comedy of human undress and nakedness of which the Jewish writers are the world's masters. The other gift of Mr Bellow is his power of fantastic invention. He has hit upon a wonderful device for conveying Herzog's nervous breakdown. How to deal with his paranoia – if that is what it is – how to make it contribute not only to the character of Herzog but also to the purpose of the book? Mr Bellow decides that Herzog's dottiness shall consist in writing unfinished letters to all kinds of people living and dead, known and unknown – to his women friends, to editors, tutors, professors, philosophers, to his dead mother, to the President. It is the habit of the mad and Moses is not mad; but he at once is comically and seriously disturbed by every kind of question. Is romanticism 'spilt religion'? 'Do the visions of genius become the canned goods of intellectuals?' He writes to Eisenhower asking him 'to make it all clear in a few words'. He begins addressing M. de Jouvenal about the aims of political philosophy. The letters are really the scribbles of an exhausted mind. Travelling in the subway Moses evokes the dream figure of a Dr Shrödinger at Times Square:

> It has been suggested (and why not) that reluctance to cause pain is actually an extreme form, a delicious form of sensuality, and that we increase the luxuries of pain by the injection of a moral pathos. Thus working both sides of the street. Nevertheless, there are moral realities, Herzog assured the entire world as he held his strap in the speeding car.

Since Moses is a man of intellect these addresses are often interesting in themselves; but chiefly they convey the dejected larking of a mind that has been tried by two contradictory forces: the breakdown of the public world we live in and the mess of private life. In which world does he live? He is absurd yet he is fine; he is conceited yet he is raw. He is a great man yet he is torpedoed by a woman who 'wants to live in the delirious professions' – trades in which the main instrument is your opinion of yourself and the raw material is your reputation or standing. At times he lives like a sort of high-class Leopold Bloom, the eternal Jewish clown; at others he is a Teufelsdröckh; again he is the pushing son of the bewildered Polish-Jewish immigrant and failed boot-legger, guilty about his break with the past, nagged by his relations, his ambitions punctured.

As a character Moses is physically exact – we know his domestic habits – but mentally and emotionally amorphous. Any objection to this is cancelled by his range as an observer-victim. It is a triumph that he is not a bore and does not ask our sympathy.

The outsize heroes of Bellow's long novels are essentially moral types who have been forced by the American scene to behave like clowns. They are the classic American monologue in person, elephantine chunks of ego. In *Humboldt's Gift* we meet the clown as performing poet:

> A wonderful talker, a hectic non-stop monologist and improvisator, a champion detractor: to be loused up by Humboldt was really a kind of privilege. It was like being the subject of a two-nosed portrait by Picasso or an eviscerated chicken by Soutine . . .

One recognises the voice at once: it has the dash, the dandyism, the easy control of side-slipping metaphor and culture-freaking which gives pace to Saul Bellow's comedies. He is above all a performer, and in *Humboldt's Gift* he tells the story of performance in the person of Citrine, Humboldt's worshipper, disciple and betrayer.

As a youth Citrine had kneeled before the great manic depressive who had passed the peak of his reputation and was left, gin bottle in hand, cursing American materialism for what it does to genius and the life of the imagination. Humboldt was shrewd enough to see that the young Citrine was on the make, but was glad to have an ally among the young: everything went well, in a general alcoholic way, until Citrine did a frightful thing: he wrote a Broadway success which made him a sudden fortune. He had gone straight to the top of the tree. This was more than the crumbling, middle-aged poet could bear: he did not mind that Citrine had portrayed him as a knockabout Bohemian character; what he resented was the money going into Citrine's pocket. By this time Humboldt has become the classic American drunken genius and hospital case who shows up American philistinism. Getting out of Bellevue, Humboldt has a delightful time with the psychiatrists:

> Even the shrewd Humboldt knew what he was worth in professional New York. Endless conveyor belts of sickness or litigation poured clients and patients into these midtown offices like dreary Long Island potatoes. These dull spuds crushed psychoanalysts' hearts with boring character problems. Then suddenly Humboldt arrived. Oh Humboldt!

He was no potato! He was papaya, a citron, a passion fruit . . . And what a repertory he had, what changes of style and tempo. He was meek at first – shy. Then he became child-like, trusting, then he confided . . . He said he knew what husbands and wives said when they quarrelled . . . People said ho-hum and looked at the ceiling when you started this. Americans! With their stupid ideas about love and their domestic tragedies. How could you bear to listen to them after the worst of wars and the most sweeping of revolutions, the destruction, the death camps, the earth soaked in blood . . . The world looked into American faces and said: 'Don't tell me these cheerful, well-to-do people are suffering . . . Anyway I'm not here to discuss adolescent American love-myths' – this was how Humboldt talked. Still, I'd like you to listen to this.

And, suddenly blazing up, he howled out all the melodramas of American scandal and lust. The lawyers had heard it a thousand times – but they wanted to hear it again from a man of genius. He had become what the respectable professionals long for – their pornographer.

As admirers of Saul Bellow's work know, he is a master of elaborately patterned narrative that slips back or forward in time, circulating like Sterne, like Proust even. Sterne did this because he loved human inertia: Bellow is out for every tremor of the over-electrified American ego: he is expert in making characters disappear and then reappear swollen and with palms itching for more and more instant life. Humboldt will die in an elevator, but he will haunt the novel to the end like Moby Dick: even contemporary ghosts are jumbo size. The story moves to Chicago and there, on native ground, Citrine fills out. He is Cleverness and Success in person:

> It was my turn to be famous and to make money, to get heavy mail, to be recognised by influential people, to be dined at Sardi's and propositioned in padded booths by women who sprayed themselves with musk, to buy Sea Island cotton underpants and leather luggage.

His troubles with the tax man, with his ex-wife's lawyers who are stripping him of everything they can get hold of, seem to excite rather than depress him. His sexual life is avid and panicky: he hopes to outsmart middle age. He has bouts of hypochondria. These are enjoyable because he is very frank about his vanity: his touchiness, as middle age comes on, is the making of him as a comic figure. Gleam as he may with success, he cherishes what his wife calls his 'cemetery bit'; he has a bent for being a victim: ironical and sentimental, he also knows he is as hardheaded as that other famous twelve-year-old charmer, David Copperfield.

Once Humboldt is dead, Citrine is without a necessary enemy, and here Mr Bellow makes a very interesting find: Rinaldo Cantabile, a small crook with the naïve notion that he can 'make' the top Mafia. Unlike Humboldt, there is nothing myth-attracting in Cantabile. He is a loud, smart, nasty smell; he understands the first lesson of gangsterdom: to humiliate your victim; but he is an ass. We remember that Citrine is out to explore the American love-hate of Culture and Genius and indeed takes us round colleges and foundations: Cantabile is introduced to suggest that the Mafia might get a foot in here. Cantabile even thinks he can terrorise Citrine into seeing that Cantabile's wife gets a Ph.D. by fraud. My own view is that he does not make the grade as a compelling menace: he is without the extra dimension given to Bellow's strongly felt characters.

However, good comes of Cantabile, for he gets Mr Bellow back to Chicago. That city is the hero of *Humboldt's Gift*. No American novelist surpasses Bellow in the urban scene. He knows Chicago intimately from the smell of old blood in the hot nights to the rust on its fire escapes and the aluminium glint of the Lake. He knows the saunas:

> the wooden posts were slowly consumed by a wonderful decay that made them soft brown. They looked like beavers' fur in the golden vapour . . . The Division Street steam-bathers don't look like the trim proud people downtown . . . They are vast in antique form. They stand on thick pillow legs affected with a sort of creeping verdigris or blue-cheese mottling of the ankles . . . you feel these people are almost conscious of obsolescence, of a time of civilisation abandoned by nature and culture. So down in the super-heated sub cellars all these Slavonic cavemen and wood demons with hanging laps of fat and legs of stone and lichen boil themselves and splash ice-water on their heads by the bucket. Upstairs, on the television screen in the locker room, dudes and grinning broads make smart talk or leap up and down . . . Below, Franush, the attendant, makes steam by sloshing water on the white-hot boulders.

The secret of Mr Bellow's success is that he talks people into life and never stops pouring them in and out of his scenes. In this book the women are particularly well-drawn. Citrine's sexual vanity is a help here: once satisfied, he is taken aback by the discovery that women have other interests – the delightful delinquent Demmie is reformed, but in sleep at night her buried life comes out in groans and howls as she wrestles with the devil, and she wakes up next day fresh as a daisy to get down on her knees for redemption by scrubbing floors. Denise is the climbing wife of the climbing man. Vassar girl, seductive and respectable – what more does she want? The ear of top people at the White House; she wants to tell them what she has just read in *Newsweek*! And then Renata – a fate for more than one Bellow hero – Spanishy, flamenco-ish, vulgar, genial, sexually voracious, knows her Ritzes, and while willing to listen to high-class intellectual talk for a while, makes it clear that her price is very high and her fidelity at perpetual risk. These women are real, even likeable. Why? I think because in some clever way Mr Bellow shows them moving through their own peculiar American day, which is unlike the day of Citrine. One might press the point further and say that Bellow's characters are real to us because they are physical objects – Things. What other tenderness can a materialist society contain?

It says a great deal for Bellow's gift that although he can raise very boring subjects and drop names like an encyclopaedia or a digest, he has tact and irony. He is crisp. But two-thirds of the way through this novel he lands himself with a tangle of dramatic situations as complex as, say, the last act of a Restoration comedy. Here he lost me. Humboldt – it turns out – had repented of calling Citrine a Judas and traitor; had even left him a money-making film script – put into the hands of the right phoney director it should make a fortune. It does. Citrine does not take the money, indeed he behaves so well that it looks as though in saving his soul from corruption he may lose Renata. One curious act he does perform: he has Humboldt and his mother disinterred and re-buried in a decent cemetery. That's one thing you can do for artists.

A Quiet American

The title of Mary McCarthy's *Birds of America* makes clear that this is an ironical ornithology of certain American species on their contemporary feeding grounds in New England, Paris and Rome. It is really an *éducation sentimentale* of a young American bird-watcher, Peter Levi. He is literally that. From boyhood his lonely, seeking mind is haunted by the lusts of the Great Horned Owl, the ancient knowledge of the cormorant. His talented twice-divorced mother, who is 'perfect' in her divorce – no alimony – and who is 'too good to be true' is, for him, a rose-breasted grosbeak; the hard-drinking local Admiral with his horrible curries and his telescope has 'the hoarse voice of a sea bird'. Not for nothing is the cormorant dying out. Not for nothing at the end of the book has young Peter Levi, lying in a fever at a Paris hospital, been injured by an angry swan in the Jardin des Plantes. Not for nothing in his delirium does he see his favourite philosopher, Kant, crawling up the coverlet with the news that God is dead – everyone knows that – but that nature is dead too.

As a bird himself Peter belongs to the tame young American Candide group. Well-educated by elusive academic parents, intelligent, driven by conscience and maxims – Treat no one as a Means: Not to Care is a Sin – without vanity or conceit trying to make up a virginal mind, Peter has, for the moment, the neutered air of his type. He has a much better brain than Candide had but he suffers from the fact that his bustling elders have gobbled up the store of family passion and vitality for the moment. All their passions have left him with is Reason.

Rosamund, his mother, the grosbeak, has had two Jewish husbands, the second a German physicist. She has separated from them – one never hears what went on – and is seen early on scrupulously trying not to be married to her son. She will find a third partner and become a famous international harpsichord player. An old American story: the boy is left serious but happy in his loneliness, for personal relations have been disinfected. By the time he is nineteen the youth has an elderly view of his mother. 'Her faults pleased him' but

> . . . he had become cautious about her, not trusting her sweetness and unruffled temper. Besides her faults were no longer familiar. He recognised them in himself. Her zeal to please had set him a bad example. It made him placatory. Her scruples in him had become irresolution and an endless picking at himself like masturbation – a habit he had not completely outgrown and which seemed to him ignominious, even though she and the *babbo* [his father, the Italian Jew] had said it was natural in puberty; on that score he felt they had given him a wrong steer. Moreover her good qualities [she was generous to a fault] did not inspire imitation. Rather the contrary . . . He admired his father for having the strength of his defects.

Peter 'really loved his mother for having the faults of America', summed up in the word 'extravagance'. Puritanism was an extravagance, like Prohibition. Americans, the Babbo said, were logicians with no idea of limit.

So there at Rocky Port, Peter stands 'quarantined in history' in a fading New England where his mother is beautifully stirring up trouble because the old foods and recipes are giving place to awful packaged mixes. The old New England is being replaced by the commercially historic for the summer residents. Tradition itself has become a product.

> The word *tradition* was often heard at Rocky Port cocktail parties, usually on the lips of a woman with blue hair or a fat man in Polynesian shorts. The village was protecting its traditions, Peter was repeatedly told, as though Rocky Port were a sanctuary of banded birds, threatened with extirpation. He wondered what had been handed down to these people and what they were safeguarding – except money. There was nothing distinctive about Rocky Port's way of life, unless it was the frequency of gift shops for selling 'gourmet' foods, outsize pepper mills, 'amusing aprons' and chefs' costumes, bar equipment and frozen croissants 'just like in France' . . . Rocky Port was a museum.

All this is Miss McCarthy with the claws just showing and it is very funny but what will happen to the innocent Peter when he gets abroad? He is wide open to disaster and in a vulgar way we hope for it. He is rather

English public schoolboy, Huxley type, *circa* 1925. He will have small misadventures, like failing to realise his dream of crossing France on his motor bike and other comedies of youthful shyness, but Miss McCarthy is out for his education. The book is partly a *Bildungsroman* of the young man who meets the wrong people abroad and who will discover that the modern world is polluted by unsolved questions. Human beings themselves are becoming a kind of mass garbage.

We settle down to one of Miss McCarthy's sharp-eyed commentaries of travel. Peter asks questions about equality, education, politics, mass society, and so on, and since he is a touching, fidgeting and exceptional young man, he finds more and more to worry about. We are on his side all the time. When goaded he can burst out at an awful Thanksgiving dinner in Paris – one of the high satirical moments of the book – and he is a wicked listener. (Getting information embarrasses him because it feels like espionage: this is one of Miss McCarthy's excellent insights into a thoughtful young man's mind and indeed, throughout, in preserving its elderliness, she has really brought out the half-resentful charm of youth.)

Although it can be said that his scruples insure him against any danger of chancing his arm, Peter is an extremist in his own way. He has inherited the national obsession with plumbing from his mother and, in Paris hotels, has a comic and philosophical bout of compulsive toilet cleaning. He is certainly not earthy about 'night soil'; but he does wonder whether his cleaning up after others isn't undemocratic, i.e. being cleaner than others. If he is a prig he is an original. There is his care for a Fatsheara, a plant, a species of ivy which he tries to keep alive in his dark room. It begins to get leggy. The scene that follows might come out of that delightful Victorian conversation piece, *Sandford and Merton*:

> The leaves at the base were falling off one by one, and though he had been carefully irritating the stem at the base to produce a new sideward growth, it had been ignoring this prodding on his part and just getting taller, weed-like, till he finally had the idea of taking it for walks, once or twice a week, depending on the weather . . . He thought he was beginning to note signs of gratitude in the invalid for the trouble he was taking . . . there was a detectable return of chlorophyll, like a green flush to the cheeks of the shut-ins. He spoke to it persuasively –

sometimes out loud – urging it to grow. So far, he had resisted giving it a shot of fertiliser, because a mildewed American manual he had acquired on the *quais* – How to Care For Your House Plants – cautioned against giving fertiliser except to 'healthy subjects'. That would be like giving a gourmet dinner to a starving person – the old parable of the talents.

This plant-walking saves him when he runs into a student riot. The thing has grown tall and guarantees his innocence to the bored *flics*. Naturally he has already got in touch with French bird-watchers, most respectably, through the Embassy. How odd that regard for embassies strikes a European! Practical, of course.

But the American bird abroad tends to the flaunting species of the turkey. Peter soon runs into it gobbling in its European farmyard. He goes to an awful Thanksgiving dinner given, without the art that conceals art, by a general who would like to swap the war in Vietnam for the real thing. Here the narrative breaks into broad farce. The general's son – a problem boy who has failed college, can't get a job: he simply collects parking tickets – has volunteered for Vietnam. His mother drinks his health:

'It was Benjy's own decision. "I've got to go, Mom," he said. Leonard wanted us to refuse our consent though he's only Benjy's stepfather. "Let him wait till he's drafted," Leonard said. But I couldn't say "No" to Benjy . . . I guess I've spoiled him: he's my only child.' Her face, which might have been pretty when she was young, crinkled and puckered like a wide seersucker bedspread.

Benjy is guzzling pie and ice cream: his 'wine-intake had been monitored by his mother'.

It came as a surprise to Peter that contrary to what you would expect in such a milieu, Benjy's parents were far from being proud of the patriot they had fledged. Even if he came back covered with medals he would not get the fatted calf. To hear his mother tell it, she spent most of her time on her knees praying for peace. 'Though Benjy doesn't like me to do it. He hates it if I go into some little church and light a candle.' 'Yeah, I want to get some of those gorillas fast'. '*Guerrillas*, please, Benjy.' She gave the 'l's' a Spanish pronunciation. 'He used to think they were real gorillas,' she explained with a little gurgle of a laugh. 'He got it from listening to the radio.'

In the same scene there is a vegetarian girl, a heretic at the national feast; Peter rather falls for her and 'has a new worry: as an animal lover how can he justify eating meat?' We also get a glimpse of private life in NATO. Peter's neighbour at the dinner is a leathery lady whose husband has gone off with a German.

'He wants a divorce, but if I give him a divorce, they'll take away my PX card and my Q.C. privileges. You can smile, Peter, but to me it's a tragedy . . . Civilians don't dig what it means to us. Chuck and Letitia can entertain lavishly because, unlike you and me, they don't buy a thing on the French market. Not even a stick of celery.'

Ordinarily Peter would have felt sorry for this coarse-grained Donna Elvira. Maybe she loved the guy and was ashamed to mention that: it was odd what people were ashamed of, sometimes the best part of themselves.

The Sorbonne, so far as Peter's fellow Americans are concerned, is a shambles. The University cynically takes the fees, knowing the students will do nothing, but will kid themselves that they are absorbing something or other unconsciously. Peter can't make up his mind about this. In Rome, which he enjoys more than Paris, he meets a real stinker in the mean figure of Mr Small. Mr Small hangs about the galleries and cafés, insinuating himself among the young and getting information about student life and needs. At the right point, he takes down what they say on tape.

He quickly decides Peter is so abnormal that he needs a psychiatrist, but Peter is now in good condition for an argument. He discovers Mr Small is doing research for a foundation which has a tie-up with hotels, travel agencies, advertisers and airlines. The motive? To follow and quietly direct the migration routes of these young birds and to capture and exploit the student traffic. Mass student transport under the direction of mass society, the old conference trick!

The dreadful question of tourism arises. The Sistine Chapel is full of garbage – human garbage. An art lover cannot see the pictures. People are polluting the planet, because it pays to pollute it. Peter thinks enviously of Milton who was said to have travelled with a hermit. Doesn't Mr Small occasionally get scared, asks Peter, the protector of the human bird sanctuary. Mr Small replies:

'Scared? I can't think of a more challenging time to be alive for an American. All the options are open. No society in history before our own has given so-called mass man such opportunities for self-realis-ation.' 'To me everything is closing in,' Peter argued. 'If I were a Russian or a Pole at least I might have the illusion that things would be better if there was a revolution. Or even gradual evolution. But here evolution just means more of the same . . .'

Peter does adroitly prevent Mr Small from putting down his lunch to Mr Small's expense account. The scrupulous have to rely on a small victory here and there.

One is waiting for Peter to commit at least one rash act. Love has escaped him. While he wavered, his vegetarian girl has gone off with a Frenchman and one half-expects the boy to rescue a fallen woman. He does – but she is no more than a reeking female *clochard* whom he allows to spend a night on the floor of his room. She rewards his charity by stealing his door knob, a clever move in a small-minded way. (Strange that it should puzzle him.)

So we leave this quiet American to be rescued by his immensely successful mother and the dream figure of Kant. He points out to her irritably that he was not *bitten* by a swan; swans strike, they do not bite. (Not, I believe, true; I was bitten by one when I was eight.) He will return home from studying the American bird abroad to face college and the Army.

Miss McCarthy has really rediscovered an old form of travel commen-tary in giving Peter her own critical detachment and knowledge; but it doesn't matter that Peter is too precocious and, like his mother, too good to be true. He is a relief after the showy, self-dramatising confessionals and sexual loud-mouths. A late developer, he enjoys and profits by the virginity that his learned and irresponsible, rational parents have unwit-tingly loaded him with. If he is a tame bird, he is very touching in his dignity. He is too absorbed by what he sees to be self-pitying. Goodness knows how he has missed the morbidity of youth – perhaps that is a loss for him and even a mistake on Miss McCarthy's part, but one is glad to be spared it. He is just the shy young pedant to keep a topical allegory about intellectual pollution from being a bore. In a novel he would be thin, as he is; but in the Euro-American laboratory he is a ready piece of Puritan litmus.

Satan Comes to Georgia

On the whole, English writers were slow starters in the art of the short story. Until Stevenson, Kipling and then D. H. Lawrence appeared, our taste was for the ruminative and disquisitional; we preferred to graze on the large acreage of the novel and even tales by Dickens or Thackeray or Mrs Gaskell strike us as being unused chapters of longer works. Free of our self-satisfactions in the nineteenth century, American writers turned earlier to a briefer art which learned from transience, sometimes raw and journalistic but essentially poetic in the sense of being an instant response to the exposed human being. Where we were living in the most heavily wind-and-water-proofed society in the world, the American stood at the empty street corner on his own in a world which, compared with ours, was anarchic; and it was the opinion of Frank O'Connor, the Irish master, that anarchic societies are the most propitious for an art so fundamentally drawn to startling dramatic insights and the inner riot that may possess the lonely man or woman at some unwary moment in the hours of their day.

All the characters in the very powerful stories of Flannery O'Connor – *Everything That Rises Must Converge* – are exposed: that is to say they are plain human beings in whose fractured lives the writer has discovered an uncouth relationship with the lasting myths and the violent passions of human life. The people are rooted in their scene, but as weeds are rooted. It would be fashionable to call her stories Gothic: they certainly have the curious inner strain of fable – replacing the social interest which is a distinguishing quality of the American novel. (She herself was an invalid most of her life and died in her native Georgia in 1964 at the age of 38.) The Southern writers have sometimes tended to pure freakishness or have concentrated on the eccentricities of a decaying social life: but this rotting and tragic order has thrown up strong, if theatrical, themes. Flannery O'Connor was born too late to be affected by the romantic and nostalgic legend of the tragic South: the grotesque for its own sake means nothing to her. It is a norm. In the story called *Parker's Back*, an ignorant truck-driver has indulged a life-long mania for getting tattooed and in a desperate attempt to reawaken the interest of his pious wife who had once been captivated, as other women had been, by this walking art gallery, he has one final huge tattoo done on his naked back which up till then had been a blank wall. He pays for the most expensive tattoo there is: a Byzantine Christ. She throws him out because he has revealed himself as an idolater. The point of this story is not that it is bizarre: the point is that, perhaps because of the confused symbols that haunt the minds of the Bible Belt people, an inarticulate man can wish to convey to her that, as a graven image, he is indifferent to God and the Day of Judgment. He has some claim to an inner life of his own. He wishes to show that he is someone. He has burst the limits imposed on him. The act is an agonised primitive appeal. It is also a childish act of defiance and hatred.

The passions are just beneath the stagnant surface in Flannery O'Connor's stories. She was an old Catholic, not a convert, in the South of the poor white of the Bible Belt and this gave her a critical skirmishing power. But the symbolism of religion, rather than the acrimonies of sectarian dispute, fed her violent imagination – the violence is itself oddly early Protestant – as if she had seen embers of the burning Bible-fed imagery in the minds of her own characters. The symbols are always ominous: at sunset a wood may be idyllic, but also look blood-sodden. They usually precede an act of violence which will introduce the character at the end of the story 'into the world of guilt and sorrow'. This is her ground as a fabulist or moralist. We are left with an illusion shattered, with the chilly task of facing our hatreds. In one story, a priest comes to visit an unbeliever who is fanatically keen to die in order to punish his mother for having emasculated him. The man is cured by the local doctor whom he despises. We leave him on his deathbed but not dying:

> He saw that for the rest of his days, frail, racked, but enduring, he would live in the face of a purifying terror. A feeble cry, a last impossible protest escaped him. But the Holy Ghost, emblazoned in ice instead of fire, continued implacably to descend.

The essence of Flannery O'Connor's vision is that she sees terror as a purification – unwanted, of course: it is never the sado-masochist's intended indulgence. The moment of purification may actually destroy; it will certainly show someone changed.

Symbolism has been fatal to many writers: it offers a quick return of unearned meaning. I am not convinced by the theatrical entrance of the Holy Ghost in the above quotation. But elsewhere, whenever one detects a symbol, one is impressed by Flannery O'Connor's use of it: it is concrete and native to the text. Take the title story of the book: a middle-aged widow, dressed up in an awful new hat, is seen going with her son to a slimming class in order to get her high blood pressure down. She is a 'Southern lady' in reduced circumstances and now, bitterly but helplessly opposed to Negro integration, she sticks to her dignity. 'If you know who you are, you can go anywhere . . . I can be gracious to anybody. I know who I am.' This is true, in a way, but it is also a cliché, as her son tells her while they travel on the integrated local bus. Here a disturbing figure appears: a Negro woman with her child.

> She had on a hideous hat. A purple flap came down on one side of it and stood up on the other; the rest of it was green like a cushion with the stuffing out.

The hat is exactly a replica of the white woman's hat. To her son this is comical; it ought to teach his silly mother a lesson in racialism. The Negro woman's child sees the joke too. The white woman becomes gracious to the child and prepares to do a terrible, gracious thing: to give the little child a bright new penny. When they all get off the bus she does this. The huge Negro woman, seeming 'to explode like a piece of machinery that had been given one ounce of pressure too much', knocks the white woman down. Her son, who has hated his mother for years, sees a reality kill his mother and his own guilt.

Many of the stories are variations on the theme of the widowed mother who has emasculated her son; or the widower who is tragically unaware of what he is doing to his child. In one instance, a widower destroys his grandchild. These stories are not arguments; they are not case-histories or indignation meetings. They are selected for the claustrophobic violence which will purify but destroy. The characters are engaged in a struggle for personal power which they usually misunderstand. A mature and sensible young historian living with his mother is maddened by her naïve and reckless do-gooding behaviour. She rescues an amoral girl who calls herself a 'nimpermaniac' and has her to stay. The girl instantly makes a set at the historian who shows her that he hates her. There is a revolver in the house. Who will be killed? A probation officer – a widower – in another rescue story, takes into his house a young boy crook who introduces his son to fatal Bible Belt fantasies about Heaven and Hell – again, who will be killed? This story, particularly, is an attack on practical ethics as a substitute for religion: in another Art is shown to be inadequate as a substitute.

If these stories are anti-humanist propaganda one does not notice it until afterwards. Like all Gothic writers, Flannery O'Connor has a deep sense of the Devil or rather of the multiplicity of devils, though not in any conventional religious sense. To the poor-white Gospellers, Satan has become Literature. For her the devils are forces which appear in living shape: the stray bull which kills the old farming widow whose sons let her down; the criminal child who is proud of being an irredeemable destroyer because he has been called a child of Satan, and looks forward, eagerly – it is his right – to an eternity in the flames of hell which he takes to be literal fire; the delinquent girl who has been taught by psychiatrists to regard her vice as an illness sees this as an emancipating distinction. The author is not playing the easy game of paradox which is commonly a tiresome element in the novels of Catholic converts: for her, the role of the diabolic is to destroy pride in a misconceived virtue.

A short story ought to be faultless without being mechanical. The wrong word, a misplaced paragraph, an inadequate phrase or a convenient explanation, start fatal leaks in this kind of writing which is formally very close to poetry. That closeness must be totally sustained. There are no faults of craftsmanship in Flannery O'Connor's stories. She writes a plain style: she has a remarkable ear for the talk of the poor whites, for the received ideas of the educated; and she creates emotion and the essence of people by vivid images. We see all the threatening sullen life of a poor farmer in this sentence: 'His plate was full but his fists sat motionless like two dark quartz stones on either side of it.' Since a short story must plant its situation – and promise another – in its opening lines, the passage at the beginning of *The Comforts of Home* is a model:

Thomas withdrew to the side of the window and with his head between the wall and the curtain he looked down on the driveway where the car had stopped. His mother and the little slut were getting out of it. His mother emerged slowly, stolid and awkward, and then the little slut's slightly bowed legs slid out, the dress pulled above the knees. With a shriek of laughter she ran to meet the dog who bounded, overjoyed, shaking with pleasure, to welcome her. Rage gathered throughout Thomas's large frame with a silent ominous intensity, like a mob assembling.

Thomas, an educated man, will find in fact that he has a mob buried in his unconscious. Flannery O'Connor is at pains to make us know intimately the lives of these poor white and struggling small-town people. They are there as they live, not in the interest of their ignorant normality, but in the interest of their exposure to forces in themselves that they do not yet understand. Satan, they will discover, is not just a word. He has legs – and those legs are their own.

The Great Snail

It is obvious from the three opening volumes that the new complete eleven-volume edition of Pepys's Diary is an excellent effort of Anglo-American scholarship. The omissions in earlier editions, whether from prudery, accident or fear of tedium, have been put back. The great difficulties of transcribing Pepys's shorthand with its curious half-words 'in clear' have been mastered as far as they can be; the innumerable notes are irresistible, and Robert Latham's introduction of 120 pages is by far the most searching and graceful essay available on the Diary in relation to Pepys himself and to history. It is particularly valuable on Pepys's methods. In short full justice is done to the Great Snail of English diarising.

The only serious rival to Pepys is Boswell, but Boswell is a snail without a shell. He trails through life unhoused and exclamatory, whereas Pepys is housed and *sotto voce*. Boswell is confessional before anything else, whereas, though he too tells all, Pepys is not; he records for the sensual pleasure of record. Boswell adores his damned soul to the point of tears and is in shameless, ramshackle pursuit of father-figures who will offer salvation. Unlike Pepys, he has above all a conceit of his own peculiar genius. Pepys has no notion of genius. Where Pepys is an eager careerist, struck by the wonder of it, Boswell has no career; he has only a carousel, and it is odd that the careerist has a more genuine sense of pleasure than the Calvinist libertine. Although both diarists are lapsed Puritans and owe something to the Puritan tradition of the diary as a training of conscience, Pepys writes without appealing to some private higher hope. He is as obsessional as Boswell, but to whom is the secretive Admiralty official talking as his shorthand flicks across the page? To no person, not even to himself, even when he adds a remorseful groan or two, after running his hand up the skirt of a servant girl or the wife of an officer who has come to bribe him for a job for her husband. Even the groan is record rather than adjuration. He is simply amazed that life exists in days, hours and minutes.

He is transfixed by wonder at the quotidian of his bodily and working existence, as part of history. He is a man (as Arthur Bryant has said in his well-known Life, which must be read as a companion to the Diary) to whom the most common things were wonderful:

> At night, writing in my Study, a mouse ran over my table, which I shut up fast under my shelfes upon my table till tomorrow. And so home and to bed.

No, he is not addressing a person. He is not even addressing God. It may be that he is addressing history, for he left the Diary to his college at Cambridge: yet the bequest may be due to his passion for preserving papers, for property, an act of vanity in administrative tidiness. No longing for immortality there. If he addressed anything, the future Fellow of the Royal Society was blamelessly addressing the new Curiosity, science itself. It was fashionable to be a Baconian, a virtuoso, to potter on the new outskirts of invention, to catalogue as the Victorian botanists did two centuries later; and this new itch for documentation does strongly influence the diarist as it also influences Defoe. The random private trait comes to life when it is a response to a consciousness of one's times.

Pepys was astutely aware that he was the success thrown up by a revolution which had got rid of its leaders and its dogma and now offered the technologist a fortune: in this he is very modern. The son of a tailor – outside the reactionary Guilds and therefore in the black market – to be shrewd and efficient enough to rise and become the friend of the King! To have erotic dreams about Lady Castlemayne, to become Head of the Navy – and rich! To be the all-powerful valet! Pepys has the essential and topical character of the hero of a picaresque novel like *Gil Blas*. His is the secrecy of the indispensable.

Yet as a careerist and an importance the little man who lets his hair go long is not a bore; he is large and various. His 'morning draught' at the tavern, his drunken evenings, his sing-songs, his playing of the lute, his dancing, his love of pretty well all women, his love of show, the theatre, silver plate; his martinet behaviour with his wife who leaves her clothes on the floor, but whom he adores – a myriad small interests keep him spry. One sees him boring holes into his office wall so that he can spy on his clerks, worried by playing the lute on Sundays, hitting his wife by accident when he wakes up in the morning, boxing his manservant's ears, being forced to leave the Abbey at the high moment of the Coronation because he is bursting to pee. He never misses a public occasion: there is an unmoved account of the execution of Sir Harry Vane. He stayed in London for the plague. His early life in the Admiralty has a low social note which the rising man begins to disapprove – how long a tradition lower-middle-class comedy has!

> In the morning to my office, where after I had drunk my morning draught at Will's with Ethell and Mr Stevens, I went and told part of the excise money till 12 o'clock. And then called on my wife and took her to Mr Pierces, she in the way being exceedingly troubled with a pair of new pattens, and I vexed to go too slow, it being late. There when we came, we found Mrs Carrick very fine and one Mr Lucy, who called one another husband and wife; and after dinner a great deal of mad stir; there was pulling off Mrs Bride's and Mr Bridegroom's ribbons, with a great deal of fooling among them that I and my wife did not like; Mr Lucy and several other gentlemen coming in after dinner, swearing and singing as if they were mad; only he singing very handsomely.

Two years later, when he has cut down his oysters and his wine-drinking, moved into a grander house and doubled his time at the office, there is a memorable Sunday, beginning with church, sermon and an excellent anthem and symphony, the organ supported by wind instruments, until:

> Thence to My Lord's, where nobody at home but a woman that let me in, and Sarah above, whither I went up to her and played and talked with her and, God forgive me, did feel her; which I am much ashamed of, but I did not more, though I had so much a mind to it that I spent in my breeches. After I had talked an hour or two with her, I went and gave Mr Hunt a short visit, he being at home alone. And thence walked home-ward; and meeting Mr Pierce the Chyrurgeon, he took me into Somerset House and there carried me into the Queene-Mother's presence-chamber, where she was with our Queene sitting on her left hand . . . here I also saw Madame Castlemayne and, which pleased me most, Mr Crofts the King's bastard, a most pretty sparke of about 15 years old.

Then the King, the Duke and Duchess came in, 'such a sight as I could never almost have happened to see with so much ease and leisure'. The only thing that worried him on the way home was that he had promised his wife to be there before she got back. Yet he had not done this 'industriously' but by chance. There we have the Puritan, a bit of a cautious rake, a bit of a voyeur, a bit of a romantic snob; but, as he says, his great fault (which he will try and amend) is that he can never say 'No' to anyone. Enormous industry – starting work at four or five in the morning – and temptation are his fate: the Puritan syndrome.

The most absorbing historical part of these three early volumes concerns Pepys's modest, canny but courageous part in the crisis of getting Charles II over, seeing him crowned, and the religious manoeuvres as the Cromwellian revolution was liquidated. Such things in the Diary have been enormously important to historians and there is no more intimate guide to London life at the time. The city streets, taverns, theatres, courts, docks, the business of fitting out ships and paying for it, and political gossip live minutely in the pages. We simply follow in hundreds of journeys down streets or by water to Greenwich, because he is so busy. Why is he so alive, what has given this fat, slightly pompous and fussy little man an edge to his record? Obviously he worked at his desk longer than anyone else in the city, and because of that huge labour we know him. But what made him more than a recorder, and such a recorder? Vitality and curiosity, of course. Three other things are suggestive. First, he had nearly died of the stone when he was very young and he never stopped regarding himself as a miracle because he survived. Maybe – to judge by the case of Montaigne, which perhaps one should not do – the disease has something of the phenomenal in it that encourages a deep physical curiosity. Grave early danger stimulates the appetite for pleasure. Every minute is a gift: catching sight of Lady Castlemayne, 'I glutted myself with looking at her.' Then he was a linguist, which certainly diversifies personality and even offers disguises. The Puritan intensifies his secrecy and his pleasure in using dog-French, Spanish and Dutch in his erotic passages:

nuper ponendo mes mains in su des choses de son breast mais il faut que je leave it lest it bring me alcun major inconvenience.

Finally, in his indiscriminate dabbling in science there is not only his shorthand – the miraculous means of catching life as fast as it flows – but his microscope, which makes life stand still so that it can become as large as life is. Pepys's mind was genial because it was also a microscope. By magnifying, the glass defeated time, it gave an overpowering vividness to memory. Take the example of the ship auction:

> Where pleasant to see how backward men are at first to bid; and yet when the candle is going out, how they bawl and dispute afterwards who bid the most first.
>
> And here I observed one man cunninger than the rest, that was sure to bid the last man and to carry it; and enquiring the reason, he told me that just as the flame goes out the smoke descends, which is a thing I never observed before and by that he doth know the instant when to bid last – which is very pretty.

At night, under his own dying candle, Pepys systematically 'bid last'.

Mr Latham has gone deeply into Pepys's shorthand system and into his methods. His normal prose was the ornate style of the organisation man of the period; in the Diary, as if sharing in the Royal Society's new programme for the prose of the new age, he used the plain, rapid, talking language. It catches the instant, saves time and catches time. But were there earlier notes and drafts? There is evidence that there were; that he wrote up the Diary from them days later. (It is known that his famous account of the Fire, which will appear in the later volumes, was done months after the event.) In other words – and this was to be true to Boswell also – the immediacy is in part the effect of revision. Good diaries are good because they are not left in a flabby state of nature, but have been worked on; they are not verbatim or documentary, they are works of art. And to become this they must be obsessional. This was tragically true for Pepys. After eight years he was threatened with blindness. He had to give up the Diary. True he could dictate, but how much he would have to leave out! The only thing was to get the clerk to leave a wide margin in which Pepys could add notes of his own, notes not suited to delicate ears.

'And so', he ends,

> I betake myself to the course which is almost as much as to see myself go into my grave; for which all the discomforts that will accompany my being blind, the good God prepare me.

The human microscope had given up. The snail retired to his official shell.

The Infantilism of Genius

T hose who have read Dr A. L. Rowse's little masterpiece of auto-biography *A Cornish Childhood* will guess why that romantic and petulant historian had for over forty years hankered after writing a biographical portrait of Jonathan Swift. An outsider in the political acrimonies of the nineteen-thirties, an early 'Leftist' who has turned against 'Leftist liberal cant', Dr Rowse, in his new book, *Jonathan Swift*, portrays Swift as a fellow-recalcitrant whose ammunition is useful to his biographer in a one-man war against old appeasers and new fanatics: ex-Whig, high Tory, man of crusty common sense – what could be closer to our combative Cornishman? It is indeed likely that Swift, who hated mankind as a generality but said he loved the individual Jack, William, and Tom, would have found our world third-rate and obscene beyond expression. It is con-ceivable that Swift would have raged against the appeasement of Hitler, the humbug of Baldwin's England, the errors of the American 'computerwar' in Vietnam, the belief in the educability of everyone, the political fancies of Laputa-like philosophers such as Bertrand Russell, and (of all petty things) even the Value Added Tax, which torments the British of today. (Probably the author of the *Drapier's Letters* would have hated that most.) But when Dr Rowse drags such matters into what is elsewhere a very lucid and moving study of the terrifying Dean of St Patrick's, he reduces him to the level of an irritable writer of letters to *The Times*. To take Swift out of his century is to cloud him and distract us from the incessant pride, passion, and imagination of our supreme satirist and his truly tragic person.

Although Swift struck nearly everyone – especially women – as the most dazzling, robust, and naturally open man, and one irresistible in his rudeness, he was deeply secretive and evasive. His practice of anonymity in his plain, ferocious writing was not simply a caution before the threats of imprisonment for libel; it was meant to be a momentous underground game. His exhaustive biographers have found it impossible to make their minds up about the myths and gossip that surround his life – and not only because so much of it comes from Dublin, the most malicious city in Europe. One half hoped that Dr Rowse would start one of his well-known hares, but he does not: he ignores, for example, wild stories like the suggestion that Swift was Sir William Temple's bastard and the half brother of Stella (Esther Johnson) and confines himself to what the best scholars have suggested, sensibly and kindly weighing the possible against the probable. He bows to Harold Williams and follows Middleton Murry's much fuller and very feeling *Life*, although, unlike Murry, he regards Vanessa (Esther Vanhomrigh) as a devouring female egotist and an impossible plague. As he rather coarsely puts it, Vanessa was an instance of the unspeakable in pursuit of the uneatable. Whatever else may be said against the passionate Vanessa, she was not a fox-hunting girl.

It is agreed that Swift's humiliating failure as a very young man to persuade Jane Waring (Varina) to marry him set him violently against marriage for good, and that the words of his insulting farewell to her hardly suggest that he was impotent. If we are unlikely to know whether the tale of the secret marriage to Stella is true, it does seem very possible. Stella knew Vanessa was in pursuit; she could guess Swift had had his head turned. Stella's jealousy – and a very rational and Swift-like poem of hers expresses the feeling with extraordinary and painful detachment – may have made her insist upon a belated marriage in order to insure her position; Swift may very well have agreed to it as a secret trump card to play against Vanessa. We shall never be sure about Scott's tale that Vanessa found out and wrote to Stella, and that in a rage Swift rode out to confront Vanessa with the letter, threw it in her face, and never saw or wrote to her again. The scene is in character – supposing Swift to be a personage in one of Scott's novels. Dr Rowse makes much of the difference in social class between Stella and Vanessa. Once educated by Swift, Stella was well fitted to please in the retired life of clerical society in Ireland. But the gifted Vanessa belonged to fashionable society, which Swift adored, and in training her he made her much more intelligent than the usual run of fashionable women. The core of the comedy, which became a tragedy, is clear in Swift's private poem 'Cadenus and Vanessa', which she allowed to circulate after her death, as a vengeance. The insulting Dean was a practical feminist who in curing his two pupils of female silliness found that his Galateas had perfected their minds but retained their natures. Reason was not all. Stella and Vanessa were rival works of art who came only too powerfully to life when they were fighting for possession of him. His gift for intrigue and self-protection had failed him. What is truly horrible is that after their relatively early deaths, and for reasons of guilt, shame and probably a sexual repression we can only guess at, he became obsessed by the dreadful image of the female Yahoo and the scatological nightmares. Even here we must not be too sweeping. We know that the commonest sight of eighteenth-century streets was excrement; that society stank, and even elegant society was blunt in language; and that one or two men with a skin too few – Smollett, for example – may have revelled in dirt but also, like the scrupulous Dean, preached against it.

If Swift seemed a dull, cold, calculating man – as the bland and censorious Victorians thought – and something of a monster, he was pitiable. If he did not love, he was tender and craved tenderness and cleverness in women. As Dr Rowse says, everything in his life put him apart from other men. His father's death before he was born was surely one decisive factor. That he was kidnapped as a baby in Ireland and taken to England by his nurse, with whom he lived for three years, is strange. That his mother is shadowy and that he was sent away to school at Kilkenny – the best Ireland offered at that time – are pointers to an absolute loneliness. His uncle and cousins could claim connections, but only as poor and distant relations. By the time he was taken in by Sir William Temple at Moor Park, in England, the young egotist was formed. Temple became the father figure to an uncouth boy who had stood on his own in the rough Anglo-Irish world – and what a rough lot the Cromwellian colonists must have been, freed as they were from their native English restraints, their liberty based on stolen land! What heady luck for a clever youth to go to a great English house like Moor Park and find a protector in one of the most cultivated and eminent men in English public life! It was a leap from barbarism to the graces of civilisation. What a reinforcement for a poor boy's will to power and ambition! There was a price, of course, and one slowly learned: the great and powerful are wayward and lazy, especially when a difficult young man becomes importunate. Swift wanted spectacular advancement at once; with his eyes on the main chance he was disappointed by queen, kings, lords and archbishops throughout his life.

The touching thing is that Moor Park became a lasting dream of the good life. When, in a simple, practical way, he persuaded Stella and her companion, Miss Dingley – poor fellow relations – to settle in Dublin after Temple's death he was carrying an imaginary Moor Park in his head.

It strikes one that Swift is an instance of the infantilism of genius: he was a self-regarding child-egotist all his life. The will to instant power may not succeed, but intellectually it is devastating. In a rather schematic inquiry written in the Thirties Mario M. Rossi and Joseph M. Hone have the following words about Swift's egotism which exactly convey his attitude to the great and to Stella and Vanessa:

> From Swift's assertion that he loathed humanity and yet loved Jack, William and Tom we are not to suppose that he loved them for what they were, nor indeed that he had even *knowledge* of them as they were. He loved them in so far as they surrendered to his whim, he loved them for being a sort of extension of himself, other bodies of his overlapping self. He disliked humanity because it was a number of extraneous selves; the egotist cannot identify himself with a mass. He identifies himself with individuals in so far as they are his servants.

In its drastic fashion this seems to me true; one has only to look at Swift's purely practical and self-protective attitude to Stella and Vanessa when emotionally they were in extremes, and indeed when they were dying. The two women loved him in their differing ways and were grateful to him. He was not cold, but – like a child – he was incapable of facing or under-standing what *they* felt. And, like a child, he was an expert politician in playing where adults do not play. For example, the baby talk in the *Journal to Stella* so skilfully, to all appearance, addressed to Stella and Miss Dingley for respectability's ingenious sake, is not a lover's baby talk but a brilliant raillery which imitates Stella's lisping habit of speech with everyone when she was a backward child at Moor Park. It is a clever, affectionate, but daring mockery of her childhood, designed to keep her *in statu pupillari*. The baby talk – which he used with no other woman – is, so to say, a juvenile exercise in the art of philandering, at which he was notoriously expert.

Swift's hardness to Stella and Vanessa has often been described as mean, calculating and, at heart, frightened; but, as Dr Rowse can easily show, in Swift's relationship with everyone an exorbitant, ingrained pride – the

[1065]

pride of the solitary who will not give himself – is always there. As an unknown cleric, he forced the great Harley to walk halfway to meet him – not that Harley would notice: he would be either well-mannered or merely drunk in an aristocratic way. Such a pride looks almost insane; it was in fact the source of Swift's genius as a satirist. He did not simply hate; he drew upon all the minutiae that buried hatred makes vivid and effective. It is clear, plain, merry obloquy, as unremitting and unanswerable as a day's rain. What Dr Rowse does not go into – and a biography that makes us feel sympathy for a maimed character may not require this literary comment – is the curious influence of that new fashionable and scientific toy, the magnifying glass, on Swift's imagination. Perhaps that simple instrument played as great a part as pride when he came to assuage his passions in *Gulliver's Travels*. How monstrous or tiny it could make his disgusts or his fears, even his own ego. How right that the elderly child should have written a child's book.

I must say that for the first time in my reading, Dr Rowse has made the factional quarrelling of Queen Anne's London clear and even gripping. We are made to see it and feel it and want to be in it, for the moment, as Swift himself so avidly did. After all, he was trying to stop the slaughter of Marlborough's war. And Dr Rowse is even better on Swift's 'conversion' (if that is the word for it) to Ireland. Hated in Ireland, slandered in Ireland, he became eventually the spokesman for Irish (colonial) liberty – although he despised the Irish for their refusal to help themselves. In one way, little Dublin was just the place for the egotist so passionately and, above all, so pedantically concerned with his own liberty. The city was and is a place where one can exist as an irredeemable personality, giving and receiving blows and becoming notable as a protest at having been born – that splendid Irish grudge. Though Swift was elsewhere regarded as avaricious and as counting every penny, his continual and thoughtful charities in Dublin to those whose needs were real or bizarre made him at one with that charitably uncharitable city, a testy and at last a senile saint.

When one looks back on him again what strikes one is that he recorded the multitude of his daily acts pretty well as closely as Pepys did. He belongs to that very small number of famous people whose daily life is visible to us from hour to hour. That may be, as Rossi and Hone have said, because egotists of Swift's kind have instant passions but no lasting aim, grow tired when there is no one about and turn to telling us even about such silly things as how they get up in the morning.

So I'll rise, and bid you good morrow, my ladies both, good morrow. Come stand away, let me rise: Patrick, take away the candle. Is there a good fire? So – up adazy.

It all comes as sweetly to him as handling a prime minister or terrorising a duke. The terrible child will play his private games for ever, until playing games drives him out of his mind.

Ruffian Dick

===

The Burtons? Those people with the two delinquent boys who looked
like gypsies and who could be seen annoying the inhabitants of Galway,
Boulogne, Tours, Pisa and Pau in the 1830s. They were the Galway
Blazers abroad. There was father, the Colonel, the soul of honour, pacing
up and down. He had wrecked his career by refusing to give evidence
against Caroline, the wife of George IV. In a family crisis, the Colonel
breaks up camp and moves on. The mother? Docile. The boys? Duellists,
beaters-up of tutors and foreign maids, known to the brothels and the
police; fiends, liable to hit out at their elders if called arch-fiends. They
don't like the word 'arch'. (However, later on in life, one of them does get
such a knock on the head that he is dead silent for forty years. One is sorry
and hopes he was not a genius like his brother Richard.) The West of
Ireland, with a lot of eighteenth-century hell-fire still left in it, perhaps also
some delayed Rousseauism, like Major Edgeworth's, and the colonial
precocity, produces in Richard Burton a noble savage who has brains.

Very early on Richard Burton was uttering Latin in the Italian style to
annoy the English; very early he could speak Béarnais, French and Italian,
a little later, German. All very well. But one day the Colonel rushes home
to find the usual story of girls and police and learns the boy is dying of
fever. He listens to his snores and says: 'The beast's in liquor.' The Colonel
breaks camp once more. There is some smuggling in Pau, more duelling
and attempts to clip off the opponent's nose or tonsils in Heidelberg, and
then Richard is sent to Oxford. To him this is the final blow. He takes up
with a gypsy girl in Bagley Wood, learns Romany and reads falconry.
Soon he is sent down to study astrology, alchemy, gambling, Hindustani
and Arabic. Pushed into the Indian Army, he turns to Gujarati and Persian
in Bombay. Languages are a new appetite. In no time he learns snake-
charming from a master, also hypnotism; he has an Indian mistress, goes in
for native disguises and is known in the mess as 'ruffian Dick' or the 'white

nigger'. In a year or two, by the time he is twenty-eight, he has written two short books of travel, one describing an attempt to abduct a nun in Goa; another on falconry and a standard army manual on the bayonet. Then – but this is the ruin of his military career – a report on pederasty. The General had asked for it, but had not expected it to be so enthusiastically complete.

Born today in another class Burton would be in borstal. In his own period, he is simply an Anglo-Irish Elizabethan, born out of time. As Mr Farwell, his American biographer, says, he was a great adventurer rather than one of the great explorers like Speke, Livingstone or Stanley; he did not make the one extra and disciplined effort that would get him over the next hill. At the penultimate moment, on the shores of Tanganyika, he lacked the obsessive quality of Speke and let this tedious man go on to discover the source of the Nile.

The odd thing is that though Burton had the Elizabethan courage and wild, animal energy, he was checked by a taste that is purely Victorian – the taste for documentation and cataloguing. He could always be driven on but was always eventually held up by an appetite for bizarre fact. Indeed Burton is even less an adventurer than an appetite. He is Appetite itself. Quarrelsome, autocratic, with no notion of how to control men on an expedition, Burton was best on his own where, born mimic and actor that he was, he could disappear into a disguise and glut his voracity for people, customs and all physical sights. He is an almost pestiferous pursuer of whatever can be turned into a footnote. He has no sense of proportion and therefore no sense of theme. He is always salivating at the news of a detail and there is nowhere he won't stop in order to ask a question. Burton's is an appetite for life not for nature, though when he is an actor in his surroundings, as he is when riding in the desert, he can describe splendidly. The appetite turns the romantic into a pedant. One has often seen this happen to adventurous men. Alas, his miscellaneous learning did little for his fame; it is only in fairly recent times that he has been recognised as an early anthropologist and that his eccentric 'pornography' – as he was truculently fond of calling it – has been properly instead of improperly appreciated.

If Burton desired Fame, appetite made him neglect the process by which fame is acquired. He would do the dramatic things, like the famous

journeys to Mecca and Harar – which are his best – but he just did not
bother to rush back home at once with his tale. He was absorbed in his
notebooks, filling up more and more of them for his own sardonic pleasure.
He enjoyed also what the Arabs call their *Kahl* – just sitting and doing
nothing – which, for him, meant derisively scribbling down any fact. It was
the hanging around and questioning that kept him at Tanganyika, when he
ought – if he wanted Fame – to have gone on.

For an adventurer, Burton is strangely literary and he even has the
writer's complacency. When Speke returned to camp after his discovery,
Burton fell back on literary egotism and refuted Speke's claim by argument. In Speke's shoes one would have found this intolerable, backed as it
was by Burton's bullying and superior airs; one can understand how
Speke, a dull, shy man, must have built up a boiling resentment. It was
shabby of him to bolt home quickly and claim the credit but the great
explorers have usually been great publicity-hunters and sometimes cads;
and Burton had only his own intellectual vanity and indolence to blame.
One is sorry for the arch-fiend because his total confidence in his power to
dominate anybody made him naïve in personal relations: he had no real
belief in the existence of anyone but himself.

Burton's sweeping disregard of other people, even when his interests
demanded the opposite, is an aspect of his passion for freedom and his love
of risk. He had the true adventurer's love of raising the stakes and of
imperilling his own situation. In the planning of his journey to Mecca one
sees all his virtues and weaknesses at work. He went out to Alexandria
disguised in order to train himself thoroughly. As patiently as an actor he
studied Moslem behaviour; he perfected his languages; he threw himself
into theology and religious observance. He had decided to go as a Persian
but, always making casual acquaintances and picking brains, he found out
that Sufism was more dangerous than Christianity on this pilgrimage and
he switched, in a scholarly way, to the right sect. Irreligious but superstitious, he knew how to dabble successfully in a modicum of faith.

So far, all Burton's thoroughness is evident. Then suddenly – perhaps it
was due to the strain or to natural devilment – he risked his plan and his
life. On the eve of his departure, he went off on a drinking bout with a
lapsed Moslem, and in their cups they tried to force a devout Moslem friend
to drink. He screamed blue murder. The night was wild and when Burton

came round, he had to make a run for it. Again in Mecca, the peril of taking notes was extreme and, like many serious travellers, Burton was a public note-taker. He held himself in but in the end his nature was too much for him. He had the nerve to make a surreptitious scribble in the midst of a religious ceremony, relying on the blindness of ecstasy in the people surrounding him. The trick came off, but he might have been killed on the spot.

When one reads of his adventures – and Mr Farwell's account of them is clear and lively – one realises that Burton was lucky and that, probably by boldness, he made his own luck. His sombre appearance and above all something magnetising and frightening in his gaze must have given pause when he drew pistols or raised his fists. He had not graduated as a *maître d'armes* in France, nor trained himself as a wrestler, nor written on the bayonet for nothing. He was able to stick terrible physical suffering. He could stand any fever. He had little need of sleep. He could drink like a fish. He created drama or was always at the centre of it. There was something cheerfully appropriate – from Burton's point of view – in the manner of Speke's death. After years of public controversy and accusation, the two antagonists were to meet on a public platform and decide the issue of the Nile once and for all. All was set for the fight – and then Speke couldn't be found. He had shot himself. It was not a suicide but an accident. Burton appears merely to have snorted. In Brazil, Arabia, Beirut or Africa, one had seen deaths just as bizarre as that, and in more interesting circumstances.

And what can have been more bizarre than Burton's marriage? Mr Farwell has nothing new to say about it, but he appreciates the comedy. There was a lot of nonsense in Burton; he was superstitious, he was an actor, his fact-hunting led him to imaginative generalisations about anything. He was very much a man to have his cake and eat it, which meant that his mind delighted in living a double life. On a different level, Isabel Burton matched her nonsense with us. She was infatuated with Burton and the idea of romantic adventure. She was also obstinate. As fast as she filled his pockets with Catholic beads, medals and protective objects, he flung them out of the window. He put *his* faith in horse chestnuts and, during attacks of gout, tied silver coins to his ankle. She made him sign for a Catholic burial; Burton would sign anything, and laughed. What religion had he not had a go at?

The marriage worked very well. And it certainly consoled him in the long period of failure, neglect and defeat that marks his middle life – before at last the gods, if not the British Foreign Office, smiled on him. The gods murmured to him that although he was a failed official, a dull writer, a broken adventurer, there was one more country he could ransack without moving from his room in Trieste. He could rediscover and expound a literature. The translation of the *Arabian Nights* is his most eloquent journey. There, at last, his habit of being distracted from his objective could bear fruit. Let Arabia produce the theme, but leave Burton to add himself and the thousand and one experiences of his life to the Thousand and One Nights.

The Crab's Shell

Reading Miriam J. Benkovitz's life of Frederick Rolfe, who called himself Baron Corvo, one spots in him a Gissing turned inside out. Corvo was all shady personality and Gissing, the real novelist, was scrupulously without it. Their basic resemblance is in original circumstance. Both were lower-middle-class casualties, trained by Puritan poverty for self-righteous failure; both are emotionally arrested or diverted from the norm. Gissing first marries a prostitute and, after, a virago-servant; Corvo is a pederast; both are underdogs. Gissing has no influential friends, Rolfe-Corvo loses his; the pair are naturals for the future of the snubbed hack and the unsaleable 'masterpiece', but are imbued with the pride of the artist-prince which was the cult of *fin de siècle* Bohemia. They belong to the period when the gifted became obsessed with the defeat of aristocracy (i.e. genius) at the hands of Demos, the hooligan mob with its prolific diet, the new popular journalism.

And it is here they part. Gissing, the truth-telling realist, drudged and drew directly on the lives around him, though privately he thought of himself as an ancient Greek; Corvo was rigid in his personal dream and quarrelled with those who disturbed it. He cadged a living – also an honorary title from a rich Anglo-Italian patroness – and turned into a small fantastic with a studied Oxford accent. His first eccentric gesture, not without germs of self-interest and pretence, was to turn Roman Catholic and to leave school at fifteen; at twenty-five he began a long struggle to enter the priesthood. His faith seemed to have been genuine to the frantic point of pedantry; he became more papist than the Pope and such a prayer-wheel that he was soon at war with his fellow Catholics, high or low. His vision of himself was paranoid: as Miss Benkovitz says more sympathetically, he made the impossible demands of a child in an adult world. He was generally accused of lying and sponging, but if he was continually slapped down by people who were exasperated by him, even reduced to semistarvation and self-imposed vagrancy, he always rose again indomitably, convinced of himself as a genius and an enterprise. *Hadrian the Seventh* is an inspired piece of vengeful autobiography; and *The Desire and Pursuit of the Whole* a half moving, half absurd psychological give-away. It explains his pederasty: he deeply felt that puberty is a child's most dreadful experience, for the indeterminate wholeness of boyhood and girlhood sex is destroyed. For him, to remain the boy-girl is the only wholeness: he is in a search for complete identity with a friend who embodies this peculiarity.

The quest – as we know from A. J. A. Symons's classic portrait, *The Quest for Corvo* – was fanatical and went floundering into the farcical, the picaresque and finally ended in squalor. Although Miss Benkovitz spells out the story in minute detail and writes very well, I do not think her long book tells us essentially any more than Symons has done, although certain episodes of his career do benefit by expansion; one must grant that the pettifogging of deep neurotics is an important part of their case. And if the detail of Rolfe's dreary and perpetual quarrels as a downtrodden tutor or schoolmaster is tedious, the account of his emotional and financial crushes catches the point that he had a changing image and that he depended, as an actor does, on being seen, heard and talked about. His quarrels also led to amusing changes of company. It is strange to see this man who cultivated archaic prose and speech, and who could almost pass as a priest, ghosting a book on African agriculture for a colonel, flirting with Hugh Bland and E. Nesbit about Socialism – which he detested, but he sent £5 to Bernard Shaw as a contribution to the Fabian Society (hardly the home of the True Church).

Rolfe was a poseur or, more sympathetically, one can say he projected images of himself which for the time being he idealised and believed. His expectations, once friendship had been given, were preposterous: if he was an adventurer, he really lived or half-lived in the imagination and was self-deluded. When the illusion dissolved because he asked too much he became quarrelsome, litigious and scarifying. His rage at having his vocation denied went deep and by the time he settled down to his notorious Venetian period in middle age, he let himself go.

Miss Benkovitz's skill in threading her way through a minutely entangled story comes into its own as Rolfe-Corvo's life did in Venice. He had called himself variously the Raven, the crab of unbreakable shell, the master of felinity and, after thirty-five years of failure as a writer, his nerve hardened. The sense of 'peerless difference' from other men which he had ingeniously constructed was now absolute and sustained by long training in a kind of animal cunning. It is not enough to call him a poseur: in Venice he lived the image he had projected. One reason was the beauty of Venice itself; but the private reason was that the twenty years of celibacy required by his attempt to be acceptable to the priesthood had lapsed. He had not lost his faith; he was still ardent in trotting to his prayers. Rome, or rather the clergy and the Catholic laity, had betrayed him. He still had his debts, and his insulting begging letters: he went after the well-off among the English residents and the old story of viciously biting the hand that fed him began once more. But now he was a pagan. His worship of young men and boys was excited by the young gondoliers. He had always kept himself strong by exercises, but now he became an oarsman on the canal; the young gondoliers were his friends and teachers. He had his own little boat in which he would sleep out in the winter, plagued by the rats of the canals, when he was evicted from his lodgings or dropped as intolerable by the residents. He was writing *The Desire and Pursuit of the Whole* and caricatured his benefactors. Of one, a long-suffering Dr Van Someren, he wrote that he was dishonest in mind, a bore and a hypocrite. His savaging of this dietician is very funny: 'I never want to see your food-splashed face again, you have had your chance and you have mucked it up most magnificently.'

But if there were months of desperation, Rolfe-Corvo went on with his literary work in his painful beautiful handwriting, and there are an adventurer's spells of fortune. At one time he had a gondola equipped with sails on which he had painted crabs and ravens, a heraldic device at the prow and 'a great Saint George (a Perseus-Poseidon-Hermes kind of nudity) at the poop'. It was lined with the skins of leopards and lynxes and was handled (John Cowper Powys wrote) by 'a Being who might have passed as a faun', while at rest upon the leopard skins lay Corvo, 'one of the most whimsical of writers'. That was glory. But the notorious Venice Letters written by Rolfe to Masson Fox between 1909 and 1910 tell the story of moral disintegration which shocked A. J. A. Symons. They appear to show Rolfe as a pimp, enticing a pederast, offering to supply boys; and one letter describes what purports to be one of his own sexual encounters. As Miss Benkovitz says, there is a case for thinking Rolfe was chaste but that, if this is not accepted, then the Letters are in fact pornographic letters designed to entice by imagined accounts of lust, and are a disguised form of begging. This, knowing his skill and history, they may very well be. What they do reveal, as she says, is the 'rampant sexuality' of a man living in his imagination. How can one tell? One can only note that his chief gift as a writer was his visual power, his invention of startling if affected images. He is a man for sensations and the physical surfaces – not for nothing had he started life as a photographer, colourer of photographs and designer of emblems – as this random example from *Hadrian the Seventh* shows when he writes that the Pope's voice: 'was a cold white candent voice which was more caustic than silver nitrate and more thrilling than a scream'.

Miss Benkovitz's *Life* does not claim to be a critical biography and, as she says, there can be no complete understanding of Rolfe without an examination of the work in relation to his period. Still she tells one enough. It is a matter of taste, but for myself the affectations and insinuations of his Huysman-like world have no appeal. One has the impression of surfeit fake and even of hysteria loitering in the wings. I have read no more than *Hadrian the Seventh*. It is dashing in its semi-learning. For a man who was rejected by the Church in which he saw his salvation, to hit upon the notion that he has, in proper fashion, been elected Pope and is sought out by the crowned heads of Europe is brilliant. And, at any rate in the early chapters, the book is ingeniously convincing in all its sardonic detail. Rolfe had an actor's detachment from his own character and played many parts with an effrontery which amounts to courage. The weakness of *Hadrian the Seventh* as a chronicle is that it eventually becomes a shrewd journalist's 'think-piece'. Still, as we know, the boldness of the fantasy is excellent pantomime. How far away we are from the sight of poor self-pitying Gissing turning out the blameless papers of Henry Ryecroft by the Ionian Sea, and mildly wishing he was a respectable ancient Greek, yet a writer far more diverse, and fuller than Rolfe-Corvo ever was.

The Tale of Genji

When Arthur Waley's translation of *The Tale of Genji* came out, volume by volume, in the late Twenties and early Thirties, the austere sinologue and poet said that Lady Murasaki's work was 'unsurpassed by any long novel in the world'. If we murmured, 'What about *Don Quixote* or *War and Peace?*' we were, all the same, enchanted by the classic of Heian Japan which was written in the tenth and eleventh centuries, and we talked about its 'modern voice'. What we really meant was that the writing was astonishingly without affectation. Critics spoke of a Japanese Proust or Jane Austen, even of a less coarse Boccaccio. They pointed also to the seeming collusion of the doctrines of reincarnation or the superstition of demonic possession with the Freudian unconscious – and so on.

Arthur Waley admitted a remote echo of Proust, for there was a nostalgia for *temps perdu* in a small aristocratic civilisation; but he was quick to point out that the long and rambling *Tale* was hardly a psychological novel in the Western sense. The Chinese had excelled in lyrical poetry, but despised fiction outside of legend and fairy tale; in Japan, Lady Murasaki's contemporaries were given only to diarising. What she had contrived was an original mingling of idealising romance and chronicle, but a more apt analogy was with music: the effect of her classical and elegant mosaic suggested the immediate, crystalline quality of Mozart. Evocations of instrumental music and also of things like the music of insects occur on page after page: at one point Genji floods a garden with thousands of crickets. The more one thinks about this, one sees that Waley's insight contains a truth: it is music that steps across the one thousand years that separate us from Lady Murasaki.

A translator like Waley would have European reasons for thinking her 'modern': Japanese art had played its part in the revolution that was occurring in European painting – see Van Gogh, and Picasso in the early

1900s – and English prose was ceasing to be Big Bow Wow. Both the sententious and the precious were yielding to the personal, the conversational, the unofficial, the unaffected, and the fantastic – one sees this in Forster and, above all, in Virginia Woolf, who had contrived an ironical mingling of the formal and natural. Such a change reflects the moment when a culture reaches a sunset in which private relationships are given supreme importance and when there is leisure for wit and perspective and an intense sensibility to the arts for their own sake.

I think this may go some way to explain why the post-1914 period in England produced admirable translations like Waley's, Beryl de Zoëte's *Confessions of Zeno* (which may have improved on the regional prose of Trieste, but captured the marked Viennese spirit of the original), Scott Moncrieff's Proust, and Constance Garnett's Chekhov and Turgenev. Their translations are gracefully late-Edwardian, and are, of course, metaphors; the translators felt an affinity of period, even though (as we are now told by critical scholars) they made serious mistakes or generalised and embroidered in such a way as to mislead. Since translators are bound to work in images, and not only sentence but paragraph by paragraph or page by page, generalisations tend to drift off course, and in some translators, the act of re-creation, though often inspired, is not self-effacing.

As both poet and scholar, Arthur Waley has often been suspected of re-inventing with the wilfulness of the poet. He was never in China or Japan: his enormous knowledge was that of the hermit of the British Museum. The generation that followed him are far from any *belle époque* and are dedicated technicians strictly bound to their texts. Professor Edward G. Seidensticker, an American scholar, belongs to this school. In his translation of *The Tale of Genji* he tells us that he owes his admiration for the *Tale* to Waley's often wonderful translation and says that Waley often genuinely improved on the original (with one or two exceptions) by drastic cutting when the book bored him. It has its *longueurs*. Seidensticker's chief criticism of Waley is that he embroidered (as an admirer of Virginia Woolf might well do), that his language is far less laconic than the original Japanese, and that, more seriously, he did not catch the rhythm of Japanese prose. I would guess on rereading Waley that this may be true. Seidensticker's translation, which gives the whole uncut, is still shorter than Waley's! There was indeed a languor in his prose.

It is impossible to do more than point out a few of the 800 characters of the story which passes from episode to episode. The main dramas move among the large number of Genji's love affairs, which are as various as those in Boccaccio. Princes and their trains move from the capital, where all is ambition and court gossip, to the country, where mysterious girls, usually of noble connection, have been hidden, protected only by corruptible or sentimental nuns or servants. There are soldiers but they do not fight. There is no violence. There are no crimes of passion. There are a few rather unpolished provincial governors – a despised caste. Lady Murasaki is as sensitive as Jane Austen is to rank and status, noting drily the pretentious who have come to nothing and the common who have risen. There are priests in their temples, soothsayers, exorcists who are called in to throw out demons, which are, as a rule, projections of jealous passion.

We see a society ruled by ceremonies and rituals and checked by taboos. Ill-luck, bad behaviour, tragedy may be caused in one's life by influences from a previous incarnation for which one cannot be held responsible. Lady Murasaki's temperament is not religious: for her, religion is a matter of proper observances and manners. She has a taste for funerals properly conducted.

The sexual act is never described; the ecstasies of physical love are not even evoked conventionally as they are rather tiringly in *The Arabian Nights*. We see the lovers meet with a screen between them. They strike the string of the koto or exchange short poems to show their artistic skills. The touching of an embroidered sleeve causes alarm and desire; when the lover is admitted or breaks in, the servants retire and we have a full description of the lady's clothes and her hair, but not her body. A coverlet is removed and the next thing we know is that night has passed and the lover is required to leave at dawn under cover of the perpetual mist, his sleeves washed by the dews. He hands the lady a sprig of blossom and sends her a two-line poem with a conversational postscript. The book is almost entirely concerned with the interplay of feelings, joyful, sorrowing, and longing. All is rendered with classical restraint.

The magnificent and always engaging Genji dominates two-thirds of the book and then with little explanation fades out of it. (Perhaps the manuscript has been lost.) He is incurably susceptible and unfaithful, but he makes amends to his conscience by behaving generously. Society deplores but forgives what are called 'his ways'. He is the illegitimate and favourite son of the emperor – 'a private treasure' – and he is scarcely more than a boy when he falls in love with his stepmother, the emperor's second wife, who seems, in this incestuous society, to be an ideal. She has a child by him, but that is nothing. He is married off to Aoi, another woman years older than himself. They do not cohabit and she treats him like a schoolboy but in time he will love her deeply. Meanwhile he takes Lady Rokujō, his uncle's wife, also many years older than himself, as his mistress.

Lady Rokujō's violent jealousy of Aoi leads to one of the great dramatic scenes of the book, for if she is resigned to Genji's casual love affairs, she finds his love of Aoi intolerable. The drama comes to a head at the Festival of Kamo. An enormous crowd of all classes comes to see the nobility ride by on horseback. There is a great traffic jam of fine carriages, among them Aoi's. Lady Rokujō has gone incognito to the festival in a simple curtained carriage, to get one last glimpse of Genji, but her carriage and her attendants collide with Aoi's. There is a brawl between the rival servants and Lady Rokujō is pushed into the background.

The affront is devastating. From now on the evil spirit of jealousy becomes a demonic entity. Aoi is pregnant, indeed about to give birth, and is found to be dying. The evil spirit has indeed entered her, and when the demented Genji speaks to her, she answers in the voice of Lady Rokujō. Powerless to control herself Lady Rokujō has projected her voice into the dying woman. It is an instance of possession. Such scenes are not uncommon in romance, but this is so well done that we believe it and feel the horror. A wild emotion has been transmitted and is recognisable as an emanation of the unconscious, for Lady Rokujō, who has not consciously willed this act, nevertheless feels remorse. It drains her of all desire to continue her powerful life at court: to annul the magic that possesses her she enters a nunnery. Had the scene been done in the high manner of romance it would be as unreal as a fairy tale; in fact the writing is restrained and therefore frightens us.

Genji's 'ways' continue rashly until he sins against protocol and is obliged to go into exile in the mountains. The whole court, even the offended emperor, is upset. There are many rough journeys over muddy tracks, in fog, snow, freezing winds, across flooded rivers. The amount of rain that pours down in the *Tale* must be about equal in volume to the floods of tears, whether of joy, grief, longing, or remorse, which so easily overcome the characters. The tears themselves are a kind of music, a note of the koto. In exile, Genji thinks of his new wife, Murasaki – she seems unlikely to have been the authoress – and of his other ladies. But Genji cannot really repent. He thinks of old lovers:

> He went on thinking about whatever woman he encountered. A perverse concomitant was that the women he went on thinking about went on thinking about him.

A cuckoo calls – it is a messenger from the past or the world beyond death, not the mocking creature of Western culture.

> It catches the scent of memory, and favours
> The village where the orange blossoms fall.

Even the sinister Lady Rokujō is forgiven. She had been a woman of unique breeding and superior calligraphy. She replies in a long letter:

> Laying down her brush as emotion overcame her and then beginning again, she finally sent off some four or five sheets of white Chinese paper. The gradations of ink were marvellous. He had been fond of her, and it had been wrong to make so much of that one incident. She had turned against him and presently left him. It all seemed such a waste.

The lady of the orange blossoms, an older mistress, writes:

> Ferns of remembrance weigh our eaves ever more,
> And heavily falls the dew upon our sleeve.

A Gosechi dancer, a wild girl, writes:

> Now taut, now slack, like my unruly heart,
> The tow rope is suddenly still at the sound of a koto.
> Scolding will not improve me.

Genji spends his time among the fishermen of the wild Akashi coast and here, of course, temptation comes and he is sending messages to a girl hidden in one of the houses, a rustic, whose parents have 'impossible

hopes'. Her father is a monk, but soon stops his prayers when he sees Genji
may raise her fortunes. Genji admires beyond the protecting screen:

> Though he did not exactly force his way through, it is not to be imagined
> that he left matters as they were . . . The autumn night, usually so long,
> was over in a trice.

No hope of a respectable marriage for her. All the same, Genji will install
her in the capital later in the story and she will have her influence on his
life. As usual, he is guilty about this secret. The girl had enhanced his love
for his wife, to whom he confesses.

> It was but the fisherman's brush with the salty sea pine
> Followed by a tide of tears of longing.

His wife replies gently but ironically, in words that have a bearing on the
Calderón-like theme of the novel, i.e. that life is a dream:

> That you should have deigned to tell me a dreamlike story which you
> could not keep to yourself calls to mind numbers of earlier instances.

And politely adds to her poem:

> Naïve of me, perhaps; yet we did make our vows.
> And now see the waves that wash the Mountain of Waiting.

She knows that Genji will not stand jealous scenes for one moment.
Everyone knows it. His lasting defence of his adding new loves to old is
that he never forgets, and he adds: 'Sometimes I feel as if I might be
dreaming and as if the dream were too much for me': it is an attempt to
define what life itself, with all its happiness and disasters, feels like.

Genji's early love of mother figures perhaps necessarily accounts for the
incestuous strain in him. His second wife (i.e. Murasaki) was taken into his
mansion as a child and he has brought her up to think of him as her father.
He flirts with the little girl; then, when she reaches puberty, he can't
control himself and gets into bed with her. It is a kind of rape. The girl is
shocked and sullen. The silent aftermath is plainly and delicately shown;
but ritual saves the situation. The required offerings of cakes are pushed
through her bed curtains. Marriage follows and, in time, she adores him.
She has after all married the ruler of the country; however, in years to

come, she will find him playing the father game again. He has by this time installed his chief concubines in apartments in his mansion; each has her own superbly made garden. He is getting on – probably in his forties – and he likes dropping in for a chaste evening chat with some of the older ones. There is some discreet bitching among the women, disguised as two-edged gardening presents. One older lady sends the younger Murasaki an arrangement of autumn leaves with the words:

> Permit the winds to bring a touch of autumn.

Murasaki's garden is without flowers at this time. She replies with an arrangement of moss, stones, and a cleverly made artificial pine, with the words:

> Fleeting, your leaves that scatter in the wind.
> The pine at the cliffs is forever green with the spring.

The pine is a symbol of hopeless longing and Genji tells his wife she has been 'unnecessarily tart'.

'What will the Goddess of Tatsuta think when she hears you belittling the best of autumn colours? Reply from strength, when you have the force of your spring blossoms to support you.'

The magnificent man is fortifying because he is not only benevolent by nature, but also astute.

After the deaths of Genji and his second wife, the novel is dominated by a new generation: Yūgiri, Genji's pompous son, and the young heroes and courtiers, Niou and Kaoru. These two are friends, who laugh and drink together, and also rivals. The important thing is the marked difference of their temperaments, and on this Lady Murasaki becomes searching. Niou is the handsome and dashing Don Juan or playboy who lacks Genji's powers of reflection. Kaoru has a startling physical quality. In a story where the men are known by the scent they use, Kaoru has a body that needs none: its natural fragrance can intoxicate 200 yards away like the smell of some powerful flower. (It can of course betray where he has been!) If this perfume allures it does him no good: he is a neurotic, tormented, indecisive, and self-defeating Puritan who botches his feelings and escapes into the fuss of court administration at the decisive moment. Responsibility is his alibi and curse. The explanation of his insecure character is that he is a bastard incurably depressed because he does not know who his father is.

The rivalry between Niou and Kaoru begins with a long intrigue with two orphaned sisters who live in the Uji country, a solitude of howling winds and sad rivers. Elsewhere we hear the cheeping of the crickets, the songs of birds, but at Uji the music is the mournful, deafening, maddening music of waterfalls. Niou quickly conquers one of the sisters but only to make her his concubine and not his wife. Kaoru, who is in love with both girls, in his way, loses both. His trouble is that he is an intellectual whose real interest is religion. He will eventually take the vows of Buddhism.

The 'novel' has by now almost ceased to be a work of worldly and poetic comedy and, in its last part, becomes a fast moving drama of intrigue and passion and dementia in which lying servants and old women play their part. (The analogy is extravagant, I know, but it is as if we had moved from, say, Jane Austen to an Oriental version of *Wuthering Heights*.) This final section, along with the opening one of the *Tale*, is by far the most gripping. It excited Arthur Waley! The drama arises from one more adventure of the rivals. Niou and Kaoru are this time in love with a simple, hidden girl of mysterious parentage called Ukifune. Kaoru loves her because she reminds him of the one he had lost earlier – memory, or being reminded of earlier loves, is a continuous musical theme – Niou is out for yet another rash seduction.

The girl is too young to know who of the two she loves and who is her friend; and in her misery decides to drown herself as girls always do, Lady Murasaki remarks, in the romances she has read. The girl attempts this and disappears, and is generally supposed to be dead. Indeed the servants arrange a false funeral in order to avoid scandal. They go out with a coffin containing her bedding and clothes, and burn them on the funeral pyre; the country people, who take death seriously, are suspicious and shocked by the hurry. They watch the smoke: it smells of bedding, not of a burning corpse. In fact, unknown to Niou and Kaoru and ourselves, Ukifune has been rescued and hidden once more in a temple. We see Niou shocked by grief for the first time in his life. (Lady Murasaki is remarkable in scenes of wild grief.) The extraordinary thing is her account of Ukifune's loss of memory and speech after the 'drowning': it is done with astonishing realism and could be a clinical study.

Lady Murasaki is almost too inventive. She is, as I have said, properly class-conscious, quick to detect the vulgar, and is therefore capable of refreshing bits of farce. Pushing, common provincial governors or tomboys with bad accents are neatly hit off: 'Pure, precise speech can give a certain distinction to rather ordinary remarks,' she notes like any lady in a Boston or London drawing room, *circa* 1910. Girls who talk torrentially become 'incomprehensible and self-complacent'. Still, eventually there is a chance that being in good society will cure them. On the other hand, don't imagine that there is any deep difference between the aristocrat and the lowborn: the sorrows of life afflict all. Life is short, time swallows us up; old palaces fall into ruins, new ones take their place. Our life is a dream and, like the *Tale* itself, fades away.

As a translator Seidensticker matches Waley's excellence in detail: theirs is a ding-dong rivalry. There are Anglo-American differences in talk and if Seidensticker's manner is laconic this sometimes runs him into the heavily jaunty word. (Look back to that phrase 'perverse concomitant' in my earlier quotation.) There are many amusing episodes in Seidensticker which are missing from Waley: on the other hand one grasps the whole more easily from Waley's discursive pages even if he is artfully generalising.

In his preface Waley has more to say by way of literary judgment in his stern, sensitive manner; Seidensticker's preface is more informative about the peculiar history of the manuscripts and composition, and about Lady Murasaki herself. It is curious that literary work of this kind was solely an occupation for women in her time, and Seidensticker thinks that this may be because unlike the women of other Oriental cultures Japanese women were free of harem politics; also that they were less conventional than the men, who were tied to the bureaucracy and the endless ceremonies of the court. Lady Murasaki's contemporaries were simply diarists; she was widowed early. Perhaps, in loneliness, she took the leap from memoir into the imagination, and, looking back, felt that 'the good life was in the past': this indeed is the meaning of Genji's name.

Snares and Delusions

Ruth Prawer Jhabvala's stories have been compared to Chekhov's. She is a detached observer of what he called *morbus fraudulentus*, the comedy (in the sternest sense) of self-delusion which leaves us to make up our minds. Her novel *A New Dominion* embodies this irony, but one is more struck, this time, by the echoes of *A Passage to India*. Two generations have passed since Forster. The Westerner is not now in India to rule or give. He is either an apologetic foreign official, a tourist safe in his hygienic hotel, seeing the sights but fearful of their implications, or – more rarely – a 'seeker' in flight from the materialism of the West who is confused by the materialism of the East. But, allowing for this difference, Forster's and Mrs Jhabvala's characters are matched. Raymond, the sensitive English aesthete and inquirer, is another Fielding, plus unconscious homosexuality; his Indian friend, the ingenuous and plaguing student Gopi, is a budding, ill-educated, up-to-date version of Dr Aziz. The disturbance in the mind of the unhappy Mrs Moore becomes bold and explicit in the persons of three English girls who have recklessly gone to India on a spiritual quest. They throw themselves without defence upon India in order to attain their 'higher selfhood' and to find their 'deepest essence'. To these lengths Forster's characters never went, for the girls have come to suffer, to be destroyed so that they can be remade. Times have changed, but the theme is similar: opposites have met.

In one way, Mrs Jhabvala's book is a satirical study of the disasters that overtake those who dabble in the wisdom of the East, and one can think the lesson forced. The girls are rootless, daring, and sexually frigid. One is told little about their background. Under what circumstances in their native land did these virgins, or demi-virgins, pick up the idea of something 'higher' than sexual love? Why, one asks, didn't they become nuns at home? Or are they in some sense hippies? We do not know. And are these three not too alike? The Western characters in *A New Dominion* are denatured types. Raymond has collected his scholarly information and firmly saves his skin with Gopi's mockery in his ears: 'Sometimes you are just like a woman. Look how neat you are and tidy!' For the girls – disaster, though they are trite until disaster catches them. One of them dies of hepatitis and in squalor, because her chosen swami disbelieves in modern medicine. Another has become a pale, glazed automaton, the swami's hypnotised slave: the most truthful and stubborn of the three girls holds on to her Western will. But against her judgment and despite what she has seen, she abandons herself to a sexual experience that disgusts, terrifies and overpowers her. She craves to be dominated against her will. She has, indeed, discovered an unsuspected self – one compelled by horror. She finds 'wholeness' in degradation, a craving not for the highest but for the lowest – and with her eyes open.

Yet if Mrs Jhabvala's novel is in part satirical, it rises above satire in her patient, sensitive, and undismayed treatment of the situation. Her attitude is that of the careful truth-teller rather than of the arguer; the irony lies between the honest lines, so if we feel that the girls are bickering shadows and their behaviour is unbearably silly and pretentious, they are always explicit when, from time to time, they come on the scene. The inner subject of the book is the idea of dominion. In the foreground is the dominion of the new, rich, brash, Indian middle class, itself torn between the dominion of its traditions and the vulgar, careless ostentation now available to it. Sexuality will dominate, luxury will dominate, the gurus will dominate, squalor will dominate, servants will intrigue and be downtrodden. Yet all have their eager, dreamy eyes on the West. The girls are dominated less by the swami than by his insinuation of his belief in Fate: India, in its chaos, has its ancient belief in the domination of Fate in its bones. This is exactly the theme for Mrs Jhabvala, who probably knows more about India and *feels* it more strongly, in terms of personal conflict, than any other novelist writing in English. She has a constant power of collecting the scene in hundreds of glittering fragments – the life of Delhi, Benares, and a desert province – and of losing herself in the contradictions and ambiguities of temperament. Her prose has not the plain Chekhovian transparency, but her method is one that curbs pure satire, for the novel is built up from dozens of short passages in which each character speaks for himself. A large number of these passages are short stories in which the light changes from the bizarre to the poetic, from the comic to the horrifying, from the thoughtful to the mischievous – all with an allusivenes, a susceptibility to mood, a tenderness of which Chekhov was the exemplar. The light in which we see the people, and in which they see each other, changes every minute.

The Hindus are Mrs Jhabvala's complete characterisations – above all, the ancient Princess Asha and the impossible young Gopi. Under their impetuosity they have reserves of cynicism and passivity, and they have no dramatic notions of being 'remade' by their 'saints' and gurus. They run to them with a gambler's abandon; they are stroked, cuddled, bullied, starved into a passing repentance, until at last boredom sets in, and then off they go, to sin with greater carelessness or battered desperation. The gurus are simply islands in a flood of uncontrolled emotion. The Princess seduces Gopi out of hand, though he is a mere youth. She will never cease to be sensually frantic, unscrupulous, disorderly in her jealousy, and avid for the Western gin bottle as she heaves gorgeously on her divan, either caressing or in tears. She is also a wily judge of human nature. She will never believe that the delusions of sensual love and the delight in being adored are not worth it. When Gopi is sentenced to a traditional marriage, she is in despair, but after a spell with her 'saint' she realises that a maternal love of the young man can be a new refinement of Eros. And Gopi, after observing his Westerners, concludes that, narrowed by guilt, they know nothing of the amusing varieties of the sexual impulse. It is true that Gopi is a boaster of little accomplishment, but he is uninhibited.

The Princess is a remarkable mixture of the blowsily vulgar and the distinguished. She loves to behave atrociously at her adored brother's house – he is a rich and rising politician – and, out of jealousy, to outrage her high-minded sister-in-law, who is a stern Gandhian. The Princess always provides comedy. In their gardens, her brother and his wife stage a grand party and the very proper guests are brought out to sing Gandhian hymns. They walk out onto the moonlit lawns:

Led by the Lady Minister, they had begun to sing hymns. They started off with Gandhiji's favourite hymn – a rousing tune and heartening words about the Oneness of God whether worshipped as Ishwar or as Allah. Unfortunately most of the guests did not know these words and they trailed behind the leader, who sang in a loud and manly voice, sometimes clapping her hands to rally the others along. They kept tripping up and some of them giggled at their own ineptitude, which made others sing louder in order to cover up. They sounded terrible.

Gopi is there. He has sneaked away from Asha in order to flirt with a girl who is as pretty as an ornament. Asha has got together a rival group of musicians who are far from being hymn singers: they represent the old, wicked, malicious India, which insinuates its power through the senses:

> The tabla player had now begun to accompany the maestro, and they were working themselves up to a contest where each tried to outwit the other with superior skill. The sitar flung a phrase of unmatchable beauty towards the tabla which responded by not only matching but even surpassing it so that the sitar was forced to try again: and so they continued to cap triumph with triumph, challenging one another to soar higher and higher and up to heaven if possible. Each of them secretly smiled to himself, and sometimes they also exchanged smiles in a mischievous way for each knew what pride there was in the other's heart.

The hymn singers are forced to stop and, to complete the rout of the Lady Minister's respectable party, Asha rushes forth in a fury to drag Gopi away by the hair. Afterwards, she has one of her bouts of shame – shame itself being a luxury – and goes to see an old 'saint' she has known. But her aged servant strokes her forehead and sings her folk songs about the thighs of heroic lovers and secret passages to the bedroom. The ancient mischief of India undermines Asha's calm and revives her passions. Soon she is back with Gopi and the gin in a pleasure palace that had belonged to her old rip of a father – a place that has known all kinds of love and even murder.

Gopi is an intolerably crude yet touching young man, childishly moody and tiresome in his insecurity. He at once tempts, mocks and envies the prim Raymond who may not be willing to consider the nature of his attachment but has the strength of his inhibitions. He watches Gopi's antics with remarkable detachment and tolerance. Gopi fingers Raymond's clothes and furniture greedily; his hands covet any Western object. He has a shameless eye for the main chance. He likes to dress up, to envy, and to annoy. He passionately longs for friendship, yet is negligent in return. He makes scenes about the superiority of his feelings to anything a Westerner can match, yet he is as coarse and egotistical as a child. He is the kind of character (but this is true of everyone in the novel) who is best seen episodically, and in brief scenes Mrs Jhabvala is excellent. Each episode is framed in a passing aspect of the Indian scene: the heat of the day, the sweetness of the evening, the fears of the night, the squalid, the brutal, the absurd. And one is made to feel the tension of the senses. In Benares, while Raymond and Gopi are being rowed on the river by a worn-out old man, Gopi sings a sad love lyric:

> As soon as he was out on the water [Raymond] felt as if all the squalor of the city – the stale puddles, the rotting vegetables, the people waiting to die on the sidewalks – was all suddenly purified and washed away. Yet how could that be? How could that water purify anything? Crowds of people, many of them diseased, were constantly dipping into it – and not only living people but even the remnants of dead bodies which (on account of poverty and the high cost of wood) had not been burned up completely. But Raymond, especially with Gopi sitting opposite him singing his lyric, found it easy to ignore these facts.

Yet the contentment vanishes as they glide into one more raw scene with Asha.

All Mrs Jhabvala's scenes are so ingeniously put together that the wry, the absurd and even the terrible mingle in the space of a few minutes. One situation bears upon another, and all the more sharply because the speakers rarely answer one another but pursue what is going on in the isolation of their own minds. India is indeed evoked by non-communication. To take one outstanding example: when Raymond, in his best moral form, is trying to make Asha give up Gopi because of his coming marriage, arguing that the boy will get bored and leave her, Asha cunningly tells him of the suicide attempt of a young man who went further than Raymond has ever dared to go. In this she is covertly needling him about his repressed feelings for Gopi. Raymond counters that ma-noeuvre by saying primly, 'Asha, I don't think I need to hear this.' While they talk, the incurable Gopi is playing a raucous Western record on a tinny gramophone and trying to transpose it to an Indian scale as he sings. It sounds awful, and he laughs at himself. The incident ends abruptly:

> Raymond said: 'You really shouldn't make him drink so much. He's not used to it.'
>
> 'If you take him away, I don't know what I shall do. Can you imagine being alone here?'
>
> 'You don't have to stay here.'
>
> She said, 'It's the same everywhere. In Bombay too. Those sounds you say you hear at night, so often I hear them in Bombay. Of course I know it's the sea, really, but to me it sounds like here and then I think I am here.'

What are these sounds? They are the screams of the hyenas. Heavy, dark birds hang motionless in the sky above them.

One can see why the comparison with Chekhov has been made. Like so many of the Russians, Mrs Jhabvala 'made it strange' and has caught hours of the passing day through the comedies and tragedies of her people, especially the Indians. The hour is her measure. With her Englishman and her English girls, Forsterism comes in. Here I find her schematic, for they are outside the Indian hour; they are arguments of young and baffled shadows in a novel where the vitality is elsewhere.

Flann v. Finn

$\overline{\overline{}}$

Flann O'Brien and Myles na Gopaleen (Myles of the Little Ponies) were among the pen names disguising the comic genius of a Dublin civil servant called Brian O'Nolan who became celebrated in 1939 for the 'novel' *At Swim-Two-Birds*, the finest piece of learned comic fantasy to come out of Dublin since the Treaty. Despite the praise of James Joyce, Graham Greene, Anthony Burgess, John Updike and Dylan Thomas – the last said it was 'just the book to give your sister if she's a loud, dirty, boozy girl' – the book did only moderately well. Its successor, *The Third Policeman*, did not find a publisher in Flann O'Brien's lifetime. He turned to journalism, as Myles na Gopaleen, with a satirical column in the *Irish Times* entitled *Cruiskeen Lawn* (*The Little Overflowing Jug*). He wrote a parody in Irish, *The Poor Mouth*, and, among other things, the well-known *Dalkey Archives* which was turned into a ribald play, one of whose characters is St Augustine: he is discovered underwater off the Irish coast. After O'Brien's death in 1966, at the age of fifty-four, *The Third Policeman* at last appeared.

Flann O'Brien was a fierce, elusive and legendary figure in a city where people become legends very rapidly and bitter gossip is much admired. He seemed to inhabit a wide-brimmed black hat and disappeared and re-appeared, dissolving his anger, sorrows and learning in whisky and black porter. When, a year before he died, I was told I'd probably meet him somewhere on the street between O'Connell Street and Trinity, he seemed to me to be a vapour. We stood in the usual drizzle. His voice was soft and courteous, he had a look of pride and shy appeal in his small reddened eyes. Then he vanished: goodness knows where; down the Quays or into oblivion among his illnesses?

Now, as one can tell from *A Flann O'Brien Reader*, edited by Stephen Jones, he has an international fame. This book has the admitted disadvantage of being a collection of extracts from his chief works, but it does give a tang of masterpieces like *At Swim-Two-Birds* and *The Dalkey Archives*. Mr

Jones's introductions are a help in a discursive way; they contain also a number of O'Brien's anxious letters to his publishers and some biographical hints. As a family, the O'Nolans seem to have had the advantage of a rambling literary education in Latin, Greek and Gaelic, which sharpened their appetite for 'the word' and the distractions of haphazard learning. When I say 'rambling' I must add that at University College O'Brien did take a master's degree with a thesis on Nature in modern Irish poetry. His gentle and serious evocations of Nature are very delicate. The following sentence recalls the medallion-like landscapes in P. G. Wodehouse: 'The whole overhead was occupied by the sky, translucent, impenetrable, ineffable and incomparable, with a fine island of cloud anchored in the calm two yards to the right of Mr Jarvis's outhouse.' The comic spirit is poetic at heart.

Naturally Flann O'Brien is seen in Dublin as an heir to Joyce: nowadays critics talk of Beckett, Borges, Barth, Queneau, the *nouveau roman*, and the anti-novelists who breed fiction out of other fictions. We take the point, but this process was well known to ancient cultures like the Gaelic and, indeed – for the English contributions to Irish writing – to the Elizabethans, not to mention Sterne, who was brought up in Ireland. O'Brien's domestic desuetude and Rabelaisian innuendo are pure *Tristram Shandy*:

> Aren't you very fond of your bedroom now, my uncle continued. Why don't you study in the dining-room here where the ink is and where there is a good bookcase for your books? Boys but you make a great secret about your studies . . .
>
> My bedroom is quiet, convenient and I have my books there. I prefer to work in my bedroom, I answered . . . I know the studying you do in your bedroom, said my uncle. Damn the studying you do in your bedroom.
>
> I denied this.
>
> *Nature of denial*: Inarticulate, of gesture.

Amid belchings, scratching the lice on his person and recovering from a drinking 'bash', the young student narrator of *At Swim-Two-Birds* lies on his grubby bed discussing literature with a friend called Brinsley:

> The entire corpus of existing literature should be regarded as a limbo from which discerning authors could draw their characters as required,

creating only when they failed to find a suitable existing puppet. The modern novel should be largely a work of reference . . .

That is all my bum, said Brinsley.

The student then holds forth on *oratio recta* and *oratio obliqua* and offers several styles, including the parody of the legend of Finn MacCool:

I will relate, said Finn . . . With the eyelids to him stitched to the fringe of his eye-bags, he must be run by Finn's people through the bogs and marsh-swamps of Erin with two odorous prickle-backed hogs ham-tied and asleep in the seat of his hempen drawers. If he sink beneath a peat-swamp or lose a hog, he is not accepted of Finn's people. For five days he must sit on the brow of a cold hill with twelve-pointed stag-antlers hidden in his seat, without food or music or chessmen . . .

Likewise he must hide beneath a twig, or behind a dried leaf or under a red stone or vanish at full speed into the seat of his hempen drawers without changing his course or abating his pace or angering the men of Erin. Two young fosterlings he must carry under the armpits to his jacket through the whole of Erin and six arm-bearing warriors in his seat together. If he be delivered of a warrior or a blue spear, he is not taken. One hundred head of cattle he must accommodate with wisdom about his person when walking all Erin, the half about his armpits and the half about his trews, his mouth never halting from the discoursing of sweet poetry.

Gradually, the narrative – always alive with interjections, notes of squalor from Dublin realism, and hilarious fantasy – builds up an intrigue: the student is writing a novel about a dull novelist called Trellis who is pillaging other novels. Maimed by the banal treatment they receive from Trellis, the characters get their own back by spreading grotesque yarns about him. In the end Trellis is taken to court, with his characters as judge and jury, in a place remarkably like the bar of a pub. A tram conductor complains that as a character he was made to do a seventy-two-hour week on 'non-pensionable emoluments' and was obliged to speak to his passengers in 'guttersnipe dialect, at all times repugnant to the instincts of a gentleman'. A writer of Wild West tales called Tracy says he was obliged to lend Trellis female characters: 'He explained that technical difficulties relating to ladies' dress had always been an insuperable obstacle to his creation of satisfactory female characters and produced a document purporting to prove that he was reduced on other occasions to utilizing disguised males.' He once lent Trellis a pious girl character who came back 'in a certain condition' six months later. Tracy reinstated the girl in her employment by marrying her to an 'unnecessary person' and got her son a job with a man 'dealing with unknown aspects of the cotton-milling industry'. Some question of a potato-peeler comes up and a judge asks, 'What is a potato-peeler?' The reader notes that the prose of Trellis is a string of clichés.

The absurd trial is, of course, a send-up of the Dublin courts. Indeed, at every point there are satirical glimpses of Dublin life. If the whole were simple, broad farce, it would soon pall. What transforms it is the comic, if often maddening, influence of Irish pedantry – the comedy of hairsplitting – and O'Brien's ear for the nuances of Dublin talk: above all, for its self-inflating love of formal utterance and insinuation. His humour, as Mr Jones says, depends on the intricacy of its texture. Language is all: he is a native of a country of grammarians, thriving on the perplexities of a mixed culture, and creating, as Joyce did, vulgar or scholarly myths.

To say this is not to underrate O'Brien's superb invention in broad farce – in, say, *The Hard Life*. That book purports to describe the inspired swindles invented by the author's deedy adolescent brother, who makes a start in life by inventing a successful correspondence course in tightrope-walking. He pulls in the money through medical warnings about the dangers of the sport, in a learned pamphlet on giddiness, or Ménière's disease, caused by haemorrhage in 'the equilibristic labyrinth of the ears'. He knows the Irish worship of the grand word:

> The membranous section of the labyrinth consists of two small bags, the saccule and the utricle, and three semi-circular canals which open into it . . . In the otolith organs the hair-like protuberances are embedded in a gelatinous mess containing calcium carbonate. The purpose of this grandiose apparatus, so far as *homo sapiens* is concerned, is the achievement of remaining in an upright posture, one most desirable in the case of a performer on the high wire.

O'Brien's glee has a double edge – allegorically, Irish life is lived on a 'high wire' or the liberating hope of risk. The boy goes one better by inventing something called Gravid Water, the miracle cure for rheumatism. He achieves a grotesque interview with the Pope. Gravid Water cures rheumatism, but the patient dies of incurable overweight. *The Hard Life* was a late book and, Mr Jones thinks, a step backward – although he does not quite agree that the tale may be an 'exegesis of squalor' or mental sluggishness, common enough in Dublin's stagnant moods. O'Brien's extravagant mock encounters with Joyce (who is heard saying that *Ulysses* was smut written by American academics) and with Keats and Chapman paralytically drunk in a pub after closing time (when the landlord has to declare that the illegal drinkers are all his uncles and nieces) are fun of a journalistic order.

The Dalkey Archives is another matter. Hugh Leonard turned it into the delightful play *When the Saints Go Cycling In*. Here we find the learned De Selby who has scientifically overcome the limitations of time and is able to take his guests under the sea, in a handmade Cousteau-style tank, to meet and gossip scandalously with the Christian saints who deride the Apostles. St Augustine is the arch humbug and is exposed. De Selby is a splendid anti-Prospero who is possessed by the native desire to blow the world to smithereens. O'Brien's narrator is worried by the religious scandal but thinks that the only way to put a stop to De Selby's threat is to have him collaborate on a book like Joyce's epic – say, *Finnegans Wake* – which will so befuddle his mind that he will forget his scheme. Poor O'Brien was near death when he wrote this work and, Mr Jones says, the humour rises far above wit and cleverness and is 'beautiful'. I would have said 'calm and equable'. Another writer has quoted what O'Brien said of Joyce – 'With laughs he palliates the sense of doom that is the heritage of the Irish Catholic' – as being a summary of O'Brien's literary and personal tragedy.

The curious theme of death kept at bay by the invention of conceits underlies *The Third Policeman*, the posthumously published version of the early novel that had failed. It seems to have begun as a mock detective story, in which the author is forced to commit an appalling murder by a man who has enslaved him and robbed him of his property. This is a dark and disturbing tale. O'Brien's work is rich in distracting episodes and here we come upon a conceit that seems to point to something obsessive in his inward-turning mind. The conceit reminds one of Borges and of those figures who multiply in a series of reflections in retreating mirrors. In

O'Brien the object is a box that contains a box containing boxes, getting infinitely smaller, until they are invisible. It seems that O'Brien put off doom by retreating into a metaphysical solitude. But the scene becomes macabre. Ridiculous policemen arrive. The narrator is arrested and hears a scaffold being built, plank by plank, on which he will be hanged. As an idea, this concentrates an easily distracted mind. Bicycles – another of O'Brien's obsessive groups of objects – confuse the tale, for he cannot resist an idea. But there is no doubt of his laughter and unnerving melancholy.

Pain and Laughter

═══════

Sholom Aleichem is one of the prolific masters of Yiddish comic story-telling, an art springing from the oral folk traditions of Eastern Europe and crossed by the pain and laughter of racial calamity. Like all comics he is serious, has one foot in the disorder and madness of the world and, as a Jew, the other foot in the now perplexing, now exalted, adjuration of the Law and the Prophets. Did God really choose their fate for the Jewish people? If so, was He being irresponsible, or why doesn't He make it clear? There is no answer. The oppressed stick to their rituals and are obliged to perfect the delights of cunning, the consolations of extravagant fantasy, the ironies and pedantries of the moralist who is privately turning his resignation into a weapon. With so many insoluble dilemmas on his hands, Aleichem developed that nimbleness of mind and fancy, those skills of masking and ventriloquism, that made him the prolific 'natural' in short tales drawn partly from the remaking of folk tradition, a juggler of puns, proverbs, and sudden revealing images caught from the bewildered tongues of his people.

There are certain distinctions to be noted when we speak of the general Jewish gift for anecdote. These are made clear in the exchange of letters between Irving Howe and Ruth Wisse which introduce their selection from a striking variety of Aleichem's best work and discuss the growth of mind it reveals. Mr Howe points out that Aleichem is not a 'folksy tickler of Jewish vanities' and the Yiddish folk material he uses is not as cosy 'as later generations of Jews have liked to suppose'. Under the laughter is fright and the old driving forces of anxiety and guilt: if Aleichem is close to folk sources he escapes the collective claustrophobia of a folk tradition that was broken by the pogroms and wars that drove the Eastern European Jews to flight or death; he has let in the light of 'a complicated and individual vision of human existence. That means terror and joy, dark and bright, fear and play.'

Ruth Wisse points to Aleichem's position in the period when the Jewish moral crisis came to a head in Eastern Europe. Writing of his contemporaries, the classical masters Mendele Mocher Sforim and I. L. Peretz, she says that they are embattled writers, 'fiercely critical of their society', strong in dialectical tendency, pitting old against new; whereas Aleichem, who also felt the break in the Jewish tradition and in his own life, 'makes it his artistic business to *close* the gap. In fact, wherever the danger of dissolution is greatest, the stories work their magic in simulating or creating a *terra firma*.' I do not know the work of these writers but it is certainly true of Aleichem's work that it shows his balance and poise in tales like 'A Yom Kippur Scandal', 'Station Baranovich', the terrifying 'Krushniker Delegation', 'Eternal Life', and above all in the four grave Tevye tales. As he tries to face his daughters' rebellion against tradition Tevye becomes, tragically, something more than a folk figure: he becomes a man.

Aleichem has the style of the spontaneous talker, at home in many garrulous idioms; it is a style that plays as it moves forward dramatically and then, hit by an image or a proverb, circles back. The narrator's mind is continually split between what is happening and something else, some fear, some scheme, some hope that is going on in his mind. He acts on impulse and regrets at once; always escaping from his situation, he is back in it only to find it changed, usually for the worse. He writes as a man backing away from the next minute and going headlong into it. Nearly all of Aleichem's people are whirled around by their imaginations, addressing fate, knocked this way and then that by scripture or the proverbs – 'When a soup bone is stuck in somebody's face who doesn't give it a lick?' On second thoughts, 'You can skin a bear in the forest but you still can't sell its hide there.' Speculation is their anguish. They burn with a fever. 'My blood began to whistle like a teakettle.' Aleichem's powers of invention pour out of the language he utters. The innumerable surprises of language so entangle us that we are caught out by the vaster surprises of the tale. In catching us out, his art shows its depth.

Aleichem's people themselves belong to a storytelling culture. He is as astonished and disturbed by his bizarre tales as we are and uses the device of not bringing them to an end, sometimes in order to show that the meaning of the tale has been hidden and we must work it out for ourselves or go on making it up on our own. This is evidence of a very self-conscious art, as Mr Howe says.

A clear example is 'A Yom Kippur Scandal'. A stranger comes to the synagogue and overcomes mistrust by handing out silver coins, but when the rituals are over, he suddenly screams out that he has been robbed of 1800 roubles, on the holiest day of the year. He had put the money into the praying stand and it has gone. The rabbi and his congregation turn out their pockets. Only one person refuses. He is a young man notorious for knowing the Talmud by heart, for being a master of Hebrew, arithmetic, algebra, unequalled in chess – perfection. The congregation argue with him, he begs to be spared, but they throw him to the ground and, going through his pockets, discover only a couple of gnawed chicken bones and a dozen plum pits still wet from chewing.

> You can imagine what an impression this made – to discover food in the pockets of our prodigy on this holiest of fast days. Can you imagine the look on the young man's face, and on his father-in-law's? And on that of our poor rabbi?

But what about the 1800 roubles? Never found. Gone for ever, says the story-teller, and never explains. We can suspect, if we like, that the stranger had invented the drama, to cover up the fact that he had stolen his employer's money. But Aleichem does not explain. Why not? Because the deeper sin than the sin of theft is the sin against God and His Law? Aleichem still doesn't say. We are perhaps left to search our own souls. Who knows?

'Station Baranovich' is another tale that stops short of its ending. It is told by a Jewish stranger on a train and is an event that occurred in tsarist times. A loose-tongued bartender called Kivke starts a religious argument with peasants on a Sunday. He is reported to the police and is sentenced to be stripped naked and to run a gauntlet of cavalry officers, who will whip him. The Jews unite to plot his escape. They fake the death of Kivke in prison, arrange a mock funeral, and get him out of the country. He shows his gratitude by blackmailing them for larger and larger sums of money now that he is free. The final threat is to report the whole thing to the Russian Commissioner. But at this point the train stops at Baranovich and the teller of the story jumps out. What happened next, what is the end? the listeners shout. All they get is

'What end? It was just the beginning!'

and he is gone. Aleichem says

May Station Baranovich burn to the ground!

What does he mean? Ruth Wisse says it sounds like a protest against his own art or a defence of it. More likely it seems to me that the end being 'just the beginning' evokes the only too familiar frightful prospect that awaited the Jews of that village, a further test of their emotions, their ingenuity as an oppressed people.

Aleichem's humour has a double edge; it is concerned with a good deal of trickery or with efforts to bring off a successful or kind action which come to disaster because of some helpless absent-mindedness. In 'Eternal Life' the green young theological student who lives under the thumb of his mother-in-law volunteers, out of a desire to do a good deed that will win him Eternal Life, to take the body of a dead mother to the burial ground, because the father cannot leave the house and has no sleigh. The journey through the blizzard is terrible, so terrible that he cannot remember the name of the dead woman. So he is mad enough to make up the tale that the body is his mother-in-law's; she has died of fright. The inspector of the Burial Society asks, What sort of fright?

> My tongue seemed to stick to my palate. I decided that, since I had begun with lies, I might as well continue with lies, and I made up a long tale about my mother-in-law sitting alone, knitting a sock, forgetting that her son Ephraim was there, a boy of thirteen, overgrown and a complete fool. He was playing with his shadow. He stole up to her, waved his hands over her head and uttered a goat cry, *Mehh!* He was making a shadow goat on the wall. And at this sound my mother-in-law fell from her stool and died.

Again and again, the story-teller invents other selves when he dramatises a dilemma. Yet this story is not mechanical farce; it passes through the moods of youthful exultation and sorrow, and as the blizzard drives him almost into sleep on the sleigh, the idea of Eternal Life has the sweetness of death and then turns to terror, for the wind seems to be the voice of the dead woman on the sleigh. She seems to accuse him and say, What are you doing to me, young man? Destroying a daughter of Israel who has died?

In this story we move through joy, exaltation, fear, and farce, as if these were a weather in which the people live. Indeed in all the stories, the feelings bound from one to another. The characters repeat themselves with comic fervour, as if searching for guarantees; they dramatise themselves as if they were momentary universes. Each in turn is the only one who loves, hates, scolds, whines, tricks or believes. In their voices these people, who have no land, have their territory and thus Aleichem has written its history.

Irving Howe notes that the Mottel farces introduce a Tom Sawyer-like note, which one does not hear in the adult stories. I notice something like a theme of Flann O'Brien's in one of them, My Brother Elye's Drink – in 'Mottel the Cantor's Son'. It is about a boy out to make a fortune from homemade kvass and ink, and who even offers to rid his town of mice. One can see Aleichem's instant, restless eye unfitted him for the novel. As the Tevye stories show, he could be grave without encumbering himself with novelistic architecture. One surprise is the almost complete lack of erotic or mystical fantasy, such as we find in I. B. Singer.

Five Minutes of Life

I saac Babel was the most *telling* writer of abrupt stories to come out of the Russian revolution. This gentle Jew was a man who hit one in the belly. More important he had – what is indispensable to short stories – a distinct voice. Made famous by *Red Cavalry* and the Odessa stories – he was rewarded with a very pretty dacha – he worked under Gorky's influence and protection as a writer precariously accepted by the regime but increasingly restless and finally silent under it as a person and an artist; he was allowed to go to Paris and Italy, but his foreign contacts must have brought him under suspicion; he was arrested, secretly tried, and presumably executed, in the general Stalinist attack on the arts in 1939. A blunt story – rather like one of his own. His works vanished; references to them were cut out of histories and criticism; his manuscripts and papers were either destroyed or, haphazard, lost. Not until 1964 was he rehabilitated and there was a public celebration of his genius.

Letters written to his first family who were in Brussels and Paris have been recovered; also stories lost in periodicals or in salvaged manuscripts. Few have yet appeared in Russia or in translation. It is the same old stupid Soviet tale. The MacAndrew edition contains his letters and two early stories, including the famous 'My First Fee': the Max Hayward edition which first appeared in 1969 also contains early work like 'An Evening at the Empress's' and 'The Chinaman', and the texts of a long interview, and of the speeches made in 1964 by Ehrenburg, Paustovsky, Nikulin and Munblit. The Paustovsky piece supplements the fine portrait in Babel's *Years of Hope* and is a valuable and intimate account of his habits as a writer in the early days. He and Paustovsky belonged to the very talented group who began to write in Odessa in the terrible period of the Civil War. In spite of biographical criticisms made by Nathalie Babel, the edition of her father's stories introduced by Lionel Trilling in 1955 is important.

The subjects of a very large number of Babel's stories are primitive and direct. The war and the expropriations have turned the peasants on the Asiatic border into murderers, looters, and bandits; the new government forces are as ruthless in getting a new regime set up. Babel's prose is sharp and laconic. There is little comment. And yet within the fatalism of the tales there is the unmistakable Jewish humanity; sometimes the Jewish humour and fantasy – what one can only call the irony of recognition: the recognition of the manly or womanly essence of each briefly elicited character. Babel had a master in Gorky, but his deeper masters were Gogol and Maupassant: Gogol for the imaginative richness, Maupassant for detachment, economy, and devilish skill. Eventually Babel was to find Maupassant cold. What I think Babel meant was that the Frenchman was *outside*, whereas all Babel's characters carry some grain of the presence of Russia, the self being a fragment of the land's fatality. One says, as one sees the Kulak kill his horse rather than let it go to the Cheka people when he is turned out, when one sees him become a legend as a bandit, and when he is run to earth and killed in a pit: 'Yes, that is how it was. It was the end of an epoch, dreadful.' One has seen the rage of a lifetime.

As an artist, Babel describes himself in 'My First Fee':

> From childhood all the strength of my being had been devoted to the invention of tales, plays and stories – thousands of them. They lay on my heart like toads on a stone. I was possessed by devilish pride and did not want to write them down prematurely.

His early idea was to 'dress them in beautiful clothes' and he could write, for example:

> The flowering acacias along the streets began to moan in a low, faltering voice.

Later, in his innumerable rewritings (so that one very short tale might be drained from dozens of versions as long as a novel), his aim was to cut and cut and cut. He was tormented by the amount of words and inventions inside himself.

On the other hand, occasionally he expanded an early version. 'My First Fee' has an early laconic version called 'Answer to an Inquiry', which contains one of those brief asides which are a remarkable but traditional part of his art – an item in a prostitute's room:

> In a small glass bowl of milky liquid flies are dying – each in his own way.

and, although the end is sharper in the first version, the second and longer one is richer. The boy's lying tale is now really fantastic; and the symbol for describing the sexual act is more truthful than anything by contemporary masturbators:

> Now tell me, I should like to ask you: have you ever seen a village carpenter helping his mate to build a house? Have you seen how thick and fast and gaily the shavings fly as they plane a beam together? That night this thirty-year-old woman taught me all the tricks of her trade.

In story after story Babel worked until he hit upon the symbol that turns it from anecdote into five minutes of life. He was not a novelist. By 1937 he was being semi-officially questioned about not writing on a large scale like Tolstoy or the very *bien vu* Sholokhov. It was being insinuated that he was idle and not pulling his weight. Poor devil! Short story writers are poets. Babel could not but be opposed to the clichés of Socialist Realism and particularly to the rhetorical magazine prose it had led to. He was also asked why he wrote of the exceptional rather than the typical, and one knows what Stalinism meant by 'typical': the middlebrow ideal. He replied with Goethe's simple definition of the *novella*: it is a story about an unusual occurrence. And he went on – the interview appears verbatim in Hayward's volume:

> ... Tolstoy was able to describe what happened to him minute by minute, he remembered it all, whereas I, evidently, only have it in me to describe the most interesting five minutes I've experienced in twenty-four hours.

He was opposed to the short story as a condensed novel. The short story is an insight.

Babel, as Ehrenburg said in his speech at the celebration in 1964, 'was formed by the Revolution'. The struggle between order and anarchy nourished him, not in a thinking or philosophical way, but instantly in terms of people and events seen with the naked eye. His official work enabled him to travel restlessly. He was eager for that, but he also hid where people could not get at him; like many famous writers in Russia and the West he was overworked in the public interest. His curiosity was eccentric and endearing. In Odessa he used to treat people or pay them to get the story of their first love. In Paris he used to pay girls to talk to him. One of his favourite questions to a lady was, 'Can I see what you have got in your handbag?'

The *Letters*, edited by Babel's daughter, are moving in their unconscious self-portrait of the anxious and worried Jew, minutely concerned about the daily life of the family from whom he was separated.

> I have already learned Natasha's school report by heart and am in dire need of new spiritual nourishment. I would like very much to know how Grisha is doing, whether he is working and whether he 'is making progresses' as a certain Jewish woman in Odessa used to say.

One can see that he was a self-burdened man who could not resist more burdens, passing from euphoria to gloom:

> I've gone completely cracked with my thirst for 'work'. I want to work every hour of my life.

His last recorded utterance was in 1939, when the police came for him. He was not alarmed – one imagines him never alarmed – the mild round face, with the strong out-of-date steel-rimmed glasses, smiled. All he said was 'I was not given time to finish'. It might be the last abrupt sentence of any of his stories.

Growing Old

Simone de Beauvoir is one of those writers who dig and dig until they pile up the monumental. Faced by the stretches of dead wasteland in ourselves and our society, in which we dump our unsolved or evaded problems, she settles down to an exhaustive sifting and then rebuilds. She is sometimes portentous, and rarely witty; but her feelings are strong and she is unremitting in her concern. Her present object is to analyse our attitudes to old age. After dealing with the biology of the inevitable decline of the tissues and muscles, she moves on to the behaviour of a few primitive societies; next, period by period, from the Greeks and Romans to today; and then to old age as we know it in everyday life. She draws on the words and lives of many rancorous writers, painters, scientists, and musicians who, privileged by their vocations, have closely observed the change that old age has brought to them. Her object is to break the conspiracy of silence on a subject that has become privately and publicly taboo in the advanced countries which are governed by the values of profit-making capitalism.

The fact is that in this century traditional concepts of old age have lost their meaning: socially, old age has become the scrap heap. The irony is that the percentage of elderly people in the wealthier and more advanced countries has enormously increased since the beginning of the century. All but a few are forced to end what sentimental liars have called 'the golden years' on declining means among the middle class, and in poverty with little remedy among the workers. The affluent society is strictly for the under-fifties.

> The fact that for the last fifteen or twenty years of his life a man should be no more than a reject, a piece of scrap, reveals the failure of our civilization: if we were to look upon the old as human beings, with a human life behind them, and not as so many walking corpses, this obvious truth would move us profoundly.

And she reminds us of the Grimms' story: a peasant makes his father eat out of a small wooden trough, apart from the rest of the family. One day he finds his son fitting little boards together. 'It's for you when you are old,' says the child. At once the grandfather is given back his place in the family. But the Grimms' family home cannot survive in urban industrial life. The boy's father is liable to lose his job today, and when he applies to Situations Vacant he will find that 'no one over forty need apply'; he is many years away from his retirement pension and will certainly be unable to support either son or grandfather.

If one can think of thousands of exceptions to this threat, it hangs imminently over a large section of the working classes and has begun to affect the white-collar worker. First one is disqualified, then one moves on to the segregated condition of the old. All governments are plagued by what the machine or, rather, what the policy that runs the machine is doing; and in Western Europe, Scandinavia, and the United States – among the capitalist countries – there has been a great deal of research and some action which Simone de Beauvoir examines. Scandinavia, with few political difficulties to deal with and very drastic taxation, has easily done the best: the community is small enough to be coherent. It is hard to follow the regulations and statistics provided for the other countries: one can only say that good intentions are marred by meanness. The state puts the economy first and the economy is directed to maniacal productiveness.

One would have expected a writer with a Marxist turn of mind to make the Communist practices clearer and, above all, more living than they appear here. One is obviously better off in these countries if one belongs to the Party, and production is still the God. One cannot tell in any country how many of the aged like being institutionalised and how many hate it, or what has been lost and what gained. I have seen many 'old folks' communities in many countries, and what is depressing about them is the unnatural sight of people living entirely and perforce among people of their own age. One is in an organised ante-chamber for the dying or in the stiff, lifeless rooms of a doll's house. And the smell of old age pervades.

I do not think that Simone de Beauvoir's examination of primitive societies adds much more than exotic spice to the subject, though it is interesting that settled tribes behave on the whole better to the old than nomads do. Among the nomads the legs of the old cannot keep up, and they are often left behind or deliberately exposed to death. The elderly Fangs accept their fate and even joke about it. They take it to be natural that their heirs should get rid of them; sometimes they ask to be burned alive and go out in a blaze. The Hottentots admire the old, but hate the senile, who are sent off to starve, though with a great ritual feast of the tribe to send them on their way. Ceremonial politeness is at least a recognition that a man's dignity lies in his role – a concept that has vanished in the impersonal life we live nowadays, though one can observe it in the slums of Naples – and also, of course, it helps against magic, which, in our terms, means the retribution we ourselves invent.

We are becoming closer to the nomads, I think, simply because modern economic life forces us to be mobile; we move on from one exhausted hunting ground to another conveniently like it; the family, once the shelter of the old, is scattered. One certain thing primitive life shows: the old are better off in rich societies, but not rich societies like ours, where the wealth depends on each being out for himself.

The most urgent part of Simone de Beauvoir's survey is concerned with retirement, the modern nightmare. Only worn-out manual workers or people with ruined health look forward to it. The retirement forced on most people today is the real error of our industrial ethos, and it is made worse by the low pensions that rob the man or the woman of the rewards of their long labour and status. The white-collar worker adapts himself more easily than the labourer. Only the wealthy can assure themselves, when they are kicked out, of a pension that is close to their real salary, for neither the work nor the pay of the worker changes very much in the course of a lifetime.

The real shock lies in being disqualified. Some recover, others fall into poor health and listlessness when work stops. In all countries a very large proportion of the retired men simply hang about the house, particularly in America. An English woman said of her husband when he retired:

'That was a day to remember! He cried and the children cried too.' And the husband went on: 'I didn't know what to do any more. It was like when you're put in chokey in the army. I just sit staring at these four walls, that's all. Before, I used to go out with my mates on Saturday evening, or with my sons-in-law. I can't do that any more. I'm like a pauper. I haven't got a pound-note in my pocket . . . What I give my wife doesn't amount to anything . . . I'm ashamed.'

Another wife said of her husband: 'It's murder, having him in the house. He worries about what you're doing – and he's always asking questions.' One asked permission to cut the bread.

There is a long list in this book of these despondent stories from France and America as well. A good deal depends on whether those who retired were optimists or pessimists; but in general, those who did not dream of leisure are better off. Florida and the Mediterranean deceive – the latter is found to be bad for rheumatism and rents are too high – but the experience at Prairie City in the United States is that people who go on working have 'a much higher *tonus*' than the retired and their recreations are richer. And, to relieve the gloomy picture, there is a group of Burgundian bicyclists; their average age was eighty-six and activity kept them in spanking health. Many worked full time in their regular jobs, the rest found secondary occupations and devoted themselves to bicycling, walking, shooting and reading. They were ordinary men far above the intellectual level of their neighbours.

It is Mlle de Beauvoir's argument that a society like ours, which treats people as material instead of treating them as men and women, prepares its working population for boredom by maiming at the outset, but I have known many old coal miners, especially in Wales and in the north of England, of whom this was certainly not true fifteen years ago. Indeed, elsewhere in industrial England, wherever a trade was well-rooted and the community long established (as it often is), one could see that the body was aged but the communal pride and spirit were rich. In the new generation of huge cities like London the maiming may have begun – except in pockets like Bermondsey or among dock workers – but from this one deduces that, education or no education, it is the clan or community that is the real educator and the genuine source of a sustaining culture. In so far as it breaks up real communities the new capitalism is antihuman. It standardises the nomad.

Simone de Beauvoir is on more certain ground when she writes of old

[1110]

age as it affects us privately. There *is* a conspiracy to make us believe that the old are different from ourselves. Their passions, their sexuality, their needs are intensified by the discovery that all time does not stretch before them. Their angers and jealousies are notoriously fierce although the range is narrower. As she says, there is a return not to second childhood but to something like the wilfulness of children, and if old people are strange it is because, as Victor Hugo and the Greek tragedians saw, there is a psychological reconnection with the fantasies of childhood and adolescence. Both children and the old live on the fringes of the adult world and are therefore often mocked.

If life is tragic, society takes the view of comedy: the sexuality of old people is frequently laughed at or censured, for there is an interested reluctance in accepting that the old are like ourselves. Goethe's family raged against his love for a very young girl when he was in his seventies – they were afraid of losing their inheritance. The mocking of old men and women in their antics with people younger than themselves or with one another is natural for, like all satire, it aims at that part of ourselves that hates what we find in ourselves: the comedy of disgust is as much a purgation as tragedy is, and has the virtue of reconciliation. I am not as shocked as Mlle de Beauvoir is by the grotesque ballet of old women lifting up their skirts and pretending to be young, for the old are often used to their own half-admiring self-mockery. It is even a strength, as she indeed says about Picasso's pictures of himself as the monkeyish dwarf man pleading and fawning before a beautiful young girl: he is so sure of his strength that he is able to play with any situation in his life.

To censure elderly sexuality is to forget that in those who have had a rich sexual life, it will be prolonged. And it is at the heart of the creative imagination, whether in artists or in the ordinary man. What is difficult for the old is sexual loneliness. It is much worse for older women than for men, though I cannot agree with Mlle de Beauvoir that no one speaks of 'a beautiful old woman'. In any case, instinctive sexual attraction may not depend on beauty at all. A voice, for example, is as potent as a body.

These chapters on sex are very valuable, but we have to return to the dour fact that old age is a parody of life: 'The vast majority of mankind look upon the coming of old age with sorrow or rebellion. It fills them with more aversion than death itself.' Emile de Faguet wrote, 'Old age

[1111]

is a perpetual play that a man acts in order to deceive others and himself and whose chief drollery lies in the fact that he acts badly.' Great men and women may turn upon their own achievements, as Michelangelo did when he denounced his own sculptures as puppets. There is only one solution, Mlle de Beauvoir says: 'In spite of the moralists' opinion to the contrary, in old age, we should wish still to have passions strong enough to prevent us turning in upon ourselves. One's life has value so long as one attributes value to the life of others, by means of love, friendship, indignation, compassion.' It is not a good way of preparing for old age to brood on the money one is setting aside, on hobbies, and on one's place of retirement.

It is strange that Mlle de Beauvoir gives less attention to women in this book than to men. Certainly she quotes Mme de Sévigné at length and speaks of one or two others, but one can think of many more signal figures. I do not believe that women have been more silent than Chateaubriand, Hugo, Goethe, Tolstoy and Proust or many others whose cases she examines. It is true that women have been reserved about their emotional and sexual lives, but in all human beings of strong creative ability there is what may be called an overflow of vitality. There is a marked literary bent to Mlle de Beauvoir's mind, which is fortunate, because writers, painters, and musicians have had few reserves about their sensations as old people. Painters and musicians do better on the whole than writers, or at any rate better than novelists, in keeping, and indeed putting new life into, their talents. The failure of invention in novelists is probably due to the fact that memory overcrowds their minds, as it does the ageing minds of most of us; it suffocates the power of fantasy from which the novel springs.

All the same, it is to the novelists we must turn for the most intimate accounts of old age. Two seem to me outstanding: Italo Svevo's *Confessions of Zeno* with its astonishing portrait of Zeno's ageing father, a description which weaves clinical observation and profound imaginative sympathy together. He is dispassionate and tender, yet intellectually alert. Italo Svevo was fitted for this by his comic genius and his fervid interest in illness: life is a sickness, he said, that only death will cure, and the old know well how to mock. This cleared the ground of all conventional sentiment and morbidity at the outset and freed him to see the life of the aged in their own affronted sense of time as past and present mingled. I imagine Svevo would be too wayward for Mlle de Beauvoir – but wilfulness, after all, is one of the privileges and weapons of old age. It was Bertrand Russell in his nineties who sat down on the pavement at the CND protest in Whitehall saying, 'I am not prepared to be tolerated much longer.'

The second novel is one Mlle de Beauvoir does go into at length: *The Golovlyovs* of Saltykov-Shchedrin, which is unsurpassed in its portrait of the changing mind of a woman who passes from the bustling despotism of middle age to the muddle of timeless daydreaming and the dozing frights of old age.

> She lived as though she took no personal share in existence ... The weaker she grew, the louder was the voice of her desire to live ... Earlier she had been afraid of death; now she seemed to have forgotten it entirely. She longed for all those things she had deprived herself of ... Greed, gossip, and a self-seeking pliability developed in her with astonishing speed ... The transition from cantankerous despotism to submissive flattery was no more than a question of time ...

These are bleak quotations which do not bring out the real reason for the care and fullness of the portrait: this springs from the time sense of the Russian novelists of the nineteenth century – the sense of dwelling in the day itself, in the minutes that trickle through the fields or the empty room. That is precisely what the time-scale of advanced old age is: a life moving a day at a time, giddy with memory, waking with violence and fright, appeased by drowsiness and with strange austerity raising its startled head out of confusion.

With one exception the Golovlyov family is closer to our subject than other variations on the theme of Lear (Mlle de Beauvoir thinks Lear may conceivably have come into Shakespeare's head when he looked at the breakdown of the manorial system under the Tudors, when unemployment and beggary spread everywhere). The exception is in the work of Samuel Beckett. His writing shows how artists are more sensitive to the burning theme that is hidden or repressed in any given period than the sociologists or reformers are. And indeed see it sooner.

Beckett is not moved by meliorist ideas but presents his old men and women as creatures who have entered a culture of frenzy, complete in itself, with its own rage of inquiry, its feverish speed of acute and changing sensation. They are at war not with death but with their own vitality. His old people are agonised by the life force that prevents them from dying. 'What tedium!' cries his Molloy, continuously, contemptuously. Beckett joins those writers who reject the idea of serenity with the frightful hilarity of people forced to survive. His fever is different from the fever of Chateaubriand's eloquent self-loathing, but both contain their truth and illumination: when we recognise the inevitable, we are strengthened to bear it or (more important in a selfish society that values long life) to endure it in others.

The social aspect is one thing, but the private is another. A thousand considerations of temperament, upbringing, and chance make generalisation impossible. Some people are born older than others and become young late in life. If we are not struck by mortal disease many of us in our seventies nowadays feel little different from what we were at fifty – though this may be a delusion – except that we now know time is shorter. If by luck of vocation or temperament we are incurably active we have little time to think of our decline. But our sense of the mysteriousness of life becomes sharper and we are jarred by the death of friends, as if by the sound of a harsh forgotten chord. If we are vain of our survival we now discover a more piercing grief, for the dead have taken away a part of ourselves. Indeed it might be said that what the old learn at last is how to grieve.

We all have known intimately men and women of all social classes in their eighties and nineties who are incredibly clear in mind and vibrating with life. How much depends on our tonnage of vitality! The only thing to be said is that these old people have usually placed themselves outside the system. They have not been worn out by others; and if they have their aches and pains, they have added to their lives by increasing their work and not by rest. Perhaps they were born unresting.

The Sayings of Don Geraldo

There is a moment in the old age of a writer when he finds the prospect of one more long haul in prose intimidating and when he claims the right to make utterances. We grow tired of seeing our experience choked by the vegetation in our sentences. We opt for the pithy, the personal, and the unapologetic. For years we have had a crowd of random thoughts waiting on our doorstep, orphans or foundlings of the mind that we have not adopted; the moment of the aphorism, the epigram, the clinching quotation has come. So, in his eighties, Gerald Brenan has sat in his Spanish house, ignoring the fame that has gathered around him as the unique interpreter of Spanish history, politics, and literature, his energetic past as a sort of scholar-gypsy in Europe, Morocco, his previous hopes as a poet and novelist, and his interest as a confessional biographer, and has set about polishing his *pensées* in this miscellany which he has called dismissively *Thoughts in a Dry Season*. ('Dry' is the wrong word: the juices are very active in him.)

Brenan has always been a man of vast reading in many languages, interested in everything from religion, politics, literature, men, women, animals, down to flowers, trees, birds, and insects: he has lived for inquiry and discovery. Although he left school young and is innocent of the university, he cannot be called an autodidact. Greek and Latin came easily to him, he is not a dogmatic 'knower' but, as he says, a 'learner', and he has had the advantage of rarely having reviewed a book or given a lecture. A Chair has not allured him. None of his sayings is therefore a regurgitation. He confesses to having kept a commonplace book earlier in his life, but he did not keep it up. His only regret is that the exigencies of modern publishing have made him cut out his longer reflections on history, philosophy, politics, and the phases of the revolution we are now passing through and which have been his passionate preoccupation since, I suppose, the Spanish Civil War.

[1115]

Since Brenan, or Don Geraldo as the Spaniards call him, has been my closest friend for the last forty years, I cannot look at the present volume with detachment. I have sat by his blazing wood fire in his Spanish house listening to him talk this book into existence. I see and hear him rather than read it. The tall man whose glasses flash as if he were sending out signals, as he slippers about the room talking fast and softly while he looks above my head into a vast distance, or looks down suddenly as if puzzled by my existence, pops up between the lines of the printed page.

He is an egoist, a performer, who invites one into the upper air of his fantasies and insights. He is one of those excited conversationalists who at once define and transform the people, places, and ideas that have set them off. If he is an encyclopaedia, it is an encyclopaedia that has wings. He will punctuate his talk with the most elegant of smoker's coughs and the most enticing of suggestions or gossipy innuendo. I have often wished I could transcribe his manner of conversation, his sudden darts into some preposterous item of sexual news, his pleasant malice, the jokes that enliven the quirks of learning and his powers of generalisation, but the thing escapes me. But now, in the epigrams and discursive entries in this book, I hear his voice.

How does Brenan talk, what is his manner? Here it all is. This is Brenan, any day, on his terrace or by the fire or talking his way up Spanish paths, passing from village to village, switching, for example, from the idea that no village loves the next village, but only the next village but one, and that this may have its roots in Arab habit, to expounding on the cultivation of plants, the habits of birds, the moral and social influences of architecture, the problems of abstract art, T. S. Eliot's deficiency in historical sense, the nature of pretty girls, the ups and downs of sexual life, the phases of marriage, the patterns of theology, the difference between the nature of the poet and the prose writer, the differing formalities of the Mediterranean, the northern European, the Muslim, and the American cultures and their historical causes. Things are things and events are events, and he knows all about them, but they suddenly take off and become ideas and then become part of the flow of historic instances before they drop into some comical anecdote.

He has arranged his utterances in groups about life, love, marriage, death, religion, art and architecture, literature, writing, people, nature, places, introspection, and dreams. He has invented a terse Chinese sage, Ying Chü. In his talking life these matters will run from one to another and we shall have scarcely time to agree or disagree. Here I shall note varieties in his manner, remembering that what may sound dogmatic and like a sharp military order – for there is something of the curt soldier in him – is really put forward as a question he invites us to dispute.

Poverty is a great educator. Those who have never known it lack something.

Most of our personal opinions lie on the board like iron filings. But pass the magnet of a strong emotion over them and they will change overnight and point in the opposite direction.

On love:

Some girls only fall in love with ugly men. These are the girls who when they were children preferred golliwogs to dolls.

Love and admiration often precede sexual attraction and may even exclude it. Think of Stendhal and the fiasco. The following is a real Geraldo-ism:

But women also have their problems. Thus making love to a girl for the first time can be like going into a dark room and fumbling for the electric switch. Only when a man has found it will the light come full on.

Marriage:

In a happy marriage it is the wife who provides the climate, the husband the landscape.

On religion he is a moderate sceptic. He does not care for utilitarianism. He is not a humanist because he does not feel 'Man is a sufficiently noble animal to be given absolute power over his destiny.' He needs authority:

What authority I do not know, but my need has made me a fellow traveller of the religious, though I shall get out of their bus several stations before the end.

[1117]

(He is close to Montaigne. Above all he admires Montaigne's prose, but 'not in translation'.)

The paintings that move him most are those that express a moment in time when things seem to be arrested and made to stand still.

I am not drawn to Rubens because in his paintings every little detail is on the move. Nothing has weight, there is no rest for the mind, one thinks chiefly of the skill and mastery.

On painting, he passes from the *pensée* to the essay, but the *pensée* punctuates the essay. On the abstract painters:

there is no struggle in their canvases, no tension – only choices and hesitations.

Yet the works of the American abstract expressionists

surge up from some deep layer on the borders of the unconscious and make a strong emotional impression.

The essay goes on to architecture –

Modern States [being strictly utilitarian] are the natural enemies of good architecture.

– and an analysis of the Romanesque, the Gothic, and the Byzantine, and praise for the Muslims for their 'abnormal sensitivity to small variations'. These are intended to 'lull the senses', and he has a eulogy of the mosque of Adrianople. All this ends with an odd kind of aside that gives a sparkle to the learned phrases of his talk. The bishop who completed Salisbury Cathedral had been Queen Philippa's chaplain, a dwarf who was notoriously impotent. He built the finest spire in England.

The entries become longer when he moves to literature. He looks at Stendhal ('an amateur in a nation of professionals'), Balzac, Flaubert, Henry James, Quevedo, Italo Svevo – a talking author very close to him, indeed I often confuse my friend with him – Jane Austen and even P. G. Wodehouse, Góngora and many other poets, and each paragraph contains a startling *aperçu*. These pages are too long to quote but I have heard many of them thrown off in high moments of his talk where they were as precise as they are in print; his conversation has the glancing quality of something rapt and yet prolonged. His afterthoughts are sudden:

> Who, for example, among English writers of talent could have written a serious poem on dentifrice, as Apuleius did, except Nabokov? And in their use of erotic subjects for unerotic ends they are also similar.

Or:

> The cliché is dead poetry. English, being the language of an imaginative race, abounds in clichés, so that English literature is always in danger of being poisoned by its own secretions.

Whereas French writing – until 'Sartre eroded the language' – relied on the precision of its syntax. All the same, clichés,

> if well chosen, provide a rest for the mind and give a more leisurely movement to the sentence . . . A good deal can be done by words that are vague and plastic: consider the use that Vergil makes of the word *res*.

So one listens to Brenan's talk for its vivacity and for the extraordinary breadth of its interests. In one section he amuses himself by bringing in his imaginary Chinese sage to whom modern rulers, from Hitler onward, come to ask advice. The troubled Nixon asks whether there is any chance of being born again in another life in which he could fulfil his potentialities. The sage reminds him that if he is reborn he will find that billions of others will be reborn – 'including all your compatriots' – and suggests he will cease to be tormented by this craving for immortality if he reflects on this, before breakfast.

As for himself, there are discreet revelations: he has the writer's shame before his own writing. Out of dullness he wakes up when he gets to his desk, but cannot believe that he is the 'I' who has written and is praised. Modesty? No, he says, conceit. Fog surrounds him: only intuition can give access to the vague shapes he discerns in the fog. All his remarks on nature – on the toad, the snail, insects, and birds – are delightful to hear. He is a connoisseur of the distribution of the olive. To walk with him is to see creatures, trees, rocks, and soils come to life, not only because he knows so much, but because what he knows comes lightly to his tongue. A bore would have stunned us with more information. He does not inform: he incites. There is no melancholy in this Jacques:

Rain, rain, rain. It brings out all the scents – roses, heliotrope, lemon leaves, loquat flowers, freesias, but subduing them a little and mixing them with the smell of the wet earth. This garden is where I should like to live if I were blind, because in its soft air the sounds as well as the scents have a soothing and memory-provoking quality. Ordinarily the senses take in too much. One would better enjoy using one's eyes if they recorded fewer things, because the less clearly objects are defined, the greater is the charge of emotional associations they carry.

Brenan ends by cursing the critics of poetry who insist on 'explicating'. He is no sentimentalist. He is always exacting. Be careful: if he is drawing his portrait he may be drawing yours. It will be sharp and yet you will be enlarged by his fantasy. Thousands of Malagueños came to his funeral when lately he died.

Pioneer

In the last twenty-five years the cloak of legend – the cloak of the Red Cross Knight – has been twitched from the shoulders of Robert Browning. His romance no longer hides him; rather, it deepens the complexity of his double character; and his tortuous achievement as a dramatic or novelistic poet becomes more forceful in our eyes. His two new biographers – Park Honan has completed the biographical study cut short by William Irvine's death – are polished writers and they concede a great deal to Betty Miller's arguments of the 1950s, when, looking again at the famous elopement from Wimpole Street, she saw the Perseus–Andromeda situation was reversible: Andromeda also rescued Perseus.

There is nothing like the sickroom for building up the will and strengthening the mind, and Perseus was not quite the dominant figure the victim of Mr Barrett hankered after. In fact two invalids – and even two victims of the colonial slave trade – had found each other; or two histrionics, one successful at that time and the other not. (No modern biographer has accepted Miss Mitford's tough, spinsterly view that Browning was a long-haired, effeminate, climbing dandy who, living unscrupulously off his parents into his late thirties, was out to float on Miss Barrett's fame and money. Down-to-earth women like Miss Mitford are rarely good judges.) If we are going in for malice we prefer Miss Barrett's rival suitor who offered the typical gem of English suburban snobbery when he called Browning the 'New Cross Knight', thus pushing the Browning family out of genteel Camberwell to within close sight of the Surrey Docks.

It is very extraordinary that the elder Barrett and the elder Browning had the closest connection with the slave plantations, the former owing his personal fortune to them, the latter, in a clerkly manner, being sent out to St Kitts as a young man. The gentle bookworm came back quickly,

[1121]

shattered by the horrors he had seen. A bit of an artist, he would be caught doodling horrifying human heads in black and red ink, working off memories too awful to speak of. A meek, poorish clerk in the Bank of England, he was a childish bibliophile, a mild Voltairean, ruled by a sweet but sternly religious wife. She was of modest Scottish and German stock and – as surely as Mrs Ruskin – she knew she had given birth to a genius and was determined not to let his soul out of her command; in time, invalidism became one of *her* weapons.

One mustn't put it like this, for the boy adored her; he flourished like an ambitious mushroom in his happy prison. Only one part was mushroom; the other was restless, noisy and demanding. The mother's boy was handsome and delicate; for thirty-odd years he slept in the room next to his mother's and the door was always left open in case he or she should call. Elizabeth Barrett's door opened on her father's. Together Robert Browning and his mother had headaches and backaches and wondered at the felicity of it.

The boy refused to go to school or university after the age of fourteen, was tutored but read his way through six thousand learned books, listened to music; and got up erudite charades. Father and son re-enacted things like the siege of Troy, drawing on the furniture for battlements. The Browning cottage (Irvine writes) was a thick interior epidermis of epics, tragedies, biographies, tales, miscellanies, so that the family lived in a kind of intestine. No wonder the boy grew up to spend a lifetime turning dictionaries and encyclopaedias in French and Italian into poetry: the privacies of London suburbia have traditionally been rich in sedentary fancy. In the Brownings there seems to have been a delight in congesting the intellect and the emotions.

At twenty, the young Browning proudly refused to clerk or go into the law and decided to live by writing epics of introspection, and the parents – living on £257 a year – submitted and supported him. They even raked up money to send him to Italy and Russia. He dressed with elegance and never left the house without white gloves: they were a lifelong obsession. Why? Unclean, unclean? Here we must be cautious. The one violent disturbance in his life was his contact with the atheism of Shelley. Christian respectability had long replaced the ideas of the French Revolution and Mrs Browning drove him to recant; the guilt attached to this surrender lasted his life. Surely this has nothing to do with gloves, but Irvine takes the plunge:

> . . . Robert's zealous regard for gloves – old or new – astonished even his contemporaries. The need to conceal his hands seems to have been one feature of that larger, more intricate need to resort to camouflage in his writing; to conceal the unresolved conflicts in his own personality from the world's eye, and to live almost comfortably and respectably with his mother's religion and Shelley's poetry. Even the most autobiographical passages in darkest *Sordello* suggest that he could not bear to examine his own deepest loyalties too closely or directly.

But one remembers Balzac's passion for gloves. One surely does not argue that the English took to carrying umbrellas because they were seeking psychological shelter. Surely the glove was no more than an intimate token of elegance and sentiment in European life, an item of dandyish fastidiousness also. A naval officer was so taken by the young Browning on the voyage from London to Venice that he kept a pair of his gloves as a remembrance. At most Browning was displaying the histrionic vanity that Jung associates with introverts. The boisterous Browning was a deeply introverted and happy prisoner of his childhood, perhaps all his life. If his conflicts were insoluble, they were the source of his actor-like gift for dressing up and vicariously living in others.

The most enlightening passages in the present biography are the critical ones which go into this and into the obscurities of Browning's writings. On the Wimpole Street romance, the authors follow the story sensibly; but the courtship is really much better read in the recent Elvan Kintner edition of the letters, which bring out the important and deeply Browningesque point that the two parties are really four – their epistolary and real selves – who seem to be trying to get into a future story by Henry James. The irony was that Elizabeth Barrett sought an autocrat and Browning obstinately wanted to be ruled: he for the goddess in her, not she for the god in him. In their letters, both are cleverer – one guesses – than in life.

As for Browning's 'semantic stutter', there have been many theories about the cause. Irregular education, no logical training, is one. The chaos created by voracious and random reading; the tumbling in of images from constant listening to music; a sort of congestion of ideas in a mind isolated within a peculiar family, a conceit of originality very common in narrow religious sects; the egotism of such an isolation – these explanations have been advanced. There is the obvious influence of Carlyle: more here than meets the eye, for Mrs Browning was of Scottish and German stock and one suspects the sweet domestic lady could become flinty and ablaze with Biblical metaphor and even German grotesque if, say, the subject of Shelley and atheism came up.

But another explanation seems to me overruling: the imprisoned intro-vert was a violent man, acting out violent Calvinist fantasies in words; he was by nature, though not by gift, a man of the theatre. His words, his inverted phrases, his telescopings, his grotesqueries, are syntax as a stage cast: words are players. It is important that he spent many years writing tragedies and melodramas in verse in the hope that Macready would produce them. Of all the English poets of the nineteenth century Browning seemed the most likely to succeed on the stage; he was deter-mined on it. But, his biographers say:

> From first to last, Browning attempted to depict, as he said in the original preface to *Strafford*, 'Action in Character, rather than Character in Action.' . . . As his venture grew desperate, he turned from history to romance and violence, but action continued – ever more glaringly – to be an ironic irrelevance to character . . . He treated the theatre as a gigantic laboratory . . . Some lessons he could not learn. Browning was fascinated by motives, but seemed scarcely interested in how motives produced action or how one action must be linked logically and psychologically with another. He could depict character in iso-lation – even at a moment of crisis – but he could not easily bring one character into dynamic relation with another.

In short his gifts were those of the novelist or the poet of monologue. There is a proliferation of brilliant detail, so that the small things and psychological dilemmas become more dramatic than the main drama. He adopts the point of view of characters unlike himself, and this putting on of another's voice and life depends on a certain bouncing abruptness and on an acute sense of the mind's sensations. There is a double take: the poet is both outside and inside the husband in these lines from *The Ring and the Book*:

> Up he jumps.
> Back to mind come those scratchings at the grange,
> Prints of the paw about the outhouse; rife
> In his head at once again are word and wink,
> *Mum* here and *budget* there, the smell o' the fox,
> The musk o' the gallant.
> 'Friends, there's falseness here!'

Difficult rather than obscure, simply because deviousness and the 'impossible' perversely attracted him, Browning is one of those who, except in direct dramatic song, are travelling underground with torches of imagery in a mind that is often too continuously vivid. The effect is of broken mosaic, thought and feeling turned into broken-up things and events:

> Till sudden at the door a tap discreet,
> A visitor's premonitory cough,
> And poverty had reached him in her rounds.

The symbols 'tap', 'cough', and 'door' are stronger than 'poverty' because exact. A stuttering demagogue, said Chesterton. A crowd of arguments, theories, casuistries, images in physical shape rush together to the point of his pen at once. Our first impressionist? Irvine points out, what one easily forgets because of Browning's originality, that he did not invent impressionism or the dramatic monologue. The most interesting suggestion is that what he does not owe to Carlyle, he owes to Burns. (Mrs Browning the elder would have been pleased to hear this.)

The Ring and the Book – despite what Henry James called its 'inordinate muchness' – *is* in advance of its time. It *does* look forward to twentieth-century impressionism, as the poetry 'deprecates itself by prose expressions . . . and even by unmelodious strings of compound epithets'. Another source of difficulty is that life is embedded in a dense texture of historical reading. So much of Browning was refracted through the medium of other arts, particularly music and painting, as well as through antiquarian vestiges. Browning was tremendously a Victorian in that he was a collector; his ego also colonised history, particularly the medieval, with something of the Protestant mercantile aggression. Another excellent point is that (possibly like some ornate ham) Browning turns himself into a myth. He wrote to a prim admirer:

> We differ apparently in our conception of what gross wickedness can be effected by cultivated minds – I believe the gross*est* – all the more, by way of reaction from the enforced habit of self-denial which is the condition of men's receiving culture.

Mr Honan suggests in the later chapters that *The Ring and the Book* nevertheless marks a decline – too much of the didactic, lack of self-confidence or faith, which lead him to blare too loudly on his trumpet.

The wall between Browning's public and private selves becomes thicker as time goes by. The commonsensical and sanguine man of the world becomes stronger. He was loud and seemed more like a prosperous grocer than a great poet. Presumptuous, he was more than once inept in his relations with the adoring women who surrounded him after Elizabeth's death. Grief had left him hardened. He felt no longer. He became, as these biographers note, a sort of Richard Feverel with a System in his attitude to his son; indeed there are close resemblances in life and language, and fundamental lack of invention, with Meredith, the novelist, another adept of idealism and the grotesque.

One can suspect that as a poet Browning was drawn to Elizabeth Barrett by her remarkable facility, by the lack of confusion in her feeling, even by the easy popular spontaneous throb of her coloured verse. Invalidism had in fact matured her. One can also see that she must have been one more mother figure; in his later poems there are moments when he resents, now she is dead, that memory chains him; love and hate run close in an angered mind. Yet the chains were also a protection to a poet who seems always to have wished to mask his own life so that he could pour himself into the skins of others. In this he was undoubtedly a novelist – perhaps the earliest to move towards the twentieth century.

Welsh Peasants

After the excellent book on his travels, *In Patagonia*, it is at first surprising to find Bruce Chatwin writing a novel about the small sheep farmers at home on the hills of the Welsh Border country of England. On reflection, sheep-farming is a natural link. In the nineteenth century, as if drawn to the isolation, the rains, the snows and stern conditions they knew at home, large numbers of tough, poor and thrifty Welsh migrated to Patagonia, where they were free of the alien gaze and rule of the despised Sassenach conquerors. The people of *On the Black Hill* are part of this sturdy remnant who toiled and haggled at home. But if the novel is a watchful traveller's journey through peasant life during the first eighty years of this century, its characters are strong enough to burst the bond of local record and fortune. They are carrying with them the inner life of their race. *On the Black Hill* has been compared to works like Thomas Hardy's *The Woodlanders* or *Tess of the D'Urbervilles*, because it comes so close to the skin of its people, but the comparison is misleading. Chatwin dispenses with grand tragic plot and the theatrical use of coincidence. Above all there is no classical President of the Immortals, indifferent to human fate; there is no Victorian pessimism.

The imagination of the Border people is mythical and Biblical: it has been lit by the torrential eloquence of their dissenting preachers. (The exception among Mr Chatwin's people is an Anglican clergyman and Greek scholar who scorns the Bible and who distributes the *Odyssey* to his parishioners. He was also joint master of the local hunt and was continually called upon as the only man who could save a swarm of bees barehanded. He tipped them into hives which he compared to Athens.) The Bible people see themselves as descendants of Abraham – the man of flocks – and look upon the money-making English cities across the Border as examples of the corruption of Sodom. They see themselves as travellers to the 'Abiding City' of God.

[1127]

Strangeness plainly stated is the key to the book, the mingling of outward and inner life. The story is dominated by two bachelor brothers who are identical twins. They are thrifty farmers who slave until late old age on poor mountainy land in an isolated farm originally called Ty-Cradoc – the name of Caractacus, the Welsh hero who fought the Roman invaders is still evocative in the Border country – but now known as The Vision because a country girl saw the Virgin there in the eighteenth century. Benjamin and Lewis Jones are old men who have shared the same bed and worn-out bedclothes since the death of their parents and we go back over their lives. They are normal shrewd hard-working men but they are magnetised by their likeness to each other and their awareness of each other's minds. Very important to them is that they were born of an unlikely marriage. Their father was a hot-tempered labourer who had married the educated and lonely daughter of an eccentric scholarly clergyman who had suddenly died. She had spent her childhood in India, seemingly in an Anglican mission. It is she who fights to stop her two sons from becoming village dolts. They get a little schooling – much against their father's will – but she brings them up on Shakespeare, Euripides, Hardy and – of all people – Zola – perhaps because of *La Terre*. But the Bible is still their mainstay and her education has an odd effect on them. Late in life they will eagerly turn to Giraldus Cambrensis and to Froissart's *Chronicles*. If the mother had to put up with brutality from the husband she loved and who loved her she never left him. The sons worshipped her, loved the Indian relics she brought with her and in old age slept out of piety under the worn-out coverlets she had stitched together.

When they were born the mother could not tell her sons apart and indeed throughout their lives they gazed mystified by each other. They were never to go away further than Hereford thirty miles off and once only, in 1910, to the seaside. Lewis, the elder by half an hour, was tall and stringy. At the age of eighty he could walk miles over the hills easily or wield a heavy axe all day. 'He gave off a strong smell. His head would wobble as he spoke: unless he was fumbling with his watch-chain, he had no idea what to do with his hands.' The two men would often take out their watches, not to tell the time, but to see whose watch was going faster. Lewis would say no more than 'Thank you!' or 'Very kind of

[1128]

you!' if anyone made a statement of fact to him. He was brilliant with sheep dogs. Benjamin grew up to be shorter, pinker and neater, rather bald with an aggressive long nose. His chief skill was delivering lambs. After their mother's death he did the cooking, the darning and the ironing, kept the accounts and, like his brother, was an extremely hard bargainer and stingy, except with their hay which he gave away to any neighbour in need, saying it was 'God's gift to the farmer'. Lewis was the restless one. Among the pictures in their home there was one of a Red Indian in his birch-bark canoe, and this, together with the memory of learning to recite Longfellow's *Hiawatha* from their mother, gave Lewis a restless desire for far-off places. He was mad about geography.

> He would pester visitors for their opinions on 'them savages in Africky'; for news of Siberia, Salonika or Sri Lanka; and when someone spoke of President Carter's failure to rescue the Teheran hostages, he folded his arms and said, decisively, 'Him should'a gone to get 'em through Odessa'.

He developed in time a fascination for air crashes and kept a record of them. At the end of his life he even took a short trip in a plane.

It was Lewis who hankered after girls – a danger to their closeness and once the cause of a violent quarrel which their mother had always feared. (There is an account, strangely close to the horse-riding seduction scene in Turgenev's *Torrents of Spring*, in which a local artist's wife seduced Lewis, having betted her husband that she would.) Benjamin guessed this at once: the twin brothers knew each other's thoughts; they could even quarrel without speaking. In middle life Lewis outraged Benjamin by buying a tractor which he thought of as a woman and wanted to give a woman's name. He worshipped it, loved its noise and thought the engine as perplexing as a woman's anatomy.

In their early childhood Benjamin was stung by a wasp but it was Lewis who cried and who showed a curious life-long power of taking his brother's pain on himself. They used each other's names. Benjamin screamed when they were separated and ran away from people who could tell them apart. They had curious games, such as standing forehead to forehead staring into each other's eyes in wonder. When their sister was born they hated her and played at having babies – their mother had to stop them; so they played at being new-born lambs – not so strange perhaps: children often play at being animals. At school when they played football, it was fatal to put them on opposite sides: Benjamin would dash across to Lewis's side. In the classroom they gave identical answers to questions. Their most agonising time came with the 1914 war, when conscription started. Lewis was allowed to go off and work on another farm: Benjamin had to join the army. Benjamin pined. He gave up washing for fear of reminding himself that – at the same moment – Lewis might be sharing someone else's towel. He hated Lewis for leaving and suspected him of 'stealing his soul'. One day, staring into the shaving mirror he watched his face growing fainter and fainter, as if the glass were eating it. Later, in the army, Benjamin deserted and was arrested. Lewis knew by the pains in his own coccyx that his brother was being beaten up in the Detention barracks.

Around the brothers are their strange neighbours, notably the Watkins family at the Rock. Watkins is a coffin-maker. The son of that family is a notorious thief who seduces his own sister. After the father's death the mother sees money in fostering the bastard children of the countryside, a bedraggled bemused collection who come and go as the years pass. As the two brothers prosper the Watkins family collapse into rural misery. There is a suicide and there are awful deaths when the farms are isolated in bad winters. We are watching strange processions of raw people as they grope their way fiercely and sometimes comically through their lives: they are neither the poeticised people of early nostalgic novels about peasant life, nor are they crude and Zolaesque. They take their open sexuality for granted. Mr Chatwin is not an erotic novelist but he does convey the ruling sexual excitement. There is a robust account of a lusty Welsh Fair where Lewis, who is after the girls, makes Benjamin take a spin on the Wall of Death and Benjamin has to face the sight of the girls with their dresses flying over their faces and sees bare flesh. He staggers into the street and vomits into the gutter. After that the girls could not get Lewis away from him.

Mr Chatwin's writing is plain and direct. He has perhaps learned from the Russians 'to make it strange'. He is delicately true to changes of sky, weather and landscape and is remarkable in his power to bring human feeling to the sight by some casual action.

[1130]

I find the following simple incident remarkable. Lewis has gone to see Rose Fifield who had rejected him as a lover when she was a maid at the Big House and was willingly seduced and abandoned by the son of the family. She has turned into a broken, oldish woman and Lewis goes to see her out of charity because she is ill and in want; there is nothing but some jars of pickled onions in the house. She does not thank him for the food he has brought and there is little in their monosyllabic chat:

> Before leaving, he foddered her sheep which had gone a whole week without hay. He took the milk-can and promised to come back on Thursday.
>
> She clutched his hand and breathed, 'Till Thursday then?'
>
> She watched him from the bedroom window walking away along the line of hawthorns, with the sunlight passing through his legs. Five times, she wiped the condensation from the pane until the black speck vanished from view.
>
> 'It's no good,' she said out loud. 'I hate men – all of them.'

That phrase 'with the sunlight passing through his legs' is an example of Mr Chatwin's ability to catch the evanescent detail that lights not simply the act of parting but a moment in the life of the heart. He is a master of catching the day itself passing through his people. He is not a professional sorrower at the toils of the peasantry.

The modern world comes slowly in with its trippers and its week-enders, its washing machines, its cheating antique dealers who try to strip the old farmers of their treasures; but the Bible is the ruling consolation. The mythical world lives side by side with reality. The Border people live by their imagination. We shall see Theo, the Afrikaner, at a Harvest Festival reading from the Book of Revelation at the Chapel. Preaching has done something for him. With fervour he lists the jasper and jacinth, the chrysoprase and chalcedony, without misplacing a syllable. The visiting preacher cried out that he felt he could reach out and touch the Holy City:

> [But this was] not a city like Rome or London or Babylon! Not a city of Canaan, for there was falsity in Canaan! This was the city that Abraham saw from afar . . .

[1131]

The preacher is a Welsh nationalist of extreme views but, in the cautious Welsh way, 'expressed these views in so allusive a language that few of his listeners had the least idea what he was talking about'. He was (Mr Chatwin notes) wearing a suit of 'goose-shit green' and had the habit of 'cupping his hands in front of his mouth, and gave the impression of wanting to catch his previous statement and cram it back between his teeth'. Droll and yet manly he is storing his breath up, perhaps, for the moment when he would let out thunder so that Abraham would become indistinguishable from a traditional Celtic giant.

Spectators

━━━━━━

What are the bonds between pairs of inveterate bachelors? For the rest of us, such men are a rare, protected species. In her introduction to *Flaubert & Turgenev: A friendship in letters*, Barbara Beaumont quotes the French critic E. M. de Vogüé: 'There can only be close friendship and solidarity between two men when their intellects have made contact.' The bond between Flaubert and Turgenev was their common belief in the primacy of art, and their innate role as spectators of events outside it. They were to be friends for seventeen years, from their forties until Flaubert died, in 1880. There was little of the attraction of opposites. The stout and bellowing Norman saw himself as a sedentary Viking and was corpulent and tall. Turgenev was dubbed 'the gentle giant' or 'amiable Barbarian' at the famous Magny dinners in Paris where they first met, and if his voice was quiet it could quickly rise to almost hysterical shrillness when he was excited. He was continually mocked for this in St Petersburg society. If giant faced giant, it is important that they seemed exotic to each other. Bald, red-faced, bourgeois Flaubert, with his Oriental affectations, faced a soft, heavy man with thick white hair, the melancholy Russian landowner and aristocrat. They enormously admired each other's work. On Flaubert's side – and he flattered himself on his powers of research – there was awe before the range of Turgenev's knowledge. Turgenev seemed to have read everything of importance, 'even the darkest recess of every literature in the world'. He could speak, read and write, translate at a glance anything in French, German, and English as well as the Classics. He could declaim from Voltaire's tragedies – from Goethe, too – from memory. He was the finest of critics, and yet he could write *Fathers and Sons*, and could give himself intensely to *Salammbô* and *Madame Bovary*. Both men loved food and wine, and talking long into the night.

If the decisive bond was of congenial minds, there was also a bond of private history. When they were younger, both men had been dominated by their mothers. Flaubert loved his mother deeply. He lived with her in Croisset. Turgenev's mother had been a barbarous and thrashing monster to her serfs and her sons, and only he, the favourite, had been able to placate her. If he hated her, he pitied her. She had been outraged when he fell under the spell of Pauline Viardot, the world-famous Spanish opera singer – 'That ugly gypsy!' she shouted. And, indeed, Pauline Viardot had enslaved and never rewarded him. If Flaubert boasted of his feats when he was free of his mother, in Paris, or on his travels in North Africa, he stuck firmly (as all the French did at Magny's) to the idea that love was of passing importance to the artist. But Turgenev, himself believing that marriage was disastrous to art, declared that all his life he had been 'steeped in feminality'. No book, or anything else, had 'been able to take the place of a woman for me', he wrote. 'How can I explain it? I find that only love produces a certain fulfilment of one's being.' He went on to tell the story of an affair with the poor miller's daughter who had refused all presents and had asked him merely for a bar of soap, so that 'she might make herself worthy of her lover's caresses'. There had been nothing in his life, he said, to compare with that moment. Flaubert, Gautier, Daudet, Sainte-Beuve, and the Goncourts were astounded. How naïve, how Russian, the gentle Barbarian was in his *aperçus*. The touching thing in the lives of the two bachelors is that they were united in their devotion to a mother figure whose Radical politics shocked Flaubert particularly – 'poor old mother Sand'. Eagerly they went to her exhausting parties at Nohant.

Of the two friends, Flaubert the hermit is the lonelier, the jealous and more demanding one. From year to year, he is begging the Russian to stay with him at Croisset, but there are Turgenev's annual trips to Russia. In France, there are his violent attacks of gout and his gadabout social life in Paris which delay him at the last minute. If he agrees to meet, he is inevitably hours late. The habit of carrying a dozen watches on his person is clearly an affectation; he has no sense of time at all. He carries them simply to amuse Pauline Viardot's children. Flaubert is convinced that the Viardots will not allow Turgenev out of their sight; he is jealous. After all these years, to be the slave of a woman who has turned you down!

In the late Sixties, there is a long separation. Turgenev leaves Paris, as it seems, for good. Viardot trouble again! Pauline Viardot's great voice has gone: she can give no more performances. She and her husband settle shrewdly in fashionable Baden, where she gives expensive lessons to the daughters of the rich and the princely. Turgenev joins them, builds a house there, and even a little theatre for her, and settles to writing *Torrents of Spring*, and his stories. Flaubert delights in the stories, picking out the exquisite sentences that Turgenev writes so easily, while he is left groaning for days over phrases of his own. Suddenly, the war of 1870 breaks out. The Germans shell Strasbourg. The Viardots are ruined and flee to London, and Turgenev joins them. Here we fear a serious rift in the friendship, for Turgenev has been distinctly pro-German. But no, for Flaubert is angry with the irresponsibility of the French government: its conduct confirms his belief in the corruption of the hated French bourgeoisie. He has suffered the humiliation of having Germans billeted in his house and admits that the sight of their helmets on his bed has angered him but says that the foreigners behaved well. Still, 'seeing my country die has made me realise that I loved it'. But he *is* distraught enough to hope that Turgenev's Russia will avenge the French defeat! Then comes the awful rioting of the Commune. 'Oh we have hard times,' Turgenev writes, 'to live through, those of us who are *born spectators.*'

The Viardots return to Paris, and Turgenev with them. There are long conversations; Turgenev continues to be late. As the years pass, there is a common cause not only in literature but in family disasters. Russia may be 'green and gold, vast, monotonous, gentle and old fashioned and terribly static', but Turgenev is in trouble with his brother, who is cheating him out of his income from the family estate. The husband of Flaubert's niece has gone bankrupt and is slyly robbing him. Flaubert writes:

> Are you like me? I prefer to let myself be robbed rather than act in self-defence, it's not that I'm not interested, but it all bores and wearies me. When it's a question of money, disgust and rage seize hold of me and I go almost out of my mind.

And he goes on, 'Ah! Dear friend, how I should love to stretch out alongside you on your great haystacks.'

The letters turn to their binding enthusiasm for each other's work. The two writers examine sentences. They praise. Letters talk for them. Turgenev has done an introduction for a Russian translation of Flaubert's '*Un Coeur Simple*', but the Russian censor has banned it: there can be no possibility in Orthodox Russia of publishing the story of an old servant who has come to believe a parrot is the Holy Ghost! While Turgenev – the faster writer – has started his last novel, *Virgin Soil*, Flaubert has begun the encyclopaedic *Bouvard and Pécuchet*. Turgenev begs him, very wisely, to cut it to the length of a short satire by Voltaire or Swift, but Flaubert obstinately makes his two clowns go on to geology and archaeology, in their quixotic obsession with the quest for book-learning. 'What an abyss (a wasps' nest or a latrine) I have stuffed myself into!' he tells Turgenev. 'By the autumn you must come and stay.' Turgenev fails once more – his gout is terrible but he sends Flaubert a new Oriental dressing-gown to make up for his absence and Flaubert is ecstatic: 'This royal garment plunges me into dreams of absolutism and luxury. I should like to be naked underneath and harbour Circassian women inside it.' The two friends send each other enormous parcels of exquisite food.

Turgenev is still grappling with *Virgin Soil*, a work also too long. (If it failed in Russia, it was a huge success outside Russia and, above all, in America.) Flaubert's little fortune is vanishing. The sales of his books are small, and his friends, with Turgenev and Maupassant in the lead, attempt to get him a comfortable sinecure – a delicate matter, for the Norman is proud. He refuses to be 'a State pensioner'. In the end, he gives in. His friends call on the powerful minister Gambetta, who refuses them. The pension is reserved for the son of a politician! Turgenev's account of the interview in the corridors of power is masterly. Gambetta says merely two words as he leaves the room with his sycophants and waves the party away.

In collections of letters, the minor domestic events, the odd little details give the accidental human piquancy. Turgenev worries about Flaubert's weight and tells him to walk more. He says that when he was in prison – indeed, in solitary confinement – in Russia he had saved his own life by making four hundred and sixteen trips up and down his cell every day, achieving two kilometres in all. This was carefully calculated. He had used playing cards for counting his steps. The gadabout – 'a squirrel in a cage', as he called himself – an outsize squirrel – had his resources. Flaubert replied that five minutes after getting this advice 'I broke my leg'. This was almost true. The press got hold of the story, and he raged against the vulgarity of an age without privacy: 'I found that paragraph *very distasteful.*'

The two gourmets indulged themselves on Flaubert's fifty-eighth birthday. Soon afterward, Turgenev had to go to Moscow to attend a banquet at the inaugural celebrations for a statue of Pushkin. He knew Flaubert would not join him but begged him, 'the greatest novelist in Europe', to send a telegram, which would be read to enthusiastic public applause. He thought continually of his friend's fame. But now Flaubert is the defaulter. In his penultimate letter, he says he is 'principally indignant against Botanists. It is impossible to get them to understand a question that seems as clear as anything to me.' Turgenev replied from Russia, but the letter was delayed. His friend was dead when it arrived.

Universal Man

A lexander von Humboldt is one of the irresistible scientific brains of the late eighteenth century. Born in 1769, he died at the age of ninety, a year before the publication of the *Origin of Species*. He aimed at nothing less than universal knowledge and as an explorer he was Napoleonic: he invaded the natural sciences and remade their foundations. Napoleon himself hated and suspected this conquering intellect and commanding personality. Kings, presidents, governments and scientists consulted Humboldt obsequiously on everything from the geography of their countries to the natural resources, and he was a social idol too. As for his feats, like his climb of Chimborazo (for which he held the record in high climbing for a generation) or his disappearance for years in the forests and mountains of Venezuela, Ecuador and Peru, they appealed to the popular imagination everywhere; and though he did not discover the Humboldt current off the South American coast, it was spontaneously given his name after he had made his famous oceanographic survey there. His grand work *Cosmos*, which set out to depict in 2,000 pages and in detail

> the entire material universe, all that we know of the phenomena of heaven and earth, from the nebulae of stars to the geography of mosses and granite rocks – and in a vivid style that will stimulate and elicit feeling,

defines the range of his confident and armoured nature which, like that of almost all explorers, had its strange reserves.

Well known to the general reader of the nineteenth century, Humboldt is one of those heroes of science who are inevitably superseded and become remote to all except specialists as time goes by. Douglas Botting's new popular biography reintroduces us to the career and the writings. There is, as he says, a difficulty about the latter. The man of feeling was

[1138]

tortured by the failure to 'elicit' it. He was an exhaustive fact-collector but in prose imagination failed him. He lacked the grace and idiosyncrasy that make great scientists like Wallace and Darwin and the self-effacing Bates delightful; and one cannot but think that he knew the private reason for this. It was strange that a man who charmed men and women with his spell-binding monologues, whose passionate spirit gave such pleasure in his friendships, should harden in writing. There is a personal mystery here which is linked with the dilemmas which set genius on its course. Douglas Botting's Life is interesting about this. He has gone to the proper sources, the text is well organised, and as a traveller in South America and Siberia, he has often found himself on Humboldt's paths. But the book does suffer from lapses into the breezy and blokey style of the broadcasting studio. Humboldt is seen 'bumping into' and 'catching up' with people; when he is nearly drowned off Cartagena we are told 'clearly it was not Humboldt's night'; in London the East India Company drop him because he is a 'hot potato'. Still, the travels have been skilfully drawn from Humboldt's narratives, and the dilemma of Humboldt's character, as he goes from success to success and rises above seemingly disastrous political setbacks, is given its dignity.

Humboldt was born with great advantages. A young aristocrat, handsome and rich, he was sure of privileged position whether he had gifts or not. (These appeared late because he was a slow learner.) But his disadvantages were serious as well. He was born into a dull provincial society – Berlin was a backward city of 140,000 people, scientific education scarcely existed, science was half-superstition: he did not even hear of botany until he was eighteen – and he was brought up by an unfeeling mother who thought little of him. The emotional check in his childhood was critical to a man of strong passions and dominant character. He turned, inevitably, to romantic friendships with men and, once feeling was aroused, the energies of will and mind were released. Women excited him, but his affections ended in wariness. One woman, the young wife of a Jewish professor who had led him to science, did dazzle him; he was almost in love with her and she became his first confessor. He revealed to her one of his startling dreams in which men became women then turned once more into men: a dream which suggests an androgynous rather than purely homosexual nature. It is probable that he remained

[1139]

chaste all his life. His passionate friendships he described as 'brotherly'. They were profound and invigorating, even if they eventually led to despair when, through marriage or some other reason, they had to break. (With one couple he travelled on their honeymoon.) It may be that the curious interest in the hermaphrodite which appeared in Europe at the time of the French Revolution may have caught his mind and encouraged him; he certainly held to the political idea of the brotherhood of man with something more than intellectual conviction. What seems certain is that he turned to ambition, hard work and encyclopaedic knowledge, as Mr Botting says, to escape from the temptations of the flesh.

Sublimation, masochism or the firm shutting of the door on the private self? The dilemma was scotched by Humboldt's efficiency, his determination and his confidence in himself as a superior being. His mother had forced him into the dull life of the civil service. He chafed at it but, once there, he soon surpassed his older colleagues by his ability and leapt to the rank of Assistant Inspector of Mines. Wealth and influence helped but he now outdid anything influence expected. He went to the derelict mines of Bayreuth, documented the forgotten sixteenth-century workings and was down in the pits from four in the morning till ten at night, applying his mind to every detail. His success was spectacular. In one year the yield of gold approached what had previously taken eight years, and at half the cost. At twenty-six he was famous. His health, which had been delicate, improved and from that time on it became impervious. And he had added humanity to a far-seeing intelligence. The wretched miners needed education and protection. He started a mining school which was thronged by the men. He analysed the gases at great risk to himself, invented a form of breathing apparatus, paid for the school out of his own money and refused the State's offer to repay him, asking instead for the money to be put to creating a pension fund for the old and sick miners. The task had not only been one of applying scientific knowledge; it also came out of a determined social conscience which, in later years, made him suspect to reactionary governments. He wrote that

Steben had such a strong influence on my ideas, I worked out so many of my greatest plans there and abandoned myself so completely to feeling that I almost dread the impression it would make on me if I ever saw it again. During my stay there, especially in the autumn and winter of 1793, I was kept in a state of such nervous tension, that I could never see the lights of the cottages at Spitzberg shining through the evening mist without emotion. On this side of the ocean no place would ever seem to me its equal.

Having succeeded, he was restless and he resigned his post. He was looking for the chance of scientific travel. There was also an emotional crisis. He suffered when his love for an officer in the Prussian army was frustrated by the young man's marriage. There is evidence that he may have thought of ending his life. But his mother died, and an immense fortune came to him. He went to Paris. He hoped to go with Lord Bristol to Egypt, following Napoleon's train of scientific experts, but the war stopped that. His imagination was stirred by a meeting with Bougainville, who had sailed round the world. Then he found Bonpland, the botanist, already experienced as an explorer; after many failures they walked from Marseilles across Spain to the court of Carlos IV, and in this unlikely place their luck turned, and they were granted the royal permit to explore the resources of South America. The future course of Humboldt's life was settled.

The explorer appears: the tall, almost elegant man in the high hat, surrounded by his scientific instruments, pushing on indefatigably every day, making his notes in the forests of Venezuela, arriving at the cataracts of the Orinoco, moving to the upper Amazon and that dramatic moment when the needle of the compass turns from north to south, climbing volcanoes in Ecuador, the first to be let into the secret of the preparation of *curare* and to observe the scarcely known value of guano as a fertilizer. He was enraged by the treatment of the Indians at the Christian missions:

> To say that the savage, like the child, can be governed only by force, is merely to establish false analogies. The Indians of the Orinoco are not great children; they are as little so as the poor labourers in the east of Europe, whom the barbarism of our feudal institutions has held in the rudest state.

He went on to the silver mines of Mexico and to the United States, where Jefferson was one of the earliest to get as much as he could out of him, for political reasons of his own, and got back to Paris after five and a half years with his fantastic collection, to become thereafter the scientific adviser to the world.

As an explorer and as a temperament, Humboldt was a man of iron, without physical weakness. Of course, he pushed himself forward and saw to it that Bonpland took second place in the fame of their South American travels – still, the egotist was naïve. He was ambitious, he monopolised, was often arrogant and bellowed, in the German way, but it did not greatly offend because of his charm. His 'love affairs' with men continued, and so did his philanderings with women.

Mr Botting's book is beautifully illustrated with excellent and out-of-the-way colour plates and drawings of the period in the best Rainbird manner. They are especially worth having in the book of a traveller, and few are well known.

Irish Behaviour

After the Treaty in the Twenties the Anglo-Irish gentry – the 'Ascendancy' as they were called – rapidly became a remnant. Some stormed out shouting insults at the receding Wicklow Hills. Those who stayed on resorted to irony; for centuries they had been a caste in decline on a poor island-within-an-island in Britain's oldest colony. They stuck to their wild passions for huntin', shootin', fishin', the turf, drink, and, above all, genealogy, as the damp rose in their fine but decaying houses. Debts and mortgages gathered around them, but they had long settled for not knowing history socially except when it presented itself in the form of family trees (sometimes done in tapestry) going back to the Normans, the Elizabethans, even to Charlemagne.

The snobbery approached, as Stendhal would have said, the Sublime. In their time this race had produced great generals, clever colonial servants, excellent playwrights, writers in prose and poetry. In these last, their particular gift lay in clear swift writing, in the unrelenting, almost militant comedy of manners or in uproarious farce. How often, in the expectant stare of their eyes, one noticed a childlike or raging innocence and the delight in mischief. Their condition was the nearest thing in Western Europe to, say, Gogol's or Turgenev's Russian landowners, and this in the ever-changing light of an often graceful landscape, and in a climate that either excited the visionary in them or drove them in on themselves.

As one who knew something of the period of Molly Keane's *Good Behaviour* I was astonished to find there no hint of the Irish 'Troubles', the Rising of 1916, the later civil war, or the toll of burned-down houses. Was this an instance of the Anglo-Irish, indeed of the general Irish habit of euphemism and evasion? What, of course, is not unreal to Molly Keane is the game of manners, the instinctive desire to keep boring reality at bay, yet to be stoical about the cost.

[1143]

The Victorian and Edwardian codes stayed on far longer in southern Ireland than in England. *Good Behaviour* was less a novel than a novelised autobiography which exposes the case of Anglo-Irish women, especially in the person of the narrator, a shy, large, ungainly, horsey girl. The males, young or old, are always away, either fighting in the 1914 war or shooting and fishing or dangling after less innocent girls abroad. For the women at home sex is taboo, yet marriage is the only hope – so long as you remember that by their nature 'It's a thing men do, it's all they want to do, and you won't like it.' Love, like sex, is really a state of cease-fire. One of the rules of good behaviour is that you say nothing about *it* unless it is done by animals. The native Catholic servants, untroubled by the use of euphemism or 'place', burst with gaudy oaths to your face. They are chiefly excited by illness and death and are passionate adepts at wakes and the 'last rites'. The young girl has to rise above it all. Her duty is to know the voice of command that 'puts people in their places'.

So the amiable war hero and landowner, the girl's father, reckless in the saddle, will have a heart attack in mysterious circumstances; he is a charming drinker and accepted pursuer of young girls when he goes to London. When he is dying his freezing wife is indifferent; her role is to conserve the 'things' of the family – pictures, silver, fine inherited furniture, and the remains of the status and money. The role of the young girl is to control the war between wife, nurse, and the head-tossing servant who sneaks into the sickroom with fatal draughts of whiskey. She is the peasant with the pacifying art of giving sexual relief under the sheets: she pretends she is warming the old man's feet. What does the daughter crave? All the excitements of the freedom she has heard of in the Twenties: to be loved by the young man who has merely flirted in a gentlemanly way at a dance or two, and has vanished. She is red-faced, gauche, and clumsy in society, and has scarcely been educated by an ignorant governess hired mainly to teach her a few phrases of French as an item of gentility. What she craves is the assurance that her father is convinced of her virginity and that he loves *her*: he certainly hates his selfish wife. In the end he *does* show that he loves his daughter. He punishes his wife by leaving the girl the property. And the book ends with that great national festival, the classic Irish funeral at which the girl gets majestically drunk.

This book is an entertainment which in part recalls the one outstanding Irish novel of the nineteenth century, *The Real Charlotte* by E. O. Somerville and Martin Ross – the latter was the more sensitive and serious partner in the collaboration of Somerville and Ross in, for example, *Further Experiences of an Irish R.M.* Somerville was the mistress of country house farce and its metaphors ('Birds burst out of holly bushes like corks out of soda water bottles.' We remember old Flurry Knox whose 'grandmother's curry' was so powerful that 'you'd take a splint off a horse with it'.) Ross was the subtler social moralist who could almost match Mrs Gaskell's *Wives and Daughters* or, on native grounds, Maria Edgeworth.

Molly Keane's real novel, substantial and ingeniously organised, is the more recent *Time After Time*. It is more Ross than Somerville in temper than the earlier book. Now good behaviour is in abeyance, although its shadow is there. We are now in a period closer to the present day. Still no politics, though there is a horrified glance at a political crime abroad, the Holocaust.

For the rest, the Irish imbroglio tells its own tale. Elderly Jasper Swift and his three sisters look back on past glories as they quarrel in the Big House while its remaining acres have become a wilderness. The family are all old, the youngest in her sixties, the others in their late seventies. There are no comic servants, there is little money. Jasper, once at Eton, paces about in the patched clothes of his dressy youth: he has been left the terrible legacy of looking after his bickering and pitiless sisters. His realm is in the kitchen. He does the cooking, specialising in dubious menus with strange sauces which he recalls from his gourmet past; some of the stuff has been rescued from the dogs and cats and is made anonymous by a last-minute scattering of herbs. He is a quiet, nervy fellow and doesn't bother now to conceal his faintly homosexual past; a sort of half-fey cunning saint whose main relief – apart from cooking – is ruling his sisters by getting his own back. They are tough, high-spirited, unsexed ladies but bottled in illusions about their youth. In a confusing narrative which ingeniously brings back glimpses of the family past – and without any clumsy use of flashback so that the past secretes itself in fragments – we are grateful that the ladies are conveniently called April, May and June.

Fiercely they lock their bedrooms against one another. They have all, including Jasper, been emotionally maimed by the monstrous, possessive will of their 'darling Mummie', long ago dead. We are back in a forgotten Anglo-Irish, perhaps totally Irish, puzzle: how do the women survive? The answer is by secretiveness, rancour; liberated by isolation, they go 'underground' and 'make do', all expert in the 'home truth'.

Shut up in her room, seventy-five-year-old April, the ex-beauty, lives among the beautiful dresses of her past. She is a childless widow – she knows what the others don't, that 'thing men do'. (Her husband, a pornographer, liked 'doing it' on trains.) She lives in the past, and is deaf and carries a pad on which the others have to write down what they have to say. Her chief occupations are weight-watching and push-ups. Her deafness seems to enhance what was once beauty: she is 'armoured for loneliness'. She sips vodka and is bemused by tranquillisers.

May's room is as bleak as a room in a nursing-home. She looks and lives like a robot, has never been desired, but is frantically busy as a bad artist. She makes pictures out of tweed, grasses, dead flowers, and leather. She loves to collect china rabbits – her obsession. She is also light-fingered where bright little objects are concerned: tinsel, marbles, anything that shines – a jackdaw. Her dexterity with her hands is astonishing for she was born with a 'cropped right hand with only two fingers'. She knows how to conceal this wound at local talks on flower arrangement. She is in conspiracy also with the local antique dealer – a new type in modern Ireland – and is not above some skilful stealing.

Baby June, the youngest, aged sixty-four, has reverted to the peasant condition and is indeed a by-blow. Fit to do the work of two men, illiterate, she is a powerful girl in the stables and has been, in her time, a rider who was the terror of every point-to-point in the country and was 'the shape and weight of a retired flat race jockey'. She is an expert at delivering calves, killing lambs, knows how to deal with farrowing pigs. She clumps into the house, satisfied by the blood on her hands and clothes. Her closest friend and pupil is a pious Catholic stable-lad she is training to become a jockey. Around the sisters crowd their lascivious dogs and cats in Jasper's filthy kitchen. (*His* cat sits on the bread board.)

And then, a pitiless figure descends on them – old indeed, fat but in gorgeous clothes, reeking of Paris and insinuation. She is Leda, half-

Jewish, the daughter of a famous restaurateur in Vienna who had married into the family before the 1940 war. To her cousins she brings back the childhood memories of past wealth and pleasure. Miraculously they feel rejuvenated. They had never liked to talk about her because of her Jewish blood, for they were sure she had been trapped by the Nazis and had died in Belsen. They half-remember that, when staying with them as a girl, she had been suddenly, without explanation, and in one of the high moments of 'good behaviour' – 'so sorry you cannot stay' – firmly sent off at a moment's notice by 'darling Mummie', a genius of the final goodbye. Perhaps it was something to do with Daddy or Jasper? It doesn't matter now: they are ravished by her miraculous chatter. They are overcome by pity for her state: she is blind. Only Baby June, illiterate, dirty, has no time for her. Jasper himself, the man who had always longed to be 'more of a Human Being', is excited. He returns to compete with Vienna in his kitchen. Leda, in short, brings the family to life. They put her in Mummie's sacred room and thenceforth she worms their secrets out of them. It is a seduction with a special compensation: her blindness. She cannot see how aged they all are, any more than she can know her own ugliness.

But when we see Leda installed alone in Mummie's sacred room we watch her do a strange thing. She gropes towards the wardrobe where Mummie's beautiful dresses still hang and, fingering the material, pulls the finest one out and spits all over it. Leda, we see, is here for vengeance. (Here is the real echo of the appalling jealousy Martin Ross evoked in *The Real Charlotte*.) One by one she worms out the eager secrets: April, full of erotic notions, picked up from her dead husband the pornographer; May the artist and nimble shoplifter; guilty Baby June who once shot Jasper in the eye when she was a child of seven; and Jasper, with his peculiar meetings with a local monk. At a terrible breakfast scene she comes out with all of it. Jasper in his lazy, evasive, semi-saintly way gladly makes himself out to be worse than the sisters who drive him mad, in order not to look nicer than they are.

There is more to this thoroughly well-organised traditional study of intrigue, malice, and roguery. It is rich and remarkable for the intertwining of portraits and events. It is spirited, without tears. The ingenious narrative is always on the move and has that extraordinary sinuous, athletic animation that one finds in Anglo-Irish prose. Mrs Keane has a delicate sense of landscape; she is robust about sinful human nature and the intrigues of the heart, a moralist well weathered in the realism and the evasions of Irish life. No Celtic twilight here! Detached as her comedy is, it is also deeply sympathetic and admiring of the stoicism, the *incurable* quality of her people. When Leda herself is exposed and is taken off and put back with her nuns again, a helpless, cynical, evil creature, April relentlessly goes with her, almost like a wardress, to make her do her slimming exercises. Jasper, who has never quite been able to become a 'human being', has one less sister to torment and turns once more to his cooking and gardening. So Irish realism, with the solace of its intrigues, dominates this very imaginative and laughing study of the anger that lies at the heart of the isolated and the old, and their will to live.

Medieval Voices

At the beginning of the fourteenth century, the Inquisition set out to crush the Albigensian, or Cathar, heresy in one of its last resorts, the tiny mountain village of Montaillou, on the French side of the Pyrenees, in what is now the Department of Ariège. In medieval times, the region was an independent principality ruled by the Comtes de Foix. A verbatim report of the proceedings of the Inquisition lies in the Vatican Library and had long been known to historians, who apparently regarded it as worthy of not much more than a footnote in their studies. History has traditionally been concerned with great persons and central political situations, but in recent years a number of French historians associated with the journal *Annales* have taken another view. They have turned from public life to the intimate and natural life of people caught as they live through events: to the daily habits, the superstitions and beliefs of anonymous men and women. The Inquisitor's report on Montaillou turned out, quite unintentionally, to be a mine rich with the everyday habits of an isolated group of peasants given idealistically to human error. Emmanuel Le Roy Ladurie, a fine and original historian – well known for his *The Peasants of Languedoc* – saw the peculiar value of the document, and although one might think an exhaustive study of Pyrenean peasant life in the fourteenth century to be outside the common interest, his *Montaillou: Cathars and Catholics in a French Village 1294–1324* was a best-seller in France. The English translation, by Barbara Bray, is an abridgment of the French, but it is well done and irresistible.

M. Le Roy Ladurie conveys his wide and searching scholarship in a graceful, clear, and witty prose. His intelligence sparkles. One reason for the book's success is overwhelming: the Inquisitor's verbatim report enabled the author to give us what history so rarely can – the real voices and phraseology of a people lost for hundreds of years. We hear them talk of their village, crops, families, animals; their attitude to love, sex, marriage, death; their superstitions, their friends and enemies; their religious speculations. One is listening to an artless, sometimes sturdy, sometimes cunning confession. The whole might be the puzzled confession of a culture and an age. It was winkled out of them by the sly Inquisitor Jacques Fournier, Bishop of Pamiers, later Pope Benedict XII, who might almost be called the hostile co-author of Le Roy Ladurie's book. Fournier, we are told, was the 'very devil of an Inquisitor' – a remorseless psychologist and deadly theologian, a terrible sifter of souls. No detail of his victims' lives was too small for his attention. Had he not been a theologian, he might have been a novelist collecting his material. He also resembles the contemporary commissar, depending on spies and informers, and determined to destroy heterodox Error. Although Fournier was rarely a torturer, he had the sadistic pleasure of sending his victims to the stake or to be fettered in prison, where they were forgotten, and of sending the minor sinners to homeless ruin and the wearing of a yellow cross as a penalty for heresy.

It is not necessary for Le Roy Ladurie to go deeply into the Cathar heresy except in so far as it reveals the daily life of Montaillou, which became its last refuge; over the passes, the fugitives could get to the relative tolerance of Catalonia and the Mediterranean. The heresy was Christian and appeared originally in Languedoc, northern Italy, and the Balkans. In an eccentric form it foreshadowed the great Protestant revolt in Europe two centuries later. Catharism is evidence of a slowly growing change of heart and mind among the common people. It accepted the Manichaean doctrine of two opposite principles; one of good, one of evil – light and darkness, the spiritual and the carnal. God and Satan were equal or nearly equal gods. Cathar belief distinguished between believers, or *crédentes*, and an élite of personal righteousness – the *parfaits*, or *bonshommes*. The *parfaits* were commonly said to be 'hereticated' – an equivalent of 'baptised'. They had to refuse to eat meat or to unite with women. Conversion assured them of immortality in a peasant Heaven; they were missionaries and could bless bread. Baptism was by book, not by water. The cult was practised without Church ritual, in the privacy of the home. At death, the *parfaits* entered into a state of ascetic *endura*, or suicidal fasting. Less austere believers had a more agreeable life. They profited by one of the paradoxes of dualism: when everything is forbidden, everything becomes allowed (as the 'justified' sinners among Calvinists later discovered) until the last moments before death. Then ordinary believers might also become 'hereticated', and would be assured of the consolations of forgiveness and immortality – in which reincarnation played an ingenious part. The soul became part of a multitude of spirits that fill the air or enter animals:

> When the spirits come out of a fleshy tunic that is a dead body [said Belibaste, one of the villagers interrogated], they run very fast for they are fearful. They run so fast that if a spirit came out of a dead body in Valencia and had to go into another living body in the Comté de Foix, if it was raining hard, scarcely three drops of rain would touch it! Running like this, the terrified spirit hurls itself into the first hole it finds free! In other words into the womb of some animal which has just conceived an embryo not yet supplied with a soul; whether a bitch, a female rabbit or a mare. Or even in the womb of a woman.

Bad souls become devils, entering wolves, snakes, toads, flies, and all poisonous beasts, inedible or inimical to man.

The peasants were less hostile to religion than they were to increases in Church tithes, to the greed and worldliness of powerful priests, to taxes on humble foods such as cheese, beets, and turnips, to the rising price of Indulgences. Official Christianity became a political ideology. The peasants, weavers, and shepherds of a remote mountain village like Montaillou may have been in fee to the Comte de Foix, but the village was almost classless. The small castle that stood above the community, which hung down the mountainside, one house above another, had its châtelain, but the nobles were almost indistinguishable from the rest of the people. One of the most compelling women in this book is Béatrice de Planissoles, the châtelaine, who had had two 'noble' husbands and also several village lovers outside her caste. She could pass for a primitive village woman, as dirty in body as everyone else was, though not in hands and face, and, like the others, she would sit by the hearth delousing her husbands, her lovers, and the assembled family. Delousing was a common social way of passing time. Caste feeling was far slighter in the south of France than in the north, and in Montaillou poverty excluded it. The village had little dependence on the châtelain. The peasant did not feel inferior to the artisan, nor did the artisan feel inferior to the often ragged noble. The poverty was not wretched: the village lands were too cold for the vine, but there was wheat. The people lived on bread, smoked pork, the trout of the mountain streams, snails, and the squirrels in the forests. The familiar terraced plots of Southern Europe grew enough. Money was scarcely used; barter replaced it. Domestic utensils being scarce, too, these were borrowed. To be free of temptation and spies, the *parfaits* lived a good deal in the forests, chopping timber, which the women carried home. There was a tailor who was a *parfait* and a cobbler who distinctly was not. It was a general rule in such villages that the cobblers and the priests were the Don Juans and contributed to the supply of bastards, who often became domestic servants. The rate of mortality was very high, especially among infants.

The moral centre of the society was the *ostal*, or *domus* – or, as we would say, the hearth. A family was not simply the persons in it but the stone, wood, or daub that housed them and their beasts, and the energies that sustained them. To protect these energies in the future, the hair and the fingernails of the corpse were preserved when the head of a family died; these were known to grow after death and were kept to stop the dead taking away the vitality of the *domus*. Another danger to the *domus* was the loss of women by marriage: they took their dowry with them. The villagers therefore negotiated marriages with the care of auditors making a balance sheet. Some, including the priest, inclined to the day-dream of incest between brothers and sisters as a guarantee, but the defence of the family introduced subtler rules; marriage between first cousins was prohibited. Outside of this, Catharism was permissive without being promiscuous. There was a distinction between what was shameful and what was sin. Raymond de l'Aire, a peasant – and a confessed atheist – said:

> To sleep with one's mother, sister or first cousin is not a sin, but it is shameful. On the other hand, to sleep with second cousins and other women I do not consider a sin, nor a shameful act either; and I hold firmly to this view, because in Sabarthès there is a proverb which says, 'With a second cousin, give her the works'.

The *parfaits* of Montaillou were revered as the 'goodmen', the bearers of virtue in a primitively Christian faith. But not all the inhabitants were heretics, and the Inquisition turned the place into a web of spies and informers. In Fournier's report, three or four figures come vividly to life. First, the brothers Clergue. Bernard was the tax collector and bailiff of the Comte de Foix. Pierre was the priest. He is the complex exemplar of the man who runs a protection racket – the godfather, or spider at the centre of a complex web. A short, frightening, blackmailing seducer of the women of his parish but a very able man, he was the son of a Cathar father, who detested him, and a Cathar mother, whom he adored. In his early years, he seemed to be a genuine heretic, but, intent on power, he soon became a double agent, and his brother co-operated with him. Bernard collected tithes and, to keep in with both sides, shared them between the Cathars and the orthodox Catholics. Neither brother saw himself as a renegade; rather, each saw himself as carrying out a justified vendetta against his family's enemies. Although the Clergues' evidence led many to be condemned, the Inquisition sent the brothers to death in prison when their dirty work was done.

Then, there is Béatrice de Planissoles. She would never consent to bear a child outside her own caste. She endured rape by the priest's cousin, a bastard, but does not seem to have been greatly distressed. Her love affairs were public; she was a sensual and passionate creature. Even the priest would not give her a child, for he recognised that he was lowborn and knew that she would be shamed. Yet he would sleep with her secretly, before the altar, on a bed brought into the church. He also practised a form of birth control, using a package of herbs containing the rennet of a hare.

> One day [said Béatrice] I asked the priest: 'Leave your herb with me.'
> 'No,' he said, 'I won't, because then you could be united carnally with another man, and thanks to the herb avoid becoming pregnant by him!'
> The priest said that out of jealousy of Pathau, his cousin, who had been my lover before him.

Although the strength of the *domus* lay, as everyone knew, in marriage, the interrelationships often made marriage difficult. Concubinage was

[1153]

acceptable, and distinctions were made about the nature of love. The daughter of a sheep farmer formed a temporary union with Arnaud Vital, the cobbler. She said:

> I was very fond of Arnaud, with whom I had established a dishonourable familiarity; he had instructed me in heresy; and I had promised him to go and see my mother to persuade her to agree that my young brother [he was very ill] should be hereticated.

Le Roy Ladurie notes that she did not think her life anything to hide or to be ashamed of – this was a real love affair, a matter of inclination. Arnaud remained on good terms with his mistress's mother. Many women thought carnal love no sin so long as one made love for pleasure. When pleasure ceased, it became sin. The Inquisitor unearthed the astonishing variety of influences, whether realistic, religious, or simply innocent, on human feeling. It was considered no sin to go with a prostitute so long as one paid: the payment absolved.

Le Roy Ladurie is not an anecdotalist. Every word spoken adds something to our knowledge of how the people lived and felt. He notes how the women married many years earlier than the men, who aged rapidly, so that if women had a hard life when they were young they survived much longer and came to formidable positions of power as mothers-in-law and grandmothers. He notes that the women were great gossips (dangerous in this period of religious persecutions) but that there was no educational difference between the sexes – neither had any education. Discrimination did not appear until parish schools were introduced: these schools were attended only by boys. The women liked firing off questions to one another about their relatives, about childbirth, and, always, about who was or who was not a heretic. It was not until the coming of a more bourgeois civilisation, with its concern for privacy, that this kind of watching, eavesdropping, and spying chatter decreased.

The most attractive human being among the enlightened families of the narrow *domus*-dominated village is Pierre Maury, the shepherd. The shepherds, who drove their flocks in the seasonal migrations across the Pyrenees into Catalonia, had the unsettled character of nomads. They were great bread eaters. They might stay in houses for a while or sleep in barns. They changed their masters often, preferred their freedom to money, rarely married, and scorned to accumulate goods. Pierre Maury was, it is true, once tricked into a marriage – which lasted three days – by a delinquent *parfait* whose mistress was pregnant. The *parfait* missionaries had a technique of preaching to the shepherds as they trudged on their journeys. Though Pierre Maury dabbled in heresy, he was soon bored and sly. He would lead the preacher up the steepest paths of the mountain, so that he was too short of breath to preach:

> But the shepherd and the goodmen used to stop for a pleasant, if not always very liturgical, snack on the journey: galantine of trout, meat, bread, wine and cheese. They had a Cathar good time, while the tentacles of the Inquisition had not yet extended to an altitude of 1,300 metres.

At one time, Pierre dared to rescue his sister from her husband, who was beating her. Pierre was a free man who did not bear malice for long. When ridiculed for being tricked by the *parfait* into the false marriage, he continued to be friends with the man who sponged on him:

> ... this unrequited friendship was not only the result of individual magnanimity. It belonged to a general background of Occitan [i.e. Provençal] culture and artificial relationships in which total brotherhood between friends unlinked by blood, who shared everything equally without hesitation, was institutionalized in the ritual forms of fraternity (*affrèrement*), recorded from the beginning of the fourteenth century.

An informer called Sicre – a man as repellent as Pierre Clergue, the priest – pretended to enjoy Pierre Maury's popularity and friendship; Maury was imprisoned by the Inquisitor. Maury was a happy fatalist. He believed in freedom, preferring a full network of human relations – casual women picked up in taverns – to a wife he could not, he said, 'afford' (though he was often wealthy, in a haphazard way). He chose a life based on Fate freely accepted. Le Roy Ladurie adds, 'is this not the very definition of Grace?' Pierre Maury had only one luxury – 'a pair of good shoes of Spanish leather' – and he was careless of arrest by the Inquisition, 'leading a life that was both passionate and passionately interesting'.

[1155]

Montaillou was concerned, as the author says at the end of this absorbing book, with the physical warmth of the hearth and the promise of the Albigensian peasant Heaven 'one within the other'. Now the terraced plots of such villages, as one can see everywhere in the mountains of Southern Europe, are being abandoned. The stability of an ancient world has gone. Our own world's new peasantry is in the factories, and, unlike the people of Montaillou, belongs to a society of competitors and consumers.

The Death of Lorca

Thirty-seven years after the killing of the poet Federico García Lorca, whose fame had already spread far beyond Spain at the time of his death, it is still impossible to be absolutely certain of the accomplices in the crime and the exact motives for it. Even now, when Lorca's name is rehabilitated in Spain – owing to foreign opinion – and the act has been officially deplored because of the damage it did (and still does) to the image of Franco's 'National Cause', the blame is shifted from one group to another, without naming names. People who might have told much have died; some who could tell have grown old, memories have become vague or evasive. In Granada people waver between caution and fantasy. As in southern Ireland after the civil war of the Twenties, among those once close to the crimes committed there are embarrassment, the wish to forget, generalised talk of personal jealousies and 'uncontrollable elements' that 'come to the surface' in such times.

In Granada, where Lorca died, there was for example a 'Black Squad' of lawless killers who were given *carte blanche* by Valdes, the civil governor, to terrorise the city. They mainly butchered workers in the streets or dragged the wounded from the hospitals. The names of many of these monsters are well known: many died violently, one committed suicide, one still thrives as a timber merchant, another became, of all things, a university professor. When the Franco apologists speak nowadays of 'uncontrollable elements' they half hope we shall think Lorca fell to them. In fact it has been established that the arrest and shooting were very much a hysterical official affair and the work of 'respectable' people in the quarrelling groups who were important in Granada. The moderate CEDA blames the Falange, the Falange blames the CEDA or the Acción Popular, and the story becomes a triangle of factions and provincial personalities. In any case the Andalusians are spontaneous inventors of hearsay and love to dramatise it. They play up, as the Irish play up to Joyce scholars.

Ian Gibson is the latest foreign investigator to go into the mystery. The pioneer, of course, was Gerald Brenan (the Spanish scholar who lived in Andalusia most of his life) in his *Face of Spain*, published in the Fifties. Since then the French writer Claude Couffon, like Brenan, thought the murder might have been a reprisal for the death of Benavente. However, this suggestion came from a hysterical speech by the blood-thirsty Queipo de Llano, who was trying to excuse his blunder in giving the order: Benavente lived long after the civil war. Queipo de Llano may very well have believed the rumour and it seems probable – and is indeed reported – that he told the hesitant governor of Granada to 'give him [Lorca] coffee, plenty of coffee' – Queipo's favourite euphemism when ordering an execution. Enzo Cobelli, an Italian, came to the conclusion that Lorca was a pawn in the struggle between the Falange and the Army represented by a Captain Nestares, who was in charge of the executions at Viznar. (Nestares is still alive, very rich, but Mr Gibson could get nothing out of him.)

A third work, by Marcelle Auclair, seems to Mr Gibson to come closer to probability. It is well established that an informer or agent called Ruiz Alonso played a part in the arrest of Lorca, who was hiding in the house of a close Falangist friend, Rosales. The Rosales family were political enemies of Ruiz Alonso, who was a religious fanatic, and he decided to get them into trouble for hiding the poet. A fourth work, by Jean-Louis Schonberg, argued that there was nothing political in the arrest and that it was a vengeance springing out of homosexual jealousy. (Lorca was indeed homosexual, though he regarded himself as one of the 'pure' as distinct from the 'impure' homosexuals.) In Schonberg's argument Ruiz Alonso was also homosexual and was jealous of the poet. This was exploited by a Granadino painter, in order to save his own skin. (When Gibson put this to Ruiz Alonso he made a dramatic rhetorical scene, proclaimed his heterosexual virility was famous, and offered to seduce the women folk of the critics who denied it.) I agree that Schonberg sounds like an erotic sensationalist taking advantage of the myth of Spanish *machismo*.

Mr Gibson's patient examination of the known evidence and his own further, persistent inquiries, which include interviews that were very bold, have led him to believe that the persecution of Lorca was initiated:

> ... not by any one man but by a group of ultra-Catholic and like-minded members of Acción Popular, among whom Ramón Ruiz Alonso, as an ex-deputy of the CEDA, was the most influential.

The men who took Lorca off from the Rosales house with Ruiz Alonso included a rich landowner called Trecastro and one other. All were members of that fanatical religious group. All, except Alonso, are dead. Trecastro, a roystering Andalusian womaniser and therefore a hero of the Granada cafés, boasted of his part in the arrest and, seemingly, the execution. These things do not constitute proof but there is no doubt that the Acción Popular hated Lorca for his family contacts with the liberal intellectuals of Granada who had brought a celebrity to the city which is now lost and sold to package tourism.

The labyrinth to which this book introduces us is incomprehensible without knowledge of Spanish history, the conflict of the intellectuals with the Church in the nineteenth and twentieth centuries, and the politics of the Second Republic after 1931. Fortunately Mr Gibson is succinct about these matters and is particularly good on the situation in Granada. The picturesque and moribund city had become attractive to distinguished foreigners and Spaniards, and a centre for artists and intellectuals drawn first by the beauty of the Alhambra, which was being intelligently restored, and by Andalusian music. By the end of the century the university had an enormously influential figure in the person of the socialist Fernando de los Ríos, whose family were closely connected with the brilliant anti-clerical educationalists and writers known as 'the generation of '98'. They have had no successors.

At the same time, the city had become rich by the introduction of the sugar beet into the fertile *vega* outside it; a new, wealthy bourgeoisie grew up and *their* Granada, already deep in the fame of being a symbol of the defeat of the Moors, the persecution of the Jews, and the unification of the country, was now about the most obdurately conservative city of the south and beginning to feel the world-wide economic depression. Conditions of life for the peasants were bad; they had begun to organise themselves politically; the middle classes were undoubtedly terrified. It is interesting that Ruiz Alonso – not a native of the province – came from a family that had gone downhill; he had become a printer. His resentment was the classic fascist one of the lower-middle-class 'chip'. The established rich in Spain have always held to the traditionalist Catholicism and the militant and violently intolerant spirit of the Counter-Reformation. From the early nineteenth century onward they have been totally opposed to liberal reform, especially in education.

By the Twenties – when I first went to Granada and spent some time with Fernando de los Ríos – I was, like most foreigners, astonished by the absolute division between the Catholic and the liberal groups. There was not merely hostility of opinion, there were personal hatred, social ostracism, and undeclared civil war. The hatred was for the intellect, especially for an intellect which had contacts outside Spain. The Acción Popular would hate Lorca simply because he was a playwright and poet, famous everywhere and connected with the intelligentsia in Granada, Madrid, Paris, and New York. Politically he was naïve: he was simply and generously on the side of the poor, for his art derived from the popular culture of the *vega*. But he had no party connections; for him 'the people' did not mean 'the People' of left-wing politicians. He was closely related to the de los Ríos family, but he was equally a friend of the Falangist Rosales and of the young José Antonio Primo de Rivera, leader of the Falange.

To Lorca, as to hundreds of gifted and independent people like him, the anarchic state of Spain was a torment that frightened him. It was in deep depression and fear that he went home to his family in Granada when the rising was about to break. It seems that Ruiz Alonso was on the night train that took Lorca to Granada. When, weeks later, Alonso came to the house of Rosales where Lorca was hiding and Rosales asked what charges were made against the poet, Alonso's reply was, 'He did more damage with his pen than others with their guns.' In that there is all the rancour of the slave turned informer.

One of Mr Gibson's achievements is to have secretly taped Alonso's rambling rhetorical attempts in old age to blow up his importance and disown his responsibility. There are streams of religious justification and self-praise. If in the end Mr Gibson's indefatigable inquiries bring no certainty, they have led him through the ghastly scenes of the Franco terror in Granada. Over 4000 people were shot in the city alone. The trucks loaded up the prisoners, among them a large number of famous lawyers, doctors, surgeons, university professors, and carried them out night after night to be shot against a country wall.

Readers of this book may think of it as an exercise in detection, and a very able one, and may be tempted to say, with the Franco sympathisers, that the same went on on both sides. It did. But as Mr Gibson says:

> Had Federico not died that morning at Víznar, the thousands of other innocent, but less well known, *granadinos* liquidated by the rebels might have been forgotten. As it is they will be remembered long after those responsible for the repression have passed into oblivion.

Seen in this light of course Lorca's death has a symbolic significance that goes far beyond Granada to the thousands who fell to the ferocity which Franco awakened in a nation notoriously prone to it.

Malraux and Picasso

In his essays on painting and sculpture André Malraux was a master of
eloquence and aphorism. He had been a Marxist, drawn romantically to
revolutions – first in the Far East and then, as a soldier, in the Spanish
Civil War. He was also, mysteriously, a collector and an entrepreneur,
and, finally, a Minister of Cultural Affairs whose hero was de Gaulle.
Malraux was deeply a hero-worshipper. His famous novels were laconic.
Later, flights of pugnacious rhetoric came to illuminate his polemical
writing like flashes of lightning, by which his subjects jumped into sil-
houette out of what one can only call a landscape of generalisations. This
quality dominates *Picasso's Mask*, the essay he wrote in the last year of
his life. The book is a moving and pointed recollection of talks about
painting that he had with Picasso over the years. It is also a fighting
commentary on the 'Copernican revolution' that changed the direction
of Western painting and sculpture after 1900, when the West made its
contacts with Asian, African, and prehistoric art. Added to this, there is
a very personal campaign for what he calls the Museum Without Walls,
in which certain works of genius can look across the centuries and, as
he puts it, 'whisper' to one another. Such a museum, it is agreed, must
ideally exist in the mind; artists, in any case, fear museums. Malraux's
first flash of lightning makes this distinction:

> What did the Louvre assert? What was Giotto's response to Cimabue
> and to the Byzantine mosaics of the baptistry in Florence, which he
> passed each day? Art is an interpretation of nature – of what men can
> see . . .
>
> In many respects the Renaissance was a resurrection of the visible.
> In many respects, the Museum Without Walls is a resurrection of
> the invisible.

In a famous phrase – an echo of Dostoevsky's 'Without art a man might not find his life worth living' – art, for Malraux, is 'a revolt against man's fate'. It is 'a manifestation of what men are unable to see: the sacred, the supernatural, the unreal . . .'

Picasso, parodist, destroyer and creator, the most prolific inventor of styles and forms, was exactly the figure to attract Malraux's electricity. Of the private Picasso he says little, though what he does say is touching and vivid: we see Malraux after his escape from Spain in the Civil War talking to the painter while he is working on 'Guernica'; we see them again in the studio in the Rue des Grands-Augustins, and still later in Provence. There is little about politics. After Picasso died, Malraux went down to the farmhouse, Notre-Dame-de-Vie, at Mougins, in which each room was the painter's workshop and where one walked as on a jungle path through canvases stacked everywhere. He was called in to help the grieving Jacqueline Picasso – the pretty girl from Arles, 'a Roman medal with an aquiline nose' – in her difficulties about housing the painter's work and collection. Appropriately near to Mougins, the first experimental embodiment of a Museum Without Walls, which he and Picasso had often discussed, was opened in 1973, at the Fondation Maeght. There, in 'secret confabulation' across time, were the pieces of Asian statuary, the 'Penelope' looted from the Acropolis, the 'Kacyapa' of Lung-Men, Manet's 'Berthe Morisot', the Beauvais 'King', Rouault's 'Worker's Apprentice', some Fauves, and, of course, Braques and Picassos, and much else. Missing were Courbet's 'Portrait of Baudelaire' – one of Malraux's 'saints' – and there was no Monet. Picasso had no Realists or Impressionists in his personal collection. For Picasso, 'the saints acting as intercessors' were Cézanne, Van Gogh, and Douanier Rousseau.

The word 'intercessors' is arresting. When Picasso was painting 'Guernica', he spoke of the influence of Japanese painting on his immediate predecessors, and of his own encounter with Negro sculpture:

The [Negro] masks weren't just like any other pieces of sculpture. Not at all. They were magic things. But why weren't the Egyptian pieces or the Chaldean? . . . Those were primitives, not magic things. The Negro pieces were *intercesseurs*, mediators . . . They were against everything – against unknown, threatening spirits. I always looked at fetishes. I understood; I too am against everything. I too believe that everything is unknown, that everything is an enemy! Everything! Not the details – women, children, babies, tobacco, playing – but the whole of it! . . . all the fetishes were used for the same thing. They were weapons. To help people avoid coming under the influence of spirits again, to help them become independent. They're tools. If we give spirits a form, we become independent. Spirits, the unconscious (people still weren't talking about that very much), emotion – they're all the same thing. I understood why I was a painter.

And this led him on to the disputes with Braque: Braque wasn't afraid of the masks, didn't even find them foreign to him; he had not a trace of superstition. Also Braque *reflected* when he worked. Picasso put curiosity before reflection:

Personally, when I want to prepare for a painting, I need things, people. He's lucky: he never knew what curiosity was . . . He doesn't know a thing about life; he never felt like doing everything with everything.

The pair had, said Jacqueline, awful rows. Picasso hated continuity of style; his successive periods follow one another 'like outbursts within rage'.

He grumbled: 'Down with style! Does God have a style? He made the guitar, the Harlequin, the dachshund, the cat, the owl, the dove. Like me. The elephant and the whale – fine – but the elephant and the squirrel? A real hodgepodge! He made what doesn't exist. So did I. He even made paint. So did I.'

Picasso's condemnation of style, Malraux says, was more profound and also more obscure than his remark 'I have no real friends. I have only lovers! Except perhaps for Goya, and especially Van Gogh.' In later life, he would have added Rembrandt. What a painter had to do, Picasso argued, was to revolutionise people's way of identifying things – create images they wouldn't accept, a world that was not reassuring. He liked to think of himself as a 'sorcerer' (and some have thought of his works as acts of exorcism); Malraux notes that the word 'was in keeping with the trancelike states of some of his forms'. His figures come out of 'black magic, his power of metamorphosis'. Picasso knew that 'his genius had a mysterious side to it; he was aware of his malarial fits of invention'. He had, Braque said, a sleep-walking side. Of course, if one is conscious of violence and anarchy – which strike me as having deep roots in the Spanish tradition – there is also something of the child's free imagination, inventiveness, and feeling for play, the child's impatience. One day, Malraux recalls, Picasso took out of a metal cupboard a violin-shaped idol from the Cyclades and two casts of a prehistoric statuette – the Lespugue Venus. One was of the mutilated statuette. The other was of the statuette restored: '. . . her bust, and her legs joined together, sprang forth symmetrically from the lusty volume of her rump and her belly.' A grotesque? No. A new object buzzing with its new life. Picasso said, darkly, 'I could make her by taking a tomato and piercing it through with a spindle, right?' He sounded, Malraux says in another connection, as if he were poking fun at himself, though often he seemed to be jeering at the human form: 'His jokes were grating.'

This essay is not the work of an art historian, or even of a critic, but, rather, the rhetorical response of a man of action to some of the artist's innumerable acts with his hands. (Like others of his generation, Picasso rejected the word 'artist'. He hated 'professionalism'. The professionals were just turning out cakes and confectionery of the required kind. Aesthetics were an irrelevance.) To Malraux, who had a lot of the old Marxist left in him, evaluation and the question of beauty are matters of history, and history has now become much wider in our own minds. How does he relate Picasso, the genius of metamorphosis, to our need for art, and how do we know our standards? How is it that we can tell the difference, say, between Surrealism and Picasso's fantastic invention, between the *tableau vivant* and folk invention, between accident and design? These are questions of value that writers have put to painters hotly since the 'Copernican revolution' – questions notoriously futile from the painter's point of view. Painting and sculpture cannot be translated into words. One art cannot evoke another.

We have to turn to the very long and sweeping speech that Malraux made when his idea of a Museum Without Walls was modestly realised at the Fondation. The address is the brilliant glissade of a mind through the sacred and profane phases of Western art from pre-Christian times to the paganism of today. His aphorisms and paradoxes cut like forked lightning. One has to be quick to see the silhouettes of artistic crises as they jump out and pass. His mind is combative. To those who may be thinking of Spengler, the decline of the West, and that all is chaos, Malraux replies that 'the Museum Without Walls is based on the assumption that the destiny of all great styles is metamorphosis'.

> Artists had represented the characters of Classical mythology in accordance with faith, but they then came to represent the characters of the Christian faith in accordance with Classical mythology.

With Romanticism, the whole world of art changed: 'The glory of the word "beauty" came to an end with Delacroix.' The painters no longer said, 'It's beautiful'; they said, 'It's good.' Realism, for Malraux, derives from the idealism and spiritualism of the Romanticism that preceded it, and against which it fights. Manet's 'Olympia' did away with 'the illusion and the poem' in Titian's 'Venus of Urbino', and is a reincarnation. The power to create may originate, as we know well,

> from the most disquieting unpredictability, from a madman's inspiration, from the naïveté of the naïve, or from the patience of a shepherd . . .

but it 'harmonises its own elements in a way that life never does'. All historical civilisations have carried on 'a dialogue with the unknowable', and the unknowable 'encompasses death, sacrifice, cruelty . . .'; it is 'a mixture of what man hopes to know and what he will never know'. Finally:

> Our civilization, which now sees that of the nineteenth century as a hesitant and optimistic preface to it, is not devaluing its awareness of the unknowable; nor is it deifying it. It is the first civilization that has severed itself from religion and superstition. In order to question it.

> And the forms of our art 'have become as arbitrary as the forms of the sacred . . .'

What would Picasso, the painter who worked all day and half the night, sometimes in a fever, sometimes humorously and ingeniously at play – what would he have made of this speech? I think he would have been struck by precise instances rather than by argument. From what Malraux says in an aside earlier in the book, both he and Picasso seem to have been astonished that a form like the stained-glass window, 'which awoke and fell asleep in accordance with the passing of day', was forsaken. It gave in and died when painting turned to the discovery and innovation of shadow. Five hundred years passed before painters rediscovered 'the arbitrary element' in the stained-glass window, and in mosaics. Whimsically, but with dire meaning, Malraux adds, 'When stained-glass windows vanished, clocks began to reign over the churches.' The epigram allows a laugh of pleasure to the reader of a strenuous book that rather overpowers the subject. (Malraux was equally overpowering in his well-known essay on Goya.) Malraux engages us most when he digs up the dear old rows about art which kept Paris alive until, after the last war, they moved on to New York.

The Romantic Agony

Thomas Mann was one of those formidable novelists who strike us as being men of iron, locked in ambition, eloquent on the podium, cold in detachment, and brimming with erudition. He is the high-bourgeois artist who claims the rights of the artist-prince yet nevertheless looks down with the melancholy of the artist-surgeon seeking intimations of our mortality. There are glints of a romantic sadism in that gaze, which has come to be thought of as a characteristic of 'the Romantic Agony' common in his generation. He himself knew that this tormented spirit was penetrated by the strong influence of the Protestant work ethic, which he inherited from his mercantile forebears, who had been eminent in Lübeck for generations. He can indeed be thought one of the great martyrs of that ethic, but it is untrue to add, as some critics have, that 'he starved his life to feed his art'. In an Afterword to the biographical study *Thomas Mann: The Making of an Artist 1875–1911*, by Richard Winston, the biographer's widow writes that Thomas Mann was 'bewilderingly caught up in life'. 'He had fought with great energy on literary and political battlefields. Several times over he had seen the stable world around him crashing to pieces. He had had more than his share of acquaintances, alliances, loves, hates, tragedies. In fact, Mann's personal history had all the elements of a great novel.' Alas, Mr Winston died in 1979, halfway through that 'novel'. But he did reach the period of *Death in Venice* and was already aware of the sources of the masterpieces of old age, *Joseph and His Brothers* and *Dr Faustus*. Winston's book establishes 'the making', and, if it is rather crowded in detail, it is persuasive in its good sense and free from jargon – as indeed Mann himself was – and is fascinating as a human portrait and a literary inquiry. Mr Winston had translated some of the works and letters, had read Mann's very private diaries, and is always persuasive in his conclusions.

[1168]

About Mann's famous 'cold' detachment: the accusation of coldness stung him. In 'Der Bajazzo' ('The Dilettante'), an early story, he wrote, 'It almost seems, does it not, that the quieter and more detached a man's outward life is, the more fierce and exhausting are his inward struggles.' But, as Mr Winston says, those early lines about himself turn halfway into a story about his elder brother, Heinrich, with whom Thomas's life was so entangled in their early years. They aimed their books at each other. The two young men united in their rebellion against the family – Heinrich the dashing leader at first, Thomas the more jealous in the bond. They were obsessed with each other even in their long quarrel in middle age. Heinrich was to pass from the dilettantism of the neo-Romantic into something closer to the social revolutionary. Thomas's own conservatism would eventually soften. If the Dilettante is Heinrich, the delightful childhood scenes in 'Der Bajazzo' are Thomas's. As for intellect, Thomas is at first the backward schoolboy, idle and dreamy; like Tolstoy, almost an autodidact. He is intoxicated by the myths and erotic sensations aroused by Wagner's operas, by Nietzsche's superman. As for the gloom of Schopenhauer, who captivated so many nineteenth-century novelists, Thomas was no philosopher yet believed that '. . . the will to live perpetually seeks to cancel out the results of its own blind strivings . . .'. For both youths, this was evident in their distinguished family's history: their wealthy father closed down his business in the Baltic grain trade when it showed signs of decline before the influences of the new 'imperialist capitalism'. The moral was that the belief in Will and the work ethic had created a longing for rest, for nirvana and death – a theme to become strong in Thomas, though taking a different direction in Heinrich. The message of Thomas's superb *Buddenbrooks*, written in his twenties, was not shirtsleeves to shirtsleeves in three generations but shirtsleeves to decadence and art.

The artistic impulse seems also to have had sources outside the North German tradition. The mother of the boys was solidly German, but she had been brought up in Brazil by a Portuguese mother; Mr Winston speaks of her as a kind of Latin mermaid who beguiled with her taste for music. Thomas was vain of this exotic foreign strain – talk of inherited 'blood' was a nineteenth-century obsession; also he was eager to call himself a 'philo-Semite', because he was strongly drawn to the cultivated

Jewish circles in Lübeck, and in fact eventually married a rich, beautiful, intellectual Jewess.

Add these influences together, impose the torrential influences of Wagner's operas, and we have an imaginative artist who was his mother's son and an inveterate, if melancholy, disciple of the father's gospel of work. He said of himself in one of his intensely explicative essays, 'as a guardian of myth the writer is conservative. But psychology is the keenest sapper's tool known to democratic enlightenment.' He was certainly a master of irony and a mediator. One has to be wary of Mann's Flaubertian comments on art. There is always a mocking spirit in them. The most committed of artists, he saw the artist almost as a harlequin or a not-to-be-disturbed wanton – a man who turned from real life to 'puppets'. He wrote that he had no desire to deny or betray his vocation, but he held that fiction could be a serene, even sacred game, yet still a game. His erudition itself, he said, was a game or a feat of opportunism. He just 'worked things up':

> ... that is to collect information in order to play literary games with it – or strictly speaking, to scandalously misuse it. Thus I became in turn an expert in medicine and biology, a firm Orientalist, Egyptologist, mythologist and historian of religions, a specialist in medieval culture and poetry, and so on ... I forget with incredible speed everything I have learned.

Death in Venice is most delicate and exact as it catches the literal pleasure evoked by Venice and the Lido, but he carefully researched the cholera and the sinister Eastern winds that brought the plague to stagnate there; he researched the city's official policies in hushing up the rumours of the plague. In *Buddenbrooks*, he documented the rise and fall of the Baltic grain trade, the changes in real-estate values, the role of married women in sustaining the bourgeois ethos of the merchants, and their weariness of the cult of achievement. Not only did he document as required but, as many other artists have more accidentally done, he stored up passing experiences for use in the far future. When Thomas and his brother were in Italy as young men, they saw the famous Roman *Mosaico del Nilo*, with its fantastic crowd of elephants and crocodiles, in the medieval city of Palestrina; the experience came back to his mind in old age when he was reconstructing the anthropological myth that gives powerful meaning to *Joseph and His Brothers*. Documentation was not fact fetishism, as it was so often in the novels of Zola; it was not an aspect of Balzac's speculative greed. Facts turned into the myth that lifts one out of reporting and journalism into the images of art by which we live.

Yet if Thomas liked to think he had inherited a Latin strain through his mother, he was inescapably the prudent North German. He was both a Naturalist and a mythmaker: an ear man, he said, rather than an eye man. The brotherly rivalry came to a head when Heinrich wrote his extravagant novel *Die Göttinnen* as a fashionable erotic counterpart to *Buddenbrooks*. Thomas was appalled by Heinrich's paganism, and by the reckless prose and syntax, which he called bombast. When they were entranced by Italy, Heinrich felt at home there, Thomas was soon bored. Thomas was distinctly his own psycho-analyst: the affectionate sensuality, the conscienceless comedy of Neapolitan life, drove his young Northern mind inward. His sexuality froze. He wrote in his diary:

> What am I suffering from? From knowledge – is it going to destroy me? What am I suffering from? From sexuality – is it going to destroy me? – How I hate it, this knowledge which forces even art to join it! How I hate it, this sensuality, which claims that everything fine and good is its consequence and effect. Alas, it is the *poison* that lurks in everything fine and good! – How am I to free myself of knowledge? By religion? – How am I to free myself of sexuality? By eating rice?

Yes; at least rice was cheap, and he had little money. Get back to the desk and work to drive away temptation. In Naples, he wrote a glum monologue called 'Disillusionment', which no one – except a curious biographer like Mr Winston – need read now. Yet – and this is Mr Winston's point – there was rarely any grist lost to Thomas Mann's mill. He would wait forty years until the pimps who had tormented him in Naples were ready to be used in *Death in Venice*.

This brings us to what Mann called his secret homoeroticism, which came to light in the diaries published after his death, and which – to the happily married man – seemed a 'defect' in his nature. In his boyhood, he had passionately loved one or two of his school friends and in later life he had strongly erotic but entirely innocent attachments to young

men. These attachments were, he said, a secret source of pleasure, interest, and creative power – the last, we must suppose, their most important
aspect. Mr Winston thinks that Mann may have exaggerated the importance of the 'defect' as he exaggerated his headaches, his colds, his neurasthenia, his exhaustion, and that longing for nirvana, sleep, even death
which derives from an excess of work and will. And Mr Winston notes
that the attraction of young men or boys, or what Mann called *Knabenliebe*,
was generally acceptable as a sort of education in the years of the Weimar
Republic, and turned quickly to a greater attraction to women: the diagnostician was very familiar with Freud on the erotic spell of the mother-
son relationship. *Death in Venice* derives from Mann's sense of his personal
'defect' and, such was public opinion at the time, the story caused a
scandal when it was published. But stories rarely if ever spring from a
single impulse. A work of art is a transposition, even an evasion: real life,
as it is, is no good. *Death in Venice* is a masterpiece not only because of
its exact evocation of the scene but also because the writer drew on a
variety of sources. Mann said that the book started in his head as a story
based on the aged Goethe's disastrous passion for a very young girl,
hardly more than a child. If Aschenbach in Venice is a tired old writer,
he is neither Goethe nor Mann; he is even given the strange head of
Mahler, the composer. The only intimate links with Mann are the Socratic
dialogue from the Phaedrus (which Mann reread) and the use of obscene
nightmare – a truly Wagnerian saturnalia that enabled him to make
the carnal insinuation clear but blameless. Still, Mann *was* the perpetual
autobiographer simply because he was not writing literal autobiography.
Years later, a middle-aged Polish gentleman, living in Warsaw, wrote to
Mann's daughter enclosing photographs of a boyhood holiday on the
Lido. He claimed that he had been the original of the charming boy in
Death in Venice. There he was, again and again, in the very clothes Mann
had described. There stood his Polish mother and her family. Even the
scrimmage on the beach had occurred. He said he remembered that there
was a peculiar, puzzling old man who kept staring at him and following
him about. The Warsaw gentleman was delighted to be so immortalised
in a masterpiece.

Both Heinrich and Thomas, but especially the latter, were ruthless in
their portraits of their families and intimates, exposing the secrets of those

close to them, and, Mr Winston says, there is sometimes a suggestion of cruelty in this. Most novelists find that a character does not come to life until blended with others or altered by context. Mann's defence was very different:

> I should like to point out the error inherent in making a literal identification between reality and its artistic image. I should like to have a work of art regarded as something absolute, not subject to everyday questions of right and wrong.

Goethe, he said, had not insulted the real people portrayed in his *Werther*: On the contrary, Lotte and her husband

> ... realized that it would have been petty to hold a grudge against the writer who in his book had conferred upon them a life a thousand times superior, more intense and lasting than they were leading in their ordinary respectable reality – and they held their peace.

And, he added, if a portrait was hostile in any respect, the author was inevitably self-portrayed and attacking himself with the same detachment. We might add to this the self-irony in the reflections of Aschenbach, as Eros drives him to his desk:

> Verily it is well for the world that it sees only the beauty of the completed work and not its origins nor the conditions whence it sprang; since knowledge of the artist's inspiration might often but confuse and alarm and so prevent the full effect of its excellence. Strange hours, indeed these were, and strangely unnerving the labour that filled them.

Such hours, sometimes mundane and crowded with the agitations of German life of the period, have been skilfully sought in Mr Winston's biography. The disaster of the 1914 war, the rise of Hitler, Mann's flight from Germany, were yet to come, and Winston did not live to show Mann embattled.

Iran and Pakistan

In 1979 and '80 V. S. Naipaul travelled through Iran, Pakistan, Malaysia and Indonesia, in an attempt to get into the minds of students, villagers, traders, teachers and missionaries who had been swept emotionally into the Islamic revival. Some of the young students had been at British or American colleges and they particularly were convinced of the 'sickness' of the West – no religious faith – and of the evils of Western 'material-ism'. Most had put their faith in the literal guidance in the primitive oracular work, the Koran, and its minute system of rewards and punish-ments and were preaching revolt by regress; others were revolutionary Marxists, above all in Teheran. We are faced in Iran by scenes of sav-agery, faction and ruin; underlying this is the belief that the Muslim faith contains the secret of spiritual 'wholeness' which the West has lost. At the same time, all are eager for the skills and, above all, the rewards of Western science and technology. In this confusion the mind is split. As Mr Naipaul goes eastward he is among peoples who are racially divided and they feel themselves to be lost and 'displaced'. When Muslims spoke to him of this he reminded them that he was a native of Trinidad whose family traditions were those of displaced Hindus, now without faith, and that the Western ethos had equipped him with the will to strive intellectually.

Mr Naipaul is a remarkable diagnostician and, above all, a fertile novel-ist. These gifts are the making of him as an admirable, thinking traveller who exposes himself to the scene. He is a born narrator in the small or large scene. Every place and person and mind comes to life. Like most travellers he uses all his wits to make people talk of themselves and he is so persistent in this that, again and again, it strikes us that they would not have known how to do so without his ingenious Socratic questioning. He is not out for 'copy' but to explore states of experience and mind. He is fully tutored in religious and secular history. He knows the Islamic past. He understands, for example, why the upheaval in Iran (up to now, in many respects, a civilised society) was possible because of its distance from the desert tradition. But, although sharp and decisive, he has a temperamental sympathy and even tenderness for his often intractable people.

Naipaul is far from being a fundamentalist. The Muslim fundamentalist, he notes, seeks to work back to a whole 'with the tool of faith alone – belief, religious practices and rituals. It is like a wish – with intellect suppressed or limited, the historical sense falsified – to work back from the abstract to the concrete, and to set up the tribal walls again.'

But he knows the Muslim mind is split and even idle:

The West, or the universal civilization it leads, is emotionally rejected. It undermines; it threatens. But at the same time it is needed, for its machines, goods, medicines, warplanes, the remittances from the emigrants, the hospitals that might have a cure for calcium deficiency, the universities that will provide master's degrees in mass media. All the rejection of the West is contained within the assumption that there will always exist out there a living, creative civilization, oddly neutral, open to all to appeal to. Rejection, therefore, is not absolute rejection. It is also, for the community as a whole, a way of ceasing to strive intellectually. It is to be parasitic; parasitism is one of the unacknowledged fruits of fundamentalism.

In the empty Hilton in ruined Teheran no sermons were too long for the idle desk clerk. Having got rid of the Shah the people believed that 'oneness was all that was still needed...'

What, after the centuries of despotism, they really believed was that the state was something apart, something that looked after itself and was ever restored. And even while with their faith they were still pulling it all down – a hotel, city, state – they were waiting for it to start up again, to be as it was before.

His first interpreter in Teheran was a young science student, Behzad. He was not religious. He was a Communist, the son of a Communist father who had been imprisoned in the Shah's time, and had inherited his father's

[1175]

dream of social justice. Behzad kept away from mosques and the observances and was forcing himself to see in Khomeini's religious fervour the outline of the social revolution he wanted. For him the Ayatollah was a *petit bourgeois*. Behzad was a tormented young man because the revolution, except in its proletarian aspect, was not his: his hero was Stalin! He was compassionate and had the old Persian delicacy, but he hated Revolutionary Guards and mullahs. He warned Naipaul never to describe himself as having no religion. In the holy, learned and therefore dangerous city of Qom, Behzad took him to see the Ayatollah Shirazi, a benign teacher in the theological college. It had 14,000 students who would remain there for anything from six to fifteen or twenty years: 'as in medieval Europe, there was no end to theological scholarship'. Thinking had been reduced to the repetitious. One of the lecturers had produced material for a twenty-five-volume commentary on the Shia idea of the Imam. (The Ayatollah Khomeini, known for his studies in jurisprudence and Islamic philosophy, had also produced eighteen volumes on other topics!) Shirazi's accent was more Arabic than Persian as he intoned his conversation. And then came the crucial question 'What is *your* religion?' There were Pakistani students present and Naipaul felt he had to be wary before them: his own forebears were Hindus. Behzad told him to say he was Christian. Shirazi asked, 'But what kind of Christian?' Luckily Naipaul said, 'Protestant.' This half pleased the Ayatollah Shirazi who said, 'Then you are closer to the truth. Catholics are inflexible'; but as Naipaul acutely notes he was merely giving a Shia twist to Christian divisions. The Persians are Shias; with their heretical line of succession to the Prophet they see themselves as 'an embattled minority'. This, combined with the industrial wealth of the Shah's dispensation, gave the startling Persian revolution its hysteria and fanaticism: they saw themselves as the true heirs of the Faith. It struck me, twenty years ago when I was in Iran, that a pride in primitive tribal violence was just under the skin, even of the Westernised; and that it was blatant among the poor in the countryside.

At Qom Naipaul thought he had no chance of seeing the notorious hanging judge Khalkhalli but the message came back that the judge 'would *love* to see you'. The famous slaughterer was merely five feet tall, a quick-stepping little clown of a man with merry eyes and wearing glasses, crumpled clothes and a couple of cotton garments hanging over his slack white trousers. He boasted that he had started life as a shepherd – 'right now I know how to cut off a sheep's head' – and added that he had sentenced and killed the Shah's Prime Minister, Hoveyda. This was a joke, put on to make the crowd in his room roll with laughter.

'You killed him yourself?' the author asked, through his interpreter. (In fact Hoveyda had been killed by the son of an ayatollah.)

'But I have the gun,' the judge said. He said he had it in the next room: a treasure.

Foreign interviewers, as Naipaul says, are easy money; he knew the judge was a comedian and was using him as a straight man. He and Behzad returned to Teheran. There the student was to hear that the left-wing paper he worked for had been closed down; by the end of the book this earnest worshipper of Stalin finds his political group defeated for the moment: many of his friends are in prison, many are dead. 'We have to kill *all* the bourgeoisie. All the bourgeoisie of the oppressor class,' he said (with a sweet smile) as Naipaul left him to his mathematical work – done in his fine Persian script, with Western (or Arabic or Indian) numerals. Many of his textbooks were American. Behzad had been fed by so many cultures, Naipaul reflects, but now, at what should have been the beginnings of his intellectual life – like the Muslims to whom he was opposed – he had cut himself off.

In Iran one felt that money, foreign goods and tools gave the illusions of Islamic power, for unearned dollars kept an idle country and its revolution 'on the boil'. In much poorer Pakistan, the tensions of poverty and political distress were falsified by crude rhetoric. Once more, in this book, Naipaul makes individual people bring the dilemmas of Pakistan to life. A shrewd businessman pours out the history of the pre-Aryan race of Sind (creators of the Indus valley civilisation) 'in one gulp'. He was agonised by dreams of fortune; haunted by general dishonesty. The beauty of Islam, he says, lay in its mixture of law and compassion and in its charity. He recommended the author to the shrines of Sind.

At the end, with a tenderness for which I wasn't prepared, he pressed his forefinger to the middle of my forehead. He said, 'That is where it gets you. If you were a businessman you would get blood pressure. You're an intellectual. You are concerned with the truth. So it gets

[1177]

you there, in the eyes. You must rest your eyes. You must look at green things.'

Several of Naipaul's acquaintances remarked on the tired look of his harassed eyes. There was relief for him when he went up to the Kaghan valley in sight of the Himalayas with a science student called Masood. They saw the migrating Afghan shepherds – one of the spectacles of this part of the world – where 'the busy little trotters of the sheep ground the fine dust of the road finer'. This long chapter is indeed the most refreshing in the book, largely of course because we are out of the conflicts of the cities far below where the mixture of old and new is grotesque to the point of vulgarity. Here the effect was of tribal gorgeousness and the certainty of usage and tradition in everyday things:

> One woman walked with one shoe on, the other off, and on her head.
> It was a style – the shoe on the head: later we saw women with both
> shoes on their heads, the heels fitted one into another to form a little
> arch. Shoes were worn when the ground was pebbly; when the ground
> was smooth or soft with dust it was better to walk barefooted.

To Malaysia, Islam had spread from India and Pakistan as an idea. There had been no planting of Arab colonies, no sending back of treasure and slaves and, up to now, religion was simply the old village tradition. Now that has changed: Islamic missionaries from Pakistan bring in the sense of a world movement: the village Muslims now feel the awakened rage of passive pastoral people against the rich in the towns, above all the incessantly active Chinese. There were leaders of the younger generation who had been to England for education, one to Bradford. He disapproved of Bradford. The people there 'are too individualistic . . . They're trying to say be together with others, but not with your family. They are created by their own technology.' Modern Malaysia must not copy that. Free-mixing of the sexes, the use of alcohol are the great Western evils. There were 'brave' independent girls here, but they had covered hair. The face may be seen, but the hands only from the wrist. What did the girls read in their English classes? Thomas Hardy! But, more avidly, Barbara Cartland, Perry Mason, James Hadley Chase. This is pretty comedy. More serious is Shafi, the guide and mentor who – like

Behzad – loved a long quiet soul-searching. He had first lost his village, travelled to America and then had lost the last of his traditions. 'I could see how, without Islam,' Naipaul says, 'he would be lost.' Shafi was trying to run a Muslim commune. Was it possible to be close to Nature without exploiting it? he anxiously inquired. An ecologist might sympathise.

When Naipaul gets to Indonesia he finds a people stunned by foreign occupations, by memories of the massacres of 1965 and now, clamped under army rule – like people 'looking, from a distance, at a mysterious part of themselves'. Islam was the formal faith, but below that were relics of the Hindu-Buddhist animist past, 'no longer part of a system'. The reader himself cannot hold in his mind the world Mr Naipaul asks us to see in a new light, but his strength lies in the tense pitch of his inquiry and in his narrative that brings people and landscape to life in flashes of telling detail, and gives them meaning as, also self-portrayed, he passes through.

The Crystal Spirit

══════

The eccentric, the crank, and the thorn in the flesh turn up regularly in British life and in war many of them come into their own. This was certainly true of George Orwell, who, in addition, was two persons: the suppressed figure of Eric Blair, once a police officer in Burma, old Etonian, and poor Scot, briefly soldier of misfortune in the Spanish Civil War; and George Orwell, amateur outcast, Bohemian, and journalist who, as Herbert Read said, raised journalism to the dignity of literature. He was a familiar London figure in BBC circles during World War II – he was in charge of broadcasts to India – in the Soho pubs, the offices of *Horizon*, and in many districts where poor writers settled in those hungry and seedy times. There is considerable Orwell anecdotage. It was impossible to know such a complex, straying, and contradictory man well, but George Woodcock, who became a friend after the usual quarrel which established one with Orwell, gives a good account of his personal spell, and has written a very penetrating personal study.

Orwell looked, as Mr Woodcock says, like Don Quixote and he was haunted by his Sancho Panza; better still, like a 'frayed sahib' in shabby jacket and corduroy and betraying his class by his insouciance. Tall and bony, the face lined with pain, eyes that stared out of their caves, he looked far away over one's head as if seeking more comfort and new indignations. He had a thin-lipped, hard mouth; his general bleakness was relieved by sudden smiles and by a vigorous shock of wiry hair *en brosse*. The voice had the lazy, almost spiritless, Cockney drawl, but had something like a rusty edge to it that suggested trouble and had been used to authority. He seemed more at home than we were in the bleak no-man's-land that war creates in the mind and in life in general.

Among my encounters with him three stand out. I once went back to a half-empty flat he had taken on the top floor of a high and once expensive block of flats in St John's Wood. He pointed out that the building was half empty because of the Blitz, the rents had dropped low, and that it was lucky to be able to live close to the roof because you could get out quickly to deal with the fire-bombs. He seemed to want to live as near to a bomb as possible. Another time we stood for a long time in a doorway off Piccadilly while he told me about the advantage of keeping goats in the country with full details of cost and yield – for he was a born smallholder and liked manual work. While at the BBC he spent his evenings in a part-time job making small parts for aircraft. He tried to get me to bring my family and join him in the disastrous migration to the island of Jura. The attraction of the island seemed to be that it was out of touch with the mainland for long periods because of storms, that one would be scrabbling along the rocks and shores for food and fuel, and would be free of the competition of modern totalitarianism. We were eating and drinking expensively and well in Percy Street at the time, for a genial Sancho Panza would unexpectedly take over from the gaunt Quixote. One of the things that made him hate industrial capitalism was that it fed its people so badly on the ersatz and had so demoralised them that they could not cook. But, at the same time, he would stuff his pipe with cheap shag bought at miserable little shops and drink strong tea out of its saucer – in the romantic belief that this was what the decent British workman did, and point out the moral advantages of dossing down in 'working-class discomfort'.

These habits led to charges of affectation. Certainly there was a streak of moral vanity in Orwell; but, as Mr Woodcock says, the charge of affectation is superficial. There was an element of inverted dandyism in Orwell and it is indicated by his surprising admiration for Oscar Wilde and especially for Dorian Gray. Orwell was not at all interested in homosexuality but he was fascinated by Dorian's double personality and his impulse to go native in his own country. The other statement, made at the time of his death, was that his opting out of our kind of society, and his eagerness to suffer – as in the harsh experience in Jura – were suicidal. He was already tubercular. It is true that there seemed to be a core of exhausted indifference or something like a gambler's neutrality of spirit in him; but the belief that one could find the comely, natural life in primitive surroundings among simple people was central to him. 'Comeliness' was one of his favourite words. He certainly would not have taken the adopted son, whom he adored, on an expedition directed to a suicide. We cannot know much about this because Orwell insisted that no biography should be written about him. He was secretive and liked to keep his friends and his life in different compartments.

It is well known that Orwell's political conscience and interests were precocious and that his ideas grew out of action. He was closer to Camus, Silone, and Koestler than he was to any English contemporaries who were not blind to Continental politics but hated to believe they were real. He had resigned from the Burmese police on principle, but unlike many romantic rebels, he respected the need for authority, as one can see in the passages where he defended Kipling. In many ways, the Radical was conservative – as English radicals have often been. For him, Victorian colonialism and Victorian England were bad, but, at any rate, concealed a core of personal decency. This, he believed, would have little chance of surviving in our period of disintegration in which we were bent on saving ourselves through an authority that was impersonal, totalitarian, non-human, and dishonest. We were condemned to Newspeak.

Orwell's pictures of England are a mixture of sarcasm, pragmatism, and sentiment. One must treat his writings as one treats Shaw's: collect the fragments of good sense. The Burmese experience led him to suppose, as Mr Woodcock says, that the attitude of the colonial rulers to ruled was identical with the attitude of the English and European ruling class to its workers. They were outcasts too and he sought to join them. This diagnosis was extravagant and his personal renunciation led him to meet outcasts only, the down-and-outs. In this he was as romantic as Dorian Gray. For the main body of the British working class have been respectable and self-respecting since the Industrial Revolution. They were educated by their unions. The class barrier was absolute on their side. Their obsession with sport, beer, gambling, and bad newspapers did not affect their tenacious political puritanism. They too, like Orwell – this is their one link with him – had a double mind; but they were not *déclassés*. In his slapdash book about English life, *The Lion and the Unicorn*, he made a tolerably good picture of the truculent and lazy-minded English muddle.

The value of Mr Woodcock's study lies in the care with which he picks his way among Orwell's self-contradictions and follows his progress from work to work. This is a difficult task, for Orwell was not one for organised abstract thought. He is as drastic but as variable as a Cobbett or a Dickens – even, it has lately struck me – as Carlyle. His essay on Dickens is about the best thing done by an English writer since Gissing. It is important to understand how seriously Orwell worked at finding a style that would reflect his attempt at a *natural* attitude to his subjects, his curious humour, and his realism. From the coloured uncertainties and guesses of journalism, he advanced to a prose as clear as rain, Swift-like in passages of *Homage to Catalonia* and *Animal Farm*. Mr Woodcock is very interesting on the links between the early *Burmese Days* (the work of liberation), the childhood passages in *Coming Up for Air*, and the fantasies in *1984*; and in the sadistic images which crop up mysteriously. It is also instructive to see how his interest in the abuse of language grew from his work in the BBC. He was not a good novelist, but he was 'in life' and an intrepid pamphleteer.

A Better Class of Person

John Osborne has always been a master of spoken diatribe, whether it is of the 'bloody but unbowed' kind or the picturesque confessional of wounds given and received. In his vigorous autobiography *A Better Class of Person* he has the wound-licking grin of the only child who has been through the class mill and is getting his own back – very much a comic Mr Polly or a Kipps reborn in 1929, if less sunny and innocent than Wells was. Osborne adds to the rich tradition of English low comedy, which draws on the snobberies and vulgarities of lower-middle-class life, with its guts, its profligate will to survive despite its maudlin or self-pitying streak. He calls his people Edwardian, for manners drag on long after their presumed historical death; really his family were on the bohemian verges. Both the Welsh and the Cockney sides – the latter known in the family folklore as 'the Tottenham Crowd', with some sniffing of the nose – had a racy leaning towards pubs, music halls, and theatre. (All, except his sad father, lived to a tremendous age.) His two grandfathers were well-established if secretive rakes; one was the man-ager of a once famous London pub in the theatre district and had an early-morning spat with the lavishly seductive Marie Lloyd. Osborne's Welsh father was a self-taught pianist who could sing a song. He earned his living as an advertising copywriter of sorts until his health collapsed. He first met Nellie Beatrice Grove, who was to be the playwright's mother, when she was a barmaid in the Strand. She had left school at twelve to scrub floors in an orphanage, had quickly bettered herself as a cashier in a Lyons Corner House, and eventually went on to the bar of a suburban hotel. She resented her sister Queenie putting on airs because she had, by some family accident, been 'educated' and worked in a milliner's. (The class struggle has its nuances.) If one uncle was a stoker in the Navy, another had an admired connection with Abdulla cigarettes. Was he a director? Goodness knows, but he smoked the expensive things all day. Bids for gentility were natural in a family that, on both sides, took some pride in having 'come down in the world'. Osborne writes:

... the Groves seemed to feel less sense of grievance, looking on it as the justified price of profligate living or getting above yourself, rather than as a cruel trick of destiny ... They had a litany of elliptical sayings, almost biblical in their complexity, which, to the meanest mind or intelligence, combined accessibility and authority. Revealed family wisdom was expressed in sayings like, 'One door opens and another one always shuts' (the optimistic version – rare – was the same in reverse). 'I think I can say I've had my share of sorrows.' Like Jesus they were all acquainted with grief. 'I can always read him like a book'; 'I've never owed anyone anything' (almost the Family Motto this); 'You can't get round him, he's like a Jew and his cash box'; 'Look at him, like Lockhart's elephant.'

The last was a characteristic piece of poetic fancy by which the Londoner draws on local history. The words meant that someone was relating the young Osborne to times before his own; he was 'clumsy'. The elephant evoked a popular large bun sold at a cheap and now extinct eating-house in the Strand. I believe the American equivalent would be Child's.

Osborne was an only child, and for long years he was too sickly to be sent to school. No adult spoke to him much, so he listened, puzzling his way through the family babble. Religion was remote. Comfort in the discomfort of others, he remarks, was the abiding family recreation. 'Disappointment,' Osborne adds, 'was oxygen to them.' The Family Row at Christmas was an institution, the Groves shouting, the Osbornes calmer and more bitter in their sense of having been cheated at birth. Nellie Beatrice, the barmaid mother, mangled the language with her Tottenham mispronunciations – very upsetting to the precise and eloquent Welsh. As she complained, they 'passed looks' when she spoke. Her genius shone at the bar:

Quick, anticipative with a lightning head for mental arithmetic, she was, as she put it, a very smart 'licensed victualler's assistant' indeed. '*I'm* not a barmaid I'm a victualler's assistant – *if* you please.' I have seen none better. No one could draw a pint with a more perfect head on it or pour out four glasses of beer at the same time, throwing bottles up in the air and catching them as she did so.

She was known as Bobby, and was noted for shouting out her wartime catch phrases: 'Get up them stairs'; 'The second thing he did when he come home was to take his pack off'; or 'I couldn't laugh if I was crafty.' At home, her energies were restless. She was a relentless cleaner, whether she lived in digs in dreary Fulham or in a snobby suburb, and never stopped stripping and cleaning the few rooms they lived in, taking up all the carpets and taking down all curtains once a week. She loved moving house. Meals, such as they were, were made to be washed up rather than to be eaten. She was a mistress of the black look. She was hungry for glamour, not for bringing up children, and certainly not a sickly boy who caught every illness going. Her ideal – after the father died and the war filled her purse with wartime tips – was to 'go Up West', walk round the big London stores without buying anything, complaining of her feet, and have a lunch at the gaudy Trocadero, where she could look suitably stand-offish. She was deeply respectable. This is the half-cruel portrait by her son, who was to become a 'better class of person'. He confesses to a struggle against a shame of her:

My mother's hair was very dark, occasionally hennaed. Her face was a floury dark mask, her eyes were an irritable brown, her ears small, so unlike her father's ('He's got Satan's ears, he has'), her nose surprisingly fine. Her remaining front teeth were large, yellow, and strong. Her lips were a scarlet-black sliver covered in some sticky slime named Tahiti or Tattoo, which she bought with all her other make-up from Woolworth's. She wore it, or something like it, from the beginning of the First World War onwards. She had a cream base called Crème Simone, always covered up with a face powder called Tokalon, which she dabbed all over so that it almost showered off in little avalanches when she leant forward over her food. This was all topped off by a kind of knicker-bocker glory of rouge, which came in rather pretty little blue and white boxes – again from Woolworth's – and looked like a mixture of blackcurrant juice and brick dust. The final coup was an overgenerous dab of California Poppy, known to schoolboys as 'fleur de dustbins'.

What froze him was that she was incurious about him.

The frail short-lived father had been white-haired since his twenties.

> His skin was extremely pale, almost transparent. He had the whitest hands I think I have ever seen; Shalimar hands he called them. ('Pale hands I love beside the Lethe waters', of Shalimar. It was one of his favourite Sunday ballads.)

But his long fingers were stained by nicotine. His clothes were unpressed and his bowler hat and mac were greasy, but he was particular about his cuffs and collars and his highly polished, papery shoes. A gentle, sad creature, he is oddly described as being like a 'Welsh-sounding prurient, reticent investigator of sorts from a small provincial town'. For some reason unknown – not only because of his long spells in hospital – the couple were mostly apart.

For the only child, schools were places of pain and humiliation. Certainly they were often rough. He had to discover cunning. At one mixed school, the adolescent girls turned out to be the thumping bullies of the smaller boys, preparing them for the sex war. Still, in the suburbs, there were sympathetic, literate families who helped the backward autodidact. He was nothing more than a nuisance to his energetic mother, and by now they almost hated one another. He was luckier than he thinks to be sent to a third-rate boarding school, for he did at least read a lot and did pretty well with his belated education. But he was laughed at for saying he wanted to be a historian and go to a university. All he was fit for, he was told, was journalism. He was sacked for hitting a master who had slapped him and for writing love-letters to a girl there. Schools took a stern line on that. The sexual revolution, though rife elsewhere, did not easily penetrate the semi-genteel regions of provincial life. So journalism it was. The Benevolent Society to which his father had subscribed and which had paid for his schooling completed its obligations by getting him introduced to a publisher who produced trade journals like the *Gas World*. He had to prepare himself for this by going to typing and shorthand classes.

Folly is often a salvation in such dreary circumstances. Osborne was eighteen, spotty, shy, and longing for friends, especially girls. It occurred to him that a course of dancing lessons at a school that put on amateur

theatricals was a likely chance. He became a dim star and sent his photograph to a theatrical agent; the bohemian traits of his upbringing sprang
up in his sullen, slightly flashy being. He had first to disentangle himself
from the usual sentimental suburban engagement to a nice enough girl
who took her reluctant boyfriend (earning two pounds a week) to the
windows of furniture shops. The warning was clear. He jilted her, wrote
her remorseful, high-minded letters, was tormented by guilt and by
threats and denunciations from the parents. But he was soon out on tour
with a third-rate company and learned about theatre without training
from the bottom, starting with the job of assistant stage-manager and
understudying the five actors, aged between twenty-five and seventy.
What is clear from the long picaresque experiences with this down-at-
heel and hungry company is that he was really a writer and, despite
poetising ambitions, had a marvellous ear for real speech. The book is
punctuated by passages from his plays that hark back to what he heard
'on the road'. The 'real' life is in fact the overflow of theatrical life
evoking people outside. On that first long tour, sexually starved, he
simpered after a fluttering actress called Sheila but soon had the simper
knocked out of him by a formidable actress called Stella, an aggressive
thirty-year-old, with 'the shoulders of a Channel swimmer' and a body
that 'looked capable of snapping up an intruder in a jawbone of flesh'.
She was 'arrogantly lubricious' and had 'an almost masculine, stalking
power'. She was not put off by his sickly appearance and his acne;
she expertly detected the writer in him, and was after him to revise his
first attempt as a collaborator, on a play that she and her husband wanted
to put on. When she and Osborne became lovers, they quarrelled incessantly about dramatic construction; she was out for the commercial success
of another *Autumn Crocus* or *Dinner at Eight* – what he calls 'a Nice
Play' about middle-class gatherings. She in fact woke up his independent
intelligence. He discovered he had his own ideas about the theatre. She
said he was a lazy, arrogant, dishonest amateur – not only that but
ungrateful to her complaisant husband, who tolerantly rescued them
when the company's run stopped and the money ran out. She had to
take a job as a waitress and Osborne became a dishwasher. She eventually
left him for a job in the north, and he admits that he spitefully left her
door unlocked and her electricity turned on when he left the flat she had

[1188]

lent him. Rightly, she never forgave him. Years later, the play did run for a week, with Osborne trying to recognise some lines of his own in it.

The knockabout theatrical chapters tend to be repetitive, but they are rich in sharp, short portraits, especially of the theatrical landladies. They end with his runaway marriage with one Pamela, a capable young actress. He was tactless enough to carry on this passion when the company got to her own home town, in the face of her hostile family. They were well-established drapers. The correlative scripture of what went on in real life will be seen in the quotations from *Look Back in Anger*, notably Jimmy Porter's speech about the wedding:

> Mummy was slumped over her pew in a heap – the noble, female rhino, pole-axed at last! And Daddy sat beside her, upright and unafraid, dreaming of his days among the Indian Princes, and unable to believe he'd left his horsewhip at home.

Osborne says that this is a fairly accurate account of the wedding, except for the references to the Indian Princes. They seem unlikely in the life of a local draper. Daddy has in fact been elevated socially by the 'angry' exposer of class consciousness. Osborne is safer as a guide to congealed suburban or theatrical snobberies. He now writes about the episode:

> I was aware that I had left behind the sophistication and tolerance of the true provinces. Sprung from Fulham and Stoneleigh, where feelings rarely rose higher than a black look, the power of place, family, and generation in small towns was new to me. In the suburbs, allegiances are lost or discarded on dutifully paid visits. The present kept itself to itself. In such a life there was no common graveyard for memory or future. The suburb has no graveyard.

Just before the end of the book there is a collection of extracts from Nellie Beatrice's letters. Years have passed, but she's still on the move, saving up gift stamps for a new carpet-shampoo cleaner, washing down the ceiling, though 'I never did like Housework'. She just wanted things clean. And then comes her crushing phrase:

[1189]

I'll say that for him – he's never been *ashamed* of me. He's always let me meet his friends – and they're all theatrical people, a good class all of them, they speak nicely.

And to his notebook Osborne groans:

I am ashamed of her as part of myself that can't be cast out, my own conflict, the disease which I suffer and have inherited, what I *am* and never could be whole.

About that time, 1955, George Devine rowed out to Osborne, who was living on a barge on the Thames, and offered him a twenty-pound option on *Look Back in Anger*. English theatre changed in a night. I look forward to Volume Two.

Clowns

The hero as the clown. It is not a new idea, but it can be given a new twist if he is sick and if the 'normal' world is more absurd, more dangerous, and sicker than he is. *That* sickness comes from the normal man's refusal to face the facts; the clown's sickness comes from a morbid awareness of them. Having gone through so much, he is clever and stoical. He pesters himself to the point of laughter. After all, he is the comedian of the clinic; and, in Walker Percy's novels, the clinic is sex-mad, science-mad, pleasure-mad contemporary life.

Why is the clown sick? After reading *Love in the Ruins*, which is a satirical fantasy set in the United States twenty or thirty years ahead, one sees that the basic reasons have been developed since that very seductive first novel, *The Movie-goer*. In this work the clown is a prosperous young broker and lapsed Catholic in New Orleans, pursuing happiness in the civilisation which has stretched that piece of elastic until it snaps back on him. Caught by the itch for instant sex, new things, and the general go-go, he is unaccountably trapped by malaise. Buy a new car, try a new girl, and there is the instant 'pain of loss'. He is no longer 'more able to be in the world than Banquo's ghost'. He becomes 'abstracted from reality' and can be said to be 'orbiting in limbo' between 'angelism and bestiality'. In *The Movie-goer*, he is a nice, clever, unreliable young man. The movie ideal of the car and the girl never quite works:

> . . . I discovered to my dismay that my fine new Dodge was a regular incubator of malaise. Though it was comfortable enough, though it ran like a clock, though we went spinning along in perfect comfort and with a perfect view of the scenery like the American couple in the Dodge ad, the malaise quickly became suffocating. We sat frozen in a gelid amiability. Our cheeks ached from smiling. Either would have died for the other. In despair I put my hand under her dress, but even such a homely little gesture as that was received with the same fearful

politeness. I longed to stop the car and bang my head against the curb. We were free, moreover, to do that or anything else, but instead on we rushed, a little vortex of despair moving through the world like the still eye of a hurricane.

In *The Last Gentleman*, the sense of loss becomes literal amnesia. He has lost identity, but that is rooted of course in the past and there, somewhere lying about, was the religion he no longer believes in; also the security of a shady but settled way of life in the South. To devote oneself blindly to another's pain is worth a try; but shy of a moral so schematic, he turns this into a wandering adventure all the way from New York to Louisiana with the bizarre family of a dying youth. The sick make good picaresque figures, for sickness gives one the sharp eyes and freedom of fever.

Walker Percy's gift is for moving about, catching the smell of locality, and for a laughing enjoyment between his bouts with desperation and loss. As in pretty well all intelligent American novels, the sense of America as an effluence of bizarre locality is strong. The hero is liable to sexual hay fever. This book ends with him racing after his sinful psychiatrist, in desperation. Case unsolved, but he has travelled like mad, his eyes starting out of his head: a comedian.

In *Love in the Ruins*, the sick hero is older. He is in his disgraceful forties, a brilliant alcoholic and girl-chasing doctor, liable to depression and bowel trouble most of the week. But war and general disaster have an appeasing or stimulating effect upon neurotics. The sense of a loss beyond his own wakes up his eccentric faculties; now he sees that the world is more farcical than he is. For the America of (I suppose) the 1990s is breaking up. There have been outbreaks of civil war for years, brought on by Negro risings and the fifteen-year war in Ecuador:

> For our beloved old U.S.A. is in a bad way. Americans have turned against each other; race against race, right against left, believer against heathen, San Francisco against Los Angeles, Chicago against Cicero. Vines sprout in sections of New York where not even Negroes will live. Wolves have been seen in downtown Cleveland . . .

Poison ivy grows up the speaker-posts in drive-in movies, vegetation grows through the cracks in the highways, and – greatest of all symbols of disaster – many a Howard Johnson motel has gone up in flames. Of course there has been nuclear fallout here and there. The hero has hives.

A disastrous story, but not very tragic for the doctor, although his wife has run off with an English Buddhist and his daughter has died. A shrewd irony, helped by a mixture of bourbon and self-interest, pulls him together. Not only that: he is lucky to live in a suburban town which survives in a state of respectable paranoia on the edge of a swamp inhabited by murderers and other disaffected people. Occasionally the murderers come out for the kill, but golf staggers along. In the Fedvil complex, the hospital still stands, the Masters-and-Johnson-style Love Clinic – now run by a lapsed Irish priest – is packed every day with experimental copulators who earn fifty dollars a go; the Geriatric Rehab buildings keep people alive until they are a hundred, and euthanasia does well at Happy Isles. You press the Euphoria button.

The American way carries on, but the evasions, the unaccountable rages, and the tendency to be abstracted from reality and orbit in limbo and to alternate between bits of meaningless idealism and bestiality have increased. Cunningly the doctor has patched up a corner of a wrecked Howard Johnson where he plans to store three girls he will save in the next wave of destruction. Sniping has begun again, there are rumours of a new rising of blacks, and there is a sodium cloud in the distance.

The doctor, known to be a crackpot genius and no more than a nuisance when in drink, has a consolation. The study of sodium and encephalology has led him in the course of years to create an instrument called the lapsometer. It measures the electrical activity of the separate centres of the brain. Can the readings be correlated with the causes of the woes of the Western world, its terrors, rages, and impulses, even the perturbations of the soul? Up to a point they can be. There are comic successes with the impotent, the frigid, the angry, the passive: the medical comedy is very good. The hospital suspects the metaphysical turn of its drunk genius, but the Director sees what a political weapon the lapsometer can be. What a gift for Washington, this machine that can, at any rate, manipulate people if it can do no more.

This theme of science fiction is crossed with the drama of the community's situation. The riots are beginning, murders increase, the sodium cloud comes nearer, the sand in the golf bunkers is on fire. Saved by his lapsed Presbyterian secretary, the lapsed Catholic stays on in the wrecked community, now largely taken over by the blacks who copy English accents from their English golf pros on the course. The intellectual blacks have fled to Berkeley, Harvard, and the University of Michigan, to scowl at the mixed-up population who, as well as they can, get on with ordinary life. The doctor is nearly off the bottle and nearly off chasing girls.

To satirise the present one pretends it is the future. Mr Walker Percy's present is limbo; a scene of wicked comedy, sharp portraits of types, and awful habits of mind. The religious and political mix-up is very funny. He is a spirited and inventive writer and there is a charred hell-fire edge to his observation. Exactly what, as a moralist, he wants us to do, I'm not sure. Join the remains of the Church, get back to the doctor's ancestor Sir Thomas More? Or simply rejoin ordinary life? Or is middle age the ideal to be aimed at? He is more interested in the state of sex than in the state of the Union: but isn't sex just the latest item of conspicuous waste in Western society? I am afraid that in the eye of this hurricane of laughing anger, there is a sentimentalist. Still, a very clever one, full of ideas. As always in American novels, the impedimenta are good. Sears Roebuck has made its contribution to literature.

Escaping from Belfast

Early in 1923, when I was a very naïve and untrained newspaper correspondent in Dublin, it was my duty to take a regular trip to Belfast and to find out what was going on politically in that depressing and bigoted city of linen mills and shipyards. The Orangemen were contemptuous of the Southern Irish and had a blustering condescension to Englishmen like myself, and one of the few people whose talk was a relief from this was Forrest Reid, a novelist and critic in his late forties, admired by Yeats, Forster and Walter de la Mare, but almost ignored in his own city at that time.

His family had belonged to the merchant class, who were relatively free of the political stubbornness which was extreme among the industrialists and their workers. He himself was totally indifferent to Irish or to any other brand of politics. He had broken with the Christian faith and was a professed pagan of the Classical Greek persuasion – certainly without the Gaelic nostalgia of the South, despite his friendship with Yeats. I found him living alone on the top floor of a shabby house in a noisy and dirty factory district. His room was bare and poor, and only packed shelves of books, carefully bound in white paper covers to protect them from smoke and smuts, suggested the bibliophile and the scholar. A pile of novels for review stood on his table, alongside his papers and pencils, and the remains of a cold leg of mutton which, I imagined, had to last the week, and during our talks he would sit near to a miserable little fire, shyly drawing intricate patterns with a poker in the soot on the back of the fireplace. I had never met a book-reviewer before, had not read any of his novels, and though by this time I had heard talk of mysticism, the supernatural, visions, and of reality dissolving into dreams, these subjects were above my head and beyond my inclination.

But his talk was quiet and enlightening. He did once or twice mention that E. M. Forster was a friend of his and that he knew Cambridge, and

[1195]

this explained why his speech was free of the mournful glottal-bottle blurting of Ulster address; as I had not heard of Forster at the time, this made Reid even stranger to me. The certainty was that he was one more example of the 'quare fellow' or of the large population of Ireland's eternal bachelors. He was forty-eight. I left Ireland, and not until years later, when I read *Apostate*, the account of his upbringing in Belfast, did I understand that he was more than a shabby and kindly eccentric schoolmasterish man. He was ugly in a fascinating way because of his high block-like forehead and his broad nose that turned up at the tip as if in ironic inquiry, but there was a kind of genius in his truthful portraits of boys as the wary or daring young animal grows up.

His present biographer mentions that Reid's small feet had high insteps, which – to me, at any rate – suggests someone capable of springing into some other air. I had not noticed his feet, nor did I know that this lonely and engaging man was a pederast – one who found the homosexual and heterosexual acts 'disgusting' and who had sublimated his desires in tutorial friendships that, perforce, would die as those he loved grew up, got tired of him or married – the last hard for him to bear.

An earlier biographer of Forrest Reid – Russell Burlingham – found this subject difficult to discuss in 1953. So, even now, does Brian Taylor, but he has treated it with delicacy and understanding. If Forrest Reid was 'a case', Taylor shows that 'a case' is in itself a crude simplification of life. All 'cases' are different: Reid was an instance of the man whose desires are overruled by his affections and his principles. He spoke frankly of his 'arrested development', and, as Taylor shows, it led to a lifelong preoccupation with the intervention of dream-like moments in reality. As a youth – in Belfast of all places – he had been under the influence of Henry James to the point of writing to the Master boldly and getting flattering replies. As for the 'pagan supernatural', that had been stimulated by Forster's *The Celestial Omnibus* and the stories and poems of Walter de la Mare. The latter pair had become his literary counsellors and friends. He rather daringly sent his first novel to Henry James, who responded seriously: but when the Master read Reid's second novel, *The Garden God*, based on an incident noted by Reid in which the portrait of a beautiful boy by G. A. Storey in the Royal Academy dissolves, and the boy turns into a phantom dressed in a silver suit riding in a forest, so that 'something told me that I was looking on either the boy's innermost life, or on some former life of his', James was embarrassed and angered by the platonic eroticism of the book and broke off the relationship in a panic. Edmund Gosse was not disturbed. He detected the pain in Reid's isolation and added that 'for people too obstinately *themselves*, there is always dreamland'. A rather Barrie-like observation: but if Reid was timid and not without self-pity, he was not a sentimentalist. He found a complex resource in a Proustian obsession with memory, and a curiosity about Time. In one of his much-praised later novels, *Uncle Stephen*, there is a passage:

> *Could* you be in two times at once? Certainly your mind could be in one time and your body in another ... Somebody might come to you of *his* time into yours. You might, for instance, come face to face with your own father as he was when he was a boy. Of course you wouldn't *know* each other: still you might meet and become friends, the way you do with people in dreams.

Reid seems to be stating, as Brian Taylor suggests, 'his perennial concern with a boy's search for a father, a childless man's search for a son, and the reaching out of both for companionship and understanding'.

Forrest Reid was the youngest and not much wanted son of a Belfast merchant whose business was failing and of a mother of an old aristocratic English family who could not conceal that she had married beneath her. This story is told in *Apostate*. Reid's passionate love was given totally to his nurse, Emma, who after a few years left home: he could love no woman after that. After his father's early death, the family went further downhill, the neglected boy played with 'rough' boys in the streets and was a pain to his older sisters. He was ugly, but his boyish animal spirits were high and he was clever. He left a good school early and was put to work in a tea merchant's office, an easy trade, for he found it simple to hide in a storeroom and read Greek and was determined to write. In loneliness, his search for friendships was fierce and possessive. He was already a Platonist. His mother's death freed him from the tea trade, for he was left a small legacy, and, at last, got what he wanted – a place at Cambridge – but far too late. (He was nearly thirty and said he got little out of his time there.) He can be said to have been penned in by autobiography all his life, writing version after version of his boyhood experience, in nearly all his novels, and becoming obsessed about 'getting it right' while evading – as was inevitable in his time – the sexual dilemma. Perhaps the pagan did not quite suppress the Presbyterian, and he was left, as he said, 'intractable' in his companionship with the one or two men with whom he lived in a tutor–pupil relationship.

The striking things in Reid's writing are the clarity of his descriptive style, his fervid response to landscape and his totally unsentimental, almost minute-to-minute evocations of the changes in a boy's real and imaginative experience as he passes from childhood to youth and the loss of wild innocence. He recalls what the day brought and felt like without affectation and what most of us have inevitably generalised or forgotten in growing up. We have forgotten, also, the passing dreams that suddenly came and abruptly vanished. His obsession, or perhaps a half-humorous pedantry, obliged him to try and try again exactly to recover those moments – which of course narrowed his scope – and the many quotations here from scenes in his novels and from his letters make this point. One is especially struck by the curious fact that Aksakov's memoirs of *his* childhood under the rule of a dominant mother was one of Reid's favourite books – one more example of a natural sympathy between some Irish writing and the Russian feeling for the vivid and troubled hour of the day. The pagan Greek ideal has something precious and Ninetyish in it, and this Russian naturalness seems to me a more valuable influence on his talent, although Reid's Irishness was almost non-existent, except in that pure, direct response to the natural scene, whereas Aksakov's Russianness was historically Slavophil and innate.

Reid has been thought of as a provincial and escapist: he accepted that. He wrote in a letter that he 'preferred the literature of escape and what *I* should call the literature of imagination for the escape is only from the impermanent into the permanent'. Brian Taylor refers to Russell Burlingham's *Forrest Reid: A Portrait and a Study* for purely literary criticism. Taylor's is a sensitive and intelligent study of Reid's dilemma without the dramatising aid of Freudian or sociological fictions. As a person, Reid becomes very clear, sad and droll. He was soon to leave that bare room where I first listened to his talk and his friendly silences.

He moved to a council house outside Belfast with his adored dogs and his current friend, perpetuating a kind of boyhood, smoking his pipe as though he were a Belfast chimney. He could be testy at the card-table. He was barricaded by an ever-growing pile of first editions, he pondered his stamp collection, and was loftily resigned to being more avidly read for his excellent book reviews than – as far as the large public was concerned – for his admired and not very saleable novels. He did attain a local fame. One claim he could make: the scrupulous artist had reserves of sudden extrovert fierceness and triumphant skill and cunning – he could win Challenge Cups at croquet all over England and Ireland. No sublimation there: he was certain to get through those hoops.

Midnight's Children

In Salman Rushdie, the author of *Midnight's Children* (Jonathan Cape, 1981), India has produced a great novelist – one with startling imaginative and intellectual resources, a master of perpetual story-telling. Like García Márquez in *One Hundred Years of Solitude*, he weaves a whole people's capacity for carrying its inherited myths – and new ones that it goes on generating – into a kind of magic carpet. The human swarm swarms in every man and woman as they make their bid for life and vanish into the passion or hallucination that hangs about them like the smell of India itself. Yet at the same time there are Western echoes, particularly of the irony of Sterne in *Tristram Shandy* – that early non-linear writer – in Rushdie's readiness to tease by breaking off or digressing in the gravest moments. This is very odd in an Indian novel! The book is really about the mystery of being born. Rushdie's realism is that of the conjuror who, in a flash, draws an incident out of the air and then makes it vanish and laughs at his cleverness. A pregnant woman, the narrator's mother, goes to a fortune-teller in the Delhi slum:

> And my mother's face, rabbit-startled, watching the prophet in the check shirt as he began to circle, his eyes still egglike in the softness of his face; and suddenly a shudder passing through him and again that strange high voice as the words issued through his lips (I must describe those lips, too – but later, because now . . .) 'A son.'
>
> Silent cousins – monkeys on leashes, ceasing their chatter – cobras coiled in baskets – and the circling fortune-teller, finding history speaking through his lips.

And the fortune-teller goes on, sing-songing:

> 'Washing will hide him – voices will guide him! Friends mutilate him – blood will betray him . . . jungle will claim him . . . tyrants will fry

him . . . He will have sons without having sons! He will be old before he is old! *And he will die . . . before he is dead.*'

Outside the room, monkeys are throwing down stones on the street from a ruined building.

This is pure *Arabian Nights* intrigue – for that son, Saleem Sinai, now thirty-one, is writing about what he is making up about his birth; he is dramatising his past life as a prophecy, even universalising his history as a mingling of farce and horror and matching it with thirty years of the Indian crowd's collective political history. The strength of a book that might otherwise be a string of picaresque tales lies in its strong sense of design. Saleem claims that it is he who has created modern India in the years that followed Indian independence – has dreamed into being the civil strife and the wars – as a teller of stories, true or untrue, conniving at events and united with them. Central to this is the fantasy that the children born at midnight on the day of liberation, as he was, have a destiny. The Prime Minister himself pronounces this: 'They are the seed of a future that would genuinely differ from anything that the world had seen at that time.' Children born a few seconds before the hour of what Saleem calls Mountbatten's 'tick-tock' are likely to join the revelling band of conjurors and circus freaks and street singers; those born a few seconds after midnight, like Parvati, the witch, whom Saleem eventually marries, will be genuine sorcerers. Saleem himself, born on the stroke of the hour, will be amazingly gifted but will also embody the disasters of the country. The novel is an autobiography, dictated by a ruined man to a simple but shrewd working girl in a pickle factory – to this Saleem's fortunes have fallen. (She is addressed from time to time as if she were Sterne's 'dear Eliza'.) The fortune-teller's words 'washing will hide him' point to Fate. The prophecy was not a joke.

The rich Delhi Muslims who raise him are not his parents: he is a changeling, and not their son. The wrong ticket has been tied to his toe by a poor Goanese nurse, who, demented by the infidelity of her husband, a common street singer, had allowed herself to be seduced by a departing English sahib. Saleem is ugly, dwarfish, with a huge snotty nose, and is brought up rich; the real son is Shiva, brought up poor. Years will pass before the nurse confesses. The point of the political allegory becomes clear. Shiva, like the god, will become the man of action, riot, and war – the bully, cunning in getting to the top. Saleem's gift will be the passive intellectual's who claims the artist's powers of travelling into the minds of people. The rival traits will show in their school days. Proud of being midnight's children, the boys form a privileged gang. Saleem sees the gang as a gathering of equals in which every one has the right to his own voice. Shiva, brought up on the streets and refusing to be a whining beggar, rejects Saleem's democratic dream:

> 'Yah, little rich boy: one rule. Everybody does what I say or I squeeze the shit outa them ... Rich kid, you don't know one damn thing! ... Where's the reason in starving, man? ... You got to get what you can, do what you can with it, and then you got to die.'

The effect of Indian independence on the rich family is to give them the opportunity to buy up the property of the departing British cheaply, and speculation drives Saleem's 'father' to delusion. When he ages, he shuts himself up to fret about getting the words of the Koran in the right order. Then the riots of partition begin; there is the war in Kashmir; identifying himself with mass-consciousness, Saleem declares the war occurred because he dreamed it; Gandhi is assassinated; there is the war between India and Pakistan. In Bombay, where Saleem's family have migrated to make money, the bombing smashes their houses and kills off several of them. These events are evoked in parodies of news-flashes from All India Radio. Saleem, indeed, sees himself as a private radio sending out his satirical reports; once they are issued, the narrative returns to his story. He has a strange sister – a delightfully mischievous girl, known as the Brass Monkey, whose main sport is setting fire to the family's shoes. When Saleem discovers the truth about his birth, he falls in love with her; she turns him down and becomes pious, and Saleem henceforth believes all his failures in love are due to the sin of a meta-physical incest. The girl eventually becomes a superb cold-hearted singer and is 'the darling of the troops' in the war. Failure in sexual love haunts all the family. The more his 'parents' disappoint each other sexually, the more they apply themselves to loving each other. Saleem grows up to be something of a voyeur or vicarious lover.

In his attitude to love, Saleem is very much the ever wilful, inventive, teasing Scheherazade, prolonging the dreams of his people and puncturing them at the point of success. For example, his Aunt Pia, notorious for making emotional scenes, may be seen wantonly going through the motions of seducing Saleem – who is only ten at the time – but the act is physical charade: her extreme sexual provocation is put on as a 'scene' in which she rids herself of a private grief. Love is a need and custom, sexuality is play-acting. Towards the end of the book, Saleem will refuse to consummate his marriage to the witch Parvati (who has saved his life and who loves him), but not because she is pregnant by another man – in fact, his brother and opposite, the womanising Shiva. Saleem pretends he is impotent. Why this self-love? Is it possible that – too entranced by his fantastic powers of invention – he is the artist in love with storytelling itself? Or do such episodes spring from a fundamental sense that India is a chaos in which no norm can be realised? What a Westerner would call Saleem's self-pity is the egoist's devious and somehow energising passivity and resignation. It is, at any rate, the obverse of Shiva's grossly self-seeking attitude to life. Shiva is not a man to spend himself in a breathless stream of words.

All this is brought to life by Rushdie's delight in ironies of detail, which is entirely beguiling, because the smallest things, comic or horrible, are made phenomenal. But when we come to the war in East Pakistan the narrative takes on a new kind of visionary power. Saleem is a soldier, and in defeat and flight he leads a tiny group of men into the jungle – see the sorcerer's prophecy! – where he sometimes calls himself 'I', sometimes 'he' or 'buddha', and maybe also Ayooba, as if desperation had become a fever that burns out his identity. The soldiers are diminished by the rain forest, which has become a phantom personage who arouses in them all the guilt they have hidden, and punishes them for the horrors they have committed.

But one night Ayooba awoke in the dark to find the translucent figure of a peasant with a bullet-hole in his heart and a scythe in his hand staring mournfully down at him ... After this first apparition, they fell into a state of mind in which they would have believed the forest capable of anything; each night it sent them new punishments, the accusing eyes of the wives of men they had tracked down and seized, the screaming and monkey-gibbering of children left fatherless by their work – and in this first time, the time of punishment, even the impassive buddha with his citified voice was obliged to confess that he, too, had taken to waking up at night to find the forest closing in upon him like a vice, so that he felt unable to breathe.

The forest permitted a 'double-edged' nostalgia for childhood, strange visions of mothers and fathers; Ayooba, for example, sees his mother offering her breasts, when she suddenly turns into a white monkey swinging by her tail high up in a tree. Another lad hears his father telling his brother that their father had sold his soul for a loan from his landlord, who charged three hundred per cent – 'so it seemed that the magical jungle, having tormented them with their misdeeds, was leading them by the hand towards a new adulthood'. But there are worse tests to come: in a ruined temple the soldiers are deluded by lascivious dreams of houris, evoked by a statue of a savage multi-limbed Kali. The men wake up discovering the meaninglessness of life, the pointless boredom of the desire to survive.

The experience of these very ordinary men is a purgation but not a salvation. As in an opera – and perhaps that is what *Midnight's Children* really is – the next grand scene is of comic magic. The conquering armies enter Dacca, led by a vast company of ghetto minstrels, conjurors, magic men. Marching with the troops come the entertainers:

> ... There were acrobats forming human pyramids on moving carts drawn by white bullocks; there were extraordinary female contortionists who could swallow their legs up to their knees; there were jugglers who operated outside the laws of gravity, so that they could draw oohs and aahs from the delighted crowd as they juggled with toy grenades, keeping four hundred and twenty in the air at a time ... And there was Picture Singh himself, a seven-foot giant who weighed two hundred and forty pounds and was known as the Most Charming Man In The World because of his unsurpassable skills as a snake charmer ... he strode through the happily shrieking crowds, twined from head to foot with deadly cobras, mambas and kraits, all with their poison-sacs intact ... Picture Singh, who would be the last in the line

of men who have been willing to become my fathers . . . and immediately behind him came Parvati-the-witch.

She was rolling her magic basket along as she marched, and – would you believe it? – eventually helped Saleem to escape by popping him into it. After her magic, the allegory: it is Shiva who seduces Parvati and deserts her, and Picture Singh who makes Saleem marry her, in the ghetto where Picture Singh draws the crowd with his snakes while Saleem, the man of conscience, shouts political propaganda. (Mr Rushdie has already told us that the magicians are all Communists of every known hue and schism.) This episode, like so many others in the book, is almost delicately touching, but, of course, there is disaster in the next act. Back in India, Saleem is a political prisoner and is forced to submit to vasectomy. The man who lied to Parvati when he said he was impotent is now truly impotent as he dictates this long story to Padma, the working girl, who has got him a job in the pickle factory. He loves inventing chutneys – they have the power of bringing back memories.

The novel is, in part, a powerful political satire in its savaging of both political and military leaders. The narrator's hatred of Mrs Gandhi – the Widow (that is to say, the guillotine) – is deep. But I think that as satire the novel is at variance with Mr Rushdie's self-absorption and his pursuit of poetic symbols: the magic basket in which one can hide secret thoughts, and so save oneself, is an example; another is 'the hole', which recurs, and suggests that we see experience falsely, because in a little over-excited peep at a time. These symbols are rather too knowing; he is playing tricks with free association. Padma, the not-so-simple factory girl to whom the ruined Saleem dictates the book, pities his wretchedness but often suggests that he is piling it on, and is suspicious of his evasiveness. So much conjuring going on in Saleem's imagination *does* bewilder us. But as a *tour de force* his fantasy is irresistible.

Lost in the Stars

Antoine de Saint-Exupéry belonged to the heroic age of aviation, and in *Night Flight* he created its legend. In doing this he became, very willingly, a legend himself. The life by Marcel Migeo, *Saint-Exupéry*, sets out to separate fact from fantasy and to expound his character. The author is well placed for the task. He was a friend of Saint-Exupéry from the time they did their flight training at Neudorf, near Strasbourg, two years after the First World War. The gladiatorial period of flying was over; the first dangerous attempts to civilise flying, which began with carrying the mails, were being made. Saint-Exupéry took to the air when planes were flown by compass, map, and eye, without radio; when the top speed was a hundred miles an hour and the range no more than three hundred. Engines stalled 'with a crash as of broken crockery'. Casualties were severe. When Saint-Exupéry, failing to get into the Ecole Navale, joined what became known, almost religiously, as 'the Line', a forerunner of Air France that essayed to fly mail from Toulouse to Dakar and ultimately extended its route to South America, he faced another hazard. Pilots forced down in Africa were set upon by Moorish tribes and either tortured and killed or else held for ransom. This happened so frequently that pilots hopefully preferred to take with them an interpreter instead of a mechanic. After a year of routine flying in this service, Saint-Exupéry was stationed at a lonely desert refuelling outpost that had to deal with this hazard, and for this reason the French were later on to compare him with T. E. Lawrence.

What sort of a man was Saint-Exupéry? The first legend to go in M. Migeo's book is that he was one of the great pilots and a man for whom flying was a vocation. It is an illusion easily brought about by the overtones of mission and dedication in *Night Flight* and *Flight to Arras*. He was, this experienced friend says, an adroit pilot but too absent-minded and eccentric to be great. He had no sense of time. He was careless.

Once he left the door of his plane open and it was torn off by the wind. His attempts at long-distance records, like his flight from Paris to Saigon or from New York to Patagonia, were badly prepared and disastrous. In the cockpit his mind wandered. He was, before anything else, a writer, and he sought in flying a liberation from the boredom of city life and its worries (he was always in debt and entangled with women), as well as a spiritual liberation.

Saint-Exupéry was a very tall and eventually rather hulking man, and very plain, with a small, round head, a comically tipped-up nose, and a fixed, upward look to his eyes. (At school they called him Pique-la-Lune.) He came of a poor but aristocratic family. His father died when Saint-Exupéry was a child, and he became its dominant, restless, quarrelling, and cajoling leader, full of ideas and conversation. There is nothing, M. Migeo says, in the legend of early struggle and hardship. There were distinguished relatives to help him. He wheedled money out of his gifted mother for years. He liked to live in style. He was a gourmet. Some of his flying friends thought him a snob in the early days; if he was, snobbery was knocked out of him when he went to work for 'the Line', because men of all classes had to knuckle under to the hard work and severe discipline of that organisation. His greatest friend was a fellow-pilot, Henri Guillaumet, a peasant by origin, and a prudent, courageous, plain chap whom Saint-Exupéry pretty well worshipped. 'The Line' settled his character; his devotion to the group diminished his eccentric isolation and created in him the profound sense of the overwhelming value of duty and necessity that gives gravity to a sparkling imagination.

Saint-Exupéry's fame as a writer and his success in organising airfields in South America for his company were not of great help to him when, in the early Thirties, 'the Line' was reorganised. The honeymoon with adventure was over. He entered what he called his 'blue epoch', in which he lived by journalism and film-making. His long flights failed. Saint-Exupéry the solitary lived sometimes in a blaze of publicity; occasionally he might be seen sitting at Lipp's or Les Deux Magots, pudgy and dejected, scribbling notes on bits of paper and feeling that at thirty he was finished. These notes and random articles were eventually put together, and after enormous labour they became *Wind, Sand and Stars*. This often brilliant but contrived work got the Académie award, and in

America it made his fortune – a meaningless word to a man so hopelessly extravagant. Saint-Exupéry had meanwhile married a vivid, birdlike, and tempestuous Argentine widow who turned out to be a mixture of the unmanageable, the uneconomical, and (after bouts of violence) the pathetic. They frequently separated. He was a difficult man, but M. Migeo points out that this marriage at any rate satisfied the writer's need for '*inquiétude*'.

When the Second World War came, Saint-Exupéry was nearly forty. Courageously, he flew reconnaissance planes over the advancing Germans. After the fall of France, he went to New York, unluckily stopping on the way in Vichy and meeting the reputed collaborator Drieu La Rochelle. He was soon involved in those dismal slanders that affected so many Frenchmen at the time. He was at odds with de Gaulle, who he felt 'was asking the French to fight a war of fratricide', and was accused of being a Pétainiste. M. Migeo disposes convincingly of this accusation. When de Gaulle refused him any assignment during the North African campaign, he went with the American forces into Africa and, after some high-level wirepulling, was charitably allowed to fly on photographic reconnaissance over Occupied France. His eccentricities continued; many times he forgot to lower or take up his landing gear. On what was to have been his last operational flight, he disappeared. He was, it is assumed, shot down between Nice and Corsica. A German intelligence officer who was a great admirer of him has provided evidence that his death occurred off Corsica, but M. Migeo suspects that a woman who saw two planes in combat near Nice is the true witness of his death. He was forty-four.

M. Migeo is a patient and readable biographer. He has drawn a detailed account of a brilliant, charming, ruthless egocentric who made exhausting demands on his friends, who kept them up all night while he read them his latest pages, and who was always the last customer to be tactfully edged, still talking at the top of his voice, out of *brasseries* and restaurants. Women made a set at him; he had not the art of shaking them off. M. Migeo thinks that he was not much interested in them; a writer, he was much more interested in himself. The austere, ascetic man of action, the servant of fidelity and duty, whom we picture from his writings is very different from the ebullient, self-dispensing, sensual man of real life.

When M. Migeo considers Saint-Exupéry's writings, he is less rewarding. He echoes all the contemporary praise and rejects all criticism, especially the idea that there is anything derived in his work. He makes one important but, I think, disputable reflection on *The Wisdom of the Sands*, arguing that the crucial experience of Saint-Exupéry's life was the loss of his faith in Catholicism when he was seventeen. One catches a note of regret, but the loss was permanent. Yet M. Migeo sees in Saint-Exupéry's religion of Man and his mystical humanism the line of a quest for a lost faith. I do not believe that the loss of faith had this importance. The vital event occurred, surely, much earlier, in his early boyhood: it was the death of his father. Saint-Exupéry felt deeply the need of male authority and the ruling of self and others. In *Night Flight*, Rivière, the stern builder of 'the Line', who never forgives a pilot a mistake, puts the claims of duty against the claims of love and ordinary human happiness. He is a father figure. Rivière is a portrait drawn from life, and the original saw no resemblance and did not much care for it. He was no poet and no metaphysician. He was embarrassed. Good chiefs and good pilots were not like that.

Saint-Exupéry was a poet and a man of contradictions. He was, in fact, two styles. One is plain and noble, breaking into often superb and original imagery. It is seen in *Night Flight*, in *Flight to Arras*, and in the fragments of actual experience – the crash in the desert, Madrid under bombardment – that appear in *Wind, Sand and Stars*. The other is his stained-glass-window style. Here rhetoric and mysticism conjoin. One even hears echoes of Kipling and the jingles of the Law, and one loses the traditional, singeing psychological sensibility of the French moralist. The stained-glass Saint-Exupéry is a proverb-maker writing in tiresomely archaic language (in his last book) and a conjuror of truisms. It is a curious fact that in life he was an irresistible diplomat and a mystifying adept at card tricks.

The French, when they are looking for a myth, compare Saint-Exupéry to T. E. Lawrence. As a writer, the Frenchman is by far the superior. Both men were seized upon as possible blueprints for a contemporary hero, the technician-leader. Both were romantics. And it can be said that Saint-Exupéry got as much out of the Moroccan desert as Lawrence got out of Arabia. But Lawrence was a man of action who was able to act out his Hamlet part. He was alone. Saint-Exupéry, though he wrote much of the solitude of the airman, was not really alone. He had the group. He was – it is his favourite statement about human beings – 'a tangle of relationships'. Lawrence flattered the undisciplined instincts of his horde and their love of being hypnotised by a leader. Saint-Exupéry comes closer to the contemporary man who depends on the intricately worked-out technical order. Lawrence was conscious of guilt; one finds no trace of it in Saint-Exupéry. Both men had to consider the ineluctable, but where Lawrence, in his vanity, assumed guilty introspection, Saint-Exupéry had a far more humane insight into tragedy. But both may have been said, in Saint-Exupéry's phrase, to have 'bartered' themselves for an idea. Yet Saint-Exupéry's idea was not really to submerge himself in 'the service'. One has the impression that he was bored by it and that his mysticism was an evasion. His fundamental idea was aristocratic and French. 'What I value,' he said, 'is a certain arrangement of things. Civilisation is an invisible boon; it concerns not things we see, but the unseen bonds linking these together in one special way and not otherwise.'

Comic Genius

===

The ridiculous or preposterous father is a subject irresistible to the comic genius. The fellow is an involuntary god, and the variety of the species extends over the knockabout and the merely whimsical to the full wonder of incipient myth. To this last superior class the fantastic father invented by Bruno Schulz in *The Street of Crocodiles* belongs; the richness of the portrait owes everything to its brushwork and to our private knowledge that the deepest roots of the comic are poetic and even metaphysical.

Few English-speaking readers have ever heard of Schulz, and I take from his translator, Celina Wieniewska, and the thorough introduction by Jerzy Ficowski, the following notes on a very peculiar man. Schulz came of a Jewish family of dry goods merchants in the dull little town of Drogobych in Poland – it is now in the USSR – where he became a frustrated art master in the local high school and lived a solitary and hermetic life. The family's trade separated them from the ghetto; his natural language was Polish. The only outlet for his imagination seems to have been in writing letters to one or two friends, and it is out of these letters that his stories in this and other volumes grew. They were a protest against a boredom amounting to melancholia. He became famous, but found he could not live without the Drogobych he hated and he was caught there when the war began and the Nazis put him into the ghetto. It is said that a Gestapo officer who admired his drawings wangled a pass for him to leave the ghetto; one night when he took advantage of his freedom and was wandering among the crowds in the streets he was recognised and shot dead in a random shooting-up of the crowd. He was fifty years old.

It is not surprising to find comic genius of the poetic kind in serious and solitary men, but to emerge it has to feed on anomalies. We might expect – or fear – that Schulz would be a Slavonic droll in the Polish folk

[1211]

tradition, but he is not. Distinctly an intellectual, he translated Kafka's *The Trial* and was deep in *Joseph and His Brothers* – to my mind the most seminal of Thomas Mann's works; hence his sense of life as a collusion or conspiracy of improvised myths. Note the word 'improvised'.

Drogobych had suddenly become an American-type boom town owing to the discovery of oil, and the fantasy of Schulz takes in the shock of technology and the new cult of things and the pain of the metamorphosis. His translator is, rightly I think, less impressed by his literary sources in Kafka or surrealism than by the freedom of the painter's brush – his prose, she says, has the same freedom and originality as the brush of Chagall.

'Our Heresiarch' – as Schulz calls his secretive father, in *The Street of Crocodiles* – blossoms into speeches to his family or the seamstresses and assistants in his dress shop. He rambles into theories about the Demiurge and our enchantment with trash and inferior material. He discourses on the agonies of Matter:

Who knows ... how many suffering, crippled, fragmentary forms of life there are, such as the artificially created life of chests and tables quickly nailed together, crucified timbers, silent martyrs to cruel human inventiveness. The terrible transplantation of incompatible and hostile races of wood, their merging into one misbegotten personality.

Misbegetting is one of his obsessions.

Only now do I understand the lonely hero who alone had waged war against the fathomless, elemental boredom that strangled the city. Without any support, without recognition on our part, that strangest of men was defending the lost cause of poetry.

The awed seamstresses cutting out dresses to fit the draper's model in their room are told the model is alive.

Where is poetry born? In the solitary imagination of the child who instantly sees an image when he sees a thing, where the wallpaper becomes a forest, the bales of cloth turn into lakes and mountains. In this way, the father has the inventive melancholy of Quixote. The delightful thing about him is that he is the embarrassing, scarcely visible nuisance in shop and home. It is hard to know where he is hiding or what he is up to. He is an inquiring poltergeist, coated with human modesty; even his faintly sexual ventures, like studying a seamstress's knee because he is fascinated by the structure of bones, joints, and sinews, are as modest as Uncle Toby's confusion of the fortress of Namur with his own anatomy. A minor character, like Adela the family servant, sets off the old man perfectly. She comes to clean out his room.

He ascribed to all her functions a deeper, symbolic meaning. When, with young firm gestures, the girl pushed a long-handled broom along the floor, Father could hardly bear it. Tears would stream from his eyes, silent laughter transformed his face, and his body was shaken by spasms of delight. He was ticklish to the point of madness. It was enough for Adela to waggle her fingers at him to imitate tickling, for him to rush through all the rooms in a wild panic, banging the doors after him, to fall at last flat on the bed in the farthest room and wriggle in convulsions of laughter, imagining the tickling which he found irresistible. Because of this, Adela's power over Father was almost limitless.

This is a small matter compared with his ornithological phase when he imports the eggs of birds from all parts of the world and hatches them in the loft. The birds perched on curtains, wardrobes, lamps. (One – a sad condor – strongly resembles him.) Their plumage carpeted the floor at feeding time. The passion in due course took an 'essentially sinful and unnatural turn'.

... my father arranged the marriages of birds in the attic, he sent out matchmakers, he tied up eager attractive brides in the holes and crannies under the roof . . .

In the spring, during the migration, the house was besieged by whole flocks of cranes, pelicans, peacocks. And father himself, in an absent-minded way, would rise from the table,

wave his arms as if they were wings, and emit a long-drawn-out bird's call while his eyes misted over. Then, rather embarrassed, he would join us in laughing it off and try to turn the whole incident into a joke.

[1213]

It is a sign of Schulz's mastery of the fantastic that, at the end of the book, he has the nerve to describe how after many years the birds returned to the house – a dreadful spectacle of miscegenation, a brood of freaks, degenerate, malformed:

> Nonsensically large, stupidly developed, the birds were empty and lifeless inside. All their vitality went into their plumage, into external adornment... Some of them were flying on their backs, had heavy misshapen beaks like padlocks, were blind, or were covered with curiously coloured lumps.

In a curious passage the father compares them to an expelled tribe, preserving what they could of their soul like a legend, returning to their motherland before extinction – a possible reference to the Diaspora and the return.

Like an inquiring child, the father is wide open to belief in metamorphoses as others are prone to illness: for example he has a horror of cockroaches and, finding black spots on his skin, prepares for a tragic transformation into the creature he dreads by lying naked on the floor. But it is in the father's ornithological phase that we see the complexity of Schulz's imagination. The whole idea – it is hinted – may spring from a child's dream after looking at pictures of birds; it is given power by being planted in the father; then it becomes a grotesque nightmare; and finally we may see it as a parable, illustrating the permutations of myths which become either the inherited wastepaper of the mind or its underground. Incidentally – and how recognisable this is in childish experience – there is an overwhelming picture of the ragged idiot girl of the town sleeping on the rubbish heap, who suddenly rises from the fly-infested dump to rub herself in terrible sexual frenzy against a tree.

Under the modesty of Schulz the senses are itching in disguise. Each episode is extraordinary and carried forward fast by a highly imaged yet rational prose which is especially fine in evoking the forbidden collective wishes of the household or the town: when a comet appears in the sky and a boy comes home from school saying the end of the world is near, the whole town is enthusiastic for the end of the world. When a great gale arrives, the town becomes a saturnalia of *things* at last set free to live as matter wants to live. There is the admonitory farce when loose-living Uncle Edward agrees to reform and to submit to the father's discovery of mesmerism and the magic of electricity. Uncle Edward is eager to shed all his characteristics and to lay bare his deepest self in the interests of Science, so that he can achieve a 'problem-free immortality'.

> The dichotomy 'happy/unhappy' did not exist for him because he had been completely integrated.

Schulz's book is a masterpiece of comic writing: grave yet demented, domestically plain yet poetic, exultant and forgiving, marvellously inventive, shy and never raw. There is not a touch of whimsy in it.

The Stamp of the Puritan

The first volume of Bernard Shaw's collected letters – there will be three more – opens in the mid-1870s when he is seen, aged eighteen, living with his drunken father and sacking himself from the job of 'accountant' – i.e., office boy – he has held for three years in Dublin, because he finds 'he has nothing to do'. This is, of course, an early Shavian gesture; really he wants to go to London.

The volume ends, 700 letters and 22 years later, when he is famous; now he is trying to rescue an actress from morphia and brandy, and insulting an Irish millionairess with an eye to wedlock. To give value for money and to expect money for value has the strong stamp of the Puritan which was primitively imbedded in Shaw's character, as was his horror of human stagnation and self-destructiveness. To the actress, Janet Achurch, he wrote that he had seen 'the process in my father; and I have never felt anything since. I learnt soon to laugh at it; and I have laughed at everything since. Presently, no doubt, I shall learn to laugh at you. What else can I do?' The loss of heart is the point, but Shaw's Bohemian family hardly encouraged that luxury. Someone wrote of his 'hard, clear, fleshless voice'.

His own addictions were the Irish addiction to words and the Puritan's to work. Add to his early novel-writing, his journalism, his musical and dramatic criticism, his pamphlets, his mass of plays with their enormous prefaces, his lecturing, his speechifying to the Fabians, his letters to the press, his active work as a borough councillor – add to these more than a quarter of a million letters full of zest and vitality and we see a man who is doubling his life.

He is a feverish and compulsive letter-writer. Like Dickens, he has no sooner finished his work than he is up half the night writing letters and postcards to his professional friends and fans, until his eyes run with exhaustion. It is all business of some kind. Even his love-letters are that.

[1216]

He has a manic capacity for endless self-perpetuation as a public fantasy.

His work was not enough. Like many other Irishmen, he turned his ego into a profession. His habit was to carry his correspondence about in a sack wherever he went and to answer a handful of letters at a time while he was in buses, on trains, even when he went for a walk and sat down in a field. Like Dickens, he set up as tycoon and public performer, not only managing all his immense theatrical, literary and political business himself – and always the financial side of it with great acumen – but managing other people's as well. Unlike Dickens, in whom artist and tycoon were separated, Shaw is a single show always inseparably on the road.

There is scarcely a letter in this first volume that does not do a stage turn in order to get across some 'adamant' point. The Irish are almost always shy, almost always trying to conceal, and they have notoriously been apt to produce a stage personality to do so. Shaw's exhibitionism, his enormous vanity, his wild philanderings and gallantries are (as he often said, especially to his women correspondents) indications that he is heartless, cold, self-interested. That too is untrue: he was simply determined to preserve his freedom at all costs. Otherwise, how could he do his 18-hour day? The moment he lived by the underlying shyness – in his early days in London he was ashamed of his poverty and too frightened and gauche to go to a party – he would be bogged in Irish stagnation.

In the preface to one of his novels, 'Immaturity', he wrote about the weekly parties given by his London friends the Lawsons:

I suffered such agonies of shyness that I sometimes walked up and down the Embankment for twenty minutes or more before venturing to knock at the door: indeed I should have funked it altogether, and hurried home asking myself what was the use of torturing myself when it was so easy to run away, if I had not been instinctively aware that I must never let myself off in this manner if I meant ever to do anything in the world. Few men can have suffered more than I did in my youth from simple cowardice or been more horribly ashamed of it ... The worst of it was that when I appeared in the Lawsons' drawingroom I did not appeal to the goodnature of the company as a pardonably and even becomingly bashful novice. I had not then tuned the Shavian note to any sort of harmony; and I have no doubt the Lawsons found me discordant, crudely self-assertive, and insufferable.

He dropped the parties because it was wasteful to fail like that.

Success was everything, but it had, for this most austere and chaste of Irish Puritans, to be a 'clean' success; that is to say, what he and he alone would accept. No compromises. The absence of compromise in Shaw's career, as it is shown in his letters, is remarkable. He would, from sheer necessity, take on temporary commercial jobs – one was to obtain sites for telephone poles on commission at half a crown a time – but that was to keep his mother quiet while he wrote novels no one would publish.

When he got a foot in the door of journalism and lecturing, he slaved for next to nothing – at one time he was giving a hundred ill-paid lectures a year – and once he had decided on the then exceedingly unremunerative belief in Fabian Socialism, he stuck to it ruthlessly: 'If . . . a man is to attain consciousness of himself as a vessel of the Zeitgeist or will or whatever it may be, he must pay the price of turning his back on the loaves and fishes, the duties, the ready-made logic, the systems and the creeds. He must do what he likes instead of doing what, on secondhand principles, he ought.'

On second-hand principles, he goes on, he ought to have got a safe job to save his dear old mother from living on a second floor and teaching schoolgirls to sing. He refused, and what is the result? ' . . . my mother, the victim of my selfishness, is a hearty, independent and jolly person, instead of a miserable old woman dragged at the chariot wheels of her miserable son, who had dutifully sacrificed himself for her comfort.'

This is well-known Shavian stuff: Shaw's socialism got a strong boost from his dislike of family strangulation. The theory of the pursuing female evidently arises, as the letters show, because he was much pursued, philandered to escape and, if caught, refers (with an eighteenth-century gallantry) to the lady as his 'seductress'. (He was, as all the Anglo-Irish were, a throwback to the eighteenth century.) He often remarks that his Irish gallantry to women takes the English aback: it does. It indicates mystification rather than performance.

Shaw falls back on the idea that women rarely love – which his one or two complete love affairs violently contradict – but, rather, affectionately pity men for falling in love with them, and treat them like babies. This argument was hopelessly out of date in Victorian times and prepares the way for the enslaving of women.

So, shifting his ground again, Shaw takes the genial line with actress after actress, to the woman who became his wife, that he is going to get what he can out of them and throw them aside; and that they will benefit by having worked with him! This was, of course, the rude-shy approach. A letter to his future wife, who had invited him to go on holiday to Dieppe, at a moment when 'the sprite', as Beatrice Webb called him, was worn out with overwork – and really scared – illustrates the point:

> I am to embark in a piercing wind, with lifeboats capsizing and ships foundering in all directions; to go to a watering place in the depth of winter with nothing to do and nowhere to go; I am to be chaperoned by two women, each determined that the other shall seduce me and each determined that I shall not seduce her . . .
>
> No use in looking for human sympathy from me. I have turned the switch, and am your very good friend, but as hard as nails.

The joke did not succeed. There are times when artificial comedy annoys. The future Mrs Shaw was as Irish and shy as he was, and he had a hard time living this letter down.

Shaw's letters are good because they are sharp, shrewd about people, comic, direct, always good-natured, contain news and have a core of purpose. He is the plausible speaker convincing an audience, and that core of seriousness is flattering. His letters are as lively when he is writing to the Webbs and the other Fabians as when he writes to his theatrical and literary correspondents. Shaw says in one of them that as a writer he sees life less as people than as fragments of situation. For this reason alone he was a born playwright, and it is odd that a man as experienced in the theatre as William Archer was should not have spotted it; but Archer was stuffy.

There is a situation in every letter; and in spite of what he says, a very subtle sense of character and its relation to the possible actor or actress, in his plays. The letters of outright criticism or advice to famous people like Ellen Terry or Mrs Patrick Campbell are incisive. The letter to

Charrington, Janet Achurch's husband, tactfully suggesting that he is unsuitable for the part of Morrell in *Candida*, is a masterpiece.

There is always the tenderness of play in the letters to Ellen Terry (the next volume, I presume, will contain the bulk of them), but in the letters to Janet Achurch there is more than tenderness: there is a deep concern, an expression of the humanity and seriousness that Shaw would sometimes allow to come out; in her case because she has come so wretchedly close to his own, never-forgotten, wretched home background.

The glimpses of a concealed inner Shaw are rare – some lines in the long correspondence with Janet Achurch, the Ibsen actress, a very old friend, are among the few instances. They contain a glimpse of the inciting misery, shame, loneliness and frustration of his early Dublin life, and then quickly the shutter closes with the laugh that enables him to escape onto the stage.

An early boyish letter to his sister Lucinda, the singer, shows him preternaturally sagacious and ruthless for his years: '. . . you have only to be immoveable, polite, generally amicable, and adamant . . .' 'You ought to laugh at Mamma more than you do.' That is the Shavian essence: Stand on your own, laugh at everyone but heal the wound by the skill of your laughter. Shaw enraged, yet he never made an enemy. Perhaps because he went beyond enraging into the fantasy world of outrage.

One long grave letter takes Janet Achurch, as it were, aside, and talks privately to her, quietly turning over the case for the advantages and disadvantages of religion. In its real sense – the Puritan argues – it is re-creation, the remaking of the self; it can arise from formal religion, from love, from art. We must have recreation or else stimulation. 'The question is, how am I to make Janet religious, so that she may recreate herself and feel no need of stimulants. That is the question that obsesses me.'

It did obsess him, and people have often wondered at it. The fact is that, in another way, his own case was like hers. His addiction was to words and his cleverness with them; but like her, he depended on an audience and knew the price this exacted. I am not sure that he was a great letter-writer; but his letters must have been delightful to receive; unlike Voltaire, who was called a chaos of clear ideas, he was a chaos of clear arguments. They become monotonous, and in letters his pre-dictability shows up. Strangely, it is not the performer who dazzles here, for he repeats his tricks. The happy shock of the unfair argument wears off.

What really gets us is that the performer is at heart the industrious apprentice – one whom we indeed see at the end of this volume winning the great gamble and about to marry the capitalist boss's daughter. It is a moral story.

Getting Richer

The key to John Updike's 'Rabbit' novels is in the last phrase of this opening passage from *Rabbit Is Rich*:

> Running out of gas, Rabbit Angstrom thinks as he stands behind the summer-dusty windows of the Springer Motors display room watching the traffic go by on Route 111, traffic somehow thin and scared compared to what it used to be. The fucking world is running out of gas. But they won't catch him, not yet, because there isn't a piece of junk on the road gets better mileage than his Toyotas, with lower service costs. Read *Consumer Reports*, April issue. That's all he has to tell the people when they come in. And come in they do, the people out there are getting frantic, they know the great American ride is ending.

We don't suppose Rabbit is all that rich – not as rich as the old Pennsylvania mineowners were – but as a lower-middle-class citizen of the shrewd kind he has done pretty well, marrying the boss's daughter, in the manner of the industrious apprentice. In a beautiful scene of furtive comedy, we see him buying Krugerrands. Still, there is alarm in that last phrase of his. It contains something like a metaphysical message. Huck Finn's classic American dream of 'lighting out for the territory' – into whatever wilderness of contemporary *moeurs*, or even of the spirit, one likes to think of – is done for. That 'ride' as pure escape sets the pace in the first of the 'Rabbit' novels, when Harry Angstrom swung impulsively on to the highway, heading south, away from Janice, his tippling, muddling 'mutt' of a wife. He is dragged back by news of tragedy at home: befuddled, she had drowned her baby, as we read in Updike's carefully documented account of the awful physical conditions of the case. If Rabbit was guilty by association, he had at any rate left her a car, that secondary sexual organ of our contemporary life. In *Rabbit Redux*, he was reduced to guilty matrimony, and it was Janice who lit out – with Stavros, her father's Greek assistant – and with even more appalling results. That volume seems to me the most impressive of the chronicle: it had Thomas Hardy-like items in it. In the present one, it is Rabbit's son who lights out – of college, to accuse the forty-six-year-old father he loves and hates. Here Updike's difficulty is to find a means of insinuating the sins of the past without recapitulating them and to make the novel something more than a job of clearing up. All his astonishing technical virtuosity as a poet, chronicler, moralist, and story-teller is called for. I detect some change of tone, but he has at any rate escaped the journalistic telegraphese that ruined, say, the later 'Forsyte' and other sagas. And if *Rabbit Is Rich* is in danger of becoming an essay in latter-day Babbittry, the author does fill out a man ashamed of his shamelessness; Rabbit is shown puzzled by his inescapable Puritan guilts, and relieved by bursts of rancour. As a one-time basketball hero, he has not much more in his head than the ethos of the 'achiever': you must 'win'. Beyond that, he is so cloudy in mind that he never really knows whether, morally speaking, he is lighting out or lighting back. Some critics have called him a monster, but he is far from that. Even in his tiresome sexual obsession he is excusable, having come to sex later than the young do today. He is really a deedy infant, and moderately decent: he'd like to learn. If he doesn't quite know how to love his wife, he is sentimentally protective; in the common love-hate between father and son, he is honest, though his methods are risky. The son swings between thinking of his father as a murderer of a baby and a wacky girl (but by default) and thinking of him as a comforting shadow. The curse of the cult of 'achievement' has its misleading aspects.

If we look first of all at Updike as a chronicler, we have to say that he was dead right in choosing the minor provincial city of Brewer, Pennsylvania, and putting Rabbit into the motor trade. That trade is the source of inner-city decay. This kind of ad hoc city has become international; horrible world news pours in via 'the boob tube', and adds new fantasies to what one has to call the 'ongoing' private stream of domestic consciousness – one recalls that in Joyce, to whom Updike has a debt, that stream mainly flowed back. The next element is native American, even though it has spread: television's real contribution to the mind comes from the Things in the commercials, with their awful jollities.

Updike has the extraordinary gift of making the paraphernalia of, say, the Sears Roebuck catalogue sound like a chant from the Book of Psalms turned into vaudeville. Industrialised society consumes and worships what can be bought. As Henry James once told us, 'the shopping' is in the blood. Updike knows, for example, every gadget in a car, from the engine to the coachwork, even to the point of giving us the useful information that it is not easy to perform the act of lust on vinyl seating.

It has always seemed to me that in his preoccupation with the stillness of domestic objects Updike is a descendant, in writing, of the Dutch genre painters, to whom everything in a house, in nature, or in human posture had the gleam of usage on it without which a deeply domestic culture could not survive its own boredom. The stress on paraphernalia, even the label on the product, has put something vivid into American comic writers as well as serious moralists. By extension, the clothes and underclothes of people, the parts of their bodies – heads, faces, ears, noses, legs, arms, hands, toes, complexions, and the hungrier organs – are minutely noted. (Rabbit's son is upset because his wife has one nostril larger than the other.) I don't mean that these things are catalogued by Updike; they simply give the ripple of ballad-like vividness to the stream of consciousness. If downtown Brewer looks as if it had been bombed by its loving inhabitants, Updike is as exact as a war artist who rises far above the documentary and the unfelt. Like Eliot, he is moved by the waste land. Where Sinclair Lewis's clutter of mind and matter pushed at us the brutalised pathos of accepted vulgarities, Updike is a poet. He loves words and images. If his sexual curiosity runs to the clinical, he relieves us with gnomic sentences; perhaps the closeups of sex, the private porn, are 'a kind of penance at your root'. There is a preacher inside him who says that if 'anything goes', there is a price, which, for some unfair reason, a Mediterranean like Stavros never has to pay; unlike the Puritan Rabbit, and knowing he will die, Stavros has a 'superior grip upon the basic elements of life'. If he is compelled in his pursuit of pleasure, he knows how to give it; in bed, he loves a distracting chat and the small talk of the affections, the fun of taking sex as friendship, not a climax. He has the old Greek sense that 'nothing too much' lasts longest. This is what charms Rabbit's wife.

One sees the ex-athlete Rabbit closer to his particular norm as he takes up jogging when that absurd craze comes to the health-clowns of Brewer. Updike is the poet of physical action:

> [Rabbit] begins to run. In the woods, along the old logging roads and bridle trails, he ponderously speeds in tennis shoes first, orange with clay dust, and then in gold-and-blue Nikes bought at a sporting goods shop in Stroudsburg especially for this, running shoes with tipped-up soles at toe and heel, soles whose resilient circlets like flattened cleats lift him powerfully as, growing lighter and quicker and quieter, he runs.

The one-time athletic Puritan is all conscious of the 'murderous burden swaddled about his heart and lungs' in the early days of these desperate bids for immortality. He experiences fanaticism about his body but eventually finds himself 'casting his mind wide' and becomes aware of the country, and, indeed, more:

> There is along the way an open space, once a meadow, now spiked with cedars and tassle-headed weeds, where swallows dip and careen, snapping up insects revived in the evening damp. Like these swallows Rabbit, the blue and gold of his new shoes flickering, skims, above the earth, above the dead. The dead stare upwards. Mom and Pop are lying together again as for so many years on that sway-backed bed they'd bought second-hand during the Depression and never got around to replacing though it squeaked like a tricycle left out in the rain and was so short Pop's feet stuck out of the covers. Papery-white feet that got mottled and marbled with veins finally: if he'd ever have exercised he might have lived longer. Tothero [the sports coach] down there is all eyes, eyes big as saucers staring out of his lopsided head while his swollen tongue hunts for a word. Fred Springer, who put Harry where he is, eggs him on, hunched over and grimacing like a man with a poker hand so good it hurts. Skeeter, that that newspaper clipping claimed had fired upon the Philly cops first even though there were twenty of them in the yard and hallways and only some pregnant mothers and children on the commune premises, Skeeter black as the earth turns his face away.

(Skeeter we remember as the mixture of Negro religion and conspiracy, on the run in *Rabbit Redux* – the one profoundly tragic character in that book.)

Rabbit is running silent as an Indian when he gets into the pine needles of the woods:

> Becky [his drowned baby], a mere seed laid to rest, and Jill [burned to death in a fire], a pale seedling held from the sun, hang in the earth, he imagines, like stars, and beyond them there are myriads, whole races like the Cambodians, that have drifted into death. He is treading on them all, they are resilient, they are cheering him on, his lungs are burning, his heart hurts, he is a membrane removed from the hosts below, their filaments caress his ankles, he loves the earth, he will never die.

He gets home, and his wife says, 'For heaven's sakes. What are you training for?' He says the thing is to press against your limitations. 'It's now or never... There's people out to get me. I can lie down now. Or fight.' And when she asks who is trying to get him, he says, 'You should know' – it's that damn son of theirs. 'You hatched him.' She is an incompetent woman, who can't shop, cook, or keep a house even fairly clean, and he does not know whether he loves her or not, but he'll never leave her. I quote these long passages because they are examples of Updike's mastery of allusive narrative, which mingles past guilts and mistakes with the going world of the present.

In this volume, we realise that the women, even when they are victims, are stronger than Rabbit is, for a reason he somehow stumbles on. Men are solitaries and egotists; foolish or not, they see themselves as born to be alone. The women are not solitaries. Their strength lies in their capacity for assimilating personal relationships, in living for the primacy of family and accepting its hierarchies. Rabbit may earn the money, out of compulsion; the women control the capital, real or emotional. They live by arrangements among themselves and never forget a nourishing jealousy.

The two earlier novels had a tight, dramatic tension. In the present one, the tension is looser, because the elders are getting fat and middle-aged, but there is the new drama of the puzzled father and the son who too much resembles him. The 'four o'clock garbage' of television still filters in from the outside world. There is comedy: the scene with the 'broad-minded' young minister who is called in to marry the unbelieving young people in church. The son is ashamed among his shacking-up friends, who are often high on pot or beer, for weakly marrying a girl merely because she is pregnant by him. Worse, she is not a student from the college he has dropped out of but is a mere secretary – loss of group caste there. But she is strong enough to call her young macho a 'twerp', to have her baby, and to let her husband go back to college. He makes the startling discovery that since she has been obliged to cut education and to work for a living, she is more grown up, more independent than his student friends. Among the young women, she is the fullest and most subtle portrait in the novel.

Janice, Rabbit's wife, in her devious way, grows stronger the more muddled she is. And, of course, Grandmother Springer, with her split-minded sentences, is the confident voice of Fate itself. But the clinching final incident is Rabbit's sentimental journey to see Ruth, the wronged woman of *Rabbit, Run*. She belongs, in the American class system, to the stoical, rural, hard-tongued poor. Rabbit burns to know, in his shame-faced sexy way, whether she bore him a daughter or whether she had an abortion. He hints at putting his hand in his pocket. With the mastery of the Sphinx, she evades telling him. Or, indeed, us. This scene has the wit of a Molière comedy. She tells him, quietly, that her dead husband was the best father her children could have had and more of a man than Rabbit could hope to be. She had been a used woman, but she had known, in her grim way, how to become unused. In the meantime, the middle-aged friends of Rabbit have drifted into the pricey hedonism of trying to copy the young. They drink rather too much. There is a muddled wife-swapping holiday for these 'oldies' in the Caribbean in which the women put their heads together and see that Rabbit, especially, does not get the partner he had hoped for. After this, the porn magazines lose their spell; the elders return making moral grimaces. A phrase about shadows falling – they 'sneak in like burglars' – evokes the emotional experience of so many of the inhabitants of Brewer.

There is nothing in this volume as searing as the Skeeter episode in *Rabbit Redux*, but that in fact enhances the conviction that these three books of Updike's are a monumental portrayal of provincial and domestic manners. He is both poet and historian, so various in observation and so truthful, so inventive and adept, that he leaves us brooding on his scene and remembering his epithets.

One of Nature's Balkans

She 'lived her life operatically and tinkered endlessly with the story-line, the score and the libretto'. These frank words come from Victoria Glendinning's sympathetic and searching life of Cicely Fairfield, known to us as Rebecca West. Operatic? The mind wanders to the stormy life of George Sand, who had also been a combative journalist and a richly textured novelist reckless in her passions, and of whom her daughter wrote, 'It will take a clever fellow to unravel the character of my mother.' It would appear that Rebecca West felt in her old age that the story of her life required two clever fellows. In Ms Glendinning's introduction we read that Rebecca West left 'a signed request' that Ms Glendinning, who had known her well during the last ten years of her life, should write a short biography while we were waiting for a fuller life by Stanley Olson. The choice was happy. Ms Glendinning is a well-known, prize-winning biographer of such difficult ladies as Edith Sitwell and Vita Sackville-West and of the admirable Elizabeth Bowen. In this last, she seemed somewhat nervous of that electric Anglo–Irish brain, but with Rebecca West she is alert to the pathos, the grand drama of sweeping judgment. She understands how the tunes of temperament change.

Why did the young Miss Fairfield choose to be Rebecca West? (She disliked Ibsen's plays.) To re-imagine herself? To catch attention? To stand apart from her sisters, one of whom was already making an impression as a distinguished doctor and would eventually become a barrister, while the other sister was blamelessly conventional? We must look back to Rebecca's Puritan Scottish mother, of crofter stock, and her fantasising Anglo–Irish father. The parents met in Australia, where they were poor immigrants. He had become a painter and a clever, restless journalist, inclined to parlous mining speculations and casual love affairs. The marriage was a union of two lonely people. Hating Australia, he brought her back to Scotland. No Puritan he. He came from wild Kerry, and his fancy was filled with talk of rank and with Anglo–Irish obsession with grand cousinage. The daughters listened in their childhood to his tales of an ancestor who had been a cousin of Sir Walter Raleigh, of a connection with the great Sackvilles which somehow gave them all descent from an aunt of Anne Boleyn. Even Rebecca's older and sterner sister, Lettie, the distinguished doctor, when she turned Roman Catholic spoke of the family connection with a procession of saints – St Margaret of Scotland, St Louis of France, two Russian saints, and a Spanish one.

More interesting was the father's political talk. He was an admirer of Edmund Burke and corresponded with Herbert Spencer. When he brought his family back to Scotland, he worked in Glasgow on the *Glasgow Herald*, and then moved them to London. Eventually, he vanished abroad on some speculative pharmaceutical deal, pursued women, and abandoned the family completely for five years – it is possible that his wife threw him out – and was found dead in lodgings in Liverpool. In the meantime, the mother raised the family in Edinburgh. Her gift was musical, and her taste for Schumann and the influence of music in general were to be strong in Rebecca's writing. In Edinburgh, the Athens of the North, the clever girls soon won scholarships to excellent schools. Rebecca's desire was to become an actress, and when she was seventeen she went to London to the Academy of Dramatic Art. There, for all her gifts and although she did get one or two minor parts, she failed. Why? The beautiful girl was histrionic. The victim of high-strung nervousness, she reacted to strain with involuntary grimaces and was plagued by uncontrollable itchings. In short, she could not unself herself and become other people.

She inherited from her father a literary gift, but it would have startled him to see her succeed as an ardent feminist. He had been a strong Tory, and loathed the notion of women's suffrage: suffragettes, he said, were 'unsympathetic and repellent'. He would have been shocked by the articles she wrote for *The Freewoman*, though he certainly would have admired her mastery of the irreverent metaphor, which caught the attention of Bernard Shaw. We hear her dismissing the British intelligentsia as 'the left-wing carriage trade'. (Much later in her life, at the time of the abdication of Edward VIII, she was to write of the King that his mind seemed to be like 'a telephone exchange with not enough subscribers'.) Such wit in her writing and conversation led the young woman to the famous, but it had its price. One of her lifelong friends, the distinguished journalist Charles Curran, who was of great help to her when she was writing her long, incisive investigative studies of crime and treachery, said of her that she 'has several skins fewer than any other human being, it's a kind of psychological haemophilia, which is one reason why she writes so well, and why she is so vulnerable'.

Vulnerable especially in love, as we see in the notorious and painful affair with H. G. Wells. How could she have ignored the warnings of his disastrous public affair with the young Amber Reeves? How could the young Rebecca not perceive or understand Wells's gratitude to his wife? Rebecca's headlong ambition in love led to neurotic illness, and this was to be repeated in her love affair with Beaverbrook, the newspaper tycoon. The extravagance of feeling was certainly operatic in the sense that it was orchestrated and, in fact, led to disturbing, and even fantastic, illusions.

The young woman, who had been a 'displaced person' as a child, not unnaturally sought the glamour of wealth and respectable certainty. We come at last to her marriage with Henry Andrews, notoriously a pedant, apparently rich, and a bore. He passed as a solid English country gentleman, but he, too, had been a displaced person. He came of Polish or Lithuanian stock, had been educated in Great Britain, and had spent several years in a prison camp in Germany during the First World War. He dabbled in merchant banking, not always happily: he was really by nature a fussing academic. (When he and Rebecca set up in a rather grand country house in Buckinghamshire, the local villagers were mystified by him and lightly called him 'a comical old bugger'.) For Rebecca, he had one valuable gift: he was a linguist. This was indispensable to her on her visits to Yugoslavia before 1939, when she wrote what is thought by many to be a masterpiece of romantic travel, *Black Lamb and Grey Falcon*. As her biographer says, Rebecca became 'one of nature's Balkans', and, indeed, at one point in *Black Lamb and Grey Falcon* her chatty husband is heard saying to her, 'As for your other demands that from now on every day will be an apocalyptic revelation, I should drop that, if I were you!' But she didn't. John Gunther, her great friend, said the book was not so

much about Yugoslavia as about Rebecca West. She herself wrote in a
well-known passage:

> Only part of us is sane: only part of us loves pleasure and the longer
> day of happiness, wants to live to our nineties and die in peace, in a
> house that we built, that shall shelter those who come after us. The
> other half of us is nearly mad. . . . [This fight] can be observed con-
> stantly in our personal lives.

True or untrue, the overtone is operatic: even the scenery, the archaeology, the history, and many of the people seem to be stage chorus.

Ms Glendinning has made much of Rebecca West's admiration for
Proust and the music of his long-winded and branching sentences, and
of his influence on her. This is true up to a point; in her novels (except
in *The Fountain Overflows*) we often have the sensation of claustrophobia.
Wells complained that in the narrative of her early novel *The Judge* she
was dilatory and began too far back. This is also true of her last novel,
The Birds Fall Down – an ambitious historical story in which an innocent
girl is used to carry a message to tsarist dissidents. We are soon lost in
the décor and the overfurnishing of the intrigue. Too many people
appear, too completely. The whole story is too brilliantly laboured. It is
astonishing that while she was working on this very long book the manic
side of her temperament was driving her to write scores of letters to
friends, explaining here, attacking there, as she poured out the wrongs
of her personal life: the tedium of her marriage; the persisting quarrel
with her son, Anthony; her feuds with her critics, who rightly accused
her of political extremism. Her health was bad. After a serious operation,
she had hallucinations: she said that the wretched Henry Andrews was
trying to poison her with doctored soup sent over from a London restaurant.

In 1968, Henry died. His organised fussiness was revealed. In the
waistcoat pockets of thirty Savile Row suits – all the suits the same – a
hundred and eighty-seven pounds was found: money the prudent man
had reserved for tips! A more disturbing discovery was that he had been
in the habit of casually picking up girls. Rebecca was enraged. She had
only briefly been unfaithful to him – once with a doctor and once in
Nuremberg, with a judge at the trial. In itself rather an odd choice.

[1232]

Rebecca West lived on until she was ninety. She sold the Buckingham-shire mansion and moved to a terrace in Kensington, a few doors from the Iranian Embassy that later sheltered terrorists. A highly trained anti-terrorist squad attacked the building, and she eagerly watched the affair from her window until she was dramatically rescued in a scene of gunfire. The incident is an ironic and unexpected crown of her career. She could almost have invented it.

An Anglo–Irishman

T he late Richard Ellmann's *Oscar Wilde* runs to nearly 600 pages, is exhaustive but not in the leaden manner of the fact-fetishist, but in the humane spirit of fervent inquiry. In Wilde he has an Anglo–Irishman who acts his reckless way through the hidden intimacies of late Victorian society, a man brimming with wit, images and inventive afterthoughts in his progress to fame and his own undoing. When reporters crowded round Wilde on his arrival on his first trip to New York and asked the dandy what impression the stormy Atlantic Ocean had made upon him, Wilde replied that it seemed tame to him. The reporters cabled to London: 'Mr Wilde Disappointed with the Atlantic'; but Ellmann reminds us that Wilde had once denounced the sea as being 'unvintageable'. He was a man who could always outdo himself. Yet Mr Ellmann shows, Wilde is also the classic tragic hero, self-destroyed at the height of his fame, 'refulgent, proud and ready to fall'. The fall is dreadful but it is perfect that it begins when the greatest of his comedies, *The Importance of Being Earnest*, is entrancing London audiences and masks his own secret life as a homosexual. It is perfect also that when Wilde returns one night to his club he finds a card from the Marquess of Queensberry containing the fatal ill-spelt words: 'To Oscar Wilde, posing Somdomite' – a blow below the belt from the author of the world-famous Queensberry rules for boxers, also the father – himself a minor poet – who is determined to rescue his son, Lord Alfred Douglas, from Wilde's love and influence. Wilde loses his head, brings an action for libel against the rough and noble fox-hunter and in the following trials Wilde is at the mercy of deadlier actors than himself: the lawyers. They have collected evidence from male prostitutes and in the trial that follows for 'indecent behaviour' Wilde is done for. Almost two generations will pass before that particular law, now known as the 'blackmailer's charter', is repealed.

Wilde's father was a fashionable and distinguished Dublin eye surgeon and had been knighted: he founded St Mark's Hospital in Dublin for special treatment of the eye and ear. He was also a scholarly authority on the neglected, prehistoric Barrows of Ireland and an outstanding expert on Irish folklore. A scholar, he was no saint: he had fathered three illegitimate children before his marriage and his wife was far too proud or indifferent to complain. She was an Irish patriot, she stood for Irish freedom and was also a poetess who felt herself 'destined for greatness'. She claimed to have been an eagle in an earlier life on earth; that her family, the Elgees, were of Italian origin, called herself Speranza and was as famous for her flamboyant clothes as her son was for his. When Oscar was born in 1854 she gave him operatic names – Oscar Fingal O'Flahertie Wills Wilde – the O'Flahertie in honour of her supposed family connection with pre-Norman Kings of West Connacht who had provoked the famous Galway prayer 'From the wild O'Flaherties good Lord deliver us'. Convinced of the genius of her son she saw to it that he was sent to a school known as the 'Irish Eton' near Enniskillen, then on to Trinity, Dublin, where he became an excellent classicist. The youth was already an aesthete. He went on to Magdalen, Oxford, where despite some delinquencies, he triumphed by winning the Newdigate Prize for poetry and indeed got a Double First.

Mr Ellmann writes:

And so Wilde created himself at Oxford. He began by stirring his conscience with Ruskin and his senses with Pater; these worthies gradually passed into more complicated blends of Catholicism, Freemasonry, aestheticism . . . Initially he tried to resolve his own contradictions. But gradually . . . he came to see his contradictions as a source of strength rather than of volatility.

He will have the art of becoming other people.

At Oxford he lost, or was careful to lose, his Irish accent. On his successful lecture tours in America the actor in him brought it back when he left the east and faced the descendants of poor Irish emigrants. They were not much interested in the pre-Raphaelitism or the House Beautiful, or even his socialism. For them he became the poetic Speranza's son, the Irish patriot. One had supposed that his extraordinary clothes –

the romantic cloak, the extravagantly wide collar, the velvet knickerbockers and the silk stockings – not to mention the touches of jewellery –
that his tall massive figure would draw ridicule. Far from it. Americans
delighted in fantastic clothes in their parades. Wilde's costume was not
an eccentricity: he was more than half an actor and he was also protesting
against the heavy frock coat of conventional Puritan success. Still, he
was not a man to be taken by surprise. Hearing that some students
intended to jeer, he adroitly appeared in conventional dinner-jacket. The
revolt was killed. In his private meetings with famous American writers
Longfellow and, above all, Whitman were impressed. Only Henry James
– who was to have his own secret – felt there was something 'unclean'
in him.

We come to Wilde's return to Great Britain and his marriage to Constance Lloyd. It seems certain that he had had homosexual contacts in
Oxford where they were tolerated and even fashionable. Ellmann says
that Wilde had caught syphilis there and thinks that the marriage to
Constance could have been long delayed on this account. The courtship
of Constance was indeed slow. Her mother had died, her father had
remarried and the girl lived with her grandfather, a lawyer. She was shy
and said by Ellmann to be 'logical, mathematical, shy yet fond of talking',
could read Dante in Italian – '(and did)'. There are touching lines in a
letter she wrote to her future husband about the failure of his early play
Vera in America. She says, with a ring of truth, about her life:

> The world surely is unjust and bitter to most of us; ... There is not
> the slightest use in *fighting* against existing prejudices ... I am afraid
> you and I disagree in our opinions on art, for I hold that there is no
> perfect art without perfect morality, whilst you say that they are dis-
> tinct and separable things. ... Truly I am no judge that you should
> appeal to me for opinions.

She was (as Ellmann says) 'intelligent, ... capable and independent'.
She was certainly well-read in French and Italian literature and 'learned
German so they could enjoy reading new books in the language together'.

When at last they married they moved into 'the House Beautiful' Wilde
had planned and which is described in detail. We note that the library
where he worked had pale gold walls and that 'along two sides of the

room was a low divan, in front of which were ottomans, lanterns, and hangings, an Eastern inlaid table and – no chairs.' And in one of the drawing rooms upstairs, appropriately, a small bronze figure of Narcissus. Wilde was indeed in love with himself and 'played the married man with a flair which suggested that for him it was an adventure rather than a quiescence'. Even more a dangerous display of the double nature of the born wit.

The sudden success in the theatre with *Lady Windermere's Fan* and *A Woman of No Importance* splits his emotional, social and sexual life. The homosexuality which had been stirred at tolerant Oxford puts him at the mercy of the young Alfred Douglas and, as Ellmann says, if Wilde was bold, Douglas was totally reckless – 'reckless and unmanageable... Since neither Wilde nor Douglas practised or expected sexual fidelity, money was the stamp and seal of their love.' And 'like a figure in Greek tragedy, Wilde had allowed his success to make him overweening'. And Douglas was a young man who, like his father, thrived on quarrels. As we follow the detail the sole comfort in a tangled story is Wilde's generosity to the spendthrift young man who is destroying him.

What we have forgotten is that there were three trials: Wilde's defiance of Queensberry failed. Wilde's wife and friends urged him to go to France. He refused to take his chance. Boy prostitutes saw immense prospects of blackmail and he was easily trapped.

Ellmann writes:

A half-packed suitcase lay on the bed, emblem of contradictory impulses. He was tired of action. Like Hamlet, as he understood that hero, he wished to distance himself from his plight, to be the spectator of his own tragedy... He had always met adversity head on... It was like the history of Timon of Athens or of Wilde's old admiration, Agamemnon, yet meaner.

In London his two plays *An Ideal Husband* and *The Importance of Being Earnest* were taken off. The same happened in New York. At the second trial the jury disagreed. At the third trial he was done for.

We know the rest. In Reading Gaol the Governor ruled by the book and it was a long time before Wilde was permitted to read anything.

[1237]

Later conditions were a little easier and his warders were distinctly sympathetic. *The Ballad of Reading Gaol* tells his story. We may have become
dubious of the famous line 'Each man kills the thing he loves' as a tragic
utterance but the portraits of his awed fellow-prisoners are not easily
forgotten. His life in France after his release is a life without a role. We
see him uncertain and dismayed, when, by accident, some old acquaintance hesitates to recognise him; he can only beg with his eyes or turn
away. In the final scene in the little hotel in Paris the proprietor is decent
but the death of Wilde is horrible. He is living on lethal draughts of
absinthe and brandy and dies horribly of syphilis. (His body burst.) He
was buried in the cemetery of Bagneux. In 1909 the body was moved to
Père Lachaise and has Epstein's famous monument and lines from *The
Ballad of Reading Gaol*:

> And alien tears will fill for him
>   Pity's long-broken urn,
>   For his mourners will be outcast men,
>   And outcasts always mourn.

He belongs to our world, Ellmann says, more than to Victoria's: I am
not sure what that sentence means unless it is that we share in the general
vengeance of the gods?

Never-Never-Land

Among the writers who are celebrating the centenary of the birth of P. G. Wodehouse this year, Benny Green seems to me the most spirited and cogent to have appeared so far. He calls his book 'a *literary* biography' (my italics), which is exactly what is called for in dealing with a surprisingly scholarly master of comic folly, who in spite of poor eyesight seems to have done nothing but write all day, almost from the cradle until his ninetieth year. If he had another secret life behind his writing he was preoccupied enough to make it impenetrable. He was clearly a professional but one with the gift of imperturbable and deedy innocence.

He remained a schoolboy for life but without the sentimental morbidities of, say, Barrie or Milne's tinklings from the kindergarten. If he has a literary coeval, this is 'perhaps' – as Mr Green says – the Max Beerbohm of *Zuleika Dobson*. Not perhaps at all: this is real insight. Wodehouse was certainly an Edwardian and much influenced by the D'Oyly Carte opera, and one recalls that the age was remarkable for producing a number of comic writers of ingrained 'English light humour'; like a dry white wine it nourished the assumptions, malice, and comforts of F. Anstey, Saki, one book of Jerome K. Jerome's, the Grossmiths, and W. W. Jacobs. They were 'English' in the very sap of that conceit: they travelled well in America in their time, especially Wodehouse himself, though I have found lately that flocks of American students have never heard of him. This is sad but understandable. The age of light-headed imperial innocence began to vanish after 1914 and we have grown up in the black laughter of outrage, enhanced by the obsession with sex. One can only say that laughter for its own sake is never *passé* for very long: we still laugh at Goldsmith and Restoration comedy after a spell of sneering at their subjects, their oaths and delivery.

It has been said, especially of light comedy, that its writers are apt to be trapped by period and the presumptions of its manners and vernacular;

that none of us has known a butler or 'gentleman's gentleman', a rich silly-ass with a monocle, like Wooster, or a barmy peer like Lord Emsworth; that their idiotic world is dead. One has heard it scathingly argued that these fools are socially and politically deplorable, propaganda for reactionary causes and against what used to be called 'the challenge of our time'. Our nostalgia ought to be for the future. The argument is crabbed. The kingdoms of fantasy and mirth are long-lasting and not of this world; and their inhabitants make circles round our respectable angers. The strength of Wodehouse lies not in his almost incomprehensibly intricate plots – Restoration comedy again – but in his prose style and there, above all, in his command of mind-splitting metaphor. To describe a girl as 'the sand in civilisation's spinach' enlarges and decorates the imagination.

Of course the society into which Wodehouse was born in 1881 has its importance either as an influence or as a springboard. I am old enough to have known the rather rueful beginning of the end of his period and, by chance, to have lived in his sainted Dulwich, and to have been briefly educated at what was called the Lower School – lower in social class, and more productive of bank clerks than colonial governors, than was his Dulwich College, the subject, incidentally, of one of Pissarro's romantic Anglophile paintings. The 'romance' and pleasances of what was then one of the most vernal London suburbs, and the niceties of its local snobberies, are well known to me. (The college's second cricket team would condescend to play our first once a year and often beat us. They, we used to say, had expensive coaches!) We belonged to the same Elizabethan foundation, Alleyn's College of God's Gift.

I felt the Dulwich dream of the time and did not much repine because it was certain not to be realised, though we copied items of its swank. One or two of our senior boys would cause a stir by playing at being dressy Bertie Wooster and putting on a monocle to annoy the masters. (Some learned writers to the London *Times* have claimed that the monocle was added by vulgar illustrators – probably from the Lower School – and not by Wodehouse himself.) Our envy – when we were schoolboys – was chiefly centred on the illusion that at the college they could get away with more 'ragging' and more extravagance of a gentlemanly kind than we ourselves could. Mr Green has a delightful account of the prospects before our betters in Wodehouse's day. Both father and son were destined for Hong Kong:

> By 1867 imperial traffic was brisk, as the British wandered the surface of the planet in search of either divine missions or increased dividends, or, better still if it could be arranged, both at the same time. Off they sailed down the sea lanes ... the brevet colonels flushed with the proud apoplexy of a recent mention in dispatches; horse-faced subalterns whose toothy sibilance would soon be whistling across the promontories of the North-west Frontier; staff majors grimly pursuing the carrot of a KCIE; ruddy adjutants whose leaden gallantries might before long be rattling the teacups of some half-forgotten hill station; reverend gentlemen dedicated to the export of their religion to areas which had known their own when the English were still daubing their rumps with berry juice ... all these men resolved to reconciling somehow the opposing ideals of playing the game and pinching someone else's property, and miraculously succeeding, at least in part.

Public schools with their devotion to sport and their insistence on a solid grounding in Greek and Latin and even modern languages – Mr Green mentions the effect of this excellent education on Raymond Chandler, who was at Dulwich after Wodehouse. (Chandler remarked that a classical education saves you from being fooled by pretentiousness.) The creator of Wooster was a star athlete and boxer and editor of the school mag to whom the composition of crisp rhymed couplets in Latin and Greek was second nature. Characteristically the eupeptic Wodehouse thought the college was bliss, boyhood was bliss, the suburb of Dulwich heaven, and he scorned people who said life at English public schools was hell. There were only two flaws. His father lost his money, and he was forced to chuck Oxford or Cambridge and to go and earn his living in a Lombard Street bank, from which he was sacked early on for an outrageous act in the tradition of Dulwich 'ragging': he defaced and tore out the first page of that sacred object in banking life, a new ledger. Clearly, like his insuppressible Psmith, he had been taught nerve.

The other flaw – if it was really a flaw, for, a eupeptic by nature, he scarcely mentioned it – was that like so many of the imperial sons he was sent home from abroad to be boarded out at holiday institutions or other families and especially with aunts. One thinks of the long list of English writers to whom this occurred: Kipling, Maugham, Saki, Orwell, wounded men all who scarcely knew their mothers. Did Wodehouse settle for a paradise of childlike laughter because of this deprivation? Does his general ferocity about aunts – except the one called romping Aunt Dahlia – come from this? Perhaps so.

On the other hand many of those half-abandoned boys were not as afflicted as some critics think they ought logically to have been. The only faint distress Wodehouse records is boredom with his elders, which is surely a normal affliction. The only places he liked, after Dulwich, were places like rural Shropshire, Lord Emsworth's moss-eaten paradise. One thing about the eternal schoolboy was his exceptional spryness in plotting his own cheeky and ingenious way, doing what he liked at once, which was to scribble and earn his living. He got off the ground in early school stories. Mr Green says:

> By a freakish collusion between temperament and experience, those schooldays left Wodehouse with a commitment to the schoolboy sensibility to which he remained forever steadfast, and which had the unexpected effect of making his work unique. For although Psmith insisted on breaking out, he took with him the intellectual and emotional luggage of a schoolboy. He and his followers may have been at large in the world of great affairs, but they arrived there still acting and reacting like the fifth-formers they would always remain. That is why there can be no sex in Wodehouse's world, only romance, no morality, only posture, no dogma, only laughter ... only Wodehouse [among scores of writers] pursued the odd idea of disguising his fifth-formers as responsible citizens and letting them loose among grown men and women.

And he quotes J. B. Priestley's admiring judgment about Wodehouse's lifelong character:

> ... there is no sign of a mature man here. Together with his talent for the absurd, this explains his success.

The Drones Club was a schoolboy's ideal. So is every pretty, sly,

sexless girl who knows how to make circles round any romantic fool –
provided she does not wear glasses and has not been to the London
School of Economics or Cambridge and has not read Freud. From housemaid to debutante – she has to retain the *savoir-faire* and the legs of the
chorus.

The prestige of the school story – in which Wodehouse began his
career – seems to be a special curiosity of English life, for generations.
I rather think the taste has now gone, but it harks back to Victorian
traditions of character building: *Tom Brown's Schooldays* and most obviously Frederic Farrar's book *Eric, or Little by Little*. When Wodehouse
tore that page out of the sacred ledger at the London bank he tore
up the old school tradition. Mr Green detects a moralistic opponent in
Wodehouse's work: the famous but distinctly down-market stories of the
Magnet and *Gem* examined by George Orwell and written for us lads of
the Lower School who would never be more than pseudo gentlemen or
'cads'. But when Wodehouse left the bank to write popular sketches and
quips for the newspapers and then went off to New York, on a boyish
impulse, nominally because he wanted to meet a few American boxers,
he in fact turned his skills to writing lyrics for the new kind of musical
comedy.

Mr Green is an authority on this arcane aspect of his hero's life, which
is little known to fans of his subsequent novels. On reflection, one sees
that a classical scholar would have his sort of skill in playing with language of all kinds, and knowing how to make the lines short but true,
light humour being one of the graces of a good education of the classical
kind. But when he broke into the impertinent joy and invention in *Carry
On, Jeeves*, he found himself as a writer. The pompous Sir Roderick is seen
'wolfing' a plateful of chicken fricassee and 'handing up his dinner-pail for
a second instalment'; the awful Honoraria Glossop, who has the voice
of 'a lion tamer', appals Wooster because she looks like what the law
calls an 'Act of God. You might just as well blame a fellow for being
run over by a truck.' A professor has an eye 'like a haddock' and his wife
the look of a woman who 'had had bad news round about the year 1900
and never really got over it'. (The phrase 'round about' has that sense
of a great leap into timeless space which is present in all his fantasies.)
Wooster worships his brainlessness as he worships his ties and is given

[1243]

to prosaically knowing *obiter dicta* passages that end in grotesque explosions of precision:

> It is a peculiar thing in life that the people you most particularly want to edge away from always seem to cluster round like a poultice.

When he meets a girl at a station in *Leave It to Psmith*, Wooster's clichés are lyrical:

> . . . you are as fresh and blooming as – if I may coin a simile – a rose. How do you do it? When I arrived I was deep in alluvial deposits, and have only just managed to scrape them off.

Comic writing, at its best, is an inverted poetry. As for blasts of introspection, does anything equal Lord Emsworth's discovery that the one thing his ancient family had somehow lacked was 'a family curse', but now, thank God, he has got one: his son.

Mr Green quotes Frank Swinnerton as saying that Wodehouse's great gift in language and invention is 'an irresistible air of improvisation' which has the paradoxical effect of putting dash into the sly sententiousness of Edwardian prose. In sheer pace he outdoes his contemporaries. It is in this and his stirring-up of fantasy, as A. J. P. Taylor rightly says, that Wodehouse ranks with Firbank and Congreve. One of the tests of such a remark is to see Wodehouse slowed down on television. This is a visual and oral disaster. His people were not meant to be seen or even heard, but have to be inducted from the ridiculous page; and anyway his people completely fox the modern actor or actress, who overdress the accents.

Mr Green goes carefully into the row about the notorious broadcasts to his American friends from Germany when he was taken prisoner in France. The talks were harmless, innocent, and Wodehouse has long ago been forgiven even by the official classes and the law. He was as foolish in this episode as any of his grown-up schoolboys. He suffered and saw what an ass he had been. It is to the great credit of Malcolm Muggeridge that he came intelligently to Wodehouse's defence; but in Orwell's defence of Wodehouse Mr Green acutely sees that Orwell errs when he says that Wodehouse had an upper-class blindness to the threat of Nazism. Long before, in one of his stories, Wodehouse had made a savagely hilarious attack on dictators. Benign as he was, Wodehouse got his own back on enemies like the one-time ambassador in Paris and on A. A. Milne.

It does strike one that his time in the German prison camp unseated Wodehouse's judgment: also that in his long years in the United States he lost something of his native ground – as indeed the great Henry James may be thought to have done in Britain and Europe. Yet, when we think of Wodehouse's long and flourishing years in the United States, it strikes us that his fantastic England depended on his being distant from it, and even if not copied the American vernacular does loosen the waistcoat. His England, his romantic fools and villains, depend for their lives on being absurdities. If this is so, why do the British, who devoured and still devour his books, recognise themselves? I heard Auberon Waugh say the other afternoon that perhaps in their poetic moments the British secretly idle in the dream of being Psmiths, Woosters and Jeeveses and Emsworths in disguise. The never-never-land is irresistible. It abounds also in Dickens. Even the pose of making fun of ourselves may disguise a private ideal. All nationals seem to have another self, preoccupied with sustaining illusions. Isn't this what comedy is about?

The Strength of an Injured Spirit

$$\rule{3cm}{1.5pt}$$

Biographies of Mary Wollstonecraft have usually dwelt, quite properly, on the historical influences that favoured her leap from a statement of the Rights of Man to her book *A Vindication of the Rights of Woman*, first published in 1792. Her new biographer, Eleanor Flexner, looks rather to those things in her upbringing and private character that turned a neurasthenic into a pioneer of feminism. The driving force, as in other outstanding founders, sprang from a sense of personal injustice and family torment; her vision was intimately connected with the wrongs of childhood.

If she is a sad figure she grasped the luck that was going in the century of her birth. The rise of Puritan individualism worked for and against women but it did create a new concern for education as the eighteenth century invented its modernising revolutions. The class conflict between the new middles and the aristocracy put vehemence into controversy. Piety swept forward into scorn. More important, this was the time when the woman reader and the woman writer appeared, either as the author or reader of trashy novels, religious tracts, and copybook guides or, more preciously, as the bluestocking. What a weapon intellectual snobbery is!

Even if the writers did nothing for female emancipation, they were *paid* for their work and, in this sense, emancipated themselves. Indeed women authors owe it to the eighteenth century that they have been liberated for pretty well 200 years in the profession and are in many respects better placed than men. Mary Wollstonecraft began her life as many poor, unmarried women did, by governessing and teaching, but she was able to migrate to literature with relative ease. Her school handbooks did well and the famous 'bible' – *A Vindication of the Rights of Woman* – ran to several editions. Godwin, the philosopher, whom she eventually married, had been forced to become a sponge on aristocratic Shelley.

In her first book, *Thoughts on the Education of Daughters*, published in

1786, she aimed 'to teach women to think' and 'to prepare a woman to fulfill the duties of a wife and mother . . . No employment of the mind is a sufficient excuse for neglecting domestic duties, and I cannot conceive that they are incompatible.' If she is remote from us, she put her finger on the central issue of her time. A marked boredom and often a disgust with domesticity are noticeable in the English novelists of the eighteenth century. Marriage is so often seen as a stagnant and even squalid condition for both sexes. Who, outside the Widow Wadman, would have cared to marry into the Shandy family and share its ill-managed torpor? And although Mary Wollstonecraft would not have agreed, the gallantry and frivolity of the upper classes which she denounced were also, in a sense, a protest. Better to sin than to suckle until the state of medicine improved.

The eighteenth century was the classic period of the standing army; one of the witty passages of the *Vindication* contains a comparison of married women with soldiers:

> Standing armies can never consist of resolute, robust men; they may be well-disciplined machines, but they will seldom contain men under the influence of strong passions, or with very vigorous faculties. And as for any depth of understanding I will venture to affirm, that it is as rarely to be found in the army as amongst women; and the cause, I maintain, is the same. It may be further observed, that officers are also particularly attentive to their persons, fond of dancing, crowded rooms, adventure and ridicule . . . They were taught to please.

The consequence (says our educator) is that they acquire manners before morals and a knowledge of life before they have reflected on it.

> Satisfied with common nature, they become a prey to prejudices, and taking all their opinions on credit, they blindly submit to authority.

Men who are slaves to their mistresses tyrannise over their sisters, wives and daughters. The famous jeer that women cannot resist a uniform is refuted by Mary Wollstonecraft: 'Has not education placed them more on a level with soldiers than any other class of men?'

The *Vindication* is a passionate, assertive, headlong, slapdash book, terribly repetitious and exclamatory. The author flings herself whole upon the reader; anger is mixed with a piety that hardly conceals a long, personal pain. It is a book written out of unhappiness and frustration. The merit of Miss Flexner's study is that it examines a vigorous if unstable character with sympathy and patience.

Mary Wollstonecraft came from the rising middle class. The rise was effected by her grandfather, an ambitious weaver who, having established himself as the landlord of useful London properties, devoted the rest of his life to the ruling fantasy of his class: setting up as a country gentleman with a small estate. He wished to be like his betters. His son, Mary's father, inherited the fantasy but not the acumen; weaving went downhill, and after failing in the townee's dream of farming he became a careless speculator and a violent, spendthrift drunk who could not keep his hands off his children's money. Mary's childhood was wrecked by the scenes of violence between her father and her Irish mother, a woman beaten down who nevertheless obviously had some power of moral survival. The effect of the family drama was to arrest the emotional development of a girl who was well above the norm in intelligence. She made a stand for independence. She was a second child, a beauty of the heavy kind, not the favourite, but the most capable. She had a defiant self-knowledge and in a letter written when she was sixteen to a friend she says unpleasingly:

> I am a little singular in my thought of love and friendship. I must have first place or none.

This was ominous. She was already, says Miss Flexner,

> possessive, and highly sensitive. The slightest affront, often fancied rather than real, caused intense feelings of rejection and anger ... she wrote bitter letters raking up past grievances.

But as the family went to pieces it was she who energetically took command of her sisters and emerged as strong and masterful. The effort of will, as with many domineering people, had its price in sudden losses of confidence and in lonely pathos. Her passionate friendships with one or two girls of her own age were part of a search for an alternative family, but they were dangerously demanding. The pattern remained in her relations with men later on in her life; she asked too much, either out of blinding innocence or the ineptitude that sometimes affects the brilliant. Miss Flexner says:

> Modern psychiatry has identified some of the symptoms of which Mary constantly complained – lassitude, depression, acute headaches and digestive difficulties – as symptoms of deeply repressed anger. She had ample reasons for it – at a society that thwarted women; at a father who had thrown away a comfortable endowment and mistreated both wife and children; and at a mother with inadequate understanding.

Another symptom of this formless anger was anxiety, 'the sense of I know not what'. It was to explode at a crisis in her thirties in a thorough attempt at suicide after she had been abandoned by one of the father figures – this time only too like her father – to whom such a temperament would be drawn.

The fatality of such a temperament in a woman of intelligence and charm is sad. Her high-mindedness was apt to be ruthless and her naïveté hard to credit. When she saw her sister miserable after a forced marriage and the birth of a child, she obliged the not very bright girl to leave her husband, leaving the baby behind! It is not surprising that the 'rescued' sister was embittered for the rest of her life. One must admire the vitality of the bossy girl who took over her family, but one is struck by her lack of knowledge of the heart. When in a gush of juvenile feeling she herself adopted a little girl she quickly grew tired of the responsibility. And, of course, having made her sisters dependent on her help in their school teaching, she aroused their sneers and jealousies when at last she gave up her schooling and governessing and courageously turned to her ambitions as a writer. They thought she had grown too big for her boots.

Her story, of course, makes clear the exasperating burden of petty domestic trials upon an independent intelligence. It is the old tale – brothers could get away, for better or worse, and were not much help. Mary Wollstonecraft's salvation and her belated growth into adulthood began when her publisher, Joseph Johnson, took paternal charge of her. A man of extraordinary benevolence, he took her in for a time and gave her literary work – a good deal of it translation. He saw the born journalist who needed the education of his clever, radical circle. Blake, Fuseli,

[1249]

Tom Paine and eventually Godwin belonged to it. She threw over the governessing and, intoxicated by good talk, her mind came to life.

True, she was reckless in judgment, not to say unscrupulous – she accused Burke of being bought by a government pension – but she succeeded to the point of notoriety. At thirty she was emotionally a schoolgirl liable to crushes; she developed a passion for Fuseli, and when one considers her Puritan hatred of sex and of her father's rage it is strange that she seems not to have been put out by Fuseli's temper and the blatant sexual imagery of his work. He was, of course, expert in disengaging the unconscious. His brilliant talk carried her away. She seems to have been unaware of her repressed sexuality. She pestered Fuseli as George Eliot – if she was indeed innocent – pestered Chapman, with a swamping superego. Still, it may not have been quite like that: Fuseli was happily married and Mary was showing a girlish hunger to belong to a family. She had the simplicity to propose to Mrs Fuseli that she should come and live with them. Mrs Fuseli discerned the egotist and showed her the door.

As Miss Flexner says, the friendship with Fuseli seems not only to have aroused her intellect but to have awakened her to the emotions that lay behind her earnest daydreaming. What followed was an emotional disaster. The French Revolution was in its idealistic phase and many English radicals rushed to Paris. Her reputation as an educationalist was well known but surely she went rather far in offering to advise the French authorities on the education of French women! The Terror stopped that. She was horrified and frightened. As an Englishwoman she was in danger of arrest. She turned to an American speculator and plotting political agent, Gilbert Imlay, a liaison began, and he saved her by saying she was his wife.

Imlay was in fact a charming rascal. He was a fugitive from justice in Kentucky and one can see that an inexperienced, intellectual woman of her kind was likely to fall for the dubious gallantry she had always attacked. Imlay was not one to stay long with any woman; he was always disappearing. Mary was soon pregnant and his absences grew longer. He tricked her into going on a mission for him in Scandinavia – a quarter of Copenhagen had been destroyed by fire when she got there – and on her return she found him living with another woman in London.

It was now that the basic rage of her nature (the inheritance, no doubt, of her father's rage) burst out in a very determined attempt at suicide by drowning. She planned it thoroughly, even going to the length of letting the rain soak her clothes so that she would sink at once. Fortunately she was rescued. It was Godwin's friendship that saved her mind. When she was thirty-seven she married him and then, once more, she was a victim. Her death in childbirth is the final injustice. Her daughter by Godwin grew up to be Mary Shelley, who, tormented in her turn, revered her mother's work but refused to have anything to do with female emancipation. The idea faded until Mill's essay on the *Subjection of Women* – a far better book than the *Vindication* – vigorously revived it for the mid-Victorians.

Miss Flexner has gone carefully into Mary Wollstonecraft's writings and, as she says, her distinction is that her opinions came from her experience of ordinary people she knew. But when she turned to novel-writing she could not make such people live. Earnest, bold, a teacher to the backbone, she was really self-absorbed, too little resilient to allow other people to exist except as generalities or projections of her opinions. Her tale is painful but she made a great deal of an injured spirit. The tragedy is that under Godwin's influence her powers might have grown; he certainly conquered her touchiness after a patient struggle.

Dostoevsky's Wife

═══════════

The story of Dostoevsky's extraordinary second marriage during which he wrote his greatest novels is a novel in itself. He was forty-five and a widower; his first marriage and his love affairs had been disastrous; he was bankrupt; he had assumed the heavy debts of his dead brother and responsibility for the family, also for the predatory and offensive son of his own first wife by a previous husband. Dostoevsky was ill and drowning in a sea of promissory notes, and had had to stop writing *Crime and Punishment* because he had been trapped by a publishing rascal into another novel. A penalty clause had been put into the contract which would bind his earnings to the man for nine years if he failed to deliver the book within four weeks. He was exhausted and ill, and he had no clear story in his head beyond his experiences as a ruined gambler tormented by a neurotic young mistress.

In his plight he was persuaded to call in a girl stenographer – a new career for women in the 1860s – and a plain, awed girl of twenty arrived. He stared at her with embarrassment and in silence for two days and then suddenly found he could dictate. The novel was *The Gambler*, it was finished within two days of the deadline, and, as the girl had sharply foreseen, the publisher had disappeared into the country in order to dodge delivery and close the trap. Dostoevsky was forced to go round from one police station to another in St Petersburg before he found an officer willing to give him a receipt for the manuscript. In the meantime the novelist had fallen in love with the stenographer – to whom he had nothing but his calamities to offer – and was astounded to find she had fallen in love with him.

Such young daydreamers as this Anna seemed to be do not usually last the course, but Anna did. The fact is that her obscure family and especially her father and herself were old admirers of Dostoevsky's work: he was a hero before she met him. She was no intellectual; her one pride was that she was the prize pupil of the stenography school. It is interesting that her mother came of stolid Swedish Lutheran stock and her father, who was a reading man, from the Ukraine: a uniting of efficiency and fantasy.

Anna inherited her mother's independence and her matter-of-fact temperament, and under the influence of the feminism of the Sixties (and in the manner of the nihilists whom she defended, though she disapproved of their rude manners and their affectation of sloppy clothes) she believed a girl should earn her living. If she was literal-minded and frankly said she did not understand Dostoevsky's ideas, even when he tried to put them simply to her, she revered his work and gave him total devotion and family happiness for the fourteen years left to him. She saw at once that he had to have peace of mind for his work and that she must behave with total self-abnegation, even at the cost of her own feelings; yet if she might appear to him as one of his 'meek' characters, she was far from that.

It was soon evident to her that the immediate enemies of her marriage were the leechlike family and especially the arrogant stepson. They saw Anna as a frivolous young intruder who would take the bread out of their mouths. When she fought back they sneered and told her that the family – and not she – had the first claim on her husband's time and money. The course of the battle is set out in the *Reminiscences* which after Dostoevsky's death she tried to put together from the daily shorthand notes she made about every detail of their life together.

As Helen Muchnic says in her introduction to the present revised edition – the first appeared in 1925 edited by Leonid Grossman – it is a plain, straightforward, honest, and moving account of a happy if reckless marriage, a record tritely and exactly domestic. The tone is neither boastful nor fulsome. She says little or nothing about his work, and is unique in offering no theories about his genius. Dostoevsky appears as the childlike, toiling, anxious, and affectionate father who has to be protected from the world and whose inner tumults – his gambling for example – are understood without being censured. She is perhaps a little proud of his ludicrous jealousy. The brave, simple young adorer has written the only really intimate portrait of him that we have.

There is something more than his portrait and the joys and great sorrows and struggles of a marriage, the misery of the loss of two children. She evokes, without trying, what everyday Russian life in shabby districts was like, without dramatising it as the Russian realists do: the grey exposure to lies, meanness, trickery, cheating, and stealing, the dangers of the streets at night where violence and robbery were taken for granted, the rule of the pawnshop, the cult of begging, the flooding in of hungry hangers-on in every family, the fights with the landlords, the clumsy difficulties of getting about from one district to another, the damp, unhealthy climate of Petersburg which killed off the weak, the collusion of police with thieves. Her book makes one understand why Dostoevsky's novels are choked with people whose lives are hanging out on their tongues and whose only role seems to be to drag in others, living by custom at one another's expense. Into his own flat the relatives swarmed to borrow and be fed and to shout and cry in each others' faces by divine right. There is no privacy in Dostoevsky's novels and Anna had to fight for that above all, so that he could work.

And then, during the dragged-out and drunken jollities of their wedding, Anna had to face the shock of his epilepsy. He seems not to have told her of it. Suddenly he fell roaring to the floor and at once the family ran away, noses in the air, and left the 'silly girl' to deal with his fits as best she could. After this experience, she guarded her tongue and became the constant watcher for the rest of his life. She saw that the first step must be to free him from his family and that the only way to do this was to get him out of Russia. The relations came round whining, threatening, and defying her at once. They waylaid him to get his money from him and he was too weak to stand out against them. Her master-stroke was to use the money of her own small dowry: even the stepson saw that they could not touch that – and for the four years during which she and her husband were travelling in Europe the family were defeated and the marriage became unshakable.

Despite the dislike of Europe which was – and is still – a religion among Russians and in Dostoevsky's writings particularly, both he and Anna were deeply happy. She was, of course, seeing an entrancing new world for the first time. Dostoevsky was a tireless walker, a firm visitor of art galleries. Anna walked, listened, and marvelled; but also noted down the prices in shops and was overcome when she saw her genius fussing about new underclothes for her at the draper's or choosing hats. From Dresden they went to Wiesbaden and Baden-Baden. But she noticed he was not writing. She had not transcribed *The Gambler* for nothing. She saw the gambler's passion stir when their money began to go. She was sensible enough not to try to stop this obsession from bursting out when it did, though it soon brought them to the pawnshop and to desperate letters to her mother and his friends. She listened to his mad hopes and remorseful sobs: she gave in when he begged again. She even writes:

> All of Fyodor Mikhailovich's rationalisations about the possibilities of winning at roulette by using his gambling system were entirely correct. His success might have been complete – but only on condition that this system was applied by some cool-headed Englishman or German and not by such a nervous and impulsive person as my husband, who went to the uttermost limits in everything.

But she adds shrewdly:

> In addition to cool-headedness and perseverance, the roulette player must have substantial means in order to be able to hold out through unfavourable turns of the wheel.

He came home in despair after one more ruinous evening, saying that just as he was winning he caught sight precisely of one of those cool-headed Englishmen at the table – this is much better reported in the shorthand notes, of the 1925 edition – and at once lost his nerve and everything he had won. (One sees how visual his disturbed mind was: calamity was a person.) Anna was proud of keeping her own domestic head and of not uttering a word of reproach. The passion did at last burn out and suddenly he began to write.

The return to Russia had its traditional risks that have lasted until today. Knowing that his manuscripts and papers would be taken from him at the frontier and that, as a one-time political prisoner and still under surveillance, he might not get them back, he decided to burn his drafts of *The Idiot* and his notebooks. Anna argued him out of that; her mother had come to stay with them and they got her to smuggle his notebooks in.

Back in Russia Anna took one more bold step. She knew that he was incapable of dealing with money and with publishers, and when *The Devils* was written she decided to get his work printed, published, and distributed by herself. She knew nothing of the trade. She was ignorant of the Balzacian nature of Russian commerce, and that it depended on the

promissory note and on dealing in discounted bills. She had the house-
wife's suspicion of a practice so mystical but soon mastered it.

> The bookseller Kozhanchikov came to us with an offer to buy 300 copies
> on a four-month promissory note. He asked for the regular discount of
> 30 percent . . . What troubled us was that he would be taking them on
> Notes . . . I had no idea what a commercial Note was at that time and
> therefore suggested to my husband that he should chat for a while with
> the buyer while I would drive over to the printer . . . He assured me that
> Kozhanchikov's Notes were good and that he would be willing to accept
> them in payment of our printing debt.

She was amused when buyers came in and did not know the title of the
book: 'Sometimes they called it "the Evil One," sometimes they would say
"I came for the devils," and sometimes "Let me have a dozen demons."'
She took over the business of dealing with people who, at several
removes, had taken up his own promissory notes: a crowd of widows,
landladies, retired officers, and frauds arrived, threatening attachment and
prison. Put him in prison and he will earn nothing, she said. That brought
them to compromise, and after thirteen years of embittering struggle she
paid off the debts which Dostoevsky had taken over from his dead brother
and their own: 20,000 roubles. Her only bitterness is that burden. When
she looked at the easy lives of Turgenev, Tolstoy, and Goncharov, all
of whom had money, she was indignant when critics complained of
Dostoevsky's repetitive and clumsy style:

> How many times did it happen in the last fourteen years of his life that
> two or three chapters [of a novel] had already been published in the
> journal, the fourth was in the process of being set up in type, the fifth
> was in the mail on its way to the *Russian Messenger*, and the rest had not
> yet been written down and existed only in his head.

And, as we know from his notebooks, only in a confused and speculative
state.
Their holidays in the country were as perilous as their life in St
Petersburg. In a country of wooden buildings disastrous fires swept
through villages and towns. The Dostoevskys scrambled into the streets
with their belongings and then scrambled back when the fire stopped short

of their dwelling. The carting about of luggage by road, steamer, or ferry was a nightmare. Landing at Novgorod from Lake Ilmen one night they lost the suitcase containing the manuscript of *A Raw Youth*, for which they were frantic to collect the money next day. Anna guessed it might have been stolen at the docks, a neighbourhood noted for armed thieves and hoodlums, and herself drove there with a scared driver who was afraid a dock gang would seize his cab. They ran off when they saw Anna, who had found the case. It took courage for a woman to go into these slummy neighbourhoods at night. It is characteristic of their life that she left Dostoevsky standing with the children while she herself went off on the search.

The present edition of the *Reminiscences*, revised by the Soviet scholars S. V. Belov and V. A. Tunimanov, was published in 1971 and was based on over thirty notebooks of rough drafts, in confused chronological order. Anna rewrote, duplicated, and had not arrived at a definitive text. There were 800 pages of manuscript and it is now at last in order. Certain things from the shorthand notes in the Leonid Grossman edition have been smoothed away or have vanished: the direct explosive account of the famous quarrel with Turgenev about *Smoke* which Dostoevsky gave when he returned from his row has gone, perhaps because it has been described by other hands or because Anna had come to idealise the past. The only faults she allows her husband are the irritability natural to writers, and his absurd and violent fits of jealousy or terror when he saw her speaking to other men. In a giddy moment she once provoked his jealousy by faking an anonymous letter: he nearly strangled her.

Her shocked refutation of Strakhov's attack on her husband after his death, in which he insinuated that Dostoevsky had seduced a child in a bath house, is printed in full. In an early version of *The Devils*, Stavrogin is said to have done this, and the publisher made Dostoevsky cut it out. But, Anna said, she had learned enough about the artistic imagination to understand that an artist does not need to be a criminal in order to describe a crime. She defends him, too, against the common charge that he was a nasty, suspicious whisperer of malicious things when he was in company: he came into crowded rooms and flopped down 'not in arrogant silence', she says, but because his incurable emphysema left him struggling for breath. The marriage succeeded, she wrote, because neither of them tried to meddle with the other's 'soul'. 'In this way my good husband and I both of us felt free in spirit.' And as Helen Muchnic adds in her feeling introduction to this book, Anna did not pry. He was her idol, she said. Perhaps because, unlike the idols of a young girl's dreams, she saw an idol who worked like a demented slave and was helpless without her.

Playing Stendhal

'I would be rather taken for a chameleon than for an ox': one of Stendhal's pungent remarks, uttered, no doubt, in some Paris salon where he was, as usual, posing, and where his scornful wit was making its random hits. Someone who heard the phrase noted that the stocky, rather overdressed and ugly, timid man had made a studied effort to pass as 'an ungraspable, conjectural figure'. In early portraits he looks bluff, even doggish. Silvestro Valeri's picture of him in consular uniform in 1835 gives him a bitter mouth.

A great talker, something of a coxcomb, yet also a dreaming, drastic adolescent when he was a young man, at heart a solitary, Stendhal certainly played studied roles, as later generations know from his letters and his journals. They are so full of strategies that his continuously autobiographical writings give him the air of a man writing a manual in the art of seduction. He set out at an early age to scrutinise his character, to experiment with it and remake it. He was, in one sense, an artifice. Born bourgeois, he sought to break with his class and to become an aristocrat, even to the length of intriguing for a barony; at heart he was a man of superior sensibility and feeling, a mixture of artist and man of the world.

He had felt the release of the Revolution, the elation of the Napoleonic glory, and the disillusion of Napoleon's eclipse and saw himself as one caught in 'an age of transition', between two dispensations – the classical worldliness of the eighteenth century and the romantic energies of the nineteenth – an outsider in both or, as he put his ideal, an exceptional soul, one of 'the happy few'.

As everyone knows, to his contemporaries he was an eccentric. The nature of his genius as a novelist was not understood until after his death when he was eventually recognised as a precursor of the psychological novelists Proust, Henry James, Gide, and even, today, of Joyce and the novel 'without a centre'. Julien Sorel and Fabrice seem to us to have uncertain temperaments close to our own. In one of the many good essays on Stendhal written in the last few years Robert M. Adams, for example, says:

> Perhaps the most enchanting yet terrifying thing about the heroes of Stendhal's novels is that they define themselves provisionally, in conflicts of thought and action, in negations; without enemies, they are almost without natures and wither away, like Fabrice when deprived of danger.

The biographer of Stendhal faces tantalising competition in the auto-biographer. The unfinished *Vie de Henri Brulard*, published after his death, is one of the finest terse and ruthless autobiographies ever written, reckless or careless as it may be in its detail. The indefatigable Beylists seem to have traced every moment of a man who was always on the move. They know, within a day or two, how long he spent with his many mistresses, every person he met, and where he lodged. One of his stormier mistresses hid him in the cellar of her château, out of fear of her violent husband. That was a coup.

A plain narrative of his life is as diverting as any picaresque novel. But as Robert Alter in his new biography says, as others have done before him, the life is so entwined with his work as a writer that the significance is lost without a critical attempt to interpret it. There is hardly a scene in his novels without its echo of inner or active experience. This is true but I fear one more portentous psycho-analytical analysis of the Oedipal aspects of his character or another obfuscating examination of myths and symbols suggested by towers, the Alpine summits, prison, the hermitage, and the mire of vulgar life. Mr Alter is tactful about these inescapable matters. He is a perceptive biographer, sensible, fresh, fairly free of academic jargon – though he is overfond of that newish academic technological cliché 'stance' and there is the horrible package word 'complementarity'.

In his lively narrative Mr Alter is good on the natures of the women Stendhal successfully or unsuccessfully pursued in the cause of what he called his profession: 'the study of the human heart'. He is sound about the novelist's changes of character, mind, and feeling in each important phase of his life. He does not miss Stendhal's surprising efficiency as an administrative officer in Napoleon's army in Germany and Russia, and is very good on the influence of his journalistic habits, including his plagiarisms, on his practice as a great novelist. If Stendhal's own character is provisional, like that of outstanding characters in his novels, we see how important improvisation was – as important as his powers of minute scrutiny were to his work. As a man he is separated from observing his dreams and sensual desires by an almost military concern for strategies and inventing obstacles. The obstacle provokes the psychologist. In life his stratagems often misfire, in love and politics: in art – as he would say, the thing that alone can make experience 'real' – they lead to the rewards of reverie he had caught from Rousseau.

Stendhal's finest work was written late because, as he said, he lived first. He was a refractory son, careless of education. He broke with his father and sought the important influence of his well-placed relations in Paris. He was not as uncouth an outsider as the half-self he projected in Julien Sorel – but he strikes one as standing in his own light and naïve. He was after a comfortable job and rising fortune so that he could dress well, conquer women, and devote himself to playwriting and literature. He was conscientious in his boring offices and fixed in his mistaken belief that he was a playwright: it took him years to see that Napoleonic times did not provide the stable society, set manners and morality on which eighteenth-century comedy depended.

Luckily the romantic young man got into Napoleon's army in Milan and he found in Italy a spiritual home. Like the pushing young Boswell in London, he found actresses and opera singers who so often played the parts of great ladies were surrogates for aristocratic women in Society; but the calculating and timid Stendhal was given to something like seizures of romantic feeling which dissolved in tears, before the moment of achievement. He was driven to brothels. In Paris he did not impress his benefactors, but at last he did manage to cadge his way into administrative rank in Napoleon's Russian adventure, though not as a fighting soldier. He was again efficient but spent his time toiling at his impossible play, and reading. He saw Moscow burn, managed barely to survive the appalling retreat, and lost for good the illusion of Napoleonic glory which so deeply affected his generation. This is all well known. More interesting is Mr Alter's comment:

[1261]

Whatever Beyle actually saw [he was not yet disguised as Stendhal] of cowardice, crudity, savage egoism in the masses of men fleeing across the frozen Russian countryside conveyed to him an abysmal vision of human nature (parallel in a way to what many sensitive writers experienced in World War I) for which the polished precision and the cool confidence of the language of the *Philosophes* were somehow beside the point.

The idea of a rational control over personal relationships was chimerical. After the Russian experience where he had been flung into the mire,

Beyle would tend to place himself as much as he could within the civilised, protected perimeter of that symbolic clean well-lighted place . . . the ballroom of a high culture that knew how to translate desire into a perfectly choreographed pattern of repeated fulfilment.

This is the point where Stendhal's doctrine of 'the happy few' was shaped.

The next point at which Mr Alter does well is on Stendhal's attitude to women as it appears in that eccentric essay 'De l'Amour'. He was a feminist and, being an Anglophile who had read of Bentham, he held that to deprive women of education 'deprives society of half its potential for intellectual achievement'. The argument was not original, but Stendhal made it witty as he drifted from theory to anecdote. His work is (Mr Alter notes) free of the female stereotypes – the patient sufferer, the gentle paragon of redemptive virtue – which were found later in the novels of Balzac, Dickens, and Dostoevsky. The memorable women in Stendhal's novels have the 'same qualities of energy, wilfulness, self-dramatising extravagance, physical daring, and intelligence' that are present in his male heroes.

On the puzzling idea of 'crystallisation' which 'De l'Amour' advances, and which we could perhaps call the igniting power of 'idealisation', Mr Alter notes the importance of Stendhal's change of heart about the merits of Don Juan and Werther. Don Juan had been his guide as a youth, first as the eighteenth century's adaptation of the myth in Valmont of *Les Liaisons dangereuses*. In maturity he changed his mind. Don Juan paid too high a price for his useful virtues of daring, resource, and wit, and Stendhal turned to the nineteenth century and Werther, 'who opened the soul to all the arts, to all the soft and romantic impressions.' Mr Alter writes, 'The plots of his two greatest novels are a kind of derailing of Don Juanism and the discovery of a Wertherian dénouement.' There is a romantic withdrawal from the world. Don Juan kills love.

We come closer to the writer at his desk when we turn to the origins and side effects of Stendhal's habit of borrowing and improvisation. Despite his class – perhaps because of his rejection of it – Stendhal was so at odds with the education he had that he was, like so many other great writers, really self-taught and therefore, for all his enormous reading, a guesser who relied on dash, impulse, and wit.

He became a very clever and readable journalist, notably as a correspondent of the *Edinburgh Review*, for that paid well; at times he lifted other people's ideas as it suited him and notoriously lifted the text of other people's work. He had two hundred pseudonyms and these, if they protected him politically – for the Austrian police kept an eye on him in Italy – also covered his plagiarism. This, as Mr Alter says, is deplorable and uncovers the marked strain of opportunism in his character. But if he was guilty of this, what at once strikes one in his works of travel is the presence of his person, his sharpness of sight and ear, the sound of the journalist's voice, disputing, asserting, generalising. He loves pungent anecdote, he catches character and dialogue. Mr Alter quotes one passage which has all the anecdotal undertone of *La Chartreuse de Parme*:

> We were told the touching anecdote of Colonel Romanelli who killed himself in Naples because the Duchess C had left him. 'I could easily kill my rival,' he said to his servant, 'but that would distress the Duchess too much.'

Fabrice has a very similar reflection when he steals a horse from a stranger who he thinks threatens his life as he escapes across the Swiss frontier.

The plain writing that winds back and forth in time as it runs through the mind enables Stendhal when he moves into longer analyses of feeling to be crisp and exact – to see Count Mosca moving from day to night about his house tormented by jealousy yet coming slowly upon the proper strategy to adopt. Yes, we say, that is what jealousy is like, it moves from hour to hour, from room to room. The plain style is essentially conventional, but when rapture has to be evoked it comes spontaneously. In one sense his novels are as declamatory and yet as flat as opera. More important, in the great novels, the talker makes no bones about the point of view: he can be the narrator outside the character and yet drop into direct dialogue and slip into words of interior monologue between utterance and thought so easily that we hardly notice it. What we do notice is that the people have become, as in life, many-dimensional: they seem to be singing and moving in Mozartian arias among themselves.

Where did he acquire this fluency and domination? His adoration of operatic music plays its part. But strangely, from Fielding in *Tom Jones*, a novelist who, as Mr Alter says, invents 'a genial expatiating narrator who casts a finely woven net of cultural, social, and political commentary over the narrated events; enriches our perception of the characters through a shifting play of ironies.' Stendhal wrote in the margin of *Lucien Leuwen*, after rereading *Le Rouge et le Noir*: 'True but dry. One must adopt a more ornate, less dry style, witty and gay, not like the *Tom Jones* of 1750, but as the same Fielding would be in 1834.' There is an additional reason for the speed he puts into his circuitous inspections and the dominance of the conversational style: he dictated his work; his hand could not be deciphered. After the five weeks in which he is said to have 'written' *La Chartreuse de Parme* his amanuensis must have been a wreck.

It seems to me that Mr Alter's interpretation weakens at one critical point: the significance of *Armance*, Stendhal's first novel written in his forties. The subject is surmised sexual impotence. It was a fashionable subject borrowed from another novelist. (That, by the way, is all we mean when we say he lacked invention: in the borrowed subject he acquired the necessary freedom which enables the novelist to invent a deepened self and to pour in random echoes of his own experience.) It is agreed that Stendhal was far from impotent despite his fascination with the experience of fiasco. In the *Promenades dans Rome*, and in his own peculiar mixture of French and English, he had written: '*Enfin Dominique regarde* love as a *lion terrible* only at forty-seven.' But in the far more detailed and searching examination of *Armance* by Martin Turnell (*The Novel in France*, 1951) one understands that Armance is the first of Stendhal's 'outsiders' whose singularity points less to a sexual or social context than to a haunting psychological and moral dilemma: the conflict between misanthropy, duty, and sensibility. And Turnell's writing is superior to Mr Alter's.

[1264]

Mr Alter is more acceptable on that other difficult unfinished novel *Lucien Leuwen*, which becomes tedious and breaks in two: the subject of French bourgeois politics killed Stendhal's Italian brio and blurred his real powers of self-invention. The portraits from provincial life are nevertheless very freezing examples of his ideal of 'exact chemistry'. Mr Alter does his best with *Lamiel*. Here Stendhal was nonplussed by his real-life model: she was to be a female Julien Sorel who lived for active political conspiracy and danger – things which had an uncomfortable bearing on the pursuit of happiness and the rewards of reverie. Perhaps he was too old and too embittered and melancholy in his humiliating role as a mere consul in Civita Vecchia to 'see' this book. He went to Paris briefly and died of a stroke as he came out of the office of the foreign ministry. A year before, maintaining his irony as an enigma, he had said: 'I find that there is nothing ridiculous in dying in the street, so long as one does not do it deliberately.'

Camille Pissarro

The exhibition which celebrates the 150th anniversary of Pissarro's birth has now travelled from London to Paris and is soon to arrive in Boston, and three stout, handsomely illustrated and scholarly volumes are here to inform a layman like myself. They also test and enlarge our response to a restless and prolific artist of very complex character. The introductory essay to the general catalogue by John Rewald is a rhetorical attempt to revive the history of the long battle between the Impressionists and the Salon. He appeals to Nietzsche and grinds his teeth at the name of Gérôme. Two other contributors, Richard Brettell and Françoise Cachin, are more inquiring and more nourishing. The Ashmolean volume reproduces an enormous number of Pissarro's drawings and working sketches; we see Pissarro's foundations as a graphic artist who came to painting late. And Ralph E. Shikes and Paula Harper are very searching and enlightening on the relation of the life and work.

A literary person, venturing to write on a delightful art, can, at any rate, be fortified by some words of Walter Sickert – I take them from Françoise Cachin – partly because Walter Sickert was a painter who was also dashing and got to the heart of the matter in print; partly because he liked to make the then unfashionable assertion that he was a literary painter, which was almost true: 'Pissarro . . . remains the painter for those who look at, rather than for those who read about, painting.'

We have read; but we have also looked, and Pissarro does take one clean through the surface of his pictures into their depth and architecture. Sickert's word, 'remains', has exactly the overtone of ambiguity to which we respond. Pissarro does distinctly 'remain' in our visual sense and minds. Other Impressionists give us sensations of evanescence and the dance of suffused light; Pissarro seems to convey the haunting permanence of an hour that has been lost.

The distinguished writers who rallied to the Impressionists were, like ourselves, in the usual literary difficulty of seeing the ostensible subject as 'the hero' of the painting whether it is person, action, or landscape; we are also apt to see analogies between the manner of prose and paint, each arrangement of brush strokes being a possible phrase. For us the famous *Young Girl with a Stick* is 'the dawn of adolescence'. George Moore was lyrical about those dream-like apples that would 'never fall'. Hostile critics who were bored by Pissarro's fields of cabbages and who called him 'a market gardener' got the tart reply that the Gothic artists were bold enough to use the humble cabbage and the artichoke as ornaments in their cathedrals.

As a firm atheistical materialist Pissarro hated being credited with penetrating 'the soul of nature', but none of our literary tribe went so far as Zola, in his later years, when he inflated Cézanne in *L'Oeuvre* and turned the painter's life into a typical Zola-esque melodrama. For myself I am tempted to see Pissarro and other Impressionists as artists who retrieve that forgotten storyless hour of the day in which the clock has beautifully stopped. One of the merits of Ralph E. Shikes and Paula Harper's *Pissarro: His Life and Work* is the following statement that puts the hour back into paint – look again at the early and Courbet-like *Côte du Jallais near Pontoise*:

> It is often perceived that Pissarro was consistently interested in firmly structured compositions, in itself a visual statement of permanence. His perspectives imply a single, fixed viewpoint; if the world of nature is in flux, the one who views it is stable. Monet, by contrast, in many of his last paintings, dissolves the viewer into the scene; there are few reference points that relate to space on a human scale or gravity as a human experience. But Pissarro constantly reasserts the fact of human-kind interacting with the natural world both in his subjects and in his insistence on a logically constructed space seen from a still point.

Yet there was a transformed prose in Pissarro's mind; it lay in his political convictions. He had read Property-is-Theft Proudhon, Elisée Reclus, and Kropotkin. He was called 'the poet-logician' by Gauguin. Like more than one of the Impressionists, but more lastingly and even in a practical way, he was imbued with the innocent millenarian dream of Anarchism. He had an active hatred of the centralised bourgeois state. Vague though the dream was – and he was never able to define what he precisely meant by it beyond talking about the joyful liberation of perpetual creative work that would insulate us from the sorrows of life – the dream gave a grace to his sense of the need for social justice. His anarchism was not sentiment: it is related to his particular kind of humanism, an earnest of manna for the humble worker at a period when Guizot was telling everyone to 'get rich'; it was also perhaps a spur to his changes of style and the eagerness to try new means. Yet also, in some intimate way, it was connected with what he called, with some irony, his 'Creole passivity' or foreignness; in the sense that Chekhov was a passive artist, i.e. one who chooses to be hidden in his work.

It is clear that Pissarro, who appeared simple to the point of sanctity, was a deeply complex man. Some believed he was naïve and self-taught: he was not. Far from being a peasant, he was distinctly a bourgeois and had little in common with the peasants he lived among in the valleys of the Seine and Oise. He rarely individualised the peasant. His revolt against the bourgeois was (he always said) a personal family affair but not violent as Cézanne's was in his relation to *his* banker father.

Pissarro's own upbringing had anomalies. Born in 1830 in the Danish island of St Thomas in the West Indies, he was a child of one of the Sephardic families of part French and part Portuguese Jews who had emigrated to the island because it had become the most prosperous entrepôt for trade in the days of sail. His parents were successful general shopkeepers, mainly in cloth. Money-making (as Trollope said when he went to St Thomas) was the sole preoccupation of the colonial population, and the strong Jewish colony benefited from the religious tolerance of the Danes.

The colonial wealth had also drawn a shrewd itinerant Danish painter, Fritz Melbye, who did well out of the European demand for exotic topographical landscapes, and it was he who noticed and first tutored the young Pissarro's remarkable and lasting graphic talent there, and indeed made possible his eventual freedom from the detestable fate of keeping shop.

Pissarro had two particular gifts: intense concentration in sketching the humble mestizos and Indians, and an eye for intimate rather than panoramic landscape – as one can see in the exhaustive store of drawings in the Ashmolean collection. He had also power as a colourist. One picture,

[1268]

Carnival Dance, has the verve of Goya in his *maja* period. (This picture was done when he and Melbye went to Venezuela.) What really released him from his years in the shop was an economic crisis: the sudden change from sail to steam which killed the St Thomas trade. The crowded Pissarro family returned to their relations in France in 1855 and were prosperous enough to live in Rue de la Pompe in Passy. At the age of eleven Camille had been sent to school in Paris, as was common for colonial boys. But now he was in France for good to study Courbet and get the friendship of Corot, but bringing with him his 'Creole passivity' which for him meant, by a paradox, a dedicated and intellectual absorption in work. He had in mind a revaluation and revival of the French landscape tradition which was at first stimulated by the then unfashionable Barbizon School. He had also arrived in the Paris of Napoleon III and Baron Haussmann and the triumph of the bourgeois reaction.

Pissarro's was the classic rejection of the bourgeois ethos by a dissident son. He went so far as to quarrel with his dominant mother, a woman given to hysteria, because of his liaison (which eventually became a much opposed civil marriage) with the family servant. He went off to live close to rural poverty in Pontoise and then Eragny, painting peasants at work in the fields; moving to the logical link of the peasant with the market, on to the appearance of the factory in the rural scene, and to daily labour on the docks of Rouen.

All the critics in the present volumes point out that Pissarro was not really close to peasant life – even his wife, a country girl whose family had a little land of their own, 'came to have marked bourgeois leanings'. He rarely notes the harshness of field labour. He can even be said to have generalised those awkward bodies as they bend to the pattern of work.

Richard Brettell's long essay on each phase of Pissarro's art says his upbringing in a Jewish bourgeois family 'did little to equip him to understand or sympathise automatically with the peasantry,' and if he made obvious gestures to Millet he in fact reversed Millet's tendency to 'aggrandise' the peasant monumentally. Yet, although in many pictures his peasants are seen pausing or resting in the private satisfactions of being simply alive, there are many others who are the half anonymous shapes of a team enclosed in the geometric trance of a habitual drama. I am thinking of *The Harvest* (1882) and *The Gleaners* (1889). The superb apple gatherers *are* working, but their work is stylised, almost arrested; and from the arms of the figures reaching up to the tree one gets the sensation of a moment slowed down, explored, even enlarged and enriched as if caught, as Brettell says, in a pavane in which the grasses, the trees, the flowers and fruit, the light and shadow of the hour have merged with the bodies of the gatherers in a conspiracy of nature with man; yet without any intrusive suggestion of allegory. We are in that '*plein air*' which annoyed the Salon.

The critic Mirbeau put Pissarro's manner in excellent words: 'Even when he paints figures in scenes of rustic life, man is always seen in perspective in the vast terrestrial harmony like a human plant.' On the other hand, as Brettell says in another connection, Pissarro's innate sense of social history emerges in his market pictures, where the figures *are* individual, talking shapes:

> These pictures suggest that it was the economic inter-relationship between the fields and the town which fascinated Pissarro and that for him the life of the peasant was not a seasonal cycle of sowing and harvesting, but rather one of events that ended with the market . . . These images form the necessary bridge between 'la vie agreste' and 'la vie bourgeoise', and complement Pissarro's landscapes with factories.

The peasant turns into 'the *petit commerçant*'. (However, *The Harvest* does seem to contradict this theory.) I incline to the belief that what drew Pissarro and others to the country factory was the novel arrangement of shapes that had to be assimilated to the rural scene and even tamed. Industrialism came late to rural France. There is nothing Satanic in the well-known chimneys of the factory near Pontoise. Satan comes later in Pissarro's political cartoons.

Like all important artists Pissarro feared to repeat himself. A painter's painter, he was preoccupied with experiment in style and means to the point of anxiety and restlessness. There is an exchange of influences in his responses to Cézanne, Monet, Degas, Gauguin, and Seurat particularly. To some contemporaries, most of whom became famous before he did, his changes of style marked him as a conservative who had become derivative and undecided in his objectives. Modern critics like Rewald and Brettell reject this view and see the intellectual vitality of a man remaking himself.

The passion for increasing the difficulty year by year was indeed innate from the beginning. If there *is* self-doubt it is of the studied fertilising kind; if there is anxiety it is the anxiety of an ambition which had to endure many harsh setbacks. Monet and the others became successful long before he did, partly because they were consistent and also – Shikes and Harper say – because Monet was a man of spontaneous passion and immediate conviction, if in the end he repeated himself, whereas Pissarro sought renewal in the temptation to see reality through many windows, and yet wavered because he was essentially a 'balanced thinker'.

Yet the contradictions in his character, the pervasive strength of his philosophy, the simplicity of his life, do not affect the serenity of his work, whether he is painter, etcher, or lithographer, whether he is painting on window blinds or designing fans to make money. Brought up in a crowded family, he turned by nature to begetting a crowded family of his own; no solitary artist he – rather the pedagogic patriarch who, to his wife's despair, was determined to turn the whole family into painters. The primacy of art which he firmly believed in had to carry the Pissarro tribe with it. The family became a kind of school, even a cooperative.

He could not bear the quarrels of the Impressionists: he was the pacifying friend with the long white beard of 'le bon Dieu' and the beautifully modulated voice; in old age as ardent as a young man. One gets a very amusing guess at his character from a comical incident in his warm friendship with Gauguin, to whom he was a father figure. Gauguin claimed to be able to analyse character from handwriting and his report, of course, tells as much about Gauguin as it does of his victim. Gauguin said, as most people did, that Pissarro was 'simple and frank' but added that he was 'not very diplomatic', 'more poet than logician'; had 'great ambition', 'stubbornness and softness mixed'; was 'enthusiastic' yet 'mistrustful', 'egotistical and a little cold'; wrote in 'graceful letters'; was a 'little eccentric'. It was rather silly of Gauguin, who was rich and a wild spender, to say that Pissarro was 'parsimonious' and 'money hungry'. He was often driven to borrow money, but he was a firm repayer of debts.

The one serious crisis in Pissarro's painting life occurred when he turned, almost against his nature, to neo-Impressionism under the influence of Seurat and pointillism. Under that influence some think his scenes became static and flat, so that for all the skill in perspective we are not borne into them. The scientific theory has displaced the human. His natural mode prevented him from continuing in this manner for long. And there is something almost droll in the seriousness with which the painter thought the solution to his torment was to put the pointillist dots further apart, so as to leave some larger gap for reflection, or the human throb; thus destroying the point of pointillism and the exhilaration of its blinding chemical noonday glitter. (Pisarro had always held that the noonday sun neutralised colour and Seurat had outbid Pissarro's doctrine.)

For a period the demand for his work collapsed; his self-confidence was baffled. In his depression he turned to suspicion. Perhaps – he wrote to his niece Esther, who lived in England – his failure

> was a matter of race. Until now, no Jew has made art here, or rather no Jew has searched to make a disinterested and truly *felt* art. I believe that this could be one of the causes of my bad luck – I am too serious to please the masses and I don't partake enough of the exotic tradition to be appreciated by the dilettantes.

Although, as Shikes and Harper say, anti-Semitism was common in France, there is no evidence that Pissarro suffered because of it, despite his public defence of Zola and his own political cartoons. He had indeed more to fear personally when the militant anarchists turned to violence and President Carnot was murdered. For Pissarro terrorism was a betrayal of the Anarchist dream. In old age his imagination made one of its magnificent leaps when he painted his extraordinary Parisian panoramas – the Place du Theâtre Français, for example – in which he looked at Paris from a high window and tipped the city almost on end with powerful effect.

There is much more to be got out of these immensely informative volumes than I have space or judgment to suggest, for Pissarro grows as an artist and a man as the reader looks and reads and looks again. There is one curious period in his later years, however, that still puzzles me: his people are rarely seen enjoying careless pleasure except in some very late drawings when he attempts *baigneuses* as if he recalled Cézanne. It is true that it was difficult for him to get models for the nude in the country, and that he found contemporary nudes lubricious. His figures may be shown undressing to go to bed or even washing, by domestic habit; then suddenly we have a few surprising drawings of a naked country bather confronting geese in a pond, and in another a group of women wrestling and larking in the water or sprawling as they gossip on the bank. The bodies are plain enough but we have what seems to me the first sight of laughter. He had refused earlier to paint the cheerful bourgeois weekend holiday on the Seine, but now he catches the wanton country women. They are very individual. The poet-logician lets himself go, as he had done once, many years before, in his pictures of the carnival dance in Venezuela.

Albert Camus

═══════

Albert Camus is one of those writers who are idolised in their lifetime and then are trapped by their legend. Now he is neglected in France, though he is still admired in Great Britain and the United States. He was entangled in the fierce and barren quarrels about political and moral commitment during and after the Second World War, and allowed himself to appear as a hero of the Resistance from the beginning, though in fact he did not join it until eight months before the Liberation. He came to be thought of as a 'lay saint' and as 'the moral conscience of his generation'. His famous novel *L'Étranger* (*The Outsider*) seemed to put the bleak halo of existentialism above his head, although, as he said and Sartre feelingly agreed, he was no existentialist. His world-famous novel *La Peste* (*The Plague*) passed as an allegory of the Nazi Occupation. He, indeed, said it was, and most readers of the time thought so, too. We can now see that the matter was more complex. In time, the hero from Algiers who believed in justice and assimilation for the poor Arabs disconcerted his admirers by siding with the *pieds noirs* against Algerian freedom. Camus was really a kind of liberal who had a lifelong horror of bloodshed, terrorism, and war. To the next generation of French writers, for whom the doctrine of political commitment has burned itself out, Camus has some interest because of his experiments in multiple narration and language. A new critical biography – *Camus*, by Patrick McCarthy – attempts to sort out facts from prejudice. For McCarthy, Camus was no 'saint' (though many saints have been as ambiguous and as devious as he was); a poor philosopher and no political thinker, his temperament being religious but not god-seeking; a wooden playwright and a fine novelist. It strikes me that Camus's real distinction is that of the mythologising autobiographer, the essayist and probing talker; that the man himself is more interesting than his legend. In personal life, he had a spell that was half physical. Compared with the immensely well-educated, upper-middle-class Sartre,

Camus is the proletarian and near-autodidact – part journalist, part artist, and, above all, the uprooted colonist, on his own. He was also an instinctive actor who was a collector of roles. McCarthy concludes:

> Camus's life was almost the opposite of what it seemed to his contemporaries: a long, losing battle against wars and terrorists, tuberculosis and fame. French Algeria, which had offered him instincts, passions and happiness, however tangled with poverty and prejudice, almost destroyed him along with itself.

The tuberculosis seems to have been responsible for his euphoric excesses, his sexual promiscuity, his gallows humour, and his obsession with death.

Camus was the son of an Algerian labourer of French descent who was killed in the 1914 war. The son had not known him. He *did* know that his father had been obliged to see a man guillotined, and that stuck in the mind of father and son. The mother was a charwoman of Minorcan descent, one of the thousands of poor workers of mixed Mediterranean races in the Algerian colony – a real *pied noir*. Camus was very proud of his Spanish connection, and as he grew up he cultivated the impassive Spanish pride and macho bearing. (However, note that the Minorcans were not Spanish but energetic Catalans.) The mother brought up her son in the slums of Belcourt, outside Algiers. She was simple and illiterate and was known for her stunned silences. The household, Camus said, was a speechless solitude. He saw her silence as an act of revolt against her life. Close to the home was the Arab slum, more wretched than their own. Camus said there were no words of affection between mother and son; he simply worshipped her. She became mythical in his eyes. It does not seem that McCarthy goes too far when he remarks that 'their bond lay in their joint indifference, the badge of the suffering and the knowledge that they shared.' Camus spoke of inheriting a 'profound indifference which is like a natural infirmity.' Eventually, as McCarthy points out, 'her suffering assumed a religious form. Her stoicism was not merely a rebellion; it was an ascetic rejection of the things of this world.' 'A God is present in her,' Camus wrote when he was young. This God, McCarthy says, was 'remote and uncaring' yet was the source of Camus's own 'strong, ever-frustrated religious impulse'.

McCarthy is excellent on the Algerian boyhood and, indeed, on the history of French rule in Algeria. The colony had something of the quality of a frontier or pioneer state. The colonists had the colonial 'chip', the colonial loneliness and violence, the colonial fear of the conquered Arabs. Algiers was a city where robbery, murder, and death were brutally familiar. At the carnival, it was normal that one float should contain a man stretched out in a coffin, acting the corpse. The colony

> drew on cultures which had known centuries of bloodshed and had turned fighting into a ritual . . . But the main cause of violence lay, inevitably, in the colonial situation, in that secret, unavowed fear. Algeria was becoming [in Camus's boyhood] ever more a frontier country because the European population was retreating into the coastal cities.

Camus was the complete wandering street kid, the tough and personable young proletarian, always ready to fend off a blow, fanatical about soccer and swimming and bodily fitness. The solid, communal ethos of the working class was to remain with him all his life, even after his two middle-class marriages and his final wealth. It was soon clear to his alarmed mother that he was a passionate reader and very intelligent. He was helped by a remarkable schoolmaster who was a dogged philosopher and a minor writer. The boy easily got through the lycée; he read Nietzsche and Dostoevsky, and at the university he distinguished himself by his thesis on St Augustine. But the soccer and the swimming went on, the lonely wanderings in the countryside and the low quarters of Algiers, and presently the easy sexual encounters on the idyllic Mediterranean beaches with the girls from the cigarette factories. He saw himself as the impassive Spanish Don Juan to whom girls and women flocked. He turned to journalism and was also soon working with poor theatrical groups; and, with his chosen friends, was for a time involved in Communist politics. It was natural to be a left-winger and to feel that something ought to be done about the Arabs who were the victims of the rich French farmers and entrepreneurs. He read and argued about the mixed cultures of the Mediterranean. He deplored the ruthless Roman influence that had prevailed rather than the Greek sense of limits and 'nothing too much'. Algeria was mindless, exploited by France, and was barbarous, but the barbarity was of nature and could be called primitive and innocent. His senses responded to the harsh mountain landscape, the stony plateau, and the desert that was another sea; to the clear sunlight, the brassy heat, and the seductive silence of the evenings. The deep sense of 'indifference' in him responded to the indifference of nature, but not in a Northern, Words-worthian way: there was nothing 'deeply interfused' here. Each stone or tree was an object: his visual sense of the 'things' of landscape is intense in all his writing. Mortality was a presence as unanswerable as rock. His work as a journalist would eventually lead him to lapse sometimes into rhetoric and sentimentality, but his best manner is plain, detached, lonely, and laconic: abruptly lyrical and briefly sensuous. There is a sentence in his *Notebooks* – 'One of our contemporaries is cured of his torments by contemplating a landscape' – that marks his identification with his country. What are those torments? Not of conscience or poverty alone. At the age of sixteen, he had become tubercular. The disease never left him; it is at the heart of his 'indifference', and the almost too vivid sense of the instants of hope.

A large part of McCarthy's book is given to the story of Camus's career as a polemical journalist, first in Algiers and then in Paris during the German Occupation. One marvels that, coughing out his lungs, Camus was able to work and quarrel so hard and carry on with his compulsive drinking and his part as habitual seducer – who tried desperately to save his first wife, a morphia addict; who loved his much-tried second wife and their children, and was capable of tortuous passion in his liaison with the Spanish-refugee actress Maria Casarès. In love, Camus was a gambler but (as McCarthy says) a prudent one.

I find McCarthy helpful about *The Outsider, The Myth of Sisyphus, The Rebel,* and *The Fall,* and especially *The Plague.* Defoe's *Journal of the Plague Year* was, of course, the literary source of *The Plague.* In Defoe, the story-teller is omniscient. In Camus, the real narrator is concealed in the voices of Oran, the city of the plague; the use of many narrators is a success because it 'flaunts' the limits of the people's understanding and says 'less' to suggest mysteriously 'more'. 'Anonymity' and 'amputation' remain, McCarthy writes, 'the watchwords of Camus' art'. The aim is to offer a collective view and to make it more positive than a single narrator can; the remote, invisible 'narrator who puzzles' is, to McCarthy, a 'thoroughly modern achievement'. It seems to derive from Camus's inheritance of the

[1277]

communal mind. Only short passages of his journalistic rhetoric break the spell for a moment. Outside of his political polemical writing or works like *The Rebel*, which are rather lumbered up with research (which is, in fact, sketchy), Camus is a natural personal essayist.

McCarthy thinks the last book, *The Fall*, is a far better book than *The Plague*. *The Fall* was written in defiance of the writer's block that paralysed Camus's imagination during the Algerian conflict, and at a time when he had no hope of recovering his health. The remedy for the artist was to transfigure his evil by attacking himself. Simone de Beauvoir thought that the story was a confession of a hidden guilt – the guilt that the Don Juan, the habitual seducer, felt towards his wife. It is true that in his *Notebooks*, which I find very revealing, he does groan and lacerate himself on this score. But *The Fall* goes far beyond the personal. Camus was a great mimic and talker, and in this tale he magnifies these gifts: the verbosity of a hypocrite at the confessional. Camus has a strong sense of the French classical tradition, and McCarthy says that Clamence, the penitent lawyer, 'is a pessimistic moralist in the long French tradition that goes back to La Rochefoucauld and La Bruyère. Like them, he attributes all man's actions to egoism.' Clamence feels himself justified by his resemblance to all mankind. But Camus undercuts the language of Clamence with the irony that is the classical French gift. McCarthy's final word is that 'despite the lack of redemption' *The Fall* is a piece of religious writing about man's fallen state: 'It is a superb novel written from the viewpoint of a world without men.' Clamence is indeed as isolated as Tartuffe. By a stroke of genius, Camus sets the confession not in the clear light of Algeria but in the deceiving fogs of Amsterdam, with its concentric circles of canals, which are the inescapable circles of Hell. The place is 'hemmed in by fogs, cold lands, and the sea streaming like a wet wash'. Holland is a country where 'everything is horizontal, no relief; space is colourless, and life dead. Is it not universal obliteration, everlasting nothingness made visible? No human beings, above all, no human beings! You and I alone facing the planet at last deserted!' With an awful glee, the penitent lawyer, who has himself committed a crime that will implicate anyone so foolish as to discover it, talks his way into moral complacency by incriminating mankind. What an irony that 'the outsider' of Algiers should turn up as 'the insider' in Amsterdam!

Among the Ruins

In person Cyril Connolly was a gift to the rueful moralists and extravagant gossips of every kind in his generation, but above all to himself. He was an egoist and actor with many parts and impersonations. I often thought of him in middle age as a phenomenal baby in a pram, his hands reaching out greedily for what he saw, especially when it was far beyond him, or, if he got it, delighted for a moment and then throwing it out and crying to get it back. Marvellous at amusing us, lost or sulky when alone: a baby talked about by the nannies, principled, spiteful, or bemused, who, of course, gathered around the resourceful only child. He disarmed by parodying others and himself. He had his moods. 'I have always disliked myself at any given moment,' he wrote. 'The total of such moments is my life.' Yet soon he would be saying that his life was 'a chain of ecstatic moments'.

One of his roles was the bohemian. Not as bohemian as all that, as David Pryce-Jones notes in his portrait, but rather dressy, a man who knew his tailors, almost a dandy, negligently upper-class. At his best, charming, formidable in knowledge, at his worst bad-mannered when he did not like his company. In these middle years he turned on himself. 'A fat, slothful, querulous, greedy, impotent carcass,' he wrote in *The Unquiet Grave*; 'a stump, a decaying belly washed up on the shore'. But, as David Pryce-Jones continues, there was pleasure in the words: the festive pleasure 'latent in the vocabulary . . . suicide by aphorism . . . He was not going to deprive himself either of the joys of excess or of the atonement which topped them off.' He could be very grave.

A fine critic, compulsive traveller, and candid autobiographer, author of *Enemies of Promise* and *The Unquiet Grave* – vocabulary was the making of him. It fitted him to crave, at least, to write 'a masterpiece'. On that he laid down the law for all writers who wanted to count. He was extremely well educated. The Latin classics had been drummed into him at Eton, he had read widely in French, Spanish, and other languages. It would be a crime, he held, not to be a Baudelaire, a Flaubert, a Rochester, a Pope, Congreve, or Dryden, even a Sterne, where his English tastes lay, or an elegiac Roman poet. He had read them all and – as his critical writing shows – he had imagination and decisive images flashed with the speed of wit in his mind. What checked him? The pursuit of pleasure, dining out, chasing women, his spendthrift habits, even his love of conversation – he lists all the notorious traps. He adds his life's grudge: writers without private means or patrons fall back upon reviewing other people's books and it stultifies their creative gift. Like himself, they become, at best, men of letters; at worst, newspaper hacks who go public.

But, as David Pryce-Jones says, there is another buried theme in *Enemies of Promise* – the loss of will-power and failure of nerve in the upper-class English of his generation, who had exhausted that will after the huge achievement of the Victorian age and the 1914 war. By the Thirties the high bourgeois culture had lost its place and its grip. It had become a minority affair of coteries on the one hand – Connolly was a natural coterie figure – or had drifted into commercialism on the other. Not to mention the rise of fascism. A putative Connolly of today would groan that the man of letters is now 'out' and that the sciences and, above all, the levelling effects of technology are driving out any hope of the masterpiece. Its public has gone.

The most startling and effective chapters in *Enemies of Promise* are those in which he analyses the state of English prose and its past cycles: 'The vocabulary of a writer is his currency but it is a paper currency and its value depends on the reserves of mind and heart which back it.' Journalists, politicians, and advertisers devalue this currency:

> There was a time . . . when it was impossible to write badly. This time I think was at the end of the seventeenth and the beginning of the eighteenth century, when the metaphysical conceits of the one were going out and before the classical tyranny of the other was established . . . To write naturally was a certain way of writing well.

Until Addison ruined everything by making prose 'artful, and whimsical . . . sonorous when sonority was not needed, affected when it did not require affectation'. Connolly's early tastes were for the natural mandarins: for Dryden, Pope, Congreve, and Rochester. Addison turned it into a popular industry. 'The quality of his mind was inferior to the language which he used.'

At this we turn to Peter Quennell's selection of Connolly's essays, to one on Sterne written when the critic was a mere twenty-three. He knew all about Sterne's insincerity and smirking and that *Tristram Shandy* 'must be the slowest of any book on record', so that it often

> reminds one . . . of the youthful occupation of seeing how slowly one can ride a bicycle without falling off; yet such is Sterne's mastery, his ease and grace, that . . . [we feel] he will always keep his balance and soon there will follow a perfect flow of words that may end with a phrase that rings like a pebble on a frozen pond.

The clinching gift for images like that is one that Connolly never lost, when he cleared up his own early mandarin passages. If slothful, he was not so as a reader or in what he wrote. Rather, he was a perfectionist of a special kind: 'I stay very close to the text – no soaring eagle, but a low-swung basset who hunts by scent and keeps his nose to the ground.' And so much depends on style,

> this factor of which we are growing more and more suspicious, that although the tendency of criticism is to explain a writer either in terms of his sexual experience or his economic background, I still believe his technique remains the soundest base for a diagnosis, that it should be possible to learn as much about an author's income and sex life from one paragraph of his writing as from his cheque stubs and his love letters.

Enemies of Promise was a book of warnings. From the mandarins, as he said goodbye to them, one could 'borrow art and patience, the striving for perfection, the horror of clichés, the creative delight in the material, in the possibilities of the long sentence and the splendour and subtlety of the composed phrase.' We must reject such things as 'woolly profundities . . . whimsy . . . archaism, pedantic usages'. The list is long. There should be no 'when all is said and done', no 'to my way of thinking', no 'I must aver', no 'adventurers among their books', no coy references to personal habits, no armchair. Among 'the realists, the puritans, the colloquial writers' one must reject 'the flatness of style . . . the cult of a violence and starkness that

[1281]

is masochistic'. 'Construction' is what we can learn from the realists, 'that discipline in the conception and execution of a book, that planning which gives simply-written things the power to endure.' And 'pruning': without that 'the imagination like a tea-rose reverts to the wilderness'.

It is very odd indeed that, except for a reference to Tolstoy, he has nothing to say, in the books before me, on the Russian novelists, little about the Victorians. He was thinking only of his English contemporaries – Forster, Joyce, Firbank, Virginia Woolf, Lawrence – and always under the shadow of Flaubert.

Did Connolly think of his own 'masterpiece' as being a novel? He wrote one, *The Rock Pool*, and is said to have tried another. Reading it again, one sees that it keeps to the text of his addiction to the fashionable Mediterranean and the passing dissipations of foreign artists in Cagnes. It shocked English publishers in the Twenties because it portrayed one or two lesbians. It caught the jargon and the spell under which the dizzy exiles of this Rock Pool lived. It is more interesting for its send-up of the typical sententious English youth down from public school and Oxford on his first spree; its theory of the permanent adolescence of this English type, pompous, snobbish, and mannered. The story connects with the attack on the concern with 'character' and preparing for high office and rule at these schools in his time and fits very well with Connolly's response to his and Orwell's youth at Eton in *Enemies of Promise*. But if *The Rock Pool* dates it does establish lasting matters in his life: his inherited restlessness and love of travel; the obsession of aggressive or romantic islanders. (Always make your fortune overseas and release your 'id' abroad. Even left-wing 'little Englanders' have adopted Blake's wish to establish a mystical Jerusalem 'in England's green and pleasant land' as their ideological anthem.)

Connolly's forebears were English military men, always on the move, with Anglo-Irish, i.e., colonial, connections. Travel began when he was a child sent on long stays to southern Ireland where he was spoiled, and where he found Anglo-Irish castles and ancestral talk of Norman blood romantic. He even started to learn Gaelic but came to fear the lowering influences of the Celtic Twilight. He was taken twice to South Africa and often to France. These places, and particularly their landscape, with everything luscious and strange in nature, intensified his powers of minute observation. Exotic flowers, fruits, animals, birds, and insects were, so to say, his first 'texts'. When he grew up he longed to return to the privileges of the Grand Tour; he tried a 'modern' Grand Tour. He loved modern luxury. The great sights excited: he had little interest in the inhabitants. And despite his lifelong complaint that Eton's old method of teaching Latin concentrated on endless construing of the sentences of the ancients, he identified himself in Italy with the Rome of Virgil, Tibullus, and Petronius: every site brings the art and literature and the importance of history to life.

So he is a discursive traveller, and those who condemned him for being a self-indulgent French and Mediterranean buff will find from his diaries and notebooks that he was a close observer of the streets of London, and not only the fashionable or elegant: he was often doing an anti-Grand Tour in the East End, not as a topographer and social observer, but more as a collector of life stories.

He is always present in these wanderings, a man with an eye on his dinner, but bent on the great extraordinary site – see the excellent essay 'In Quest of Rococo'. He is always candid when he is bored or disappointed, very briskly himself, speculating on the relation of art to life and life to art. He never leaves out his own nostalgias and guilts, so that we come to see that if he ever wrote the indispensable masterpiece that 'will last ten years' it would not be a poem or a novel but something compulsively auto-biographical: the exposure of a temperament.

On mature travel, as Peter Quennell says in his introduction to the essays, a piece called 'The Ant-Lion' is striking. Connolly is on the edge of Provence. At Albi he is looking at the extraordinary blood-red cathedral. Inside 'the pious buzz like cockchafers.' The landscape is magnificent, the site on the cliff looking down on the Garonne is dramatic. But outside, Connolly, the naturalist, has been distracted by the gruesome sight of a fight to the death between two insects – the 'ant-lion' and a gadfly. He goes on to the Bishop's Palace. It is attached to the cathedral and astonishingly houses the pictures of Toulouse-Lautrec. The collector of the bizarre wakes up. The powerful mother of the painter had obliged the cathedral to turn the palace into a *musée* for the work of her dwarfish son: La Goulue, the Moulin Rouge in this holy place! The painter, he notes, is to Degas what Maupassant was to Flaubert, not of the first rank; he recalls an 'artificial' world because 'it excludes the sun,' and yet for all that he had 'force and intelligence'. But an ant-lion on holy ground!

The wandering moralist lets his speculations run on. Holy ground? This is the country of the Albigensian heresy, the Cathari, who were massacred, who believed in abstinence from food. The Elect or Perfecti held procreation to be evil, were heretics who dreamed that when all men were equal and free they would live in static bliss and would cease to kill for a living. Well, lately we have had the story from Ladurie's *Montaillou*, but Connolly's imaginative leaps of association dramatise the scene. Characteristically, the cathedral, which had amazed, now disappointed him.

It turned out, indeed, that Connolly's 'masterpiece' was to be a travelling affair, an autobiographical myth, one of his own fables.

> 'Dry again?' said the Crab to the Rock-Pool. 'So would you be,' replied the Rock-Pool, 'if you had to satisfy, twice a day, the insatiable sea.'

Forty years after it was published, we come again to *The Unquiet Grave*, Connolly's mythical confession and elegy which we notice he very characteristically called 'A Word Cycle'. In the Fifties it was attacked as being a mere anthology, done by a lazy man, borrowing from others and his hoarded notebooks. It was abused for *outre-mer* snobbery and self-indulgence by the colloquial generation who found it morbid and depressing. In a revised introduction Connolly pointed out that it was written during the war when Londoners were indeed tired, depressed, and battered. But why drag in Virgil and the Palinurus myth? It turns out that Connolly had been haunted by it when he was a young man and had even mentioned Palinurus in his very first essay. Reading the book again Connolly did not find it morbid. He excused what he rightly considered the weakest part – the speculative passages concerned with depth-psychology; still they were worth it, 'even if a loss to literature'. He denied the morbidity: he had set himself free.

> All grief, once made known to the mind, can be cured by the mind, the manuscript proclaimed; the human brain, once it is fully functioning, as in the making of a poem, is outside time and place and immune from sorrow.

In Dryden's translation of Virgil, Palinurus is the pilot of the ship that carries Aeneas away from Dido. He falls asleep during a storm and is thrown overboard, taking the rudder with him. It becomes his raft. The ship founders on the shore and the gods do not save the crew, who with Palinurus are butchered by the inhabitants. Later the gods repent and allow a minor Cape to be named after him. The juxtaposition of Connolly's own griefs and tastes, his lusts, his failures, his moralisations, with the long quotations from the masters that orchestrate or comment on his experience enhances his private dilemmas. (Mere anthologies do not orchestrate.) His wit and his fantasies have their play: 'My previous incarnations: a melon, a lobster, a lemur . . .' or 'It is better to be the lichen on a rock than the President's carnation.'

His curiosity, especially in natural history, flashes out:

> Why do ants alone have parasites whose intoxicating moistures they drink and for whom they will sacrifice even their young? Because as they are the most highly socialised of insects, so their lives are the most intolerable.

There is the satire in bravura passages on the Thirties:

> Ah, see how on lonely airfield and hill petrol-station the images of Freud and Frazer are wreathed in flowers! From Wabash to Humber the girls are launching their fast-perishing gardens of Adonis far out on to the stream; with sacred rumbas and boogie-woogies the Id is being honoured in all the Hangars.

Or 'Our memories are card-indexes consulted and then returned in disorder by authorities whom we do not control.' Or more piercing, at the age of forty:

> Everything I have written seems to date except the last lines I set down. These appear quite different, absolute exceptions to the law – and yet what dates in them does not vary but remains the same – a kind of auto-intoxication which is brought out by the act of writing.

Was *The Unquiet Grave* a work of auto-intoxication? Yes, but also an ordered cure by mythologising in four parts, curing himself of guilt. The terrible sayings of Pascal dominate the first; in the second there is grief and remorse over loss of love and youth; in the third Sainte-Beuve (whom he more than half resembles) and Chamfort bring cynicism, philosophical

[1285]

resignation, and drive off the suicidal ravings of Nerval; in the final section of catharsis he relives the early stages of his love affair. Goodbye, Sainte-Beuve. There is an apology for the pursuit of happiness and he affirms the values of humanism. The epilogue is a pastiche of psycho-analytical jargon and Jungian exegesis, and then he fusses happily with the scholarly disputes about the story of Palinurus. For example – how did Palinurus, the pilot, manage to fall off the ship? How could he so conveniently carry the rudder with him so as to be able to use it as a raft?

Connolly has earned his minor cape.

Proustifications

As a young letter writer Proust is already talking himself into what would eventually become autobiography as a continuing art. There will be no stopping the rush. He is about seventeen, still at the Lycée Condorcet –

> Forgive my handwriting, my style, my spelling. I don't dare re-read myself. When I write at breakneck speed. I know I shouldn't. But I have so much to say. It comes pouring out of me.

He is sending a younger friend one or two tips about half a dozen of the teachers he will have to face and issuing a warning:

> Well, I beg you – for your own sake – don't do what I did, don't proselytise your teachers. I could do it, thanks to an infinitely liberal and charming man, Gaucher [he had lately died]. I wrote papers that weren't at all like school exercises. The result was that two months later a dozen imbeciles were writing in decadent style, that Cucheval thought me a troublemaker, that I set the whole class about the ears, and that some of my classmates came to regard me as a poseur. Luckily it only lasted for two months, but a month ago Cucheval said: 'He'll pass, because he was only clowning, but fifteen will fail because of him.' They will want to cure you. Your comrades will think you're crazy or feeble-minded . . . If it hadn't been for Gaucher, I'd have been torn to pieces.

What is he up to? His friends called it Proustification. Earlier we've seen him dazzling his adored grandmother with phrases swearing 'by Artemis the white goddess and by Pluto of the fiery eyes', paraphrasing Musset – it will please her generation – and 'consoling his woes' with 'the divine melodies of Massenet and Gounod'. He will soon be sagely worshipping Anatole France from whom he seems to have learned what was to fertilise him as a novelist: that each human being is made up of many selves. He is classicist, romantic, and exotic at will. In his introduction to Philip Kolb's

[1287]

selection of the early letters from the Plon edition, written before Proust remembered tasting the madeleine, J. M. Cocking remarks that Proustifying is a flexing of the linguistic muscles by a youth of enormous reading who seems to know more about literature and the arts than can be good for any novelist to know. He is experimenting not only with the actual use of words, but with thought, too. He is attempting to analyse and understand his own spontaneity, his cascading hyperbole, his outrageous flights of social flattery as exercises of the 'imagination and sensibility'.

Later Proust called that divine pair 'the two ignorant Muses which require no cultivation'. The young man fears the dilettante in himself, but that will not prevent him from going all-out for the flowery manners of the *belle époque* and their sinuous pursuit of paradox. (Here Ralph Manheim's translation is excellent.) What an up-to-the-minute chaos the young Proust is. He is drunk on Emerson, for example, as he was to be on Ruskin, having glided over the moral content of these misty figures, yet (as Mr Cocking shrewdly says) Proust was a sort of transcendentalist without belief in any definable metaphysic. He transcends in person. The *sound* of the music was enough. Music, as we soon see in his letters, was the art apart. He reproached one of his early lovers for having a literary view of it.

The letters are also a kind of open, floating notebook in which he hopes to delight his correspondent, not only by the sight of his passing selves, but by his fascination with theirs. The letters are also displays. He is passionate in those written to his mother and his grandmother, but to others, men or women, he can be bold. To Mme Emile Straus, the family friend who seems to have been one of the models for the Duchesse de Guermantes, he risks saying:

> At first, you see, I thought you loved only beautiful things and that you understood them very well – but then I saw you care nothing for them – later I thought you loved people, but I see that you care nothing for them. I believe that you love only a certain mode of life which brings out not so much your intelligence as your wit, not so much your wit as your tact, not so much your tact as your dress. A person who more than anything else loves this mode of life – and who charms. And because you charm, do not rejoice and suppose that I love you less . . .

To practise writing love letters, as Balzac said, improves a writer's style.

But Proust's turn out also to be a store of fragments that will find their way, years ahead, into *A la recherche*. Proustian detectives have noticed that the nose of the Marquis de Cambremer (in *Cities of the Plain*) – the nose being 'the organ in which stupidity is most readily displayed' and which in this instance was moujik-like and suggested an artifact imported from the Urals – was noticed years before in 1903 and is therefore evidence of the victory of *Time Regained*. The nose transcends.

The young climber is a romantic snob and a moralist as he notes class habits. Unlike the admired Balzac he is uninterested in social forces. At one of Mme Alphonse Daudet's parties, he notes (sadly) the 'frightful materialism, so surprising in "intellectuals". They account for character and genius by physical habits or race.' Mme Daudet was 'bourgeois' and had no manners, not even bad ones. 'From the viewpoint of art, to be so lacking in self-mastery, so incapable of playing a part, is abominable.' As for the aristocracy – pre-Napoleonic, of course,

> they certainly have their faults, but show a true superiority when thanks to their mastery of good manners and easy charm they are able to affect the most exquisite affability for five minutes, or feign sympathy and brotherhood for an hour. And the Jews . . . have the same quality though in another way, a kind of charitable self-esteem, a cordiality without pride, which is infinitely precious.

By this time he has become the journalist writing the witty sketches for *Le Banquet* that will become *Les Plaisirs et les jours*. He has met and flattered the fantastic Montesquiou and has been caught out mimicking his stormy voice and mannerisms. Montesquiou is no fool. The youngster is put in his place. The count tells him 'he does not need a travelling salesman for his own wit'.

Presently Proust's adored mother steps in and puts the young butterfly on to a more serious task. She does a rough translation of Ruskin's *Bible of Amiens* to help him and makes him work on it. A grind. His English is not good, yet he does claim to have read *Praeterita*, which, on reflection, might come too close to his relations with his mother. But what a stroke of genius on her part: the influence of Ruskin's metaphors, his labyrinthine sentences, his imaginative flights, and his melodious pedantries will be so beguiling that years will pass before he notices the intransigent and

Protestant moralist. Marie Nordlinger, the young English scholar and minor poetess, comes over to help him. In return he is moved to become her critic. We see that the word 'memory' is already planted in his mind.

Don't complain of not having *learned*. Strictly speaking, no knowledge is involved, for there is none outside the mysterious associations effected by our memory and the tact which our invention acquires in its approach to words. Knowledge, in the sense of something which exists ready-made outside us and which we can learn as in the Sciences – is meaningless in art. On the contrary, it is only when the scientific relationships between words have vanished from our minds and they have taken on a life in which the chemical elements are forgotten in a new individuality, that technique, the tact which knows their repugnances, flatters their desires, knows their beauty, plays on their forms, matches their affinities, can begin. And that can happen only when a human being is a human being and ceases to be so much carbon, so much phosphorus, etc.

He worked on *The Bible of Amiens* for four years. There were many mistakes, but some were due to the irreducible obscurity of the text. It turns out that his translation of *Sesame and Lilies* was excellent. About this time he seems to have been bowled over by *Middlemarch*. He sees that translation is not his real work. He writes to Antoine Bibesco:

It's enough to arouse my thirst for creation, without of course slaking it in the least. Now that for the first time since my long torpor I have looked inward and examined my thoughts, I feel all the insignificance of my life; a thousand characters for novels, a thousand ideas urge me to give them body, like the shades in the *Odyssey* who plead with Ulysses to give them a little blood to drink to bring them back to life and whom the hero brushes aside with his sword. I have awakened the sleeping bee and I feel its cruel sting far more than its helpless wings. I had enslaved my intelligence to my peace of mind . . . So many things are weighing on me! when my mind is wholly taken up with you. I never cease to think of you, and when I write to you I keep talking about myself.

Ruskin dragged on and on. We pick our way forward to see Proust at odds with his invalid life, his travels, his appetite for society, and his absorption in the intrigues, jealousies, suspicions, and almost comic fusses of his homosexual love affairs. His love for Antoine Bibesco is a strange mingling of adoration and the strategies and practical pedantries of jealousy. We laugh at the comic word *tombeau* – 'silent tomb' – which occurs even in telegrams as a warning to 'keep this to yourself'. This is Albertine without the tedium. The letters written by the sick writer about a proposed journey to Constantinople, the where, how, and when of it, the changes of mind, the splitting of hairs are fuss raised to the point of sublimity, yet to be taken seriously. Proust is a tyrant in love. He is frank. One never desires to fight off an affection, yet 'You know in me, no affection can withstand absence.' On the other hand, 'Some affections go on too long. They must be dropped before they become too important.' 'A year or a year and a half is the term beyond which affection or, I should say, infections, abate and die away.' The bother is that discarded lovers may 'register an upswing', some 'bring on a slump'. The more serious trouble is that Ruskin has slumped. So no trip to Constantinople. He will finish with a hysterical joke: 'I shall not see the Golden Horn, a thought which gives me palpitations.'

The 'real work' is presumably *Jean Santeuil*, the 'straight' autobiographical novel which he came to see was following the pedestrian course of voluntary memory. (The madeleine has not yet been tasted.) His father dies and he is caught by grief and guilt at being the invalid son who has caused nothing but sorrow to his parents. We read his pathetic, self-pitying outbursts against his mother, which begin fiercely and end in the miserable fretfulness of a baby.

The selection inevitably ends too soon, that is to say years before *A la recherche* begins. For the moment we seem to be in the midst of an enormous web of glittering intrigue in which Proust clings to his friends and rules them by his demands and charm.

For the reader the letters improve as Proust approaches his discovery of what he must do. His health is worse, he is already forced into the necessary solitude, but his Proustifications are calmed by his sense of serious purpose. At two key points we have seen the thinking political moralist strongly appear: scathingly on the scandal of the Dreyfus case; with wisdom in his reaction to the anticlerical ban on teaching by the religious orders. What he fears in both cases is the perversion of justice, the loss of the lasting images of a civilisation. He is both Catholic and Jew. Looking back on the letters to his mother one realises the enormous, protective, nourishing influences his grave and gifted family had on his conscience and on his formation as both man and artist.

Stories

═══════

The reader who knows no Russian is cut off from Pushkin as a lyrical poet and yet can respond to a narrative poem like *Eugene Onegin* in, say, Sir Charles Johnston's recent Byronic version and to the volatile wordplay of Nabokov's translation. Like Byron, Pushkin is one of the world's greatest letter-writers, open and impromptu in all his moods. He is the sunniest of devils. We can see from the narrative poems that he is the forerunner of the great Russian realists of the nineteenth century. Yes, he is the Russian Shakespeare or Cervantes. 'Not a giant' – as John Bayley defined him a few years ago in *Pushkin: A Comparative Commentary* – 'but a Proteus': like Shakespeare, presenting new forms with the laughing boldness of a Renaissance figure. In his translated fictions, especially those written between 1830 and 1837, when he was killed in a duel, we have the superb short stories 'The Queen of Spades', 'The Stationmaster', and 'The Undertaker', the unfinished and spirited 'Dubrovskii', and the gripping, if sometimes melodramatic, novella 'The Captain's Daughter'. They have delighted us, but have we understood what Pushkin was doing with their late-eighteenth-century manner? First of all, his prose has struck us as formal and expository, as parts of Scott do. The bother is that the reader allows the Classics to stale in the memory. We respectfully fail to see the artist in the act of writing. One can easily be caught taking *The Queen of Spades* as a set piece by Mérimée or a conceit by Hoffmann, an ingeniously designed ornament. Yet it comes straight out of the Russia of Pushkin's time.

Two volumes by Paul Debreczeny – *Alexander Pushkin: Complete Prose Fiction* and *The Other Pushkin* – are a scholarly examination of the poet training himself to write prose. The *Complete Prose Fiction*, which Mr Debreczeny has edited and translated, contains some remarkable unfinished exercises. One, 'The Guests Were Arriving at the Dacha', is said to have given Tolstoy his start when writing *Anna Karenina*. This volume ends with notes for stories that were never written or took some other course. One is startling, because, as we are apt to say, it is 'so Russian': 'N. chooses Nevskii Avenue as his Confidant – he confides all his domestic troubles and family grievances to it . . . They pity him . . . He is satisfied.'

But this is by the way. Debreczeny's interest throughout these books is this: how scrupulously the poet trained himself to cut out the exotic images of poetry and write plain prose. 'A continuing tension between two trends – one toward a sparse, austere style, the other toward poetic techniques,' he says, 'produced the rich variety of Pushkin's prose fiction.' We are in the writer's workshop. The subject is not as academic as it sounds: the speed of Pushkin's narratives and the surprises of his changing tune give zest even to his formal writing. The poetry turns into élan. He is a cheerful pillager of styles, a parodist and an eager borrower of plots, a master of the sly art of frustrating the expectations of the unwary reader who is too excited to foresee the psychological design. Pushkin was deep in English, French, and German literature. He had read Voltaire, Rousseau, Stendhal's *Le Rouge et le Noir*, Hoffmann, Richardson, and Scott. He was an excellent critic. The tame love affair that is said to spoil 'Dubrovskii' may very well be an artful parody of the sentimental fiction imported from Europe. The penultimate scene of 'The Captain's Daughter' seems to have come from *The Heart of Midlothian*. Debreczeny is good on the tension and on the development of Pushkin's experiments, on the use of many voices breaking the surface of a story. Yet what Pushkin is really doing in his dramas and comedies is giving us the sensation, distinctive in the later Russian novelists, that 'the doors and windows of the human house are wide open': that if only one person lives there he is many inconsistent persons, or that more than one person tells the tale. Everything is, as Bayley suggested, provisional and open-ended. The dismissive endings of Pushkin's completed stories are ironical, and they are therefore still open, as art stops and life goes on. The impersonality is warm, if not altogether heartening. What everyone has noted is the tender or spontaneous tone of his famous letters, his extraordinary power of self-control. His wild or his worldly genius is governed by the skills of the craftsman who laboriously sharpened as he rewrote. We need not believe entirely the last phrases of Pushkin's exclamation 'I sing as a baker bakes, as a tailor sews, as Koslov writes, as a doctor kills – for money, money, money. Such am I in my cynicism.' He was fly enough to see that the novel was the new and popular thing; but, like Stendhal when he wrote *Le Rouge et le Noir*, he made no concessions to popular taste. The laconic style, the disabused and offhand wit unite the two novelists.

The *Complete Prose Fiction* opens with *The Tales of the Late Ivan Petrovich Belkin*, done very much to the recipe of Scott's *Tales of My Landlord*. Pushkin is the simple raconteur of another man's tales, a man looking back on his time, and the dialogue is dull and largely indirect and generalised, even though the stories amuse us. Pushkin's early prose is still expository, and even scholarly. In fact, he had a natural bent for exposition: his *History of Pugachev* is almost official and neutral in manner, and was carefully reconstructed from historical documents; yet out of this sprang 'The Captain's Daughter', a Romantic and vivid story of spun-out suspense. Debreczeny seems to me too much a structuralist in reading Oedipal complexity into the tale. The ironical beginning – the wilful hero, a young officer, and the morally rebuking family servant in their journey through a blizzard to a military station on the frontier – seems to promise the conventional theme of headstrong master and testy servant. But it suddenly breaks with the eighteenth-century tradition. By the time we get to the wretched fort where the young man has been sent to be broken in, we are alarmed. The modest commander at the absurd fort is a man risen from the ranks and too self-effacing to drill his troops properly; his nice wife and their daughter are charming – too charming for their dangerous life. The young man is soon quarrelling with an unpleasant officer about the commander's daughter. They all forget they are facing a savage rebellion led by the primitive Pugachev and his tribesmen. Then comes the attack and Pushkin's mastery of intrigue. The commander has at any rate the wit to hide his daughter, an obvious prize. But horror ensues. Pugachev captures the place, kills the commander's wife, hangs the commander and a lieutenant, and *leaves them hanging* in order to cow the villagers at the fort. The young officer boldly demands a safe conduct for the girl. The crucial scene is the meeting with Pugachev, who has him at his mercy. Pugachev is suddenly obliging. Critics have found this unbelievable in a cruel and savage leader. Why? So well is this incident managed that we are convinced: the double self is not unknown. Then, the two men have met before, in the blizzard, without knowing each other's names. The young man had given Pugachev a hareskin coat. If we don't accept this as a bond, surely it is plain that a daring rebel would admire a daring man, or a man of honour. Moreover, Pugachev has proclaimed himself King of Russia and can be expected to indulge the mercy of a king. Or maybe he is feeling the melancholy that has come after an easy victory. Perhaps in the self-command of the young man the rebel sees that his own successes with his ungovernable tribesmen will soon run out. Possibly he is a gambler vain of playing with risk. Pushkin is drawn to the mysteries of honour. Any one of these motives seems more than plausible. More serious is the criticism of the cruel and disgusting exposure of the bodies of the commander and his lieutenant. We have not seen them hanged, but worse – they are left obscenely hanging, and Pushkin does not miss a shocked glance at them. The sight indeed haunts the reader with a kind of shame at seeing it. Surely the contemporary reader in our far more cruel and violent times has seen or heard worse. But has the tone of the story been broken – a false note struck, not in life but in art? One Russian writer, the poet Marina Tsvetayeva (Mr Debreczeny tells us), has argued that we can accept the scene as children accept horror in a fairy tale. Pugachev, she says, 'is not an ordinary human being in our perception, but an incarnation of the evil of popular imagi-nation, the wolf or robber of folklore'. And, in fact, a Russian of Pushkin's generation was closer to the figures and emotions of folklore than we are. The Flaubert of *Salammbô* would not have objected. Romanticism could not resist the macabre.

The unfinished 'Dubrovskii' is also a story of outlawry, which starts – almost as a document of social protest – with a quarrel between a villainous landowner and his humble, decent neighbour and turns into a tale of ingenious revenge and a charade of disguises. The helpless lover of justice, who has the oppressed peasants on his side, turns into an elusive Robin Hood, cleverly righting public wrongs. This story was founded on real court cases, and was no myth. Pushkin used all his skill in playing with it and then suddenly tired of his ingenuity.

The one certain triumph of the collection is, of course, 'The Queen of Spades'. It is hard to think of a short story so shapely, so diamond-like, a dire comedy so full and so ingeniously concentrated, and so morally convincing. The poet has written a sonnet – a series of interlocking sonnets – in prose. His tact is perfect. We are left astounded at 'the pack' of characters, the moments of society life, phases of gambling fever, times of day and night that glitter beneath its deceiving surface. The weather itself is alive, and the story is as visual as a Vermeer. Moments are caught and held and pass, just as ordinary life passes, and now Pushkin becomes, at last, a connoisseur of the kind of natural talk that, like a played card, has a new meaning as it falls on the table. The superstition of the magic hand of three cards suggests a fairy tale, yet the real subject is the fever of greed. (Freud, Mr Debreczeny notes, said that gamblers seek self-destruction.) It is interesting that Hermann, the German gambler, is a little Napoleon in appearance, the very model of the upstart of enormous will: men of will are the most likely to become irrational. So the story is not artificial; nor is it a fantasy, asking us to suspend disbelief in magic. It is intensely real as a study of Petersburg types, and its predominant interest is psychological. Pushkin is a great painter of the miniature portrait that appears to be still and fixed yet becomes fiercely alive and moves, changes, and reveals what is hidden the closer we look. Pushkin, the craftsman-gambler, knew that the cards are not cards only but emblems of risk and passion. Like other things of Pushkin's, the story was not invented by him; such tales of magic sequences of cards go the rounds of those who are fevered by the game. Once more, the curt speed of Stendhal is seen in the writing. The German is a tedious little man, too cautious to play until he is equipped to cheat. No poet he. The old Countess, with her secret of the winning sequence and her history, is a superb creation. She is believable when she dies of sudden shock after the young gambler threatens her and begs for her secret, in the rightly famous bedroom scene. She simply dies, like a dropped card, in four simple lines. She is also believable after her death, when she 'walks' as a ghost. Her 'walk' is, of course, in the young German's guilty mind. It is a marvellous observation of Pushkin's that as an imagined ghost she is 'seen' still wearing her bedroom slippers and can slam a door loudly when she leaves. The very detail of the screens, the corridors, the staircase of her apartment dramatises the phases of the gambler's desperate secretiveness. Pushkin has learned how to make the detail of furniture and passages briefly work for him. His passing talk creates the crisis. If there is symbolism in it, it is beautifully concealed. I am not sure that it is safe for critics like Mr Debreczeny to dig it out; it is really an aspect of reverie. Again and again, as they looked at life, the Russian novelists thought the 'real' was not real until it was seen to be strange.

[1297]

Temperament of Genius

To the present-day reader who can know 'Bloomsbury' only by hearsay, and for a critic like myself who read Virginia Woolf's works as they came out but who had no acquaintance with the older survivors of the set until their middle age in the Second World War, they must seem like the natives of some lost tropic of this century's early history. One is apt to forget that they were not the only distinguished writers, artists, thinkers, Puritans, or hedonists of the time. After 1939 that phase of our civilisation, sometimes known as the sunset of the high bourgeois culture of Europe, had clouded over. As the dramatis personae reappear in *The Diary of Virginia Woolf*, patiently annotated by Anne Olivier Bell, in the *Letters*, edited by Nigel Nicolson and Joanne Trautmann, and in Quentin Bell's *Life*, their voices, with their cool antique accent, come back.

We now have the sixth and last volume of the wonderfully talking *Letters*; we have already had the third volume of the *Diary* covering the years 1925–1930: the final volume is yet to come. (It is therefore impossible to match the *Letters* with the *Diary*, in which Virginia talks to herself, but events rarely correspond with her private musing.) In the *Letters* she carelessly and hastily gave away the projected self of the hour; in the *Diary* she contemplated herself and her work more searchingly, often more gloomily. Her truthfulness was, as is usual in diaries, a truth to the moment, as her observation of people changed from one day to the next. The unguarded candour on which 'Bloomsbury' prided itself had the malice of artificial comedy, and she was known to have the sharpest tongue of all. But the cult of friendship was reckoned to be strong enough to stand the militancy. The artist was forgiven, the Kensington lady not always.

Virginia Woolf was a compulsive letter-writer. The 'humane art', as she once wrote in an essay on letter writing, was a way of warding off loneliness by keeping conversation going with the absent, at a time when conversation had revived as an art in itself. She did not much care for the

[1298]

solitude she needed but lived for news, gossip, and the expectancy of talk. She was a connoisseur of manners and gestures, and had the habit of asking a question and breaking off to ask another. If she wrote to captivate her friends and to keep the affection she so strongly needed, the other purpose of letter-writing was to stir the mood for serious writing (Balzac also recommended this). Nigel Nicolson adds a passage that cannot be bettered:

> She described people as if they had no substance until their differences from other people had been analysed, and events as if none had really taken place until it had been recorded, in a manner unmistakably her own, imagining the smile, the frown, of the recipient, rarely repeating a phrase, so grateful for the wealth of the language that she scatters it wilfully, as lavish with words as a pianist is with notes, knowing that it is inexhaustible.

It must be said that if her pace had always been fast, it often became a shade frantic in her fifties. This is because she worked harder than ever when she became famous, as gifted writers do – what else is there to do but write? – but also because for everyone younger or older than herself the Thirties were a period of oppressive anxiety. The *fear* of yet another great war was at any rate removed when war became real, though – as she noted in an ominous phrase – it was henceforth impossible 'to lift the fringe of the future'. Her history of madness, the tragedies of her early life had made her familiar with terror. One may even feel that her imaginative prose has wildness in it and that her laughter, as she breaks life down into moments, is a skirmish with alarm. In the third volume of her *Letters*, in which her great energies are more robust than in the present one, her will was on terms with the venture she was committed to. To Vita Sackville-West she wrote in 1928:

> I believe that the main thing in beginning a novel is to feel, not that you can write it, but that it exists on the far side of a gulf, which words can't cross; that it's to be pulled through only in a breathless anguish . . . Only when one has forgotten what one meant, does the book seem tolerable.

There is confidence and experience in those words.

[1299]

In 1936 she had finished *The Waves* and *Orlando*, a volume of *The Common Reader* was behind her, and she was struggling with the enormous novel *The Years* and her tormenting biography of Roger Fry. It tormented because biography has to bow to research and fact. (Those who sneered at her, as Q. D. Leavis did, as 'an idle social parasite' might bear in mind the immense reading her criticism in *The Common Reader* demanded and that, for example, even a short essay on Mrs Thrale was rewritten eight times. If she could not resist society, which her husband thought dangerous for her, her plunges were not pure vanity and may have relieved an overactive brain.) And London was not all vapid dissipation: her own circle were deep in political committees – she could hear them droning away in the next room at Tavistock Square – as Hitler went into the Rhineland and the Spanish Civil War began and was brought close to home by the tragedy of Julian Bell's death there. There was the relief of the guilt, the fear, the hysteria of Munich as she went back to Rodmell to her familiar headaches. Civilisation, said Leonard and everyone else, was at an end. 'Bloomsbury' was coming to an end. The younger generation questioned the solitary obsession that kept her going.

In the third volume of the *Diary* (1925–1930) we do hear of a 'brush with death' when she falls down unconscious during a walk with Lydia Keynes. She writes:

> Had I woken in the divine presence it wd. have been with fists clenched & fury on my lips. 'I don't want to come here at all!' So I should have exclaimed. I wonder if this is the general state of people who die violently. If so figure the condition of Heaven after a battle.

Earlier still she had felt 'that old whirr of wings in the head which comes when I'm ill so often.'

If violence was latent in her genius and nature, the letters show her as the mistress of comedy. It is the one certain excellence, and perhaps supreme, in the English essayists and novelists, for our affections are entwined with our militancy. In the present volume, as the familiar Bloomsbury chatter goes on, the startling figure of Ethel Smyth thumps in and out. This seventy-year-old feminist and musician who is at war with the whole male sex and whom Virginia freely addresses as 'my uncastrated cat' falls in love with her. Ethel Smyth is a sort of deaf Britannia who bawls out her hatred of Bloomsbury like some blustering figure out of Rowlandson.

'What a rackety race you Smyths are,' Virginia writes to her. 'Bankruptcy, Sapphism, hunting, suicide, all in one gulp. How then did you keep so d – d military upright and brass-buttoned? Explain.'

At first afraid that Ethel will put a portrait of her in one of her autobiographical works and maddened by the almost daily bombardment of letters, Virginia fights back in defence of her friends. Ethel is quite unlike the adored Vita Sackville-West who can be called upon to 'pluck a swan and dip its feather in green ink' and touch mind and heart in her letters. Virginia writes to Vita:

> Oh Ethel! I could not face her, though she was passing our door. Her letters sound as if she was in a furious droning mood, like a gale, all one note . . . [All about the hostility of the male-governed world] Deafness I daresay . . . She can't get rid of her mind in talk.

But she excuses herself to Ethel when *The Waves* is getting out of focus:

> But this explains perhaps certain absences of mind, and cannon bolts down the telephone – Lord! how I like the thud of my abuse upon your hide. I think I shall make a practice of it. 'Ethel, d'you know you're a damned Harlot – a hoary harpy – or an eldritch shriek of egotism – a hail storm of inconsecutive and inconsequent conceit. That's all.' And I shall ring off.

But, cooling down after a row about Maurice Baring:

> How you grow on me. Isn't that odd? Absence; thinking of someone – then the real feeling has room to expand, like the sights that one only sees afterwards. Is that peculiar to me, or common to all? Anyhow, lying in bed, or listlessly turning books I could hardly read, over and over again I've thought of you, and dwelt on your affection . . . And then how I adore your broad human bottom – how it kindles me to think of you, worried and bothered, yet lunching at a party of 12 and I'm convinced keeping the table in an uproar; and plunging like a blue Italian Dolphin into all the nets of the Sitwells, always battling and battering – and with it all keeping a mushroom sensibly intact.

All the letters are fictions in embryo – this particular running portrait Dickensian caricature. She is treating Ethel with far more affection in her wicked wit than Dickens showed Americans in his *American Notes* or *Martin Chuzzlewit*, for Ethel was half an outsider, and escaped the fate of what the Woolfs called the underworld beyond their circle.

We notice deep unchanging devotion towards her husband, her sister, her nephew Julian, and her adored niece Angelica. She fought back hard when Benedict Nicolson – Vita's son – attacked Roger Fry for his supposed failure to 'educate the masses' – that general charge of social isolation and lack of committed social conscience which the young were bringing against their elders.

The war-time letters are valuable as historical day-to-day evidence. The war frames the letter to Benedict Nicolson so that it is like a long short story, for as she takes up Fry's defence, bombers come over: 'I went and looked at them. Then I returned to your letter.' Her defence begins to blister with sarcasm about Ben's privileges, which Fry had not had. 'The raiders began emitting long trails of smoke. I wondered if a bomb was going to fall on top of me; I wondered if I was facing disagreeable actualities; I wondered what I could have done to stop bombs and disagreeable actualities . . . Then I dipped into your letter again.' The argument continues as she is telling him she admires his honesty but warns him against looking for scapegoats. It was particularly searing for her to have to remind Ben that Fry had to deal with insanity and death in his own home. 'I know you're having a worse time [in London] than I am . . . Another siren has just sounded.' The letter is fierce as argument and story. It worried her afterwards that perhaps she had misunderstood his argument.

Being in the 'front line' for air raids and possible invasion at Rodmell gave her, as it did elsewhere to others, a gambler's exhilaration to her fears: there was the awful sense of 'the suspended sentence', the possibility that 'the sense of the future by which we live' had gone. The most shattering intimate aspect of the war for her was the destruction of the little streets and great sites of ancient London which, more than any other place, and far more than the serene marshes and Downs of Sussex, had fed her sparkling sense of people and place. The London of her late Victorian girlhood, of the talkers of the eighteenth century and the gestures of the gorgeous Elizabethans, had been the mother of her genius.

What was the future? One has the impression that what haunted her at this time was another fear, the one that haunts the gifted as they age: that their talent may be vanishing whether their world is or is not collapsing. Illness, exorbitant, compulsive work might perhaps be exhausting not her talent, but the great strength of her will, except the will – and that would be rational – to kill herself. But the noises and dreaded voices in her head had begun.

When we turn back to Volume Three of the *Diary* we see her at the height of her matured powers, wryly conscious of the deceits of fame. She was basking in the lark of *Orlando*, the fantastic love-letter to Vita Sackville-West, and was agonising as she went on to *The Waves*, a very different matter. The 'tug and suck' are at her; why, she asks, could she not be as spontaneous as she had been in *Orlando*? But,

> . . . the idea has come to me that what I want now to do is to saturate every atom. I mean to eliminate all waste, deadness, superfluity: to give the moment whole; whatever it includes. Say that the moment is a combination of thought; sensation; the voice of the sea. Waste, deadness, come from the inclusion of things that don't belong to the moment; this appalling narrative business of the realist: getting on from lunch to dinner: it is false, unreal, merely conventional. Why admit anything to literature that is not poetry – by which I mean saturated?

She is disquieted by 'the remorseless severity' of her mind. It never stops reading and writing. Is she too much a professional, 'too little any longer a dreamy amateur'?

She goes to see Thomas Hardy, who impresses by his vitality. Writing poetry, he flatly said, was a question of physical strength. A kind, sensible, sincere man, who held his head down like a pouter pigeon, he made one good Hardyesque remark: 'None of my books are fitted to be wedding presents.' She goes to see H. G. Wells, who had the red cheeks and jowls of a butcher, liked rambling and romancing about people, but who reeked of lust. The virtues he admires, he says, are courage and vitality. ('I said how ghastly.') He replies nothing is ghastly where there is courage. He gets drowsy after lunch. She goes to see Arnold Bennett – no love here. He's too pleased with his clothes.

'And you drop your aitches on purpose,' I said, 'thinking that you possess more "life" than we do.' 'I sometimes tease,' said B. 'But I don't think I possess more life than you do.'

She is blind to Bennett and certainly didn't grasp that *Riceyman Steps* is a masterpiece that has lasted. The old men she likes best are those like George Moore and Yeats who kept their minds flying.

There is a painful meeting with Eliot and his first wife. Mrs Eliot, who is 'sane to the point of insanity', all suspicion and looking for hidden meanings, says Virginia has made a signal for them to go. When they've left Virginia says, 'This bag of ferrets is what Tom wears round his neck.' And there are the weeks of long personal gloom.

One goes down the well & nothing protects one from the assault of truth. Down there I can't write or read; I exist however. I am. Then I ask myself what I am? & get a closer though less flattering answer than I should on the surface – where, to tell the truth, I get more praise than is right. But the praise will go; one will be left alone with this queer being in old age. I am glad to find it on the whole so interesting, though so acutely unpleasant.

The next day she cheers up a little, reflecting on the mystical side of solitude.

How it is not oneself but something in the universe that one's left with . . .

And out comes that sudden, wild, mysterious image –

One sees a fin passing far out.

Perhaps that shark-like fin is a hint of how the impulse to write *The Waves* first came to her. Quentin Bell calls the *Diary* a masterpiece: it is, indeed, among the great diaries, and is a huge, sharply peopled autobiography of the temperament of genius.

List of sources and dates

In My Good Books – 1942

Gibbon and the Home Guard; A Conscript; A Swiss Novel; The First Detective; *Germinal*; Sofa and Cheroot; A Russian Byron; A Comic Novel; A Hero of Our Own Time; *Faits Divers*; The Clown; The Nobodies; A Victorian Misalliance; The First and Last of Hardy; A Curate's Diary; The Great Flunkey; The South Goes North; The Proximity of Wine; An Anatomy of Greatness; The Dean; The End of the Gael; The Steeple House Spires; One of Our Founders; The American Puritan; The Quaker Coquette

The Living Novel – 1946

The Ancestor; *Clarissa*; The Shocking Surgeon; The Crank; A Scottish Documentary; Scott; Our Half-Hogarth; Disraeli; *Edwin Drood*; George Eliot; An Irish Ghost; A Victorian Son; A Plymouth Brother; The Scientific Romances; The Five Towns; *Sons and Lovers*; A Pole in the Far East; The Irish R.M.; An East End Novelist; An Amateur; Two Writers and Modern War; *Cavalleria Rusticana*; Poor Relations; The Bohemian; The English Frenchman; The Centenary of Anatole France; The Russian Day; The Hypocrite; The Great Absentee; The Minor Dostoevsky; A Russian Cinderella; A Russian Outsider

Books in General – 1953

The Poet of Tourism; Cellini; An Italian Classic; Verga; The Early Svevo; Galdós; A Portrait of T. E. Lawrence; *The Notebooks of Henry James*; Butler's *Notebooks*; A Victorian Child; The Carlyles; Boswell's London; Swift to Stella; The Unhappy Traveller; Maupassant; A Love Affair; Zola; A Political Novel; André Gide; The Act of Believing; Tolstoy; The Art of Koestler; *Tristram Shandy*; The Roots of Detection; The Poe Centenary;

Oliver Twist; Meredith; Poor Gissing; An Émigré; The Octopus; Firbank; W. W. Jacobs; The Hill-Billies; The Eye-Man

The Working Novelist – 1965

Fordie; The Forsytes; The Knightsbridge Kennels; An Irish Oblomov; Alexandrian Hothouse; Kipling's Short Stories; El Cid; Mr Forster's Birthday; Pain and William Golding; Grub Street; *Miss Lonelyhearts*; Henri de Montherlant; The Tin-Openers; The Brutal Chivalry; The Performing Lynx; Hugo's Impersonations; Trollope Was Right; Ross at the Depot; *The Military Necessity*; The Major's Daughter; The Young Gorky; New York, 1900; A Viennese; *Quixote*'s Translators; The Bored Barbarians; Meredith's Brainstuff; Conrad

A Man of Letters – 1985

Lewis Carroll's Inkpot; The Con-Man's Shadow; *La Cousine Bette*; Goya; Turgenev in Baden

The Myth Makers – 1979

Unsafe Conduct; The Gulag Circle; A Doctor; The Despot; The Dream of a Censor; The Early Dostoevsky; Founding Father; A Bolting Horse; Estranged; A Modern Nihilist; Zola's Life; And *Lélia*; The Quotidian; An Early Outsider; A Portuguese Diplomat; A Spanish Balzac; A Brazilian; The Myth Makers; Medallions

A Man of Letters – 1985

The Supreme Fairy Tale; Lord Byron's Letters; A Rough English Diamond

The Tale Bearers – 1980

A Dandy; Fairy Tales; Still Riding; A Pre-Raphaelite's Son; A Moralist of Exile; The Aesthete in War; The Private Voice; Disloyalties; Club and Country; Going Downhill; In the Echo Chamber; Birth of a Hermaphrodite; Towards Revolution; Jumbos; A Quiet American; Satan Comes to Georgia; The Great Snail; The Infantilism of Genius; Ruffian

Dick; The Crab's Shell; *The Tale of Genji*; Snares and Delusions; Flann v. Finn

Lasting Impressions – 1990

Pain and Laughter; Five Minutes of Life; Growing Old; The Sayings of Don Geraldo; Pioneer; Welsh Peasants; Spectators; Universal Man; Irish Behaviour; Medieval Voices; The Death of Lorca; Malraux and Picasso; The Romantic Agony; Iran and Pakistan; The Crystal Spirit; *A Better Class of Person*; Clowns; Escaping from Belfast; *Midnight's Children*; Lost in the Stars; Comic Genius; The Stamp of the Puritan; Getting Richer; One of Nature's Balkans; An Anglo–Irishman; Never-Never-Land; The Strength of an Injured Spirit

A Man of Letters – 1985

Dostoevsky's Wife; Playing Stendhal; Camille Pissarro; Albert Camus; Among the Ruins; Proustifications; Stories; Temperament of Genius

Index

All major references to authors and works are in **bold**.

Index

Index

About the Author

_____

V. S. PRITCHETT is one of the great literary men of our time, a critic, novelist, writer of short stories, biographer, and autobiographer. His most recent work is *Complete Collected Stories*. Now in his ninetieth year, he is president of the Society of Authors, and a foreign honorary member of both the Academy of Arts and Letters and the Academy of Arts and Sciences. Pritchett was knighted in 1975. He lives in London with his wife, Dorothy.